CW01305006

Encyclopedia of
Jamaican Heritage

Encyclopedia of Jamaican Heritage

Olive Senior

TWIN GUINEP PUBLISHERS

Published by
Twin Guinep Publishers Ltd
PO Box 34, Red Hills PO, St Andrew, Jamaica, W.I.
www.twinguinep.com

Copyright text and captions
© **Olive Senior 2003**

Copyright for all photographs/illustrations
resides with the individual owners

First published 2003

All rights reserved
No part of this book may be reproduced, stored in a retrieval system, or transmitted in any form or by any means, electronic, electrostatic, mechanical, photocopying, recording or otherwise, without prior permission of the copyright owner

---

ISBN 976-8007-14-1

Cover and book design Dennis Ranston

Pre-press Book Art Inc., Toronto, Canada

Printed in Hong Kong, China

Contents

Acknowledgements vii

Introduction ix

How the Encyclopedia is arranged x

Abbreviations xi

Weights and Measures xii

Subject Index xiii

Map of Jamaica xx

Bibliography 535

Entries

	page		page
A	1	N	343
B	35	O	355
C	85	P	365
D	145	Q	404
E	167	R	407
F	179	S	431
G	205	T	473
H	227	U	498
I	241	V	501
J	249	W	505
K	263	X	523
L	273	Y	524
M	295	Z	533

Acknowledgements

I am a child of Jamaica who was fortunate enough to be born in a time when I was free to wander, look, and ask questions – of family, friends, or total strangers. It seems that that is mostly what I did. For, although I soon claimed the world of books or it claimed me, my first primer was the natural world of rural Jamaica, my first teachers the sometimes unlettered folk who were nevertheless capable of 'reading' the world around them in sight, sound, colour, gesture, meaning, utility and relationship to mankind. Thus my first demands as to 'who, what, why, when, where, how' were answered not by books but by my parents, teachers and people of the various communities on the Manchester/Trelawny and Westmoreland/Hanover borders where I spent my childhood, virtually all of them now gone. I hope that my debt to them is somewhat repaid by those elements of their teachings that I have managed to capture in this book which serves as a testament to their generosity in allowing me to witness, perceive, enjoy and grow up to be passionate about Jamaica.

My first book on this subject was the *A-Z of Jamaican Heritage* published in 1983. I would like again to acknowledge the contribution of those who were my colleagues at the time at the Institute of Jamaica who read and commented on that work so long ago – especially Mrs Beverley Hall-Alleyne, Dr Ena Campbell and Miss Cheryl Ryman of the African-Caribbean Institute of Jamaica and Dr Thomas Farr and Dr Peter Bretting of the Natural History Division, Institute of Jamaica. It was only so much later that I understood how much I owed them not only for reading and commenting on that manuscript, but for their graciousness in not commenting also on my obvious ignorance or naivety about so many things. That process helped enormously to clarify and develop my understanding of Jamaican culture in its various aspects and in shaping my world view. The fact that this much larger project grew out of that one is a reflection of how much that earlier exercise taught me about what I didn't know, and how much more there is to learn. I'm still walking on that path.

Obviously this book could not have been written without the many scholars in the various disciplines who have gone before me and whose work I have also heavily drawn on.

I am greatly indebted to the many specialists in the various fields covered by this book who generously responded to my request to read and comment on entries. Some were old friends, some are people I have yet to meet – all are named below. Their knowledge contributed greatly to what I hope is the accuracy and authority of this work. It goes without saying that all errors, omissions, or misinterpretations are entirely my own.

The following individuals read and commented on one or more entries in the following fields:

ART – Dr David Boxer, Miss Gloria Escoffery, Mrs Veerle Poupeye Rammelaere, Dr Anne Walmsley, Mr Deryck Roberts.

LANGUAGE, LITERATURE, EDUCATION – Professor Edward Baugh, Mrs Jean D'Costa, Dr Hyacinth Evans, Dr Ruby King, Dr Pamela Mordecai, Professor Mervyn Morris, Dr Velma Pollard.

SOCIOLOGY AND ANTHROPOLOGY – Dr Erna Brodber, Professor Barry Chevannes, Mr Herman McKenzie, Professor John Rashford.

HISTORY – Mr G.A. Aarons, Mr Brett Ashmeade-Hawkins, Dr Pamela Beshoff, Dr Nigel Bolland, Mr Ainsley Henriques, Dr Howard Johnson, Mr Easton Lee, Mr Patrick A. Lee, Mr Martin Mordecai, Mrs Jacqueline Morgan, Mr Guha Shankar, Mrs Carmen J. Thomas, Revd Clarence Thomas, Miss Judith Washington and members of the Jamaican Historical Society.

CULTURE, MUSIC, DANCE AND SPORTS – Mrs Sheila Barnett, Mr James Carnegie,

Dr Carolyn Cooper, Mrs Honor Ford-Smith, Dr Olive Lewin, Mr Hartley Neita, Professor Rex Nettleford, Miss Cheryl Ryman, Professor Maureen Warner-Lewis, Miss Marjorie Whylie.

SCIENCE AND NATURAL HISTORY – Dr Karl Aitken, Professor Brendan Bain, Dr Eric Garraway, Mrs Catherine M. Levy, Dr L.E. McLaren, Mr Andreas Oberli, Mrs Emma Ranston-D'Oyen, Professor E. Robinson, Dr Peter Vogel, Dr Margaret Williams, Miss Gillian Young.

I owe a special debt to those who read substantial portions or the entire draft of the manuscript at various stages and made helpful comments, in particular members of the Jamaican Historical Society, Mr G.A. 'Tony' Aarons, Mr Andreas Oberli, Dr Margaret Williams, Mr Herman McKenzie and especially Mrs Jean D'Costa who rescued me with wit and wisdom from my various entanglements. Mr Martin Mordecai and Dr Pamela Mordecai took on the arduous task of editing the manuscript, the final editing (and much else!) was undertaken by Mrs Jackie Ranston, the general editor. The unenviable task of graphic production and general marshalling of all the elements fell to Mr Dennis Ranston.

Thanks as well to Professor Reginald Carpenter, Mr Ivor Conolley, Mrs Denise Gray Gooden, Miss Shivaun Hearne, Mrs Mary Langford, Miss Maxine McDonnough, Mr Ross Murray, Mrs Faith Myers, Miss Audrey Pinto, Mr Jamie Ranston and Miss Zoe Ranston.

In addition to those acknowledged as the source of illustrations used throughout the text, I would like to acknowledge the assistance of Mrs Valerie Facey and The Mill Press for the colour photographs by Kent Reid of the Taino artifacts at the National Gallery of Jamaica and the illustration of Nutmeg by Juliet Thorburn; and of Dr Owen Minott and Mrs Marjorie Minott, Mrs Marjorie Tyndale-Biscoe and Mr Lascelles Samms, Mr M. Blake of the Jamaica Tourist Board library, Dr David Boxer and the National Gallery of Jamaica, the Gleaner Company reference library and the photographic archives of the National Library of Jamaica and the UWI library. For time, trouble, generosity and advice I am especially indebted to Maria LaYacona. Some Jamaica Government offices and agencies were helpful in supplying information, especially the Meteorological Office, the Jamaica Government Railway, the Jamaica Bauxite Institute and the Jamaica Statistical Institute. I am also grateful to the Jamaica National Heritage Trust and the University of Technology.

Special thanks also to the following for the material specified:
Professor Diane Austin-Broos for quotations from *Urban Life in Kingston, Jamaica: The Culture and Class Ideology of Two Neighbourhoods* in Caribbean Studies Series 3, New York and London: Gordon & Breach Science Publishers. The Sandberry Press, Kingston, Jamaica and Toronto, Canada for the quote from the poem 'Sunday Afternoon Walks with my Father' by Edward Baugh in *It was the Singing*. Trojan Records, London for the quote from 'Rivers of Babylon' by The Melodians and Aquarius Recording Studio, Kingston for the quote from 'Blackheart Man' by Bunny (Livingston) Wailer.

I would like to acknowledge the facilities offered by libraries in many countries, but especially those of the National Library of Jamaica, the former director Mr John Aarons and Mrs Eppie Edwards; the UWI Library and especially the director, Miss Stephney Ferguson, the African Caribbean Institute of Jamaica and Metro Toronto Reference Library and Toronto Library Services.

Over time I have obviously incurred many more debts of a more general and intangible kind, among family and friends – too numerous to name – in the Caribbean, the USA, Canada and Europe, for accommodation, meals, conversation, entertainment and moral support over the long process of completing this book which spanned not just years but continents. I apologize to all whose names are not inscribed here.

This project would probably not have been completed without the steadfast support, tolerance, encouragement, hard work and unflagging commitment of Jackie and Dennis Ranston. Their overall contribution to this volume is immeasurable.

Thanks to all for sharing the vision.

Olive Senior, Kingston and Toronto
2002

Publisher's Note

Every effort has been made to trace the copyright holders of illustrations used in this book, but in a few cases this has not proved possible. We would appreciate any information that would enable us to do so.

Introduction

What do I mean by Heritage?

There are varying definitions of what 'heritage' means, and readers will no doubt have their own. For me, it is everything from the past (our inheritance) that shapes us and serves as pointers to who we are, both as individuals and a nation. This includes the good and the bad, the serious and the frivolous. Obviously, not all the elements in this book are known or shared by all Jamaicans; indeed, they reflect our great diversity. What is important is the points at which many of these elements do intersect and how these feed into the formulation of national identity.

In this book I considered heritage in terms of:

1. Place: Heritage has to do with what we can see and touch and how these influence or reflect us. These include (a) the natural environment – the sea, the land, geological and geographical features, plants and animals; (b) the built environment – historic and symbolically important sites, buildings, places.

2. Creative activity: Heritage is what we create – our social, political and economic systems and activities, our intellectual life, our music, art, literature, dance, drama, religion, education, sports, healing and the magical arts, crafts, foods, and what we express in verbal art and artistry – our speech and our oral culture – our folklore, stories, songs, games, sayings, proverbs, etc.

3. History: Heritage is what we experience – our history, our heroes and heroic deeds, our charlatans and villains. And what we achieve – in all fields of endeavour, over time.

4. Rituals and Traditions: Heritage is what and how we celebrate, in groups, or nationally – our holidays and feast days, our family and community gatherings, births, weddings, deaths, anniversaries and how these sustain and reflect collective beliefs and practices.

My own view of our national heritage is holistic, that is, that the whole is greater than the sum of its parts. I believe that those of us who call ourselves Jamaican are shaped by a unique set of circumstances that are intrinsic, even as we belong to distinctive racial or ethnic categories.

Jamaica as a nation is a recent invention, born in 1962. But our natural heritage – the emergence of our island from the sea, the formation of our mountains and rivers, the arrival of flora and fauna, go back much further in time, beginning some 10-15 million years ago. And the Jamaican people have been in the process of fashioning a heritage since the first Native American settlers of whom we have a record, the Tainos of Arawak descent, arrived around 1000 AD (displacing even earlier peoples of whom little is so far known). Since the earliest European 'discovery' in 1494, successive waves of people have contributed to our formation – a variety of Europeans, Africans, North and South Americans, and Indians, Chinese, and Middle Easterners.

We are not newly minted and fashionably 'multicultural'. We have been the meeting ground, from our earliest history, the coming together of peoples (and their cultural baggage) from all over the world. Jamaicans since earliest times have in turn spread out across the globe to the extent that today, more of us reside abroad than in our island. And though we might be able to trace this or that element of our heritage to Africa, or the British Isles, the transforming genius of place is such that we have over centuries managed to infuse whatever we import with our own desires, adapt it to our needs, graft it on to what is indigenous, so that ultimately it becomes a reflection of who we are, our 'version', named with our own names.

Part of my own formation has been the realization that we also share much of what is contained within this book with other members of our Caribbean 'tribe'. British West Indians, Guyanese and Belizeans, should have no difficulty in recognizing many of the artefacts, the plants and their uses, the 'folkways' and the historical streams that intersect. We might do things differently and we often call things by different names (as the *Dictionary of Caribbean English Usage* attests) but the common ground we share is as remarkable as our differences.

I hope this volume will contribute to that pluralist perspective on the past that is a necessary factor in shaping who we want to be, contributing to the public discourse about a national identity. For me, breaking down complex information and reassembling it in this fashion (alphabetically) opened up new connections and facets of experience and provided fresh perspectives on many of the subjects contained herein. I hope that dipping into this book at random, and sampling Jamaican culture in a non-hierarchical way, might provide the same experience for others. Then 'heritage' might be seen not as something exclusively encoded in great houses or the arts of one set of people, but as that to which each of us can lay some claim. Such a sense of possession should also elicit from us the consciousness of what is urgently in need of our attention, to treasure, to conserve, and to protect, for future generations.

OS

How the Encyclopedia is arranged

Entries are arranged alphabetically. Words in small capital letters within entries indicate that there is also an entry on that topic.

'See – ' or 'See also' before a cross-reference, for example:

> A system of healing widely practised in Jamaica. (See also MEDICINE, Folk.)

tells where additional information on the topic may be sought. The list at the end of most entries indicates sources of information (author's surname and date of publication) and suggestions for further reading on the topic. The surnames can be checked against the alphabetical listing in the Bibliography to obtain publication details. The Subject Index is meant to point readers to topics that go together.

Although I have tried to make this work as comprehensive as possible, it was quite evident that in one volume I could give only passing reference to some topics that might loom large in people's minds. Ultimately, the choices made here are my own, though I hope my justification for whatever is included will be evident. I should underscore the point that this is an Encyclopedia of Jamaican Heritage, not The Encyclopedia of Jamaica. While there is an enormous need for the latter, such an undertaking is far beyond my scope and ambition. Neither is this book a Dictionary of National Biography, so my entries of historic or distinguished Jamaicans is also limited.

I would certainly appreciate hearing from readers (via my publishers) with comments on any inaccuracies and omissions as well as suggestions for future editions.

Bibliography

Astute readers might note some of my sources in the Bibliography as ancient or ephemeral publications, but in some cases these were the only sources of information available. I have listed whatever sources I have consulted. Some of the basic information regarding Jamaica's traditional culture is based on my personal knowledge or from interviews I have conducted over the years. Nevertheless, I also set out to verify all of my information by reference to written sources and in virtually all cases succeeded in doing so, at times having to patch together what might be a very brief entry with bits and pieces from many different sources. Certain publications were virtual source books to me and were always consulted though not always cited, principal among them, Cassidy and LePage's *Dictionary of Jamaican English* (DJE).

Abbreviations

ACIJ	African Caribbean Institute of Jamaica
AD	anno Domini
anon.	anonymous
API	Agency for Public Information
b	born
BA	Bachelor of Arts
BBC	British Broadcasting Corporation
BC	before Christ
B Ed	Bachelor of Education
BITU	Bustamante Industrial Trade Union
BI	Bustamante Institute
BM	British Museum
BMS	Baptist Missionary Society
BWIR	British West Indies Regiment
c.	circa
C	centigrade
Capt	captain
Caricom	Caribbean Common Market
Carifesta	Caribbean Festival of Arts
Carifta	Caribbean Free Trade Association
CEE	Common Entrance Examination
comp.	compiler
cm	centimetre
Col	colonel
CUP	Cambridge University Press
CQ	Caribbean Quarterly
CXC	Caribbean Examinations Council
d	died
DCC	Dunlop Corbin Compton
DCEU	Dictionary of Caribbean English Usage
dj	disc jockey
DJE	Dictionary of Jamaican English
E	east
ed.	editor
et al.	and others
F	farenheit
Fr	Father
GOJ	Government of Jamaica
GSAT	Grade Six Achievement Test
ha	hectare
HM	His or Her Majesty
HMS	His or Her Majesty's Ship
Hon	Honourable
HRH	His or Her Royal Highness
IAAF	International Association of Athletics Federations
IMF	International Monetary Fund
IOJ	Institute of Jamaica
IOJP	Institute of Jamaica Publications
ISER	Institute of Social and Economic Research
JA	Jamaica Archives
JAMAL	Jamaica Movement for the Advancement of Literacy
Jampro	Jamaica Promotions Corporation
JAS	Jamaica Agricultural Society
JBC	Jamaica Broadcasting Corporation
JCDC	Jamaica Cultural Development Commission
JDF	Jamaica Defence Force
JFM	Jamaica Federation of Musicians
JHR	Jamaican Historical Review
JHS	Jamaican Historical Society
JIS	Jamaica Information Service
JJ	Jamaica Journal
JLP	Jamaica Labour Party
JLS	Jamaica Library Service
JMB	Jamaica Memory Bank
JNA	Jamaica Netball Association
JNHT	Jamaica National Heritage Trust
JNTC	Jamaica National Trust Commission
JPM	Jamaica People's Museum
Jr	Junior
JSM	Jamaica School of Music
JTB	Jamaica Tourist Board
kg	kilogram
km	kilometer
km^2	square kilometre
kph	kilometres per hour
KRC	Kingston Restoration Company
KSAC	Kingston and St Andrew Corporation
lat	latitude
LTM	Little Theatre Movement
long	longitude

lb	pound
Ltd	Limited
£.s.d.	pounds, shillings and pence
m	metre
MA	Master of Arts
MC	Mico College
MD	medical doctor
mm	millimeter
NAM	National Army Museum
n.d.	no date
NHD	Natural History Division
N	north
NE, NW	north-east, north-west
NDTC	National Dance Theatre Company
NG	National Gallery
NHC	National Hurricane Centre
NLJ	National Library of Jamaica
NPG	National Portrait Gallery
NWU	National Workers Union
OECS	Organization of Eastern Caribbean States
OM	Order of Merit
PNP	People's National Party
RA	Royal Academy
RAF	Royal Air Force
Revd	Reverend
Rt	Right
Rt Hon	Right Honourable
S	south
SE SW	south-east, south-west
SAT	Scholastic Achievement Test
SES	Social and Economic Studies
Sgt	sergeant
SAJ	Shipping Association of Jamaica
SM	Smithsonian Institution
sp	species
Sr	Senior
St	Saint
STATIN	Statistical Institute
STINAPA	National Parks of the Netherlands Antilles Foundation
t	tonnes
trans.	translator
UAWU	University and Allied Workers Union
UK	United Kingdom
UNIA	Universal Negro Improvement Association
UP	University Press
US, USA	United States of America
UTech	University of Technology
UWI	University of the West Indies
VC	Victoria Cross
Ven	Venerable
VIP	very important person
vol	volume
W	west
WHO	World Health Organization
WIMJ	West Indies Medical Journal
WIR	West India Regiment
WIRL	West India Reference Library
WISCO	West Indies Sugar Company
WPJ	Workers Party of Jamaica

WEIGHTS AND MEASURES
Imperial Equivalents

1 millimetre	=	0.039 inch
1 centimetre	=	0.394 inch
1 metre	=	1.094 yards
1 kilometre	=	0.6214 mile
1 square centimetre	=	0.155 sq inch
1 square metre	=	1.196 sq yards
1 square kilometre	=	0.386 sq mile
1 hectare	=	2.471 acres
28.35 grams	=	1 ounce
1 kilogram	=	2.205 pounds
1 tonne	=	0.984 (long) ton
1 millilitre	=	0.002 pint (British)
0.0284 litre	=	1 fluid ounce
1 litre	=	1.76 pints
0.473 litre	=	1 pint (16 fluid ounces American)
4.546 litres	=	1 gallon

To convert Centigrade into Fahrenheit: multiply by 9, divide by 5, and add 32.

Olive Senior/Encyclopedia of Jamaican Heritage   xiii   **Index**

Subject Index

1 The Natural World

ANIMALS
Alligator *see* Crocodile
Anansi
Ant
Bat
Bees
Boa *see* Snake
Bullfrog
Butterflies and Moths
Camel
Cattle
Chigger
Codfish *see* Fish, Salt
Conch
Coney
Coral
Cow *see* Cattle
Crab
Crocodile
Dog
Donkey
Dragonfly
Duck Ants *see* Ant
Fauna
Firefly
Fish and Fishing
Frog
Galliwasp
Goat
Horse
Iguana
Jackass *see* Donkey
Jangga
Jellyfish
Jigger *see* Chigger
Lizard
Lobster
Macaca
Manatee
Mongoose
Moth *see* Butterflies and Moths
Mullet
Pedro Seal
Peenie *see* Firefly
Pig
Pond Turtle
Rain Fly
Sea Shell *see* Shells
Shells
Shrimp
Silkworm *see* Silk
Snail *see* Shells
Snake
Spider
Tiki-Tiki
Toad *see* Bullfrog
Turtle
Turtle, Pond *see* Pond Turtle
Yellow Snake *see* Snake

BIRDS
Birds
Birds in Folklore
Blackbirds
Booby Eggs
Cattle Egret
Cling Cling *see* Blackbirds
Doctor Bird *see* Hummingbird
Dove and Pigeon
Dove and Pigeon in Folklore
Gaulin
Gimme-me-bit *see* Duppy, Money
Guinea Fowl
Hummingbird
John Crow
Loggerhead *see* Petchary and Loggerhead
Mockingbird
Nightingale *see* Mockingbird
Owl
Parakeet *see* Parrot
Parrot
Patu
Pelican
Petchary and Loggerhead
Pigeon *see* Dove and Pigeon
Senseh Fowl
Solitaire
Tody
Water Birds *see* Gaulin
Woodpecker

BOTANIC GARDENS
Bath
Castleton
Cinchona
Hope
Liguanea, the Botanic Garden *see* Gordon Town

GEOGRAPHICAL AND GEOLOGICAL FEATURES
Antilles
Blue Hole
Blue Mountains
Booby Cay
Bowden
Caribbean
Catherine's Peak
Caves
Cay
Climate
Cockpit Country
De la Beche *see* Halse Hall
Earthquake
Forest
Glistening Waters
Geology
Goat Islands
Hellshire Hills
Hurricane
Jamaica
Judgement Cliff
Latitude and Longitude
Limestone
Low Layton
Lovers' Leap
Moneague Lake
Morant Cay *see* Cay
Mount Diablo
National Parks
Navy Island
Ocho Rios
Palisadoes
Pedro Cay *see* Cay
Rio Cobre Gorge
Runaway Cave
Spur Tree Hill
Seasons
West Indies
Yallahs Ponds

MINERALS
Alumina *see* Bauxite
Bauxite
Copper
Gold
Guanín
Limestone
Salt

MINERAL SPRINGS
Bath Fountain
Black River Spa
Milk River Bath
Rockfort

PARKS AND SCENIC ATTRACTIONS
Bamboo Avenue
Black River
Blue Hole
Blue Mountain and John Crow National Parks
Boston Beach
Cockpit Country
Doctor's Cave *see* Montego Bay
Dunn's River
Emancipation Park *see* Emancipation Day
Fern Gully
Glistening Waters
Hellshire Hills
Hollywell
Kingston Race Course
Lovers' Leap
Montego Bay Marine Park *see* National Parks
National Heroes Park
National Parks
Negril
Ocho Rios
Oracabessa
Parade
Park, St William Grant
Rio Grande (Rafting)
University Campus, Mona
Victoria Park *see* Park, St William Grant
YS Falls

PLANTS
Ackee
Agave
Allspice *see* Pimento
Almond
Aloe
Anatto

Antidote Cacoon
Apple
Arrowroot
Avocado
Bamboo
Banana
Barringtonia
Basil, Wild
Bauhinia
Beads
Bissy see Kola
Blue Mahoe see Mahoe
Bougainvillea
Breadfruit
Bromeliad
Bush
Cacoon
Cactus
Calabash
Calalu
Cannabis see Ganja
Cannonball Tree
Cashew
Cassava
Cassia
Castor Oil Plant
Cedar
Ceiba see Cotton Tree
Cerasee
Cherry
Chewstick
Chocho
Chocolate see Cocoa
Cinnamon
Citrus
Cockroach Poison
Coco
Cocoa
Coconut
Coffee
Cohoba
Coolie Plum see Apple
Coratoe see Agave
Corn
Cotton
Cotton Tree
Cowitch
Crab Apple see Apple
Croton
Cuscuta
Custard Apple
Datura
Dodder see Cuscuta
Duppy Fly Trap
Ebony
Fennel
Fern
Fever Grass
Fig, Wild
Flora
Forest
Frangipani
Fustic

Ganja
Ginger
Golden Apple see Apple
Gourd see Calabash
Grapefruit
Grave Plants
Guaco Bush
Guango
Guava
Guinea Grass
Guinep
Gum Trees
Gungo Pea
Hibiscus
Hog Plum
Irish Moss
Irish Potato see Potato
Jackfruit
Jew Plum
John Crow Bead
Junjo
Khus-Khus
Kingston Buttercup
Kola Nut
Lace Bark
Leaf of Life
Lemon Grass see
  Fever Grass
Lignum Vitae
Lime
Locust
Logwood
Love Bush see Cuscuta
Macca
Macca Fat see Palm
Madam Fate
Mahoe, Blue
Mahogany
Majoe Bitter
Mammee Apple see Apple
Manchineel
Mango
Mangrove
Marijuana see Ganja
Maypole see Agave
Mimosa
Mint
Mountain Pride
Naseberry
Navel String Tree
Nunu Bush
Nutmeg
Okra
Orange
Orchid
Ortanique
Otaheite Apple
Overlook Bean
Palm
Papaw
Passion Fruit
Peanut
Peas and Beans

Pear see Avocado
Pepper
Periwinkle
Piaba
Pigeon Peas see Gungo
Pimento
Pineapple
Pingwing see Bromeliad
Plantain
Plum see Apple,
  Jew Plum, Hog Plum,
  Plumb Point
Poinciana
Poinsettia
Potato
Poui
Pumpkin
Quaco Bush see
  Guaco Bush
Quassia
Quick-stick
Rose Apple see Apple
Saman see Guango
Sandbox Tree
Sarsaparilla
Sea Grape
Sensitive Plant see Mimosa
Shoeblack see Hibiscus
Silk Cotton see
  Cotton Tree
Sinklebible see Aloe
Soap Plants
Sorrel
Soursop
Spathodea
Spirit Weed
Starapple
Sugar Cane
Susumba
Sweet Cup see
  Passion Fruit
Sweet Potato see Potato
Sweet Sop
Tamarind
Tangerine
Tea
Thatch
Tobacco
Tom Cringle's
  Cotton Tree
Toona
Torch-wood
Trumpet Tree
Tuna see Toona
Ugli
Velvet Apple see Apple
Wangla
Water Hyacinth
Watermelon
Wild Pine see Bromeliad
Wis
Woman's Tongue
Yam

Yampi
Yuca see Cassava

RIVERS
Black
Cabaritta
Cane
Dunns
Ferry (Fresh)
Hope
Martha Brae
Milk
Ocho Rios
Plantain Garden
Rio Cobre
Rio Grande
Rio Minho
Roaring (St Ann)
Roaring (Westmoreland)
Wag Water
White
Yallahs
YS

2 Economic Life

COMMUNICATIONS AND TRANSPORTATION
Airports see Aviation
Aviation
Banana Loading
Broadcasting
Canoe
Cycling
Donkey Cart see Dray
Dray
Ferry
Gleaner
Horse
Jackass
Kingston Industrial
  Garage
Latitude and Longitude
Mandela Highway
Panama Canal see Panama
Postal Service
Queen's Highway
Rafting see Martha Brae,
  Rio Grande
Railway
Rio Cobre Gorge
Telephone Service
Tethering Post
Toll Gate
Tourism
Tramcar
'Trunk Fleet'
Windward Road

ECONOMIC ACTIVITIES
Agriculture
Banana Trade
Bauxite

Cement Company *see*
  Rockfort
Conuco
Cotton
Croptime
Day Work
Digging Match *see* Day
  Work
Encomienda
Fish and Fishing
Fish Farming
Forest
Gangs, Jobbing
Gangs, Slave
Goat
Ground
Head Sugar *see* Sugar, Wet
Jackass
Jackass Rope
Jerk
Logwood
Markets
Money
Pardner
Pig
Provision Ground
Quattie *see* Money
Red Mud Lake
Rum
Seasoning
Silk
Sugar Cane
Sugar Plantation
Sugar, Wet
Susu *see* Pardner
Tourism
Victoria Market

TRADES AND OCCUPATIONS
Blacksmith
Book-Keeper
Cooper
Cabinet-Maker
Carpenter *see* Cabinet-
  Maker
Higgler

3 Cultural Activities

CULTURAL ACTIVITIES
Art
Broadcasting
Dance
Dancehall
Drama, *see* Pantomime,
  Theatre
Festival, Jamaica
Festivals
Folk Music Research *see*
  Music
Folk Tales *see* Anansi

Language
Literature
Musgrave Medals
Music
Music, Folk
Pantomime
Reggae

CULTURAL ARTEFACTS AND NATIONAL SYMBOLS
Abeng
Bells of Port Royal
Coat of Arms
National Anthem
National Awards
National Flag
National Symbols
Shark Papers
Tethering Posts
Treadmill
Victoria Cross

CULTURAL INSTITUTIONS AND ORGANIZATIONS
African Caribbean
  Institute of Jamaica
  (ACIJ)
Arawak Museum *see*
  Taino Museum
Archaeological Museums
  see Old King's House;
  Old Naval Hospital,
  Taino Museum
Archives
Art School *see* Edna
  Manley College
Cultural Training Centre
  see Edna Manley College
Dance Company *see*
  National Dance Theatre
  Company
Dance School *see* Edna
  Manley College
Drama School *see*
  Edna Manley College
Edna Manley College
Folklore Collections *see*
  ACIJ
Folk Museum *see* Kings
  House, Old
Friendly Societies
Georgian *see* Cabinet-
  maker, Falmouth, Great
  House
Hanover Museum
Institute of Jamaica
International Reggae
  Studies Centre *see* Reggae
Jamaica Council of
  Churches *see* Religion

Jamaica Cultural
  Development
  Commission *see* Festival,
  Jamaica
Jamaican Folk Singers
Jamaica Library Service
  see Libraries
Jamaica Memory Bank
  see ACIJ
Jamaica Military Band
Jamaica National
  Heritage Trust
Jamaica National Trust
  Commission *see* Jamaica
  National Heritage Trust
Library of the Spoken
  Word *see* Broadcasting
Libraries
Little Theatre
Money Museum *see* Money
Museums *see* Institute of
  Jamaica, Jamaica
  National Heritage Trust,
  Hanover, German,
  Money, Bob Marley, Taino
Music School *see* Edna
  Manley College
National Council for
  Indian Culture *see* Indian
National Dance Theatre
  Company
National Gallery *see* Art
Natural History Museum
  see Institute of Jamaica
Olympia Art Centre *see* Art
Registrar General *see*
  Archives
Seaford Town Museum
  see German Heritage
UNIA *see* Garvey, Marcus
Ward Theatre

EDUCATIONAL INSTITUTIONS
Agricultural Training *see*
  Agriculture
Alpha
Beckford and Smith *see*
  Beckford
Calabar
Edna Manley College
Education
Hampton *see* Black River
  Anglican Church
Immaculate Conception
  see Constant Spring
Jamaica College *see* Drax
  Hall
Knibb Memorial High
  School
Mannings School
Martí, José, Secondary
  School

Mico College
Munro College *see* Black
  River Anglican Church
Northern Caribbean
  University *see* Seventh-
  Day Adventist
Queen's College
Rowe's Corner
Rusea's School
St George's College
St Jago School
Titchfield School
University of Technology
University of the West Indies
Westwood *see* Stewart
  Town
Wolmer's

RELIGIONS – AFRICAN-JAMAICAN
Bedwardism *see* Bedward
Kumina
Missionary
Myal
Native Baptist *see*
  Missionary
Pocomania
Rastafari
Revival
Zion

RELIGIOUS DENOMINATIONS
Anglican
Baptist
Ethiopian Orthodox
Friends, Society of
Jews
Methodist
Moravian
Muslim
Pentecostal
Presbyterian
Religion
Roman Catholic
Seventh-Day Adventist
Quakers *see* Friends,
  Society of
Salvation Army
United Church
United Congregation of
  Israelites *see* Jews

4 Domestic and Leisure Activities

CEREMONIES AND CELEBRATIONS
April Fool's Day
Areito
Ash Wednesday
August, First of, *see*
  Emancipation Day
Bruckins

Buru
Christmas
Cropover
Easter
Emancipation Day
Festivals
Good Friday
Groundation
Hosay
Independence Day
Jonkonnu
Myal
Nine Night
Palm Sunday
'Pickni Christmas'
'Play'
Rally
Seating, Ceremonial
Set Girls
Set Up
Tambu
Tea Meeting
Weddings, Country
Work Songs
Yam Festival
Zemi

DOMESTIC ACTIVITIES AND OBJECTS
Bandana
Barbecue
Basket
Bead
Cacoon
Calabash
Castor Oil Plant
Chewstick
Clothing see Bandana, Osnaburgh
Coal-pot
Cooking Pot see Dutchie
Cotta
Crocus bag
Cutlass
Dutchie
Filtering Stone
Fireplace
Floor Cleaning
Folk Medicine see Medicine, Folk
Gourd – see Calabash
Great House
Guinea Fowl
Jackass Rope
Kitchen Bitch
Lace Bark
Laundry
Machete see Cutlass
Monkey Jar
Mortar
Osnaburgh
Pottery see Art, Monkey Jar, Yabba
Puss-boots
Schoolgirl
Seating, Ceremonial
Senseh Fowl
Shut Pan
Spanish Wall
Stand-pipe
Stick
Thatch
Thunderball
'Trunk Fleet'
Yabba
Yard
Zinc

FOOD AND DRINK
Ackee and Codfish see Ackee
Bammy
Booby Eggs
Bread
Bulla
Bun see Easter Bun
Calalu
Cassava Bread see Bammy
Chaklata Ball see Cocoa
Chocolate see Cocoa
Chewstick
Christmas
Christmas Pudding
Coal-pot
Cocoa
Coco-bread see Bread
Coconut
Codfish see Fish, Salt
Corn dishes see Corn
Crab
Curried Goat see Goat
Dip an' Fall Back see Run Dung
Dokunu
Dumpling
Dutchie
Easter Bun
Escoveitch
Festival
Filtering Stone
Fireplace
Fish see Fish and Fishing, Fish Farming
Fish, Salt
Fu-Fu
Ginger Beer
Gizada
Goat
Grater Cake
Grog
Gungo Pea
Hard-dough Bread see Bread
Head Sugar see Sugar, Wet
Irish Moss
Jackass Corn
Jangga
Jerk
Jerk Pork
Johnny Cake
Junjo
Lime
Lobster
Macaca
Mannish Water
Mullet
National Dish see Ackee
Patty
'Pear' see Avocado
Peas and Beans
Pepper
Pepper-pot
Planter's Punch
Poco-mungee
Pone
Rice and Peas
Rum
Run Dung
Salt
Salt Fish see Fish, Salt
Sangaree
Shrimp
Shut-pan
Snowball
Solomon Gundy
Sorrel
Stamp-and-Go
Sugar, Wet
Sweets
Tamarind
Tea
'Tonic'
Turn Cornmeal see Corn
Turtle
Wangla
Wedding Cake see Christmas Pudding

GAMES AND PASTIMES
see also SPORTS
Alphabet, Jamaica
April Fool's Day
Anansi Stories
Autograph Album
Batey
Bessy
Big Boy
Dinki Mini
Dominoes
Drop Pan
Games
Lying Stories
Moonshine Baby
Nine Night
Peaka-Peow
'Play'
Riddle
Sally Water
Set Up
Stick
Tea Meeting
Wake
Warri

MUSIC, MUSICAL INSTRUMENTS AND DANCE
Abeng
Areito
Bamboo
Banjo
Bells of Port Royal
Benta
Bessy
Bruckins
Buru
Calabash
Calembe
Catta Stick
Conch
Coromantee
Cropover
Dance
Dancehall
Day Work
Dinki Mini
Drums
Dub see Dancehall, Reggae
Etu
Festivals
Folk Music see Music, Folk
Games
Gerreh
Goombay
Gourd see Calabash
Hosay
Jamma Song
Jawbone
Jonkonnu
Kumina
Limbo
Maroons
Mayohabo see Areito
Maypole
Mento
Music
Music, Folk
Musical Instruments
Nine Night
Pantomime
'Play'
Pocomania
Quadrille
Rastafari
Reggae
Revival
Rumba Box
Set Girls
Shay-Shay
Stick Dance see Stick

Street Cries
Tambu
Tea Meeting
Theatre
Trumpet Tree
'Version'
Wake
Work Songs
Yanga

SPORTS
Athletics
Batey
Boxing
Cricket
Cycling
Football
Golf
Horse Racing
Netball
Soccer *see* Football
Tennis, Lawn

5 Folklore

BELIEFS
Albino
Archway
Babylon
Bat
Bible in Folklore
Birds in Folklore
Birth
Charm
Cocobay
Conch
Cotton Tree
Cow in Folklore
Dog in Folklore
Dove and Pigeon in Folklore
Duppy
Firefly
Frog in Folklore
Galliwasp
Goat Mouth *see* Goat
Good Friday
Guava
Guinea Fowl
Jackass in Folklore
John Crow Bead
Kingston Buttercup
Legend and Myth
Lizard in Folklore
Obeah
Ol'Hige
Overlook Bean
Papaw
Pigeon in Folklore
Pumpkin
Salt
Senseh Fowl

Shipmate
Spider in Folklore
Thunder-ball
Token
Tody
Wangla

CUSTOMS
Birth
Bush Fighting
Corn
Coyaba
Cranial Deformation
Day Names
Death Rituals
Dinki Mini
Etu
Gerreh
Ground
Kumina
Maroon, To
Navel String Tree
Nine Night
Set-up
Tambu
Wake
Wedding, Country
Zella

HEALING ARTS, MAGIC AND SORCERY
Amber
Balm
Birth
Bush
Castor Oil Plant
Charm
Chigger
Cocobay
Cotton Tree
Doctor Bird *see* Hummingbird
Duppy
Ganja
Goombay
Grave Plants
Graveyard
Guinea Fowl
Kumina
Majoe Bitter
Medicine, Folk
Medicine, Taino
Nunu Bush
Myal
Obeah
Overlook Bean
Pocomania
Quassia, Jamaica
Revival
Salt
Senseh Fowl
Spirit Weed
Stick

Thunder-ball
'Tonic'
Vomiting, Ritual
Wangla
Whip
X

LEGENDS AND LEGENDARY BEINGS
Black-heart Man
Gold, Legends of
Legend and Myth
Long Bubby Susan
Lovers' Leap, Legend of
Martha Brae, Legend of
Mountain Pride, Legend of
Ol'Hige
Panya Jar
Rolling Calf
Rose Hall, White Witch of
Three Foot Horse
Warner
Whooping Boy

MYTHS AND MYTHICAL BEINGS
Amazon Women
Antilles
Atabeyra
Baibrama
Baraguabael
Boinayel
Cave of Emergence
Coatrischie
Corocote
Creation Myth
Flood Myth, Taino
Guabancex
Guahayona
Guataubá
Legend and Myth
Maquetaurie Guayaba
Márohu
Matininó
Opiyel Guobirán
Water Spirits
Weather Spirits
Yaya
Yucahú
Zambi
Zemi

ORAL CULTURE
Address, Terms of
Anansi Stories
Birds in Folklore
Big Boy
Charms
Day
Dove and Pigeon
Games
Jamaica Alphabet *see* Alphabet, Jamaica

Kiss-teet
Language
Legend and Myth
Literature
Lying Stories
Memory Gem
Proverb
Riddle
Street Cries
Yanga

6 Historic People

HEROES, NATIONAL
Bogle, Rt Excellent Paul
Bustamante, Rt Excellent Sir W. Alexander
Garvey, Rt Excellent Marcus
Gordon, Rt Excellent George William
Manley, Rt Excellent Norman Washington
Nanny, Rt Excellent
Sharpe, Rt Excellent Samuel

HISTORIC GROUPS, OFFICES AND ORGANIZATIONS
Buccaneers
Burial Societies *see* Friendly Societies
Cacique
'Colón Man'
Colonial Church Union
Custos
Government
Jamaica Welfare
Jonkonnu
Maroons
Militia
Missionary
Parish
Pirates *see* Buccaneers, Calico Jack Rackham, Henry Morgan, Port Royal
Pirates, Women
Set Girls
Trade Unions
West India Regiments

HISTORIC PERSONS
Accompong
Baker, Lorenzo Dow *see* Banana Trade
Baker, Moses *see* Adelphi
Barrett
Beckford
Bedward, Alexander
Benbow, Vice-Admiral John

Index

Bolas, Juan de *see* Lubolo, Juan
Bolívar, Simón
'Calico Jack' *see* Rackham, Jack
Campbell
Canoe, John *see* Jonkonnu
Colbeck, Col John
Columbus, Christopher
Cowen, Sir Frederic
Cubah (Cornwallis)
Cudjoe, Captain
Dallas
DeBolas, Juan *see* Lubolo
De la Beche *see* Halse Hall
Dupont, Fr Joseph
Edinburgh Castle, Mad Doctor of
Edwards, Bryan *see* Bryan Castle
Esquivel
Finlayson, James *see* Brown's Town
Galdy, Lewis
Gosse P.H. *see* Bluefields
Grant, St William *see* Park Haughton
Hope
Johnston, Dr James *see* Brown's Town
Jordon, Edward
Knibb, Revd W. *see* Baptist, Knibb Memorial, Missionary
Kojo *see* Cudjoe
Las Casas, Bartolomé de
Lewis, M.G. *see* Hordley
Liele, Revd George *see* Adelphi, Baptist, Missionary
Lubolo, Juan (de Bolas)
Maceo
Manchester, Duke of
Mandela, Nelson *see* Mandela Highway
Marley, Robert Nesta
May, the Revd *see* May Pen
Metcalfe, Sir Charles
Morgan, Henry
Nelson, Admiral Horatio
Nugent, Lady *see* Kings House, Old
Pané, Friar Ramón
Penn, Admiral William
'Peter Pindar' *see* Alley Church
Phillippo, Revd *see* Baptist, Missionary, Spanish Town Baptist, Free Villages
Plato, The 'Courtly Bandit'

'Princess of Port Royal' Quaco
Rackham, Jack ('Calico Jack')
Rodney, Admiral George
Rose Hall, White Witch of
Seacole, Mary
Sloane, Sir Hans *see* Flora
Tacky
Three Finger Jack
Venables, Gen Robert
Vernon, Admiral Edward
White Witch *see* Rose Hall
Williams, Dr Cecily
Wolcot, John (Peter Pindar) *see* Alley Church
Ysassi, Don Cristobal

RACE, ETHNIC AND CULTURAL GROUPS
African Heritage
Africans, Indentured
Albino
Arawak 'Indians'
British
Bungo
Carib
Chinese
Ciboney
Coloureds
Congo
Coromantee
Creole
East Indian *see* Indian
English *see* British
Etu
Free Coloureds, *see* Coloureds
French
German Heritage
Guinea
Hosay
Ibo
Indian
Irish
Jews
Lebanese
Mandingo
Miskito Indians
'Mosquito Indians' *see* Miskito
Nago
Paratee
Portuguese
Quaco
Quashie
Scots
Spanish Jamaica
Surinam Quarters
Syrian *see* Lebanese
Tainos
Welsh
Yoruba

7 Historic Events

HISTORIC EVENTS
Apprenticeship System
August, First of, *see* Emancipation Day
Capture of Jamaica
Carlisle Bay, Battle of
Columbus in Jamaica
'Christmas Rebellion' *see* Sharpe, Samuel
'Discovery' of Jamaica
Earthquake
Emancipation
Free Villages
Hurricane
Independence Day
Jamaica
Middle Passage
Morant Bay Rebellion
Panama
Port Royal Earthquake *see* Port Royal
Rio Nuevo, Battle of
Runaway
Slavery
Spanish Jamaica
Tacky's War *see* Tacky
World Wars
Xaymaca

HISTORIC EVENTS – MEDICINE AND DISEASE
Chigger
Cholera
Cocobay
Dirt-Eating
Fever, *see* Yellow Fever and Malaria
Seacole, Mary
Smallpox
Williams, Dr Cecily
Yaws
Yellow Fever and Malaria

8 Historic Places

HISTORIC HOUSES
Admiral's Pen *see* Admiral Town
Bluefields
Bryan Castle
Cardiff Hall
Cinnamon Hill *see* Barrett
Colbeck Castle
DeMontevin Lodge
Devon House
Folly
Good Hope
Gordon House
Great House

Greenwood *see* Barrett
Halse Hall
Headquarters House
Invercauld *see* Black River
Jamaica House
King's House
King's House, Old
Mandeville Rectory
Rose Hall Great House
Seville Great House
Stewart Castle
Stokes Hall Great House
Trafalgar House
Vale Royal
Waterloo *see* Black River

HISTORIC PLANTATIONS
Albion
Bowden
Bybrook
Constant Spring
Dallas
Drax Hall
Frome
Holland
Hope
Hordley
Ironshore
Kenilworth
Lyssons
Montpelier
Orange Valley
Pepper
Richmond-Llandovery
Spring Garden
Tryall
Worthy Park
YS

HISTORIC STRUCTURES – MONUMENTS
Bogle's Statue *see* Bogle, Paul
Bolívar Monument *see* Bolívar, Simón
Cenotaphs *see* World Wars
Coconut Tree, Monument to the
Cross Roads Clock Tower
Dupont, Fr Joseph
Half Way Tree Clock
Jordon Statue *see* Jordon, Edward
Kingston Parish Church
Lucea Clock
National Heroes Park
Park, St William Grant
Rodney Memorial
St James Parish Church
St Peter's, Port Royal
Samuel Sharpe Square

Soldier's Stone
Victoria Statue
Wolmer's

HISTORIC STRUCTURES – RELIGIOUS
Alley Church (St Peter's)
Annotto Bay Baptist Church see Annotto Bay
Black River Anglican Church
Burchell Memorial Church
Christ Church (Port Antonio)
Coke Methodist Church
Falmouth Baptist see Knibb Memorial Church
Falmouth Parish Church
Falmouth Presbyterian Church
Half Way Tree see St Andrew Parish Church
Hanover Parish Church
Holy Trinity Cathedral
Jewish Synagogue
Kettering Baptist Church
Kingston Parish Church
Linstead Anglican Church
Mamby Park Church
Manchester Parish Church
Rio Bueno Anglican Church
Rio Bueno Baptist Church
Salters Hill Baptist see Adelphi
Scots Kirk
Spanish Town Baptist Church
Spanish Town Cathedral
St Andrew Parish Church
St James Parish Church
St Peter's (Port Royal)
St Peter's, Clarendon see Alley Church
Tamarind Tree Church (St Dorothy)
University Chapel

HISTORIC STRUCTURES – SECULAR
Cage, The
Dome, The
Falmouth Courthouse
Falmouth Police Station
Ferry Inn see Ferry
Flat Bridge
Folly Point Lighthouse
Fort Augusta
Fort Charles
Fort Charlotte
Fort Clarence
Fort Dundas
Fort George
Fort Haldene
Fort Johnston
Fort Lindsay
Fort Montego
Fort Morant
Fort Nugent
Galina Point Lighthouse
General Penitentiary see Penitentiary
Giddy House
Gordon House
Half Way Tree Clock
Hope Aqueduct
Iron Bridge
Jubilee Market
Kenilworth
Lucea Clock
Mandeville Court House
Mandeville Hotel
Mandeville Jail and Workhouse
Mandeville Rectory
Morant Point Lighthouse
Morgan's Harbour
National Stadium
Negril Point Lighthouse
Newcastle
Ocho Rios Fort
Old House of Assembly
Old Naval Dockyard see Morgan's Harbour
Old Naval Hospital
Penitentiary, General
Portland Point Lighthouse
Plumb Point Lighthouse
Rockfort Mineral Spring
Rodney Memorial
Spanish Town Court House
Spanish Town Square
St Ann's Bay Fort
St Catherine District Prison
Victoria Market
Ward Theatre
Water Square, Falmouth

PARISHES
Clarendon
Corporate Area
Hanover
Manchester
Parish
Portland
Trelawny
St Andrew
St Ann
St Catherine
St Elizabeth
St James
St Mary
St Thomas
Westmoreland

SITES, TOWNS AND VILLAGES
Accompong
Adelphi
Admiral Town
Albion
Alley
Annotto Bay
August Town
Banbury Cross
Bath, Town of
Black River, Town of
Bluefields
Brown's Town
Bull Bay and Cow Bay
Constant Spring
Cross Roads
Dallas
Denbigh
Discovery Bay
Doctor's Cave see Montego Bay
Don Christopher's Cove
Easington
Esquivel
Falmouth
Ferry
Free Villages
Geffrard Place
Goat Islands
Gordon Town
Half Way Tree
Harbour View see Fort Nugent
Hellshire Hills
Hope
Hope Tavern
Jamaica
Kingston, city of
Lacovia
Liguanea
Linstead
Lititz
Llanrumney
Lucea
Lyssons
Manchioneal
Mandeville
Martha Brae
Matilda's Corner
May Pen
Middle Quarters
Mocho
Moneague
Montego Bay
Morant Bay
Mount Diablo
Mulberry Gardens
Naggo Head
Nanny Town
Navy Island
Negril
Newmarket
Ocho Rios
Old Harbour Bay
Oracabessa
Palisadoes
Paratee
Passage Fort
Pepper
Port Antonio
Port Henderson
Port Maria
Port Royal
Porus
Quaco Point
Quaw Hill
Rio Bueno, Town of
Rio Cobre Gorge
Rockfort
Rowe's Corner
Runaway Bay
Santa Cruz
Savanna-la-mar
Samuel Sharpe Square
Seaford Town see German Heritage
Sevilla la Nueva see New Seville
Seville, New
Sligoville
Spanish Town
Spur Tree Hill
St Jago
Stewart Town
Stony Gut
Surinam Quarters
Titchfield
Toll Gate
Tom Cringle's Cotton Tree
Tryall
University Campus, Mona
Up Park Camp
Vere
Vernamfield
Villa de la Vega
Water Square, Falmouth
White Horses
Windward Road
Xaymaca
Yallahs
YS

Jamaica

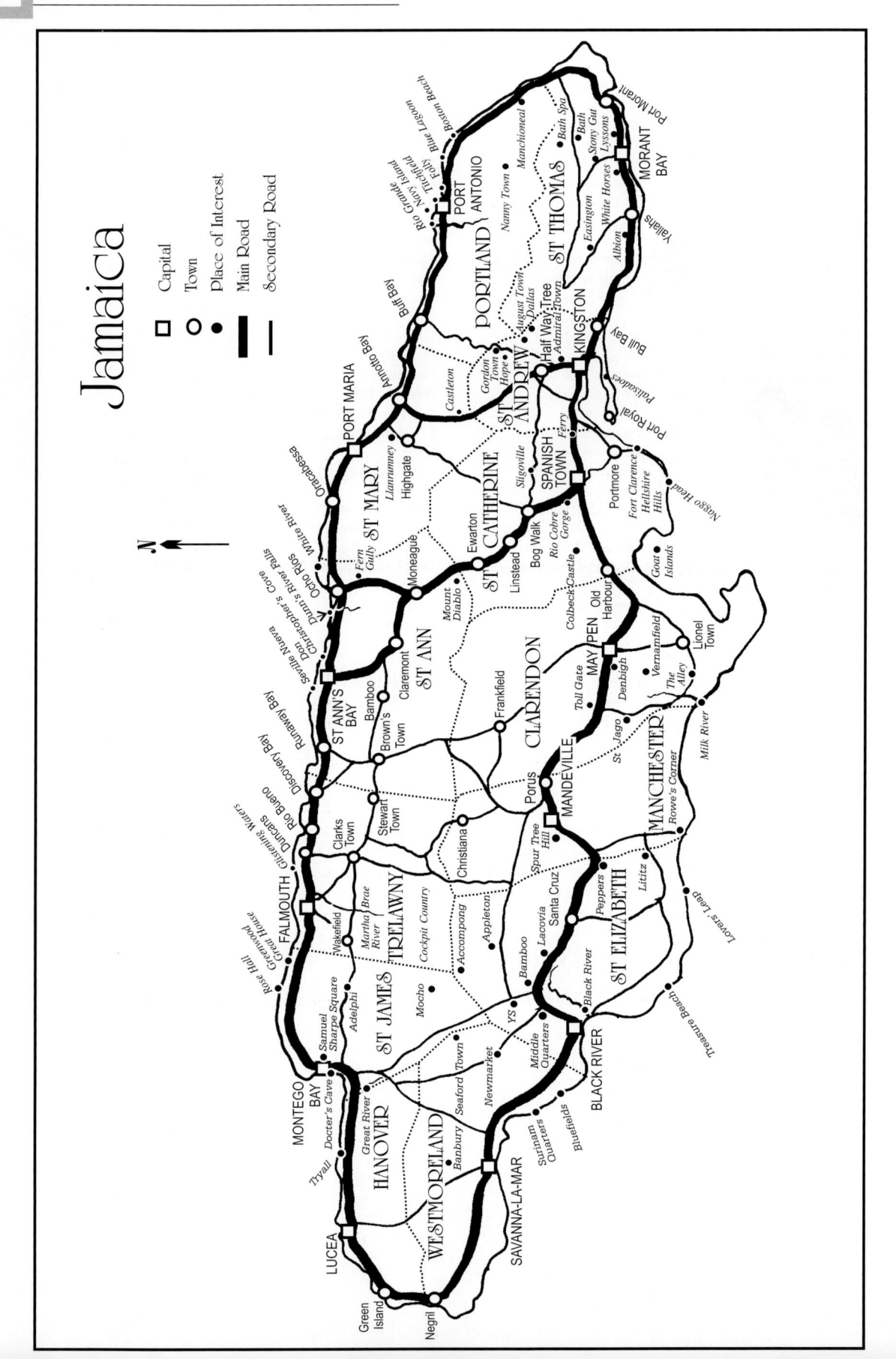

A

ABENG

Animal horn used as a means of communication by the MAROONS, an important element in their culture. The horn is blown by putting the lips to a hole in the concave side and working the thumb over a small hole in the tip to produce variations in tone. The word *abeng* comes from the Twi language of the Akan of Ghana and means an animal horn or MUSICAL INSTRUMENT. The Maroons used the abeng to keep in touch with each other during their wars, hence it has by extension come to be a symbol of freedom; for instance, a radical newspaper in the 1960s was called *Abeng*.

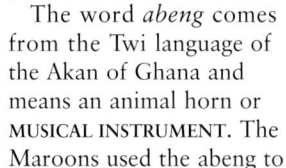

Abeng player

Through the abeng, the Maroons could communicate with one another over great distances in ways that would not be understood by outsiders. As Mavis C. Campbell describes it: 'This instrument can utilize a wide range of notes; thus it was capable of transmitting complicated messages, intelligible only to the Maroons, informing them of the size of the approaching troops, the amount of armaments they possessed, the path they were using, and the like. Similarly, directions regarding Maroon strategies would be given on the abeng by their chief of operations. Once the alarm was sounded everyone [warriors, women and children] knew what to do.' She adds that the abeng was also a source of terror to the enemies: 'The Maroons soon became aware that the British parties found its sound "hideous and terrible", and they exploited its use to the fullest extent, by blowing on it continuously when the parties were close to their towns, thus creating confusion and in some instances flight among the soldiers.'

The American dancer Katherine Dunham who visited the ACCOMPONG community in the 1940s said the Colonel of the Maroons told her that, 'When expertly blown, the message is transmitted not by a signal or code but by the actual pronunciation of the words and by tones which are easily distinguishable by a trained ear'. He explained that if a person died, a relative at market at BLACK RIVER 38.6km away could hear the signal of the horn and by listening intently to the spoken words hear the message as though it were delivered conversationally. Dallas in his *History of the Maroons* (1803) tells us that the Maroons had a particular call on the horn for each individual.

In the old days, the 'horn man' had to undergo a long and arduous training, and still does, but the skill for sending 'talking messages' seems to have died out. Today the abeng (made from the horn of CATTLE) is used in the Maroon towns to summon residents to meetings and announce important news. On some national occasions, the abeng is also blown by a Maroon.

[Beckwith 1929, Campbell 1990, Dallas 1803, DJE, Dunham 1946]

ACCOMPONG

MAROON settlement in ST ELIZABETH Parish named after the founder of the town, Accompong, brother of the great Maroon leader CUDJOE (or Kojo). The name is derived from Acheampong, a personal name among the Twi speaking people who were brought to Jamaica in large numbers in the 17th and 18th centuries from the area that is now Ghana. Most of the Maroons came originally from this group – referred to locally as COROMANTEES.

Accompong is now the only Maroon town left on the western side of the island. It was officially founded in 1739 when land was ceded to the Maroons as one of the terms of the peace treaties with the English which ended the Maroon wars. The Maroon signatories of the treaty of 1 March 1738 were the brothers Cudjoe, Accompong and Johnny, along with Cuffee and Quaco – all styled 'Captain' in the articles of pacification. The village was built on the site of the camp chosen by Accompong from which he had raided the surrounding countryside.

As at other Maroon towns, the leader at Accompong today is called the Colonel. A Festival (open to the public) called 'Cudjoe's

Day' is held here every 6 January to celebrate the signing of the treaty and the founding of the town. For an insight into the Accompong Maroons, see Col Martin-Luther Wright's article in Agorsah 1994.

[Agorsah 1994, Campbell 1990, Dallas 1803, DJE, Lewin 2000, Williams 1934]

ACKEE (*Blighia sapida*)
National fruit of Jamaica and one-half of the 'national dish' – ackee and salt fish (see FISH, Salt). The representation of the beautiful ackee fruit is nowadays widely employed as a motif in art and popular culture, celebrated by poets and folk singers. 'Carry me ackee go a Linstead Market, not a quattie wut sell' is the plaintive lament in the folk song 'Linstead Market' but the fruit is mentioned in many other popular songs such as 'Jamaica Farewell' and 'Big Sambo Gal'. The culinary inadequacy of the latter is marked by the accusation: 'Im tek ackee mek soup, im tek natta (ANATTO) colour it. Gal yu want fi come kill me?'

Perhaps because Jamaicans are among the only people who eat ackee, the fruit has over the years come to assume significant cultural importance. As anthropologist John Rashford has pointed out, Jamaicans have come to associate ackee 'with pleasure, overall well being and national identity. The ackee is indeed the island's colourful tree of life'. All this despite the fact that ackee also has the reputation of being a poisonous fruit if proper care is not taken in harvesting and preparing it. For many years it was banned from entry into the United States of America, but the ban was lifted in 2000. Canned ackee is much in demand by expatriate Jamaicans.

The tree is a familiar sight in many Jamaican yards, including urban areas, and is naturalized or cultivated from sea level to over 900m, but is rarely grown in the other CARIBBEAN islands. It will grow up to 15m under favourable conditions and bears large red to yellow fruits 7.5-10cm long which when ripe will burst into three sections, each revealing a shiny black, round seed atop a bright yellow aril which is the part cooked and eaten.

Jamaicans believe the ackee must not be used before the pods have opened on the tree, the aril must be properly cleaned of red fibre, and the water in which it is cooked must be discarded. 'Ackee poisoning' (called 'vomiting sickness' before the cause was identified – see WILLIAMS, Dr Cecily) may result in some circumstances when ackees are improperly handled. According to the *Jamaica Farmer's Guide*, the aril contains 'hypoglycine, an amino acid which can cause vomiting and lowering of the blood sugar and, potentially, death if ingested by malnourished children. The hypoglycine content falls as the fruit matures and is present in harmless concentration in fully ripened fruit when the pods dehisc (split) naturally'. A riddle conveys this information: 'Me fader send me to pick out a wife; tell me to tek only those that smile, fe those that do not smile wi' kill me.'

Ackee

The colour of the aril helps to identify the two main varieties. That with a soft yellow aril is popularly called 'butter' while 'cheese' is hard and cream-coloured. Ackee grows naturally from seed, but in recent years it has also been propagated from tip-cuttings to provide seedlings for orchard culture. The result is a short compact tree which fruits in 1-2 years, compared to the usual 3-4 years, and is popularly (though wrongly) regarded as a 'dwarf' variety.

The tree comes from West Africa, its introduction recorded in 1778 when some plants were purchased from the captain of a slave ship. However, one story relates how once long ago a man in Africa was picking ackees when he was captured by slave traders. He had one of the fruits in his hand and he clutched it so tightly he never let it go throughout his terrible journey all the way to the coast and on the slave ship across the Atlantic, thus bringing the fruit to Jamaica. Its long importance in the diet is attested by the fact that archaeological explorations of African-Jamaican slave culture by Douglas V. Armstrong have revealed that 'The presence of ackee is a strong indicator of the location of abandoned slave village sites throughout Jamaica'.

The name Ackee or *Akee* is from the Twi language of Ghana. Captain Bligh, who brought the first BREADFRUIT to Jamaica, in turn took the first ackee from Jamaica to London, and in 1806 it was officially described and given the botanical name *Blighia sapida* in his honour (*sapida* referring to its savoury taste).

The plant has in the past been used in traditional folk MEDICINE, ackee leaves being boiled to make a rub for pain and a tea for colds. In Jamaica as in parts of West Africa, the inside of the shell surrounding the aril has been used as a soap (see SOAP PLANTS) and to scour pots, and pulverized ackee has been used as a fish poison. It should be noted that what is called 'ackee' in Barbados is the Jamaican GUINEP (*Melicoccus bijugatus*).

[Adams 1972, Armstrong 1991, Asprey and Thornton 1953-55, Baccus and Royes 1988, Campbell 1974, Rashford 1995b]

ADDRESS, Terms of

The warning to Jamaican children up to recently to 'always give a handle to the name' sums up the attitude that still persists among many people. In direct address or in reference, the name of an adult is preceded by a courtesy title; obligatory for children and frequent even between adults who know each other well. Failure to give a title can be taken as a sign of deliberate discourtesy, contempt, or undue familiarity and some people will defend their right to be addressed in what they construe as the proper manner. In the formal workplace and other non-domestic settings the use of a title and surname is still the norm, unlike the practice in some industrialized countries. Children addressing adults by their first names are frowned upon as 'rude' and 'facety'.

First names alone were once used only between intimates and to make class distinctions. Nowadays, the use of a first name without a 'handle' is still employed to denote a disparity in social and economic status, in the domestic and less formal work spheres. Thus a domestic worker will be called by her first name though she is expected to give the adult members of the household a 'title' before first or last name, and the same will apply to some workers in relation to management, especially in small and family owned businesses. In the past, even small children of a higher social status had to be addressed as 'Miss' and 'Master'.

This class-based formality can be seen as a legacy of BRITISH colonialism but the courtesy implied in the use of titles is also a reflection of the formality of Africans and the respect paid to older people by the younger.

While in modern times the universal titles of 'Mr', 'Mrs', 'Miss' and nowadays 'Ms' are used or first names exchanged, in rural Jamaica especially, outside of the elite, it was common practice to address older people as 'Aunt' and 'Uncle' whether or not they were related. This is a possible African survival since it is noted among people of African descent in the American South and elsewhere. Barry Higman has commented that the creation of 'fictive kin' by slaves lacking real kin in the West Indies refers back to 'the great value placed on kinship' by the African societies from which the slaves came. (See AFRICAN HERITAGE, SLAVERY.)

'Auntie' or 'Grannie' even today imply not only female relatives but are titles given to older women, and are so used in folk tales and folk songs. 'Ta' or 'Tata' were respectful terms of address to an older woman or man in or outside the family (though now considered old-fashioned) as are terms like 'Nana' or 'Grandy'. Other terms of address used in former times included 'Co' or 'Coz' for cousin or any relative other than immediate family and 'Bra' (brother) and 'Sta' (sister) used for equals, whether family or friends. Today, 'Brother' or 'Bredda' is still used informally in addressing an equal, reinforced by Rastafarian usage of Brother or 'Brother Man', 'Bredda' or 'Bredren' originally referring to an adherent of RASTAFARI. Thus 'Dawta', also taken from Rasta usage, and referring to their women, is now applied in familiar address to any young woman while 'Queen', another Rasta term for his female partner, tends to be used jocularly in the wider society.

'Mistress', 'Missis' and 'Mam' were once terms of respect applied to women of higher status, now little heard, though 'Chile' (for child or girl or, familiarly, an adult woman) is still widely used, 'Son' less so. Among rural women, even friends, it is common practice to use the title 'Miss' with the first name, regardless of marital status. School children nowadays seem to apply 'Miss' to all females older than themselves and universally to their female teachers. 'Mass' and 'Massa', formerly respectful titles for the boss, are also terms of address to older people or equals. 'Bass' (boss), 'Busha' (from 'overseer'), Bukra Massa ('white master') are also still used, the last two nowadays derisively.

The most commonly used term by Jamaicans of all classes is 'man' (frequently written 'mon' by foreigners) and is used without regard for sex or age.

Divine personages were also formerly accorded the same respect as the human, God being referred to as 'Big Massa', or 'High Massa', Jesus as 'Massa Jesus'.

Some terms refer to ethnicity – 'Babu' is a derogatory term for an East INDIAN male, 'Baba' a respectful term applied to an older Indian man. Indian women tend to be addressed as 'Miss Coolie' or 'Mai', younger girls as 'Bibi' and 'Beti' though the latter three terms are also used as girls' names in the wider community. 'Missa Chin' and 'Miss Chin' are generic terms of address for CHINESE. F.G. Cassidy reports 'Mushé' as an old-fashioned title applied usually 'to an Oriental' or a Syrian (see LEBANESE) – it appears in the song 'Quattie a yard O, Salo' in the second verse: 'Mushé a come O, Salo' (see MUSIC, Folk). Cassidy says the word 'is undoubtedly from French Monsieur, which was also borrowed in this form into the Hausa language. It may have come thence to Jamaica or directly – probably the latter'.

Some kin terms have been appropriated by organizations. 'Brother' and 'Sister' are also used to designate religious connections in some churches, and leaders in BALM and REVIVAL are addressed as 'Mother' or 'Mada' and 'Faada' (as well as 'Shepherd' and 'Captain'). Some powerful community leaders – obeah-men or others – are sometimes respectfully addressed as 'Papa'.

[Baxter 1970, Cassidy 1961, Higman 1979a, Jackson 1967]

ADELPHI

Village in ST JAMES Parish which was the first place on the north side of the island where religious instruction was given to the slaves during the BRITISH period. It was formerly part of an estate known as 'Stretch and Set', a name derived, it is said, from the brutal punishment inflicted on the slaves there. The estate was acquired by George Lascelles Winn, a Quaker planter (see FRIENDS) who renamed it 'Adelphi'. In 1786 Winn purchased some slaves in KINGSTON among whom were members of the BAPTIST church founded by the Revd George Liele. Winn later persuaded Moses Baker, a member of Liele's church, to come to Adelphi to minister to his slaves.

Baker, like Liele, was a free black from the United States. He was converted after his arrival in Jamaica in 1783 and commenced his ministry at Adelphi in 1788, setting up a church at nearby Crooked Spring in 1791, to be followed by other churches in the area. Baker, a former barber, was already an old man when he started his ministry and was so successful that he contacted the Baptist Missionary Society of Great Britain requesting help with the work. As a result, in 1814 the BMS sent the first white Baptist MISSIONARY, John Rowe, from England. The young man was advised by his employers: 'You are going to unite with an aged man, in the work of instructing negroes, a man whose character and conduct, according to all the information we have been able to obtain, as well as his years, will entitle him to your Christian respect. In many things you may find him inferior to you in knowledge, but never make him feel himself to be so, and in those things wherein his age and experience will naturally give him the precedency, you will, we trust, as naturally yield it. Let there be no strife between you, and if he be more tenacious of some peculiarities than you may think necessary, yet if they are not evil, for love's sake bear with them.'

In the present Salter's Hill Church near to Adelphi can be seen a memorial to Baker who died in 1828 at the age of 97.

[Cundall 1915, Gayle 1982, Wright and White 1969]

ADMIRAL TOWN

Place name in KINGSTON, which recalls the earlier name of Admiral's Pen which embraces what is now the 'town' and adjoining areas. The residence was one of Jamaica's historic buildings, immortalized by the visiting English painter James Hakewill (1778-1834). Admiral's Pen was the residence of the commander-in-chief of BRITISH naval forces in Jamaica at a time when this station was one of the most important in the British Empire. Among its illustrious visitors was the future Admiral Lord NELSON.

When the house and pen near to Greenwich on the western side of the harbour were purchased by the government in 1774, it was already called Admiral's Pen, three admirals having lived there in succession, the dockyard at Greenwich being the naval embarkation point. As the official residence, Admiral's Pen became a centre of colonial social life and is one of the places frequently mentioned by Lady Nugent, wife of the governor of Jamaica 1801-05, in her famous *Journal*. But by 1829 the house was described as 'ruinous and uninhabitable'.

In the 1840s Admiral's Pen was used to house IRISH immigrants on arrival, five shiploads of them staying there at one point in time. In 1863 the property was acquired by the civic

Admiral's Pen, 18th century

authorities for use as a poor house and was known as the Union Poorhouse for Kingston and ST ANDREW. Attached to the poor house was the burial ground; the area now known as 'Ghost Town'.

[Cundall 1915, Nugent 1839]

AFRICAN CARIBBEAN INSTITUTE OF JAMAICA

Established in 1972, the African Caribbean Institute of Jamaica (ACIJ) is the principal cultural agency for the study and dissemination of research on Africa and the AFRICAN HERITAGE and culture as manifested in Jamaica and the rest of the CARIBBEAN. A merger in 1990 with the Jamaica Memory Bank (JMB) which was started in 1980, strengthened the institutional mission to collect, research, document, analyse, preserve and disseminate information from oral and scribal sources. The ACIJ is a division of the INSTITUTE OF JAMAICA.

ACIJ research topics have included traditional DANCE forms, LANGUAGE, folktales, traditional and popular recorded MUSIC, social movements, traditional healing practices and the history of village developments. The Memory Bank has been engaged in recording the memories of older Jamaicans and these are part of a growing audio-visual archive. The ACIJ also conducts outreach programmes that include published and audio-visual material. Its principal publication is an occasional Research Review.

AFRICAN HERITAGE

The majority of the Jamaican population is of African descent (classified in the 1991 Census as Negro/Black – 90.5 per cent, and Mixed/Negro – 7.3 per cent).

Africans first arrived in Jamaica in 1513, having been forcibly captured in their homelands, sold as slaves and brought to the New World by SPANISH settlers. They served as body servants, cowboys, hunters and herders of wild HORSES, PIGS and CATTLE. The knowledge these Africans acquired of Jamaica's interior was later to prove invaluable to them, for when the English took the island in 1655, many escaped into the mountains. From their forested hideaways they first assisted the Spanish resistance fighters who had set them free (see LUBOLO, YSASSI) and later fought to retain their freedom from the BRITISH colonizers. Self-liberated Africans, like the escaped TAINOS before them, were called by the Spaniards *cimarrón* ('wild') and from this the English derived their word MAROON. These early Maroons were a mixture of Congo, Angolan, Akan and mixed-race people of Taino and Spanish origin, probably speaking a Spanish CREOLE. SUGAR CANE had been introduced from the early 16th century by the Spaniards who had small sugar mills (*ingenios*) and from this base the English began to establish the plantation system, a process aided by the arrival of experienced sugar planters who had previously settled in Barbados. The enormous labour force required by the SUGAR PLANTATIONS was supplied by the slave trade through which millions of Africans were forcibly brought to the New World. Although no exact numbers are available, estimates of the numbers of slaves brought to Jamaica from the mid-17th century until 1807, when the slave trade was abolished, range from 750,000 to one million (see SLAVERY).

Full freedom for the enslaved did not come about until 1838 (see EMANCIPATION) although, from the Spanish period onwards, a small number did secure their freedom by various means and functioned within the society as free people, though with limited civil rights. The Maroon element was also continuously augmented by African RUNAWAYS who opted for a life of freedom in the bush. With Emancipation, many of the formerly enslaved left the sugar plantations and their negative associations and established themselves as free settlers in the mountains or in FREE VILLAGES, forming the backbone of the Jamaican peasantry. (See AGRICULTURE.)

From the very start of the Africans' arrival in the New World, there was intercourse with the rest of the population. Initially, with the surviving Tainos, and over a much more extended period, with the Europeans, leading to the rapid development of a group intermediate in colour and status which was usually referred to as the 'coloured' population. Although under slavery a child automatically assumed the status of its mother, some of these coloured children of

Young revellers dance to the Festival '79 song 'Born Jamaica'

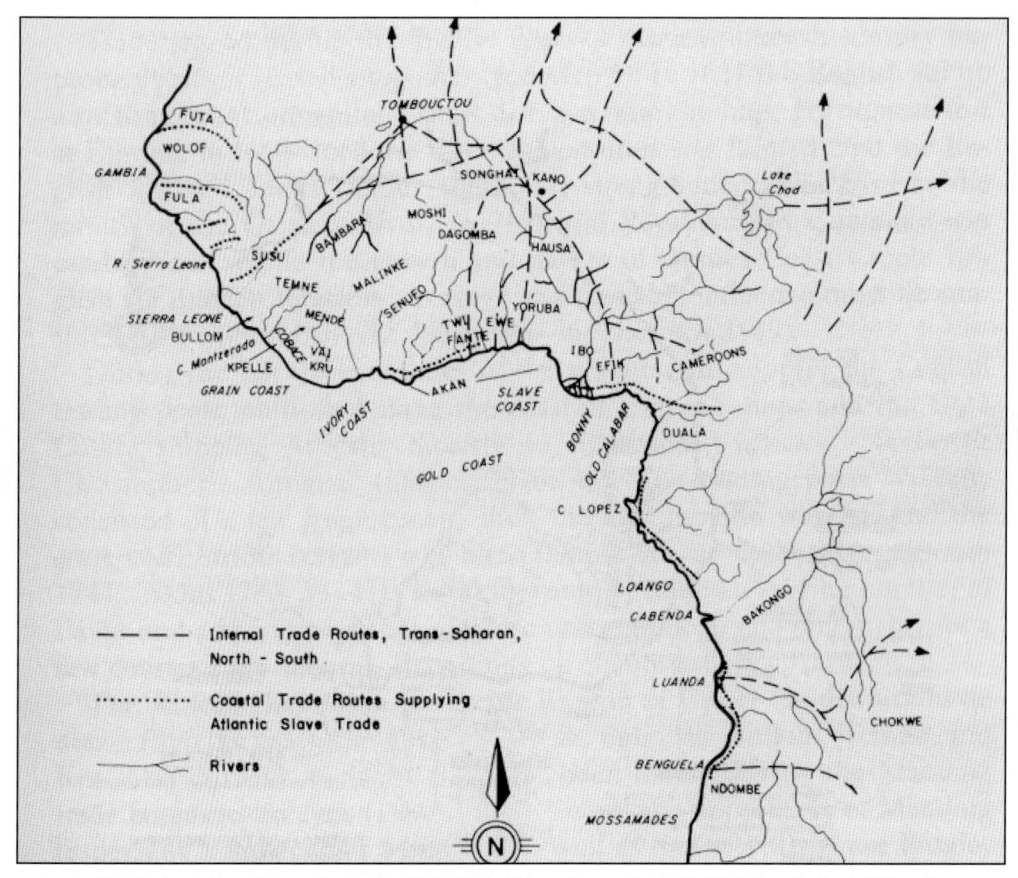

Principal peoples and routes involved with the West African slave trade, 1600-1800 (from Lalla & D'Costa)

slave mothers and white fathers were freed by their fathers, and enjoyed the status of 'free coloureds', being granted in 1830 the same civil rights as Europeans. (See COLOUREDS.) The arrival of later immigrant groups – particularly CHINESE and INDIAN in the 19th and early 20th century – led to further racial and ethnic mixtures in the population.

Not all Africans came to Jamaica in bondage. In the years 1837-67, some 11,000 arrived to work as wage labourers on the plantations. (See AFRICANS, Indentured.)

Most of the Africans who came to Jamaica were from the Gold Coast eastward to the Niger Delta on the Gulf of Guinea and from West Central Africa. Among such peoples were the Akan (including the Ashanti and Fanti of present-day Ghana – see COROMANTEE), the Aja-Fon from today's Republics of Togo and Benin, the IBO and Calabari of southern Nigeria, the Yoruba (called NAGO) from southwestern Nigeria as well as from the southern Republic of Benin, the CONGO, Ndongo and other ethnic groups from the hinterland of today's Congo Brazzaville, Democratic Republic of Congo, and Angola. Smaller numbers of people from the Upper Guinea coast also came, such as the Temne, MANDINGO, and Limba. Many of the later indentured Africans were Congo, Ibo and Yoruba.

In the process of enslavement and forcible removal from their homelands, the Africans were stripped of virtually all their physical possessions, although they retained knowledge

The slave-traders' greatest fear was of ship board rebelllion

Slave gang at work

of their languages, customs and beliefs.

If they survived the horrors of the journey to the coast, imprisonment in the slave 'castles' and shipment on the MIDDLE PASSAGE, they were faced with a lifetime as the property of another, being sold as soon as possible after arrival. Although some were sold to town dwellers, the majority was destined for the rural plantations on which a variety of crops were grown, with sugar predominant.

On the plantations, the enslaved first went through a process of SEASONING and were forced to become 'creolized' as soon as possible. Attempts were made to suppress many of the traces of their former culture. However, we now know that the enslaved Africans kept many of their traditions alive, usually in great secrecy, and their beliefs, customs and cultural practices can be discerned in present-day Jamaica. Increasingly, researchers are finding more and more of these African 'retentions', that is, what is remembered or retained of the African heritage. This heritage is revealed most strongly in Jamaican speech (see LANGUAGE), the foods grown and eaten, folk beliefs and customs, MUSIC and DANCE, and aspects of family and community life. Specific concentrations of African retentions may still be observed in Jamaica today among the Maroons, KUMINA practitioners and the Nago people (see YORUBA).

The principal agency for the collection and dissemination of information on the African Heritage is the AFRICAN CARIBBEAN INSTITUTE OF JAMAICA.

[Adetugbo 1996, Afroz 1995, Agorsah 1994, Alleyne 1988, Bilby 1985a, Brathwaite 1970, Curtin 1969, GOJ -STATIN 1999a, Hall-Alleyne 1982, 1996, Higman 1976, Morales Padron 1952, Patterson 1973, Warner-Lewis 1996]

AFRICANS, Indentured

Between 1837 and 1867 over 11,000 free Africans arrived in Jamaica to work on the SUGAR estates. Although a few eventually returned home, most were denied the opportunity of return and had to remain to be absorbed into the mainstream of Jamaican life. Most of these immigrants were from Central Africa, the Yoruba and Dahomey coasts, and the Niger Delta. Some of the YORUBA settled in WESTMORELAND Parish and formed the village of Abeokuta. Those in HANOVER Parish contributed to the ETU tradition. Monica Schuler has argued that KUMINA also owes its impetus to these arrivals, many of whom were concentrated in ST THOMAS Parish. The African immigration was part of a general policy of encouraging immigration to the British West Indies in order to provide a reliable labour force for the plantations following EMANCIPATION. (See also CHINESE, GERMAN, INDIAN, IRISH, PORTUGUESE, SCOTS.) The Africans were persons who had been liberated by the BRITISH from slave ships of nations still engaged in the slave trade, Britain having abolished the slave trade in 1807 and slavery in 1834. Some of them came directly from Cuba as *emancipados* (1,388 between 1837-39), but the majority of the liberated Africans were taken to Sierra Leone or St Helena (an island in the southern mid-Atlantic) and it is from these two places that most of the emigrants embarked for Jamaica. Some had been settled in Sierra Leone for some time after being disembarked there from captured slave ships. The first group of these immigrants to reach

Jamaica were 266 landed from the *Hector* in 1841 and they continued to arrive intermittently until 1867, numbering 10,003.

All these various categories of Africans were hired under a system of indenture by which they were transported free of charge but were expected to work for a number of years at a set wage.

At first the Africans showed great reluctance to emigrate, partly because they were fearful that it represented another kind of enslavement. The government representatives had to wage a propaganda campaign to convince them of the attractions of life in Jamaica. Respected members of the local communities, village headmen and the like, were hired as 'delegates' and given a free round trip to Jamaica. They were treated well, loaded with gifts and were expected to 'sell' the virtues of the island to their fellow villagers on their return home. Island products such as enormous YAMS, COCONUTS, etc., were also sent back with them to demonstrate the fruitfulness of the country. On the whole, these efforts were not very successful and the level of immigration remained a disappointment to the British authorities even after they resorted to coercion. In the end, they had far more success in encouraging indentured immigration from India. In the 1860s, the African and Indian immigrants shared the same ships.

What is remarkable is the extreme youthfulness of many of the 'Free Africans' who came. In one case an entire shipload consisted of 85 boys from a government school in Sierra Leone, all under 14 years of age. Because of their age, special provision was made for them. They were placed in selected estates in close proximity to one another, and so ended up in Hanover Parish at Lethe, Copse, Content, Chester Castle, Argyle, and Plum Pen.

The Africans were landed at virtually all the ports of the island and were widely distributed in each parish. However, it was usual for large groups to be taken by each estate owner so that they were concentrated in small pockets. Many of the early arrivals ended up in the PLANTAIN GARDEN RIVER Valley in St Thomas. Among them were persons from the Kru Coast who provided the labour for building the MORANT POINT LIGHTHOUSE.

Among the first set of arrivals too, was a group of 60 MAROONS who came from Sierra Leone, where the Trelawny Town Maroons had ended up, having been transported first to Nova Scotia, Canada in 1796 following the second Maroon War, and from there to Sierra Leone. Some members of this group took the opportunity to return to their homeland.

For the most part, the newly arrived Africans were highly regarded by their employers and were seen as good, steady workers. At first they kept mainly to themselves or communicated with older Africans resident on the island, mixing very little with the CREOLES (Jamaican born). As their indenture ended, many moved off the estates and settled down in their own villages.

One of these villages near BATH, St Thomas, is today called Rhine and was part of Rhine Estate, which was one of several bought at rock-bottom panic prices following the economic crash of 1846 by an enterprising young man named George William GORDON. A Quaker visitor (see FRIENDS) in 1850 visited Rhine estate and found there 40 African labourers, some Congo. They had been released from captured slave ships between one and two years previously. He reported:

'All of them were indentured to G.W. Gordon for three years, on the condition of receiving lodging, food and clothing. They seemed to have found out that their indentures are not binding in law, as they now refuse their food and refuse to work and insist on money wages.'

They seemed to have all been herded together to live – 30 men and 10 women – in one large room, though barracks for them were under construction. The visitor noted that some of them wore no clothing but a blanket, but was assured by the overseer that they all possessed good clothing. It appeared that their strategy was to 'refuse for a time the accustomed portions of food, and the clothing provided by the estate, that they may bring their masters to terms'. He regarded their situation as 'lamentably poor and wretched'.

The visitor found the situation different on HORDLEY and Amity Hall estates in the Plantain Garden River Valley where a large number of Sierra Leone immigrants were employed. Of 100-150 labourers on Amity Hall estate, 80 were Africans. He commented:

'They had been well taught in the mission schools of that colony and can read and write; they are more moral than the creoles, they marry early, live reputably and work industriously. No barracks had been provided for them, as on some other estates, but good cottages, such as the creole laborers build for themselves.'

[Candler 1850, Roberts 1957, Schuler 1980, Thomas 1974]

AGAVE

Called Coratoe, Karato or Maypole, the local species of Agave in Jamaica (*Agave sobolifera*) is highly visible on well drained hillsides from 30-900m though nowadays nowhere as abundant as in the mid-18th century, when Patrick Browne could say: 'There are few plants more common than this in Jamaica.' It is easily identified from its large, succulent, strap-like leaves that are edged with prickles, with a sharp spine ('macca') at each tip. Arranged in a tight spiral at their bases, the leaves will grow up to 2m long and 25cm broad. But the plant's most remarkable feature is its flowering.

The plant is monocarpic, flowering and fruiting only once from each growth, after which it dies. This feature has given Agave its other popular name of 'Century Plant' though the process takes not centuries but decades; the local species is believed to complete its growth and flowering cycle in eight to ten years. The plant uses this time to manufacture and store enough food in its leaves for its one grand effort – a spectacular inflorescence. The central stem will suddenly and rapidly elongate 5-10m in height and send out large golden yellow flower clusters along its length which can be seen from quite a distance, attracting the admiration of humans and the patronage of numerous insects and HUMMINGBIRDS. February to April is the usual flowering time. Instead of fruits and seeds, bulbils are formed on the inflorescence, developing into miniature plants that will eventually fall to the ground where they readily root.

The dried stem is light and strong and was used as the central pole for the once popular MAYPOLE dance. Nowadays the dried inflorescence is sold as a tropical 'CHRISTMAS tree', frequently sprayed silver.

A. sobolifera ('Maypole') is also found in Cayman Brac. *A. sisalana* (from Yucatan) which yields the useful sisal fibre, is found in cultivation.

A. americana and other species were introduced as ornamentals and have escaped. Agave is a large family, the members of which are sometimes confused with the ALOE as well as CACTUS, though they are not related. Agaves are native to the Caribbean and Central and South America.

Like Sisal, the Maypole or Coratoe is an extremely useful plant. The pulp of the thick leaves was formerly used to clean pewter, the soapy juice can be used as a soap and as bleach, the fibre provides thread, ropes and WHIPS, and is used to make handicrafts, and the whole plant is frequently planted out as a live fence. It is also used in folk MEDICINE. The fibres were used by the TAINOS to make ropes, baskets, etc.

[Adams 1971, 1972, Browne 1756, DJE, Long 1774]

AGRICULTURE

Before the newer sectors such as BAUXITE, TOURISM and manufacturing were developed, Jamaica's economy was based almost entirely on agriculture. Although the relative contribution of agriculture has declined, it is still of considerable importance and remains a way of life for large numbers of people. Roughly 50 per cent of Jamaica's population is still rural. Agriculture is also a significant employer of labour; agriculture, forestry and FISHING in 1997 accounting for over one-quarter of the employed labour force.

Jamaica's agricultural production has always been export-oriented, though the production of food for domestic consumption has also been significant. The principal export crops are SUGAR (and by-products molasses and RUM), BANANAS, COCONUTS, COCOA, COFFEE, CITRUS and spices, especially PIMENTO ('allspice') and GINGER and food colouring such as ANATTO. Jamaica also has well developed fishing, livestock, poultry and dairy industries, though production is not enough to meet demand and a great deal of food is now imported. The country is also blessed with a wide variety of root crops (see, e.g. CASSAVA, COCO, YAM) as well as tree crops (see, e.g. ACKEE, AVOCADO, BREADFRUIT, MANGO) though orchard-type cultivation of a few crops to meet export and manufacturing demands is recent. While some export crops are produced on large farms and plantations, the food consumed locally (domestic crops) has remained mainly in the hands of small farmers.

Despite Jamaica's small size, the island exhibits great variety in soil, climate, terrain, and virtually all tropical and sub-tropical crops can be grown. Some temperate crops will thrive in the cool mountain areas. However, the island has fairly limited land space for agriculture, mainly because of its mountainous terrain, over

Agave leaves and flowers

Yam planted on contoured hillside

50 per cent of the total land area lying above 300m. Of the total acreage of 1.08 million ha, less than half is suitable for some kind of agriculture, though the acreage under cultivation is actually less and shows continual decline. The Jamaican small farmer frequently cultivates on hillsides so steep that in many other countries such plots would be regarded as unsuitable for any form of agriculture. Jamaica's rugged topography and steep slopes combined with the intensity of tropical downpours have made soil erosion a serious problem, aggravated in recent years by deforestation.

Although other crops such as indigo (see VERE), COTTON, TOBACCO and ginger were also cultivated for export, sugar remained king from the 17th to the 20th century. Sugar interests had an inordinate influence in determining the course of the island's social and economic development, contributing, some critics have argued, to its under-development.

The post-EMANCIPATION period was marked by the decline of sugar, the break-up of the plantations, the growing diversification of the economy and the introduction of indentured workers (see AFRICAN, CHINESE, INDIAN). They made their own substantial contribution to agriculture, especially in the growing of rice, vegetables and flowers by Chinese and Indians. But the most significant development of that period was the establishment of the small farming class (see FREE VILLAGES). By the 1950s, thousands of small farms (10ha and under) had been created, occupying 38 per cent of the land in agricultural use and providing almost one-half of the total agricultural product.

As the *Farmer's Guide* notes: 'By the beginning of the twentieth century, small farming was an essential part of the Jamaican society. The traditions of the small farmer had become deep and established. Separate cultural practices of coffee, sugar and banana zones began to develop and lifestyles were equally affected. In the yam-growing areas there were traditions such as "digging matches" [see DAY WORK, digging songs, MUSIC]: days when the whole communities worked together to dig yam hills. The men dug, the children pushed the barrels with yam "head" and the women cooked a giant meal.' To this might be added now-vanished community activities such as CORN shelling and ginger peeling or the making of lime kilns (see WHITE LIME).

The life style of the rural dweller, regarded as the backbone of Jamaican society, came to be much studied in books such as Madeline Kerr's *Personality and Conflict in Jamaica* (1952), Edith Clarke's *My Mother Who Fathered Me* (1957), David Edwards' *An Economic Study of Small Farming in Jamaica* (1961), and in other sociological and anthropological works. The rural landscape and the rural way of life have also continued to feed the imagination of artists and writers.

Yet the reality is harsh, especially for those with very small plots of land; subsistence farming is now the preserve of mainly old people. Many of the younger generation show little inclination to be farmers, having witnessed their parents' unrewarding way of life. Younger people tend to leave the farms for urban areas and overseas. Some put their efforts into the quick and lucrative returns from GANJA cultivation, probably Jamaica's most successful agricultural crop, despite prohibition. There is evidence that the face of farming is changing, with many non-farmers now buying property and investing in agricultural enterprises and some young, well-educated farmers turning back to the land. But overall, agricultural productivity shows continual decline.

Since INDEPENDENCE in 1962, there have been efforts to develop a planned economy. But the

Aquaculture

decline in agricultural output and the rapid increase in food imports is an indication of the failure by successive governments either to alter massive structural problems that have handicapped the farming sector over the years or to invest in research to develop new technology. Contradictory policies have veered from an import-substitution approach to an export-oriented approach, to a free market approach that allows the open importation of fresh farm produce in direct competition with local farmers.

As the *Farmer's Guide* puts it: 'Agricultural practice today is an interesting combination of the old, the new and many grades in between. While many farmers still use implements and techniques dating back centuries, mechanical harvesting, grading and packaging have been recently introduced into larger farms, and flowers and foliage are being flown by jet to North America.' In the process, Jamaica has made what has been called 'an uneven transition from the CUTLASS to the computer'.

Twentieth-century agricultural developments have been in export crops such as flowers and tree crops and in developing products aimed at local consumption such as vegetables and the poultry, dairy and PIG industries. A large market exists among expatriate Jamaicans overseas for island produce and culinary by-products such as sauces, drinks and spices, but this is being met only to a limited extent.

Farmers are served by a number of commodity and special interest organizations of which the oldest is the Jamaica Agricultural Society formed in 1895.

Agricultural training in Jamaica is provided at the College of Agriculture, Science and Education (CASE) at Passley Gardens, PORTLAND Parish, and regionally, in the Faculty of Agriculture at the Trinidad campus of the UNIVERSITY OF THE WEST INDIES. Three agricultural schools in rural Jamaica: Elim, Knockalva and Ebony Park, provide agricultural training at a lower level.
[Baccus and Royes 1988, JAS 1954, Jamaica GOJ 1971, GOJ - STATIN 1999a]

AIRPORTS see AVIATION

ALBINO

The albino (defined by *Collins English Dictionary* as 'a person with congenital absence of pigmentation in the skin, eyes and hair') obviously attracts considerable popular attention in Jamaica if names are anything to go by. The DJE lists 39 descriptive terms and a riddle: 'cheap cherry bears cedar'. The riddle, like most of the terms, is derogatory, referring to the fruit of the cedar that resembles a cherry plum but is inedible. One folkloric belief in Jamaica is that albinos are born to women who have engaged in sexual relations during their menses.

Some of the terms used in Jamaica are African, for instance *kwao* and *dundus*, though like many other African terms still in use, e.g. DAY NAMES, they seem to have lost their original meaning. Dundus is derived from Kongo *ndundu*.

Albinos are viewed ambivalently in Africa. In some societies they are regarded as abnormal and therefore expendable while in other societies this abnormality strongly suggests their kinship with the spirit world, with which the colour white is associated. As such, among the Mande, they could be objects of human sacrifice, and among the Kongo their hair was used in sorcery. In other parts of West Africa, albinos are favoured, for instance, by the YORUBA god Obatala as well as Lisa, one of the major gods of the Ewe people. However, to judge from the terms recorded in Jamaica, that high esteem did not travel to the New World or became lost over time.

The arrival on the music scene in the 1980s of Winston Foster, an albino deejay who achieved fame as 'Yellowman' (see DANCEHALL) has certainly helped to create a more favourable image. In literature, the novel *Black Albino* by the MAROON artist and writer Namba Roy (1910-1961) deals with the theme, and in Jean D'Costa's children's book, *Escape to Last Man Peak*, Wuss-wuss, an albino boy, is a pivotal (and positive) character.

The first listing of the word albino in the English language comes from a Jamaican source, Edward Long in 1774, according to the DJE. Long described in unflattering terms a male child born in ST CATHERINE Parish, adding that albinos were called 'Dondos' in central Africa and

'King' Yellowman

were said to be 'educated in the science of priestcraft or witchcraft'.

In earlier times, albinos were exhibited abroad as freaks at circuses and fairs though the word albino was not used. A Jamaican girl was taken to England in 1754 at about the age of five and offered for sale (for 400 guineas) as 'the greatest Phænomenon ever known'. A year after her arrival she was being exhibited at Charing Cross where people paid a shilling a head to see her. In 1788 she was again exhibited at Bartholomew Fair. Named as Mrs Amelia Lewsam (or Newsham) she was described as 'the White Negro Woman' having 'all the features of an Ethiopian, with a flaxen woolly Head, a Skin and Complexion fair as the Alabaster'. Also exhibited was 16-year-old Primrose, 'The Celebrated PIEBALD BOY' born in Jamaica of African parents, as well as a 'beautiful spotted negro boy' taken from his African parents in St Vincent at the age of 15 months and brought to England for exhibition by a travelling showman.
[Balandier 1968, D'Costa 1975, DJE, Fryer 1984, Long 1774, Roy 1961]

ALBION

Place name in ST THOMAS Parish, about 27km from KINGSTON, which recalls a historic estate on the delta of the YALLAHS RIVER about 1.6km off the main highway on the turning to EASINGTON. It gave its name to Albion SUGAR, a light coloured sugar first manufactured here in the 1870s. Albion in the 1880s was Jamaica's leading producer of sugar and RUM, and according to historian Barry Higman 'played an important role in the introduction of new sugar technology'. Like many other estates, Albion found it increasingly difficult to compete with European beet sugar and produced its last crop in 1928, when it was sold to the United Fruit Company and converted to BANANA cultivation.

The 18th century GREAT HOUSE and old factory are now in ruins, though the aqueduct that brought water from the Yallahs River can still be seen. The aqueducts and ruined mill house are listed as historic monuments by the JNHT. Albion was once owned by Simon Taylor, the richest man of his day. (See VALE ROYAL.)
[Cundall 1915, Higman 1988]

ALLEY (or THE ALLEY)

Former capital of the old parish of VERE (now part of CLARENDON Parish), once known as Withywood ('with' pronounced WIS) because of the thick bush of the area in the early days of settlement.

ALLEY CHURCH (St Peter's)

St Peter's Church in ALLEY (CLARENDON Parish) is the third oldest ANGLICAN church in Jamaica, built between 1671-75 as the Parish Church of VERE, which was once a separate parish. The present brick building was erected around 1715 on the old foundation. Gigantic COTTON TREES in the churchyard were, according to legend, already growing when the French Admiral DuCasse attacked in 1694 (see FRENCH invasion). The organ was built in 1847, which makes it one of the oldest in the Commonwealth Caribbean. The church bell was cast in 1857 by Messrs Mears of Whitechapel, London, the same foundry that made 'Big Ben' for the English parliamentary buildings at Westminster. The church has a slate roof, one of the few remaining in Jamaica. Slate – quarried in Wales – was formerly widely used as construction material, since it was brought as ballast in sailing vessels. Almost all the buildings in PORT ROYAL at one time had slate roofs; several in the old Naval Hospital complex still do.

One of the famous rectors of this church was Dr John Wolcot (1738-1819) whose conduct provided the most outrageous example of how lightly the pastorship of a church was taken in the early period of Jamaica's history. Wolcot first came to Jamaica in 1768 with Sir William Trelawny, the new governor who was his kinsman and patron. He was the Trelawnys' doctor and 'grand master of ceremonies' among other posts, but decided that religion would be more lucrative. He returned to England in 1769 and took holy orders and on two successive days was ordained deacon, then priest, by the Bishop of London. He returned to Jamaica in 1770 and was appointed Curate of Vere, a post he held for two years. He actually lived in SPANISH TOWN and deputized some of his church duties, rarely conducting services. While curate of Vere he published a book of poems called *Persian Love Elegies*. This was printed in 1773 and is one of the oldest books printed in Jamaica in the National Library collection. After Wolcot returned to England, he became a well-known satirist, writing under the name 'Peter Pindar'.
[Cundall 1915]

ALLIGATOR see CROCODILE

ALLSPICE see PIMENTO

ALMOND *(Terminalia catappa)*

The almond that grows in Jamaica is a species popularly called Seaside Almond or West Indian

Almond, and its nut is used as a substitute for the almond of commerce. The fleshy fibre outside the nut is also edible. The tree, which grows 5-16m high with spreading branches, is commonly planted for shade. It grows from sea level to 200m and is naturalized in wet areas and near the sea where it tolerates salt spray. A characteristic of this tree is that each leaf turns red before falling, usually a small number on each tree at any one time. The Seaside Almond is a native of SE Asia, N Australia and the Pacific, and was introduced into Jamaica in 1790.
[Adams 1972, NHSJ 1946]

Almond tree and nuts (inset)

ALOE *(Aloe vera)*
Succulent plant, bitter to the taste, known in Jamaica and other islands as Bitter Aloe or Sinkle Bible (*Sinterbibu* in the Dutch islands), believed to be a corruption of another name of the plant, Sempervivum, (from Latin *semper vivens* 'ever living'). Its healing properties are mentioned in the Bible and it is still regarded as a medicinal plant. The jelly-like substance in its leaves is taken internally, being widely regarded as a tonic and laxative, or used externally for burns, cuts and bruises. It provides the commercial product aloin that is used in the pharmaceutical and cosmetics industries for the treatment of skin disorders. In commercial operations, the sap is reduced by evaporation to crystals, whereas in home use, the outer layer of the leaf is peeled to reveal the jelly that is applied or ingested. Aloe is traditionally one of the plants used in embalming; its bitterness makes it a symbol of penitence and suffering. In former times, bitter aloe was rubbed on the mother's breast as a means of weaning infants or on a child's finger to discourage thumb sucking.

Aloe

Aloe originated in southern Africa but has been long established in the New World tropics, where it has been cultivated for its importance in the pharmaceutical industry. As early as 1693, 'Barbados aloes' was offered for sale in London where it was used as a powerful purgative.

In Jamaica, aloe grows from sea level to 100m and is easily grown in containers.
[Adams 1972; Asprey and Thornton 1953-55, Fraser et al. 1990, Robertson 1982, 1990]

ALPHA
A complex of religious and educational institutions in KINGSTON operated by the ROMAN CATHOLIC Sisters of Mercy. Alpha was started in 1880 as an orphanage by three lay sisters, and took its name from 'Alpha Cottage', their 16.8ha site on South Camp Road. They raised funds for their orphanage in various ways; these included selling firewood from the forests then surrounding them, and offering pasturage for a small fee. In 1890 they were joined by Sisters of Mercy from Bermondsy, England. Today, the Sisters of Mercy operate islandwide with mainly Jamaican members, and lay and religious representatives from many countries. While the various institutions at Alpha have played a notable role in Jamaica's cultural and social life, the band of the Alpha Boys' School is especially noted as the cradle for many of Jamaica's finest musicians. (See MUSIC, REGGAE.)
[Osborne 1988]

ALPHABET, Jamaica
Known nowadays only from the written record, what is called the Jamaica Alphabet arose from the oral tradition and was part of a popular

game, played in the following way, according to Martha Warren Beckwith: 'Any number of players sit in a circle. As a letter falls to each player in its order of succession in the alphabet, he must match the letter with an object with the same initial by reciting a verse from some familiar alphabet or inventing one impromptu in the same form. A forfeit is demanded as the penalty for failure.' Players also stood in a circle and played the game to the sound of rhythmic hand clapping. Beckwith published (in 'Folk Games of Jamaica') three alphabets from informants, and one that had been printed in the *Gleaner* as the 'Jamaica Kitchen Alphabet' – 'taken down from the lips of servants in the country'.

Various other written versions of the Jamaica Alphabet exist. Aston W. Gardner, who had a stationery, book selling and printing business and published tourist guides, published the *John Canoe Alphabet* in 1896 and *The Negro Alphabet*, illustrated by Violet Heaven in 1897, as well as a series of postcards with the illustrated rhymes. Samples of the Alphabet have been published in *Jamaica Journal*, 17:3 and 18:1 and a text with Violet Heaven's illustrations as *The Jamaica Alphabet* by Jamrite Publications in 1990.

Although the rhymes seem to have been popular up to at least the early 1920s when Beckwith visited, they do not appear in later collections of Jamaican folklore. Olive Lewin in discussing BRUCKINS party suggests that such rhymes were part of the entertainment segment of those events. Below are two versions, the first from Beckwith, the second from a printed version by Gardner, which is almost identical to one collected by Beckwith in Mandeville.

Jamaicans today would recognize many of the terms in Beckwith's version. ACKEE, bammie (BAMMY), calallue (CALALU), DUMPLING, guzu (CHARM), JACKASS, Pear (AVOCADO), QUASHIE, YAMPI all appear in this Encyclopedia. Puncheon-water (which Beckwith defines as RUM), Tackoomah (ANANSI's son) and fungi (which she does not define) are probably the only exceptions. Fungi is close to what is called 'turn cornmeal' (see CORN). Its characteristic – 'it choke fever' – is puzzling, but the DJE's entry for 'fungee' quotes Moreton (1790): 'For the pains in their stomachs, to eat plenty of homony and fungee.' In the Gardner version, Asoonoo refers to the elephant in ANANSI STORY; for other Jamaican creole terms see entries for DUPPY, JOHN CROW, monkey, Pattoo (PATU) and quattie (MONEY).

Jamaica Alphabet Game

A signify ackee, qualify fish,
B signify bammie, work proper with pear,
C signify callalue, eat very nice,
D stand for dumpling, if it ever tie you 'teet',
E is for elephant, big like Tacoomah,
F is for fungi, it choke fever,
G is for Goozoo, all nigger papa,
H is for Heaven where gran'ma gone,
I is for the pronoun that you must learn,
J is for jackass, plenty go to school,
K is for Katy, – she make me fool,
L is for lawyer, them never walk straight,
M is for money, make you feel first-rate,
N is for Nancy, – that's a girl have a mouth!
O favour C but a little more stout,
P for Puncheon-water, let you fight one another,
Q is for Quashie, Quabina oldest brother,
R is for room, let the best man fool,
S is for sugar, eat all you can,
T is for Thomas, is very unbelieving,
U is for Uncle Jacob, is very deceiving,
W is for women, – follow them you fret,
X is a cross will favour ten,
Y is for yampe, a poor man's friend,
Z is for Zacheus, the smallest of men.
(Beckwith's printed version omitted 'V')

Jamaica Alphabet card

Jamaica Alphabet (Gardner version)
A fe Asoonoo, koo how him tan!
B fe Backra – very bad man!
C fe Puss, him name Mariah,
D fe Duppy, fe him yeye tan like fire.
E fe Eel, live in a Ferry,
F fe Fiddle, play sweet merry.
G fe Governor, live in King's House,
H fe Old Harbour, place poor like a church mouse.
I is a gentleman, very well bred,
J fe John Crow, him have a peel head.
K fe Kalaloo, sinting sweet when it bwoil!
L fe Lizard, fe him tail 'pwoil.
M fe Monkey, koo him face!
N fe Nana, fe him cap trim wid lace.
O fe Oliphant, koo him mout'!
P fe Pattoo, night time him come out.
Q fe Quattie – beg you one Massa, please,
R fe Ratta – tiptoe pon cheese.
S fe Sinake, live in a grass,
T fe Toad, forrad and fas'.
U is me Uncle, him I'm gwine to see,
V fe Vervaine, boil very sweet tea.
W, X, Y - 'top – me figget!
Z fe Zebedee, a men' him net.

[Beckwith 1928, Jamrite Publications 1990, Lewin 1984, Robertson, 1985]

ALUMINA see BAUXITE

AMAZON WOMEN

The Amazons were a legendary nation of women warriors, a myth of the Old World brought to the New World by COLUMBUS and his crew. When they heard from the TAINOS the story of the mythical island of MATININÓ, which was peopled exclusively by women, they took it as corroboration of the ancient myth of Amazon women. The explorers left determined to find them among the islands to the south and when they failed to do so, took the myth with them to the American continent. As time went on, the home of the Amazons was pushed further and further west, Sir Walter Raleigh in 1595 claiming to have found it in Guyana. Though these 'Amazons' were never found, the Europeans pursued them into the middle of the continent of South America, where they found the mighty river that they named the Amazon after the women believed to have their kingdom there.

[Alexander 1920, Morrison 1955]

AMBER

Ritual object, talisman, guzu or CHARM widely used in MYAL and OBEAH for divination. Although an actual amber bead might be employed, 'amba' as used by Jamaican practitioners refers to a variety of magical objects. R.T. Banbury writing in the 19th century, tells us that 'anything through which they look at the obeah either in the ground or skin is called an "amber", the name is not confined strictly to the substance so called', and M.W. Beckwith noted the use of a glass marble. An amber bead along with 'jiggey' which she describes as the seeds of a herb, were the principal 'fetishes' or ritual objects used in curing rituals by the Myalists she met in the COCKPIT COUNTRY in 1924. These objects were obtained by the Myal man after he had danced in the bush, and were used to 'pull' the disease planted in the patient by an obeah-man. Securing and protecting this principal magical object were important elements in ritual practice. The amber, her informants said, should be kept in a thread bag or better still, in RUM, since 'spirits love rum'. Beckwith recorded several Myal songs that referred to the use of the amber.

In using amber, Jamaican practitioners share in a universal practice. The actual substance called amber is the fossilized resin of the sap of ancient pine trees and is one of the oldest talismatic objects known to man, being used for protection against dangers and a prevention and remedy against illness. Partly because of its electrical properties, amber will develop a static charge when rubbed. Pliny, in his *Natural History* (AD 77), mentions Roman matrons wearing amber beads for 'remedial virtues', and in 1942, researchers in England found amber beads being sold as cures for croup, whooping cough and asthma.

[Banbury 1894, Beckwith 1928, Opie 1992]

ANANSI

Jamaican name for the SPIDER (also spelled Anancy). It comes directly from the Twi (West African) name *Ananse*. An Anansi rope is a spider's web, and ANANSI STORIES feature the spider as the chief character. The spider most closely identified with Anansi stories is the common 'house spider', a large brown spider which enters houses and feeds on cockroaches, but doesn't construct a web.

ANANSI STORIES

Many of the folk tales of Jamaica (and other

Caribbean countries) were brought from West Africa and are called Anansi stories (Nansi 'tory) after the spider-hero ANANSI – even when he does not appear in them. (See SPIDER IN FOLKORE.) In Ashanti they are called *Anansesem* (literally, 'words about the spider'). Of course the tales have become 'Jamaicanized' over the centuries, and though much of the old has survived, many new elements and characters have been introduced. Among the old characters are Anansi, his wife Crooky, his son Tacoomah (from the Twi *ntikuma*), and Asunu the elephant.

B'rer or Bra (Brother) Anansi is a trickster hero. In the Jamaican tales, he is sometimes a man (portrayed as short and small) but more often is a spider with human qualities and characteristics, the most outstanding being his greed. Anansi survives by 'working brains', i.e. by cunning, helped by his glibness of speech despite his 'tie-tongue' (lisp) and a falsetto voice. He personifies the qualities of survival and the triumph of the weak over the strong, attributes which the enslaved Africans, torn from their homelands and forced to labour in a foreign land must have found particularly satisfying (see AFRICAN HERITAGE, SLAVERY). If they themselves could not triumph over 'bukra massa' – the white man – their imaginative creation Anansi could triumph over everyone.

Anansi stories were, up to recently, frequently told to children at bedtime. But modern inventions such as electric light, radio, television and the cinema have facilitated competing attractions. The telling of Anansi stories is part of the tradition of African villages where everyone gathered around a fire at night to hear the old tales. In Jamaica, as in Africa, Anansi stories were in the past never told in the daytime. Among adults, they are still told at WAKES and moonlight gatherings.

Song is usually an integral part of the tale, Anansi himself frequently featuring as the composer of songs for the occasion, as fiddler or singer (though from time to time he will find other animal musicians). Several well-known songs (see MUSIC, Folk) have come down through Anansi stories, e.g. 'Wheel O Matilda' or 'Ride through, Ride through the Rocky Road'.

Each story is ended with the words 'Jack Mandora me no choose none', the origin of which is uncertain but which is supposed to mean that the teller does not approve of Anansi's tricks.

Anansi stories provide another point of interest, the etiological or 'folk' explanations of the habits and appearance of certain animals, e.g. 'why Rat lives in a hole' (because he attempted to cut such a caper at a dance that he slid on the floor and split his trousers – to his eternal embarrassment), or 'why Anansi lives in the housetop' (because in several stories that is the only place he can go to escape the consequences of his actions).

Although traditional storytelling has virtually died out, Anansi is still a well-loved (or much derided) folk figure, 'Anancyism' representing clever rascality. The stories are preserved through literature and the stage. Anansi is often a principal character in the popular annual PANTOMIME and the Anansi archetype has inspired a number of writers, such as Andrew Salkey, who has used the character extensively in his fiction and poetry. Anansi tales have been retold by a number of writers, most notably Sir Philip Sherlock and 'Miss Lou' – Louise Bennett, Jamaica's principal folklorist, who has frequently included the spider-hero in her writings and performances. There are also recent collections of Anansi stories from storytellers all over Jamaica by Daryl Dance and Laura Tanna, and older collections by Colman-Smith, Jekyll, and Milne-Home, among others. Accompanying Tanna's collection are audio and video cassettes of local storytellers in action.

[Baxter 1970, Beckwith 1924, Bennett 1979, Dance 1985, Jekyll 1907, Milne-Home 1890, Morris 1986, Patterson 1973, Sherlock 1954, Smith 1905, Tanna 1983a, 1984]

Storyteller 'Miss Adina' Henry

ANATTO, or ANATTA *(Bixa orellana)*

Shrub or small tree, up to 6m high, which for centuries provided Jamaican kitchens with seeds for colouring foodstuffs. The use locally of cooking oil coloured with anatto (or 'natta' as it is more commonly pronounced), seems a thing of the past, but it is still common in Latin American countries.

Commercially, anatto is exported for use in the food and cosmetics industries and is shipped dry or as concentrate. Food colouring is derived from the powdery aril (which is known as the bixen) that is separated from the dry mature seeds and processed into norbixen.

The TAINOS, and virtually all other native peoples of the Caribbean and South America, regarded anatto as one of the sacred trees, a principal source of red body paint – perhaps the reason why the natives of the Americas were first called 'Red Indians' – and it is still used for that purpose by many dwellers of the tropical rain forest. The name anatto is probably an Arawak word; it is also known as *Achiote, Bixa, Bija* or *Roucou*.

A native of South America, anatto was probably brought to the islands by the Tainos, who cultivated it in their gardens, though a European observer in 1662 noted that it grew everywhere in the West Indies without cultivation. Edward Long (1774) recorded it as a common shrub in Jamaica, loving rich soil and shady locations and thriving near rivulets. It grows from 75-450m. The plant has given its name to ANNOTTO BAY in ST MARY Parish.

Anatto usually blooms from June to November and fruits most of the year, the main crop coming from December to the end of May. The attractive single pink flowers are followed by round spiny seed pods which grow in clusters atop the stem. The ripe pods split into halves, revealing about fifty seeds coated with the orange-red dye. The Africans and Europeans learnt how to harvest and use these seeds from the Amerindians.

They would collect large quantities and infuse them in water, allowing the pigment to settle before pouring the water off. This colouring matter would be exposed to the sun until dried, then made into balls or cakes. The Amerindians mixed the dried powder with oil and stored it in a reed joint or gourd for daily use and also to take on journeys; it was an essential part of their daily life, used for anointing their hair and skin. The paint provided protection against insects, the heat and the sun, but like other paints was also used for specific ritual purposes: Taino warriors for instance, painted their entire bodies red when going off to war.

In Long's time, anatto was still prepared and sold in the markets the Amerindian way, in balls or cakes. Africans and Europeans used the powder as colouring matter in food. Long tells us that the powder was regarded as cooling and cordial, and used by the Spaniards in chocolates and soups to heighten flavour and give an agreeable colour. It was also regarded as good for kidney disorders.

Anatto continued to be used in New World kitchens to impart a bright orange colour and delicate flavour to cooking oil, for the enslaved Africans simulating the rich colour of PALM oil, the cooking staple of West Africa.

[Adams 1972, Baccus and Royes 1988, Cabrera 1984, DJE, Karsten 1926, Long 1774, Robertson 1990, Roth 1901]

ANGLICAN

The Church of England was the State church from the time the Protestant English took Jamaica from the Catholic Spaniards in 1655, until the church was disestablished in 1872. (See BRITISH.) Originally called the Church of England, the term Anglican began to be used from the 19th century. During the 1960s, the Church of England in Jamaica was renamed The Anglican Church of Jamaica in the Province of the West Indies.

Jamaica was divided by the English colonists into parishes (the PARISH being an ecclesiastical division) and each was slated to have a Parish church. Nevertheless, the colonists were found to be 'either indifferent or hostile to the authority of the church or they were lax in the practice of their religion'. Few attended church, as Lady Nugent's *Journal* and other records attest. The scarcity of clergymen which led to the appointment of those poorly qualified was a contributing factor, the historian Edward Long declaring of the Jamaican clergy that some were 'much better qualified to be retailers of salt fish, or boatswains to privateers, than ministers of the gospel'. (See, e.g. ALLEY CHURCH, MAY PEN.)

Dominated as it was by the SUGAR planters and English government officials, the church was described as an 'ornamental adjunct to the State' and made little effort to minister to the majority

Anatto fruit cut (inset) to show seeds

C.D. Adams; inset, Fawcett & Rendle

of the population, which consisted of slaves and free blacks and coloured people. (See COLOURED, SLAVERY.) The Church of England's supremacy was challenged from the late 18th century by the arrival of non-conformists (see BAPTISTS, METHODISTS, MISSIONARIES, MORAVIANS, PRESBYTERIANS) and it was naturally hostile to these efforts. Such hostility reached a climax following the slave revolt of 1831-32 (see SHARPE, Samuel) when renegade Anglican clergymen and churchmen formed the COLONIAL CHURCH UNION to destroy non-conformist chapels and drive the missionaries from the island as part of a campaign to prevent EMANCIPATION. Nevertheless, there were always individual Anglican clergymen and benevolent planters who took an interest in the welfare of the slaves.

The Jamaican church was under the jurisdiction of the Bishop of London, which meant that the only clergymen in the island were priests and there was no local structure or control. The appointment of its own bishop in 1825 allowed the local church for the first time to undertake proper administration of its affairs. In later years, the church was revitalized under the leadership of Archbishop Enos Nuttall (1842-1916), and attracted new membership from all ranks of society, becoming involved in the establishment of educational institutions and social welfare activities. It remains a leading significant denomination in Jamaica: in the population census of 1991, 127,331 persons listed themselves as Anglicans.
[Bisnauth 1989; GOJ-STATIN 1999a, JIS 1975]

ANNOTTO BAY
Town in ST MARY Parish which was once an active port on the north side. It derives its name from the ANATTO that probably grew widely in the area or was shipped from here. The 16th century SPANISH settlement of Mellila was probably located near present day Annotto Bay, and Fort George in the hills above is thought to have been built on Spanish foundations. The BAPTIST chapel on the main street is the most interesting structure in the town. It was built in 1894 and is listed as a national monument. The church was designed by the Revd Charles Barron of Scotland. It is believed that he himself cut the glass for all the windows by hand and fitted them in the frames, and decorated the walls of the church with verses of scriptures. The style is unique.
[Sibley 1965, Wright and White 1969]

Annotto Bay Baptist Church

ANT
Although some Jamaican ants do inflict painful bites, they are more of a nuisance than anything else, and there is no record in the island of 'ant invasions' such as plagued other CARIBBEAN islands in the past: Barbados in 1760, Martinique in 1763 and Grenada in 1770. These invaders were 'Sugar ants' which covered everything in their path as they moved along, said to be so numerous that on the road the print of a horse's hoof would appear for a moment or two then immediately be filled in. In Grenada, fire, poison, and other methods of eradicating them were tried with no result, until a HURRICANE ended the invasion. Apparently this pest is not the same as the small 'Sugar ant' which inhabits kitchens today. But some Jamaican ants do have a reputation for fierceness, as the name COROMANTEE given to a big, black stinging ant will attest. Also named after an African group is a red ant called 'CONGO Peggy'.

A rapacious ant known as 'Tom Raffles' (after the man who imported it from Cuba) was introduced in 1762 to prey on young rats but itself became a pest. The names of other ants are fairly descriptive of their behaviour: 'Mad-ants' or 'Crazy-ants' run around but do not bite; the tiny, reddish 'Sugar ants' will go for anything sweet; the tiny, red 'Pepper-ants' sting 'hot', as do 'Fire ants' and 'Pity-me-little'. There are also two types of large black ants that are common.

What are known in Jamaica as 'Duck ants' or 'Wood ants' are wood termites that build huge nests (which end up looking like large black bags) in trees. The nests were once thrown into poultry yards as a treat. Parakeets use Duck ants' nests as their own nests, apparently without disrupting the life of the insects and without being harassed by them.

There are tens of thousands of species of ants in the world grouped under the name

Formicidae. They are related to the bees, wasps, etc. and all belong to the order 'Hymenoptera', membrane-winged insects.

F.G. Cassidy has pointed out that in Jamaica ants are called 'hants' or 'hans', a coincidence of form and meaning between English and the West African language Twi, which calls a black ant *hanii*.

[Bell 1889, Cassidy 1971, DJE, Fraser et al. 1990]

ANTIDOTE CACOON *(Fevillea cordifolia)*
Perennial climbing vine whose fruit yields seeds used in former times as medicine, oil for lamps and – because of their purgative nature – as an antidote when poisoning was suspected. The plant is also known as Sabo, Segra-seed, and Nhandiroba. It grows in wet, hilly woods and the small pale flowers give way to a shiny green fruit like a small CALABASH with a circular black line around it. The seed kernels yield oil formerly used in lamps. Edward Long tells us that for other purposes the seeds were dried and grated and infused in RUM or other spirits. Taken in small doses 'it opens the body and stimulates the appetite'. The grated nut is also used as a plaster for wounds and an emetic. The plant is native to continental tropical America and the CARIBBEAN.

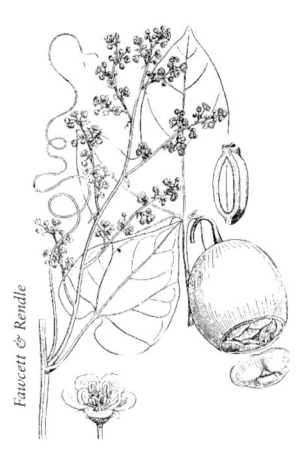

Antidote Cacoon vine and flower, fruit and seed

[Adams 19723, Asprey and Thornton 1953-55, Beckwith 1928, DJE, Long 1774]

ANTILLES
Name given to the CARIBBEAN archipelago by COLUMBUS; another example of an Old World myth brought to the New World. The original island of Antillia was a mythical island located to the west of (the equally mythical) Atlantis. Columbus applied the name in plural form (*Las Antillas*) to the archipelago of islands that enclose the Caribbean sea. The 'Greater Antilles' consists of the four large mountainous islands to the north: Cuba, Hispaniola, Jamaica and Puerto Rico; the 'Lesser Antilles' refers to the islands to the east and south of these. In the English-speaking islands, the terms have never been as widely used as 'Caribbean' or WEST INDIES.

[Jobes 1961, Morrison 1955]

APPLE
While the familiar apple of more northern latitudes does not thrive in Jamaica, there are seven or eight edible 'apples' to choose from, as well as a few inedible ones (see, e.g. MANCHINEEL). The edible apples are of varied origins, flavours and appearances, the most popular being OTAHEITE, STARAPPLE and CUSTARD APPLE, the latter a member of the Annona family which includes SWEET SOP (also known as Sugar Apple) and SOURSOP. Less well known is the Mammee Apple (*Mammea americana*) which bears between June and August an edible thick-skinned brownish fruit on a tree 8-18m high. Crab Apple (*Ziziphus mauritiana*) is probably better known by its other name of Coolie Plum – a fleshy, brownish orange fruit that appears September to December. The prickly, drooping branches help to identify this small tree.

Rose Apple (*Syzygium jambos*) is not often seen in the markets, but grows wild along rivers and streams, the low bushy tree bearing throughout the year a pale yellow egg-shaped fruit that is piercingly sweet and highly scented (and therefore objectionable to some). Its pom-pom like flowers, yellowish white, mark it as a close relative of Otaheite. A native of the East Indies, Rose Apple was introduced in 1762 by Zachary Bayly, and was found useful not so much for its fruit as for its value as a windbreak in hill COFFEE plantations, and in binding the soil on hilly slopes.

The attractive flowers of Golden Apple (*Passiflora laurifolia*) mark it as a member of the PASSION FRUIT family. It is closely related to the Sweet Cup, which it resembles, but with a less hard shell. The golden egg-shaped fruit encloses a sweet jelly-like substance filled with small black seeds, all of which can be eaten as is, or made into a drink with milk and sugar (or sweetened condensed milk) and flavourings. Golden Apple grows on a vine in hilly districts. It is a native of tropical South America and the West Indies.

The most fascinating – and rarest – is the plum-coloured Velvet Apple (*Diospyros discolor*) whose lush ripe fruit can often be seen fallen beneath the tree in the upper section of CASTLETON GARDENS. An introduction, this apple is also known as the Philippine persimmon, and is edible, though not widely known.

Since the apples of more northern latitudes (known in Jamaica as 'American apple', in Barbados as 'English apple') do not thrive in the Caribbean, they were once regarded as rare and special imports sold as a treat only at Christmas.

Today, such apples are commonly sold in supermarkets and even local fruit stands, now competing with home-grown 'apples'.
[Adams 1972, DJE, Eyre 1966]

APPRENTICESHIP SYSTEM

What was called the Apprenticeship System was a transitional period for the slaves of the British West Indies (see SLAVERY) who were set free on 1 August 1834 under the Imperial Abolition Act, but did not achieve full freedom until 1838 in most of the colonies (see EMANCIPATION).

The Act made provision for a period of apprenticeship before 'full free', whereby the former slave was required to labour for his or her former owner for 40½ hours a week without wages; payment for work after that was to be negotiated. Praedials, those directly involved in production on the estates, were to be apprenticed for six years, non-praedials for four. Children under six years (and those born after 1 August 1834) were granted unconditional freedom and could only be employed if their mothers agreed. Adults could purchase their own freedom before the end of the apprenticeship or could be manumitted (legally freed) by their masters. Disputes at the workplace were to be settled by a newly created stipendiary magistracy.

However, the system failed to work and it was terminated after four years, having been characterized by suspicion and misunderstanding on both sides, and serious abuses. Many apprentices were to bear the brunt of their master's wrath at the change in the system, experiencing much more punishment than during slavery; the TREADMILL, introduced as a humane method of punishment, was merely added to other tortures in the workhouses, as the slave prisons were called. Publicity in England regarding some of the more notorious cases helped to speed up the termination of the system.

The planter-dominated Jamaica Assembly was the first to enact the Emancipation Law but they did so unwillingly. Conflicts arose over wages, rents, hours of work and access to PROVISION GROUNDS. Many of the workers continued to agitate for better treatment or simply quit the plantations. (See FREE VILLAGES.) The period saw the beginning of efforts to import labour for the estates. (See AFRICANS, indentured; CHINESE, GERMAN, INDIAN, IRISH, PORTUGUESE, SCOTS.)
[Wilmot 1984]

APRIL FOOL'S DAY

Jamaican schoolchildren are used to taking part in this widely celebrated day by playing jokes on unsuspecting people, though perhaps with no knowledge of its true significance. April is derived from the Latin *aperire* 'to open', and was so-called because it was the month (in northern latitudes) for planting, when the earth opens.

The first of April was celebrated as All Fool's or April Fool's Day when people were given licence to act foolishly. It is practised in other English speaking lands, much of Western Europe and India and remains 'one of the most flourishing of all BRITISH customs'. Popular jokes include sending 'the fool' for imaginary objects such as left-handed screwdrivers or 'sending the fool a little further' by giving him or her a note to deliver to someone which says precisely that. The recipient then dispatches the fool on another fruitless errand, and so it goes. In Scotland it is called 'Hunting the Gowk' (Cuckoo). The news media sometimes get involved in April Fool's pranks and hoaxes. One of the rules is that all foolery should cease by midday.
[Jobes 1961, Kightley 1986]

AQUACULTURE see FISH FARMING

ARAWAK 'INDIANS'

The aboriginal people who inhabited the CARIBBEAN islands when COLUMBUS arrived are commonly referred to as 'Arawaks' and 'Caribs', though we now know that the cultures (and languages) that developed on the islands were different from those of the mainland groups from which both people came. This book follows the now accepted practice of referring to the people of Arawak stock who created their own society in the islands as the TAINOS.

The word Arawak most correctly describes a language group –

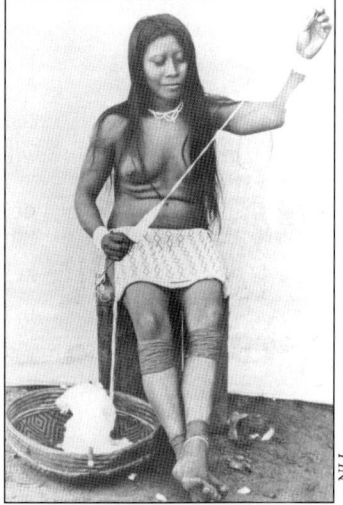

Arawak Woman (Guyana)

the Arawakan-speaking people of northern South America, i.e. Venezuela, the Guianas and Brazil, from whom the islanders descended. Those closest to the island Caribbean refer to themselves most commonly as the *loko* or *lokono*, meaning 'the people', while their Caribbean relatives in the Greater ANTILLES referred to themselves to Columbus as *taíno*, meaning 'good person' or 'good people'. The Tainos of the Bahamian archipelago called themselves the *lokono kairi* – corrupted by the Spaniards to *Lucayano* or *Lucayo*, meaning: 'the people of the islands'. Ironically, the 'Island CARIB' of the Eastern Caribbean (*Kalina, Kaliban* as described by the Taino) spoke (and still speak) an Arawakan language, while the 'Mainland Carib' spoke a 'Cariban' language. In Trinidad, there were representatives of both groups at the time of the contact.

The people Columbus encountered in the New World came to be called 'Indians' because on his arrival in the Caribbean Columbus thought that he had reached the Indies. In this book, the term INDIAN is used only in reference to those people who came to the Caribbean in the 19th and 20th centuries from the Indian subcontinent; the indigenous people of the Caribbean and the rest of the Americas are referred to as 'Amerindian' throughout.

[G.A. Aarons, personal communication; Rouse 1992]

ARAWAK MUSEUM see TAINO MUSEUM

ARCHITECTURE see GREAT HOUSE

ARCHIVES

The Jamaica Archives and Records Department, SPANISH TOWN, contains the largest collection of historical records in the English-speaking Caribbean. It is the government institution responsible for preserving for posterity archival official and other records, and making them available to researchers. It preserves all government documents and papers no longer in current use by the various departments, as well as non-official but significant historic documents. Among examples of non-official records are estate records – such as those of WORTHY PARK – and records of some religious denominations such as ANGLICANS and METHODISTS. There are also records of some individuals and organizations.

Among the fascinating documents in the Archives, according to the former government archivist, Clinton Black, 'are records relating to the early settlers, to BUCCANEERS, pirates, admirals, generals and governors, and to ordinary people as well. Here are documents signed by signatories of the Declaration of American Independence, documents signed by George Washington, Louis XVI, Toussaint L'Ouverture, Queen Victoria, Queen Elizabeth II and Haile Selassie. Here may be seen the marriage record of Annee Palmer the "White Witch" of ROSE HALL, a handbill with precautions to be taken against CHOLERA and the Proclamation of INDEPENDENCE which confirmed Jamaica's sovereignty in 1962'.

The Government Records Centre in Kingston provides storage for temporary, official records, and offers consultancy services and training in records and information management for the public sector.

Records of official documents and certificates, e.g. births, deaths, wills, etc., are kept at the Registrar General's Department, now located at Twickenham Park, east of the old capital, Spanish Town.

[Black 1968, Robertson 1959]

ARCHWAY

A ceremonial archway of PALM fronds crossed at the top, often decorated with flowers, used to be a common feature of country WEDDINGS and other celebrations, providing entrance to the YARD or to the BAMBOO booth that is usually erected to house the affair. Regarded by many as a purely decorative feature, the ceremonial archway also serves to form a protective barrier against evil spirits, palm fronds being regarded as especially efficacious for this purpose in various cultures. Hindus and Buddhists erect demon-repelling ceremonial archways of crossed palm fronds, sometimes across roadways. Such archways are also common in West Africa as a protective device at religious ceremonial sites, shrines, etc.

That some of the ritual function of such archways was retained in Jamaica is suggested by this description of a wedding in ST MARY Parish attended by the American anthropologist Zora Neale Hurston in the 1930s: 'Just around a bend in the road we came to an arch woven of palm fronds before a gate. There were other arches of the same leading back to a booth constructed in the same manner.' She noticed that three women 'with elaborate cakes upon their heads were dancing under the arch at the gate. The cakes were of many layers and one of the cakes was decorated with a veil. The cake-bearers danced and turned under the arch, and turned and danced and sang with the others something about "Let the stranger in".' This continued until one of the elderly women present touched one of the dancers. 'Then the one who was touched whirled around gently, went inside the yard and on into the house. Another was touched and she went in and then the third.'

Nowadays, archways are sometimes constructed around balmyards (see BALM) and people entering are required to spin counter-clockwise as they pass under, presumably to deflect evil forces.

[Hurston 1938, Leach and Fried 1972, Parrinder 1961]

AREITO

Communal ceremony performed by the TAINOS to mark the great events of their lives. Areitos were held to mark individual rites of passage. These included birth, first cutting of hair, initiation or puberty rites, marriage and death; curing rituals for the sick; national crisis events such as going to war, ceremonial activities such as first clearing of land, building of CANOES, the making of a chief or CACIQUE. Through areitos the people also prayed for rain and the growth of crops. The size of these ceremonies varied, the biggest being held annually in honour of the ZEMI of Yuca, the staff of life (see CASSAVA, YÚCAHU).

The areito consisted of MUSIC, DANCE and ritual in which special songs (called areitos) played an important part. These songs were part of the memorized oral tradition of the Tainos which recorded their histories, origins, and the myths of their gods, and it was part of the duties of the caciques (who presided over the ceremonies) to learn them in childhood. There seem to have been two categories of these songs, some so sacred they were forbidden to women, children and commoners; the others were sung at the great festivals with all present. They served as laws, when sung to a sacred drum called a *mayohabo*, a large slit drum made of a hollowed tree trunk turned on its side. It was said that when this instrument was played, it would be heard 8km away. (It was also the drum played at curing rituals.) The chiefs or nobles would lead the ritual dances that accompanied the songs, each song-dance lasting several hours at least. They dealt with warfare, mourning, love, the power of the zemis, and the history and deeds of the ancestors.

A European's description of an areito ceremony held in the post-conquest period in the middle of the 16th century has come down to us. He described how the ceremony (to Yúcahu) was attended by all the people. The zemis were elaborately decorated. The priests arranged themselves around the cacique, who sat at the entrance with a drum by his side. The men came painted (red, black, blue, etc.) covered with branches and garlands of flowers or feathers and SHELLS, wearing shell bracelets and little shells on their arms, and rattles on their feet. The women arrived naked and unpainted (if unmarried) or wearing breechcloths if married; all wore rattles. They approached dancing and singing to the sound of shells. The cacique saluted them with his drum. Entering the temple they vomited, using a small spatula (see VOMITING, Ritual). They seated themselves tailor fashion and prayed with a low voice. Then a large number of women approached bearing baskets of cassava cakes on their heads, and flowers and herbs. They formed a circle and prayed and chanted songs in praise of the zemi. All rose in response at the end. The tone changed, and they sang another song in praise of the cacique, after which they offered bread to the zemi, kneeling. The priest took the bread, blessed it and shared it out, each person taking a piece home to preserve it until the next festival, as protection against accidents.

[Alexander 1920, Arrom 1975, 1990, Fewkes 1907, Lovén 1935, Radin 1942, Rouse 1992, Steward 1948]

ARROWROOT *(Maranta arundinacea)*

Herbaceous perennial whose underground stem or rhizome was once commonly grown in Jamaica for its starch. The plant, which grows to about 1m, originated in tropical South America and was taken to the CARIBBEAN by pre-Columbian populations. The earliest uses of arrowroot seem to have been religious and medicinal, being highly regarded as a poison antidote. Its name is supposedly derived from its use in curing wounds inflicted by poison arrows. By the 18th century it was an important plantation food, especially as a thickener and a substitute for other starches. In the 19th century it was exported as a starch, for the most part produced by small farmers.

Arrowroot is nowadays used mainly as a food for babies and invalids, and a thickener for soups and sauces.

In Jamaican folk MEDICINE, a paste made from the water mixed with starch is applied to cuts, sores or pimples. In manufacturing, it has been used as an ingredient in face powder and glue and in the manufacture of computer paper.

[Asprey and Thornton 1953-55, Beckwith 1928, Handler 1971, Lovén 1935, Robertson 1982, 1990]

ART

The beginnings of what may be called modern Jamaican art date only from the 1930s, yet the speed and scope of this movement and its subsequent development are extraordinary. Jamaica by the 1980s not only had a fine National Gallery, but an outstanding privately-owned gallery at A.D. Scott's Olympia Art Centre and many smaller commercial galleries. Patronage by the commercial sector put art in public spaces such as banks and corporate offices. There was a growing number of private collectors. A well-established School of Art existed, and a public that was becoming steadily more knowledgeable and appreciative of Jamaican art. For a while, Jamaican artists could make a living from their art. By the late 1990s, however, the fortunes of the art world had come to reflect the general economic condition of the island as well as governmental attitudes and support (or lack of it) for the arts. Yet up-and-coming artists have the privilege of building on what might be called the Jamaican art tradition. Unlike earlier artists who – in the words of Dr David Boxer – had 'no living tradition of their own', yet 'were able to provide the birth of a true movement – a true "school" of art, that is now perhaps unrivalled in the entire CARIBBEAN'.

The First Decades The creative explosion of the 1930s coincided with the political and social ferment of the times; this in turn contributed to the development of an indigenous iconography and gave the movement its energy and forward momentum. Like the writers (see LITERATURE), the artists felt that they had a significant role to play in the process of decolonization and the creation of a national identity. Jamaican art in the succeeding decades also owed its dynamism to the simultaneous development of what might be called two schools, distinct and yet interdependent. One was that of the trained 'mainstream' artists. The other was that of the self-taught, visionary artists whose

John Dunkley – 'Banana Plantation', c. 1945

David Miller Sr polishes head by David Miller Jr

dreams were ignited by Marcus GARVEY, or fuelled by popular religions such as REVIVAL and RASTAFARI, and who were to gain recognition in the 1980s as the Intuitives. On the international scene, it is these Intuitive artists who have attracted the widest attention.

Yet the vigour of the early mainstream artists also came from their identification with the black working class that was throwing off its chains politically (see BUSTAMANTE, FROME, MANLEY, TRADE UNIONS). The catalyst for the creation of an art movement in the twenties and the thirties was Edna Manley (1900-1987), who had married one of the architects of political decolonization, Norman Manley. Born in England of a Jamaican mother and an English father, and trained at English art schools, Edna Manley herself was to create a work of sculpture now regarded as the icon of that early movement, 'Negro Aroused' (1935), which is in the National Gallery of Jamaica. It was to be the first of a series of explicitly political carvings that celebrated the black peasantry and working class. Edna Manley's talents and training in three-dimensional art forms influenced, and in turn was influenced by, contemporary self-taught Jamaican sculptors. Art historian Veerle Poupeye has noted: 'The dominance of sculpture and specifically, woodcarving in early modern Jamaican art is exceptional, even in the Caribbean context, and may be attributed to the revival of the African traditions in Jamaican culture that accompanied cultural nationalism.'

Apart from Manley's own extraordinary series

Henry Daley, by Vera Alabaster   *Albert Huie*   *Ralph Campbell*   *Edna Manley*

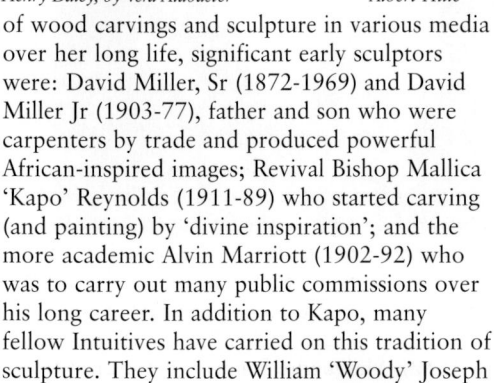

of wood carvings and sculpture in various media over her long life, significant early sculptors were: David Miller, Sr (1872-1969) and David Miller Jr (1903-77), father and son who were carpenters by trade and produced powerful African-inspired images; Revival Bishop Mallica 'Kapo' Reynolds (1911-89) who started carving (and painting) by 'divine inspiration'; and the more academic Alvin Marriott (1902-92) who was to carry out many public commissions over his long career. In addition to Kapo, many fellow Intuitives have carried on this tradition of sculpture. They include William 'Woody' Joseph

Edna Manley – 'Negro Aroused', 1935

(1919-98) and Everald Brown (1919-2002), better known for his paintings but also the creator in wood of carvings and of exquisitely made and decorated musical instruments such as his 'dove harps'. Two noted Jamaican sculptors who spent most of their lives in England should also be mentioned: the MAROON Namba Roy (1910-61); and Ronald Moody (1900-84),

whose distinguished work features in leading British art galleries and collections and is renowned internationally. Several fine sculptors also developed in the later period, among them Christopher Gonzalez (b 1943) and Winston Patrick (b 1946).

But the majority of the early artists were painters, several of them students at the art classes that Edna Manley started in 1940 for a small group of adults at the Junior Centre of the INSTITUTE OF JAMAICA. When the classes outgrew this space, the Jamaica School of Art and Crafts was established, becoming in 1956 a full time institution (and now a part of the EDNA MANLEY COLLEGE). Artists associated with these early beginnings who achieved prominence included Henry Daley (1919-51), Albert Huie (b 1920), Ralph Campbell (1921-85) and David Pottinger, (b 1911) a painter of the downtown Kingston scene. Other key artists of this early period who developed outside the Institute group included: John Dunkley (1891-1947), who worked independently and left a small but highly significant body of works; Gloria Escoffery (1923-2002) who went on to immortalize her adopted Parish of ST ANN and its inhabitants, and Carl Abrahams (b 1913), one of the towering figures of Jamaican art.

Post-Independence   A few of these early artists received training in English art schools. The important figures of the post-INDEPENDENCE art

Karl Parboosingh   *'Barrington' (Watson), self-portrait*

Gloria Escoffery *Colin Garland* *Dawn Scott* *Laura Facey*

movement were trained abroad, in Europe and North America, and were to bring an internationalist and at times a more iconoclastic vision to their work. They included Barrington Watson (b 1931), Eugene Hyde (1931-1980) and Karl Parboosingh (1923-1975) who formed the Contemporary Jamaican Artists Association in 1964; Alexander Cooper (b 1934), Karl 'Jerry' Craig (b 1936), Osmond Watson (b 1934) – who continued to explore his African heritage in both sculpture and painting, George Rodney (b 1936), Milton George (b 1939), Hope Brooks (b 1944), Judy Ann MacMillan (b 1945), David Boxer (b 1946), Kofi Kayiga (b 1943) and Cecil Cooper (b 1946) to name a few.

Christopher Gonzalez, self-portrait

A large number of young artists have since emerged, many like those of the 1930s using their gifts to wrestle with contemporary political issues such as race, poverty, neo-colonialism, and social injustices. Prominent among a group that emerged in the 1980s working in neo-expressionist style but with a 'black nationalist perspective' are Omari Ra ('African', formerly known as Robert Cookhorne b 1960) and Stanford Watson (b 1959). Like earlier artists such as Laura Facey (b 1954), Margaret Chen (b 1951) and Eric Cadien (1954-1993) they received their early training at the Jamaica School of Art which Poupeye describes as 'the hub of the Jamaican art world' under Karl Craig as principal in the early seventies. This is not to suggest that all Jamaica's artists have expressed their vision in a nationalist/political context. Hope Brooks, Milton Harley and Margaret Chen, for instance, are three influential artists who work in a predominantly abstract mode.

Among the numerous fine artists working in the closing decades of the 20th century, a few of the outstanding ones not so far mentioned are: Stafford Schliefer (b 1939), Judith Salmon (b 1952), Marguerite Stanigar (b 1952), Petrona Morrison (b 1954), Roberta Stoddart (b 1963), Nicholas Morris (b 1967), Anna Henriques (b 1967), and Charles Campbell (b 1970).

Albert Chong (b 1958) who lives in the USA but has intermittently worked and exhibited in Jamaica is only one of several contemporary internationally successful artists of Jamaican ancestry. Others include Keith Morrison (b 1942), Peter Wayne Lewis (b 1943), Nari Ward (b 1963) in the USA, and Eugene Palmer (b 1955) in England. At the same time, a significant contributor to the dynamism and eclectic nature of Jamaican art over the years has been the presence of many artists born elsewhere who have made the island their home.

Carl Abrahams, self-portrait

These include artists such as Michael Lester (1906-1972), Seya Parboosingh (b 1925), Susan Alexander (b 1929), Jonna Brasch (b 1930), Valerie Bloomfield Ambrose (b 1935), Colin Garland (b 1935), Rex Dixon (b 1939), Tina Matkovic Spiro (b 1943), Graham Davis (b 1944), Samere Tansley (b 1944), June Bellew (b 1945), Fitz Harrack (b 1945), Prudence Lovell (b 1949), Rachel Fearing (b 1949), Susan Shirley (b 1950). Women artists are prominent among them. On the whole, women came

Milton George (L) and Stanford Watson

strongly to the fore in the seventies, part of a process that was also occurring in literature and other fields, and has continued.

The Intuitives The art scene was enlivened in the 1980s by the institutional and public recognition of the Intuitives as a distinctive group of artists, mainly due to the key exhibition called 'The Intuitive Eye' mounted by David Boxer at the National Gallery in 1979. In addition to Kapo and Brother Brown, who were already prominent, many other self-taught, visionary artists gained their first exposure or greater recognition at that time, including Gaston Tabois (b 1931) Ras Dizzy (b 1930), William 'Woody' Joseph (1919-1998), Sydney McLaren (1895-1979), Leonard Daley (b 1930), Albert Artwell (b 1941), John 'Doc' Williamson (b 1911); their ranks were later swelled by recognition of Allan 'Zion' Johnson (1930-2001), William Rhule (b 1956) and Errol McKenzie (b 1954).

In justifying his choice of the term 'intuitive' over 'primitive', 'naïve' or 'folk art' to describe the work of the Jamaicans, David Boxer noted in the catalogue to 'The Intuitive Eye' exhibition: 'It is a difficult art to characterize, but there are certain elements that bind these works and their creators together. These artists paint, or sculpt intuitively. They are not guided by fashions. Their vision is pure and sincere, untarnished by art theories and philosophies, principles, and movements. They are for the most part, self-taught. Their visions as released through paint or wood, are unmediated expressions of their individual relationships with the world around them – and the worlds within. Some of them – Kapo, Everald Brown, William Joseph in particular – reveal as well a capacity for reaching into the depths of the sub-conscious to rekindle century-old traditions, and to pluck out images as elemental and vital as those of their African fathers.'

Allan 'Zion' Johnson

Other Art Forms Another art form based on indigenous traditions which has developed and won acceptance is that of ceramics, spearheaded almost singlehandedly by one man, Cecil Baugh (b 1908). Baugh learnt his craft at an early age from Jamaican traditional potters (see YABBA) and went on to explore and develop on his own an extensive knowledge of Jamaican clays and

William 'Woody' Joseph and work

glazes. He later studied with the English master potter Bernard Leach, and returned to Jamaica to continue his own explorations and to pass on his knowledge at the Jamaica School of Art, all the while lifting pottery to an art form. Many of the fine Jamaican potters today acknowledge their debt to Baugh, among them Norma Harrack (b 1947), Gene Pearson (b 1946), and the many others featured in Tanna and Baugh, 1999.

Likewise, much of the work of photographers in Jamaica in recent times may be placed in the category of art, though at the time of writing there is no gallery dedicated to photography. Evidence of the long tradition of this art form on the island may be found in the extensive photographic collection from the 19th century onwards in the National Library.

There have been a few practitioners of fibre art, the most noted being Dawn Scott, (b 1951) acknowledged for her outstanding batik paintings (among other art) and Sharon Chacko (b 1950).

Also prominent in the last decades of the 20th century is Yard or Street Art, seemingly spontaneous mural compositions that enliven city streets in poverty-stricken neighbourhoods, as well as a more decorative style of painting to be seen in city and country bars and other public places. A specific style of RASTAFARIAN art also emerged, some of it expressed in the paintings and sculpture of the leading Intuitives, but also in the pencil portraits (reproduced and sold as prints) of artists like Ras Daniel Heartman, who might not be exhibited in galleries but who provide the only art work found in many a home.

Cecil Baugh

The National Gallery

The National Gallery was established in 1974, based on about 200 presentable paintings and thirty sculptures in the Institute of Jamaica collection. Under the direction of its first curator/director, the artist and art historian Dr David Boxer, the Gallery has helped to develop an historical framework for viewing Jamaican art and, more than any other institution, has contributed to the art education of the general Jamaican public.

The Gallery's permanent collection provides a brief historical tour of the art movement. It also includes – on permanent view – the Edna Manley Galleries, the Kapo Collection, the Cecil Baugh Ceramic Gallery, and the A.D. Scott Collection. The National Gallery has a continuous roster of temporary exhibitions, some from abroad and some thematic. Once a year it opens its doors to all Jamaican artists and mounts the mammoth Annual National Exhibition.

National Gallery of Jamaica

Portrait by Ras Daniel Heartman

Another public collection is the sculpture park established in 1999 at the UNIVERSITY OF TECHNOLOGY. The UNIVERSITY OF THE WEST INDIES, Mona, also has a fine collection of Jamaican and Caribbean art, though these works are scattered around the campus and not grouped for public viewing.

The British Tradition The development of Jamaican art in the 20th century is especially remarkable, given the stultified, Eurocentric nature of the island's culture, steeped as it was in the very narrow, hierarchical racial and class structures which existed under colonialism and SLAVERY. In his *Journal*, Monk Lewis (see HORDLEY) mocks his slave's attempt to create a portrait of Massa, saying that the other slaves admired the work but that it bore no resemblance to anything human. Such art as existed was, like much of the literature, a pale imitation of the European. The birthpangs of Jamaican art were not easy, nor were they predictable.

David Boxer

Teachers noted that for years, Jamaican children drew best what they saw in books but somehow could not draw what they saw before their eyes every day. Trained in an imitative tradition of European art, early 20th century Jamaican artists found themselves hemmed in by unhelpful techniques based on concepts of light, landscape, skin-tones and anatomy all foreign to Jamaica: as portraitist Judy Macmillan explains, the underlying tones for portraying black and brown skin-tone differ utterly from those useful

A new generation, L-R: Naÿr, Stanford Watson, Paul Smith, Jeffrey Cameron, Cheryl Phillips, Clinton Pink, Andy Jefferson, Cheryl Daley-Champagnie, Walford Campbell, Michael Layne, Anna Henriques, Sherida Levy

Cecil Baugh – stoneware pot, with zirconium trailed decoration over a shale glaze from Hardwar Gap, 1978. Peter King Collection

Philip Wickstead – 'Richard and Jane Pusey and servant', 1775

to Rubens. Not until the social and economic ferment beginning in the 1920s did Jamaicans begin to discover that their art forms could and should be used to celebrate themselves. Even so, the artists were way ahead of the general population, for resistance continued for a long time in those quarters that saw art that rejected the European academy as sacrilege. Such resistance reflected the severance from their roots experienced by generations of Jamaicans, for little outside of pottery and a few carvings remained of the magnificent art of the TAINOS or of African-Jamaican artists which would have shown that this earlier art too was a celebration of the indigenous. All that Jamaicans knew of 'art' were the monumental English sculpture in churches, graveyards and public squares, illustrations in books, and the paintings of itinerant foreign artists who left behind exquisite views of Jamaican GREAT HOUSES and landscapes commissioned by the local plantocracy. The works of such artists as J.B. Kidd (1808-1889), James Hakewill (1778-1834), Philip Wickstead (active in Jamaica 1780s-1790s), George Robertson (1748-1788) and Isaac Mendes Belisario (1795-1849) is still treasured today (and much reproduced), Belisario especially leaving behind the best known images we have of long-established, Africa-rooted festival arts such as JONKONNU. All this work can now be viewed as part of a historical continuum. Nevertheless, European art served Caribbean art well.

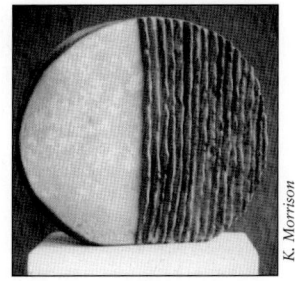

Norma Harrack – 'Circular Form', 1981

Publications Up to the time of writing, there is no single comprehensive publication on Jamaican art. Aspects of this art have been documented and discussed in the few publications cited below, in the many articles over the years in *Jamaica Journal* and the short-lived *Arts Jamaica*, and in the catalogues faithfully produced to accompany every exhibition held at the National Gallery, some with extensive essays. (Poupeye 1995 lists all publications up to that date.)

[Boxer 1990, Boxer and Poupeye 1998, Lewis 1972, Poupeye 1995, 1998, Straw and Robinson 1990, Tanna and Baugh 1999, Walmsley 1992]

ART, School of
see EDNA MANLEY COLLEGE

ASH WEDNESDAY
Religious holiday observed in Jamaica as a public holiday. Since the 6th century, Ash Wednesday has been observed in the Christian church as the first day of Lent. The celebration was originally connected with public penance, the name coming from the practice of the priest placing ashes in the form of a cross on the foreheads of worshippers with a verbal reminder of man's mortality: 'Dust thou art, and to dust thou shalt return.' The ashes came from burning the palms used in the previous PALM SUNDAY. The first day of Lent signifies the beginning of a period of penance and culminates in the EASTER celebrations on Sunday when Christ arose; thus the choice of Sunday as the day of worship for the majority of Christian religions.

ATABEYRA
One of the 12 major ZEMIS of the TAINOS, and the female fertility symbol. She had many other names, but PANÉ, the chronicler, tells us that, *Attabey* means 'first in being'. In Jamaica her name was recorded as Atabex, Mother of God, and the noted mythologist Joseph Campbell identifies her as Mother of the High God (YÚCAHU), and also as Water Mother and sister

Petroglyph at the Taino site of Caguana, Puerto Rico

of Guacar, the Moon. As such she is identified with many South American legends regarding the Moon and the Water Mother, and is associated with fresh water in rivers and ponds. Atabeyra is often represented as a woman giving birth (squatting figure) and was prayed to by women in childbirth.

[Arrom 1990, Campbell 1989, Morales Padron 1952, Stevens-Arroyo 1988]

ATHLETICS

Jamaica's prominence in international athletics is completely out of proportion to its size. For instance, at the Seoul Olympics in 1988, Jamaica was the only country other than West Germany to make all four relay finals for men and women.

At the Sydney 2000 Olympics, Jamaica won seven medals: Silver – Lorraine Graham (400m flat); Deon Hemmings (400m hurdles; women's 4x100m relay; women's 4x400m relay). Bronze – Tanya Lawrence (100m); Gregory Haughton (400m); men's 4x400m relay. The women's 4x100m relay was anchored by Merlene Ottey who has been the dominant female sprinter for 20 years, representing Jamaica at her fifth Olympics and winning her eighth Olympic medal at age 39.

Jamaica's strength lies in track and field, but the island has also achieved competitive heights in other sports, especially in competitions such as the Pan-American and the Commonwealth Games. At the Olympic level, David Weller's bronze medal for cycling at the 1980 Moscow Olympics made him, up to the time of writing, the only non-track athlete to win an Olympic medal for Jamaica. Jamaica's bobsled team entry in the Winter Olympics of 1988, while regarded as a novelty, gained the participants high marks for courage and inspired the Walt Disney film *Cool Runnings*. In 1994, at the Lillehammer Olympics, the Jamaican four-man team beat the USA and several leading European countries.

While the female athletes dominated the scene in the closing decade of the 20th century, it was the male athletes who first brought the island's prowess in track and field to world attention. It began with Herb McKenley, who in 1947 became the first sportsman from the English-speaking Caribbean to set a time or distance-

Hometown heroine – Merlene Ottey

measured world record (in the 440 yards at Berkeley, California). McKenley, like many athletes since, was a product of the Jamaican athletes' nursery, the Boys' Track and Field Athletics Championships (known as 'Champs'), which has fostered intense school rivalry. (The Girls' Champs was a later development, but both Boys' and Girls' Champs have now been unified.) McKenley also won an athletic scholarship to a university in the USA, setting a pattern for the progression of athletes which continues to this day. The Gibson Relays (contested by secondary, primary and preparatory schools each year) have also contributed to the healthy spirit of rivalry from which champions can emerge.

McKenley was Jamaica's first outstanding international athlete, and continued to be so for the next few decades. At the 1948 Olympics in London, England, he qualified for the finals in both the 200m and the 400m, and took the silver in the 400. He was, however, beaten in the 400m by another remarkable Jamaican, Arthur Wint, who became the Caribbean's first gold medallist in track and field and won silver in the 800m. Both men continued to excel at the next Olympics, at Helsinki in 1952. McKenley reached the finals in the 100m and 400m events, winning silver in both. Another Jamaican, George Rhoden, won the gold in the 800m. But it was in the 4x400m relay that the Jamaican team shone, the foursome of McKenley, Wint, Rhoden and Leslie Laing setting a world record, the only such ever set in the event by a team from outside the USA.

The era of the late fifties and sixties brought a new crop of world-beaters, including Keith Gardner, the twins Mal and Mel Spence, and George Kerr. They were never Olympic medallists, but they dominated the Commonwealth and Pan American games at their distances. In the late 1960s emerged the man sometimes called 'Jamaica's greatest ever track and field athlete' – Donald Quarrie. He has certainly been one of the most lasting: at the Los Angeles Olympics of 1984, at the age of 33, he became the first male sprinter to earn a medal in his fifth Olympics (as a member of the Jamaican men's team which won the silver in the 4x400m relay).

Quarrie won three gold medals at the 1970 Commonwealth Games in Edinburgh, in the 100m and 200m and as part of the winning 4x100m relay team (which also included Errol Stewart, Carl Lawson and Lennox Miller). By 1976, he was ranked number one in both the 100m and 200m rankings by *Track and Field News* and was the Olympic 200m gold and 100m silver medallist. In that year, he became Jamaica's third individual Olympic champion.

The other outstanding male athlete of the era was Lennox Miller, who won the silver in the men's 100m in the 1968 Olympics and the bronze at the 1972 Games. (In the 1996 Olympics, his daughter Inger Miller won a relay gold medal for the USA.)

The establishment of the IAAF World Championships in 1983 created another platform for Jamaican stars, with Bert Cameron winning the first world title in the men's 400m. But the dominant Jamaican athlete since then has been Merlene Ottey. She was one of several women who came to the fore in the 1980s, but has been by far the most outstanding, winning the 200m World titles in 1993 and 1995 as well as several medals at Commonwealth and Pan American Games.

Four Jamaican women – Cynthia Thompson, Vinton Beckett, Kathleen Russell and Carmen Phipps – made the finals in the 1948 Olympic Games and a 16-year-old high school girl, Una Morris, finished 4th in the 200m at the 1964 Olympics in Tokyo. But Merlene Ottey was the first woman to win an Olympic medal with a bronze in 1980. She continued to dominate her events, becoming one of the world's leading athletes and being named Female Athlete of the Decade by *Track and Field News* in 1999. Ottey has competed successfully in the 100m, 200m and 400m, but is best known for the 100m and 200m events. She has three Olympic silver medals and five bronze, though no gold.

Other outstanding women athletes have included Grace Jackson and Juliet Cuthbert who won Olympic silver medals in 1988 and 1992, and Deon Hemmings. Although Jackson failed to win a medal at the 1984 Olympics at Los Angeles, she achieved the feat of running in four Olympic track finals in the same Games – 100m and 200m and the 4x100m and 4x400m relays. Deon Hemmings won the 400m hurdles and set an Olympic record at Atlanta in 1996, the first female Olympic champion from the English-speaking Caribbean. She won silver in the event at Sydney.

Helsinki, 1952

Donald Quarrie (L) and Herb McKenley

Deon Hemmings (left) sets an Olympic record when she wins the gold medal in the Women's 400m Hurdles, Atlanta 1996

While only the top world beaters have been mentioned above, Jamaica's successful athletes who have turned in good performances at international competitive levels number in the hundreds. What is significant is their fighting spirit, given the limited material resources of the island and of many of those individuals.

Many Jamaicans have also achieved world prominence on the teams of their adopted countries such as England, Canada and the United States. Jamaican-born world champions have included Donovan Bailey, Linford Christie, Tessa Sanderson and the controversial Ben Johnson (athletics), Louis Martin (weight lifting), and Patrick Ewing (a member of the USA basketball 'dream team' at the 1992 Olympics).

[Carnegie 1996]

AUGUST, First of
see EMANCIPATION DAY

AUGUST TOWN
This village on the bank of the HOPE RIVER in ST ANDREW Parish is supposed to have been so named to commemorate the date of the EMANCIPATION of the slaves on 1 August 1838, which thereafter became a notable holiday (see EMANCIPATION DAY). The village is also associated with the great Revivalist Alexander BEDWARD.

AUTOGRAPH ALBUM
Personal books called albums with blank pages in which friends and acquaintances were invited to write verses have been popular in Jamaica (as elsewhere) from time to time. Many of the verses attest to friendship, offer good wishes or predictions and most strive to be witty and amusing. Many autograph verses are in fact very old and by some mysterious method seem to travel from country to country. Such books have a long history, appearing in the mid-16th century among German university students who took to carrying around a leather bound book called an *album amicorum* in which they invited patrons, companions, friends to write their names and good wishes. Since students in those days travelled about a great deal the craze for such books spread in Europe. In the 1820s autograph albums first became widely known in America. It was only later that the autograph book came to contain signatures of celebrities. Some examples from a local autograph book:

> There are tulips in the garden
> There are tulips in the park
> But the best kind of tulips
> Are your two lips in the dark

• • •

> You are going through life
> You will need an umbrella
> May yours be upheld
> by a handsome young fella

• • •

> Whenever on this page you look,
> Whenever on this page you frown,
> Remember the fellow who spoilt your page
> By writing upside down.

[Leach and Fried 1972]

AVIATION
Commercial air service was inaugurated in Jamaica on 3 December 1930, when a Pan American Consolidated Commodore twin engine flying boat landed in KINGSTON harbour,

Flying boat in Kingston harbour

bringing mail but no passengers. It had flown from Miami, Florida. After refuelling, the pilot inaugurated a non-stop Kingston to Panama flight, the longest non-stop flight over water to be attempted by a commercial airline, the journey of approximately 1,085km taking 16 hours and 17 minutes.

The following year Pan American introduced Sikorsky S-40 Clippers on the Miami-Kingston-Cristóbal (Panama) route. The first clipper was piloted by the famous US aviator Col Charles Lindbergh who, along with Igor Sikorsky, the designer of the flying boats, was given a tumultuous welcome when he landed at Bournemouth Baths in Kingston on 23 November 1931. Thereafter, amphibian planes ('flying boats') landed in Kingston harbour until 1941 when Palisadoes Airport (now Norman Manley International Airport) was built. In those early days, vendors selling straw goods and souvenirs would row out to the flying boats and try to sell their wares before the passengers got to land.

Air Jamaica plane coming in to land in the early 1970s (top) and the newest A340 Airbus (below). Air Jamaica was established by the government as the national airline in 1969; the company was reorganized in 1994, when 70 per cent was transferred to private ownership

Today, Jamaica has two international airports – Norman Manley International in Kingston, and Sangster International in MONTEGO BAY. There are also a number of smaller landing strips. Both international airports were owned and operated by a single government body, the Airports Authority, but in 2002 the House of Representatives passed the Airport (Economic Regulation) Bill which permits a private company to operate the island's international airports. At the time of writing negotiations were in progress for the divestment of the Sangster International Airport.

Norman Manley International is named after the National Hero and former Premier, the Rt Excellent Norman Washington MANLEY. The airport is located at the widest part of the narrow strip of land known as the PALISADOES, – where it is 1.6km across – and was formerly known as the Palisadoes Airport. It was developed from a naval station built on the site during the Second WORLD WAR. Sangster International in Montego Bay, named after a former Prime Minister, Sir Donald Sangster (1911-1967), was first established as a United States Army landing strip during that war.
[Hanna 1992; KSAC 1952]

AVOCADO (*Persea americana*)

Popularly called 'pear' in Jamaica, avocado is a native of Mexico, where it was first cultivated around 7,000 BC and from there spread throughout the Americas. It was taken to Europe by the Spaniards. The Spanish term avocado was 'substituted by "popular etymology" for Aztec *ahuacatl* . . . of which a nearer form in Spanish is *aguacate*' [OED], hence 'alligator pear' in Jamaican usage.

The avocado is of the family Lauraceae and is a close relative of CINNAMON and other aromatic trees. It grows up to 15m high and is common in cultivation up to 1,000m. Pear grows wild in Jamaica, though many varieties are also cultivated. The large seeds grow easily, though hybrids will not come true.

Eaten as a salad vegetable when ripe, in Jamaica pear is most often peeled and sliced lengthwise as an accompaniment to a meal. BULLA or BAMMY with sliced pear is regarded as an especially delightful culinary combination. Two proverbs attest to pear's popularity: 'Ripe pear nuh know danger till mout' ketch 'im' and, in tribute to its popularity with cats: 'Puss laugh when pear tree fall.' Indeed, pear, which tends to fruit liberally, is also used to feed other animals, especially pigs.

Avocado

During 'pear season', August to December, the markets are usually flooded with the fruit in every combination of shape and size – round, oval, pear-shaped, or the easily identified 'alligator', which has a long neck. The skin of the ripe pear is either green or deep purple to black, depending on variety, and may be highly smooth and shiny or rough and bumpy. The general appearance of the skin is not necessarily a good indicator of the texture and quality of the pear inside. To judge the degree of ripeness of a green-skinned pear requires long practice. Usually, the skin loses much of its gloss and becomes duller; the tip of the fruit near the stem usually ripens first and light pressure there may be used as a test. The flesh varies a great deal in depth and texture, thick, blemish-free 'butter' pear being held in the highest esteem. As with MANGOES, there are pear 'aristocrats' and common pears, the supply and price varying accordingly. Alligator and Simmonds pears are usually expensive, and so are the commercial out-of-season varieties – Lulu, Collinson and Winslowson, which ripen between December and February and so extend the traditional season.

In the old days, avocado was known as 'Midshipman's Butter' or 'Subaltern's Butter', because it was such a good substitute for the real thing. Charles Rampini, an English visitor, recorded in his *Letters from Jamaica* (1873) an anecdote about an irascible old planter who nearly dismissed a BOOK-KEEPER on his estate for eating butter at breakfast during pear season, asserting that 'a man who can do that . . . upon the wages I give him, cannot possibly be honest'.

Rampini, like Hans Sloane who visited in the 17th century, said pear was eaten as a fruit, mixed with sugar and wine (or lemons), a usage which does not persist in Jamaica today (though Brazilians and Filipinos do eat avocado sweet). He also noted that the seeds contained a large amount of tannin, which could be used for the same purpose as indelible ink. Avocado has also been used in traditional medicine, Asprey and Thornton noting that the leaves used to be boiled to make tea thought to be 'good for the blood', as a lotion for colds, and as a drink for pains. Jamaicans for centuries have also used avocado pulp as a skin softener and hair rinse, usages that now have found commercial applications by the international cosmetics industry. Sloane also noted that avocado was regarded as 'a great incentive to venery', i.e. had aphrodisiac properties. Edward Long was more explicit. The fruits, he said, were considered 'great provocatives; and, for this reason, it is said, the Spaniards do not like to see their wives indulge too much in them'.

[Asprey and Thornton 1953-55, Baccus and Royes 1988, Campbell 1974, Long 1774, Nugent 1839, Rampini 1873, Robertson 1990, Sloane 1725]

B

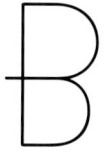

BABYLON

In RASTAFARI usage, symbol for the oppressor or the place of oppression, widely used from the 1960s and appearing in many popular songs. Although the DJE records the term from the early 1940s in reference to the police, Horace Campbell attributes its popular usage to a famous Groundation (Rasta gathering) organized by Prince Emmanuel Edwards in Kingston in March 1958. 'Babylon' became the forces arrayed against Rasta, symbolized by the army and police as representatives of the State, but in time the epithet came to include all those perceived as exploiters of the poor and 'downpressed'.

The concept of Babylon as the symbol of the debasement of the human spirit, of the material world versus the spiritual, is an ancient one. It was used by Old Testament writers who saw Babylon – which Herodotus called the most splendid city on earth – as the antithesis of Paradise and the Heavenly Jerusalem. The best known reference is Psalm 137 written by the Jews during their Babylonian captivity around 586 BC. Rasta (for whom the Bible was a foundational book) saw a parallel in the oppression of black people brought to the New World as slaves and their yearning for their African homeland. The song 'Rivers of Babylon' by the Melodians (which topped the charts in 1969 and was part of the sound track of the film *The Harder They Come* in 1972) drew heavily on the Psalm and made explicit the Rastas' sense of spiritual exile in 'Babylon': 'By the rivers of Babylon/Where we sat down/There we wept/When we remembered Zion/Carried us away captivity/Required from us a song/How can we sing King Alpha's song/In a strange land?'
[Campbell 1985, DJE, Murrell et al. 1998]

BAIBRAMA

One of the major ZEMIS of the TAINOS, the spirit of vegetation and fertility, associated with cassava or YUCA; thus Baibrama means 'Lord of the Harvest'. Usually represented with a small bowl on his head that was used to hold offerings, Baibrama is also portrayed with a frightening expression and erect penis for he is associated with war and warriors as well. He had two other names that meant 'ugly' and 'bad'. One of the finest examples of this figure was found in Jamaica.
[Alegría 1990, Arrom 1990, Fewkes 1907]

Jamaican Taino carving

BALM

A system of healing widely practised in Jamaica. (See also MEDICINE, Folk.) The practitioner is called a 'balmist', 'balm lady' or 'balm man'. Most balmists maintain their own healing centre in a compound called a 'balmyard' (which is usually identified by a cluster of flags) though some will also travel to nearby places to hold services. Success is based on the ability of the balmist to 'read' or diagnose the patient by various means and prescribe the correct treatment. This treatment is usually based on 'bush baths' as well as herbal and other remedies. Balm continues to thrive because of the persistent belief that illness usually has a spiritual cause that needs to be addressed; resort is often had to the balmist when standard medical procedures have failed. The best balmists rely almost exclusively on native herbs (called 'BUSH') of which they have a thorough knowledge. Some balmyards have been passed on from one generation to the next; one in MANCHESTER Parish has been in existence for over one hundred years.

The practice of balm derives from the old religion of MYAL and is today identified with two systems, REVIVAL and OBEAH. It should be noted, however, that a balmist might be a revivalist and/or an obeah practitioner, or might not be identified with either system. Some balmists see their role as removing the evil spirits 'set' by obeah.

There used to be many specialists in balm, including 'bone men' who treated fractures, 'burn men' who treated burns, 'cuppers' who treated ailments by using a coconut shell or similar cup-like device to produce suction. While herbal treatment is the most prevalent, items purchased from the drugstore, especially popular over-the-counter medication, are sometimes recommended. In the past, drugstore purchases were far more esoteric, old-time druggists being able to interpret exactly the identity and combination of substances wanted in such prescriptions as 'oil of madness', 'oil of keep the dead', or 'oil of deliver me'. Those who rely too heavily on drugstore prescriptions are referred to as 'paper woman' or 'paper man', implying that they have no real knowledge of herbs. Many of Jamaica's herbs that have been used in balm and traditional medicine are now being studied for their medicinal properties by scientists both in Jamaica and abroad. (See, for example, CERASEE, GANJA, PERIWINKLE.) The song 'Man Piaba Woman Piaba' also known as 'The Weed Woman' celebrates the vendor of a long list of medicinal herbs.

[Barrett 1973, 1976, Beckwith 1928, Cassidy 1971, DJE, Kerr 1952, Lowe 1972, Seaga 1968]

BAMBOO (*Bambusa vulgaris*)

Giant grass originating in the Far East which is now naturalized all over Jamaica. It is one of 250 species of grass found on the island from sea level to 1,100m, the most important commercially being SUGAR CANE. Several ornamental bamboos of smaller size have also been introduced.

Bamboo is recognized as one of the most useful plants in the world, and is utilized in many ways in Jamaica. In times of drought, bamboo shoots provide fodder for animals. Bamboo roots hold the soil together so the plant is used in conservation work. Bamboo joints are used to carry water and as planters; they are also carved and decorated to make ornaments. Perhaps the bamboo's greatest use is as construction material – to make pig sties and other animal enclosures, wattle for homes and kitchens, 'bamboo booths' for country WEDDINGS and other affairs, BASKETS, furniture, and screens. Bamboo is also made into MUSICAL INSTRUMENTS such as the BENTA, Bamboo Tamboo – a length of bamboo which is stamped on the ground, and the bamboo saxophone of the late Mr W. 'Sugar Belly' Walker. In folk MEDICINE, bamboo leaves boiled with GUINEA GRASS and mixed with white rum were used in the treatment of malaria and other fevers.

A unique feature of bamboo is the speed with which it grows, sometimes over a metre a day; it is regarded as the fastest-growing plant in the world. It is also noted for its lengthy flowering cycles, plants of the same species all flowering at the same time, in whatever part of the world they happen to be.

A grass (*Chusquea abietifolia*) which is found in Jamaica only in the BLUE MOUNTAINS area between 1,100 and 2,250m and is called Climbing Bamboo is not a true bamboo though, like the bamboo, it flowers rarely. Adams (1971) has calculated that it flowers every 33 years.

[Adams 1971, 1972, Asprey and Thornton, 1953-55, Huxley, 1978, Rashford 1995]

Bamboo furniture

BAMBOO AVENUE

A 4km scenic drive through an archway of living BAMBOO, on the main south coast highway between MIDDLE QUARTERS and LACOVIA in ST ELIZABETH Parish. The species planted here is *Bambusa vulgaris*, the largest species of bamboo in Jamaica, originally brought from Haiti. The avenue which is also known as 'Holland Bamboo' was planted by the owners of Holland estate, a sugar estate of some 1,780ha which once belonged to John Gladstone (1764-1851), the father of William Gladstone, the 19th century British prime minister.

BAMMY

A flat round BREAD made of CASSAVA flour, probably the oldest prepared food in Jamaica. As *casabe*, it was the staple of the TAINOS (and other native peoples of tropical America) and is still widely eaten today. In Spanish-speaking countries, bammy is still known as *casabe* and the cassava plant as *yuca*, both ARAWAK names. The word bammy is derived from the Taino Arawak *guyami*.

The making of cassava bread in Jamaica follows the same method used by the Tainos and other native Americans. The bitter cassava tuber is dug out of the ground, the skin is peeled or scraped off, and the tuber is grated. The pulp is put into a contraption (called a 'bammy presser' in Jamaica) to express the juice, which is poisonous. The remaining dried mass (cassava flour) is sifted for lumps. For cooking, it is spread thinly inside an iron hoop on a hot metal griddle or baked in a cast iron pot. Since the flour is virtually all starch, the heat causes it to quickly coalesce and the bammy is turned so both sides are cooked.

Bammy, or flour made from bitter cassava, will last for a very long time if kept dry, a factor that has contributed to its popularity down the centuries. It was offered to Christopher COLUMBUS and his crew at virtually their first meeting with the native peoples and thereafter became the staple food of the Europeans in the islands until they established their own food supplies. Bammy played its part in conquest and empire-building as it became a staple in provisioning the ships of the *conquistadores* travelling to and from the Spanish Main. Much of it probably came from Jamaica which, during Spanish times, served as a provision depot. In the early days of English settlement, cassava bread continued to be part of the diet of sailors because of its excellent keeping qualities. It was also the bread of the early settlers.

D. Ranston

Bammy

The Amerindians passed on their bammy making skills to the Europeans and Africans. In the days before wheat flour or wheat bread were widely available, bammy was the standard bread of poorer folk. ST ELIZABETH Parish was the 'bammy capital' since the cassava plant thrives on the dry southern plains and the women there became particularly skilled in the art of bammy making. However, much of the bammy offered for sale today is factory made.

A thick, flexible bammy about the size of a dinner plate was the standard hand-made one; those currently sold are much smaller and thicker. Tiny, paper-thin bammies are called wafers or cassava bread and are eaten as snacks. In the old days, the Tainos (and Island CARIB for whom it was also a staple) dipped the dried bammy into their PEPPER-POT to soften it, a method still used by contemporary Arawaks on the mainland. Jamaicans today soak the dried bammy in water, milk or coconut milk until it absorbs a fair amount of moisture before draining and preparing it for eating by frying, steaming or baking. It is usually served as a starchy accompaniment to a meal, bammy and fried fish being a popular combination.

[Lathrap 1970]

BANANA (*Musa acuminata x balbisiana*)

The banana is actually a large herb 33-82m tall with a narrow 'true' stem and a sheaf of overlapping leaf bases. The fruit originates from a small flowering shoot rising from the middle of the leaves in mature plants. The shoot develops into a long stalk that eventually bends downwards, sending out a large red bud which gradually opens up to reveal rows of tiny flowers. As the corollas of some of these are shed, they leave behind small 'fingers' that grow to form bananas.

The banana's growth (from Leader)

The fingers are clustered together into 'hands', several hands making up a 'bunch'. One bunch grows to each plant. After bearing, the plant dies, but new plants develop from suckers at its roots; in cultivation most of these are removed. In commercial operations, plantlets produced by tissue culture are used. The life cycle of the plant takes from 15 to 18 months.

The Latin name originally given to the edible banana (*Musa sapientum*) means 'food of the wise'. Bananas have been cultivated from earliest times and there are hundreds of edible varieties, including the PLANTAIN. The banana originated in Asia and was brought from the Canary Islands to the West Indies by the Spaniards. It was first grown in Santo Domingo in 1516 and is believed to have reached Jamaica around 1520.

The plant on which the BANANA TRADE was based, the Gros Michel, was introduced in 1835 from Martinique by Jean François Pouyat who planted it at his Bel Air coffee plantation in ST ANDREW Parish. This fine variety spread throughout the island and from there was taken to Central America where it became established as the preferred variety.

In Jamaica, the Gros Michel was at first called 'Martnik' or 'Pouyat' but later became known as the 'Go Yark' banana, i.e. 'Go to New York', meaning the fruit was the best for export. The Gros Michel proved susceptible to Panama Disease and was succeeded by more hardy varieties of the Cavendish group such as the Robusta (introduced in 1909 from Guatemala), the Lacatan (introduced from Trinidad in 1926) and the Valery (introduced in 1963). The most recent variety developed in Jamaica is RG1. This variety is resistant to yellow and black Sigatoka disease, tolerant to nematode infection, and sturdy. It does not suffer from 'finger drop' like other varieties, produces a good bunch, and is very tasty when boiled.

All parts of the banana tree are useful, yet the value of the fruit was not recognized until recent times when ripe bananas became popular. Formerly in Jamaica they were used in tarts and fritters but hardly eaten, and the unripe 'green' banana was scorned by humans and fed to PIGS (the plantain being preferred). But like the ripe fruit, cooked green bananas eventually became an important article in the diet of all Jamaicans, a process speeded up by the Second WORLD WAR which cut off supplies of imported starches such as rice, hence its jocular name of 'long grain rice'. Indeed, the green banana is now believed to be full of iron, and to obtain the greatest benefit, some drink the water in which it is boiled (called 'benefit' or 'pot likker'). Popular dishes such as curried GOAT or mackerel rundown (RUN DUNG) are almost unthinkable without boiled green bananas as an accompaniment. Green bananas are also grated to make porridge and puddings. Ripe bananas are consumed as fruit and used in many desserts.

The dried bark of the tree ('trash') is useful for tying and forms a rough and ready packaging material; mats and other craft items are also made from banana bark, and it is used to create decorative pictures for framing and on cards. Green banana leaves can be cut up to make dining plates when no other type is available and, singed, they are wrapped around a pudding mixture to make DOKUNU. In times past, patients suffering from SMALLPOX or fevers were wrapped in green banana leaves as a cooling measure. In folk MEDICINE ripe bananas are used for constipation, and green banana skin or grated green banana mixed with kerosene oil is a remedy for removing poisons, inflammations, or splinters from the skin. The sap of the leaves as well as roast banana sucker mixed with other ingredients is a burn remedy. Whole green bananas or the discarded skins are also used to feed farmyard animals, especially pigs.

[Asprey and Thornton 1953-55, Black 1965, GOJ JIS 1968, Hart 1967, McKay 1979, Robertson 1982, 1990]

BANANA LOADING

Although the BANANA loaders' song 'Day-O' has become internationally known (thanks to a version sung by Harry Belafonte), the activities celebrated in that song which date from the time when bananas were loaded on to the ships by hand, have long faded into history. Nowadays, bananas are not checked 'six hand, seven hand, eight hand, bunch!' (not 'foot' as the popular version of the song proclaims) but are reaped, cut into hands, packed into boxes, and taken straight to the ship to be mechanically loaded. For the export trade, banana yield is now calculated by weight rather than 'hands' and 'bunches', each box weighing 15.6 kilos. The old expressive terms are still used in the local markets, though giving way to measurement by the dozen or number of 'fingers' on a 'hand', as well as by weight.

In the post-EMANCIPATION years, the BANANA TRADE became the island's most important enterprise, an activity around which economic as well as social life revolved, and the summons to reap the fruit and load the ships brought intense excitement to banana-growing areas. For many, it represented their only means of livelihood. While there were many large landowners among the growers, it is the 'small man' (and woman) who planted, reaped, and loaded the bananas on to the ships who is celebrated in story, in songs such as 'Day O', and mythologized in poems such as 'Song of the Banana Man' by Evan Jones. Jones's Banana Man proudly asserts: 'Praise God an' m'big right han/I will live an die a banana man.'

In the early days when word was received from abroad that a ship would arrive on or about a given day, the sound of the CONCH shell would be taken up and echoed throughout the hills. Excitement gripped the area as all hands rushed to cut the perishable green fruit. Each bunch was tenderly wrapped in dried banana leaves ('banana trash') to protect it during its journey to the sea.

This journey involved a long human chain. First, the bunches were carried on the workers' heads along tracks to the main roads. There they were collected by trucks or, in earlier days, by 'wains' – large wagons usually drawn by oxen. A boy ran ahead blowing a conch shell to warn others off the road. (Wain Road which leads into the town of PORT ANTONIO recalls this mode of transportation). The bananas were then taken to the RAILWAY station yards for selection and purchase by the fruit companies.

Each stem was offloaded on to the head of a worker, part of a long line that went past two checkers who checked the 'stem count'. Nine hands and over on each bunch were paid for as a 'bunch', eight hands were counted as three-quarter bunch, seven hands as half. Anything else was rejected for export. Each carrier was given a metal disc showing the bunch count, to be redeemed later for payment. The bananas were loaded on to railcars that eventually were hitched to an engine that collected all the cars along the line and took them to the wharf where the fruit were offloaded to await the ship.

The ship's arrival sent another round of signals into the hills to alert the carriers and stevedores to come rushing down to the wharf. In places where there was no deep water pier, the fruit were carried to the ship in lighters. But at wharves such as the big Boundbrook pier in Port

Banana loading, early 20th century

Antonio, a frenzied scene would be enacted. The banana carriers were mostly women and young girls. Each grabbed a banana bunch and, swinging it on to her head, set off at a running pace up the gangplank, snatching from the 'tallyman' as she passed, a metal check or tally to be redeemed later for pay. As she reached the ship's hold, the bunch was snatched from her head by a loader (always a man) who stacked them in the hold, and the carrier without breaking stride would loop around to secure another bunch. Poet Edward Baugh who grew up in Port Antonio graphically recalls (in 'Sunday Afternoon Walks with My Father') 'the intense knee-dipping canter of the bearers,/a human millipede hurrying the green/bunches into the sure hands of stevedores/who know the secrets of the dark hold'.

During peak periods, this work was carried on into the night. Between the loading of one ship and the next, the workers snatched what sleep they could, lying on the banana trash on the docks.

In his book *Jamaica, the Blessed Island* (1936), a colonial governor, Sidney Olivier, about to sail on one of the banana boats, left this word picture of banana loading on to ships in Kingston harbour:

'I waited a little to watch the loading traffic. The sheds on the wharf were stacked with tiers of white barrels and long, flat boxes; in bins along the farther wall were ranged great piles of heavy stems of green bananas, carefully sorted in sizes and laid to await our arrival. Between these piles and the ship, diverging to the fore hatch and the after hatch, there coursed uninterruptedly two circulating double streams of dingy, ragged figures, girls and women. Such rags – such dirt – they wore. I watched them from above as they hurried to and from the iron-jawed hatches that gaped in the side of the ship, clear as day under the glare of the arc lights.'

The women loaders carried the bananas on their heads, placed there by the men who offloaded them from the bins.

'The women came at a smooth, noiseless double across the planking towards the ship, the heavy head-load poised, just steadied with a touch of the fingers, the face thrown a little forward, the chin raised, the eyelids dropped to

Banana loading, c. 1962

the level, intent, expressionless, all but for a kind of unquestioning patience of beasts of burden, the look of all yoked animals, in their eyes. On each side of the doorway where they issued stood a negro lad with a cutlass; the runners slackened pace as they passed him, approaching the gangway bridge; if a stalk were too long at either end of the bunch, a flick of the blade and off it flew on the planking, or sometimes there was only a pat on the bum with the flat of the cutlass. They strode down the gang-plank slower. Their dresses were festooned bundles of rags that had once been decent cotton Sunday gowns. They were spotted and streaked now from shoulder to hem with dark stains of banana juice. They hung in tattered fringes, disguising all human form, except where too full a bosom strained their holding. Their colours were all the imaginable shades of dinginess.'

Many photographs of these workers in their tattered garments exist, as banana loading was a popular tourist attraction and in the daytime the wharves were often crowded with visitors with cameras taking pictures of these 'human millipedes' and listening to their **WORK SONGS**. It must have been humiliating for the workers to be photographed in their work clothes. The juice from the cut stem and green fruit permanently stains clothing, so banana workers wore the same clothing week after week for this dirty work.

Carriers were paid half a penny for two bunches. A gang of 14 loaders and a boss could load 5,000 bunches in a day, earning 22 shillings for 1,000 bunches. While the wage of the banana worker was considered good compared to the wage of the average rural labourer, the work was essentially casual in nature, dependent on the arrival of ships and competition with others for jobs. Many often worked only one or two days per week. But when work was available, there could be no slackening in the carrying and loading until each boat was filled: 'Mi back dis a bruck with the bare exhaustion', the banana workers sang. Not surprisingly, banana carriers and dock workers were in the forefront of the labour struggles of 1937-38 (see BUSTAMANTE, FROME) which resulted in the formation of TRADE UNIONS and political parties. [Baugh 2000, Olivier 1936, Post 1978]

BANANA TRADE

The trade in what has become one of the world's most popular fruits actually began in Jamaica, and from 1876 until 1929, when it was overtaken by Honduras, the island remained the world's largest banana producer. It was from Jamaica that the Gros Michel (the main BANANA variety on which the export trade was based until replaced by the Cavendish) was taken to Central America to develop the industry there.

Although the banana has been grown in Jamaica for centuries, it had no commercial importance until the late 19th century and was not highly regarded as food until the mid-20th century (the closely related PLANTAIN being preferred). When the trade did begin, it brought 'boom times' to many parts of the island (see, for example, PORT ANTONIO) and prosperity to a great many people. The demand for the ripe fruit that developed in North America and Europe turned the banana into 'green gold' for Jamaica and many Latin American countries. So powerful did banana-growing interests become in Central America that many of these countries used to be scornfully referred to as 'Banana Republics'.

The originators of the trade were American sea captains who on their trips to Jamaica in the 1860s began to see the potential in the fruit. One of these men, a Captain George Busch, who had been selling Cuban bananas to the United States, took some of the Jamaican fruit back with him in 1866 and quickly sold it in Boston at a profit. With the help of Jamaican businessmen in the Oracabessa-Port Antonio area, he made arrangements to buy the fruit regularly. They held meetings around the countryside urging peasant settlers to grow bananas. But the trade did not take off until another sea captain,

Lorenzo Dow Baker (from Johnston)

Lorenzo Dow Baker, master of the 85-ton schooner *Telegraph* arrived in 1870. Baker put in at Port Morant and was struck by the quantities of fruit he saw lying around. He loaded up with a cargo of COCONUTS and 160 bunches of bananas, which he bought at one shilling per bunch. Eleven days later, he sold these in Jersey City at two dollars (about eight shillings) per bunch, thus proving that bananas could be shipped to the USA without excessive spoilage and for a huge profit. He filled his ship with salted cod, shoes, gay cotton prints and other 'Yankee notions' for which he found a quick sale in Jamaica. A two-way trade had begun. Baker and Busch kept on supplying bananas on a small scale until 1877 when a regular trade was started.

In Baker's own words (at a function held in Kingston to honour him on his 65th birthday in 1905): 'It was 35 years ago when I first dropped anchor in the harbour of Port Morant where I first got the first bunch of bananas I ever got from Jamaica.' He was told that at the time there was some shipping of bananas from Port Antonio 'in a very feeble way'. The next year, 1871, Baker went to Port Antonio. 'I was not and do not claim to be the first shipper of bananas from Jamaica', Baker said, but his efforts were certainly the most successful – 'From a rowboat we went to a cutter and then to steamers.' Baker himself seemed to have been well loved by Jamaicans for his personal generosity and philanthropic activities. He was widely mourned on the island when he died in Boston in 1908.

Baker's small efforts were to grow into the Boston Fruit Company which in 1899 merged with the Keith and Lindo interests in Costa Rica to become the United Fruit Company of New Jersey. By the early 20th century, that company controlled most of the banana trade in the West Indies and Latin America. Although several fruit companies operated in the island, it remained a stronghold of United Fruit until the Second WORLD WAR. Principal among the independent Jamaican businessmen active in the trade was the Montego-Bay-based John Edward Kerr who ran his own line of banana ships and was the first to ship fruit by steamer.

Between 1870 and 1932, the United States was the major market for the Jamaican fruit. The first shipment to England was made in March 1895 on the *Port Pirie*. The fruit arrived in good condition at the West India docks on 5 April, and shipments continued thereafter at irregular intervals. In 1901 the first full cargo of bananas left for England, utilizing a specially developed cooling device to keep the fruit at a low temperature on long distances to prevent premature ripening. Later that year, a regular fortnightly service in specially refrigerated ships was started by the British company Elders and Fyffes. (Elders and Fyffes was later absorbed by United Fruit.) In 1932 the trade to Britain overtook that to the United States, encouraged by new tariff protection, and the American trade declined as the British grew. By 1938 Jamaica was producing 78 per cent of British banana imports.

The banana industry developed at a time when the SUGAR industry was seriously in decline and in the early days, everyone – big landowners as well as small farmers – dropped everything to grow the 'green gold', so quick were the returns. There were 'banana wars' in which the big shippers fought to get supplies and prices to growers escalated. While the small farmers were actively engaged in banana growing at the start, their participation was reduced after a severe hurricane in 1903, followed by Panama Disease, wiped out the crop. Many could not afford to revive their cultivation as the large growers could.

United Fruit itself grew bananas on the enormous acreage it had come to own while maintaining a virtual monopoly on shipping. Fruit produced by the individual grower was contracted to the company but would be bought only if space was available on the ships and there were markets overseas. Growers sometimes watched all their bananas rotting at railway stations because they were squeezed out of the market. The years 1900 to 1929 were marked by several attempts to break this monopoly on shipping. But it was not until Jamaican growers formed the Jamaica Banana Producers' Association in 1929 that this step was achieved. The Association established its own marketing organization in Britain and its own line of ships carrying bananas to that country. Operating as a cooperative, 'Producers' shared profits with all those who supplied it with bananas and, competing successfully with United Fruit, was able to raise the price to Jamaican growers to the highest in the world. In 1936, under pressure from United Fruit and near bankruptcy, the Producers' Association ceased to be a cooperative and became a company with shareholders, the shares available to any banana grower in the island. The Association was able to provide a secure market and stability for the grower.

Although banana growing is still of some importance in Jamaica, the boom times did not last beyond the late 1930s, when the crop was almost wiped out by Panama Disease. Banana cultivation has also been susceptible to severe damage by HURRICANES and by Leaf Spot disease. During the Second World War, the export market collapsed owing to lack of shipping, but the industry was kept alive by the UK government subsidizing the purchase of fruit. In recent years, the industry has been affected by developments in international trade, including the European Union and the World Trade Organization.

Today, bananas still constitute the second most important agricultural crop in Jamaica, next to sugar. However, the presence of small farmers in the trade has declined, owing to the cost of cultivation. The fruit for the export trade is nowadays grown only on large plantations though bananas for domestic consumption continue to be easily grown on small farms or even in back yards.

The start of the banana trade brought an additional advantage to Jamaica: the banana boats brought the first tourists to the island. (Captain Baker was one of the earliest promoters of TOURISM in Port Antonio, then the headquarters of the banana trade.) The banana boats also facilitated travel abroad by Jamaicans, providing the main means of transportation to England until the development of air travel.

[Black 1965, Brown 1976, GOJ JIS, Hart 1953-1964, 1954, 1968, McKay 1979, Post 1978]

BANBURY CROSS or BANBURY

Village a few miles north of SAVANNA-LA-MAR that was the site of Queen's Town, once the chief settlement of WESTMORELAND Parish. In the burial ground at the crossroads is the tomb of John Guthrie (d 1739) who lived at Banbury Great House nearby and who, as colonel of the Westmoreland militia, signed the Treaty of Pacification with CUDJOE, the great MAROON leader, in 1739. Guthrie came to Jamaica as a small boy with the Darién expedition. (See CAMPBELL.)
[Cundall 1915]

BANDANA

Characteristic plaid cotton material (with principal colours of red, yellow and white) incorporated into Jamaica's national costume. Also known as 'native woman plaid' and 'Madras handkerchief', bandana has traditionally been used to make the head-dress ('head-tie') and aprons of Jamaican peasant women and is most closely identified as the occupational badge of HIGGLERS or market women, though it is nowadays seldom worn. Today, the use of bandana plaid is largely ceremonial and symbolic. Revivalists (see REVIVAL) often use bandana plaid to make their turbans, and it is incorporated in a 'Jamaican costume' when such is required, e.g. for participants in the 'Miss World' or 'Miss Universe' beauty contests. It is also frequently used in the costuming of singers, storytellers, and other performers of 'folk' material.

The original bandana was a square of cloth (slightly less than a square metre) of tie-dyed silk, imported from India in the 18th century. The word is derived from *bandhna* which means 'tying' in Sanskrit. The 'bandana' handkerchief was originally made for home use and later exported. Advertisements in the Jamaican press (reproduced in Murphy and Crill 1991) show that the genuine Bengal bandanas imported in the late 18th and early 19th century were 'spotted silk handkerchiefs', the tie-dyed pattern consisting of white spots on a chocolate-coloured background.

Over time, the name 'bandana' became transferred to the plaid patterned Madras or Pullicat handkerchief which was worn as a head-

Dancers from Port Antonio Infant School in bandana costumes

wrap by working class females of African and INDIAN descent. It was known as 'Madras handkerchief' from the Indian city and province in which it was made and from which it was exported. When the material became available by the yard, its usage extended from head-ties to aprons and other articles of dress. African women in Jamaica have always worn head-wraps, in the style of their West African homelands, but the wearing of the now-familiar Madras cloth seems to have become common among women of both African and Indian origin in the years following EMANCIPATION. Tied the traditional way, the bandana head-tie usually has two ends sticking stiffly into the air. Although different styles of tying have been identified, the tying of the head-tie does not seem to have been used as a 'language' here as in the French islands, where women signalled their marital status by the arrangement of their head-dress.
[Murphy and Crill 1991]

BANJO

The first written reference to this popular MUSICAL INSTRUMENT comes from Jamaica in 1739. In those early days it was recorded as Banja, Bonjour, Banjee, Banjaw, etc. until the name became standardized as Banjo, though 'banja' has remained the common pronunciation in Jamaica. The DJE says the word is probably African and the instrument itself is regarded as an African contribution to world music. An early version of the instrument (called a Strum-Strum) had a gourd resonance chamber, as shown in an illustration in Sloane (1725). Sloane said: 'They have several sorts of instruments in imitation of lutes, made of small gourds fitted with Necks, strung with Horse Hairs, or the peeled stalks of climbing plants or withs. These instruments are

Banjo (20th century) made in Brampton, St Elizabeth Parish, for a village band

sometimes made of Hollow'd Timber covered with Parchment or other skins wetted, having a Bow for its Neck, the strings ty'd longer or shorter, as they would alter their sounds.' William Beckford (1790) described the instrument as a 'bonjour'. Bryan Edwards (1794) called it a 'banja' or 'merrywang'.

The Banjo's existence on the American mainland was also recorded early. Thomas Jefferson asserted in his *Notes on Virginia* (1784) that 'the instrument proper to them is the Banjar, which they brought hither from Africa, and which is the origin of the guitar, its chords being precisely the four lower chords of the guitar.'

[Beckford 1790, DJE, Edwards 1794, Jefferson quoted in Jackson 1967, Long 1774, Sloane]

BANKRA see BASKET

BAPTIST

This denomination represents one of the largest organized religious groups in Jamaica. According to the census of 1991, there were 203,135 Baptists. The significance of this church in Jamaica's history is attested to by the fact that three of seven NATIONAL HEROES were Baptists.

The Baptist church was brought to Jamaica by black American ex-slaves who, like the white Loyalists, had settled in the island after the American War of Independence. The first and most illustrious was the Revd George Liele (to use the spelling he himself used, according to his biographer Clement Gayle, though in the historical records the name is also spelled variously as Leile and Lisle). George Liele (1752-1828) was baptized in Savannah, Georgia and obtained a licence to preach to his fellow slaves and was later ordained a minister. He secured his freedom, but with the ending of the war and defeat of British forces, he brought his family to Jamaica in 1783 and shortly after began his ministry, his preaching at KINGSTON RACE COURSE attracting hundreds. He built the first Baptist chapel in Jamaica and commanded a wide following among the black and coloured population; indeed, he was the first person in the island to convert a significant number of slaves. There were a number of other black itinerant preachers such as George Gibb and George Lewis. The most illustrious, next to Liele, was Moses Baker (see ADELPHI) whom Liele had baptized. It was Baker who contacted the Baptist Missionary Society of Great Britain requesting help with his work. As a result, the first British Baptist MISSIONARY came from England in 1814.

The Revd George Liele

Because of their stand against SLAVERY, the Baptists soon became the most popular religious group in Jamaica, gaining large numbers of converts among the slaves and free black population. Like the other non-conformists (METHODISTS, MORAVIANS, Congregationalists), the Baptists were extremely unpopular with the establishment, especially in the aftermath of the slave rebellion of 1831-32 (see SHARPE, Samuel) which was known as the 'Baptist War'. Despite severe persecution of themselves and their followers, the missionaries continued to participate in the struggle against slavery both in Jamaica and in the English Parliament. (See also BURCHELL, KNIBB, PHILLIPPO.)

After EMANCIPATION, the Baptist missionaries were instrumental in assisting the former slaves in establishing themselves in FREE VILLAGES. They were also pioneers in education. Baptists built the first theological college in the West Indies for the training of a local Ministry. (See CALABAR.)

In 1842 the Jamaica Baptist churches became independent of British Baptists. They formed a Missionary Society, sending missionaries from Jamaica to Africa and Central America. They also pioneered Baptist work in Haiti and Cuba, among other places. 'Native Baptist' churches, i.e. indigenous churches that grew out of the orthodox Baptist church but became independent of it, also still flourish.

[Gayle 1982, Knibb-Sibley 1965]

BARAGUABAEL

One of the principal ZEMIS of the TAINOS and the most mysterious. We know little about this zemi except that it was a tree spirit, a living bough that continually escaped into the forest, no matter how often it was caught. One scholar has suggested that this spirit is the guardian of plants, animals, and fish and symbolizes the regenerative powers of nature. *Bara* means 'the sea'.

[Arrom 1990, Fewkes 1907, Stevens-Arroyo 1988]

BARBECUE

In Jamaica, barbecue in the past referred to a flat paved area used for drying crops such as PIMENTO, COFFEE, CORN, COCOA or beans, though nowadays it also refers to a contraption for cooking. The traditional barbecue is still used to dry crops in the sun. The crop is spread out during the daytime and is turned regularly with rakes. At night, or during rainy weather, the crop is raked up and stored indoors or a waterproof covering is spread over it. Barbecues on large plantations can be elaborate structures made of mortar or concrete which may be divided up into several separate compartments. Each is slightly slanted with a hole on the lowest side through which water that has collected can be swept. The barbecue in the yard of the small farmer is often a small rectangle made of earth pounded flat and smoothed over.

The original barbecue (like that used for cooking) was a platform made of sticks and comes from the TAINO Arawakan *barbacoa* ('heated stick'), corrupted by the French to *babrecot* from which the English is derived.

[DCEU, DJE]

Plantation barbecues

BARRETT

Large landowning family that left its mark on western Jamaica in the BRITISH colonial period. At one time, it was claimed, the Barretts owned all the property from Little River (near ROSE HALL, ST JAMES Parish) to the TRELAWNY Parish border.

The first Barrett came to Jamaica with the army of conquest sent by Cromwell (1655) and received land grants, his grandson settling on the north side in 1715. This is the family from which the famous poet Elizabeth Barrett Browning is descended. (Her husband Robert Browning also had West Indian connections: his great-great grandfather was a shoemaker and tavern keeper in PORT ROYAL.)

Elizabeth's father, Edward Barrett Moulton-Barrett (formerly Edward Barrett Moulton 1785-1857), known as 'the tyrant of Wimpole Street', was born at CINNAMON HILL (above Rose Hall GREAT HOUSE). Although he left for England at the age of seven for his schooling and never returned, he secured the surname of Barrett in order to inherit the family's vast northside estates. There is a memorial to him in the family burial ground at Cinnamon Hill as well as at another family property, Retreat Pen, ST ANN Parish. At the time of EMANCIPATION, Edward Moulton-Barrett owned Cinnamon Hill and six other large estates and over 2,000 slaves (inherited from his grandfather). Elizabeth wrote to a friend in 1833 regarding the Emancipation Bill: 'The West Indians are irreparably ruined if the Bill passes. Papa says that in the case of its passing, nobody in his senses would think of even attempting the cultivation of sugar, and that they had better hang weights to the sides of the island of Jamaica and sink it at once.' (See SLAVERY, SUGAR PLANTATION.)

Richard Barrett, estate owner, represented the Jamaica Legislature before the British Parliament during the Emancipation debate

The fact that Moulton-Barrett received only £20,000 in compensation instead of the £140,000 he expected no doubt contributed to his bitterness. Elizabeth later developed abolitionist views in regard to American slavery (which continued long after it had ended in the West Indies), writing at least one anti-slavery poem, 'The Runaway Slave at Pilgrim's Point'.

Edward Moulton-Barrett's sister Sarah was also born at Cinnamon Hill and was the subject of the famous portrait 'Pinkie', much reproduced on chocolate boxes. She died at age 12 in 1795, the same year the portrait by Sir Thomas Lawrence was shown at the Royal Academy in London. The portrait now hangs in the Huntington Library and Gallery in California. This painting lived on in the Caribbean Victorian and early 20th century sensibility, Pinkie appearing in Derek Walcott's autobiographical poem 'Another Life'. This unrecognized but real connection between Britain and its Caribbean world characterizes to a not inconsiderable extent the cross-cultural ties between colony and colonial power.

Cinnamon Hill was built by Edward Barrett (1734-98), Moulton-Barrett's grandfather who was exceptional for his time in that he chose not to be an absentee proprietor in England but to spend his days in Jamaica. The last Barrett to live at Cinnamon Hill died there in 1870. This was Edward Barrett who sold the land on which the town of FALMOUTH was laid out and donated the plot on which the Falmouth Parish Church was built; his town house stood at 1 Market Street. A more recent owner of Cinnamon Hill is the American country and western star Johnny Cash.

A cousin of Moulton-Barrett's, Richard Barrett (1789-1839), built Greenwood House, also in the Rose Hall area around 1810. Greenwood has been restored and furnished in period style, with mementos of the Barrett family, and is open to visitors. Richard Barrett's main house was Barrett Hall (on the hill behind Greenwood).

[Marcus 1995, Marks 1938, Shore and Stewart 1911, Walcott 1986, Wright and White 1969]

BARRINGTONIA (*Barringtonia asiatica*)

Huge spreading evergreen tree of the Old World tropics, growing up to 21m with a trunk 9m or more in diameter. Not as striking perhaps as its relative the CANNONBALL TREE, it is noted for its large fruit surrounded by a thick husk like a coconut which has given it the popular name of Duppy Coconut. These fruits will stay buoyant in water for up to two years and often take root when washed ashore, hence the tree is naturalized in some coastal areas, especially in PORTLAND Parish. Huge specimens can be seen at BATH GARDENS (estimated to be 220 years old)

Barringtonia fruits

and at BLACK RIVER courthouse. The glossy, thick evergreen leaves are similar to ALMOND.
[Rashford 1989]

BASIL, Wild (*Ocimum micranthum*)

Herb that grows wild in Jamaica, more popularly called Barsley or Baazli. It is a perennial bush with small, extremely pungent leaves that are used in cooking but are more importantly used in folk MEDICINE, as a drink for fever and pains, and in baths and body rubs. See also NUNU BUSH.
[Asprey and Thornton 1953-55]

BASKET

Local basketwork not only delights visitors as an interesting craft, but once played an important role in the lives of the folk. 'Bankra', the most popular Jamaican name for 'basket', is of West African origin (Twi language). Nowadays, baskets have been largely replaced by other containers such as 'scandal bags' – as semi-transparent plastic shopping bags are jocularly called because they expose their contents to public view (hence the introduction of opaque black bags by the local manufacturer).

Basketwork was one of the crafts pursued by the TAINOS. *Jabas*, as baskets were called, were widely used for domestic and other purposes. The twilled basketwork was woven so tightly that they could be used to hold liquids. Baskets were used for carrying, spherical ones sometimes being attached to the ends of sticks that the Amerindians balanced on their shoulders. *Cibucanes* were used for expressing juice from bitter CASSAVA. Offerings of cakes and cassava bread were carried to the ZEMIS in baskets and they served another ritual purpose, to hold skulls and bones of dead ancestors that were sometimes kept in the huts. Basket-making material came from Sisal or AGAVE, Wild Banana leaves, and wicker, as well as COTTON.

Basketry and straw plaiting were also important skills among the African Jamaicans who produced baskets as well as bed mats, ropes and wicker chairs for their personal use, for the plantation, and for sale in the markets. Before the advent of modern transportation, much of the food consumed in the cities and towns was brought from the countryside in baskets on the heads of market women and men, or in panniers borne by DONKEYS. Even today the basket remains a favourite container of some market folk.

Food is still transported from the fields in baskets and they are used for storage and other purposes such as smoking meat, pressing the juice from cassava to form the flour used for BAMMY and sifting the flour. Fishermen use shrimp and lobster traps ('pots') made of baskets. Their shapes and names bear a close relationship to their functions and several reflect their African origin. The styles of baskets in use today are as numerous as the names given to them. The material used in making them also varies widely, including BAMBOO, WIS or withe, Thatch PALM, Sisal, Agave, and Jippi Jappa.

The most common baskets are those used by the HIGGLERS in the markets. One called 'market basket' is round with a concave bottom so it will fit firmly when carried on the head. Another is the 'hamper basket' which, like the hamper itself, comes divided into two, though with the basket the division is more suggested than real. The hamper basket has a strong handle across the middle and echoes the shape of the hamper or wicker pannier used in pairs across the back of the donkey or mule. Similar to the market basket is the 'ground basket' that is taken to the fields to bring back produce and is built for carrying on the head. These are all heavy duty baskets and are usually made of strong material such as Bamboo or wicker and built with 'bones' or ribs made of Supple Jack (Wis), Rose Apple or Hook Wis. Often the bones are reinforced with metal strips to make them stronger. Heavy baskets usually rest on the head on a circular pad made of grass or banana trash called a 'cotta'. In the days of SLAVERY, it is said that when a couple cut a cotta in two, it was taken as a sign of separation and division of property.

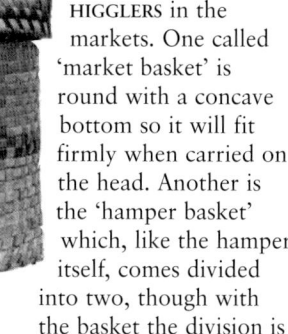

Probably the best known basket is the 'bankra', so much so that the word bankra has become synonymous with basket. According to the DJE, the original bankra is the same as the 'travelling' basket that is called *bonkara* in Twi. The bankra is made of woven thatch palm and is rectangular with square corners, handles, and a cover.

Smaller baskets used for travelling include the 'hand basket' – a small, round wicker basket – and the 'heng pon me' or 'cutacoo' (from the Twi *kotoku*). This is a rectangular flat basket of woven thatch, with a close fitting cover and a handle of rope running along the sides and across the bottom of the basket. The 'heng pon me' is usually taken by the farmer or hunter to the fields and is worn slung across the shoulder and hanging down by the side. A version made of cloth, crocus or other material is called a 'namsack', which word probably derives from both the English 'knapsack' and 'nyam' since it usually contains things to eat (and is no doubt the bag carried by the trickster-hero ANANSI on his foraging expeditions). Finally there is the pretty basket made of Sisal or fine straw such as Jippi Jappa and decorated, usually with raffia. These are the baskets seen in our crafts markets and they are referred to as 'lady basket'.

[Bercht et al. 1998, Cassidy 1971, DJE]

Decorated basket

Bankra

BAT

In Jamaica this animal is known as 'rat bat', the term 'bat' often being mistakenly applied to the moth. Twenty-three species of bats are known from the island, including four species found nowhere else. The majority of Jamaica's bat species roost in CAVES.

The bat is neither a bird nor a reptile but a fur-bearing mammal, i.e. an animal that bears its young alive and nourishes them on mother's milk. Because bats are active at night, spending their days hidden in dark places such as caves, people feel an unreasoning fear of them. In Europe they were identified with demons (which in art are often given bat wings). In Jamaica, as elsewhere, they are death-images. There are many beliefs about blood-sucking bats, but most in fact eat only insect or plant products.

Jamaican bats are varied in their diet but the insect eaters are the great majority and serve a useful purpose in controlling night-flying insects. Other bats live on fruit, some sip nectar from flowers, and one species lives on fish as well as insects.

Flowers and fruits patronized by bats have special features to attract them. Flowers visited by bats open at nights and often have a revolting odour. Since bats are colour-blind, these flowers are often white or in a range of dark colours – purples, browns or dark reds. They have large openings for the beakless creatures and are strong enough to withstand their clutches. Bat-pollinated flowers must also make a great deal of pollen and nectar for these voracious feeders. Jamaican flowers pollinated by bats include many trees of the bombax family, such as Baobab and COTTON TREE as well as CANNONBALL TREE and Queen of the Night CACTUS.

Fruit-eaters seem to prefer soft, pulpy fruits such as SWEET SOP, MANGO, ripe BANANA, and NASEBERRY. Bats will transport fruit considerable distances, sometimes between islands.

The unusual fish-eating bat (*Noctilio leporinus*) is a large light-coloured bat that is sometimes seen swooping over harbours at twilight.

The majority of bats bear one young at a time but the babies are quite large at birth, about one-quarter the size of the mother. The fact that these heavy babies are carried about by the mother for some time, on all her flights, attests to the flying prowess of the bat. Also astonishing is the bat's ability to fly at high speeds in total darkness without crashing into objects, guided by a sort of radar.

Tree-dwelling bats are solitary in habit, but those that live in caves are gregarious, forming large colonies. Bat dung or droppings is called guano and is a fertilizer rich in nitrates that is sometimes exploited by small farmers.

In Toronto, Canada, at the Royal Ontario Museum, one of the attractions is the reconstruction of a Jamaican bat cave.

[Bain 1985, Baker and Genoways 1978, Bretting 1983, Fincham 1997, Goodwin 1970, Huxley 1975, JJ back cover 18:2 1985, NHSJ 1949]

Pregnant bat in flight

BATEY

The TAINOS were fond of athletic contests – running, wrestling, fighting – but above all, of the ball game which they called *batey*. (*Pelota* that is played by Latin Americans is said to be a modern form.) The popularity of the game is attested to by the number of ball courts (also called batey) discovered in the Greater ANTILLES by archaeologists; it is believed that by the time of the conquest, every large village had one of these courts. Although no ball court has been discovered in Jamaica, we do know the Tainos here also played the game.

The game played by the Tainos was similar to the one played in Mexico and Middle America by the Aztecs and Mayas. Two opposing teams attempted to advance a ball to goals at either end of the field, keeping it in the air without crossing a line, knocking it out of the court or touching it with the hands or feet. Each time one side failed to do this, the opposition scored. It was a game played by men and women, usually separately. Each side could have 10-30 players.

Playing batey required enormous strength as the hips, thighs, and shoulders alone were used

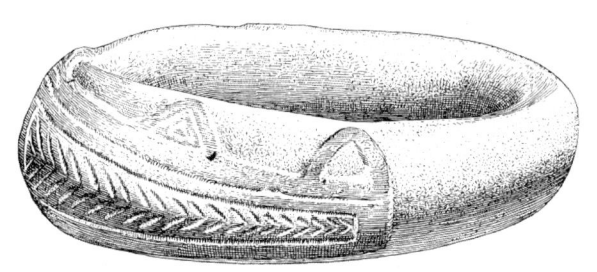

Taino 'stone collar' (from Fewkes)

and it could be quite dangerous to the players, a heavy ball of rubber or other resinous material being used. This astonished the Europeans who were not familiar with rubber. Many artefacts discovered in the CARIBBEAN which archaeologists call 'stone collars' and whose purpose has been a mystery are now believed to have been belts worn by the players to deflect the ball and provide protection, rather like the yokes worn by Mexican players.

The ball games sometimes represented contests of rival teams loyal to competitive CACIQUES. The Taino ball courts so far unearthed show they were large level spaces, usually rectangular and enclosed by a ring of stones.

[Bercht et al. 1998, Fewkes 1907, Rouse 1992, Stevens-Arroyo 1988, Steward 1948]

BATH FOUNTAIN

'The Bath of St Thomas the Apostle' is the official name for Bath Mineral Spring (or Bath Fountain) in ST THOMAS Parish. The spring was discovered around 1695 by a runaway slave named Jacob, on the backlands of the estate of his master, Col Stanton. When he found that the warm waters of a pool deep in the forest healed ulcers on his legs that had plagued him for years, he braved his master's wrath and returned to tell him about the marvellous discovery.

News of the spring spread but only the most daring – or the most desperate – at first went there, for there were neither roads nor shelter. However, in 1696 two persons built huts to stay in and regained their health after ten days at the spring. This spurred development. In 1699 the owner of the land sold the spring and 457ha to the government for £400 and the Bath of St Thomas the Apostle was formed. However, it does not seem to have been developed before 1731 when an Act was passed and £500 voted by the House of Assembly for the development of Bath. The town of BATH was laid out, a road was built, and buildings erected, including a hospital in the town square, on the spot later occupied by the courthouse.

Bath Mineral Spring is located on the east bank of the Sulphur River about 180m north of the guest house which is itself about 2.4km north of the town of Bath. The water comes from both cold and hot springs (temperature 46-54°C) which issue from the rocks over which the bath house has been built. The water is mixed before being piped into the baths to attain the

Caricature of the planter's life by William Holland, 1807-1808

proper temperature. Bath mineral water is high in sulphur and lime and is regarded as of special value in the treatment of rheumatic ailments and skin diseases. It is mildly radioactive.

Shortly after it was opened, Bath began to record cases of people cured there, like Mr Watson whose 'dry bellyache was eased by the first draught of the water'; or Mrs Forbes who was cured 'of the hysterics and loss of appetite and spleen'; or Mr Gordon who was cured 'of lowness of spirit and depraved appetite'. Many writers of this time claimed that in planter society, Bath was almost a necessity because of the general over-indulgence in food and drink by both men and women for, as a governor's wife (Lady Nugent) later described them, 'they ate like cormorants and drank like porpoises'. One doctor claimed that the 'dry bellyache' for which many came to be cured was caused by nothing more than an over-indulgence in RUM punch.

A stay at Bath usually involved a change of diet and habits and some found drinking Bath water a substitute for alcohol. According to the historian Edward Long (1774), the water at first drinking, 'diffuses a thrilling glow over the whole body; and the continued use enlivens the spirits, and sometimes produces the same joyous effects as inebriation. On this account, some notorious topers have quitted their claret for a while, and come hither, merely for the sake of a little variety in their practice of debauch, and to enjoy the singular felicity of getting drunk with water'.

Succeeding generations have continued to sip and dip in Bath water, ascribing to it powers as varied as the patronage.
[Handbooks of Jamaica, Long 1774, Porter 1990]

BATH GARDEN

Located in ST THOMAS Parish, this botanic garden was established by the government in 1779 and is said to be the second oldest one in existence in the Western Hemisphere. (The oldest, established in 1765, is on the island of St Vincent.) When the town of BATH was laid out, a piece of land was put aside for a botanic garden and Dr Thomas Clarke, 'Practitioner in Physic and Surgery', came to the island in 1777 as its first superintendent. He was also the doctor in charge of Bath hospital. Later, the garden and hospital came under the care of Dr Thomas Dancer, Island Botanist. (See MEDICINE, Folk.) At this garden, many of the plants introduced to Jamaica were first planted, among them CINNAMON, JACKFRUIT, CROTON, Jacaranda and BOUGAINVILLEA. The most important plant ever introduced here, however, was the BREADFRUIT.

The garden is much smaller today than when it was established and bears little trace of its former glory having been repeatedly flooded by the Sulphur River. There is a fine stand of Royal PALMS at the entrance and a splendid example of BARRINGTONIA. There is also the Screw Pine with stilt roots that was among the plants on board a French ship captured in 1782 by HMS *Flora*, a ship in Lord RODNEY'S squadron at the Battle of the Saints, St Lucia, the last Anglo-French battle in the Caribbean. Finally, descendants of at least two varieties of the original Breadfruit trees can be seen in one corner of the garden.
[Cundall 1915, Eyre 1966]

BATH, Town of

Village located in the interior of ST THOMAS Parish that owes its origin at the beginning of the 18th century to the discovery and development of BATH FOUNTAIN. In 1731 an Act was passed by the government that led to the development of the town. Public buildings were erected and lots sold to the fashionable who built town houses there. Twice a day they would ride up the hill to the spring, sheltering from the sudden rain showers at sheds conveniently placed by the road.

At nights, Bath – like its famous English namesake – was the scene of gaiety and amusement: there were balls, card games, and billiards. However, Bath's splendour was extremely brief. One reason frequently cited for its rapid fall from fashion is the fact that the atmosphere there was ruined by the clash of political factions, and people began to stay away. This turmoil apparently reflected overseas loyalties, specifically the split between Jacobites

Town of Bath, 18th century

and Hanoverians. (Jacobites were members of the Catholic Stuart dynasty, supporters of James II who had abdicated in 1688 and his descendants who included Bonnie Prince Charlie; Hanoverians were Protestant supporters of the Hanover dynasty which began with King George I in 1714 and ended with Queen Victoria in 1901.)

Bath soon lost its influx of seasonal residents and became a ghost town with ten inhabitants. The hospital was turned into barracks for soldiers and goats gambolled on the billiard tables. Bath developed as a village but never regained its former splendour, though the spring has remained an attraction for visitors to this day.
[Cundall 1915, Long 1774]

BAUHINIA (*Bauhinia spp.*)

Beautiful leguminous flowering shrubs or trees popularized only recently as public ornamental plants, especially in town house and apartment

Bauhinia – Poor Man's Orchid

complexes. Bauhinia includes many species and varieties found in tropical regions. Some species are indigenous to the CARIBBEAN and in Jamaica have been cultivated in gardens for a long time; several species can be seen growing wild in hilly areas. The plant's recent popularity owes much to imported hybrid varieties, especially the purple, though there are several other colours, especially pink, lavender, and white.

All bauhinias have flowers and leaves of characteristic shapes, the flowers well described by the popular name, Poor Man's Orchid. Another common name for the plants, Bull Hoof, describes the cleft shape of the leaves. The twin lobes of the leaves also symbolize the brothers Jean and Gaspard Bauhin, FRENCH herbalists of the 16th century after whom the genus was named.
[Adams 1972, Kingsbury 1988]

BAUXITE

The raw material from which the metal aluminium is made. Bauxite ore occurs in red earth found in the LIMESTONE areas of Jamaica, high grade deposits occurring in the parishes of MANCHESTER, TRELAWNY, ST ELIZABETH, and ST ANN. Lower grade but exploitable deposits occur in the uplands of ST CATHERINE, CLARENDON, and ST JAMES parishes. At one time the country was the world's largest producer of bauxite.

The existence of red ferruginous earth in Jamaica was known from the late 19th century though its potential importance as an ore of the metal aluminium was not recognized at the time, commercial production of aluminium from bauxite beginning only in the late 1880s. It was not until the middle of the Second WORLD WAR that exploitation of the mineral was first considered. New interest in bauxite came about when a local planter, Sir Alfred D'Costa, sent soil from sections of a property he owned in St Ann for analysis, since it yielded poor crops. Back came the answer – it was almost pure bauxite. A Canadian company began prospecting and proved the existence of significant deposits in the parishes of St Ann, Manchester, and St Elizabeth. In November 1942 under wartime regulations, the government declared all bauxite in Jamaica the property of the Crown. Extensive exploration work was begun in 1943 leading to the first test shipment to North America that year. Because of the war, commercial exploitation was delayed, the first shipment being made in 1952.

Reynolds Metal Company of America bought Sir Alfred D'Costa's properties of Lydford and Crescent Park and was among the pioneers of bauxite exploitation in Jamaica. (Reynolds has put up a plaque to Sir Alfred at Crescent Park, near to the MONEAGUE roundabout.) Reynolds Jamaica Mines Ltd sent the first regular export shipment of bauxite in 1952 and the industry developed rapidly from this start.

Bauxite is currently mined by subsidiaries of North American multinational firms. The companies either dry the ore and ship it in its raw state for processing overseas or they process the raw bauxite into alumina, a second stage on the way to making aluminium. The alumina is then shipped overseas for smelting. Bauxite companies operating in Jamaica include Kaiser

Bauxite mining c. 1962

Jamaica Bauxite Company; Alumina Partners of Jamaica (ALPART); JAMALCO, Clarendon Alumina Works (formerly ALCOA) and the West Indies Alumina Company (WINDALCO, formerly Alcan Jamaica).

[Hose 1950, Porter 1990, Wright and White 1969]

BEADS

Jamaican craftwork employs a wide range of decorative beads derived from indigenous plants. Among beads used in necklaces are Soapberry (*Sapindus saponaria*) which is hard, black and perfectly round and Job's-tears (*Coix lacryma-jobi*), a hard mottled grey and brown triangular seed which grows on a water grass and is often dyed in bright colours. JOHN CROW BEAD (*Abrus precatorius*) which is small and shiny red with a black spot, used to be very popular in craft items but its use for that purpose has been banned because of its poisonous nature (though the poison is killed when the hard seed is boiled before being pierced for stringing). There is also the seed of the Circassian or Red Bean Tree (*Adenanthera pavonina*). Its remarkable feature is that each seed is usually the same in weight (just under four grams) for which reason it has traditionally been employed in other countries as a jewellers' or apothecaries' weight. The seed of CACOON (*Entada gigas*) is very large, flat, chocolate brown. Horse Eye Bean is round and flat with a black band around it and grows on a climbing vine similar to COWITCH (*Mucana pruriens*). Nicker or nicol (*Caesalpinia spp.*) is a polished yellow or grey seed much valued in the game of marbles and attractive in necklaces.

Certain leguminous plants also yield attractive beads – POINCIANA that has flat, long seeds, Wild Tamarind (*Pithecellobium arboreum*) which yields similar smaller seeds, and Barbados Pride (*Caesalpinia pulcherrima*). The huge Sandbox Tree (*Hura crepitans*) yields circular flattish fruits that contain numerous flat, crescent-shaped seeds; Elephant Ears (*Enterolobium cyclocarpum*) is a brown fruit with a light yellow rim, also suitable as a bead. The hard fruit of certain PALMS (e.g. Sago and Talipot) are also employed in ornamental work, and beads have also been strung from the hard, shiny brown seeds of the Canna or Indian Shot (*Canna spp.*).

Beads such as these, used in craftwork and decoration by enslaved Africans, have been found in excavations at their settlements dating from the mid-18th century and were certainly in use earlier. Many have also been found in TAINO sites. Taino beads were made mainly of stones, shells and fish bones. Those of stone were called

Early 16th century Taino beaded cotton zemi (front and back views) Dominican Republic in the Museo Nazionale Preistorico/Ethnografico L. Pigorini, Rome reproduced with permission from the Ministero per i Beni e le Attività Culturali. (Below) Beaded belt with zemi in the Museum für Völkerkunde, Vienna

ciba; long strings of stone beads called *colecibi* were much prized. Among the presents the CACIQUE Guacanagarí on Haiti gave COLUMBUS were 800 of these beads. One description of beads as body ornament is that of 'the elder daughter and most beautiful' of a Jamaican cacique. She 'walked completely naked except for a pretext of a belt made of very small and black stones girdling only the waist from which dangled a thing shaped like an ivy leaf made of green and coloured stones fastened onto woven cotton'. (This belt or 'skirt', worn by married women only, was called a *nagua*.)

Glass beads that were among the first trade items offered by the Europeans became highly popular with the Tainos and incorporated into their work. Among the finest examples of Taino art are a beaded ZEMI in the Pigorini Museum in Rome, Italy, and a beaded belt in the Museum für Völkerkunde in Vienna, Austria, their similarity in style suggesting the same maker.
[Adams 1972, Alegría 1985, Bercht et al. 1998, Cassidy 1971, DJE]

Bead vendors and tourist

BECKFORD

One of the famous English planter families in colonial Jamaica. They were the island's biggest landowners during its heyday as the world's largest SUGAR producer. At one time four Beckford brothers owned over 16,800ha of land, of which one-third was in WESTMORELAND Parish. Williamsfield and Petersfield are among the places in that parish named after Beckfords. (See also DRAX HALL.) Petersfield was named after the founder of the family in Jamaica, Peter Beckford, who was descended from a family long established in Gloucestershire and who is mentioned in Pepys' *Diary*. He came to the island in 1655 as an officer in Penn and Venables Army (see CAPTURE OF JAMAICA) and soon restored the family fortunes, becoming one of the wealthiest planters. It is said that he made his start by hunting wild horses and selling them. His son, Col Peter Beckford Jr, was matriculated at Oxford (the first Jamaican-born person to be admitted) and became lieutenant governor of Jamaica, speaker of the House of Assembly, and president of the Council.

West Indian sugar grown and reaped by the blood and sweat of slaves (see SUGAR PLANTATION, SLAVERY) enabled the establishment in England of a powerful West India lobby which mounted a formidable defence of planter interests in and out of the BRITISH parliament. Sugar not only made planters like the Beckfords rich, it enabled them to buy their children entrance into fashionable society in England at a time when the phrase 'rich as a West India planter' was commonly used. Since

William Beckford, Lord Mayor of London

Fonthill Abbey

at the time it took a great deal of money to 'buy' an English parliamentary seat, Beckford money also 'talked' in this area. In 1754 the Independent Merchants and Traders of London complained to the House of Commons that absentees were able to 'support contests in some of the richest and most populous cities in this country' and referred specifically to the Beckfords. Three brothers of them at one time held three of the most fashionable and expensive parliamentary seats. They were Peter Beckford Jr's sons: William Beckford (1709-70), born in Jamaica and owner of 8,900ha in the island in 1750, a successful London merchant and city Alderman and twice Lord Mayor of London who was MP for Shaftesbury from 1747-54 and London from 1754-70; Richard Beckford (owner of 3,740ha in Jamaica), MP for Bristol 1754-56, and Julines Beckford (owner of 3,317ha) who sat for Salisbury from 1754-64.

William Beckford's illegitimate son Richard was also a West Indian planter and MP (Bridport 1780-84, Arundel 1784-90, Leominster 1791-98). William Beckford Jr (1759-1844), the Lord Mayor's legitimate son, never came to Jamaica but inherited a 'princely fortune' at the age of 11. Called by Byron 'England's wealthiest son', he later became notorious for his personal lifestyle, his eccentric residence, Fonthill, built in the form of a Gothic abbey, and the sensational novel that he wrote called *Vathek*. He was an absentee MP for Wells from 1784-90 and Hindon (1790-94 and 1806-20) during which time he squandered a large fortune.

Another William (1744-99), an illegitimate son of the Lord Mayor's brother, inherited some of the vast Westmoreland properties including Fort William, Williamsfield, and ROARING RIVER, and spent four years in Jamaica as a planter. However, he got seriously in debt and spent some time in the English debtor's prison, the Fleet. There he occupied himself writing the two-volume *A Descriptive Account of the Island of Jamaica*. William Beckford was also the patron of two English artists who left behind paintings done in Jamaica in the late 18th century, George Robertson, who painted landscapes, and Philip Wickstead, a portrait painter. The Beckford family graves are in the chancel of the SPANISH TOWN CATHEDRAL.
[Cundall 1915, Fryer 1984, Wright and White 1969]

BEDWARD, Alexander (1859-1930)

Popular folk hero and leader of a messianic cult movement ('Bedwardism') which attracted thousands of followers from all over Jamaica, Cuba, and Central America from the late 19th century. The movement was centred on the Jamaica Native Baptist Free Church in AUGUST TOWN, ST ANDREW Parish, on the bank of the HOPE RIVER.

Bedward was converted by H.E.S. Woods, better known as 'Shakespeare', a remarkable prophet who founded the church. Among Shakespeare's prophecies was one that a great religious leader and movement centred at August Town would arise from among the ranks of the church elders. It would be some time before Bedward fulfilled this role.

Bedward was born of poor parents and worked as a farm labourer at Mona Estate. From all accounts he had no special claim to righteousness or virtue. In the 1880s he emigrated to Colón, along with tens of thousands of other Jamaicans in search of work on the PANAMA Canal, then under construction by a French syndicate. (See also COLÓN MAN.) While in Colón, Bedward had a vision or 'religious crisis' that made him return home. He was baptized by Shakespeare and became actively involved in the August Town church.

It was not until 1891 that he actually began his Mission, having been 'called by God'. Bedward's fame as a preacher and faith healer soon spread far beyond the little village, and thousands came to be cleansed of their sins by being 'dipped in the healing stream'. Miracle cures were attributed to the Hope River water that was also taken home in containers.

But Bedward was more than a REVIVAL preacher for he boldly challenged secular authority as well as the religious establishment, and the colonial government soon became anxious about the 'goings on' at August Town. They kept a close watch on the Prophet and his followers and in 1895 arrested him for sedition following his prophecy that 'the black wall shall

Alexander Bedward, December 1920

crush the white wall' and, even more alarming, his references to the 'Morant War' (see **MORANT BAY REBELLION**). Bedward was declared insane and committed to the lunatic asylum but was soon released on the intervention of his lawyers. (It should be pointed out that committal to the asylum was not infrequently used by the authorities against perceived 'troublemakers', i.e. those who engaged in anti-colonial rhetoric, such as Leonard Howell, one of the founders of **RASTAFARI**.)

Bedward resumed his activities and between 1895-1921 the phenomenon of Bedwardism grew. In 1920 he announced that he would ascend to Heaven on 31 December and descend on 3 January 1921. Thousands of persons in Jamaica and from Panama, Cuba and other parts of Central America disposed of their belongings and came to camp at August Town to wait for the 'miracle'. It failed to take place and Bedward announced that the time was not yet right.

On 21 April 1921, Bedward decided to lead a march of his followers from August Town to Kingston for a 'manifestation'. The police and soldiers were waiting for him, a warrant having been issued for his arrest. The march was intercepted and Bedward was arrested and so were 685 of his followers (many dressed in white robes and carrying wooden crosses and palm leaves). The followers were charged under the Vagrancy Law and many were jailed; others (mainly women and children) were discharged, and a few were remanded for trial. Bedward was ordered committed to Bellevue once again and there he remained until his death on 8 November 1930.

The American anthropologist Martha Warren Beckwith was one of those who interviewed Bedward at the height of his fame, visiting him on the morning of 26 December 1920. 'I looked into his face in vain for any trace of an imposter', she asserted. She described him as 'a large fine-looking Negro with the rapt brightness on his face of a visionary' and believed him to be, not a 'scheming pretender' as some said, but 'a dreamer'.

A doctor who gave evidence at his trial in 1895 was quoted as saying: 'I think witness not as responsible as very sane men. He can realize right and wrong when explained to him, but when on his legs preaching he has no conception of what he is saying; that is not an uncommon thing. He suffers from amentia rather than dementia.'

Ken Post has argued that 'Whether he was certifiably insane or not is from our point of view probably immaterial. What is important is that for nearly thirty years his church attracted the support of large numbers of the sufferers of Jamaica, and that their support was an expression of protest against prevailing conditions. Bedwardism was . . . a vital link in the continuity of protest from Morant Bay onwards'.

Bedward's true role in Jamaican history is still to be assessed. A mad man to many, to others he was a political visionary preaching black nationalism and black redemption, drawing on the traditions of the Native **BAPTIST** church, providing for some a bridge to Garveyism (see **GARVEY**) and Rastafari. His church functioned according to an elaborate organizational structure and he had a distinct theology.

Regardless of the ultimate judgement of history, Bedward's place as an authentic folk hero seems secure. He inspired a number of songs, two of which at least are still well known. One goes:

Dip dem Bedward, dip dem
Dip dem in de healing stream
Dip dem sweet but not too deep
Dip dem fe cure bad feeling.

The other, more derisive, is 'Sly (or Slide) Mongoose' which tells of how a scheming young man made off with one of Bedward's flock:

> Mongoose go inna Bedward kitchen
> Pluck weh wan a him righteous chicken
> Put i' inna him waistcoat pocket
> Sly Mongoose!
>
> Mongoose seh him a Bedward member
> Bedward seh him nuh quite remember
> Mongoose seh him join last December
> Sly Mongoose!

[Beckwith 1929, Brooks 1917, Chevannes 1994, Post 1978]

BEES

The domesticated honeybee was brought to Jamaica by the Spaniards. There is a record of honey being produced at New SEVILLE in 1534 but bee-keeping might have been established before that time. Many excellent varieties of honey are produced in Jamaica today, the most esteemed being LOGWOOD.

The imported honeybee displaced most native bee species that were believed to be stingless. These were relatively small bees that generally nested in tree hollows, a hive numbering hundreds of individuals, and were the bees of the native peoples of Central and South America and the Caribbean. The TAINOS of Cuba brought honey from these bees to COLUMBUS and those of Hispaniola brought beeswax. They also occurred in Jamaica but seem to have vanished, either much reduced or made extinct as a result of the raids on the hives by ants or the imported honeybees.

Dr T.H. Farr, late entomologist of the INSTITUTE OF JAMAICA asked in 1967: 'Where have all the stingless bees gone? We used to have them here; Richard Hill saw them in 1847 "at Skelton Pen on the banks of the Rio Cobre",' and specimens were collected by a scientist in 1923. Dr Farr himself though constantly on the lookout, never saw a single specimen.

[Facey 1993, Farr 1967]

BELLS OF PORT ROYAL

Two sets of church bells are associated with LEGENDS of PORT ROYAL. It is said that in rough seas, fishermen can hear the tolling of church bells beneath the sea from the direction of Church Beacon, a permanent navigational marker. It is believed that this is where St Paul's Church sank beneath the sea during the EARTHQUAKE of 1692 that destroyed the town. Despite the fact that underwater explorations have shown that the building beneath Church Beacon is not that of the church at all, but Fort James, some still claim to hear the ghostly church bells.

Also associated with Port Royal is a large Spanish-made bronze bell that was dredged up after the earthquake. Although cracked, the bell was hung in the new church built at Port Royal, but the crack widened and it was taken down and sold for scrap. The bell eventually ended up in a junk shop in Kingston and was purchased by the government as an important historic relic. It is now in the INSTITUTE OF JAMAICA. On the day of the earthquake, 7 June 1692, there were several 'Spanish prizes' at dock in Port Royal harbour awaiting auction, and this bell is probably from one of them. Until recently it was one of the few SPANISH relics ever found in Jamaica above ground, despite the fact that the Spaniards occupied the island for over 150 years. (Numerous Spanish artefacts have been found in archaeological excavations, especially at SEVILLE.)

[Cundall 1915, Marx 1967]

BENBOW, Vice-Admiral John (1653-1702)

One of the famous 'English sea dogs' associated with Jamaica's early history. In 1697 Benbow was stationed at PORT ROYAL as commander of the King's Ships in the West Indies. He later returned to England but was sent back to Port Royal in 1702. Benbow is remembered for his courageous conduct in a battle that year. This was during the War of the Spanish Succession when England and the Netherlands declared war on France and Spain. CARIBBEAN territories

Admiral Benbow

belonging to these nations immediately became targets for enemy attacks. Benbow sailed for NEGRIL with a large fleet in search of the French Admiral Du Casse. He found and engaged him in a battle lasting for five days, but was forced to give up when several of his captains refused to fight any longer and deserted him. He continued to direct operations for some time after one leg was shattered by a shot.

On his return to Port Royal, Benbow courtmartialled his officers and as a result two were sentenced to be shot. He died of his wounds two months after the battle and was buried in KINGSTON PARISH CHURCH. His tombstone is near the High Altar.

[Cundall 1915]

BENTA

MUSICAL INSTRUMENT made of BAMBOO with a gourd (CALABASH) resonator; along with TAMBU, the principal instrument at a DINKI MINI or death observance in ST MARY Parish.

Musician Marjorie Whylie points out that the benta is a glissed instrument related to other instruments in the region such as the *berimbao* of Brazil. It is constructed using a length of thick bamboo consisting of two or three joints, with a string lifted from the outer bark and carefully tied at either end to prevent further stripping. For playing, the benta is laid horizontally with a piece of wood holding the string out from the body.

A player at one end slides the dried gourd resonator along the string to produce a 'heavy, low and twanging note on the first and third beats of each bar' as Olive Lewin describes it, while a player at the opposite end uses two slender bamboo sticks to play 'an ostinato rhythm' on the string. The benta is believed to have CONGO antecedents. The NATIONAL DANCE THEATRE COMPANY has choreographed a dance called Gerrehbenta which takes its name from the death celebration GERREH, found in western parishes, and dinki mini/benta found in the east, where a benta is played to accompany the dance.

The instrument has come to public attention fairly recently and the benta as we know it today is not listed in the DJE though there is reference to an instrument called a 'bender' by William Beckford (1790) which had become 'benta' by 1868 (defined as 'a rude musical instrument'). Beckford described what seems to be a musical bow, the simplest of all stringed instruments, being developed from a hunting bow, and commonly found in Africa, Asia and the Americas. The addition of a resonator is a later development. Beckford described the bender as made of 'a bent stick, the ends of which are restrained in this direction by a slip of dried grass; the upper part of which is greatly compressed between the lips, and to which the breath gives a soft and pleasing vibration'. The player pressed a slender stick to the string a little below his mouth to graduate the vibration. The instrument, according to Beckford, produced 'a trembling, a querulous, and a delightful harmony'.

[Cassidy 1961, DJE, Lewin 2000, Musical Instruments 1976, Tanna and Ramsay 1987, Marjorie Whylie, personal communication]

BESSY

Term used in several different senses, which are perhaps not unconnected. 'Bessy' is used to describe a busybody, someone who always puts in an appearance, such as 'Burying-', 'Funeral-' or 'Wedding-Bessy', similar usage being found in England and the USA. In Jamaica the term has also come to be applied to birds and other animals that display what is construed as exaggerated and stereotyped 'female' characteristics, for instance 'Bessy-kick up', a bird which, according to the DJE 'flirts or bobs its tail as it walks'. In old English folk dances 'Bessy' is a female impersonator who no doubt mimics the busybody female.

However, when applied to movement, bessy means 'bend' according to F.G. Cassidy. In the ring GAME 'Bessy Down', the child playing Bessy stoops and juts or bobs her bottom and it is in this sense that the term appears in one version of the folk song and game 'Hill an Gully Rider'

> Hill an Gully Rider, Hill an Gully
> An a ben dung low dung Hill an Gully
> An a low dung bessy dung Hill an Gully

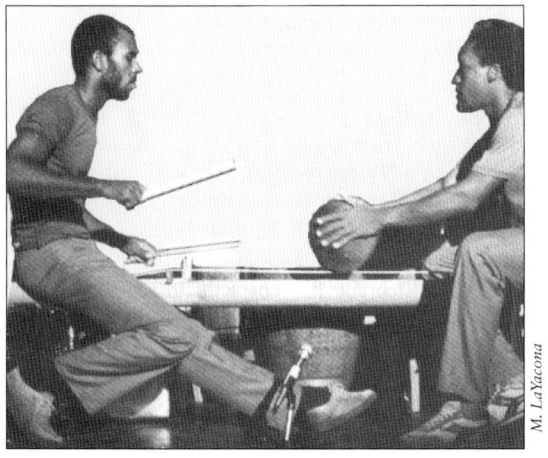

Benta players

The DCEU ascribes the name to a French source, bésé-dòng being used for the ring game which is also played in Trinidad, bésé in French creole meaning 'bend down', from French baisser, meaning to lower, to let down.
[Cassidy 1961, DCEU, DJE, Leach and Fried 1972]

BIBLE IN FOLKLORE

The Bible is often used by Jamaican folk as a ritual object. G.E. Simpson in *Black Religions* says this is a trait borrowed from Europeans and reinterpreted throughout America and the Caribbean. Opie's *Dictionary of Superstitions* confirms this, with many entries regarding the use of the Bible in European divination, for instance 'Book and Key' which is well known in Jamaica and other Caribbean countries (and described in V.S. Naipaul's novel *The Suffrage of Elvira*). This is a kind of trial by ordeal in which a key is inserted at an appropriate text in the Bible (relevant to the case) and the Bible and key tied with string. Two persons then place their fingertips on either side of the key to balance the Bible while they call various names including that of the suspect person. Or, in other versions, the accused swears an oath while touching the Bible or holding the key. Details vary, but generally the Bible and key will give a sign to indicate guilt – by swinging around or falling to the ground, for instance.

In Jamaica, the Bible is also used to protect from DUPPIES or harmful spirits, by inserting a knife inside a page, reading it backwards, placing it under a pillow or carrying it ahead of a newborn child when it is moved from one room to another. Specific Bible verses, especially the Psalms, are also used for conjuration to secure desired ends. Jamaica is not alone in this, Zora Neal Hurston in *Mules and Men* which describes the folklore of the American south, said of her informants: 'All hold that the Bible is the greatest conjure book in the world.'
[DJE, Madden 1835, Opie 1992, Puckett 1926]

BIG BOY

Traditional jokes about this mythic figure beloved of school children have circulated for generations. Big Boy is the over grown, over aged, over sexed prankster who remains in the lower grades forever, unable to pass his exams but always able to pass remarks intended to shock. The jokes deal with rebellion against authority, scatological humour, and sexual matters. A typical example: A little boy is telling the teacher that his father lives abroad and wrote a letter to his mother, after which she had a baby, to which Big Boy comments: 'A woulda like see de pen him take fe write dat letter.' Many variants of the jokes exist.
[Dance 1985]

BIRDS

About 280 species of birds have been recorded from Jamaica. Of these, 30 species and 19 subspecies are endemic, i.e. they are found nowhere else. Among the endemic birds is the national bird of Jamaica, the Streamer Tail HUMMINGBIRD, better known as Doctor Bird. All but one of these endemic birds are protected by Jamaica's wildlife laws. In the past, bird hunting was a popular pastime but it is now severely restricted, the government declaring the dates of the season, setting bag limits, and so on.

Eight species of birds have been successfully introduced into the island (in addition to domestic fowl that are all introductions). They are the Starling, the Saffron Finch (also called Wild Canary), the House Sparrow, the Guiana Parrotlet and more recently the Nutmeg Mannikin, Chestnut Mannikin, Golden Bishop and Red Bishop. Two other species are self-introduced, that is they extended their range and found suitable habitat on the island (probably owing to man's destruction of natural vegetation). These are the CATTLE EGRET and the Shiny Cowbird. It is believed that within historic times three (possibly four) species of birds have become extinct. Several others are at risk, being endangered or vulnerable.

Jamaica's bird population consists of residents and winter and summer visitors. There are 116 breeding species and over 80 winter visitors. The island lies on one of the main migration routes between the north and south and migrating birds frequently stop here on their journeys. In the winter months, some birds that breed in the north migrate southwards. A large number of birds arrive during August to November. Many of these visitors spend more time here than they do on their breeding grounds. The majority of the winter visitors are shorebirds and warblers. A smaller number of bird visitors arrive in the summer. These come from their homes further south to breed in Jamaica. Among these well-known visitors is a vireo known as John-to-Whit that comes around March, and the PETCHARY. A number of birds that spend most of the year far out in the ocean also arrive on the CAYS near Jamaica to breed. Among them are the sooty and noddy terns, known locally as BOOBY Birds. Some birds are also passage migrants. They pass

through the island on their journeys north or south.
[Bond 1960, Downer and Sutton 1990, Gosse 1984, Jeffrey-Smith 1972, Raffaele et al. 1998, Smith 1968, Taylor 1955]

BIRDS IN FOLKLORE

In Jamaica, BIRDS are often seen as the symbols of departed souls or as spirit messengers – an ancient, world-wide concept. Their eggs and feathers are also assigned significance.

Among contemporary Jamaicans, the OWL ('Patu') symbolizes death or witchcraft. (See OL-HIGE.) Other birds such as the Ground-dove, White Belly, and the Gimme-me-bit are associated with spirits (see DUPPY). Spiritual significance is also given to the Doctor Bird (see HUMMINGBIRD) and the JOHN CROW. Of yard fowl, the SENSEH is believed capable of scratching up any hidden secrets, e.g. bad 'guzu' or CHARMS. In African-Jamaican religions, birds – most often DOVES or pigeons but also yard fowl – are used in blood sacrifice.

Feathers and eggs are sometimes associated with the spirit world and are used in OBEAH practices. R.T. Banbury, writing in the 19th century, noted that eggs were much dreaded, being considered an embodiment of obeah, and that few would steal eggs out of the nest. Egg stealing in any event was discouraged by the belief that if someone stole an egg, he would keep on stealing till he died. In 'shadow-catching' exercises by MYAL men and women, the COTTON TREE was sometimes pelted with eggs to release the spirit, the eggs presumably a payment or offering to the tree.

Among the native peoples of the Americas, feather ornaments and garments are symbols of spirituality. The shaman (the principal religious figure of native Americans) serves as an intermediary between man and the other worlds and he or she often does so in the guise of a bird able to fly between realms. In CAVES in Jamaica where TAINO pictographs and petroglyphs have been found, birds or humans with bird heads are frequently depicted, and birds are often portrayed on carvings, etc. Although we cannot be sure of their meaning, these depictions might well be associated with spirituality. One of the most important Taino carvings ever discovered was the so-called 'Bird Man' found in a cave in Jamaica at 'Spots', Carpenter's Mountain.

Bird feathers were also used as personal adornment by the Tainos, among other South American peoples and were perhaps symbols of authority and power. Tyrrell and Tyrrell (1984) note that: 'The Aztecs, for example, adorned the ceremonial cloaks of Montezuma with the brilliant plumage of hummingbirds. Statues of deities . . . were fashioned so as to display the stunning metallic hues in the bird's feathers.' On his first visit to Jamaica, COLUMBUS was greeted at OLD HARBOUR by a CACIQUE wearing 'a cloak of coloured feathers of a shape like a coat-of-arms and on his head, a large feathered headdress'. Peter Martyr also tells us that on going to battle and on festive days, the men (who otherwise went about naked) put on feather tufts and feather cloaks of various colours.

'Savacou' by Ronald Moody (UWI campus)

Birds, e.g. hummingbirds, are also connected with TOBACCO, of great spiritual significance to the Tainos, tobacco smoke being the food offered by the shaman to the spirits that help him. This close connection to the shaman offers one possible explanation for the Doctor Bird's popular name (see HUMMINGBIRD).

Water birds are also depicted frequently in Taino art, symbolizing rain and fertility. The woodpecker is another spiritually significant bird for native Americans and in the myths is the one that assisted men in the creation of women (see WOODPECKER). Spiritual qualities were also attributed to PARROTS; they were frequently kept as pets and taught to speak and their feathers valued for adornment.

Bird symbolism also appears in the Christian religion in Jamaica as elsewhere, especially in church decoration and architecture. The dove

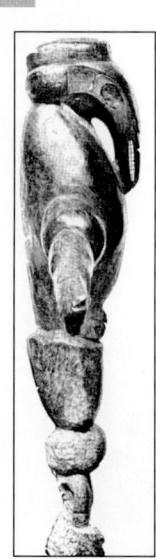

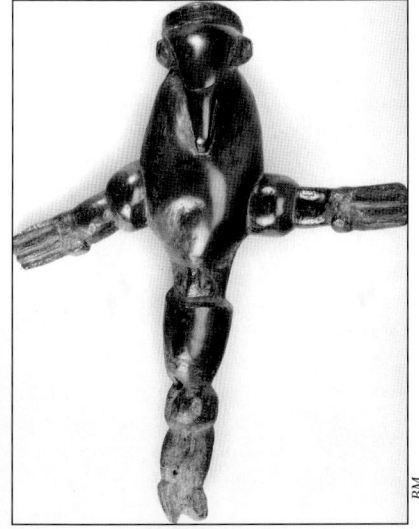

Jamaican Taino 'Bird man' carving, side and front view

frequently represents the Holy Ghost, a role played by the PELICAN at the University chapel, that bird being the symbol of the university. In European folklore the pelican symbolized unstinting self-sacrifice, hence its association with Christ. It was thought to pluck out its own breast in order to feed its young, its method of regurgitating pre-digested food having been misunderstood.

Birds have found their way into numerous PROVERBS, sayings and songs, 'Chi Chi Bud-O' – which lists an endless array of birds – being one of the best known folk songs. In religious hymns, the REVIVAL 'I saw a parakeet in the garden' is an outstanding example of the bird metaphor, likening the betrayer Judas to the talkative parrot. There are also many folk tales featuring birds, 'Bird Cherry Island' being one of the best-loved ANANSI stories. In this story, each bird lends Anansi a feather so that he can fly with them to their favourite feeding ground. Anansi, as usual, becomes too greedy and the angry birds remove their feathers, leaving him stranded.

Like peoples the world over, Jamaicans use bird behaviour as a weather prognosticator. (See, e.g. GAULIN.) The close observation of birds over many centuries has also led the countryman to attribute articulate sounds to many bird cries, and give birds names such as Gimme-me-bit and John-to-Whit, based on these cries. Many interpretations of bird sounds have been recorded by May Jeffrey-Smith and by visitors such as Charles Rampini and M.W. Beckwith. The Gimme-me-bit or Night Hawk is supposed by its cry to warn fishermen, 'Turtle inna net'.

Others say it screams 'Gimme-me-bit' (see MONEY) at humans to demand payment for ridding the night of mosquitoes. The Pea Dove's mournful cry says either, 'Mary dead, who kill im?' or 'Mary boil brown rice'; for church-goers it says, 'Moses preach God word'. The harsh guttural tones of the elusive Jabbering Crow were interpreted to P.H. Gosse as saying: 'Walk fast, Crab, do Bukra work. Cutacoo better than wallet.' (Cutacoo is a kind of BASKET.)

There are even domestic bird dialogues. The female Bald-pate coos: 'Sairey coat blue' while the male agrees: 'For true, for true, for true.' The Hen Turkey complains: 'We poor black people hab bery bad time' while the male Turkey gabbles out his counsel: 'Take heart, Take heart, Take heart, Take heart.'

[Alegría 1985, Banbury 1894, Beckwith 1924, Cassidy 1971, DJE, Jeffrey-Smith 1972, Mico 1896, Rampini 1873, Tyrrell and Tyrrell 1984, 1990]

BIRTH

African beliefs associated with birth were especially prevalent in rural areas in the days when children were delivered at home by the village midwife or Nana. These practices of course varied from place to place, and according to class and race. But some were fairly well known and might still be practised in some parts, though birth in a hospital is now the norm and children are more likely to be born and raised according to conventional western practices.

Isolating the mother and child for eight days after birth was fairly common. Once the Nana was summoned, she took charge of the household during birth and for the extended period following, when both child and mother were regarded as extremely vulnerable. Steps would be taken to protect them from spiritual harm as well as the physical dangers accompanying childbirth. The room was swept with a special broom and the sweepings not thrown out during this time; the child was marked with blue, and the scissors or knife used to cut the umbilical cord would be guarded. On the ninth day the child and mother were brought outdoors, to be greeted by family and visitors and given presents. The child would also be named on that day.

This probably stemmed from the West African belief that until the eighth day, the fate of the child is uncertain and its personality-soul is not localized until then. More significantly, the child might be a visitor from the spirit world in which case it should not be welcomed. Such a belief might explain the seeming neglect of slave children by the old Nanas for the first eight days of life. The child dying during that time would be taken as proof that it was an evil spirit or, as it is known in parts of West Africa, a 'born-to-die' child.

The treatment following birth is similar to that brought to the Caribbean by INDIANS from the sub-continent. Information is not available for Jamaica but Moore (1995) noted for Guyana that the child is not regarded as a separate being distinct from its mother for the first five to twelve days. During that time both are polluted and kept in isolation. Should the child die before being named, it would not have become a social personality. The naming ceremony took place 10-12 days after birth.

In preparing for the birth, the Jamaican Nana would anoint the mother's belly with CASTOR OIL; castor oil would also later be given to the child and castor oil and NUTMEG used to dress the navel. The child would be born into the Nana's hands and she would often blow smoke into its eyes – from the old clay pipe these women habitually smoked. (TOBACCO smoke is regarded in native American and African-Caribbean cultures as food for the (good) spirits). She would wash her face with RUM and sometimes drink some. According to informants of Fernando Henriques in PORTLAND Parish, this was done to give her 'eyesight' since every time she witnessed a birth her sight was affected. The newly-born was bathed in cold water into which rum and a silver coin from the father were thrown. The water and coin were buried in the yard along with the afterbirth, the Nana first counting the knots on the umbilical cord to determine how many children the mother was destined to have. The navel string was also buried and a tree planted on the spot. (See NAVEL STRING TREE.)

Aside from the protection offered by washing blue and an open BIBLE, the child might also be protected with a 'guzu' or CHARM of some sort, usually a strong-smelling substance like asafoetida. It is believed that a child born with a caul is able to see DUPPIES (the caul being a part of the inner membrane surrounding the foetus that is occasionally found on a child's head at birth).

[Clarke 1957, Henriques 1953, Kerr 1952, Moore 1995, Parrinder 1961, Patterson 1973]

BIRTH TREE see NAVEL STRING TREE

BISSY see KOLA

BLACK RIVER, The

Described as Jamaica's finest river, the Black River was originally named Rio Caobana by the Spaniards, *caobana* being the TAINO Arawak word for Mahogany.

The river, as the Hector's River, begins near to Coleyville, MANCHESTER Parish, and travels westerly for about 20km, forming the boundary between Manchester and TRELAWNY Parish. Shortly after passing Troy, Trelawny, the river sinks in wild cockpit country to reappear at Oxford, Manchester. Here it officially becomes known as the One Eye River, though local residents call it Noisy River from the sound of the cataracts where it emerges. After this it sinks underground again, passing through a ridge to the north of Bogue Hill.

When the river re-emerges at Siloah, ST ELIZABETH, it officially becomes the Black River, meandering through Siloah, Appleton, and Maggotty. In its 53.4km journey southwards from its source to the Caribbean Sea, the river grows to considerable size as it is joined by many tributaries, including the YS, Broad, Grass, Horse, and Savanna Rivers. In its lower reaches the river with tributaries drains an area of 88km^2 at elevations only slightly above sea level. Here it has created Jamaica's largest wetland, the Lower Black River Morass, consisting of MANGROVE, morasses, reeds and floating vegetation. The Lower Morass is rich in BIRDS and FISH, and it provides a habitat for the fast-disappearing TURTLES, CROCODILES and MANATEES. Shrimping is still an important industry.

The Black River was once the lifeline for prosperous activities along its basin. LOGWOOD was a thriving industry from the late 1800s to the early 1900s. There were also SUGAR estates

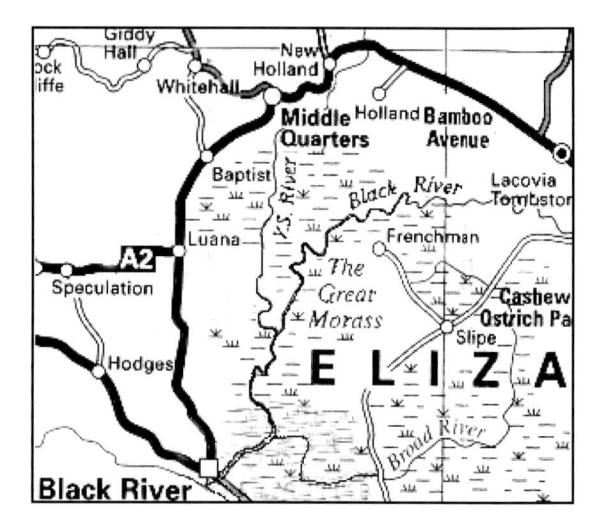

and large CATTLE farms nearby. Goods and people were transported on the river, in former times by lighters. Nowadays, river CANOES are still used, as well as boats for pleasure. There are commercial boat tours for visitors into the mangrove forests along the river.
[Handbooks of Jamaica, Jamaica 1946, Wade 1984, Wright and White 1969]

BLACK RIVER ANGLICAN CHURCH
The Parish Church of St John the Evangelist in BLACK RIVER, ST ELIZABETH Parish, was built in 1837. It contains marble monuments to Robert Hugh Munro (d 1798) and Caleb Dickenson (d 1821) who left money for the education of the poor children of the parish. The Dickensons owned Appleton estate. For several years the money was misused until the 1850s when the Trust was reorganized. The Munro and Dickenson Trust was used for the establishment of two schools, Munro College for boys and Hampton School for girls, both located in the hills near Malvern.

Munro was founded in 1856 with 12 pupils and Hampton in 1858. Shortly after its opening the boys' school was transferred to a place called Potsdam in the SANTA CRUZ mountains and the school was known as 'Potsdam' up to the First WORLD WAR when German names became unpopular. It was then changed to the name of one of its benefactors.

Potsdam property was so named by Henry Cerf, the pseudonym in Jamaica of a German aristocrat who sold all his properties when he returned to Europe to be the adviser of his cousin, the first King of the Belgians. Cerf was the surname of his Jewish grandmother.

BLACK RIVER SPA
Mineral spring located just outside the town of BLACK RIVER, ST ELIZABETH Parish. Up to the 1930s the spa was a fashionable watering place. Several cold sulphurous springs rise from a pool near the seaside and, as in the case of Jamaica's more famous mineral springs, miraculous cures have been attributed to its waters. The spa has now fallen into disuse.

BLACK RIVER, Town of
Principal town of ST ELIZABETH Parish, population 3,590 (1991), located on the shore at the mouth of the BLACK RIVER. The original name of the town was Gravesend, probably because of its unhealthy location. (See YELLOW FEVER AND MALARIA.)

There is little economic activity in the town nowadays but Black River was once a prosperous place, the inhabitants deriving their wealth mainly from the export of LOGWOOD. Black River was the main port from which this once valuable commodity was shipped, the logs being brought down the river. While the logwood boom lasted, it brought prosperity to the town that had its brief glory in the late 19th century, becoming the first town in Jamaica to have electric lights. A local family called Leyden installed lighting in 1893 at their house that was called 'Waterloo'. Waterloo is now a guest house as is another stately home in the town called Invercauld, built in 1890.
[Wade 1984, Wright and White 1969]

BLACKBIRDS
Jamaica's most endangered bird, an endemic genus, is known as the Jamaican Blackbird, or Wildpine Sargeant (*Nesopsar nigerrimus*). It is found only in mature forests where it is often seen feeding in wild pines. (See BROMELIAD.)

Two other birds called Blackbird are much more common, social birds, encountered year-round in Jamaica: the Cling-cling, Tinkling Grackle or Greater Antillean Grackle (*Quiscalus niger*), and the Smooth-billed Ani (*Crotophaga ani*) known as Savanna Blackbird or Tick-bird. The birds resemble each other superficially in many ways but belong to different families. Both Blackbirds follow cattle about to feed on the cattle-parasites. Both are also very gregarious and travel, roost, and nest in flocks, incubating and rearing their offspring collectively. What really distinguishes one from the other is the very different beak and their personalities.

The Ani belongs to the Cuckoo family. It is a medium-sized bird and its very long tail and short rounded wings provide a way of telling it apart from the Cling-cling. It uses its parrot-like beak to search for ticks on cattle, its name *Crotophaga* meaning 'tick-eater'.

In the matter of personality though, it is the Cling-cling that attracts attention with its noisy, raucous cry. 'It tinkles', says one writer, 'like coins thrown down, and its manner is that of a clever sharper'. With its glossy coating, bright eye, and stuck out angled tail – like the keel of a boat says one observer, like a vertical fan, says another – it is often an amusing sight in the garden. As May Jeffrey-Smith describes it: 'The cling-cling swaggers about on the ground fussily jerking its folded tail, flies up hastily to snatch at a tick, but even if the bird alights on the cow it soon descends to the ground.'

The Ani on the other hand has 'a queer, loping walk, a lazy slouch, and almost seems to be apologizing for its existence', according to Jeffrey-Smith. And writer Adolphe Roberts described it as looking 'rusty as a coat out of storage' with clumsy movement, curving beak and raucous voice. P.H. Gosse's description in the mid-19th century of the Ani still holds good today: 'Familiar and impudent, though very wary, they permit a considerable acquaintance with their manners, while an approach within a limited distance, in a moment sets the whole flock upon the wing, with a singular cry.'

This bird sets a 'look-out' and warns the others of approaching danger, a habit which gained it the name of 'Informer' as it apparently revealed the runaway slaves' hiding places to pursuers.

Cling-Cling (top) and Ani

Neither Blackbird is much thought of for eating by the folk as attested by the saying, 'Nuh waste shot pon blackbird', or 'Nuh waste powder pon blackbird'.

[Gosse 1984, Jeffrey-Smith 1972, Roberts 1955, Taylor 1955]

BLACK-HEART MAN
Sinister legendary figure also known as 'Black Art Man'; supposedly a sorcerer who travels up and down the countryside looking for victims so he can procure their hearts for evil purposes. The threat of the Black-heart Man was used as a way of warning children to be careful in accepting lifts from or having anything to do with strangers on the road. The term is also applied to an OBEAH-man. 'Blackheart Man' was the name of a popular song and album by REGGAE artist Bunny (Livingston) Wailer who sang:

> Tek care the Blackheart Man little children
> Me sey 'Don't go near him'
> Tek care the Blackheart Man little children
> For even lions fear him . . .

A similar legendary figure in Barbados is called Heartman.

BLACKSMITH
Before the ascendancy of motor transport in the 20th century, the blacksmith was an essential craftsman, making and maintaining shoes for horses and metal parts for carts and DRAYS. His services were also constantly in demand to make or repair tools and metal parts for boats. In the plantation era, each plantation had at least one blacksmith and in the post-EMANCIPATION years, the blacksmith was a vital part of town, and sometimes village, life. Today, only one or two blacksmiths exist in Jamaica.

Michael Craton has described how indispensable the smith was on the plantation. He worked at his forge either with charcoal or coal specially imported from England and spent his time shaping individual barrel hoops, wain tyres, horseshoes, from scrap or imported bar iron. He also made the basic tools needed on the plantation. As Craton describes the situation at WORTHY PARK estate, 'the blacksmiths quite often made replacement parts for the machinery of mills, boiling-house, and still, as well as wain parts, special tools, brackets, hinges, hooks and large nails. Besides ironwork they were also expected to work items in copper, tin, lead, and brass and be experts in brazing and soldering. Presumably it was also the blacksmiths who were responsible for unshackling and branding the new slaves and for fitting anklets and chains to the recalcitrants in the Vagabond Gang'.

Iron work represents one area of technology transfer from West Africa where metallurgical craft was highly developed by the end of the 16th century; African blacksmiths and metal workers were among those forcibly brought

Blacksmiths in Africa (from an old print)

Instruments of slave torture L-R: a pair of ankle irons, a punishment 'necklace', stock fetters and punishment bit

from that continent as slaves. As in Africa, New World smiths were accorded high status, occupying elite positions in the plantation hierarchy of slaves. By their own countrymen they were regarded as workers of magic. Outside of the plantations, the MAROONS were noted ironworkers. According to Edward Long: 'The rebellious negroes . . . forge their own ironwork, making knives, cutlasses, heads of lances, bracelets, rings, and a variety of other kind of necessaries, they have bellows which are made of wood.'

Research by Candice L. Goucher of an 18th century foundry established in ST THOMAS near to MORANT BAY, showed that the owner, John Reeder, relied heavily on the skills of African and African-Jamaican metalworkers, both slaves and Maroons.

[Craton 1978, Goucher 1990, Long 1774]

Blacksmith at Ginger Ridge, St Catherine

BLUEFIELDS

Fishing village in WESTMORELAND Parish. This was the site of Oristan, one of the three principal towns founded by the SPANISH settlers in Jamaica. It was named after a town in Sardinia, then under Spanish rule. The settlers had first established Oristan at PARATEE in ST ELIZABETH Parish, before relocating it at Bluefields. From there it was connected by road to the north coast town of Sevilla la Nueva (SEVILLE, New) reached via MARTHA BRAE (Para Mater Tiburon), then a hacienda. It was also connected to Santiago de la Vega (SPANISH TOWN) via a south coast route through Cagua (PORT HENDERSON). Possibly owing to the raids of the French and English corsairs, the Spaniards abandoned Oristan before the English conquest, but its ruin could be seen up to the 19th century.

The beautiful Bluefields Bay is connected with many naval exploits, since it was for a long time the rendezvous for ships sailing in convoy to England and elsewhere. It was from Bluefields Bay that the BUCCANEER Henry MORGAN sailed in December 1670 to sack the city of PANAMA. Some associate the name with the famous Buccaneer Bleevelt (Blauvelt, a Fleming) who gave his name to Bluefields, Nicaragua.

The old Bluefields House is associated with the inventor of the marine aquarium, Philip Henry Gosse (1810-88), an English naturalist who stayed in Jamaica for 18 months in 1844-45. Gosse gathered samples of Jamaica's FLORA and FAUNA and collected material for two charming books on the island's natural history – *A Naturalist's Sojourn in Jamaica* (1851) and *The Birds of Jamaica* (1847). *Illustrations of the Birds of Jamaica* was published in 1849. An edition combining excerpts from all three books was published by Institute of Jamaica Publications as *Gosse's Jamaica 1844-45*.

[Cundall 1915, Gosse 1984, Wright and White 1969]

BLUE HOLE

'Blue hole' is a term used to describe a point of emergence for water welling up gently from the underground, such submarine springs near the shoreline being characteristic of LIMESTONE areas. The water is usually a mixture of ground water and sea water. The blue colour comes from the depth of the hole; some 'blue holes' can be green. The best known 'Blue Hole' is a beauty spot in PORTLAND Parish which falls under the JNHT. Also called Blue Lagoon, it is over 55m deep and 90m in diameter and is popular with water skiers, swimmers, and divers.

In the COCKPIT COUNTRY, blue holes may also be deep pools formed by waterfalls, or pools marking the point where a river goes underground. Both types of pool are associated with mystery and the presence of WATER SPIRITS or ghosts. Runaway slaves and MAROONS are said

to have studied such blue holes in order to find chains of secret caves leading underground to safety. Children were often forbidden to play in or near such blue holes.
[Porter 1990]

BLUE MAHOE see MAHOE

BLUE MOUNTAINS
Jamaica's highest and most extensive mountain range, much of it forest-clad, appears blue from a distance. The mountains dominate the eastern parishes, forming the interior of PORTLAND, ST THOMAS, and ST ANDREW. Blue Mountain Peak at 2,556m is the highest in the island. The peak itself is one of a series of peaks over 1,820m high which rise swiftly from the coast, providing a spectacular backdrop for beaches and plains and bringing a cool mountain climate within minutes of the city of KINGSTON. The mountains rise 2,100m from the coastal plain in only 16km, 'a general gradient that has few equals anywhere in the world', according to the official *Handbook*.

Indeed, the entry to Kingston by sea or air affords a striking perspective of the mountains and explains the fascination they exert on travellers and residents alike. For a good part of the day, the higher peaks are covered in mists, adding to their mysterious and compelling beauty. Although much of Jamaica is mountainous, it is the lofty eminence of the Blue Mountains that dominates the imagination. 'I shall be quite at home with the mountains of Heaven' wrote a colonial governor (Sir Sidney Olivier) after a tour of duty in what he called 'The Blessed Island'. And, concluded Jamaican writer Roger Mais, 'All men come to the hills/finally'.

The highly dissected ridges of the Blue Mountains alternate with steep sided valleys and gorges, forming a rugged terrain with a variety of soil types and luxuriant vegetation. Radiating from the central highlands are a number of large rivers, principally the RIO GRANDE which drains the north-east slopes and the YALLAHS RIVER which drains the central southern slopes. In the east, the character of the mountains changes after Corn Puss Gap, and the LIMESTONE formation of the John Crow Mountains develops. In the west the main ridges throw out other spurs of lower elevation which form the central backbone of the island. (See GEOLOGY.)

The Blue Mountains have a tremendous effect on the climate, temperature and rainfall in the

The Blue Mountains

eastern parishes. For one thing, temperature drops with altitude, and the hills become much cooler as one climbs. Thus while the average temperature on the coast is 26.2°C at elevations over 610m, minimum temperatures of 10°C have been reported, and at Blue Mountain Peak, temperatures below 4.4°C have been recorded.

The mountains also have a significant effect on rainfall, the lush canopied interior of the north eastern side presenting a striking contrast with the hills and plains of the south. These are in what is called the 'rain shadow', a phenomenon brought about by the fact that the moisture-bearing winds, the north east trades, approach from the Portland side and on meeting the mountains in their path are forced to rise. As they do so, they meet increasingly cooler air and rain-bearing clouds are formed. These drop their load on the 'windward' side, leaving the 'leeward' or south east side relatively dry. Thus, in the rugged interior the rainfall is usually torrential, some mountainous places in the north east receiving more than 5,080mm annually. Here, the mountains present a lush appearance of still largely natural vegetation, the very rugged and wet nature of the terrain preventing exploitation. The southern coastline will get as little as 889mm of rainfall per year and the hillier areas, though wetter, get much less than the mountains on the north side. The southern-facing slopes of the mountains have also been much exploited and abused by man over the centuries. A great deal of the forest cover in rural St Andrew, in particular, has been removed. In the Yallahs Valley area, all the land below 1,524m is believed to be of secondary growth. For conservation measures, see NATIONAL PARKS.

[GOJ Handbook of Jamaica 1961, GOJ STATIN 1999a, Mattley 1951, Porter 1990]

BLUE AND JOHN CROW MOUNTAINS NATIONAL PARK see NATIONAL PARKS

BOA see SNAKE

BOGLE, Rt Excellent Paul (?-1865)

National Hero of Jamaica. Paul Bogle, a deacon of the Native BAPTIST Church of Stony Gut, ST THOMAS Parish, a small mountain village about 6.5km from MORANT BAY, was the leader of passive resistance to oppression and injustice in this parish. When this approach failed, he (along with his brother Moses) led the active resistance movement that culminated in the so-called MORANT BAY REBELLION of 1865.

Bogle was an independent peasant proprietor and one of only 106 inhabitants in the parish who had the right to vote. Very little is known of his life before the rebellion. Clearly, he had strong leadership qualities. He was the political agent for George William GORDON to whom he also had religious ties, and is said to have organized the people of Stony Gut not only in religious activities but in a military form of organization. However, what Bogle's intentions were was never made clear as he and his followers never had their day in court. After the disturbances at Morant Bay, Bogle was captured by the MAROONS near Torrington in St Thomas on 23 October and taken to Morant Bay where he was swiftly tried by court martial and hanged, along with other leaders of the rebellion.

Bogle was named one of the first five National Heroes of Jamaica when the Order was established in 1969.

A statue to this National Hero stands in front of the Morant Bay courthouse and was erected on the centenary of the rebellion in 1965. It is the work of noted sculptor Edna Manley, OM (see ART), who was the widow of another National Hero, Rt Excellent Norman Washington MANLEY.

[Heuman 1994, Robotham 1981, Wynter 1965]

BOINAYEL

One of the 12 principal ZEMIS of the TAINOS. Represented as a twin with Márohu; associated with the weather. (See WEATHER SPIRITS.) While Márohu's name (meaning 'No Clouds') suggests that he was the bringer of sunny weather, Boinayel's name suggests the opposite – 'Son of the Grey Serpent' – or dark rain clouds. As such, he was the bringer of rain and therefore associated with good weather for agriculture.

Jamaican zemi

Paul Bogle

BOLAS, Juan de, see LUBOLO, Juan

BOLÍVAR Simón (1783-1830)

Famous South American liberator who had a short – but significant – stay in KINGSTON. The north west corner of Princess and Tower streets was the site of Raphael Poysas' lodging house where Bolívar stayed and survived an assassination attempt. The lodging house no longer stands but the KSAC erected a plaque to mark the historic site. While active in the struggle to free the Spanish-American colonies from Spanish rule, Bolívar came to Jamaica to seek help from the British. He stayed from May to December 1818. Spanish loyalists in Kingston bribed his servant to kill him but the assassination attempt failed. Bolívar was out and a friend who had come to visit was lying in his hammock while waiting for him. The friend was mistaken for the liberator and knifed to death. While in Jamaica, Bolívar wrote his famous Jamaica Letter (*Carta de Jamaica*) which is regarded as one of the great documents of his career. The final years of the liberator are recorded in the novel *The General in his Labyrinth* by the Columbian Nobel Laureate Gabriel García Márquez.

A monument to Bolívar can be seen at the southern end of National Heroes Circle in Kingston, in front of the Ministry of Education. It was presented by the Government of Venezuela (where Bolívar was born) in gratitude for his safe exile in Jamaica and is one of the few representations of the hero that does not show him on horseback.

BOOBY CAY
Islet at the northern end of Long Bay, NEGRIL, which was used for filming the South Sea scenes in Walt Disney's *Twenty Thousand Leagues Under the Sea*. The CAY is probably named after the Booby Bird. (See BOOBY EGGS.)

BOOBY EGGS
Speckled eggs once hawked on the streets of KINGSTON as a popular delicacy, but little seen today since the numbers of BIRDS have declined severely, and some nesting sites are protected. Though called 'booby eggs', they are not those of the Booby Bird but of species of terns which spend most of the year far out at sea, coming to the CAYS offshore Jamaica to breed. They are also known as Egg Birds. James Bond (in *The Birds of the West Indies*) lists eight different species of terns that have 'Egg Bird' as one of their common names. Most eggs were collected from the Sooty Tern (*Sterna fuscata*), a bird closely related to the seagull and a smaller number from the Brown Noddy (*Anous stolidus*).

Booby Bird and egg

Booby eggs were collected by fishermen on the cays, particularly the Pedro and Morant Cays, a practice that was followed from the time of the TAINOS until the early 1960s when the supply dwindled to almost nothing, with increasing encroachment on the birds' habitat by commercial FISHING and other activities. One of the Morant Cays (South East Cay) has now been designated a bird sanctuary to protect the nesting birds.

The true Booby Bird is rarely seen on the mainland in Jamaica. There are three species in the CARIBBEAN, the Brown Booby (*Sula leucogaster*), Red-footed (*Sula sula*) and Masked (*Sula dactylatra*). Their eggs are bluish, covered with a white chalky deposit, and slightly larger than a fowl egg. The bird was called 'booby' by sailors for the same reason that they call it 'crazy bird' – it is so easily captured. As COLUMBUS neared landfall in the Caribbean on his first voyage, the first bird to come to the ship was a Booby, as he recorded in his journal, 19 September 1492.
[Bond 1960, Jeffrey-Smith 1972, NHSJ 1949]

BOOK-KEEPER
Term formerly used in Jamaica to describe the assistant to the overseer or manager of a SUGAR estate; large estates employed several who came from the British Isles (see IRISH, SCOTS). These were the men who went into the fields and factories and supervised the work. Each work GANG had a headman or driver (usually black or COLOURED) who reported to the book-keeper.

In the early days, book-keepers were often poor white indentured servants, little more than boys, whose lives, from all accounts, were a form of hell, being circumscribed by harsh rules and tyrannical overseers. The death rate was extremely high. While a few might be fortunate enough to graduate to overseer or even proprietor class (see BROWN'S TOWN), most were transient, leaving little record of their passing. The poet Robert Burns was contracted to come to Jamaica as a book-keeper but fortunately for him and the Scots, he cancelled out at the last minute.

The term 'book-keeper' is a misnomer since, according to the planter-historian William Beckford: 'There are many so little deserving the name they bear, that so far from being able to calculate accounts they cannot many of them even read.' In the post-EMANCIPATION period, the word continued to be employed on sugar estates to denote an employee who was subordinate to the overseer but who often was literate and numerate, and able to keep crude

records of workers' names, shifts, and rates of pay.
[DJE, Shore and Stewart 1911]

BOSTON BEACH
Public beach in PORTLAND associated with JERK PORK since this is the place where it first gained widespread popularity. Pork is still 'jerked' here in the old way right beside the beach. Boston property was once owned by the late, flamboyant movie star, Errol Flynn, who bought several properties in the PORT ANTONIO area including NAVY ISLAND, and visited frequently for many years until his death. His widow Patrice Wymore Flynn continued to farm some of their properties in the parish.

BOUGAINVILLEA
Straggling shrub of intense coloration – reds, purples, oranges and creamy-whites – which grows in profusion across the island. Bougainvillea is so ubiquitous it is hard to imagine Jamaica without its hot tropical colours. It was introduced in 1849 by the curator of BATH GARDEN. The original bougainvillea that came from South America bears purple flowers and has thorns.

Bougainvillea thrives in the summer months, often providing the only burst of colour to be seen when everything else is dry and parched. Its intense colours do not come from its flower that is creamy white and inconspicuous but from three coloured tissue-paper-like bracts that surround it, their purpose being to act as a signal or flag to insects which pollinate it. The plant originated in tropical South America and is named after a FRENCH navigator, Louis de Bougainville (1729-1811), who discovered it in Brazil and took it to Europe.

Bougainvillea flowers and bracts
D. Ranston

In cultivation, bougainvillea is carefully trained in hedges or as a specimen plant, otherwise it runs wild, covering fences, banksides, and even fully grown trees with its showy splendour. Miniature varieties are also cultivated as pot plants. Apart from its showiness, bougainvillea is a favourite among gardeners because of its liking for dry conditions and its many varieties.

According to Bannochie and Light, three species, *B. glabra*, *B. spectabilis* and *B. peruviana* have given rise to the several hundred cultivars recorded by the International Registration Authority for Bougainvillea, New Delhi, India. A popular cultivar (protected in the USA by plant patent rights) is called 'Surprise' because the plant bears both brilliant magenta and white flowers in dramatic contrast, sometimes on the same branch. Double or multi-bracted forms were first developed in the Philippines.
[Bannochie and Light 1993, Webster 1965]

BOWDEN
Area in ST THOMAS parish which takes its name from a former owner, William Bowden, a late 17th century settler from Nevis. (See STOKES HALL.) It has also given its name to the 'Bowden formation' of Port Morant, a thick deposit of extensive fossil remains from the late Miocene geological period. Some of these fossils are in the collection of the British Museum of Natural History, American Museum of Natural History and Johns Hopkins University. Fossils – the remains of animals and plants preserved in rock that existed millions of years ago – are important to scientists studying natural history. The Bowden Formation has one of the richest late-Miocene deposits in the world. Species of marine SHELLS have been described from this formation, many still retaining their distinctive colours and patterns. There are also fossils of higher plant remains.
[Hose 1951]

BOXING
Jamaica in the 20th century contributed significantly to the sport of boxing at an international level. Men who had an impact since the 1930s include Kid Silver and Lefty Flynn. It was during this period that Norman Washington MANLEY was instrumental in forming the Jamaica Boxing Board of Control, which oversees both the amateur and professional aspects of the sport.

Next to track and field ATHLETICS, boxing is the sport in which Jamaica has most often competed at the Olympic Games, beginning in 1948 and in every summer Olympics between 1964 and 1996. Jamaica has never won a boxing medal in these games, but Michael McCallum in 1976 and Dwight Fraser in 1984 both reached the quarter-finals. At the Moscow Olympics in 1980, McCallum was a favourite to make the welterweight final and thus win at least a silver medal when he suffered an attack of appendicitis and could not compete. Trevor Berbick also competed for Jamaica in 1976. Milo Calhoun (fighting then as Cephas Calhoun) and Ronald Holmes have won gold medals for Jamaica at the Commonwealth Games.

As a professional, McCallum earned recognition as one of the world's great fighters. In a professional career lasting over fifteen years, he has suffered less than a handful of defeats and has never been knocked out. He was only the 14th man to win three or more world titles at different weights – junior, middle, and light-heavy, and he also fought for the cruiserweight title. He was undefeated as a junior middleweight and was chosen by *The Ring* magazine, the self-described 'Bible of the sport', as the second best junior middleweight champion of all time. Nicknamed 'The Body Snatcher', he was often chosen as among the best fighters in the world, pound for pound. He has won Jamaica's Sportsman of the Year Award more than any other athlete, and is regarded as one of the region's leading sports personalities of the 20th century.

McCallum has won one title each from the World Boxing Council, the World Boxing Association and the International Boxing Federation, the three most widely recognized governing bodies. Five other Jamaican born fighters have also won world titles in various mixes of what has been referred to as the 'alphabet soup' of controlling bodies, since a fighter is only recognized as undisputed champion when he has won all three versions, which happens very rarely. (A fourth body, the World Boxing Organization has also gained increasing acceptance but is not as recognized as the other three.)

The boxer next in significance to Kingston-born McCallum would be Simon Brown who came from CLARENDON Parish originally but was much more 'Americanized' after service in the US Armed Forces. He won world titles in both the welter and junior middle divisions for two of the world bodies. He also had the distinction of being the only Jamaican to win a world title fight at home, when he defended his welterweight title successfully against Jorge Vaca of Mexico at the NATIONAL STADIUM in Kingston before spectators who included at least one busload from his native village.

Before Brown, Lloyd Honeygan, based in Britain but born in ST ELIZABETH Parish, and Trevor Berbick, who also served in the US Armed forces, and resided in Canada, both won world titles. Honeygan's was in the welterweight division and was a big upset at the expense of Don Curry, who was touted at one time as the best fighter pound for pound in the world. (Curry was also later to fight McCallum and was knocked out by what was perhaps one of the most spectacular left hooks ever delivered.) Berbick won a version of the heavyweight title against Pinklon Thomas for what was once one of the biggest prizes in sport. Unfortunately devaluation had set in and he may be largely remembered almost as a curiosity, as the boxer who beat Muhammad Ali in that giant's last fight, when he was a mere travesty of himself.

Mike McCallum

Several other Jamaicans have also fought unsuccessfully for three world boxing titles, while, it should be noted for the record, Gerald Gray was the first Jamaican to earn a top-10 world ranking in the welterweight division (1958). Three Jamaican fighters lost world title fights at home. Bunny Grant in the junior welterweight division lost to Eddie Perkins of the USA (a loss that he was eventually to reverse in a non-title bout). Percy Hayles (Grant's great rival) lost to Carlos Hernandez of Venezuela in the lightweight division. Richard 'Shrimpy' Clarke put up a most creditable showing against Sot Chitalada of Thailand – regarded as one of the greatest flyweight champions ever – for eight rounds before being knocked out in the eleventh.

Interestingly, Jamaicans have won world titles which cover the entire upper weight range, from welterweight to heavyweight – the dividing line being the upper limit of the welterweight, 66.68kg or 147lb – but the island has not produced any world champions at the lower end of the scale.

Jamaica has also had some notable boxing promoters, including Puckoo de Souza, Stanley Mair, Felix Smith, and Lucien Chen. Chen was a factor in the most important fight promotion ever held on the island (co-promoted by the government company, National Sports Ltd, the predecessor of the present Institute of Sports Ltd). This was the 'Sunshine Showdown' in 1973, when George Foreman knocked out Joe Frazier in the second round to become the

Lloyd Honeygan

undisputed world heavyweight champion. This is still the only heavyweight boxing title fight held in the CARIBBEAN since Jess Willard beat the famous Jack Johnson, the first black heavyweight champion, under dubious circumstances in Havana, Cuba, in the midday sun nearly sixty years before.

Aside from the Jamaican based boxers, there have been several recent champions of Jamaican parentage or Jamaican birth who have received their training and fought in other countries, especially England. The world heavyweight champion Lennox Lewis was born in England of a Jamaican mother, and has lived in both England and Canada.

[James Carnegie, personal communication; Golesworthy 1988]

BREAD

In *The Red Book of the West Indies* published in 1922, the author made this extraordinary statement: 'The economic problems of Jamaica are based on its bread supply, to which all its commercial and industrial activities are really subservient; for bread enters probably more largely into the dietary of the great bulk of the inhabitants of the island than in that of any other people.'

There might have been some truth in this for the poorer people, but mainly those living in the towns, for commercially made wheat bread was not widely available throughout the countryside until the development of modern transportation in the 20th century. Nevertheless, the almost Biblical esteem for bread is attested to by the fact that country-folk refer to their starchy foods (such as BREADFRUIT, YAM or COCO) as 'bread-kind', for they also serve as cheap, filling, nutritious food and the farmer can grow them himself.

Sweet and hard biscuits and crackers that could last for a long time without refrigeration were more available than wheat bread in the deep rural areas, bought at the small country shops supplied by a travelling 'bread van'. Popular with early travellers were bread substitutes made of wheat flour such as DUMPLINGS, especially JOHNNY CAKE, fritters such as STAMP-AND-GO, biscuits and cakes such as BULLA, toto, JACKASS CORN, and, of course, the PATTY.

Although several types of bread are now widely available, the most popular has for a long time been hard-dough bread, a fine-grained, dense white loaf made by all the island's bakeries and noted for its keeping qualities. The origins of this bread are obscure, but food historian Norma Benghiat reports encountering hard-dough rolls in southern Spain and points to a possible Cuban source for Jamaica. She says what is called the 'dough break machine', important for achieving the right texture, is utilized only in Jamaica, Cuba and Haiti.

Also popular is Coco-bread that was originally made from spreading out dumpling dough, folding it over and baking. It was once common at small bake shops throughout the countryside but is now made commercially and is a lunchtime favourite, sometimes served plain with butter or filled with bully beef. A 'patty and coco bread' is a common combination for city office workers and schoolchildren alike. The origin of the name coco-bread is unknown. Perhaps it was the quick bread made at home in the mornings to drink with COCOA-tea?

In the past, a much greater variety of bread was found in the towns, made mainly by the smaller bakeries which have almost disappeared, replaced by large commercial establishments. *The Red Book* took note of the number of bakeries in towns such as SAVANNA-LA-MAR, but while it lists some of the bakeries around the island and their machinery and volume, it does not, unfortunately, tell us about their products. Popular wheat flour breads of the past (now rarely seen) included krispy crust, grotto, peg bread, and gatta-cake, the latter a semi-sweet, moist, twisted roll; its name is apparently a combination of French *gateau*, or cake, and the

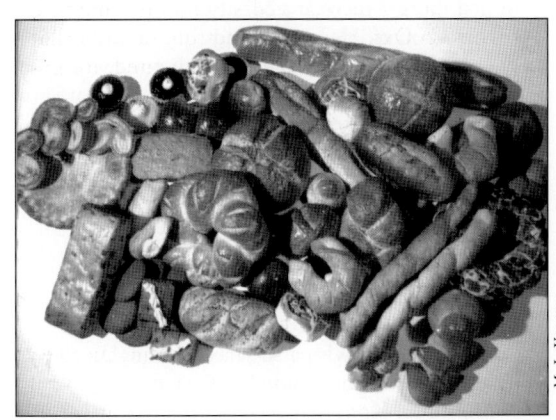

Bread

English word cake. Such terms (and the recipe) may have been brought from Haiti by FRENCH refugees in the 1790s and later. There were also regional specialities, like the large Pomona biscuit developed and manufactured by Salmon's Bakery of MONTEGO BAY. According to *The Red Book*, it was so named by its creator because 'on the day the manufacturing process was first completed one of the first steamers that carried BANANAS from Jamaica docked in the harbour, and was named the "*Pomona*".'

Before electricity, these early bakeries used fire-brick ovens, and some had steam-driven machinery. The fact that a grand house such as DEVON HOUSE has a brick oven suggests that some of the elite ate homemade bread.

In the early days of BRITISH settlement at PORT ROYAL, bread was hardly eaten as the imported wheat flour usually arrived in a rancid state. Though we are told that the cravings of those with a sweet-tooth were satisfied by a large variety of English-style cakes and confections whipped up by the local bakers. The merchants, like the sailors and BUCCANEERS as well as the black population, took to cassava BAMMY as their staple bread and this remained the popular bread for centuries with rich and poor alike.

Nevertheless, bread (presumably made of wheat) was a significant factor in the lives of the early settlers for whom it had been the 'staff of life' at home. One of the earliest regulations of the Vestry, the governing body of the city of Kingston formed after the destruction of Port Royal, was the Assize of Bread, a regulation which fixed the weight of a loaf which was to be sold for a bitt, or 7½d in Jamaican currency of the time, as we are told by H.P. Jacobs. In the mid-18th century, Edward Long noted that 'the flour comes for the most part from New-York, inferior to none in the world; and the bread is excellent', though the imported butter was rancid. Jacobs records a Mrs Brandon running a bakery on Oxford Street, Kingston, in 1824. But the bread supply must have been limited, for in the numerous accounts we have of the fare of the plantocracy over succeeding centuries, there is virtually no reference to bread, even the elite apparently adapting to Bammy and 'bread-kind'. Caroline Sullivan in her cookbook of 1893 provides daily menus for a small (and, presumably, elite) family, but lists no bread to be eaten with the rest of the breakfast fare (though she does give recipes for breakfast rolls and homemade bread using soda as a raising agent). There is, however, a prevalence of 'bread-kind' such as 'mashed yam', 'roasted coco', 'boiled yam', 'toasted coco', 'roasted breadfruit', 'grated yellow yam', 'roast PLANTAIN', 'johnny cakes' and 'yampee' along with fried plantain.

According to Benghiat, the yeast-leavened bread was a late development in Jamaica, and until the mid-19th century, bicarbonate of soda was used as the leavening agent. She notes that 'Fresh yeast had a short life span in the days before refrigeration, and it was probably after compressed yeast was developed that yeast-leavened breads made their appearance in Jamaica'.

Popular with all levels of society for hundreds of years have been the sweet 'breads' made from local provisions, such as sweet potato bread, CORN bread, banana bread, COCONUT bread, and GINGER bread, usually leavened with soda. Buns are also popular, plain ones as everyday fare as well as the more elaborate EASTER BUN. (For sweet confections see SWEETS.)

The arrivals of different ethnic groups have contributed other types of bread, such as 'Pow' associated with the CHINESE, 'Syrian bread' with the LEBANESE, and Roti with the INDIANS.

Showbread, or Shewbread, a large, elaborately decorated bread made for special occasions, is now rarely seen, though it was once an essential part of the EASTER and GOOD FRIDAY fare, and is still much used by REVIVAL Tables. The bread is often made in the form of animals, religious symbols such as the DOVE being most popular. The name and origins of the bread date back to the Old Testament, referring to the loaves of bread placed every Sabbath in the temple of the ancient Israelites. Used for secular purposes such as the TEA MEETING, such large, decorated loaves were called Crown Bread from the most popular shape.

[Benghiat 1985, 1987, Cassidy 1961, Jacobs 1976, Long 1774, Macmillan 1922, Sullivan 1893]

BREADFRUIT (*Artocarpus altilis*)

A large tree up to 20m which grows widely in Jamaica, especially at lower elevations in sufficiently rainy areas, from sea level to 450m, its fruit providing a staple of the diet. This tree was unknown on the island before 1793 and its arrival is bound up with one of the most famous sea stories of all times – the story of the mutiny on the *Bounty*, subject of numerous books and several films.

Seeking a cheap source of food for the slaves in the West Indies (see SLAVERY, SUGAR PLANTATION), the planters in 1775 had offered to pay 'all reasonable costs' to anyone who would supply them with plants of the tree that produced 'bread' all year round for South Sea islanders. They might have been influenced by descriptions such as that by William Dampier who had first encountered the breadfruit in his journey around the world in 1688: 'The natives of Guam use it for bread. They gather it, when full-grown, while it is green and hard; then they bake it in an oven, which scorcheth the rind and makes it black; but they scrape off the outside black crust, and there remains a tender thin crust; and the inside is soft, tender, and white like the crumb of a penny-loaf. There is neither seed nor stone in the inside, but all is of a pure substance, like bread.'

Since the breadfruit does not bear fertile seeds, it must be propagated by suckers. Despite the planters' offer, plus a gold medal promised by the Society of Arts, no one came forward with plants. The project languished until the 1780s when famine in the West Indies stimulated new interest. Food imports from the North American colonies were cut off during the American Revolutionary War (1775-83) in which the colonies fought to gain their independence from Britain. In Jamaica, a HURRICANE every year between 1780-86 destroyed the PROVISION GROUNDS. In between there was drought. In the years 1780-87, 15,000 slaves are said to have died on the island from famine or malnutrition and resultant diseases.

This time the planters persuaded the King of England to mount a special expedition to obtain the breadfruit. In 1787 an English sea captain named William Bligh was appointed commander of the HMS *Bounty* and charged with the task. He sailed to the islands of Timor and Tahiti where he obtained the plants and set sail for the West Indies, but one month out of Tahiti the crew mutinied, threw the plants overboard, and set Bligh and a few members of the crew adrift in an open boat. Bligh managed to navigate 5,760km across the South Pacific, making landfall in Timor and eventually make his way back to England.

Undaunted, he set out once more and in 1793 successfully brought the first breadfruit plants to Jamaica and St Vincent, along with a host of other valuable plants on the HMS *Providence*. (On his return journey Bligh loaded the ship with tropical plants, including 800 from Jamaica, for Kew Gardens in England, and one of these, the ACKEE, was to be given the botanical name *Blighia sapida* in his honour.)

Captain Bligh's ship with the breadfruit had first stopped at PORT ROYAL, the deck covered with growing plants, and the slaves rowed out in CANOES to see 'the ship that have the bush'. Then he sailed for Port Morant and other ports to unload his precious cargo. The first trees were planted at BATH GARDEN, ST THOMAS Parish, where descendants of these trees can still be seen. For his first attempt to bring the breadfruit, Bligh was awarded 500 guineas by the Assembly of Jamaica and 1,000 guineas for the successful effort. Although the breadfruit immediately flourished on Jamaican soil, it was many years before the population would attempt to eat the strange fruit. Today the breadfruit – roasted, boiled or fried – is one of the favourite starches of Jamaicans.

Breadfruit

Observation of the breadfruit tree's longevity and its way of propagating itself by sending up suckers from the root, has led Jamaicans to see it as a symbol of perseverance, encoded in the saying, 'the more you chop breadfruit root, the more it spring'. In folk MEDICINE, breadfruit leaf tea is believed by some to relieve hypertension and the gum from the green fruit 'makes an effective dressing for the contagious skin disease *Tinea versicolor* or liver spot', according to Asprey and Thornton.

[Asprey and Thornton 1953-55, Bligh 1792, Campbell 1974, Powell 1973]

BRITISH

Strictly speaking, the term 'British' is both misleading and correct when applied to colonial Jamaica: misleading because it suggests a unity that did not exist in the 17th century, and correct because it points to the presence of England's lesser partners in the making of Jamaica. The term British is correctly applied after 1706 when the Act of Union was passed declaring that England and Scotland (which had been united under one sovereign since 1603) should have a united Parliament from 1 May 1707.

Although James I technically ruled over England, Ireland, Scotland and Wales, the four nations barely formed a political whole, and strongly resisted being a cultural whole. Centuries of bitter warfare between them would not cease for generations: Catholic Irish, Presbyterian Scots and Catholic Scots resisted English Protestant power.

In 16th century expansion, it was the English – sailing from London, Plymouth, Portsmouth and Bristol – who laid down their language, their customs and their forms of culture in those countries to which they went. On the American continent, for example, Virginia was named after the Virgin Queen, Elizabeth I, while Pennsylvania was named after William PENN, son of the English admiral who invaded Jamaica. New England was exactly that: England, not Britain. Still, the four partners in what is now the United Kingdom had already started to merge in the 17th century, with England as the dominant power.

As far as any colony was concerned, at the centre there stood English LANGUAGE, government, law, naval and military power, merchants, MONEY, EDUCATION, fashions, and social behaviour. Jamaica, like other colonies, has retained the stamp of the Church of England (see ANGLICAN), of English common law, of parliamentarian GOVERNMENT and many other purely English cultural features.

Interwoven into this English fabric are the Celtic languages, dialects, sayings, names, tales, and beliefs of the SCOTS, IRISH and WELSH who took part as managers, artisans, soldiers, servants, sailors and, to a lesser extent, as landowners in the new colonies. These Celtic peoples had to assume the roles given them by English power, but they left their British, non-English stamp on countries like Jamaica. 'I'm gone now' is a literal translation of an Irish sentence; the names Lloyd, Hugh and Gwen are Welsh; CAMPBELL (Scots) and Williams (Welsh) are two of the most common surnames in Jamaica, rivalling Smith (English) and Jones (Welsh).

Although Jamaica has been an independent nation since 1962 (see INDEPENDENCE), many of the island's institutions and much of its way of life have been shaped by its status as a British colony for 307 years. Technically, Jamaica became an English colony when the island was captured from the Spaniards by Cromwell's forces in 1655 (see CAPTURE OF JAMAICA) and remained so until 1707 when the term 'British' came into use. The average Jamaican probably makes little distinction between English, Scots, Irish and Welsh. But from the English point of view, these distinctions in the colonies were quite acute, class consciousness, with the English at the top of the hierarchy, being rigidly maintained.

A Jamaican Chief Justice (Hon. Sir Herbert Duffus) in formal dress

While many of the early English settlers were small farmers (with 20-80ha), as a class they disappeared in a generation or two, with large plantations and landowners coming to dominate after the sugar boom began in the late 18th century.

With the pressing need for colonists to settle the newly captured island, settlers were encouraged by the promise that they would be 'free denizens of England and shall have the same privileges to all intents and purposes as our free-born subjects of England', by a royal proclamation of 1661. This allowed for some religious tolerance in the island for JEWS and non-conformists such as Quakers (see FRIENDS) who at the time suffered religious persecution in England and elsewhere. But civil liberties had to be fought for, the free COLOUREDS and Jews achieving full civil rights in 1830 and 1831, respectively.

Of course the vast majority of the population, the black AFRICANS brought as slaves (see SLAVERY) to meet the demands of the plantation system, had no rights whatsoever, being property of their masters and governed by a slave code. With the slaves, the Irish were the most popular, as many Irish in the early days were actually little better off than Africans. The Scots accounted for most of the 'bushas' and BOOK-KEEPERS, agents and attorneys, and were both respected and feared, as it was they who literally handled the whip on behalf of absentee English owners.

While slavery was maintained by the British and the demands of the mercantile system, it was also British men and women who led the fight to end the slave trade (1807) and in England threw their energies behind the agitation of the slaves themselves for full EMANCIPATION which came in 1838. (See MISSIONARIES.) Still later, Irish Jesuits and other Irish Catholics came to Jamaica to serve their fellow believers and to work among the poor.

Part of the movement associated with political independence has been the recognition and elevation of other aspects of the Jamaican heritage. (See, e.g. AFRICAN HERITAGE, GARVEY.) Nevertheless, the British heritage remains strong. The Jamaican Parliament, judiciary, the civil service, military and police forces are still based on the English model, as is the educational system. The official language remains English and up to recently it was the English canon that influenced Jamaican LITERATURE. Though there is discussion from time to time about making Jamaica a republic (like the former BWI territory of Trinidad), the Head of State is still the Queen of England acting through her representative, the governor-general. Jamaica remains a member of the British Commonwealth.

The main Christian Protestant churches are all offshoots of British churches and retain some of these connections though they have been somewhat displaced by the rise of indigenous RELIGIONS and American denominations such as PENTECOSTAL and SEVENTH-DAY ADVENTIST. Architecture (see GREAT HOUSE) and ART before the 20th century betray British origins; and MUSIC and THEATRE owe a great deal to the British Isles. Sports, GAMES and pastimes are largely British derived, CRICKET being an institution. Jamaicans drive on the left, as in Britain, and the road system is a legacy of the British. So are many crop plants that they introduced, such as COFFEE, commercial varieties of SUGAR CANE, and many fruit and ornamental trees and flowers, facilitated by the establishment of botanic gardens in the 18th and 19th centuries. Jamaican cuisine can be described as a PEPPER-POT or heterogenous mixture, but many popular dishes betray their British ancestry – among them EASTER BUN, CHRISTMAS PUDDING, SOLOMON GUNDY and the Sunday roast.

Attachment to, combined with continued ambivalence towards things British continues, despite the increasing leanings towards (and economic and cultural penetration by) North America.

Parliament – the mace bearer leads the Speaker into the House

Governor-General (Sir Clifford Campbell, the first Jamaican Head of State) takes the salute

BROADCASTING

Broadcasting, especially radio, remains Jamaica's most popular means of communication. It is estimated that 96 per cent of all homes are equipped with radios and there are 1,639,000 radio sets in use (including car radios). Especially appealing are radio talk shows when popular personalities field telephone calls from a wide cross-section of listeners.

In the closing years of the 20th century, television gained in popularity, especially with the access to foreign programmes through cable and satellite communications and the advent of several new services in place of what used to be a one-station government monopoly. At the time of writing, Jamaica has three television stations – Television Jamaica (TVJ, formerly the JBC), CVM Television and Love TV – and a number of radio stations. These were: RJR and Fame FM, JBC FM, Power 106, Love FM, and Zip FM, all broadcasting from Kingston, Radio West broadcasting from Montego Bay, KLAS FM from

Mandeville and IRIE FM from Ocho Rios.

Broadcasting began during the Second WORLD WAR on 17 November 1939 using the 'ham' shortwave radio equipment of John Grinan, an American resident in the island who handed over his station to the government in compliance with wartime regulations. Station ZQI – as it was renamed – went on the air for one hour per week and for a while continued to broadcast from Grinan's house. The chief organizer and manager of station ZQI was an Englishman, Dennis Gick, a skilled professional photographer. In addition to re-broadcasts of BBC news and other programmes, Gick gave excellent commentaries on the progress of the war and there was also considerable input by local artistes and amateurs, notably Archie Lindo and Molly Ward-Johnson. The former organized cultural programmes while the latter was responsible for the broadcast of play readings. By 1947 the station was broadcasting four hours daily, in the daytime only. There were 22,920 radio sets in 1950, with an estimated listening audience of up to 100,000.

Ten years after ZQI started, financial constraints prompted the government to grant a licence to Rediffusion International on condition that it took over the station. Commercial broadcasting began 9 July 1950 when the Jamaica Broadcasting Company, a wholly-owned subsidiary of the Rediffusion Group of London, went on the air as Radio Jamaica. In 1951 the company started operation of its Rediffusion service and the station became RJR – Radio Jamaica and Rediffusion. Rediffusion was a wired speaker service carrying RJR's programme to subscribers throughout the 19½ hours of radio broadcasting and continuing throughout the night after radio signed off at midnight, with uninterrupted recorded music. With the advent of transistor radios, consumer demand for Rediffusion fell and the service was discontinued in 1968.

In 1959, the government organized the Jamaica Broadcasting Corporation (JBC) on the lines of the BBC and the Jamaica Broadcasting Company changed its name to Radio Jamaica Limited. JBC Radio was joined by the first television broadcasting station, JBC TV in 1963. In the 1970s both JBC and RJR radio added FM services, providing virtually islandwide radio service on both bands, 24 hours a day. Although the JBC was originally intended to follow the unbiased pattern set by the BBC, it was misused by both political parties and lost favour with the listening public. JBC Radio and TV were sold to RJR in 1997, the government retaining one radio station which at the time of writing is slated to become a public broadcasting station. In the 1990s, several new radio stations were licensed and a new TV station (CVM) started, funded by local private sector interests. In 1998, a consortium of religious denominations and groups that had established Love FM in 1993 inaugurated Love TV.

Broadcasting is licensed by the government, the Broadcasting Commission being the regulatory body.

While radio continues to generate programmes with Jamaican content, cultural penetration continues with the growing popularity of TV satellite receivers and cable companies which bring foreign broadcasts, especially American, directly to Jamaican homes. Additionally, local television stations fill much of their time slots with imported fare. However, both radio and television have over time contributed to the writing and production of local dramatic material for broadcast. (See LITERATURE.) At the time of writing, *Royal Palm Estate* is a popular locally produced soap opera on CVM TV that has already lasted for several seasons, as did *Lime Tree Lane* produced by JBC TV.

In the 1950s, as part of its outreach programme, the UNIVERSITY OF THE WEST INDIES established a Radio Unit to develop programmes that were broadcast by radio stations in the various territories served by the university. They covered a wide range of material on art, dance, language, folklore, poetry, philosophy, history and current affairs. The valuable archive of some 5,000 reel and cassette tapes generated by this unit has now been collected into a Library of the Spoken Word housed on the Mona Campus. This non-print audio library is the most comprehensive in the Commonwealth Caribbean. The UWI also operates a local radio station – Radio Mona – out of Carimac.

[Baxter 1970, Chang and Chen 1998, GOJ STATIN 1999a, Mordecai 1991]

BROMELIAD

Jamaica has a large variety of Bromeliads – 63 species – mostly epiphytes that attach themselves to trees or shrubs without drawing sustenance from them, to rocks, and even power lines. Plants of this huge family (over 1,000 species) are confined to the New World though in recent years some species have become popular internationally as houseplants.

The name Wild Pine was first applied to them in Jamaica from their resemblance to the most famous member of the family, the PINEAPPLE which, like the Ping Wing (often planted as a 'living fence'), grows on the ground. Both are introductions. Jamaica's native Wild Pines are commonly seen festooning the trunks and branches of trees, and a large tree, such as the COTTON TREE, might accommodate hundreds at a time.

Because the formation of their spiky leaves creates a hollow rosette where they meet, water collects here and in the wild, this natural 'pond' in turn becomes home to numerous creatures. For this reason, one writer has called the Wild Pine a 'free lodging house', another a 'community centre'. Inside these plants might be found tree FROGS including egg and tadpole stages, mosquitoes, DRAGONFLIES, beetles, SPIDERS, etc. as well as algae, microscopic animals, water bugs and a unique CRAB.

Wild Pines have also provided water for humans in extreme cases, the larger species holding as much as half a gallon. T.H. Farr once sampled it and commented: 'The flavour of this water isn't too bad, at least if you are as thirsty as I was.' During the second MAROON war, it was noted that once the Maroons had exhausted water left by rain in the hollows of rocks in their COCKPIT COUNTRY fastness, their only recourse was the water in the Wild Pine.

[Adams 1971, 1972, Edwards 1796, Farr 1983, Vogel 1993]

Bromeliads (A. Hawkes)

BROWN'S TOWN

Large inland market town in ST ANN Parish named after its founder, Hamilton Brown (1776-1843), an Irishman. Brown started out humbly as an estate BOOK-KEEPER and rose to become a large landowner, representing the parish in the House of Assembly for 22 years. He is buried in the churchyard of St Mark's Church (ANGLICAN).

Brown's Town was one of the centres of early MISSIONARY activities. The BAPTIST church there was served for nearly a century by two men, the Revd John Clarke (1809-80) followed by his son-in-law, the Revd George E. Henderson (1849-1931) who recorded their struggles in a book called *Goodness and Mercy: A Tale of a Hundred Years*. From Brown's Town they established many churches in the surrounding area.

The first church was established in answer to a call from James Finlayson, a slave who was converted in the town one market day when he heard a Baptist preacher. He gathered around him a nucleus of believers who induced a minister to come in 1830, Finlayson becoming the first deacon. Their newly built Brown's Town chapel was among the 13 destroyed by the COLONIAL CHURCH UNION in the wake of the Christmas rebellion of 1831-32. (See SHARPE, Samuel.) Hamilton Brown was then a colonel of the MILITIA and a leader in the Union.

The Brown's Town Baptist Minister had left after the destruction of the church but the congregation was kept going by the slave Finlayson who conducted secret services in a cave until discovered. His subsequent brutal punishment by his master and his trials in the Workhouse (slave prison) were recorded by the Quaker visitor William Sturge and used as propaganda in England for the EMANCIPATION of the slaves. Finlayson who had learnt to read and write kept a notebook in which he recorded how, 'In the time of Mashal (Martial) Law when pasucution arises, all the Chappel was pulled doun to the ground, and I took my Bibel and all my Books and put them in a box, and carry it to a cave; and, when I get a little time, I go to the cave and set myself down, and try to rede my Bibel, the little that I could rede, and it was very little, but it make me happy. When I go into the cave, and set me down, I feel that God is with me there'.

The Brown's Town Evangelist Tabernacle on Top Road was founded by Dr James Johnston, MD (1854-1922) as a breakaway from the Baptists. The colourful Dr Johnston became a leading citizen of Brown's Town, presiding over his Evangelistic mission, representing the Parish in the Legislative Council, practising medicine as well as photography. A collection of his photographs of Jamaica was presented to Queen Victoria. He was one of the earliest promoters of TOURISM in the island, in 1903 publishing *Jamaica: the new Riviera: a pictorial description of the island and its attractions* and accompanying postcards. Earlier, he led an expedition across Africa, with six young Jamaicans, publishing a book called *Reality versus Romance in South Central Africa* (1893).

Brown's Town and its environs today is the

location of several educational institutions including St Hilda's High School for Girls, Brown's Town Community College, St Christopher's School for the Deaf, and the Servite Convent School among others.
[Henderson 1931, Wright and White 1969]

BRUCKINS

Celebration marrying dancing, singing, speechmaking, feasting and friendly rivalry that originated as an event held to mark the anniversary of the EMANCIPATION of the slaves. (See AUGUST, First of.) Traditionally the celebrations started 31 July and continued to the early hours of 1 August so the revellers could 'bring in the August morning'. Although Emancipation occurred in 1838, Olive Lewin's informants told her that the first celebration was actually held in 1839, since (according to the story passed down by their elders), after the disappointment of 1834 (see APPRENTICESHIP), they waited a year to see if 'full free' had really come.

Although the Bruckins tradition died out in other parts of the island, it survived as a dance in two villages, MANCHIONEAL and Kensington in PORTLAND Parish, and was performed in public for the first time in 1966 as part of the Jamaica Festival of Arts. At that time, most of the performers were old people. Since then, Bruckins has been seen at the annual FESTIVAL events, being kept alive by the very old or by the young school children of these districts.

Bruckins is a mixture of European and African influences, part of it an imitation of English royal pageantry, the rest exuberantly African in style and execution. The Bruckins dance that survives is a long processional dance. It makes use of long, gliding steps that Ivy Baxter suggests were derived from the Pavane, a European court dance of the 15th and 16th centuries, along with forward and backward movements of the body and other dance expressions that are African-derived.

Performers consist of two rival sets, the Red and the Blue, wearing costumes in imitation of a royal court, the colours probably derived from an older tradition, the red and blue SET GIRLS. Each set of dancers is led by a King and Queen and accompanied by attendants such as Queen Granddaughter, princesses, captains, soldiers, each wearing appropriate headwear and carrying a sword or sceptre. Each set comes out and shows off their costumes and dancing skills to their rivals, the 'bruck' by each Queen, a special move, being the highlight.

In earlier times Bruckins was widely celebrated as an elaborate village pageant called Bruckins Party or Queen Party and included the costumed participants, processions, set dances, as well as a TEA MEETING, an element that is not a part of the contemporary bruckins.

A traditional Bruckins Party started in the evening, the two sets of dancers parading through the village, revealing their costumes to their rivals for the first time and showing off their dance skills. Blue Granddaughter came out first and danced, followed by Red Granddaughter, and so on, with all the women in order until the Blue Queen and then the Red Queen appeared. As each appeared, 'clappers' (firecrackers) would be fired in imitation of gun salutes, as one of the performers in 1966 explained to Ivy Baxter. The highlight was the 'Queen Party figure', with the queen of each set coming out to dance, each queen seeing who could 'bruck' the better, that is move the lower part of the body in elaborate movements, making it seem as if it were broken at the waist. Marjorie Whylie describes 'the bruck', since the 1980s, as a 'somewhat forcible forward contraction of the pelvis accompanied by a rowing motion of the arms'.

The males would come out to dance in the same order, ending with the Kings. Then the processions of male and female pairs would continue in stately fashion around the village. Dancers would add to the long gliding steps a movement of bending the body alternately backward and forward in intricate variations, what Ryman calls the 'thrust and recovery action of the hip and leg which are initiated by a subtle upper-torso contraction'. The processions would continue until around midnight when the song 'We are going out to the supper room' would announce the break for the next phase of the night, the Tea Meeting. This was usually held in a bamboo booth, a temporary structure enclosed with split bamboo and interwoven palm leaves constructed for special events such as dances, wedding celebrations, and religious rituals. The Tea Meeting would be conducted with great ceremony and included elaborate or bombastic speeches or 'speechifying' and 'cutting English' by the Chairman, auctions, and the unveiling of the queen and showbread. (See BREAD.)There would also be communal feasting.

After the Tea Meeting, the dancers would exit the booth in the reverse order to that in which they first appeared, with Blue Granddaughter coming out first. There were set songs for each element in the evening and the celebrations

Bruckins performance

would continue until the new day dawned. Bruckins songs were topical or referred to the progress of the dance and its various figures, such as 'Decent marching around the throne', 'Pick up yu foot an Siloh', 'Rally around' and 'Fall back me da hol de line fe go dance me Jubilee'. Of the topical songs, one – 'Yu nuh yeary whe me yeary' – referred to the turbine explosion at the Duckenfield sugar factory.

Although the Tea Meeting elements have not been preserved, the traditional songs are still sung at these events, the most popular of them referring to Queen Victoria, during whose reign the slaves were freed:

> Jubilee, Jubilee, this is the year of Jubilee
> August morning come again
> Queen Victoria set we free
> This is the year of Jubilee, etc.

Bruckins dancers nowadays are accompanied by singers and musicians playing instruments that Marjorie Whylie describes as European-derived. They consist of a double-headed bass drum played with a stick in a fairly slow march-like pattern, a rattling (side) drum played with two slender sticks in phrases of alternating syncopated and triplet patterns and a pair of shakkas (CALABASH rattles), usually played by the lead singer.

The word 'bruckins' in Jamaican creole has also come to mean any lively dance party.

[Baxter 1972, Henry 1984, Lewin 1984, Lewin 2000, Ryman 1980, Whylie 1994]

BRYAN CASTLE

Residence in TRELAWNY Parish located about 5km from RIO BUENO, built in the late 18th century and – until it was destroyed by fire in the 1990s – an interesting contribution to Jamaican architecture (see GREAT HOUSE) and plantation history. Lady Nugent, the governor's wife, dined there in 1802 and wrote in her *Journal*, 'It is really a beautiful place; the house is a good one, and tolerably well furnished, and has a Turkey carpet in the drawing room – an extraordinary sight in this country.' It was one of the houses appearing in the artist James Hakewill's *Picturesque Tour of the Island of Jamaica* (1825).

It was here that Bryan Edwards (1743-1800), merchant and planter, wrote *The History, Civil and Commercial, of the British Colonies in the West Indies* (1793) which was for a long time the standard work. Born in Wiltshire, England, Edwards was sent out to Jamaica in 1759 to his wealthy and influential uncle, Zachary Bayly, planter and CUSTOS of ST MARY and St George (a parish later absorbed into PORTLAND), from whom he inherited several properties, including this one. Edwards became a member of the

Bryan Castle in 1820 by James Hakewill

House of Assembly, first for St George and later for Trelawny. He eventually returned to England in 1792 and settled at Southampton, where he died.

[Cundall 1915, Nugent 1839]

BUCCANEERS

The 'Brethren of the Coast' are a significant element in the history of old PORT ROYAL that became their base. The original buccaneers were a mixture of men of every nation, the outcasts of society, who flocked to the unsettled parts of Hispaniola where they hunted herds of wild PIGS and CATTLE. From the native peoples they learnt a method of curing meat on a contraption which they called a boucan from which the name 'buccaneers' (*boucaniers* to the French) was derived. Eventually the buccaneers moved to the island of Tortuga (near to Haiti). To resist the efforts of their dreaded enemies, the Spaniards, to drive them off, they formed themselves into 'The Confederacy of the Brethren of the Coast'. Under strong leaders they began to carry out many daring acts of piracy against Spanish ships.

Since Spain was also the traditional enemy of England, the English governor of Jamaica, Lord Windsor, in the late 1650s, invited the buccaneers to come and use Port Royal as their base for attacks against the French and the Spaniards. The buccaneers were given licences to attack enemy shipping and towns in return for which the Crown got one-tenth of all booty captured. These buccaneers who were licensed became known as 'privateers' and contributed greatly to making Port Royal both the wealthiest city of its time and 'the wickedest on earth'. The most famous buccaneer was Henry MORGAN who topped his career by the capture of the City of Panama in 1671.

Eventually, though, England made peace with her old enemies and outlawed the buccaneers. In fact, Morgan's capture of Panama had taken place after the signing of a peace treaty (the Treaty of Madrid, 1670), with Spain and to appease the Spaniards both the governor of Jamaica and Morgan were recalled to England. The governor, Sir Thomas Modyford, was shut up for a while in the Tower of London, but Morgan was knighted and returned to Jamaica as lieutenant-governor. In this new respectable role, Morgan turned around and savagely suppressed those buccaneers or privateers who refused to give up their old ways. They were now outlawed and regarded as pirates.

Gallows Point

Pirates continued to haunt Caribbean waters but were ruthlessly hunted by the British Navy. Those caught were hanged at Gallows Point on the PALISADOES. The last of these pirate executions took place in 1831. (See also RACKHAM, Jack.) A description of such an execution is given in Michael Scott's *Tom Cringle's Log*. A first-hand account of the buccaneering life by a contemporary of Henry Morgan is *The Buccaneers of America* by Esquemeling, first published in 1678.
[Black 1989]

BULLA
Small, flat, round cake about 10cm in diameter, made with flour, molasses (or very dark sugar) and baking soda, sometimes flavoured with ginger. Bullas used to be sold very cheaply and were much enjoyed by schoolchildren and poorer folk, being sweet and filling. They were made and baked in home-made tins and sold at all church fairs and from simple glass cases at the side of the road and could be bought in every village shop. Bullas seemed to have disappeared for a while, but have made a comeback and can sometimes be purchased in local supermarkets. They are also much consumed by expatriate Jamaicans in North America and the UK.

Bulla

BULL BAY and COW BAY
Adjoining bays in ST THOMAS Parish, so-called because CATTLE used to be slaughtered and cured nearby, according to some authorities, probably by the BUCCANEERS who were originally known as 'cow-catchers'. Others say that the 'cows' and 'bulls' were MANATEES or sea cows that were harpooned in the bay and brought here for butchering. In 1694 when a French invasion of Jamaica was attempted (see CARLISLE BAY), the French Admiral DuCasse's fleet anchored at Cow Bay, landed, and plundered for several kilometres. However, they were routed by the local MILITIA. From here the fleet sailed west and attacked at Carlisle.

BULLFROG (*Bufo marinus*)
What is called the 'Bullfrog' in Jamaica is really a giant toad. This species was introduced from Barbados in 1844 by Anthony Davis, planter-

owner of Molynes estate, ST ANDREW parish, in the hope that it would destroy cane piece rats. The 'bullfrog' quickly spread to become a familiar sight all over Jamaica. It is one of the largest species of toads in the world and is the only toad found in Jamaica, being well established all over the island to 750m. It is native to Central and South America and the southern United States. Because of its usefulness in destroying insect pests, the bullfrog, according to Bernard Lewis, has been distributed by man over a greater part of the world than any other animal. (See also FROGS.)

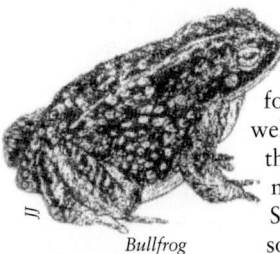

Bullfrog

[NHSJ 1949]

BUNGO

The DJE says the word 'Bongo' or 'Bungo' possibly derives from one or more tribal names for Bantu, Semi-Bantu or Pygmy peoples between the Niger Delta and the Congo. For instance, Bongo or Bungu or Vungu was the name of a Congo sub-group in the Yombe region and was considered the birthplace of the Congo nation sometime before 1200. 'Bongo' may also derive from Congo (m)*bongo* (money) and thus may have functioned as a self-ascription and ascription for a bought person, a slave.

In the CARIBBEAN, people from Central Africa were held in contempt by more north-westerly nations and this attitude continued to prevail in Jamaica long after SLAVERY ended. Thus 'bungo' like CONGO is in general Jamaican usage nowadays to describe uncouth people, a bungo-story (like congosaw) tells of the stupidity of the Bungo or Congo people, and Bungo talk is uncultivated speech.

However, among Kumina practitioners (regarded as strongly influenced by Congo arrivals in the mid-19th century), the dancers are regarded as 'Bungo men' or Africans and sing songs in 'Bungo' language; early Rastafarians also affirmed the 'Bungo' element in their heritage, being also called 'Bungo men'. Some, like the poet 'Bongo Jerry', assumed it as part of their names and Bob Marley (in 'Natty Dread') affirmed 'Dread Natty Dread now/Dreadlocks Congo Bongo I'.

A cult from eastern Jamaica is called Convince or Bungo and engages in spirit possession with music in African call and response style accompanied by polyrhythmic clapping and percussive sticks (CATTA STICK). In Trinidad, the Bongo dance is a dance of African origin performed at wakes to placate the ancestral spirits and is said to share many musical traits with Convince of Jamaica.

[Bilby 1985, DCEU, DJE, Herskovits 1976, Vansina 1990, 1996]

BURCHELL MEMORIAL CHURCH

This BAPTIST church in MONTEGO BAY, ST JAMES Parish, was established in 1824 with 12 members under the care of the MISSIONARY the Revd Thomas Burchell. The original church was destroyed by mob action following the Slave Rebellion of 1831-32. This was the church at which Samuel SHARPE, the great slave leader, was a deacon. Burchell himself was saved from personal violence by the intervention of the Collector of Customs who found him temporary refuge on board a warship in the harbour. The cornerstone of the present church was laid in 1835.

BURIAL see DEATH RITUALS

BURIAL SOCIETIES see FRIENDLY SOCIETIES

BURU

Recreational African-based dance and drumming style associated with secular KUMINA entertainment. It is also associated with RASTAFARI music and with the masquerade tradition (see JONKONNU) especially in CLARENDON and ST CATHERINE parishes. Buru is believed to derive from WORK SONGS from the days of SLAVERY. It was carried by rural dwellers to KINGSTON where it was danced

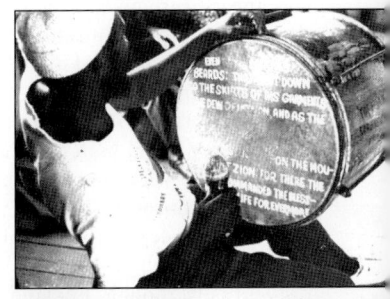

Players of bass (top) repeater (left) and funde (righ[t])

mainly on holidays and to celebrate the return of discharged prisoners to their slum communities. In the *Daily Gleaner* of the 1940s occur accounts of people 'dancing the buru' on moonlight nights. The songs of Buru relate to Christmas and New Year celebrations, the masquerade figures, and songs of praise and derision, their lyrics often dealing with subject matter that is taboo in the context of polite speech.

Some researchers have argued that the Rastafarian Nyabinghi drumming style resulted from a fusion of Buru and Kumina secular drumming. Buru music is accompanied by three DRUMS, along with scrapers, rattles and other percussion instruments. The drums are called funde, bass and repeater. The funde and repeater are small open ended instruments, the bass is double headed. The repeater is used to play the melody while the funde is used to give syncopation.

[Bilby and Leib 1986, Reckord 1977, Marjorie Whylie, personal communication]

BUSH

The word is applied to wild or uncultivated land as well as to a cultivated plot a long distance away from the yard or home, one that is 'in the bush'. The saying 'bush have ears' or 'bush have eye' cautions discretion, as 'bush' in this sense can be any wild plant. But the word is most commonly applied to any plant or part of a plant, including root, stem, bark, seed, leaves, or flowers, used in folk medicine (see MEDICINE, folk) in an infusion ('Bush-tea') or bath ('Bush bath') or to the names of particular plants, e.g. 'Asthma bush'. An obeah-man or folk healer is sometimes called a Bush Doctor or Bush Man since bush is also used in BALM or OBEAH for healing or protection. A 'bush bath' is used by traditional healers to drive out evil spirits.

The 'bush bath' is also a traditional home remedy for fevers or other illnesses (also called fever-bath). Caroline Sullivan in *The Jamaica Cookery Book* published in 1893 gives a recipe for a bush bath and states: 'This bush bath is firmly believed in by all Jamaicans. In fact it is considered absolutely necessary after fevers or other illnesses.'

The bushes are usually boiled together and strained into the bath that contains hot water and the patient is placed to sit over the bath under a covering so that profuse sweating is induced. Leaves to be boiled in Sullivan's recipe ('a few of each or as many as you can get') included: ACKEE, SOURSOP, Joint-wood, PIMENTO, Cowfoot, Sage, Velvet leaf, GUAVA, Jack-in-the-bush, Thistle, CERASEE, Elder, LIME leaf, Liquorice bush.

BUSH FIGHTING

A term used in two different senses in Jamaica. As originally used in the Americas, the term referred to the activities of native Americans from the 'Mosquito Coast' of Nicaragua (see MISKITO) brought to Jamaica to hunt down the MAROONS. An account from the 1730s noted that the Amerindians were formed into companies under their own officers, allowed 40 shillings a month pay, shoes, and other articles. White guides were assigned to conduct them to the enemy. It was remarked that they observed the most profound silence in marching and once they hit a trail, they were sure to discover where it led. The authorities observed with satisfaction that they were the most proper troops to be employed in 'bush fighting'. But the Maroons too, engaged in 'bush fighting', both in terms of their knowledge of the bush and the guerrilla tactics they employed, and also in the fact that they often draped themselves with 'bush' – vines and branches, as camouflage. (See CACOON.)

[Edwards 1794]

BUSTAMANTE, Rt Excellent Sir Alexander (1884-1977)

National Hero of Jamaica. First prime minister, labour leader extraordinary. Founder of the Jamaica Labour Party and the Bustamante Industrial TRADE UNION, Bustamante is honoured in his homeland as a champion of the poor and oppressed, for his role in organizing labour, and for his part in furthering the nationalist movement by his challenge to colonial authority.

'Busta' as he was familiarly referred to by everyone, was born at Blenheim, HANOVER

Reconstruction of Bustamante's birthplace

Sir William Alexander Bustamante dances with HRH Princess Margaret at Jamaica's Independence celebrations, 1962

Parish, on 24 February 1884, the son of a modest pen-keeping family and was christened William Alexander Clarke. His education and opportunities were limited and in 1903, like tens of thousands of his compatriots, he left Jamaica in search of adventure overseas (see COLÓN MAN). He lived and worked in many countries, acquiring a dashing Latin style of dress and behaviour as well as the name Bustamante by which he was known thereafter, formally changing his name by deed poll in 1944.

Historians have not yet managed to totally untangle the reality from the myths and legends of Bustamante's foreign sojourn.

Bustamante returned to Jamaica for good in 1933 and tried his hand at several occupations, eventually becoming a money-lender and was well into his fifties when he entered public life. He first attracted attention by a series of letters he wrote to the newspapers attacking the social and political conditions of colonial Jamaica. Soon he began speaking on public platforms, particularly at meetings at North Parade in Kingston (in association with St William Grant – see PARK).

In 1937 Bustamante got into the business of organizing the labour force and his charismatic personality soon won him a huge mass following. As Sylvia Wynter has expressed it (in *Jamaica's National Heroes*): 'if the word "charisma" had not existed, the eruption of William Alexander Bustamante on the Jamaican scene in the 1930s would have caused some political scientist or other to have invented it . . . In the life and time of William Alexander Bustamante we see the word "charisma" made flesh.'

For his role as the spokesman and champion of labour, he was imprisoned during the islandwide riots of 1938 (see FROME). He also spent 17 months (1940-42) in detention camp during the Second WORLD WAR. It was during the '38 labour ferment that Bustamante formed the Bustamante Industrial Trade Union (BITU). In 1944, Jamaica's first general election was held under Universal Adult Suffrage granted by a new constitution. Bustamante formed the Jamaica Labour Party (JLP) to contest the election and led it to victory, gaining 23 out of 32 seats. He thus became Jamaica's first chief minister. The JLP held power until 1955 in which year Bustamante was knighted by the Queen.

Jamaica became a part of the WEST INDIES Federation that was established in 1958 and Bustamante was Jamaican leader of the Democratic Labour Party that came to power in the Federal elections. However, he soon changed his policy and advocated the withdrawal of Jamaica from the Federation and a move towards INDEPENDENCE. Jamaicans voted to secede from the Federation in a special referendum and the island became Independent in 1962. The JLP won the election held that year and Bustamante became the first prime minister. In that year, he married his private secretary of many years, Miss Gladys Longbridge. Bustamante retired from active politics in 1967, but until his death in 1977 continued to be an influential figure in both the party and the union. Sir Alexander Bustamante was proclaimed a National Hero during his lifetime, the only living National Hero Jamaica has had. Port Bustamante, Bustamante Children's Hospital and Bustamante Bridge (St Thomas) are among the places named in his honour.

[Eaton 1975, Hamilton 1978, Hill 1975, Ranston 1977, Shearer 1978, Wynter 1971]

BUTTERFLIES AND MOTHS

At least 134 species have been described from Jamaica, of which 20 are endemic (known only from Jamaica), and there are probably others waiting to be discovered. Jamaicans still frequently call both butterflies and moths 'bats' (real BATS being called 'rat bats'). Much is known about Jamaican butterflies; little about its moths.

The division into butterflies and moths is an artificial one. The popularly perceived difference between the two is that butterflies are gaily coloured and fly by day, moths fly at night, though there are exceptions. There are gaily coloured moths, drab butterflies, day-flying moths, dusk-flying butterflies. Close relatives, they both belong to the order of insects known as *Lepidoptera*, a Greek word meaning 'scaly winged', their colouring and patterning deriving from tiny scales arranged over the transparent wing-membranes. The most noticeable structural difference is in the antennae – in butterflies each feeler ends in a knob or hook, in the moth the feeler is either thread-like or feathery and tapers to a point.

The infancy of both is spent first as a caterpillar, then in a cocooned stage, the winged creature emerging when fully grown. Each species of caterpillar has its own preferred plant. Butterflies and moths live chiefly on nectar sucked from flowers and always lay eggs on the plant the particular species prefers.

The most spectacular butterfly in Jamaica is the Giant Swallowtail (*Pterourus* [formerly *Papilio*] *homerus*) with striking yellow and black colouring, which is found nowhere else. It is one of the largest butterflies in the western hemisphere, with a wing span of 15.2cm. Since its discovery in the 18th century it has been much sought after by collectors. It is not widely distributed; its main habitat is in the John Crow

Giant Swallowtail

Mountains although it is found elsewhere, especially in the COCKPIT COUNTRY. *Pterourus homerus* tends to fly high and is encountered in rugged terrain, hence it is not easily collected.

The most striking of the moths are the Hawk-moths (*Sphingids*) that resemble HUMMINGBIRDS as they hover over flowers. The tongue of this moth is a long flexible tube that it uses to suck up juice and keeps coiled up in front of its head when not in use.

A white species of butterfly (*Kricogonia lyside*) is remarkable for its swarms around the LIGNUM VITAE trees from time to time.

Lady Edith Blake, the wife of a governor of Jamaica, spent her time in the island between 1889-98 creating a remarkable record of Jamaica's butterflies and moths, now in the collection of the British Museum of Natural History. Almost all of her 196 illustrations show a complete life cycle, and depict the preferred food plants of the species, complete with larval damage.

[Barnes 1988, Brown and Heineman 1972, NHSJ 1949]

BYBROOK

Place name in ST CATHERINE Parish, near to Bog Walk, it was one of the first to go into SUGAR cultivation in the island, around 1667. Bybrook estate was first patented and named by an adventurer named Carey Helyar who, accompanied only by his dog, paddled down the RIO COBRE and discovered the fertile valley beyond. This was shortly after the English CAPTURE OF JAMAICA and settlement at that time ended at Angels (from the Spanish, *Los Angelos*) just outside SPANISH TOWN.

CABARITTA RIVER

Chief river of WESTMORELAND Parish, rising in the parish of HANOVER near to Cascade and flowing 39.7km to the sea at SAVANNA-LA-MAR. The Cabaritta is navigable by small boats for about 19.2km. The name might be a version of Cabonito which is a name mentioned in SPANISH accounts of the island. There is also a Cabaritta island in PORT MARIA bay.

The rich alluvial plain built up by this river and its tributaries, as well as the knowledge and skill brought by the Suriname settlers (see SURINAM QUARTERS, BANBURY) made Westmoreland Jamaica's foremost SUGAR growing parish. In the lower reaches, rice was cultivated by descendants of the INDIAN indentured workers who introduced cultivation of the crop to the island.

CABINET-MAKER

The craft of woodworking has a long tradition in Jamaica, though the demand initially was for carpenters rather than for cabinet-makers, those craftsmen who specialize in the making of fine furniture, or joiners who specialize in finished woodwork (e.g. windows, doors). Such craftsmen were present in PORT ROYAL at the time of the 1692 earthquake, but we are told that while the houses in this rich merchant city were elaborate, the furniture was scant. Thus skilled craftsmen often had to turn their hand to more utilitarian work, in response to demand.

One outlet for a variety of woodworking skills has always been in church building and decoration. Excavations of the sunken city of Port Royal yielded fine wooden pews and decorative wood carvings that were done locally for the church of St Paul's, built shortly before the earthquake, and the demand for such work continued over many centuries. Today, the work of these unknown craftsmen can best be seen in the island's older churches, such as SCOTS KIRK or Phillippo Baptist Church, or in former grand residences, such as HEADQUARTERS HOUSE. The work of contemporary skilled craftsmen can be seen in the fine reproductions in places such as DEVON HOUSE, ROSE HALL Great House and Half Moon Hotel.

Carpenters were of great importance on every SUGAR PLANTATION. While the early craftsmen came from the British Isles, over time their skills were transferred to slave craftsmen (black and COLOURED) as well as freedmen. Slave craftsmen were the most valuable of the human property on the estates (see SLAVERY). Craton tells us that 'An ordinary carpenter was thought to be worth more than a head driver, and a head carpenter might command . . . the value of four healthy male field slaves'.

In a situation where wood was widely used in construction, including parts of the mills and estate buildings and for the carts and drays used in transport, carpenters had to master a very wide range of skills. There is little evidence of estate carpenters building more than the most basic furniture, though, as Craton remarks, 'men who could fashion louvred windows, bannistered stairways and decorated porches were quite capable of producing furniture'. (See GREAT HOUSE.)

Furniture At the height of the plantation era, much of the furniture for the elite was imported from England. One important supplier from the mid-to late 18th century was the Lancaster firm of Waring and Gillow. K.E. Ingram's research into their files reveals some of the tastes of the plantocracy. Much of the furniture was made of MAHOGANY shipped from the West Indies to England. In addition to the standard furnishings, gentlemen's travelling desks, telescoping tables, as well as billiard and backgammon tables were popular, for the West Indians kept up with the

Scots Kirk interior showing fine woodwork

height of fashion in furniture as well as clothing. In a climate where so much drink was consumed, a popular Gillows item was the cellaret with compartments for bottles.

At first, locally made furniture were copies of British and, later, North American styles. But with such a wide range of beautiful woods available, a local vernacular style developed, especially in the manufacture of sideboards, wardrobes and presses, couches and four-poster beds, adapted to the architectural spaces and the climate. Often, upholstery was replaced by cane seating, and heavier mahogany or CEDAR preferred to veneering over soft woods, as these were subject to termites.

The fine furniture produced by Gillows left a lasting impression on local cabinet-makers. According to Ingram: 'Perhaps the most marked influence may be seen in the bureau bookcases or wine glass or plate cabinets of nineteenth century Jamaican manufacture with glazing held in place by delicate lattice work strips suggestive of Chinese influence and with plain solid or dentilled cornices, also in the ubiquitous sofa with its carved backrest and scrolled headrest, in the sofa table with its reeded legs, claw-tipped or square-ended and covered in brass. The elegantly fluted reeded bedposts such as Adam or Gillows designed had few imitators in Jamaica, where bulbous cup or pineapple motifs predominated.'

Local Craftsmen In the late 18th century, we know of a GERMAN joiner named Blenchenden who operated a cabinet making establishment in Kingston with over 30 workmen, including 19 black slaves 'who worked naked making the most beautiful tables and turned work from the lumber of mahogany and cedar'. By the early 19th century, cabinet-making was a well established craft, the introduction of French polish – which helped to bring out the grain and beauty of local woods – contributing to that development.

Cellaret in Devon House

Unfortunately, most of the master craftsmen have remained anonymous. One who became well known was Ralph Turnbull, who had a manufacturing establishment in KINGSTON from 1820-40, employing 60 journeymen and apprentices; his work was noted for its fine inlays. The House of Assembly presented Turnbull with a reward for his research into local woods. Another master cabinet-maker of the time whose name we know is Henry Page of FALMOUTH, a former slave.

While the patrons of the cabinet-maker and consumers of imported furniture were the wealthy or upwardly mobile, the majority of the population relied mainly on the village carpenter who, in the tradition of the earlier plantation carpenter, built everything from houses and furniture to coffins. Village carpenters in 19th and early 20th century Jamaica also built small wooden churches decorated with fine trellis-work. For funerals, the carpenter sometimes accepted lumber from the family of the deceased but charged nothing for his labour, which might include French polishing, carving, and adding a bronze plate etched with the dead person's name. Some of these skilled men travelled the island so as to get

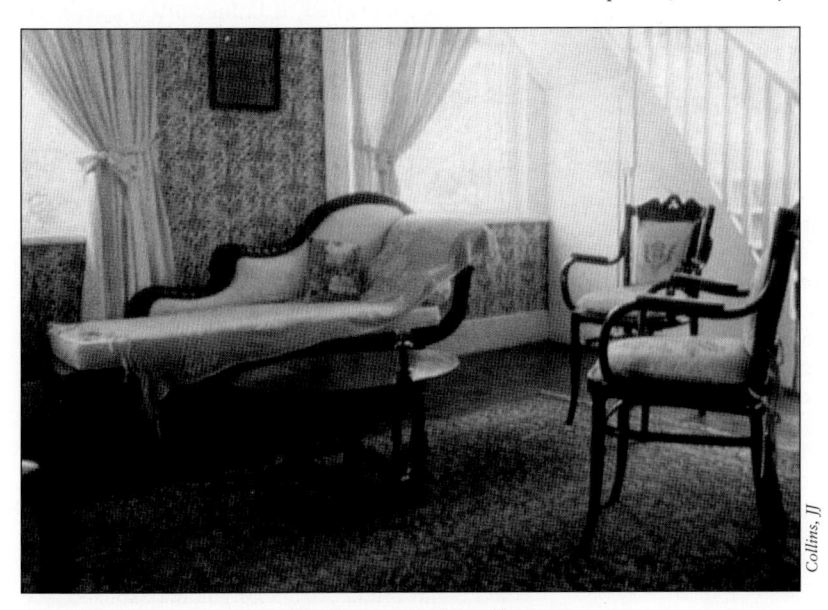

The sewing room, Devon House

Four-poster bed

work. When emigration overseas began with the construction of the Panama Railroad in the mid-19th century, these craftsmen were among the first to go. In the 20th century, many others returned with a trade acquired from their years spent on the construction of the PANAMA Canal and other industrial undertakings in the Americas. (See COLÓN MAN.)

Some of these early craftsmen, known and unknown, left behind not just beautiful examples of their work, but the legacy of their skills passed on, through their apprentices, to succeeding generations. The well-known Jamaican writer Claude McKay (see LITERATURE) was just such an apprentice, his Trades Master, as he called him, being located in BROWN'S TOWN. Though his Master was 'a jack-of-all-trades – a wheelwright, a carriage builder and an excellent cabinet-maker', perhaps fortunately for literature he seemed to have imparted little of his vast knowledge to McKay, who left after two years. This was shortly after the 1907 EARTHQUAKE and McKay recalled that 'Those were the days . . . when people indulged in their fancy homemade furniture. We certainly had some wonderful native workmen. That was the period before the invasion of the modern Grand Rapids American furniture'.

[Carson 1994, 2000, Craton 1978, Ingram 1992, Jacobs 1976, McKay 1979, Pawson and Buisseret 1975]

CACIQUE

Name for the political and religious leader or chief of the TAINOS. The Taino homelands were organized into chiefdoms (*cacicazgos*) or provinces, each ruled over by a cacique. Some of these caciques became famous in the SPANISH chronicles, as they welcomed (or resisted) the Europeans. We have the names of only a few caciques in Jamaica at the time of the conquest: Ameyro, Aguacaciba, Maima, Aomaoqueque, Huareo.

The development of a hierarchical society led by a cacique is regarded as one of the distinguishing marks of the Tainos. Each grand cacique would have under him sub-chiefs in charge of local districts, and within each district there would be a headman or cacique for each village. Thus caciques varied greatly in rank and prestige, but the rule of each was absolute over the people he (or sometimes she) governed. Caciques came from the ruling class (called *nitaíno*), inherited their office and were set apart by many signs of special status: they were entitled to special food, housing, dress, ornaments, mode of transportation and death rituals. They lived apart from the general population in a large rectangular house called a *bohío* which contained the large village ZEMIS (the commoners, called *naboría*, lived in round houses called *caney*) and they owned the largest and most elaborate CANOES. Their symbol of office was a neck plate of GUANÍN. Caciques were carried about on litters; in death their bodies were not allowed to touch the ground: they were interred seated on special stools called *duhos* (see SEATING, Ceremonial).

Contact among the caciques extended between the islands. The paramount cacique of Jamaica, a rank which rotated between the major *bohíos* of the island (but at the time of COLUMBUS' arrival was centered on White Marl, ST CATHERINE Parish), was suzerain to the paramount chief of Hispaniola. The name of this paramount chief at the time of Columbus was Guarionex, followed by Caonabo-Anacaona and Cotubanama. Alliances could be powerful when there were disputes; caciques sometimes declared war on each other over matters such as trespass on hunting or fishing rights or a breach of marriage agreements.

Caciques were expected to be good organizers, brave and courageous, since they led their people into battle. They were also spiritually powerful through their contact with the supernatural power of the zemis. They were expected to go into trances to gain prophetic insight that was applied to decision-making. Great caciques were immortalized in the AREITOS or oral histories, and could become zemis or guardian spirits.

Each village cacique was responsible for organizing the daily routine regarding work such as hunting, fishing, tilling, etc. He also organized the storage and distribution of extra provisions. He acted as host to visitors and conducted relations with other villages and caciques. He was responsible for leading the songs and dances, memorizing the areitos or oral histories in childhood as part of his training. His zemis were the most powerful in the village, and he organized their worship. He presided over the COHOBA rituals. He could be despotic, since he had the power of life and death over his people who were expected to obey him. He judged disputes and crimes and imposed punishment, including the death penalty, which was reserved for theft (regarded as the most serious of crimes) and adultery. Village chiefs were expected to provide more powerful chiefs with provisions and services as agreed, such as yuca, manpower or military support. Those belonging to the naboría class were the cacique's to command and could be sent from one chief to another (and later, were sent as labourers to the Spaniards under the ENCOMIENDA system).

Like many Taino words first heard on the islands, the term cacique was applied by the Spaniards to rulers of the other native peoples they encountered on the islands and mainland.
[Fewkes 1907, García Arévalo 1977, Stevens-Arroyo 1988, Steward 1948]

CACOON *(Entada gigas)*
Rampant vine (also known as Kakoon and Mafoota WIS) found on trees on riverbanks and wet areas between 100-600m. It bears what is probably one of the largest bean pods in the world. The pod averages about 10cm in width and 1-2m in length. It was used as a container by the MAROONS (and before them, the TAINOS); the Maroons during their wars also draped the vines about themselves as camouflage. A recent description by Colonel Harris of the Moore Town Maroons, of the preparation of the kernel to make delectable dishes, also indicates its usefulness as food. The seed kernel is also used in folk MEDICINE.

The seeds are probably best known from their utilization in craft work, especially necklaces, but they are also used to make yo-yos and music shakers. The seeds are flat, chocolate brown, about 3-5cm in diameter and are sometimes found washed up on beaches. Ten to twelve seeds are found in a pod.

The plant is found in other parts of the CARIBBEAN, tropical America and tropical Africa.

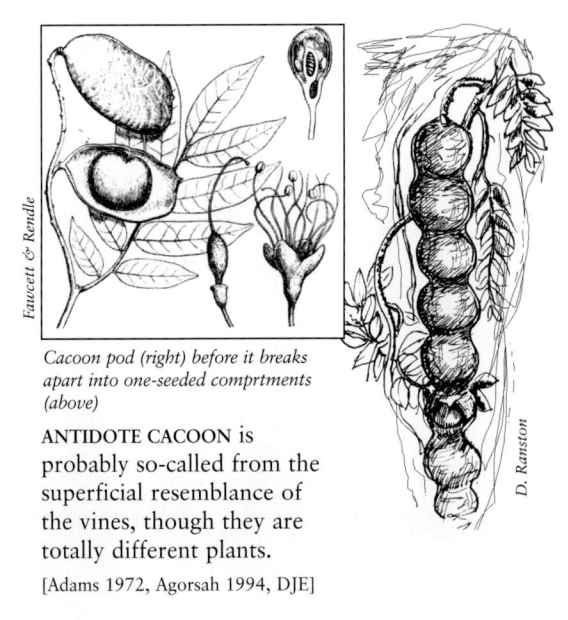

Cacoon pod (right) before it breaks apart into one-seeded comprtments (above)

ANTIDOTE CACOON is probably so-called from the superficial resemblance of the vines, though they are totally different plants.
[Adams 1972, Agorsah 1994, DJE]

CACTUS
Cacti are a family of plants native to the Americas that have developed special features adapted to their habitat in dry and inhospitable areas, such as jointed and fleshy stems without leaves that enable them to conserve moisture. Many species of these succulent plants occur in Jamaica, including several endemics. Cacti flourish in the drier coastal area of southern parishes, although climbing species are found inland at higher elevations.

TOONA, Prickly Pear and Roast Pork are the popular names given to the best known cacti, the genus *Opuntia*. These are widely used for medicinal and other purposes, the names being variously applied to different species. Typically, these fleshy cacti have many branches that are covered in large hairy spines surrounded by barbed bristles. For this reason they are sometimes planted as barriers or fences. The *Opuntia* also bear attractive flowers and edible pear-like fruit.

There are at least six species of *Opuntia* in Jamaica, of which four are endemic.

The popular Toona or Tuna (*O. tuna*), and the Seaside Tuna or Prickly Pear (*O. dillenii*), are found in rocky and sandy places from sea level to 100m and are widely used in folk MEDICINE. Toona produces a soapy juice which can be used as a hair rinse, hence its other name of Swipple (*slippery*) Pole. The name Prickly Pear derives from the prickly, pear-shaped, edible fruit of these plants. There is also a Prickly Pear Tree (*O. spinosissima*), a shrub that finally grows into a tree, its black and spiny trunk up to 30cm thick.

Olive Senior/Encyclopedia of Jamaican Heritage 89

CACTI IN JAMAICA

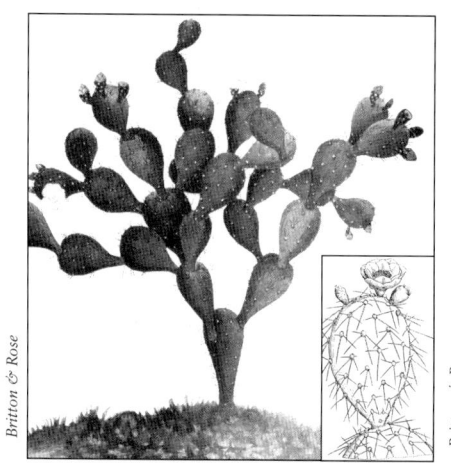

'Toona': Opuntia jamaicensis and O. tuna showing (inset) shoot with flower bud and fruit

Prickly Pear, O. dillenii – flowering joint

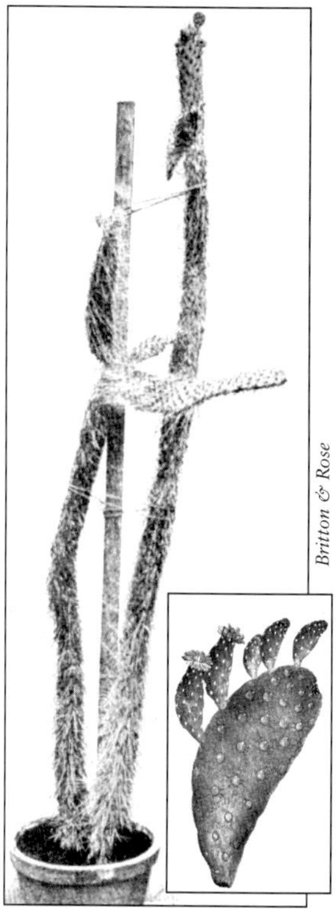

Prickly Pear Tree – O. spinosissima with flowering joint

Cochineal cactus: O. cochenillifera – upper part of flowering joint

Torchwood: Harrisia gracilis with fruiting branch (inset)

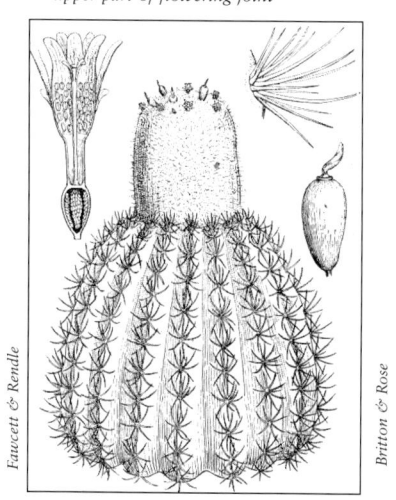

Turk's Cap: Melocactus communis

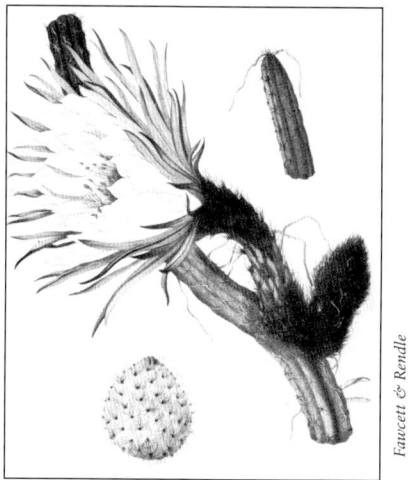

Queen-of-the-night: Selenicereus grandiflorus with flower and fruit

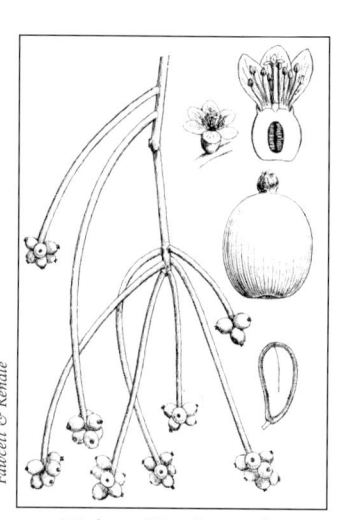

Mistletoe: Rhipsalis cassutha

Prickly Pear Tree is found in coastal parts of southern parishes. The many-branched Cochineal cactus (*O. cochenillifera*), a native of Mexico, is found in gardens at low elevations, cochineal dye being obtained from the bodies of insects that feed on it. However, in Jamaica it is prized for its medicinal properties. It is called Roast Pork or Smooth Pear, because for home remedies the fleshy part is roasted and is then said to resemble pork.

Also well known are the tall Dildos, that will grow to over 6m, column-like cacti common in coastal areas from sea level to 50m and frequently used as hedges, a practice that is common throughout the Caribbean. There are two species, the smaller being called Torchwood (*Harrisia gracilis*), since the woody centre of the stem is used as a torch, especially by fishermen. This shrubby cactus is common in arid areas on the south coast from sea level to 200m and is found only in Jamaica and the Cayman Islands, the botanical name honouring William Harris, a former Superintendent of Public Gardens and Island Botanist. The Torchwood bears a fruit that is yellow when ripe, while the fruit of the Dildo Pear (*Stenocereus hystrix*) is red.

Also common in the southern coastal areas is the Melon Cactus or Turks Cap (*Melocactus communis*), this species growing only in Jamaica. Large, rigid spines form a melon-like base that is eventually topped by a magenta cephalium that looks like a woolly cap, hence its popular name.

In the higher elevations are found the spectacular climbing Cereuses, including the Queen-of-the-Night (*Selenicereus grandiflorus*) which is known for its enormous, powerfully scented white blooms that open only for one night. Also native to Cuba, it is found from sea level to 800m, and is sometimes cultivated in gardens.

An endemic climbing cactus known as God Okra or Supple Okra, Prickly WIS or Vine Pear (*Hylocereus triangularis*) is found at higher elevations up to 1,200m. Aerial roots rise from the triangular stem that sprawls over trees, thickets and rocks without apparently touching the earth, a fact that is regarded as supernatural. The name 'okra' is said to derive either from the fact that the cut stem is slippery like OKRA, or that its scaly buds cooked in soup are similar to okra. It bears a large cream flower that opens at night, and a scarlet edible fruit called a 'vine pear'. The centre of the stem yields a strong wis called 'puss gut'.

A hanging cactus known as Mistletoe looks similar to the universally known parasite of that name, and like it has acquired mystical and supernatural properties, but the Jamaican 'mistletoe' is in a very different plant family. Known also as Currant, Spaghetti or String Cactus (*Rhipsalis baccifera*), it is a well-known epiphyte seen throughout the countryside hanging on rocks and trees. Its limbs are like lengths of green spaghetti up to 2m and it bears tiny white flowers that are followed by white berries. The other popular name for the plant – God-bush – recalls its connection with the supernatural while Scorn-the-Earth describes its habit of growing not by roots in the ground but by attaching itself to other plants.

In addition to these familiar or relatively common cactus species, other less well known species occur in the wild, or are cultivated as introduced ornamentals, such as the West Indian Gooseberry (*Pereskia aculeata*) grown for its fruit.

Many plants that are called 'cactus' are unrelated, though like cacti they have adapted to life in more arid regions. Among these are the Maypole or AGAVE, Yucca or Dagger Plant and Sinkle Bible (ALOE).

[Adams 1971, 1972, Bannochie and Light 1993, Honeychurch 1986, Marshall 1952, NHSJ 1946, Robertson 1990]

CAGE, The

Historic stone structure in the heart of MONTEGO BAY, ST JAMES Parish. The Cage was built in 1806 and was originally used as a temporary lockup for runaway slaves, disorderly seamen and other vagrants. At first the Cage was of wood, but apparently was so damaged by its occupants that a stone structure had to be built. In 1811 a belfry was installed, and the bell was rung as a warning for country slaves to leave town. The bell was rung at 2:00pm and again at 3:00, after which any vagrant blacks found on the streets were locked up. Since the days of SLAVERY, the Cage has served many purposes – it has been a clinic, a dispensary, the office of a travel agency, of the Montego Bay Chamber of Commerce, and a museum.

[Wright and White 1969]

CALABAR

Boys' school in ST ANDREW Parish that was named after Calabar in north eastern Nigeria from where many AFRICANS who came to Jamaica originated. The name was first attached to a property near RIO BUENO, TRELAWNY Parish, where the BAPTISTS established Calabar College to train Jamaican Ministers. The college was opened in 1843. In 1869 it was moved from Rio

Bueno to KINGSTON, first to the East Queen Street Baptist Church premises, then to Chetolah Park lands, and finally to the Red Hills site where Calabar High School now stands. The high school itself was opened in 1912. When the United Theological College of the West Indies was established in 1964, the Baptists decided to join this venture and phased out Calabar College. The high school, however, remained.
[Sibley 1965]

CALABASH (*Crescentia cujete*)

Small spreading tree 6-10m high, a native of tropical America, which bears on its trunk and main branches large round or oval fruits with a thick skin; when emptied out and dried, they serve as containers.

The fruit is called calabash or gourd, but among the folk is better known as Packy or Goady. In the past, this was one of the most useful fruits in the domestic economy, and for many peoples, including the TAINOS and other native peoples of the Americas, also the most important spiritually. The name *higüera* or *jigüera* that is used in the Spanish Antilles, reflects the original Taino name of *güira*.

The tree gourd or calabash should be distinguished from the gourd that grows on the vine, *Lagenaria siceraria*. *Lagenaria* is widespread in Africa and parts of the Americas, and although it grows in Jamaica, it is not well known. On reaching the New World, the AFRICANS who were accustomed to using tree gourds in their everyday life, adopted the calabash gourd as a substitute and transferred to it the name – packy (from Twi *apakyi*) – by which the gourd is known in West Africa. The calabash in Jamaica has several other names: Cuppy is a small calabash provided with handles, usually used for dipping up water, soup etc. similar to a packy-spoon. Cutta-Cutta or Took-Took is a large calabash that is used by the countryman to carry water to his field; it is usually slung over his shoulder by a cord. When used for this purpose, a small hole is bored and a stopper, often a dried corncob, is inserted; the names echo the sound made when water is poured from it.

That the calabash is a metaphor for something hidden is expressed in the advice: 'Keep yu secret inna yu own goady'. If you don't, then you 'open packy.'

There are several varieties of packy yielding fruit of varied sizes and shapes. Both the Island CARIBS and the Tainos used calabashes for dishes, spoons, basins, plates, drinking vessels, and for storage. (An Island Carib name, *couyes* or *couis*, is still used in Haiti today for a gourd bowl; the Caribs also used the name *güira*). The Africans too, in the New World as in their homelands, emptied out the dried calabash and used its hard waterproof shell in as many ways as the indigenous peoples. For the slaves, there was no other tableware, and packy was also used for cooking, and for carrying and storing liquids and other goods.

Small calabashes dried and filled with pebbles or seeds and equipped with a handle form a traditional musical instrument called a Shake-shake, Chak-chak or Maracca. Gourds are used as resonators in other MUSICAL INSTRUMENTS, for instance in the earliest BANJO and the BENTA. The calabash fruit is also carved and decorated to make attractive craft items. When dried, the calabash can be highly polished. Green calabash leaves are used to boil a tea for colds. The tree yields a tough and durable wood that has been used to make CATTLE yokes, tool handles, felloes of wheels, and ribs in boat building.

Calabash trees used to be planted to mark family grave sites.
[Arrom 1990, DJE, Rashford 1988b, Roth 1927]

CALALU

Name (also spelled callaloo) applied to several kinds of green potherbs, the most popular being *Amaranthus* species which provides the principal cooked 'greens' or 'spinach' in Jamaica, and the main ingredient for the thick soup known as Calalu or PEPPER-POT. The leaves and stripped stems are used to provide other types of

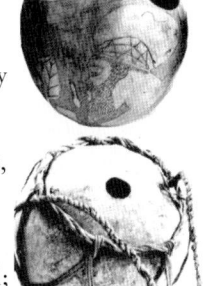

Calabashes on tree

tasty dishes elsewhere in the Caribbean, calalu and crab being a favourite in some islands. It is also called *calalú* in Spanish-speaking countries and in Haiti. The name is West African, from the Akan. In Jamaica, RASTAFARI have given a new impetus to the consumption of calalu. It is prepared without salt to form a side dish of an ital meal.

'Calalu' seems from earliest times to have been applied to four species of plants. First is the cultivated *Amaranthus* species. In addition to *Amaranthus viridis*, or green calalu, there is a wild edible species, *A. spinosus*, a perennial with red stems and sharp spines located in pairs at the base of each leaf. Also known as Duppy Calalu, it is eaten when the better sort is scarce.

The word calalu is also applied to *Phytolacca*, a wild variety of edible spinach with fat leaves and stems found in the cooler hills or mountains; it is also known as Mountain calalu, Surinam or Jocato calalu or Poke-weed. It seems to be a native plant.

A third type is Riverside calalu or Indian kale (*Colocasia sp.*), also known as Coco calalu. Unlike COCO, which produces an edible root, it is the leaves and stems that are eaten, forming an important ingredient in pepperpot soup.

Finally, there is the branched calalu, known as Guma, Gooma, Black Nightshade or Wild Susumber. The plant is a species of Solanum (*S. nigrum*) to which family belong edible plants such as the tomato, Irish POTATO, as well as the deadly nightshade which it closely resembles. It is said that in strong doses branched calalu can be cathartic and narcotic, and it has acquired sinister overtones from its use in MYAL ceremonies, frequently cited in the historical literature. There is a suggestion that its narcotic qualities are destroyed in boiling but retained in cold infusions such as RUM. The black berries are not eaten, and are said to be very poisonous. The young leaves can be eaten as calalu, and an infusion is said to be good for the blood. The leaves are also applied to the head for easing fever. Guma can also act as a purge, the saying, 'Ol lady swear fe guma, guma a swear fe ol' lady' describing this characteristic. The word 'guma' is an African one, deriving from the Yoruba *ogumo*, or the Igbo *ugumakbe*.

Amaranthus viridis is the most widely used of the plants for food, and is also employed in folk MEDICINE, Asprey and Thornton noting that it is regarded as 'good for the bowels'. As a drink it is used to clear up skin conditions.

[Adams 1972, Asprey and Thornton 1953-55, Beckwith 1928, Cabrera 1982, DJE, Hall-Alleyne 1996, Long 1774]

CALEMBE

Stick dance performed at wakes (see WAKE), now part of the DINKI MINI tradition. The term calembe, calemba, or variants such as calinda, describe a complex of dance and ritual activities throughout the CARIBBEAN and imported from there into Louisiana, but is most commonly applied to a stick dance or mock battle dance done at wakes. (See also LIMBO.)

In the Jamaican Dinki Mini, two men hold a pair of sticks horizontally between them while a third dances on them while displaying great acrobatic skills. M.W. Beckwith who also called it 'cumbolo' described seeing an old woman who 'danced to the song with a queer jumping motion like boys playing leap-frog and with all the agility of a young girl'. She noted that it was a men's dance when done at wakes but a song-dance otherwise.

Cheryl Ryman describes calembe as an acrobatic dance for men still performed on the north coast, known as the Bamboo Dance. The dancer jumps in and out of two sticks held horizontally and parallel to the ground, which are snapped together and released to a rhythm and song accompaniment, the act signifying death and resurrection. The dancer also balances on the sticks as they are raised from the ground, a feature described from elsewhere and highlighted in the NATIONAL DANCE THEATRE COMPANY'S 'Gerrebenta'. Nellie Payne in discussing the history of masquerade in Grenada, described the identical dance as 'Cha Cha-O', remarking that it was regarded as 'a dangerous dance', since the performer dancing between the sticks can be injured.

[Beckwith 1924, DJE, Payne 1990, Ryman 1980]

CALICO JACK see RACKHAM

CAMEL

The 'ship of the desert' was once found in Jamaica. In the 18th century, camels were brought here as beasts of burden to carry SUGAR and RUM on the estates. The animal was known to be far more tractable and docile, and better able to bear heavy burdens, than the mule. But the disadvantages proved too many, and the animal came to be an embarrassment.

The camel, it soon became apparent, was more suited to the long sandy stretches of the desert than to Jamaica's mountainous terrain. The roads were too rocky for its hooves, and the hills too steep. In time, camels became nothing more than road hazards, for their sudden appearance

Camel in Jamaica

would terrify HORSES, causing them to bolt and overturn their carriages. Writing in the late 18th century, the historian Edward Long found them 'the most useless animals belonging to the island'. The camels eventually died out.

The camel belongs to the family Camelidae, in which there are two species of camel – *Camelus bactrianus* and *C. dromedarius* (plus three species of llama and one of vicuna). The Westmoreland planter Thomas Thistlewood recorded in his diary seeing the camels in SAVANNA-LA MAR in 1753: 'Friday 20th: Went to see the camels at Wade's (in Wade's yard) about 40 of them, and in very good order. I take them to be dromedarys, though all the Bay hold them to be camels.'

Jamaica was not the only New World country in which camels were tried out; they were introduced into Barbados in the mid-17th century (and depicted on an early map by Ligon) and to the arid areas of the American southwest. They had earlier been tried out by the Spanish settlers in the coastal deserts of Peru in the mid-16th century, but lasted for only 60 years, dying out by 1615. In all these places the camels were abandoned after being found to be 'only theoretically valuable' in the words of Alfred W. Crosby Jr, and might have suffered the fate of those of Peru that were killed by escaped slaves for food.
[Crosby 1972, Hall 1989, Long 1774]

CAMPBELL

One of Jamaica's most popular surnames, a reflection of the Scottish heritage. (See SCOTS.) At the Old Works, Hodge's Pen (near to BLACK RIVER, ST ELIZABETH Parish), is the tomb of John Campbell, the inscription on which claims that he was the first Campbell to settle in the island. Colonel John Campbell (d 1740) came with a group of Scottish people who settled in the St Elizabeth-Westmoreland area after the collapse of the Darién expedition in 1699. This heritage is still evident in the many place names in this area that indicate a Scottish origin: e.g. Culloden, Auchindown, Craigie, Aberdeen and Ben Lomond.

Darién, now in Panama, was the site of a Scottish settlement that failed. (Their leader was William Paterson, who later founded the Bank of England.) Colonel Campbell was a captain of the troops at the Darién settlement, and he came to Jamaica with the rest in 1700. He was luckier than most, for he ended up marrying a rich woman and gained a great deal of land. He became prominent in Jamaican life, was a member of the Assembly, CUSTOS of St Elizabeth, and a member of the Privy Council. It is inscribed on his tombstone that he helped many to settle in Jamaica, thus no doubt helping to spread the Campbell name. Campbell was descended from the ancient family of Auchenbreck and was born in Inverrary in Argyllshire, Scotland.
[Cundall 1915, Wright 1966]

CANE RIVER

The Cane River enters the sea at Seven Miles on the KINGSTON/ST THOMAS highway. It is formed from several small tributaries that drain the area between DALLAS Mountain and Good Hope Mountain in ST ANDREW Parish, the chief of which are the Mammee and Barbecue rivers. At the Cane River Falls, the river changes direction as it begins to flow through a deep gorge with cliffs up to 305m in the white limestone range of Dallas Mountain.

Cane River Falls is associated with the legendary 18th century highwayman THREE FINGER JACK, who had his lair in a cave nearby. The Falls have also been used in the filming of several movies, most notably *Dark of the Sun* (1968), starring Rod Taylor and Jim Brown, about civil war in the Congo.

CANNABIS see GANJA

CANNONBALL TREE *(Couroupita guianensis)*

Huge ornamental tree (up to 20m) of bizarre appearance that attracts attention wherever it grows with its striking flowers and enormous fruit, and by the vile smell emitted by the ripe fruit. Fine specimens can be seen in the botanic gardens at CASTLETON, BATH and HOPE, and on the UNIVERSITY CAMPUS at Mona. In public places the ripe fruits are usually cleared away before they cause offence.

As Alan Eyre describes the tree: 'In May it puts forth on a jumbled mass of woody twigs which emerge from the bark of the tree near the ground (having no connection with the wood of the trunk) a mass of beautifully scented flowers of striking appearance. Each is several inches across, in colour a strange mixture of browns, yellows and white. Few of the flowers are fertile but the few that do develop become transformed over eighteen months into the oddest feature of the tree, the heavy cannon-ball . . . sometimes as big as a man's head.'

The tree is pollinated by BATS attracted to the saucer-shaped flowers with their off-centre brush of stamens. A native of northern South America, related to BARRINGTONIA and the Anchovy Pear Tree, the Cannonball Tree was introduced into the CARIBBEAN as an ornamental.
[Adams 1972, Eyre 1966]

CANOE

A boat originally made from a hollowed tree-trunk, now commonly made of fibreglass, part of the long sea-faring tradition of coastal America. The dugout canoe was known and used by native Americans such as the TAINOS and CARIBS, but was also part of the African tradition. It should be viewed as an artefact common to both the Old World and the New, deriving elements from both, including the name.

The word canoe was applied by the Tainos to a 'boat without decks' or a 'dugout', made from a hollowed-out tree trunk. COLUMBUS first heard the word from the islanders, and introduced it into European languages. It underwent various changes of meaning, the word canoe coming to mean any type of aboriginal boat. Coincidentally, in some West African languages the word *kunu* also means 'boat'. This is the pronunciation still used in Jamaica by the descendants of the AFRICANS who brought their maritime and riverine traditions, including the construction and navigation of the dugout canoe.

Long before Europeans arrived, sub-Saharan Africans had developed extensive commercial

Taino dugout canoe

Canoe on the African coast

networks by water, relying on their great river systems. European explorers from the 15th century described meeting huge canoes made from the COTTON TREE, including one carrying 120 warriors on the Sierra Leone river, about 1506. In dugout canoes of various sizes and designs, the Africans conducted commerce and war.

The New World plantation system 'relied on canoes and pettiaugers to transport supplies and plantation products; and African boating skills kept that plantation system afloat', according to W.J. Bolster. He concludes that 'American small boats and the skill necessary to build and handle them were truly creole – an amalgam of West African, European and North American technologies'.

Nevertheless, it is with the native American that the dugout canoe in the New World is most closely identified. The Tainos and Caribs originated among peoples who were accustomed to using dugout canoes on the large South American rivers, and it was in ocean-going versions of these boats that they set off from the South American mainland, discovering the islands where they eventually settled.

The islanders' boats ranged from small dugouts paddled by a single person to large ocean-going vessels capable of holding up to 200 persons. They were used for travel on larger rivers, for inter-island travel, and for larger trading voyages. A symbol of the office of the CACIQUE was a large, beautifully decorated ocean-going canoe, such as the one that greeted Columbus at OLD HARBOUR. However, not all Tainos were maritime peoples; some settled along the river valleys high up in the mountains. The word canoe probably applied only to dugout boats, while the larger boats, called *piraguas*, were used for sea voyages and trading.

The method used by the Tainos to make their vessels was similar to that of continental Arawaks. A large tree was selected, in the Caribbean the Cotton Tree or CEDAR being preferred. A fire was built at the base of the tree, and it was covered by moistened moss, to prevent the fire from ascending. According to a description from the method of the Island Caribs (which was the same as the Tainos), this process was done little by little over a period of some months. After burning, the forest giant was left standing for some time to 'season'. It was eventually felled, and hollowed out by fire, and a hatchet or wedge made of dark green stone.

For ocean-going boats, the sides were built up with sticks and reeds, fastened with fibres and pitched with gum to make it watertight. It would be painted and ornamented with carved images. Later descriptions of the pirogue or piragua said they were squared off at each end like punts. The boats were propelled by wooden oars with a crosspiece at one end and paddle at the other. Before the arrival of Europeans, the Tainos did not use sails.

When the Africans came to the New World and met the aboriginal canoes, they introduced features of their own. Among the Africans, people of the Gold Coast were specially noted as canoe makers and seamen.

Shrimp fisherman in his dugout on the Black River

It is hard to imagine today how important boats once were in the rivers and sea around the island – not just for fishing but for transporting produce and people. The island's rivers then contained much more water in their lower reaches. Boats were widely used by the sugar estates to float produce to the chief ports. Flat-bottomed barges and canoes were used on the larger rivers for conveying items such as grass, wood, limes and stone. These boating activities provided employment for a wide class of slaves and free blacks – as boat operators, fishermen, etc., giving them a level of freedom otherwise unknown on the plantation.

The tradition of building canoes from Cotton Trees and other wood continued until fairly recently in Jamaica, but is now a dying art, the dugouts being replaced by boats constructed of wood or fibre glass. Trees large enough to be used as dugouts are also not easily accessible.

[Beckwith 1929, Bolster 1997, DJE, Fewkes 1907, Long 1774, Roberts and Shackleton 1983, Roth 1901]

CANOE, JOHN see JONKONNU

CAPTURE OF JAMAICA

Jamaica was captured from the Spaniards by English forces in 1655, ushering in over 300 years of BRITISH rule until the country became an independent nation in 1962. (See INDEPENDENCE.) The 'capture' was effected by a joint army-navy force headed by Admiral William PENN and General Robert VENABLES. This attack was a part of the grand Western Design conceived by Oliver Cromwell, who was Lord Protector of England from 1653-58, and his advisers, to establish British rule over the CARIBBEAN down to the Isthmus of Panama.

The expedition – organized by Cromwell's brother-in-law – was described as 'perhaps the worst equipped and organized that ever left England'. A participant said that the majority of soldiers were 'Common Cheats, Thieves, Cut-purses, and such like lewd persons'. Mrs Venables, who accompanied the fleet, described it as a 'wicked army'. The fleet stopped off in the eastern Caribbean to recruit more men, and thousands joined up from Barbados, St Kitts and Nevis. The admiral and the general did not get on and the Lord Protector had not clarified who was senior in command of this motley crew. They first attempted to take Santo Domingo in April 1655. It ended in a complete rout by Spanish lancers and roving bands of CATTLE hunters. A third of the English army was left behind as dead or missing.

'The Lord hath greatly humbled us', murmured the Lord Protector when he heard. But before the news actually reached his ears, Penn and Venables had decided to take another SPANISH island as consolation prize. They chose nearby Jamaica because it was known to be poorly populated and weakly defended, with fewer than 200 men able to bear arms. The English fleet with about 7,000 men sailed into what is now known as KINGSTON harbour on 10 May 1655, and after a few shots dispersed the defenders at PASSAGE FORT, then the disembarkation point for the capital of SPANISH TOWN. The next day they marched the 9.6km into the town. By this time the Spaniards had been alerted and had packed up all their valuables. Most fled to the coast and some eventually sailed for Santiago de Cuba, a Spanish possession, but many were to die on the island, some from disease brought by the invading army. The English served harsh surrender terms on those remaining, led by the governor Don Juan Ramirez, who was old and sick and who was to die on the trip from

Oliver Cromwell (centre) with Lord Venables (left) and Admiral Penn

Jamaica. Those Spaniards who wished to leave were allowed to do so, with only the clothes they wore on their backs. Most left, but some of the younger men refused to give up without a fight for the place they called home, and under the leadership of Don Cristobal Arnaldo de YSASSI, were to continue guerrilla warfare for another five years. They were aided by the enslaved AFRICANS whom they had freed upon the arrival of the English (see, for example, LUBOLO). It was not until 1660 that the conquering army was truly in control of the country.

Soon after the capture, Admiral Penn chose to return to England to explain himself. The suspicious Venables was not far behind. They were both interned in the Tower of London for deserting their posts. Eventually, both were freed, Venables to sink into obscurity, Penn to rise again under the monarchy to the august position of Captain of the Fleet. He was also knighted, and the American colony of Pennsylvania (founded by his son William) was named after the family.

Despite the ease of the initial capture, things did not go well with the English. They were constantly harassed by the Spanish and African guerrillas. Food and medicine were scarce, and the soldiers began to die in droves from tropical fevers and hunger. Within the first 10 months it is estimated that 5,000 men died. The rest were close to starvation for the next few years until they began to settle down to farming. By the time civil government was established (under D'Oyley in 1660), settlers had already begun to arrive to people the new English colony. Jamaica was formally recognized as an English possession by the Treaty of Madrid, 1670.
[Taylor 1965]

CARDIFF HALL
Private residence in ST ANN Parish (off the main road from Cardiff Hall Development), which has been in continuous use as a home since about the middle of the 18th century. The GREAT HOUSE, which is one of the best preserved old houses in Jamaica, was for over two centuries owned by the Blagrove family who were large landowners. (See also KENILWORTH, Hanover.) Daniel Blagrove was one of the regicides, members of the court which condemned King Charles I to death, and the Cardiff Hall property was a reward from Cromwell. (See CAPTURE OF JAMAICA.)

John Blagrove, the owner in the late 18th century was famous for improving the breeds of both CATTLE and HORSES on his pens, importing some of 'the best-bred horses England ever produced', according to Cundall. He died in 1824. He was noted also for his benevolent attitude towards his slaves, unusual for the time. In his will he left a dollar for every man, woman, and child on his estates, 'as a small token of my regard for their faithful and affectionate service and willing labours to myself and family, being reciprocally bound in one general tie of master and servant in the prosperity of the land, from which we draw our mutual comforts and subsistence'.
[Cundall 1915, Wright and White 1969]

CARIB
Native American from whom the word CARIBBEAN is derived. Along with the TAINOS, the Caribs were the principal inhabitants at the time of COLUMBUS' arrival of what became known as the Caribbean.

The Caribs inhabited the southern islands, and strongly resisted the Europeans from their first contact, unlike the hospitable Tainos, who at first welcomed the invaders, too late turning to resistance. The people of the Bahamian archipelago and the Greater Antilles whom Columbus first met, displayed great fear of their Carib neighbours, portraying them as warlike savages and evil spirits. That image, coupled

Carib war dance (after Pickard from Fewkes)

with the strong Carib resistance to European conquest, was used to justify their later enslavement by the Spaniards as more and more Carib territory was conquered. The Caribs were nevertheless able to keep the Spaniards out of their territories for some hundred and fifty years, losing control after the French and English invasions; even so, they remained active defenders of their homelands until the end of the 18th century.

The Island Caribs inhabited the southernmost islands, while the Tainos occupied the islands to the north. It is believed that successive waves of Carib warriors pushed the Tainos in this direction and away from earlier settlements on the smaller islands. At the time of the conquest, the Carib were in fact moving towards the Taino islands and already had a foothold in northern Puerto Rico and the island of Vieques. They had started to raid the other islands; in 1547 they were reported as a threat to Jamaica and Hispaniola.

Carib basket, with weight for expressing juice from bitter cassava (from Fewkes)

The word Carib derives from the name these people called themselves, rendered as *Calina* by the Dutch, in English Carib, in French *Galibi* and in Spanish *Caribe*. The Island Carib had two languages, a Cariban language spoken by the men, and an Arawakan language spoken by the women and children. Boys, on reaching puberty, were inducted as warriors and thereafter lived with the men and spoke only Carib. This peculiar arrangement arose because as the Carib emigrated from their original homes deep in the rain forests of tropical South America, they did not travel in family groups. Usually, roving bands of young men broke away and moved on to raid the peoples they came across, killing the males and taking the younger women as wives. These women transmitted their own language and culture to their offspring. In the islands, the captured wives were Taino-speaking, thus the Island Carib were a mixture of both peoples.

All Carib men were warriors, achieving that route by undergoing great endurance and suffering as part of their rituals, to demonstrate their extreme bravery.

Contemporary Caribs include the Karina of Venezuela, Carib of Guyana and Calina of Suriname and Cayenne. Small remnants of Island Carib populations still exist in Trinidad, St Vincent, Guadeloupe and most importantly in Dominica, where an elected CACIQUE rules over a full-blooded community of several thousand people. In Belize, the Garifuna (Carifuna or Black Carib) are a mixture of Carib and African.
[Fewkes 1907, Lathrap 1970, Rouse 1992]

CARIBBEAN
The archipelago of islands from Cuba to Trinidad; also taken to include the parts of South and Central America washed by the Caribbean Sea as well as the Bahamian archipelago and Bermuda in the North Atlantic. 'Caribbean' is used to describe this geographical unit, the Caribbean Sea, and the peoples of these islands who form a cultural unit. It is now the preferred designation. WEST INDIES, the older term, usually refers to the English-speaking territories only, all former BRITISH colonies. The word Caribbean is derived from CARIB. According to the DCEU, the Spanish 'Islas de los Caribes' came into 16th century English as 'Isles of the Caribees', in reference to the Carib people inhabiting the eastern islands of the archipelago; later 'The Caribbees' came to refer to the islands, then to the whole area.
[DCEU]

CARLISLE BAY, Battle of
Located at the mouth of the RIO MINHO on the south coast (near Rocky Point – CLARENDON Parish), Carlisle Bay was the scene of the principal military engagement with a foreign foe that took place in the island during the BRITISH occupation. In the late 17th century, England and France were at war and the hostilities spread to the CARIBBEAN area. This was only two years after the great EARTHQUAKE that had destroyed PORT ROYAL in 1692. Jean duCasse, governor of the FRENCH colony of St-Domingue (now Haiti), believed the island to be still weak from the effects of the earthquake and easily captured. However, an English sailor, Captain Elliott, then

a prisoner in St-Domingue, escaped in a CANOE to bring the news of duCasse's fleet to Jamaica.

The island was immediately put on a war footing. When duCasse and a strong fleet consisting of three men-of-war and 23 transports arrived, they first attacked the coastline along ST THOMAS Parish, plundering and killing and carrying off many slaves (see BULL BAY). A month later they sailed past the heavily fortified Port Royal and dropped anchor at Carlisle Bay, then described as a 'pretty town', probably intending to march through VERE.

The English governor, Sir William Beeston, had guessed their intentions, and the militia and trusted slaves had built a fortification at the bay, about 270m from the seashore. Meantime, reinforcements set off from SPANISH TOWN. On the morning of 19 July 1694, the French landed 1,400 men at Rocky Point, a little to the east of Carlisle Bay, and began to attack the breastwork. The militia held out as long as possible, but the men were forced to make a last stand with their backs to the Rio Minho. At the critical moment the militia from Spanish Town arrived, having marched 58km. Without stopping to rest, they immediately charged the French and forced them to retreat. The brave defenders then withdrew about 3km, leaving some 25 men in a brick house that belonged to one Mr Hubbard, halfway between Carlisle Bay and ALLEY. On the following day there were skirmishes as the French tried to capture the house. But the people inside resisted so strongly that the French, after losing many of their men, gave up in defeat and sailed off, after firing the small town of Carlisle. Carlisle Fort was built the next year, but fell into ruins that cannot now be seen. Carlisle Bay continued to be important in the days when sea transportation around the island was relied on. The bay was named after the Earl of Carlisle, governor of Jamaica 1678-80.
[Buisseret 1983, Cundall 1915]

CASHEW (*Anacardium occidentale*)
Tree that grows 4-8m high and produces the well-known cashew nut, often pronounced 'kushu' by the folk. What is called the nut is actually a fruit that becomes edible after roasting. The so-called 'fruit' is an edible fleshy stalk that grows above the nut. This is sometimes eaten raw but is best roasted or stewed; aphrodisiac properties have been claimed for the punch made from the ripe fruit.

Cashew is a native of the CARIBBEAN and Central America, but has been naturalized in parts of Africa and elsewhere in the tropics. Its use in Jamaica dates back to the TAINOS. The plant seems to thrive best on poor soils in areas of low rainfall from sea level to 300m, and fruits in the summer months. Cashew leaves are widely used in folk MEDICINE, in combination with other 'BUSH' in baths for fevers. Cashew nuts in their shells were also once used in several children's games. Like other trees of the same family, such as MANGO and HOG PLUM, the cashew contains tannins, resins and pigments. Sap from the bark of the tree produces an indelible ink.
[Adams 1972, Asprey and Thornton 1953-55, Beckwith 1928]

Cashew nuts and fruits

CASSAVA (*Manihot esculenta*)
One of the most popular root crops of the CARIBBEAN and Central and South America, from where it was taken to the East and Africa. Its high carbohydrate yield has made it one of the staples of the tropical world. It is also known as Yuca, Tapioca, and Manioc. The cassava root is unusual in that it is a source of both poison and food. The natives of tropical America developed techniques for making it suitable for consumption thousands of years ago, and this method of preparation and the equipment used have become more or less standardized throughout the region. (See BAMMY.)

Cassava occurs in two varieties, the 'bitter' and 'sweet' and the plants are difficult to tell apart. The root of the sweet variety can be boiled or baked, since the glucoside is concentrated in the skin that is peeled and discarded in preparation for cooking. In the bitter variety, the poison (hydrocyanic acid) is found throughout the root. However, it is the bitter variety that has been most valued, mainly because the starch content is higher and more suitable for the production of BREAD or flour, which will keep for a long time. Edible starch (farina or tapioca) and laundry starch are also obtained from the root, as well as a kind of beer made by Amerindians and cassareep, a flavouring and preservative. (See PEPPER-POT.)

Cassava was one of the three important agricultural crops of the inhabitants of the hemisphere when COLUMBUS arrived (the other crops being POTATO and maize – see CORN). Cassava was the staple of the ARAWAK-speaking

Cassava root and stem

peoples. When these peoples began to leave the South American mainland for the Antilles, before the time of Christ, they took cassava with them, and distributed it throughout the islands. Although cassava can be harvested within a year, it can also be left in the ground for two or more years, thus providing a kind of food bank. The TAINOS called the crop *yuca*, and so important was it to them that they formed the name of their supreme ZEMI – YÚCAHU – as well as of spirits and villages, from the word.

Although cassava became the popular name in the English-speaking islands, the earliest names used in Jamaica were also forms of Yuca; 'Yucam' and 'Yaccu' being recorded. The Taino word *cazabe* is still used today in Spanish-speaking islands for cassava bread or bammy.

It has been suggested that the fruitfulness of the Greater Antilles, which led to flourishing and relatively easy yuca production, enabled the Taino society on these islands to rapidly develop certain characteristic features, and move beyond those of the Lesser Antilles and parts of the tropical mainland.

Yuca was the principal crop of the Tainos and cassava bread their 'staff of life'. They made offerings of it to their zemis, and at religious festivals to celebrate the harvest, cassava bread was blessed by their CACIQUES and then shared out among those present. Each person kept his or her piece until the next festival, as a charm. The Amerindians also recognized the other side of cassava – its death-dealing qualities. Under SPANISH domination the drinking of bitter cassava juice became a popular method of suicide and of poisoning the oppressors.

DJE, Lathrap 1970, Lovén 1935, Saur 1966, Stevens-Arroyo 1988]

CASSAVA BREAD see BAMMY

CASSIA

Leguminous flowering trees and shrubs common to the tropics. Some species are planted as shade trees in downtown KINGSTON, where they sometimes provide the only burst of colour in the dry summer months. Twenty-nine species occur in Jamaica, several of which are endemic, but the showiest are the introduced ones.

The most common though not the most spectacular is *Cassia siamea*, which was formerly much planted as a public ornamental because of its hardiness and quick-growing character and ability to accept severe pruning. The main entrance to HOPE GARDENS is lined with stands of these trees. The erect yellow flowers grow on a spike. The plant is a native of East Asia.

Another yellow-flowering species is *Cassia fistula*, whose common name of Golden Shower describes its spectacular pendant clusters that appear April-July when the tree is bare of leaves. Like all cassia, this bears prominent seed pods, in this case cylindrical black pods 30-50cm long. A native of India, it is also known as Indian Laburnum. Pink cassias include the striking *Cassia nodosa* that is massed with flowers in the summer. *Cassia grandis*, or Horse Cassia is a large spreading tree with smaller flowers of coral pink which bloom February-April.

Several species of cassia have economic and medicinal use, *Cassia italica* being used as a substitute for senna. Known as Jamaica Senna or Port Royal Senna, it was introduced in the 17th century by a slave, and at one time was cultivated on the PALISADOES. In folk MEDICINE, perhaps the best known is the native species *Cassia occidentalis*, a common shrub known as Yellow Candlewood whose variety of other folk names – Dandelion, Piss-a-bed, Stinking Weed, Stinking Peas and Wild Coffee – attest to its popularity. Its seeds, dried and beaten, have been

Cassia seed pods

used as a coffee substitute. A small tree that bears yellow flowers, it grows near the coast and is sometimes used for firewood. In folk medicine, a drink prepared from the leaves is used in kidney and bladder complaints, the name Piss-a-bed referring to its diuretic qualities.
[Adams 1972, DJE, NHSJ 1949]

CASTLETON GARDENS

Botanic gardens on the bank of the WAG WATER RIVER in ST MARY Parish. The main KINGSTON to ANNOTTO BAY highway (called the Junction Road) runs through these gardens. Once said to be 'one of the great gardens of the Hemisphere', Castleton has lost much of its former glory and has suffered from periodic flooding, HURRICANES and general neglect, but still remains one of the most beautiful gardens and a popular place for picnics.

Established in the 1860s and stocked by Nathaniel Wilson, Castleton included 400 specimens sent from Kew Gardens in England. In 1897 there were 180 species of PALMS in the palmetum. Many beautiful and valuable trees introduced to the island were first planted here. They included the flowering trees SPATHODEA and POINCIANA, and Bombay MANGO (introduced 1869 – though more 'common' mangoes were introduced a long time before).

Among the interesting trees still to be seen in the upper section are the Strychnos, from which the medicine (and poison) strychnine is obtained, the Velvet APPLE – which describes its fruit which is often seen lying on the ground, and the Pride of Burma with its spectacular orchid-shaped flower. In the lower garden, Pandanus with stilt roots, Burma Teak, West Indian MAHOGANY and specimens of COFFEE can be found. This section of the garden was at first planted out in trees that could be of economic value to Jamaica.
[Eyre 1966]

CASTOR OIL PLANT (*Ricinus communis*)

Small shrub that grows wild from sea level to 800m, especially along river banks; a native of the Old World tropics. A member of the Euphorbia family that includes Physic Nut and CASSAVA, it is also known as Oil Nut tree, Castor Bean or Palma Christi. The seeds produce oil that was formerly much used in folk MEDICINE since it could easily be prepared by the householder. The seeds are gathered after the pods break open, and are beaten and thrown into a large pot with water and boiled until the oil rises to the surface, where it can be skimmed off and strained. One gallon of nuts yields one quart of oil. In the old days it was also used as

Castleton Gardens

Castor oil plant

lamp oil, and was said to give a clear odourless light that would reportedly burn for hours.

Castor oil was dreaded by generations of children to whom it was given as an obligatory purge or 'wash out' before returning to school each term. Home-made (unrefined) castor oil is a thick, black, smelly, evil-tasting liquid. Castor oil was also given to newborn children (see BIRTH). Castor oil is believed to encourage hair growth, and was often applied to skin and hair to promote a healthy shine. As a home remedy, warm castor oil is applied in a poultice to the affected parts to ease pains and swellings, for arthritis and ear infections. The leaves are also applied to painful areas. The seeds are poisonous, though poison does not remain in the expressed oil.

Internationally, castor oil is used as a lubricant in aeroplane engines, as it has a lower freezing point than mineral oils.

[Adams 1972, Asprey and Thornton 1953-55, Robertson 1990]

CATHOLIC CHURCH see ROMAN CATHOLIC

CATHERINE'S PEAK

Hill immediately overlooking NEWCASTLE. This is one of the highest points in ST ANDREW Parish (1,541m) and was named after the first woman to climb it. She was Catherine Long, a lieutenant-governor's wife and sister of the historian Edward Long. She made the ascent in 1760.

CATTA STICK

Rhythmic percussion stick (also called Catatick, Katatik, or Kyata), 'catta' also refers to the playing. During SLAVERY, 'catta' was made from old chairs and pieces of board, according to Patterson. In 1823, Cyrnic Williams described a JONKONNU dancer accompanied by music from shak-shak, GOOMBAY and the 'katty', a windsor chair taken from the piazza to serve as a secondary drum. 'Kitty-katty' is described by the DJE as a simple percussion instrument of wood, beaten with two sticks. Nowadays, Catta stick is used in KUMINA ceremonies. Moore described it as the stick that is beaten against the centre pole of the dancing booth. In more recent times, Catta sticks, or 'kyatas', are used by the 'rackling men' to play a rhythm on the backs of the Kumina drums. Catta stick is also used in TAMBU. The name and instrument are also known in Haiti, the *catalier* described as the man who leads songs and *catas*, i.e. beats a rhythm on his hoe or machete with a stone.

[Courlander 1973, DJE, Moore 1953, Patterson 1973]

CATTLE

Today, cattle serve mainly as beef and milk producers. But in their long history in Jamaica, these animals have been far more valued for other purposes; first, for providing hides to make leather and suet for tallow used in candle-making; later, as draft animals, providing motive power for plantation mills and to transport goods and people. Development of cattle primarily as beef-providers only came about in the 19th century, and as providers of milk on a commercial scale in the 20th. The breeds of cattle have changed and developed in response to these changing needs over time. Jamaica itself has contributed to international cattle breeding four breeds of animals adapted to tropical conditions, which were developed by Dr Thomas P. Lecky. They are the Jamaica Hope, a dairy breed, and three beef breeds – the Jamaica Red Poll, the Jamaica Brahman and the Jamaica Black. They have not only won wide acceptance in Jamaica, but are in demand as breed stock in the CARIBBEAN and Latin America.

Cattle were first brought to the Caribbean by COLUMBUS on his second voyage in 1493, and like the other domesticated animals found the Antilles to their liking, an environment with sufficient fodder and free of major animal diseases. The cattle multiplied and ran wild, in time providing food for marooned sailors who smoked the meat on a wooden grate called a *boucan*. Eventually, the men (originally known as 'Cow-catchers') evolved into *boucaniers* (see BUCCANEERS).

Many of the SPANISH colonists had been cattlemen at home, and they took to ranching in the Caribbean, rearing the cattle on open ranges on the savanna lands. The hides and tallow the cattle yielded were far more important economically than the meat. As Alfred W. Crosby Jr points out: 'It was an age in which leather served many of the functions for which we use fiber, plastics and metals today: armor, cups, trunks, ropes.' Demand for hides in the Americas and Europe was immense, and the cattle were often slaughtered for their skins, their carcasses left to rot. Tallow was used for making candles, the main means of lighting in the Americas, also providing light for the development of mining.

Dr T.P. Lecky — Gleaner

In Jamaica the development of the SUGAR industry led to a demand for motive power, using water, wind or cattle. Cattle were also used to haul stones and logs to build factories, houses and fences, and were used for the opening up of the interior.

A demand for steers as draft animals led to a shift from ranching in unfenced enclosures to cattle farming or penning. In the BRITISH plantation era, the livestock farm came to be enclosed with walls of stone or wood and was called a 'pen'. Most of these were at higher elevations than the SUGAR PLANTATIONS, which were located in the river valleys and lowlands. In 1842, there were some 400 rural pens. (For city pens see KINGSTON.)

The island had valuable native grasses for fodder, such as Scots grass, Crab and Pimento grass. The introduction of the valuable GUINEA GRASS contributed greatly to the development of the cattle industry after 1800, as did that of Pangola and Star Grass in the 1950s.

The rearing of livestock for sale was avidly pursued by some of the slaves and continued as an activity of the small farmer after SLAVERY ended, cattle, like GOATS and PIGS, serving as a kind of bank. As T.P. Lecky reminds us: 'When money was required to do major repairs or meet large bills a cow or bull was sold. They also acted as a form of insurance against crop losses in times of hurricanes. On the small to medium sized farms they were the chief source of animal protein.'

Cattle breeding The original CREOLE or Spanish cattle were over time replaced by pedigree breeds that were developed in England in the late 18th century to meet the demand for meat and milk brought about by the Industrial Revolution. Well known breeds such as Aberdeen Angus, Holstein, Hereford, Guernsey and Jersey cattle came into being.

Jamaican plantation owners were more interested in draft animals and they turned to India, where such animals were long in use and breeds developed to withstand drought and heat. The MONTPELIER and Shettlewood estates of Lord Seaford were pioneers in the development of the Jamaican cattle industry, and first imported the Zebu from India in 1850. These animals were crossed with the local creole cattle to produce a serviceable breed, ushering in the practice of experimental breeding.

This early interest was later carried on by scientists at the government stock farm at HOPE, led by H.H. Cousins, an Englishman who was the first director. When Thomas Lecky joined as a young graduate of the Jamaica School of Agriculture, Cousins involved him in the work he was doing of testing imported European breeds of cattle for adaptation to the tropical environment. Lecky was to continue and bring new insight to this work, his efforts crowned with the successful development of the four new breeds. While studying agriculture and animal husbandry in Canada, he developed his idea that line-breeding rather than the cross-breeding, which was then the method being pursued, was the answer. His continued experiments at Hope led to his path-breaking doctoral dissertation at the University of Edinburgh, 'Genetic Improvement in Dairy Cattle in the Tropics'. He returned to Jamaica with plans for the development of an indigenous Jamaican breed of dairy cattle; in 1949 he produced the Jamaica Brahman and in 1952 the Jamaica Hope, the first breed of tropically adapted dairy cattle, followed by the other two beef cattle breeds.

During the plantation era, the consumption of fresh beef by the slaves was discouraged; such beef as was available came from old cows or steers – hence the heavy reliance on preserved meat (see SALT) and salted FISH. With freedom and the growth of an urban population came the growing demand for fresh beef and milk, though this was at first confined to the wealthier section of the population. To satisfy this demand, European dairy breeds such as Jerseys and Guernseys were imported, as well as beef breeds such as Herefords, Aberdeen Angus, Red Poll and Devon. Before refrigeration, many of the pens and dairies supplying fresh beef and milk were located within the suburbs of Kingston. Today there is a well organized dairy industry

Jamaican bred bull (from Mona MacMillan)

producing fresh, packaged ('long-life') and sweetened condensed milk, though butter and cheese continue to be imported. Much of the locally produced beef today comes from farms operated by large landowners and one BAUXITE company.
[Crosby 1972, Higman 1998, Lecky 1996, Shepherd 1989]

CATTLE EGRET (*Bubulcus ibis*)
This snowy white heron, a native of tropical Asia and Africa, is noted for its migration from its original homelands, undertaking a crossing of the south Atlantic Ocean to South America in the late 19th century. It spread to the CARIBBEAN islands from the mainland, having reached Guyana and Surinam in 1948 and arriving in Jamaica sometime in the late 1950s.

It is one of four resident herons and egrets in the island, the others being the Great Egret (*Ardea alba*), the Snowy Egret (*Egretta thula*), and the Little Blue Heron (*Egretta caerulea*). The immature of the Little Blue Heron is white, thus adding to the confusion among these species, which are all referred to as GAULIN. Nowadays the Cattle Egret is by far the most common.

Although the egrets roost in MANGROVE forests and big trees near rivers and swamps and feed on a variety of fish, Cattle Egrets make their way early in the morning to pastures with large mammals – CATTLE, HORSE, DONKEY or mule, and

Cattle egrets

agricultural lands where they follow ploughing machines. As their name implies, they are commonly seen on cattle, either perched on the resting animals and grooming them for ticks, or following closely behind the animals as they move around, positioning themselves to grab insects, frogs or other small creatures which the bigger animals disturb.
[Terres 1980]

CAVE OF EMERGENCE
The TAINO myth of origin, as told to Friar Ramón PANÉ, describes the emergence of the first peoples from a CAVE and their acquisition of various items of culture. The origin myth tells of two caves in the mountains. One was called *Amayauna*, meaning 'of no importance'. The other, *Cacibajagua*, was of great importance, presumably because it was from this that the Tainos, the people who used *jagua* in their ceremonies emerged – hence 'Cave of the Jagua'. Jagua or *yagua* was the Taino name for GUINEP, which they used for black (sacred) body paint.

Caves in all the islands inhabited by the Tainos were used as sanctuaries where religious artefacts were preserved for ritual purposes, and where important burials took place, reflecting perhaps the beliefs shared by many other peoples that the cave is the threshold or gateway between worlds. Not surprisingly, the most significant Taino artefacts found in Jamaica, the so-called 'Bird Man' carvings (found in 1792), and the more recent cache of carvings from Aboukir, were found in caves.
[Arrom 1990, Stevens-Arroyo 1988]

CAVES
Caves of varying sizes and attractions are found all over Jamaica, especially in the white LIMESTONE that covers two-thirds of the island. More than 1,200 caves and shafts are known, with many more waiting to be discovered. Much of the island's water flows underground through cave systems.

Explorations of Jamaica's caves over the years have yielded much interesting scientific information, such as the fossil (first discovered in 1920) of a Jamaican species of monkey (*Xenothrix mcgregori*), which became extinct after the arrival of Europeans in Jamaica, and of a flightless ibis (*Xenicibis xympithecus*). New species of animals are also being brought to light by scientific cave explorations. Much of this information is contained in the study *Jamaica Underground* by Alan G. Fincham, who is also maintaining a Jamaica Cave Register database.

The longest known river cave is Gourie Cave near to Dump, MANCHESTER Parish. So far, some 3,505m have been measured. High altitude caves include Mt Rosanna at 1,200m. Outstanding sea level caves include Portland Ridge and Jackson's Bay Caves in CLARENDON Parish. Located not far from the seashore at Portland Bight, the southernmost extension of the island, Jackson's Bay Caves are regarded by caving enthusiasts as among the finest in Jamaica. Nine entrances lead to a labyrinth of chambers; some 7.25km of passage have so far been explored. Spectacular formations are to be found, as well as immense caverns with flowstones. TAINO carvings can be seen in one of the entrances. It is in these caves that palaeontologists located remains of pre-historic fossil primates.

Another outstanding cave is the Grand Cave at Riverhead, ST CATHERINE Parish, from which the RIO COBRE emerges. The RUNAWAY CAVE ('Green Grotto') in ST ANN Parish, and Nonsuch Caves, PORTLAND Parish, have been developed as visitor attractions.

Many of these caves have played a role in Jamaica's history, starting with the mythological CAVE OF EMERGENCE. They have served as ceremonial and burial sites for the Tainos, and rock carvings (petroglyphs) and paintings (petrographs) can still be seen in some of them, e.g. Pantrepant, TRELAWNY Parish and Mountain River Cave, St Catherine Parish. Caves were also used as secret churches by MISSIONARIES and slaves at a time when such meetings were illegal, and as secret meeting places by both the slaves and the MAROONS. No doubt BUCCANEERS and pirates also used caves near the coast to hide their loot; tradition associates a cave in the PORT HENDERSON area with the noted buccaneer Henry MORGAN, who supposedly used it to conceal men and booty.

Jackson's Bay Cave

People still believe that the Spaniards hid their treasure in caves before leaving the island (see CAPTURE OF JAMAICA). Thus many LEGENDS have sprung up about the guardians of the caves, such as the legend of MARTHA BRAE. Earlier historians such as Edward Long reported the finding of large quantities of human bones in some Jamaican caves. Although their origin was not determined, it has been suggested that these might have been of Tainos who retreated there to escape European domination, similar events having been recorded in other islands. Modern cave explorers have reported very few findings of human bones, and most of those found have indicated Taino ceremonial burials of individuals.

Some of Jamaica's caves such as Cousin's Cove in Green Island, HANOVER, have been exploited for the fertilizer guano that builds up after centuries of occupation by BATS. In recent times, caves have been used by GANJA producers for temporary shelter and storage of their crops, and for the guano that they use as a fertilizer.

[Ashcroft 1969, Fincham 1997, Long 1774, Porter 1990]

CAY

The name that is applied to low-lying offshore islets in the CARIBBEAN (derived from the TAINO word *kairi* meaning 'island'). It is pronounced 'key' and so called for example in the Florida Keys.

The principal cays around Jamaica are Morant and Pedro. Morant Cays lie 53km to the south east of Morant Point, and consist of four islets encompassing 15ha.

Pedro Cays lie 64-80km south of Portland Point and include four islets with a total area of 38.9ha. The islands are now used as a base by commercial fishermen (see FISH AND FISHING), but in former times they were exploited for guano, the valuable fertilizer derived from the excreta of BATS and sea BIRDS. In fact, in the mid-19th century, Jamaicans and Americans often came to blows on the cays over the guano deposits. The Americans were the first to dig for guano on the cays, but the islets had been taken over by the British Crown in 1862-63 and placed under the authority of the government of Jamaica. Thus when Jamaicans decided to exploit the guano, they regarded the Americans as interlopers. Following complaints by Jamaicans that they had been subjected to 'outrages' by the crew of an American vessel, the cays were formally annexed to Jamaica in 1882. Eventually the guano of the cays was exhausted, but a brisk trade developed in BOOBY eggs and TURTLES that were sold in KINGSTON.

Pedro Cays also used to be the haunt of the PEDRO SEALS, now believed to be extinct.

There are several small cays outside Kingston Harbour, including RACKHAM Cay, Lime Cay, Maiden Cay, etc. and off Portland Bight, the most important being Great, Little, Goat and Pigeon Islands. Other small cays include BOOBY CAY (near NEGRIL), Green Island opposite the town of the same name in HANOVER Parish, the Bogue Islands off MONTEGO BAY (some of which now form Montego Freeport), Cabaritta Island off PORT MARIA, NAVY ISLAND off PORT ANTONIO, and Bush Cay off FALMOUTH.

Lime Cay is associated with Vincent 'Rhygin' Martin, a notorious criminal of the 1940s on whose real-life story Jamaica's first full-length feature film *The Harder They Come* was based.

[GOJ Handbook of Jamaica 1961, Lethbridge 1996]

CEDAR (*Cedrela odorata*)

The West Indian Cedar is a deciduous tree up to 25m high, widely distributed from sea level to 1,200m. A native of tropical America, it is a close relative of the MAHOGANY. The new wood, freshly picked leaves and stems give off an unpleasant odour, but the cured wood is aromatic and is popular for making chests of drawers and linen cupboards, since it repels insects. It was one of the sacred trees of the TAINOS who used it to make dugout CANOES, a usage that continued until recent times when large enough specimens were still available. The tree used to be common in pastures and along roadsides but most specimens have been harvested for CABINET-MAKING. The wood is also used to make shingles for roofing, in house construction and for home-made coffins. Cedar is also used in the manufacture of cigar boxes.

Juniper Cedar (*Juniperus lucayana*) is a native conifer restricted to the BLUE MOUNTAINS, and is also a good timber for furniture and construction.

[Adams 1972, NHSJ 1946]

CEIBA see COTTON TREE

CERASEE (*Momordica charantia*)

A climbing vine of the cucumber and PUMPKIN family, Cerasee is probably the most popular of Jamaica's tea bushes (see BUSH, folk MEDICINE) its bitter taste notwithstanding, or perhaps because of it, since Jamaicans believe the more bitter the bush, the greater its efficacy. There is a thriving trade in shipping the dried bush to Jamaicans overseas. Research is now underway to investigate the medicinal properties of the plant. Cerasee is said to give false negatives in common (urine) tests for diabetes, apparently masking sugar in the urine.

The vine is common on fences and hedgerows from sea level to 1,200m, and fruits and flowers all year round.

Cerasee (vine and leaves) is commonly used in infusions or as 'TEA' for a wide variety of ailments, including colds, fevers, acne and as a general tonic. But it is most popular for complaints connected with the belly – stomach ache, constipation, for menstrual troubles, for birth control, to assist mothers after childbirth. The song 'Helena' recounts the experience of a girl who went to boil cerasee tea for a bellyache but did not know what the bush looked like. Her mother admonishes her:

> Look good pon cerasee Helena
> De leaf an de vine an de berry
> Come know cerasee, for oh cerasee
> A it cure you bad pain a belly.

The orange fruit when ripe splits open to display its seeds in a red fleshy covering, apparently to attract animal pollinators.

To call someone 'Ol Cerasee' is to comment on their bitter qualities.

[Adams 1972, Asprey and Thornton 1953-55, Lewin 1974b, Robertson 1990]

Cerasee fruit and seeds

CHARM

Magic charms are very much a part of Jamaican FOLKLORE and can be both defensive (providing protection for the user or his or her property) or offensive (used against someone else). They can be vocal (like repeating 'Our Father' when confronted by a centipede), or employ rituals or material objects, natural or man-made.

Material objects can be specially created by a ritual specialist, e.g. OBEAH-man or -woman, and imbued with 'power'; the process might also include vocal and ritual magic. Charms are often identified with those objects that are associated with spirits of some kind, e.g. plants such as the COTTON TREE as well as CAVES, GRAVEYARDS, BIRDS, SNAKES, etc. Relics associated with the dead, such as grave-dirt, small coffins, etc. are considered particularly potent.

Defensive guards can be specially created or be ordinary household objects believed able to 'cut' evil, such as scissors; those derived from Christian religious power, e.g. holy water, crucifixes, the open Bible; or those considered distasteful to spirits, e.g. SALT, LIMES, washing blue, sulphur or asafoetida. Limes, garlic cloves and WANGLA (sesame seeds) were especially used by higglers against those who used 'draw money' charms to steal from them.

Used for protection, these objects are usually termed 'guard'. A charm used for offensive purposes is sometimes called a 'trick'. The popular term 'guzu' is applied to charms both defensive and offensive, thus one can be protected by one's guzu or one can 'work guzu' against another.

Charms can be worn on the person, e.g. household 'blue' and 'coolie red' used to protect babies, or they can be placed in an appropriate location, for example 'guards' placed in fields against thieves (see OVERLOOK). When used offensively, the guzu is usually hidden, for example buried in the victim's yard so that counter-measures such as SENSEH fowl are employed to expose or unearth them. Objects associated with a person can also be used in charms against them, for example fingernail pairings, hair cuttings; such objects in the old days were carefully disposed of so that they could not fall into the hands of enemies. Hair cuttings are also used to make protective charms.

Of course there are many 'charms' used in everyday life, such as placing a broom upside down behind a door to make an unwanted visitor leave, or various rituals used to secure love. The folklorist M.W. Beckwith collected several complicated charms for such matters as soothing someone's anger or preventing someone from working.

[Banbury 1894, Beckwith 1929, DJE, Mico 1893, 1896]

CHERRY *(Malpighia glabra)*

Shrub or tree up to 6m high that grows wild from sea level to 900m. It is also cultivated in gardens for its fruit, which is the richest natural known source of Vitamin C. Too tart for some people's taste, the cherry is usually made into a drink or used in jams and preserves. Also called West Indian Cherry or Barbados Cherry, the fruit is the size of the cherry of northern climes and goes from pale orange when young to dark red when fully ripe. It is native to continental tropical America and parts of the CARIBBEAN.

[Adams 1972, Baccus and Royes 1988]

CHEWSTICK *(Gouania lupuloides)*

Climbing plant or WIS, the stem of which is used to clean teeth; also called Chaw Stick. Small pieces are cut from the stem, one end is soaked in water to soften it and generate foam; when it is chewed, it forms a soft brush. A toothpaste has also been made commercially using Chewstick. In the past, Chewstick was used in the making of a popular drink called 'Cool Drink'. Sugar, LIGNUM VITAE chips and GINGER were infused in hot water and the mixture beaten with Chewstick. This apparently produced froth and, according to Edward Long, imparted a slightly bitter but agreeable flavour. Up to recently Chewstick was used to ferment GINGER BEER and other drinks, though nowadays yeast or cream of tartar is used. The plant is found from sea level to 1,000m and is native to tropical America. It was also used by the TAINOS for the purposes described above.

[DJE, Long 1774]

Chewstick
Faucett & Rendle

CHIGGER

Tropical disease of the New World which spread to the Old (appearing in Africa about 1872, according to bio-historian Alfred W. Crosby Jr), common in Jamaica up to a few generations ago and frequently encountered in the literature and oral culture. Also spelled Chigoe and Jigger.

The chigger is actually a skin-burrowing flea (*Tunga penetrans*), which can infect humans and PIGS. After mating, the female penetrates the skin of the host (often between the toes or under the toenails), where she lays her eggs. The danger from the infection (which itches and causes acute discomfort) is that the site can let in bacteria, which can cause secondary infection. In the pre-antibiotic era, secondary bacterial infection was a serious problem that could lead to gangrene. Until the wearing of shoes became universal, many became infected with the dread disease, which was first reported from Hispaniola in the 16th century by the Spanish chronicler Oviedo, who remarked that men who caught chigger could 'remain crippled and lame forever'.

In the plantation era in Jamaica, it was cited as causing 'the most general of negro infirmities', and 'chiggerfoot' came to refer to poor (barefoot) people. The name was applied to markets in ST THOMAS, KINGSTON and elsewhere, apparently frequented by such people; 'Chiggerfoot Market' (also called Solas Market) in Kingston became JUBILEE MARKET in 1897. The word also appears in several folk songs such as 'Jigger Nanny mek the ball gawn round' in 'Pass the Ball'.

[Cassidy 1971, Crosby 1972, DJE]

CHINESE

The Chinese represent a very small proportion of the Jamaican population (0.2 per cent in 1991). However, their impact has been great, particularly in the development of commerce in the island. Many individual Chinese Jamaicans have achieved prominence in the country's civic, industrial, political and cultural life, and since the 1960s there has been increasing visibility of Chinese professionals.

The Chinese were first brought to Jamaica and other parts of the British West Indies in the 19th century as contract labourers to work on the sugar estates following EMANCIPATION. However, the majority of the Chinese arriving in Jamaica came in the 20th century as free immigrants through family and other connections, especially in the years 1910 to 1940. By the late 1930s, Jamaica had the second largest Chinese community in the CARIBBEAN (next to Cuba). There were 11,700 Chinese in Jamaica in 1970, but by 1980 the community had declined to a little over 5,000 following large scale emigration, especially to Canada and the United States, largely as a response to political conditions. In the 1990s, there has been a small inflow of China- and Hong Kong-born immigrants.

Early Arrivals The first Chinese came to Jamaica in 1854 on the *Epsom*, arriving 31 July after a three month voyage, having left Hong Kong with 267 men, of whom 43 died at sea and scores more soon after arrival. Another group came from Panama in November; 195 men arriving on the *Vampire* on 1 November and 10 on the *Theresa Jane* on the 18th. The arrivals from Panama were the remains of a larger group who had been taken from China to work on construction of the Panama Railroad, but who died out rapidly as a result of disease and the harsh conditions there. Although a large number of Chinese were brought to the rest of the Caribbean in subsequent years, only a small number came to Jamaica, some 200 from Guyana, Trinidad and Panama in the 1860s. The next set of indentured workers to Jamaica arrived in 1884 on the *Prinz Alexander*, with 680 landing on 12 July. This marked the first arrival of Chinese women (122 among the group) and children (3). They had started the voyage at Macao on the *Diamond* but a mast on that ship was broken in a storm and they were transferred to the *Prinz Alexander*.

The newcomers were mainly poor villagers with a farming background, especially from the southern province of Guangdong. The majority of those who came to Jamaica were Hakka speakers from Fui Yung, Dung Gon and Pao Onn, near modern Shen Zhen. They were lured by recruiting agents who offered a rosy alternative to the harsh conditions of their existence, brought on by years of drought, floods, famine and civil war.

Like other indentured workers of the time, they found the reality to be quite different from the promise, and as field workers on the sugar cane plantations they were subject to exploitation and abuse. On arrival, they were bound to work for five years on a specific estate for fixed wages, and could not travel more than

Rural Chinese shop

A Chinese Jamaican family visit their ancestral village

two miles beyond its boundaries without first obtaining a pass. Failure to perform their work satisfactorily could land them in prison and they were subject to harsh discipline, often with no means of appeal.

Some deserted the plantations, but many worked out their contracts, striking out on their own as soon as they could, remaining highly visible from their appearance, language and habits. For many decades, these early Chinese arrivals continued to wear their traditional dress consisting of a loose jacket and cotton trousers for both men and women; the men also wearing their hair long and plaited in pigtails.

Shopkeeping The earlier arrivals were joined in the 20th century by free immigrants. Some started to grow rice and went into market gardening but the vast majority found their niche by setting up small grocery shops the length and breadth of Jamaica, until the food retail trade became synonymous with the local 'Chiney shop'. So ubiquitous did the Chinese presence in rural Jamaica become, that the belief was prevalent that no village would prosper if it didn't have a Chinese shop, for they were the hub of village economic activity and development.

These shops were popular because the proprietors catered to the poor: they gave credit (though Jamaicans prefer the archaic English word 'trust'), and sold goods in very small amounts. A common sight was the Chinese shopkeeper and members of his family spending their time between customers measuring out small quantities of items such as salt, sugar, flour and placing them on squares of paper which they dextrously wrapped into cones ready for sale. Some were willing to barter shop goods in exchange for local produce, a boon to the poor farmer without ready cash. Since the family dwelling was usually part of the shop, they could also be relied on for purchases on Sundays, holidays and late at nights when the shops were officially closed. Although the Chinese for the most part lived peacefully in their communities, from time to time they have been targets of attacks.

Over time, many of the small family groceries grew into large enterprises embracing not only retailing but wholesaling and manufacturing, the Chinese becoming particularly active in the development of the bakery, ice cream and bottling industries, and catering and hardware.

Since in the early days few Chinese women emigrated, many of the men found local wives, which gave them a closer connection with Jamaicans than other immigrant groups and added to the racial mixture of the country. Regardless of their circumstances, many never lost contact with their homeland, and as they grew more prosperous, were able to bring wives and family members over from China or Hong Kong, or themselves return home.

By the 1940s, the Chinese in Jamaica had established a Chinese-language newspaper, a school, and a community centre – the Chinese Athletic Club – in KINGSTON, and there were freemasonry and benevolent societies. The illegal gambling games of PEAKA-PEOW and DROP-PAN that they introduced flourished at Chinese groceries and bars. Chinese restaurants appeared in the 1950s and became popular within a decade. The Chinese also represented a substantial part of mercantile activity. In the 1950s the Chinese broke the colour bar in the white banking world, Chinese tellers being among the first non-whites to stand behind the counters in the British and Canadian banks of colonial Jamaica. This cultural heyday lasted until the 1970s.

[Chinsee 1968, Lee 1963, Lee 1998, Levy 1972, Look Lai 1998, Osborne 1988, Roberts 1957]

CHOCHO *(Sechium edule)*
A type of squash growing on a perennial climbing vine that bears prolifically all year round on arbours in many a yard (also called 'chota' by some old fashioned Jamaicans, and known elsewhere as Christophene or Chayote). The large pear-shaped fruit has a single soft seed in the centre; the bland flesh is eaten as a vegetable, being especially relished in soups and stews or stuffed with meat or cheese for a main dish. It is also used as a substitute for APPLE in 'apple pie'. Raw chocho sliced thinly is used as a crudite with dips and is a vital ingredient in ESCOVEITCH fish and in pickles. It is claimed that the juice of the fruit relieves hypertension,

especially the white-skinned variety. The plant is a native of continental tropical America and the CARIBBEAN and was part of the TAINO garden landscape, maintaining its popularity to this day.
[Adams 1972, Robertson 1990]

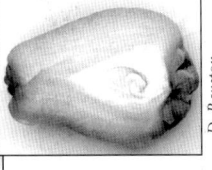

Chocho

CHOCOLATE see COCOA

CHOLERA

The island's single greatest catastrophe in terms of human life came in the form of cholera epidemics in the mid-19th century. Though the final number of deaths was never known, some estimates put it as high as 50,000 – eight to ten per cent of the population. The only grim reminders of those years are the old cholera cemeteries; KINGSTON'S May Pen Cemetery began as one.

The first and most serious outbreak of Asiatic cholera began in India and spread across Europe by the end of 1848, and from there to much of the USA, Canada and the Caribbean, reaching Jamaica in 1850. It spread rapidly across the island, but abated by the following year, by which time it had killed an estimated one in ten. Four years later, during another world epidemic, Jamaica was again attacked, this new epidemic taking an estimated 4,000-5,000 lives. The last case reported was in March 1855, also the last ever confirmed in the island.

Cholera attacked all sectors of the society but took its greatest toll among the poor, black population. In the overcrowded tenements of cities and towns, the corpses piled up. The spread of the disease is facilitated by poor sanitary arrangements, but recent research has also found a link between malnutrition and fatalities from cholera. Rural dwellers were not spared. According to C.H. Senior: 'Perhaps the most severely struck villages in the entire island during the 1850-1851 epidemic were Braziletto in the parish of VERE and Golden Grove in St-Thomas in the East. At Braziletto some fifty of the inhabitants died in as many hours and at Golden Grove eighty were said to have died within a week of the onset of the disease.'

The suddenness of the disease contributed to the panic and fear, death sometimes occurring within hours. Often there was no one to tend the sick or bury the dead. In Kingston, army and prison gangs were brought in, to undertake wholesale burial at KINGSTON RACE COURSE and other special cholera burial grounds, including one at May Pen, then an estate. In the panic, some were believed buried alive. As the epidemic spread, people fled their homes and abandoned their businesses. WHITE LIME was scattered on the streets and houses daubed with whitewash. There was hunger and starvation as provision GROUNDS were not tended and workers abandoned estates. Country HIGGLERS brought no food to the MARKETS and ships with supplies stayed away.

In the 1850 epidemic, the first case was a black woman of PORT ROYAL – called 'poor Dolly Johnson, the washerwoman whom we all knew' by Mary SEACOLE – who succumbed on 6 October, having taken in clothes for washing from a ship which came from New Orleans. The disease spread rapidly at Port Royal, especially among the poor population, and by the time it ended in mid-November, over 300 were buried along the PALISADOES.

By 10 October, the first death occurred in Kingston, the death rate rising to over 150 a day by the second week of November. By December the disease had run its course in Kingston and SPANISH TOWN, though it continued in eastern parishes. Early in the new year it travelled to the western parishes, LUCEA, the capital of HANOVER Parish being particularly hard hit. Though a cordon was thrown around WESTMORELAND, the last parish to experience the disease, it also broke out there. As the cholera abated, it was followed by outbreaks of SMALLPOX and three other epidemic diseases – influenza, measles and scarlatina.

During and after the first epidemic, there was much talk of sanitation and preventive measures but little was done and four years later the island was attacked again. This time the first victim was a seaman who arrived from Halifax, Canada, bringing the disease with him. The epidemic spread first through the hospital, the lunatic asylum and the GENERAL PENITENTIARY in Kingston, and by early March to the general population. The impact, though terrible, was less than the previous round, people apparently having developed some immunity.

Mary Seacole on her travels in Panama and, later, the Crimea, was able to put to good use what she had learnt during the cholera outbreaks in Jamaica. In Panama she even conducted a post-mortem on a dead child to further her knowledge of the disease.

These were the only cholera outbreaks in Jamaica's history. Despite their impact, improvements in the island's sanitary arrangements only began as part of the general reconstruction following the MORANT BAY REBELLION of 1865.

[Kiple 1984, Seacole 1857, Senior 1997]

CHRIST CHURCH (Port Antonio)
The Parish Church (ANGLICAN) of Portland, built around 1840 is a striking building, designed in neo-Romanesque style by English architect Annesley Voysey. A tablet inside the church records that he was 'induced to leave England in 1837, for the purpose of erecting this edifice and in the hope of otherwise contributing to the extension of the gospel of Christ'. Voysey died in Jamaica after only two years. The building was severely damaged in the 1903 hurricane but was rebuilt. The lectern was donated by the Boston Fruit Company (see BANANA TRADE). The communion vessels are from the original Parish Church, which was located at Richmond Hill Road.

CHRISTMAS
The celebration of the Christmas 'SEASON' (which goes into the New Year) is taken very seriously by many Jamaicans and has always been the island's most important holiday. The day following Christmas Day (Boxing Day) is also a public holiday and so is New Year's Day.

In modern times the celebrations have become more Europeanized, with strong religious overtones as in other Christian countries. The event is usually marked by church services, Christmas carols, much visiting and exchange of gifts and greetings, family celebrations and special food and drink, as well as partying. Many people mark New Year's Eve by attending midnight mass or church services in addition to private house parties or elaborate public balls that have become a fairly recent feature. Some have taken on the practice of decorating their house or yard with coloured lights and having lavishly decorated Christmas trees.

Despite the many imported elements, there are still some features of Christmas that are unmistakably Jamaican, starting with 'Christmas breeze', a special light and welcome wind that signals the imminent arrival of the favourite time of year. In the countryside, the SUGAR CANE sends up its feathery plume to signal its ripeness and in gardens everywhere, lavish POINSETTIA, red and white, burst into bloom, as does a wild vine known as Christmas Pop. While today children might expect to receive manufactured and imported toys, in the past Christmas was more associated with noisemakers, balloons, coloured paper hats with amusing sayings and special sweets. Firecrackers would be bought and set off from weeks ahead of the holiday (a practice introduced by the CHINESE). Firecrackers were, however, banned in the 1970s. A promenade down King Street on Christmas Day was once a feature of KINGSTON, along with the tradition of Christmas MARKET or Grand Market, and a Christmas Morning concert, now all vanished.

Special foods are associated with Christmas. Ripening in back gardens and making its appearance in the markets to herald the season is SORREL, to be made into the red-coloured drink without which Christmas is unthinkable, as well as GUNGO peas to be made into soup with the bone left over from the Christmas ham. A sweet yam called YAMPI also available at this time is regarded as a special treat. In the old days, householders cured their own hams, but now prepared hams are readily available. This is the favourite Christmas meat, though turkey is becoming popular. Earlier in the 20th century, Christmas beef or a specially raised chicken honoured the day. Among the better off, the meal must be finished off with CHRISTMAS PUDDING, sometimes doused in RUM and brought flaming to the table in the English manner.

Many people begin to celebrate Christmas well in advance of the actual event, especially since many Jamaicans living overseas try to return home, and the 'season' is not regarded as well and truly over until the second of January.

Plantation Era Christmas in the pre-EMANCIPATION era was celebrated even more intensively, since it represented for the entire population, slave and free, the longest break from labour, vacations being unknown. The three-day holidays beginning on Christmas Day took on a carnival-like atmosphere in the towns, and for a brief while a period of licence on the SUGAR PLANTATIONS. The festivals were the occasions for the slaves to dress in all their fine clothes and jewellery, paying visits to the GREAT HOUSE, on Boxing Day playing masquerade or JONKONNU. They could look forward to an abundant supply of fresh beef (denied them during the year – see SALT), and other special rations. (EASTER, the only other holiday, with one day's break, came to be known as 'Pikni' or 'Pickanni', i.e. small, Christmas.) New clothing was among the treats eagerly awaited (see OSNABURGH), hence the song: 'Christmas a come me want me lama.'

Christmas in fact signalled the end of a period of food scarcity and deprivation for the slaves. As Richard B. Sheridan in his study of slave medicine and demography has pointed out, the period July – November was generally one of scarcity and malnutrition, called by the slaves 'hard time' or 'hungry season', as few crops were in and few or no provision ships arrived. It was with a sense of hope and excitement then that the slaves awaited Christmas, for it was truly their season of plenty.

'After long months of deprivation and hunger, slaves were surfeited with food and drink during the Christmas season. For one thing, such food crops as maize, YAMS, PLANTAINS, BANANAS, and sweet POTATOES matured during December and January. Another nutritional increment came from CATTLE that were slaughtered, providing several pounds of meat to each adult black. Ships and convoys carrying plantation supplies for the sugar harvest left ports in North America and Europe so as to arrive in the West Indies after the hurricane season and by the beginning of the Christmas holiday.'

The slaves went from famine to feasting in preparation for croptime, which began shortly after the holidays and continued without a break until the end of July, a time of continuous labour as the sugar cane was reaped and processed into sugar, molasses and rum. Croptime nevertheless was a season of relative food abundance. The slaves were permitted to drink liberally of cane juice and chew newly cut cane, vitamin-rich molasses was plentiful, ground provisions and fruits were available, and ships continuously arrived with provisions. As the season (and Sheridan) concluded: 'Hunger and destitution then stalked the blacks intermittently until the next Christmas holiday, when they were once again fattened for another harvest.'

[Baxter 1970, Cassidy 1971, DJE, Patterson 1973, Sheridan 1985]

CHRISTMAS PUDDING

A reworking over the centuries of the traditional English plum pudding, Jamaican Christmas pudding is sweet and strong from lashings of RUM in which the dried fruit is put to soak months in advance of baking. The pudding is steamed. It is usually served cold, with hot brandy sauce or rum butter. The puddings will keep for several months, and are often sent to relatives and friends overseas. Puddings are made the first week in December, to allow them time to 'ripen' or mature for the Yuletide season, according to Enid Donaldson. In some Jamaican homes, fruit is kept soaking in rum all year round, always ready for use; fruit for the pudding must be soaked at least one month before use. The fruits traditionally used are ground raisins, currants, dates, and prunes soaked in rum and port wine. Spices and citron may also be added. The same recipe, with the pudding baked instead of steamed, is used for the traditional WEDDING cake, which is covered with a layer of marzipan (almond paste) and decorated with royal icing.

[Donaldson 1993, Facey 1993]

'CHRISTMAS REBELLION'
See SHARPE, Samuel

CIBONEY

Ciboney was the name given by the TAINOS to the people of the CARIBBEAN islands whom they displaced; they are called 'Archaic Indians' by archaeologists. We know little about them except that they settled in the Caribbean some time between 5,000 and 2,000 BC. The Spaniards were told by the Tainos that they had driven most of these people from the islands, though remnants probably continued to live in isolated places and in CAVES in Cuba and Hispaniola. Ciboney probably derives from the Arawakan words *ciba* (rock) and *eyeri* (man).

The Ciboneys were hunters, fishers and collectors. Theirs has been described as a 'conch shell culture'; the CONCH shell supplied them with axe blades as well as vessels and drinking cups, since they did not make ceramics. They also used hematite (ochre) for red colouring. This latter habit, as well as the conch shell drinking cup, point to North America, although northern South America and Central America have also been posited as likely places of origin. Some scholars have given the name *Guanahatabeys* to these people, but according to Irving Rouse, that name refers to remnants of another people who lived in the far end of Cuba and spoke a different language from Taino when Columbus encountered them. Both Ciboneys and Guanahatabeys might be considered the pre-Taino occupiers of the Caribbean who became extinct before they could be studied.

[Lovén 1935, Rouse 1992, Steward 1948]

CINCHONA GARDENS

Established in 1868 on a ridge in ST ANDREW Parish that rises to 1,500m, Cinchona has one of the most spectacular settings anywhere. The gardens afford varying perspectives of plunging valleys below and beyond, views of Sir John's Peak (1,930m), the main ridge of the BLUE MOUNTAINS and, when the mists lift, part of KINGSTON, PORT ROYAL and the sea. Although somewhat neglected over the years and hard to reach, this botanic garden has remained a haven for those who take the trouble to go there. It is most easily reached either on foot or by well-sprung vehicle.

The garden was established by the government for the development and propagation of the cinchona plant from which the medicine quinine is obtained. Before the advent of modern drugs it was most useful in the treatment of malaria (see YELLOW FEVER AND MALARIA) and was traditionally used for this purpose by the Amerindians of the Andes. The Spanish priests obtained the knowledge from them, and the plant came to be called Jesuit's bark. It was renamed for the Countess of Cinchón, wife of the Spanish viceroy of Peru, who was one of its beneficiaries.

Cinchona was planted in Jamaica at a time when the bark of the tree was fetching high prices on world markets and at first, large sums were made. But the project eventually failed, mainly because of the poor roads and transportation into the area. A section of the gardens had also been planted out in another economic crop – Assam (Indian) TEA. The tea thrived, but Jamaica could not compete on the English market with tea from India. A third section that was established as a 'European garden' is virtually all that remains. Here can be seen the cinchona tree, the native juniper CEDAR, and exotics such as mulberry, camphor, rubber, cork oak, and garden flowers from northern climates as well as European fruits and vegetables. The gardens today consist of about 15ha.

[Eyre 1966, GOJ Handbook of Jamaica 1961, Mordecai 1984]

Cinchona house (A. Oberli)

CINNAMON *(Cinnamomum zeylanicum)*

The bark of this large tree (up to 15m) yields the well-known spice. Native to Sri Lanka and India, it was introduced to Jamaica in 1782, one of the plants brought by Lord RODNEY'S fleet from a French ship captured in CARIBBEAN waters. Little bundles of cinnamon bark and leaves are sold in Jamaican MARKETS and are a vital ingredient in such traditional foods as chocolate tea and cornmeal porridge, as well as cakes and puddings. A close relative is the Camphor tree *(C. Camphora)* which can be found at CASTLETON and CINCHONA Gardens. Jamaica Cinnamon or Wild Cinnamon are names for another plant, Canella Bark, which is used for medicinal purposes. It is from the Canella family, is indigenous to the island Caribbean, and was known by the TAINOS.

[Adams 1972]

CITRUS

Many species of citrus thrive in Jamaica, a tree or two of the most popular being often grown by householders, though commercial orchards are located at higher elevations, away from the coastal plains. All citrus are similar in structure, differences arise in the size of the plants (which can be shrubs or trees), and in the leaf and fruit. Some also have spines or prickles on the stems.

Citrus plants originated in the Far East and were brought westwards to the Mediterranean; the first plants arrived in the CARIBBEAN with COLUMBUS on his second voyage in 1493 from the Canary Islands. These included the Sweet ORANGE *(C. siniensis)*, the Sour or Seville orange *(C. aurantium)*, Lemon *(C. limon)*, TANGERINE or Mandarin *(C. reticulata)*, LIME *(C. aurantifolia)* and Citron *(C. medica)*.

Descendants of the original Seville orange trees planted in Jamaica, probably in 1507, can still be found at New SEVILLE and, according to former government archaeologist G.A. Aarons, are noted for their 'sublime bitterness'.
GRAPEFRUIT *(C. paradisi)* is believed to have developed in the Caribbean from the Shaddock *(C. grandis)* which came via the Pacific. In recent times, several new hybrids have been developed

commercially or spontaneously, among them ORTANIQUE and UGLI.

[Adams 1972, Baccus and Royes 1988]

CLARENDON, Parish of

Area 1196.3km², population 227,500 (1999). Named in honour of an English Lord Chancellor, Clarendon incorporates VERE, which was once a separate parish. The southern plains of this parish were first occupied by the TAINOS and later by the Spaniards who established CATTLE ranches, called 'hatos' or 'haciendas'. It was the Spaniards who named the principal river of this parish Rio de la Mina or River of the Mine (now RIO MINHO). It is said that they washed for gold on this river at Longville, near to what is now MAY PEN, the capital.

Later, the English settlers developed plantations on the plains. COTTON and indigo (from which a dye is obtained) were their principal crops, until these were superseded by SUGAR CANE. Despite the natural dryness of the plains, this area has remained one of extensive sugar cane cultivation, since the cane grown here is found to be extremely high in sugar. During the early part of the 20th century an extensive irrigation scheme was introduced to make the savannas fruitful. At first, water for the irrigation canals came from the MILK RIVER but it went dry frequently. Water was then taken from the Cockpit River. Extensive deposits of underground water were later tapped, providing water for irrigation from wells. The first well was dug in 1929.

The parish that is known as Clarendon was first developed in the 17th century from land grants given by Charles II to former Commonwealth troops who established sugar estates along the Minho valley. Many places along this valley still bear the names of these original settlers such as Sutton, Pennant and Ballard. Peter BECKFORD owned acreage here, as did Henry MORGAN who owned Morgans Valley and Danks, which Morgan gave to his wife who was of German nationality. The German word for thanks is *danke* – thus providing the name for the property.

After EMANCIPATION, Upper Clarendon became an area of extensive peasant settlement, the extension of the railway from May Pen to Chapelton facilitating its development.

The first MAROONS surfaced in the northern part of this parish when Spanish slaves settled in the Cave River Valley at a place called Los Vermejales (now rendered as Vera Ma Hollis). Later, they were joined by slaves escaping from the English-owned plantations. One of the earliest recorded slave rebellions in Jamaica occurred at Suttons plantation in 1690. The runaways from here joined the Spanish-speaking free Africans in the north of the parish, and the whole group came to be known as the Maroons. In time, these Maroons were driven out of Clarendon and, led by CUDJOE or Kojo, said to be the son of the leader of the Suttons uprising, settled eventually in the COCKPIT COUNTRY.

[Cundall 1915, Taylor 1976]

CLIMATE

Although Jamaica lies in the tropics, extremes of climate are modified by the sea and by the mountainous nature of the country. The eastern portion of the island is crossed by the BLUE MOUNTAIN range, rising from 900m to 2,256m; the central and western portions consist of interior mountain ranges surrounded by high LIMESTONE plateaux 305m to 900m and the south side of extensive plains less than 152m high. There is considerable variation in the climate of the different regions. The coastal plains are hottest and driest, the climate of the limestone plateaux sub-tropical and the higher areas much cooler.

Jamaica's climate contributes to a comfortable and healthy environment. Because of the year round effect of sea breezes, there is little variation between summer and winter temperatures, the coolest months being December to March. However, there is a variation in day and night temperatures and greater variation between temperatures at high and low altitudes. For example, the 30 year mean temperature for CINCHONA (1,524m) is 21°C, and for MONTEGO BAY (less than 1m above sea level) is 29.5°C. August is generally the warmest month of the year and February the coolest. Seasonal differences between these two months are usually less than 10 degrees, being often in the order of 5°C.

Relative humidity is fairly high although not as much as in places nearer the equator. In KINGSTON it ranges from 63 per cent in February to 75 per cent in October. Montego Bay is rather more humid, with an annual range between 71 and 77 per cent.

There is a marked variation in rainfall, some coastal areas to the south receiving as little as 889mm annually and some mountainous areas to the north-east more than 5,080mm annually. Most of Jamaica can be said to receive moderate rainfall, the long term (1881-1980) annual mean being 1,895mm. Most parts of the island have two wet seasons, May-June and September-November and these annual seasons occur as regular cycles, though the pattern varies significantly from year to year. Short duration rain showers can also fall at any time, mainly in the afternoon. The driest period is usually December to March. Most of the rainfall between November and March is associated with cold fronts migrating from North America.

The HURRICANE season runs from June to November.
[GOJ Handbook of Jamaica 1961, GOJ STATIN 1999a]

CLING-CLING see BLACKBIRD

COAL-POT
Not a pot but a small charcoal stove, its other name of 'coal-stove' being more accurate. The coals are placed in the basin-like top, and the ash falls through a grill into the hollow cylindrical foot that is about 15cm deep. Pots (usually round and blackened like the stove) are perched on the coals and meat can be grilled on sticks laid across the top. It was also widely used for heating flat-irons for ironing clothes. (See LAUNDRY.) The stoves were once made of clay but now are made of cast iron.

Coal pot (clay version)

Although replaced whenever possible by kerosene, gas and electrical stoves, the coal-pot is still the only cooking device in many families. Even in households with modern appliances, the coal-pot might still be used for special tasks such as roasting BREADFRUIT, and it is popular with street food vendors. It was probably introduced into the CARIBBEAN by the Dutch in the 17th century, hence its other name of Dutch stove (see also DUTCHIE). 'Coal-pot' is supposedly derived from the Dutch *kool pot*, i.e. a pot for charcoal.
[DCEU]

COAT OF ARMS
The Jamaican Coat of Arms consists of a shield that bears a red cross with five golden PINEAPPLES, flanked on either side with a male and female TAINO. The male is shown carrying a bow and arrow, weapons unknown to the Tainos until the European contact. The crest is a Jamaican alligator (but see CROCODILE) surmounting the royal helmet and mantling. The motto 'Out of Many One People' – adopted at the time of INDEPENDENCE – appears below.

The modern Coat of Arms is a variation of the original that was given to the island as an English colony in 1661 and designed by the Archbishop of Canterbury. The two natives being described as 'Indians', the original motto of the colony was: 'Indus Uterque Serviet Uni'. This is translated as 'The Indians twain shall serve one Lord' or, in a rendition given by Theodore Sealy who was Chairman of the Independence Committee which chose the national symbols, 'both Arawaks, male and female, serve one nation'.
[Cundall 1915, GOJ Handbook of Jamaica 1961, NLJ Historical notes – National Emblems]

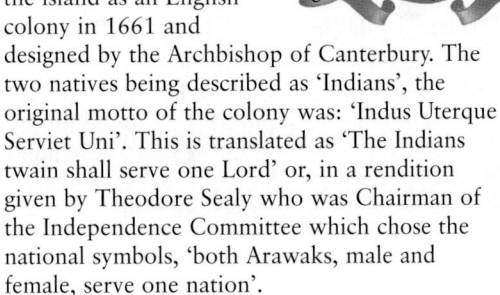

COATRISCHIE
One of the 12 principal ZEMIS of the TAINOS, Coatrischie (or Coatrisquie) is a weather spirit whose name means Flood and along with GUATAUBÁ (Thunder), is the subordinate of and assistant to GUABANCEX, Lady of the winds. Coatrischie's other names mean 'the carrier of water to the mountains', 'drifting storm clouds', 'sweeper or ruler of waves', signifying a spirit that gathers water in the mountain valleys to cause the floods that accompany the HURRICANES. There is the suggestion that the representation of water birds can be identified with this zemi.
[Arrom 1975]

COCKPIT COUNTRY
Geographical area encompassing 1,300km^2 of the parishes of ST ELIZABETH and ST JAMES, regarded as Jamaica's most inhospitable region. Few roads cross the territory and much of it remains unexplored.

'Cockpit' type terrain exists in several other parts of the LIMESTONE region of Jamaica, though nowhere as developed as in the eerie and unusual landscape of the Cockpit Country. The cockpits are steep sided valleys that alternate with conical hillocks to form a peculiar type of terrain known as Karst topography. Limestone cannot retain surface water and rain water immediately percolates below ground through cracks and fissures, widening these over millions of years until the pits or valleys are formed. The

Cockpit Country

conical shape of the hills comes from the effect of weathering. Although there is no surface water, streams and rivers flow underground, and sinkholes and CAVES are characteristic of the area. The area influences the BLACK RIVER, the Great River and the MARTHA BRAE.

In the 18th century the Cockpit Country became the stronghold of the MAROONS led by Captain CUDJOE who had his headquarters in a cockpit near the Petty River. The Maroon village of ACCOMPONG is located in this country, named after a brother of Cudjoe. The southern section is known by the picturesque name of 'Land of Look Behind', which probably dates from the Maroon wars. Another place name in the region, 'Me No Sen Yu No Come', records the sentiment of a group of runaway slaves who had established themselves there.

Most of the Cockpit Country today still remains virtually uninhabited and difficult to access, though some of the valley bottoms have been cultivated by farmers from the surrounding areas. Much of the natural vegetation still remains, especially on the hillsides. The Cockpit Country is the area with the highest number of endemic plants in Jamaica and has a rich diversity of FLORA and FAUNA. At the time of writing, efforts were underway to create a Cockpit Country NATIONAL PARK to conserve some of this unique natural heritage.
[Fincham 1997, GOJ Handbook of Jamaica 1961]

COCKROACH POISON *(Solanum aculeatissimum)*
A member of the Solanum family that includes tomatoes, Irish POTATOES and the deadly nightshade, this plant is noted for its orange-red fruit like a small tomato, which is broken open and placed in closets and is supposedly effective against cockroaches. In folk MEDICINE, the plant pounded with LIME juice has been used for ringworms. The fruit is poisonous if eaten.
[Adams 1972, Asprey and Thornton 1953-55]

COCO
The name coco is applied to a number of similar root crops grown in the tropics, referred to as cocoyam in West Africa. In Jamaica the most popular coco is *Xanthosoma sagittifolium*, a hard white tuber that is widely eaten, especially in soups. This coco is the Taro of Polynesia and was brought to tropical America by the Portuguese, probably as a by-product of their 16th century Asiento slave trade with the Spanish colonies, as an inexpensive food source for their human cargo. It is also known as Tannia and Yautia. Similar plants are the Badu, Eddo and Dasheen (*Colocasia esculenta*) though in this case it is the rhizome or 'head' rather than the tuber that is eaten. The leaves of coco plants, especially dasheen, are also consumed, and are a vital ingredient in PEPPERPOT soup.

Coco

In the 1920s M.W. Beckwith found coco next to YAM in importance to the small settler, attested to by the saying: 'When man have coco-head in barrel, him can pick wife.' Its utilitarian value is signified by the saying 'One-one coco full basket'. The tubers are valued for their keeping qualities after reaping.

The coco is one plant that Jamaica has given to Africa. The plant was taken to West Africa in 1843 and the Jamaican name – koko – is the one by which it is known there.
[Beckwith 1928, DJE, Hall-Alleyne 1996]

COCO-BREAD see BREAD

COCOA *(Theobroma cacao)*
The tree (cacao) which produces the beans that yield cocoa and chocolate grows well in Jamaica. Though exported on a small scale, Jamaican cocoa is regarded as of high quality on the world market.

Cocoa was cultivated in the tropical American

Cocoa pods on tree and cut pod showing beans

forests long before the arrival of Europeans. The beans provided more than beverage; they served as a medium of exchange from pre-Columbian times up to the late 19th century in some parts of South and Central America. For the Aztecs, chocolate was the 'Food of the Gods' (which is the meaning of the Latin name *Theobroma* that was later given to the plant). The Aztec emperor Montezuma offered the Spanish *conquistador* Hernando Cortez a drink called *xocoatl* that was prepared from cocoa beans flavoured with capsicum peppers. Although this was not quite to European tastes, cocoa, which was introduced to the Spanish court by COLUMBUS in 1502, was to become a staple of Spanish commerce and consumers learnt to mix chocolate with sugar, making it more palatable.

Invention of the milk chocolate drink is credited to the English doctor, Sir Hans Sloane (see FLORA), who encountered chocolate in Jamaica but found the local drink 'nauseous'. He started the practice of boiling the beans in sugared milk. On returning to London, Sloane sold the recipe to an apothecary who marketed it as 'Sir Hans Sloane Milk Chocolate'. The advertisement claimed that 'several eminent physicians' recommended it for 'its lightness on the stomach, and its great use in all consumption cases'.

However, until the early 1800s, the cocoa product continued to be a fatty drink prepared from the whole bean, not relished by everyone. Refinements in processing in Europe led to the extraction of cocoa butter and the development of cocoa powder and chocolate. The manufacture of the chocolate bar in the 1840s created a worldwide demand for the product. However, Sloane's invention had continued to be sold, and the Cadbury Brothers bought the recipe and marketed it from 1849-85 as 'Sir Hans Sloane's Milk Chocolate'. This time it was squares of chocolate that were melted in boiling water to which sugar and milk were added.

By the late 19th century chocolate had developed as one of the world's most popular foods. This spurred the development of cocoa plantations throughout the tropical world, especially in West Africa, and led to the expansion of the crop in Jamaica and elsewhere in the Caribbean where it had been grown and exported since SPANISH settlement. Trinidad became a centre for breeding and improvement of the crop.

Jamaicans from earliest times were fond of the fatty chocolate drink, and the Spanish cocoa plantations were continued by the English after the island changed hands in 1655. Edward Long said that in 1671 there were 60 fine 'cocoa walks' in bearing and many new ones in cultivation, but a blight was to destroy these early efforts. The English governor, Colonel Beeston attributed the blight to the appearance of a comet which he said had 'blasted' the cocoa trees in Jamaica, Cuba, and Hispaniola. Cocoa continued to be grown and exported on a small scale, until the revival of the 'cocoa walks' by English cocoa companies in the late 19th century.

The handsome small tree (up to 7.5m) thrives in hot, wet areas, especially under the shade of taller trees. It bears on its branches and trunks the red or orange fruits called pods. When these are ripe they are harvested and broken open to reveal a collection of cocoa seeds or 'beans'. These are extracted from the pods, fermented, dried, roasted and ground to form the cocoa, cocoa butter and chocolate of commerce.

Chocolate or more frequently 'chaklata' in Jamaica was the name applied to the tree, the beans and the drink or 'TEA' made from them, nowadays more commonly called cocoa-tea. Chaklata was up to recently the name given by country folk to breakfast or the first meal of the day.

Although chocolate is processed locally in a few factories some people grow trees in their plots and from them prepare 'chaklata' by hand in the traditional way. The outer pod is cracked and discarded, the beans taken out and fermented, then dried in the sun. They are parched or roasted in a hot iron pot, the skin is removed, and the beans are pounded in a wooden MORTAR until a paste-like consistency is reached and they exude oil. The chocolate is then scraped out and formed by hand into balls or cigar-shaped rolls. Air-dried, these can be kept for a long time. To prepare chocolate for drinking, the ball is grated and the chocolate boiled with water and milk, sweetened and flavoured with CINNAMON. Chocolate balls are usually sold in the markets and supermarkets, often with a stick or leaves of cinnamon included.

In folk MEDICINE, cocoa butter is used for eczema and other skin problems.

[Adams 1972, Beckwith 1928, Long 1774, Robertson 1990]

COCOBAY

Word used to describe leprosy or any disfiguring skin disease; commonly believed to be caused by a whitish poisonous substance found in the skin of the BULLFROG and thus to be avoided, since anyone coming in contact would end up having skin like a toad. The proverb says, 'Nuh shake cocobay man hand fe tek shame outa yu eye', i.e. do not do something dangerous out of shame. The word comes from the Twi (West African) *kokobe*, meaning leprosy.

[DJE]

COCONUT *(Cocos nucifera)*

PALM of tremendous importance to Jamaica, widespread in its distribution and usage. The nuts are usually carried by the world's oceans and washed up on sea shores. Although there are many palms indigenous to the New World, the coconut is believed to be of Old World origin. The name is from the Portuguese word *coco* for grimace or grinning face, from the resemblance of the nut with its three 'eyes' to a monkey's face. It is from one of these eyes that a new coconut plant shoots when a ripe coconut falls to the ground. The shoot takes nourishment from a small amount of water left inside the nut. The root will eventually force itself through the bottom of the hard shell.

Scientists are undecided about the original source of the coconut in the Americas, but the trees were common in Jamaica and the other West Indian islands by the 17th century as Hans Sloane noted. (See FLORA.) In Jamaica it did not become a commercial crop until the mid-19th century when the first plantation was established at PALISADOES, on the land now occupied by the Norman MANLEY International Airport. (See COCONUT TREE, Monument to.) Coconuts thereafter began to be planted along with BANANAS wherever there was plenty of rainfall on lands unsuitable for SUGAR CANE, to meet the growing demand in the British and American markets. Though this remains an important economic crop, the plantations have been much affected by HURRICANES, which in some instances have destroyed all bearing trees, as well as by lethal yellowing disease, the seriousness of which was first recognized in MONTEGO BAY as early as 1891.

The original variety, the Jamaica Tall, once grew in profusion along the sea coast, and gave

Coconut palms

to the shoreline its postcard prettiness. But that seascape has changed in recent decades as the Jamaica Tall has been virtually wiped out by lethal yellowing. It has been replaced by the Maypan variety, a hybrid of the Malayan Dwarf and the Panama Tall, which is believed to be more resistant to the disease, the Malayan Dwarf also having proved susceptible. The skin of the new variety varies in colour from green to yellow and orange.

Up to the Second WORLD WAR, coconut meat (copra) was an important export crop. In the postwar years most of the nuts have been consumed locally, since production has been seriously reduced by lethal yellowing. Whereas most of Jamaica's yield formerly went into the production of oils and fats and coir from the husks (used for stuffing mattresses and furniture), in recent years the widespread drinking of 'coconut water' from the fresh young fruit has generated competing demand.

The coconut water industry like JERK pork or 'drum' or 'pan chicken', is an example of grass roots entrepreneurship, for makeshift stands on roadsides and city streets or itinerant vendors now make this thirst quencher, packaged by

Coconut vendor

nature, almost as accessible as bottled drinks. Coconut vending spots are usually recognized from afar by a trimmed coconut leaf stood upright. On request, the coconut vendor will split the hard covering of the green nut from which the water has been drunk to make available the young flesh or jelly. In recent years, bottled coconut water has also become widely available.

Coconut water should not be confused with coconut 'milk', which is extracted from pouring hot water over the grated flesh of the dry nut. The flesh and milk from dry (i.e. mature) coconuts play an important role in Jamaican cuisine, as they do in many tropical countries. The milk is an essential ingredient in RICE AND PEAS and RUN DUNG ('run down') sauce; a thicker cream is served with baked bananas, COFFEE, stewed fruit, GUAVA cheese, etc. Coconut is also a notable ingredient in cakes and puddings and is used to make popular SWEETS such as coconut drops, GRATER CAKE, GIZADA and ice cream.

Most importantly, the milk is the source of coconut oil that was formerly the staple cooking oil of Jamaica. With the shortage of coconuts, the local factory switched to making most of its oil from other sources such as soybean and corn, and popular taste has changed accordingly. But coconut oil is preferred by many for imparting a special flavour to Jamaican dishes, and some people still make their own by boiling down the milk until it is reduced to oil, which is then separated from the solids. The popular Run Dung is made by this process, though it is taken off the fire before the separation occurs.

Extracting coconut meat (copra)

The coconut palm is one of the most useful trees of the world, bearing for some 30-40 years. It furnishes food and drink; oil for soap, cosmetics and cooking; mats, hats, and shelter from its fronds; novelties, jewellery and decorations from the hard shell of its nut; wood from its trunk and coir fibre from the husk covering the outer shell. Formerly used to stuff mattresses, coir is now more frequently used as a growing medium for anthuriums and as an ingredient in potting mix for other plants. Even the dead trees can yield benefit, for the trunks of those killed off by disease have been used to manufacture parquet flooring and furniture.

Coconut water is also used in folk MEDICINE: a source of potassium, it is used to treat hypertension and considered good for the bladder.

Coconuts are often among the fruits on REVIVAL 'Tables' and are used in KUMINA rituals.

[Asprey and Thornton 1953-55, Baccus and Royes 1988, Harries 1980]

COCONUT TREE, Monument to the

This marker is to be found on the PALISADOES Road (Norman MANLEY Highway) and dates to a time when this strip of land leading to PORT ROYAL (including what is now the Norman Manley International Airport) was covered in COCONUT trees. The vegetation of much of the spit was cleared, and an extensive coconut plantation of 91ha was established there in 1869 on orders of the governor, Sir John Peter Grant, as part of his drive to stimulate agriculture. (He was also responsible for the creation of the public gardens at what is now St William Grant PARK, the plantations at CINCHONA, and for importing many plants for CASTLETON.) With the Palisadoes plantation, one of the governor's objectives was 'to show the people on the coast how, at small cost, the waste and sandy shores of the island could be converted into land yielding a very high rate of annual profit'.

Within 20 years, some 20,000 coconut trees were flourishing on the Palisadoes, but they were eventually attacked by disease and died out. Today, the only trace of the coconut plantations remaining is the stone monument near Plumb Point which records that 'The first coconut trees were planted 4 March 1869 by John Norton, Esquire, Superintendent of the GENERAL PENITENTIARY'. Inmates of the prison were used to plant and maintain the trees.

[Harries 1980, Marsala 1972]

CODFISH see FISH, Salt

COFFEE (*Coffea arabica*)

Coffee originated in Ethiopia and was eventually taken to the Mediterranean, thence to western Europe. It was introduced into Jamaica in 1728 when a former governor, Sir Nicholas Lawes, planted it at his Temple Hall plantation, ST ANDREW Parish. The industry in Jamaica got a boost when FRENCH planters fled nearby St-Domingue (now Haiti) at the end of the 18th century during the revolutionary wars there and settled in Jamaica, bringing their superior knowledge of coffee culture. However, the industry declined rapidly after the Napoleonic Wars since the duty on coffee had been increased to help finance the war. This encouraged the demand for coffee substitutes such as tea, and made coffee from non-British territories cheaper. In time, most of the coffee plantations were abandoned and coffee thereafter became a small settler crop. In the mountains, especially in St Andrew and ST THOMAS parishes, can be seen the ruins of many coffee works, including the stone BARBECUES on which the beans are dried. Today, coffee cultivation in the mountains has again been taken up by large growers.

Jamaica's coffee production is low by world standards (approximately 2.72 million kg) but it ranks high internationally in quality and flavour, especially that grown on the slopes of the BLUE MOUNTAINS which commands a high price on the world market. Coffee labelled 'Blue Mountain' has to be grown within a 16km radius of the Peak. The other generic category of coffee is Jamaica Prime, grown on the mountains of the central parishes but outside the Blue Mountain range. It also is regarded as a gourmet bean. Most of Jamaica's coffee is exported and cheaper varieties imported and blended for local consumption. Japan is Jamaica's best market for unroasted coffee, and the Japanese are involved with the expansion of the industry. The Coffee Industry Board, established by the government in 1950, is the centralized facility for processing and quality control.

Excellent liqueurs are made from Jamaican coffee, the oldest of which is the world famous Tia Maria, developed on the island.

The small coffee tree – 2-4m high – bears attractive glossy leaves and fragrant white flowers that look like its close relative, the gardenia. The hard, green berries grow on the limbs in clusters and each ripens at a different time, turning cherry red to signal that it is ready for picking, which is done by hand. The beans have to be carefully handled to ensure maximum flavour and the age-old methods of processing – pulping, washing, curing, hulling, and sorting are still used.

Though most people today get their coffee from the supermarket, up to recently many country people grew and processed their own for home use. In home processing, the ripe beans are put through a contraption called a pulper that breaks the pulpy skin to loosen it, its removal hastened by washing. The beans which come in pairs are then spread out to dry in the sun, being turned each day to prevent mildew. Once they are thoroughly dried, the beans (known as green coffee) can be kept in that state for some time. They will then be roasted and ground to provide the favourite brew. Rats will sometimes get to the ripe berries before the reaper does, and eat off the sweet outer pulp, leaving the berries intact. Such coffee was known as 'rat-cut coffee' and not marketed commercially. In the countryside where coffee was often grown as part of the kitchen garden, rat-cut coffee was regarded as the preserve of the women and children to gather and dispose of as they wished; they usually sold it locally for pocket money. Rat-cut coffee was also kept for household use.

Coffee berries and flowers

Hand operated coffee pulper

The popularity of coffee among the country folk (usually boiled up and poured through a home made calico filter) is asserted in the song which claims: 'The only thing for me/is mi bowl a bwiling cawfee in the mawning.'
[Baccus and Royes 1988, Cundall 1915]

COHOBA
Ritual snuffing of narcotic powder to induce hallucinations, initially witnessed by COLUMBUS in Cuba and Hispaniola in 1492 on his first voyage. Since then, the use of narcotic snuff has been observed to be widespread among the native peoples of South America.

Scholars have disputed whether the TAINO word *cohoba* referred to a plant or to the ceremonial practice of ingesting powders produced by a plant, and if so, what plant. The plant was originally identified as TOBACCO (which the Tainos called *tabaco* and also used for ritual purposes and as snuff). But based on knowledge of similar practice in South America in the contemporary period, it is now identified as *Anadenanthera peregrina* (formerly called *Piptadenia peregrina*) which is native to the CARIBBEAN and elsewhere in the tropical lowlands. It is a member of the mimosa family and bears long black pods filled with seeds (perhaps like Wild TAMARIND) that are used by tropical American tribes to produce a hallucinogenic powder. Indeed, the Spanish chronicler Oviedo had identified this tree as cohoba, noting: 'And this cohoba bears peas whose pods of roughly palm's length contain lentil-shaped seeds which are inedible; and the wood is very good and tough.'

To make snuff, the cohoba seeds (or tobacco leaves) would be dried and crushed in a MORTAR and mixed with lime which was usually produced by burning a special species of snail's shell and grinding to a power. For personal use the snuff would be carried in a small bag.

The Tainos seemed to have used cohoba in three ways: (1) ritual smoking to induce visions by the CACIQUES and nobles; (2) curing rituals used by the *behique* or *bohuti* (shaman); (3) as offerings to visitors (along with CASSAVA bread) but more importantly, as offering to the ZEMIS. Some zemis were carved with a type of tray on their heads that are believed to have been stands for such offerings, e.g. BAIBRAMA.

The cohoba ritual accompanied major events in Taino life and served as a kind of oracle: the chiefs and nobles would gather in the bohío (chief's house) to sniff cohoba and enter into trances in which coming events and their solutions would be revealed. The presiding cacique sat on a ritual seat called a *duho* (see SEATING, Ceremonial). The cohoba was placed on a special table described by Columbus as round and finely wrought, from which it was sniffed up into the nostrils through forked tubes that were called *tabaco* by the Tainos; many examples have been found by archaeologists. Sniffing of the powder or smoke from burning tobacco leaves would bring on a condition that struck Western observers as 'drunkenness', 'madness' and 'going out of one's senses'.

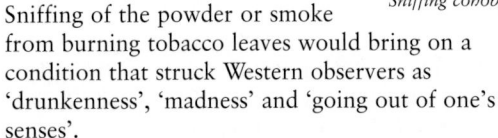

Sniffing cohoba

In curing rituals, the cohoba was ingested by the shaman or behique and he would feed some to his patient as well.
[Arrom 1975, Fewkes 1907, Reichel-Dolmatoff 1975, Roth 1901, Rouse 1992, Stevens-Arroyo 1988, Wilbert 1987]

COINAGE see MONEY

COKE CHURCH
Famous KINGSTON landmark located at East Parade. The steps of the old church used to be a favourite platform for politicians in the early days of national political awakening. Coke Church stands on the site of the first METHODIST chapel built in Jamaica. The chapel was originally a merchant's house that was remodelled. The first chapel was opened in 1790 but this was a time when MISSIONARY activity was frowned upon. Some time after its opening, a Grand Jury in Kingston found the chapel 'injurious to the general peace and quiet of the

Coke Church

said town', and ordered it closed. It stayed closed for seven years, but when it reopened in 1814, the congregation had trebled. Coke Church was built on the same site in 1840 and named after Dr Thomas Coke, founder of the Methodist missions in the British West Indies who arrived in Jamaica in 1789 and preached around the island, afterwards arranging for 12 Methodist missionaries to be sent from England. This church was severely damaged in the 1907 EARTHQUAKE and the present building dates from that time. It is one of the few brick buildings in the city, the use of this material being frowned on after the earthquake.

COLBECK CASTLE

Located 2.4km north-west of OLD HARBOUR, ST CATHERINE Parish, this is the ruin of what was the largest building of its kind in Jamaica, measuring 27.4m by 34.7m and consisting of

Colbeck Castle

three stories with square towers at each corner connected by arched arcades. Colbeck Castle is Jamaica's 'mystery building' for there is virtually no information about its origin. It is generally supposed to have been built by Colonel John COLBECK. However, no one is sure if it was ever completed or lived in, or even when it was built, its construction being variously ascribed to both the 17th and 18th centuries though c. 1670 is believed to be the most likely date. This is listed as a national monument by the JNHT.
[Buisseret 1969, 1980a]

COLBECK, Colonel John (1630-82)

Colonel Colbeck's name is perpetuated in Jamaican history mainly because of his association with COLBECK CASTLE. Colbeck came with the English army of conquest in 1655 (see CAPTURE OF JAMAICA) and became a big landowner in ST CATHERINE Parish. He was active in the civic, political and military life of the young colony, but little is known of his life and less about the building of what must have been once a magnificent house. One historian has noted that there is a tradition in Lincolnshire, England, that Colbeck came from a branch of the family there and was transported to the CARIBBEAN for cutting down an elm tree.

Colbeck died in 1682 and there is a monument to him in the SPANISH TOWN CATHEDRAL. In his will he left nothing to any relatives he might have had. Among his bequests was £20 to the parson to preach his funeral sermon, and money to purchase rings to be given to several prominent persons including the famous buccaneer Henry MORGAN, who owned land in the area. To the TAMARIND TREE CHURCH he left money to put in glass windows and iron bars. After his death the name Colbeck does not appear again in Jamaican history until its recent resurrection as the name for a locally made sherry.
[Cundall 1915]

'COLÓN MAN'

While present-day Jamaicans are among the most travelled people anywhere, large scale emigration actually began in 1850, to Latin America, and the icon of the foreign experience from that time until well into the 20th century was 'Colón Man'. He inspired many folk songs (see MUSIC, Folk), the most popular of which is still sung:

One-two-three-four
Colón Man a come
With him watch-chain a lick him belly
bam bam bam

Ask him for the time
and he look upon the sun
With him watch chain a lick him belly
bam bam bam

Colón (named after Cristóbal Colón – or COLUMBUS) is now a town in Panama at the Atlantic end of the Panama Canal. But long before the birth of the Republic of Panama or the construction of the Canal, it was (under a succession of different names) the disembarkation point for travellers and therefore the port Jamaicans aimed for.

Jamaicans had flocked there in their tens of thousands for work on the construction of the Panama Railroad (1850-55), for the French attempt to construct the Panama Canal (1880-

1904), for the final and successful American construction of the Canal (1904-14), and for construction and defence works on the Canal in the 1940s. Up to the world-wide depression of the 1920s and enforced repatriation, Jamaicans had also found work all over Latin America in constructing railways, in banana and other plantations, in mining, and in Cuba during the SUGAR boom there. Between 1881-1921, Jamaica experienced a net loss of 146,000 persons.

But it was Colón that came to be not just a synonym for Panama but for the style of some of those who had travelled to 'farrin'. The visible Colón Man was only a small part of the migration story (which also included a significant number of women and children and many men who shunned the flashy image), but it was this image that prevailed. Though viewed with ambivalence, as the song indicates, Colón Man was the hero of the folk.

It was to Panama that the first migrants had gone and Panama became an embodiment of the myth of El Dorado. If it were believed that the streets of London and New York were paved with gold, it was in Panama that a man could actually get his hands on the stuff and return home draped with gold watches, gold chains, sporting gold jewellery, gold teeth, gold-capped walking sticks and umbrellas, and actual gold coins to shower on friends and relatives. The very act of travelling imbued the traveller with a quality of glamour. After the Americans took over the Canal in 1904, the American values, speech patterns, gestures and commodities the emigrant brought home, helped to contribute to the aura.

To understand the impact of Colón Man one has to understand the nature of the society that he left. Jamaica was long past its days as a rich sugar colony and bananas had not yet been developed as the new source of wealth (see BANANA TRADE). It was a colonial backwater with extremes of poverty or wealth, with few economic opportunities or social outlets and a rigid and stifling caste system based on colour. Ambitious young people literally fought to get on to the ships that were leaving for places abroad where opportunities beckoned.

Though most ended up in the most arduous jobs of ditch digging, those going were not all wage labourers. A significant number were craftsmen and professionals, including carpenters, teachers, doctors, pharmacists, ministers of religion and business people. An untold number also travelled back and forth with goods to sell, including YAM, JACKASS ROPE, RUM, sugar, and 'BUSH medicine'. They included Mary SEACOLE in the 1850s, and P.A. Benjamin with his newly invented Benjamin's Healing Oil during the US construction period and a host of other commercial travellers and HIGGLERS.

Nevertheless, the majority were poverty-stricken young people from rural areas, a significant number of whom were to die or suffer destitution abroad and never return. But those who were successful came back to be seen and admired. Claude McKay in his novel *Banana Bottom*, captured the essence of Colón Man with the character Tack Tally 'proudly wearing his decorations from Panama: gold watch and chain of three strands, and a foreign gold coin attached to it as large as a florin, a gold stick-pin with a huge blue stone, and five gold rings flashing from his fingers. He had on a fine bottle-green tweed suit with the well-creased and deep-turned pantaloons called peg-top, the coat of long points and lapels known as American style. And wherever he went he was accompanied by an admiring gang'.

Tack Tally wasn't far removed from the real life 'big swell' described by a Jamaican planter in the 1870s, who swaggered in with 'a watch and gold chain, a revolver pistol, red sash, big boots up to his knees'.

No less striking to the beholder was the appearance still later of another, now more famous, returning emigrant – Alexander BUSTAMANTE, who like the other young men of his time had gone to Latin America and elsewhere. He had been a rather wild young man when he left, but as his cousin Norman MANLEY was to recall of a visit from him in late 1922, he returned: 'Such a dandy! Oh, dressed with the most immaculate care – with all the airs and graces of a Cuban grandee. His ties matched the handkerchief in his pocket and that matched his

West Indian wedding party on the Canal Zone, 1913

socks – his hair was pomaded and he was full of airs and graces – he was a real la-d-da.'

The presence of the returnees was regarded as a mixed evil by the elite, who nevertheless benefited from the money they brought or sent back and injected into the economy. Every village had a Colón Man or Cuban Grandee. He had a style of walking (called after 1904 'the Yankee strut'), of talking (the 'Yankee twang' salted with Spanish words and phrases), of dressing, and, most important, of behaviour. In its most extreme forms, this behaviour seems to have either reeked of Latin pseudo-gentility or savoured of rudeness. The most significant aspect of this behaviour was that he was no longer servile or subservient in his manner. As such he represented a challenge to existing social mores and to imperial authority, an authority that rested on repression, subordination, and subservience.

Not surprisingly, it was the people who had travelled to Panama and elsewhere and returned to their colonial island homes throughout the British WEST INDIES who were to become catalysts for change. Many were in the forefront of the social and political upheavals in the 1920s and 1930s that led to political decolonization. Many activists of the time had been forged in the crucible of American style racism (see PANAMA) and Latin revolutionary violence, as well as the racist experiences as soldiers during the First WORLD WAR. They brought back new ideas of race and class, of republicanism, of egalitarianism, of union organization, worker solidarity, all of which fused with the domestically nurtured drive for constitutional change. Many who were not activists went on to play leadership roles in community and commodity organizations. Others simply applied to business and occupations the valuable skills and discipline of work they had acquired, the new ways of thinking and getting things done. All contributed to the modernization process which, it is safe to say, would not have occurred or been substantially delayed, without this energizing force. It was the 'Colón' experience that enabled many to improve their lives, school their children and rise in society.

While many returned home, others stayed on in Latin America and contributed a strong British Antillean influence. They left an important (and often unacknowledged) legacy behind, for it was emigrants from the Anglophone Caribbean who were responsible for starting schools, churches, business and social organizations in many of the places to which they went. Those who left Jamaica at this time represented not just the Colón Man of song and legend and story. Even more than later emigrants, they were builders of their own and other societies; true agents of transformation.

[W. Brown 1975, McKay 1933, 1979, Senior 1977, 1978, 1980, Waldron 1926]

COLONIAL CHURCH UNION

An extremist organization formed on 26 January 1832, shortly after the 'Christmas Rebellion' (see SHARPE, Samuel). It was dedicated to maintaining slavery and silencing the non-conformist MISSIONARIES by destroying their churches and expelling them from the island. The actual objectives claimed were 'to defend by Constitutional means the interest of the Colony (in the maintenance of slavery), and to expose the falsehoods of the Anti-slavery Society and to uphold the Established Church'. Formed in ST ANN Parish, the CCU included the leading men of the western parishes – planters, magistrates, Anglican clergymen and MILITIA officers. The founders were Col Hilton, a planter and head of the St Ann Militia and the Revd George W. Bridges, Rector of St Ann. The renegade ANGLICANS did not have the support of the church and the clergymen involved were hostile to the new Anglican Bishop of Jamaica for his appointment of curates who were instructed to give education to the slaves.

In the CCU's brief but notorious career which lasted for a year and a half, mobs of prominent white men resorted to violence, tearing down and burning churches and rectories, physically attacking the missionaries and their families, arresting missionaries on trumped-up charges and intimidating and persecuting their followers. (See BROWN'S TOWN.) All non-conformist chapels in the parish of St Ann were destroyed, as were chapels at Salter's Hill, STEWART TOWN, LUCEA, SAVANNA-LA-MAR, and other places. Effigies of three non-conformist ministers whose chapels had also been destroyed were hung on a shaddock (GRAPEFRUIT) tree and the island's governor who dared to oppose them was burned in effigy on the streets of ST ANN'S BAY.

Though condemned by the authorities, CCU members continued their violent activities that brought fear and terror to a considerable part of the island, branches of the society being formed in most of the parishes. They had strong support from sections of the Press and the courts. Edward JORDON, the COLOURED editor of *The Watchman* was jailed for daring to speak out against slavery. The Union was broken only by the decisive action taken by the new governor, the Earl of Mulgrave in May 1833. The drama took place at Huntley Commons near Brown's Town (the regular parade ground of the St Ann Militia). Here, in front of their assembled company, the governor in his capacity as captain-general cashiered the top militia officers who were active in the union and forced the others to resign their posts. Although the Union was declared an illegal organization, the agitation continued and was only quelled by the dispatch of regular troops to the parish. In 1837, the House of Assembly voted compensation for the churches destroyed and most of the non-conformist church buildings in the west date from after that time.

Ironically, the activities of the CCU might have contributed to the EMANCIPATION process, for the missionaries dispatched William KNIBB to England to lobby on their behalf. His vivid first-hand accounts of the outrages perpetrated against the slaves and missionaries added fuel to the anti-slavery debates in and out of the British parliament.

The subsequent fate of one of the leading figures in the Union, the Revd Bridges, was seen by some as retribution. Bridges, an Englishman, was a colourful figure in Jamaica for many decades, a rigorous defender of the planter class and the author of a history called *The Annals of Jamaica* (1814) and other works. His first appointment was to Manchester Parish (see MANDEVILLE RECTORY) and from 1823-37 he was rector of St Ann. His personal history after the CCU became a tragic one. In 1834 his wife abandoned him and returned to England. In 1837, from his hilltop home in St Ann's Bay, he witnessed the drowning of his four daughters and their friends when a boat capsized in the bay. After these tragedies, he locked himself up for a time, issued a Confession of Faith to his parishioners and headed for the wilds of Ontario, Canada, with his surviving child, a son. The move was inspired by his reading *The Backwoods of Canada*, by Catherine Parr Trail, an English immigrant, about her experiences as a homesteader there. Bridges claimed to have lived in a cave before building a home at Rice Lake, Ontario, and had other adventures before returning to England where he became a country curate and his son joined the navy.

Bridges seems to have repented his actions before leaving Jamaica, for he met with the QUAKER abolitionist Joseph Sturge when he visited the island and presented him with a copy of his book. He inscribed on the flyleaf: 'The unworthy author in presenting this work to Joseph Sturge hopes that he may be allowed to solicit his prayers for one under the heavy hand of an offended God – and to subscribe himself his afflicted friend Geo W. Bridges. Jamaica 25th Feb., 1837.'

[Henderson 1931, Olivier 1936, Wright and White 1969]

COLOUREDS

In the plantation era, the official designation for a section of the population who were the progeny of white masters and black slaves. (See SLAVERY, SUGAR PLANTATION.) Some remained slaves all their lives, but those who gained their freedom were known as 'Free Coloureds' or 'Free Persons of Colour', a class whose status was between masters and slaves.

Although the free coloureds could work for themselves and own property (including slaves) they could not vote or hold office and were, like the free blacks, hampered in their civil liberties, such as having to travel with a certificate of freedom. The free coloureds nevertheless had opportunities for advancement denied the black and coloured slaves, and as a class they became increasingly wealthy and powerful. They came to own land, including many of the PIMENTO and COFFEE estates, and others of their number became successful businessmen and educated professionals.

Civil rights were gradually denied as the free coloureds grew in numbers and in wealth. There was a tendency for white elite fathers to leave property to their coloured offspring but legislation was passed to limit the amount of property they could inherit.

By 1820 the coloureds were powerful enough to form a secret society through which to carry on the struggle for equal rights. Leading lights were Richard Hill, Robert Osborne and Edward JORDON, who was proprietor of the free coloured newspaper *The Watchman* started in 1829. In 1830, the free coloured and free blacks gained full equality with whites with the passage of an act abolishing all legal discrimination on the grounds of colour. By this time the free coloureds outnumbered the white population, who feared that they would otherwise join with the slaves and incite revolt.

Once they had won their own battle, men like Osborne and Jordon became part of the anti-slavery struggle, Jordon himself being imprisoned for sedition in the wake of the 1831-32 rebellion (see SHARPE, Samuel). Later, a free coloured, George William GORDON, led the struggle in Parliament for the rights of the free black population in the post-EMANCIPATION years, which culminated in the MORANT BAY REBELLION and his execution.

Race relations (and the definition of 'coloured') during slavery were complex, and are perhaps best explained by historian Barry Higman in his book, *Slave Population and Economy in Jamaica 1807-1834*: 'In the United States of America all persons of African ancestry, of whatever proportion, were lumped together as 'Negro' both socially and legally. In the Hispanic American colonies, on the other hand, the range of gradations of colour and racial mixture was almost infinite. The BRITISH colonies in the Caribbean fell into an intermediate position between these two extremes. In Jamaica there were generally recognized to be four grades of colour between black and white and two between white and black.'

The child of a union between black and white was called a 'mulatto', of a mulatto and white a 'quadroon', of a quadroon and white a 'mustee' and of a mustee and white a 'musteephino'. In Jamaica the child of a musteephino and a white could legally pass as white. A child of a mulatto and a negro was a 'sambo' and that of a negro and sambo a 'negro'. With the possibilities for increased status and opportunities associated with whiteness, there was a strong desire among coloured women to 'raise the colour' by mating with men lighter than themselves. Marriages between black men and white women were rare.

Colour distinctions were maintained in the records of slaves, black slaves being classified as black or Negro, African slaves often given their 'country' designations; coloured slaves were classified as 'mulatto', 'brown' or 'yellow'. It has been estimated that 10 per cent of the slaves were

Coloured lady at the racecourse

coloured, most of them concentrated in urban areas. Many of these slaves were given privileged positions as household servants or functioned as hucksters and jobbers (see GANGS, Jobbing). Some of the free women of colour became mistresses of white men and as such used their power to enhance their status and that of their children. In time, these women came to dominate certain occupations such as hotel and tavern keeping.

Black or coloured slaves could secure their freedom through manumission by their owners or by purchasing their own freedom. Slaves who performed some essential service for the State could also be given their freedom as a reward. Coloured children were sometimes freed by their owners who happened to be their fathers, and sometimes benefited from an education and their father's estate. They were also given their father's name. Though coloureds might be educated and rise in society, colour distinctions were sharply maintained and people known to have coloured blood were not accepted into white society, J.B. Moreton in 1790 writing that 'in my opinion, Mongrels, though thirty generations distant from black blood, cannot be real whites'.

The reality though is that many of these coloured as well as white daughters of the plantocracy – 'creole heiresses' as they were called – and some of the sons were enabled by their vast wealth to marry into the British middle and upper classes. The classic Caribbean novel, *Wide Sargasso Sea* by Jean Rhys, tells the story of Bertha, the (white) Caribbean heiress who marries Mr Rochester, the hero of Charlotte Bronte's *Jane Eyre* and becomes, not 'the skeleton in the closet' that some of these alliances produced but 'the madwoman in the attic'. Thackeray's *Vanity Fair* features a coloured Kittitian heiress, Miss Swartz, who attends a select London seminary for young ladies and later marries into the aristocracy.

[Campbell 1976, Craton 1978, Heuman 1981, Higman 1976.]

COLUMBUS IN JAMAICA

Christopher Columbus 'discovered' Jamaica in 1494 on his second voyage (see DISCOVERY OF JAMAICA). But Jamaica is also the place where the explorer once spent a full year, 25 June 1503 to 29 June 1504, the longest time he stayed in one place on any of his voyages. He spent the year marooned at ST ANN'S BAY.

Columbus had first seen St Ann's Bay on his second voyage and named it Santa Gloria. Nine years later, on his fourth and last voyage, after exploring the Caribbean coast of Central America, he was hoping to make Cuba or Hispaniola with his two remaining worm-eaten and leaking ships, the *Capitana* and the *Santiago de Palos* (also called the *Bermuda*). But he was forced to put in at Santa Gloria. The boats were sailed as far as they could go into the bay and then beached side by side. The crew built thatch huts on the decks to live in.

Columbus was accompanied by his brother, Bartolomé, his young son, Ferdinand, and a crew of 113.

Columbus expected that help would be soon forthcoming from the nearby Spanish colony of Hispaniola. But he and his crew were to spend one year and five days in this location before a rescue ship arrived.

On landing, all they had to eat were oil, mouldy biscuits and vinegar. Diego Mendez, the boatswain, immediately set out to make arrangements to be supplied with food by the TAINOS living in large villages nearby, including Maima (on SEVILLE plantation just north of the GREAT HOUSE), Aguacadiba (present day Windsor) and Mellila (near present-day ANNOTTO BAY). The CACIQUES agreed to the following exchange: one CASSAVA cake for two glass beads; two Hutias (CONEY) for a lace point; large quantities of FISH or maize (CORN) for a hawk's bell (a tiny bell that was tied to the leg of a trained hunting bird in Europe and brought to the New World in large quantities for trade with the natives).

His food supply organized, Mendez fitted a CANOE he had purchased from one of the caciques with a mast and sails, and set out with six Taino paddlers and another Spaniard for Hispaniola. Forced to return, on his second attempt he was accompanied to the point of departure from the island by a Spanish force. Mendez and his crew were at sea five days and four nights, enduring many hardships before they hit the coast of Hispaniola (he was to ask for a canoe to be carved on his tombstone). Eventually he met with the governor Nicolas de Ovando (who was then pacifying the province of Xaragua, during which he burned and hanged 84 caciques, including Queen Anacaona). A sworn enemy of Columbus, Ovando refused to aid him though he did send a small ship to Jamaica that dropped off a package containing a letter of condolence, some wine and a slab of bacon. Mendez had to spend the next several months on his own trying to buy a ship to rescue Columbus, which he eventually did.

In the meantime, things were going badly in Jamaica. The Tainos were refusing to supply more food, for they found that satisfying the huge appetites of Europeans was more than they had bargained for. Columbus himself was confined to bed with illness (believed to be arthritis). Sickness broke out among the crew. Soon, there was open revolt. Led by the Porras brothers, 50 of the crew mutinied, seized canoes and provisions and set out to reach Hispaniola on their own. They failed and were forced to return to the island where they went on a rampage, brutalizing, raping and killing the Tainos, who retaliated by cutting off Columbus' food supply. To bring them back in line, Columbus interpreted an eclipse of the moon as a sign of punishment from their gods for their unwillingness to help him, and frightened the caciques back into submission.

Columbus monument in St Ann

By this time, the rebels had found their way back to the St Ann's Bay area. Columbus sent messengers with offers of pardon, which they refused. The admiral's brother, Bartolomé, then set off with 50 men and engaged the rebels in a fight just west of the present Seville Great House. The Porras brothers were captured and their followers surrendered. All were brought back to the ship where Columbus pardoned them, though the ringleaders were confined aboard ship. In June 1504, the rescue ship organized by Mendez finally arrived and took Columbus and the surviving crew, about 100 men, off the island. In November 1504 Columbus returned to Spain, dying there in 1506. His son and heir, Diego Colón, in 1509 sent the first Spanish governor, Juan de Esquivel, to establish a city on the site where Columbus had his enforced sojourn. (See, SEVILLE, New.)

Work has been underway for some time to locate the remains of the two ships of Columbus, beached at St Ann's Bay over 500 years ago.
[Aarons 1983-84, Goodwin 1946]

CONCH *(Strombus gigas)*
Large shell fish (pronounced 'konck' in Jamaica) which from the earliest settlement of CARIBBEAN

islands, provided food from its flesh and from its attractive pearlescent shell, utensils, weapons, and MUSICAL INSTRUMENTS. So useful was the conch to the CIBONEYS, the first inhabitants of the Greater Antilles that we know of, that theirs has been described by archaeologists as a 'conch-shell culture'. They had virtually no other tools or equipment but those they fashioned in a crude way from conch shells – axes, drinking cups and vessels. The people who succeeded them, the TAINOS, also made extensive use of the conch for food, jewellery, utensils and implements as is evidenced by its frequent occurrence in their middens (rubbish dumps unearthed by archaeologists). Tainos also used conch shells to carve representations of their ZEMIS.

The use of the conch shell as a musical horn or trumpet also dates to the Tainos, who were led into battle by warriors blowing trumpets of large conch shells. The shell was also carved into a horn (*fotuto*) which was used in special rites. Amerindian chiefs used large shell trumpets to give orders from boats to people on land or for communication between boats.

Later, the shell was to serve as the alarm for work and other activities from the earliest days of plantation SLAVERY until recent times. Workers got up at 'shell blow' and toiled or ceased labour according to its signals until (in the 20th century) shell blow was replaced by steam whistles at the sugar factories. These warning whistles are called 'kachee', the word (from American Spanish) originally applied to the conch shell (or animal horn) blown as a signal. The word in different forms survives elsewhere in the Caribbean.

In Jamaica in the old days, a blast of the shell was used to warn users on the roads when a team of mule or oxen approached with loads, and in remote areas to call villagers together or generally to sound alarms, such as fire. When the BANANA TRADE superseded SUGAR as the main economic activity, the conch shell was used to alert growers in the hills when it was time to cut the perishable fruit for shipment. Vendors who carried fresh fish from the coast at Alligator Pond up the hill to MANDEVILLE some 30km away, also used to blow a conch shell as they ran, to signal their passing to customers, their fish in trays carried on their heads or suspended in a cutacoo (see BASKET). This widespread use of the conch for signalling is immortalized in the saying: 'Trouble da come, him never blow conch shell.'

During the revolutionary wars in Haiti, the conch shell served as the principal means of communication among the slaves, as the ABENG was used by the MAROONS in Jamaica. The famous Haitian statue to 'The Unknown Maroon of St Domingue' by Albert Mangones shows the way in which the conch was blown – with the lips pressed to the hole at the base and the tip held high. The shell continues to be used in religious and secular African Caribbean rituals such as the Haitian Ra-ra, the Trinidadian Shango, among Jamaican Maroon celebrations and in JONKONNU bands. Musicians are also incorporating the shell into modern music. On Monty Alexander's *Stir It Up: The Music of Bob Marley*, for instance, one track features Steve Turre playing the conch shell.

As a decorative object, conch shell is used to outline flowerbeds in rural areas, though its rich pearly pink or peach colouring will fade in the sunlight. It also serves as a grave decoration, a usage that goes back to Africa and the shell's mystical connection with water. For this reason, many people will not have these shells inside the house. Conch flesh is also eaten, though it is not as widely available or as popular in Jamaica as in some other Caribbean islands.

[Beckwith 1929, DJE, Fewkes 1907, Lovén 1935, Stevens-Arroyo 1988]

Conch shell blown by Maroon (statue in Haiti by Albert Mangones)

CONEY

The Jamaican Hutia (*Geocapromys brownii*), locally known as the Coney, is the island's only surviving ground dwelling mammal (the only native mammals are BATS). The hutia family is limited to the West Indies, and other species are found in the Bahamas, Cuba, Hispaniola, and other islands.

Conies shelter underground in crevices and burrows, and emerge only at nights, to feed on

Coney

leaves, shoots, fruit and bark. Thus few Jamaicans have ever seen the animal in the wild.

A brown-coloured rodent, the coney was once abundant in Jamaica and a favourite food of the TAINOS. Hunting of the coney has continued down the centuries (though now illegal) and this has contributed to reduce its numbers. The introduction of the MONGOOSE has also been blamed for the reduction of coney populations. But the biggest threat to their existence in recent times has been the modernization process, as more and more of their habitat has been encroached upon by expanding towns and cities and the clearing of forests for cultivation.

The animal now seems to be confined to a few forests, its strongholds include WORTHY PARK hills in ST CATHERINE Parish, HELLSHIRE HILLS, and John Crow Mountains.

In recent years, coneys have been successfully bred in captivity at the Jersey Wildlife Preservation Trust (on Jersey, Channel Islands). Coupled with recent studies of coneys in their native environment, this has enabled scientists to build up a picture of the biology and behaviour of these animals. Based on this research, we know that coneys are highly social creatures, will live in family groups, love close physical contact with each other, are long lived, have small litters (not more than three) but produce young that are born in an advanced stage of development. The knowledge gained about the coney will no doubt help in planning strategies to ensure its survival, and hopefully give Jamaicans greater understanding and appreciation of this link with the past.

[Oliver 1983, Wilkins 1991]

CONGO

'Congo' is an omnibus term for many ethnic groups of West Central Africans from the extensive Congo river basin who were forcibly brought to the island as slaves during the plantation era and as free people during the post-EMANCIPATION period (see AFRICANS, indentured; SLAVERY). Kongo properly is the name given by the BaKongo to the land they occupied which was the Kingdom of the Kongo before 1200 and up to 1702. This area in modern times includes Congo (Brazzaville), Republic of Congo and Angola. Although in Cuba and Haiti, Congo were highly valued as domestic slaves, in some other Caribbean territories including Jamaica, they were looked down upon during slavery, stereotyped as backward and stupid. However, they were very influential in the musical sphere, as regards rhythm, instruments and DANCE. They have also impacted the religious sphere, and arrivals in the 19th century are believed to have heavily influenced such practices as KUMINA and TAMBU.

The expression 'congosaw' or 'konkosaw' for a tall tale or 'sweet mouth', is not derived from 'Congo' but from a Twi word meaning falsehood, deceit or hypocrisy.

[DJE, Patterson 1973, Schuler 1980]

CONSTANT SPRING

Busy suburban centre in ST ANDREW Parish that takes its name from a SUGAR plantation through which ran a reliable spring which still exists. The plantation was first settled by Col Archbould, who had come with the English Army in 1655 at the same time as Richard HOPE (See CAPTURE OF JAMAICA.) Col Archbould's first crop was indigo, but he soon switched to sugar, and Constant Spring continued as a sugar estate until the late 19th century.

In 1770 the then owner, Daniel Moore, got permission to bring water to irrigate his property from the WAG WATER RIVER. This water was carried by a tunnel through the mountain and through an aqueduct that still forms part of the CORPORATE AREA water supply system.

Immaculate Conception High School, one of the leading girls' schools, is housed in what was the main building of the Constant Spring Hotel that was built in 1888, one of the first large hotels in the island. The school is run by the ROMAN CATHOLIC Franciscan Sisters who opened their first school on East Queen Street in 1857. They later moved to Duke Street but those premises were destroyed by fire in 1937. They bought the old hotel from the government of Jamaica and established Immaculate there in 1940.

Two early literary works by foreign visitors are set in Constant Spring: *The Captain's Story*, or *Jamaica Sixty Years Since* (1880) by Captain Brooke-Knight, which describes the estate in the 1830s, and *A Study in Colour* by 'Alice Spinner' [Augusta Zelia Fraser] (1894), a guest at the hotel.

[Cundall 1915, Osborne 1988]

CONUCO
TAINO name for their agricultural plots in which seeds and cuttings were planted in mounds – a practice followed by Jamaican farmers, who still make 'hills' for root crops such as CASSAVA and YAM. The name as *cunucu* has persisted in the Dutch Leeward Islands to describe the flat countryside and during SLAVERY was applied to the slave's plot of land (equivalent to the PROVISION GROUND in Jamaica).
[Gastmann 1978]

COOLIE PLUM see APPLE

COOPER
The cooper – as a barrel-maker is called – was an important skilled worker when SUGAR and RUM were shipped in hogsheads and puncheons that were made on each SUGAR PLANTATION. A large estate such as WORTHY PARK, which made its own barrels, produced 500 hogsheads of sugar and 300 puncheons of rum per year. Such an estate could have up to six skilled coopers; they were among the most highly valued slaves. Each served a long apprenticeship, graduating from making hogsheads to puncheons. A practised cooper was expected to make between 3-4 barrels a week.

Some estates brought in 'shook' or broken down barrels that were assembled as needed. Others were made from scratch, requiring the greatest skill to make the barrels watertight. Staves had to be split from CEDAR logs, which were shaped with adzes, draw knives and spoke-shaves while held in a vize. The flat heading was shaped and fitted with pins and binding rope. With the help of the BLACKSMITH, four riveted iron hoops were slipped on while red-hot, constricting the joints watertight as they cooled.

Coopers, like other craftsmen, were among those who found little employment in the post-EMANCIPATION period with the failure of many sugar estates, and they were among the earliest emigrants when opportunities opened up elsewhere in the mid-19th century (see COLÓN MAN).
[Craton 1978]

Present-day coopers at work making rum barrels — Appleton Estate

COPPER
Metal that has been mined in Jamaica several times in the past. For instance, Edward Long claimed that the bells that hung in the SPANISH church in St Jago (SPANISH TOWN) when the English took the island, had been cast of copper produced in Jamaica. Unique TAINO copper ingots were taken from Jamaica by German archaeologists Reichard and Bastien in 1937, and can be found at the Museum of Folk Culture in Berlin. The prized Taino ornament called GUANÍN, which was worn by the CACIQUE, was made from an alloy of gold and copper.

The most important copper deposits occur in upper CLARENDON and ST CATHERINE Parishes, as well as in PORTLAND and ST ANDREW and a number of mines have been worked in these areas in the past. The Charing Cross Company north east of MAY PEN in Clarendon shipped 207t of copper ore to Liverpool in 1857. Copper mines have also been worked south of PORT ANTONIO, Portland parish, by the Rio Grande Mining Company which shipped the ore from here before the American Civil War. The Mount Vernon Mine, south-east of Good Hope Mountain in St Andrew parish, has also been worked.

The RIO COBRE (i.e. Copper River) was so named by the Spaniards, but whether it has any connection with the metal is not known. It is more likely that the river was so called from the colour of the silt-laden stream when in flood. The Spaniards were on the whole disappointed by the lack of precious metals in Jamaica, which contributed to their failure to develop the island.

However, LEGENDS about the existence of such metals persisted, and in the 1850s, Jamaica had a 'copper rush'. It occurred at the same time as the California, Alaska and Australian gold rushes and though on a minute scale compared to these, offered no less in individual excitement.

As part of the international fever, fresh rumours began to circulate about the island's mineral wealth. Many normally sane and serious persons took to the hills to prospect for GOLD, iron, lead and, most of all, copper. A spate of companies was formed with local, English and American capital. According to Douglas Hall, at one time shares in the Job's Hill Mines in ST MARY Parish sold at a premium of £18 on the London Stock Exchange. Miners were imported from England to work the copper mines here. However, a proper mining survey of the island was not completed until the 1860s. This showed that although rich copper veins exist in Jamaica they are so located that profitable extraction is not feasible. By the time these facts were known, the prospectors, disappointed in their search for quick riches, had long departed.

[G.A. Aarons personal communication, GOJ 1973, Hall 1959, Porter 1990]

CORAL

Beaches of white coral sands and coral reefs offshore are part of Jamaica's attraction, but only now is the importance of the living creatures responsible for such beauty being recognized. Coral reefs are constructions that are built up slowly over a long period of time by living organisms but can be quickly destroyed, hence the need for protective measures.

A coral is a sedentary marine invertebrate that belongs to the phylum Coelenterata (pronounced see-len-terata). A coral colony consists of individual polyps that live within a protective skeleton that they secrete. The skeleton of stony or true corals is made up of pure calcium carbonate (LIMESTONE) and forms the large structures we know as coral reefs.

Corals feed on minute plankton brought by currents, and are found in tropical and sub-tropical regions, usually where the water is no colder than $20°C$.

The size of each coral polyp, as the individual is called, varies from a pinhead to a foot. Coral polyps have the ability to extract calcium from the water and simultaneously absorb carbon dioxide; in time these elements are combined and deposited as a protective limestone container each creature erects to live in, consisting of an oral cavity surrounded by tentacles at the top.

Coral polyps form colonies consisting of thousands of individuals, and as they die they leave behind their skeletons; new polyps continue to grow on top. Polyps can branch and form other polyps, eventually becoming a large structure of tree-like branching colonies or massive domes. Coral reefs are built up in this way, from billions of polyps over time. In the tropical Atlantic and elsewhere, thousands of islands have been created by constant growth of

Coral colony (left) and coral polyps (below)

coral polyps, e.g. Bahamas, Bermuda, and the Florida Keys.

Although Jamaica is not a coral island (i.e. built up exclusively from the activities of corals), examples of all kinds of coral are found here, and part of the island's beauty and attraction derives from their presence. Forty-three species of reef-building corals have been found in the coral reefs and sea gardens off the coast, with great variation in shape and size. As one naturalist has said, 'the corals are artists, their shelter, sculptures'.

The coral reefs are not only a unique marine attraction for tourists and locals alike, they are a vital element in the coastal environment. FISH and marine creatures in the reefs provide a living for fishermen; collectors in the past have enjoyed acquiring species of coral, craftsmen have fashioned jewellery and other objects from the beautiful black coral. Now there's a ban on the sale of both black and white coral, and other activities on the reef are being monitored because Jamaica's coral is fast disappearing. Protection of the reefs is one of the objectives of the Montego Bay Marine Park (see NATIONAL PARKS).

As in many parts of the world, the reefs are under severe threat from the growing activities of man and from natural disasters. The rate at which this vital natural resource is vanishing is alarming, on Jamaica's north coast, researchers in DISCOVERY BAY have measured a 60 per cent decline in living coral cover between 1980-83 alone.

The presence of the living coral is vital because the reefs provide a home for plants and animals, sand for the beaches and protection of the beaches from erosion by waves.
[Bruckner 1993, Mendes 1994]

CORATOE see AGAVE

CORN
Referred to simply as corn, both maize ('Indian Corn') and what is called Guinea Corn (sorghum) have been cultivated in Jamaica, and formerly played a significant role in the diet and domestic life of the countryman. With pre-packaged cornmeal and other substitutes now widely available, homegrown corn is not as important as it was in the past in feeding both humans and animals.

Maize (*Zea mays*) is a New World crop, unknown outside the Americas before COLUMBUS' arrival; today it is one of the world's four most important food plants. Next to CASSAVA or yuca, maize was the most important crop for the TAINOS, whose word *mahiz* made it into European languages; by the middle of the 16th century it had superseded cassava as the most important food crop in Hispaniola.

Maize in Jamaica yields two or three crops per year and can be planted at any time if the soil is moist. As a quick cash crop, it is sometimes planted between slower growing crops, such as YAMS. Guinea corn is usually planted in September and yields only one crop – in January – but it gives at least twice the yield of Indian corn. Guinea corn grains are mottled in colour while maize grains are a uniform yellow.

Guinea corn is an Old World crop; under the name millet or sorghum it was a staple of sub-Saharan Africa for over a thousand years. The cereal was called Guinea Corn in the New World, having been brought from Africa as provisioning for the slave ships, as the favourite article of diet of Africans from what were called the Slave Coast and the Gold Coast. The cereal has continued to be of significant nutritive and ritual value to their descendants in the CARIBBEAN.

One of the few songs which has come down to us from the days of SLAVERY (recorded in 1797) celebrates the Guinea corn and was probably sung as a WORK SONG, with a call and response pattern:

Guinea Corn, I long to see you
Guinea Corn, I long to plant you
Guinea Corn, I long to mould you
Guinea Corn, I long to weed you
Guinea Corn, I long to hoe you
Guinea Corn, I long to top you
Guinea Corn, I long to cut you
Guinea Corn, I long to dry you
Guinea Corn, I long to beat you
Guinea Corn, I long to trash you
Guinea Corn, I long to parch you
Guinea Corn, I long to grind you
Guinea Corn, I long to turn you
Guinea Corn, I long to eat you.

Until recent times, corn was important to the small farmer because it could be easily grown and, once harvested and dried, would keep well, usually being hung up by the husks inside the kitchen or buttery. Young corn, cobs as well as green husk, could be chopped up and used in animal feed, and the easy availability of dried corn grains provided the housewife with the means to feed the chickens she invariably raised. Around the house, dried corn husk was used for stuffing mattresses in poorer homes. The dried cob was used as a pot scourer or in the LAUNDRY to scrub clothes. Corn cob dolls were made to amuse children, and the smaller cobs provided stoppers for bottles and gourds, a welcome addition in places where cork was hard to come by, though the saying warns, 'When bottle hold RUM, corn stalk get drunk'.

In former years, large quantities of corn would be grown on big properties, especially for animal feed. After the corn was reaped and dried, the grains would be scraped from the husk and stored in CROCUS bags. 'Corn shelling', which was usually held inside a large barn or storeroom, was one of the big communal events of the year. It attracted shellers from all over with the promise not only of payment but of food, drink, ANANSI STORIES, RIDDLES, songs and laughter, with everyone competing to shell the most corn. Whole families would attend.

As a cheap, healthy food that could be prepared in so many ways, corn was especially popular with the poor farmer who could easily produce his own. It can be eaten on the cob boiled or roasted, grated and made into meal, or parched and pounded into powder in a MORTAR. The fresh young corn on the cob is known as 'green corn' or 'sweet corn' and sold as such in the markets and wayside shops; the older dried corn is used for household use, animal feed and for planting.

Most rural children grew up on thick cornmeal porridge – flavoured with SUGAR, NUTMEG and CINNAMON, with milk or COCONUT milk, promoted as health-giving and consumed at breakfast and other times. A thinner gruel of usually grated green corn mixed with milk and sugar, called 'pap', was the food of babies and old people.

Cornmeal DUMPLINGS were a soup-filler and when the larder was empty of everything else, 'turn cornmeal', similar to Italian polenta, could be made from a few dried ears of corn ground into meal and mixed with hot water. The mush would be stirred or turned in a cast iron pot until it became thick. To this mixture would be added, depending on availability, seasoning such as onion, tomatoes, coconut milk or butter, and codfish, but OKRA was a required ingredient. Turn cornmeal could be dressed up or down. It developed from African dishes which were called *fufu, fungee, couscous* or *musa*; in the Eastern Caribbean, a version is known as 'coo-coo'.

Several kinds of corn puddings were also made, the most popular being DOKUNU. Corn pone was made of cornmeal, grated coconut and seasonings topped with coconut milk and baked – where no oven was available – in a covered iron pot (DUTCHY) placed on the fire, with hot coals or firesticks also placed on the top. This arrangement led to the riddle: 'Hell a bottom, hell a top, hallelujah in the middle.' Hominy (like pone, of American origin) was another popular dish, the corn grains being soaked in a lye of ashes and water to soften the skin which was removed by beating in a mortar. The hominy would be boiled with milk and sugar.

In the old days parched corn was a favourite, a quick snack food that could be prepared by anyone. Dry corn would be shelled and the grains parched in a hot pot and then pounded in a wooden mortar and sifted until it was the consistency of sand. Mixed with SALT or sugar, the dark mixture could be eaten dry or water added. It was called Brown George, Asham or Sham sham, 'asham' derived from the Twi word for 'parched and ground corn'. Parched corn ground and mixed with sugar and made into balls (sometimes coloured) provided another confection known as Coction. Nowadays, packaged asham can sometimes be purchased in supermarkets.

Among New World peoples of African descent, parched corn (without salt) was used in DEATH RITUALS, the Ashanti regarding asham (*sansam*) as special food for the spirits. Parched corn, ground and sifted, has also been used as a COFFEE substitute. In folk MEDICINE, corn silk infused in water is drunk for bedwetting and other bladder problems and for cleansing the skin.

Nowadays, a treat for travellers is to stop at roadside stands on the highways to eat boiled or roasted corn on the cob.

[DJE, Beckwith 1928, Brathwaite 1971, Dallas 1803, JAS 1954, Lovén 1935, Robertson 1990, Steward 1948, Viola and Margolis 1991]

COROCOTE
One of the 12 principal ZEMIS of the TAINOS. Corocote images were made of COTTON, and only a few examples have been recovered. This seems to have been the spirit of unbridled sexuality and male fertility; Corocote is associated with amorous escapades, having a fondness for lying with women.

[Arrom 1975, Stevens-Arroyo 1988]

COROMANTEE
Term used to describe many of the enslaved AFRICANS brought to Jamaica, mainly from the Gold Coast (present-day Ghana), who were shipped from a slave 'castle' or fort called Koromantine which was established by the English on that coast in 1651. In the literature the word is spelled in many ways, including Cromanty, Koromantee, Kromanti, etc. Although Coromantee was not a tribe or nation, it was first used to describe all the slaves shipped from that port, regardless of their origins (present-day inhabitants of the African town call it 'Kromantse'). Later it came to describe a culture group with distinct characteristics, most pronounced in Jamaica and the Guyanas, which were the colonies that received a large number of these Africans. Some colonies would not have them since they were from the warlike Akan-speaking peoples (especially Ashanti and Fanti) and were fierce, proud fighters. Many were of warrior stock, prisoners taken in the constant wars between the Akan tribes on the coast that led to the emergence of the powerful Fanti and Ashanti states. In the Guyanas and Jamaica they came to form the core of the MAROONS, and were leaders of most of the slave revolts.

In the first few decades of BRITISH rule, many Coromantee slaves came with settlers arriving from Barbados and so were already 'seasoned' to life in the West Indies. They ended up occupying the important slave posts by the time the others started to arrive and thus had a dominant position from the start.

Between 1702-76 the majority of the slaves brought in by the British were also Coromantee. However, contrary to popular belief, Coromantees did not constitute the majority of Jamaican slaves. Barry Higman indicates that over the entire history of the slave trade to Jamaica, 46 per cent of the slaves came from the Bight of Biafra (IBO) and Central Africa (CONGO). Approximately 83 per cent of the slaves entering Jamaica in the last years of the slave trade (1792-1807) were from these areas. Philip Curtin estimates that a quarter of the slaves imported during the British period (1655-1807) were Coromantee.

On the plantations the Coromantees tended to keep to themselves and were generally disliked by the other slaves. Despite their warlike disposition – they were described by Edward Long (and others) as 'haughty, ferocious and stubborn' – they were a favourite of the Jamaican planters because of their hardiness and courage. Many other European nations refused to have them because of their involvement in revolts. The incidence of slave revolts in Jamaica was particularly high between the 17th and 19th centuries, almost all of them involving 'Coromantees' or Akan-speakers.

The terms Karamanti, Kromanti or Cromanty are still preserved among the Maroons of Jamaica and Suriname, especially in reference to warrior spirits, and also refer to the secret language of the Jamaican Maroons. Katherine Dunham refers to a 'Coromantee War Dance', and there is also mention in the literature of a 'Cromanty flute' which is made from the TRUMPET TREE and, according to Lady Nugent, 'has a plaintive and melancholy sound'. She also mentions that it was played by the nose, a fact not recorded by anyone else (though a BAMBOO flute blown by the nose by the ARAWAKS of Guyana is mentioned by Roth, and one by the Suriname maroons by Stedman. Stedman, writing in the 18th century, lists a musical instrument called the 'kiemba-toetoe, or hollow reed, which is blown through the nostrils, like the nasal flute of Otaheite: it has but two holes, one at each end, the one serving to sound it, the other to be touched by the finger').

Among contemporary Maroons, the Kromanti-dance or Kromanti-play are ceremonies that revolve around possession of participants by ancestral spirits who give them power to help the living solve problems; they are different from the 'recreational style' of Maroon MUSIC and DANCES that are open to the public. Among Suriname Maroons, Kromanti is the word for the powerful magic force believed to protect warriors.

[Agorsah 1994, Bilby 1985, Curtin 1969, DJE, Dunham 1946, Herskovits 1936, Higman 1976, Long 1774, Patterson 1973, Price 1973, Stedman 1796]

CORPORATE AREA

This is the local government term for urban and suburban parts of the Parishes of KINGSTON and ST ANDREW which were amalgamated for administrative purposes in 1923 when the Kingston and St Andrew Corporation (KSAC) was created. A definition of the current boundaries of what is now called the Kingston Metropolitan Area can be found in the *Statistical Yearbook of Jamaica*, 1998. The population of this area in the 1991 census was 538,144 out of a total island population of 2,314,500.

[GOJ STATIN 1999a]

COTTA

Thick circular pad (also called catta) made of PLANTAIN leaf or cloth, about six inches in diameter, placed under loads carried on the head. To cut a cotta in two was a symbol of the breaking of a marriage or partnership.

COTTON (*Gossypium sp.*)

One of the staple commodities of Jamaica from the time of the TAINOS, now hardly cultivated; the occasional plant can still be seen growing wild in the dry southern plains. A member of the HIBISCUS family and therefore easily recognized by its flower (which is pale yellow) the dry pod bursts open to reveal the fluffy cotton of commerce. The plant which thrives on rich gravelly soil was planted in walks and yielded two crops, in May and September.

Roth recorded that the cotton would be picked, put into the sun to dry for a day or two and stored in open BASKETS; great care would be taken to keep it dry. When needed, the seeds and foreign matter would be picked out and the cotton teased out bit by bit and wound on a

Ashanti war dance drawn by 19th century missionary

spindle. The cotton was woven to make a short skirt (*nagua*) worn by the married women, ZEMIS, headbands, belts and loincloths which were worn occasionally by the men, sails for the CANOES (in the post-Columbian period), and hammocks (derived from the Taino word *hamaca*). Among the Tainos, Jamaica was noted for its cotton. The crop continued to be grown by the SPANISH settlers and, later, the English. The cotton grown in Jamaica is the variety called 'Sea island'.
[Roth 1901]

COTTON TREE (*Ceiba pentandra*)

The Cotton Tree (also known as Silk Cotton or Kapok) is a huge, majestic tree, probably the largest in Jamaica, formerly used for making dugout CANOES. A canoe 29m x 2.4m was reported by COLUMBUS from Jamaica.

The COTTON Tree is regarded as a sacred tree in both Africa and the Americas, a symbol of long life and continuity, traditionally held in awe and reverence as the dwelling place of spirits. The Lokono ARAWAKS of Guyana call it the *komaka* and say that living creatures were formed from its scattered twigs and bark. The TAINOS of the islands referred to it as *guasina*, meaning 'the dwelling place of spirits'. It is also regarded as sacred by the Mayas of Guatemala and is the national tree of that country. The Ashanti of Ghana call it the 'God tree', a name by which it is also known in Jamaica. MYAL ceremonies were traditionally conducted around the Cotton Tree, and specific types of DUPPIES such as WHOOPING BOY are said to dwell at its roots. 'Even in a state of decay', we are told, 'it is an object of . . . superstitious fears'. In former times before a Cotton Tree was cut down, permission would be asked of the spirit believed to dwell within the tree and an offering made; RUM would also be poured. There are many stories of mishaps occurring to people who cut even a limb of the tree before taking such precautions.

Its girth and height (up to 40m high) make the Cotton Tree an imposing and conspicuous element on the landscape wherever it grows. From its huge, straight trunk, it sends out spurs in all directions; its crown rises high into the air above surrounding trees. Thus it can be seen for miles around and from far out at sea; indeed, Cotton Trees used to serve as markers for sailors. The tree harbours on its branches a great variety of wild life – ORCHIDS, WILD PINES, parasites, birds' nests, creepers – which contribute to its almost supernatural appearance.

Some Cotton Trees in Jamaica have been notable for their age and size, one of which was the so-called TOM CRINGLE'S COTTON TREE on the Spanish Town Road at FERRY on the border of ST ANDREW and ST CATHERINE parishes. A visitor in 1850 described his encounter with another giant, this one at YALLAHS, ST THOMAS Parish, which was claimed to be the largest in the island:

'Many of its branches are as large as good sized English oaks and elms, as are also its roots which rise above the ground and run on the earth's surface. I paced the ground under its branches that made a diameter of 240 feet [73m], and of course a circumference of more than 800 feet [248m]. We measured its trunks, four feet [1.2 m] from the ground by a string, which encompassed the buttresses as well as the trunk itself, and found it 72 feet [22m].'

The fact that these trees will live for hundreds of years contributes not only to their size but to their legendary nature. It was one of those giants that came to be called HALF WAY TREE, the name of the capital of St Andrew Parish. The Cotton Tree growing within FORT CHARLES at PORT ROYAL is at least 300 years old; its roots extend beneath the foundations of the 1699-1702 structure. The historic treaty between CUDJOE of the MAROONS and Colonel Guthrie on behalf of the English forces was signed 'and all the solemnities attending it' under a large Cotton Tree growing in the middle of Maroon Town at the entrance of (what was later called) Guthrie's Defile. 'The tree was ever after called Cudjoe's tree, and held in great veneration', we are told.

Unlike most tropical trees, the Cotton Tree sheds its leaves and for several months presents a bare appearance. In spring, the creamy-white flowers appear, closely followed by the young leaves. Next come the green pods which eventually ripen and burst, revealing the silk

Cotton Tree

cotton or kapok of commerce. It was once widely used for stuffing pillows and upholstery. The silky creamy cotton (enclosing black seeds) will often be seen floating in the vicinity of the tree before descending to earth. Cotton from the Silk-cotton Tree as well as from the Sea-island COTTON shrub was spun into cloth by the Tainos.

Associated with the tree is the giant beetle *Euchroma gigantea* whose larvae feed exclusively on its bark.

[Adams 1972, Banbury 1894, Candler 1850, DJE, Rashford 1985]

COW see CATTLE

COW IN FOLKLORE

Numerous PROVERBS attest to the popularity of 'cow' in folk culture – the term applied to CATTLE in general. The importance of minding one's business is frequently expressed in the saying 'You come to drink milk, you don't come to count cow', the declining powers of old age as 'Bull old, you take plantain bark tie him', while respect for elders is taught by, 'Ol'cow a pasture a bull mumma', or 'Don't mock maugre cow, a bull mumma'. Perhaps a lesson in genetics is passed on in 'You can't hate the mother and love the calf'.

Because of their habit of sitting quietly and chewing their cud, cows are perceived as 'deep' or symbols of prudence and wisdom, hence the saying: 'Is not for want of tongue mek cow no talk. Them read them law book inna them belly', the law-book being its tripe, known in England as its 'leaves'.

The behaviour of cows, like that of BIRDS and other animals, can give TOKENS or warnings of death, hence the superstitious belief in the 'talking cow' – particular animals that are known to give the sign by their extraordinary vocal behaviour. One of Frank Cundall's informants also told him that 'If cows surround a bull lowing sadly while the bull ploughs the earth with its horns, it is an omen of death'.

Among creatures of LEGEND, the ROLLING CALF was once the most feared. Cows also feature in several folktales – see Dance 1985 and Tanna 1984.

COWEN, Sir Frederic Hyman (1852-1935)

Musical composer who was born in Jamaica. A plaque on the wall at 90 Duke Street (corner of Charles Street) KINGSTON marks it as his birthplace. Sir Frederic was taken at an early age to London where his father became treasurer of Her Majesty's and Drury Lane Theatres. The young Cowen was a musical prodigy, composing a waltz at age 6, an operetta at 8, and a symphony at 17. He later gained fame as composer and conductor and received many honours in his lifetime, including a knighthood in 1911. In 1929 he was honoured by the INSTITUTE OF JAMAICA while on a visit to the island. For many years, a music store run by Astley Clerk on King Street, Kingston was called 'Cowen's Music Rooms' in his honour. Some recent recordings have been issued in England of Cowen's music.

Another famous resident at 90 Duke Street was Emperor Faustin I of Haiti, better known as Soulouque who was exiled in 1858 and lived in Kingston for some time. He was one of several Haitian ex-presidents who sought exile in Jamaica at one time or another. (See also GEFFRARD Place.)

[Andrade 1941, Jacobs 1976]

COWITCH

The name is applied to several plants with one characteristic – they have parts covered with stinging hairs that inject an acid in the skin when touched, causing great itching and discomfort – similar to stinging nettle. One (*Mucuna pruriens*) is a twining vine, common in cultivations, thickets, and woodlands from 75 to 750m, whose leaves and brown beans are covered with stinging hairs. In another, the stiff stinging hairs occur over the entire plant while in a third, they are confined to the margins of the leaves.

Cowitch

[Adams 1971, 1972, Hawkes and Sutton 1974]

COYABA

Coyaba or *Coaybay* was the name given by the TAINOS to their residence after death. The lord of this land was MAQUETAURIE GUAYABA (Lord of GUAVA) for the dead were believed to come out at night and feast on this fruit. The Tainos' afterlife offered neither punishment nor reward, it was simply another form of living. So the spirits at nights arranged feasts, AREITOS, danced, sang and enjoyed themselves till dawn when they returned to their hiding places in the forest. The

Taino dead were called *opía* and like DUPPIES today, were much feared; people did not walk about at nights if they could help it.
[Arrom 1975]

CRAB
Crabs used to be plentiful and much consumed. Especially favoured was the land crab of the Antilles (*Gecarcinus ruricola*) which, as Black Crab or Mountain Crab, was a culinary delicacy, favourably mentioned in chronicles of plantation life including Lady Nugent's *Journal*. When fat and in a perfect state they were said to be 'of surpassing flavour and delicacy'. These crabs live in the mountains far from the sea but go to the water once a year in March or April to spawn or lay their eggs. This practice gave rise to perhaps some exaggeration as to their numbers and habits, R.C. Dallas saying they marched in a body of 'some millions at a time'. It was claimed that they marched in a direct line and would crawl over any obstacle in their path, attempting to scale even houses. Such marching crabs were still a remarkable sight some forty to fifty years ago.

Also popular is a white land crab (*Cardisoma guanhumi*) which is edible. During the rainy season many people still go out hunting for crabs, a favourite dish being stuffed crab back, that is, seasoning the cooked crab meat, putting it back into the shell, and baking it. Once caught, crabs are usually kept alive for several days, fed on pepper leaves and cornmeal to cleanse and flavour them, before being cooked.

There are many species of land crabs, occupying MANGROVE marshes, river estuaries, and streams, as well as sea crabs, though the latter are not held in as high esteem as the former.
[Dallas 1804, Facey 1993, Nugent 1839]

CRANIAL DEFORMATION
Called *bilobé*, the practice of modifying the angle of the forehead of a newborn child by binding on it a small board in oblique position was common to both TAINOS and CARIBS, the pressure forcing the cranium into the desired form, that of a high forehead. This was regarded as a sign of beauty, and was also common to the ancient Olmecs and other Meso-American cultures. Although the reasons for the practice are obscure, the Mayas, for whom maize was their

Device for flattening head (from Argentina)

staple food, are believed to have desired the shape of the forehead to resemble a CORN cob. European observers also noted that a high forehead had practical advantages for the rain forest Amerindians, making it easier to shoot arrows overhead, for example.
[Stevens-Arroyo 1988, Larousse 1987]

CREATION MYTH, Taino
The TAINO creation story tells of two pairs of twin brothers who, at the end of a divine journey in which they acquired the arts of civilization – fire, CASSAVA and TOBACCO – built a house and mated with Turtle Woman, engendering the human race. The chief of the brothers was Deminán. It is one of the myths that was told to Friar Ramón PANÉ in Hispaniola in the first decade of the 16th century.
[Arrom 1975, Stevens-Arroyo 1988]

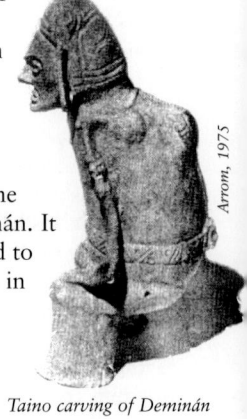

Taino carving of Deminán

CREOLE
Term used in the English-speaking CARIBBEAN in several different senses. Historically, it referred to persons born in the colonies and was originally used by European white colonists to refer to themselves, the word coming from the Spanish *criollo* meaning, 'a committed settler'. It was also used by New World blacks to distinguish themselves from those born in Africa ('Guinea born') and to describe animals bred in the island, e.g. creole CATTLE, to distinguish them from the imported.

Today, creole is also used to refer to the distinct culture that has evolved in the former plantation societies of the Caribbean. A leading exponent of the creole society model of Caribbean society is the poet and historian Kamau Brathwaite.

The word is also used to describe the distinct speech that has evolved in the islands. There is a Francophone creole that is spoken in Haiti, Guadeloupe, Martinique, St Lucia and Dominica. In the last two, it shares places with an Anglophone creole that is spoken in all the former BRITISH colonies. (See LANGUAGE.)
[Brathwaite 1971, 1974, DCEU, Shepherd and Richards 1998]

CRICKET
Game universally played in the Commonwealth CARIBBEAN though its popularity in Jamaica has been somewhat eroded in recent years by the rise of FOOTBALL and the attraction of games such as

basketball, through the influence of American television. Nevertheless, productivity drops and absenteeism continues to be rife during international cricket matches, and cricket commentary blares from every radio. Up to 1960 in Barbados, where cricket is described as a religion, business closed and Parliament adjourned when international teams came to town.

For many, cricket is not simply a game but a potent symbol of the struggle by the black man for recognition, enacted on the sports field. In recent years, many scholars have written on the sociological aspects of the game, starting with C.L.R. James's classic, *Beyond a Boundary*. Jamaica's former Prime Minister Michael Manley also published a book on the game and historian Hilary Beckles has produced several volumes, to name a few authors. The fortunes of West Indies cricket on the international scene might wax and wane, but cricket writing is a growth industry.

A quintessentially English game from the 16th century, cricket remained firmly associated with that country and, later, with the larger colonies such as India and Australia, being seen as an extension of the British Raj.

Cricket became popular in Jamaica and the rest of the WEST INDIES during the Victorian era. At first played exclusively by Englishmen in the colonies it was quickly taken up by the non-white populations, though until the late 19th century it remained a game that was as segregated as the rest of society. The earliest cricket clubs were formed by white plantation owners and non-whites were excluded. This led to the establishment by coloured and black Jamaicans of their own clubs, though over time, such barriers were eroded.

The first clubs were rural: the ST JAGO, VERE and CLARENDON Cricket Clubs were established by the white plantocracy in 1857. The first urban club was the Kingston Cricket Club formed in 1863 by a group of young men who had as their first patron governor Edward Eyre, later the villain of the MORANT BAY REBELLION. They first met at KINGSTON RACE COURSE then moved to rented premises at Sabina Park Pen in 1880. Since that time, Sabina Park has been developed as one of the foremost cricket grounds in the West Indies. Other urban clubs soon followed: Kensington, founded in 1878, Melbourne in 1892, Garrison Club at UP PARK CAMP and Lucas in 1898, and St George's in the 1890s, Clovelly and Railway around the turn of the century. Lucas was named after R. Slade Lucas, the first Englishman to bring a team to Jamaica (in 1895) and was started by a hackney carriage driver named David Ellington.

For many years cricket was more of a social activity than anything else, but it became firmly established as a sport by 1900. Cricket was taught in exclusive boys' schools as a tool to inculcate the noble values of English culture, including fair play and gentlemanly conduct. Nevertheless, the increasing success of blacks in the game mirrored the other changes that were taking place in Caribbean society.

According to Beckles, West Indian cricket by the end of the 19th century 'had been transformed from a minority elite "English" sport into the region's first expression of popular mass culture. By the mid century it had broken out of the mould represented by garrisoned English military men, and had spread into the plantations, villages and towns of the colonies. In so doing, cricket traversed a wide geographical space and slowly embraced all social classes and races in ways never before witnessed in the region'.

West Indians not only played the game, they transformed it, the players bringing style, speed and elegance, the crowds substituting carnival spree for English reticence, bringing 'spectator theatre and participatory festiveness to bear upon the idealization of the physical and artistic elements of cricket'. Successful cricketers became heroes.

Jamaican teams took part in territorial competitions from the late 19th century, and in 1896 Jamaicans were part of a West Indies team that toured Canada and the USA (cricket then being a Canadian national sport). Before the First WORLD WAR, various English sides visited the West Indies, and in 1906 and 1923 West Indian sides played first class matches in England. The West Indies Cricket Board of Control, the sport's governing body, was formed in 1926 and the West Indies team played its first Test match in 1928 against England and in 1930-31 toured Australia. In these formative years of

Jamaican cricket greats – George Headley (L) and Collie Smith

West Indian cricket between 1928 and 1939, Jamaican George Headley became the island's first cricket hero and one of the greatest batsmen in the world. He was the first man to score two centuries in one test match at Lord's in London, the world centre of the sport.

It was the success of men such as Headley and the Trinidadian Learie Constantine (who was an outstanding cricketer between 1923 and 1939 and ended up as the first fully black member of the British House of Lords) that inspired young men of all classes to take up the game and reap the professional and monetary rewards. Constantine was also the first of several outstanding West Indian cricketers to be knighted by the Queen.

The fortunes of the West Indies have waxed and waned, a high point being the years 1962-67 when the team ranked no. 1 in the world of Test cricket. In the 1950s cricket was dominated by the 'Three Ws' – batsmen Frank Worrell, Clyde Walcott and Everton Weekes (all Barbadians). The sport's best all-rounder, Garfield Sobers, also Barbadian, recorded his first triumph in 1958 at Sabina Park with the highest individual score then made in Test Cricket, 365 runs, only one of several world records that have been made at the historic grounds. More recently, in April 2000, fans at Sabina had the thrill of witnessing Jamaican Courtney Walsh beat the previous world record as the most prolific wicket-taker in Test cricket history. Among the other outstanding cricketers produced by Jamaica is Michael Holding, once the no.1 fast bowler in the world. In 2000, as many as five Jamaicans played on the Test team at the same time, including Walsh and team captain Jimmy Adams.

The West Indies cricket team has continued to be one of the few links between the countries of the Anglophone Caribbean. Cricket between the Caribbean territories (including Guyana) got a boost in 1965-66 with the introduction of the Shell Shield tournament (now the Red Stripe Cup tournament).

Although the formal game of cricket requires prescribed clothing and equipment, lack of these has not prevented anyone from playing the game. Algernon Aspinall, writing in 1898, noted that 'It is quite common to see tiny black children innocent of clothing indulging in it with all the assurance of their elders, using, however, SUGAR canes for wickets, a COCONUT palm leaf for a bat and whatever they can lay hands on for a ball'; such improvisations continue to the present day. One attraction of cricket is that it can be played almost anywhere, from city lanes to country yards to international venues, and the sport has helped to foster community spirit, teams existing at all levels of the society. Although a game associated with men, cricket has also for a long time been played by women: the first women's cricket match was played in England in 1745. A Jamaica women's team has played in regional competitions since the 1980s.

To the uninitiated, cricket is incomprehensible, and the terms used in the game – 'silly mid-off', 'fine leg', 'bowl a maiden over', 'googly' or 'bowled for a duck' – are a cause of great hilarity to outsiders. But cricket can best be understood if it is seen as a cultural and social ritual. International matches run from 10:30am to 5:30pm each day for up to five straight days (eight days in the past) and even then might end in a draw. The players break each day for lunch and tea and the spectators must fuel themselves, hence the rituals of picnic baskets and afternoon tea. When the action is sluggish, diversion is mandatory. Limited overs, one-day cricket matches have become popular universally over the last 30 years. The West Indies team won the first two One Day World Cups in 1975 and 1979 and reached the finals of the third in 1983. The West Indies is also scheduled to host the ninth World Cup in 2007.

Cricketers can also laugh at themselves, as in this famous description of the game attributed to an English cricket club:

'You have two sides, one out in the

Courtney Walsh

Michael Holding

field and one in. Each man that's in the side that's in, goes out and when he's out he comes in and the next man goes in until he's out. When they are all out the side that's out comes in and the side that's been in goes out and tries to get those coming in out. Sometimes you get men still in and not out. When both sides have been in and out including the not outs, that's the end of the game.'

Howzat!

[Arlott 1975, Beckles 1998, Carnegie 1983, Cozier 1995, Delapenha 1993, Manley 1995, Soares 1989]

CROCODILE *(Crocodylus acutus)*

The American Crocodile is a reptile found in coastal wetlands of tropical America, Florida, the Cayman Islands, Cuba, and Hispaniola as well as Jamaica where it lives in low-lying swampy areas. In the literature and popular speech it is often referred to as an alligator, which it resembles but which does not occur on the island. The chief superficial difference between the two is that the alligator has a short head with a blunt flat snout while the crocodile has a long tapering snout.

The confusion between the two creatures goes way back in Jamaica's history, for one of the earliest laws decreed that the island's COAT OF ARMS should have an alligator for its crest. The alligator is also enshrined in tales, sayings, and PROVERBS, such as 'nuh cuss alligator long mout' till yu cross river', and in the place name Alligator Pond (MANCHESTER Parish). Milne-Home (1890) recorded that an alligator tooth was worn as a CHARM, supposedly to prevent one from seeing DUPPIES and to avert bad luck in love affairs.

Crocodiles are found mainly in the MANGROVE swamps of the south coast and the BLACK RIVER, where they can be seen by visitors on boat tours. Their main diet is fish. They will lie quite still for long periods with only their eyes and nostrils showing and can also capture unwary BIRDS and mammals. They were once numerous but over the years have been much reduced in numbers through illegal hunting and loss of habitat. Since 1971, they have been protected by the wildlife law. They are potentially dangerous, and may attack if they are provoked, especially at their nesting sites.

Crocodiles are among the world's oldest living animals: they coexisted with the dinosaurs. However, while dinosaurs and others have become extinct, the crocodile continues to survive, providing one of the few remaining links with our earlier past.

CROCUS BAG

Sack made of unbleached jute, formerly much used for storing and shipping crops such as PIMENTO, COFFEE, CORN, and SUGAR. The bags came with a different coloured vertical stripe to denote the size of each and so they were known as 'blue seam', 'red seam', etc. When filled, the open side would be sewn up so the bags could be stacked and transported. Crocus bags are still used for transporting and displaying goods in the market and in the GANJA trade. They are also used by householders for a wide variety of purposes.

The DCEU suggests that the word probably derives from *corchorus* (the shortened form of the botanical name for the jute plant, *Corchorus capsularis* or *C. olitorius*). It was used in the plantation era in ordering this merchandise from India before the Hindi word jute replaced it in English in the mid-18th century.

[DCEU]

CROPOVER

The term that is common throughout the CARIBBEAN for the end of the SUGAR CANE harvest (see SEASON) and the celebrations attached to it; in earlier times it was also called Harvest Home from the English celebration attached to bringing in the last of the harvested CORN.

During SLAVERY, Cropover marked one of the main seasonal FESTIVALS. With the cutting of the last canes on each plantation (often with a contest between cutters to see who would cut the last), there would be general merriment as flags were displayed in the fields. In some accounts, the slaves would all then gather in the boiling house and DANCE to the sound of the GOOMBAY. The stores were opened by the overseer and special rations handed out: each slave got provisions of salt FISH, sugar, RUM and santa (a mixture of rum and fruit juice).

Cropover

It was a time of celebration for the masters too, as the overseer would be visited by the neighbouring whites to celebrate in feasting. Some time in the evening the overseer would send to the slave village for the fiddlers, a signal to the slaves – now dressed in their finery – to run in a body to the GREAT HOUSE. The fiddlers would strike up and black and white would dance together till suppertime, when the whites returned to the dining room, leaving the hall to the slaves where they would continue dancing till morning.

After EMANCIPATION, the biggest celebration became the First of August – EMANCIPATION DAY – and Cropover, which was usually held in the first week of August, became absorbed into it. However, Cropover dances and other sorts of celebrations have continued to be a feature of sugar estates till the present time.
[DJE, Patterson 1973]

CROPTIME see SEASON

CROSS ROADS
Busy centre in the CORPORATE AREA, the name Cross Roads coming into use around the beginning of the 20th century. It was formerly known as Montgomery Corner, supposedly after a Lieutenant Montgomery, who was thrown from his horse while near the west gate of UP PARK CAMP and dragged to this spot, where he died. But long before the episode of Lieutenant Montgomery, this location was a busy cross roads, and a place of public hangings. There seem to have been no buildings here for some time; it is said that at the turn of the century Cross Roads had one CHINESE shop surrounded by bush. At that time much of the area around was taken up in 'pens', i.e. townhouses of wealthy gentlemen surrounded by enough land for them to pasture their cows and HORSES. The names of many of these old pens or properties are preserved in nearby street names, among them Eureka, Swallowfield, Ripon, Worthington, Knutsford, Kensington and Retreat.

The most imposing building in Cross Roads was the Carib Cinema that was built in 1936, then one of the largest cinemas in the Caribbean. It burnt down in 1996 and was rebuilt with five cinemas within the former walls of the old Carib. The clock tower was erected by public subscription in memory of the servicemen of KINGSTON and ST ANDREW who died in the Second WORLD WAR. It was handed over to the Kingston and St Andrew Corporation in 1956.

CROTON
Decorative shrub with leaves of many interesting shapes, patterns and colours, widespread throughout Jamaica. About 15 species occur on the island, several of them endemic. Some species are aromatic and some are valued in folk MEDICINE. Jamaican crotons called 'rosemary', are true crotons in the genus *Croton*; the ornamental crotons belong to the related genus *Codiaeum*. 'Rosemary' is strongly scented when the shoots are broken and is boiled for BUSH

Crotons

baths and TEA for colds and fevers. Like the herb rosemary, it is used as a shampoo and is burnt to drive away DUPPIES.

Croton is often planted on graves in rural Jamaica, its hardiness and the fact that it will spring again after drought emphasizing its everlasting qualities. REVIVALISTS also consider the croton an indispensable part of their church decoration, especially the 'Jeremiah' variety. In some forms of folk healing, the healer will diagnose by 'reading' the spots on the leaf. In recent times, croton has been cross-bred quite extensively in Jamaica.

[Adams 1971, Hawkes and Sutton 1974, Rashford 1988c]

CUBAH CORNWALLIS (? – 1848)

Before the advent of hospitals, several black and COLOURED women achieved fame as healers (see MEDICINE, Folk) and their lodging houses also served as private hospitals and nursing homes (see e.g. Mary SEACOLE). Cubah Cornwallis was one of these free coloured women, famous for having saved the lives of many naval officers at her PORT ROYAL establishment.

She boasted among her patients the future Admiral Lord NELSON as well as the future King William IV, who fell ill when he visited the island as a midshipman (becoming the first member of the British Royal Family to visit Jamaica). It has been claimed (though so far unverified) that Cubah was later sent an expensive gown by Queen Adelaide, wife of King William in appreciation of her services. She refused to wear it in her lifetime, reserving it for her funeral. She died in 1848.

Cubah might have been of Ashanti stock, Cubah being the Akan DAY NAME for a girl born on a Wednesday. However, her name also appears in the historical literature written as 'Cuba'. We do know that she assumed the name Cornwallis from her benefactor, the Hon William Cornwallis, captain of the *Lion*, a BRITISH frigate based at Port Royal and who in some accounts is said to have secured her freedom. He was a son of the 1st Earl Cornwallis and brother of the famous General Charles Cornwallis who commanded British forces against the American rebels in the American War of Independence. Captain Cornwallis became Nelson's messmate at the Port Royal station and cared for him aboard the *Lion* on which the sick Nelson travelled back to England in November 1780, having spent 30 months on the Jamaica station. Cornwallis, then in his mid-thirties, was described as 'fat', and so red-faced he was known among seamen as 'Billy-go-tight'. He was also known as 'Blue Billy', 'Coachee', and 'Mister Whip', but was apparently a popular man and remained a lifelong friend of Nelson.

[Cundall 1915, Oman 1996]

CUDJOE, Captain

Freedom fighter, military strategist and warrior, regarded as one of the great MAROON leaders. His name is an Akan DAY NAME and means 'male child born on a Monday', spelled also as Kojo and Kwadwo but written in the contemporary literature as 'Cudjoe'.

Cudjoe was one of many runaway slaves who roamed the CLARENDON hills (near to Cave Valley) in the late 18th century. He soon emerged as a leader and welded together all the Clarendon Maroon bands. So great did his fame become that many Maroons made their way from other parts of the island to place themselves under his leadership.

When pressure from the planters and soldiers grew too great, Cudjoe led his people to the COCKPIT COUNTRY, where he set up his main camp at the Petty River Bottom, a steep-sided valley. From here the Maroons waged guerrilla warfare against the English settlers and soldiers for many years. The English authorities were

Captain Cudjoe and Dr Russell exchange hats as a token of friendship during the peace-making negotiations (from Dallas)

forced to sign a treaty with Cudjoe, and he and his people were given 1,500 acres of land (600ha), with an additional 1,000 acres (400ha) to the ACCOMPONG band. Cudjoe's settlement was named Trelawny Town after the governor, and Cudjoe was made chief of his community for life, with a clear line of succession established. It is not known when Cudjoe died, but he was still alive in 1764 when he was probably in his eighties. Captain Cudjoe came of Ashanti warrior stock (as did many of the Maroons) and remains a legendary figure to this day. A contemporary tale of Cudjoe can be found in Tanna (1984).
[Dallas 1803, Robinson 1969]

CULTURAL TRAINING CENTRE
see EDNA MANLEY COLLEGE

CUSCUTA *(Cuscuta americana)*
Commonly called Love Bush, this parasitic climber of the Convolvulus family is used in love charms and divination. As a test of love, a piece of the bright orange stem is thrown while saying the name of the love object; it is believed that if it grows the love will flourish. However, Love Bush always flourishes for it is a notorious parasite, probably the reason for its other common names: Strangle Weed, Hell Weed and Devil's Guts, the latter describing its string-like appearance. It is also known as Dodder.

Love Bush occurs from sea level to 365m. Its leaves absent or reduced, it is visible as a network of bright orange thread that climbs on herbs, shrubs and low trees, totally covering them if left unchecked. It is extremely difficult to eradicate since even the smallest piece will form a new plant. Love Bush fruits and flowers throughout the year.

The plant has large reserves of food in its seeds, which it sends into the air in the hope of finding suitable hosts. If the seed fails to do so, it will send out roots which enable the seedling to live up to seven weeks without a host. During that time, the rapidly growing stem sends out spirals seeking a suitable host stem to which it attaches itself as soon as contact is made. Once attached, the plant loses its root and grows an extensive network of very thin stems that it attaches to the host by spiralling until it completely enmeshes it. The stem contains very little chlorophyll once it becomes attached to a host, and the leaves are reduced to scales.

In folk MEDICINE, Love Bush is made into tea as a general beverage and for colic in babies, and mixed with other bush, is used for asthma,

'marasma' (marasmus) and other ailments.

A native of Central America, it is now found throughout tropical and southern sub-tropical America.

It was celebrated in Erasmus Darwin's 18th century *The Botanic Garden*:

> Two Harlot-Nymphs, the fair Cuscutas, please
> With labour'd negligence, and studied ease;
> In the meek garb of modest worth disguised,
> The eye averted, and the smile chastised,
> With sly approach they spread their
>   dangerous charms,
> And round their victim wind their wiry arms.

[Asprey and Thornton 1953-55, Beckwith 1924, DJE, Huxley 1978]

CUSTARD APPLE *(Annona reticulata)*
A native of the American tropics and the CARIBBEAN, this is another well loved member of the family that includes SWEETSOP and SOURSOP, and was used by the TAINOS. Custard Apple, as its name suggests, yields fruit with a sweet, custard-like, granular pulp. The smallish tree (5-10m high) grows from sea level up to 550m, and is found in gardens and waste places where seeds have been thrown. It fruits in February. The stem

D. Ranston

Custard apple

of the reddish-brown fruit contains an alkaloid. The fruit was formerly used in treatment of dysentery and diarrhoea, and the mashed leaves applied to sprains.
[Adams 1972, Asprey and Thornton 1953-55]

CUSTOS

The principal magistrate of a PARISH, appointed by the governor-general who is the Queen's representative; the name and office are derived from the English Custos Rotulorum (from the Latin 'Keeper of the Rolls'). The plural is custodes. The post is an honorary one and dates from the earliest days of English settlement. (See BRITISH.) The earliest recorded custos was BUCCANEER-turned-worthy-citizen Henry MORGAN, who was custos of PORT ROYAL in 1680.

In earlier times, before representative government, the custos would have presided over the vestry – the local government authority which managed the affairs of the parish. The importance of the office was much greater in the past; today it is largely ceremonial. As the governor-general's representative, it is the duty of the custos to receive the sovereign, any member of the British royal family, the prime minister on an official visit, or any other important personage commended by the governor-general. The custos also chairs the committee that makes recommendations for the appointment of justices of the peace for each parish. JPs carry out lay magistrate duties assigned to them, for which no charge is made.

In the absence of the governor-general, his role is filled by the senior custos.
[GOJ STATIN 1999a]

CUTLASS

Used interchangeably with machete, the principal agricultural tool of Jamaica, particularly among small farmers (see AGRICULTURE) and SUGAR CANE workers. A cutlass was originally a weapon, especially of sea fighters such as pirates and BUCCANEERS.

According to the DJE, there are 10 distinctive types of cutlasses, differing according to shape, method of sharpening, etc., and there are more than 60 individual names for this tool – and sometime weapon – of the Jamaican farmer. Although in earlier times there seems to have been a distinction between a cutlass (popularly shortened to 'lass') and a machete (the final 'e' is not pronounced in Jamaica) no such distinction exists today, though the use of one term or the other will prevail in different parts of the island. The term 'Spanish machete' signifies a double-crosser, a blade sharpened on both sides.
[DJE]

Cutlass

CYCLING

The late 19th century was the age of the bicycle, cycling becoming the latest craze of the upper and middle classes in Jamaica as elsewhere. Riders at first risked their lives on the high wheel bicycle – later called the penny-farthing – which was developed in Europe in 1869 and introduced to the USA in 1876. In 1885 came the Rover 'safety' bicycle, similar to the bicycle of today, its popularity enhanced by the successful commercial application of the inflated or pneumatic tyre by Dunlop in 1888.

Cycling parties vied with horseback riding as popular pastimes for both men and women. Young men toured the island by bicycle and also rode to work, and tourists brought their bicycles for local rides. The fact that the Jamaica Bicycle Club, formed in 1886, was under the patronage of the then governor of the island shows the elite status of the riders: the average cost of a bicycle was £8. In 1897 the Victoria Cycle Club was formed and inaugurated cycle races at a track at Newton Square in KINGSTON.

According to historian Patrick Bryan: 'By the end of the nineteenth century the novelty of bicycle riding seems to have worn off, and the functional rather than the leisure value of the bicycle was coming to be exercised.' An unofficial count showed 531 bicycles in Kingston in 1903 when an effort was made to establish a Cycling Association.

In 1908 the firm of L.K. Brandon was formed in Kingston, and for the next 50 years until its closure in 1964 was synonymous with the bicycle. The import business was run by the brothers Kenneth and, later, Keith Brandon who recalled that the First WORLD WAR curtailed business but that it boomed in the 1920s as the bicycle became the main means of transportation of the man on the street. When there was petrol rationing during the Second World War, many car owners rushed to obtain bicycles. In the post-war years sports models came in and there was professional racing. Although bicycles continued to be popular for some time, after 1959 the introduction of hire-purchase put the motor car within easier reach of many people, and the self-propelled machine lost its place. At a time when cycles were in use all around Jamaica, the main activity of the village constable appeared to be the prosecution of riders for travelling without lights at night, or not having brakes or a bell.

Cycle racing began in Jamaica as a lowly-paid semi-professional sport at Kensington Park and the Town Moor, located at the famous KINGSTON RACE COURSE where Lance Hayles, Frankie Minott and the Blissett brothers became local stars.

Cycling since then has continued as a popular sport. The cyclist David Weller won a bronze medal at the 1980 Moscow Olympics, making him, up to the time of writing, the only non-track athlete to win an Olympic medal for Jamaica (see ATHLETICS), and the only competitor from the English-speaking Caribbean to win such a medal.

[Arlott 1975, Bryan 1991, Gregory 1964]

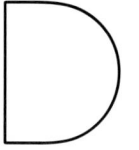

DALLAS

Place name in ST ANDREW Parish, ancestral home of the man after whom the USA city of Dallas, Texas, was named. The founder of the Jamaican branch of the family was Dr Robert Dallas, a physician of Scottish birth (see SCOTS) who emigrated to Jamaica in 1730. His Jamaican SUGAR PLANTATION was originally known as Boar Castle, but he renamed it Dallas Castle when he purchased it in 1758. One of his sons, R.C. Dallas, wrote the first *History of the Maroons* (published in 1803), and was uncle by marriage to and literary assistant of Lord Byron, the poet. Another son, Alexander Dallas, emigrated to the USA and founded the Pennsylvania branch of the family, becoming secretary of the US Treasury (1814-16). His son, George Mifflin Dallas, became United States vice president 1845-49 under President Polk, and the Texas city was named after him. Another grandson of Dr Dallas, Samuel Jackson Dallas, became speaker of the Jamaica House of Assembly (1842-49). The Dallas family eventually lost their Jamaican plantation and it came under the ownership of Joseph Gordon, father of National Hero, Rt Excellent George William GORDON. The name Dallas survives in both a village (Dallas Castle) and the surrounding hill (Dallas Mountain). There are still descendants of the Dallas family living in Jamaica.

[Ashcroft 1980]

R.C. Dallas

DANCE

Dance has been a popular pastime from the earliest days of settlement in Jamaica, indulged in by the TAINOS in their AREITOS, and later, by the Europeans and Africans alike.

For the BRITISH settlers, balls were the centrepiece of the social season which coincided with the sitting of the House of Assembly in the capital of SPANISH TOWN and the holding of the Grand Court in PARISH capitals. Dancing was almost obligatory at house gatherings and parties. The *Journal* of Lady Nugent, wife of the English governor at the beginning of the 19th century, is filled with such activities, and many visitors in the plantation era commented on the dancing propensities of the settlers.

The English novelist Anthony Trollope who visited in 1851 claimed that: 'The soul of a Jamaica lady revels in dance. Dancing is popular in England – is popular everywhere; but in Jamaica it is the elixir of life, the Medea's caldron, which makes old people young, the cup of Circe, which neither man nor woman can withstand . . . It is singular how the most listless girl, who seems to trail through her long days almost without moving her limbs, will continue to waltz and polk and rush up and down a gallopade from ten till five; and think the hours too short!'

Taino dancing

Festival dance troupe

The European dances were observed and later imitated by the slaves, often evolving into completely new dances – such as the QUADRILLE, which is a creolized version of the European original. The musicians at the dances too were often slaves or free COLOUREDS who brought the music and the European styles back to their own communities.

The enslaved AFRICANS too were said to be 'passionately fond of dancing' – music and dance being the only recreation they had from back-breaking labour. (See GANGS, SLAVERY.) The song 'Quaco Sam', preserved from the early 19th century conveys the sheer joy that could be obtained from MUSIC and dance as a momentary distraction from the hardship of servitude, the ever-watchful eye of the slave-driver, and beatings ('fum-fum'). It says in part:

> Me yerry say one dance deh a Berry Hill:
> Unco Jack fe play de fiddle, one hog deh fe kill;
> Come tell me, cousin Cuba, how ebery ting 'tan
> Mek me ax sista Susan, me me call sista Ann.
>
> Cho: Wid me ring ding ding an me pam pam pam
> Me nebber see a man like-a Quaco Sam
>
> Oh Lard! How me wi dance when me yerry fiddle and drum!
> Me no tink pon backra wuk, me no care fe fum-fum
> Me wi dance de shay-shay, me wi dance de 'cotch reel,
> Me wi dance till ebry craps a me foot-battam peel.

On Monday morning, despite driver Harry and his whip, the dancer still has her memories to sustain her in the SUGAR CANE fields:

> Me tek me road da cane-piece, weh de people-dem da run,
> An all come behin' me, get de fum-fum.
> Wid de centung da me back, chacolata da me pan
> Me da wuk, me da laugh, me da tink pan Quaco Sam.

For the enslaved, dancing was not only a means of recreation but of making connection with their former lives, with the ancestors, and was used for religious ritual as well as satirical purpose. It was one activity that never ceased on the Atlantic crossing from Africa to the New World, for on that MIDDLE PASSAGE, slaves were frequently forced to dance on board the slave ships, as a means of exercise and as offering amusement for the crews.

The enslaved Africans were stripped of all their physical possessions on leaving their homelands, and the aspect of their culture that remained strongest was what they could carry in their memories and bodies – music, dance, and the making of MUSICAL INSTRUMENTS. Since in Africa these were all associated with religious activities, they probably also served as a memory aid in the reconstruction of such practices. Even today, music and dance are important elements in African-Jamaican religious activities.

Slaves dancing aboard ship

The Jamaica School of Dance, now part of the EDNA MANLEY COLLEGE, is the leading institution for dance training, and the NATIONAL DANCE THEATRE COMPANY the leading company.

[Barnett 1982, Baxter 1970, Brathwaite 1970, Handler and Frisbie 1972, Lalla 1981, Nettleford 1986, Patterson 1973, Ryman 1980, Trollope 1860]

DANCEHALL

Originally meaning the place where dances are held, from the 1980s onwards Dancehall came to refer to the dominant popular MUSIC which developed from REGGAE, as well as a whole sub-culture that has grown around it. At the centre of the Dancehall music and drama is the DJ or deejay, who has replaced the singer as the star performer. The accent is on the 'riddim' and the word as the deejay chants over a popular rhythm, cultivating his or her distinctive style that will appeal to the masses or 'massive'.

Originating in the poorest communities (called the 'ghettoes') of KINGSTON, Dancehall provides a stage for men and women to profile and strut in an explicitly sexual manner and to comment on the social and political conditions of their communities. 'Dancehall' refers to the music as well as the dances, dress, language and behaviour

Dancehall fashion (C. Wilmot, Gleaner)

of this sub-culture. In the early stage of its evolution, sexuality ('slackness') dominated the discourse but over time explicitly political issues ('culture') have come to the surface and the repertoire of, for example, Yellowman (Winston Foster), exemplifies this diversity. Slackness usually wins out since it is the most in demand commercially. Though in Jamaica much of it is deemed by the local radio stations not fit for airplay, it is played on stations abroad (many foreigners not understanding the lyrics though some do master the language). And while some Dancehall artistes have signed huge international recording contracts, it is success with the local 'massive' that really measures the winners and losers in the competitive deejay game.

The Dancehall itself is not usually a hall, it is often a large open space or a performance stage used for commercial shows. Each deejay adopts a theatrical name and personality, the more flamboyant the better: Tiger, Bounty Killer, Admiral Bailey, Yellowman, Beeny Man, Buju Banton. As Carolyn Cooper points out, the deejay needs to sell himself in a competitive field and elaborately declare his mastery. Dancehall fans are not averse to 'bottling' off the stage those who fail to 'tear-it-down' (give a top performance). By the same token, in imitation of the 21-gun salute given by the state to its heroes, 'lick shot' (gunshots or their sound imitation) is used to salute a ranking dancehall Don.

Chester Francis-Jackson who compiled *The Official Dancehall Dictionary* in 1995, explains: 'in the specific area of Dancehall music, DJs who created and maintain this style of music do so in a very competitive environment, which demands of its exponents lyrical dexterity in order to survive. Reputations, and consequently the all-important recording contract, are secured by the DJ who is best able to chat lyrics from night till morning in the dancehall.'

Deejaying involves skill with language and engaging in tongue-twisting and ear-bending vocal improvisations. Cooper has noted the subversive quality of dancehall, in which performer and audience collude in creating new language shifts, giving new meanings to standard words, e.g. 'trash' meaning 'dressed'.

As Chang and Chen explain: 'The deejay's art consists primarily of an ability to "ride" the riddim, that is to chant in tune with the beat. Next comes a fluency in varying timbre, tone and speed of speech. The knack of creating intelligent and witty lyrics, while always a welcome bonus, seems to rank relatively low in the hierarchy of dancehall skills. Many big deejay hits have been based on nonsense rhymes.'

The deejay style started in the actual dance halls of the 1960s when the turntable operators of sound systems would chant-toast-scat over the music. One of the first of the system deejays to record was U-Roy (Ewart Beckford), and his immediate success with hits like 'Wear You to the Ball' (1970) set off a rush of imitators. The sound became popular in the USA; from it, some have argued, hip-hop and rap developed. However, in Jamaica the 'roots' reggae singer continued to rule the mainstream music scene, while the popularity of the deejays for the most part was confined to the ghetto, until the emergence of Yellowman in 1982 ushered in the era of 'slackness' and the ascendance of Dancehall.

While Dancehall is perceived as elevating a macho culture, Cooper argues that female fertility rituals dominate the discourse. The greatest supporters of dancehall are women, some – such as Carlene, a stage dancer – developing such a public persona they are given the title of 'Queen' which they then find marketable in the wider community, as in advertising. (*Dancehall Queen* was the name of a feature film in 1999.) Women – such as Lady Saw – are also among the most enthusiastic performers of 'slackness'. Dancehall dance styles have explicit names and moves, such as the Butterfly, the Bogle, Della-move, Bubbling, Jockey Fashion, Water-pumpy, Slide'n'wine and Batty-rider.

Since being 'trash' – fashion conscious – is part of the dancehall ethos, it has generated its own style in fashion, make-up and hair dressing for men and women.

[Barrow and Dalton, 1997, Chang and Chen 1998, Cooper 1993, Francis-Jackson 1995, Stolzoff 2000]

DATURA *(Datura stramonium)*

Annual herb that bears white or purple-tinged trumpet shaped flowers, also called Devil's Trumpet, Jimson Weed and Thorn Apple, the latter describing its fruit that is about 30cm in length. Datura is of the same family as the tomato, Irish POTATO and eggplant. A tall, pungent smelling, poisonous weed, in Jamaican folk MEDICINE it has been used to make an ointment for scalds, burns and painful sores – hence its other name of Burn Weed.

All parts of the plant are narcotic and hallucinogenic, and it has been one of the plants used by Native Americans (including the TAINOS) to produce altered states of consciousness. The Lokono ARAWAKS of South America boil the fruit of the Datura and use the juice thus derived to make a hot poultice in the treatment of asthma. This practice was likely taken to the CARIBBEAN and passed on in the heritage of folk medicine, as it is still widely practised by rural folk in the Greater ANTILLES including, significantly, SEVILLE Plantation peasant farmers. The closely related Angel's Trumpet (*D. suaveolens*) is an ornamental cultivated in gardens.

Datura flower and fruit

[G.A. Aarons, personal communication, Adams 1971, Asprey and Thornton 1953-55, DJE]

DAY

Certain days have been given an identity by their lack of plenty. 'Banyan (or Benian) Day' is a nautical term brought ashore, a day on which (as on shipboard) no meat is served, hence a day of fasting or austerity. The sailors borrowed the term from the Banyan, a caste of Hindu traders who ate no meat. A lack of plenty is also known as 'Ben Johnson Day' – the day before payday when money is short, hence, a meatless day. F.G. Cassidy in *Jamaica Talk* suggests that the latter might be derived from the former; there is no evidence of who 'Ben Johnson' might have been.

'Barefoot Sunday', describing the Sunday after EASTER, suggests poverty of a different sort. As Jean D'Costa recalled, on Easter Sunday when parson came and gave communion, everyone who could do so, went to church and wore shoes, often putting them on in the yard at the last minute. The Sunday after Easter was the plainest Sunday of the church's year, with no visit from parson, and hence no need to wear shoes. A similar idea persists in England, where the Sunday after Easter is called 'Low Sunday', in contrast to the 'high' feast of Easter Sunday.

[J. D'Costa, personal communication]

DAY NAME

Also known as 'Born Day Name', this refers to a specific name given to a child according to the day of the week on which he or she was born. It is a custom of the Akan or Twi-speaking peoples and of the neighbouring Ewe peoples of West Africa that was followed by their descendants in Jamaica, particularly during SLAVERY. There does not appear to have been any resistance by Europeans to the use of these names for Africans and their children, perhaps because they were short. These names also came to be used by persons who were not necessarily Akan or Ewe descendants and who were also CREOLE.

Today, the names are still in use, but as descriptive terms, not usually complimentary, e.g. a 'cuffee' is a stupid or ill-bred person; a QUASHIE is countrified, and QUACO is ignorant and foolish. The day names for males and females were as follows (spelling variations given)

Day	Male	Female
Mon	Cudjoe/Kojo	Juba or Adowa
Tue	Cubbenah/Kubi	Beneba
Wed	Quaco/Kwaku	Cuba
Thurs	Quao/Kwao	Abba
Fri	Cuffee/Kofi	Phibba
Sat	Quamin/Kwame	Mimba
Sun	Quashee/Kwasi	Quasheba

[DJE, Williams 1934]

DAY WORK

System of informal labour exchange, once common. It is also known in different parts of the island as Digging-Match, Work Sport, Morning Work, Day for Day, etc. In former times, persons in a community got together to work on a specific task, e.g. clearing a field, digging YAM hills, planting, reaping, house building, house moving, on the understanding that the host would in turn give the others his day's work. The host's obligations for the day included provision of adequate food and drink. There would also be pleasurable communal activity to lighten labour, such as singing. Many of Jamaica's folk songs (see MUSIC, Folk) originated from day work, especially those called JAMMA SONGS.

Edna Manley – 'The Diggers'

These communal activities were also called Banter-sing, the latter probably referring to the topical nature of the songs, led by a 'professional' song-leader called a 'bomma' or 'singerman', someone whose sole job was to lead the songs and keep the activity going. The traditional call-and-response pattern – the leader singing the lines while the rest sing the chorus, to the rhythm of their work activity – is AFRICAN derived.

In the post-EMANCIPATION years, when MISSIONARY activity was high, such activities were also church-sponsored, a 'Wesleyan' being a METHODIST-sponsored collective labour activity. At church concerts, a self-selected bomma often led from the back, beating time with a club on the floor, calling out to the performers and causing much hilarity. The bomma sometimes had to be removed by the church wardens for bad behaviour.

Horace Campbell has noted that the traditional concept of sharing a reciprocal day's work was effectively abandoned by young farmers after the police repression of the 1950s against the growing of GANJA.

'Day work' also refers to the activities of workers such as labourers or domestics who hire themselves out by the day.
[Baxter 1970, Campbell 1985, DJE]

DEATH RITUALS

Death and burial are still treated with great reverence and seriousness by many, one of the few events nowadays that serves to bring people of a district together, along with those from far distances. With families now scattered over many countries, a burial will usually be delayed until as many relatives as possible can come from abroad and from other parts of the island, and it often serves as the only opportunity for family gatherings. The WAKE, funeral arrangements, and size of the funeral are seen to reflect on the prestige and status of the family, as well as that of the deceased.

Because death observances were not banned during SLAVERY as were other AFRICAN cultural practices, they served as a means of preserving the old customs among African descendants throughout the Americas. Death rituals also

Monumental tombs in the Jewish cemetery (above) and St Andrew Parish Church (below)

incorporate many European practices, especially those brought by the IRISH, SCOTS and WELSH to the English-speaking CARIBBEAN.

Beliefs Death rituals in Jamaica today are a mixture of African and European custom and Christian practice. People of all classes share certain beliefs regarding death rituals: for instance, covering mirrors in the house; stopping the clocks; telling the bees; ensuring that the corpse is taken out feet first, and rearranging furniture so that the ghost will not recognize the place if it returns. The mourning colours of black, purple and white up to recently were the only colours approved of for funerals and for the period of mourning by close family members, though this is less widely observed today.

TOKENS of approaching death include birds or moths flying into the sickroom, or into the house where the dying person lies. Birdsong in the dark of night is a similar warning. (See BIRDS IN FOLKLORE.) Up until the 1950s, the nursing staff of country hospitals discouraged visitors from bringing either highly scented flowers or worse, arrangements of red and white flowers – a harbinger of death.

Monuments The monumental tombs and family vaults of planter families (see BRITISH) may be found in many parts of rural Jamaica, some of them in land now ruinate or given over to modern development. Built of bricks or cut-stone, these tombs often measure 2m long, 1-1.2m wide, and may stand as high as .60m. Inscriptions set into the mortar on the surfaces (or in a few cases, into a marble inlay) declare the names, dates and memorials of the deceased.

The Jarrett family vault at ORANGE VALLEY, TRELAWNY Parish, was typical of the more elaborate mausoleum: it consisted of a stone-laid chamber set into the side of a small hill a few hundred yards from the GREAT HOUSE. Lead coffins stood on a stone shelf, or lay on the ground: holes measuring a few inches in width had been cut into all of them by grave robbers searching for the gold and gems thought to be buried with such people. Such tombs evoked great fear in many Jamaicans, who avoided those places (see DUPPY). It was believed that touching a coffin or skeleton could result in paralysis of the guilty hand, or even death. Children were warned never to climb or sit on tombs for fear of the dead.

Other elaborate tombs and monuments of the elite can be found inside many of the old ANGLICAN churches and GRAVEYARDS (see e.g. KINGSTON PARISH CHURCH, SPANISH TOWN CATHEDRAL, ST ANDREW PARISH CHURCH). A record of the island's monumental inscriptions has been compiled by Philip Wright (1966).

Despite these signs of opulence associated with the burial of the elite, in the 17th and 18th centuries it was rare that a minister of religion could be found to conduct a funeral, for Jamaica did not rank such ceremonies highly. On the plantation, the master or overseer pronounced a few words over the body at burial, perhaps the Lord's Prayer and extracts from the Bible, if such were available. Burials took place on the day of death or the next, given the nature of a tropical climate and the real terror of epidemic diseases. Few markers remain for the white indentured servants, artisans, BOOK-KEEPERS, and others who also died in Jamaica; the high death rate among the white population is attested to by the military cemeteries such as those at NEWCASTLE. (See also YELLOW FEVER.)

No slave cemeteries have so far been found in Jamaica. Although they undoubtedly existed, much of the material used would have been ephemeral. In Barbados archaeologists have discovered a slave cemetery dating back to the 17th century; a unique find. For some dead slaves, the only ritual might be, being thrown into a gully to nourish the crows, a practice recalled in a song recorded in 1788, 'Carry him along':

'Take him to the Gulley! Take him to the Gulley!
But bringee back the frock and board!'

'Oh! massa! me no deadee yet!'

'Take him to the Gulley! Take him to the Gulley!
Carry him along!'

African Custom During slavery, Africans took care of their own, and burial rites were according to African custom. Although today most people are buried in Christian church rites, remnants of these customs still prevail, though not as strongly as in the old days, when preparations for the burial would have been made at home rather than through a professional undertaker, the corpse staying in the house until burial. Before the coffin left the house, adults would stand on either side of it and pass the young children of the family across it three times, to prevent, it is said, the spirit from harming them. This ritual is sometimes still observed.

There were always older people in each village who knew the 'correct' way of doing things when a person died, and 'correctness' was important every step of the way in order not to offend the dead. For the African belief in the multiple soul or three components of the individual persisted. While the physical body died it was believed that the spirit returned to God (hence embarked on a journey) while the duppy or shadow lived on, and could become a menace to the living if not accorded proper respect. Funeral rites therefore served to ensure the safe journey of the spirit as well as placate the duppy. Because of the belief in the old days that the spirit on death returned to Africa,

The carrying of the coffin (from Phillippo)

messages to loved ones there were sometimes sent by this route and the process of death and burial became a prolonged event (see NINE NIGHT, WAKE).

Among people of African descent, as was the practice in Africa, it was incumbent on survivors to try to discover the cause of the death and, if witchcraft was suspected to be involved, to punish the perpetrators. In the old days, the corpse would be equipped with weapons to avenge a death that was believed caused by malice or witchcraft. It might be given a knife, razor, or money with orders to 'go do your work'. It might be armed with broomweed tied in white cloth to 'sweep the yard clean' (harm the entire household), or a horsewhip with a spur on one of his boots to 'ride' or kill the killer. Ordeals to prove innocence or guilt could be administered to persons believed responsible for a death, especially to family members.

The corpse itself sometimes participated in the inquest as the coffin was borne by pallbearers from the home to the church or burial site. There are many stories of the coffin forcing the bearers to stop before the house of the enemy and refusing to budge no matter how hard they tried to move it, and even spinning them around. It was also believed that the coffin would get heavier before a door where a debt was owed, if the murderer was one of those carrying the coffin, or if the dead was due to be buried in a place where it did not want to go.

Burial Just as certain rituals had to be observed in preparation of the body for burial, in funeral processions, in the demeanour and dress of family members, so too care had to be observed in grave preparation and burial. In digging the grave, a libation of RUM is still poured on the ground to ask permission of the earth spirit before the first sod is cut, and sometimes the earth is knocked as well. Graves are dug east to west and the body placed to face the sunrise. In past times, after the ceremony, mourners would take a little of the grave dirt and, with back turned to the grave, throw it between their legs to prevent the dead from following them home.

Certain precautions had to be taken to keep the dead in the grave, especially with plantings. (See GRAVE PLANTS.) Often personal belongings of the deceased would be placed on the grave. However these items were always damaged. One explanation for this practice comes from the Sea Islands (Georgia and South Carolina, USA): 'Yuh break duh dishes so dat duh chain will be broke', with the suggestion that if this isn't done, a 'chain' of family deaths will follow.

The grave would sometimes be outlined with SHELLS, most notably CONCH, until, for those who could afford it, a tomb was erected. For some people, memorials for the dead would be held after 30 or 40 days and the erection of a tomb the opportunity for a final leavetaking. For KUMINA practitioners, the 'Tombing' one year after death is a significant rite.

[Banbury 1894, Beckwith 1929, D'Costa and Lalla 1989, Handler and Lange 1978, Henriques 1953, Hurston 1938, Kerr 1952, Mico 1893, 1896, Pigou 1987, Wright 1966]

DEMONTEVIN LODGE

One of the attractive old houses of PORT ANTONIO, PORTLAND Parish, now operated as a guest house. It was built at the turn of the century by the Hon David Gideon, who became CUSTOS of Portland in 1923. Some of the decorative ironwork might have been brought on the banana boats which regularly plied between

Demontevin Lodge

Boston and the town (see BANANA TRADE). The structure is said to bear a striking resemblance to the sea captains' houses of the Massachusetts coast, as well as town houses in Limón (Costa Rica), the Bay Islands (Honduras), Colón (Panama), Livingston (Guatemala), Bluefields (Nicaragua) and Santiago de Cuba, all enclaves of English-speaking CARIBBEAN migrants in Spanish-speaking countries. (See COLÓN MAN, PANAMA.)

DENBIGH

The permanent headquarters in CLARENDON Parish of the Jamaica Agricultural Society's annual show. The fair is held over the long INDEPENDENCE weekend in early August and is a showcase for Jamaica's farmers and agricultural activities. (See AGRICULTURE.)

DEVON HOUSE

Historic building on Hope Road, ST ANDREW Parish, regarded as one of the finest examples of 19th century domestic architecture in Jamaica. The ambience is that of a GREAT HOUSE. Now open to visitors, it is furnished with antiques of Jamaican and CARIBBEAN origin as well as reproductions by Jamaican craftsmen. (See CABINET-MAKER.)

The house was built in 1881 by George Stiebel, a COLOURED Jamaican wheelwright who became a millionaire through gold mining in South America. He subsequently became a figure of note in Jamaica, and was CUSTOS of St Andrew. Devon House was sold by Stiebel's grandson in 1923. After a succession of owners, the house was threatened with demolition to make way for a housing development. The government of Jamaica placed a preservation order on the property and acquired Devon House for the nation in 1967. It has since then been carefully restored. For some years, it was the home of the National Gallery of Jamaica (see ART), which in 1983 moved to the Roy West Building on the KINGSTON waterfront.

Devon House

Devon House is now the centre of a complex that includes crafts shops, restaurants and other attractions, all contrived to create a Jamaican ambience in a gracious setting. The grounds are a popular site for wedding photographs and Sunday afternoon picnics.
[Cundall 1915, Dello Strollogo 1984, Shields 1991]

DIALECT see LANGUAGE

DIGGING MATCH see DAY WORK

DINKI MINI

Wake observance, nowadays known mainly from ST MARY Parish (see WAKE). The dinki is always a joyous occasion, with singing, dancing and ring GAMES, the purpose being to cheer the bereaved (see DEATH RITUALS). Central to the dinki is a dance (called 'dinki mini') in which the male dancer bends one leg at the knee and makes high leaps on the other foot, and with male and female dancing together with very suggestive pelvic movements. A MUSICAL INSTRUMENT called the BENTA is played.
[Tanna and Ramsay 1987]

Dinki Mini dance

DIP AN' FALL BACK see RUN DUNG

DIRT-EATING

A practice known as pica or geophagy, referring to an addiction to eating a type of clayey earth. It was common during SLAVERY, though it frequently led to serious illness and sometimes death.

Richard Sheridan calls pica 'one of the most obstinate and troublesome disorders that afflicted blacks. It disabled slaves for a considerable time, sometimes years, and often terminated in dropsy'. On some plantations, dirt-eating was treated as a crime and those who indulged were forced to wear a face mask or mouth piece secured with a padlock. Slaves who were victims to the pica habit ate a wide variety of substances. In Jamaica the favourite earth was called 'aboo earth', or 'clammy marl', which tasted sweet and dissolved easily in the mouth. Those bent on self-destruction consumed other substances. The craving affected children as well as adults. The practice was also called mal-d'estomach or 'stomach-evil', though Kenneth Kiple suggests that the terms cover illnesses that were not caused by dirt-eating.

Doctors then and now have been perplexed by the practice which still continues in many parts of the world. One theory holds that the craving to eat clay has a nutritional base and arises from deficiencies of essential mineral nutrients in the body which are supplied by the clay.
[DJE, Kiple 1984, Sheridan 1985]

DISCOVERY BAY

Coastal town in ST ANN Parish, part of which was originally called Puerto Seco or Dry Harbour. In recent times the name was changed to Discovery Bay to commemorate the first place Christopher COLUMBUS set foot on Jamaican soil. Some authorities, however, believe that this claim rightly belongs to RIO BUENO. Both bays are of similar shape, but Rio Bueno has fresh water whereas Discovery Bay has none; Columbus called it Puerto Seco for this reason.

The port operations of Kaiser BAUXITE company are located in this bay at Port Rhodes. The company operates Puerto Seco beach (open to the public) and is responsible for the development of Columbus Park nearby. The UNIVERSITY OF THE WEST INDIES operates a marine laboratory in the area and the Jamaican Coastguard has a sub-station here as well.

'DISCOVERY' OF JAMAICA

On 6 May 1494 Christopher COLUMBUS landed on Jamaican soil and took possession of the island on behalf of the Spanish sovereigns King Ferdinand and Queen Isabella, naming it Santiago after the patron saint of Spain (see JAMAICA). He was on his second voyage to the New World (which began in Spain, 25 September 1493) and had sailed from Cuba to explore the island to the south that Amerindians in Cuba and the southern Bahamas had told him about from his first voyage. They assured him that it was full of GOLD. In his caraval *Niña*, accompanied by the *San Juan* and *Cardera*, he had spent the night of 4 May anchored off a bay which the next morning he named Santa Gloria (ST ANN'S BAY) declaring the island itself 'the fairest that eyes have beheld'. The natives appeared hostile, but the TAINO warriors making warlike gestures from their fleet of painted CANOES were sent scurrying back to shore by a cannon shot. Columbus did not land as there was no water evident at St Ann's Bay. He continued to sail west, noting that Jamaica was the most heavily populated of the islands of the Greater Antilles, the coastline thickly dotted with villages and so many Tainos it seemed 'the earth was covered with them'.

On the 6th he found suitable anchorage at what is now believed to be RIO BUENO, though claims have been put forward for DISCOVERY BAY. Here the natives again set out from the shore in great numbers in their canoes, making hostile gestures, but Columbus sent off the ships' boats with crossbowmen who killed and wounded many of them. For good measure, they let loose a huge DOG as they landed. This was the Tainos' first glimpse of this terrifying creature that attacked and bit several of their number, and the rest fled. Pacification completed, Columbus landed and took possession. The CACIQUES came in submission, bringing gifts of provision and fruit, receiving in exchange beads, bells, mirrors, and other trinkets. Columbus stayed for three days while his ship was repaired, enjoying the Tainos' hospitality, and sailed westward again on 9 May. He stopped long enough to name El Golfo de Buen Tiempo (MONTEGO BAY) and then sailed along the south coast as far as Port Morant

The 'discovery': dogs and guns trained on the fleeing Tainos, at left

before returning to Hispaniola.

In July he again returned to Jamaica, reaching El Golfo de Buen Tiempo on the 21st. He spent the next two months exploring the western and southern coast. A high point occurred at Bahia de las Vacas (COW BAY – Portland Bight, CLARENDON Parish), where he was met by a fleet of canoes including one 27m long containing a splendid cacique and his retinue (see OLD HARBOUR). He continued eastwards and on 19 August cleared Cabo de Farol (Morant Point, ST THOMAS Parish) for Hispaniola. Columbus did not visit Jamaica on his third voyage and was stranded on the island on his fourth. (See COLUMBUS IN JAMAICA.)

[Aarons 1983-84, Osborne 1968]

DOCTOR BIRD see HUMMINGBIRD

DOCTOR'S CAVE see MONTEGO BAY

DODDER see CUSCUTA

DOG *(Canis familiaris)*
The dog was introduced into the ANTILLES by COLUMBUS whose fleet on his second voyage to the New World was equipped with 'a pack of twenty purebred mastiffs and greyhounds'. Their main purpose was to subdue the native peoples. Varner and Varner in their book *Dogs of Conquest*, assert at the very beginning: 'Historians have agreed that the Spanish conquest of the Indies was accomplished by men, HORSES and dogs, in that order.'

In Europe, voracious dogs formed a part of the nobleman's equipment for hunting both animals and men, and had been used by the Spaniards against the Canary Islanders and the Moors. This was good preparation for what Varner and Varner called their role as 'lethal weapons of war' in the conquest of the Americas, beginning with their subjugation of the TAINOS of Jamaica: 'the first incident recorded in which a dog served a military purpose in the Indies'. (See 'DISCOVERY' OF JAMAICA.) Dogs in the employ of the *conquistadores* were thereafter to lay a bloody trail across the islands and mainland.

The Tainos did have a variety of

Cuban bloodhounds and handler (from Dallas)

Pre-Columbian clay dog in Museo Nacional, Mexico

dog, but it was a hairless, barkless animal, similar to that found in Mexico (and China) which served as both a pet and food. Although it did not bark like the European dog, it was not mute, but 'did yowl, grunt, and make other guttural sounds'. These dogs learned to bark after coming into contact with the European dogs, which were initially purebred but soon interbred with the local dogs.

The Tainos' first bloody encounter with the European dog was to set the pattern for centuries to come. The use of dogs as anti-personnel weapons continued in the BRITISH colonial period. One year after the English CAPTURE OF JAMAICA, in response to the Spanish ex-slaves who continued to harass them, an English soldier wrote home requesting 'a couple of whelps of the bloodhound strain, for I can think of no better way to clear the black rogues from this place'. Nevertheless, both African and Amerindian runaways adopted the animal for their own purpose, especially the MAROONS, who employed dogs in hunting the wild pig (see JERK) and the CONEY.

The historian Edward Long writing in the 18th century said that the introduced English breed of dogs became degenerate in size but did not lose their character. Those belonging to the hog-hunters he described as a mongrel mixture between the mastiff and greyhound, swift and fierce. The brindled were esteemed the best. They were similar to the Spanish breeds and much taller, like a greyhound. The Spanish dogs were much feared; in Jamaica they were bloodhounds imported from Cuba and used against the slaves and freed people, a reference as late as 1862 referring to 'a brace of Spanish dogs to be let loose on the next OBEAH gathering'. But the most chilling memory of dogs is of the 100 Cuban bloodhounds brought into the island with their 40 handlers in 1796 to track down and put fear into the hearts of the Trelawny Town Maroons.

There are no longer any wild dogs in Jamaica, but the ambivalent nature of Jamaicans' relationship with this animal continues. (See DOG IN FOLKLORE.)

[Crosby 1972, Long 1774, Varner and Varner 1983, Viola and Margolis 1991]

DOG IN FOLKLORE

In Jamaica, the word 'dog' has many connotations, usually negative in the mind of the folk. DOG is often a reviled creature, but at the same time it is immortalized in folk songs and sayings. Among published collections of Jamaican PROVERBS, there are more about dog than about any other creature or object. Part of the reason might be that dog is often used as a metaphor for the poor, the downtrodden, the suffering, or the stupid: 'Hungry dawg nyam roas corn'; 'If yu sorry fe mawga dawg he will turn round bite yu'; 'Puss and dog don't have same luck'; 'Every dog have him day, every puss him four o'clock'. Sometimes a person will refer to him or herself as 'dawg', ironically to signify poor treatment by someone else, suggesting, 'Am I worthy of this?' If a third party describes someone as being 'treated like a dog' it implies very bad treatment. 'To feel like dawg' means to feel terrible indeed. To 'not even say "dawg" ' to someone is to ignore that person, treat him or her lower than a dog is treated.

On the positive side, dog is credited with being non-complaining, as in the saying, 'Dog sweat but tek hair kibba it'.

The view that the male dog is sexually promiscuous was in the 1990s given expression by popular singer Beenie Man with a song called 'Ol'Daag'.

The word dog is used metaphorically in many ways; for instance, 'dog cornpiece' denotes a dangerous place in which to find oneself, dog being a good watchman; the phrase 'dog nyam yu supper' denotes a threat of punishment. Ironically, the popular phrase 'To swap black dog fe monkey', denoting an exchange from which one derives no benefit, does not refer to the animal at all. According to the DJE, 'black dog' was a cant phrase in Queen Anne's reign for a bad shilling or other base silver coin, and 'black dog' according to the OED was a coin of the lowest value current in the West Indies in the 18th century. Rampini, who visited Jamaica in the 19th century, makes the money connection explicit in quoting the proverb: 'Black dog (a small coin) buy trouble; hundred pound no clear him.'

While dogs today are given simple names like 'Tarzan' or 'Bingo' or 'Rover', dog names in the old days were often used to express their owners' aspirations or fears (in the same way that 'Try-see' was a popular name for a PIG). Edward Long noted that blacks 'gave their dogs as many names as a German prince', frequently calling them by a whole sentence such as 'Run-bruk-you-catch-um-good'. Another source claims that a woman scorned, called her dog 'Little-did-I-thought-that-man-was-so-deceitful' and a meek woman whose husband had a wicked temper named her dog 'Begin', and would thus call out each time her spouse began to work himself up to a shouting match.

Thomas Thistlewood, an 18th century planter in WESTMORELAND, noted that his mulatto slave driver had six dogs that he used to chase after trespassers and hunt in the morass. The names he gave them are no doubt suggestive of his past experiences: 'Gainst Me', 'Creold Woman', 'Fair to My Face', 'Good Women's Scarce', 'Woman Worst All', and 'Help Myself'.

Today, almost every Jamaican household has its dog, ranging from the mangy or common dog – sometimes called 'bruck-kitchen' – to the pedigreed and well-fed watchdogs or pampered pets of the wealthy suburbs. Whatever their pedigree, dogs in Jamaica are given to much barking throughout the night.

Despite its usefulness and closeness to man, the creature does call up ambivalent responses in the hearts of most Jamaicans, for dogs in the island have always been used and viewed as an extension of the ugly side of 'Massa'. Dogs were used to subdue and savage the TAINOS, and to track down (and savage) runaway slaves and MAROONS. Even today, dogs are sometimes conditioned to make class and racial distinctions between visitors who are welcome in the home and those who are not.

The ambivalence towards dogs might also be part of a universal mixture of fear and respect accorded to a creature that has been worshipped and portrayed from earliest times as dangerous, nocturnal and punitive on the one hand, and protector against forces of evil on the other. Dogs are credited with sensing DUPPIES and

foretelling death by howling. Perhaps because of the keenness of their sense of smell, dogs have always been associated with the dead, serving as guardians of the gates to the underworld. The Tainos had a dog-like four-footed ZEMI, OPIYEL GUOBIRÁN, lord of the underworld.
[Arrom 1990, Cassidy 1971, DJE, Edwards 1796, Hall 1989, Long 1774, Robinson 1987]

DOKUNU

A pudding that is wrapped in BANANA or PLANTAIN leaf and tied in little packages before cooking, hence its other name of Tie-leaf. Dokunu is made in small individual portions, and from the blue colour that the leaves turn when heated, it is also known as Blue Drawers. The main ingredient is grated CORN or cornmeal, though grated green banana or CASSAVA flour is also used, mixed with COCONUT milk, sugar and

Dokunu and ingredients

spices. Dokunu can be boiled or thrown directly into a fire or baked in the oven. The word dokunu betrays its origin as a West African dish, meaning in the Twi language, 'boiled maize bread'; it is still found in Accra, Ghana. (Another Twi-derived term, Conkie, is used in some of the other West Indian islands.) Dokunu's popularity is celebrated in an ANANSI story of a fabulous dokunu tree.
[DJE, Donaldson 1993, Facey 1993]

DOME, The

Structure in MONTEGO BAY erected in 1837 over the creek that supplied the town with water. An official called the Keeper of the Creek lived in the upper floor of the Dome. Legend has it that the water of the creek was discovered during Spanish times by two little girls hunting shrimps who lifted a stone and heard underground water flowing. The townspeople obtained water from

The Dome c. 1920 by Wells Elliott

the creek until 1894, when piped water was introduced. Until that time, a common sight was the long line of servants with YABBAS on their heads, waiting to collect water. The Dome still exists as a city landmark and has given its name to Dome Street.

What is called the Dome in FALMOUTH (Thorpe and Upper Harbour Streets) is a dome-shaped structure that was constructed around 1801 as an iron foundry, The Phoenix Foundry, much of its work being the repair of sugar machinery.

DOMINOES

One of the most popular pastimes in Jamaica. Players of all ages can often be seen throughout the island in bars, under trees, outside shops and on verandahs, or – more usually – heard, for the slamming of the dominoes on the playing surface seems an intrinsic element of the game. There are domino tournaments and clubs, and in 2000 the island was host to a World Domino Tournament. Though played by some women and sometimes by mixed groups, the game is very much the domain of men.

There is no clear indication of when the game was first played in Jamaica and indeed, very little has been recorded or written about it. However, anthropologist Diane J. Austin who studied a working class and a middle class neighbourhood in KINGSTON had interesting observations to make on the nature of the game and especially on the noise and exuberance that are generally associated with it. First she observed of the working class neighbourhood: 'Within the context of bar life, the major games are dominoes, cards and race tipping. Dominoes is by far the most important of these games . . . The champion domino player is generally a quiet and sometimes older man. He will reach a pitch of voluble excitement only occasionally. Perhaps a major contender has beaten him and his partner a number of times and a match or rubber is in danger. Then if the man wins a series of games to save the situation, perhaps in the very last game he will slam his dominoes down on the table, cry out and tease the opposing pair to illustrate that he after all is the master.'

She adds that 'Although the crowd around a domino game may be noisy, serious players generally revere their concentration and seldom make extreme claims for their prowess. The attraction of the game for the good player is in the excitement of playing an evenly matched pair and thus for the players the game is first and foremost an exercise of high skill and only for observers and adolescents a time for boisterous boasting. A boastful player is generally not a good player, and if he is good, is likely to be resented by his peers'.

In the bars of the middle class neighbourhood that she studied, Austin found dominoes to be 'simply a game rather than a ritual of excellence and prestige'. The boisterous conversational style of the working class neighbourhood is absent 'for these bars do not constitute a proving ground for men, but simply a location for relaxation away from home and office. Certainly Jamaican idiom and the game of dominoes have become increasingly prevalent in Jamaican middle class life since Independence, and especially during the 1970s. It appears as if the middle class have heaved a sigh of relief, acknowledged their indigenous rural background and thrown off some of the social pretensions of colonial life'.

Dominoes originated in China perhaps as far back as 2000 years ago. The Chinese game, however, is different from that played in the western world and the domino set differs from the set used in western games. The game is believed to have been taken from China to Europe by Venetian traders in the 14th and 15th centuries. The game spread to France and was introduced to the English by French prisoners-of-war during the Napoleonic wars. Since then it has spread throughout the world.

In England the game achieved great popularity in the late 18th and early 19th centuries when it was played in coffee houses. Dominoes became especially popular among working men; one explanation is that while the upper class had cards, dominoes carved from bone, ivory or wood (and later, plastic) were cheaper and more durable than paper cards, which in earlier times were very expensive.

The domino pieces are called in different places by different names, such as 'tiles' and 'bones'; in Jamaica, 'cards' seems to be the most common term.

[Arlott 1975, Austin 1984]

DON CHRISTOPHER'S COVE

Beautiful inlet on the shoreline of DRAX HALL property, ST ANN Parish, which is associated with Don Cristobal YSASSI, leader of the SPANISH guerrillas who kept up resistance against the English for five years after their CAPTURE OF JAMAICA. In this scenic area a number of early Hollywood films were made, including *Daughter of the Gods* with Annette Kellerman, and *Saturday Island* with Linda Darnell. Ysassi is also associated with another Don Christopher's Cove at Robin's Bay, ST MARY Parish, the reputed site of his final departure from Jamaica in 1660.

[Wright and White 1969]

DONKEY (*Equus asinus*)

This popular 'beast of burden' is also called Jackass, a term used by countrymen to refer to both the male and female donkey or ass, though 'Jenny' or 'Jenny-ass' is sometimes used. Rural Jamaicans once relied almost exclusively on this animal for transport, donkeys carrying much of the food to market in their sturdy hampers (panniers) before road and rail transportation systems became widespread. The MARKET woman (HIGGLER) wearing her traditional BANDANA and riding on or walking behind her donkey was a common sight and has been much used as a motif in folk art and souvenirs. The farmer also depended on the animal to transport loads to and from his field, often several kilometres away from his dwelling, a use that persists.

Domino players

Farmer with donkey transporting produce from his field

The donkey, like the HORSE, was brought to the New World by the Spaniards, the first arriving in 1493 on COLUMBUS' second voyage. Like the other quadrupeds brought on that voyage – the DOG, GOAT, PIG and CATTLE – it thrived in the fertile Antilles.

The donkey belongs to the horse family Equidae but has a much longer historical association with humans. Wild asses from early times were found in the dry parts of East Africa and Arabia, and were domesticated from the time of the Roman Empire. Since then, the donkey has proven a most useful assistant of mankind, providing transportation, motive labour (i.e. in turning mills), as pack animals, and in producing mules, by mating a jack (male ass) with a mare (female horse). Mules are sterile (i.e. cannot reproduce their own) but are regarded as genetically superior to parents on both sides, being stronger and of greater endurance. (See also JACKASS IN FOLKLORE.)

DONKEY CART see DRAY

DOVE AND PIGEON (Columbidae)

Ten kinds of these closely related BIRDS are native to Jamaica, and there are two introduced species. Many are well known, since among them are game-birds as well as the birds that are most commonly kept in captivity, their cooing often heard from trees, dovecotes and 'pigeon coops' even in city yards. Their abundance in the past is attested to in the name Pigeon Island (*Cayo de Palominos*) given by 16th century Spanish settlers to a large CAY south of Jamaica which was usually 'covered in doves'. On St John's Day the entire population would go there, returning with their boats laden with the birds.

The universal religious symbolism of these birds is also expressed in art and iconography in Jamaica, in religious songs, and in blood sacrifices in African-Jamaican religious and cultural expressions (see DOVE AND PIGEON IN FOLKLORE).

The different doves and pigeons are easily recognizable as their popular local names refer to their habits or appearance. Their mournful calls are also distinctive enough to provide identification even when they cannot be seen, and country people have put words to these calls, many of which are listed by May Jeffrey-Smith in her book, *Bird-Watching in Jamaica*.

The local names of the Columbids with their English names in brackets, are as follows:

Ring-tail	(Ring-tailed Pigeon)
Mountain Witch	(Crested Quail-Dove)
Bald-pate	(White-crowned Pigeon)
Pea Dove	(Zenaida Dove)
Long-tail Pea	(Mourning Dove)
White Belly	(Caribbean Dove)
White-wing	(White-winged Dove)
Ground Dove	(Common Ground Dove)
Red Partridge	(Ruddy Quail-Dove)
Blue Dove	(Plain Pigeon)

Two species are among the earliest birds introduced into Jamaica, the Rock Dove ('Pigeon') and the Ringed-turtle Dove ('Barble Dove'). They are not found in forests or woodlands, and only occur around human habitation.

Of the native species, the Mountain Witch and Ring-tail are found only in Jamaica.

The Ring-tail (*Columba caribaea*), which is so-called from its black-banded long tail, occupies the dense mountain forests and is not often seen by casual observers. According to P. H. Gosse, the English naturalist who studied Jamaica's birds in the 1840s, this arboreal bird is 'never seen to put his feet upon the earth', or at any rate chooses to do so when no one is about. Gosse failed to collect a single specimen. Also called Mountain Pigeon or Mountain Dove, the Ring-tail has in the past been regarded as a culinary delicacy; today, it is among the birds considered vulnerable.

The Mountain Witch or Crested Quail Dove (*Geotrygon versicolor*) is also difficult to see, as it is a terrestrial bird that inhabits well-developed wet forest. It is known for its haunting cry described as 'mournfully human'. This beautiful ground dove is also called Blue Dove or Blue Partridge.

The Bald-pate, Long-tail Pea Dove and White Wing are game birds; like other birds they are protected by law and can only be shot during the bird-shooting season, the dates and the bag limits of which are set and monitored through the Natural Resources Conservation Authority (NRCA).

The Bald-pate (*Columba leucocephala*) is a medium size dark blue-gray pigeon with a conspicuous white (not bald) head; it is a high flyer that is rarely seen on the ground. Usually found in larger numbers in lowlands and MANGROVE swamps, this is one of the birds frequently captured illegally and reared as a cage-bird.

The Pea-dove (*Zenaida aurita*) is so called from its habit of eating peas planted by the farmer, and can be identified by its sweet, mournful, cooing. Closely related to, and resembling the Pea Dove, is the Long-tail Pea Dove or Mourning Dove (*Zenaida macroura*).

The White Wing (*Zenaida asiatica*) is so-named from the conspicuous white band extending across its wings; it is also called Lapwing. It is said to be the only gregarious dove, liking to move about in flocks.

The White Belly (*Leptotila jamaicensis*) is found only in Jamaica and Grand Cayman and is a ground dweller, a shy bird of woodland and forest given to 'sobbing' notes.

The Ground Dove (*Columbina passerina*) is the smallest – a little bigger and more rounded than the sparrow – and the most familiar, so-called from its habit of feeding on the ground. It is almost always seen in pairs, on roadways or in gardens, or in small flocks. Described as 'neat' and 'perky', it is a common sight all over the island and indeed is the most widely distributed of its family in the West Indies. It also occurs in North and Central America, Mexico and the southern USA.

The Partridge (*Geotrygon montana*), also known as Red Partridge or Ruddy Quail Dove, is a ground dweller of the woods and forests and is rarely seen.

The Blue Dove or Plain Pigeon (*Columba inornata*) occurs only in the Greater ANTILLES. It is slightly larger than the Bald-pate, and its numbers have been declining throughout its range, probably owing to hunting, loss of habitat and predation by introduced mammals (e.g. MONGOOSE). It flies high and is more often seen in flocks.

[DJE, Espinosa 1628, Gosse 1984, Jeffrey-Smith 1972, Raffaele et al. 1998, Taylor 1955]

DOVE AND PIGEON IN FOLKLORE

The words pigeon and dove are used interchangeably in Jamaica. The BIRDS they describe are used in African-Jamaican religious rituals and for sacrifice by, for example, Revivalists, flocks of doves being kept in the Shepherd's yard. One Revival officer is called a Dove and coos like one. (See REVIVAL.) As in other cultures the birds are used symbolically. In medieval art, the dove is pictured as an emblem of divine benediction and in Christianity it represents the Holy Ghost. In Revival and other indigenous churches, the dove is also widely used as a religious icon, painted on walls of churches, carved on the Shepherd's staff, etc. It also frequently appears in the paintings and sculpture of intuitive artists. (See ART.) Showbread (see BREAD) in the shape of a dove is also baked for religious occasions.

The Ground Dove and White Belly (which are frequently found in GRAVEYARDS or walking over graves in rural areas) are regarded as DUPPY birds.

DRAGONFLY (*Libelinlina*)

The swift flying, graceful insect commonly seen darting over streams and ponds is known in Jamaica as Needlecase, supposedly from the shape of its body. Jamaica has over sixty species of Dragonflies plus the closely related Damselflies that are smaller and thinner; two dragonfly species are known only from the island.

As in other places, the dragonfly is also called Devil's Darning Needle from its supposed habit of sewing up the ears and mouths of naughty children. Water Dipper, Needle Pointer and Snake Doctor are other, less well known names, the latter because the creature is believed to minister to SNAKES. In folk MEDICINE, Needlecase is preserved in RUM against aches, pains and stings.

The insect is characterized by its long slender body, two pairs of large reticulated transparent wings, and huge, bulging eyes that form the bulk of its head. Each eye is made up of as many as 1,500 tiny six-sided facets, fitted together like the cells of a honeycomb and looking out in all directions.

The female lays eggs in a huge mass on the water surface, on damp moss or attached to underwater stems or leaves. Each egg hatches out a tiny nymph that has no internal skeleton but a tough supporting exoskeleton that it periodically bursts out of and discards, growing another one, consuming enormous quantities of mosquito wrigglers and other water animals in the process. This continues for several months until the insect acquires wings, at which point it ceases to grow.

Though most Dragonflies fly by day, there are three species in Jamaica that fly at dusk. Dragonflies eat voraciously, on the wing, and are of great benefit in keeping down insects.
[Cassidy 1971, DJE, NHSJ 1949]

DRAMA see PANTOMIME, THEATRE

DRAMA SCHOOL
see EDNA MANLEY COLLEGE

DRAX HALL
Old SUGAR estate in ST ANN Parish, near to ST ANN'S BAY, which was first settled by Charles Drax, an immigrant from Barbados (where there is still a Drax Hall). By his will dated 1721, Drax left Drax Hall and other property for the founding of a charity school in the parish, with detailed instructions for its conduct. He stipulated, for instance, the diet of the students: fresh meat on Sunday and Thursday, fresh or salt fish on Wednesday and Friday, beef and pudding on Monday, pork and beans on Tuesday, and 'pot luck' on Saturday. But nothing was done immediately after his death to establish the school, for by various underhand means 'that excited the indignation of every honest man who became acquainted with the transaction' the estate was 'captured' by one of the richest families of the day, the BECKFORDS. After years of litigation a settlement was arrived at (for a greatly reduced sum) and in 1802 Drax's Free School was endowed.

In 1806 the school was transferred to Walton, MONEAGUE, and later renamed the Jamaica Free School to indicate its broadened scope. It was merged in 1883 by the governor, Sir John Peter Grant, with the Jamaica High School which was established at HOPE in ST ANDREW Parish. A college called University College was attached to the school in 1890 and enabled students to take degrees of London University externally. A number of Jamaicans did gain degrees in this fashion, including one MA. However, the college and school were amalgamated in 1902 and became Jamaica College, a boys' secondary school.

In this century, the old sugar works at Drax Hall were used first as a lime factory and later as a soap factory. The soap factory was to be absorbed into what later became the Seprod group that manufactured soap and edible products, and 'Drax' was retained as a brand name of soap for some time. Recently there have been plans to develop Drax Hall as a resort area.

Drax Hall has in recent times been the site for archaeological investigations, particularly of the AFRICAN slave settlements (see SLAVERY) and later free settlement on the estate. These investigations were conducted by the INSTITUTE OF JAMAICA and the JNHT in association with the University of California at Los Angeles. In 1983 Drax Hall was the venue for the first field school in Afro-Caribbean archaeology in the Caribbean.
[Armstrong 1991, Cundall 1915, Wright and White 1969]

DRAY
A low cart without fixed sides, drawn by mules or HORSES, formerly much used to transport goods such as grass for animal feed, coal, SUGAR CANE from field to factory, and sugar to the wharf. Now rarely seen, the dray was once a familiar sight in the country as well as on urban streets. The open drays were built with two or four wheels. A smaller two-wheeler cart with fixed sides and a removable rear panel was popularly known as 'donkey cart'. These carts were locally made. They were a collective effort of the carpenter (see CABINET-MAKER) who made the wooden body of the cart and the driver's seat, the wheelwright who made the wooden wheels that were reinforced with iron bands and covered with iron tires, and the BLACKSMITH who made the axle and other metal parts.

Dray

DROP PAN

Folk lottery brought by CHINESE immigrants, an illegal game that is still played though not as widely as it once was. This is a numbers game: books of tickets numbered from 1-36 are sold by vendors working for the 'banker' who is the person running the game. Each numbered ticket sold is dropped into a pan for the draw, each draw or play being called a 'pan'. All holders of the number drawn become winners. Each number is assigned a special meaning or several meanings ('mark'), some originally brought from China, others developed in Jamaica, e.g. the number 1 signifies 'white', 18 'doctor', and so on. Purchases are therefore often based on dreams, guesses, signs ('rakes') or TOKENS of the number or symbol, and Dream Books are sometimes consulted. Drop Pan is also called Tyshin and Woppy and in other parts of the CARIBBEAN, Whe-whe. The game apparently is still popular in the DANCEHALL environment, with specially coded meanings assigned to the numbers. (See also PEAKA-PEOW.)

[Chevannes 1989, DJE, Francis-Jackson 1995]

DRUM

The fact that African-style drums and drumming were frequently banned during SLAVERY is indicative not only of the instrument's importance in the lives of the enslaved AFRICANS but of the fear it engendered in their white owners. More than anything else, drums were viewed by the planters as instruments of communication among the slaves and therefore significant factors in fomenting revolt. The 'noise' of the drumming was also an irritant to European ears. The WESTMORELAND planter Thomas Thistlewood, for instance, complained that his slaves, to whom he'd given permission to gather and not make noise, 'transgressed, by beating the Coombie [Goombay] loud, singing high, &c.' Drums were also later discouraged by the Christian MISSIONARIES who saw them as 'heathen' instruments. While the drums might have gone underground, drumming did not, as the many improvisations in percussion, then as now, indicate, for example: the bamboo stamping tubes in GERREH, gourd bass in KUMINA in ST MARY Parish, and handclapping and bamboo clappers in DINKI MINI.

The drum has remained the key instrument in virtually all forms of African-Jamaican music making, as central to religious and healing rituals as to secular 'play'. In the past, the traditional drums were made by the users, though with the easier availability of factory-made instruments the craft is dying.

Among the many drum types today are the side drum of JONKONNU, REVIVAL bass and rattling drum, BURU funde (or fundeh), bass and repeater, kumina kbandu and playing cyas, BRUCKINS drum, TAMBU drum, bongo and conga and GOOMBAY. Some are single-headed, others stopped at both ends. Both sticks and hands are used, and styles and rhythms vary considerably.

The various types of hollowed out wooden drums as well as the goombay represent

Marjorie Whylie (above) and a class of her students at the Jamaica School of Music

Tivoli Gardens Drum Corps, 1971

the African element, but the prevalence of naval and military forces during the plantation era also introduced the military drums and drumming styles still seen, e.g. the fife and drum elements of Jonkonnu. In recent years, American-style marching drum corps have become popular among schools and youth groups, and the bands attached to both the military and police have contributed to the training and employment of many professional musicians. The INDIAN tradition of HOSAY also introduced the tasa and nagara drums in the 19th century, though many of the players today are African Jamaicans.

In religious and popular music, the drums come in sets of two or three, the most common number for the core group of drums in the West African style. Usually the lead drum improvises and one or two others play contrasting rhythmic patterns. The role of the drum is to give directions to the dancers and/or stimulate worshippers to ecstasy (e.g. Kumina, Revival). In religious rituals, the drums themselves have a sacred function and are built and prepared according to specific rites. Ritual drums are usually kept separate from those used for secular purposes.

Although drums and drumming styles display West African features and even names, these are syncretic or blended New World creations, not traceable in their entirety to any specific region or ethnic group in Africa. For instance, the drum language of the Akan has not survived; it is said that Jamaican drummers who went to an international arts festival in Lagos were asked: 'Why do your drums not speak?'

While the drum has always been a significant element in the folk culture, its use was practically unknown in the schools, churches, concert halls and 'respectable' arenas until the 1970s, when the Jamaica School of Music decided to change the British derived curriculum to better reflect Jamaican needs. Conga drumming became a compulsory part of the training of all students, based on the argument that while European music is melodic and vocal, Jamaican music is essentially percussive and rhythmical. As Pamela O'Gorman, then head of the school explained it, drumming was insisted on 'in much the same way as European institutions insist on compulsory choir or keyboard proficiency – not to produce advanced practitioners, but to give "hands on" experience of the musical behaviours that are integral to the culture'. Jamaican musician Marjorie Whylie, then Head of the Folk Music Research Department, was responsible for teaching drumming as a systematic element in music education. In the process she influenced scores of musicians and music teachers who passed on their skills and made the instrument as widely accepted 'above ground' as it is today.

[Bilby 1985, Hall 1989, JSM 1972, 1976, O'Gorman 1991, Whylie and Warner-Lewis 1994]

DUB see DANCEHALL, REGGAE

DUCK ANTS see ANTS

DUHO see SEATING, Ceremonial

DUMPLING

Dumplings made of flour and water used to be the staple food of men who did heavy manual labour. A gang going out to work often carried a clean 'kerosene tin' – an empty five gallon oil pan – to do what was called 'bush cooking'. Sometimes they would make red peas or GUNGO peas soup (the thicker the better) to which they added dumplings. But if there was nothing else, they would put a pan of water on the wood fire and throw in flour dumplings of an enormous size, kneaded until they were very hard and shaped flat and round. If there was no pot, they would be thrown directly into the fire and roasted until they were crisp and blackened on the outside. The DJE lists many names attached to these dumplings, such as 'cartwheel'.

In the home, soups and stews are unthinkable without small cigar-shaped dumplings called 'spinners'. Dumplings made with a baking agent are usually fried and are called JOHNNY CAKE. Flour is the basic ingredient in dumplings, but other starches such as cornmeal, CASSAVA flour, grated green BANANAS or PLANTAIN are sometimes added.

[DJE, Donaldson 1993]

Dunn's River falls

DUNN'S RIVER
The cataracts on this river near to OCHO RIOS, ST ANN Parish, form one of Jamaica's most beautiful sights and the island's most popular tourist attraction. The falls are usually crowded with visitors and locals alike who seek the thrill of climbing up its 183m waterfall. Dunn's River is part of a landscaped park that includes the beach where the river enters the sea. Dunn's River falls is one of several beautiful waterfalls along the north coast (see ROARING RIVER, ST ANN) but is now the only one maintained as an attractive site.

DUPONT, Fr Joseph (1806-1887)
This ROMAN CATHOLIC priest is the only clergyman to have a statue erected to him in Jamaica. Originally located at the Parade (see St William Grant PARK), the statue was in 2000 moved to SS Peter and Paul Church at MATILDA'S CORNER, one of the churches he founded.

Fr Dupont was born in Savoy, France and came to Jamaica in 1847. He devoted the next 40 years ministering mainly to the poor and needy who inhabited Kingston's lanes and tenement yards. His outreach activity made him a legendary figure and he was mourned by the whole island when he died. A statue was erected to his memory by public subscription in 1892 at the Parade and was destroyed by the EARTHQUAKE in 1907. It was again replaced by public subscription.
[Osborne 1988]

DUPPY
Restless ghost or spirit of the dead. While the term 'duppy' is commonly used to describe anything that is connected with the supernatural, some people make a distinction between the 'duppy' as evil spirit and other types of 'good' spirits, sometimes called ancestral spirits. This is based on the widespread belief that dead family members live on in the spirit world and continue to take an interest in the welfare of the family. (See DEATH RITUALS, WAKE.) These spirits (in the old days referred to as 'Ol'people') can appear of their own accord, or be called upon for help in time of trouble. In African-based religious and cultural practices, e.g. BALM, GOOMBAY, KUMINA, MAROON, MYAL, REVIVAL, they can be invited to come by various means, including spirit possession. Information transmitted by these spirits is usually interpreted for the benefit of the group or of individuals in the way of healing or advice. These spirits are cared for through offerings, sacrifices, feasts and general recognition. Family spirits will also appear to individuals in dreams to give warnings and advice. The verb 'dream' in Jamaican creole means 'to call on the living through a dream', hence 'my granny dream me last night'.

While the ancestral spirit is known, the duppy is usually an unnamed and unidentified human dead that is unhappy and unsettled ('restless') and believed capable of doing harm, sometimes assuming demon-forms such as ROLLING CALF. These spirits, regarded as the 'shadow' side of the human personality, can hang around to haunt the living but even worse, they can be summoned by the OBEAH-man or woman from the GRAVEYARD and employed to work for them (in exchange for payment of food, and drink, especially RUM). Obeah-men, it is believed, can 'set duppy' on people to alter their behaviour, drive them insane, or even kill them; duppies are said to 'knock' such people. The duppy may also be cast into a rat, crow, MONGOOSE, FROG or reptile which then takes the curse to the intended victim. It may occasionally miss the victim and attack whoever happens to be where it expected to find its prey: this innocent person then becomes the target. Specialists under various names ('Four-eye people') who can see duppies are employed to get rid of such spirits, or special Kumina or Revival services are held.

Duppy Lore Stories about duppies are very much a part of Jamaican FOLKLORE. Some people seriously believe in and are terrified by the notion of duppies. Others are sceptical but tell 'duppy stories' to entertain. Jamaica is said to have a very high frequency of noisy, troublesome ghosts (called poltergeists) – the ones that throw stones on houses, set fires, break crockery and furniture, make rapping sounds and are otherwise physically active. One Catholic priest who was also an anthropologist, Fr J.J. Williams, wrote a book called *Psychic Phenomena in Jamaica* based on some of the cases of poltergeist and other ghostly activities he investigated.

Duppy is frequently invoked in Jamaican sayings. A well known expression is 'Bull buck and duppy conquerer', i.e. someone who is the biggest and the baddest. One of Bob MARLEY'S early hit songs was called 'Duppy Conqueror'. A popular PROVERB is 'Duppy know who fe frighten an who fe tell "goodnight", (i.e. we do not provoke those whom we know will retaliate, instead, we treat them with respect). The folk song, 'You want to hear duppy laugh', advises that to do so, you must 'go down a river early morning'. Many 'duppy stories' are among Jamaican folk tales and can be found in collections of these tales. (See ANANSI STORIES.)

The 'duppy' is believed to be the spirit of someone who was wicked in life or who was not accorded proper memorials or who has unfinished business on earth and so has stayed around to haunt the living. These are the spirits that can be seen (or felt) by anyone, especially in the darkness of night and at certain dangerous venues, e.g. the root of COTTON TREE and BAMBOO.

Duppies are believed to possess certain common characteristics: they all speak in high nasal voices and are repelled by SALT; someone seeing a duppy should eat salt right away. One can tell when a duppy is near by the feeling of heat that duppies 'throw' on people and by a feeling of the head 'growing big'. But in some cases, duppies cause a feeling of cold and numbness, signs more associated with European folklore.

Duppies are believed to have powers to hurt; especially by 'blowing', i.e. breathing, on a person that will make them get sick; a person touched by a duppy will have fits. An eruption on the skin may be diagnosed as 'duppy box you there'.

These ghosts are said to feed on FIG leaves, bamboo roots and duppy PUMPKIN. If they are to be placated with offerings of cooked food, no salt must be used; they also enjoy such sweets as molasses and condensed milk.

Duppy lore is so well known that the individual doesn't have to appeal to a specialist to avoid or deflect attentions of spirits (assuming he or she is not already protected by a CHARM or Guard). Inversion is a good way of fooling the duppy: put your cap on back to front or turn your clothes inside out. You can also shame a duppy: a woman can throw her skirt over her head, or a man can unzip his pants and show himself; 'bad language' (cursing) can also be used.

Other precautions include striking two matches, blowing each out saying 'One', then 'Two', and throwing them down. After lighting the third match, one says 'Three', blows it out, but keeps it. The duppy will stay all night searching for the third match in that spot while its intended victim runs away. You can take a hair from the middle of your head and put it in your mouth; make the sign of the cross; walk with small objects to throw so the duppy will be forced to stop and count while you make your escape; or burn something with a strong odour: horn, Rosemary (see CROTON), SPIRIT WEED, Worm Weed (See-me-Contract), Death Weed or sulphur. Barking DOGS will drive duppies away also. Stopping-up every nook and cranny, every keyhole and crack will keep duppies out of the house at night.

Strangers who knock on one's door late at

night are almost certainly duppies, and even a friend or relative remains suspect until clearly identified.

Duppy Plants Night scented plants such as the jasmine are thought to attract duppies, and so are avoided. Scented lilies are regarded as death or duppy flowers for the same reason and some people would never bring them inside a house; the same belief attaches to sea SHELLS: they are believed to attract duppies to the house and empower them. During the day, duppies take the form of large green lizards; it is very bad luck to have such LIZARDS nearby, and many Jamaicans kill them on sight. (See LIZARD IN FOLKLORE.)

Duppy has given its name to a host of objects whose characteristic is that they are an imitation (or 'shadow') of the real thing. Thus Duppy Soursop or Duppy Peas closely resemble the SOURSOP or peas but are not edible; a 'duppy game' is a drawn game. In other cases the object has uncanny characteristics, e.g. 'Duppy Fee-fee' for the Monkey Fiddle plant that makes a squeaking sound when its stems are rubbed together; Duppy Gun is a plant with seed pods that burst explosively; Duppy Riding-horse is the praying mantis; Duppy Umbrella is the wild mushroom or fungus. Some BIRDS are known as 'Duppy birds' especially the Gimme-me-bit and the Ground-dove, and are regarded with suspicion.

[Adetugbo 1996, Banbury 1894, Beckwith 1919, DJE, Dunham 1946, Henriques 1953, Mico 1893, 1896, NHSJ 1949, Patterson 1973, Perkins 1969, Rashford 1984, 1985, 1988a, Rattray 1927, Williams 1934]

'Duppy plants' drawn by Lilly G. Perkins: top, L-R: 'Overlook Bean' (Canavalia ensiformis), 'Duppy Rattle' (Crotalaria retusa); below, L-R: 'Duppy Tomato' (Solanum ciliatum), 'Duppy Cherry' (Cordia collococca)

DUPPY FLY TRAP *(Aristolochia grandiflora)*

Husky climbing vine that bears the largest flower to be found in Jamaica. The perianth is up to 20cm broad, with a spur of 50-60cm. The flower itself is of mottled light purple and buff, becoming solid purple as it nears the stem. Its strange appearance is matched by its habit of trapping insects – hence its popular name. At times the flower exudes an unpleasant odour which attracts carrion flies (so it is sometimes called Poison Hog Meat). Once inside, the flies are trapped by a profusion of hairs turned inwards – until they have served their purpose which is to become covered in pollen. For the flower does not consume the insect as is sometimes supposed, but uses it to carry out pollination. When the insect is covered with pollen, the hairs collapse and enable it to escape, hopefully to pollinate another flower. The plant is found usually along rivers, gullies and water courses from 360m to 800m and is used in folk MEDICINE. It is a relative of Dutch-man's Pipe (*A. ringens*) which is sometimes cultivated in gardens.

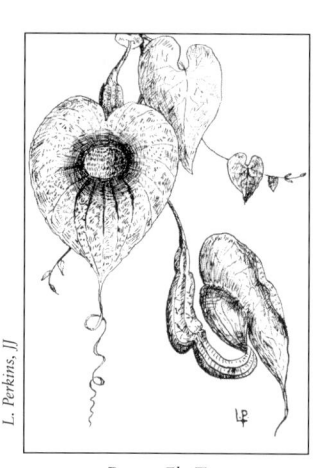

[Adams 1972, Perkins 1969]

Duppy Fly Trap

DUTCHIE

Short for 'Dutch pot' – a heavy cast iron pot with three small feet, handles, and a cover (known in some other CARIBBEAN islands as 'three-foot pot'). This was once an essential item in every household, placed on the FIREPLACE or three firestones. It was the all-purpose cooking utensil, used for frying, boiling and baking, as a coal or wood fire could be placed both underneath and heaped on its top. Many

Dutch pots

Jamaicans still swear by their old Dutchies for baking dishes such as sweet potato and cornmeal puddings: 'Hell a top, hell a bottom, hallelujah in the middle' is the resulting riddle. The pots come in different sizes, and some were hung by hooks over the fireplace. Like the COAL-POT, the Dutchie was probably imported from Holland. During the plantation era, throughout the Caribbean these were the cooking pots distributed by the owner to each slave household and listed in the plantation records, along with slave clothing. (See SLAVERY.)

Another popular cooking pot of times past was a Jesta (from 'digester'), a large iron or enamel pot with a long handle. Any large pot is jocularly called a 'bella gut'.

The role of the Dutchie or other large pots in communal eating took a modern turn in the 1980s when the British group Musical Youth had a major hit with the song, 'Pass the Dutchie' (1982). The original Jamaican version of the song by The Mighty Diamonds had enraged the moral majority, for it celebrated not communal cooking but communal GANJA smoking with a chillum pipe. Their song was called 'Pass the Kutchie'.
[Cassidy 1971, DCEU, DJE, Higman 1998]

EARTHQUAKE

Although Jamaica is in a seismically active region, seismologists claim that large earthquakes are comparatively rare though usually of relatively high intensity. The majority of earthquakes are minor ones of low intensity. The island experiences much less seismic activity than the Eastern Caribbean or Central American region. Jamaica's reputation for earthquakes rests on two major disasters, those of 1692 and 1907.

The earthquake of 1692 occurred on 7 June and was sufficiently large to rank as one of the great earthquakes in history. Within the space of less than 30 seconds, it destroyed the city of **PORT ROYAL**, then the most important and prosperous English city in the New World. Several eye-witness accounts of the horror have come down to us, telling of the two slight shocks before the third which caused the earth to open and swallow people alive and throw up long-dead bodies from the cemetery. Two-thirds of the city was sunk beneath the sea and the rest of the buildings crashed to the ground, burying hundreds under the falling masonry. Many were drowned as houses were moved intact from dry land to the bottom of the sea. Some time after the earthquake, a monstrous wave rolled over the surviving part of the city, drowning the survivors. About 2,000 people were killed. (See eyewitness accounts in Marx 1967a and by Quakers in Langford 1997.)

Though the earthquake is associated with the destruction of Port Royal, its origin was under the sea off the north coast and even more severe damage occurred in the rest of the island. While the tsunami or sea-wave generated by the earthquake struck Port Royal some time after the quake, the two events were almost simultaneous on the north coast. According to John Shepherd, 'to make matters worse, the wave was reflected between the coasts of Jamaica and Cuba and returned to Jamaica at least eight times in the five hours after the earthquake'.

Part of the heavy destruction on Port Royal was due to building practices, the rich merchants erecting multi-storey heavy brick buildings on unstable, waterlogged soil close to the sea. The only buildings surviving the earthquake were the huts of the slaves in which the wealthy survivors were forced to seek refuge.

The earthquake of 14 January 1907 destroyed

Destruction of Kingston by earthquake and fire, 1907

a large part of the city of KINGSTON, killing over 600 out of a population of 40,000, though much of the damage was done by fire which broke out during the earthquake, destroying some 22.6ha of the city. As before, the damage reflected the type of buildings: brick and stone buildings suffered most, cement and wooden buildings least. East and west walls of buildings collapsed, while those facing north and south were less damaged, suggesting that the shock ran east and west. Reinforced concrete has been favoured for construction since that time and regulations governing construction of new buildings are based on the California earthquake building code.

Nevertheless there was extensive property damage in the next serious earthquake, which occurred on 1 March 1957 at about 7:30pm and was felt all over the island but most intensively in western parishes. Three people were killed and several rendered homeless. In Port Royal, a stretch of beach 2.4m wide by 183m long broke off and disappeared into the sea. But the greatest effect was felt in MONTEGO BAY and environs. Electricity, telephone, and telegraph services all failed and water mains were broken. Many of the older buildings suffered destruction, especially the churches; in Montego Bay these included Holy Trinity, St Paul's Kirk, Burchell Baptist as well as the parish church. The clock tower of the parish church was completely destroyed and all the walls of the main building and the altar cracked. The RAILWAY line from Kingston was blocked by boulders between Anchovy and Montego Bay.

According to the Earthquake Unit at the UNIVERSITY OF THE WEST INDIES, the total number of quakes located from 1976 up to 1998 in the parishes of Jamaica and offshore within the local region grid was 1,071.

A magnitude 5.4 earthquake – Modified Mercalli intensity (MM)7 – occurred near Kingston at 12:11pm on 13 January 1993 causing significant damage in Kingston and ST ANDREW. The main shock was near to Silver Hill Peak, PORTLAND Parish; the hypocentres of 32 aftershocks were determined. What is significant about this earthquake is that it indicated that land-based faults in Jamaica can produce events with damaging intensities whereas previously damaging earthquakes were perceived to have offshore origins.

Counting the January 1993 event and those recorded in the Tomblin-Robson Catalogue (1977), 13 earthquakes with intensities of MM7 and greater have been documented in the past 326 years. All intensities are on the 1956 version of Modified Mercalli Scale. Ten of these affected the eastern part of Jamaica more severely than the western parishes. The 13 January event was the tenth eastern Jamaican earthquake in the known history to have caused intensities of MM7 and higher. On average, therefore, Jamaica can expect one such event every 33 years though the length of time between these events has been from one to 82 years.

[Langford 1997, Marx 1967a, Parkes and Stewart 1999, Shepherd 1968, Wiggins-Grandison 1996, Wright 1976]

EASINGTON

Small village on the bank of the YALLAHS RIVER that was the capital of the parish of St David from 1836-67 before it was merged with ST THOMAS. A plaque erected by the Jamaica National Trust Commission records this fact and also pays tribute to National Hero the Rt Excellent Paul BOGLE who is associated with this area. Easington overlooks JUDGEMENT CLIFF and a plaque to this effect has also been erected in the village by the Jamaican Historical Society.

EAST INDIAN see INDIAN

EASTER

One of the principal holidays of the year, when Jamaicans enjoy a long weekend of four days' holiday. For Christians, GOOD FRIDAY is a day of sober worship, followed by the quiet of Holy Saturday, and then the rejoicing and fine new clothes of Easter Sunday, and the popular entertainments of Easter Monday.

Under MISSIONARY influence, Good Friday came to be set aside in many communities as a day on which no work should be done, no food cooked or fires lit, and servants should be freed from tasks. Attendance at Three Hour service (noon to 3:00pm, the period of the crucifixion of Christ according to the Bible) was obligatory. The main food allowed was EASTER BUN and cheese, which could be discreetly munched in church during the long service. Those who went to the beach on Good Friday or Holy Saturday – or even on Easter Sunday – were viewed with disapproval by religious Jamaicans though nowadays many treat the entire long weekend as a secular holiday.

Even before African and black CREOLE Jamaicans had created their own Easter traditions, the irreligious pirates and planters of white 17th century Jamaica held holidays on the two great festivals, CHRISTMAS and Easter. Easter was one of the few times that some churches opened their doors for the year. (See ANGLICAN, RELIGION.) So during the centuries of SLAVERY, the enslaved shared the three days' holiday of Christmas as well as 'Pikni Christmas', the name they gave to the one-day holiday at Easter which seemed a small or 'child' holiday. Easter falls during croptime when the SUGAR CANE is reaped and factories operate at full blast (see SUGAR PLANTATION, CROPOVER, SEASONS), so time off would have been the bare minimum. The holiday probably did not become generally known among the slaves as Easter until well into the missionary era in Jamaica, perhaps by the beginning of the 19th century.

EASTER BUN

Sweet buns are popular all year round in Jamaica, 'bun and cheese' being fairly common fare, but the spicy and fruit-rich 'Easter bun' is special, the commercial bakeries competing to create more and more elaborate buns, the cost depending on the quantity of fruit. Easter buns (like CHRISTMAS PUDDINGS) are usually sent to relatives overseas. Individuals who make their own have their favourite recipes, with choices of whether to use yeast, baking powder, baking

Easter bun and cheese

soda or stout, Enid Donaldson giving recipes for all four in her cookery book. Easter Bun derives from the English tradition of Hot Cross Buns at GOOD FRIDAY which became popular during Tudor days. According to Norma Benghiat, even today, 'some of the Yorkshire buns are identical to our Easter buns'.

[Benghiat 1985, Donaldson 1993]

EBONY (*Brya ebenus*)

West Indian Ebony is a shrub or small tree, up to 8m high, found only in Jamaica and Cuba (although other woods called 'ebony' are found elsewhere). Its dark heavy wood was once exported, known as 'Cocus wood' on the world market to distinguish it from other ebonies, and used for making brush backs, parts of musical instruments and inlay work, among other things. Nowadays the ebony is probably better known as a garden ornamental shrub whose brilliant burst of orange-yellow flowers after rain makes it easily identified. The flowers last for a few brief days and are a powerful attraction to bees. Ebony grows wild up to 600m in dry areas, especially in the southern plains and foothills, and is sometimes used for fence posts. In former times, the slender but flexible green branches, like those of the TAMARIND, were used to make switches.

[Adams 1972, NHSJ 1946]

EDINBURGH CASTLE, Mad Doctor of

Lewis Hutchinson, the 'mad doctor', was an 18th century mass murderer whose motive was never established. He disposed of his victims in a sinkhole, near his 'castle', the ruins of which can still be seen half-way on a rough road between Kellits (CLARENDON Parish) and Claremont (ST ANN Parish).

Hutchinson was born in Scotland in 1733, was well educated, having spent some years in medical school, and came to Jamaica in the 1760s. Soon after, he built his 'castle' – a small two-storied house with two circular loop-holed towers placed diagonally at opposite corners. From here he had a good view of the road and those who happened to pass by alone he would kill with a single shot. His slaves were forced to dispose of the bodies in the sinkhole. In his more playful moods, Hutchinson would invite the victim to his house, entertain him royally, bid him godspeed on departure, and shoot him dead as he rode off. No one knows the final count of his victims but after he was arrested a search made of his house revealed considerable amounts of clothing and belongings of others, including 43 watches.

Although Hutchinson was unpopular with his neighbours because of an unpleasant personality and was the subject of countless rumours, no move was made against him for some time because there was no evidence of his involvement in criminal activity. In those unsettled days people frequently disappeared and his slaves were too terrified to speak out. In any event, slaves were not allowed to give testimony against a white man. Finally, Hutchinson went too far, and attacked Dr Jonathan Hutton who owned a nearby property. A warrant was issued for his arrest and he promptly shot a soldier who was sent to serve the warrant – in full view of several Europeans.

With the authorities aroused at last, the 'mad doctor' abandoned his castle and made his way to OLD HARBOUR where he took to sea and attempted to board a ship about to sail. But the navy had been alerted and he was captured by sailors from Lord RODNEY'S ship. Hutchinson was brought to trial and sentenced to death. He was hanged at the SPANISH TOWN gallows on 16 March 1773, aged 40.

Much of what occurred at Hutchinson's 'castle' was revealed by his slaves who felt free to speak after his capture. No one ever discovered what psychological quirk was responsible for him becoming a mass murderer. Even as he went to the gallows he showed no remorse, as the Revd G.W. Bridges recorded in his *Annals of Jamaica*, 'nor can the annals of human depravity equal the fact that, at the foot of the scaffold, he left an hundred pounds in gold to erect a monument, and to inscribe the marble with a record of his death'. His wishes were never carried out. The epitaph he composed ended:

> Their sentence, pride, and malice, I defy;
> Despise their power, and, like a Roman,
> die.

In 1895 Sir Henry Blake, governor of Jamaica, along with the superintendent of Public Works, was lowered to the bottom of Hutchinson's hole. No bones or other relics of Hutchinson's victims were found but the bottom of the hole appeared to have been flooded at some time and this was taken to account for their absence. Although legend has it that the hole is 'bottomless', a depth of 98m was established by cavers in recent times.
[Bridges 1828, Cundall 1915, Fincham 1997]

EDNA MANLEY COLLEGE

The Edna Manley College of the Visual and Performing Arts (formerly the Cultural Training Centre) is the main institution for training in the arts in Jamaica; it also serves other CARIBBEAN territories. The college is located at 1 Arthur Wint Drive, Kingston 5, close to the LITTLE THEATRE and the Kingston and St Andrew Parish LIBRARY.

As the Cultural Training Centre, it was established in 1976. The government-funded complex brought together four institutions: Jamaica School of Art, Jamaica School of Dance, Jamaica School of Drama and Jamaica School of Music, each of which had been formed at a different time and was up to then in a different location. In 1995, the centre was renamed the Edna Manley College in honour of renowned artist and cultural icon, the Hon Edna Manley, OM (see ART). It was moved from the aegis of the INSTITUTE OF JAMAICA and the Office of the Prime Minister to that of the Ministry of Education. A BA in visual arts, dance, drama or music is offered in collaboration with the UNIVERSITY OF THE WEST INDIES, as well as diplomas and certificates. Part-time and children's programmes are also offered by some of the schools.

The School of Visual Arts, the oldest in the institution, was itself founded by Mrs Manley in the early 1940s as the Jamaica School of Art and Crafts. Over the years it has played a major role in the development of art in Jamaica, including the training of art teachers for schools. The School today offers programmes in painting, sculpture, ceramics, history, photography, textiles, jewellery, design communication, and art education. There is an annual show of work by final year students that is a well-known event on the Jamaican art calendar, attended by art enthusiasts, connoisseurs and critics. There is also a collection at the School of the work of outstanding graduates.

The School of Music is noted for pioneering a cross cultural approach to music education, offering training in classical as well as folk, jazz, and popular music. It trains not just practitioners and performers but also helps to satisfy the demand for trained music teachers in secondary and primary schools. The school was founded in 1961 on the model of the British royal schools for the training of classical musicians. In 1976 when it became part of the Cultural Training Centre, the curriculum was revised to make it more responsive to the needs of Jamaicans. While the classical department was retained, the school also began to offer courses in the other areas of music, bearing in mind the need for trained musicians to make a living. Drumming became a compulsory part of the curriculum. A Folk Music Research Department became an integral part of the school, with responsibility not just for collection in the field but for developing a folk music syllabus. (See also DRUM, MUSIC, MUSIC, Folk; MUSICAL INSTRUMENTS.)

The School of Dance was founded in 1970 by members of the NATIONAL DANCE THEATRE COMPANY. The School trains performers and teachers in classical and folk technique and choreography and has its own performing group called Danceworks.

The School of Drama was established in 1976 to train teacher/artists. From the outset the curriculum of the school was conceived as a blend of theatre, social and cultural research, and community service. The School grew out of the work of the Little Theatre Movement which set up a part time evening school then called The Theatre School to teach basic theatre skills to potential cast members of its annual PANTOMIME. A drama-in-education programme later developed for teachers who wanted to use drama as a part of their work within the school system.

EDUCATION

Jamaica's educational system over the years has produced not only a body of educated citizens but many outstanding individuals of national and international stature. In recent times, the island's record in the education of women has been exemplary, the enrolment of females at the time of writing surpassing males at all levels of the system. High school graduates now routinely sit the American Scholastic Aptitude Test (SAT) as they are courted by elite American universities and colleges at which they tend to do well. The Jamaican Spelling Bee champion Jodi Ann Maxwell went on to win the US competition in 1998. Many Jamaicans who emigrated still send their children 'back home' to be educated, believing that they will not only do better academically but that the good 'old-time discipline' of their own schooldays still exists. Education for many has been the route to improved socio-economic status and upward social mobility.

The public education system in the 1996/7 school year facilitated approximately 660,000 students and 25,000 teachers in over 2,500 institutions. Some 294,000 are found in grades 1-6 of Primary, All-Age, and Junior High Schools. There were about 210,000 students aged 9-19 in grades 7-13 in public sector secondary schools, representing five different types of institutions – New Secondary, Secondary High, Technical High, Comprehensive High and Vocational. Enrolment in tertiary or post-secondary education was 24,852 in 1995/6.

At the tertiary level, there has been considerable expansion and the creation of more diverse opportunities for further education in recent times. Jamaican based universities have recently grown to three. In addition to the regional UNIVERSITY OF THE WEST INDIES (UWI), there are also the UNIVERSITY OF TECHNOLOGY (UTech, formerly the College of Arts, Science and Technology) and Northern Caribbean University (see SEVENTH-DAY ADVENTIST). Tertiary Education is also offered at the College of Agriculture, Science and Education (CASE), the G.C. Foster College of Physical Education and Sports and the EDNA MANLEY COLLEGE of the Visual and Performing Arts. There are seven teacher training colleges (Shortwood, Mico, St Joseph's, Church, Sam SHARPE, Bethlehem and MONEAGUE) and five community colleges (Montego Bay, Portmore, Exed, Brown's Town, Knox). Bethlehem and Moneague are classified as multi-disciplinary colleges, combining teachers and community colleges. These offer pre-university and general education as well as professional and para-professional and skills training. They offer courses leading to the associate degree level and also prepare students for selected UWI certificate courses. Selected UTech courses are also offered at the community colleges. In association with UWI, a BEd in early childhood education is offered at Shortwood Teachers' College and in special education at Mico College. The G.C. Foster College offers a degree in physical education under the aegis of the University Council of Jamaica. A bachelors degree in technical education is offered at UTech. Many Jamaicans also take advantage of opportunities offered by American universities' off-shore programmes to improve their education.

Decades of hard work by CARIBBEAN-based educators have helped to transform the curriculum of primary and secondary schools, moving from the old English-based curricula to a more Caribbean-based and child-centred one. The Caribbean Examinations Council (CXC) has been fulfilling its mandate to reform the upper secondary school curriculum (grades 10-13).

All of these advances nevertheless obscure a paradox of the educational system – that while some students continue to do well, especially those privileged to attend the so-called elite schools, education for the masses of children is still second-rate or beyond their means. Despite

Kingston Technical High School class in session

Moravian school house, 19th century

all the efforts made by successive governments since 1953 to make education truly democratic and accessible to all, many of the problems continue to be rooted in the inability to break truly free from a colonial past that articulated a distinct policy of social bias in education. Only a look at the way education developed historically can explain the complexities of the educational system today.

Education in colonial days From the days of earliest BRITISH settlement to the end of the 17th century there is little reference to education in Jamaica. Education for the masses of the population (the enslaved Africans and indentured whites) was unthinkable. Indeed, education for the masses was not thought of in England at that time.

The crassness that pervaded colonial society was reflected in the lack of interest in learning. Up to 1740 when Leslie published his *New History of Jamaica* he could say that 'Learning is here at the lowest Ebb; there is no publick School in the whole Island, neither do they seem fond of the thing; several large Donations have been made for such Uses, but have never taken Effect. The Office of a Teacher is looked upon as contemptible and no Gentleman keeps Company with one of that Character; to read, write and cast Accounts, is all the Education they desire, and even these are but scurvily taught'. Books then as now were never regarded as prime property, indeed there is the saying: 'If you want to hide something in Jamaica, put it in a book.'

The wealthy whites who desired learning for their children did not look to providing schools in the colony. Some hired tutors and governesses from England; others sent their sons and daughters to school in England. In time, wealthy fathers educated both their white and COLOURED children abroad. Edward Long (1774) laments the uncaring attitude of the Jamaican ruling class towards providing good education for the island and the deleterious effect on the children themselves who were sent to England for their schooling 'like a bale of dry goods, consigned to some factor'. From the late 17th century it was also the habit for sons of the wealthy to attend Oxford and other British universities and those who did return formed part of the small upper crust elite. (One free black Jamaican, Francis Williams, in the mid-18th century received both grammar school and university education in England, thanks to an aristocratic patron, the Duke of Montagu, who wanted to prove that blacks were as capable of higher learning as were whites. Williams graduated from Cambridge University and, denied an official post by the governor, established a private school in SPANISH TOWN.)

Many private schools appeared and disappeared during the plantation era but many children of overseers, resident owners, and other rural whites received little or no education, especially if they were girls. Visitors in the 18th and early 19th centuries describe these white Jamaicans as no better than their black slaves, and sometimes worse. On the other hand, some slaves brought from Africa were educated men, literate in Arabic and students of the Koran. (See MANDINGO, MUSLIM.)

The 'large Donations' that Leslie refers to were in the nature of bequests to establish schools from the 18th to the early 19th century. Though some endowed schools were eventually established (see e.g. MANNING'S, RUSEA'S, WOLMER'S) many such bequests were thwarted by a dilatory Assembly and corrupt trustees (see e.g. DRAX). These early endowed schools were for poor whites or coloureds only; they were not established for black children. Most of them fell under the control of the PARISH vestries. After 1879, the residual funds from the 18th century trusts were used to establish a secondary school system.

The start of public education With EMANCIPATION for the slaves approaching, attention turned for the first time to public education. The Emancipation Act provided for the 'religious and moral education' of the ex-slaves with an annual grant of £30,000 from the British government through the Negro Education Grant of 1835, marking the start of elementary education. Jamaica's share was used to establish schools around the island. These were mainly denominational schools for the newly freed, many developing from the mission schools which at first catered to adults and children alike, funded by religious and philanthropic groups in England and their local supporters (see

MISSIONARIES). Under the Mico Charity, Mico Training College was started for the training of teachers. The Negro Education Grant was reduced after 1841 and ceased altogether in 1845. The local legislature provided virtually no funds.

Nevertheless, the number of schools grew steadily. The *History of Mico College* published on its 125th anniversary notes that in 1837, the year after Mico was established there were 183 primary schools in the island. By 1864 there were 490. Since the elementary school system was established through the churches, missionaries and Anglican clergymen were given a free hand and popular education was seen as the 'path to moral reformation', as Carl Campbell has argued. The schools were regarded as recruiting grounds for church members and the accent was on the number of schools rather than the quality. The planters on the whole continued to be hostile to education for the ex-slaves as they saw it as corrupting the labouring population.

Following the MORANT BAY REBELLION of 1865 and the institution of Crown Colony government, the new governor, Sir John Peter Grant had stronger powers than his predecessors and was able to reorganize elementary education and provide a higher per capita allowance. Grant in his enthusiasm also established the tertiary institution, QUEEN'S COLLEGE, at Spanish Town, long before the island was ready for such a step. However there continued to be harsh criticism of the elementary schools, of their curricula, the quality of the teachers and the poor results obtained. As late as 1883, exactly 10 pence was being spent per child per year for public education.

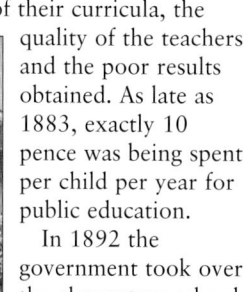

In 1892 the government took over the elementary school system which until then had remained under church auspices, and began to provide funding and direct policies. From 1897, the government also took over construction of all new elementary schools, the churches owning those already built. Nevertheless, this had little impact on the development of an educational system suited to the colony's needs. Crown Colony rule meant official rule by expatriate department heads and a British curriculum that has been satirized in recent times by the Calypsonian Sparrow and others. Genuine educational reform would not begin until the constitutional changes of 1944 that gave Jamaica some measure of self-government.

As Campbell points out: 'The fundamental obstacles to qualitative and quantitative development of education in post-Emancipation Jamaica were social and economic. Like the mass of the English people, the negro ex-slaves never evolved genuine schools of their own . . . The denominations, Anglican and dissenters, which undertook to build schoolhouses and conduct schools for the masses in Jamaica were the same agency which had pioneered popular education in England [scarcely thirty years before]. They did not feel the necessity to think out an original philosophy of education for Jamaica because they already had one for the English masses which was applicable, so it was thought, to the Jamaican masses.'

One result of the philosophy was the development of primary and secondary education along separate lines, controlled by two different bodies, which served to reinforce the race, class and gender biases of colonial society.

Elementary Education After 1892, primary schools were under the authority of the Education Department. Elementary education for the masses was intended to 'civilize' and make them good and faithful servants – a pliable labour force. They were taught the three Rs, some craft work, a great deal of moral and religious instruction with a strong emphasis on the virtue of obedience to social superiors.

The elementary schools from the late 19th to the mid-20th century catered to children age 7-15 and a constantly growing number attended. By the 1940s some 70 per cent of the age cohort were enrolled, though, then as now, absenteeism was a significant factor. Between 1861-1921, the basic literacy rate rose from 31.3 per cent of the population over the age of 5 to 60.9 per cent. But a significant proportion of the school age population continued to be untouched, since the attendance rate of those enrolled was only 59.1 per cent in 1871 and 61.4 per cent in 1921. Absenteeism was often due to poverty, rural children especially being needed to help out at home.

St George's College

Despite the inadequacies of the system, bright and ambitious individuals found ways of fulfilling their thirst for schooling. However, the opportunities education offered to escape from the backbreaking toil of their parents were limited to a small number, the brightest and the best, especially those from families with ambition for their children and the vision and capability to spur them on.

Opportunities for promising teenagers were provided by the pupil-teacher system which was a form of apprenticeship for students who completed their own schooling and learned to teach in the school while taking a series of Jamaica Local Examinations. Those who were successful could enter a teachers' training college or qualify for a clerkship in some firm. Up to the first six decades of the 20th century, many of the most effective Jamaican professionals and business people – at home and abroad – took this alternate path to success. The British-based curriculum was rigid and demanding. Parallel to these institutions were a number of private 'colleges', some good, some indifferent, which offered secretarial, technical and business training at fees which lower and middle class families could afford. Many took correspondence courses offered by British institutions, and at least one minister of education gained his university degree by this avenue. The rest went to labour in the fields, were apprenticed to trades or seized opportunities for migration that increasingly opened up. (See COLÓN MAN, PANAMA.)

The development from the 1830s onwards of colleges for the training of local teachers and local ministers of religion (see e.g. CALABAR, MICO, MORAVIAN) provided a niche for upward social mobility for some black Jamaicans who were excluded from the secondary schools. By the late 19th century, the local elementary school teacher and the parson were the grass roots community leaders of Jamaica, playing a central role in the formation and development of influential organizations such as the Jamaica Union of Teachers (1894) and the Jamaica Agricultural Society (1895).

Secondary Schools In 1879 a Jamaica Schools Commission was established to organize and manage a system of secondary schools, utilizing funds and other resources from the 18th century endowments and trusts. The secondary grammar schools that were created catered at first to white and increasingly brown elites, the boys receiving training for leadership roles, the girls to be 'good wives and good mothers'. Religious institutions once again became heavily involved in the creation of new schools. The ROMAN CATHOLIC church which had not been part of the initial missionary activities was a pioneer of secondary education, establishing several institutions in the 19th century, including ST GEORGE'S COLLEGE and Immaculate (see CONSTANT SPRING), and many more in the 20th century. The other denominations also established secondary schools; indeed few secondary schools were established by the government itself until the 1960s and most of the traditional high schools (now called secondary high) are still denominationally owned though government funded. In the 20th century some schools established by private individuals grew into lasting institutions, such as Excelsior and Camperdown.

The thrust to establish secondary schools aggravated the divide between rich and poor since there was no system whereby children could automatically pass from one level of the educational system to the other. Children of middle and upper middle class parents often attended private preparatory schools before going on to secondary schools which until the 1960s were staffed to a large degree by British expatriates. The fact that these schools were fee-paying effectively excluded the majority of the population; in addition, many of the schools practised selectivity based on class, colour, and the moral as well as social status of parents. Many were boarding schools and, following the British pattern, were single-sex schools. These schools were rigidly academic, based on the structure and curricula of English grammar schools. Students sat external examinations of Cambridge University (introduced in 1882) and London University (introduced in 1891) set and marked by English examiners. Together, they catered to a small minority of the total school age population. In 1929, only 2,677 were enrolled in secondary schools, representing one school place for every 25 enrolled in primary. Over time, there was an increasing number of government and other scholarships to these fee-paying schools though as late as 1948, only six boys and six girls were granted government scholarships out of the hundreds who sat the examination.

One important function of colonial education was to produce loyal British subjects. As Errol Miller expresses it: 'British culture was dominant in all schools. To participate in the school system of any type and at any level was to be anglicized.

The common Anglo-culture was the glue that united the dual system of colonial education which reflected the plural nature of colonial society.' By the same token: 'All other cultures were not only made improper but illegitimate in the school systems. Mastery of the Anglo-culture, particularly mastery of the English language, became the most important criterion of upward social mobility through education.'

Education Today In 1953, the Ministry of Education was created and the first minister appointed, signalling the beginning of the transfer of power from colonial administrators. This transfer included the development of local leadership at the top rungs of the educational hierarchy to replace leadership that had been almost exclusively expatriate

Since INDEPENDENCE in 1962, successive governments have made flawed but persistent efforts to widen the scope of secondary and tertiary education. The Ministry of Education oversees four levels of schools: early childhood, primary, secondary, and tertiary.

Privately funded secondary schools are now the exception; most secondary schools have been government funded since the 1994-5 school year on a cost-sharing basis. Government allocations cover teachers' salaries and related expenses as well as major repairs and infrastructural development. The fees that parents pay are used to defray operational costs.

The main problem continues to be the lack of enough places in the secondary system for elementary school leavers, despite a massive school building programme since the 1950s. In 1957 the Common Entrance Examination ('Eleven-plus') was instituted as the means by which the children competed for the limited number of high school places available. The provision of so-called government 'free places' opened up the formerly elite schools to a wide cross section of society, as did the development of new schools such as comprehensives which provide a greater mix of academic and vocational subjects than the traditional secondary high. The 2,000 'free place' holders of 1960 increased to many thousands, but in 1999 when the Eleven-plus was abolished, those securing secondary school places still represented only one-third of their age cohort.

In addition to the secondary high (still regarded as the most desirable option) successive governments have created a proliferation of other types of secondary schools under many different names, and there are a number of private fee-paying institutions, all of varying quality. The government schools include a small number of new secondary schools (grades 7-11) to which access from nearby primary schools is automatic and there are also vocational and technical schools where entry is by other forms of testing.

In 1999 the dreaded Common Entrance was replaced by the Grade Six Achievement Test (GSAT) in order to make the selection more based on the curriculum studied rather than an intelligence test, which the CEE was. The claim is also made that there is now a 'place' for every child to continue in the system. While the CEE selected students only for the high, comprehensive high and technical high schools, the GSAT allows placement for all of these plus the all-age schools (which terminate at grade 9). However, this has not solved the fundamental problem, that the quality and offerings of the different levels of schools – and thus the educational opportunities for each child – vary widely. The children with the highest marks still go on to the elite schools as they did under the CEE.

The basic division continues to be between the high schools and the all-age schools. These are the elementary schools that were established in the 19th century for the children of the ex-slaves. Today, as educator H.E. Evans explains in her book, *Inside Jamaican Schools*: 'High schools provide the most certain avenue to a university education, and are valued as educational institutions by employers and parents alike. The all-age school on the other hand, is attended mainly by children of the poor . . . Although 40 percent of Jamaican students enrolled in grades 7-9 are in all-age schools or those upgraded to primary and junior high

Priory Prep School students

schools, these schools are sometimes dismissed as an anachronism – an institution that should be abolished. Unlike the high schools, many of whose graduates can go on to a university, students who attend the all-age school and the primary and junior high school have limited educational opportunities. Those who have not already dropped out are forced to leave school at an early age with little hope of gaining entry to a secondary school.'

Examinations On the whole, the curricular of the schools remain academically challenging and cover a wide range of subjects. Children usually attend secondary school for five years (grades 7-11) and the secondary high schools offer a further two grades (12-13), normally regarded as preparation for university. At the end of five years, students sit external examinations. Until 1980 this was the University of Cambridge Ordinary level (O-level) exams. Those who stay on for the extra two years sit the advanced or A-level exams. Since 1979, students at the Ordinary Level in the Caribbean region have also been able to sit parallel examinations set by the Caribbean Examinations Council (CXC) and the advanced level CXC exams have more recently been introduced. In time, the English examinations will be phased out.

The CXC was established in 1973 to devise a Caribbean-based curriculum, offering syllabi that were in many ways more advanced than the watered down colonial syllabus emerging from Cambridge. This is only one of several initiatives taken on a regional basis to improve the educational system inherited by the British West Indian colonies. These initiatives began in 1939 with the revision of curricula and the creation of

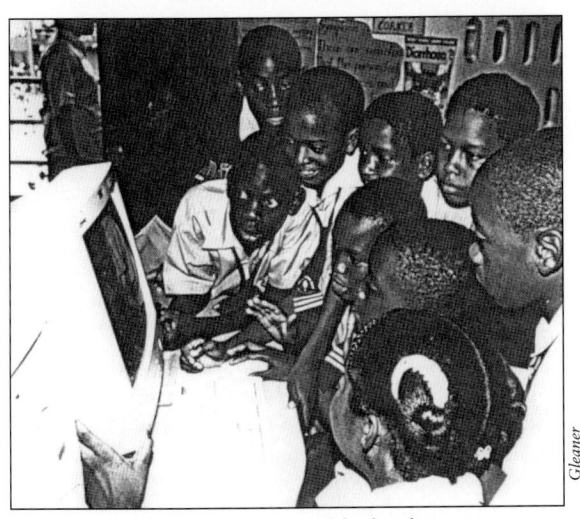

McGrath Secondary agricultural students

textbooks especially written for Caribbean students. And Independence of the various territories, beginning in 1962, brought new blueprints for education. The UWI contributed to these developments, helping to design new syllabi for history, social studies, and mathematics. Emphasis on Caribbean LITERATURE emerged, and in the 1960s, children began reading the works of such writers as Michael Anthony, V.S. Naipaul and Vic Reid. Work has also been continuing on English LANGUAGE studies. For the elementary schools, a set of language arts textbooks designed especially for Jamaica's language culture emerged after years of work from the UWI School of Education and was introduced in schools by the Ministry of Education in 1981-82.

Despite these developments, there is a continuing high failure rate at the school leaving exams. There are multiple factors impacting on education, beginning at the primary level where children are supposed to obtain the basic preparation they need for advancement through the system. One significant factor continues to be poor attendance. In 1994-5 the percentage attendance in primary schools was only 68 per cent and in all-age schools 66 per cent. This means that a third of school time is lost. Large classes in the schools for the poor and the quality of teaching are other factors. Teachers are now among the worst paid professionals, and the classroom is no longer the attractive option it once was. In 1996, one-fifth of the teachers in the system were untrained and these were mostly

Half Way Tree Primary School students

to be found in the primary, junior high and all-age schools. Overall, education has been severely affected by economic factors influencing the country as a whole, especially the impact of IMF-mandated restructuring policies and the heavy burden of foreign debt repayment.

Even if a child does succeed in securing a place in a secondary school, only tuition is free (although there is a special welfare fund to assist needy parents). Poor parents find it increasingly difficult to meet the cost of transportation, books, lunches, school uniforms, and those extras charged by schools to make up for inadequate funding. The universities also charge fees and obtaining a university education requires a great deal of sacrifice on the part of students, many of them parents themselves. What has always been remarkable is the level of personal sacrifice that parents are willing to make to improve their children's opportunities through education. Despite the inadequacies of the system, there is much achievement to celebrate.

[Augier and Gordon 1962, Campbell 1996, Eisner 1961, Evans 2001, GOJ Ministry of Education 1996, GOJ STATIN 1999a, Miller 1989]

EMANCIPATION

Word used to refer to the freeing of the slaves (see SLAVERY) in the British West Indies, numbering at the time nearly three-quarters of a million men, women and children. The law that was passed by the British Parliament was called the Emancipation Act (also known as the Abolition Act). It provided for freedom for the slaves from 1 August 1834, but with certain conditions attached under a transitional period of APPRENTICESHIP. Full freedom for the 311,000 slaves in Jamaica was not achieved until 1 August 1838.

EMANCIPATION DAY

Popularly known as 'First of August', EMANCIPATION Day was first celebrated to mark the freeing of the slaves, 1 August 1838, and was formerly one of the most important holidays. It was discontinued after Jamaica gained political independence in 1962 and Independence Day, the first Monday in August, replaced it. Since 1997, Emancipation Day has again been celebrated in Jamaica, after a break of 35 years, and INDEPENDENCE DAY has been fixed as 6 August.

The return of Emancipation Day in Jamaica and other CARIBBEAN countries is a reflection of a new generation's desire to mark this important event in their history.

Apart from the emotional fervour associated with the early celebrations of Emancipation Day, the fact that it coincided with the CROPOVER celebrations that marked the ending of the SUGAR CANE harvest contributed to its importance. However, as Barry Higman points out, by the 1850s Emancipation lost ground in favour of CHRISTMAS. Nevertheless, as can be observed from events such as BRUCKINS, for many of the older folk, First of August continued for a long time to be a memorable day. It was established as a public holiday in 1893, as the first Monday in August, but from 1895 to 1962, the year Jamaica gained Independence, 1 August itself was celebrated unless it fell on a Saturday or Sunday.

On 31 July 2002, Emancipation Park was opened on the former Knutsford Park lands in New Kingston. The 2ha site which sits in the heart of Kingston's financial and hotel district provides a welcome recreational space with its sprawling lawns, water fountains, jogging trails, variety of flora and historic symbols in keeping with the spirit of Emancipation.

[Higman 1979b]

Entrance to Emancipation Park, New Kingston

ENCOMIENDA

Term used to describe the status of TAINO Indians under SPANISH colonial rule, a status which made them virtual slaves. The word means a permanent dividing up, in practice a portioning out of the Amerindians to the service of the Spaniards. The theory was that the Amerindians were to be 'committed' to Christian masters. Lots of natives under a CACIQUE were *encomendados*; each lot constituted an *encomienda*; their masters were *encomenderos*.

[Wright 1910]

ENGLISH see BRITISH

ESCOVEITCH
Method of marinating fish in a spicy sauce, from the Spanish *escabeche* (popularly 'scaveech') meaning pickled, one of the island's oldest dishes, probably brought by Spanish or Portuguese JEWS who first came in the early 16th century. (The Spanish-American dish of *ceviche* probably derives from the same source.) Its popularity no doubt owes much to the fact that it does not have to be refrigerated as the marinade acts as a preservative, hence it was a boon in the days before electricity. It was often eaten on religious days for the Jews or religious holidays for Christians (e.g. ASH WEDNESDAY, GOOD FRIDAY) when no cooking was done. Nowadays escoveitch fish is standard fare on Jamaican restaurant menus and is popular with beach-goers and picnickers.

The fish (sliced or left whole) is lightly fried and drained and then put into a marinade of vinegar boiled with onions, CHOCHO, carrots, hot peppers and PIMENTO grains. It can be left for some hours or overnight. Very hot pepper is liberally used with an escoveitch which can be eaten at any time of day. A favourite accompaniment is BAMMY.
[Benghiat 1987, DJE, Donaldson 1993]

ESQUIVEL
Place name (near OLD HARBOUR BAY) in CLARENDON Parish which recalls Juan Esquivel, the first SPANISH governor (1509-19) of the island. The shipbuilding port the Spaniards established on the south coast was named in his honour. From Esquivel, the Spaniards had a trail across the island to their capital of Sevilla la Nueva (see SEVILLE, New). In recent times, Alcan Jamaica Limited has built a shipping terminal – named Port Esquivel – on the site of the old Spanish port.

ETHIOPIAN ORTHODOX CHURCH
This religious denomination was established in Jamaica in 1970 by the head and administrator of the church in the USA. However, local groups had begun to hold services along the lines of this church before that. Local adherents are mainly RASTAFARI.

ETU
A group of YORUBA ancestry, found on the western side of the island, referred to as NAGO people. They exhibit a strong cultural

Etu dancers and Achaka player

resemblance to the Nago people of Abeokuta, Waterworks, WESTMORELAND. Anthropologist Kenneth Bilby found the group singing Yoruba migrant songs in both CREOLE and Yoruba and exhibiting a distinctive style of drumming found nowhere else on the island. The HANOVER Etu group exhibits strong African Yoruba retentions in LANGUAGE, food and DANCE.

Etu musical events might be part of a 'PLAY' held on the occasion of a dinner feast, wedding, or forty night memorial (i.e. the fortieth night after a person's death – see DEATH RITUALS). In the Yoruba language, *etu* does not designate a Yoruba sub-group but is the shortened form of *etutu* meaning 'peace, atonement, placation' and names a ceremony for placation of the souls of the dead relatives.

Each family exhibits a different dance style accompanied by two DRUMS – an Achaka (kerosene tin) which is played as a lead drum while held between the knees in horizontal position and an Irre (two-headed oval shaped drum). 'Shawling' – a ritual throwing of shawls or scarves around the neck of another dancer as a sign of appreciation – forms an integral part of each Etu performance.

Detail of Etu dancing

[Adetugbo 1996, Baxter 1970, Bilby 1985a, Lewin n.d., Ryman 1980, Tanna 1983b]

FALMOUTH

The capital of TRELAWNY Parish, Falmouth (population 7,955 in 1991) is the town in Jamaica that has best maintained the features and ambience of the past, and has been declared a Historic Town. Most of its old buildings are in an advanced state of dilapidation and though its restoration has many times been proposed, nothing on a large scale has been tackled. T.A. Concannon, an architect who did much to preserve other aspects of Jamaica's heritage (e.g. DEVON HOUSE, ROSE HALL GREAT HOUSE, PORT HENDERSON) observed that Falmouth remained

A view of Falmouth c. 1844 by Adolphe Duperly

'perhaps the only town where the spirit of eighteenth century Jamaica can still be felt, and to some lingering extent seen in brick, stone and timber'. He described its architectural importance as follows in *Falmouth 1791-1970*:

'Enthusiasm in the colonies for buildings in the Georgian expression was very much alive during the late eighteenth and early nineteenth centuries when Falmouth came into being, a small town on the coast where an abundance of domestic buildings was created in a simple yet charming vernacular using classical elements adapted to local conditions . . . The conception of Falmouth in its grid plan, and construction in stone, brick, and timber seems to have resulted in a . . . complete and comprehensive small town with its own distinctive environment.'

Aside from the surviving examples of domestic architecture, Falmouth also has a number of public buildings of historic interest. Among them are the FALMOUTH COURTHOUSE, FALMOUTH PARISH CHURCH, Cornwall District Prison which now houses the FALMOUTH POLICE STATION, FALMOUTH PRESBYTERIAN CHURCH and the KNIBB MEMORIAL CHURCH, named after BAPTIST missionary William Knibb (1803-45).

The old Falmouth hospital, located by the sea, used to be valued as a fever hospital (see YELLOW FEVER AND MALARIA). As late as the 1920s, European techniques and CREOLE medical practices combined to save patients suffering from malaria, one of the diseases indigenous to Falmouth and its environs. This building was abandoned in 1955 when a new government hospital opened on another site.

Falmouth was laid out as a parish capital in 1790, superseding MARTHA BRAE when silting at the mouth of that river made it unsuitable for shipping. The new town was named after Falmouth, England, which was the birthplace of the governor, Sir William Trelawny, after whom the PARISH was named.

The land on which Falmouth was built was bought from Edward BARRETT, who also donated the land for the ANGLICAN church. His townhouse at 1 Market Street, built in 1799, was one of the original buildings of the town. Falmouth is one of the few towns in the island that was laid out according to a plan. Lots were sold and the rich planters and merchants eagerly bought them. A few years after it was founded Falmouth had 150 houses, and was steadily built up over the next 40 years until around 1830, when its steady decline began.

Falmouth was created at the height of the prosperity that came from SUGAR. The parish was one of the richest sugar areas in the island, at one time having 88 estates. When the sugar industry declined in

Duke Street house under restoration and traditional cut-stone boundary

Corner of Newton and Cornwall Streets

the mid-19th century, coastal towns such as Falmouth declined in importance also.

In its heyday, the town was economically and socially on a par with KINGSTON. It supported many businesses and more than one weekly newspaper, the most widely read being the *Falmouth Post* (1835-76). Falmouth was noted for the introduction of anaesthetics in the extraction of teeth and scientific experiments by David Lindo (1833-89), a Jewish merchant and self-taught chemist. He developed a method of determining the total nitrogen in fertilizer (the Lindo-Sladding method), adopted by the US government.

The remains of old wharves and warehouses along the sea are among the reminders today of the town's former importance. It was the port from which sugar was shipped and at which all the imported goods needed at the estates in the interior were landed. Sometimes as many as 27 ships would be in the harbour at one time. (Of course, these were small sailing ships – the largest were 612t barques.)

Sugar in those days was shipped in large barrels called hogsheads (and RUM in puncheons). (See COOPER.) Each hogshead weighed 1.02t. Mule or ox-drawn carts brought the hogsheads into town for loading on to the ship – it would take six men to put one on board.

The ships depended on the trade winds to blow them back home. They would sometimes have to wait in the port for up to one month until they got the right breeze. Each ship carried about twenty sailors and while they waited they would create an uproar in the town, so much so that the town fathers decreed that sailors could not stay in Falmouth later than six o'clock in the evening. If caught, they were to be jailed for the night. This seemed to have had little effect, for in 1803 the town had a stone cage built to lock up drunken sailors. The cage cannot now be seen as it was torn down to make way for the market, but was probably similar to the CAGE in MONTEGO BAY.

Aside from the sailing ships from North America or England, Falmouth harbour was alive with a great deal of local traffic, including the CANOES of fishermen. In the old days, water transportation between coastal towns was of great importance (especially since few roads existed) and canoes plied for hire between Falmouth and the neighbouring harbours. The harbour would also be thick with a special kind of boat called a drogher. The droghers distributed goods brought in by the sailing ships between Falmouth and the other towns, serving the same purpose as delivery trucks and vans today.

The advent of the steamship was a heavy blow to the town. The first steamship came to Jamaica in 1837, and after that steam gradually replaced sail. But the Falmouth harbour could not handle big ships without expensive improvements. More and more of the coastal trade was diverted to towns with good natural harbours or to Kingston itself. Falmouth was further bypassed with the extension of the RAILWAY in 1894 from Kingston to Montego Bay. By the 1890s Falmouth had become almost a ghost town. After decades of population decline, the population has been increasing, one cause being proximity to tourist resort areas.

The very isolation of Falmouth has helped to preserve its historical heritage. In 1990, a team of conservationists (Binney et al.) described the significance of Falmouth in this way: 'No town of the Georgian era besides Falmouth has retained its ancillary and dependent buildings, most of which were slave quarters attached to the planters' town houses. At Colonial Williamsburg these had to be reconstructed from archaeological evidence, but here in Falmouth many are intact and are a remarkable display of what might be called the cabin style of Georgian vernacular architecture. Herein lies the supreme architectural importance of the model town of Falmouth.'

[Binney et al. 1991, Georgian Society n.d., Ogilvie 1954, Wright and White 1969]

FALMOUTH BAPTIST CHURCH see KNIBB MEMORIAL CHURCH

FALMOUTH COURTHOUSE

The original courthouse in the town of FALMOUTH was built in 1815 but was later destroyed by fire. The present courthouse – built in 1926 – is a replica of the original Palladian style building, except for the roof line and windows.

Falmouth courthouse

FALMOUTH PARISH CHURCH
The ANGLICAN church of St Peter's located on Duke Street, FALMOUTH, was built in 1795. It is both the oldest public building in the town and the oldest church in the parish of TRELAWNY. The land for the church was donated by Edward BARRETT, part of whose estate had been bought to lay out the town. In 1842 the church was enlarged, with a western extension which now forms the nave.

FALMOUTH POLICE STATION
This building on Rodney Street in FALMOUTH occupies the former Cornwall District Prison and is one of the historic structures of the town. It was constructed in 1814. In the old days the prison consisted of a jail and a workhouse or 'house of correction', as the slave prisons were called. There was also separate accommodation for debtors. The houses of correction were notorious places of torture. A favourite method of punishment in this and other slave prisons was the TREADMILL, introduced during the APPRENTICESHIP period (before full abolition of SLAVERY).

After EMANCIPATION, Falmouth's house of correction, like all others became a prison for criminals, while the jail was reserved for debtors and minor offenders. The prisoners had heavy iron bolts attached to their legs and were compelled to lift them while walking. Black prisoners wore iron collars round their necks and were chained two by two when they were sent out to maintain the roads of the parish. A visitor to Falmouth in the 1860s found prison discipline poor, and prisoners sentenced to hard labour enjoying a 'soft' life. He claimed that of the two hard labour prisoners in the jail, one kneaded BREAD while the other cleaned shoes.

FALMOUTH PRESBYTERIAN CHURCH
Scotsmen who were prominent in TRELAWNY Parish built St Andrews Kirk at the corner of Rodney and Princess Streets in the town of FALMOUTH in 1832 (See SCOTS.) Alterations have been made to the original building.

FAUNA
While Jamaica has a relatively small number of large animal species, it has an exceptionally high number of endemic fauna, that is, animals that are unique to the island. Scientists attribute this to the fact that Jamaica emerged as an island 10-15 million years ago and has never been connected to any other land mass. (See GEOLOGY.) This isolation has resulted in unique genetic developments and along with size, range of elevation and diversity of habitat has provided the island with a unique biodiversity and an exceptionally high rate of endemism. As a BBC film (*Spirits of the Jaguar*) expressed it, Jamaica emerged as virgin soil for new arrivals, resulting in 'vacancies' on this new land, waiting to be filled.

Among the groups with a particularly high ratio of endemic species to total of native species are BIRDS (30 to 116 breeding species), terrestrial mammals (1 of 1 – see CONEY), BATS (2 to 21), LIZARDS (20 to 26), FROGS (21 to 21), BUTTERFLIES (20 to 134), SNAKES (6 to 7), jumping SPIDERS (20 to 26), hoverflies (15 to 56), robberflies (14 to 24), hawk moths (4 to 40), fireflies (45 to 48), caddisflies (28 to 39) and land SNAILS (514 to 555).

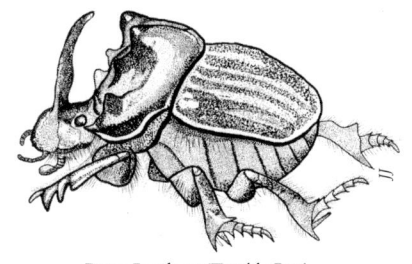

Dung Beetle or 'Tumble Bug'

Some animal species also become diversified over time, separating into sub-species that might reflect their different habitats and adaptation to micro conditions. Thus the Doctor Bird (see HUMMINGBIRD) is black-billed in eastern Jamaica, red-billed elsewhere. There are hundreds of different species of land snails, evolving over millennia isolated on separate LIMESTONE outcrops.

Of greatest interest to biologists is a velvety caterpillar-like creature referred to as Peripatus

Fiddler Beetles

Jamaican peripatus

(Phylum Onychophora) which belongs to a group of animals of such great antiquity they are known as 'living fossils', having undergone no change in form in over 500 million years! The first museum specimen was collected in Jamaica by Sir Hans Sloane (see FLORA) and the largest in the world – over 13cm long – occurs on the island. Five species of Onychophorans have been found in Jamaica, of which four are endemic.

The question now is, if Jamaica arose from the sea, how did the animals get to the island in the first place? The answer is, the same as humans do today: by sea or air. Some animals travel on sea currents and by what is called rafting, that is drifting on logs and other plant parts; others are airborne by air currents, caught up in winds and HURRICANES. In later times, many accompanied humans. Some, such as the CATTLE EGRET, arrived in ways not yet understood.

Though animals have arrived from all directions, the highest number of near-relatives is found in what is today Central and South America. It is believed many species originally came from there at a time during the last ice age when the seas were shallower and there might have been a land bridge with what is now Honduras (along what is now the shallow areas of the Mosquito, Rosalind and Pedro banks). However the poisonous spiders and snakes and the large cats of the American mainland have never reached Jamaica.

Many animals were deliberately introduced by man – cats, chickens, HORSES, CATTLE, PIGS, DOGS, by the Spaniards. Rabbits have never become native to Jamaica, unlike Australia. Some less useful animals arrived accidentally as passengers on ships from earliest times: lice, and fleas (those which infest either animals or humans), as well as cockroaches, and ticks, which probably came with the cattle since none of the island's 7 species is native. Of the island's 72 species of mosquitoes, only 2 seem to have been introduced, including the *Aëdes aegypti*. (See YELLOW FEVER AND MALARIA.)

Various animals have been introduced to combat rats (themselves introductions), especially those destructive of canefields, including the Tom Raffles ANT, the notorious MONGOOSE, and the giant toad or BULLFROG. Other introductions include the Lady Blake toad that is a tiny 'whistling frog' that occurs throughout the island in deforested areas. Few efforts have been made to stem the inflow of possibly dangerous new animals.

The human colonization of the island and the associated introduction of a large number of exotic species had a severe impact the native fauna. Several species ha not been observed for over one hundred years and are believed extinct, including the PEDRO SEAL, Giant GALLIWASP, the Black Racer, Jamaican Petrel, the Jamaican Pauraque, and the Jamaican Rice Rat. Known from the fossil record only, a unique Jamaican monkey may also have gone extinct as a result of human influence. (See CAVES.) Except for the Pedro Seal, these animals occurred nowhere else than in Jamaica.

A number of species have become rare and limited to the last remaining natural forests and wetlands. These animals are greatly endangered and may soon disappear unless their habitat is properly conserved. They include the Giant Swallowtail Butterfly, the Blue Mountain River Frog, the Jamaican IGUANA, and the Jamaican BLACKBIRD, all of them endemic to Jamaica. Several non-endemic species such as sea TURTLES and the MANATEE are threatened worldwide and in need of conservation programmes in Jamaica and elsewhere.

Land Snails

Many more animals survive to some degree in degraded wood- and wetlands, but are absent in areas converted for agriculture, settlement and industrial development. While they are not immediately threatened by extinction, their long-term survival will depend on the conservation of significant areas of forests and wetlands as well as healthy rivers, beaches and marine environments.

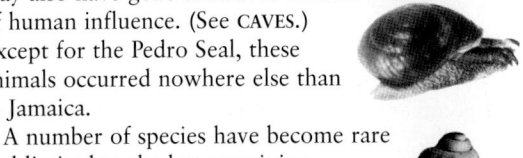

Various animals are sensitive to pollution. The Peenie-Wallie, a nocturnal click beetle (see FIREFLY) is rare today in some areas. Like many other species, it fell victim to the heavy use of insecticides. Similarly, animal diversity of coastal waters and rivers has greatly suffered due to pollution. Once teeming with calipever MULLET (prized for its delicacy) and JANGGA (a large crayfish), the lower regions of many rivers are nearly dead.

Overall, much of the Jamaican fauna has survived the arrival of the human species for now, but is in dire need of greatly extended conservation efforts to ensure long-term survival.
[Brown and Heineman 1972, Farr 1967, 1984a, 1984b, 1990, Schwartz and Henderson 1991, Woodley 1968]

FENNEL (*Foeniculum vulgare*)

Perennial aromatic herb, also called Aniseed, popular as a home remedy. The leaf is made into a TEA as a cold remedy for babies and as a general beverage, and the seeds used to aid digestion. A drink made from Aniseed and RUM (called 'anisou') is used as a medicine for coughs and fevers. The plant grows up to 2m high and can be found growing wild along road banks and in open waste places at medium to high elevations (especially in MANCHESTER, ST ANDREW and TRELAWNY Parishes). A member of the carrot family, the plant is native to Europe and the Mediterranean region and has become naturalized in Jamaica and other islands to which it was introduced.
[Adams 1972, Campbell 1974, DJE]

Fennel

FERN

Botanists believe that Jamaica for its size probably has more species of ferns than any other country in the world. So far 579 species and 30 varieties have been identified; of these 82 are known only from Jamaica. The diversity of this fern FLORA is also remarkable. Ferns are found almost everywhere, from the rain forests to the swampy coastlands, and range from majestic tree ferns with trunks over 9m tall, to the filmy fern which has leaves that are only one cell thick and are as thin as tissue paper. There is the walking fern that sends up new plants wherever the tips bend over and touch the ground, and the shoestring fern that looks just like the object after which it is named. Silver fern and gold fern are so-called from a waxy coating on the underside of the leaves that makes impressions in gold or silver when pressed

Tree ferns

against dark material. There are also water ferns, including water clover, which looks like a floating four-leaf clover.

The world famous 'Boston fern' is said to have originated from the common 'sword fern' (*Nephrolepis exaltata*) that was introduced from Jamaica to the USA in 1793. About forty years later, the first variation appeared and was named *bostoniensis* in honour of the neighbourhood in which it was discovered. Still later, the first of several new variants of this 'Boston fern' appeared, many of which have achieved widespread popularity in the plant world.
[NHSJ 1949, Proctor 1972, 1985]

Silver fern

FERN GULLY

Scenic 4.8km drive near to OCHO RIOS, ST ANN Parish, on the main KINGSTON to northcoast highway, its attraction deriving from the profusion of FERNS and other vegetation which forms a cool damp archway on both sides of the road. Fern Gully originated

Fern Gully in earlier times (from Leader)

Fern Gully today

as a river course in an underground tunnel in the LIMESTONE. Over time, the water eroded the roof, which eventually disintegrated. It was first planted out in the 1880s by a superintendent of Public Gardens. The gully has been ravaged more than once by HURRICANE and flood, and the character of the vegetation keeps changing.
[Powell 1974]

FERRY

Area on the highway between KINGSTON and SPANISH TOWN, once celebrated for its inn. It was once part of a swamp and in 1677, the concession was given to one William Parker to operate a ferry across it. The charges for using Parker's Ferry were seven pence half-penny for a person on foot or grown beast without a rider, fifteen pence for man and horse, and sixpence for every sheep, calf or hog. The ferry keeper was also instructed to capture runaway slaves. By the ferry, Parker constructed an inn that for centuries thereafter remained the place for breaking the journey between Kingston and Spanish Town.

Ferry Inn was at various times in its chequered history a highly fashionable establishment, attracting the patronage of such as the snobbish Lady Nugent, the governor's wife who recorded some of her visits to the inn in her *Journal*. The building that was once the historic inn still stands (beside the police station) having been rebuilt several times on the original foundations. But its charm, so faithfully recorded by painters of the early Jamaican scene such as Kidd, and photographers such as Duperly, has been lost under constant changes to the façade.
[Cundall 1915, Nugent 1839]

FERRY (FRESH) RIVER

River in ST CATHERINE Parish between KINGSTON and SPANISH TOWN, regarded by geologists as a fine example of a karstland or LIMESTONE river. The river originates in underground reservoirs and water courses in the Red Hills. These hills are of white limestone which catches and temporarily stores rain water. Some of this water emerges as a series of springs on both sides of the small hill known as Ferry Hill. The springs to the west of Ferry Hill are fresh while those on the east are salt. The Fresh River is joined by the Salt River before entering the sea at Hunts Bay in Kingston harbour. When BANANAS were widely grown on the St Catherine plain at the turn of the century, water for irrigation was drawn from Fresh River. Drinking water for parts of Kingston has also come from this river.

FESTIVAL

Fried DUMPLING of cornmeal and flour, associated with the famous HELLSHIRE Beach near KINGSTON where the women there first cooked it to go with their fried fish. The name celebrates the Jamaica FESTIVAL, the big August INDEPENDENCE celebrations.

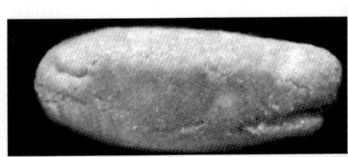

Festival

Ferry Inn

FESTIVAL, Jamaica

The Jamaica Festival is a multi-cultural event that provides a platform for local talent in the performing arts (MUSIC, drama, DANCE, speech), LITERATURE, the visual arts (fine arts, craft and photography) and the culinary arts. It is through

Festival that Jamaicans of all ages, in all walks of life and from city or remotest village, have the opportunity to display their skills and talent. Festival events are competitive, taking place at different levels, the best going on display during Festival Week, which coincides with the annual INDEPENDENCE celebrations in August. Gold, silver and bronze medals are usually awarded in the different competitions, along with other prizes donated by the corporate sector. 'Festival' in its present form has existed since 1963 and is administered by a government agency, the Jamaica Cultural Development Commission (JCDC).

Organized competitions in arts and crafts, speech and music have a longer history, growing out of earlier efforts including those called *eisteddfod* after the WELSH model. These early competitions demanded high standards, and adjudicators for some events such as music were brought from England. Marcus GARVEY through the local UNIA also staged music, elocution and debating competitions as part of his 'upliftment' programmes. Cultural elements were also an integral part of JAMAICA WELFARE, established in the 1930s. Jamaica Welfare made such events accessible to people across rural Jamaica, most previous events being localized or confined to the city of KINGSTON.

In 1946 the Parish of PORTLAND organized a huge festival event with week-long competitions culminating in a grand prizegiving, and other parishes soon followed. The Parish LIBRARIES, then as now, played a leading role in their organization. The first large island wide festival was 'Jamaica 300' of 1955, held to mark Jamaica's tercentenary as part of the British Empire. For the event, competitions were first organized at school and village level, with finalists moving on to zone and parish levels and eventually to the national finals, a pattern that continues with the Jamaica Festival today. Various national arts festivals continued to be held until 1963 when Festival was established on an annual basis.

The Festival movement has made some lasting contributions to the development of Jamaican artistic expression, providing the cradle for talent that subsequently achieved fame in many areas. Festival owes its success to thousands of volunteers along with corporate sponsors, as well as its specialist officers who provide training and upgrading of skills in the different areas. One of the most significant contributions of the Festival movement has been the growing appreciation of traditional expressions of Jamaican culture first exposed to a wider public on the Festival stage, especially in dance and music. (See e.g. BRUCKINS, QUADRILLE.)
[Baxter 1970, JCDC 1988]

FESTIVALS

In the plantation era, the three holiday periods were CHRISTMAS, EASTER (called by the slaves 'pikni Christmas') and CROPOVER or Harvest Home, the latter usually held at the beginning of August. A YAM FESTIVAL was also celebrated by people of African descent. The JONKONNU celebrations include remnants of all of these great festivals of the past.

In the autumn months, many village churches still hold Harvest Festivals, a Protestant religious festival brought from the British Isles. During Harvest Festival, the churches are decorated with flowers and produce; the climax is a procession of children carrying offerings of baked goods, eggs or prize vegetables to lay around the altar. A sale follows, often with competitions between gardeners, bakers, and confectioners.

FEVER see YELLOW FEVER AND MALARIA

FEVER GRASS (*Andropogon citratus*)

Important oil grass, also known as Lemon Grass from its scent. It is widely used in folk MEDICINE and in cooking. In Jamaica it is infused as a TEA for fevers and colds, and drunk with GINGER for diarrhoea. It was introduced into the island around 1800.
[Asprey and Thornton 1953-55, Robertson 1990]

FIG, Wild

Plants (mainly of two genera: *Ficus* and *Clusia*) which grow on and eventually strangle host trees, becoming in time independent flourishing trees with huge interlacing networks of roots, in Jamaica commonly called 'Fig' or, in former days, 'Scotchman'. This latter reference was to the apparent success of the SCOTS attorneys (estate managers) in the island during the colonial era, the tree being likened to 'the Scotchman hugging the CREOLE to death', or the mortgagee strangling the proprietor.

The Fig has been called a vegetable boa constrictor, for it literally crushes the host tree to death. As 'The Strangler Tree', it was sensationally featured in the first edition of Ripley's *Believe It or Not! A Modern Book of Wonders, Miracles, Freaks, Monstrosities and almost-Impossibilities . . .*

Each fig starts life from a seed dropped into

Wild figs among the ruins, Hyde Hall

the crown or bark fissure of an established woody tree by a BIRD, BAT, or other animal. The young fig begins life as an epiphyte, i.e. a plant that lives on but does not take nutrients from the host. Once it has attached itself firmly the fig will begin to send down roots into the soil, giving it the opportunity to derive sustenance for itself and develop a huge network of roots which will eventually strangle the host at the trunk while its leaves choke it at the crown. By the time the host dies, the strangler will be able to stand alone, its roots forming a cylinder up to 30m high. Its killing of the host is a slow and insidious process, in the case of huge forest trees such as the COTTON TREE, taking, it has been estimated, up to one hundred years. A common sight on old estates is the fig growing out of the chimney of abandoned SUGAR works.

One of the typical stranglers, *Ficus benjamina*, is popular as a house plant but as such presents no threat, since it develops strangling tendencies and forms its huge trunk only if it happens to germinate in a tree.

[DJE, Huxley 1978, Kingsbury 1988]

FILTERING STONE

A device made of hollowed out LIMESTONE that was commonly used to filter drinking water of solid impurities in the days before piped water was widely available. Water would be placed in the porous stone bowl and slowly filtered into a jar underneath, or in more elaborate cases, would filter through a second, shallower limestone bowl before falling into the jar. Both filter and jar would be housed in a framework made of wood or stone, the jar having a square flange at the top to support it in the frame. Such stones were in use from at least the 18th century and, according to F.G. Cassidy were borrowed from the Spaniards (see SPANISH). Indeed, filtering stones and fragments thereof have been found in the archaeological excavations of 16th century New SEVILLE. A fine example of a limestone water filter showing a lattice-work housing is in the Jamaica People's Museum in SPANISH TOWN.

[Cassidy 1971, DJE]

FIREFLY

Nearly fifty species of fireflies (*Lampyridae*) occur in Jamaica and one species of luminous click beetle (*Elateridae*). The fireflies are actually beetles, called Blinkies, and their lights turn off and on repeatedly. The click beetle is called Peenie-Wallie or Peeny, and its light is a steady glow. However, the names are used interchangeably. The flashing lights seen as they dart about at night are for courtship purposes – so that males and females can find one another in the darkness. Each species flashes a light of different duration, frequency, and brightness and groups of fireflies will sometimes flash in concert. The lights are situated in special luminous organs, the brightest lights being visible in flight.

The female, which is usually the bigger of the two, has only one lighted segment and her role in the courtship game is largely passive. She sits quietly in a prominent spot – some cannot even fly – while the male flits about searching for a mate. When he flies nearby and flashes his light, she gives an answering flash. The lights of each species are synchronized differently, and females of the same species flash in a different sequence from the males so there is no chance of confusion. As soon as two fireflies get together, courtship begins; they mate, and eventually the female lays her eggs. After this, there is no further use for the adults. So far as anyone can discover, propagating the species is all that they live for, though scientists – and lay persons – are intrigued by their marvellous ability to produce light without heat.

Visitors to the island are often fascinated by their first contact with fireflies, which were once plentiful inside houses as well as outdoors, country children often collecting them in glass jars to provide illumination. Lady Nugent, the governor's wife noted their presence at Clifton, in ST ANDREW: 'October 1st. Up at 4, and dress by candle-light. The fire-flies looked beautifully in the hall, as we passed through to our carriages. The walls were quite illuminated.' And the next day, again at 4:00am: 'The morning darker than usual, and the fire-flies more brilliant; all the walls seem covered with gold spangles.'

In FOLKLORE, fireflies or Blinkies seen inside the house in the daytime are taken as a sign of a visitor arriving.

[Farr 1984b, Mico 1896, NHSJ 1946, Nugent 1839]

FIREPLACE

In the past, cooking was done on wood burning fireplaces which ranged from the elaborate ones in the plantation house to more modest ones consisting of rocks and mortar forming a raised platform called a 'fireside', or, in some places, 'firewall'.

In GREAT HOUSE or hut, the fireplace was always in a separate building from the house. The more elaborate kitchens were vented with chimneys; those in poorer households had no such outlet for the smoke, which in time coloured the room black, the same colour as the iron or clay pots that were used for cooking. Sometimes the fireplace had a long hook or hooks hanging from the ceiling so pots could be hung over the fires; also hung over the fire was a basket or basket-like arrangement called a 'kreng-kreng' or 'hankra' which was used to smoke and preserve meat.

Fireplace with Kreng-kreng

The fireplace arrangement gradually gave way to the use of the COAL POT and the 'Dover' stove, and eventually to modern gas or electric appliances. The cooking arrangement of the poorest has always consisted of a wood fire built between three large stones arranged on the ground so that a pot can sit comfortably on top. The fire is set on a smooth cleared space in the yard or, when available, a ZINC sheet. The pots traditionally have rounded bottoms – see DUTCHIE.

FISH AND FISHING

Fish is a favourite food of Jamaicans, and commercial fishing provides a livelihood for thousands of people. There are 200 known fishing beaches around the island with some 3,000 CANOES operating along the coast (called inshore fisheries). In addition, some 150-200 canoes engage in 'cay fishing' on the Pedro and Morant CAYS, the banks here providing the best fishing areas. In recent times, villages of commercial fishermen living on the cays year-round have developed. They are served by 'packer boats' from Jamaica that take them supplies and bring back iced-fish to the island. A few vessels operate (with permission) in foreign fishing grounds, especially the rich Honduran and Nicaraguan shelves. Most fish are caught by traditional Z-traps (fish-pots) but handlines, troll lines, seine nets, gill nets and spear guns are also used. There have also been initiatives to develop inland fisheries by stocking ponds with fresh water species such as Tilapia (see FISH FARMING) in order to relieve the very high levels of fishing pressure on marine fisheries.

Fishing is one of the oldest occupations in Jamaica and up to recently was undertaken from dugout canoes. The dugout boats are now uncommon, having been largely replaced by fibreglass boats with outboard engines, except on the north coast.

The dugout boats, fishing techniques and many of the fish species would have been familiar to the West AFRICANS who were brought to the West Indies as slaves (see SLAVERY). It is they who took over the job of fishing Jamaican waters, a task carried on by their descendants to this day, as a living for some and to supplement the domestic diet of others.

Much of the fishing takes place close to shore in the shallow seas adjacent to the island, the much wider shelf on the south coast being the most important. All along the north coast from NEGRIL to MORANT POINT, the deep water mark (the contour line from 200m) is found 1.6km from the shore, giving easy access to big fish such as Blue Marlin, Dolphin and Tuna which are attractive to sports fishermen. This aspect of

M. LaYacona

Fish pots

Tarpon caught on the Black River c. 1930 (from Olley)

fishing has developed since the 1950s, with sports fishermen from Florida and elsewhere arriving in pursuit of Blue Marlin, leading to the development of local charters for tourists. Nowadays, there are several well organized fishing tournaments around the island, the best known being the PORT ANTONIO International Fishing Tournament first held in 1959, an event targeting Blue Marlin when they are most plentiful, in September and October. Fish under 100lb caught at the tournament are released for conservation reasons, but enough are caught not just for fresh eating but to provide a Jamaican delicacy, smoked Blue Marlin. Blue Marlin are caught year round, along with Wahoo, King, Mackerel and other big fish.

A huge variety of fish are caught and sold in the local markets, many of brilliant colours and varied shapes. They come with an enormous range of local names, most based on minute observations of the colours and other physical attributes as well as the behaviour of the fish. The fact that F.G. Cassidy in his *Jamaica Talk* devotes several pages to these names attests to their richness. For example, names of the popular Jack fish based on colour include silver, yellow or butter, yellow-tail, green, green-back, burn-fin, black, and amber jack, while other characteristics of the same fish yield round-head, swine-head, point-nose, pig-nose, goggle-eye, horse-eye, crab-eye, mule or mule-back, wire-back, hard-bone, and streamers jack, among many others.

Although the local catch nowadays is supplemented by imported fish, Jamaicans still prefer fresh fish, which in pre-refrigeration days was not available to people in the mountains. If close to a stream, inland dwellers nevertheless had access to freshwater fish including one that is regarded as an island delicacy, now rare, in the Mountain MULLET or Tum Tum, as well as fine Hognose and Calipever mullet. Snook, Tarpon and Jack are still taken at river mouths and bays, especially of the larger rivers such as the RIO GRANDE and the MARTHA BRAE, and the lower reaches of the BLACK RIVER, along with crustaceans.

Each person has a favourite fish, but the most popular probably are King, Snapper, Butterfish, Parrot, Doctor, Grunt and Sprats. Freshly cooked fish (with a favourite accompaniment of BAMMY) can often be had in traditional fishing communities such as PORT ROYAL and OLD HARBOUR and at HELLSHIRE and other beaches patronized by locals. Jamaicans believe in the efficacy of 'fish TEA', as a soup cooked with fish head and bones is called, and many like to eat all of the fish, including the head and eyes. Fish is regarded as 'brain food'.

Before cooking, fresh fish is always washed in LIME juice to 'cut' the fishy smell. Frying and steaming are favourite cooking methods, there being numerous recipes; ESCOVEITCH or 'scaveech' is a popular pickled fish dish.

The earliest inhabitants of the CARIBBEAN lived on shellfish (see CIBONEY) and the people who supplanted them, the TAINOS, also had a diet that was rich in seafood, the Caribbean sea at that time also teeming with CONCH, TURTLE, MANATEE, Oysters and other shellfish. Hans Sloane, who spent some time in Jamaica in the late 17th century (see FLORA), wrote: 'I know not, neither have I heard of any place where there are greater plenty of fresh Water and Sea Fishes, than in the island and on the coast of Jamaica.'

Nowadays the manatee and turtle have virtually disappeared and their hunting is forbidden, and the CRAB, JANGGA, LOBSTER,

Fishermen landing their catch

Oyster and other crustaceans are no longer found in any great abundance. Conservation measures to protect the island's resources have only recently begun. But Jamaicans' great liking for imported salted fish, a taste shaped by history, continues undiminished. (See FISH, Salt.)

[Cassidy 1971, Donaldson 1993, Facey 1993, GOJ STATIN 1999a, Lethbridge 1996, Munro 1969, Patterson 1964, Sloane 1725]

FISH FARMING

Commercial FISH farming (Aquaculture) is a relatively new development, using scientific methods to produce freshwater fish for both export and the local market. In Jamaica the fish is mostly Tilapia, but Carp, Oyster, and freshwater prawn are also grown.

Tilapia mossambica was first introduced to Jamaica in the early 1950s and stocked intensively in rivers and ponds, but the project was unsuccessful for various reasons. In 1978-79, the *Tilapia nilotica* (Silver Perch) was introduced. Then in the 1980s came the even more preferred Red or Pink Tilapia (Red Snapper). Commercial production of Tilapia began in 1976 under a project jointly undertaken by US-AID and the Government of Jamaica; the Inland Fisheries Unit that oversees the industry was created in 1977. Fish farming has grown significantly since then. In 1995, with 675 pond hectares in production, approximately 214t of fish were exported to Europe, 79t to the USA, and 6.5t to Canada, in addition to supplying the local market.

[GOJ Jampro 1997, Ross 1985]

FISH, Salt

A statement by a 19th century cookbook writer would certainly hold good today: 'It is surprising to most newcomers to find that in Jamaica there is hardly a more popular dish among the natives, and often among the upper classes, than the despised salt fish, eaten at home [i.e. England] not from choice but as a sort of penitential dish.' So wrote Caroline Sullivan in *The Jamaica Cookery Book*, adding: 'Here it is the almost daily, and certainly the favourite, food of the people generally, and cooked as they cook it cannot fail to please the most fastidious.'

The salt fish was cod, nowadays virtually out of reach because of price and scarcity, the fish stocks being almost depleted. Pickled and salted mackerel, herring and shad have also played and continue to play their role in the Jamaican diet, along with pickled and salted meats such as pig's tail and salt beef and pork. These were all imported in former times, but meat from the hunt and domestically reared flesh were also salted and cured in the days before refrigeration. In the 1920s, isolated coastal villages such as NEGRIL caught and salted many local varieties of fish. And almost every kitchen had a contraption above the FIREPLACE called a 'kreng-kreng' or 'hankra' into which meat was put for smoking, and a large jar or YABBA for salting the meats in brine. Of course, JERK was an even earlier method of preserving meat, the PIMENTO and other flavours making up for a scarcity of salt in the earliest days of settlement.

Cod fish

Such a heavily salt-based diet goes back hundreds of years to when the West Indian SUGAR CANE planters sought a cheap protein food for the enslaved AFRICANS they were importing for plantation labour. (See SLAVERY, SUGAR PLANTATION.) With all hands put to planting cane, there was little time or inclination to provide fresh meat, and cheap cod from the New England colonies was the answer, salted and dried hard to survive the tropical climate. In exchange, the boats took back molasses and RUM. The cod that was not acceptable to the discerning Mediterranean market was sold to the plantations, and 'West India' became the commercial name for the lowest quality. Soon, Nova Scotia was specializing in this product. The West Indian planters came to refer to the fish as 'Halifax Mutton' and enjoyed eating it as much as their slaves did.

Salt fish was supplemented by other pickled

Icelandic fisherman with cod c. 1925

fish that up to recently were regarded exclusively as 'poor man's food'. Yet even a small amount of salted fish or meat provided a relish to an otherwise bland meal of starches; perched on top of a large plate that might be full of boiled YAM, COCO, breadfruit, PLANTAIN and dumpling, the savoury tidbit was called the 'watchman'. Although the slaves reared poultry and livestock, most of this seems to have been sold to the white inhabitants and transients, leaving them heavily reliant on imported protein. Famine occurred when wars and embargoes cut off food from abroad and local crops failed, as occurred for several years in the 1780s (see BREADFRUIT). There was a severe shortage of salted provisions during the wars of the French Revolution and the Napoleonic wars which lasted, with brief intermissions, from 1793 to 1815 and had a considerable impact on the West Indies where some of the battles were fought.

Some of Jamaica's most popular dishes today are made with salt fish – including ACKEE and saltfish, a fritter called STAMP-AND-GO and a dish of salt mackerel or codfish in COCONUT milk called RUN DUNG (run-down). SOLOMON GUNDY is a popular relish made with red herrings.

Although salt fish is soaked in water to remove much of the salt before cooking, the prevalence of this condiment in the diet is believed to contribute to the island's extremely high incidence of hypertension. (See SALT.)
[Kurlansky 1997, Sheridan 1985, Sullivan 1893]

FLAG, Jamaican see NATIONAL SYMBOLS

FLAT BRIDGE
One of Jamaica's oldest and best known bridges, constructed without railings to facilitate the flow of water during the rainy season when the RIO COBRE is in spate, or 'come dung' as it is described locally.

Flat Bridge in 1773 by George Robertson

Flat Bridge today

The bridge in ST CATHERINE Parish has been the main north-south link since the 1770s (see RIO COBRE GORGE), when the road was built along a mule trail which followed the river through its gorge. The river road was called Sixteen Mile Walk and maintained by the owners of the 16 plantations in the area who sent their produce along it to the wharves on the south coast. They were required to send one slave in every fifty to work on the River-Road, as it was also called.

The earliest bridges were made of logs and earth. Even with modern construction techniques, the bridge has been built without railings, as these have been found to disappear in flood waters which rise in the gorge with alarming rapidity, making crossing the bridge impossible. The fact that only vehicles going in one direction can cross the bridge at a time sometimes leads to altercations and worse when two drivers 'buck up'. Confrontations were reduced by the installation of traffic lights at either end in 1998. To make up for the inconveniences, the bridge and its setting in the spectacular gorge with high cliffs on one side of the road and the swift flowing river on the other, offer motorists a thrilling ride.
[Cundall 1915, Porter 1990]

FLOOD MYTH
In TAINO mythology, the sea and fish come from a broken CALABASH gourd. The Taino CREATION MYTH tells of four twin brothers who in their wanderings stole food from the gourd of YAYA, the creator, and in their haste, failed to hang it back securely. It fell and broke apart. According to the story that was told to PANÉ, 'so much water came from that gourd that it covered the whole earth and from it came many fish . . . this is how the sea took its origin'. In another story, YaYa and his wife take down a gourd to see the bones of their dead son that were kept there and they accidentally spill the bones that turn into fish.
[Arrom 1975]

FLOOR CLEANING

Up to recent times the main flooring material in Jamaica was wood. The bare floors of native hard woods, sometimes arranged in beautiful patterns and with an impeccable shine, were often the feature of Jamaican houses most remarked upon by visitors. Thus floor cleaning was an important household chore. Before the advent of electric floor polishers, the wooden floor was cleaned and polished with a COCONUT brush, that is, the husk of a dried coconut sawn in two, which, along with native beeswax as polish, gave to floors a marvellous shine and, over time, a rich patina. (Such brushes are still sold in the markets.)

Various agents were used to give a rich colour to the wood. The most popular were red ochre or tree bark (in the old days MAHOGANY) which imparted a rich, dark red colour. A 19th century cookbook recommends throwing a roasted CALABASH into the water the floors are wiped with, to give 'a very handsome dark stain'.

Usually the floor would be wiped dry, the dye applied and left to dry. The beeswax would be warmed and rubbed on the brush and applied to the floor, the cleaner kneeling on a piece of cloth and moving around, both to apply the polish to the floor and later to shine it.

The English naturalist P.H. Gosse made the following interesting observation on floor cleaning at a house he stayed at in WESTMORELAND in the mid-19th century: 'Scarcely anything surprises an European more than to tread on floors as beautifully polished as the finest tables of our drawing rooms. The mode in which the gloss is daily renewed is curious: if the visitor should peep out of his bedroom about dawn of day, he would see some half a dozen sable handmaids on their knees in the middle of the floor, with a great tray of sour ORANGES cut in halves. Each maid takes a half-orange, and rubs the floor with it until its juice is exhausted; it is then thrown aside and the process is continued with another.' The wood was then polished with coconut-brushes, as described above, the maids afterwards walking on pieces of cloth as they moved around to maintain the floor's shine. All these practices are still current today when no electric polisher is available, though store-bought polishes will be used. A well-shined floor is still a matter of pride among the folk as among the elite.

Experienced cleaners would knock the back and sides of the brush on the floor in a rhythm known as 'Johnny-Coopa-Lantan', a name derived, says the DJE, from its imitation of the rhythmic sound made by a COOPER (barrel maker) fastening hoops on RUM casks. With more than one cleaner at work, there could be competition in beating out rhythms such as 'Mosquito One, Mosquito Two, Mosquito jump inna hot callalu', a way of making lighter an arduous routine task.

Olive Lewin has pointed out that sometimes groups of women would get together to clean each other's houses, the group moving from house to house, turning hard labour into conviviality. This led to floor cleaning song types such as 'Mr Potter'.

[DJE, Gosse 1984, Lewin 2000, Sullivan 1893]

FLORA

Jamaica exhibits great variety of terrain, soil and climate and a correspondingly diverse plant life. According to C.D. Adams, about 3,000 species of flowering plants have been discovered. ORCHIDS, FERNS and BROMELIADS are extremely well represented among native plants, there being over 230 species of orchids, over 550 native ferns, and about 60 species of Bromeliads or Wild Pines. There are also 200-odd species of grasses, though most of these have been introduced. Eight hundred endemic species of plants (i.e. those which occur nowhere else in the world) have been discovered so far, representing 27.2 per cent of all flowering plants. (See also FAUNA.)

Hans Sloane

Jamaica's flora is closest to that of its nearest neighbour, Cuba, and next, to the other islands of the Greater ANTILLES. The island also has a wide variety of native timber trees, indeed the

House cleaners

The genus Portlandia was recently discovered in Jamaica. Above, two of the native species – P. coccinea (L) and P. albiflora

original vegetation of Jamaica was virtually all FOREST, with some marshland here and there. Despite the profusion of native flora, it is of interest to note that virtually all of Jamaica's economic plants are introductions, though many have become naturalized (i.e. can propagate themselves without the assistance of man).

Jamaica's flora has been well studied over a long period of time. Botanic gardens began to be established in the 18th century (see BATH, CASTLETON, CINCHONA, HOPE GARDENS and GORDON TOWN) and helped to encourage the introduction and propagation of plants from virtually every corner of the world. Jamaica has also been a source of plants for many world famous collections, including Kew Gardens and the British Museum of Natural History. Indeed, this museum was founded with a collection of Jamaican plants made by Sir Hans Sloane. He arrived in the island in 1687 as physician to the governor and in 15 months collected 800 plant species, many of which were new to science. Sloane also published two illustrated volumes of his collections.

The first systematic study of the Jamaican flora was done by William Fawcett, who came from the British Museum in 1886 as director of Public Gardens. Fawcett and Rendle's *Flora of Jamaica* has been published as a multi-volume series by the British Museum. C.D. Adams's *Flowering Plants of Jamaica* is today's standard reference work.

[Adams 1971, 1972, Bretting 1983a, 1983b, NHSJ 1946, 1949, Sinha 1972]

FOLKLORE

Although there are many definitions of what constitutes 'folklore', it may be defined as the tales, legends, sayings, customs, beliefs and practices of a group of people, constituting a common core of traditions which have been handed down orally from generation to generation. The term 'folk' can refer to any group, so long as they share some common customs. This group may be as small as the family or as large as the whole country. Sometimes the tradition is common only to the small group; at other times, the lore is known to the whole country, to other territories which share a common heritage, or it might be known throughout the world. Some of the beliefs pertaining to, e.g. SALT, would fall into this latter category. What is significant is that over time the 'folklore' becomes accepted and recognized as part of the cultural heritage of the community. Two recognized features of folklore are that (a) it is anonymous and (b) it exists in many variations.

Many of the things that Jamaicans do habitually and cannot explain, probably once had significant meaning which has been lost over time. For instance, pouring RUM on the earth before first digging into it to make a grave, a house, etc. might in the past have reflected deference to the African spirit of the earth of whom permission had to be obtained to avoid her vengeance.

The term 'folklore' is never applied by people themselves to what they do; it is a term used by scholars to indicate material in the traditional oral culture that can be collected and classified in a scientific manner for the use of researchers and students. Thus what might be part of the everyday life of one set of people might be 'folklore' to another. In the past, many visitors (and some Jamaicans) have taken part of this folkloric material and, tearing it from its roots, projected it in a sensational or one-sided manner. Some Jamaicans also tend to sensationalize aspects of the lives of people different from themselves. Often, the practices, beliefs, and customs of the poorer people have been derided by the elite. Some wanting to appear 'modern' will dismiss folklore as 'ol'time sinting' while others will view 'ol'time sinting' with great nostalgia.

Jamaica shares elements of folklore with the rest of the CARIBBEAN and parts of the Americas to which Africans were transplanted as slaves. However, many elements from the European and other groups that make up our society have been incorporated into this body of knowledge, so it sometimes becomes difficult to trace precise origins. Many have argued that there are in fact 'Two Jamaicas' existing side by side, and two cultural traditions: one western and urban representing the culture of the elite; the other rooted in the countryside and largely African based. However, it might be more useful to see folklore, like the Jamaican LANGUAGE, as existing on a continuum where the two Jamaicas often meet (e.g. WEDDING or CHRISTMAS customs, folk MEDICINE), each segment of the society at the same time preserving something of its own 'folklore' that is not shared by the other elements.

The earliest written records of Jamaican folklore and folk life were by Europeans – visiting travellers, resident planters and missionaries and other churchmen who wrote down what they heard and observed. Although these are often the only records Jamaicans have of their past, and they are valuable for that reason, the early European observers also applied their own bias in presenting this material as 'quaint' and laughable or 'sinful' and worthy of condemnation.

During SLAVERY and after, there were legal bans on some elements of folk life, for instance, the DRUM was prohibited during the plantation era. Some of the banned elements went underground and continue to thrive there, e.g. OBEAH. Others later resurfaced but in a fragmentary form, e.g. JONKONNU.

Because of disapproval by others, some people suppressed aspects of their heritage and refused to pass information on to their children, or questioned the children's 'readiness' to receive 'secret' information. In this way, some things never get passed on (as researchers found, for instance, among the old YORUBA in WESTMORELAND). Others have given up their inherited beliefs and customs on changing their lifestyle. This occurred, for instance, during the widespread conversion to Christianity during the 19th century MISSIONARY era when many practices brought from Africa were dismissed as 'pagan', and precious artefacts identified as 'idols' destroyed, an attitude that still persists in some quarters today. A move 'upward' in society or from country to town can also result in a deliberate shedding of past beliefs and practices, and invariably impacts on the use of language. Since much of the folklore employs the Jamaican language – 'patwa' or 'creole' – disapproval of the use of such language in the past also meant the suppression or denial of what the language contained, e.g. folk songs, tales, beliefs, proverbs, etc. Even today, some people mistakenly believe that to be 'respectable' means pretending not to know anything that could be identified with the Jamaican 'folk'.

It is only since the latter part of the 20th century that researchers have begun to collect and analyse Jamaican folklore within a historical framework, providing a better understanding of its meaning and its role in national cultural heritage. Unwritten aspects of the past are no longer presented as 'backwardness' or 'superstition' but as an integral part of the fabric of the nation. Folkloric elements are also being continually renewed, revitalized and extended in the literary and performing arts. In recent times, collections of stories and songs have been able to utilize modern technology of tape recording and film to record and preserve. Many recordings of Jamaican folk music now exist, and the recollections of many Jamaicans have been obtained and preserved in the Memory Bank at the AFRICAN CARIBBEAN INSTITUTE OF JAMAICA. (See also DANCE, LITERATURE, MUSIC, REGGAE, THEATRE.)

Since folklore is a part of living, its elements have to be kept alive by people or they will die out or disappear. This happens when there is no longer any strong feeling associated with what gave rise to the belief, activity or event. FESTIVALS, songs and celebrations associated with EMANCIPATION provide a good example. The First of AUGUST celebrations and the BRUCKINS tradition associated with it were once large and elaborate events among the generation who had experienced slavery and desired to commemorate freedom. But celebrations to mark the events and the stories, songs, dances associated with them faded away as later generations preferred to forget this painful past. At the end of the 20th century, a generation with a new perspective on the past brought back the celebration of EMANCIPATION DAY.

Much of the folklore arising from the AFRICAN HERITAGE has been kept alive through religious activities associated with life cycles such as BIRTH and DEATH and associated rituals including DINKI MINI, ETU, GERREH, KUMINA, NINE NIGHT, ZELLA and aspects of MAROON culture. Many of these elements remained hidden from outsiders in deep rural Jamaica and have only recently come to light. Though almost vanished traditions themselves, TEA MEETINGS and country weddings helped to preserve the older traditions of lengthy and elaborate and playful speech, and testimonials known as 'speechifying' and toasting. One could argue that such practices have been brought to life again by the Deejays of DANCEHALL and Reggae.

Some of the elements of folklore scattered

throughout this Encyclopedia are listed in the Subject Index under Folklore. It should be borne in mind that the breakdown into categories is only for the sake of convenience, as any given item can fall into several categories.

While there is no one general collection of Jamaican folklore, references to publications relating to specific aspects of folklore are given at the end of the individual entries. The most comprehensive general collections are: Banbury 1894, Barrett 1976, Beckwith 1924, 1928, 1929, Bennett 1979, Brathwaite 1970, Dance 1985, Jekyll 1907, Lewin n.d., Lewin 2000, Sherlock 1954, Tanna 1984, Williams 1934.

In addition, Baxter 1970, Clarke 1957, Kerr 1952, Cassidy 1971, DJE, D'Costa and Lalla 1990, Lalla and D'Costa 1989, Patterson 1973, also contain material on folklore, as does as some of the historical literature listed in the bibliography.

FOLK MEDICINE see MEDICINE, Folk

FOLK MUSIC see MUSIC, Folk

FOLK TALES see ANANSI

FOLLY

Ruined mansion at Folly near PORT ANTONIO, PORTLAND Parish, the subject of LEGEND. The chief belief is that sea water was used in its construction – hence its ruined state – and that the mansion started to crumble from the moment the owner stepped over the threshold with his bride. She burst into tears at this omen and fled, never to return. The property fell into neglect and ruin, testament to a rich man's folly.

Folly mansion was in fact built by Alfred Mitchell of New London, Connecticut, USA in 1905, and he and his family lived there on and off until his death in 1912. He was originally buried at Folly but his remains have been removed to Connecticut. Although the legends say that Mitchell built the house for his bride, he and his wife were already grandparents when the house was built, and it was very much a family residence. The house continued in use until 1936. Although sea water was used in mixing the cement, it was not the cement that crumbled but the steel that rusted.

The building was designed by Boston architects Chapman and Fraser as an adaptation in concrete of a Roman villa. The sixty-room mansion had two stories and a basement and was about 60m long. Everything but the doors,

Ruins of Folly mansion

windows and marble staircase was of concrete. To build Folly, Mitchell first had to drain the swamps in the area, and he installed his own lighting plant and water system, including a reservoir. There is no doubt that Mitchell's extravagant life style, including the monkeys and other animals he kept on a small island off the beach, impressed Portlanders at the time.

Mitchell's wife was of the famous Tiffany jewellery family of New York. One of their daughters married Sir James Jeans, the British astronomer, and another married Hiram Bingham, the American archaeologist who rediscovered the 'lost city' of the Incas, Machu Picchu in Peru, in 1911.

The name 'Folly' was applied to the area long before Mitchell came – FOLLY POINT LIGHTHOUSE was built in 1888. One of the early owners of the property was a Revd James Service, a BAPTIST minister. Apparently he bought the property in small lots over a long period of time. This gave rise to a Portland saying: 'A no so Savis did get Folly', in other words, 'Be thrifty'. Folly property is now owned by the Jamaican government.

[Wright and White 1969]

FOLLY POINT LIGHTHOUSE

Located in PORTLAND Parish, this lighthouse was built in 1888. It flashes a white light of 2 seconds duration followed by 8 seconds of darkness. The light is visible up to 19km.

Folly Point lighthouse

FOOTBALL

Jamaica was ignited by the success of its 'Reggae Boyz' football (soccer) team that in 1998 made it the first country in the English-speaking CARIBBEAN to qualify for the World Cup Soccer Finals. Although the team was knocked out in the preliminary round of the competition in France, they continued to be hailed as sporting heroes, for this was the best that the island had ever done at football.

The success of the team owed much to the Brazilian soccer coach Rene Simoes and national coach Carl Brown who were determined to produce a world class team in four years and did so. While for many years Jamaica had played friendly international matches (starting with a game against Haiti in 1925), this was the country's first major success at the international competitive level. It was a long road to France during which time the country built up experience, a pool of talent, and widespread interest in the game that is Jamaica's most popular spectator sport. The NATIONAL STADIUM is usually packed to capacity (32,000) when international games are played.

Football was first played in the island towards the end of the 19th century – Jamaica's first football club was formed in 1893. The sport became popular and many clubs were established, including Kensington, Melbourne, Kingston, Lucas and St George's College Old Boys. But the real football excitement has for a long time been provided at the secondary school boy level. Rural schools compete for the DaCosta Cup and those in the CORPORATE AREA for the Manning Cup; the winner of each cup then competes in two matches for the Olivier Shield, usually providing one of Jamaica's most exciting sports event. A competition originally for the elite schools, much fresh talent was brought in by the newer schools such as Tivoli Comprehensive High School, Excelsior School, Camperdown High School, Charlie Smith Comprehensive and Trench Town Comprehensive. Much of the talent for the Reggae Boyz team came from such schools. Players were also drawn from the UK among footballers playing for English teams who were born in Jamaica or were of Jamaican descent.

Aside from the Reggae Boyz, individual Jamaicans have in the past achieved outstanding success overseas, including Lindy Delapenha, England's first professional Jamaican footballer, and John Barnes who played with great distinction for England in the 1980s and 90s. In 1998, Barnes was selected by the English Football League as one of its 100 Legends of its first 100 years.

[Carnegie et al. 1998]

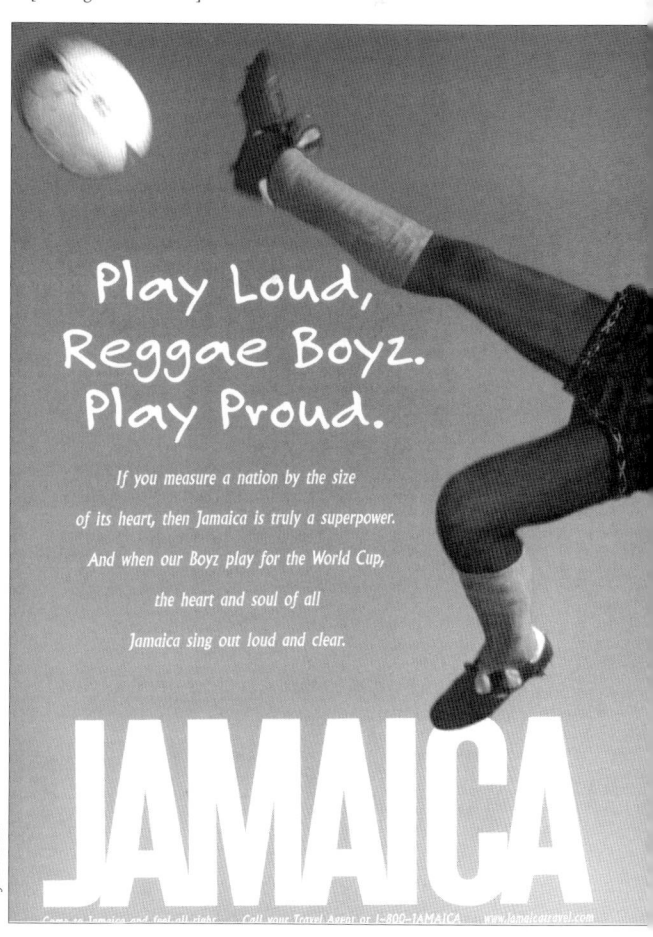

FOREST

The natural vegetation of Jamaica consists of woodland or forests; at the time of COLUMBUS' arrival such forests around the island came down to the sea, the aboriginal inhabitants the TAINOS settling mainly along river valleys.

Much of the natural forest has been cleared for cultivation and settlement. Twenty-four per cent or 265,000ha of the total land area of the island remains in forest, of this 40,500ha as state forest, administered by the Forestry Department. Much of the remaining deciduous forest is in difficult mountain terrain where it cannot be economically exploited. The undisturbed forests in the higher reaches of the BLUE MOUNTAINS and Port Royal Mountains are important for protecting the watershed but they are also of interest to botanists for their unique FLORA; some 41 per cent of species here are considered to be endemic (i.e. found nowhere else). Attempts are being made to protect these areas with the establishment of NATIONAL PARKS. Even so, they remain under threat from human encroachment.

Jamaica's vegetation is very diverse because of high variations in rainfall, altitude and soil. It includes: the montane cloud forest and elfin woodland of the Blue Mountains, the rainforest of the John Crow Mountains, cactus-thorn scrub, palm thickets, dry tropical forest on LIMESTONE, mostly along the south coast, forest on limestone hills (mogotes) which form plateaus in the west and centre, savannas, and the littoral swamp and MANGROVE forests (see GEOLOGY).

Jamaica at present supplies only a small portion of its requirements for forest products and relies heavily on imports. Commercial forestry has been supported by the government since the 1960s. Caribbean Pine, Blue MAHOE, and Honduras MAHOGANY have been the principal species planted.
[Thompson et al. 1986]

FORT AUGUSTA

This imposing structure is located off the road that leads to Portmore, ST CATHERINE Parish. Now a prison for women, it was formerly a fort guarding the western end of KINGSTON harbour. The fort was planned in 1740 by Admiral Sir Charles Knowles (later governor of Jamaica 1752-56) and built under extremely difficult conditions in what was a swamp; the land was known as Mosquito Point. The fort was finally completed in the mid-1750s and named Augusta in honour of the mother of King George III. It was fortified with about 80 large guns.

As a safety measure, ships would discharge ammunition at Fort Augusta before entering Kingston harbour. In 1782 the magazine with 300 barrels of gunpowder was struck by a bolt of lightning. Three hundred persons were killed and windows up to 27km from the resulting blast were broken. The building was torn from its foundations and the masonry destroyed. The shocks created a huge crater that soon filled with water. It eventually took 9,180t of rubbish to dump up the hole so the fort could be rebuilt on a raft of palmetto logs (Thatch-pole PALM).

One of the major events here was the mutiny of recruits of the 2nd WEST INDIA REGIMENT in 1808, leading to the death of three officers.

Fort Augusta was abandoned for some time in the late 19th century before being taken over by the Prisons Department in the early 20th century.
[Buisseret 1969, Cundall 1915]

FORT CHARLES

Built immediately after the English conquest (1655) as Fort Cromwell on Cagway. On the restoration of the monarchy in 1660 it was

Fort Charles

renamed Fort Charles, and Cagway became known as PORT ROYAL. It is not only the oldest standing fortification in Jamaica dating from the English period but one of the oldest in the Western Hemisphere and remains a visitor attraction.

FORT CHARLOTTE

Located at LUCEA, HANOVER Parish, this fort was named after the consort of King George III in whose reign it was built. Like other forts, it has been declared a national monument by the JAMAICA NATIONAL HERITAGE TRUST. The

Fort Charlotte, Lucea

battlement is in good repair and two of the early cannon can still be seen. RUSEA'S School occupies part of the old fort.

FORT CLARENCE

Fort Clarence beach in the HELLSHIRE HILLS, ST CATHERINE Parish, preserves the name of one of a ring of forts and batteries that protected KINGSTON Harbour. This fort at the foot of PORT HENDERSON hill was originally named Fort Small, after its builder. Around 1799 it was renamed Fort Clarence, possibly after William, Duke of Clarence.

FORT DUNDAS

The ruins of this fort can still be seen behind the government school at RIO BUENO, TRELAWNY Parish. It dates from 1778 and was named after Henry Dundas, British secretary of war.

FORT GEORGE

This fort was begun in 1729 to protect PORT ANTONIO, PORTLAND Parish, at a time when Spanish attacks on the north coast were feared. But the threat from the MAROONS in the interior was more real, and two British regiments were hastily sent from Gibraltar, arriving before the barracks were finished. Forced to live in thatched huts with earthen floors (which was common housing for troops at the time), many of the soldiers soon contracted fevers and died. (See YELLOW FEVER AND MALARIA.) The survivors were returned to Gibraltar. One of the officers was Lieutenant Roger Sterne, father of the English novelist Laurence Sterne, author of *Tristram Shandy* and other books. Sterne Sr died in Port Antonio on 31 July 1731 within a few months of his arrival.

Fort George has 3m thick walls. It was built to hold 22 guns and several George III cannon mounted in the original emplacement can still be seen. One of them bears the date 1813 and the name of its maker: Carron Ironworks near Edinburgh. The fort functioned up to the First WORLD WAR and is now part of TITCHFIELD School.

FORT HALDANE

Ruins and cannon of this fort in PORT MARIA, ST MARY Parish, can still be seen at Gray's Charity, an old people's home. The fort was named after General George Haldane, governor in 1759.

FORT JOHNSTON

Located on the coast in HELLSHIRE HILLS, ST CATHERINE Parish, one of a ring of forts that protected KINGSTON harbour in the 18th century. Like FORT CLARENCE, it was constructed at a time when England was threatened by both France and Spain, and extra efforts were made to strengthen its important overseas possessions.

FORT LINDSAY

Fort Lindsay was erected in 1745 at Morant Point, ST THOMAS Parish with a magazine and barracks attached. At Prospect – at the point opposite Fort Lindsay – are the ruins of Fort William that guarded the western side of the entrance to Port Morant harbour. The road to Blue Mahoe at Prospect is called Fort Drive and the island in the bay is Fort Cay. After the First WORLD WAR, the government rented out the lands near the barracks and used the money to help war veterans in the PARISH.

FORT MONTEGO

This fort once guarded the approaches to the town of MONTEGO BAY, ST JAMES Parish. What can be seen of the fort today is the battery with three old cannon and the powder magazine. Although Fort Montego was large, it was apparently most inefficient. In 1760 one of the rusty guns exploded and killed a gunner while firing a salute to celebrate the surrender of Havana to English forces. The only record of the guns actually being fired at a ship entering the harbour showed that the vessel was the schooner *Mercury* coming in at dawn in December 1795 with a cargo of bloodhounds and their handlers from Cuba (see DOG), brought to hunt down the MAROONS. The officer in charge of the fort thought the vessel was an enemy ship and ordered the guns to be fired. This was done, but probably because they worked so poorly, there was no damage.

Guns have been fired in the direction of the fort. In 1779 a warship with loaded guns pointing at Montego Bay caught fire in the harbour, a steward having upset a lamp among casks of liquor. As the guns started to go off, the shots damaged several houses on shore. The situation was saved by the future Admiral Lord NELSON, British naval hero of Trafalgar, who as a young man was in port on his ship the *Badger*. The crew of the stricken HMS *Glasgow* were about to abandon ship – and the town to the guns – when Nelson came up in his boats. He ordered the crew to cast their powder overboard, point their guns skyward and jump into the water, where they were rescued and taken on board the *Badger*. Montego Bay legend has a more romantic version, that the incident occurred while Nelson was attending a dance at Grove Hill House on the bluff overlooking the town, from which he dashed to save the situation.
[Oman 1996]

FORT MORANT
Remains of this old fort can still be seen in the town of MORANT BAY. It was built in 1773 and designed for nine guns. The three guns that remain are twenty-four pounders manufactured in the early 19th century. Each gun would have fired a solid shot weighing 11kg. At one time there was also a magazine and barracks attached to the fort.

FORT NUGENT
Harbour View Housing Estate is located on the site of this fort that once guarded the eastern approach to the city of KINGSTON. The first fortification was put up by the Spanish slave agent in Jamaica, James Castillo (who died in 1709) to guard his home there against enemy attacks. This fort was later strengthened by Sir George Nugent, governor (1801-1806) and commander-in-chief of the island, and named after him. All that can be seen of the fort today are the ruins of the Martello Tower that was built around 1806. It follows the plan of similar towers that were built in England at the time when an invasion was feared. The first such tower was built at Cape Mortella in Corsica, from which the name of the structure is derived.
[Buisseret 1971b]

FRANGIPANI (*Plumeria*)
Small shrub or ornamental tree that will grow up to 6m, native to Central America and the CARIBBEAN. Its waxy, fragrant flowers were used by the Aztecs in their religious rites. The

Frangipani

Martello Tower, Harbour View

botanical name of the plant celebrates the FRENCH botanist Charles Plumier, who made voyages to the Caribbean in the 17th century and introduced the plant to the rest of the world. It came to be so valued for its beauty and fragrance, that it was planted near to temples and burial grounds, especially in the East, acquiring its name of 'Temple Tree'. It is also used in the Pacific islands to make leis or flower garlands for visitors. The common name Frangipani comes via French from the Italian, and was first applied to a perfume for scenting gloves, named after its inventor, the Marquis Muzio Frangipani, a 16th century Roman nobleman.

The wild Frangipani of Jamaica and other Caribbean islands (*P. obtusa*) is common in thickets and woodlands of LIMESTONE, often in exposed situations near the sea from sea level to 900m. Several other species are cultivated in gardens. The showy, funnel-shaped flowers of red, orange or white all have yellow centres and five petals. The leaves are shed in the dry season, the flowers appearing soon after. The white milky sap is poisonous.

[Adams 1972, Bannochie and Light 1993, Kingsbury 1988]

FREE AFRICANS see AFRICANS, Indentured

FREE COLOUREDS see COLOUREDS

FREE VILLAGES

Many of Jamaica's village settlements were established by the formerly enslaved and their non-conformist MISSIONARY supporters following EMANCIPATION, when they took the matter of social reconstruction into their own hands.

Emancipation had been forced on the Jamaica Assembly by the British Parliament, bowing to public pressure in England, and most members of the Assembly were opposed to the idea and hence unwilling to give much thought to the requirements of a free society. The imposition of a period of APPRENTICESHIP between Emancipation in 1834 and full freedom in 1838 merely added to the antagonism between planters and ex-slaves. The owners of the slaves were compensated to the tune of £6.6 million for the inconvenience of losing their slaves. But for the 311,000 slaves, there was neither compensation nor preparation for the sudden transition to full freedom. (See SLAVERY.)

Indeed, the planters placed severe obstacles in the way of freedom. Previous to Emancipation, the slaves lived on the plantations to which they belonged, usually in plantation villages or 'slave yards'. No matter how terrible the condition of these YARDS, the slaves were attached to their homes there, for some had been occupied by the same families for generations. In addition to their PROVISION GROUNDS on the backlands of the estates, they were allowed to cultivate the land around their huts and, most important, they buried their dead nearby. But since the planters opposed Emancipation and the demand for money-wages by the formerly enslaved, many drove the newly freed people from their former homes on the estates through ejectment, the imposition of high rents and the institution of vagrancy and trespass laws. Since they had nowhere else to live, the planters reasoned, the ex-slaves (now a landless proletariat) would remain a captive and cheap work force.

But the ex-slaves wanted to be in a position to bargain for adequate wages and security of tenure and many began to buy up small plots of land for themselves. The settlements for the most part were haphazard and unplanned and determined by the availability of land in the area. In some cases, abandoned SUGAR PLANTATIONS were cut up and sold. In other places, only poor backlands were available. Some who could not purchase land simply squatted far into the bush. They had, after all, the example of Jamaica's first free black citizens, the MAROONS and other runaways who had been establishing their own settlements in the bush for some hundreds of years. Additionally, many Jamaican slaves had developed a spirit of working for themselves and providing by their own effort, through the cultivation of their provision grounds and the sale of the produce (see HIGGLER, MARKET).

With Emancipation, many people preferred to settle down in towns and villages, on freeholds that ranged in extent from one to ten acres. The process was captured by Hall Pringle, an observer writing in 1839: 'On the borders of Clarendon and Manchester, a town is springing up at Porus, by the unaided energy and industry of the negro settlers, of whom there is now, as near as I can guess, 1,500 including the females

Spanish Town Square, 1 August 1838, Emancipation Day (from Phillippo)

and children. Within an area of two miles, several proprietors are selling land for the purpose.' Most of the freeholds were under two acres. Pringle observed that, 'The quality of the land is so bad, and freeholds so small . . . that it is almost an impossibility that they can reap any produce from them, and this the settlers know well; I was informed by them they only wished for homes where they could not be troubled, and that they might have the liberty of working where they might choose for their livelihood'.

This subdivision of landed property continued at a great pace in the immediate post-Emancipation years. It led to a situation where, according to Hugh Paget, 'the population which had hitherto been grouped artificially on a purely economic basis on the sugar estates, had for the most part settled themselves on a social basis in the districts, villages and on their own scattered individual freeholds'. The present social structure of Jamaica dates from that period. (See also AGRICULTURE.)

The name 'free village' was given by the missionaries to those sub-divisions that took place under church sponsorship. The first such free village to be established in the West Indies was SLIGOVILLE, ST CATHERINE Parish, in 1834. Other well-known free villages include Sturge Town, Bethel Town, Mt Carey and Islington. These villages were founded mainly by BAPTIST church members. Foremost among the missionaries were the Revd J.M. Phillippo (see SPANISH TOWN BAPTIST CHURCH) and the Revd William Knibb (see KNIBB MEMORIAL CHURCH).

Even before Emancipation, the missionaries had begun to buy up old estates that they subdivided into lots that were sold to the ex-slaves. The early history of these church-sponsored villages is a story of cooperative effort, the villagers helping each other in clearing the land, in building, and in preparing their fields. (See DAY WORK.) Since each village was settled by members of a congregation, they also contributed their time and effort to building a church and a school (often the first buildings). Only six years after Emancipation, over 19,000 freedmen and their families were settled in these church-sponsored villages. Some were named after the emancipators – Clarksonville, Buxtonville and Wilberforce, but others were given names such as Content, Mt Horeb, Happy Valley and Harmony.

Sir Charles Metcalfe, who arrived as governor in the unsettled year of 1839, in his first despatch to London makes an interesting commentary on the formation of the Jamaican character: 'The generally tranquil state of the country without any police is a strong proof of the present peaceful disposition of the inhabitants. The character, however, acquired by the people in their transition from slavery to freedom, seems to be more that of independence than of submission to the will of others. They are, I imagine, as independent and thriving, and as little subservient, as any labouring population in the world.'

[Carnegie 1987, Genovese 1976, Hall 1953, Paget 1954, Phillippo 1843]

FRENCH

To the Jamaican folk, 'French' used to be more associated with the neighbouring country of Haiti than with France. The vast majority of French-speaking settlers arrived in the island in the late 18th century as refugees fleeing revolution in what was then the French colony of St-Domingue, the defeat of the French there by black and coloured forces leading to the establishment of the free Republic of Haiti. Probably because of its proximity, Jamaica as a BRITISH colony also continued over many years to offer refuge to deposed Haitian presidents (as it did to the Cuban revolutionaries of the 19th century such as MACEO and Martí). (See GEFFRARD PLACE.)

Approximately 1,200 white émigrés sought refuge in Jamaica during the revolution, along with thousands of their black slaves and untold numbers of free COLOUREDS. The first refugees came at the start of the revolution in 1791 when the slave uprising against the French plantation owners of the island began, but the bulk arrived 1793-98 as civil war raged after the defeat of French forces. While Jamaica opened its doors, there was nevertheless considerable nervousness about the new arrivals on the part of the authorities and the planters, who feared contamination of their own coloureds and blacks with the spirit of revolt. In 1799 Sas Portas, a Haitian spy, was hanged at the Parade in KINGSTON. There were numerous rumours of Haitian plans to invade the island and free the black slaves, and of Haitian links with the rebellious MAROONS.

The authorities were especially suspicious of the free coloureds, some of whom were accused or suspected of subversive activities and expelled; for a time there was an attempt to confine the non-whites to Kingston. The authorities went as far as deporting as 'aliens engaged in revolutionary activities' two British subjects of Haitian descent, born in Jamaica,

Edward Escoffery and Louis Lecesne, their expulsion and subsequent return becoming a celebrated case. In 1803 all the French 'aliens' and their slaves were rounded up and offered free passage to New Orleans, though some refugees by this time had become naturalized and were allowed to settle. It should be pointed out that from the French Revolution of 1793 to 1815, England and France were at war, with the CARIBBEAN the scene of major naval engagements. In addition to the French from Haiti, some had been brought to the island as prisoners of the Anglo-French wars, and some refugees from the revolution in France had arrived via America.

The bulk of the white émigrés had been planters in St-Domingue, and many of those who settled in Jamaica bought land in the mountains, especially in the parishes of ST ANDREW and what are now PORTLAND and ST MARY, contributing to the expansion of the COFFEE industry. Others became established city merchants or manufacturers, of which the best known names today are Desnoes, Malabre and DuQuesnay. While some of the immigrants brought skills and capital, many had escaped with nothing but the clothes on their backs and were in fact destitute, contributing to the city's poor. Some of the émigrés settled the village of Above Rocks in ST CATHERINE Parish.

The French infusion had an impact on the cultural life of Kingston especially. According to Errol Hill, among them were 'people of culture, musicians especially, who gave concerts and had found employment in theatre orchestras'. In the military too: Patrick Bryan notes that 16 boys aged 9-17, all mulattoes or blacks previously attached to a French regiment in Haiti, had found employment in Jamaica as band musicians with the Twentieth Regiment of Light Dragoons. In the Jamaican theatre there were for a while French companies 'in residence', including for two years a French operatic company under Mr and Mrs Armand, as well as other companies providing lighter fare. Especially light was the entertainment cited by Clinton Black of a 'Monsieur du Mulin . . . whose main act was to dance on a tight rope with two children tied to his feet!'

The public scene was also much enlivened by the arrival of the French SET GIRLS, first recorded in 1794, becoming a part of the JONKONNU festival. For those who trafficked with the occult, the practitioners of 'French OBEAH' were regarded as the most powerful (a belief, by the way, which persists, while Haitians regard Jamaican obeah as more powerful and sinister than their own practices). The infamous Annee Palmer, the legendary White Witch of ROSE HALL, was said to have been schooled in Haitian vodun.

While the French arrivals were of different races, classes and political persuasions, they were united by one institution, the ROMAN CATHOLIC church. There were several Roman Catholic priests among the refugees and it was they who revived the church in Jamaica in 1791. For many years thereafter it was known as the 'French church', both the early priests and most parishioners being French speaking. The dispersal of the French émigrés to rural Jamaica led to the spread of this religion outside of Kingston. As late as 1872, there was objection by a Catholic (who claimed he spoke for many) to the appointment of an Englishman to head the church in Jamaica.

Prior to the arrival of the Haitians, the French connection was mainly a military one, as antagonists to British

French Set Girls by Belisario

forces at a time when the Caribbean was known as the 'cockpit of Europe', fought over by the European powers. (For some notable battles against French foes or the threat of invasion, see CARLISLE BAY, NELSON, RODNEY.)

On a more pacific note, several of the island's most popular decorative plants owe their names to French navigators or naturalists who first introduced them to Europe, among them BAUHINIA, BOUGAINVILLEA, Plumeria (FRANGIPANI) and POINCIANA.

Prominent Frenchmen connected to the island in earlier times included Lewis Galdy (see PORT ROYAL), Martin RUSEA, a benefactor of education, Father DUPONT, and Jean François Pouyat, a Haitian refugee who became famous for his introduction of the Gros Michel BANANA. The most famous today are the Duperlys of photography fame.

The eminent artist and photographer, Adolphe Armand Desiré Duperly, was born in Paris in 1801, the son of Jean François Duperly and his wife, Marie Elizabeth. He left France for Haiti where he taught lithography before travelling on to Jamaica by way of Santiago de Cuba. Following his arrival in Kingston on 7 August 1824, Duperly set up his studio to become a pioneer of the photographic art.

Duperly is best known for his 1844 set of 24 Jamaican scenes called *Daguerrian Excursions in Jamaica*. These pictures were lithographs on stone, taken faithfully from the daguerreotype that was a precursor process of what was to become photography as we know it today. The daguerrotype was invented in 1839 in France and Duperly was one of the first to use the process. He married Louise Desnoes (daughter of Joseph Desnoes and Marie-Charlotte Bouilly, a Haitian creole) in Kingston on 11 August 1832. The Desnoes family originally came from the parish of St Brice, near Bordeaux.

Duperly died in Kingston on 4 February 1864, and was buried in the churchyard of Holy Trinity Church, Kingston. His sons and grandson carried on the famous photographic family business in Kingston until 1933.

[Black 1965, Bryan 1973, Campion Jesuit Community, Hill 1992, Jamaica Archives, Nugent 1839, Osborne 1988]

FRIENDLY SOCIETIES

Mutual-aid organizations called Friendly, Benevolent or Burial Societies were once widespread all over the English-speaking CARIBBEAN, including Jamaica. These indigenous lodges date to the mid-19th century and were based both on the lodges derived from Europe

Friendly Society parade

and the African idea of secret and mutual aid societies. Their main goal was to provide relatively poor people with financial assistance in illness and with a decent burial. Members paid dues as a form of insurance for themselves and their families. The societies also provided moral support and social activities for members. Each lodge had an elaborate name, elected officers – some with grand titles, ritual secrets, regalia, banners and so on, and often engaged in grand public displays, especially at the funerals of members. Many such societies were also started by Jamaican emigrants to PANAMA and elsewhere in Latin America, or brought back to Jamaica by those returning.

[Bryan 1991, Herskovits 1958]

FRIENDS, Society of

Religious group, popularly known as Quakers, who were among the religious non-conformists persecuted in 17th century England, leading to the migration or transportation of many to the colonies. Within two years of the English CAPTURE OF JAMAICA in 1655, Quakers were settled on the island. George Fox, the founder of the Society of Friends, an unusual group who lived an extremely simple, non-violent, almost Christ-like life, visited the Friends in Jamaica in 1671, along with Elizabeth Hooten, his first female convert. He found the local Quakers living 'in unity and peace . . . and the seeds for future progress sown in good soil'.

There was a Quaker Meeting House in PORT ROYAL on part of the land which sank in the 1692 EARTHQUAKE and several Quakers left first-hand accounts of the catastrophic event. But with the passing of the Toleration Act in England (1689) and the remarkable success of the Quaker merchants in Pennsylvania (see PENN), by the end of the century the majority of Quakers in Jamaica had moved north. They left behind abandoned Meeting Houses and Quaker burial grounds in KINGSTON, LACOVIA in ST ELIZABETH and SPANISH TOWN. A few Quakers such as George Lascelles Winn (see ADELPHI) remained on the island and gave considerable assistance to the BAPTISTS in their religious work among the slaves.

In England, Quakers were prominent in the movement to abolish the slave trade, and later SLAVERY itself. After EMANCIPATION, individual members of the Society visited the island to ascertain for themselves the success or otherwise of the APPRENTICESHIP period (1834-38), and the state of religion and education throughout the island after the disturbances of 1865. (See MORANT BAY REBELLION.)

Towards the end of the 19th century, Quakers in the mid-west United States were moved not only to work with the native peoples and freed African-Americans but to spread Christianity in the wider world. In 1881, Evi Sharpless, followed by a small band of missionaries, many of them women, began to 'labour in Gospel Love' in Jamaica under the sponsorship of the Iowa Yearly Meeting of Friends. Friends Jamaica Mission worked mostly in the eastern parishes of ST THOMAS, PORTLAND and ST MARY, establishing Day Schools, Sunday Schools and Monthly Meetings. The Happy Grove Industrial School (later Secondary School), the Lyndale Girls' Home and the Swift-Purcell Home for Boys, developed out of the missionary interest in the children of INDIAN indentured labourers.

In 1941, the indigenous Jamaica Yearly Meeting of Friends was inaugurated and has continued, with expansion into Kingston, the institutions and Monthly Meetings started by the Americans. Membership does not now exceed 500. In all services, periods of silent worship, as observed by Quakers the world over, remain a distinguishing feature.

[Cadbury 1971, Langford 1997]

FROG

Jamaica has 21 species of native frogs, all endemic to the island. However, the local name for these animals is usually 'toad'. They fall into two groups.

A first group of 17 species belongs to the genus *Eleutherodactylus* (whistling frogs). These frogs have evolved within the island from a single ancestor arriving in Jamaica from across the sea. Most species have a restricted distribution. Some are confined to western and central sections of the islands, and others to the east. Also, they show certain altitudinal preferences though much overlap exists. Each species has its very distinct call.

Unlike most other frogs, *Eleutherodactylus* frogs do not have tadpoles. The female lays her eggs in a cool and moist place, usually in the leaf litter or under stones. She usually guards the clutch until the tiny froglets hatch from the eggs. In one species of a Jamaican *Eleutherodactylus*, the frogs have been observed to enter CAVES for mating and nesting. Again, the female remains with the clutch. As soon as the froglets hatch, they climb on the back of the mother who then carries them out of the cave.

A second group of four frogs belong to the family Hylidae. Inhabiting BROMELIADS, the Jamaican species have evolved a unique life style. The females deposit the eggs into the water tanks that form between the leaves of large bromeliads. These tanks provide the aquatic habitat for the tadpoles. However due to a scarcity of food in the tanks, the mother has to feed the young, which she accomplishes by laying additional unfertilized eggs that are gulped up by the growing tadpoles. The two larger of the four species reach a length of up to 8cm. They have very loud voices, reminding of a laugh and a snore, respectively. Thus, they are sometimes referred to as the Jamaican Laughing Frog (*Osteopilus brunneus*) and the Jamaican Snoring Frog (*Calyptohyla crucialis*).

Five species of amphibians were introduced to Jamaica, including the Marine Toad (*Bufo marinus*, locally called 'BULLFROG'), the proper Bullfrog (*Rana catesbeiana*), and two species of *Eleutherodactylus*. These introduced species are now the most common amphibians in the deforested areas, and may pose a threat for the native FAUNA.

The introduced frogs did not live up to the expectations that led to their introduction. The Marine Toad was brought to fight the introduced rats in the cane fields – without success (see MONGOOSE). *Eleutherodactylus* were brought in from Barbados to help control ticks, which bother CATTLE, to no avail. Large edible frogs were thought to provide a delicacy, but nobody eats them in Jamaica.

Remarkably, no tailed amphibians (salamanders) occur in Jamaica or elsewhere in the West Indies, though they are common on the nearest continental mainland. The

Whistling frog

salamanders simply did not manage the journey across the sea.
[Bäuerle and Vogel 1995, Diesel, Mahon and Aiken 1977, Schwartz and Fowler 1973, Thompson 1996]

FROG IN FOLKLORE
In TAINO mythology, the FROG is connected with female fertility and with rain, and was a motif commonly used in Taino art, especially on roller stamps which they used to decorate their bodies. In one Taino myth, the women went off leaving their children. When they became hungry and began to cry for their mothers they were turned into tree frogs. The Taino name for frog and child is *toa*, commemorating the LEGEND. Today, on CARIBBEAN islands, the croaking of the tree frogs is still believed to herald rain. (See also COCOBAY.)
[Garcia Arévalo 1977, Lovén 1935]

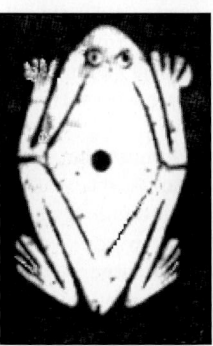

Taino frog amulet

Taino frog petroglyph

FROME
Large SUGAR estate and factory in WESTMORELAND Parish, once the centre of the region's economic life, processing cane grown on its own lands as well as that supplied by thousands of individual small growers from surrounding areas. As a result, for a while, 'Frome' and 'Westmoreland' were almost synonymous.

To establish Frome, the BRITISH sugar manufacturers of Tate and Lyle through their subsidiary, the West Indies Sugar Company (WISCO), bought up 16 estates in Westmoreland and HANOVER, with seven small and largely obsolete factories. When Frome Central Sugar Factory was opened in 1939, it was the most modern sugar factory in the CARIBBEAN and the first central factory to be established in the island.

During the construction period, Frome became one of the flash points of the widespread labour disturbances of 1938. Construction of the factory and consolidation of the small farms began at a time of severe unemployment and social discontent, and thousands seeking work converged there from all over the island. Most could not gain employment but stayed on in the vicinity. Those taken on as construction workers were also dissatisfied with the living and other conditions, and with the fact that their wages fell short of the magical 'dollar a day' which they had expected. A dispute with wage clerks flared into a violent strike in April-May 1938. Canefields were set on fire and a riot broke out on 3 May. The police fired into the crowd, killing four people and wounding thirteen. Over 100 persons were arrested.

Labour leader Alexander BUSTAMANTE arrived the following morning from KINGSTON and identified himself with the cause of the workers. Frome was only one of such clashes between workers and the authorities that were to take place all over the island during the ensuing weeks. (The first disturbances had occurred at Serge Island sugar estate in ST THOMAS Parish and the Kingston waterfront.) Out of these disturbances were to come Jamaica's first mass-based TRADE UNIONS and organized political parties.
[Eaton 1975, Hill 1975, Post 1978, Wright and White 1969]

FU-FU
West AFRICAN dish brought to the New World and once popular, though hardly found in Jamaica today. To make Fu-fu a starchy food such as YAM, PLANTAIN, or CASSAVA is boiled and then pounded up in a MORTAR. The mass is then made into balls and put into soup or dipped in a rich stew or sauce.

FURNITURE see CABINET-MAKER, GREAT HOUSE

FUSTIC (*Chlorophora tinctoria*)
Spreading tree, up to 15m tall, common to the CARIBBEAN and Central America, which provided one of Jamaica's earliest exports. Fustic dye was formerly used to give the characteristic colour to military khaki. Like many dye plants, its importance was reduced with the introduction of synthetic dyes. Fustic is also used as a furniture wood. The fruits resemble green raspberries and are edible though not much eaten. This plant was also used by the TAINOS.
[Adams 1972, NHSJ 1946]

FUNERAL see DEATH RITUALS

G

GALDY, Lewis (1659-1739)

A FRENCH Huguenot (Protestant) immigrant who had one of the most miraculous escapes in history during the EARTHQUAKE that destroyed PORT ROYAL in 1692. Galdy was swallowed by the earth, then thrown up again and flung into the sea by another shock. He kept afloat until rescued by a boat. Galdy had been among those expelled from Montpelier, France, because of their Protestant religion. He lived to be 80, becoming an affluent merchant, churchwarden and member of the Assembly. Galdy's wealth came from the slave trade since he was a factor (agent) for the Asiento – the suppliers of slaves to Latin America. He died in 1739 and was buried at Green Bay across the harbour. The story of his miraculous escape was engraved on his tombstone. Galdy's tomb can now be seen at ST PETER'S, Port Royal, where it was transferred in 1953 to facilitate viewing by HM Queen Elizabeth II during her coronation year visit to Jamaica.

Galdy tombstone

GALINA POINT LIGHTHOUSE

The lighthouse located at Galina Point near PORT MARIA, ST MARY Parish, consists of a white concrete tower 12m high and has a white flashing light with a range of 19km. There is one flash of 1.2 seconds followed by 10.8 seconds of darkness.

GALLIWASP

LIZARD that is the subject of many superstitious beliefs in Jamaica. Although the galliwasp is harmless, its bite is considered fatal by many unless certain precautions are taken. The principal belief is that if one is bitten by a galliwasp, one should immediately run to reach water. The galliwasp will do the same, and only by reaching water before the galliwasp can the intended victim survive. In that case, the galliwasp dies. The belief comes directly from an AFRICAN tradition and was apparently applied by enslaved Africans to the Jamaican galliwasp. The original galliwasp was a large lizard, now extinct, which was nearly 60cm in length. The name and superstition were afterwards transferred to lizards of the genus *Diploglossus*. These are smooth-scaled lizards that live in or along the ground or in stone walls.

GAMES

In the past, the traditional games of Jamaica were preserved not only by children but by adults as well. Known as 'ring game' or 'ring play', they were an integral part of such activities as DINKI MINI and other NINE NIGHT observances, or of song and game sessions called 'Ring Ding', done purely for enjoyment at nights. (The name and concept were used in a television programme hosted by folklorist Louise Bennett.)

Now, the old games are hardly played and represent one aspect of the folklore in danger of dying out. Many of the songs however, live on, sometimes in a pure form such as 'Manuel Road', or in pop versions such as Boney M's recording of 'Brown Girl in the Ring'. Fragments of games are also included in popular MUSIC and poetry. A notable example is the poem by the late Michael Smith, 'Mi Cyan Believe it'. He uses a skipping rhyme 'Room for rent/apply within/when I run out/another run in/' for social commentary: 'Room dem a rent/ me apply widin/ but as me go een/cockroach rat and scorpion/also come een.' Novelist Erna Brodber titled her first novel *Jane and Louisa will soon come home* after a song that is a popular ring game as well as a figure in QUADRILLE, which is used as a motif throughout the book.

Often, children's games are versions of adult ones. The majority appear to have been derived from BRITISH games, adding local variants over time. Some were clearly introduced by MISSIONARY schools; others, such as 'Here we go loo-by loo' (known by children throughout the English-speaking world), had a level of obscene adult innuendo unknown to Jamaican children of the 1930s and 40s. In Dominica in the 1890s, well-bred children did not dance or sing the 'Looby-loo', according to Jean Rhys. The meaning of the words and gestures has been lost.

But as in other aspects of music and DANCE, youthful players have brought to the games a performance style that is clearly African-derived. Many are known in slightly different versions throughout the English-speaking Caribbean and in parts of the American South (see SALLY WATER). A feature of these games is the call and response style that is used, a leader calling out a line and the rest replying in chorus. Common to many of the ring games is the requirement to 'show your motion' or 'wine' the body, often the only opportunity in the past for children to do just that, such movement being frowned on otherwise as 'rude'.

Among the schoolyard games still played, popular are the lively stone-passing games such as 'Manuel Road' or 'Cobally' (which is the subject of a painting 'Kuballe' by intuitive artist Kapo – see ART). The stone-passing games, like the LIMBO, were originally part of African-derived rituals played by adults at wakes. (See WAKE.)

Also popular at Dinki Mini, as among schoolchildren, were courtship games such as 'Sally Water', 'Jane and Louisa' and 'Brown Girl in the Ring'. The folklorist Alan Lomax encountered the ring-game 'Brown Girl in the Ring' sung and played by children all over the West Indies but not in the United States nor anywhere else in the English-speaking world. He believes it to be a 'genuinely original contribution by Caribbean children'.

Many of the traditional games show either verbal or physical dexterity. Popular in the old days with adults and children was a game called 'MOONSHINE BABY' and the Jamaica ALPHABET rhyme.

Finger games were also popular, such as the universally known string game 'Cat's Cradle' or the game 'Peter and Paul' done to amuse small children. The adult or older child would stick a piece of paper on two fingers to represent Peter and Paul, saying:

Two little blackbirds sat on a wall
One name Peter, one name Paul (showing fingers)

Then saying, 'Fly away Peter, Fly away Paul' the player would substitute two plain fingers, and finally saying 'Come back Peter, come back Paul', show the marked fingers. Only the very young would be fooled by this game for long.

Another finger game consists of a dialogue:

- See me basket
- Wha fe do?
- Fe go tief backra peas and corn
- Suppose them catch you?
- Me wi jump
- Jump mek me see

The game is played by crossing the third and fourth fingers. At the last line, they must be quickly uncrossed. If they stick, the thief is caught.

Foot games also existed: this boys' game popular in the 1940s was never shared by girls, and was said to be 'dirty'. A circle of boys surrounded one player at a time: he stood on one foot, while tossing a small light object (such as a bit of orange peel) with the side of the other foot up in the air to a definite rhythm. The game called for great co-ordination and balance by the central player. As each one tried to keep going, the others chanted: 'See well lash!/Jimmy (or name of player) batty waan wash/In im mada calabash.' If a teacher or monitor appeared, the game stopped at once.

While universal games like skipping rope, hopscotch, jacks and tic-tac-toe, have been popular with Jamaican girls, marbles, gigs (as home-made spinning tops are called) have been popular with boys, as well as spinning hoops and racing home-made go-carts.

Among adults, popular games are DOMINOES and, to a lesser extent, darts and card games.

[Beckwith 1928, Cassidy 1971, DJE, Lomax, Elder, Lomax Hawes 1997]

GANGS, Jobbing

Not all slave owners were landowners, some made a living from hiring out their slaves to the estates or other enterprises to perform specific tasks. (See GANGS, Slave; SLAVERY.) These so-called 'jobbing gangs' or 'jobbers' were often skilled workers who might also be hired for individual tasks. They could live away from their owners for the duration of the task but were expected to remit to him or her a fixed portion of their pay. Often, owners of jobbing gangs were town dwellers and many were free COLOUREDS.

GANGS, Slave

During SLAVERY, the workforce on each plantation was divided into 'gangs', groups that worked on tasks together, graded according to age and or fitness. Usually there were three gangs, sometimes a fourth if very small children were counted separately from older children. In any event, children started work as early as age three or four. Up to the age of nine or thereabouts, they belonged to what was variously called the 'small gang', 'hogmeat gang' or 'pickney gang', or on some of the other islands, 'chip-chip' or 'vine' gang. Supervised by an old woman, their principal duties were to gather grass for animals and green slips and vines to feed the hogs – such plants being called 'hogmeat' or 'vine'. The older children also ran errands and engaged in tasks such as cleaning paths, carrying firewood, etc.

The third gang consisted of older slaves and children; elderly females would be assigned lighter field tasks such as grass cutting, as cooks attached to various gangs, as nurses in hothouses (as the slave hospitals were called), or as midwives in charge of children. Men of the third gang would be assigned duties as watchmen or as tyers who collected and bound cut cane for carriage, both tasks requiring lengthy hours of duty. Although this gang was assigned the lightest work, it too proved to be arduous. 'Even the third gang, consisting of young children from nine to twelve years of age, were tasked to do an amount of work which kept them from dawn of day till dark,' one observer reported.

After puberty, boys and girls were put into the second gang and assigned various tasks – as field workers, working with livestock or in the GREAT HOUSE as domestics, depending on their strength, endurance and other attributes such as their skin colour, lighter-skinned negroes being favoured for domestic work. Also in the second gang would be those slaves demoted from the first gang after the age of 45. The planter-historian Bryan Edwards noted: 'The second gang is composed of young boys and girls, women far gone with child, and convalescents, who are chiefly employed in weeding the canes, and other light work adapted to their strength.'

The first gang or great gang consisted of the fittest and strongest slaves on the estate – men and women – who formed the backbone of plantation life. They worked in the fields planting and reaping SUGAR CANE and then in the factory during the 'crop' or cane grinding SEASON. Like other gangs, they would be subdivided into smaller work groups, each under a separate driver. Slaves in this gang were the most highly valued of the field slaves. Fit slaves would usually be put into this gang in their late teens and reach their peak at age 25. Unless burnt out in the interim, some could continue in this gang until the age of 45 or so, when they would be demoted to the third gang.

[DJE, Edwards 1793, Patterson 1973]

GANJA (*Cannabis sativa*)

Narcotic herb, popularly known as marijuana elsewhere. The 'weed' or 'herb' produced in Jamaica is regarded as particularly potent, especially the sensemilla variety, and it finds a ready market both in Jamaica and overseas. Ganja is in fact regarded as Jamaica's most valuable unofficial export, and the plant is nowadays cultivated using the latest scientific methods of agriculture.

Ganja might have been introduced into Jamaica long before official notice was taken of it in the 19th century, since it is a universal source of hemp. But the practice of cultivating, smoking and otherwise consuming the herb is believed to have been popularized by the INDIAN indentured immigrants who began to arrive from 1845. The local name 'ganja' is Indian, as are other associated words such as 'chillum' (and the use of the chillum pipe) and the name 'collie' (*kali*) weed. The concept of ganja as a holy herb is a Hindu one; it is widely used to enhance the religious experience in parts of India (despite

Ganja

government prohibition). But the use of Indian hemp for narcotic purposes was also known in Africa. In the Kingdom of the Congo (from which many enslaved Africans arrived in the New World), Indian hemp was called 'Congo tobacco' and used as a narcotic named *dyamba*. In colonial Brazil, *diamba* or *maconha*, as cannabis was called, was widely used by black slaves and might well have been known and clandestinely used by other slaves in the New World. It is interesting that when the ganja plant flowers, indicating high potency, in Jamaica it is said to 'makoni'.

The rise of RASTAFARI since the 1930s has contributed to the widespread use of the herb, since Rastas regard it as an integral part of their religious worship. However, consumption and sale of ganja in Jamaica were declared illegal in 1913 and remain so. The widespread cultivation and export of cannabis dates from increased usage and demand internationally, particularly in the United States.

Long before its international popularity and notoriety, the herb was for generations consumed by Jamaicans as a drink or infusion ('ganja TEA') for medicinal purposes, especially for the treatment of asthma. More recently, three medical preparations have been developed by two Jamaican scientists (Professor Manley West and Dr Albert Lockhart) from cannabis and manufactured locally: Cantimol that replaces an earlier drug, Canasol, for the treatment of glaucoma; Asmasol for bronchial asthma and coughs, and Canavert for seasickness. Dr Manley West is professor emeritus and head of the pharmacology department of the UNIVERSITY OF THE WEST INDIES (UWI) Mona Campus in Kingston. Dr Albert Lockhart is a researcher and opthamologist. Their pioneering research began after West noticed that Jamaican fishermen who used ganja before going out to sea had very good vision. An observation supported by Dr Lockhart indicating that persons using cannabis had lower intraocular pressure than non-users. (Increased intraocular pressure damages the eye's optic nerve causing partial vision loss and eventually blindness in glaucoma.)

[Anon 1993, Balandier 1968, Bilby 1985, DJE, Robertson 1990, Rubin and Comitas 1976]

GARVEY, Rt Excellent Marcus Mosiah (1887-1940)

Black internationalist and National Hero of Jamaica. Marcus Garvey was born of humble parents in ST ANN'S BAY, ST ANN Parish. On leaving elementary school, he worked as a printer in KINGSTON and at an early age became involved in movements aimed at improving the lot of black people. In 1910 Garvey left Jamaica and travelled throughout Central America working and observing the conditions of blacks throughout the region. He went to England in 1912, where through personal contact and extensive reading he deepened his knowledge of Africa and further refined his philosophy for uplifting the black peoples of the world.

On his return home in 1914 he formed the Universal Negro Improvement Association (UNIA) to unite 'all the Negro peoples of the world into one great body to establish a country and a government exclusively their own'. The motto was: 'One God! One Aim! One Destiny!' But it was not until Garvey went to the United States in 1916 that his ideas caught fire. From the first United States branch of the UNIA formed in New York in 1916, Garvey was to build an enormous mass movement that would number millions of supporters in North America, the Caribbean and Latin American countries where many emigrant British West Indian workers lived, as well as in Africa.

Part of Garvey's plan to secure black independence was to establish black-owned business enterprises, and several efforts were made in this direction. The most significant was the steamship company known as the Black Star Line. However, largely because of poor management, this and other business ventures were to fail. Garvey, seen as a 'dangerous agitator' by American authorities and the British colonial administrators, was increasingly harassed and eventually indicted in the USA for using the mails to defraud. He was found guilty and sentenced to Atlanta Federal Prison, where he served two years of a five-year sentence and after an Executive Pardon, was deported to Jamaica.

In spite of considerable opposition to him on his return home, Garvey continued to challenge the system and organized the People's Political

Marcus Garvey statue by Alvin Marriott

Party on a reformist platform. He ran for a seat in the legislature but lost, especially since most of his supporters in those days of restricted franchise did not have a vote. Garvey did gain a seat on the Kingston and St Andrew Corporation (KSAC) – while in jail for contempt of court – but was unable to make any headway against the established system in achieving the changes he sought. In 1935 he again left Jamaica for England and died there in 1940.

Garvey was named one of Jamaica's National Heroes and in 1964 his remains were brought back from England and re-interred with full national honours in NATIONAL HEROES PARK. On 17 August 1980 a bust of Garvey was unveiled at the Hall of Heroes of the Organization of American States, the first national figure from an English-speaking nation to be so honoured. A statue of Garvey can be seen outside the parish LIBRARY in St Ann's Bay.

Although he was denigrated and ridiculed by many in his lifetime, in recent years there has been serious reconsideration of Garvey and his role in the international liberation of black peoples. He is now regarded as the father of the concept of 'black power'. His writings and teachings also provided inspiration to many of the young nationalists in the emerging nations of Africa. But Garvey was to die a frustrated man, recognition of his visionary qualities and the acceptance of his ideas coming only long after his death.

Garvey, his teachings and the iconography associated with his movement have continued to inspire Jamaican creative artists, especially REGGAE singers such as Burning Spear, as well as painters and writers. Garvey has also inspired many LEGENDS which are still current in Jamaica (see Hamilton 1991).

[Cronon 1955, Garvey 1970, Hill 1983-1990, Jamaica Journal special issue 1987, Lewis and Bryan 1988, Martin 1976, Vincent 1975]

GAULIN

Name applied in Jamaica to ten different herons. They are distinguished by colour – White Gaulin (of which there are several), Blue or Black Gaulin, and the Red-necked Gaulin. Two are 'Night Gaulin' since they fly after dark. All belong to the family *Ardeidae* that includes herons and egrets.

They are tall birds on stilt legs with long necks and sharp bills, and a tall, ungainly person with a long neck might be unfavourably called 'gaulin'. The birds on the ground are quite graceful, though the naturalist P.H. Gosse found the flight of herons 'flagging and laborious'.

'Gaulin' drawn by May Jeffrey-Smith, L-R (1-5): Great Blue Gaulin (Heron), White Gaulin (American Egret), White Gaulin (Snowy Egret), Blue Gaulin (Little Blue Heron), Great White Gaulin

Gaulins are seen along the coast and salt marshes or by inland ponds and river-banks. They are considered weather prognosticators and when seen inland far from water are taken to signal rain, as they tend to fly before an approaching storm. Fishermen also take the flight of these birds to predict good or poor fishing conditions.

Most Gaulins roost and build in colonies and huge flocks are sometimes seen roosting in trees at evening time, for instance along the RIO COBRE GORGE.

[Gosse 1984, Jeffrey-Smith 1972, Taylor 1955]

GEFFRARD PLACE

Street in ST ANDREW near the western end of NATIONAL HEROES PARK which commemorates the name of General Nicholas Fabre Geffrard, a former president of Haiti (1859-67) who resided in this area for many years. Geffrard abdicated as president in 1867 and came to Jamaica, living here until his death in 1878, his granddaughter marrying a prominent Jamaican. Geffrard's house was later demolished and the land subdivided.

General Geffrard was not the only exiled Haitian president to live in Jamaica. Among the others were Jean Paul Boyer, second president of the Republic (1818-43), who abdicated in 1843 and lived in exile at 98 East Street, KINGSTON for a while until he left for Paris; Emperor Faustin I (F.E. Soulouque) who was exiled in 1858 and lived in the city at 90 Duke Street; and General Nord Alexis who was exiled to Jamaica in 1908, and died here in 1909 (his body being taken to Haiti for interment).

Another famous resident of this section of the city was General Antonio López de Santa Anna (1794-1876), former President of Mexico who was defeated in a war with the USA and retired to Jamaica in 1847, moving on to New Granada (Colombia) in 1853.

[Jacobs 1973, Who's Who 1909]

GEOLOGY

The oldest part of Jamaica is at least 120 million years old, judging from the age of the oldest rocks. However, the island as we know it is no more than 10-15 million years old, following its final emergence from the sea, a phenomenon that has led to the development of some unique FLORA and FAUNA.

Geologists tend to divide Jamaica's geological history into three phases, the first occurring in early Cretaceous times when the island emerged as one of a chain of active volcanoes thrust up from the sea. This phase of volcanic activity continued intermittently until about 45 million years ago when volcanism ceased and the landmass became submerged. During this period of submergence, thick layers of sediment mainly in the form of calcium carbonate accumulated. When the third phase, final uplift of the island, occurred about 10 million years ago, the land was covered with these deposits of white LIMESTONE – up to 1,500m thick in places. Since then, some of this limestone at higher elevations has been eroded, exposing the older Cretaceous rock.

Three distinct types of landscapes have emerged from the geological past. They include: (1) the highest elevations (see BLUE MOUNTAINS) consisting of the older exposed igneous and metamorphic rock, with high serrated ridges alternating with deeply eroded river valleys; (2) the limestone plateaus of the central areas; and (3) the gently sloping alluvial plains, less than 200m above sea level, of the south, including the LIGUANEA Plain on which the city of KINGSTON is located. The plains have been built up of sediment brought down from the mountains by the rivers, especially the CABARITTA, BLACK RIVER, RIO MINHO, RIO COBRE, HOPE, YALLAHS, Morant and PLANTAIN GARDEN.

Though the island is no longer subjected to volcanic activity, it is affected by the activities of EARTHQUAKES and HURRICANES, which can alter the landscape. The geological process is continuous, though perhaps not immediately perceptible, with severe erosion in the upland areas and sedimentary deposits below, as well as the slow build up of CORAL on the coast.

The first geological survey of Jamaica was undertaken in 1823 by Sir Henry de la Beche. (See HALSE HALL.)

[GOJ Handbook of Jamaica, Hose 1950, Matley 1951, M. Morrissey 1983, Porter 1990]

GEORGIAN see CABINET-MAKER, FALMOUTH, GREAT HOUSE

GERMAN HERITAGE

The most visible evidence of the German heritage in Jamaica is the village of Seaford Town in WESTMORELAND Parish that was settled by immigrants from northern Germany in 1835. Seaford Town was part of a larger effort to establish European settlements in Jamaica as freedom approached for the enslaved AFRICAN population. (See IRISH, PORTUGUESE, SCOTS.) In all, over 1,500 Germans came and were settled in various parts of the island, including LACOVIA, ST ANN'S BAY, Dry Harbour Mountains, MONTEGO BAY, BLACK RIVER, Spauldings and the CLARENDON mountains. Place names that are the result of their presence include Bremen Valley, New Brunswick, Schellenberg, Stettin, Hessin Castle, etc. There are also surnames such as Groskopf, Sauerlinder, Wehrman, Niemier, Eldemire, Stockhausen, Santfleben, Eberle, Schlieffer.

The settlers were brought by several entrepreneurs including John Myers, a ST ANN

German family at Seaford Town

pen-keeper of German origin. In May 1834 Myers brought 65 German immigrants composed of 13 families from Wesel. The idea was to establish a white labouring community of farmers and artisans to provide the Negroes with 'an example of European industry and skill'. But the 18 adult males included among their trades 'that of loom-maker, two weavers of linen and one of damask, a miner, lapidary, coppersmith, and gunsmith', the rest being farmers. All the women were skilled spinners and knitters. Myers settled these Germans at Pleasant Mount and New Brunswick, on condition that they would reimburse him for expenses incurred or work for three years without pay.

In December 1834 another group of 506 Germans arrived on the *Olberes* from the port of Bremen, and were distributed over the western parishes.

Another entrepreneur was Dr William Lemonius, also of German origin, who was commissioned by the Jamaica House of Assembly to engage German immigrants, and imported 800 between 1835-37. These were to become the Seaford Town settlers.

Seaford Town was founded on 200ha of MONTPELIER Mountain and named in honour of the donor of the land, Lord Seaford, owner of Montpelier estate. When the first Germans arrived, lured by promises of land, work, and houses, they found instead a wilderness with only a few of the promised houses ready. For the first 18 months of their stay, they were provided with free rations, including a daily supply of RUM. Many emigrated to the United States as soon as they could. But enough settlers remained in Jamaica's 'German Town' to leave their distinctive stamp to this day. Many of the people of the area are still blond and blue-eyed, and the ROMAN CATHOLIC faith of the original immigrants is still strong.

The majority of the Seaford Town settlers were from Westphalia, with 28 from Waldeck. Very few were accustomed to agricultural labour; most were disbanded soldiers and craftsmen. Settled far into the bush and left mainly on their own, the Germans were isolated by geography, culture, religion, LANGUAGE and race.

Most were Catholics but they had no priest, and it was not until late 1839 that a 28-year-old English-speaking catechist named John Bierbusse left Seaford Town and made his way across the island to KINGSTON to make contact with the Catholic church there. It took time for a priest to be sent and in the meantime Bierbusse continued to function as lay preacher and schoolmaster. He did his best to maintain morale among the Seaford Town settlers, many 'soured with bitterness at the slave-like treatment afforded them'. As Fr Francis Osborne described their situation: 'In a strange land, among a strange people, unable to understand, they learned the negro patois and forgot their native German after a generation or so. Their children grew up completely isolated from the town life of the island and lost all contact with Germany.' Starting in the 1940s, many of the younger German descendants of Seaford Town emigrated to Canada.

Of the actual German heritage, little remains except surnames, a few of the old houses which display a distinctive architectural style, and some old folk customs, particularly those relating to the preparation of food. A historical museum is located in the Sacred Heart Catholic Church compound at Seaford Town.

Although in Jamaica the word 'Jarman' became a pejorative synonym for 'poor white', descendants of many of the German immigrants have become leading citizens in their communities, serving as custodes (see CUSTOS), becoming doctors, lawyers, scientists, businessmen and politicians.

Aside from the 19th century immigrants, German MISSIONARIES were also in the island from the 18th century, attached to the MORAVIAN church. Individual Germans also settled from time to time, some achieving prominence such as Baron von Ketelhodt (a naturalized British subject married to a Jamaican landowning widow) who was custos of ST THOMAS at the time of the MORANT BAY REBELLION and among those killed (See also LUCEA CLOCK.)
[Hall 1974-75, Osborne 1988]

GERREH

The NINE-NIGHT observance called 'Gerreh' is found mainly on the western side of the island in HANOVER and WESTMORELAND Parishes. On the first two nights after death, members of the community come together to 'jump gerreh', as it is called. The activity is secular and is characterized by ring GAMES, special songs and DANCES including a dance on two pieces of BAMBOO (see BENTA, CALEMBE). The after-burial observances when Sankey and Moody hymns are sung are more typical of Nine-Night elsewhere.
[Lewin 2000, Ryman 1980]

GIDDY HOUSE

A popular attraction at PORT ROYAL, behind FORT CHARLES, this building leans at an extreme angle,

Giddy House

producing an effect of 'giddiness' in the visitor. It is the former Royal artillery store of the British Navy, built in 1888 and thrown out of line in the 1907 EARTHQUAKE.

GIMME-ME-BIT see DUPPY, MONEY

GINGER (*Zingiber officinale*)

The ginger of commerce is an underground stem (rhizome) of a perennial plant that grows widely in the tropics. Jamaican ginger is highly regarded in world markets. Ginger was introduced from the East Indies by Francisco de Mendoza, a Spaniard, and became one of the island's earliest exports, having been first shipped to Spain in 1547. Locally, ginger is regarded as a vital ingredient in many traditional foods and drinks such as GINGER BEER and SORREL, and is widely used in folk MEDICINE, especially for stomach ailments.

Ginger is usually planted in the spring months, and matures and flowers after about six months. The plant begins to fade around September and dies down by the end of the year. After the stalks wither, between January-March, the roots are dug up and are cleaned of dirt and peeled. The spice is then scalded in hot water and laid out to dry in the sun. For most uses, the local housewife prefers 'green ginger', the freshly dug, unpeeled root. Peeling ginger requires a great deal of skill and for commercial operations was done by gangs of women armed with thin and flexible sharp knives. In the old days, ginger peeling, like CORN shelling, was a communal activity, providing the opportunity for songs, gossip, and stories.

Turmeric (*Curcuma domestica*), a closely related plant, is also cultivated for export. Larger and milder in flavour than ginger, which it resembles superficially, turmeric is an ingredient in curry and is used as a colouring in this and many other edible products.

Several species and varieties of ornamental gingers are also to be found, many growing wild in the cool hilly areas. The highly scented ginger lilies (*Hedychium gardnerianum*) have become in recent years an aggressive invasive species in the BLUE MOUNTAINS. Red ginger, a much prized garden specimen, is a recent introduction.

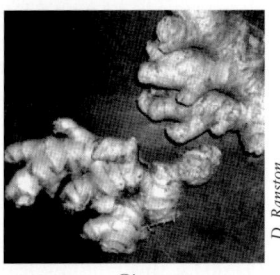

Ginger

GINGER BEER

A spicy, slightly fermented drink made from peeled GINGER root, one of the oldest drinks in Jamaica and for a long time one of the 'cool drinks' vended in markets and on the streets. Many people still make their own. Chopped or crushed ginger, water, sugar and LIME juice and cream of tartar and/or dried yeast are the basic ingredients, which are mixed together and left for a day or two before being strained and bottled. In the traditional recipe, CHEWSTICK is added to give body and flavour.

GIZADA

Popular confection, a pastry tart filled with sweet and spiced grated COCONUT; the edges of the open tart are always crimped, hence its other name of 'pinch-me-round'. The confection is believed to be of Spanish or Portuguese origin from Arabic sources via North Africa.

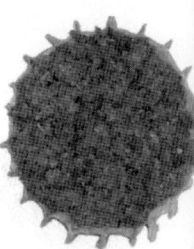

Gizada

GLEANER

Jamaica's oldest existing newspaper first appeared as a weekly on 13 September 1834, the successor to *deCordova's Advertising Sheet*, eventually becoming a daily. Nowadays it is one of several publications of the Gleaner Company Limited.

The *Gleaner* was founded by the deCordova brothers whose family continued to maintain an interest in the publication for several generations. Jacob deCordova, the younger brother, has, however, greater claim to fame outside of Jamaica and is closely identified with the history of the state of Texas, USA.

Jacob deCordova was born in SPANISH TOWN in 1808 of a Jewish family that had settled in Jamaica for many generations (see JEWS), but was taken by his parents to the United States at an early age. He became a major real estate dealer, publisher and promoter in Texas and represented Harris County in the state legislature. Jacob deCordova also laid out the town of Waco,

Texas, drew the first map of the State of Texas, and introduced the lodge, the Independent Order of Odd Fellows, to the state. While on a visit to Jamaica in 1834, he joined his brother Joshua in founding the *Gleaner*. There is a public memorial to Jacob deCordova (who died in 1868) in the State Cemetery at Austin, Texas.
[Andrade 1941]

GLISTENING WATERS
Scenic attraction located at Oyster Bay, TRELAWNY Parish, near to FALMOUTH, the water sometimes becoming fluorescent. The phenomenon is caused by a micro-organism called dinoflagellate (*Pyrodinium bahamense*) that gives off a light when the water is disturbed that is similar to that given off by FIREFLIES.

GOAT (*Capra hircus*)
The goat is a ubiquitous presence in Jamaica; flocks of these animals can always be seen wandering around, even on city streets, living up to their reputation as legendary consumers of just about anything. Goats out of control do much damage to gardens and cultivated plots, and end up causing erosion of hillsides in areas where they overcrop. It is believed that the goat's mouth is so potent, just its breath on a plant will kill it, a belief which has given rise to the notion of 'goat-mouth', that by referring to something in advance, one can 'kill' it, or guarantee its failure.

Like other domestic animals brought by COLUMBUS on his second voyage in 1493, goats found in the Greater ANTILLES an extremely favourable environment and began to multiply from the moment they arrived. They took to the mountainous interior (where they were also out of the way of the DOGS brought by the Spaniards that also went wild) and went on to populate the offshore islets, Jamaica's GOAT ISLANDS owing their name to these early inhabitants.

The goats, like the wild PIGS and CATTLE, provided food for sailors and *conquistadores*, runaway Amerindians, slaves, BUCCANEERS, pirates, and other castaways. They provided clothing too: in the early 17th century in Jamaica, the Spanish chronicler Vasquez de Espinosa noted that from the goats running wild

Sheep and goats

the colonists got 'excellent cordovan leather'.

Within the plantation economy, the slaves raised goats and other livestock for themselves, and from earliest times the MARKETS were crowded with animals as well as produce. No doubt goat flesh formed the central dish for many a slave feast, and was (and still is) a principal offering to the ancestors. Goat skin then as now was found a most useful material for shoes, bags, belts and drum heads (see MUSICAL INSTRUMENTS).

The rearing and sale of goats enabled some slaves to accumulate money, just as their descendants continue to raise goats to provide cash for feeding and educating their children.

The goat has always been the preferred livestock of the 'small man' because unlike cattle or even pigs, it requires a much smaller outlay to acquire and care for. Often, children or housewives are given a goat or two to raise around the yard, part of the chores of country boys and girls of past generations being the gathering of bush for 'goat feedin' before going off to school. Spanish Needle is the favourite of the family goat, which is kept tied on a long string to prevent it from raiding the garden or the neighbour's field – a certain cause for ill-will.

Goat on top of building

Boy with goats

Goats tend to be associated with feasts since they are easily obtainable for special events such as WEDDINGS, funerals or religious feasts, or for Christmas and other festivities. The INDIANS who began to arrive from 1845 also took to goat rearing, and added a new dimension to Jamaican cuisine, one of the island's most popular dishes today being curried goat. Goat's head soup (see MANNISH WATER) is associated with virility.

The raising of goats has in recent times been given a boost by the rise of RASTAFARI; Rastas do not eat pork, preferring goat's flesh. This has led to several popular sayings and songs about goats, one by Pluto Shervington called 'Ram goat liver' achieving immense popularity in the 1960s and 70s.

In ancestral rituals such as KUMINA, goat is the preferred animal for sacrifice. The animal is killed ritually by a specialist, the blood drunk and offered as libation to the spirits, some of the flesh cooked without SALT as offering to the ancestors, the rest eaten by participants.

A goat's horn used to be a favourite container for their 'things' by OBEAH-men and -women and Myalists (see MYAL), for instance, THREE FINGER JACK.

[Espinosa 1628, Viola and Margolis 1991]

GOAT ISLANDS

Two islets in OLD HARBOUR BAY, ST CATHERINE Parish, nowadays used mostly by fishermen, probably so-called because they were originally the haunt of wild GOATS. In 1941 during the Second WORLD WAR, under the lend-lease arrangement between Britain and the USA, the US established bases at Little Goat Island, and nearby Salt Creek and Sandy Gully on the mainland. These strategic areas were occupied by the Americans up to 1949. A special post office was set up at Portland Bight for the use of United States personnel only. Mail bearing United States stamps – with a Jamaican cancellation mark – could legally be sent from here.

GOLD

Gold occurs in Jamaica in such minute quantities as to make mining unfeasible, although there are stories of SPANISH 'gold mines' and even more importantly, of golden treasure. (See GOLD, LEGENDS OF.) Despite the absence of native gold, the metal has been valued here as elsewhere for its symbolic properties, and the TAINOS of Jamaica, like those in the other islands, wore gold ornaments, most likely acquired by trade.

It was the European greed for gold that led to the conquest of the Americas and the decimation of their populations, a greed first fuelled by the gold ornaments which COLUMBUS saw being worn by the CARIBBEAN islanders. Each set of Tainos told him the gold came from an island to the south that was filled with gold, and Columbus sailed further south on each voyage in his quest for the precious metal. Gold was found in significant quantities on the other Caribbean islands of Hispaniola, Puerto Rico and Cuba and the Tainos there became forced-labour in the mines, a fact that contributed to their annihilation. LAS CASAS blamed the decimation of Hispaniola (an estimated eight out of ten Tainos having died within five years of the Europeans' arrival) on the tribute system imposed by the Spaniards.

Under this system the little *cascabeles*, the hawk's bells brought to the New World in large quantities and used to trade with the native peoples, were to acquire a sinister meaning. Adult Tainos (14 years and older) were expected to fill a cascabel with gold every three months and give it to the Spaniards as forced tribute. The CACIQUE was expected to provide a half-calabash full of gold; all who did not live near the mining areas were forced to bring in a half-arroba of COTTON each, all on pain of death. The demands affected the Amerindian way of life, including their planting and fishing routines,

Tainos mining for gold (from Oviedo)

and famine combined with newly-introduced diseases and other factors led to the terrible decimation of that colony. It is believed that one of the reasons the Spaniards did not develop Jamaica as a colony was their great disappointment in not finding gold.

On the islands where gold did exist, the Amerindians did not mine the metal but scrabbled for gold nuggets among the gravel in certain rivers, using their fingers. They hammered these nuggets into very thin flat shapes using heavy stones and shaped this gold foil into ear and nose ornaments and as decoration in ceremonial belts and masks; sometimes they used gold in the eyes of the ZEMIS. One such gold ornament has been found in Jamaica at Bellevue Plantation, ST ANN Parish, and donated to the nation by the owners, Maurice and Valerie Facey; it has been mounted by Swiss Stores and put on display at the Bank of Jamaica MONEY museum.

[Alegría 1985, Fewkes 1907, Rouse 1992, Sauer 1966, Wright 1910]

GOLD, Legends of

Much of the European exploration of the Americas was fuelled by the pursuit of the many legends concerning fabulous GOLD treasure to be found in the New World. The most famous of these legends was the myth of El Dorado ('The Golden One'), a king of the Guyanas who was supposed to be covered in pure gold. The English adventurer Sir Walter Raleigh was one of those who set off in fruitless pursuit of this objective. The source of this legend is probably an Amerindian nation of modern Colombia which, from ancient times to the present, in one of their rituals cover their chief in gold dust.

Another legend of gold pursued by the Spaniards was that of the Seven Cities of Cibola, supposedly founded by Portuguese bishops fleeing the Iberian peninsular in order to escape the Moorish invasions and taking all the golden church ornaments with them.

Perhaps because of the intensity of the SPANISH search – and the fabulous gold treasures that did eventually flow from South America – legends of gold in Jamaica continue to be associated with the Spaniards, beliefs passed on from the earliest times to present-day inhabitants.

Several popular legends centre on mythical golden objects, such as the 'golden table' or the RIVERMAID'S 'gold comb'; but also popular are beliefs about fabulous treasures left by the fleeing Spanish colonists (see CAPTURE OF JAMAICA) which are still there, waiting to be found. Often these treasures are guarded by an Amerindian (TAINO) woman, or by Amerindians or slaves who were killed so that their DUPPIES can protect the treasure (see MARTHA BRAE). There are several stories of mysterious Spaniards turning up with maps, seeking permission to dig for treasure on old estates. Treasure is also believed buried in PANYA JARS.

The legendary golden table is made of pure gold and lies at the bottom of certain rivers or ponds. It appears briefly, and tantalizingly, from time to time, glistening in the sunlight. Whoever glimpses it will be haunted forever by the notion of obtaining it. Many stories have been told of efforts to secure a golden table, but there is no record of any having succeeded, the seeker more often than not coming to a bad end. One persistent story states that the golden table (or altar) lies within Seville Blue, the ocean-hole sitting on the edge of the SEVILLE Lagoon in ST ANN'S BAY.

Of course the fabulous treasures which fell into the sea during the EARTHQUAKE that destroyed PORT ROYAL continue to haunt the imaginations of people the world over.

GOLF

An ancient game, golf was first established in Scotland and spread throughout the world by expatriate SCOTS, frequently army officers. By the early 1880s it was played in every corner of the BRITISH Empire. In countries such as Jamaica, it became an attraction for wealthy British visitors. Not surprisingly the earliest golf course in Jamaica was the Manchester Club opened around 1895, and catering no doubt to the many British people who had retired in that parish. Other early clubs were Constant Spring (1906), Liguanea (1911), Malvern (1929), St James (1931), Westmoreland (1933).

Of these, the Constant Spring and Manchester

Golfers at Constant Spring Golf Course

Clubs were still operating into the 21st century. The Caymanas Golf and Country Club is located close to the KINGSTON metropolitan area and like the Constant Spring Club in the city, caters mainly to local residents.

Of the 13 golf courses in Jamaica in 2001, several are of championship level and are operated by resort hotels. These include Negril Hills, Sandals Golf and Country Club, Half Moon Golf Club, Ironshore Golf and Country Club, Breezes Runaway Bay Resort, Wyndham Rose Hall Golf and Beach Resort, Tryall Club, Grand Lido Braco. In August 2000 the White Witch Golf Course attached to the Ritz-Carlton Rose Hall Hotel was opened. The name celebrates the White Witch of ROSE HALL whose domain the property once was.

The Johnny Walker World Golf Championship was played at Tryall in Jamaica for several years.

Jamaican golf champions have included players who were more famous in other sports, including D.M. Clark in TENNIS and Lindy Delapenha in FOOTBALL.

GOOD FRIDAY

This most solemn holy day in Christian worship (the day of Christ's crucifixion) is a public holiday in Jamaica. While some churchgoers still maintain this as a holy day, most people now treat it as any other secular holiday, a time for relaxation and enjoyment. This was not so in the past, when the religious aspect was rigidly observed, the only activity being a church service lasting for three hours, starting at midday. The funeral colours of black, white or purple were usually worn. Often, all cooking was done the day before, since there was a tradition of not lighting fires on Good Friday. Many Christians abstain from eating meat during Lent and fish is still popular on Good Friday, fried sprat or ESCOVEITCH fish being prepared in advance to be eaten with hard dough BREAD, as well as Bun and Cheese.

Several beliefs are associated with this day, for instance that it always rains on Good Friday. Others believe that the rain water should be caught in one's hand and drunk, in order to 'cleanse' one of vices. Rain water was also efficacious if used to cleanse one's face and eyes. A lack of rain on Good Friday was taken to signify hard times for the rest of the year.

While this was seen as a day on which one should not work or even (for children) play GAMES but be quiet and reflective, certain types of work were specifically proscribed since they were identified with the Lord's suffering on the cross. These included the use of sharp cutting implements such as gardening tools. Sewing was also forbidden – on the grounds that Christ wore a seamless garment and the making of a garment would demonstrate forgetfulness of this.

Another belief is that if the bark of the Physic Nut Tree (*Jatropha curcas*) is cut around noon on this day it 'bleeds', i.e. its white sap turns red (though it will in fact do so at any other time).

A Good Friday egg was used to divine one's fortune for the rest of the year, an old English practice. An egg was set in a glass of water and punctured so the white flowed into the water. The glass was put away in a place safe from interference and periodically checked to see what shape the egg white had assumed, e.g. ship, cake, and there would be speculation about its meaning. The time the egg should be set out and taken in varied: some swore that it should be put out at sunrise, others from noon until three o'clock, and some that it should be taken up at midday.

[NLJ historical notes 'Ja Social Life and Customs', Opie 1992]

GOOD HOPE

Estate in TRELAWNY Parish that was first settled in 1741, in modern times operated as a hotel and a GREAT HOUSE museum. Good Hope has some of the best examples of Georgian architecture in a state of good repair in the island, including the great house (built around 1755), the counting house, ice house, and estate offices and sugar works. The old slave hospital was turned into a chapel (St Peter's – ANGLICAN) in 1836 by a former owner and continued in use until 1867 when the estate was sold. It is said that one of the subsequent owners was an atheist and he used wooden sections and pews of the church to make barrels (hogsheads) for shipping SUGAR. In 1905 another owner sold the church bell to the FALMOUTH PARISH CHURCH for £50. Interesting tombstones have been found in the churchyard, including one 'In Memory of A.E. Esq., who died half drunk'.

Physic nuts

Good Hope

Good Hope was once owned by John Tharp (1744-1804) after whom Thorpe Street, Falmouth, was named. (Thorpe was the original spelling; 'Tharp', the way the name is pronounced, also made its way into many manuscripts.) Tharp, the richest man of his time, had four sons, but since they all displeased him, he decided to leave his immense fortune to his only grandson. The fact that the grandson was 'feeble-minded' didn't stop many women from wanting to marry him – and his fortune – and a wedding was arranged with a titled lady. However, the experience proved too much for the 21-year-old heir and he became hysterical on his wedding night, never recovering his wits thereafter. The marriage was annulled and he lived to be well over 80. Lawsuits continued for much of his life over the immense Tharp fortune.

[Wright and White 1969]

GOOMBAY

A DRUM, and/or ritual drumming on it, used in a healing ceremony (with singing and dancing) to counteract the work of evil spirits; the 'Goombay dance' has been practised in remote parts of the island, especially in upper ST ELIZABETH Parish. Goombay is also associated with the Maroons and Myalists. (See MAROON, MYAL.) The Goombay is regarded as the purest dance retention of the once popular Myal dance. The dance is characterized by fast and seemingly violent motions that include extensive use of space, throwing of the body on the ground and acrobatic feats.

Goombay drummer

The name (spelled in various ways e.g. 'gombay', 'gumbay') has been applied to different types of drums in the literature; nowadays accepted as describing a small, square or stool-like goat-skin drum with legs, also called a bench drum. It is played with the hands. The drum has clearly religious overtones and a long history in Jamaica. Similar drums are found in West Africa.

In other parts of the CARIBBEAN, e.g. Bahamas and Cuba, Goombay applies to a drum; in Bermuda to their masquerade festivity.

Recent studies have extended our knowledge of Goombay, Judith Bettelheim exploring its possible linkages with Africa, Kenneth Bilby tracing its continued present-day linkages with both Myal and JONKONNU through 'Gumbay play', a religious ritual he discovered still being observed in upper St Elizabeth.

[Beckwith 1928, Bettelheim 1999, Bilby 1999, DJE, Dunham 1946, Roberts 1972, Ryman 1980]

GORDON, Rt Excellent George William (1815-65)

National Hero of Jamaica. Gordon was born at Cherry Gardens (now a ST ANDREW suburb), the son of a quadroon slave and the Scottish owner of the estate, Joseph Gordon. Young Gordon taught himself to read, write and do accounts and was freed by his father and sent to live with his god-father, James Daley, a businessman of BLACK RIVER. While still in his teens, Gordon went into business for himself and was to became for a time a highly successful businessman and landowner. But he always retained a passionate interest in politics and religion, and became the champion of the poor and oppressed, vigorously defending their rights in and out of the Assembly to which he was elected in 1844 at the age of 29. His battles made him unpopular with the establishment and he failed to gain a seat again until 1863 when he

George William Gordon

became representative for St Thomas-in-the East, a parish in which he owned considerable property. In the meantime as a Justice of the Peace he continued his political advocacy, making deep enemies of the CUSTOS and other prominent citizens. In time this would include the new governor, Edward Eyre, who became a target for Gordon's verbal attacks when he regained his seat in the Assembly.

Gordon's fearless fight for justice made him the champion of the small settlers, especially in ST THOMAS Parish, where their spokesman and leader emerged in the person of Paul BOGLE. Gordon had various connections with Bogle but religion was a central one.

Gordon was baptized an ANGLICAN, he later became a Baptist, and then during the 1860-61 religious revival that swept the island, was converted to a Native Baptist sect. (See BAPTIST, REVIVAL.) He established his own Native Baptist chapels in KINGSTON and St Thomas. This adherence to what was regarded as 'lower class' RELIGION further alienated him from the white establishment as well as from his own class, that of the prosperous free COLOUREDS. Gordon ordained Bogle as a deacon of his Native Baptist church and Bogle in turn established his own chapel at his village of STONY GUT which, some have argued, was also a cover for revolutionary activities.

When Bogle led the march on MORANT BAY courthouse that turned into what was termed the MORANT BAY REBELLION, Gordon was immediately branded as the leader of the conspiracy and though there was no evidence against him, Governor Eyre had him taken illegally from Kingston to Morant Bay where martial law was in force. There he was court-martialled and sentenced to death. He was hanged from the yardarm of HMS *Wolverine* at Morant Bay on 23 October 1865. Bogle's capture and death followed shortly after. For their struggles against injustice, both men were declared among the first of Jamaica's National Heroes when the Order was established in 1969.
[Hart 1972, Heuman, 1994, Wynter 1971]

GORDON HOUSE
Building at the corner of Duke and Beeston Streets, KINGSTON, where Jamaica's House of Representatives meets, named after the National Hero, Rt Excellent George William GORDON. Before Gordon House was built in 1960, the legislature met at HEADQUARTERS HOUSE on the opposite side of Beeston Street.

Gordon House

GORDON TOWN
Large township in the HOPE RIVER valley in ST ANDREW Parish that was built on what was Jamaica's first botanic garden. The garden was established privately at a property called Spring Garden around 1770 by Hinton East, attorney and member of the Assembly who also served the government in various capacities.

East's garden was regarded as the most magnificent in the CARIBBEAN. His collections included plants from all over the world; he alone was responsible for introducing some 600 new plants to the island. Among them were Garden Egg (eggplant or aubergine), Oleander, CASSIA, Seaside MAHOE and HIBISCUS. Many plants introduced by others were also planted for the first time in East's garden. The most famous example is the MANGO, which was captured from a French ship in Caribbean waters. The plants were numbered, hence one variety is still called 'Number Eleven'. Plants were also exported from East's garden to gardeners in other places.

Hortus Eastensis, an official catalogue of the garden, was published in 1793, the same year the property was acquired by the government following East's death the previous year. The garden became public property, known as The Botanic Garden, Liguanea. However, very little attention or expense seems to have been expended and in 1811 the entire property, some 78ha with buildings and 44 slaves, was sold for £4,500 to Dr John Gordon, whose name was given to the town that eventually developed there.

The gardens were not kept up and entirely disappeared, a visitor from Kew Gardens in 1843 describing the site as 'a complete wilderness'. Yet some hint of East's garden remains to this day, in the abundance of plant life in the naturally beautiful setting at the intersection of the Hope River and two small streams. One appreciative temporary resident in the late 19th century was Marianne North, an intrepid Victorian Englishwoman who travelled the world making a pictorial record of tropical and exotic plants. Her astonishing collection of 800 paintings can be seen in the Marianne North Gallery at Kew Gardens, London, among them paintings done in Jamaica.

As she recounts in her autobiography, *Recollections of a Happy Life* (published in 1892), she arrived in Jamaica on Christmas Eve, 1871 and stayed until 24 May 1872, travelling the island and recording her delight in both words and pictures. Travelling to NEWCASTLE one day (then approached via Gordon Town), 'I saw a house half hidden amongst the glorious foliage of the long-deserted botanical gardens of the first settlers, and on inquiry found I could hire it entirely for four pounds a month. It had twenty rooms altogether, and offices behind, and had been a grand place in its day. So I did hire it, and also furniture for one bedroom'. The house she stayed in, known as 'The Garden House' was destroyed in the 1907 EARTHQUAKE and rebuilt.

Hinton East had been one of the promoters of the voyages to obtain the BREADFRUIT plant for Jamaica, but died the year before it arrived on the island. James Wiles, one of the two botanist-gardeners on board the HMS *Providence*, which successfully brought the breadfruit plants following Captain Bligh's aborted first attempt on the *Bounty*, was hired by the government as supervisor of the garden at LIGUANEA. He remained in Jamaica for the rest of his life, becoming a COFFEE planter in the mountains. Both his name and the Liguanea garden were to be immortalized on the Australian coast through the explorer Matthew Flinders, who charted it. Flinders had sailed as an 18-year-old midshipman on the *Providence*, and named a small cape in South Australia, Cape Wiles, and the tiny, neighbouring island, Liguanea Island, after his friend and the Jamaican garden.

[North 1892, Powell 1972, 1973]

GOURD see CALABASH

GOVERNMENT

On 6 August 1962 the Jamaica (Constitution) Order in Council came into effect establishing Jamaica as an independent nation. The structure of government that was chosen is similar to that of other members of the British Commonwealth with a parliamentary democracy. Government is carried on in the name of the British monarch, though the monarch's parliamentary functions as head of state are formal and limited. The monarch's personal representative is the governor-general, whom she appoints on the advice of the prime minister.

Parliament consists of a majority party that is the effective government, and a minority party called the opposition. The maximum life of a government is five years, with the majority party having the right to call elections at any time during its term. Universal adult suffrage was introduced at the 1944 election; in 1979 the voting age was lowered from 21 to 18 years.

Up to the time of writing, the government has alternated between the two major parties which first contested the 1944 election: the People's National Party formed in 1938 and the Jamaica Labour Party established in 1943. Though from time to time there have been third parties, they have been unable to erode the solid base of the two leading parties, which is founded on TRADE UNION support.

Jamaica's parliament consists of an elected House of Representatives (currently with 60 members) and a nominated Senate of 21 representatives from both the government and the opposition. The role of the Senate is to review legislation passed by the House, with some limitation of its powers regarding money bills.

The initiation of government policies and programmes and responsibility for general direction and control of government rests with the cabinet, which consists of the prime minister and not less than 11 other members.

The business of the government is conducted by ministries headed by ministers who are appointed by the prime minister from members of the House of Representatives and the Senate.

Local government refers to the provision of services and amenities at the local or PARISH level, and is the oldest form of government, dating to the earliest days of English settlement in the late 17th century.

GRANT, St William see PARK

GRAPEFRUIT (*Citrus paradisi*)
This widely known CITRUS fruit originated in the CARIBBEAN. It is believed to have developed as a hybrid of the sweet ORANGE (*C. sinensis*) and the citrus plant Shaddock (*C. grandis*), which is supposedly named after the BRITISH sea captain who first brought it to the Caribbean from Polynesia around the turn of the 18th century. Claims have been made for Barbados as well as Jamaica to be considered the original home for

the Grapefruit whose scientific name means 'citrus of paradise'. The first written record of the name Grapefruit comes from Jamaica in 1814. It was so called from the fact that the fruit grows in clusters, like grapes. However, the original name Forbidden Fruit was recorded in Barbados in 1750 and according to Sloane, 'The seed was first brought to Barbados by one Captain Shaddock, Comander [sic] of an East-India ship' on his way back to England.

Although Grapefruit was first established in the Caribbean, commercial production was first undertaken in the USA. The two main varieties grown in Jamaica today are the Marsh (seedless) and the Duncan (seedy).

[Baccus and Royes 1988, DJE]

GRATER CAKE

Confection made of grated COCONUT and SUGAR (sometimes flavoured with GINGER), boiled and dropped on to a sheet where it is spread out to harden. It is cut into triangles or squares. Made of brown 'wet sugar' in the old days, today white sugar is used and grater cake is coloured pink and white. It is still sold by street vendors but is also found in supermarkets and grocery shops.

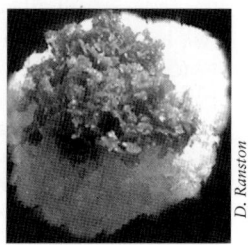

Grater cake

GRAVE PLANTS

Throughout rural Jamaica, several plants are common as grave decoration (see GRAVEYARD), two of the most popular being CROTON (the native varieties) and Coffee Rose (*Tabernaemontana divaricata*), probably because they symbolize everlasting life since they will survive the longest drought and 'rise again' to thrive and bloom. Other plants, such as peas and beans (see OVERLOOK BEAN) are more sinister and are usually planted soon after burial. Their purpose is to 'tie' the spirit (DUPPY) and ensure that it stays in the grave and does not wander around to haunt the living. Such practices were more common when the dead were buried close to the home in the family plot (see DEATH RITUALS).

GRAVEYARD

A burial ground, the residence of spirits, was once regarded as a place filled with power, where practitioners such as OBEAH-men frequently resorted to conduct ceremonies or secure important ingredients for rites and CHARMS, such as grave dirt. Graveyards were therefore seen by many people as places to be avoided, even in the daytime, though such does not seem to be the case today. Many Jamaican ghost stories (DUPPY stories) have graveyards as their settings. BIRDS which frequent graveyards are regarded as 'duppy birds' or spirits of the dead.

Though there are public cemeteries as well as those attached to churches, graveyards can be encountered anywhere, since in the old days it was the practice to bury the dead on family land. Many of these old family graveyards still survive in the BUSH or can be seen along roadsides (see DEATH RITUALS).

GREAT HOUSE

The residence of an estate-owner during the plantation era (see SUGAR PLANTATION), usually on a grand scale. The great house was often built on an eminence overlooking the SUGAR CANE fields and works, commanding fine views and positioned to catch the breeze. Over time, most of these houses were built in an architectural style that came to be called the Jamaican Vernacular, with many features adapted to local conditions.

Plantation houses served as centres of hospitality and entertainment for local and visiting whites. The richer planters kept open house and entertained lavishly and even those of more modest means freely offered hospitality, which was just as freely accepted and returned. A relatively lowly penkeeper such as Thomas Thistlewood records in his diary many instances of his entertaining or being entertained. With few inns in the country parts, 'it was not unusual for entire families, with their servants and personal belongings, to move for a stay of a month or longer in a friend's house'. (See TRUNK FLEET.) Lady Nugent's *Journal* is enlivened by the various visits she and her husband, the governor, made to plantation houses around the island. Even for BOOK-KEEPERS and humbler white folk, acceptance at a 'backra house' was a necessity. As an old slave informs an early 19th century visitor: 'Never mind ask – buckera in this country just go up and sit down in 'tother house, and go n'yam with them, and nobody ask where they come from. Tavern no de in a country place.'

Development of the Great House Few grand houses were erected during the first hundred years of BRITISH settlement, the planters being

Marlborough

more concerned with developing their plantations. An outstanding house of the earliest period was STOKES HALL (now a ruin but occupied up to the 20th century). Although there is no evidence of when COLBECK CASTLE was built, it too is believed to date from the 17th century. Like other great houses of the period, Stokes Hall was fortified, built with square towers at the four corners and loopholes to provide supporting fire in case of attack, presumably by pirates or enemy nation invaders from the sea, or MAROONS.

Charles Leslie in the 1730s informs us that 'the buildings are neat but not fine . . . the gentlemen's houses are generally built low, of one storey, consisting of five or six handsome apartments, beautifully lined and floored with mahogany'. Writing 30 years later, Edward Long said it was not unusual to see a plantation 'adorned with a very expensive set of works, of brick or stone, well executed, and the owner residing in a miserable thatched hovel, hastily put together with wattles and plaster'. (The ruins at KENILWORTH are outstanding examples of one 'expensive set of works'.) Long commented on the 'vast improvement' in residences over the previous 20 years and indeed, by 1755, some KINGSTON merchants felt confident enough to take a bet to see who could build the finest town house. The one house remaining of the four built, now HEADQUARTERS HOUSE, has excellent examples of some common great house features, such as a semi-spiral staircase with turned balusters and moulded handrails.

The most outstanding great houses were built during the 'Golden Age of Sugar', from the mid-18th to the early 19th century. Existing examples include ROSE HALL (restored), Marlborough in MANCHESTER, GOOD HOPE in TRELAWNY, and CARDIFF HALL in ST ANN. (The period also saw the construction of the fine public buildings surrounding the Georgian square in SPANISH TOWN.)

As the sugar industry declined in the 19th century, few great or grand houses were erected. Two notable exceptions were reflections of new sources of wealth. DEVON HOUSE in ST ANDREW Parish was built in 1880 as the residence of George Stiebel who emigrated to South America and made a fortune from gold mining. Agualta Vale in ST MARY Parish was built in the early 20th century for the Pringle family, a new aristocracy based on wealth derived from the BANANA TRADE. Agualta Vale was constructed in 1914 on the foundation of the original great house built c. 1760 by Sir Thomas Hibbert (builder of Headquarters House). Of reinforced concrete, the new house was said to be 'representative of the Victorian eclecticism of that era, combining successfully the classical grandeur of the Georgian, features of the Jamaican vernacular and the modern conveniences of the industrial age'. (The house was partially destroyed by fire in the 1980s.)

The Jamaican Vernacular The era of West Indian prosperity coincided with the Georgian Age in England (1720-1850) and the associated architectural style. But though the early buildings were essentially English in character, the traditional forms became modified and a local style developed. In identifying the buildings of 'architectural or historic interest in the British West Indies', Ackworth in 1951 concluded that 'Jamaican architecture is particularly interesting since from Georgian beginnings it developed a distinct line of its own, so that by 1846 there was to all intents and purposes a Jamaican style, a "vernacular".'

For the early great houses, much of the furniture and some special building materials (including stone, brick, and slate) came from Britain, and at a later period pitch-pine was imported from North America. Local craftsmen (see CABINET-MAKER) at first copied the imported furniture, modifying them for local conditions and using the superb local woods for tables, chairs, sideboards and beds. The four-poster bed was a favourite, according to T.A.L. Concannon, 'made wide and large for comfortable sleeping under a mosquito net. Rooms were high and sometimes open to the underside of roof boarding or shingles, thus able to accommodate these vast beds'. A truckle bed under the fourposter often accommodated a slave and later

Townhouse in Spanish Town with louvred window-coolers

a servant, usually a young 'SCHOOLGIRL' in attendance on the lady of the house.

Concannon, an architect who was responsible for much historical restoration in the island, has commented that, 'From Georgian-inspired beginnings, architecture in Jamaica, both in the plantation great house and the humbler village building, developed in a style of its own from which a recognizable vernacular emerged. Features such as the louvred window, projecting louvred window-cooler, and ingenious treatments of pitched shingled roofs became characteristic in town and country. Houses were embellished with simple but decorative fretwork to eaves, bargeboards and balcony railings,

The Jamaican vernacular

which were often adorned with graceful wrought ironwork. With HURRICANE, EARTHQUAKE, fire, flood and human indifference much of all this has inevitably disappeared'.

In addition to the JAMAICA NATIONAL HERITAGE TRUST, a government body, there is also the Georgian Society dedicated to the preservation, restoration and maintenance of Jamaica's historic buildings, monuments and artefacts, particularly those belonging to the Georgian period, and an active group in the UK called the Friends of the Georgian Society of Jamaica.

[Ackworth 1951, Binney et al. 1991, Brathwaite 1971, Concannon 1965, Hall 1989, Long 1774, Nugent 1839]

GROG

A RUM and water mixture so called by the sailors of PORT ROYAL after the nickname of Admiral Edward VERNON who introduced it. Vernon was called 'Old Grog' from his habit of wearing a boat cloak of grogram, a coarse fabric. Sailors in the Royal Navy used to get their rum rations neat until Vernon, who was in charge of the Port Royal station in 1740, became tired of his sailors 'stupefying themselves in rum' and issued an order forbidding the raw liquor. The order was soon adopted throughout the Royal Navy. It was decreed that the daily allowance of half-pint of rum should be diluted in a quart of water to be publicly mixed on the deck of every ship in a 'scuttle butt' kept for the purpose, and issued twice a day. The annoyed sailors called the mixture 'grog', a name that soon came into the language all over the world, and taverns and rum shops came to be called 'grog shops' (hence 'The Grog Shop' at DEVON HOUSE).

GROUND

This term was last recorded in English meaning 'a cultivated plot' back in the 11th century but is in common usage in Jamaica, showing perhaps how archaic the speech was of the English who first came. The word retains a special meaning of 'field' or 'cultivation' of the small settler. Hence to 'go a grung' means to go to one's field, which is usually some distance from the house plot or YARD (see also BUSH). The food planted in one's ground are 'ground provisions', usually root crops such as YAM, COCO, CASSAVA, sweet POTATO and dasheen.

The countryman of the past built on his ground a lean-to shelter or hut, called in some places a 'tatu'. He took water to his ground in a gourd or CALABASH with a CORN cob stopper that he carried slung over his shoulder along with a flat covered plaited straw BASKET called a 'heng pon me', 'namsack' or 'nambusack' containing his lunch, or his seeds. Also ever-present was a CROCUS bag that was used for carrying crops and would make do as a rough coat or head covering in inclement weather. In the absence of a crocus bag, a PLANTAIN leaf served as an umbrella. Tools for 'working his ground' (not working 'in') might include a hoe and a fork, depending on the season, but he would never be seen without his faithful CUTLASS or machete.

The usage derives from the term PROVISION GROUND or 'Negro-ground', which was used by the planters during SLAVERY to designate the areas set aside for the slaves to cultivate food for themselves. Perhaps because of its association with the small farmer, regarded in the past as the backbone of Jamaican life (see AGRICULTURE, FREE VILLAGE), the term 'grounds' in the sixties and seventies, at a time of political and social ferment, came to be an approving term for someone who was rooted or grounded, a 'true' Jamaican. 'Groundings' came to be used by intellectuals to describe gatherings (or 'reasonings') in which they sat and talked with the underprivileged, probably from GROUNDATION. The words 'roots' and 'rootsy', meaning 'down to earth' which gained popularity in the 1960s in reference (by Rastafarians) to African roots, probably derived some of their resonance from the earlier usage of 'grounds'. In the MUSIC industry, 'Roots REGGAE' has come to identify that form of popular music that is turning away from over-digitized music and DANCEHALL 'slackness' and returning to cultural roots in song lyrics and style.

GROUNDATION

RASTAFARI term used to describe a large gathering. The word (derived from GROUND) was apparently first used to describe such an event in KINGSTON in 1958 organized by Prince Emmanuel Edwards, a Rasta leader, and attended by thousands of locksmen. It is also called a 'Nyabingi' or 'Bingi'.

GUABANCEX

One of the 12 principal ZEMIS of the TAINO, a female weather spirit. She is associated with the spirit of thunder and with thunderstones, SNAKES, and lightning. In her representations, this zemi is shown with her hands positioned counterclockwise – in

Taino carving

the direction of winds in a HURRICANE. She has two assistants, COATRISCHIE (flood) and GUATAUBÁ (thunder).
[Arrom 1990]

GUACO BUSH (*Mikania micrantha*)

A member of the large Composite family that yields many medicinal plants, including Camomile, Garden Bitters, White Back, Strong Back and Jack-in-the-Bush, Guaco (sometimes 'Quaco') is a slender-stemmed twining vine that is common in wet places from sea level to 700m and grows throughout tropical America. It is widely used in folk MEDICINE, the leaves made into a TEA for colds and as a remedy for itch. A heated wad of the leaves is also used to relieve pain. The name is of TAINO Arawakan origin.

Guaco bush

B. Sutton

[Adams 1972, Asprey and Thornton 1953-55, DJE]

GUAHAYONA

Culture hero of the TAINOS; in one of the myths recorded by PANÉ, he acquired two major cultural items, GUANÍN, and sacred stones, cibas, from the Water Mother or Woman at the Bottom of the Sea whose name was Guabonito. Although this myth exists in somewhat fragmented form, if compared with similar myths from the ARAWAK-speaking peoples of the mainland, it would make Guahayona the first medicine-man or CACIQUE of the Tainos, and the story one that recorded his acquisition of guanín, TOBACCO and the gourd rattle (see CALABASH), the symbols of religious and temporal power.
[Arrom 1990, Stevens-Arroyo 1988]

GUANGO (*Samanea saman*)

Also known as Saman or Rain Tree, this is a very large, symmetrical spreading tree that will grow up to 20m high, and often spreads wider than its height, with an umbrella-shaped crown. It is commonly seen in pastures particularly in the drier southern plains and foothills from sea level to 800m. The Guango folds up its leaves at night or in cloudy weather so moisture accumulates beneath it, making the grass there greener than that round about. It shares this characteristic of folding its leaf with a relative, the MIMOSA or Sensitive Plant.

The tree sheds its leaves during the winter months, putting on new foliage in the spring. It bears pink-tufted flowers in mid-year and these

Guango tree

are succeeded by long black pods containing a sugary pulp which is avidly eaten by CATTLE. Guango yields a very attractive fine-grained, striped wood popular for making furniture and ornaments. The tree is a native of Central and tropical South America and is said to have been introduced into Jamaica with cattle from this area.
[Adams 1992, NHSJ 1946]

GUANÍN
Symbol of office of the CACIQUES of the TAINOS, guanín was a thin plate of reddish GOLD shaped into a half-moon or crescent. It was believed by COLUMBUS to be made of pure gold and helped to set off the feverish search for that precious metal. However, guanín was found to be not a pure metal but a composite alloy of 55 per cent gold, 25 per cent copper and 19 per cent silver. Its attraction for the Tainos apparently resided in its reddish colour and coppery smell. Some scholars believe the Tainos imported the guanín from the South American mainland, as they did not possess the technology for casting metal; others point out that since guanín objects were made of beaten, not cast gold, those from the island CARIBBEAN could have been made there. In any event, trading networks between mainland America and the Caribbean did exist in the pre-Columbian era.
[Stevens-Arroyo 1988]

GUATAUBÁ
One of the 12 principal TAINO zemis, a weather spirit whose name means 'thunder'. Along with COATRISCHIE, Guataubá was a herald, one of the two principal assistants of GUABANCEX, maker of wind and rain.
[Arrom 1990]

GUAVA (*Psidium guajava*)
Shrub or small evergreen tree, up to 7m high, which is occasionally cultivated but mainly grows wild in Jamaica from sea level to 1,400m producing a succulent fruit that is eaten raw. It is also used for making the popular guava jelly, guava nectar and other drinks, stewed guava, a popular dessert, and guava cheese, a confection made from boiling down the pulp of ripe guavas with sugar to a cheese-like consistency. The fruit is extremely rich in vitamin C.

The leaves are used in folk MEDICINE, in the past as a treatment for diarrhoea and dysentery and in treating ring worm and eczema. A folk song claims, 'Guava root a medicine fe cure young gal fever'.

The name guava derives from the SPANISH *guayaba* that in turn is derived from the TAINO *guaiava*. The Tainos believed that the spirits of the dead resided in COYABA and ate guavas at night (probably because it is one of the fruits eaten at night by BATS). Their ZEMI of the dead, guardian of Coyaba, was called MAQUETAURIE GUAYABA, also known in another form as OPIYEL GUOBIRÁN.
[Adams 1972, Arrom 1990, Robertson 1990]

Guava fruit and flowers

GUINEA
Term used in Jamaica (and elsewhere in the CARIBBEAN) to denote Africa, probably first used by the slave traders who called the African coast from which the slaves were taken the 'Guinea coast'. Thus 'a Guinea-ship' was a slave ship; in Jamaican creole it also came to mean 'a large crowd of people'. A 'Guinea man' was a man born in Africa, in contrast to CREOLES who were born in the Americas and who haughtily referred to the new slaves coming straight from Africa as 'Guinea birds'. The belief among some Africans that their souls on death would return to Guinea, and that the journey took nine nights, probably led to the NINE NIGHT observances.

GUINEA FOWL (*Numida meleagris*)
Type of fowl with black and white speckled plumage brought to the West Indies from Africa as early as 1508, and a common farmyard sight in former times. A saying that warns of the importance of preserving one's reputation notes: 'Seven year not enough to wash speckle off guinea hen back.'

Guinea fowls

Now domesticated, Guinea fowl would probably have reverted to a feral state if not controlled by the MONGOOSE. May Jeffrey-Smith recalled how common the wild birds were around the beginning of the 20th century: 'Housewives had no need to be anxious about an empty larder, should unexpected guests arrive, for these birds were easily obtained. At dawn the guinea fowls would leave the woods to harass the "grounds" of some poor settler, whose YAMS and COCOES they devoured. They were caught by means of CORN steeped in RUM, which like the birds was cheap then.' The Guinea fowl also served as a night watch, uttering its loud cries of 'Come back, come back' at the slightest sound.
[Bond 1960, Jeffrey-Smith 1972]

GUINEA GRASS (*Panicum maximum*)
A coarse grass that grows to 3m high and is one of the most valuable CATTLE feeds in Jamaica, accidentally introduced in the 1740s. The seeds were brought by the captain of a slave ship as feed for some rare West African birds given to George Ellis, a former chief justice. The birds died shortly afterwards and the seeds were thrown away. But they took root and flourished and attention was drawn to the new grass because cattle avidly fed on it. Eventually Guinea grass spread all over Jamaica.
[Cundall 1915]

GUINEP (*Melicoccus bijugatus*)
Common, large tree up to 20m high, bearing small, round, green-skinned fruit growing in clusters like grapes, especially popular with children who for hundreds of years have risked their lives to climb and break off the fruit-bearing limbs from the tree, the only easy way of reaping them. When in season (July to September) guinep is available in the markets and from roadside vendors. The crisp green shell is easily cracked with the teeth, revealing the peach-coloured coating on the large seed that is sweet and juicy when sucked off. The seed can be dangerous to young children if swallowed and they are warned to be careful by being told that if swallowed, it will grow inside them. It is said that the seeds can be roasted and eaten like chestnuts, though this is not a common practice.

Guinep grows wild throughout Jamaica from sea level to 1,000m, the seed easily taking root where it is thrown, though it grows into such a large tree that, unlike other fruit trees, it is not commonly cultivated in gardens. Although Browne (1756) says the plant was first brought to Jamaica from Suriname around 1750, it was in fact cultivated long before that in TAINO gardens. Guinep, or *jagua* as it is still called in the Spanish-speaking islands, was their most sacred plant, yielding black body paint used for ritual purposes. Hence the Taino's myth of the CAVE OF EMERGENCE distinguishes them as the 'People of the Jagua'. On the Orinoco even today, the seeds are bruised and macerated, yielding a colourless juice that turns blue-black through oxidation, a phenomenon known to Jamaican mothers whose children eat guinep in their 'good clothes' and indelibly stain them with its juice. Native peoples in tropical America still

Guinep

use jagua, especially in puberty and death rituals. The English variants 'guinep' or 'ginep' derive from the Arawakan word *genipa*, while the Spanish variant *jagua* is derived from the Arawakan word *yagua*. Guinep is related to the ACKEE and is so called in Barbados.
[Adams 1971, DCEU, DJE, Stevens-Arroyo 1988]

GUM TREES
Many plants in Jamaica are regarded as 'gum trees', a major characteristic being that they exude a clear resin that in former times was used as gum and for medicinal and other purposes. The best known is LIGNUM VITAE (*Guaiacum officinale*). Among the many uses of this plant, the gum mixed with RUM and tied to a bruise is a well known folk remedy. Called *palo santo* by

the Spaniards, it was also used to treat 'French pox', as syphilis was called.

Another famous gum tree is Birch Gum or Balsam Tree (*Bursera simaruba*) also called Turpentine Tree, Incense Tree, Mastic, Mulatto Tree, Red Birch or West Indian Birch. Its trunk is covered with a red, smooth bark that peels off in pieces like the birch of northern climates, hence its name. The wood was formerly used for making matches and it yields a clear transparent resin. Like Lignum Vitae it is used to treat boils on the skin. The leaves are used for toothache.

A perhaps less well known gum tree is the Coonoo-coonoo or Gracie Wood, also known as Boar-gum Tree, Boar Tree, Boar Wood, Hog-doctor Tree, or Hog-gum (*Symphonia globulifera*). A tree of the deep forest, its various names are derived from the fact that wild hogs rub their wounds against it, its copious balsam providing a cure. The wood has a caustic sap, closely related to the poison ivy of North America. The tree yields an attractive rich red timber and the fruit provides food for BIRDS, especially Bald-pate (see DOVES).
[Adams 1972, DJE, NHSJ 1946]

GUNGO PEA (*Cajanus cajan*)

A roundish pea that grows on a tall shrub, gungo is a favourite pulse of Jamaicans (see PEAS AND BEANS), particularly in soup or in RICE AND PEAS. Probably a native of the East Indies, Gungo was introduced from Africa and the name probably derives from 'Congo'; it is also called Congo Pea. Its popularity is attested by its many other names: Pigeon Pea, Christmas Pea, Angola Pea, Seven-year Pea, No-eye Pea. Gungo peas grow on a perennial shrub 1-3m in height. The grains are mottled from green to brown and are used, green or dried, in soups, stews and cooked with rice. Gungo peas usually ripen in December, just in time for 'green gungo' to be combined with the bone from the CHRISTMAS ham to make a favourite soup for the holiday season. Many people grow a bush or two in their yards just for this purpose though the dried, and nowadays canned, gungo is available all year round. In Jamaica talk, the phrase 'in yu gungo', means to be on top of the world. To 'plant gungo a line' means to be neighbourly, gungo being planted sometimes between properties and shared. The leaves of the plant are sometimes used in folk MEDICINE especially in a tea for colds and sore throats.
[Adams 1972, Asprey and Thornton 1953-55, DJE]

GUZU see CHARM

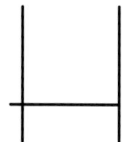

HALF WAY TREE

Busy road junction and commercial centre that originated as the principal crossroad village of ST ANDREW Parish. It got its name from the huge COTTON TREE that was standing there when the Spaniards first arrived (see SPANISH) and which died of old age in the 1870s. The tree stood near to the Parish Church at the junction of important roads between SPANISH TOWN and downtown KINGSTON as well as roads leading from the rural parishes of St Andrew and St George (PORTLAND) and ST MARY. In its shade stood a tavern. The first written record that we have of Half Way Tree is dated 1696 and notes the behaviour of some men who were drinking in this tavern. Later, the enormous roots of the tree provided a resting place for the market vendors between their homes in the hills and the MARKETS in the city.
[Cundall 1915]

HALF WAY TREE CHURCH
see ST ANDREW PARISH CHURCH

HALF WAY TREE CLOCK

The clock tower in HALF WAY TREE was erected by public subscription in 1913, as a memorial to King Edward VII of England, and has remained a major landmark, straddling as it does the junction of four major streets in the KINGSTON metropolitan area.

Half Way Tree clock

HALSE HALL

Located in CLARENDON Parish, this is one of Jamaica's historic houses listed by the JNHT. It is owned by the BAUXITE company JAMALCO. The area in which the house is located is rich in history, going back to the TAINOS who had villages nearby. The SPANISH trail across the island from ESQUIVEL to the north coast also passed within .4km of the hill on which the house is sited. When the English came, and the officers of the conquering army were awarded extensive land grants, this area was given to Major Thomas Hals (d 1701) who had come with Penn and Venables. (See CAPTURE OF JAMAICA.) It is believed that the ground floor of the present GREAT HOUSE was built by him in the 17th century. The upper floor was added by his descendants between 1746 and 1749. One owner of the house was Francis Sadler Halse, who played a leading role in the MAROON wars. In 1739 he conducted the negotiations with Colonel John Guthrie and CUDJOE which led to the signing of the peace treaties.

The most famous descendant and owner of the house was Henry Thomas de la Beche (1796-1855), whose grandfather had married the heiress of Halse Hall and whose father had changed his name from Beach to the more ancient form of the family name. De la Beche was born and raised in England. While on a visit to his Halse Hall property in 1824 he conducted a geological survey of central and eastern Jamaica and wrote the first geological account of the island. He also drew the first geological map of the eastern half of the island, believed to be the first true geological map of any area in the western hemisphere. It was published in 1827 by the Geological Society of London. In England, while still a young man, de la Beche founded the world's first geological survey (the British) and throughout his lifetime made major contributions to his field. He also published a book called *Notes on the present condition of the Negroes in Jamaica* (1825).

De La Beche

A commemorative plaque was erected at Halse Hall in 1958 by geologists from Jamaica and England to mark de la Beche's contributions to the development of GEOLOGY in both countries. The building that houses the Department of Geology, UNIVERSITY OF THE WEST INDIES, is also named in his honour.

Another famous occupant of the house was the doctor and botanist, Sir Hans Sloane, whose collection of specimens of Jamaica's FAUNA and FLORA formed the nucleus of what was to become the British Museum of Natural History.
[Cundall 1915, Porter 1990, Taylor 1976]

HAMPTON SCHOOL see BLACK RIVER ANGLICAN CHURCH

HANOVER MUSEUM
This small museum is located in the 19th century jail and prison hospital in the HANOVER Parish capital of LUCEA. The site has been recognized as a national monument and includes a display of artefacts related to the history of the Parish, Amerindian artefacts, and plants that are indigenous to the island. It is operated by the Hanover Historical Society.

HANOVER, Parish of
Area: 450.4km^2, population 67,800 (1999). This is Jamaica's smallest parish outside of KINGSTON. In 1998 Hanover held the record for the lowest crime rate in the island. The capital of LUCEA is set in one of the island's most exquisite natural bays. Hanover has been mainly agricultural but TOURISM has become important in recent years. The parish shares the NEGRIL resort area with WESTMORELAND Parish; the upmarket tourist resorts of Round Hill and TRYALL are also located in Hanover.

The parish was created in 1725 and named after the German House of Hanover. This was the Protestant German family which became the new royal line in England in 1714 with the accession of George I to the English throne after the death of Queen Anne, the last English monarch of the Stuart line.

HANOVER PARISH CHURCH
It is uncertain exactly when this 18th century building was constructed in LUCEA, the capital of HANOVER Parish. It contains a number of monuments to interesting persons such as Sir Simon Clarke, who married an heiress of the HAUGHTON family and whose grandfather, a navy officer, was supposedly transported to Jamaica for highway robbery. A monument is also here to John Castello, publisher of the *Falmouth Post* who more than any other individual helped to create the legend of the White Witch of ROSE HALL.

Walter Jekyll (1849-1929), who is buried in the Lucea churchyard, was formerly an ANGLICAN clergyman, later taught singing and interested himself in Jamaican folk life. He resided for a time at Guava Ridge in the mountains of ST ANDREW Parish where he collected the material which he published in a volume called *Jamaican Song and Story* (1907). Jekyll was a patron of writer Claude McKay (1889-1948) and it was he who encouraged McKay to write in Jamaican dialect and assisted him to go to the USA for further study. McKay draws a sympathetic portrait of him as the somewhat eccentric 'Squire Gensir' in his novel *Banana Bottom* and talks of their relationship in the autobiographical *My Green Hills of Jamaica*.
[Jekyll 1907, McKay 1933, 1979, Wright and White 1969]

HARBOUR VIEW see FORT NUGENT

HARD-DOUGH BREAD see BREAD

HAUGHTON
Place name in HANOVER Parish derived from the name of a prominent family (Haughton-James) which settled in the area. Fat Hog Quarter and Haughton Court near to LUCEA were part of the Haughton-James estates. The history of the James family goes back to Richard James who arrived with the English army of conquest in 1655 (see CAPTURE OF JAMAICA), and was given land in this area. His son, Richard James, was the first child of English parents to be born on the island. This James owned large tracts of land in Hanover and WESTMORELAND, became CUSTOS of the parishes of Westmoreland, ST ELIZABETH, and Hanover, and was colonel of the Hanover MILITIA.

Col James had another claim to fame – he is said to have lived to age 103 and attributed his longevity to a diet almost exclusively of COCOA in his later years. His second wife, Ann Haughton, came from a wealthy Barbados family. In time the local family became Haughton-James. A distinguished descendant of this family is Montague Rhodes James (1862-1936), a famous English educator who is best known as the author of *Ghost Stories of an Antiquary*.
[Cundall 1915, Wright and White 1969]

HEAD SUGAR see SUGAR, Wet

HEADQUARTERS HOUSE
Historic building located on the corner of Duke and Beeston Streets in downtown KINGSTON. Jamaica's legislature met here for nearly one hundred years, from 1872 to October 1960, when GORDON HOUSE, built across the street, became the new parliamentary building.

Headquarters House has been described as 'a tangible reminder of the wealth and opulence of the Kingston merchant in his heyday'. Built of brick, stone and timber, it has a basement and an attic as well as ground and upper floors. Although much altered over the years for office space, special features such as the elegant MAHOGANY staircase and door surrounds can still be seen.

The original owner, Thomas Hibbert (1710-80), was a prominent planter, merchant and member of the Assembly. In the 1750s, he was one of four wealthy Kingston merchants who took a bet to see who could build the most splendid town house. The other houses in the competition were Constantine House built by Jasper Hall on Highholborn Street, Bull House built by John Bull on North Street, and Harmony Hall (the name of the builder is not known) on Hanover Street. It is believed that the bet was to secure the affections of a much-married and notorious lady of the day, Teresa Constantia Phillips (see THEATRE). There is no record of the winner and Headquarters House is the only one surviving.

In 1814 the house was acquired by the military as the headquarters of the general in charge of BRITISH troops, and became known as 'General's House' or 'Headquarter's House'. When the capital was moved from SPANISH TOWN to Kingston in 1872, the house was purchased from the War Office and became the office of the colonial secretary and the seat of government. An old custom was to hoist a white flag at Headquarters House to announce the arrival of the Royal Mail boat.

[Cundall 1915, JNHT]

HELLSHIRE HILLS
Promontory in ST CATHERINE Parish on the western side of KINGSTON harbour. In recent decades, part of Hellshire has been developed as Portmore, a new urban centre or 'twin city' to Kingston. Hellshire is also popular for its beaches. The area was originally settled by the TAINOS around AD 1200 and included Great GOAT ISLAND. (Two Sisters Cave contains a Taino petroglyph.) It later became the site of runaway slave communities. There was very little activity or population until the mid-1800s when a ring of forts was built to protect Kingston harbour. This included FORT AUGUSTA, the Apostles Battery, FORT CLARENCE (now recalled in the name of the beach), etc. BRITISH settlers raised CATTLE and set up works to produce WHITE LIME, SALT from the Great Salt Ponds and indigo. By the late 18th century, PORT HENDERSON had replaced Passage Fort as the port for SPANISH TOWN, then the capital, and was developed as a holiday resort. But by the late 19th century, most of Hellshire, or Healthshire as it was sometimes optimistically called, seems to have once again become deserted, the haunt only of wild PIGS and their hunters, and fishermen.

The area is one of low rainfall, of no more than 76cm per year, with no ground water retained in the porous LIMESTONE soil, factors that retarded its development. Although various schemes were proposed for the development of Hellshire in the past, nothing was done until the large scale development strategy of the government's Urban Development Corporation, which began in the early 1960s and continues apace.

The inhospitable nature of Hellshire has proved advantageous for the development and persistence of a unique natural environment. Prior to the recent opening up of the area a scientific expedition was undertaken, and Hellshire was discovered to be the habitat of rare and fascinating FLORA and FAUNA. Botanist C. Dennis Adams noted that 'much of the vegetation of the more remote parts of the Hellshire Hills . . . is totally natural, and is a persisting example of the virgin thickets and dry woodlands of the region'. It was proposed to retain some of these areas in natural reserves.

Hellshire is the habitat of the CONEY and the

Headquarters House

IGUANA, both endangered endemic species. In the 1990s, iguanas, thought to be extinct, were found in this area. Young specimens have been taken to the Hope Zoo to be reared until they are old enough to be released safely in the Hellshire habitat.
[Aarons 1983a, Cundall 1915]

HIBISCUS

This popular garden ornamental is sometimes still referred to as 'Shoeblack' since the somewhat oily flowers of the common red variety, *Hibiscus rosa-sinensis*, were once used for polishing shoes and other leather products. Although this variety is still common, growing from sea level to 1,200m, many new varieties have been introduced into gardens, some of which have been bred in Jamaica. There are some 5,000 hybrids and cultivars world-wide, and flowers of a remarkable range of colours, sizes and shapes are now grown. They are easily identified from a 'brush' in the centre, and each flower will last for only one day whether on the plant or picked and placed in water. An interesting species is the Changeable Rose or Rose of Sharon (*H. mutabilis*) which changes colour as the day wears on.

The garden hibiscus is a native of China but now grows all over the tropical world. In the CARIBBEAN it is used for hedges and is often severely pruned; some species (*H. elatus*) will grow up to 25m.

The Hibiscus family (Malvaceae) includes many economically important or edible plants, including OKRA, SORREL that is made into drinks, and MAHOE.
[Adams 1971, 1972, Hannau and Garrard n.d., Kingsbury 1988]

HIGGLER

The word 'higgler' that is so much a part of the Jamaican economic and cultural landscape is an archaic English word meaning 'itinerant dealer' or 'huckster' who, presumably, 'higgles' and 'haggles'. The name originally referred to the Jamaican countrywoman (or, less frequently, man) who brought agricultural produce to the MARKETS to sell. In recent times it has acquired a much wider meaning to embrace vendors in many other products not traded by the original higglers, and is international in scope, as higglers now travel abroad to bring back imported goods to sell.

In addition to the original market vendors who date from the earliest settlement of the island, street or sidewalk vendors of articles such

19th century higglers

as home made confectionery (see SWEETS) also have a long history. Note was taken in the 1940s of the 'latest' higglers – those dealing in haberdashery. They sat on city sidewalks or walked up and down with their wares, earning them the name of 'walking bargain stores'. They were the forerunners of those vendors, from the 1970s onwards, whose address was known as 'Bend Down Plaza', from the fact that purchasers had to bend down to view the wares (usually imported goods) that they spread out on the sidewalk. As the civic authorities sought to regulate sidewalk vending, they gave these higglers the title 'informal commercial importers'

Market higgler

or ICIs, some of whom have turned their original street trading into well established businesses. Still, 'higgler' remains the most commonly used term.

Market Higglers The profession of buying and selling in whatever form is mainly in the hands of women and over many centuries has assisted them in forging their independence both economically and socially. The market is one place that allows women to break away from the social constraints of home and domesticity and to amass capital. Researchers such as V. Durant-Gonzalez have found that traditional higglering is a highly developed occupational skill that is often passed down from mother to daughter. The market provides the opportunity for a woman to achieve by her own abilities and build her reputation as a business woman; it is a place where her status is based on this role. In the market, the higgler is queen of her domain.

Higglers have traditionally formed the backbone of Jamaica's internal marketing system, and are regarded as a particularly tough and hardy group of women. It is a physically taxing occupation. While better transportation facilities nowadays have made their lives somewhat easier, some full time market higglers are at their posts from Wednesday evening to Saturday evening and often sleep at the market, making do with inadequate sanitary and other facilities. The higgler often acquires her special space in the market, indoors, outdoors or on the sidewalk, and maintains that spot permanently as her business address since this is where her faithful customers, the mainstay of her business, can find her.

Country Higglers Traditionally, the 'country higgler' brings produce to the market for sale either directly to the customer or to another set of higglers called 'town higglers', town dwellers who rent space in the market and sell to the housewives. The country higgler's stock comes from her own family's cultivation on their plot (see PROVISION GROUND) or she walks around and buys from other farmers in her area. Customarily, the cultivation is undertaken by the men, while women take the produce to market to sell, providing them with the opportunity to visit 'town' and do the family shopping.

In earlier times, these women travelled mainly on foot, with the goods carried on their heads, and on DONKEYS and mules over long distances, down mountain tracks and country trails till they reached the highways leading to the city and towns. These processions of higglers proceeding into the city have been much photographed and painted. Later on, mule drawn DRAYS, donkey carts and, still later, trucks laden with higglers and their goods, became a more common sight on the highways.

The old-style market woman with her proud bearing as she carried enormous loads on her head was for centuries a familiar image denoting 'Jamaica'. Her working dress consisted of a wraparound 'bib' (apron) with two large, deep pockets, and a BANDANA headtie over which she sometimes wore a large straw hat for travelling.
[Durant-Gonzalez 1983, Katzin 1959, Simmonds 1987]

HOG PLUM (*Spondias mombin*)
A native of the New World tropics, the small tree (6-16m high) bears a plum-like, oval fruit, not much eaten by humans because it tends to be wormy, but relished by hogs. Hog Plum is also used as a cure for colds, an infusion of the bark and leaves is applied to swelling; the crushed leaves and bark have astringent and germicidal properties and are used for skin diseases and infections. In former times, sufferers from YAWS would soak their feet in very hot water in which Hog Plum bush was steeped. Its close relatives are the JEW PLUM (*S. dulcis*) and Jamaican Plum (*S. purpurea*) which bears sweet yellow or purple fruit. Known by the TAINO (and today in the Spanish speaking islands) as *yobo*, the tree features in several legends and is used in Cuban witchcraft. (See also PLUMB POINT.)
[Adams 1972, Arrom 1990, Asprey and Thornton 1953-55, Cabrera 1982, DJE, Stevens-Arroyo 1988]

HOLLAND
SUGAR estate in ST ELIZABETH Parish that once belonged to John Gladstone, father of the British statesman William Gladstone (1808-98), four times prime minister of England. From humble beginnings in Liverpool, Gladstone Sr built a fortune from trade with the West Indies, America, and India. Holland Estate was established around the end of the 18th century; the factory was closed in 1982. The estate now belongs to J. Wray and Nephew, who cultivate canes here for their famous RUMS. The rows of BAMBOO trees through which the main road runs (BAMBOO AVENUE) were first planted as windbreaks.
[Cundall 1915]

HOLLYWELL
Site of a recreational park, part of the Blue and John Crow Mountains NATIONAL PARK, located

at 975m in ST ANDREW Parish. The park covers 120ha that includes scenic trails, picnic areas, and rustic cottages rented to vacationers by the Forestry Department. Hollywell lies in an area of frequent mists and vegetation here is well adapted to moisture. Tree FERNS and ginger lilies abound on the slopes.
[Eyre 1966]

HOLY TRINITY CATHEDRAL
The Cathedral of the Most Holy Trinity at North Street in downtown KINGSTON is the city's largest church and the mother church of the ROMAN CATHOLIC community. The cornerstone was laid in 1908 after the destruction in the 1907 EARTHQUAKE of the earlier Holy Trinity that had stood on the north western corner of Sutton Street and Duke Street. Shortly after the disaster, Colmar Estate, a property at the eastern end of North Street (then the city's northern boundary) was purchased for the erection of the new church. It adjoined Winchester Park, already the headquarters of the Jesuit community and including ST GEORGE'S COLLEGE. Holy Trinity was opened on 5 February 1911.

The striking Romanesque structure covers 1,115m² and remains one of city's most attractive buildings, with its large rose windows set in the massive walls of reinforced concrete that rise 26m from the ground to the summit of its copper-covered dome. The cathedral was designed by Raymond F. Almirall of New York and built by the Walker-Fyche Co of Montreal. The building, decorations and furnishings cost approximately US$150,000.
[Osborne 1988]

Holy Trinity exterior

Interior of Holy Trinity Cathedral

HOPE
Place name in ST ANDREW Parish that owes its origin to Major Richard Hope who first settled the area. He was one of the officers in the English army that took Jamaica in 1655 (see CAPTURE OF JAMAICA) and who were given land grants. Hope estate at one time extended from the hills at NEWCASTLE to the sea. At the foot of Elletson Road in KINGSTON a wharf was maintained for shipping the estate SUGAR. The estate ceased to cultivate sugar cane in the 1840s though cane was grown on the neighbouring Mona and Papine estates for much longer.

Hope was one of the most progressive estates in the island and Major Hope's descendants first used water from the HOPE RIVER to turn the estate mills, constructing the HOPE AQUEDUCT to conduct it. In 1766, Thomas Hope Elletson arranged for the city of Kingston to be supplied with water from his estate, and at his expense built a conduit into the town. In time the conduit went out of repair and the city council refused to accept responsibility for its maintenance. Meanwhile, Elletson had died and his widow married the Duke of Buckingham and Chandos. He had the concession cancelled and Kingston lost its first water supply. In the 1840s the Duke's son sold the city 253ha of the estate bordering the Hope River, from which Kingston's water supply was eventually drawn for a publicly owned system.
[Cundall 1915]

HOPE AQUEDUCT

The stone aqueduct that can still be seen at HOPE GARDENS, Mona Heights, and Mona Road, once supplied HOPE as well as Papine and Mona estates with water to turn their SUGAR mills. It was built in 1758 by descendants of Major Richard Hope.

Aqueduct, UWI campus

HOPE GARDENS

Popular name for The Royal Botanical Gardens Hope in ST ANDREW Parish. The site was formerly part of HOPE estate from which the government acquired 80ha in 1881 to establish an experimental garden. Among the attractions of the gardens are the ORCHID house and the PALM Avenue where can be seen cycads or Sago Palms that are among the oldest living trees. In 1953, to commemorate the visit of HM Queen Elizabeth II to Jamaica, the gardens were officially renamed The Royal Botanical Gardens.

Since its establishment, Hope Gardens and an adjacent small zoo have proved a durable attraction for Jamaicans in all walks of life, and Sundays and public holidays find them especially crowded, though their upkeep has been much neglected in recent years. An entertainment centre for children called Coconut Park, established to raise funds for the victims of a polio epidemic of 1952, was also located in the gardens but has disappeared. In recent years, a Plant Conservation Centre for Jamaica's rare and endangered FLORA has been established.
[Eyre 1966]

HOPE RIVER

Principal river of ST ANDREW Parish and a major source of the CORPORATE AREA'S water supply. The river takes its name from HOPE estate through which it once flowed. It rises in the hills above NEWCASTLE. Near BLUE MOUNTAIN Inn, it is joined by its most important tributary, the Mammee River, which rises near to Hardwar Gap. Hope River, like many others, has in recent years become increasingly dry, and can sometimes in its lower sections be seen as a mere trickle in its boulder-strewn bed. Nevertheless the river valley adds to the spectacular scenery of rural St Andrew which so many artists have captured on canvas. At the turn of the century Hope River became famed as the 'healing stream' of the prophet BEDWARD.

HOPE TAVERN

Village in St Andrew that is better known as 'Tavern'. Here was once located a famous tavern where travellers would leave their buggies and switch to horses for the climb to the hills. Most of the village is situated in an old bed of the HOPE RIVER, which has changed its course several times.

HORDLEY

Old estate in ST THOMAS Parish in the fertile PLANTAIN GARDEN RIVER valley; its mill like others in the valley was turned by a water wheel with water brought from the river by a series of canals. Lady Nugent favourably recorded a visit to this estate in her *Journal*; the present house dates from the mid-19th century. During the MORANT BAY REBELLION, the white residents of the estate were hidden by local blacks while the house was ransacked; the house was one of those depicted in the *Illustrated London News* with a report of the rebellion.

The estate was once owned by M.G. 'Monk' Lewis (1775-1818), an English writer and friend of the famous English poet, Lord Byron. Lewis was the author of once-popular works and a book on Jamaica (published after his death) entitled *Journal of a West India Proprietor* (1834). The book was a result of visits he made to Jamaica to inspect his estates at Hordley and Cornwall (WESTMORELAND Parish), which he had inherited. At Cornwall, he did much to ameliorate the conditions of his slaves. At Hordley, he said, he expected to find a perfect paradise, based on the reports he had been receiving. Instead, he found 'a perfect hell'. He tried to effect what changes he could in a one-week visit, especially among the slaves, leaving them in 'good humour', according to his account.

Lewis died from YELLOW FEVER on board the ship that was taking him back to England after his second visit to Jamaica and he was buried at sea. On hearing of his death, Byron penned the ditty:

> I would give many a sugar cane
> Mat Lewis were alive again.

A link between Lewis, Byron and the famous Disraeli family of England was provided by Lewis's Italian servant known as Tita, who accompanied him to Jamaica and was on board ship with him when he died. Tita, a Venetian whose real name was Giovanni Battista Falcieri, was, after Lewis's death, employed by Lord Byron. The poet is supposed to have died in Tita's arms at Missolonghi, Greece. Tita later served the family of Benjamin Disraeli, British prime minister, and ended his days as a well-known 'character' in England.
[Cundall 1915, Lewis 1834]

HORSE (*Equus caballus*)

COLUMBUS brought to Española (Hispaniola) on his second voyage in 1493 an animal that was to become one of the most significant agents of change in the New World. Spanish horses were regarded as particularly fine, and it was from the progeny of 25 Andalucian horses brought to the ANTILLES that many of the animals used in the conquest of the Americas came. In 1509 the first horses arrived in Jamaica with the settlers at Sevilla la Nueva (see SEVILLE, New), and soon began to populate the wild.

The settlers here, as on the other islands, developed huge ranches and from the horses and DONKEYS that were brought, also bred mules for export. It was horses from Jamaica that the Spanish *conquistadores* such as Cortez and Pizarro took to the mainland. The horse was regarded as an important element in the conquest: 'Horses are the most necessary things in the new country because they frighten the enemy most, and after God to them belongs the victory' said a *conquistador*.

At first the native peoples were afraid of

An early 16th century print of Spaniards using a winch to hoist horses aboard a ship for transport to the New World

Busha on horse

the horse, a fear encouraged by the Spaniards. The TAINOS, like the rest, had never seen such a creature before and LAS CASAS described the awe with which they greeted it, believing the animal to be divine; rider and horse fused into one grand creature. They also feared it fed on human flesh. The Spaniards promoted the idea of the horse's divinity as they moved through the Americas, in some cases secretly burying dead horses to hide the fact that they were mortal. But the native Americans soon discovered what kind of creature it was and, losing their fear, incorporated the horse into their own cultures, to the point where the Plains Indian on horseback became the archetypal symbol of North America and the *gaucho* of the South.

It is now believed that the horse in fact originated in the Americas, but became extinct during the Pleistocene Era, many thousands of years before Columbus sailed. But some of the original horses had crossed the Bering Strait and survived on the other side of the world, in Mongolia, from where they eventually spread throughout the so-called Old World before eventually returning to the New.
[Abbass 1986, Crosby 1972, Ranston 1993, Viola and Margolis 1991]

HORSE RACING

One of the most popular sports in Jamaica from the time it was introduced by the first English settlers in the mid-17th century. Off course and other forms of betting in modern times has sustained interest in the sport even among those who have never been to a race track, since betting shops exist in every corner of the island. While in the past there were several tracks, organized racing today takes place only at Caymanas Park near to KINGSTON.

When the English captured Jamaica from the Spaniards in 1655, there were so many wild horses that Admiral Goodson noted, 'we accounted them the very vermin of the country'. As horses thrived on the mainland, demand for those from the islands had declined. (See HORSE.) By 1545 shipments from Jamaica were almost at a standstill and from then on the horses ran wild.

Within two decades of English settlement, organized horse racing became so popular that in 1687 the governor dissolved the House of Assembly because one of the members protested against the Speaker's refusal to grant him permission to attend a race meet. The earliest races were held on the savanna west of SPANISH TOWN, then the capital. Soon, every PARISH had a racecourse, and when the races took place (at first once a year) there was a carnival atmosphere. An attraction of the races then as later was the turnout of women, dressed in their finery. The races continued over five or six days, and there were balls and DANCES every night for the fashionable crowds. The purses were usually a hundred pistoles or £100, raised by public subscription.

In Kingston, organized racing dates from the early 18th century; by 1783 a race course had been laid out to the north of the city. The first race at the KINGSTON RACE COURSE took place in 1816, run over 1.6km, for a maiden plate worth £100. From then on, racing was conducted every year without a break until the start of the Second WORLD WAR. In the old days at the Race Course, it is said that a mysterious 'Frenchwoman' occupied a house overlooking the course and greatly assisted bettors. A Frenchwoman in those days would probably have been a refugee from nearby Haiti (see FRENCH), many of whom were believed to be versed in vodun.

Early in the 20th century the major venue was moved from Kingston Race Course (now NATIONAL HEROES PARK) to Knutsford Park. The first race meet at Knutsford Park was held 26 December 1905, but racing continued at the Race Course venue for some time. Racing ceased at Knutsford Park in 1958 and found a new home in January 1959 at the modern racetrack at Caymanas Park. Knutsford Park was then turned into the commercial development of New Kingston.

Horse racing provided sport for the poor as well as the rich, and no fair or agricultural show was complete without a mule, horse, or DONKEY race. Until the widespread availability of motor transport, almost every adult male owned a horse, and there was always an element of friendly competition at social gatherings such as picnics. In the plantation era, the best jockeys were slaves. Polo was introduced in 1882 by BRITISH army officers. Estate owners had continuously imported stallions and mares to improve the stock, and English thoroughbreds were imported for racing (see e.g CARDIFF HALL). Large stud farms were developed, especially in ST ELIZABETH and ST ANN, during the 18th and 19th centuries. Jamaican horses were also exported to build up the racing stock of Central American countries.

Jamaican horses and racing personnel have continued to make their mark overseas. Jamaican horses and jockeys have twice won the Trinidad and Tobago Derby in recent years, while some jockeys and trainers have done well in the USA and Canada. Jamaican champion jockey George HoSang, for instance, was also National Champion Jockey in Canada, while Ralph Zaidie (who also kept goal for Jamaica at FOOTBALL) has been a successful trainer at Hialeah in Florida. He also had a horse in the 2000 Belmont Stakes in the USA, one of that country's Triple Crown series of races.

Popular interest in racing was stimulated by the fact that Jamaica was one of the few British countries that operated a sweepstake (a lottery based on the outcome of the races). These provided funds for the benefit of hospitals and for the development of racing. Until the 'sweeps' was discontinued, it was extremely popular and became incorporated into FOLKLORE, including a popular MENTO tune: 'Win the sweepstake/Win

M. LaYacona

Caymanas Park

New Kingston occupies the site of the former Knutsford Park racetrack

the sweepstake/Every murmur was "Do me Lord/make a me win the sweepstake".' Louise Bennett also has a poem called 'Sweepstake' in which the bettor resorts to OBEAH. (See NUNU BUSH.)

Because horse races are broadcast live on radio, the sport has had a profound impact on the popular imagination far beyond those directly involved. Chang and Chen have pointed out the way the broadcast of sport has influenced the popular MUSIC culture: 'In the old days there were only two stations and both carried live racing. Which meant no matter where you went, you were bound to hear it. This continual diet of excited "down the stretch" commentary has influenced DJ music extensively. It takes little imagination to see the inspiration of race announcers' breathless calls of close finishes in the rapid-fire speed-raps of deejays like Papa San.'

The racetrack has inspired numerous songs (including the popular mento tune 'Iron Bar' which was originally about a race horse called Barkwood, according to Olive Lewin) and the tradition has been continued by both male and female deejays (see DANCEHALL), using the racetrack metaphor for some sexually suggestive lyrics. The most enduring of the race track songs is 'Long Shot Kick the Bucket' by the Pioneers (1968). It celebrates a horse that was 'far from a champion' but caught the public imagination because of its endurance, becoming the oldest horse on the racetrack and running in 202 races, the most in local history, before dropping dead on the tracks.

[Chang and Chen 1998, Cundall 1915, Lewin 1998, Ranston 1993, Wright and White 1969]

HOSAY

Traditional annual festival (pronounced and sometimes spelled Hussay) brought to the CARIBBEAN in the 1840s by INDIAN indentured workers.

In Jamaica, Hosay used to be a common sight in large towns with sizeable Indian communities including KINGSTON, SPANISH TOWN, SAVANNA-LA-MAR, and in CLARENDON and ST MARY Parishes. In recent years, Hosay was being kept up only in Race Course and Kemps Hill, Clarendon. The procession in August attracts thousands of Indo-Jamaicans and non-Indians as observers along the route from Lionel Town to the banks of the RIO MINHO.

Hosay is the Caribbean variation of Moharram, an annual worldwide religious observance of Shi'a Muslims, who form a distinct minority community within Islam. During the Islamic month of Moharram, participants mourn the memory of the Prophet Mohammed's grandsons, Hosain and his brother Hasan, through self-flagellation, prayer, and other acts of piety. The celebrations centre on the elaborate BAMBOO and paper replica of the tomb of the slain brother Hosain that is called a Tazia or Tadjah and is built over nine days while mourning songs are sung. On the tenth day the Tazia is carried in procession through the streets and thrown into a river or the sea (or is buried in a hole in the ground when there is no access to water). The procession is led by drummers and dancers and includes stick-fighters and large crowds of worshippers.

In the Caribbean, while many of these features remain, Hosay has lost much of its religious significance. For one thing, in the New World – especially Trinidad, Jamaica, Suriname and Guyana, Hosay features the active participation of many different religious and ethnic groups other than Muslims, especially non-Indian CREOLES. (At the same time, it has been historically noted that non-Muslims were long-standing participants in Moharram, especially in areas in colonial British India from where indentured labourers were recruited for Caribbean estates.)

According to Mansingh and Mansingh: 'The process of creolization of Moharram started with a change in its nomenclature to Hosay the word which the creoles thought they heard repeatedly when the mourners loudly and repeatedly remembered the chief martyr Hosain.'

In the context of creole Jamaican society, Hosay's explicitly religious dimensions are not publicly visible, and to a large extent have gradually been abandoned. Nowadays, the few communities that still observe the event in rural Jamaica, may do so as a means of celebrating communal solidarity, proclaiming their ethnic identity in public, and affirming/remembering their ancestors' sacrifices in coming to labour on the SUGAR estates.

While the original dates follow the Islamic calendar and the festival is celebrated in the first 10 days of the lunar cycle in January-February, on Caribbean sugar plantations this coincided with the busiest period (see SEASONS). The Indians had to shift the celebration to August-September, the 'dead season' on the estates. In Jamaica the procession nowadays is held on the weekend closest to the sighting of the first new moon in the month of August.

A WESTMORELAND resident who witnessed Hosay processions as a young creole woman in the early years of the 20th century, was to recall that to her Hosay represented mystery, beauty and violence. Non-Indians, fascinated by the highly crafted Tazia, were often driven away forcefully by those in the procession. Looking or touching was forbidden, and dangerous. Fighting broke out not only from efforts to keep the ritual pure from the presence of infidels, but also from each believer's desire to be the first to launch his own shrine into the sea, an act which brings great blessing and good fortune. The police were always on alert during Hosay, and the Savanna-la-mar hospital usually admitted a number of wounded. The spectacle of the colourful 'little houses' bobbing out to sea lived on in the memories of many creole Jamaicans even when the meaning of the ceremony was unknown to them.

[Beckwith 1928, J. D'Costa, personal communication, Mansingh and Mansingh, 1995, 1999]

Tazia at Hosay in Clarendon, 1999

HUMMINGBIRD

Jamaica has three species of these beautiful BIRDS, which are found only in the New World. They are remarkable for their ability to remain stationary while on the wing or to fly backwards, their rapidly vibrating wings producing the humming sound.

The most spectacular of Jamaica's hummingbirds is the Streamer-tail (*Trochilus polytmus*), also known as Doctor Bird, Swallow-, Streamer- or Scissors-tail Hummingbird. Philip Henry Gosse, the 19th century English naturalist (see BLUEFIELDS), from his perch up in a CALABASH tree searching for ORCHIDS, described his first close encounter with this bird:

Doctor Bird (from Gosse)

'Several times it came close to me, as I sat motionless with delight, and holding my breath for fear of alarming it, and driving it away; it seemed almost worth a voyage across the sea to behold so radiant a creature in all the wildness of its native freedom.' Gosse rightly called it 'the gem of Jamaican Ornithology'.

The Doctor Bird is the national bird of Jamaica and found nowhere else in the world. Aside from the beautiful irridescent plumage that it shares with all hummingbirds, the mature male has two long tail feathers which stream behind him in flight, hence his various names. There are two forms, the black-billed that is confined to eastern PARISHES, and the red-billed that is widespread.

The other hummingbirds include the Vervain or Bee Hummingbird (*Mellisuga minima*) which is, next to the Cuban Calypte, the smallest

Mango Hummingbirds (from Gosse)

bird in the world. It is 5cm long and is sometimes mistaken for a moth, though it shares the pugnacious nature of all hummingbirds that in many Native American cultures are said to be the souls of dead warriors.

The third hummingbird was named the Mango Hummingbird (*Anthracothorax mango*) by Linnaeus though it occurs only in Jamaica and was here long before the MANGO was introduced. It is slightly larger than the Streamer-tail, about 13cm long, and appears almost black or a dusky purple all over, its beautiful iridescence showing up in bright sunlight.

Many explanations have been offered as to why these birds are locally called 'Doctor Bird'. One is their supposed resemblance to old-time doctors who dressed in black. Another is that the erect black crest and streamer-tail resemble the top hat and long tail coats that all doctors used to wear. Richard Allsopp in the *Dictionary of Caribbean English Usage* offers two other explanations for the folk-name Doctor-bird: 'from its habit of visiting from flower to flower probing with its long . . . beak, like a doctor calling on patients', and, 'due . . . to the long tail feathers suggesting a doctor's stethoscope'. The folk say it is because the birds 'medicine the plants', that is, they lance the flowers with their long, pointed bills (to extract nectar).

F.G. Cassidy in *Jamaica Talk* reminds us that 'doctor' is another name for the OBEAH-man and that the bird is an object of superstition. One folk song says, 'Doctor Bud a cunny bud, hard bud fe dead', i.e. it is a clever bird that cannot be easily killed.

The belief in the magical properties of the bird dates back to the TAINOS. They called it the 'God Bird' and believed it was the reincarnation of dead souls. It is still known by this name in Jamaica. Tyrrell and Tyrrell suggest that the concept of 'Doctor Bird' is connected with the bird's association with TOBACCO (see BIRDS IN FOLKLORE) and the Taino medicineman: 'Since the fragrant plant was their first and most important medicine, native healers relied upon its curative powers, and for this reason the hummingbird came to be associated with early medicine men, or "doctors", and earned the name "Doctor's Bird".'

[Cassidy 1971, DCEU, DJE, Gosse 1984, Jeffrey-Smith 1972, Taylor 1955, Tyrrell and Tyrrell 1990]

HURRICANE

Jamaica is in the path of the devastating tropical storms called hurricanes that cause untold

The eye of a hurricane heading for some of the Caribbean islands

damage when they make landfall, lesser damage, including wind damage, rainstorms, tidal waves or floods, when they pass nearby and, in times of drought, bring welcome rains when they pass at a safe distance.

The word hurricane comes from the TAINO *huracán*. Like other native peoples, the Tainos were great students of natural phenomena and their weather spirit GUABANCEX is portrayed with her hands positioned in the direction of the winds of the hurricane, which move counter-clockwise.

Up to the time of writing, Hurricane Gilbert in 1988 was the most costly storm of record, leaving 45 dead, one-third of the population in shelters and over US$7 billion in damage. A 1944 hurricane devastated the north and north east of the island, wiping out COCONUT and BANANA plantations in these areas and adding to food shortages caused by the Second WORLD WAR. Charlie scored a direct hit in 1951 and while Allen in 1980 passed north east of Jamaica, the island came under the influence of the circulation around the eye with resulting damage and loss of life.

These are storms within memory of Jamaicans still alive, and while the hurricane records of the Meteorological Office date only from 1871, our information on hurricanes goes back to 1559 when a hurricane did severe damage to SPANISH buildings in the island. Since then, hurricanes and accompanying tidal waves have wreaked havoc from time to time, especially on low-lying coastal towns such as PORT ROYAL and SAVANNA-LA-MAR.

Though it is foolhardy to believe that hurricanes confine themselves to rules, this reminder to prepare during the expected hurricane 'season' was once known throughout the West Indies, appearing in school books:

June – too soon
July – stand by
August – look out you must
September – remember
October – all over

The records show that direct hits to the island are seasonal, periods of active hurricane activity interspersed by periods when the island is spared. Between 1711 and 1786 Jamaica experienced 22 hurricanes, recording one every year between the six years 1780-86, these latter events leading to widespread starvation (see BREADFRUIT). Multiple hurricanes in one year are also not uncommon, as the following records show:

- 1784-85 – two hurricanes hitting Kingston, Port Royal and Spanish Town
- 1810 – two hurricanes in August and October
- 1830-32 – four hurricanes, two occurring in 1830 alone
- 1874-75 – two, in October 1874 and September 1875
- 1886 – two in August and September
- 1915 – three major hurricanes between August and September
- 1916 and 1917, two hurricanes each. (These wartime hurricanes bankrupted banana farmers in ST MARY and drove many from the land. In some places the only available food was CHOCHO.)

Names The practice of giving hurricanes names is fairly recent, though in some CARIBBEAN islands hurricanes were given the names of the Saints' days on which they occurred. Women's names for hurricanes were informally used before and during the Second World War, especially among weather forecasters who plotted the movements of storms. In 1953 the US Weather Service began using female names, a practice changed in 1978 when men's and women's names were included in the Eastern North Pacific storm lists and in 1979 in Atlantic and Gulf of Mexico lists.

Those involved with weather forecasting found the naming system much easier than the previous method of giving only LATITUDE AND LONGITUDE, especially when detailed storm information is being exchanged between hundreds of widely scattered stations, airports, coastal bases and ships at sea. Short, distinctive given names also reduce confusion when more than one storm is being tracked at the same time.

The National Hurricane Center near Miami, Florida, keeps watch on oceanic storm-breeding areas for tropical disturbances that might herald a hurricane. If a disturbance intensifies into a tropical storm – with rotary circulation and wind speeds above 39 miles (62.7km) per hour – the center will give the storm a name from one of six alphabetical lists. A separate list is used each year, beginning with the first name on the list. After all the lists have been used, they will be used again, e.g. the 1996 set repeated for storms in 2002. The letters Q, U, X, Y or Z are not used because of the scarcity of names beginning with those letters. In addition, the names of devastating landfalling storms are retired thereafter from the lists. The names, like hurricanes, are international. They are selected from library sources and the lists agreed upon by nations involved during international meetings of the World Meteorological Organization.

The resilience of Jamaicans as well as the ability to 'tek serious ting mek joke' is often brought out by hurricanes and other natural disasters. Hurricane Gilbert, the island's worst natural disaster of the 20th century, is a good case in point, as it inspired numerous hit songs, the most popular of which was 'Wild Gilbert' by Lloyd Lovindeer, a hugely comic version of the event:

> Dish take off like flying saucer
> Mi roof migrate without a visa . . .

[GOJ Office of Disaster Preparedness 1990, O'Gorman 1989, Stevens-Arroyo 1988]

IBO

AFRICANS from south eastern Nigeria (also spelled Eboe, Igbo) who were brought to Jamaica in large numbers during the entire period of the slave trade (see SLAVERY), with the heaviest importations in the period 1790-1807. Although the Ibo were an ethno-linguistic group, many other groups were subsumed under the term Ibo and some of these peoples, having come into contact with Ibo culture and traders, also spoke Ibo as a second language. Among such ethno-linguistic groups were Niger-Delta groups such as the Ibibio, Edo (Bini), Efik and Ijo or Ijaw, Kwa or Calabari, and semi-Bantu from Cameroon such as the Duala. Apart from Ibo, another umbrella term for these ethnic groups was Moco or Moko. (See MOCHO.)

From the way they are described in the historical literature, the Ibo were not popular with the planters. The fact that they had the greatest mortality rate on the MIDDLE PASSAGE combined with the bias in Jamaica towards Gold Coast slaves (see COROMANTEES) might have contributed to their negative image.

Ibo altar piece for the yam spirit

However, recent investigations into the diet of the slaves (e.g. by Kenneth Kiple) suggest that coming from a culture where YAM was the primary food, the Ibo had less protein in their diet than CORN eaters and were shorter (and perhaps not as hardy) as a result.

M.G. Lewis (see HORDLEY) at Cornwall, his WESTMORELAND estate, found that the Ibo, who formed a substantial minority, exhibited marked tribal solidarity and were organized around elected leaders. Like other Africans, the Ibo brought with them organization into secret societies and maskers who impersonated ancestors at the seasonal FESTIVALS, no doubt contributing one significant element to Jamaica's masquerade tradition. (See JONKONNU.) A major part of their celebrations occurred to mark the yam harvest. Special sacrifices to their main deity, Ala or Ani (Mother Earth: spirit of the earth and underworld) were offered at the time of planting, at first fruit and full harvest.

Some Ibo were dark-skinned but many were lighter in colour than other Africans; in New Orleans, G.W. Cable described them as 'so light-coloured that one could not tell them from mulattoes but for their national tattooing'. 'Redibo', in modern Jamaica, designates an African of reddish-yellow complexion and negroid hair, but has come to be a term of insult. A few Ibo legacies in the language are 'unu' (you, plural), ebolite (see STICK), and Eboe Drum, described as 'connected with sorcery'. The DJE also lists the word 'brechie' as 'a kind of Ibo mark denoting high rank'.

An Ibo, Olaudah Equiano, became one of the most famous Africans during the slave trade as he was able to buy his freedom and join the political movement to ban the trade. He also wrote his autobiography. Jamaica was one of the places he visited.

Olaudah Equiano

[Beckwith 1929, Cable quoted in Jackson 1967, DJE, Equiano 1789, Higman 1976, Kiple 1984, Lewis 1834, Long 1774, Parrinder 1961, Patterson 1973]

IGUANA

The Iguanidae subfamily of huge herbivorous LIZARDS includes only 31 species distributed throughout the American tropics. The Jamaican Iguana (*Cyclura collei*) occurs nowhere else in the world and its close relatives (of the genus *Cyclura*) are found only in the northern CARIBBEAN islands. With a body length reaching up to 150cm or more, the iguana is Jamaica's largest endemic reptile, yet it is on the verge of disappearing forever. Its near extinction was hastened by the introduction of the MONGOOSE which eats its eggs, but it has also suffered from the depredations of wild PIGS and the DOGS of hunters, and from more recent human encroachment on its habitat through housing developments and charcoal burning.

The Iguana's last refuges were on GOAT ISLANDS and HELLSHIRE HILLS, and even in these locations it was believed to have become extinct, with only two confirmed reports of sightings in the 20th century. The finding of a live Iguana by a hunter in 1990 spurred renewed hope for the animal's survival, and the Jamaican Iguana Research and Conservation Group was formed. Fieldwork by the group in the Hellshire Hills has confirmed that a small population does exist. Hatchlings of eggs taken from Hellshire have been successfully raised at the Hope Zoo and will be used as stock for captive breeding and for rereleasing into the wild. However, the scientists involved in the programme have warned that the survival of the Jamaican Iguana is still under severe threat, unless strong conservation measures are adopted and enforced.

Although most people have never seen an Iguana, it is a unique element in Jamaica's heritage and represents a significant link with the past. The place name LIGUANEA is believed to derive from 'iguana' which is an Amerindian name, from the ARAWAK *iwana*. Iguana was an important protein food for the TAINOS and the SPANISH settlers soon came to appreciate it, for like the MANATEE, iguana flesh was permitted on fast days to Catholics (see ROMAN CATHOLIC).

[Sauer 1966, Vogel 1994, Vogel and Kerr 1992, Vogel, Nelson and Kerr 1996]

Iguana

IMMACULATE CONCEPTION HIGH SCHOOL see CONSTANT SPRING

INDEPENDENCE DAY

The first Independence Day was celebrated on 6 August 1962 when Jamaica became an independent nation within the British Commonwealth. The most significant event of the celebrations took place at the newly built NATIONAL STADIUM at midnight on 5 August when the Union Jack, symbol of BRITISH rule for 307 years, was lowered and replaced by the black, green and gold flag of Jamaica. (See NATIONAL SYMBOLS.) Although some had feared that this day would begin an era of unrest and violence, the events of Independence went smoothly and well, with celebrations held in the bars of Gold Street – a popular working class hangout – as well as in the reception rooms of KING'S HOUSE.

Prime ministers in the first forty years of Independence. Top, L-R: Alexander Bustamante, Donald Sangster and Hugh Shearer. Below, L-R: Michael Manley, Edward Seaga and P.J. Patterson

Independence Day was at first celebrated on the first Monday in August each year, but with the re-introduction of EMANCIPATION DAY (1 August) the holiday has been fixed as 6 August. [Sealy 1982]

INDIAN

The adjective 'Indian' in Jamaica refers to (1) the aboriginal inhabitants, the TAINOS or ARAWAKS who were called Indians by COLUMBUS (and referred to in this book as Amerindians) and (2) the natives of India who first came as indentured workers in the 19th century and are referred to in the West Indies as 'East Indians'. Many compound words with 'Indian' refer to the former, e.g. Indian coney (CONEY), Indian kale (a leafy vegetable) and Indian shot (Canna). Native Americans appearing in the Wild West movies of Hollywood also influenced the development of characters called 'Wild Indians' among modern JONKONNU masquerades (though there is also an East Indian influence in characters in the sugar belt such as 'Babu'). Though many of Jamaica's plants came from India, the sub-continent is little referred to in the LANGUAGE; rather, the pejorative term 'coolie', applied to the Indian newcomers, appears in many compound words, e.g. 'Coolie Plum', 'Coolie royal', 'Coolie red', etc. This term seems not to have been applied in Jamaica to the CHINESE indentured labourers (who were also called 'coolies' elsewhere).

East Indians form the largest ethnic minority in Jamaica, representing 1.3 per cent of the population in 1991. Most of these Indians are descendants of 36,412 immigrants brought as indentured labourers for the SUGAR and other estates after the EMANCIPATION of the enslaved AFRICANS. (See SLAVERY, APPRENTICESHIP.) Indian immigration began in 1845 and continued until 1921. Later in the 20th century, another group of Indians arrived as independent immigrants, forming a part of the mercantile community. They are popularly referred to as 'Bombay merchants'. In recent years the Indian community has been enhanced by the presence of students and faculty from the other West Indian territories at the UNIVERSITY OF THE WEST INDIES.

Indentured Indians threshing rice

The workers were brought from India under an agreement or contract called an indenture, at the end of which they were promised repatriation to their homes. About one-third of them (12,109) chose to return home when their contracts expired. As the other post-Emancipation contract labourers, the Chinese, also discovered, working and other conditions were poor: they existed in a sort of semi-slavery, and the mortality rate in the early days was high. Unfamiliarity with Indian traditions led to their being branded as 'heathens'. Because of the relative smallness of their numbers in Jamaica and the imbalance in the sex ratio, it was difficult for the Indians to hold on to their cultural practices. Until 1959 every descendant of an indentured labourer from India was labelled an 'Immigrant' and had to obtain a certificate of 'no impediment' from the Protector of Immigrants before a legally valid marriage could be performed. Marriages performed according to Hindu and Muslim rites were not given legal status until 1957

Indian wedding ceremony in Jamaica with western adaptation (exchange of rings) (retroactive to 1954). As a result, many of the Indians converted to Christianity or undertook civil marriages.

The indentured workers came mainly from Uttar Predesh (UP) and Bihar provinces in northern India, the ratio of Hindus to Muslims being nine to one. Indians in Jamaica have continued to celebrate some of their traditional festivities, especially Diwali or Festival of Lights in November, Phagua or Holi, and HOSAY. People of Indian extraction are today most heavily concentrated in the old sugar parishes of WESTMORELAND, ST MARY, ST THOMAS and CLARENDON, as well as KINGSTON.

The Indian influence on the wider society can be seen in the widespread popularity of some Indian foods (curried GOAT is now a Jamaican speciality, and roti is growing in popularity). Indian jewellers, active in rural Jamaica, developed their skills into a cottage industry and encouraged a taste for jewellery among Jamaicans. Indians also introduced the growing of rice, and were once active in the growing and vending of fresh vegetables and flowers. Like other ethnic groups, Indo-Jamaicans have made their mark on every aspect of Jamaican life – 'cultural, professional, commercial, political, agricultural, sporting and spiritual', as a recent book by Mansingh and Mansingh expressed it, concluding: 'they have shown ingenuity in maintaining a distinct religious and/or cultural identity while merging their aspirations and future with the rest of their Jamaican compatriots.'

Indian elements have also been absorbed into folk consciousness, e.g. Indian spirits in KUMINA and the concept of 'coolie' DUPPY, the strongest spirit there is (though this might also have come about through the influence on OBEAH practitioners of Indian mystical writings via de Laurence publications). It is also believed that the cultivation of Indian hemp or marijuana for narcotic purposes was a habit brought by the indentured Indians. The local name GANJA is of Indian origin, as are several other names associated with the consumption of the 'weed'.

In 1983 a monument was unveiled at the Old Harbour Square to commemorate the arrival at OLD HARBOUR BAY of the first 261 Indians in 1845: 200 men, 28 women and 33 children who disembarked from the *Blundell Hunter* after a 17-week voyage from Calcutta. It was erected under the auspices of the Indo-Jamaican Cultural Society and the Jamaica National Trust Commission.

In 1995, the 150th anniversary of the arrival of Indians in Jamaica was celebrated in several parts of the island, with conferences, cultural programmes, and festivities culminating on 10 May with a staged re-enactment of the landing of the first indentured labourers at Old Harbour. The date has since been officially decreed Indian Heritage Day and is annually marked by a week of activities, including a festival and prayer services, produced by the National Council for Indian Culture in Jamaica, an umbrella organization comprising numerous Indian cultural groups.

[Cassidy 1971, CQ special issue 1995, DJE, Mansingh and Mansingh 1976, 1995, 1999, Parboosingh 1985, Shepherd 1985, 1994]

INSTITUTE OF JAMAICA

The Institute of Jamaica with headquarters in East Street, KINGSTON was founded in 1879 by the governor, Sir Anthony Musgrave 'for the encouragement of Literature, Science and Art' and was once the chief agency for the promotion and preservation of Jamaican

Institute of Jamaica

culture. The Institute comprises the National Library of Jamaica (formerly the West India Reference Library – WIRL) which has the largest collection of material relating to Jamaica and the West Indies in general; and a Natural History Division that includes museum, library, two field stations and plant and insect collections.

Also falling under the Institute's umbrella are Junior Centres, the AFRICAN CARIBBEAN INSTITUTE OF JAMAICA (ACIJ) and the Jamaica Memory Bank (JMB), a Museums Division, and Institute of Jamaica Publications which publishes the *Jamaica Journal*, a cultural periodical, as well as books and papers. The national collection of ART, formerly housed in the Institute headquarters, can now be seen at the National Gallery of Jamaica, located at the Roy West Building in the Kingston Mall.

IRISH

The 'Irish' element in Jamaican life is often remarked on by visitors who cite certain habits and attitudes: the love of storytelling and song, the rhythm of Jamaican speech, elements of folklore, the large numbers of Irish surnames and place names, including Irish Town in ST ANDREW Parish. And of course there is what Jamaicans call the 'Irish POTATO'. Joseph J. Williams, the ethnographer-priest who lived in Jamaica in the 1930s, even entitled a book, *Whence the 'Black Irish' of Jamaica?* The Irish element in other West Indian islands, especially Montserrat and Barbados, has also been noted. Many Irish were undoubtedly among the early West Indian settlers and some Irish families were landed proprietors, though the majority were bond servants, tradesmen, soldiers and – in later years – soldiers and policemen.

The English took Jamaica from the Spaniards in 1655 (see CAPTURE OF JAMAICA) shortly after Cromwell's forces had engaged in the conquest of Ireland (1641-52). This resulted in large-scale expulsion of the Irish, tens of thousands being shipped out to Barbados and the American colonies as bond servants. The English fleet that captured Jamaica stopped in Barbados for recruits, and many former bondsmen from that colony as well as the colonies of St Kitts, Nevis and Montserrat, joined them. Thus the Irish were among the soldiers who became the first settlers.

Soon, Irish women whose husbands had died in the wars, the destitute, and orphans, were shipped off to the new colony. Cromwell sanctioned the shipment to Jamaica of 1,000 boys and 1,000 girls under the age of 14 seized for that purpose by agents of the Bristol sugar planters. Hundreds of Irish men and women were transported to the island between 1671-75, carried on Bristol ships which called at southern

Shipload of emigrants to the New World

Ireland ports before sailing for the British West Indies. They were taken on board willingly or unwillingly, to be sold as bond servants.

Edward Long noted the prices paid to captains of ships that brought white servants from the British Isles in 1703: 'Every servant, English, Scotch, Welsh, or of Jersey, Guernsey, or Man: in time of war, £18; in time of peace £14; Irish servants, in time of war, £15; in time of peace, £12.' Long adds: 'The cause of this depreciation of the Irish I am not informed of; but possibly they were more turbulent, or less skilful in work than the others.' Scots were

The priest blesses Irish emigrants leaving home, 1851

regarded as more sober and industrious, the Irish as rebellious; after Cromwell's conquest of Ireland they were regarded as second class citizens. There was also religious discrimination: up to 1700 the majority of the Irish were ROMAN CATHOLICS (before the 1790s a banned religion in Jamaica as in England) and they were forced to renounce their religion.

Among the early laws of Jamaica were ones regulating the indentured white servants, who also included the Scots, especially those seized in rebellions against the English, as well as English men and women who happened to be poor, vagabonds or prisoners, and who were banished to the colonies for sale to the planters. Bond servants under 18 had to serve seven years, those over 18 four years, convicted felons for the time of their banishment. The laws regulated their clothing, diet and behaviour – a male servant who married without his master's consent had to serve two extra years. They had to obtain permission to leave their place of employment. Many failed to survive the harsh treatment, work regime and tropical climate. Some of the survivors remained as small settlers or traders, forming a category of 'poor whites'; others overcame their initial poverty and became landowners and merchants themselves. While the laws regulating indentured servants remained on the statute books, after a while the penal clauses ceased to be applied.

The Irish, like others from the British Isles, also contributed significantly to the class of tradesmen on the estates such as COOPERS, carpenters (see CABINET-MAKERS) and the like. These continued to come voluntarily as indentured servants, recruited by the planters as the plantation system expanded. Of course, some of the Irish landed families such as Sligo (see SLIGOVILLE) also owned Jamaican plantations and formed part of the island's elite.

The Irish had a significant influence on the early formation of Jamaican speech (see LANGUAGE). The incoming enslaved Africans spoke a multiplicity of languages and were forced to quickly forge some common speech on arrival on the plantations. As Cassidy and LePage (*Dictionary of Jamaican English*) explain: 'The main contact of the Negro slaves was with these indentured servants and poor whites, who acted as BOOK-KEEPERS and overseers on the plantations, rather than with the planters themselves.' Such contact helped to shape the pattern of CREOLE speech (and probably contributed to what some regard as an 'Irish lilt' in that speech). The early English speech was dominated by Western, Irish and Northern dialect speakers with, throughout the 18th century, a large proportion of Scots.

19th Century Immigrants A later group of Irish settlers came in the mid-19th century. With the abolition of SLAVERY, the House of Assembly offered a bounty for the importation of white immigrants (see GERMAN, PORTUGUESE, SCOTS) and several shiploads of Irish men and women arrived between 1835 and 1841. Many were located in ST ANN on the estates of Hamilton Brown, others in Leicesterfield in CLARENDON and Boroughbridge in St Ann. In March 1841, a group of 127 immigrants arrived, having sailed from Limerick amidst great controversy there, as John O'Connell, an MP and brother of the famous Home Rule agitator, denounced the emigration scheme as nothing but a system of white slavery. This led to strong public reaction in Limerick, and the ship had to be guarded while in the harbour. It nevertheless sailed, as did several other shiploads of migrants, those from the SS *Robert Kerr* landing in KINGSTON wearing their best clothes, some displaying 'temperance medals'. They were taken to Admiral's Pen (see ADMIRAL TOWN) where a special immigration depot was established to process them; at one point immigrants from five vessels were accommodated there.

One of the immigrants, Thomas Daly, wrote to his father informing him that 'within a week after our landing we were all employed at very high wages. In the next few days I am to enter the Police at a salary of £60 sterling. Norry [his wife] is to stop where she is, and is to get six shillings a week, her diet, and lodging for her services as cook and housekeeper and I will be permitted to live with her'. By 22 March, the governor could inform the British government that the immigrants who arrived on 8 March were all employed; 30 by Dr Hinton Spaulding on his Hermitage coffee estate, 12 by the SPANISH TOWN police, and 2 by a Kingston tailor, among others.

However, Irish immigration ceased at the end of the year, regarded as a failure by the immigrants and the authorities. While some of these newer immigrants were employed as skilled workers or by the local police, most were put to field work on SUGAR and COFFEE plantations. Finding this situation not to their liking, virtually all had left their employment. Many absconded and emigrated to other countries. Many died soon after arrival from epidemics including YELLOW FEVER. A report on the conditions of the immigrants in February of the following year stated that 'they are repeatedly intoxicated . . . drink excessively . . . are seen emerging from grog shops very dissolute and abandoned . . . and are of very intemperate habits.'

[Gleaner, 7, 11, 21 March 1841, 8 Feb 1842, Senior 1978, Williams 1932]

IRISH MOSS

Jelly-like preparation (sometimes called 'Irish mash') regarded as a particularly potent health food (see 'TONIC'), extracted from seaweed (*Gracilaria spp.*) that occurs in Jamaican waters. The seaweed is washed and dried and bleached for some time before it is boiled and strained. The resultant liquid is seasoned and sweetened and left to gel. The same seaweed is used elsewhere in the manufacture of agar-agar that has many commercial applications and is often part of the gel in which canned substances are packed. *Gracilaria* is one of nearly 300 species of seaweed found in Jamaican waters. What is called Irish Moss elsewhere is another seaweed, *Chondrus crispus*.

[Green 1968]

IRISH POTATO see POTATO

IRON BRIDGE

Historic structure spanning the RIO COBRE on the outskirts of SPANISH TOWN. No longer in use, the bridge is regarded as a national monument, sadly now in a very poor state of preservation. The bridge was erected in 1801 from cast-iron prefabricated segments shipped

The Iron Bridge by James Hakewill

from England. It is said to have been the first prefabricated cast iron bridge erected in the Americas, one of the earliest in the world, and is the only one surviving in the New World. It is also the only surviving iron bridge in the world using a construction technique called Burdon's Principle. The iron bridge was designed by Thomas Wilson, an English engineer, and cast by Walkers of Rotherham.
[Buisseret 1980b, Cundall 1915]

IRONSHORE
Place in ST JAMES Parish, formerly a large SUGAR plantation, now a resort development area outside of MONTEGO BAY. Ironshore was originally owned by a family named Lawrence, one of the landed families of English colonial times whose connection with the island lasted until 1910, when the last estate remaining in the Lawrence family (Fairfield) was sold. The original Lawrence came shortly after the English CAPTURE OF JAMAICA and soon acquired a great deal of land. His son, John Jr owned around 16,000ha and 23 plantations in the area and five of his six sons became estate proprietors.

Ironshore was one of the original Lawrence estates. It did not long remain in the family, in 1755 being exchanged for an estate in South Carolina, USA belonging to Dr James Irving, MD of Charleston whose family doings included duels and elopements. Dr Irving himself had a reputation as a duelist and one son died at age 20 in a duel. A daughter eloped with the owner of a small inland estate, the lovers being pursued by daddy armed with a couple of pistols. Dr Irving became a member of the House of Assembly and represented St James for eight years. In 1775 when he and his wife were sailing to England she died at sea. He had her body preserved in RUM (a common practice at the time) until he could reach England and have her buried at St Martin-in-the-Fields. Irving himself died in England two months later. Ironshore remained in the possession of an American branch of the Irving family until 1952.

The ruins of the Ironshore factory and the remains of the windmill that powered the factory before the advent of steam can still be seen.

It is believed that the son of the American traitor Benedict Arnold is buried on the Ironshore property, since the young Lieutenant Benedict Arnold died there in 1795. He was a volunteer in the 83rd Regiment and took part in engagements against the MAROONS.
[Shore and Stewart 1911, Wright and White 1969]

J

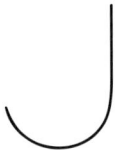

JACKASS see DONKEY

JACKASS CORN
Hard biscuit made of COCONUT, flour and sugar. Probably got its name because like the DONKEY or Jackass, it is tough and durable.

JACKASS IN FOLKLORE
An indication of the popularity of the DONKEY or Jackass is its prominence in Jamaican FOLKLORE: 'Jackass say world no level' (i.e. some people have a much harder time than others) is one much-quoted PROVERB. Another asserts: 'When Jackass carry salt, him lick the hamper', (i.e. tries to lighten his burden, or, takes advantage of a situation). Jackass is also featured in the well known song, 'Donkey want water' popularized by Harry Belafonte as 'Hol' im Joe'. Another 'jackass song' recorded by Charles Rampini (1873), and still well known is, 'Jackass wid him long tail/Bag a coco coming down'.

'Do Mr Parney Do' which was popularized by the singing group, the Frats Quintet, some years back, relates the hilarious misadventures of a man whose donkey gets loose:

> Up the hill and down the vale
> Mi donkey with the hamper
>   fe go mek a sale
> De hamper slack on the jackass back
> Down come *corpie to the attack.
>
> *policeman

An old version of the ANANSI STORY 'Anansi and Dryhead' explains certain physical characteristics of the jackass: because of his usual knavery, Anansi's tongue and ears suddenly grow to enormous length. Anansi then persuades Jackass to go to the river with him for a swim and suggests that they both take off their ears and tongues and leave them on the bank. Jackass agrees and Anansi persuades him to dive and show what a fine diver he is. Jackass does, and this gives Anansi the opportunity to make off with the shorter ears and tongue. When Jackass comes out of the water, he has to put on what is left behind. But Jackass is not really content with them, for every time he brays, he is calling out to Anansi to return his short ears and tongue. Perhaps in this lies the genesis of two other sayings: 'When you go to jackass house, don't talk bout aise' (ears) i.e. don't talk in people's hearing of the things they are sensitive about; and, 'Every time Jackass bray, him 'member something' i.e. he brays for a reason.

JACKASS ROPE
Type of crude TOBACCO once popular, especially among the peasantry. Dried tobacco leaves would be rolled together to form long ropes like those used to tie the DONKEY or Jackass, and

Jackass braying

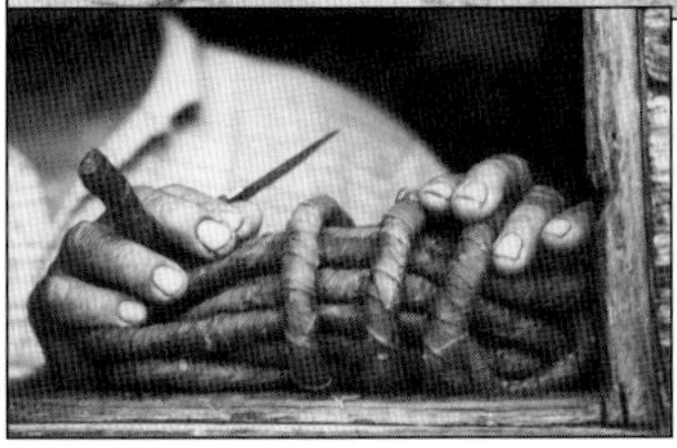

'Jackass rope' vendors early 20th century (above) and today

these would be coiled into large balls for transportation to market. There the tobacco would be cut into lengths for sale. The pungent-smelling Jackass Rope was cut finely with a very sharp knife and smoked in short clay pipes by both men and women. It can still be found in country markets.

Smoking tobacco in pipes has a long history in Jamaica, and was indulged in by both men and women. (See also COHOBA.) In PORT ROYAL in 1680 there was a pipe-maker, John Pope, who, according to Pawson and Buisseret, seems to have been the man behind the local industry of making pipes from the red clay found in the LIGUANEA Plain and around SPANISH TOWN. These locally made red pipes were reported as popular with the 'common women' of Port Royal whom a contemporary visitor observed, 'in their smockes ore linnen peticotes, bare-footed without shoes or stockins, with a straw hatt and a red tobacco pipe in their mouths'. They would 'trampouse about their streets in this their warlike posture, and thus arrayed will booze a cupp of punch cumly with anyone'.

In the plantation era, pipe smoking was popular among free people and slaves alike and large quantities of white kaolin clay pipes were imported. One observer noted that 'Negroes of both sexes regale themselves with smoking tobacco, the effect of which enables them to subsist a considerable time without food'. Pipes were sometimes imported and distributed by the planters. The scale of smoking can be gleaned from such imports of one estate, Roaring River in WESTMORELAND, belonging to William BECKFORD, whose slaves in 1807 were given 10 gross (1,440) 'Negro pipes'. This, as Barry Higman points out, worked out at approximately five per slave (though the cheap pipes were brittle and not very long lasting).
[Higman 1998, Pawson and Buisseret 1975]

JACKFRUIT (*Artocarpus heterophyllus*)
Large tree (up to 15m high), bearing on the trunk massive oval green-skinned fruits weighing as much as 13-18kg. The sweet ripe flesh surrounding the seed is eaten and relished, though some find the sweetish smell of Jackfruit overpowering. The seeds can be roasted and boiled and are said to taste like chestnuts.

Jackfruit originated in the forests of India and is a member of the fig family that includes the BREADFRUIT, which the Jackfruit resembles. The plant was first called by the Portuguese *Jaca* fruit, whence derives its present name. It was introduced into Jamaica in 1782, one of the

Jackfruit (top) with cut fruit (left), flesh and seeds (right)

plants captured from a FRENCH ship by Lord RODNEY's fleet.
[Adams 1972]

JAMAICA
Jamaica, like Cuba and Haiti, is one of the islands of the CARIBBEAN that has retained its original TAINO name. COLUMBUS on his first journey was told by the Amerindians of the island which he recorded as *Yamaye* in his log on Sunday 6 January 1493, the first written record of the place.

When the Spaniards claimed the island they named it Santiago, after St James, the patron saint of Spain. However, it soon reverted to a version of its aboriginal name Hamaika or Haymaica which the Spaniards wrote as Xaymaica or variants thereof. The Taino word is supposed to indicate an abundance of wood and springs, hence Jamaica is traditionally referred to as 'the land of springs' or, 'the land of wood and water'. (The name Santiago survives in ST JAGO, an early name for SPANISH TOWN.)

The spelling of 'Jamaica' was not standardized until well after the English period of settlement (see CAPTURE OF JAMAICA). Englishmen who wrote of the island from personal experience immediately after settlement, wrote the name variously as Gemecoe, Gemegoe, Jamico, Jammaca and Jamecah.

Jamaica, which has a total area of 10,991km^2, is the largest island of the English-speaking

Caribbean. In the Caribbean Sea, it is positioned at around 18 degrees N and 77 degrees W, inside the arc formed by the islands of the Greater and Lesser ANTILLES. Its nearest neighbours are Cuba, approximately 145km to the N, and Haiti, 161km to the E. The nearest part of the American continent is the MISKITO coast of Honduras, 499km to the SW. (See also GEOLOGY, FAUNA.) The islands of the Lesser Antilles and Trinidad with which Jamaica has strong historical, cultural and trade links, lie 1,609km to the E and SE.
[Fuson 1987, GOJ STATIN 1999a, Morales Padron 1952]

JAMAICA ALPHABET see ALPHABET, Jamaica

JAMAICA COLLEGE see DRAX HALL

JAMAICA CULTURAL DEVELOPMENT COMMISSION see FESTIVAL, Jamaica

JAMAICA HOUSE
Built shortly after INDEPENDENCE as the official residence of the prime minister, Jamaica House is now used as the prime minister's offices. It is located on Hope Road, KINGSTON, next to another public building, KING'S HOUSE.

Jamaica House

JAMAICA LIBRARY SERVICE see LIBRARIES

JAMAICA MILITARY BAND
The Jamaica Military Band is a national institution, playing on nearly all ceremonial occasions, and at different venues all over the island. They have also undertaken foreign tours, their repertoire ranging from symphonies to folk music to jazz. The band is attached to the

Jamaica Military Band (in Zouave uniform) playing for Sir Winston Churchill, on his visit to Jamaica in 1953

Jamaica Defence Force, the colourful Zouave uniform band members wear the only reminder of their connection to the historic WEST INDIA REGIMENT that was disbanded in 1927. Twenty-four bandsmen from that regiment were selected to play for the Prince of Wales when he visited the island that year and they formed the nucleus of what became the Jamaica Military Band. The band at first operated on a semi-military basis; it was given full civilian status in 1959, under the Ministry of Home Affairs, and in 1962 became part of the JDF.

The band was allowed by the imperial government to retain the Zouave uniform of the West India Regiment. The original Zouaves were a French colonial troop whose uniform caught Queen Victoria's eye, and she gave orders for its introduction into the British imperial regiments. The West India Regiment was the only regular British colonial regiment in existence at the time, so the Zouave full dress uniform was allotted to the Second Battalion in 1856.
[Cundall 1915]

JAMAICA NATIONAL HERITAGE TRUST
The JNHT is a statutory body falling under the Ministry of Education and Culture. It is responsible for the preservation and development of Jamaica's material cultural heritage. This includes all national heritage sites and monuments, which in April 2000 numbered over 300. First established in 1958 as the Jamaica National Trust Commission, the name was changed in 1985 under a new law that broadened its functions and gave it more power.

The Trust has taken over some of the

responsibilities previously falling under the INSTITUTE OF JAMAICA, including archaeology. The Archaeological Division is responsible for maintaining inventories of sites and artefacts with local and international institutions, formalizing standard agreements and regulating archaeological research in Jamaica. Over two million pieces of material have so far been recovered from several excavations. The division is located in PORT ROYAL, one of the richest archaeological sites in the western hemisphere and the most intensely excavated Jamaican site.

The Trust undertakes public education in schools and communities and has started a Heritage Register, with information on architectural sites and artefacts in Jamaica that will be made accessible to the public. Sections of the following towns have been designated Protected National Heritage: SPANISH TOWN, FALMOUTH, BLACK RIVER, PORT ANTONIO and Port Royal.

Despite these efforts, there is as yet little public consciousness of the need to preserve Jamaica's heritage – material as well as natural. Sections of many other historic towns are not yet protected, neither under a law, nor through community action. Some of the best architectural and streetscape features continue to be destroyed through unguided development, improper modification, demolition and decay, and historically important national sites are lost every year. The Trust also has to deal with the problem of theft of priceless artefacts. Not even cannon are secure; thieves tried to steal two from the Maima Seville heritage site. They had actually put the cannon into their van when they were stopped by the St Ann's Bay police.

JAMAICA WELFARE

Founded in 1937, Jamaica Welfare Ltd marked the first large-scale effort at organized social welfare in Jamaica, with emphasis on the rural poor. It developed by trial and error a community development model that came to be studied by other countries and laid the groundwork for subsequent social development programmes in Jamaica.

Jamaica Welfare was begun by Norman Washington MANLEY who also served as the first chairman. Manley had been acting as the lawyer for the Jamaica Banana Producers' Association, the growers' cooperative formed to challenge the large fruit companies that had a virtual monopoly on the marketing of bananas (see BANANA TRADE) to the detriment of the small growers. Manley's meeting with Samuel Zemurray, president of United Fruit Company, resulted in Zemurray's offer of one cent per stem of banana exported from Jamaica by United Fruit, 'to form a fund to be administered by an organization to be created . . . for the good and welfare of the people of Jamaica, with emphasis on the rural people'. This was at the height of the banana export trade and initially amounted to US$250,000 annually.

Jamaica Welfare was registered on 7 June 1937 and developed a motivated staff attracted by the idea of nation building. Much of the work was initially undertaken through community centres and cooperatives. The staff later pioneered the notion of 'community development' whereby rural Jamaicans were encouraged to themselves improve their quality of life. This involved many programmes and techniques with emphasis on savings and money management, development of cottage industries and crafts, literacy, better agricultural practices, health and sanitation, and better nutrition in the homes through a ThreeF campaign (Food for Family Fitness). Modern means of communications including a film unit and magazines and print material were also employed. The training of social workers and community leaders was an outgrowth of the programme.

When the Second WORLD WAR interrupted banana exports, the income from United Fruit dried up, but the organization was maintained by a grant from the British government in recognition of its work. After 1949, the company's work was carried on through a Statutory Board established by the government, the Jamaica Social Welfare Commission. It was succeeded by the Social Development Commission.

[Girvan 1993, Hart 1993]

JAMAICAN FOLK SINGERS

Founded in 1967 by Dr Olive Lewin, the Jamaican Folk Singers are among Jamaica's best-known cultural ambassadors, having performed to enthusiastic audiences in many countries in North and South America, the CARIBBEAN, Europe, and South Africa. In 1972 the group won gold medals at the International Festival of Folklore and Art in Mexico, and the coveted OAS Award from among 62 competitors in the world famous International Festival of Folklore in Argentina. In 1997, the group participated in the 9th International Eisteddfod of South Africa in Roodeport, Greater Johannesburg, and was awarded four gold medals for its performance

Olive Lewin (left) founder and leader, Jamaican Folk Singers

and promotion of peace through music.

The founder is a highly accomplished classical musician, who has collected and arranged many beautiful old songs once in danger of being lost. (See MUSIC and MUSIC, Folk.) In the process, the group's distinct sound has helped to create an appreciation of the aesthetic qualities of folk music, discovering the 'intuitive genius' of such music and putting it on the concert stage, according to Pamela O'Gorman. O'Gorman has noted that the presentation of the Jamaican Folk Singers 'is distinguished by finesse, precision and control. The voices are perfectly matched, without a hint of harshness. The pitching is accurate and the melodic line is delivered with a clean legato, consummately phrased to bring out every nuance and cadence. It is this tendency to move the music somewhat from its original function and to seek out its intrinsic beauty that dominates Lewin's approach'.

The group is interested not only in performance but in ongoing research into the music and those who create and maintain it, and their work is also concerned with providing a bridge between the old and the young. Thus the Singers perform items that portray various aspects of Jamaican life, including play, work, worship and celebrations. They stage an annual folk fair, called Pepperpot, and are involved in charity work in hospitals, schools, prisons, and with the aged, and provide leadership and training at many levels.

The group's over 30 members from various callings and backgrounds are all volunteers.
[O'Gorman 1987]

JAMMA SONG

Folk song, sung as an accompaniment to communal field labour (see DAY WORK) and other kinds of heavy work, also to accompany dancing and games at WAKES. The singing is led by a 'bomma' or 'singerman', the chorus sung by the workers to the rhythm of their labour. The words are usually topical, some composed on the spot. (See MUSIC, Folk.)

JANGGA

A freshwater crayfish (*Macrobrachium sp.*) of which there are several species in Jamaica. The much prized Jangga (or Jonga) is found mainly in mountain streams where it hides under rocks and comes out only at night, hence it is difficult to catch. The live crayfish is grey or black but turns bright red when cooked. A smaller version caught in the MIDDLE QUARTERS area, ST ELIZABETH Parish, is sold by roadside vendors as 'pepper shrimp'. The word 'jangga' is a West African one (Ashanti/Akan).
[DJE]

JAWBONE

Musical percussion instrument of former times, created by smoking a horse's jawbone to dry it until the teeth were loose, and passing a stick across it to produce a rattling sound. A player is depicted in Isaac Mendes Belisario's 19th century illustration of 'Jawbone John Canoe'. Jawbone is a symbol of the improvisations practised by Africans in the New World, no doubt related to the 'rattler' or 'rakler', the player accompanying the drummer in JONKONNU who runs a stick across a notched piece of wood, or the 'rackling man' in KUMINA who plays the 'cattatik'. (See CATTA STICK, MUSICAL INSTRUMENTS.) 'Jawbone' is also applied by the MAROONS to a ritual song style.
[Agorsah 1994, Beckwith 1929, Belisario 1837, Lewin 2000, Whylie and Warner-Lewis 1994]

Jawbone player (in Belisario painting of Jonkonnu)

JELLYFISH (*Medusae*)

Sea creature that is so-called because it has a soft jelly-like body; in Jamaica popularly called 'Bladder' or 'Sea-bladder'. There are many species, varying greatly in size and colour, the best known perhaps being the Portuguese Man of War (*Physalia pelagica*). It is often seen in coastal waters of Jamaica in large floating colonies composed of individuals that coordinate functions and activities. Other popular Jellyfish in local waters are the luminescent Aurelia or Moon Jelly, the Comb Jelly (*Ctenophores*) which is both luminescent and iridescent in the daytime, the Fire Horse and Puss Bladder, both *Cyanea* species.

The Jellyfish are not fish at all but belong to the family Medusae. They are abundant in warm waters, floating at or near the surface of the sea either singly or in schools. They move by rhythmic contraction of their bodies but are largely at the mercy of waves, so are often cast up on beaches. When seen alive in the water, they are quite beautiful, though their trailing tentacles can inflict painful or even fatal stings. The bowl-like body, called an 'umbrella', is both stomach and swimming apparatus and helps to keep it near the surface of the sea. The animal lives on small invertebrates that it seizes and paralyses.

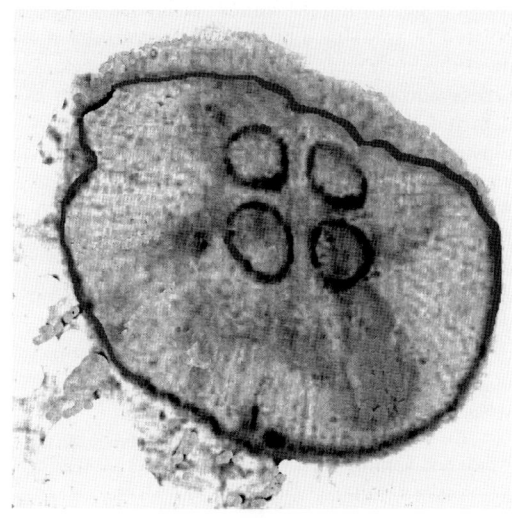

[DJE, NHSJ 1946]

Jellyfish

Jerking today

JERK

Term now widely applied to a type of seasoning or marinade for meats, perhaps Jamaica's major contribution to international cuisine. The term was originally applied only to JERK PORK originating with the MAROONS utilizing wild PIGS caught in the mountains. For a long time jerk pork was available to the general public only at one or two places, most notably BOSTON BEACH. From the 1960s, 'jerk pork', using domestic pig, began to be widely available throughout the island and the seasoning and cooking technique of 'jerking' applied to chicken and other meats.

Nowadays, chicken with 'jerk seasoning' grilled at roadside barbecues made of oil drums cut in half is a popular 'fast food' – like the widespread vending of COCONUT water, a sign of indigenous entrepreneurship. Throughout urban KINGSTON and in country towns and villages, the tantalizing aroma of 'jerking' heralds the night, for that is the time of the roadside jerk specialists. Increasingly the term 'drum chicken' is replacing the older term. In a way, the technique of present-day jerking has reverted to the original practice of grilling meat on a raised platform over hot coals – hence the TAINO term *barbacoa* from which the word and practice 'barbecue' derives.

Though jerk seasoning was for a long time a closely guarded secret, it is now on its way to becoming a new flavour in the international marketplace, and various types – wet or dry – can be purchased in large supermarkets and ethnic markets in many parts of North America and Europe. The special flavour of jerk seasoning arises from the combination of PIMENTO with other spices and seasonings.

JERK PORK

Originally, wild PIG seasoned and cooked the way of the MAROONS. The word 'jerk' is from *charqui* that derives from the Quechua language of the Incas of Peru. It means to preserve pork or beef by cutting it into strips and drying it in the sun. Hence 'jerky' is a name used for dried beef throughout the Americas, and among seamen. Sometimes meat or fish was jerked by placing it on long raised wooden racks over hot coals. The contraption itself was called by the Spaniards *barbacoa*, from the TAINO word, and from which comes the English 'barbecue'. Jerking in Jamaica for a long time continued to refer to the practice of smoking or drying meat to preserve it.

The runaway Africans called Maroons probably learnt these methods of curing meat from the Tainos, but soon developed their own techniques of seasoning and cooking (see JERK). Jamaica's mountainous interior was overrun with pigs from those first introduced by the Spaniards, but for people engaged in constant guerrilla warfare, some method had to be found to preserve the meat the hunters brought in. Jerking served the purpose.

Hans Sloane, who visited Jamaica in the late 17th century, noted 'Swine . . . running wild . . . shot or pierced through with lances, cut open, the Bones taken out, and the Flesh is gash'd on the inside into the Skin, fill'd with Salt and expos'd to the Sun, which is call'd Jirking'. R.C. Dallas in his *History of the Maroons* later described jerking as 'cutting or scoring internally the flesh of the wild hog, which is then smoked'.

Jerky was originally made with or without SALT, which, in earlier times, was a scarce commodity. For the Maroons, salt was also scarce, and they found other means of making the meat savoury, utilizing herbs and spices from the forests around them, developing a unique flavour using hot peppers and PIMENTO leaves

Amerindian barbecue, 16th century (from Drake)

and pimento wood for the fires. The preparation and cooking of the pig seemed to have moved away from the simple 'jerky' to something more complicated and infinitely more flavourful, becoming highly regarded as a culinary treat in the wider community. After the peace treaties, the selling of jerk pork in the MARKETS became a means of livelihood for the Maroons, and it was consumed even by high society – or perhaps they were the ones able to afford it.

M.G. Lewis, a visiting plantation owner (see HORDLEY), mentioned jerk pork as a speciality at the table and Lady Nugent (1802) described a dinner in ST THOMAS Parish where the first course consisted 'entirely of fish, excepting jerked hog, in the centre, which is the way of dressing it by the Maroons'. Naturalist P.H. Gosse who lived in Jamaica 1844-5, described an itinerant Maroon jerk pork vendor who sold it 'in measured slices to ready customers, as an especial delicacy for the breakfast table'.

Different methods of making jerk pork developed. Lewis described one method – cooking the meat in a covered pit. The dressed hog is seasoned inside and out, wrapped in green pimento leaves for flavour, then in green BANANA leaves. It is then placed in a cooking pit lined with stones in which a fire has been allowed to blaze and burn out, leaving hot coals and rocks. The pig is covered with more hot coals then the entire pit itself is covered. The pork would be ready in 6-8 hours.

When Zora Neale Hurston went on a wild pig hunt with the Maroons of ACCOMPONG in the 1930s, she described how the hunters built a fire and put the whole pig covered in green bush over it to 'sweat it', so that the hair could be removed. Taking it off the fire, they scraped the pig, washed it clean, and gutted it. All the bones were removed, seasoned, and dried over a fire. The meat was seasoned with salt, pepper, and spices and put over the fire to cook. The big hog took nearly all night and had to be turned by two men. The cured meat and bones were carried home. Hurston concluded: 'It is hard to imagine anything better than pork the way the Maroons jerk it.'

From the historical literature, then, there seems to have been two different methods called jerking. Either cooking the meat on a wooden grill or cooking the pig in a covered pit, both of Amerindian origin and both still utilized today, though very little hunting takes place and domestic pigs are used. The wooden grill or framework is called a 'patta' or a 'caban', the wood being specially selected to impart flavour.

Nowadays, what is popularly called jerk is closer to barbecuing – or 'drum' cooking – the name jerk describing the pimento-based seasoning used on pork, fish or chicken.

[Dallas 1803, DJE, Gosse 1984, Hurston 1938, Lewis 1834, Nugent 1839, Sloane 1707,1725, Thomas 1890]

JEW PLUM (*Spondias dulcis*)

Also called June Plum, though it appears at the end of the year, this is the island's largest plum. It has an acid flesh surrounding a spiny, fibrous seed. The size and shape of a large egg, the plum is greenish yellow when ripe and can be eaten raw. The seed softens when the plum is stewed to make a favourite dessert. It is related to two other popular plums – HOG PLUM and Jamaican plum. A native of the South Pacific now found generally throughout the tropics, Jew Plum was introduced into Jamaica in the late 18th century. This often large tree (6-20m high) which is sometimes cultivated in gardens, grows from sea level to about 600m.

[Adams 1972]

JEWS

The first persons in Jamaica believed to be of the Jewish faith came from Spain and Portugal during the SPANISH period of Jamaica's history (1494-1655). They were seeking a refuge following their expulsion from Spain by the Catholic monarchs Ferdinand and Isabella in March 1492 (only ten weeks before COLUMBUS landed in the New World).

Jews were not officially allowed in the Spanish New World colonies, but some are believed to have come to Jamaica with Spanish settlers from the earliest days of colonization by Esquivel, beginning in 1509. Because Jamaica was under the jurisdiction of the Columbus family and not of the Spanish Crown, the Spanish Inquisition was excluded and Jews lived in comparative safety, but there was nevertheless the constant fear of exposure, since the Inquisition was active on the other islands and in South America. To conceal their identities, the Jews assumed different names and called themselves 'Portugals' (as many were Portuguese). They were also known as 'Marranos', that is, Jews who had converted to Catholicism, as many had done, but who continued to practice their own religion in secret.

Tired of religious intolerance, the Jews actively helped the BRITISH fleet that landed in 1655. (See CAPTURE OF JAMAICA.) A Marrano pilot, Capt Campoe Sabbatha guided the English fleet into the harbour, and another Marrano, Don Acosta, was one of five commissioners who negotiated the terms of surrender by the Spaniards.

The Jews were allowed to remain after the conquest and began to practice their religion openly. British citizenship granted them by Oliver Cromwell was confirmed by the Windsor Declaration of 1661 that made them, like other Jamaican residents, 'full citizens of Britain'. The fact that they could own land attracted Jewish settlers of Spanish and Portuguese origin, and their numbers increased. Some were in the retail trade but many became wholesale merchants, with strong trade contacts with Spanish, Dutch, and British America.

The Jews who first came to Jamaica were exclusively Sephardi (of Spanish, Portuguese or North African descent) arriving from Brazil, Holland, England, Guyana and Surinam, among other places. After the 1770s, Ashkenazi Jews (those of Germany and Eastern Europe) also started to arrive. Although at first they maintained separate places of worship, in later years the Ashkenazim and Sephardim were united in one congregation (see JEWISH SYNAGOGUE). Immigration of Jews ceased or diminished from the early 19th century until the late 19th and early 20th centuries, when some new migrants came from Syria, Egypt and elsewhere in the Middle East (see LEBANESE).

Despite their freedom to worship openly and erect synagogues in Jamaica, Jews were nevertheless subject to discriminatory legislation, and their securing of full civil rights came after long agitation on their part. Until then, they were disbarred from public office, could not vote, serve on juries or purchase white servants. (See IRISH, SCOTS.) Jamaican Jews attained full political rights in 1831, the first British subjects of their faith to do so, 27 years before the same rights were granted in England.

Despite the constraints, their influence on the financial, economic, artistic and social development of Jamaica has always been disproportionate to their numbers. In the mid-19th century, the House of Assembly became probably the world's first legislative body to adjourn for the Jewish high holiday of Yom Kippur. This occurred in 1849 when 8 of the Assembly's 47 members, including the Speaker, were Jewish. In 1865 when the constitution was abolished after the MORANT BAY REBELLION, there were 13 Jewish members.

Jamaica's Jewish population, never large, was approximately 1,000 persons before massive emigration in the 1970s. Now their number is approximately 200. With their long history of freedom and, in later years, almost complete isolation from other Jewish communities, Jamaican Jews have become almost completely assimilated. Among the younger generations, there has been a great deal of marriage to Christian Jamaicans who have not converted to Judaism.

[Andrade 1941, Bisnauth 1989, Holzberg 1987, Scott 1981, Wright and White 1969]

JEWISH SYNAGOGUE (United Congregation of Israelites)

The synagogue 'Shaangare Shalom' – Gates of Peace – at the corner of Duke and Charles Streets in downtown KINGSTON is now the only Jewish place of worship in Jamaica. It was built in 1912 and replaced an earlier brick building dating from 1881 that was destroyed in the 1907 EARTHQUAKE. The roof, gallery and pillars of the original structure were reused in the new synagogue, which was built in reinforced concrete but followed the style of the old.

A feature of the synagogue is the floor covered with sand, a tradition of Sephardi synagogues in destinations of the Marranos. These were Spanish and Portuguese Jews forcibly converted to Christianity but secretly adhering to Judaism, who fled Spanish oppression in the 15th and 16th centuries (see JEWS). Synagogues having sanded floors include those in Amsterdam, Curacao and, until recently, one in Rhode Island, USA.

There were originally two Jewish congregations in Kingston, the Sephardim and the Ashkenazim, representing Jews of Mediterranean and Middle European origins, respectively, but they united in 1883. The synagogue was built through the combined efforts of some of the members of the two congregations, and complete amalgamation took place in 1921. Inside the synagogue, on either side of the Ark, two lights burn perpetually, symbolizing the unity here of the two congregations. The Hechal (Ark) and the Tebah (reader's platform) are in polished MAHOGANY. The Ark contains 13 scrolls of the Law from former synagogues throughout Jamaica, some of them over 200 years old.

Jamaica's first synagogue was built in PORT ROYAL 16 years before the great earthquake of 1692, probably the third oldest in the New World after those of Salvador Bahia (Brazil) and Bridgetown (Barbados), and was in a part of the town that fell into the sea. There were also at various times synagogues in SPANISH TOWN, MONTEGO BAY, and other parts of Jamaica. The

Interior (above) and facade of Jewish synagogue

old Jewish cemetery at Hunts Bay (Hunts Bay Road, Kingston) is the oldest burial ground in Jamaica. It was begun in the late 1660s, and the oldest grave there is dated 1672. Most of those buried at Hunts Bay were brought by boat from Port Royal, where the first Jewish cemetery was located.

Another old Jewish cemetery is at Elletson Road, near Windward Road. Among those buried there is Meyer Lyon (Leoni). According to J.A.P.M. Andrade, Leoni is the arranger of a piece of music that united Christians and Jews in a unique way. He was Cantor in London's Great Ashkenazi Synagogue and a singer at Covent Garden operas in the 17th century. He adapted a Slavic melody to the ancient Hebrew hymn text 'Yigdal' which is a standard in most Ashkenazi synagogues. A Methodist minister, Thomas Olivers, heard Leoni chant the Yigdal and was so moved that he asked him to write down the music. To this music Olivers wrote the hymn, 'The God of Abraham praise', which was to become a standard in many Christian churches. Leoni came to Jamaica in 1789 and became the first Cantor in the newly organized synagogue, then located at the corner of Barry and Orange Streets in Kingston.

[Andrade 1941, JJ 18:4 (back cover) 1985]

JIGGER see CHIGGER

JOHN CROW (*Cathartes aura*)
Jamaica's scavenger bird, also known as Turkey Vulture, Carrion Crow, Buzzard or Vulture, occurs throughout most of the Western Hemisphere. The bird has jet black plumage except for the featherless neck and head, which are a bright crimson. Awkward on the ground, it is most graceful in flight and can glide along for hours at a time. It is the highest flying Jamaican bird and has excellent eyesight, spying food on the ground from extremely high altitudes. It is a large bird, about 76cm long.

John Crow

The John Crow is seen virtually everywhere in Jamaica though it is reported to be far less common than it used to be. For its usefulness in eating carrion, it has been a protected bird from the earliest days of settlement. Not surprisingly, it is the subject of many folk songs (see MUSIC, Folk), sayings and tales (see PROVERBS). 'John crow seh him caan wuk pon Sunday', is a well known folk song. 'John Crow will never make house till rain come', 'John Crow seh him is dandy man when him have so-so feather', and 'Every John crow think him pickni white' are proverbial sayings. The latter arises from the fact that the newborn bird is covered with white feathers. The observation 'When John Crow see mauger cow, him roas' plantain fe him', suggests that death is imminent, and indeed, the John Crow in Jamaica as elsewhere is regarded as an omen of death, especially if one perches on the housetop (see DEATH RITUALS).

Opete, the Twi name for a carrion-feeder survived among the Ashanti in Jamaica as 'appetti', the word for a CHARM. The name harks back to the sacred function of the vulture in Africa, the bird being perceived as a messenger taking sacrifices to the gods, a role played by similar avian death symbols in other cultures. The name and sacred functions of the bird have been preserved among the MAROONS of Surinam, and Herskovits has suggested that the generalized feeling that the vulture is sacred has been carried over among West Indian blacks, who will refrain from killing or molesting it.

John Crow was originally called 'carrion crow' in Jamaica (and the John Crow Mountains first known as Carrion Crow Ridge). The name 'John Crow' was first recorded in Jamaica in 1826. F.G. Cassidy suggests that folk pronunciation reduced 'carrion crow' or 'cyancro' to 'John Crow' or 'jankro', as it is commonly pronounced. The DJE also suggests that the term 'John Crow' may have been influenced by a Ewe word *dong-gró* referring to a type of bird. Other etymologies have been suggested, including one that an Irish clergyman at PORT ROYAL named John Crow (1689) was very unpopular. The crow's black plumage and red head reminded the populace of this man and so they named the bird after him.
[Cassidy 1971, DF, DJE, Herskovits 1936, Rashford 1984]

JOHN CROW BEAD (*Abrus precatorius*)
Native pea of tropical Asia and now widespread throughout the tropics, also known as Rosary Pea, Wild Liquorice, Red Bean Vine or Crab Eye. The inconspicuous twining vine found in waste places bears leguminous pods containing shiny red seeds with a black spot, and is regarded as one of Jamaica's most poisonous plants. C.D. Adams in *The Blue Mahoe and Other Bush* notes that the seeds contain 'a protein poison which acts only through the blood stream and is destroyed by digestive juices and boiling. A small amount introduced into a wound or injected, however, could be fatal; the contents of half a seed might be sufficient to kill a man'. However, the toxin is freed only if the hard outer covering is burst. The seed was formerly much used for making necklaces. The plant is employed in folk MEDICINE, its roots formerly used as a substitute for liquorice. Listed by R.S. Rattray as one of the important plants in Ashanti medicine, the seeds in Jamaica as in Africa are also used in various rituals.
[Adams 1971, 1972, Adams et al.1963, Rashford 1984, Rattray 1927]

John Crow Bead

JOHNNY CAKE

Fried flour DUMPLING that is popular among all classes of Jamaicans, but especially at breakfast; also known as 'journey cake' because it is ideal as travellers' food. Although appearing in the historical literature from at least the mid-18th century, both terms are Americanisms, though in that country they refer to a corn cake, probably of Native American origin. 'Johnny' is apparently a corruption of 'journey'.

JONKONNU

Bands of masqueraders who appear in some towns and villages at Christmastime. The custom of Jonkonnu (or John Canoe) dates back hundreds of years and was widely indulged in by the slaves as part of their principal holiday celebration. At one time the bands were large and elaborate – an important element in CHRISTMAS carnivals. Over the years the custom has died out and Jonkonnu is hardly seen today, except at specially organized events.

Jonkonnu bands today may include a mixture of traditional and more recent characters: Cow-head or Horse-head, King, Queen (wearing a veil), Devil, Pitchy-Patchy whose vigorous acrobatics set his tatters and rags to trembling, Red Indians in mirrors and feathers, a largely pregnant 'woman' and perhaps a mock Policeman or two to keep the motley crew in check. The group is usually accompanied by musicians who play a characteristic rhythm in 2/4 or 4/4 time. Jonkonnu music is played by the fife (lead instrument), bass and rattling drums, and a grater. There are four distinct figures – marching tune, open cut out/wil'out, one drop, and fig/drille.

Although the Jonkonnu characters vary from one part of the island to the other, all characters are traditionally played by men and wear white mesh masks. If the characters speak at all, it will be in hoarse whispers for it is part of the tradition that their identities should not be known. Those who watch their antics are expected to contribute money to the band to help defray the expenses of their costumes or to provide refreshment to keep up their energy.

The Jonkonnu band today is a far cry from what it was around the late 18th century when it was at its height. The bands were first encouraged, then suppressed by the authorities that increasingly feared slave uprisings. They particularly wished to discourage gatherings of blacks, as well as the use of DRUMS, blowing of horns and CONCH shells that were not only part of the musical elements of the bands but were also instruments of communication among the slaves (see MUSIC). The question remains, where did the name and custom of Jonkonnu originate?

'Actor Boy' Jonkonnu by Belisario

Modern Jonkonnu

Secret Societies This is one area of Jamaican culture that has provided a rich field for researchers and many explanations have been advanced. The most probable explanation for the name is that offered by the DJE that the word originates from similar sounding words spoken in the Ewe language (of eastern Ghana and Togo): *dzono* (sorcerer) *kúnu* (deadly) = deadly sorcerer or *dzon'ko* (sorcerer) and *nu* (man) = sorcerer man. The sounds and related meanings of the words reinforce the hypothesis of recent scholars that Jonkonnu practices, forms, and structures, e.g. music, DANCE, characters, masquerade, secrecy, probably had their origins in West African secret societies. Thus the earliest masqueraders in Jamaica wore animal heads (often horned) and tails and were associated with fear and secrecy, elements in Jonkonnu which persist to the present day, as children frightened by the masked dancers will attest.

Jonkonnu probably became identified with Christmas festivities because Christmas was the only major holiday for the slaves. Other influences began to operate fairly early, and in addition to the African element (which is what some scholars classify as 'Jonkonnu') there was also the European masquerade tradition and, in the post-EMANCIPATION period, distinct CREOLE elements added. Despite the fusion over time, vestiges of the African, European and creole origins can still be identified in the form and practice of Jonkonnu (also called 'Masquerade' and 'Horse Head') from place to place.

The first written reference to Jonkonnu occurs in Edward Long's *History of Jamaica* that was published in 1774. He refers to what was already a Christmas tradition in all the towns of 'John Connú' dancers: 'several tall robust fellows dressed up in grotesque habits, and a pair of ox-horns on their head, sprouting from the top of a horrid sort of vizor, or mask, which about the mouth is rendered very terrific with large boar-tusks. The masquerader, carrying a wooden sword in his hand, is followed by a numerous crowd of drunken women, who refresh him frequently with a sup of aniseed-water, whilst he dances at every door bellowing out 'John Connú! with great vehemence'. Long noted that in 1769 'several new masks appeared; the Ebos, the Papaws, &c. having their respective Connús'.

European elements Jonkonnu reached its zenith at the height of the plantation era, when European slave masters actively encouraged it by promoting the festivities on their estates. Some of the European elements came from the slaves imitating – and satirizing – their masters. Among the European elements were Morris dancing, English mummery and music and dance steps – jigs, polkas, reels, etc. (See BRITISH heritage.)

By the late 18th century, the SET GIRLS began to dominate the celebrations. Once the sets came in, the Jonkonnu elements began to decline as the major features of the Christmas festivities in the towns, for the 'set girls' had the unbeatable combination of beauty and sexual rivalry. In time the carnival – as the Christmas celebration was called – included playlets and other forms of public amusements and the strictly African element was increasingly submerged, though it persisted in the deep countryside.

After Emancipation of the slaves (1838), Jonkonnu suffered a decline as the non-conformist MISSIONARIES attempted to stamp out pagan amusements and rituals among their converts. The civic authorities were also antagonistic: the most serious civil disorder in the years immediately after Emancipation was the 'John Canoe Riots' of 1841 when the Mayor of Kingston banned the Jonkonnu parade. In the ensuing clash between angry revellers in the city and the MILITIA, he was forced to take refuge on a ship in the harbour.

Later, the self-appointed censors in society saw the Jonkonnu dances as debased and vulgar and frightening to children and continued to actively discourage their appearance. Clashes between bands and the police became frequent and Jonkonnu was for a long time suppressed except in the deep countryside.

In 1951 the *Daily GLEANER* newspaper sponsored a Jonkonnu competition and the degree of participation indicated that old-timers had indeed kept the tradition alive. This renewed interest in Jonkonnu which nowadays is viewed as an important aspect of Jamaican heritage though it is kept alive mainly through government-sponsored events like the Jamaica FESTIVAL.

Through Isaac Mendes Belisario's *Sketches of Character* that was published in 1837, we have a pictorial record of Jonkonnu and the Set Girls in their prime.

[Barnett 1980, Baxter 1970, Belisario 1837, Bettelheim 1976, Cassidy 1971, DJE, Long 1774, Nunley and Bettelheim 1988, Ryman 1984, M. Whylie, personal communication; Wynter 1970]

JORDON, Edward (1800-1869)

Jamaican patriot whose statue can be seen in St William Grant PARK. Jordon was one of the most prominent public figures of his day, at various times being Mayor, CUSTOS of KINGSTON, Leader and Speaker of the House of Assembly and Island Secretary. He was also a co-founder of Jamaica Mutual Life Assurance Society.

Along with Robert Osborn, another coloured Jamaican, he was publisher of *The Watchman* newspaper that sought the extension of civil liberties to free COLOURED men. Jordon also championed the abolition of SLAVERY and the rights of the House of Assembly. Arising from an article in his paper in 1832, he was charged with sedition and treason, which were punishable by death. The article had suggested that all should 'pull together' to bring the system of slavery down. The trial was one of the most sensational to take place in Jamaica and feelings ran so high that a British warship stood by in Kingston harbour throughout. The case actually came to nothing, but Jordon was tried and convicted on another charge of libel. He served six months in prison before his appeal against the sentence was successful. Jordon's statue by R.G. Miller, RA was erected by public subscription after the patriot's death.

[Cundall 1915]

Edward Jordon

JUBILEE MARKET

Located at West Street, KINGSTON, the market occupies the site of the old Solas Market which is celebrated in the song 'Come we go down a Solas Market'. This is one of the oldest MARKET sites in the city, for vendors used to gather in an open space here from the 18th century. To commemorate the jubilee of Queen Victoria's reign, the present market was built on the site of the old Solas Market in 1887.

Jubilee Market

JUDGEMENT CLIFF

Massive scar of a landslip which can be seen across the YALLAHS RIVER from EASINGTON, ST THOMAS Parish, the only visible reminder of one of the greatest catastrophes in Jamaica's history, the EARTHQUAKE of 1692 which destroyed PORT ROYAL. In the earthquake a large part of the hillside slipped and buried beneath it a plantation and its inhabitants in the valley below. A LEGEND says that the estate belonged to a wicked Dutchman who mistreated his slaves – hence the 'judgement' on him. The scar is

approximately 300m from top to bottom and the slipped mass is estimated to contain 65 million m^3. A plaque to identify Judgement Cliff has been placed by the Jamaican Historical Society on the edge of a playing field at Easington.
[Lewis 1976, Porter 1990]

JUNJO

Any kind of fungus or fungus-like growth; the origin of the word is unknown. Edible fungus growing on the trunks of COTTON TREES and other damp places was once widely eaten, according to Patrick Browne (1756) 'washed, pounded and boiled with beef in our soups' though it is hardly consumed today. Perhaps junjo's status is summed up in the saying, 'You poor fe meat, yu nyam junjo'.

Judgement Cliff

Junjo

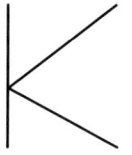

KENILWORTH

Formerly known as Maggotty, Kenilworth property in HANOVER Parish has the ruins of 'the best examples of old industrial architecture' in Jamaica. The buildings are the remains of an old SUGAR factory and include one building which housed the mill, and another complex of buildings comprising the boiling house and the distillery. The Kenilworth buildings are listed by the JNHT. There is a training school on the property that is now owned by the government of Jamaica. Beyond the works can be seen the tomb of an earlier owner, Thomas Blagrove (d 1755), whose family also owned CARDIFF HALL in ST ANN. The Blagroves were among the Regicides and first settled in Jamaica in 1665. (The Regicides were anti-Roman Catholic parliamentarians in the English civil war of 1642-44, who signed the death warrant of Charles I and were less than welcome back in England when Charles II returned in 1660.)
[Concannon 1974, Cundall 1915]

Kenilworth

KETTERING BAPTIST CHURCH

Church in Duncans, TRELAWNY Parish, (built 1893) associated with William Knibb (see KNIBB MEMORIAL CHURCH) who founded the Kettering FREE VILLAGE in 1838. The grateful ex-slaves gave Knibb enough money to build a home for himself there. He died at Kettering in 1845. Kettering was named after Knibb's native town in Northamptonshire in England. The doors from Knibb's house, which was demolished in 1953, were used in the ROMAN CATHOLIC Shrine at Seville (see SEVILLE, New).
[Sibley 1965, Wright and White 1969]

KHUS-KHUS (*Vetiveria zizanioides*)

Perennial grass, its highly aromatic roots are used as a base for a perfume and toilet water made in Jamaica. Khus-khus roots are also placed in drawers and cupboards to impart a lasting fragrance and to keep away moths. A native of Asia, the plant grows from sea level to 1,100m and is sometimes seen on country roads where it is planted to stem soil erosion. It is therefore a common sight and well known fragrance on the higher, bare slopes of the ST ANDREW mountains where, at 600-1,200m, the struggle against severe erosion is constant.
[Adams 1972]

KING'S HOUSE

Located at Hope Road in ST ANDREW Parish, King's House is the official residence of Jamaica's head of state, the governor-general. The beautiful gardens are an attraction to visitors. King's House became the residence of the BRITISH governor when the seat of government was moved from SPANISH TOWN to KINGSTON in 1872 and remained so until INDEPENDENCE in 1962. Originally 69ha of Somerset Pen were acquired, including Bishop's Lodge, formerly the residence of the ANGLICAN Bishop of Jamaica. A dining room and ballroom were added to the original building that dated from the 18th century. It was wrecked in the EARTHQUAKE of 1907 and rebuilt in 1909 from designs by Sir Charles Nicholson.

King's House

KING'S HOUSE, Old

Only the portico and façade of this impressive building can be seen today, facing the SPANISH TOWN Square, the former governor's residence called King's House having burnt down in 1925. A museum has been established in the former stables.

This is one of the few residential sites of the post-Columbian world with over 450 years of continuous occupation. The original building was the Spanish Hall of Audience to which successive BRITISH governors made changes and additions. In 1761 this building was demolished and the following year construction of a residence for the governor was begun though the entire complex was not completed until 1802. The residence of the governor in Spanish Town (and at various times, PORT ROYAL) was traditionally called KING'S HOUSE and this King's House remained the governors' residence until 1872 when the capital was transferred to KINGSTON. After that the building was for one year the home of QUEEN'S COLLEGE, Jamaica's first university.

The facade of King's House was about 61m long. It was built of freestone from the HOPE RIVER, with columns of Portland stone, and a pavement of white marble that came out as ballast on ships. A ballroom ran the length of the building and was the centre of social life in colonial times. Among the items of furniture were 13 MAHOGANY settees, 24 mahogany Windsor chairs, 60 plain mahogany chairs with fan backs and leather bottoms, and 14 large bronze busts. In 1803 the government provided 33 slaves at King's House, but the governor of the day asked the Assembly for 10 more.

The portico of King's House, and the Square itself, have provided the setting for many significant events in Jamaica's history. It was from these steps that the proclamation of the abolition of SLAVERY was read, to a vast crowd assembled, and here governor Edward Eyre delivered his final address suspending the constitution of Jamaica following the MORANT BAY REBELLION. In this square the pirate Calico Jack (see Jack RACKHAM) was brought for trial and the MAROONS brought the mutilated head of THREE FINGER JACK to collect their reward. The notorious Hutchinson, the 'Mad Doctor' of EDINBURGH CASTLE was also tried at the courthouse and hanged at the Square.

An interesting account of life inside King's House can be found in the *Journal* of Lady Nugent who was the wife of Sir George Nugent who was governor from 1801-5.

[Black 1974, Cundall 1915, Nugent 1839]

KINGSTON, City of

Capital of Jamaica, the Kingston Metropolitan Area consists of the parishes of Kingston (total area, 21.8km^2) and ST ANDREW (total area, 430.7km^2). The combined population in 1997 was 700,100 or 27.42 per cent of Jamaica's total population.

The original section of the city of Kingston was laid out some 300 years ago to house survivors of the 1692 EARTHQUAKE that destroyed PORT ROYAL. The area bounded by Harbour Street, North Street, East Street and West Street was the first settlement, part of the Parish of St Andrew known as Colonel Barry's hog crawle from the use to which it was put. The island was without a governor or lieutenant governor at the time of the earthquake and it was the council (an advisory body to the governor) that took the decision to go across the harbour from the stricken city and purchase 80ha owned by Colonel William Beeston (then absent from the island) to found a new town. A plan of the town was drawn up by John Goffe, a surveyor, and lots were sold.

For the original town of Kingston, the surveyor drew a parallelogram one mile (1.6km) in length from north to south and half a mile (.8km) in breadth bounded by the four streets Harbour, North, East and West and traversed by

Old King's House: 19th century view by Duperly (above) and 18th century interior view below

Kingston Street, c. 1846, lithograph by Adolphe Duperly

streets and lanes crossing each other at right angles. The first known resident of Kingston was a woman, Mrs Ann Louder. It was at her house in 1693 that lots were drawn in order for the council to decide on assigning land to the original settlers.

Port Royal Street was not part of the original town since the sea came up to Harbour Street which was therefore most desirable as a shipping point. But the sea kept on depositing mud and debris south of Harbour Street, and Beeston, who had returned as lieutenant governor, got hold of the land. Much to the anger of those on Harbour Street, in the early 18th century a new street named Port Royal Street was laid out on this new land, and lots were sold. This then became the principal street for shipping.

The streets within the original area of Kingston were laid out in a grid pattern that remains the same today except for the additions of Kirk Avenue off Church Street and St George's Avenue off Duke Street. Most of the early streets were named after the men who were councillors at the time of the founding of the town. In the midst of these streets, an open square was left as the Parade. (See St William Grant PARK.)

Early settlement was confined to the area below Parade. The west was near the swamps and regarded as unhealthy and was therefore the least desirable area. The most popular streets among the early settlers were Church, Harbour, and Orange Streets and those around the Parade. Here the settlers lived upstairs their business places. Behind these houses were the YARDS where slaves and poor people lived.

It wasn't until some time after Kingston was settled that the wealthy began to buy property in St Andrew and started to build residences there. Many of these properties were called 'Pen' (a Jamaican word for a livestock farm) since the owner kept his horses and probably some other livestock there. As the urban area expanded, the pens were cut up and sold, giving the name 'Pen' to many places in the Corporate Area, such as Greenwich Pen or Delacree Pen. Some of the new settlements were called 'Towns'. The first of these were Hannah Town and Rae Town, both named after the wealthy merchants who

King Street today

Aerial view of Kingston

acquired the lots that were subdivided around 1790. Rae Town was for a long time a fashionable community.

Up to the late 18th century St Andrew was still mainly rural with many sugar estates, such as HOPE, Mona, Papine and CONSTANT SPRING. But by 1890 only Mona estate was still in production and the rest had given their names to city suburbs. By that time people had started to populate lower St Andrew.

In 1802 in the reign of King George III, Kingston was granted a charter as a corporation with a mayor and council; in 1872 it became the capital of Jamaica. In 1923, the parishes of Kingston and St Andrew were amalgamated and the Kingston and St Andrew Corporation, which still administers the affairs of the city, came into being.

Throughout its history, Kingston remained principally a city of merchants and traders. Kingston harbour is one of the very best natural harbours in the world, sufficiently landlocked to provide good shelter for shipping, and with deep water for heavy freight vessels. In the Second WORLD WAR, it assumed high strategic importance but it has been valuable mainly for commerce down through the centuries. In the early years, many merchants lived near the waterfront, as commercial life centred on shipping. Houses in the city were often built with a lookout tower on the roof equipped with a spyglass from which the merchant could check on the movement of ships. (Such a tower can be seen at VALE ROYAL.)

In the early 18th century, Kingston was important as a trans-shipment port for goods from England to the Spanish colonies of Latin America. The 'goods' included people. Britain had acquired the contract (called the *asiento*) to supply slaves to the Spanish colonies, and after the human cargoes were brought across the Atlantic from Africa, they were kept in warehouses on the Kingston waterfront until they were re-shipped. This continued until 1807 when the slave trade was abolished by the British.

At the time of the American War of Independence (1775-83), as historian H.P. Jacobs recounts, Kingston had a population of 11,200 which was a little under two-thirds of the population of Boston (18,000) and roughly one-third of the English port of Liverpool (34,000). Kingston's greatest period of prosperity was during the Napoleonic Wars when trade with the Spanish colonies greatly increased. Like the rest of Jamaica, Kingston declined after EMANCIPATION (1838) and the Sugar Duties Act (1846) which ruined the sugar planters. Still, the city was never challenged as the chief port and commercial centre of the island.

In 1907 a large part of the downtown area was destroyed by an earthquake and fire, and virtually all the buildings south of Parade date from that time. After this disaster, public land was acquired on both sides of King Street and the public buildings there laid out.

In the 1960s, a major effort was begun to revitalize the old downtown areas which, like the heart of many cities, has suffered from urban blight. The first step in the redevelopment of the Kingston waterfront was the construction of a new commercial and shipping area – Newport West – on reclaimed land. This made available the old port area which has since been undergoing transformation by the Urban Development Corporation, starting with the construction of a new waterfront highway, Ocean Boulevard, and a complex of shops, office buildings, and apartments.

Since the 1960s, the urban area has been vastly enlarged by the development of new residential areas such as Portmore in the HELLSHIRE HILLS in ST CATHERINE Parish, facilitated by the construction of a causeway across the western side of Kingston harbour. At the time of writing a portion of Hunts Bay which the Portmore causeway traverses, is being filled in for the continued expansion of the Kingston port and the relocation of the causeway as part of the Highway 2000 programme.

[Clarke 1975, Cundall 1915, Jacobs 1973, 1976, Johnson 1993, KSAC 1952]

KINGSTON BUTTERCUP (*Tribulus cistoides*)

Low, spreading plant with bright yellow flowers, common in waste places, particularly in KINGSTON and along the PALISADOES. The plant was popularly called 'Kill-backra' (backra being a white man) because African Jamaicans believed it brought YELLOW FEVER which killed mainly European newcomers. Yellow fever is transmitted by mosquitoes (although this was not known at the time) and was therefore rampant after the rains when the mosquitoes were most numerous. The Kingston Buttercup also blooms profusely after the rains, hence the connection made between it and the fever. It is also known as Police Macca – presumably because of its sharp thorns, Jamaica Buttercup and Turkey Blossom, the latter from its attraction to fowls that feed on it. The plant is related to the LIGNUM VITAE. Children also played with it: if you held a flower under another child's chin and saw a yellow reflection, then that proved that your friend had a craving for butter, a belief that was brought from the British Isles where it was applied to the Buttercup.

[Adams 1972, DJE]

Kingston Buttercup

KINGSTON INDUSTRIAL GARAGE

KIG has the distinction of being the world's oldest dealer of Ford motor cars. It was the first Ford dealership to be established outside the USA and has the longest unbroken service of any Ford dealer anywhere.

According to the Henriques family who established the dealership, when a KIG representative interviewed Henry Ford's New York representative in 1907 with a view to establishing the motor car agency in Jamaica, the stipulation was that he would have to order a minimum of 25 cars per year. So when the fledgling KIG sent off their third order for 25 cars in their first year of operation, Ford himself cabled congratulations and seriously asked: 'Please advise if I should enlarge my factory to take care of your requirements.'

The firm was set up by six enterprising Henriques brothers whose construction firm built the WARD THEATRE and the old Masonic Temple on Hanover Street, among other buildings. KIG's office used to be located at 34

£180 at our Garage.

5 Passenger, Model T Touring Car.
1 Cyl : 4 Cycle. 22½ Horse Power.
5,000 Miles on 1 set tyres (over any road in Jamaica).
20 to 25 Miles to a gallon of gasolene.

Look Out for Next Saturday's Issue of the "Gleaner".

KINGSTON INDUSTRIAL GARAGE.
Sole Agents – FORD MOTOR COY.
17 West Street & 4 Pechon Street, Kingston.

Gleaner

Church Street, KINGSTON, on the site of a house where Mariana Grajales de MACEO, mother of Antonio Maceo, the outstanding Cuban revolutionary lived in exile for the last 16 years of her life.

KIG is now part of the Lascelles Group of Companies.

[JCC Journal 26:1, 1970]

KINGSTON PARISH CHURCH

Space was allotted for a parish church on the southeast side of the town square in the plan of the city of KINGSTON drawn up by John Goffe, the Church of England (ANGLICAN) then being the state religion. The original church was erected at the site of the present church before 1699 (the date of the oldest tomb there) and might have dated from the earliest settlement of the PARISH following the EARTHQUAKE which devastated PORT ROYAL in 1692. In the early part of the 18th century, the church had a seating capacity of 1,300. The building was wrecked in the 1907 earthquake and the present building reconstructed on its foundations, as much as possible a replica of the former church (except for the tower). This new building was consecrated in 1911.

Centrally situated at the corner of King Street near the PARADE, the Parish Church of St Thomas, the Apostle and Martyr, has been in the forefront of virtually all the great events connected with Kingston's history, and the church bell used to toll the 9:00pm curfew. So much was it identified with the city that 'born under the clock' came to describe those who could claim to be 'true Kingstonians' – born within sight of the large church clock.

The clock tower on the western end was erected in memory of those who died in the First WORLD WAR. The statue of Our Lady at the High Altar is a gift of the CHINESE community in Jamaica and the statue of St Thomas is a gift of the LEBANESE. The organ dates from before 1722 and is said to be one of the best in the West Indies. The church also contains some modern Jamaican ART: in the Lady Chapel is 'The Pieta' by Susan Alexander and 'Madonna and Child' by Osmond Watson with the carving of 'The Angel' by Edna Manley in the nave.

In earlier times, parishioners were buried within the church itself and there, many interesting monuments can be seen, such as those to Admiral BENBOW (forming part of the floor in front of the High Altar) and to John Wolmer (see WOLMER'S SCHOOL).

For a long time a slab inside the church which was turned downwards was believed to be that of an 18th century rector of the church who was hanged for minting counterfeit coins. Apparently the handsome young rector took to crime for the love of a beautiful lady. However, when the slab was eventually turned over, it was found to be that of a Kingston merchant. Why it was on its face, no one could tell. There does not seem to be any doubt that the counterfeiting rector existed. Historian Clinton Black suggested that the rector's story inspired the famous American novel *The Scarlet Letter* by Nathaniel Hawthorne who might have heard it from a Jamaican in London.

The church had another controversial rector. In 1818, the churchwardens of Kingston brought a series of charges against him, including refusal to bury the dead on Sunday and refusal to baptise a sick child. They claimed that he also officiated at the church before a large congregation with a bandage over his eye to cover a wound which he had received while

Kingston Parish Church

J. Tyndale-Biscoe

engaged in a boxing match – 'to the great scandal and disgrace of his sacred calling'. Finally, he had suggested that the mayor make his clerks post accounts and copy letters on Sunday. He was let off all the charges except this last one. For that, he was suspended from duty for nine months.
[Black 1952, Cundall 1915, Curtin 1984, Olivier 1936]

KINGSTON RACE COURSE

Now NATIONAL HEROES PARK, this 29ha site was purchased in 1808 by the Mayor and City Council of KINGSTON for £985 10s as a playground for the city. BOXING, ball games and other sporting events were conducted here, but mainly it became the centre of HORSERACING, and was known as Kingston Race Course. The first race was run here in 1816 and racing became a regular event until the early 20th century when it was transferred to Knutsford Park. Race Course then became a cycle racing track known as Town Moor (see CYCLING).

Aside from sporting activities, Race Course witnessed many sights and activities from the ridiculous to the sublime, from visiting circuses to visiting evangelists. After the 1907 EARTHQUAKE, its wide open space became a refugee camp for destitute people and 'Shack Town' lasted until all were able to find alternative accommodation.

It was here too that important national events were celebrated with appropriate pomp and splendour. The most elaborate of these celebrations were probably the military and fireworks displays which greeted the celebration of EMANCIPATION DAY (1 August 1838) and the jubilee of Queen Victoria's reign in 1887.

Writer Clyde Hoyte claims that in the first decade of the 20th century, differences between the people of 'east' and 'west' Kingston were settled by wholesale organized fisticuffs at the Race Course. The people from western Kingston would march in through the western gate, waving flags and brandishing sticks, while in similar warlike mood the people from the east would come via Allman Town. There would be a mighty clash in the middle of Race Course and all would let off steam. There were probably a few broken limbs and heads, but not a single fatality was recorded from the encounters.
[Hoyte 1975]

KISS-TEET

A well known vocal expression of disdain, disbelief, or annoyance, achieved by sucking in air through narrowed lips on one side of the mouth, across the side of the tongue, so as to create a coarsely hissing noise. It is of West African origin, common throughout the CARIBBEAN, and is also known as 'chups', 'steups' or 'suck-teeth'. The depth and shades of meaning depend on length, sharpness, and loudness. A good kiss-teet forms an essential act in effective cussing. Linguists describe this sound as a voiceless, lengthened, labio-palatal ingressive fricative. Regarded as highly disrespectful, it has earned many a teenager serious punishment from a parent.
[DCEU, DJE, J. D'Costa, personal communication]

KITCHEN BITCH

Small oil lamp used by the poor, consisting of a tin can filled with kerosene oil with a cloth wick, and a handle attached by the local tinsmith. Also called 'cowgut' in some localities. The kitchen bitch had no shade and was probably so called because even in homes with glass lamps it was the lamp used in the kitchen that in the old days was always in a room separate from the house. In 1973 the kitchen bitch was selected by JAMAL – the Jamaica Association for the Advancement of Literacy – as its symbol, a reflection of its motto: 'Lighten Our Darkness'.

KNIBB MEMORIAL CHURCH

This historic BAPTIST church is located at the corner of King and George Streets, FALMOUTH, TRELAWNY Parish, and commemorates the name of the famous Baptist MISSIONARY, William Knibb (1803-45) who was active in the fight against SLAVERY. The building itself dates from 1948 but it is on the site of Knibb's chapel that was destroyed in the HURRICANE of 1944. The present building was erected with the assistance of the government in recognition of its historical importance.

Knibb, an Englishman, came to Jamaica in 1825 to minister to the slaves and built his first chapel in

Revd William Knibb

Kettering, home of the Revd William Knibb in Trelawny

Falmouth. He, like the other non-conformist ministers, was viewed as a trouble maker by the planters and other privileged members of the society, and his church and life were constantly threatened. The first chapel was destroyed by the MILITIA in 1832 following a serious slave rebellion in the western parishes (see SHARPE, Samuel) – the fate of most Baptist and METHODIST chapels on the north coast. (See COLONIAL CHURCH UNION.)

On the outbreak of the rebellion, Knibb and the other ministers were arrested, since the authorities believed they were responsible for inciting the slaves. The rebellion was referred to as the 'Baptist War' from the large number of church members among the rebels. Knibb was taken by CANOE from Falmouth to MONTEGO BAY for trial but the charges were dropped.

He continued to preach against slavery in Jamaica and in England where he played a major role in lobbying for passage of the Abolition Bill. By the EMANCIPATION Act of 1834 the slaves were partially freed. (See APPRENTICESHIP.) Full freedom came in 1838. Knibb's rebuilt chapel was one of the many churches around the island where the slaves congregated all night to wait and greet together the dawning of the first day of freedom – 1 August 1838. A sculpture relief in the church depicts this scene. In the church and churchyard are monuments to Knibb (who is buried there), members of his family and other Baptist ministers.

In 1988, the government of Jamaica made a posthumous award of the Order of Merit (OM) to William Knibb.

[Sibley 1965, Wright and White 1969]

KNIBB MEMORIAL HIGH SCHOOL

The school, located at the corner of Market and Trelawny Streets in FALMOUTH, TRELAWNY Parish, is housed in one of the historic buildings of the town. The house was built in 1798 as a masonic hall but was later sold to the BAPTISTS and was the original Baptist manse. (See KNIBB MEMORIAL CHURCH.)

KOLA NUT (*Cola acuminata*)

The kola nut is called Bissy or Bisi in Jamaica, a name brought from West Africa. The Guyanese historian Walter Rodney, in his *History of the Upper Guinea Coast*, recorded the significant association of the kola nut in West Africa with religious rites, initiation ceremonies, property rights, as a symbol of hospitality, and in diplomatic relations, and noted that its spiritual and religious uses did not persist in the New World.

In Jamaica it has been used mainly as a TEA and as a home remedy for many ailments but most importantly as an antidote to poison; for this purpose, dried Bissy ready for grating was kept in every rural home. Freshly grated Bissy was used to treat cuts and bruises. It was once a popular plant in home gardens, the drink regarded as a stimulant, but it is hardly grown or consumed today. Local manufacturers of soft drinks also used it to flavour their products, before it achieved worldwide fame as a vital ingredient in 'cola' bottled drinks.

Kola nuts

The first planting of Bissy that is recorded took place on an estate near Guanaboa Vale, ST CATHERINE Parish, by one Mr Goffe, the seed having been brought on a slave ship from Guinea in 1680.

[Robertson 1990, Rodney 1970]

KUMINA

A dance-music ritual (also spelled Cumina), centred primarily on communication with the ancestors of the CONGO people and their descendants in Jamaica. Kumina is also sometimes performed for purely recreational or 'bailo' purposes.

Kumina is believed to have been brought here or to have received new stimulation from the large numbers of indentured Africans who came to Jamaica in the 1840s to 1860s, particularly from the Congo (see AFRICANS, Indentured).

Many of them settled in ST THOMAS Parish, and it is here that Kumina is strongest. However, Kumina groups are also found in PORTLAND, ST CATHERINE, and ST MARY Parishes, KINGSTON, and other areas.

Research has indicated quite clearly a Bantu, more specifically Congo, ancestry of Kumina. Among possible sources are the following Ki-Kongo words: *kumina* – to move or act rhythmically, *kumunu* – a well known traditional dance rhythm; *kumu* – to mount up. Kumina people refer to themselves as of the BUNGO nation, not with the usual negative Jamaican connotation attached to the word 'bungo', but indicative of their ancestry of which they are very proud.

Kumina is based on the Central African belief in each person possessing a dual soul: the personal spirit (which contains the personality of the individual) and the individual's shadow. On death, the personal spirit goes directly to the all-powerful god Nzambi Mpungu; these spirits can become ancestral spirits and return to earth. The shadow remains in the grave with the corpse but can leave it at will. If not given proper burial, it can become a wandering spirit (DUPPY) and a menace not only to the family but to all the people in the area.

There seemed to have been originally three ranks of Kumina spirits: Sky, Earth, and Ancestral, although contemporary practitioners acknowledge only ancestor spirits. During ceremonies, the spirits are summoned by songs and drumbeats to enter and possess the Kumina dancers. Spirit possession is called MYAL. The personal spirit of a person possessed by ancestral spirits during Kumina rituals can at death join other ancestral spirits who are able to return to earth. These ancestral spirits can be called upon and used to aid the living; to summon the spirits for assistance is the purpose of a Kumina ceremony.

Kumina dancers at Festival. Seaforth group, St Thomas Parish

Kumina ceremonies are always held for specific purposes. The most important of these are concerned with death in a family: wakes, entombments and memorials (see DEATH RITUALS). They are also performed for celebrations such as BIRTHS, weddings, thanksgivings, etc. for healing, and to remove the wrong kind of spirit from someone afflicted with 'spirit sickness'. Thus Kumina is held to mark both individual life crises and family events. In technical terms, Kumina is both a rite of incorporation and a rite of passage. Kumina DANCES might be performed at public sessions or in private ceremonies.

Singing, dancing, and drumming are the three most important elements in a Kumina session which usually begins at sundown and takes place around a central pole. As in REVIVAL, colour symbolism is important: specific colours are used for specific ceremonies, reflected in the dress of the leading participants and in the decorations of the centre pole.

Much depends on the leader of the Kumina ceremony who is called a King or Queen and is the permanent leader, with a band of disciples. The leader is expected to be well versed in the dances and rituals and usually has served a long apprenticeship before attaining the highest

Kumina drummer

Queenie Kennedy, a renowned Kumina Queen dancing with a glass of water on her head

position in the band. It is the leader who controls the spirits and therefore the success or otherwise of the ceremony. In his or her role of spirit medium, the King or Queen uses spirit conductors such as RUM (sprayed) or dances with a glass of water balanced on the head to catch the spirit. The leader will also supervise the sacrifice of a fowl or GOAT, for blood is regarded as food for the spirits. Two types of songs, associated with the main types of ceremonies, are sung: African 'country' songs which are the most sacred, and 'bailo' songs.

Central to a Kumina ceremony are the drum rhythms used to summon and control different types of spirits. Drummers, like leaders, serve a long apprenticeship and are highly respected because of their great importance to the success of a ceremony. While the leader can be male or female, only men play the Kumina drums. Before each ceremony, the heads of the drums are blessed with a libation of rum.

Two drums constitute the Kumina ensemble, each playing a specific rhythm: the Kbandu (or Bandu) and the Playing Kyas (or Playing Cas). The Kbandu is a large hollow drum regarded as the 'male' and on it is played the basic rhythm; the head is made from ramgoat skin which during construction is repeatedly stretched and sprayed with white rum to attain the proper pitch. Playing Kyas is the lead instrument, the 'female' drum, the smaller of the two, the head covered with skin of a ewe goat. It is constructed the same as Kbandu but is pitched higher and plays more complicated rhythms. Both drums are played with the hands though the tone of the Kbandu can be changed by pressure applied with the foot. The drummers straddle the drums to play. Other instruments include shakers ('shak-shak'), scrapers, clappers, and CATTA STICKS ('kyatas'). Catta Sticks are used by the 'rackling men' to play a rhythm on the body of the drum behind the drummer.

'Kumina' is one of the more spectacular dances of The NATIONAL DANCE THEATRE COMPANY.

[Baxter 1970, Bilby and Leib 1986, Brathwaite 1978, Hurston 1938, Lalla and D'Costa 1990, Lewin 2000, Moore 1953, Ryman 1984b, Schuler 1980, Warner-Lewis 1977]

LACE BARK (*Lagetta lagetto*)

Small tree, 5-10m high, so called from the fact that its inner bark can be separated into thin, web-like pieces resembling fine lace. In the past it was used in the manufacture of cordage but has also been made into clothing. In the 17th century, a cravat, frill and pair of ruffles made from this bark were sent to King Charles II by the governor of Jamaica. Edward Long noted that the ladies of the island were dextrous in making 'caps, ruffles, and complete suits of lace' with it. To bleach, they put the stretched lace in the sun and sprinkled frequently with water. The material washed well. The tree also yielded whips that were made by removing the wood from part of a small branch and twisting the lace into a leash. The tree grows on the LIMESTONE hillsides in central parishes from 400 to 1,000m. It is also found in Cuba and Hispaniola. In 1793 Captain William Bligh (see BREADFRUIT) took a plant from Jamaica to Kew Gardens in England. It was later reintroduced into England in 1844.
[Adams 1972, DJE, Long 1774, NHSJ 1946]

LACOVIA

For 50 years in the 18th century this village alternated with BLACK RIVER as the capital of ST ELIZABETH Parish. Courts and vestry meetings were held alternately in each place until Black River won out. Lacovia was once a busy place, in a central position for both road and river traffic at a time when SUGAR from the estates upstream was shipped down the Black River. It once had burial grounds for both JEWS and QUAKERS.

'Lacovia Tombstone' at the junction of the road to Maggotty is named after two tombstones at the side of the road. Tradition has it that a duel in a nearby tavern resulted in the deaths of two young men who were buried there side by side. One of the tombs no longer has any slab or inscription but the other is dedicated to Thomas Jordan Spencer (1723-38) and the arms on the slab are those of Spencer of Althorp. According to White and Wright, 'Though the arms in themselves do not prove it, recent research suggests that Thomas Jordan Spencer's father may have been a member of the Althorp family, and his mother one of the English Quaker family of Jordan (Jordans, a village in Buckinghamshire, is a well-known Quaker centre)'.

The name Lacovia comes from the Spanish *la caoba* which comes from the TAINO word for MAHOGANY – *caoba*; old residents used to call their town 'Coby'. Rio Caobana was the Spanish name for the Black River and one of the fordings across the Black River morass (which was far more extensive in those days) was near where the village of Lacovia now stands. It was the scene of skirmishes between Spanish and English forces in 1655 (see CAPTURE OF JAMAICA). In the 1880s, the Lacovia Manufacturing Company was engaged in manufacturing fibre from the BAMBOO that grew in the area.
[Cundall 1915, Wade 1984, White and Wright 1969]

LANGUAGE

Jamaicans are mainly bilingual, the extent of their bilingualism varying according to social class and educational background. For a majority of mostly working class Jamaicans, the mother tongue is Patwa (called 'Jamaican CREOLE' by

Louise Bennett (left) in characteristic pose

linguists), to which is added some competence in Standard Jamaican English. For a minority of educated middle class speakers, the mother tongue is Standard Jamaican English, with some competence in Jamaican Creole.

At one end of this linguistic continuum, we find Jamaicans who speak Jamaican Creole almost exclusively, can speak very little Standard English, but understand more than they can produce. At the opposite end, we find Jamaicans who speak only Standard Jamaican English but who understand some Jamaican Creole spoken to or around them.

Speakers of Patwa can understand (but not easily produce) the basic Standard English of church, courthouse, and formal gatherings. Speakers of Standard English can understand – and sometimes produce – the basic Creole of street, market, and farm. The Creole speaker quickly loses understanding if the discourse moves into elaborate Standard English; conversely, the Standard Jamaican English speaker quickly loses understanding if the discourse moves into elaborate Jamaican Creole.

For certain social situations, Standard English alone is acceptable: college examinations, parliamentary affairs, church ceremonies and formal occasions all demand Standard. Not to use this discourse is to offer disrespect to the situation itself. For other occasions, Creole alone will serve, as in comic and satiric exchanges, popular entertainment, informal gatherings and times when cursing ('a good tracing match') is needed. Simply put, Standard English belongs to academic and formal experience; Patwa belongs to everything else. Quite unconsciously, Jamaican speakers move between the two, using modified versions of each in order to meet the subtle demands of topic, audience and situation (what linguists call 'code switching'). What monolingual Patwa speakers offer as formal English, however, falls at varying distances from the target, confirming F.G. Cassidy's early comment that one man's English is another man's Creole.

A question such as 'Unnu nyam off de ackee?' makes

Speech competitors, Jamaica Festival, 1985

Frederic G. Cassidy

instant sense to all Jamaicans, yet the sentence cannot be defined as English: only 'off' and 'de' derive from English. In English grammar, a question normally requires inverted subject and verb ('Did you eat all of the ackee?'), while 'You ate all of the ackee' is a declarative. The Patwa question is marked simply by its rising tone at the end of the sentence, thereby changing a declarative into a question, causing a major grammatical shift. In Standard Jamaican English, this non-English grammatical feature occurs commonly even in middle class speech: 'You coming now?' instead of 'Are you coming now?'

Because some 70 per cent of Jamaican Creole vocabulary derives from dialects of the English language, Jamaicans perceive their language usage as English no matter what language they use, and classify Jamaica as an English speaking country. Both language systems however have strict grammatical rules which Jamaicans recognize instinctively, accept in English, but deny to Creole. For many, Jamaican Creole is still 'broken English'. Some of the problems of teaching English in Jamaica are directly related to this attitude.

Velma Pollard, writing about the problems, comments: 'Ask any Patwa-speaking individual what she/he speaks and you get the answer "English".' She suggests that 'if we knew that Patwa is not English we would be able to learn English more easily'.

Carolyn Cooper, crusading for the use of the Cassidy/LePage orthography (see DJE) in all Patwa writing, considers this one way that the difference between the languages might become obvious. 'The very strangeness of the orthography', Cooper writes, 'restores to Jamaican its integrity.' The increasingly popular use of the term Nation Language (following Kamau Brathwaite) to describe not only Jamaican Creole but all English lexicon creoles in the CARIBBEAN may help to affirm the distinction between English and these languages.

Historical Development Jamaica's language forms – from Standard to Creole – reflect a clear historical and socio-economic process. While several theories exist to explain how Creole arose, scholars agree that creoles arise from a limited workplace jargon, a pidgin, used by peoples of different languages to communicate in the workplace. When the workplace is a ship, a plantation, or a factory, the speakers develop a very basic means of communication, using words from the languages available. The grammar is very narrow and may show none of the complexity of the contributing languages. Speech is scaled down to suit minimum needs. As the usage for this jargon expands and as generations of children are born for whom it is the first language, it is no longer a pidgin but a creole satisfying all the expressive needs of its speakers.

In the 1660s and 1670s, the first hundreds of AFRICANS (see SLAVERY) were brought into Jamaica by a very small, mixed group of English dialect speakers – men of Bristol, Plymouth, Kent, London, Yorkshire, Ireland and Scotland. (See BRITISH, IRISH, SCOTS, WELSH.) From these sailors, servants, soldiers, white slaves, and petty merchants, the incoming Africans learned their first English. The Africans spoke many different languages, most of them unintelligible to each other. In a few short years, necessity forced all of these speakers to find a means of communicating. A workplace pidgin was born.

As time went on, the pidgin grew in importance, but it was not yet a mother tongue. When children, however, were born into this narrow community, their first language – whether they were black or white – was the pidgin that all the adults used. Some children must have learned their parents' English dialects

---

FENAY see next.

fene /féne/ vb dial; cf Twi *fḕ*, to vomit, *nḕ*, to cack, *m-fénăŋ*, bile thrown up from the stomach; Fante *fenā*, to be troubled; Limba *feño*, to faint, *feñoi*, to faint, gasp; Bambara *fono*, to vomit; Ewe (Gẽ dial) *afḛnu*, (West dial) *fḛnu*, filth, *fenyi*, trance.

1. To feel direct physical illness and show its effects: to vomit, to faint.
1943 *GL* Clar, Man, Fennay, fennea, to vomit, swoon. 1955 FGC Man, I frighten so till I nearly fene. [Some citations under sense 2 preserve some effect of this sense.]

2. In a vaguer sense: to feel intense pain, discomfort, trouble.
1941 Kirkpatrick gloss, Fenay—have a hard time. 1943 *GL* StC, Fenneh, to suffer. 1956 Mc Man /ef di gúot bók yu, yu féne/ *If the goat butts you, it will hurt*; /ef a lík yu, yu féne/ *If I hit you, you will feel it*; /mi tiit a mek mi fene/ *My teeth are giving me trouble, are paining me*.

3. Transf and neg: To treat with disdain. [There seems to be an echo of sense 1.]
1957 StE (Eld), 'She ask me a question, a wouldn't even fene on her'—*I didn't take any notice of her.*

fenɡke-fenɡke see FENKY-FENKY.

Entry from the Dictionary of Jamaican English

as well, and some blacks may have learned their parents' African languages, but all learned the pidgin and by using it as their main means of expression, they widened it into a fully developed language.

The result was Jamaican Creole, spoken fluently from the end of the 17th century by white and black Jamaicans alike. In this language one finds the vocabulary of our history: naseberry from the Spanish; Liguanea and toona from the TAINO; a host of African terms (bankra, DUPPY, cunnu, nyam); and many terms from archaic English dialects (grung, bickle, bottomside, throw (of water, meaning to pour). Reduced pronouns (*im*, *dem*), uninflected past tense (*im come las night*), adjectives acting as verbs (*Mary feeble*), serial verbs (*dem come come tell Mum*) and many other features show the varying syntactic origins of Patwa.

Over the next 200 years, more and more speakers of different English dialects and different African languages poured into the island. In addition came a few thousand GERMANS, PORTUGUESE JEWS, FRENCH Creoles, as well as native Americans from such places as Honduras (see MISKITO). Groups with limited social ties, such as the MAROONS in the mountains and the few upper class British in the towns, kept to their own language forms. On a large 18th century plantation, one might find an owner whose mother tongue was upper class British English. The overseer and BOOK-KEEPERS spoke English dialects and some Creole, and, if any had been born in Jamaica, their Creole would have been as fluent as that of a Jamaican-born field slave. All new arrivals had to come in contact with Creole, and all used it according to their status, their roles, and their needs. The CHINESE, INDIANS, and LEBANESE who came in the late 19th and early 20th centuries also learned the Creole and added to the lexicon, chiefly food items: *roti* and *pak choy* for example.

Language Today Then, as now, speech defined the speaker's social class, situation, and educational history though that started to break down somewhat in the second half of the 20th century. At that time the new social forces such as RASTAFARI and the political changes of the 1970s made for some reversal of the social order. Young people from all social strata began to adopt the language and style typical of the under class which was spread mainly through the vehicle of popular music. (See DANCEHALL, REGGAE.) A profound influence also was the language of Rastafari (called variously Iyaric, I-ance, Dread Talk – see Pollard 1994).

Rastas adjusted Patwa and Jamaican English to reflect specific social and philosophical positions, rejecting for example the word 'oppressed' to describe their situation and preferring 'downpressed' as a more accurate description. Young people across the social classes adopted that code, particularly the easily accessible 'I' category in which the initial syllable of some words is replaced by the highly valued sound representing not only 'ego' (The I, I-man) but the organ of sight, the FAR- (seeing) Eye. Words like I-tal (to describe good, vital food) and I-ree (to describe good, free feeling) have become part of the Jamaican vocabulary.

The popularity of radio talk shows has also given greater legitimacy to varying versions of Jamaica Talk. It has largely replaced Jamaican English as the language used by callers to these shows and increasingly by talk show hosts themselves (see Shields-Brodber 1997) as well as by announcers and radio deejays.

The 'breakdown' that started in the seventies has been steadily maintained, affirming Edward Baugh's claim (1986) that 'The English language is struggling for survival in this country'.

[Alleyne 1980, 1988, Brathwaite 1984, Cassidy 1971, Cassidy and LePage 1967, Cooper 1993, D'Costa and Lalla 1989, Holm 1988, Lalla and D'Costa 1990, LePage and DeCamp 1960, Morris 1999, Pollard 1993, 1994, Shields-Brodber 1997]

LAS CASAS, Fray Bartolomé de (1474-1566)

SPANISH priest appointed 'Protector of the Indians' in 1516 by the Spanish Crown who dedicated much of his life to battling on behalf of the native peoples of the Americas. His writings tell us much of what we know of the TAINOS and other Amerindians. His *Brief Account of the Destruction of the Indians* (*Breve relación de la destrucción de las Indias*) was published in Seville in 1552, but his monumental two-volume history (*Historia de las Indias*) was not published until 1875 and another volume, *Apologética Historia de las Indias*, only in 1909.

Las Casas was born in Seville, Spain and it was there that he had his first contact with an Amerindian, a Taino slave his father had brought back from the New World. Both his father and uncle had travelled

Las Casas

with COLUMBUS in 1493, his uncle remaining for three years in Hispaniola.

Las Casas himself came to the CARIBBEAN in 1502 with Ovando's fleet which conquered Hispaniola and he soon became a typical colonist, taking part in campaigns against the Tainos, using them as his slaves. He participated in the conquest of Cuba, marching with Panfilo de Narvaez through the island and becoming one of the first encomenderos (see ENCOMIENDA). While his partner was on a trading voyage to Jamaica, Las Casas had a dramatic conversion and in 1514 he renounced his estates and joined a religious order, the Dominicans, becoming the first Spanish ROMAN CATHOLIC priest to be ordained in the New World. It was in the capacity of friar that he did battle on behalf of the Amerindians, travelling throughout the Americas. He participated in an unsuccessful attempt to colonize Venezuela, lived for a time in Mexico and Guatemala and was made Bishop of Chiapas. He returned to Spain in 1547 at the age of 73 and continued work on his major books until his death in 1566.

While Las Casas battled to save the Indians, it is he who suggested that African blacks be imported instead into the Spanish colonies for forced labour in the mines and plantations. Although he recanted this view in later life, the African slave trade and SLAVERY on the plantations had by then become firmly entrenched.

[Sauer 1966, Wynter 1984]

LATITUDE AND LONGITUDE

The flagstaff at FORT CHARLES, PORT ROYAL, is the point from which Jamaica's latitude and longitude are measured. Kingston's longitude and latitude were first determined in 1875-76 by Commander F.M. Green of the United States Navy. KINGSTON station was then based at a point at the foot of King Street. From this point latitude was determined by 43 observations of pairs of stars. Longitude was determined by telegraphic signals between Greenwich, England and Kingston via a number of points in between. However, in preparing maps for Jamaica, the British Admiralty later used figures for latitude and longitude that were based on the Fort Charles flagstaff and these differ fractionally from Commander Green's. Jamaica is situated between 17° 43' and 18° 32' N lat and 76° 11' and 78° 21' W long.

Much earlier, Port Royal had played a minor role in the long quest to find a practical method of determining longitude. While latitude was easily fixed from the observation of nature, fixing longitude, which depends on time, posed the greatest technological challenge of the age. Without being able to fix their position accurately, even the best sailors could lose their bearings once they lost sight of land and many ships and lives were lost at sea. This was not just a human but an economic problem since by the end of the 17th century nearly 300 ships a year were plying between England and the West Indies alone.

The British government by the Longitude Act of 1714 established a huge prize of £20,000 (worth millions today) for a 'Practicable and Useful' means of determining longitude. A panel of judges called the Board of Longitude was set up. In order for them to judge the accuracy of any proposal 'the technique had to be tested on one of Her Majesty's ships, as it sailed over the ocean, from Great Britain to any such Port in the West Indies as those Commissioners Choose . . . without losing their Longitude beyond the limits . . . mentioned'.

As Dava Sobel tells it in her book, *Longitude: The True Story of the Lone Genius Who Solved the Greatest Scientific Problem of His Time*, the eventual winner was a humble clockmaker named John Harrison. 'He invented a clock that would carry the true time from the home port, like an eternal flame, to any remote corner of the world.' Harrison invented a series of timepieces (called chronometers) of ever-increasing accuracy (and decreasing size) that could be carried aboard ship, but it took 40 years for him to be given the prize. The prize winning piece was his fourth watch which was completed in 1759 with the assistance of his son William (and along with the other Harrison chronometers is now on display at the National Maritime Museum, London).

It was William Harrison who in 1761 carried his father's watch on a sea trial to Jamaica, embarking in November on the HMS *Deptford*. The Board of Longitude insisted that the box containing the watch be fitted with four locks, each opening with a separate key. One key went to William who had to wind the clock each day and among the other three trusted men was William Lyttleton, governor-designate of Jamaica. Two astronomers, one in Portsmouth and one sailing to Jamaica, took charge of establishing the correct local time of departure and arrival by which the watch was set. The crossing took nearly three months, the *Deptford* arriving at Port Royal on 19 January. When the watch was checked, it was found that it had lost only five seconds, after 81 days at sea. A little over a week later, Harrison and the watch left on the *Merlin* for the return voyage. Despite the watch's proven accuracy, the Board refused to give Harrison the prize (owing to the underhand machinations of the Board, which Sobel recounts in her book). In March 1764 William and the watch again embarked for another test run to the West Indies, this time Barbados.

In time, the utility of Harrison's chronometer was accepted and the instrument became standard equipment for ships.

[GOJ *Handbook of Jamaica* 1961, Sobel 1995]

LAUNDRY

Before widespread indoor plumbing or the advent of washing machines, or indeed of synthetic, colour-fast, and easy-care fabrics, wash day was a major event in the household. Washing took up a whole day, sometimes several, with ironing reserved for another day, usually a Friday. The importance of this household ritual was not lost on the Prophet BEDWARD. He explained the significance of the fasts he laid on his followers in the following terms to the visiting American anthropologist, Martha Warren Beckwith: 'A day for washing, a day for drying and starching, a day for ironing; so the heart is made clean by the fasts.'

Laundry and other household chores being so all consuming was not limited to Jamaica – indeed they were the universal lot of women, since even in the United States, in 1900, electricity was still used mainly for lighting. The advent and widespread use of appliances such as the electric stove, vacuum cleaner, refrigerator, washing machine, floor polisher, electric iron, all came after that time.

Many poor people are still unaffected by these developments and continue to wash by hand, though their chore has been eased somewhat with modern detergents and fabrics which no longer require bleaching, starching, or even ironing. In the past, 'washday' began on a Monday but because the process was so complicated, it could continue for several days. Even the poorest took great pride in wearing well-laundered clothes when they left their yard, and since the wardrobe of most people was limited, laundry was a vital undertaking each week.

In the home of rich or poor, the weekly washing would follow a regular pattern: the clothes would first be separated into 'white' and 'coloured', essential in the days before colour-fast dyes. Sometimes they were put to soak in soapy water from the night before. Boiling linen was common, especially to prevent the spread of contagious diseases such as tuberculosis and smallpox, so many households had a large iron pot set up in the yard, or a large 'kerosene tin', i.e. one that originally contained that product. Using a long stick to fish boiling hot sheets and shirts from the pot was a dangerous and skilled exercise. Clothing for everyday wear was made of heavy, durable materials such as OSNABURGH, denim or khaki and it would often be worn all week, becoming heavily soiled. Every laundress had a scrubbing board, a heavy piece of board corrugated on one side for rubbing out the dirt; a dried corncob was also sometimes used.

Before the advent of powdered detergents in the 1950s, brown (sometimes white or blue) washing soap came in three-foot long bars that would be cut by the shopkeeper to the desired length. 'Bar soap' could be melted in the water or rubbed directly on the clothes.

White clothes would be washed separately and then 'bleached' by laying them out on lines, large rocks or zinc sheets in the sunniest part of the yard and leaving them there all day. Stains were treated with a mixture of LIME juice and SALT which, aided by sunlight, removed many marks. In fact, the clothes could be laid over anything that enabled the sun to reach them, including bushes in the yard, low tree branches, hedges or pingwing fences. At the slightest sign of rain, there would be a mad rush to collect them and take them indoors.

After bleaching, the whites would be rinsed again and 'blued' to bring out the whiteness, i.e rinsed in water to which laundry blue that came in cake form, had been added.

The final step for virtually every item of laundry – including bed linen and underwear – was 'starching'. The starch was made from CASSAVA and would have to be mixed with hot water to make it liquid, then thinned to the appropriate consistency. Clothing would be dipped into it then put out to dry again.

Stiffly starched, well-ironed clothes (which in

Washing in river

M. LaYacona

some households meant virtually all the clothes, plus household linens, tablecloths and napkins, doilies, and other crocheted pieces) were a matter of pride for people of all classes.

Before ironing, each item would be sprinkled with water and rolled into a ball to keep it damp until it was ironed. Irons in the old days were either a large steam iron heated by hot coals inside it or more commonly, 'flat irons' or 'sad irons' that were heated on a stove or COAL-POT. They had iron handles, so the laundress needed a piece of padded cloth to hold them (the word 'sad' means 'heavy'). Before use, the bottom of each was wiped on a piece of cloth or, in the country, a piece of BANANA 'trash' or dried leaf to clean it and make it run smoothly over the clothes. The laundress tested whether the iron was hot enough by touching it with her finger dipped in water – it was ready when it sizzled.

Quite often, the ironing board would be made up from a piece of board laid over two chairs with layers of cloth as padding. As it was ironed, each neatly folded garment would be placed on a large, shallow wooden tray made for that purpose. The entire house would be suffused with the smell of freshly starched clothes, just in time for the weekend and the smell of wax from FLOOR CLEANING.

Washing was often done outdoors with the women stooping over the wooden (later 'galvanize') tub or standing in a special laundry room or shed in the yard of better-off homes.

In a communal YARD, washing took place – as it still does – around the STANDPIPE. In the countryside, some women still take the family laundry to a nearby river for washing; several women will get together at a shallow spot with a suitable stony bank, and make washday an occasion for song, jokes, and cooking a communal pot. The women carry the clothes to the river on their heads in huge baskets or tubs, using river sand as an abrasive agent on the 'tougher' clothes, and spread them to dry on the river-bank and nearby bushes.

The better off homes had a laundress who came in to 'do' the clothes; some professional laundresses would 'take in' washing for regular customers. In the days of sailing ships, washerwomen in coastal towns were kept busy with laundry from the ships. Indeed, it is believed that the great CHOLERA epidemic of 1850-51 was started in such a manner, as Mary SEACOLE recorded in her autobiography. When the rush to build the Panama Railroad started in 1845, Jamaican washerwomen had a thriving business taking dirty clothes from Colón (where there was then a lack of clean water) to be laundered in Jamaica. (See COLÓN MAN.)

LEAF OF LIFE
(*Bryophyllum pinnatum*)
A succulent plant much used in folk MEDICINE, especially in a TEA for colds and hypertension. The juice of the crushed leaves is also applied to insect bites and bruises. The plant is remarkable in that even a piece of leaf will grow, new leaflets arising from the indentations along its edge. A native of Madagascar, Leaf of Life grows wild in Jamaica from 200 to 1,500m and is also cultivated as a garden ornamental.

[Adams 1972, Asprey and Thornton 1953-55, Campbell 1974, Robertson 1990]

Leaf of Life

LEBANESE
Jamaica's Middle Eastern community currently numbers about 1,000 persons. They have played a significant role in the commercial and industrial development of the economy and cultural life. Most of this group came as emigrants from Lebanon, with smaller numbers from Damascus in Syria and Bethlehem in Palestine. At the time of their earliest arrival here, all of these places were part of Syria, hence the immigrants were (and sometimes still are) called 'Syrians'. They were virtually all Christians, with a few families of JEWS.

Some came to escape religious persecution since the region was then part of the Muslim Ottoman (Turkish) Empire; others came in

A gathering of Middle Easterners in Kingston. All are Lebanese except for Joseph Matalon (third left) and Mr Buzarri (third right) from Syria and Elias Issa (smoking hookah) from Palestine

search of business opportunities or adventure. Few of the earliest arrivals seem to have set out for Jamaica, though later ones did follow relatives already settled here. The first Lebanese came in the late 19th century; some were attracted by the opportunities for trade at the great International Exhibition which was held in KINGSTON in 1891 and decided to stay on.

The Lebanese started out primarily as small businessmen, especially in the clothing and the dry goods trade. With one or two exceptions, the poorer ones began as peddlers, touring the countryside with their packs of goods to sell. Because they sold goods on credit and went directly to their customers, they became a well-known fixture of Jamaican life for many decades. The folk song, 'Quattie a yard O, Salo' refers to these transactions. According to Olive Lewin, 'Salo' is apparently a corruption of 'Shalom' or 'Salaam', their traditional greetings. From these small beginnings, many of Jamaica's largest industrial and commercial enterprises have grown.

Descendants of these immigrants from the Middle East have played a major role in the development of commerce, construction and other industries (e.g. Matalon), the retail trade (e.g. Hanna, Issa), tourist industry (e.g. Issa), manufacturing (e.g. Mahfood), and politics (Rt Hon Edward Seaga, prime minister of Jamaica 1980-89). Several Lebanese-Jamaican families have been noted for their philanthropic activities.

The Middle Eastern influence on cuisine has been negligible, with the exception of the growing liking for 'Syrian bread' which for some time has been available in supermarkets.
[Ammar 1970, Issa 1994, Patterson and McDonnough 1997]

LEGENDS AND MYTHS

Legends and myths are a part of Jamaican FOLKLORE. Sometimes the two are confused and many legends are referred to as 'myths'.

Legends *The Collins English Dictionary* defines 'legend' as follows:

'1. A popular story handed down from earlier' and '4. A person whose fame or notoriety makes him [or her] a source of exaggerated or romanticized tales or exploits.'

Although every Jamaican is probably familiar with some of the stories and components of island legends, they have not been much studied. Like other aspects of the oral culture, old legends are in danger of disappearing though new ones will always arise. Some, such as the SPANISH legend of St James (see ST JAGO), exist only in the historical literature. Some extraordinary legends and legendary personalities of the past are hardly known today. Few would have heard of Admiral NELSON, THREE FINGER JACK or the Mad Doctor of EDINBURGH CASTLE. But many people would have heard legendary stories about 20th century personalities such as Marcus GARVEY, Alexander BUSTAMANTE or 'Rhygin', a criminal on whose exploits the film, *The Harder They Come*, was loosely based. Legendary stories swirled around Bob MARLEY even while he was alive. And 'legendary' sports personalities of the past, including race HORSES, are a favourite topic of conversation and disputation on verandas and in RUM bars.

Some legends are kept alive through their association with the written word. Such is the case of the 'White Witch of ROSE HALL' which might have been part of the oral culture in the western PARISHES but first received wide public attention when a journalist named John Castello (1812-77), editor of the *Falmouth Post*, wrote about it in 1868. Novels and articles, as well as its connection with a house and property that form part of a tourist attraction, have kept the legend fresh.

Another type of legend has persisted among a small group for hundreds of years, but only recently has come to wider public attention, e.g. legends associated with the MAROONS and especially with NANNY and CUDJOE.

It could be said that most of Jamaica's NATIONAL HEROES (so designated after INDEPENDENCE in 1962) have achieved legendary status quite outside of the official biographies. Many are familiar with stories about Bustamante's creative use of LANGUAGE, handy six-shooter, and huge American cars. Those who might not know about Norman MANLEY'S contribution to constitutional development have

The two Jamaicas: Cotton Tree of myth and legend and Christian Church

probably heard the stories of him as the legendary lawyer who 'never lost a case'. Marcus Garvey is the subject of numerous legends, many immortalized by musicians.

Legends involving the supernatural, e.g. stories about OL'HIGE, ROLLING CALF, BLACK-HEART MAN or Ribba Mumma (see WATER SPIRITS) were part of everyday life in rural areas in the past. In places without electricity or any form of entertainment, the dark nights were filled with threatening creatures. Unusual places (e.g. BLUE HOLES, COTTON TREES) were viewed as the abode of monsters and demons known collectively as DUPPY. Many of these legendary creatures were brought from Africa and belief in them passed on from generation to generation.

Jamaican legends collectively reflect the beliefs of the various peoples who have settled the island over time – Amerindian, Spanish, European, AFRICAN, Asian. Sometimes the origins are quite clear but many are syncretic, a fusion from several sources. The hundreds of Anansi and other tales that have been collected reflect some of this cultural blending.

The Bible itself is an object given legendary status (see BIBLE IN FOLKLORE) and Biblical stories of legendary heroes such as Moses or Daniel in the Lion's Den are widely popular. They are often incorporated into recurring cultural manifestations or given new interpretations, such as the notion of BABYLON.

Some of the people, places and objects about which stories that might be called legendary have been told are listed in the Subject Index. The reader will no doubt be able to add to the list, which is not exhaustive.

Myths Myths are often grouped with legends. *The Collins English Dictionary* defines myth as: 'A story about super human beings of an earlier age taken by preliterate society to be a true account, usually of how natural phenomena, social customs etc. came into being.'

Although we know that the Africans come from societies rich in myths, few of these have survived in the oral culture though some elements have been preserved in African-Jamaican religious rituals and stories.

Similarly, the CHINESE, INDIANS and others come from cultures that are very rich in myths and legends, but virtually none of these are known in the wider Jamaica.

Amerindian myths and legends are better known through their retelling in children's books. The TAINO myths collected on the orders of COLUMBUS have benefited from recent scholarship that has enabled interpretation of these myths, mainly by scholars from Cuba, the Dominican Republic and Puerto Rico. (See PANÉ.) For a few of these myths see CAVE OF EMERGENCE, COYABA, CREATION MYTH, GUAHAHONA, GOURD, MATININÓ, YAYA, ZEMIS.

LEMON GRASS see FEVER GRASS

LIBRARIES

Free public library facilities were first established on a small scale beginning in 1937 and became fully established with the founding of the Jamaica Library Service (JLS) in 1948 by the government of Jamaica with the assistance of the British Council, the cultural arm of the British government. The JLS Headquarters at Tom Redcam Avenue in KINGSTON is the coordinating body for the 13 parish libraries which all have branch libraries and bookmobile services. There is also a Schools Library Service.

The public library system of today began in a small way when the Revd Walter Lewis, a PRESBYTERIAN minister stationed at PORUS, asked where he could find a public library. On learning that none existed, he set about soliciting the necessary funds with the aid of prominent citizens of MANCHESTER Parish. As a result, the Manchester Free Library was started in 1937. Free libraries were subsequently established in other parishes – ST ELIZABETH in 1943 and ST ANN in 1947 – before the founding of the JLS which now serves the entire island.

Among the earliest reference libraries were those attached to the House of Assembly and to the Kingston Medical Association (1789-1823).

Circulating libraries did exist from at least the 1800s but they were limited to the small segment of the literate population who could pay the subscription fees and, even more important, be acceptable to the sponsoring organization. The Athenaeum Club, founded in 1835, established a library that existed up to the 1930s when the books were transferred to the INSTITUTE OF JAMAICA. Other subscription libraries were in existence from time to time and there were early libraries in some of the parishes. In 1884, M.M. Hicks, the director of education, organized reading clubs for small farmers' families. The subscription was one shilling a year, or half-penny per copy, for magazines imported from England. At one time the club had 1,450 adult subscribers and 1,820 children. The magazines included the *British Workman* and the *Band of Hope Review*.

The Library of the Institute of Jamaica (established in 1879) was largely the work of Frank Cundall, the secretary/librarian who assembled it during his tenure 1891 to 1937. The collection became known as the West India Reference Library (WIRL), one of the most comprehensive collections of its kind in the West Indies. In 1979, the WIRL became the National Library of Jamaica (NLJ).

Today, the National Library is the centre of a national information network system that links all the libraries of Jamaica. These include institutional libraries such as those at the UNIVERSITY OF THE WEST INDIES and other educational institutions; libraries of science and technology institutions, and industrial, commercial and cultural organizations, as well as the Jamaica Library Service, and the Jamaica ARCHIVES.

[Baxter 1970, NLJ 1983]

LIELE, Revd George see ADELPHI, BAPTIST, MISSIONARY

LIGNUM VITAE (*Guaiacum officinale*) National flower of Jamaica. The compact gnarled tree grows 4-8m high. It is native to continental tropical America and the CARIBBEAN and in Jamaica is found mainly in the dry southern plains and coastal foothills from sea level to 250m.

The attractive rounded shape of its dense crown, beautiful blue (very rarely, white) flowers and orange-yellow heart-shaped fruit make the Lignum vitae easily recognizable. Fine stands can be seen dotted around the LIGUANEA plain, especially on Marescaux Road in KINGSTON.

Lignum vitae wood, tree and flowers

When the tree is in flower early in the year, it is often for a few days surrounded by swarms of a pale yellow butterfly (*Kricogonia lyside*) newly hatched from caterpillars that feed on it.

The tree is one of the most useful in the world and was used by the original inhabitants of tropical America, including the TAINOS, for medicinal and other purposes. It was one of their sacred woods. The body, gum, bark, fruit, leaves, and blossoms all serve useful purposes though these were much more evident in former times (and the trees more plentiful). Lignum vitae continues to be used in Caribbean folk MEDICINE in many ways.'

The translation of the popular name of Lignum vitae ('tree of life') indicates the esteem in which it came to be held by Europeans. A gum (gum guaiac) obtained from its resin was long regarded as a purgative. It was exported to Europe from the early 16th century as a remedy (combined with mercury) for syphilis, and has also been used as a remedy for gout. So valuable was the gum at one time that it is claimed it reached a price of seven gold crowns per pound.

The tree also yields a valuable wood that is utilized for specific purposes such as ships' propeller shaft bearings. It is the heaviest of all woods and will sink in water. Its toughness has also made it desirable for items such as mortars and pestles, mallets, pulleys, batons carried by policemen, and wassail bowls. The wood is also used for furniture and curios.

Lignum vitae leaves were formerly used to scrub floors, and put into the weekly wash would give the same effect as high-powered detergents do today. The leaves have also been used symbolically, for example, to replace the wreath of laurel leaves traditionally used on ceremonial occasions such as the crowning of the poet laureate when that British custom existed in Jamaica.

[Adams 1972, Long 1774, NHSJ 1946]

LIGUANEA

The original name of what is now ST ANDREW Parish that still survives as the name of the plain on which KINGSTON and St Andrew are situated and in the commercial centre of Liguanea. The name probably derives from the word IGUANA (it was spelled 'Liguania' in the 17th century). The Spaniards established cattle ranches at Liguanea but it was not until after the English conquest (see CAPTURE OF JAMAICA) that the area was settled. The first settlers were English soldiers, and a regiment was quartered here. When civil rule came, the officers were granted large tracts of land, some of which – such as HOPE – bear their names to this day. In addition to Hope, the Liguanea plains had many other large SUGAR estates whose names survive in the suburbs into which they were subdivided, for example, Papine, Cherry Gardens, CONSTANT SPRING, Barbican, Whitehall, Pembroke Hall, Maverly, Cavaliers. There were also the smaller pens – where wealthier town dwellers lived and kept their horses and other livestock – and their names are preserved in place names such as Rest Pen, Delacree Pen, Cockburne Pen.

[Cundall 1915, Jacobs 1976]

LIMBO

Solo exhibition DANCE displaying strength and agility in which the dancer bends over backwards and with knees bent and feet flat, uses the toes to inch forward and under a pole held parallel to the ground, the pole being lowered after each successful attempt. Often done as a competitive dance to see who can go the lowest. Limbo is danced as entertainment nowadays, and is identified with Trinidad. However, there is evidence of this being a very old dance, known in other places before its recent proliferation throughout the CARIBBEAN as a tourist attraction. Ivy Baxter (in *The Arts of an Island*) told how she and Louise Bennett as Arts Officers went to the MAROON town of ACCOMPONG and in an exchange of songs and dances, attempted to teach the Maroons the limbo dance. She notes: 'At that time in Jamaica [in the 1960s], limbo was considered to be of Trinidadian origin, as it was from there that it was collected when it was first introduced to Jamaican theatre audiences in the performance of the Ivy Baxter Dance Group.'

In Accompong that day, 'the people dutifully attempted to learn the song, also from Trinidad . . . After a while Baba Rowe [a well-known Maroon elder] quietly took hold of the stick and said authoritatively: "This is not the way to play it. You must put it at the navel." Thereupon he took over and went under the stick himself (aged over 80 years) and two or three other old men followed him'. The song he sang was called 'Oh Mazumba' which apparently means navel. Cheryl Ryman later reported that the pole starts at navel height because the Maroons believe the strength of the body is in the navel. (It is interesting that the English word 'limber' meaning 'supple, flexible, lithe and nimble' in Jamaica talk is pronounced 'limba' and means 'to bend' as in the folk song 'Call Dinah': 'Sake a de pain a back me kean limba.')

At least two distinguished Caribbean authors have written on the significance of the limbo dance. Kamau Brathwaite who has a section

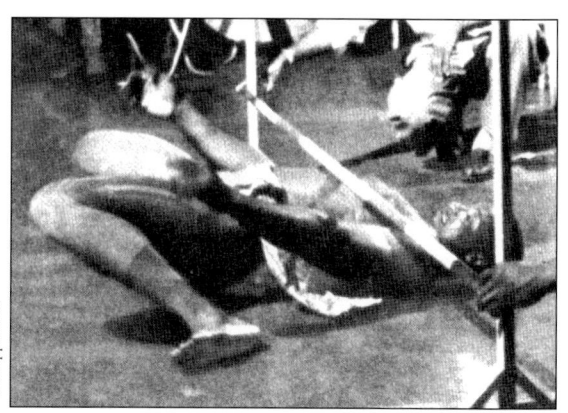

F. Stoppelman

called 'Limbo' in his poetic trilogy *Rites of Passage* notes of the dance: 'It is said to have originated – a necessary therapy – after the experience of the cramped conditions between the slave decks [on the slave ships] of the MIDDLE PASSAGE.' In his essay 'History, Fable and Myth in the Caribbean and Guyanas', the Guyanese novelist Wilson Harris makes a further connection – with the ANANSI spider of folklore. Where there was so little space on the ship, he argues, the passengers contorted themselves into human spiders – hence the limbo dancer makes himself into a spider to pass through the space between the bar and the floor. Harris sees the dance as symbolic of the need to establish 'a certain kind of gateway or threshold to a new world and the dislocation of a chain of miles' (between the Caribbean and Africa).

Others have seen the dance as symbolically establishing another gateway, that between life and death.

Recollections by the Caribbean ethnomusicologist J.D. Elder of his childhood in Tobago reinforce the connection between limbo and death observances. In his village, 'wake house' rituals were conducted by 'Bongo people' said to be of CONGO origin. Limbo competitions were very much a part of the NINE NIGHT celebrations. Elder noted that while some women did the limbo occasionally, it was 'really a man's game – an exhibition of male virility in the face of death'. Contestants from neighbouring villages would travel from 'wake house' to 'wake house' to compete. He quotes the now well-known limbo chorus as defiantly sung by the contestants:

I know nobody can limbo like-a me
Limbo, limbo like me.

Elder states that Trinidadian-born Pearl Primus was the first to choreograph the limbo for the stage, for dance students in the early fifties. It was after that that limbo became a popular entertainment in Trinidad and spread from there throughout the Caribbean, becoming an attraction for tourists.

[Baxter 1970, Brathwaite 1986, DJE, Harris 1981, Lomax, Elder and Lomax Hawes 1997, Ryman 1980]

LIME (*Citrus aurantifolia*)

CITRUS fruit widely cultivated and used in Jamaican homes, far more popular than lemons; a vital ingredient in 'lemonade' and other drinks. The fruit is bright green, turning yellow when ripe. The green, unripe lime is preferred for most uses; it is cut in two and the acid pulp used in the kitchen in preparing FISH for cooking, and for scouring to remove grease and odours. In addition to lemonade (which is called 'wash' or 'berridge' when made with brown sugar), lime juice is also widely used in PLANTER'S PUNCH and other RUM drinks.

In folk MEDICINE, lime juice is used in sponge baths to reduce fever; lime leaf TEA is taken for upset stomachs, and a rum-soaked leaf tied to the forehead is a headache remedy. Lime is also widely used to counteract (or 'cut' with its acid) the malignant effect of OBEAH and DUPPIES. It is also said to be a useful anti-aphrodisiac, 'to cut yuh courage', or reduce your sex drive.

A native of tropical Asia, the lime tree, like the ORANGE, was brought by the Spaniards in the 15th century. The tree is small, 2-5m high, and spiny, and often grown in gardens. The Caribbean lime is very acidic and is grown commercially in some islands for the export of oil of lime. Limes and lime juice were among the earliest exports of the BRITISH colonists from Jamaica to England. In Florida, it is known as the Key Lime, growing in South Florida and the Florida Keys.

[Adams 1972, Banbury 1894, Robertson 1990]

LIME, White see WHITE LIME

LIMESTONE

Sedimentary rock which makes up about one-third of the surface of Jamaica, most of the land under 900m in elevation. Limestone originates in the sea as the calcareous remains of marine animals and was deposited at various times over millions of years as the whole island was submerged and uplifted. (See GEOLOGY.) There are different types of limestone, depending on time of origin and depth of deposit, but the two main divisions are the older yellow limestone of the central and western areas, succeeded by the younger pure white limestone nearer the coast.

The rock is responsible for many fascinating geographical features (such as the COCKPIT COUNTRY, FERN GULLY and the periodic MONEAGUE 'lake') and for providing the country's most valuable mineral resource, BAUXITE, which occurs in limestone-derived soil. Other valuable limestone by-products are gypsum which is a principal ingredient in cement, white marl, which is used in road making and construction, and WHITE LIME, used in making SPANISH WALL, among other things. Limestone blocks are also quarried and were much used to make the GREAT HOUSES, churches and industrial buildings of the past.

LINSTEAD

Small inland town in ST CATHERINE Parish, celebrated in the folk song 'Linstead Market'. The MARKET was well known from at least the 19th century, having grown up in a very central location. It was described as a 'lively little market' in 1861. Apart from the weekly market held on the main street where people bought food, small-settlers coming down from the nearby hills also brought to Linstead produce such as COFFEE and PIMENTO that they sold to the local shopkeepers. They in turn would sell these goods to the wholesalers for export.

LINSTEAD ANGLICAN CHURCH

Also known as the Church of St Thomas-in-the-Vale, which was once a separate PARISH but is now part of ST CATHERINE. This church is of historical interest because all of the public records of the island were deposited here under military guard during the period of a threatened FRENCH invasion in 1805. The church was built in the late 17th century. The original church was blown down in the HURRICANE of 1822 but was rebuilt shortly afterwards. A tower was added in 1830. The church was again destroyed by the EARTHQUAKE of January 1907 and rebuilt, being consecrated in 1911.

LITERATURE

Jamaican literature encompasses written poetry, dub poetry and song lyrics; PLAYS and dramatic poetry; prose fiction such as short stories, folk tales and novels. Whether composed as oral or written, Jamaican literature reflects the power of these two traditions as well as the increasing necessity to draw the energy of the oral into the realm of the written.

Whereas in the past CREOLE or dialect was used for comic effect or employed only in dialogue (see LANGUAGE), contemporary Jamaican authors employ the full resources of their linguistic heritage, Creole and English, and the 'continuum' range in between. On occasion the alteration is dramatic, a move from one language into the other, called 'code switching'. At other times it is a gradual movement across the continuum range, referred to as 'code sliding'. It is this linguistic versatility that gives current Jamaican writing much of its energy, and engages critics and readers.

Up to the mid-20th century, most writers were expressing themselves according to the models of the English literary canon. Since then, a distinct Jamaican literature in English has been emerging out of what Gordon Rohlehr has called the ongoing 'revolution of self-perception'.

With the political, social and economic transformations following INDEPENDENCE from Britain, many formerly 'silenced' voices are being heard, and the scene is much more diverse, with writers of varied race, ethnicity, sexual orientations and social and cultural backgrounds exploring their own experiences and landscapes. With the emergence of REGGAE and other forms of popular music and Reggae-influenced 'Dub poetry', writers of rural and working class backgrounds have also found platforms for expression formerly denied them and are influencing the more literary, written tradition. A final dimension that is adding to the vitality and diversity of the literature is that with widespread emigration of CARIBBEAN citizens to metropolitan countries since the 1950s, much of 'Jamaican writing' today is taking place outside of the island.

Tom Redcam    *H.G. DeLisser*    *J.E.C. McFarlane*    *Claude McKay*    *Neville Dawes*

John Hearne    *John Figueroa*    *V.S. Reid*    *Philip Sherlock*   *Dennis Scott*

Historical Developments Jamaican literature has its roots both in the written literature of Britain and in the oral literature of Jamaica itself. In the 18th and 19th centuries, the oral tradition flourished (see MUSIC, PROVERB, RIDDLE) while books on Jamaica tended to be produced by foreigners.

Speaking of the British WEST INDIES as a whole, Kamau Brathwaite points out that: 'In the field of literature itself, a great deal of energy was given over to treatises on horticulture, fevers and diseases, SUGAR and sugar manufacture, estate management, sermons and descriptive and historical works. Some of these, like Edward Long's *History of Jamaica*, William Beckford's *A Descriptive Account of the Island of Jamaica*, the anonymous *A Short Journey in the West Indies*, 'Monk' Lewis's *Journal*, J.B. Moreton's *Manners and Customs of the West India Islands* and Mrs Carmichael's *Manners and Social Conditions of the White, Coloured, and Negro Population of the West Indies* may be classed as literary works in their own right, since they reveal the creative eye recording.'

Of the novels written during this period, a few from Jamaica by presumably non-Jamaican authors are often cited as 'being written out of the West Indian experience': *Montgomery* (Kingston 1812, 1813), *Hamel, The Obeah Man* (London 1827), *Marly: Or the Life of a Planter in Jamaica* (Glasgow 1828) and Michael Scott's *Tom Cringle's Log* (1833). Also part of this early literature but only now being recognized was the work of many women writers including the Jamaican Mary Seacole whose *Wonderful Adventures* was a bestseller in England where it was published in 1857.

There were plays reflecting the local experience by Jamaican residents about whom we know little. Errol Hill has identified some of the plays produced in the THEATRE from 1790 onwards and others published from time to time in the local newspapers. Unfortunately, up to the present time, few play scripts have been preserved, so tracing the development of dramatic writing is difficult. There is also a long history of reciters and storytellers, some of whom wrote and performed their own material in the vernacular and sometimes published it. The most prominent were the Murrays (Henry Garland Murray, the father and his sons Andrew C. Murray and William Coleman Murray) who were active from the 1870s to the early 20th century.

From the early days of settlement, elaborate narrative songs describing many a scandal made their way all over the island (see MUSIC, Folk). Folk tales from Europe and Africa also proliferated (see ANANSI STORY), as did oral histories, ghost stories, LEGENDS, myths, proverbs and rhyming sayings.

This oral tradition produced vivid imagery with ironic overtones: 'When kitchen table bruk down, maaga daag laugh.' The forces of metre, rhythm, rhyme, and other musical features of language remain highly active in the Jamaican consciousness: 'Man fi wuk an man fi nyam', and 'When me heart remember Liza/Wata come a me yeye.'

At the same time, the written tradition of British literature exerted its own profound effects. Up until the early 1960s, a significant number of educated (and some less educated) Jamaicans knew by heart large tracts of the King James Bible, numerous hymns, as well as poetry by Milton, Wordsworth, Walter Scott, Kipling, and others. Even those who never opened a book after leaving school could still recite bits of Longfellow or Ella Wheeler Wilcox (see MEMORY GEMS). Jamaicans have never been lovers of books, yet have always been lovers of words and rhetoric, of story and song. Walter Jekyll titled his 1904 collection just that: *Jamaican Song and Story*, and Martha Warren Beckwith in the 1920s also published several extensive collections from Jamaica's oral culture, including proverbs, Anansi stories, songs and games.

While up to the 19th century few attempted the high genres of the novel or tragic drama, the country was not bereft of literary interests. Although literacy levels of the population as a whole were low (see EDUCATION), there was always a class of educated Jamaicans who formed the major producers and consumers of written literature. Opinion shapers existed in the newspapers of the time, including *The Watchman*, which was the organ of the COLOURED class, and there were regional newspapers in Montego Bay and Falmouth as well as Kingston. Often these provided significant outlets for literary work. The Victoria *Quarterly*, a literary magazine appeared in 1883 and by the turn of the century two literary figures became involved in the publishing and promotion of a literature that could be truly called Jamaican: Tom Redcam, born Thomas Henry Macdermot, (1870-1933) and Herbert George DeLisser (1877-1944).

Mervyn Morris

Twentieth Century Tom Redcam was a poet who displayed a sense of historical roots and created the first West Indian novel series, the All Jamaica Library, publishing books for one shilling each, though there were only four titles. Redcam was also editor of the *Jamaica Times*. DeLisser in 1903 became editor of the GLEANER and was influential for the next 40 years, promoting writing in that newspaper and in the periodical *Planter's Punch* that lasted from 1921 to 1944. Today he is best known for his novel *The White Witch of Rose Hall* (which is still in print) but he produced a number of other novels, most notably *Jane's Career*. Other well-known writers of the early 20th century include the journalist, prolific historical novelist and nationalist W. Adolphe Roberts (1886-1962).

But the writer of this early period who would gain lasting fame was a little country boy called Claude McKay (1889-1948). Before leaving the island he published two books of poetry in dialect and went on to achieve international fame in America. His Jamaican works were the novels *Gingertown* (1932) and *Banana Bottom* (1933) and the posthumously

Velma Pollard

Olive Senior

published *My Green Hills of Jamaica* (1975). McKay's Jamaican fiction is significant for its authentic rendering of the lives of rural folk.

Marcus GARVEY (1887-1940) was active in the promotion of literature and the arts in the 1920s and 1930s and wrote poetry and plays himself. The more eurocentric J.E. Clare McFarlane (1894-1962) created the Poetry League in 1923 and for a while continued to be influential. But except for McKay, the writing produced in these formative years is mainly of historical interest, the poetry in particular being derivative of bad English poetry or 'eulogies of the newly-discovered tropical landscape'. Nevertheless, Garvey sparked an impulse that was to grow as the century wore on – 'to understand, explore and vindicate an African heritage'.

Elean Thomas

Jamaican literature, like ART, can trace the same trajectory as the nationalist political movement from colony to nation, beginning in the late 1930s. The writers who were often closely affiliated with the political movement began to explore more fully the question of what it meant to be Jamaican in a manner that was no longer a copy of the English model in diction or sensibility.

Two women who emerged in the 1930s would become influential; the first was Una Marson (1905-65), an early feminist who wrote plays and poems that for the first time dealt with the black woman. She was also important in the development of a Caribbean literature through her involvement with the BBC programme, 'Caribbean Voices', which was broadcast 1945-58. Later in Jamaica she was associated with the Pioneer Press which for a while published Jamaican works. Louise Bennett (b 1919), who started in the thirties, has continued to write, publish and perform poems and stories in dialect throughout her long career, bringing laughter and joy to several generations of Jamaicans but only in later years being acknowledged for contributing more than light hearted humour. Many of the dub or oral poets who subsequently emerged have acknowledged her as their literary foremother, especially in her persistence in going against the grain which was to

Lorna Goodison

write in standard English. Aside from her affirmation of language, as Rohlehr has pointed out: 'One of her contributions to West Indian letters was to establish the fact that the little people had not only a voice, but a way of seeing, placing and reducing the world of their social superiors.'

George Campbell (1916-2002), M.G. Smith (1921-93), H.D. Carberry (1921-89), Basil McFarlane (1922-2000) were the main poets to emerge in the period of political ferment in the thirties and forties, along with the novelist V.S. Reid (1913-87). Long before Black Power and the 'Black is Beautiful' philosophy, Campbell wrote in *First Poems* (1945):

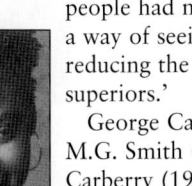

Patricia Powell

Holy be the white head of the Negro
Sacred be the black flax of a black child.

Focus, an occasional literary publication edited by Edna MANLEY, the political weekly *Public Opinion*, which encouraged the arts, and the Little Theatre Movement established in 1941 which began to stage the annual PANTOMIME, all were outlets for creative work in literature and the arts.

Jamaican literature came into its own in the 1950s and 1960s as part of a flourishing West Indian literature with many of the best known names today emerging at that time. In Jamaica, these were the novelists Roger Mais (1905-55), V.S. Reid, John Hearne (1926-94), Neville Dawes (1926-84) who was both poet and fiction writer, Andrew Salkey (1928-95), Sylvia Wynter (b 1928), H. Orlando Patterson (b 1940) and Peter Abrahams (b 1919), a South African who made Jamaica his home.

A number of outstanding poets also emerged in the sixties and seventies, among them John Figueroa (1920-99), A.L.Hendriks (1922-92), Louis Simpson (b 1923) who has spent most of his life in the USA, Edward Baugh (b 1936), Mervyn Morris (b 1937), Dennis Scott (1939-91) a playwright as well, and Anthony McNeill (1941-96).

In the 1970s too, plays such as *Smile Orange* by Trevor Rhone (b 1940), and movies such as the Trevor Rhone-Perry Henzell scripted *The Harder They Come* (later written as a novel by Michael Thelwell (b 1943) showed a growing demand at home for

Jean 'Binta' Breeze

vividly authentic Jamaican art. The demand by early radio for original work (see BROADCASTING) also challenged writers, reaching its height in the brilliant and long-running series, *Dulcimina – Her Life and Times*, by Elaine Perkins. In more recent times, television has also encouraged its own brand of dramatic writing, with a long-running series, *Lime Tree Lane* on JBC-TV and most recently in the popular romantic series, *Royal Palm Estate*, on CVM-TV. In addition, from the sixties, a number of outstanding Jamaicans have been the subjects of biography or autobiography, indicating a more self-conscious recognition of personal and national identity.

Margaret Cezair-Thompson

While for many years children's literature consisted of folktales, many retold in fine style by noted historian and poet Philip Sherlock (1902-2000), in the same period Jamaican writers began to create novels for children, the most notable being V.S. Reid, Andrew Salkey, C. Everard Palmer (b 1930) and Jean D'Costa (b 1937). A demand by the changing educational system for language arts textbooks reflecting Caribbean reality also led to the creation of many school anthologies featuring original fiction and poetry.

Jamaican Literature Today From the eighties onwards, women writers have dominated the scene, mostly in poetry and short fiction, several of them writing in more than one genre. Velma Pollard (b 1937), Hazel D. Campbell (b 1940), Olive Senior (b 1941), Pamela Mordecai (b 1942), Christine Craig (b 1943), Lorna Goodison (b 1947), Opal Palmer Adisa (b 1954), Jean Binta Breeze (b 1956), are perhaps the best known among many.

Poetry and short stories have continued to be the most popular genres among men also, Earl McKenzie (b 1943) and the US based Kwame Dawes (b 1962) and Geoffrey Philip (b 1958) also writing in both. Other recently published Jamaican-based poets include Ralph Thompson (b 1928).

Jamaica has not produced a stable of novelists as Trinidad or Guyana have done and continue to do. Few novelists with a consistent track record have emerged in the last three decades, though many novels have been written. Erna Brodber (b 1940) and Anthony Winkler (b 1942) are most popular in Jamaica, Brodber's *Jane and*

Louisa and *Myal*, and Winkler's satirical comedy, *The Lunatic*, being already regarded as local classics. Also outstanding as novelists have been Michelle Cliff (b 1946) who is also poet and essayist and Joan Riley (b 1958). Both emigrated when quite young to America and England, respectively, but have drawn extensively on the Jamaican experience in their fiction. So have more recent writers such as novelists Patricia Powell (b 1966), Margaret Cezair-Thompson, and Colin Channer (b 1963), and poets such as Claudia Rankine (b 1963), Marcia Douglas (b 1961) Shara McCallum, and Mark McMorris (b 1960), all based in the USA. Of the recent Caribbean-based novelists, Barbara Lalla's (b 1949) historical saga *Arch of Fire* continues a flirtation with the historical novel and Elean Thomas' (b 1947) *The Last Room* an engagement with alienation and exile.

Works which merge the autobiographical and fictional have begun to appear, notably *Stonehaven* by Evan Jones (b 1927) and *Drumblair*, by Rachel Manley (b 1947), each of these a study of a notable Jamaican family. Published in Canada where she now lives, Manley's book won the prestigious Canada Council Governor-General's Award. Jones who also writes for children, is far better known in the UK (where he has lived for a long time), as a screenwriter of distinction.

Dub Poets Perhaps the most striking new development since the 1970s has been the emergence of performance poets collectively called 'Dub poets', a name not readily claimed by all. This new and vital group of young artists sought to extend the oldest tradition of Jamaican literature – writing for the ear. The dub poets differ from the early reciters or storytellers in that their language is shaped by the rhythms of reggae music. Most dub poetry is best heard. Indeed, many of the best dub performers prefer to carry their message through recordings, and, in Europe especially, 'dub' performers are as popular as reggae musicians. However, several poets have successfully made the passage into written literature, producing books of their works. The best known of the oral or performance poets are Oku Onuora (b 1952), Mutabaruka (b 1952), Michael Smith (1954-83) and Jean 'Binta' Breeze who all began from an association at the Jamaica School of Drama in the eighties. In England, the best known

Mutabaruka

performer is Linton Kwesi Johnson (b 1952) and in Canada, Lillian Allen (b 1951).

Influence of Scholarship The writers of the latter decades of the 20th century – like the theatre practitioners – were undoubtedly influenced by a body of thought and scholarship in the social sciences, history and the arts, which began to emerge from the 1940s. The establishment of the University of the West Indies in 1948 created the climate for an examination from within of Caribbean culture, and the social scientists, literary critics and historians have been important in opening up the imaginative and linguistic terrain for the new generations of writers. In the 1960s, the Jamaican language, previously described as 'bad talking', gained greater recognition and respectability. Contributory factors were the formation of the Society for Caribbean Linguistics and the publication of F.G. Cassidy's *Jamaica Talk*, Cassidy and LePage's *Dictionary of Jamaican English*, and Beryl Bailey's *Jamaican Creole Syntax*, among other important works.

Political Independence in 1962 was undoubtedly a psychic watershed, and stimulated the search for national identity through the various cultural strands including traditional religion and folk culture. There was the active promotion of indigenous culture by officially sanctioned organizations such as the Jamaica FESTIVAL and the INSTITUTE OF JAMAICA. There was as well the defiant questioning of attitudes to race and class through political activism and the rise of an Afrocentric post-Garvey movement that came to be expressed mainly through RASTAFARI. A more assertive use of the Jamaican language was one signal of the social and cultural transformation that was underway, as was the implosion by the 'raw' country voices of the early Reggae singers into the hitherto middle-class-dominated culture.

Expatriate Writing In recent times, much writing by Jamaicans about Jamaica has emanated from outside the island, with poets such as James Berry (b 1924) distinguishing himself in England, and younger poets and novelists such as those mentioned above. Indeed, this expatriate writing is the fastest growing element of Jamaican literature today, and with publications from several continents, it is often difficult to keep up. As writing by a second and third generation of writers with Caribbean ancestry grows, it will bring its own impetus to the ongoing examination of exactly what constitutes Jamaican and Caribbean writing.

Publishing There has been a direct connection in the past between the vitality of Caribbean literature in general and the availability of publishing outlets. The region's potential readership is too small to support a viable publishing industry for literary work (though a great deal of other work is published locally). Creative writers remain dependent on metropolitan publishers. They are thus at the mercy of marketing trends and fashions beyond regional concerns, as well as the rapid changes and changing agendas in the metropolitan publishing world. The window of opportunity that opened in the seventies and eighties with the avid competitive pursuit of writers by the English publishers Heinemann and Longman, who both developed popular Caribbean Series, was closed by the nineties as these publishers withdrew. While foreign-based authors can try to break into the publishing industry of whatever country they reside in (itself fraught with difficulties), the Jamaican and other Caribbean-based authors are presently faced with virtually no outlet for their work. The biggest problem of Jamaican and Caribbean literature is no longer the silencing of the voice but finding the means to broadcast it.

[Breiner 1998, Brown 1978, Chamberlin 1993, Cooper 1993, Dawes 1999, Habekost 1993, Lalla 1996, Morris 1999, O'Callaghan 1993, Patteson 1998, Ramchand 1970, Rohlehr 1992a, 1992b]

LITITZ
Village in MANCHESTER Parish noted for a number of things. A large MORAVIAN mission is located here and was responsible for many pioneering efforts. For instance, Lititz was the site of Jamaica's first primary school. (See ROWE'S CORNER.) The country's first public water tank was built here in 1841 by the Moravian congregation under the supervision of their pastor. In recent years, this village has become famous as the home of the Lititz MENTO band that has won many prizes in the Jamaica FESTIVAL.

LITTLE THEATRE
Located at Tom Redcam Avenue, KINGSTON, the THEATRE was built in 1961 through the efforts of the Little Theatre Movement (LTM) headed by Henry and Greta Fowler. The LTM was founded in 1941 and since then has been a vital part of Jamaica's cultural development. It has been responsible for staging the annual PANTOMIME that has been a Jamaican CHRISTMAS tradition for many decades, a new show opening every Boxing Day. The Little Theatre is in continuous use for dramatic productions and for the annual Season of Dance put on by the NATIONAL DANCE THEATRE COMPANY. It has given birth to a Little Little Theatre used for popular theatrical productions.

LIZARD
Lizards are small to large animals and belong to the reptiles. Twenty-six species of lizards have been recorded from the island, but of these, one is believed to be extinct. The IGUANA is the largest of the lizards and the GALLIWASP is the subject of legend.

The most noticeable lizards today are the seven species of the genus *Anolis*, tree or bush lizards that are described as 'dashing, agile creatures', especially the males who provide a striking contrast to the drab females. Most anoles can change colour, some from brilliant green to dark brown or nearly black when frightened or angered, and all males possess throat fans which they can extend at will. These fans are variously coloured – yellows, oranges and browns – and are used by males for showing off before the females; they display them as a preliminary to mating or when their territory is threatened by another male, in which case they might add angry nods of their heads. Watching such lizard antics can be quite an amusing pastime. They will sometimes enter verandas and homes and (if permitted) become quite tame – though most Jamaicans will not encourage such familiarity (see LIZARD IN FOLKLORE).

These lizards occupy definite territories and will sit at the same spot day after day defending their favourite hunting grounds against others of their kind, though they seem willing to tolerate different species. Anolids have well-developed vision, identifying and pursuing prey by sight. They are also very agile, running about trees and making accurate leaps from branch to branch. Four of the seven species of anoles produce squeaking sounds when frightened or handled.

Among the most common of these lizards is *Anolis lineatopus*, which occurs throughout the island including KINGSTON residential areas and even downtown. It is mostly brown, marked with a pattern of darker brown. Another fairly common and very pretty lizard is *Anolis grahami* that has a green body, but the base of the tail may be purple. It too is fairly common in Kingston residential areas. The largest of the anoles, is *Anolis garmani*. It may reach a length of 45cm and is a bright green colour. *A. garmani* prefers large trees and is not often seen in built up areas. It feeds mostly on insects but has been known to gulp down smaller lizards.

The Ground Lizard (*Ameiva dorsalis*), common in some areas, mainly along the coast, does no climbing as its name implies. It lives in burrows and emerges in the mornings and mid-afternoons. Ground lizards eat leaves and fruit as well as insects and may lay eggs among the roots of cultivated plants. Their numbers in the countryside have been greatly reduced by the MONGOOSE and their existence in Kingston is now threatened by mongooses that have moved into residential areas, and by housing developments. (Other lizard enemies are sparrow hawks and CATTLE EGRETS.)

By far the most fascinating – and annoying – lizard is the Croaking Lizard ('Croaker') which lives in or around houses and gets its name from the loud sound it makes at nights. Croakers hide away in the daytime and come out at nights to eat insects – and to disturb householders. Croaking Lizards belong to the family Gekkonidae, also known as Gekkos. They come equipped with pads on their feet that enable them to run on virtually any surface – and walk upside down on ceilings. Croaker eggs are soft-shelled when laid and will adhere to almost any surface – and to each other.

There are at least seven species of Polly Lizards, a kind of Gekko. The Polly is a small relative of the Croaker and is sometimes mistaken for a baby Croaker. In moving, some Polly lizards undulate right to the tip of their tail. They are sometimes referred to as 'pawli'.
[NHSJ 1946, Underwood and Williams 1959, Woodley 1968]

LIZARD IN FOLKLORE

It is probably safe to say most Jamaicans, especially women, have an aversion to LIZARDS, though it is hard to explain why, especially since these creatures are so ubiquitous and harmless – indeed, they serve a useful function in devouring insects. *The Funk and Wagnalls Dictionary of Folklore* notes that where they are indigenous, lizards are always regarded as mysterious, bringers of omens and warnings, and the incarnation of a god or ancestor. In African countries the lizard is frequently regarded as a culture-hero, intermediary, or messenger of the gods. It is positively regarded in most other cultures, including early Christian theology. From its frequent appearance in TAINO art and iconography, it is clear that the lizard was accorded spiritual powers; among early inhabitants of the Americas the lizard – especially the IGUANA – is generally associated with the sun.

It is difficult to understand the unreasoning fear in Jamaica today of lizards and of SNAKES and toads (BULLFROG), all of which have come to be associated with evil magic, possibly through the use of these animals, alive or dead, in OBEAH. The more superstitious believe the green lizard to be a DUPPY. Even educated Jamaicans go to great lengths to poison and destroy lizards, and become hysterical if lizards are thought to be inside their houses. When questioned, these persons are unable to explain their phobia, one that goes back to childhood.

The green lizard is regarded as a symbol of deception because it changes colour, and a lizard dropping on a woman or walking on her dress is taken as a sign that she is pregnant (see also GALLIWASP).
[Leach and Fried 1972]

LLANRUMNEY

Village near PORT MARIA, ST MARY Parish, which derives its name from an estate which once belonged to Henry MORGAN, the famous BUCCANEER, who rose to respectability in later life, becoming lieutenant governor in 1671. This was one of the several estates he owned in Jamaica. Llanrumney, Wales, is believed to have been Morgan's birthplace.

LOBSTER

The common lobster in Jamaican waters is not a true lobster but a marine crayfish belonging to the family Palinuridae. True lobsters belong to different families and possess claws. Six types of lobsters are caught in Jamaican waters; two of them are of commercial value, the others are rare. The most common is the Spiny Lobster (*Palinurus argus*). Since 1976, laws have been passed to protect lobster supply; fishermen are

Spiny Lobster

obliged to return to the water lobsters below a minimum size and females with eggs.
[Aiken 1984]

LOCUST (*Hymenaea courbaril*)
In the CARIBBEAN this is not an insect but a large tree 10 to 30m high bearing a strange fruit, related to TAMARIND. It is better known as Stinking Toe from the fact that the toe-shaped brown-podded fruit has an unpleasant smell that is pronounced when damp. The fruit is nevertheless edible. The tree is common from 100 to 800m and is a native of Central and South America and the Caribbean.
[Adams 1972]

LOGGERHEAD see PETCHARY

LOGWOOD (*Haematoxylum campechianum*)
Dye-plant which grows wild all over the dry areas of Jamaica, from sea level to 700m, nowadays used for fence posts and fuel though of great commercial importance in the past. The heartwood of both trunk and root produces a black or dark blue dye (haematoxylin) formerly much used in the textile industry. In 1893-94 the export value of logwood from Jamaica surpassed that of the traditional leading crops of SUGAR and COFFEE. However, the trade was substantially reduced with the introduction of synthetic dyes. Jamaica still exports logwood on a small scale, the dye being used to stain animal tissue in laboratory work.

In earlier times, logwood was also found to be useful as a source of medicine, particularly in the treatment of gangrene.

The gnarled tree grows up to 10m high. In the blossoming season, December to May, logwood scents the air for miles around and BEES find the yellow blossoms irresistible. Pale amber 'logwood honey' produced in the early months of the year is regarded as Jamaica's choicest, other honey (from MANGO, ACKEE and other flowering trees) being darker in colour and less delectable in flavour.

A native of Central America, logwood is said to have been introduced in 1715 by seeds brought from Honduras on the instruction of Dr Barham, island botanist. The logwood cutters of Honduras were the pioneers of the first British colony (now Belize), then a dependency of Jamaica. Logwood from Honduras to Europe was often trans-shipped through Jamaica, even before the plant itself was introduced.
[Adams 1972, NHSJ 1946]

LONG BUBBY SUSAN
Supernatural creature of LEGEND: a woman with breasts reaching close to the ground. In case of attack, she throws her breasts over her shoulder. She is also known in Guyana.
[Mico 1893]

LOVE BUSH see CUSCUTA

LOVERS' LEAP
A sheer 480m drop where the Santa Cruz Mountains meet the sea on the south coast. This well-known beauty spot is on a property known

Lovers' Leap

as Yardley Chase, ST ELIZABETH Parish. A lighthouse was built on the cliff in 1979 with a light visible at least 35km out to sea.

LOVERS' LEAP, Legend of
During the days of SLAVERY, two young lovers used to meet secretly on the property near to what is now called LOVERS' LEAP. The owner of the property on which they were slaves lusted after the girl and arranged for her lover to be

Logwood Tree, (from Johnston)

sold. Hearing of the plot, the young lovers fled. The planter chased them and rather than face capture, they raced to the edge of the cliffs and, hand in hand, plunged to their deaths. However, an old woman who witnessed the incident said that the lovers did not die. The moon caught them up in a golden net and drew them up to it and they were last seen standing hand in hand on the moon as it sank slowly into the sea.

LOW LAYTON

Located a little beyond Orange Bay, PORTLAND Parish, this spot provides evidence of volcanic activity in Jamaica some nine million years ago, during the time when the island was being uplifted above sea level to form its present shape (see GEOLOGY). The east-west ridge about 2.4km long and rising to about 182m is composed of a solid mass of lava flow known to geologists as 'pillow lava' because of its shape; it is known to occur only when eruptions take place underwater.
[Jackson 1983]

LUBOLO, Juan

Black guerrilla leader and freedom fighter, known by the Spaniards as Juan Lubolo, by the English as Juan de Bolas. Lubolo was a slave under the Spaniards but was able to roam the woods as a wild CATTLE hunter. Following the English CAPTURE OF JAMAICA (1655), he led a group of SPANISH slaves into the mountains he knew well and established a large community in Lluidas Vale, CLARENDON Parish. This group was to play a major role in assisting a group of Spanish colonists led by YSASSI who refused to give up their island without a struggle and waged guerrilla war against the English for the next five years.

When the English accidentally discovered Lubolo's settlement, Lubolo switched sides in 1658 in return for a promise that his people would be recognized as freemen. Lubolo and his people were granted full citizenship rights and all men over 18 years were eligible for 12ha of land when civil government was established. The people in this area thus formed one of the first free black settlements in the New World. Lubolo was made a colonel of the Black Militia and given the powers of an English magistrate. Shortly afterwards, when leading his men against another group of Spanish slaves who had refused to surrender, he was ambushed and killed by them. It appears that after his death his followers were ousted from their lands by English settlers. The name by which Lubolo was known by the English lives on in the Juan de Bolas Mountains overlooking Lluidas Vale.
[Robinson 1969]

LUCEA

Capital of HANOVER Parish, population about 6,000 (1991) The origin of the name is unknown. It might have been after St Lucia, as Long (1774) refers to the harbour as Sancta Lucia. Lucea has given its name to one of Jamaica's most famous YAMS. In the days when tens of thousands of Jamaicans migrated to Latin America and Cuba (for work on the PANAMA Canal, and on SUGAR and BANANA plantations and RAILWAY construction), the people of this

Lucea in 19th century

parish grew yams which were carried from Lucea to Colón and Cuba aboard little schooners to supply the expatriate Jamaicans. (See also COLÓN MAN.)

LUCEA CLOCK

Located at the 19th century courthouse in the town of LUCEA, the clock was originally intended for the island of St Lucia but was delivered in error to Lucea, Jamaica, which had placed an order for a much more modest clock with the same English manufacturer. Once the magnificent clock arrived, the townsfolk refused to exchange it, paying for the difference through public subscription. The clock tower was erected as a gift to the town by a GERMAN landowner in the area, on condition that he should have a free hand in designing it.

Lucea clock

Thus the tower is modelled after the helmet which was worn by the Royal Guards of Germany. The clock was made in 1817.

LYING STORIES

A popular element in the oral culture, lying stories or 'tall tales' are told for sheer enjoyment. Great artistry is displayed by the inventors. Several folkloric collections contain examples of these stories, one of the most common being the 'hanging water' story. A version collected by Beckwith in the 1920s: 'Pa and I went to work GROUND, take a gourdie [CALABASH] of water, hang it on a tree, duck ANTS eat the gourdie, leave the water hang on the tree.' Daryl Dance collected a version in Kingston in 1978 in which the teller leaves a pan of water hanging up overnight and comes back to find the pan eaten away by mosquitoes and the water hanging by itself. Lying stories usually deal with 'impossibilites' and are sometimes quite elaborate but some of the shorter ones are of the formula, 'One day, I went to . . . and I saw . . .' or 'I heard . . .', e.g. 'I heard dry gungo peas talk, ask me how far I am going.'
[Beckwith 1928, Dance 1985]

LYSSONS

Village in ST THOMAS Parish named after a prosperous 17th century owner of the property, Nicholas Lycence, one of the earliest settlers in the island. He represented the parish in the Assembly. His estate was one of several in the area that was plundered and his slaves carried off by a FRENCH fleet that raided the island in 1694 (see CARLISLE BAY). At Lyssons can be seen the base of a stone windmill. Before the widespread use of steam power, wind power was used to turn the mills on the SUGAR estates and windmills were once numerous in this parish.

Also at Lyssons can be seen the tombs of Sir John Taylor (who died in 1786 on a visit to his estates in the island, including Lyssons) and his brother Simon Taylor (1740-1813). Simon Taylor was born in Jamaica and spent most of his life on the island, leaving at his death 'the largest fortune ever accumulated by a West Indian' – one million pounds sterling; he owned over 2,000 slaves on his four estates. In today's currency, Taylor was a billionaire. Both Taylors were originally buried at VALE ROYAL, ST ANDREW, Simon Taylor's residence, but their remains were removed to Lyssons on the sale of the Vale Royal property.
[Cundall 1915, Shields 1983]

MACACA

Nowadays applied to 'any grub-like worm' according to the DJE, the name formerly was used for the large fat grub of a type of wood-boring beetle that builds its nest in rotten trees, especially the COTTON TREE. These grubs were once considered a great delicacy, eaten by both native Americans and Africans; also called 'cotton tree worm'; they were recorded from Jamaica as 'macaca' from the 18th century. The other name of 'bagabu' also dates from that time. Thomas Thistlewood, a WESTMORELAND planter in the late 18th century, noted in his diary that 'Negroes fry them, and eat them, they are said to look extremely well when dressed'. Edward Long referred to the macaca beetle 'whose caterpillar, gutted and fried, is esteemed by many persons one of the greatest delicacies in the world'. There is no evidence of their being eaten today although the name survives.

This so-called 'tree worm' was relished by the TAINOS and is still eaten in some parts of tropical America. The French anthropologist Claude Lévi-Strauss leaves us (in *Tristes Tropiques*) with a graphic description of what this food tastes like. As a young man travelling in Brazil, he came across these pale coloured grubs called 'koro' which were found in abundance in rotting tree trunks. He said the Amerindians ate them but hid the fact since they were jeered at by whites for doing so. He found them to be fat, cream-coloured creatures, like a silk-worm, each one in a hollow little chamber inside the tree. He ate one. 'While the Indian looked on impassively I decapitated my catch; from the body spurted a whitish, fatty substance which I managed to taste after some hesitation; it had the consistency and delicacy of butter, and the flavour of coconut milk.'

Captain Stedman tells us in his narrative of the MAROONS of Guyana in the 18th century that the outlaws made butter by clarifying the fat of palm-tree worms, perhaps similar to the above. Finding a hidden bottle full of such butter, he reported, 'this fully answers all the purposes of European butter, and I found it in fact even more delicious to my taste'.

[Cassidy 1971, DJE, Hall 1989, Lévi-Strauss 1955, Long 1774, Stedman 1796]

MACCA

Any prickly plant or sharp thorn. People were far more aware of 'macca' in former times when most went bare-foot and so getting 'jooked' by macca was a real possibility. Today the word is used to signify any dangerous situation or person, one to be avoided. 'Every where I turn, macca jook me', someone who is finding it hard to get out of a difficult situation will say. The word was originally applied to the Macca-fat PALM (*Acrocomia aculeata*), which tree, says F.G. Cassidy, was avidly fed on by the macaw bird, a PARROT species now extinct in Jamaica whose original name *macoya* was ARAWAK. It is not clear whether the bird took its name from the tree or vice versa. In time the name came to be applied to any prickle.

[Cassidy 1971, DJE]

MACCA FAT see PALM

MACEO

Family of 19th century Cuban revolutionaries who had some connections with Jamaica. A bust of Antonio Maceo can be seen at NATIONAL HEROES PARK, presented by the government and people of Cuba in 1952 in gratitude for Jamaica's hospitality to their hero when he was exiled here. Marcus GARVEY named one of his Black Star liners the *Antonio Maceo*. Antonio and his brother José Maceo were both generals in the Cuban liberation wars against Spain. Their mother, Mariana Grajales, spent the last 16 years of her life in KINGSTON, and died there 23 November 1893, aged 85. She lived at 31 Church Street, a site later occupied by KINGSTON INDUSTRIAL GARAGE.

Born in Santiago de Cuba, Mariana, a black woman, was twice married and had 13 children, nine of whom died in the Cuban independence struggles. She herself apparently was a key revolutionary influence in

General Antonio Maceo

her childrens' lives and accompanied them in their rebel camps in the mountains until her exile. In 1957 the Mayor of Havana declared her the 'Mother of Cuba', the 'symbol of abnegation and patriotism'.

Maceo had been an outstanding leader in the Ten Years' War (1868-78) following which he and his family (including his mother) were deported to Jamaica. Maceo used Kingston as his base for travelling to nearby territories to whip up support for the revolutionary cause since British colonial governors were sympathetic to the Cuban rebels who fought against England's old rival. Jamaica became a second home for many Cuban refugees, the governor in 1872 estimating their number at 1,500. Some had settled (including TOBACCO planters) but others were engaged in raising funds and organizing expeditions to aid the Cuban cause. Jamaican merchants found gun-running to Cuban insurgents a profitable enterprise.

Mariana Grajales was visited in Jamaica by another famous Cuban exile, the liberator José Martí who was the leader of the later independence struggles (from 1895 onwards) in which Maceo fought (and in which both he and Martí were to die). In a tribute, Martí wrote of Mariana Grajales: 'the glorious old lady is dying in foreign parts, and yet still has a girl's hands to caress one who speaks to her of her country . . . She lifts her wrinkled head, wearing her headwrap like a crown.' Later, writing in *Patría* of her funeral, Martí noted that 'All Cubans attended the interment, because there is no heart in Cuba that does not feel all that is owed to this beloved old woman'.

Both Antonio and José Maceo had sons born in the island to Jamaican women, Antonio's son with Amelia Marryatt being his only surviving child.

The presence of the Cuban revolutionaries and exiles, like that of the earlier Haitians (see FRENCH) contributed not only to the arts but no doubt influenced the political climate. For instance, Errol Hill notes that on 17 February 1898 at the Theatre Royal in Kingston: 'an entertainment was given by Cuban refugees to commemorate their country's declaration of independence while the war with Spain was still being waged in their island home.' The theatre was packed for a mixed programme, including *tableaux vivants* representing the death of the patriot Antonio Maceo and a free Cuba. There were stirring patriotic orations; one by Charles Campbell took for its subject: 'Resistance to Tyrants is Obedience to God.' The central attraction was 'a thrilling one-act drama entitled *A Las Armas*, describing the outbreak of the war'. A report of the performance called the play 'a dramatic allegory of great moral and physical sacrifice, male and female, that characterized the movement'.

[Foner 1977, Hill 1992, Jacobs 1980, Stubbs 1995]

MACHETE see CUTLASS

MADAM FATE (*Hippobroma longiflora*)

Perennial herb with soft hairy stem and leaves and a milky sap, bearing singly a white tubular, star-shaped flower. It grows wild in pastures or along moist banks from 500 to 900m, and is reputedly one of the most poisonous, and also most 'magical', plants in Jamaica, much used in folk MEDICINE as well as OBEAH. Beckwith in her research in Jamaica collected several recipes using this plant. She was told among other things that 'When looking for it do not call its name or you will not find it'. Also known as Star Flower and Horse Poison, it is found throughout the CARIBBEAN and continental tropical America.

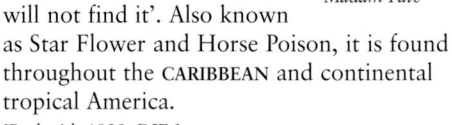

Madam Fate

[Beckwith 1929, DJE]

MAHOE, Blue (*Hibiscus elatus*)

The national tree of Jamaica. A quick-growing species that will attain 20m or more in height, Blue Mahoe is common in wetter districts up to 1,200m and is much used in reforestation. Its straight trunk, large heart-shaped leaves and hibiscus-like flowers make it easily recognizable. The flower changes colour as it matures, going from bright yellow to orange red and finally deep red before falling.

The Blue Mahoe comes from the same family as the HIBISCUS, as its botanical name indicates, and is related to vegetables such as OKRA and SORREL. The 'blue' refers to blue-green streaks in the polished wood which give it a distinctive appearance. For its beauty as well as durability, the Blue Mahoe is widely employed in cabinet-work and for making decorative objects

Blue Mahoe

Blue Mahoe flower

such as picture frames, bowls and carvings. But it has a much wider range of uses and is one of the most versatile woods.

The lace-like inner bark is known as 'Cuba bark' since it was formerly found useful for tying round bundles of Havana cigars and for making rope mats. Such 'barking', however, was responsible for killing many young trees, and the practice was made illegal. Fortunately, the Blue Mahoe is one of the fastest growing timber species.

The Seaside Mahoe (*H. tiliaceus*) is a closely related species that grows near the seashore throughout the tropics.

The name *maho* was given by the TAINOS who used the fibre of these trees for cordage and nets.
[Adams 1971, NHSJ 1946]

MAHOGANY (*Swietenia mahagoni*)

One of the beautiful native timber trees for which Jamaica was long famed. Island families still treasure their fine mahogany furniture of the past and excellent examples of mahogany work by local craftsmen (see CABINET-MAKER) can be seen in surviving GREAT HOUSES (e.g. ROSE HALL) and in many of the older churches, SCOTS KIRK being a notable example.

Carved mahogany

Mahogany was once part of the natural FORESTS on LIMESTONE hills and on alluvial plains throughout Jamaica, but few mature trees can be found today. It takes about 80 years for a mahogany tree to grow to a suitable size for most purposes, mature trees achieving a height of 30-40m. The only true mahoganies of commerce are found in Central and South America and the CARIBBEAN. The native mahogany is the West Indian Mahogany and is the most superior in quality though Honduras Mahogany (*S. macrophylla*) became more important commercially as that on the islands was overcut. Most of what is called 'mahogany' on the world market today is a cheaper substitute which comes from Africa and the East; the loss of mahogany is not confined to Jamaica; most of the world's true mahogany has long been used up.

Mahogany was one of the woods used by the TAINOS (who called it *caoba* – see LACOVIA) to make their CANOES and was taken by SPANISH explorers back to Spain. King Philip II used it for furniture and fittings in the Escorial Palace in 1563 and the wood soon became a valuable part of the trade with Europe. Jamaican mahogany was formerly shipped to Europe under the general name of 'Spanish mahogany' coming from the Caribbean islands.

The craze in England in the early 18th century for mahogany furniture led to the scouring of the island's forests for the fine quality wood that was found here. The fact that mahogany was obtainable in larger widths than cabinet wood then in use stimulated new designs in the furniture industry, and famous designers such as Chippendale, Adam, Hepplewhite and Sheraton were among those inspired to new creations.

But the trees were also being killed locally by the practice of stripping the bark from young trees to extract a dye for staining floors (see FLOOR CLEANING). In time a law was passed prohibiting the sale of mahogany bark, but it was too late to save the valuable trees.

Mahogany tree

A Taino word for the tree, *maga*, eventually became *magahoni* and evolved into *mahagoni* which was the name given by Linnaeus.
[Adams 1971, Cassidy 1971, DJE, Huxley 1991, NHSJ 1949]

MAJOE BITTER (*Picramnia antidesma*)
Shrub whose bitter bark was used in folk MEDICINE, especially for the treatment of YAWS and venereal disease. Along with QUASSIA, one of the few medicinal plants to be named after a healer, in this case reputedly a slave woman named Majoe who achieved with it notable cures in the 18th century. However, the DCEU suggests possible West African sources for the name 'majoe'. The earliest written reference to the plant – also called Macari Bitter and Mojo Bitters – is 1726, according to the DJE.

MAMBY PARK CHURCH
This BAPTIST church on Constant Spring Road, ST ANDREW Parish, is believed to have been named after a slave who discovered the Ram's Horn spring in CONSTANT SPRING estate 'through a heavenly vision'. He was given the land by the estate owner and presented it to the Baptists who built a church and named it after him.
[Johnson 1993]

MAMMEE APPLE see APPLE

MANATEE (*Trichechus manatus*)
Large herbivorous mammal that was once common in the CARIBBEAN sea from Florida to coastal Venezuela, now threatened with extinction; the population in Jamaican waters is between 13 to 100, confined mainly to the south coast. This endangered animal is protected by the wildlife protection law that makes it an offence to catch or have in one's possession the whole or any part of a manatee.

Three animals have been kept for many years in semi-captive conditions in a river at Canoe Valley, CLARENDON Parish, and are monitored and fed by the Natural Resources Conservation Authority. Boat tours are available on the river and fortunate visitors may glimpse the animals as they feed. There is also an interpretive display with information on the manatees.

COLUMBUS and his crew on first sighting these animals in Caribbean waters, thought they were the fabulous mermaids, though the admiral complained that the creatures he saw were not as beautiful as they were made out to be.

Nevertheless, manatees are considered to be very interesting. They are sea-dwelling, warm-blooded animals that are vegetarians and feed on sea grass. Manatees have large appetites, consuming about 50kg of food each day. They grow to the size of a large cow, hence they are called Sea Cows. Mature manatees can attain a length of 4m and weigh almost 1 ton. It is said that the only defence of these gentle creatures is their extreme shyness. Their main enemy in the islands is man who slaughters them for their meat or kills them out of wanton cruelty. In Florida, they fall victim to the propellers of pleasure boats, and more adult animals are killed annually than calves are born.
[Shaul and Haynes 1986]

MANCHESTER, Duke of
Governor of Jamaica, with brief breaks, between 1808-1828, Manchester served longer than any other governor. His great popularity among the island's plantocracy was attributed by a later governor (Sidney Olivier, a Fabian Socialist) to 'being himself a good type of the traditional Jamaica Grandee – a hard drinker, a hard rider, a reckless gambler, and a begetter of a numerous brown-skinned illegitimate progeny'.

The Parish of MANCHESTER is named after him and the chief town of MANDEVILLE after his eldest son. Manchester Street in SPANISH TOWN and Manchester Square and Manchester Place in KINGSTON also commemorate his name.

MANCHESTER, Parish of
Area 830.1km^2, population 185,900 (1999). The last PARISH to be formed in Jamaica. COFFEE cultivation led to its creation in 1814 and the founding of the town of MANDEVILLE as its capital. Up to the early 18th century, the hilly areas that make up the parish were largely in

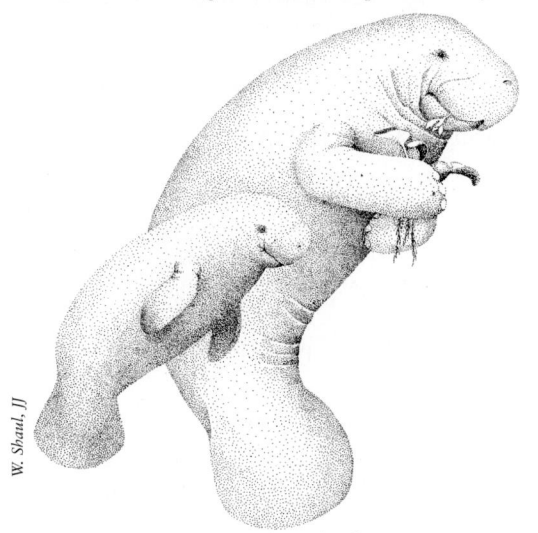

Manatee mother and calf

wilderness. Then coffee cultivation was begun on a large scale and the Manchester hills were found to be particularly suitable for the crop. Soon the area became populated with coffee growers. However, the new residents found themselves isolated from the surrounding parish capitals. On 29 November 1814 the residents of Mile Gully, May Day, and Carpenter's Mountain petitioned the Assembly to carve out a new parish and establish a town that would make religious, judicial and civic centres closer to them. The petition pointed out that no parochial or public building was closer than 64km to the majority of inhabitants of the area and there was no church. On 13 December 1814 the separate parish of Manchester was formed out of parts of the surrounding parishes of ST ELIZABETH, CLARENDON, and VERE, and named after the Duke of Manchester (see MANCHESTER, Duke of) who was governor at the time. The chief town of Mandeville was named after his eldest son.

Since SUGAR was not grown commercially in the parish of Manchester the plantation system (see SLAVERY) never took hold there. After EMANCIPATION, the newly freed slaves became independent land settlers and continued to grow coffee and other crops. (See FREE VILLAGES.)

Manchester today produces much of Jamaica's Irish POTATO crop as well as CITRUS, CATTLE, and GROUND provisions and is one of the parishes in which BAUXITE is mined on a large scale.

MANCHESTER PARISH CHURCH

ANGLICAN church in MANDEVILLE, MANCHESTER Parish, which opened its doors in 1820. The chapel and timber clerestory and tower were added later. For many years this was the only church in the PARISH. One rector was the notorious Revd Bridges. (See COLONIAL CHURCH UNION.)

In the slave rebellion of 1832 (see SHARPE, Samuel), the organ loft was used as a jail. Nonconformist MISSIONARIES were believed by the authorities to be implicated in the rebellion and many of them were arrested including the Revd H.G. Pfeiffer, a MORAVIAN. The Mandeville jail was so full he was locked in the organ loft to await a court martial. In the meantime, a sympathetic person galloped all over the parish collecting character witnesses on his behalf and they were rushed to the trial in time to secure his acquittal.

MANCHINEEL (*Hippomane mancinella*)

Tree 4-20m high, of the sandy coastal regions of tropical America which came to be known and dreaded by the early explorers who suffered the consequences of contact with it, earning it a somewhat exaggerated reputation as the 'poison tree'. Like other members of the Euphorbia family it yields a copious milky sap which, like its fruit, is poisonous, though different island populations have varying toxicity. In some places it is quite poisonous while in others it seems to have little effect. Its effects also depend on the sensitivity of the individual. The sap can blister and burn the skin and in the eyes can cause severe irritation and – it is claimed – even blindness.

Explorers and shipwrecked sailors cast up on tropical shores who ate quantities of the fruit, which looks like a small apple, sometimes died or suffered serious reactions. Combined with the pernicious effects of the sap, this led to stories that even sitting in the shade of the tree can cause death. The name is derived from the French *mancenille* and Spanish *manzanilla* for 'apple'.

Manchineel was used by the CARIBS to poison the tips of their arrows and the TAINOS their spears; COLUMBUS was the first European to record its poisonous nature. The timber yields beautiful furniture wood but has been little used. The town of MANCHIONEAL probably derived its name from the tree.

[Adams 1971, Carrington 1993, NHSJ 1946]

MANCHIONEAL

Seacoast village in PORTLAND Parish, named after the MANCHINEEL tree. For some time it was an important BANANA port. Manchioneal was also the location for some of the scenes in *Tom Cringle's Log*, a popular 19th century novel by Michael Scott set mainly in Jamaica. The hero of the book is said to have been taken to Muirton, an old GREAT HOUSE nearby (now a boys' home), when he came down with a fever.

MANDELA HIGHWAY

Named in honour of South African President Nelson Mandela who visited Jamaica soon after his release from his South African prison, the KINGSTON to SPANISH TOWN highway is the western exit from the city of Kingston and one of the island's earliest roads.

The original roadway at one time ran through extensive swamps with stands of acacia trees on the high ground that provided Kingston with firewood. High rushes bordered the road on both sides and the swamps abounded in wild life. Ducks and CRABS were avidly hunted. The swamps were created by the Fresh and Salt

Rivers (see FERRY) and the RIO COBRE. The streams were eventually bridged and the swamps drained, greatly adding to the land area of western Kingston. A turnpike was erected on what was called the Ferry road.

It was not until the 20th century that the surface of the highway was properly laid down on a solid foundation. Until that time the traveller was enveloped in dust from the white marl that was thrown on the surface, and the road was continually ploughed up by the constant traffic of heavy-laden mule-drawn DRAYS. These were the principal means of transporting goods (and MARKET vendors) across the island until the development of the RAILWAY and later, of motor transport. Today, the occasional small dray can still be seen travelling on the highway loaded with sacks of coal or bundles of GUINEA GRASS, both relics of old-time Kingston when the 'grass YARD' was an important establishment in the city.

MANDEVILLE

Capital of MANCHESTER Parish, population 39,900 (1991). Mandeville is located 609m above sea level in a cool, hilly district and offers an almost temperate ambience in the tropics. One of the most attractive towns in Jamaica, its village green and profuse flowering of blue Agapanthus and other lilies in the springtime are only two of its harmonious features. Mandeville is the fifth largest urban area in the island (after KINGSTON, MONTEGO BAY, SPANISH TOWN and MAY PEN). When the PARISH authorities first met in 1816, they purchased 40ha of land, part of Caledonia property, to lay out the town. They reserved land for public buildings and sold the rest for private dwellings. They also decided to build, in the following order, a courthouse, a parsonage or rectory, a jail and workhouse and a church. The four original buildings can still be seen in Mandeville. Also of interest is the attractive iron market.

Mandeville Square, 1930s

The town boasts several educational institutions, among them Church Teachers' College, Northern Caribbean University (formerly West Indies College), Belair School, Bishop's High School, DeCarteret College, and Manchester High School.

MANDEVILLE COURTHOUSE

Located on one side of the MANDEVILLE Square, MANCHESTER Parish, this is a fine example of indigenous architecture. It is built of LIMESTONE blocks cut by slave labour. The courthouse was one of the four original public buildings of the town and took some time to complete because the vestrymen kept changing their minds about the design; it was finished around 1820. The first school in the town was held on the ground floor.

Mandeville Courthouse, 1960s

MANDEVILLE HOTEL

Old landmark located on Hotel Street, MANDEVILLE, MANCHESTER Parish, the building was originally the barracks when Mandeville was a garrison for English troops. Many of these troops died in a YELLOW FEVER outbreak and were buried in the eastern part of the Parish Church yard. In the 1890s, after the garrison had departed, the building became a hotel called the Waverley. When Miss Jane Brooks took over in 1898, it became Brooks Hotel and finally was known as the Mandeville Hotel. It became the centre of social life for BRITISH retirees in Manchester, as well as for white Jamaicans from the area, during the first half of the 20th century. An unwritten colour bar existed there for years, enforced by various dowagers whose keen training for genetic markers could allegedly pick out any newcomer of dubious origin.

Olive Senior/Encyclopedia of Jamaican Heritage — Art

Art

Albert Huie – 'Noon Time' (1943). National Gallery collection

George Rodney – 'Packed Corner' (c. 1984). Media Mix collection

Colin Garland – 'Mr and Mrs Goose' (c. 1975). Myers Fletcher & Gordon collection

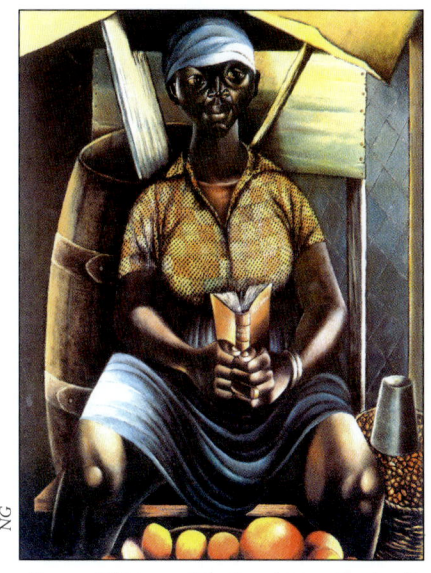

Osmond Watson – 'The Lawd is my Shepherd' (1969). National Gallery collection

Kapo (Mallica Reynolds) – 'Be Still', (1970). National Gallery collection

Gloria Escoffery – 'Habitat' (1982). Collection of the artist

Art

Olive Senior/Encyclopedia of Jamaican Heritage

Art – mixed media

Earthenware bowl by Cecil Baugh showing the effect of white and yellow trail-glaze over red iron oxide, a brown pigmented glaze. Collection of the artist

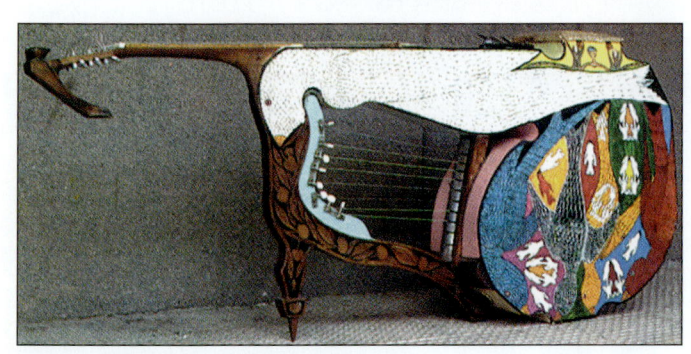

Brother Everald Brown – 'Four People Instrument' (1986). National Gallery collection

Art of Fine Jewellery – C. Garth Sanguinetti's 'Humming Bird in Flight'. A hat pin brooch created from granite and marble combined with noble metals and precious stones. A gift from the people of Jamaica to HRH Queen Elizabeth II of England, to mark her 50th Jubilee visit to Jamaica (2002)

Edna Manley – 'Moon' (1943). National Gallery collection

Christopher Gonzalez – 'Crucifix', beaten copper (1986). Hardingham collection

Olive Senior/Encyclopedia of Jamaican Heritage — Art

Pre-Columbian Art

Taino pictograph from Potoo Hole, Clarendon

Two views of Taino pictographs from Mountain River Cave, Guanaboa Vale in St Catherine

Gold disc found at Bellevue in St Ann. The only gold Taino artifact so far discovered in Jamaica. Now in the Bank of Jamaica Coin Museum

Taino 'Avian Figure' found in a cave at Aboukir, St Ann. National Gallery collection

Detail of ceremonial staff with carved male figure found at Aboukir. National Gallery collection

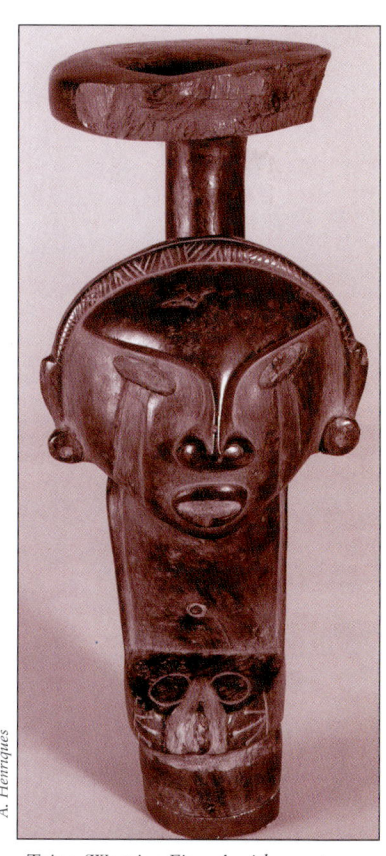

Taino 'Weeping Figure' with canopy found at Spots in the Carpenter's Mountain, Manchester

Food

Olive Senior/*Encyclopedia of Jamaican Heritage*

Food

Pepper

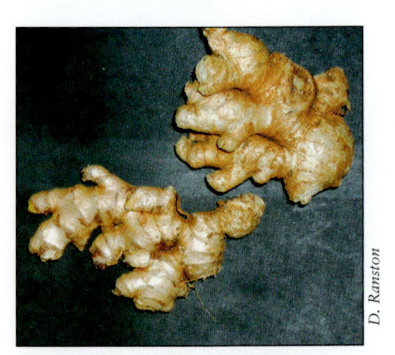

Breadfruit

Anatto

Ginger

Nutmeg

Ackee

Okra

Sweet potato

Pumpkin

Olive Senior/Encyclopedia of Jamaican Heritage   **Fruits**

Fruits

Mango

Papaw

Crab Apple (Coolie Plum)

Starapple

Jackfruit

Locust (Stinking Toe)

Otaheite Apple

Naseberry

Cashew

Passion fruit

People

Olive Senior/Encyclopedia of Jamaican Heritage

People and Customs

Carifolk singers performing at a wedding. Strawberry Hill, St Andrew (2001)

Tazia at Hosay in Clarendon (1999)

Traditional Chinese dance. Jamaica's Independence celebrations (1993)

Escoveitched fish, St Elizabeth

Faith's Pen, St Ann. A popular layby for motorists seeking real Jamaican food

Carnival queen dancing in the streets of Kingston (2000)

Roadside fruit vendors, St Catherine

Olive Senior/Encyclopedia of Jamaican Heritage — Places

Places of Interest

Downtown Kingston from Port Royal Street

Rodney Memorial, Spanish Town

St Peter's Anglican Church, Falmouth, built in 1795

Norman Manley International Airport

Liberty Hall, King Street; home of Marcus Garvey's UNIA and African Communities League

Coral reef and fish

The 18th century Hanover Parish Church, Lucea

Flowers

Olive Senior/Encyclopedia of Jamaican Heritage

Flowers

Hibiscus

Poinciana

Spathodea – Flame of the Forest

Bougainvillea

Bauhinia – Poor Man's Orchid

Cactus

Cannonball tree

Lignum vitae – the National Flower of Jamaica

Orchid, Oncidium luridum

MANDEVILLE JAIL AND WORKHOUSE
Among the first public buildings erected in the parish of MANCHESTER, this building is now occupied by the police station.

MANDEVILLE RECTORY
The house that stands to the left of the MANDEVILLE COURTHOUSE was originally the ANGLICAN rectory and is the oldest house in MANDEVILLE, MANCHESTER Parish. The rector was given 24ha of land plus 4ha for use as a plantation walk. He also got fees for baptismal certificates of one shilling and three pence for each slave and five shillings for others. In 1820 the rector (Revd G.W. Bridges) decided that the rectory was 'too public' and over the protests of some of the vestrymen, it was rented out as a tavern. It was later used as a guest house, the 'Grove Hotel'. (For more on Bridges see COLONIAL CHURCH UNION.)

MANDINGO
Known today as Mandinke but referred to in the historical literature as Mandingo, these were Africans (Mande or Malinke-speaking) from the area of present-day Senegal (formerly Mali) and (French) Guinea (Senegambia region) who were among the AFRICANS forcibly brought to the New World. They stood out in some ways, including the fact that they were Muslims,e were educated and could write and speak Arabic, knew the Koran and observed their religious practices even in SLAVERY. The planter historian Bryan Edwards had several such slaves.

Dr Robert Madden, a special magistrate sent to Jamaica during the APPRENTICESHIP period, recorded a visit from three educated Mandingo slaves, one of whom claimed there were hundreds like him in the country. A Muslim, Edward Donnelly, whose Arabic name was Abu Bakr, wrote his autobiography in Arabic for the magistrate. He came from a distinguished family in the Western Sudan and was not the only slave who claimed to be of high birth stolen by the slave traders. Dr Thomas Coke recorded the story of a member of the METHODIST congregation in the 1780s who had been a princess in her own country and whose brother ('a son of the King of Mundingo') had twice visited Jamaica in an effort to obtain her freedom. Through Dr Madden's efforts, Abu Bakr was freed by his master Alexander Anderson in 1834 and the inhabitants of KINGSTON subscribed £20 to assist him in starting life as a free man. Eventually he was able to return to his hometown of Jenne after almost 30 years. Another Muslim slave whose name we know is Muhammad Kaba whose English name was Robert Peart (also Robert Tuffit) of MANCHESTER, a member of the MORAVIAN church who nevertheless remained faithful to Islam. (See MUSLIM.)

The Almami Samori - a powerful 19th century Mandinke ruler (from an old print)

It is part of the oral tradition of Mali that in 1311 a Mandingo ruler, King Abubakari the Second, set sail from Senegal with a large fleet headed west across the Atlantic and was never heard from again. Several scholars, such as Ivan Van Sertima, have used this story (and much other evidence) to support the view that there was an African presence in the Americas long before COLUMBUS.

[Afroz 1995, Coke 1808, Curtin 1969, DJE, Edwards 1794, Van Sertima 1976, Wilks 1957]

Abú Bakr's route to the coast (from P. Curtin)

MANGO (*Mangifera indica*)

Jamaica's most popular fruit, the tree (5-20m high) is cultivated and naturalized from sea level to 1,400m. 'Mango season' in the mid-summer months is eagerly awaited by all. Numerous varieties of the fruit are to be found, each differing according to size, colour, shape, taste, texture, etc. and each with its following. The varieties Bombay, Julie, or St Julian, and East Indian are regarded as superior. 'Mi Mumma did a tell me nuh fi go mango walk/fe tief out the number leven' is a folk song which refers to the popular variety called Number Eleven.

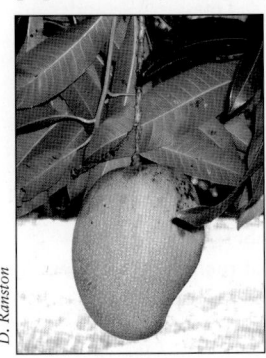

Mango is not native to Jamaica. It is commonly said to have been first brought to the island in 1782 on the HMS *Flora*, one of Lord RODNEY'S ships which had captured plants from a FRENCH vessel on the high seas, and was first planted at Hinton East's garden (see GORDON TOWN). In editing the diaries of the Westmoreland planter Thomas Thistlewood (1750-86), Douglas Hall found evidence of the fruit growing in Jamaica before that date. However, the first official notice was taken of the plants planted in East's garden. They were numbered, and 'Number Eleven' survived as a name.

Twelve years after the mango's introduction, an advertisement in the *Royal Gazette* offered 18 plants for distribution, 6 for each county. Within two decades, the mango was described as 'one of the commonest fruit trees in a great number of varieties'. F.G. Cassidy in *Jamaica Talk* has noted that there are over fifty folk names applied to mango varieties.

The Bombay mango was introduced to the island in 1869 when the governor, Sir John Peter Grant, imported from India two cases of grafted mango (18 varieties) which included the Bombay. These were first cultivated at CASTLETON botanic gardens.

The mango plant originates in India and has been cultivated for over 4,000 years. Mango is consumed both as a fresh fruit and in chutneys and sauces. It is also canned in various forms. The fruit is not only delicious, it is rich in beta carotene, and highly nutritious.

The fact that one can eat a large quantity of mangoes straight from the tree has given rise to the saying that in mango season the cooking pot is no longer needed: 'When mango plenty, woman stoccado (fence) wear black pot.'

Or as the singer expresses it in the folk song 'Mango Time':

Me no drink no coffee-tea, mango time
No care how nice it may be, mango time
At the height of the mango crop
When the fruit dem a ripe an drop
Wash yu pot, turn them down, mango time.

In folk MEDICINE, mango leaves have been used in baths and infused to prepare mouthwash, having astringent properties.

[Adams 1972, Asprey and Thornton 1953-55, Cassidy 1971, Hall 1989, Robertson 1990]

MANGROVE

Mangrove describes different plants that have developed a similar life-style adapted to the tropical shorelines and marshy areas where they live together. Several excellent examples of mangrove forests can be seen on the BLACK RIVER and its tributaries and along the PALISADOES.

Mangrove forests are extremely valuable because they play a major role in building up and protecting the shoreline and preventing erosion. They also prevent flooding by acting as a sponge when there is excess runoff from land. They harbour a variety of animal life, especially crustaceans and molluscs. Mangrove is also cut and used for fence posts, firewood and producing charcoal though this cutting is now illegal. The bark of the red mangrove is rich in tannin and is used in the leather industry. It is also used as a dye and is believed to have medicinal properties.

All four genera of mangrove that exist in the New World are found in Jamaica and all have developed remarkable features.

Red Mangrove (*Rhizophora mangle*), a tree 8-16m tall, is the one that grows most seaward and colonizes new land, and is easily recognizable by its aerial or stilt roots. It bears a remarkable seed that germinates while still on the tree, developing a long thin downward growing shoot that will eventually plunge into the mud below, planting itself. If conditions are not favourable after the seed falls, it will continue to be carried about by the

Branch of mangrove, with leaves, flowers and germinating fruit

Mangrove forest on the Black River

water until it finds a suitable place. From this new plant, true roots and leaves will start to emerge and it will eventually develop long stilt roots to support it in the mud, a characteristic feature of these plants. Over time, mud and debris trapped between these roots will form new land and the mangrove colony will move further out in the water.

Black Mangrove (*Avicennia germinans*), a shrub or tree up to 10m which is usually found growing inland behind the Red, has developed numerous pencil-like stick branches (pneumatophores or 'breathing roots') arising from the true roots which enable the plant to breathe through the mud. Like the Red, it too bears a seed that germinates on the tree. It has dark green, narrow leaves growing in pairs on the closely set branches.

The other mangroves are the White and Button Mangroves. The White Mangrove (*Laguncularia racemosa*) is a shrub or an erect tree up to 20m with leaves that are shiny and paler than the Black Mangrove and oval in shape. Button Mangrove (*Conocarpus erectus*) grows into a shrub or small tree and is common on the innermost margin of mangrove swamps and in thickets. It is so called from its small spherical fruit.

[Adams 1972, Huxley 1978, NHSJ 1949]

MANLEY, Rt Excellent Norman Washington (1893-1969)

National Hero of Jamaica, former Premier and founder member of the People's National Party (PNP), brilliant lawyer and advocate, regarded as the 'father' of the nationalist movement. Manley was born 4 July 1893 at Roxburgh, MANCHESTER Parish, the son of a produce dealer. He attended Jamaica College where he excelled in athletics. He won a Rhodes Scholarship to Oxford and studied Law at Jesus College. His studies were interrupted by the First WORLD WAR during which he saw active service in Europe and was awarded the Military Medal. He refused a commission, preferring to remain in the ranks. On his return home, Manley was called to the Jamaica Bar in 1922 and had a brilliant legal career, winning international acclaim in some notable cases. He became a King's Counsel in 1932.

Manley first became active in politics during the social disturbances of 1938 (see BUSTAMANTE, FROME, TRADE UNIONS), and in that year was one of the founders of Jamaica's first mass-based party, the PNP. As leader of the party he played a major role in the events leading toward political autonomy for the island. However, in the first election held under Universal Adult Suffrage (1944) the party won only four seats and Manley himself failed to gain one. When the PNP won the general election of 1955 he became chief minister and pressed for increasing constitutional advances, among them a cabinet to replace the executive council and reduction in the power of the colonial secretary. Under Manley's leadership in 1959 Jamaica achieved full internal self-government based on a new constitution.

N.W. Manley

When the opposition Jamaica Labour Party (JLP) announced a change of policy regarding support for the WEST INDIES Federation Manley decided to hold a referendum on the issue. On 19 September 1961 the public voted against Federation and Jamaica decided to seek independence on its own. The PNP lost the next election in 1962 and the JLP went on to form the first government of an independent Jamaica. Manley retired from active politics in 1969 and was succeeded as party leader by his son Michael, who became prime minister when he led the PNP to victory in 1972.

Aside from the significant role he played in the constitutional advance of the nation, Norman Manley also laid the foundation for social welfare development among the poor through JAMAICA WELFARE which he was instrumental in forming in 1937.

Mr Manley's memory is commemorated by the Norman Manley International AIRPORT and Norman Manley Highway leading to it, the Norman Manley Law School, the Norman Manley Foundation which presents an annual award for Excellence, among other tributes. His wife, a noted artist, is commemorated in the EDNA MANLEY COLLEGE (see also ART). His son Michael Manley (1924-97) was twice prime minister.
[JJ 1993, Manley 1973, Manley 1996, Nettleford 1977, Ranston 1999, Sherlock 1980]

MANNING'S SCHOOL

Located in SAVANNA-LA-MAR, WESTMORELAND Parish, this is one of the oldest schools in the island. It was established in 1738 after Thomas Manning, a local proprietor, left 13 slaves with land and the produce of a pen and cattle to endow a free school in the parish. (See EDUCATION.) Manning's is now a secondary institution. New blocks are grouped around the older wooden schoolhouse that was built in 1911 on the site of the original schoolhouse and is regarded as a fine example of late colonial architecture. The school buildings have been repeatedly damaged by HURRICANES and rebuilt.

Manning's School

MANNISH WATER

Popular soup served at curried GOAT feasts, believed to have aphrodisiac properties, hence its name. When served at country WEDDINGS, it is offered to the bridegroom. Made from the offal of the goat – head, legs, liver, testicles and whatever else is available – cooked with green BANANAS, other starches and seasonings. The whole is drenched in hot country PEPPERS. RUM is sometimes added to the brew.

MAQUETAURIE GUAYABA

One of the 12 principal ZEMIS of the TAINOS. Lord of COYABA (or Coaybay), Land of the Dead, his symbol is the GUAVA (guayaba) which is believed to be the food of the dead. This zemi is usually represented as a skull with wide open eye sockets, open lipless mouth and nasal cavity like that of a skeleton. The Tainos distinguished between the spirits of the living – *guaíza*, and those of the dead – *opía*; the latter lacked navels and walked at night. For that reason the Tainos walked alone at nights only with great fear. As in other cultures, the BAT and OWL were Taino DEATH symbols and might be associated with this Zemi. See also OPIYEL GUOBIRÁN.
[Arrom 1990]

Taino spoon or scoop found at Aboukir. The slightly elongated head forms the 'handle'

MARIJUANA see GANJA

MARKETS

Jamaica's internal market system is very well developed, markets having sprung up in the earliest settlements. There were three markets in PORT ROYAL at the time of the EARTHQUAKE, one for vegetables, one for fish, and one for meat. One of the first acts of the council meeting in the new city of KINGSTON 16 August 1692, following the move from Port Royal after the earthquake, was to order the erection of a market, to be held daily, and the appointment of a market clerk.

By the 18th century, an island-wide marketing system was well established, with rural slaves supplying provisions and urban hucksters supplying other goods for sale. Sunday used to be market day as it was the slaves' only day off.

Mandeville market (from Johnston)

The pattern of marketing goes back to the great markets of West Africa, the area from which most of the enslaved AFRICANS came. (See also SLAVERY.) From the beginnings of the markets, trading was dominated by women, a feature of West African markets which continues to characterize Jamaican markets to this day (see HIGGLER). Slaves in Jamaica had to cultivate their own plots of land (see PROVISION GROUND) in order to feed themselves. The surplus they sold or bartered. Thus, outside the city, the earliest Jamaican markets grew up on the larger SUGAR plantations. Other markets developed at prominent road junctions.

As the markets grew, they attracted people – enslaved and free – from far and wide. They sold foods such as ground provisions, fruits, vegetables, poultry, as well as semi-manufactured goods such as TOBACCO rolled in lengths called JACKASS ROPE, home-made chocolate (see COCOA), honey, and head sugar (see SUGAR, Wet). Both slaves and free people also handcrafted for sale products such as clay pots (YABBAS) and straw BASKETS. Some of the hucksters were urban slaves selling goods on behalf of their masters and mistresses (see GANG, Jobbing). These included provisions, handicrafts, and baked goods. In addition to fixed markets, itinerant vendors roamed the towns or travelled overland or by CANOES and coastal vessels to other towns and plantations. In the city, before the erection of the large markets, trading (often in the form of barter) took place at the 'Grass YARDS'. These were usually vacant lots where the products of cabinet-makers, yabba-makers, and dressmakers were on display, alongside the wares of country folk. Coronation Market replaced the main Grass Yard in Kingston. The lot where the chief product was charcoal for cooking was known as Coal Yard.

Some Jamaican markets still bear the names of the estates on which they were first organized. These include Papine and CONSTANT SPRING in ST ANDREW Parish, Golden Grove in ST THOMAS Parish and Darliston in WESTMORELAND Parish. After EMANCIPATION, many of the former slaves took to the hills to cultivate their own plots of land (see FREE VILLAGES) and as the pattern of settlement changed, many new markets came into being. The best known of these is NEWMARKET in ST ELIZABETH Parish.

'Grand Market' or 'Christmas Market' used to be a special market held at Christmastime, on Christmas Day or the market day immediately preceding CHRISTMAS. Grand Market was regarded as the principal social event of the towns, a time for dressing up and promenades. The tradition continued in Kingston until the early 1950s and special Christmas articles – toys, balloons, noisemakers and SORREL drink – were sold on these occasions.

[Mintz and Hall 1960, Pawson and Buisseret 1975, Simmonds 1987]

MARLEY, Robert Nesta (1945-81)

Probably the most famous Jamaican of all time, Bob Marley's name is known in every corner of the world, by people in all walks of life, through the medium of REGGAE music. Years after his death, his music, his message, and his iconic image are still universally alive, as charged with power as they were in his lifetime. Posthumously issued records, books, films have kept his memory fresh and he continues to be an influence on the musical scene. Marley achieved legendary status even in his lifetime, as the numerous stories told about him attest. As the subject of a constant outpouring of biographies, the facts of his life are common currency.

Born in ST ANN Parish, Marley moved to

Bob Marley museum

Statue of Bob Marley by Alvin Marriot outside the National Stadium

KINGSTON with his mother at an early age and lived in the impoverished area known as Trench Town. Music was always his interest and in his early teens he teamed up with a childhood friend, Bunny Livingston (b Neville Livingston 1947) and Peter Tosh (1944-1987 born Winston McIntosh) to harmonize, practising the songs they heard on radio and juke boxes but also composing and singing their own. As the Wailers, they achieved some success at home with individual records that spoke for the urban sufferers, utilizing 'roots' Jamaican symbolism and imagery in lyrical protest.

The Wailers hit it big internationally with their first album released on the Island label in England in December 1972, *Catch a Fire*. They dominated the reggae scene with live stage shows and two further studio albums. The group split in 1974, with Bunny Livingston and Peter Tosh going on to pursue their own successful solo careers. Marley teamed up with the female singing group the I-Threes – Marcia Griffiths (b 1954), Judy Mowatt (b 1952) and his wife Rita – to become 'Bob Marley and the Wailers', the Wailers being the backing musicians. Marley by then had established his own Tuff Gong label.

By 1976, Marley had a worldwide audience for his anti-oppression message, his dreadlocks RASTAFARI image, and his musicianship as singer, dancer, guitar player and composer. A triumphant tour of Europe and Africa culminated with his appearance at the Independence Day celebrations in Zimbabwe in April 1980, an event which stimulated African musicians to play reggae. Marley was poised for a major breakthrough into the American market with a tour of the USA scheduled, including three nights at Madison Square Gardens, but he was already ill from the cancer that killed him on 11 May 1981, age 36.

The Bob Marley Museum on Hope Road in Kingston is open to the public and his tomb at Nine Miles, St Ann also attracts visitors from around the world.

[Barrow and Dalton 1997, White 1983]

MÁROHU

One of the principal ZEMIS of the TAINOS, Márohu is, along with BOINAYEL, one of the 'crying twins' or WEATHER SPIRITS. This zemi's name has been translated as 'without clouds', signifying sunny weather, while Boinayel's means 'dark rain clouds'.

[Arrom 1990]

MAROON, To

For West Indian BUCCANEERS and pirates, the word 'maroon' was a verb, and described their favourite punishment for malefactors: the deliberate abandonment of someone on a desert island. The victim was usually stripped naked and left alone on a sandspit with a bottle of water, a sea biscuit, a pistol and a single charge of powder and ball. A Captain Warwick Lake, immortalized by Lady Nugent in her *Journal* as having dined with her in SPANISH TOWN in 1801 (his father was commander-in-chief in India), was dismissed from the Royal Navy eleven years later for 'having punished a seaman by marooning him on an uninhabited Caribbean islet'.

[Nugent 1839, Woodbury 1951]

MAROONS

AFRICANS who escaped from enslavement in the New World (see MIDDLE PASSAGE, SEASONING, SLAVERY) and set up their own communities throughout the Americas, fighting over many years to retain their freedom. Unconquered, Jamaica's Maroons eventually forced the BRITISH colonial authorities to negotiate peace treaties that gave them their own land and some internal autonomy in their settlements.

Maroons today

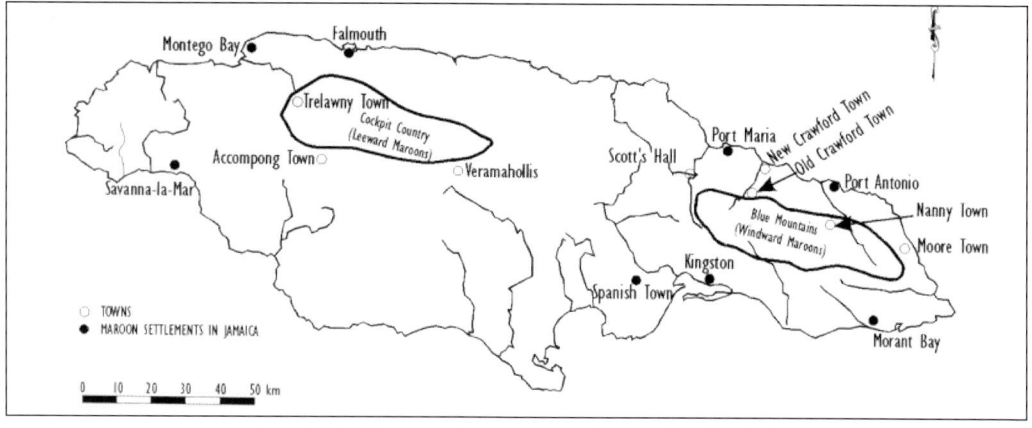

Map showing Maroon settlements, past and present (from Sherlock)

As part of the treaties, the Maroons were required to return runaway slaves to their owners, a fact that helped to widen the separation and suspicion between Maroon communities and the rest of Jamaica, as did the Maroon practice of themselves owning slaves, up to EMANCIPATION.

In recent times, much of the separation and isolation of Maroons has broken down, helped by intermarriage between Maroons and others and by the need for Maroons to leave their communities and live outside for education and work. In the wider society, it is impossible to tell a 'Maroon' apart from another Jamaican. The Maroon communities themselves that were once shrouded in secrecy, are now sharing part of their rich heritage with the rest of Jamaica and the world through their participation in international symposia and cultural events and publication of research by scholars who have lived among them. The Maroon community of ACCOMPONG now has a tour for tourists and the celebration of the town's founding and CUDJOE'S birthday on 6 January is a public one, attracting hundreds of visitors.

Nevertheless, there are still secrets that are never revealed to outsiders and Maroons preserve among themselves remnants of their sacred traditions handed down by the Maroon ancestors and preserved by each generation. Maroons are credited with being the repository of African traditions, especially those relating to healing, divination and sorcery and 'Maroon medicine' is still regarded by many in the wider society as most powerful. Farming, fishing and hunting (including the wild pig – see JERK) are still major Maroon activities. All of these elements contribute to what might be called the Maroon identity, shared by any who claim it by birth. Maroon societies have not only conserved elements of African culture but also provide a direct link with the indigenous people of Jamaica, the TAINOS. The oral culture has always held that such linkages exist, but they are now being supported by solid evidence from archaeological research in old Maroon settlements.

Maroon communities have never been large in numbers, but they have imprinted themselves on the consciousness of the wider society. In earlier centuries they created fear among the authorities and the colonists, holding up settlement of vast areas of the island through their guerrilla activities and putting military campaigns against them high on the agenda. As symbols of resistance, they have played a significant role in shaping the psyche of Jamaicans. Speaking of Maroon societies as a whole, Richard Price has observed that 'such communities stood out as an heroic challenge to white authority, and as the living proof of the existence of a slave consciousness that refused to be limited by the whites' conception or manipulation of it'.

History There are several explanations for the origin of the word 'Maroon', the most commonly accepted being that the English word maroon like the French *marron* derives from the Spanish *cimarrón* meaning 'wild'. Originally applied to CATTLE that had escaped into the wild, the word soon came to refer to the human runaways who fled to the bush and established communities in inhospitable terrain from which they resisted European forces sent against them. At first these were the Native Americans fleeing the Spaniards, but they were increasingly joined by the Africans being brought to the New World. By the end of the 1530s, the word Maroon was beginning to refer primarily to African runaways with the connotations of 'fierce', 'wild' and 'unbroken'.

Richard Price has discussed the extraordinary skills in guerrilla warfare the runaways developed: 'To the bewilderment of their European enemies, whose rigid and conventional tactics were learned on the open battlefields of Europe, these highly adaptable and mobile warriors took maximum advantage of local environments, striking and withdrawing with great rapidity, making extensive use of ambushes to catch their adversaries in crossfire, fighting only when and where they chose, depending on reliable intelligence networks among nonmaroons (both slaves and white settlers).'

When the English took Jamaica from the Spaniards in 1655 (see CAPTURE OF JAMAICA) many of their African slaves fled to the woods and played a major role in helping the Spaniards sustain the five-year struggle against the English. (See SPANISH and YSASSI.) Eventually, one band went over to the English (see LUBOLO) but others continued to resist and by the time the last Spaniard left, the remaining ex-slaves had established a life of freedom in the woods. They continued to harass the English settlers, raiding plantations for supplies, arms, and women. Over time their numbers were augmented by enslaved Africans fleeing the plantations of the English. The Maroons, as they came to be called, were predominantly Akan speakers, referred to as COROMANTEES, though other ethnic groups were also represented.

In time, there were several Maroon bands organized under strong leadership. The mountainous areas they inhabited protected their camps against the incursions of British soldiers and settlers, their trusted blacks called 'Black Shot', and from MISKITO Indians imported from Central America to track them. They lived as a fighting force so they could move quickly and were able to communicate with one another by means of their talking drums, and the ABENG, and through their secret language (shown to contain many Akan words). Over time, the Maroons developed a distinct culture.

Leeward Maroons   The Maroons split into two main groups called the Leewards and the Windwards from their geographical locations. The so-called Leeward Maroons lived at the western end of the island in the mountains bordering CLARENDON and ST ANN Parishes and were united under the great leader Kojo or CUDJOE assisted by his brothers Johnny and Accompong. In time, Cudjoe moved his band to the wild COCKPIT COUNTRY in the western parishes. From there they raided the nearby plantations for 40 years, preventing settlement of the interior. But the Maroons wanted to settle down as free people and in 1739 a peace treaty was negotiated between Cudjoe and the British government. By that agreement, the Maroons were given land and certain freedoms, including freedom from taxation. The main settlement in ST JAMES on 600ha was named Trelawny Town in honour of the governor of the day and was the headquarters of Cudjoe. Land (400ha) was also given in ST ELIZABETH Parish and the settlement named Accompong after the leader of that band.

Windward Maroons   Meanwhile, the other bands had concentrated in the eastern end, making their homes in the high mountains of PORTLAND and ST THOMAS Parishes and were called the Windward Maroons. Two of the leaders of the Windward Maroons were QUACO and Kofi. (See DAY NAMES.) But their greatest leader was NANNY whose name is recalled in their old settlement of NANNY TOWN.

Like the Leewards, these Windward Maroons were also worrying the authorities, carrying out lightning raids on settlements and retreating to their mountain fastness. The many swift rivers in Portland and the high rainfall made pursuit difficult. As in the west, they prevented the expansion of European settlement in the area, Portland Parish at the time being virtually unsettled. There were many clashes between the Maroons and government forces sent against them over the years until Nanny Town was captured in 1734. Shortly after Cudjoe signed the peace treaty for Maroons in the west, Quao signed for the Maroons in the east (on 23 June 1739). But there was a split among the eastern Maroons and one year later, Nanny signed a separate treaty for her band, founding what is now Moore Town in the RIO GRANDE Valley. It remains the principal Maroon settlement in the area.

The Second Maroon 'War'   After the signing of the peace treaties, the Maroons lived quietly in their settlements. In fulfillment of one of the conditions of the treaties, they returned runaway slaves and generally helped the authorities to maintain law and order. (See, e.g. MORANT BAY REBELLION.)

But the peace did not last forever. In July 1795 the Trelawny Town Maroons rebelled, partly in response to long-simmering grievances with the government. The immediate spark was that two of them had been convicted in the courts for pig stealing and, to add insult to injury, had been flogged by a runaway slave whom the Maroons had previously caught and handed over to the authorities. When meetings with the authorities failed to appease them, the proud Maroons took up arms again. A few of the older Maroons heeded the governor's call to surrender by 12 August (and were promptly imprisoned) but many of the young warriors once more engaged the soldiers in guerrilla warfare, raiding and plundering crops and plantations in surrounding parishes. There were only about 300 fighting Maroons in Trelawny Town but they held out against the 1,500 soldiers sent against them, supported by thousands of the volunteer MILITIA, 'black shots' or confidential slaves and the Accompong Maroons who had not joined with the Trelawnys.

The Trelawnys agreed to a truce only when DOGS were imported from Cuba (with their handlers) to hunt them down. Most of the fighting men and their families assembled in MONTEGO BAY by 6 March 1796 as demanded by the authorities, and the governor Lord Balcarres declared the war over on 16 March. The Trelawnys had come expecting to negotiate another treaty, but they were tricked by Balcarres who had personally taken charge of the war, for he ordered all of them put on board three ships he had waiting in the harbour. The ships sailed on 6 June for PORT ROYAL, and from there transported the Maroons to Halifax, Nova Scotia, Canada. Deported were 568 Maroons of whom 401 were old men, women and children and 167 arms bearing men. Their life in Halifax was never satisfactory and after two years they were sent to Freetown, Sierra Leone, in Africa. (These Maroons were to form an elite in Sierra Leone, from whom are descended many of that country's prominent families; some 60 of them returned to Jamaica in the 19th century – see AFRICANS, indentured.)

The settlement of Trelawny Town was razed and barracks built there for British soldiers who remained for many years. Eventually, when the island was more settled, the soldiers left and the barracks fell into ruin. People again settled the area and called it Maroon Town, the name by which it is known today, although it is not a Maroon settlement. Accompong remained the only Maroon settlement in the western part of the island.

Maroons Today   Maroon communities in Jamaica today are located at Accompong, St James Parish; Moore Town and Charles Town in Portland Parish, and Scot's Hall in ST MARY Parish.

Maroon 'Kromanti Play'

Each Maroon settlement is governed by a colonel, an honorary title dating from the peace treaties. The leadership is decided on among the Maroons themselves. The colonel arbitrates in minor disputes among his people. The Maroons still retain some of their old traditions and the abeng and the drums are still used on ceremonial occasions. The Maroons distinguish between their 'business dances' to which visitors are not permitted, and 'pleasure dances' which allow visitors. Researchers have argued that the isolation of the early Maroons helped to preserve many of the old African customs, among them the MYAL healing tradition. Certain types of celebrations among the Maroons also hark back to earlier times, including an 'ambush dance' in which Maroons dress in green leaves to reenact their guerrilla days in the bush and initiation dances and warrior types dances testing male courage, part of the Kromanti tradition. Music and dance styles unique to them are also found among the Maroons. A Maroon religious chant recorded in 1953 proves beyond doubt that an African-based pidgin existed alongside Jamaican Creole, and was a mixture of Akan and other African languages.

[Agorsah 1994, Baxter 1970, Beckwith 1929, Bilby 1984, Brathwaite 1977, Campbell 1988, Dallas 1803, Dunham 1946, Hurston 1938, Kopytoff 1976, Lalla and D'Costa 1990, Lewin 2000, Price 1971, Robinson 1969, 1987, Williams 1934, 1938]

MARTHA BRAE

Coastal village that was the first capital of TRELAWNY Parish. Rock, near the coast, was the shipping port. When the river silted up and made navigation at Rock difficult, the new capital of FALMOUTH was created. Martha Brae is said to have been the site of the SPANISH settlement of Melilla. Before the river was bridged, travellers used the Martha Brae ferry. Charges were five pence per head for horsekind, two pence per head for cows, and five pence for each wheel on carriage or cart. The ferry continued until 1790 when the first bridge, a wooden one, was built. In the early 1950s the river was used to irrigate rice fields around the estuary, the cultivation of rice being a government scheme intended to provide agricultural development for Trelawny. Rice-growing continued for about ten years but never prospered.

MARTHA BRAE, Legend of
Martha Brae was supposed to be a TAINO girl who was tortured by the Spaniards to reveal the location of a GOLD mine. She agreed to lead them to the mine but, calling on her powers, changed the course of the MARTHA BRAE RIVER, which drowned her and the Spaniards and closed forever the entrance to the mine.

MARTHA BRAE RIVER
One of Jamaica's finest rivers, rising at Windsor Cave in the interior of TRELAWNY Parish and entering the sea near to FALMOUTH which it supplied with water when the town was first established. The water was brought from the river by canoe until a Persian water wheel was erected in 1798 to ensure a steady supply. With its tributaries, the river is over 32km long. The sport of rafting on the Martha Brae was started in December 1970. On a map published in 1683 the river is marked 'Para Mater Tiberen Rio'.

MARTÍ, José, Secondary School
School located on the KINGSTON-SPANISH TOWN highway, ST CATHERINE Parish, a gift of the Cuban government in the 1970s. It is named after the great Cuban leader and patriot José Martí who, like other famous Cuban revolutionaries of the 19th century, at one time lived in exile in Jamaica. (See MACEO.)

MATILDA'S CORNER
Busy crossroad at LIGUANEA, ST ANDREW Parish, where Hope Road, Old Hope Road and Barbican Road converge. This remains one of the intriguing place names of Jamaica. Who was Matilda? That we do not know. Another name for the busy cross-roads was Toll Gate, from the fact that the toll gatherer was stationed here to collect from users of the road. One of the earliest structures in the area was the SS Peter and Paul ROMAN CATHOLIC Church. The original church was built in 1850 on land donated by a Frenchwoman, Madam Duval, to serve several families of FRENCH and Spanish extraction that lived nearby. It was twice closed and abandoned for lack of congregation until 1902 when the present congregation was established.

MATININÓ
Mythical TAINO island where only women lived. The Europeans hearing the story of such an island soon after their arrival in the Antilles immediately concluded that they had at last found the land of the AMAZONS. Several myths from South America where the Tainos originated tell of such an island; the women are usually guardians of the plant that became known as TOBACCO, the sacred herb. The stories tell of men's efforts to obtain tobacco, in some cases aided by the HUMMINGBIRD. The island of Matininó has also been identified with Martinique.
[Arrom 1990, Lévi-Strauss 1966]

MAY PEN
Capital of CLARENDON Parish, population 45,903 (1991), May Pen is located on the banks of the RIO MINHO and is the second largest inland town in Jamaica (next to SPANISH TOWN). The settlement of May Pen grew up from inns on both banks of the river which provided lodging for stranded travellers when it was in spate. The town grew rapidly after the railway station was built there in the 1880s.

May Pen was once an estate, named after its owner the Revd William May (1695-1754), an ANGLICAN clergyman who served in the parish and was Rector of KINGSTON PARISH CHURCH for 32 years. His first wife was a daughter of Edward and Eliza Pennant, large landed proprietors in Clarendon and his son was CUSTOS of Clarendon and Vere. He is possibly the Revd May mentioned favourably in Leslie's *History of Jamaica* (1740). Leslie is otherwise caustic regarding the clergy of the day: 'it is surprising that such worthless and abandoned men should be sent to such a place as this. The clergy here are of a character so vile, that I do not care to mention it; for except a few, they are generally the most finished of our debauchers. Messrs Galpin, Johnson and May are indeed men whose unblemished lives dignify the character they bear. They generally preach either in their own churches, or to a few in some private houses every Sunday; but for others their church doors are seldom opened.'
[Cundall 1915, Sibley 1978]

MAYPOLE
European social DANCE brought to the New World under different names, still danced in many parts of Latin America where it is usually known as 'ribbon dance'. The dance was popular in England as part of May Day celebrations and

Maypole dancers

no doubt came to Jamaica from that source. It was widely danced until well into the 20th century at outdoor events such as fairs, garden parties, picnics, and school events. Today, Maypole dancing is occasionally performed as an exhibition dance at events such as Festival. (See FESTIVAL, Jamaica.)

The dance takes place around a pole which has multicoloured ribbons attached, and as dancers weave in and out in a circle, they plait the ribbons to form intricate patterns of which the 'basket' and 'spider' weave are the most complicated. As Ivy Baxter described Maypole dancing: 'The ability of a group to plait ribbons without getting them tangled demands a certain amount of skill in cooperative movement. Besides the single and double plaits formed by couples weaving in and out in opposite directions, which becomes a close basket weave around the pole, there are other braids formed by standing or moving on the spot, while the others move in and around stationary dancers. This weave is made around their outstretched ribbons, thus giving a spider's web effect.'

Maypole dance and MUSIC in Jamaica are most often based on MENTO, but depending on the region, might include a wide variety of dance forms such as KUMINA and DINKI MINI. When maypole dancing was a popular social pastime, participants would pay for each dance. In a novel of Jamaican life at the turn of the century, *Jane's Career*, H.G. DeLisser's heroine frequented maypole or 'ribbon dances' as they were called, at which the fee was sixpence. The AGAVE frequently provided the pole in earlier times, hence the plant's other name of 'Maypole'.

[Baxter 1970, Ryman 1980]

MEDICINE, Folk

Included in the term folk medicine (also referred to as 'bush medicine') are many practices that relate to treating illness without reference to a registered medical practitioner. As H.I.C. Lowe has pointed out, while the popular conception of folk medicine is the use of 'bush' to cure illness, 'fresh air, sunlight, metallic and wooden objects, food, water, parts of animals, various chemical materials and compounds, faith healing and obeah all contribute to the practice'.

There is a vast body of lore concerning treatments, most based on plant use, but also using other simple remedies available from a 'doctor shop', as pharmacies used to be called. So home-medication is usually the first resort. Knowledge about the use of plants and treatment applications is part of the oral tradition, handed down usually from mother to daughter, passed along from house to house and village to village. Allied to actual treatments are many folk beliefs surrounding the human body and its functioning, including diet, and practices to be observed to maintain the health of the 'structure'. The link between body and mind (including one's relationships with others) is regarded as a crucial element in maintaining good health.

Folk medicine is often consumed as 'TEA', in baths (see BUSH) and by physical application such as rubbing with white RUM to forestall 'catching cold', tying a LIME leaf on the head as a headache remedy, or applying aloe or other plant material directly to a wound. There is a great deal of faith in TONICS, in the 'purge' or 'wash out' – usually by CASTOR OIL, and in the efficacy of bitter bushes, of which the most popular is CERASEE. Plants that have in recent years enjoyed a vogue in the cosmetics industry, for example aloe, have long been used in home preparations for skin and hair. Every rural household kept first aid treatments to hand, often bush growing in the kitchen garden or nearby wilderness, Bissy (see KOLA), GINGER, MINT, FEVER GRASS, Sinkle Bible (see ALOE), among the most common.

In the old days, doctors were few and far between and certainly not accessible to the majority of people who were thrown back upon their own resources for their medical needs (a situation which still holds true for some people today). The folk knowledge that has evolved over the centuries combines beliefs and practices from Africa as well as from Europe, native Americans (see MEDICINE, Taino) and the East. While there is little research available on the use of traditional medicine by ethnic groups such as INDIAN and CHINESE, and how this might have influenced or been influenced by the wider society, they no doubt brought their own knowledge and practices to Jamaica. We know that some elements of their belief systems coincided with the African, as did many of the medicinal plants used. Widespread use has also been made by Jamaicans of Chinese preparations such as 'Tiger Balm'.

Some knowledge of folk medicine is shared by people in all walks of life, though the poor are more likely to be dependent on it. The better off might resort to it when orthodox medicine has failed, or when they are in search of success in business or love, for these too have their own 'medicine'. When self- or home-doctoring, or orthodox medicine has failed, resort will be had to a traditional healer, who goes under many different names.

'Black doctors' The earliest practitioners of orthodox medicine studied Jamaican plant life and its use by local healers, doctors then being also natural scientists. Dr Hans Sloane (1660-1753) who stayed in Jamaica for 15 months, explained that 'This Voyage seem'd likely to promise to be useful to me, as a Physician; many of the Antient and best Physicians having travell'd to the Places from whence their Drugs were brought to inform themselves concerning them'. He ended up describing almost 800 new plants (see FLORA) and many other doctor-botanists followed over the years. Dr Thomas Dancer (1755-1811) who was island botanist and also practised medicine, learnt from the black people of the island as much as he could of the use of native plants, often recording such usage in his book: *The Medical Assistant*; or *Jamaica Practice of Physic* published in 1801. For instance, of Adrue (*Cyperus articulatus*) as treatment of vomiting, he notes: 'This remedy was, soon after my arrival, pointed out to me by a sensible negro, who had the charge of a hospital on a large estate.' Dancer's book was actually a medical manual intended for use by Jamaican families and planters.

Native healers were often referred to as 'black doctors' and treated whites as well. From the earliest days of SLAVERY, much of the doctoring on the estates was in the hands of these skilled slaves who were schooled in traditional African healing methods, many coming directly from that continent up to 1807, when the slave trade ended. Medicines have been named after such African healers in the New World, among them MAJOE BITTERS and QUASSIA.

In the post-EMANCIPATION period, this type of practice continued, with many people (skilled or unskilled, authentic or fake) setting themselves up as 'bush doctors' or 'balmists'. (See BALM.) There were also, both during slavery and after, free black or COLOURED women called 'doctoresses', who were noted as healers, achieving fame in the white community and caring for their patients in their own lodging houses. Mary SEACOLE and CUBAH are the most famous examples.

Many traditional healers operated as specialists, such as midwives, bone setters, cuppers, and blood letters. All acquired their skills by a combination of apprenticeship to an experienced healer, observation of the methods of a trained doctor, refinement of their own skills and knowledge by experiment and observation. Mary Seacole related that she first acquired her interest in healing as a small child watching her mother, a noted doctoress, and practised on her dolls. Some claim to acquire their healing skills through messages from the spirit world.

Mind-body connection A significant element of healing then as now is the recognition of an inseparable mind-body connection and the widespread belief that sickness always has an external source and can result from the patient having caused offence to another person or to the spirit of a dead person. (See DUPPY, OBEAH.) Thus in the popular conception, 'medicine' and 'healing' are multi-dimensional.

A healer can be a Balmist, Myalist, Obeah-man or -woman Revivalist, Maroon or Kumina practitioner or an individual with none of those connections, who might be referred to as a 'Bush Doctor'. When consulted, he or she will advise on the cause of the illness (spiritual, mental or physical) and prescribe the appropriate treatment. This might involve offensive or defensive magic (see CHARM), baths, or special ceremonies. The invocation of healing through special ceremonies involving communal MUSIC, DANCE and spirit possession is an important dimension of African-Jamaican religions and cultural expressions. (See GOOMBAY, KUMINA, MAROON, MYAL, REVIVAL.)

Many healers operate in the realm of faith healing, acquiring spirit guidance through dreams and visions. This is especially true of Revivalists. Faith healing is also a practice of more modern religions such as PENTECOSTALISM and includes the 'laying on of hands' and modes of healing that focus on the power of the Holy Spirit.

Many plants used as folk remedies have become incorporated into modern medicine though there are certain dangers in folk medication including the inability to accurately measure dosage. While claims for many medicinal plants remain unsubstantiated, others have proven their worth. One of the early activities of the medical faculty established at the UNIVERSITY OF THE WEST INDIES was a study of medicinal plant use in Jamaica, Asprey and Thornton in their path-breaking work describing hundreds of such plants. Since then, research has continued at the UWI in medicinal plants, with breakthroughs, for instance, in developing drugs from GANJA.

The present metropolitan vogue for 'alternative medicine' is also evident in Jamaica. From Sloane to the present, there has been an interplay between 'official' and 'alternative' medicine, on a continuum from rejection to incorporation. While there is no official recognition in Jamaica of folk medicine, it is deeply entrenched in the culture, celebrated in lore and song such as one listing the Weed Woman's wares. (The following verse is from a version that was collected in ST ELIZABETH Parish and not all the plants are identifiable):

She had Man Piaba, Woman Piaba
Tom-Tom Fall Back and Lemon Grass,
Minnie Root, Gully Root, Granny Backbone
Dead Man Git Up and Live On turro,
Coolie-bitter and Gorina bush, the old
Compellance Weed, Sweet-broom,
Cow Tongue, Granny Scratch-scratch,
Belly-puller and the Guzu Weed.

[Adams 1971, 1972, Asprey and Thornton 1953-55, Beckwith 1929, Campbell 1974, Dancer 1801, Genovese 1976, Hall-Alleyne 1996, Laguerre 1987, Lowe 1972, Robertson 1982, 1990, Seacole 1857, Seaga 1955, 1968, 1969, Sloane 1707, 1725]

MEDICINE, Taino

Medical diagnosis and practice of the TAINOS was similar to that of other South Americans; it employed shamanistic practice to determine the cause of illness and prescribe a cure and bears a striking similarity to the beliefs and techniques of MYAL.

Curing consisted in either removing an object from the body that should not be there, or putting back something that had left the body (the patient's soul). Harmful objects in the body were usually removed by massage and suction, a practice that is similar throughout South America and the CARIBBEAN.

The Taino medicineman was called a *bohuti* or *behique* or *piaie*, the name used by the continental Lokono ARAWAKS. The Taino practice was very similiar to that of continental

Taino healing ritual (from Oviedo)

medicinemen, the difference being that while others believed the sickness was caused by an evil spirit, the Tainos believed it was caused by the patient offending a ZEMI.

In addition to the shaman, there were also old women knowledgeable about herbs. Baths and purgatives were used. Many of the medicinal plants that are used today were known by the Tainos; some they brought with them from South America to the Caribbean. Hans Sloane, the English medical doctor who came to the West Indies in the late 17th century (see FLORA), attributed knowledge of some folk medicine he found among the black population to contact with the Amerindians because 'they use the same remedies for the same diseases in Mexico and Brazil'.

[Fewkes 1907, Lovén 1935, Sloane 1707, 1725]

MEMORY GEM

A short precept taught in Sunday school or at home based on moral or Christian principles, e.g.

Speak the truth and speak it ever
Cost it what it will
He who hides the wrong he does
Does the wrong thing still.

Such gems used to be prominently displayed on walls and blackboards and even embroidered on garments and other articles. They are still part of the memorized oral tradition of older Jamaicans.

MENTO

Traditional Jamaican dance MUSIC, as popular in its day as reggae or DANCEHALL in more recent times. Before the introduction of sound systems (see REGGAE), a mento band was a fixture at every dance. The popularity of mento faded with changing life styles, the influence of Trinidadian calypso and recorded music, and the development since the 1960s of other Jamaican popular music forms, starting with the Ska and Rock Steady. However the mento influence on these newer musical forms was strong.

Many Jamaicans of a certain age regard mento music with great nostalgia. Only a few mento bands remain today and they are composed mostly of old performers as mento no longer attracts the young. The bands have been kept alive mainly by the tourist industry, playing at north coast hotels and for cruise ships. It was also the tourist desire for recordings that stimulated the first pressing of Jamaican records. Early mento tunes (in largely expurgated versions) were recorded on the MRS label (owned by Stanley Motta, proprietor of a well known appliance store) and by the Cook Recording Company of the USA. Popular tunes were: 'Don't Fence Her In', 'Glamour Gal', 'Don't Touch My Tomato', 'The Naughty Little Flea', 'Penny Reel', 'Miss Goosey', 'Rukumbine', 'Wheel an' Tun Me'. Popular performers from the 1930s included Lord Flea, Lord Power, Sugar Belly, and Count Lasher.

The sixties and early seventies saw a revival of mento by the big dance bands of the day, including Carlos Malcolm and the Afro-Jamaican Rhythms, Byron Lee and the Dragonaires, The Sheiks, Kes Chin and the Souvenirs, and The Vagabonds. While mento as such today is infrequently heard, its musical influence persists in what Marjorie Whylie calls the 'interesting phenomenon of songs of any genre being "mentorized" – work songs, ring play, dinki mini, gerreh, pop songs and even hymns'. And Cheryl Ryman has noted the mento influence in today's dance: 'The "winey" (winding) style and intimate partner contact that are featured in this dance have been carried over into the contemporary "dry grind" or "dub".' Mento may also be performed as a 'figure' in QUADRILLE, MAYPOLE and JONKONNU. Mento, then, refers not only to the music but to the words and movement (dance steps). Mento is a complete musical form.

Mento music Whylie describes as 'a type of rhythmic organization employing syncopated melodies and the polyrhythms of traditional banjos, rhumba boxes, shakkas, drums and rhythm sticks; in fact whatever is easily accessible within the environment. Its rhythmic structure based on the 3:3:2 pattern originating in West Africa makes it related to other CARIBBEAN forms such as Goombay of the Bahamas, Calypso of the Eastern Caribbean, the Merengue of the Dominican Republic, the Bomba of Puerto Rico and many others'.

A wide range of instruments have been used in playing mento, including both the commercial and the home made. As Whylie explains: 'The lead part may be played on bamboo or wild cane flutes or fifes (very often made from lengths of PVC pipe nowadays), violins (fiddles), harmonicas, saxophones, and banjos. The music is characterized by improvisation once the melody has been stated, and solos are taken on a round robin basis.'

The words of mento songs are often humorous, topical and salacious, dealing sometimes with real people and events, though while the song lives on, the event itself is forgotten. Slim and Sam were among the early song-writers

Mento

and performers whose songs (before the days of recordings) are now part of the popular domain, everyone having forgotten the composers. Additionally, several different songs might be composed to the same tune, or new verses improvised on the spot. Topicality, satire and humour are features that mento shares with calypso.

The dance has been viewed in the past as vulgar and indecent, with its pelvic movement and intimate body contact (called 'rent-a-tile'). Typical of descriptions by foreigners (and laughable to Jamaicans today) is that in the Funk and Wagnalls *Dictionary of Folklore* (1950) which describes mento as 'An erotic Jamaican dance . . . Its music is slower and more voluptuous than that of the rumba. The woman tantalizes her partner into a frenzy with seductive rolling of the haunches and belly and works herself into a state of autointoxication'.

The origin of the word mento is unknown though a Latin American source has been suggested. It was highly popular especially in rural Jamaica from at least the late 19th century to the early 1960s and probably superseded an earlier (and similar) dance known as SHAY-SHAY. Whylie calls mento 'the first dance music to enjoy national popularity, representing the product of what had started in the seventeenth century, with the dynamic collision of the cultures of Europe and Africa'.

[Baxter 1970, Lewin 1998, 2000, Ryman 1980, Taylor 1983, Whylie 2000]

METCALFE, Sir Charles (1785-1846)

The only governor of Jamaica to have a public memorial erected to him. The statue is now located in St William Grant PARK, KINGSTON. Metcalfe was governor of Jamaica 1839-42 during a time of great social and political ferment, but by his impartial manner ended up winning the trust and affection of at least some segments of the society. The Assembly voted £3,000 for a statue of him and commended his 'wise, just and beneficial administration'. The statue was first erected in SPANISH TOWN in 1845 but was moved to Kingston when the capital was moved there. The Parish of Metcalfe was also named in the governor's honour but was later absorbed into ST MARY Parish. Metcalfe went on to become a governor-general of Canada.

METHODIST

This religious denomination has a large number of adherents in Jamaica (62,208 in the census of 1991). The evangelical movement that became

Dr Thomas Coke

Methodism was founded by Charles Wesley (1703-91) within the ANGLICAN Church to 'fortify and supplement' the work of that church. Wesley and his associates were dubbed 'Methodists' from the methodical way in which they observed their principles; adherents eventually became known as Wesleyan Methodists. The Methodists established missionary societies in the American colonies and became noted for their spiritual fervour and vigorous preaching. In 1784 there was a break with the Anglican church and the Methodist community became a separate entity though it was not established as the Methodist Church until after Wesley's death.

Dr Thomas Coke, superintendent of the American Methodists, came to Jamaica in 1789, established the first church (see COKE CHURCH) and organized for the first MISSIONARIES to come. He provoked an angry reaction from some sections of the white population when he preached on the text 'Ethiopia shall soon stretch out her hands unto God'. Like the other missionaries, the Wesleyan-Methodists persevered in their mission to minister to the non-white population, despite numerous obstacles.

In 1967 the Methodists of the CARIBBEAN and Latin America formed their own organization and ceased to be a unit of the Methodist Missionary Society. Like other churches in Jamaica, the Methodists have contributed greatly to the development of education as well as to the spread of Protestantism to nearby territories in Latin America.

[Bisnauth 1989]

MICO COLLEGE

Jamaica's leading teacher-training institution, founded in 1834. At first it was one of many schools (called Mico Schools) established throughout the West Indies to educate the former slaves (see EDUCATION, EMANCIPATION, SLAVERY) but the one that became Mico College also had a teacher-training department attached and this became its focus. It is now the only Mico institution remaining. The Mico schools were set up under a trust fund that came from the Lady Mico Charity.

Mico College

Lady Mico was the widow of a rich London Alderman, Sir Samuel Mico (of the FRENCH Huguenot family of Micault) and she left her husband's nephew an extra £1,000 in her will if he married one of her six nieces. The nephew declined and in keeping with Lady Mico's wishes, in about 1680 the money was invested in lands in East London and the interest used to free English sailors captured and held in slavery by pirates of Barbary (today's Algeria). When piracy was stamped out, the trust fund lay dormant for nearly 200 years, the interest increasing to an enormous sum. On the initiative of the emancipators William Wilberforce and Thomas Fowell Buxton, it was used to establish the Lady Mico Charity to give Christian education to the non-white population of the British colonies. The aim of the teacher training department (or Normal School as it was called) was to train a local cadre of teachers to replace those from England.

The Mico Institution was first housed in a building on Hanover Street, KINGSTON, which is now a part of Kingston Technical High School, and was moved to Marescaux Road in 1896 when the name was changed to Mico Training College. The buildings were destroyed in the EARTHQUAKE of 1907 and the present building is a modified restoration of the original. It has since been damaged by fire and HURRICANE but in rebuilding the design has been maintained.

Mico College today is co-educational, but at one time was for men only. It has played a major role in the development of education in Jamaica and produced many of the country's outstanding citizens, including two of the first three native governor-generals – the first, Sir Clifford Campbell, and Sir Howard Cooke. At one time Mico trained West Indian missionaries for service in West Africa.

[Newman 1968]

MIDDLE PASSAGE

The Atlantic crossing from Africa to the CARIBBEAN during the slave trade is referred to as the Middle Passage, the middle part of a triangular journey for the ships involved in the trade and the one in which they carried human cargo. The ships of companies such as the Royal Africa Company of England and the Dutch West India Company, as well as individual traders, sailed from Europe to the West Coast of Africa loaded with guns, ammunition and manufactured goods which were exchanged for slaves. They carried the slaves across the Atlantic for sale in the Caribbean and American colonies. (See SLAVERY.) Then they loaded the ships with colonial produce such as SUGAR, molasses and TOBACCO for sale in Europe and the profits used to purchase guns etc., for sale in Africa. This was the 'triangular trade' developed by the mercantile system.

The Africa to Caribbean leg, the so-called 'Middle Passage', was, at the best of times, a six-week journey, much longer if there were difficulties. But the capture and sale of the slaves had taken place long before they were even put on board. They were first collected in the interior, from war, capture or sale, and, fastened to one another, marched down to the coast, sometimes hundreds of kilometres, and there they were housed in buildings called 'factories' while awaiting shipment.

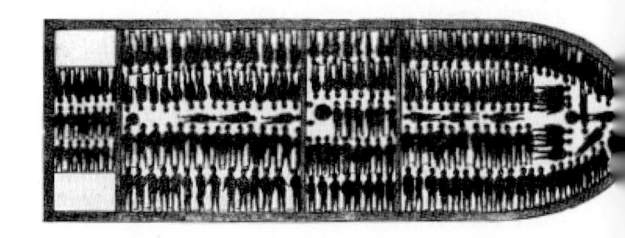

Diagram showing how slaves were stowed on slave ships. It is said that each slave had less space than a dead man in his coffin

On board the ships, the captives were packed tightly in galleries one above the other. The typical space for each person was 1.2-1.50m in length and 0.60-0.90m in height, so an adult could not lie at full length or sit upright. Because of the constant threat of insurrection, the slaves were often chained and attached in rows to long iron bars. Sometimes they undertook the entire voyage this way, being allowed up for air once a day. If the weather was bad or the cargo rebellious, they had no fresh air. As abolitionist William Wilberforce observed, 'never can so much misery be found condensed into so small a space as in a slave ship during the middle passage'. Not surprisingly, the death toll from malnutrition, sickness and disease was enormous and the Middle Passage remains a symbol of horror to this day.

Many of the slaves refused to docilely accept their position. As C.L.R. James has noted: 'They died not only from the regime but from grief and rage and despair. They undertook vast hunger strikes; undid their chains and hurled themselves on the crew in futile attempts at insurrection . . . To brighten their spirits it became the custom to have them up on the deck once a day and force them to dance. Some took the opportunity to jump overboard, uttering cries of triumph as they cleared the vessel and disappeared below the surface.'

In recent times, a number of literary works have tried to capture the experience, including *The Sure Salvation*, a novel by Jamaican John Hearne and *The Middle Passage* by the American Charles Johnson.

[Curtin 1969, James 1938, Kiple 1984]

MIDDLE QUARTERS

Highway village in ST ELIZABETH Parish, known as the 'shrimp capital of Jamaica'. Here fishermen hunt in the nearby swamp (formed by the YS and Middle Quarters rivers) for mullet and fresh river SHRIMPS. (See FISH AND FISHING, JANGGA.) The shrimps are usually caught in traps made from split BAMBOO. The shrimp is cooked with very hot peppers – thus called 'pepper swimp', a favourite of passing motorists who buy it from roadside vendors.

Shrimp vendor

MILITIA, The

Local force of volunteers formed as part of colonial self-defence, to augment activities of BRITISH regiments posted to the island. The militia included all whites and free men between 16-60; they provided the requisite accoutrements at their own expense and were obliged by law to enlist themselves either in the horse or foot. They normally paraded once a month and provided duty when summoned by the authorities.

Up to the 19th century, the class and colour distinctions of the rest of the society were maintained in the militia, with whites, free COLOUREDS, free blacks and JEWS serving in separate units. As Philip Curtin observed: 'The attorneys were officers; overseers who could supply themselves with a horse of the requisite value were in the preferred ranks of the cavalry. Book-keepers were most often infantrymen, while the coloured men and free blacks were segregated in their own units. It was a social affront for a book-keeper to step out of his station and enroll in the socially preferred cavalry, even though the overseers had lately been book-keepers themselves.' The militia drilled in the towns on a regular basis and observers (such as the English governor's wife, Lady Nugent) sometimes found their manoeuvres laughable. A militia rank was nevertheless socially important, as attested by the numerous 'colonels' in the island's plantation history.

John Jacques, Colonel of the Militia and first Mayor of Kingston, 1802

The establishment of the Jamaica Constabulary Force by Sir John Peter Grant in 1867 provided the island with a regulated peace-keeping force in place of the volunteer militia which had been implicated in the brutality of the suppression of the MORANT BAY REBELLION.

[Curtin 1955, Nugent 1839]

MILK RIVER

The Milk River is navigable for about 3.2km and used to be the principal source of irrigation for the CLARENDON plains. A considerable amount of LOGWOOD and fruit used to be shipped down it and in the 19th century, CROCODILES could be seen sunning themselves on its banks.

MILK RIVER BATH

Mineral spring said to be the most radioactive in the world, compared to world famous spas: it is 9 times as active as Bath, England; 50 times as active as Vichy, France; 3 times as active as Karlsbad, Austria and 54 times as active as Baden, Switzerland.

The Bath is located on the west bank of the MILK RIVER 21km from MAY PEN and 3.2km from Rest Village, CLARENDON Parish. It is also 3.2km from the sea at Farquhar's Beach. The waters of the bath do not come from the river but from a saline mineral spring which issues from Round Hill. The water is usually 33-34°C and flows directly in and out of the baths. Bathers are limited to 15 minutes at a time because of the high radioactivity of the water.

The land on which the Bath is located was conveyed to the Justices of VERE in 1791 by the owner Jonathan Ludford. They bought additional land and set about developing the spa, and in 1794 bathrooms were first opened to the public.

[GOJ Handbook of Jamaica 1961]

MIMOSA (*Mimosa pudica*)

Common weed, a member of the mimosa family, which can 'open' and 'close' its leaves, making it an object of endless fascination; its many common names attesting to its popularity. It is called Dead-and-wake, Sensitive Plant, Sensitive Grass, Shame-a-lady, Shame Brown Lady, Shame-lady, Shame-ol-Lady, Shama, Shamer, Shamer Macca, Shamey-bush, Shamey-macca, Shamey-Mary, Sheckel-weed, Shut-weed.

The mimosa provides a good example of self-protection in plants. The lightest touch will make the leaves snap shut, the stem then bending backward to expose its thorns, a good protection against potential enemies such as foraging animals. The plant is sensitive to the touch of raindrops, strong wind or contact by animals, including humans. The shock can be transmitted from a small segment of the leaf, to adjacent leaves, to the whole stem or plant if it is severe enough. When the plant senses that the danger has passed, the leaves will open again.

Mimosa is a native of tropical South America. It bears pink-purplish puff-ball flowers followed by brown seed pods. It is sometimes used in folk MEDICINE. The leaves, in combination with other plants, have been made into a TEA to relieve depression, and the roots, mixed with other plants, as a treatment for colds.

[Asprey and Thornton 1953-55, DJE, Huxley 1975, Robertson 1990]

B. Sutton

Mimosa

MINT

A favourite 'TEA bush', mint is consumed by many as a daily warm drink ('mint tea'), by others as a home remedy for stomach disorders such as indigestion and flatulence. (See folk MEDICINE.) Some variety of mint is found growing in most yards and in the days before packaged mint was available in the supermarket, a flourishing Peppermint bush (*Ocimum americanum*) was regarded as a great treasure, from which one met one's needs and neighbourhood requests ('Beg you likkle mint!'). Other varieties of mint are widely grown for tea, including Black or Sweet mint (*Mentha spicata*) a creeping herb, and Colon or Cullen mint (*Lippia alba*). Wild mints are also consumed, especially for medicinal purposes, in infusion or decoction, including Penny Royal (*Satureja brownei*), All Heal (*S. viminea*) and *Lantana* species, including Wild Sage. A mint called French Thyme or Soup Mint (*Plectranthus amboinicus*) is used as a seasoning in soups.

[Adams 1972, Asprey and Thornton 1953-55]

MISKITO

Peoples known in the historical literature as 'Mosquito Indians' from the English pronunciation of their homeland, the Miskito Shore of Central America (now part of Nicaragua), had a long association with Jamaica. Many were brought to the island in the 18th century to help track down the MAROONS (see also BUSH FIGHTING) and discover and destroy their PROVISION GROUNDS and settlements, and some chose to remain. Many individuals no doubt came otherwise, as there was constant traffic between Jamaica and their homeland that was for a long time a British protectorate, administered from Jamaica. In the 17th century, many were captured by pirates and brought to the island as slaves.

The association began after the BRITISH took Jamaica from the Spaniards in 1655, which gave them a base for moving on to the Atlantic coast of Central America to challenge their old enemies. They founded settlements of traders, LOGWOOD and MAHOGANY cutters, and the like, along the coast from what is now Panama as far north as Honduras (now Belize). These incursions were backed in the early days by raids on the Spanish settlements by pirates and BUCCANEERS. (See PORT ROYAL.) The British traded with the indigenous populations of the area, forming a special relationship with the Miskitos, using them in their struggles to keep the Spanish out. The Miskitos in turn sought the protection of the British Crown from harassment by pirates and the Spaniards and by 1741 there was a regular establishment of British troops in their territory. The Miskitos assisted the British in their military engagements in the area, including NELSON'S expedition against San Juan.

When the Central American colonies won their independence from Spain in the 1820s, the British kept control of Belize and maintained their claim over the Miskito 'territory' until 1860. They had established a line of English-speaking 'kings' to preside over the Miskito and maintain loyalty to the British Crown and the education of these 'kings' was the responsibility of the governor of Jamaica. One little king of about seven (whose father had just been murdered) came to be educated in SPANISH TOWN in 1804 during the governorship of General Nugent. Lady Nugent records him as throwing a temper tantrum at dinner and another a few days later when he had to be forcibly taken to school.

The last hereditary king of the Miskito territory, Robert Henry Clarence, died in KINGSTON on 10 January 1908, aged 35. According to *Who's Who*, he had been a pensioner of the British Crown, resident in Jamaica since August 1894 'in compensation for the deprivation of his former status, when the Nicaraguan government took possession of the Mosquito Shore'. Today the former Miskito territory includes the very Anglicized settlement of Bluefields in Spanish-speaking Nicaragua.

[Bridges 1814, Dallas 1803, Nugent 1839, Who's Who in Jamaica 1921-24]

MISSIONARY

Accounts of the last decades of SLAVERY in Jamaica never fail to make reference to Christian missionary activities. The names of many of these missionaries such as KNIBB, BURCHELL, COKE, PHILLIPPO, are still recalled in the names of churches, schools and villages. The missionary goal was specifically to bring the word of God to the enslaved AFRICANS and turn them into Christians; in so doing, the missionaries also unwittingly ignited the flame of freedom that led to EMANCIPATION.

Although Jamaica was nominally a Christian country, the slaves were relatively untouched by the religion of their masters (see ANGLICAN) and most still engaged in African religious practices, including the few who had been baptized and attended the master's church. OBEAH and MYAL were flourishing. Unlike the nearby Catholic countries where slaves were automatically baptized on arrival as a means of saving their souls, in the Protestant West Indies such matters were considered irrelevant by the plantocracy. The Catholic church in Jamaica which was revived in the 1790s (see ROMAN CATHOLIC) had a very limited ministry at that stage and did not proselytize among the slaves. Although in 1815 the Jamaica Assembly recognized the right of the slaves to receive religious instruction, most planters continued to deny such opportunities and little was achieved. Thus the missionaries who began to arrive in the late 18th century had a relatively untouched field to operate in.

The first missionaries in Jamaica were the MORAVIANS who arrived in 1754, but their reach was limited to a remote area in ST ELIZABETH Parish where they were first invited to settle. Dr Thomas Coke, superintendent of the American Methodists, visited in 1789 and on his return to England arranged for 12 METHODIST missionaries to be sent out. The PRESBYTERIANS also started in a small way in 1800 but their missionary activity did not effectively begin until 1824.

Baptism by missionary

A Moravian church and day school

Liele and Baker Missionary activity with a popular outreach must be said to begin with the arrival from 1783 onwards of black Baptist preachers from the southern states of America, freed slaves who like their former loyalist owners fled America after the Revolution. The most illustrious was the Revd George Liele, founder of the BAPTIST church in Jamaica. George Lewis, another American slave-preacher, Liele's converts Moses Baker and George Gibb and locals like Thomas Swigle, and other black preachers travelled around the countryside and founded churches. They were active in the conversion of the slaves to Christianity for over 30 years until, unable to cope with the demand, Baker in 1813 appealed to the Baptist Missionary Society in England for support (see ADELPHI).

The white missionaries who came were all members of the new, non-conformist Protestant sects that had arisen in the latter part of the 18th century out of the religious revivals that injected 'an active vigorous gospel' into the passive Established Church which was the Church of England. (See ANGLICAN.) From this enthusiastic movement came the volunteers 'who wanted to spend their lives preaching to the unconverted'. Baptist and Methodist missionary societies were formed and money raised by their congregations in England and America for missionary work. The first English Baptist missionary, John Rowe, arrived in 1814 and others followed, the Baptists becoming the largest and most dynamic missionary group, followed by the Methodists. With the death of the first group of black leaders, and the constant flow of outstanding British Baptists, the Baptist church was to pass from black to white leadership, and back again in the 20th century.

The years 1815-30 were the most significant for the establishment of missionary work. Impassioned preaching by black and white missionaries attracted enormous crowds to chapels in the towns and on the estates where this activity was permitted. In between, small groups led by slaves and freedmen would gather together for worship and discussion. Missionary activity undoubtedly introduced a new and – it was believed by the slaveholders – dangerous element into plantation society.

While their mission to convert the slaves to Christianity might seem simple, both black and white missionaries found themselves struggling against numerous obstacles. In the process, many of them lost their lives to tropical diseases, were punished by imprisonment, had their chapels and churches torn down, their slave congregants threatened and brutally punished, and themselves physically attacked. (See e.g. BROWN'S TOWN, COLONIAL CHURCH UNION.)

Legal obstacles The Church of England was the only church recognized by the State, in the colonies as in England. During slavery, other denominations seeking to work in Jamaica had to obtain a licence to preach from the Bishop of London. Often this was withheld or took so long the applicant sometimes died waiting. The planter-dominated Jamaica Assembly was hostile to the missionary efforts, fearful of the egalitarianism being preached and the effect it would have on their slaves. Many factors contributed to a high degree of tension and suspicion on the part of the Jamaican plantocracy, especially at this time. The American War of Independence had had a negative political and economic impact, there was decline in the illicit trade with the Spanish-American colonies and less profit from sugar. The French and Haitian Revolutions and the presence of numerous Haitian refugees and their slaves from the end of the 18th century (see FRENCH), the frequent insurrections among the Jamaican slaves, the high level of absentee proprietorship and the smallness of the white population, the increasing urbanization of the slave and freed population, all made the whites more fearful and defensive.

Among the laws passed by the Assembly to prevent the missionaries from carrying out their work was that of 1806 which prohibited 'preaching and teaching by persons

Female Negro peasant in her Sunda[y] and working dress (from Phillippo)

Salter's Hill Chapel and mission house, associated with the ministry of Moses Baker

not qualified by law'. This effectively stopped the missionary work of Liele and Baker and silenced the Moravians and Methodists who had also begun work. The consolidated slave laws of 1810 forbade the gathering of slaves 'between sunrise and sunset'. Other laws forbade the taking of money from slaves in support of non-conformist missionary work and imposed taxes on the churches. The laws were partly to prevent slaves gathering and fomenting rebellion, but a deeper fear was that the slaves might get the idea that they were in fact human beings – which is precisely what the missionary effort achieved, for what was being preached was a revolutionary doctrine.

As Shirley Gordon has expressed it: 'Where slaves heard the teaching they were attracted to a religion which recognized their humanity.' It 'made many transfer their "ownership" to God rather than to their earthly masters, and reinforced their African belief in life after death. For free coloured and blacks, who increased steadily in numbers as Emancipation approached, the dissenting missions provided an arena for self-expression and the exercise of responsibility which they did not achieve in political life until 1831.'

The missionaries not only preached the equality of man before the Heavenly Father, but some Christian practices such as baptism by immersion appealed because they were similar to African water rites. Bible stories and Protestant hymns presented the enslaved with stories and heroes with which they could identify, and the passionate preaching and emotionalism provided a new outlet for expression in their lives. As Olive Lewin has written of Jamaican religious MUSIC, 'Daniel, Jonah and David were almost folk heroes. They had to overcome what seemed to be insuperable odds: "King David slew Goliath with a sling and a marble stone." Noah was a symbol of hope, an example of the power of faith in the Almighty, and Jesus was a symbol of the conquest of death itself: "Bright angel roll away the stone/Our Lord is risen today".'

No wonder preachers could report congregations in the thousands and baptism of hundreds at a time.

Native Leaders The story is one not just of struggle by the white missionaries but of triumph for the slaves as well as the free blacks and people of colour: they flocked to the churches, suffered punishment and imprisonment for their faith and sometimes, in the absence of white ministers, kept the congregations together and the churches going. After all, at the height of missionary activity, there were only 50 white missionaries in the island. This aspect of the missionary effort is often ignored. Indeed, Gordon has argued that 'most Jamaicans first encountered Christianity through a much larger number of native leaders, deacons, elders, aides, variously named, and appointed by all missionary groups as a method of proselytization'.

The story also concerns the many white supporters in England who sustained the missionary efforts in the slave colonies and joined the struggle initiated by William Wilberforce in the British parliament to end the slave trade and, afterwards, to set the slaves free. Missionaries such as William Knibb played a major role in lobbying the English parliament for passage of the Emancipation bill, taking to England their graphic first-hand accounts from the field of battle, so to speak. While the Quakers (see FRIENDS) were not active in the missionary field at this time, their support in the struggle for Emancipation was vital.

The missionaries, especially the Baptists, were wrongly blamed for playing an activist role in the 1831-32 rebellion but there is no doubt that they presented the Christianized, CREOLE slaves with an alternative world view. (See SHARPE, Samuel.) In the post-Emancipation period, missionaries were active in the resettlement of the new freedmen and women (see FREE VILLAGES) and in the spread of literacy and education among them, for a long period providing virtually the only schools for adults and children alike. (See EDUCATION.)

Rise of Native Baptists The initial impetus and missionary ascendancy over the black population began to fade within one generation of freedom, with the rise of a new generation who had not experienced slavery and the religious struggle and saw some of the missionary intervention as paternalistic. Part of the problem arose from the schism between the missionaries and their black parishioners over the model for 'right' behaviour and the regimented life-style that the missionaries sought to impose. Much of this model clashed with the blacks' accustomed behaviour and the African beliefs to which many still clung; there was objection to the rigid Christian morality, especially over matters of sexual conduct. The rise of a trained native ministry with a greater understanding of local needs and viewpoints mollified somewhat the puritanical form of Christianity.

The native preachers or 'daddies' who first arose as converts appointed by the missionaries to take the Christian message to their fellows also began to assert their own independence over their flocks, setting up what came to be called 'Native Baptist' churches. Numerous new sects and religions were to develop from a synthesis of Christian Protestant missionary and African-Jamaican religious survivals. (See RELIGION.) The break with the purely orthodox form of Christianity became most evident with the Great Revivals which started out as Christian but by 1861 had been overtaken by African elements. (See POCOMANIA, REVIVAL, ZION.)

The poverty-stricken condition of the island as a whole and of the newly enfranchised in the years after Emancipation contributed to the growing division between two sets of Jamaicans. It might be argued that for a while, the missionaries provided a point of coherence for the 'two Jamaicas', a split again occurring under the social and economic stresses that imploded in the MORANT BAY REBELLION of 1865. On the one hand, the poorest in the land turned from supporting the churches to a more spirit-based, African-centred experience. On the other, the better off and more upwardly mobile sought the respectability of the mission chapels and the status that education and church membership brought in a free society.

[Augier et al. 1960, 1962, Bisnauth 1989, Gayle 1982, Gordon 1998, Henderson 1931, Phillippo 1843, Sibley 1965]

MOCHO

Name of several places in Jamaica (the best known, a village in Upper CLARENDON) traditionally regarded as the 'back of beyond' or as the DJE puts it: 'A place symbolic of remoteness – a rough, uncivilized place.' To describe someone as coming from Mocho is to describe that person as backward or in Jamaican terminology, 'dark'. The usage probably arose from tribal rivalry dating from the days of SLAVERY. Mocho (pronounced Moko) is derived from Mgboko, a place name of Calabar in Eastern Nigeria and suggests that the Jamaican Mochos were settled by the IBO.

[DJE]

MOCKINGBIRD (*Mimus polyglottos*)

Jamaica's sweetest songbird, whose scientific name means 'mimic of many tongues'; also called Nightingale, the name by which it is known in other countries. The bird is said to have about 30 different songs and is capable of mimicking not just other BIRDS but of adding domestic sounds to its repertoire. It sings all year round, and any time of day including midday when other birds are silent and at night-time, especially in the moonlight, hence its other name of nightingale. The Mockingbird is common in towns and countryside, preferring cultivated lands and pastures to the natural forest and woodland. It is bold and cheeky, extremely territorial, and will chase away all intruders, including humans, from its nest and pursue other Mockingbirds. It is a slim grey bird with a long uptilted tail and with white wing bars that are revealed as it jumps jerkily along the ground in search of insects and when it takes flight.

Mockingbird

[Jeffrey-Smith 1972, Taylor 1955]

MONEAGUE

Inland village in ST ANN Parish which figured prominently in the early history of the island. The old mile posts in ST CATHERINE Parish used to give the distance between SPANISH TOWN and Moneague for it was a popular overnight spot to break the three-day coach journey between the north coast and the capital.

Not surprisingly, Moneague used to be famous for the high quality of its inns. In 1860 a hotel at Moneague was described as 'the best in the island'. Around 1890 the Moneague Hotel was built, one of a number erected under government incentive to take care of the large number of visitors expected for the Great Exhibition held in KINGSTON in 1891. In 1904 the hotel was advertised as 'the most charming in the island'. It offered fresh vegetables from its gardens, pure well water, TENNIS, croquet, and shooting on the property. Visitors usually travelled by train as far as Ewarton and were met by the hotel carriage for the journey over MOUNT DIABLO. However, with the widespread use of the motor car, Moneague was no longer necessary as a stopping place and all of the inns eventually closed. The Moneague Hotel is now part of the Moneague Teacher Training College. Walton, near to Moneague, is used as a training camp by the Jamaica Defence Force.

The name Moneague is believed to be a corruption of the Spanish *mono agua* – after an underground lake in the area that rises periodically. (See MONEAGUE LAKE.)

MONEAGUE LAKE

North-east of the village of MONEAGUE, ST ANN Parish, is a low lying area which from time to time is covered with flood waters which form a temporary 'lake'. It is believed that the lake originates in periods of heavy rain from underground water that backs up and rises, the normal channels being unable to take the abnormal flow. (See NEWMARKET.)

MONEY

Jamaica uses a decimal system of currency that was introduced in September 1969. Previous to that, the British system of pounds, shillings and pence prevailed. (In writing, pounds, shillings and pence is expressed as £.s.d. For example, one pound two shillings and sixpence is written as £1.2.6. Two shillings and sixpence is written as 2/6; pence on its own is written as d, e.g. 6d. There were also fractions of pence, e.g. half-penny ('ha-penny') which was expressed as ½d, penny half-penny ('quattie') as 1½d and a quarter penny ('farthing') as ¼d.

Banknotes (paper money) were not in use until the early 19th century. Up to the mid-20th century, coins rather than paper were used for most transactions including payment to wage labourers (not surprising since in 1935, it was officially estimated that 75 per cent of those employed were receiving an average wage of only 14s.0d. per week).

Coinage From the 17th to the late 19th century coins of different denominations from many nations of the world were freely circulated – Spanish and Mexican, Portuguese and French, as well as English. The names of these old coins are still met with in the historical literature, the most popular being *pistoles*, *reales*, pieces-of-eight, and *doubloons*. The most important coins were of Spanish origin and eight silver *reales* constituted a piece-of-eight, or one dollar. *Escudos*, *pistoles* and *doubloons* were Spanish gold coins. Eventually the exchange values of all these coins were set by the colonial authorities in terms of pounds, shillings and pence.

In 1869 the first truly Jamaican coins were introduced when a Jamaican penny and half-penny were struck. In 1880 the farthing (a quarter-penny) was introduced and remained in circulation until 1952 when it was withdrawn. One hundred years after the introduction of the first Jamaican coins, the island created its own system of currency based on dollars and cents.

Folk names were often given to the coins in use and these old names live on in folk songs, tales, sayings, etc. The most popular of these names was the 'quattie' referring to the British three half-pence coin, the penny ha-penny (1½d). This coin as well as the three-pence (3d) was introduced in 1834 to provide the slaves, who were on the way to becoming wage earners (see APPRENTICESHIP), with coins of smaller denominations. The 1½d coin was of silver and was known as 'Christian quattie' from the fact that it was the coin most frequently found on the collection plate in churches.

The word 'quattie' apparently originated as a shortened form of '*cuarto* (quarter) *real*', according to Jacqueline Morgan, Bank of Jamaica archivist. The value of the *real* then was sixpence – the 1½d was a quarter of that. In folk reckoning, two quatties were equal to fippance (3d) and three quatties to a 'bit' (4½d), a bit being a fraction of the Spanish dollar which circulated widely. Eight quatties were equal to a shilling or 'mac'. These terms also appeared in combination such as 'mac-o-fippance' (one shilling and threepence or

Private banknote — BOJ Money Museum

D. Ranston

ten quatties), 'bit-an-fippance' (7½d), etc. A 'mac' ('macaroni' or maccaronie) was the name given by Jamaicans to the Mexican quarter dollar.

Many folk songs contain these terms, among them 'Linstead Market' where 'not a quattie wut sell'; the old song about the Syrian pedlar advertising cloth at 'Quattie a yard O, Salo'; 'Wheel an Tun Me' which recalls the courting 'solja man' who 'gimme one cock-eye fourbit' (i.e. 1/6d). In 'Call Dinah', the singer notes:

> Me beg Dinah buy quattie sugar
> One big gill a coconut ile
> Half penny pickle fish fe de brawta

A gill was both a measure of money (three farthings or one half-quattie) and of quantity (one-quarter pint, imperial measure).

A fascinating sentence that shows the extensive use of these terms in former times is found in Jekyll's version of the ANANCY STORY 'Tomby'. One of the characters, Miss Princess, tells what she intends to buy in the market: 'Me go buy me little salt fish an' me little hafoo yam, t'reepence a red peas fe make me soup, quatty 'kellion, gill a garlic to put with me little nick-snack, quattie ripe banana, bit fe gungo peas, an' me see if me can get quatty beef bone.'

The local name for the Night Hawk – 'Gimme-me-Bit', is supposed to reflect the bird's demand for payment, for having rid the night of mosquitoes.

Banknotes The earliest Jamaican banknotes date back to the 19th century when several private banks were established on the island. The first notes were issued by the London-based Colonial Bank that opened a local branch in 1837. These notes were unique as they were denominated in three currencies – sterling, dollars and local currency. Planters' Bank, which was in operation between 1839 and 1848, also issued its own banknotes in denominations of £1, £3 and £5.

During the late 19th and early 20th centuries, increased trade relations between Jamaica and Canada resulted in several Canadian banks opening local branches – the Bank of Nova Scotia in 1889, the Royal Bank of Canada in 1911 and the Canadian Bank of Commerce in 1920. These banks all issued £1 and £5 notes for use throughout the island. In 1925, the Colonial Bank was incorporated with Barclays Bank in London and began issuing notes under the Barclays name.

Private banks continued issuing their own banknotes until 1940 when the Currency Notes Law of 1937 was enforced, making the Board of Commissioners of Currency the government's agent with sole responsibility for issuing paper money in Jamaica.

Government of Jamaica Banknotes The government of Jamaica first released its own notes in 1920 under the Currency Notes Law of 1904 that was revised in 1918. The decision was taken to issue 10s, 5s and 2/6d, as higher denomination notes were already being circulated by the private banks. However, the 2/6d note was short-lived as it was withdrawn from circulation in 1922. Up until 1940, private banknotes circulated alongside those of the government which began issuing its own £1 and £5 notes in 1942.

When the island's central bank – the Bank of Jamaica – was established in 1960, it assumed sole responsibility for issuing Jamaican currency, and in 1961, released its first notes that replaced the original government of Jamaica banknotes. These notes were issued in denominations of 5s, 10s, £1 and £5 and remained in circulation for another eight years after which the sterling system of pounds, shillings and pence was replaced by the decimal system of currency.

Slang terms Most of the slang terms applied to money today refer to the paper notes and their worth, images, or colour, coins being regarded as of so little value they are beneath the notice of most people, including beggars. A 'Nanny' refers to the $100 bill with a picture of NANNY, also called a 'wrap-head' from the portrayal of Nanny in a head-tie. (See BANDANA.) The $50 bill is a 'Sam SHARPE' from the image of the National Hero appearing on it. The 'Concorde' refers to the $100 bill because of the speed with which it disappears, now also applied by some to the $500 bill.

Money Museum The story of Jamaica's money with examples through the ages can be seen at the Money Museum located at the Bank of Jamaica in Kingston. It is open to the public.
[Cassidy 1971, DJE, Jekyll 1966, Morgan 1979, 1984]

MONGOOSE (*Herpestes auropunctatus*)

Small furry brown animal sometimes seen scurrying across fields and highways and, more and more frequently, in suburban gardens. Its

Mongoose

bravery is legendary, immortalized in the saying: 'Mongoose seh: If you don't take chance, you nuh man.' The mongoose was first introduced into Jamaica to destroy cane piece rats but itself became such a pest that it came to be regarded as an even greater danger than the rats. Its introduction is frequently cited in textbooks as one of the ways in which the balance of nature can be so easily upset.

In 1872 a planter named William Bancroft Espeut (see SPRING GARDEN) introduced four male and five female mongooses from India to kill rats in SUGAR CANE fields that were so destructive that they actually forced some estates out of business and made the 'rat catcher' an important personage. These rats, incidentally, were introduced themselves.

From Espeut's mongooses, the animal spread all over the island, and ten years after its introduction was saving the planters £45,000 annually. However, the introduced rats remained common. Moreover, by 1890 the mongoose had itself become such a destructive pest that a commission was set up to enquire into its habits. It was blamed for diminishing the supply of fruit, fish and CRABS, capturing chickens and other farmyard animals and destroying the harmless Yellow SNAKES, ground LIZARDS, IGUANA, CONEY, and insects which were so important to the balance of nature. The mongoose is held responsible for the extinction of five endemic vertebrate species (see FAUNA).

From Jamaica the mongoose was further introduced to other CARIBBEAN islands and to the American mainland. All mongooses in the New World are presumed to go back to the nine introduced to Jamaica.

[Hoagland, Horst, Kilpatrick 1989]

MONKEY JAR

Traditional earthenware water vessel with a lidded cover, easily recognizable from its globular shape, short, upright pouring spout, and handle over the opening at the top. Once common in every home for storing and pouring water, it is nowadays regarded as a decorative object. Monkey jars incorporate both African and European ceramic features and have been made for hundreds of years; examples dating from the late 17th century have been found in PORT ROYAL.

The origin of the name is unknown but in earlier times in both Jamaica and Barbados the jars were referred to as 'monkeys' or 'water monkeys', as in, 'a monkey of cool water', and the name was also used in parts of the Southern USA. Robert Farris Thompson has noted that vessels in the Afro-Carolinas with moulded faces were often called 'Monkey jugs' after an old designation for water cooler. He cites a 1932 article that notes: 'Afro-Carolinians used to refer to the heat of the day in phrases like "monkey almost got me today". . . used in the sense of heat prostration.' On the other hand, the OED records the colloquial phrase 'to sup (or suck) the monkey', meaning to tipple, 'monkey' applying to various receptacles for liquor.

Although there are no monkeys extant in Jamaica (see CAVES), the oral tradition from Africa frequently refers to the animal which appears in numerous PROVERBS, sayings, and stories, most of which portray monkey in a negative light. Frequently the monkey symbolizes ugliness and is seen as sensitive regarding its looks. To 'make monkey-face' means to grimace or make a face at someone. This usage acquired a more sinister meaning in recent years, 'monkey lotion' being the name given to acid used to deliberately disfigure someone.

In modern popular usage, 'monkey money' is a negligible sum. Monkey is also noted for mimicry, so the proverb warns: 'Follow fashion mek Monkey lose him tail' and the more common saying 'Monkey see, Monkey do'. Thus monkey appears in compound names, e.g. Monkey BREADFRUIT, to indicate something that is an imitation of the real thing.

Monkey appears as a character in songs and folk tales, being often outwitted by ANANSI. In several of these tales, Monkey is a musician, one song concluding of Monkey the fiddler, 'Monkey draw bow so sweet'. The saying 'Monkey play fiddle mek Baboon dance' is taken to mean that families should work together.

Monkey Fiddle is the name given to a plant with smooth round stems; when two are rubbed together they produce a musical sound like a fiddle.

[DJE, Thompson 1981]

Monkey Jar

MONTEGO BAY

Capital of ST JAMES Parish, the island's second city, and the third largest urban area with a population of 82,000 in 1991. The population increased four-fold in the decades 1940-70, a reflection of the growth of TOURISM and its importance to the city.

Christopher COLUMBUS anchored briefly at Montego Bay when he first discovered the island in 1494. He called the harbour Golfo de Buen Tiempo – 'The Bay of Good Weather'. The name Montego comes from the Spanish *manteca* meaning lard. In short, the port was once known by the unromantic name of 'Lard Bay'. It was from here that the Spaniards shipped large quantities of lard or 'pig's butter' which came from the vast herds of wild PIGS that roamed the interior.

Montego Bay has been an international tourist resort since the 1920s. In the late 19th century, a local doctor, A.G. McCatty founded the Sanatorium Caribbee near the sea at what is now called 'Doctor's Cave'. Dr McCatty, who died in 1890, and his son, Dr Alexander James McCatty who died in 1923 (and donated the site in 1906 for use as a bathing club) were early advocates of the value of sea-bathing and of the efficacy of the waters of this bay in particular.

Before the First WORLD WAR, wealthy Americans began to build homes near to Doctor's Cave. But in those early days, only men went to the beach for their daily dip. When the wife of a local bank manager integrated the bathers, it caused a sensation.

After the war, two intrepid Jamaican women entered the hotel business on a small scale. They were Ethel Hart whose hotel (called Ethelhart) stood on the bluff above the town, and the legendary Maybelle 'Ma' Ewen. In 1924, Ma Ewen bought some of the American beachside houses which has been abandoned during the war and combined them to form a 12 bedroom hotel. In time, this hotel immediately above Doctor's Cave came to be known as Casa Blanca Hotel. One of the early guests was a famous British chiropractor, Sir Herbert Barker. When he published an article boosting Doctor's Cave Beach, the place became famous. Ma Ewen's early Casa Blanca was not much to boast of. It was lit with kerosene oil lamps, and water for baths was heated on a stove. The hotel was demolished in 1933 by a HURRICANE which left the beach littered with beds, bathtubs and shingles, but that only gave Ma Ewen the opportunity to improve her product.

In the early days of the industry, visitors from abroad arrived on the banana boats. (See BANANA TRADE). The hotel season lasted only for

Montego Bay beaches

J. Tyndale-Biscoe

the winter months. Most of the guests came from England and included virtually all the famous, the infamous and the mighty of their time. An aircraft landing strip was built at Montego Bay during the Second World War and after the war it was opened to commercial traffic. Montego Bay could then cater to the mass tourist market and thereafter the tourism boom was on. Some of the early Montego Bay hotels may still be seen though many new hotels have been built to cater to the visitors arriving daily in large numbers.

Some of the Bogue Islands east of the town were artificially joined in the 1980s and, as Montego Freeport, have been incorporated into the commercial and residential life of the town.
[Chapman 1958, Hart 1953-64, Wright and White 1969]

MONTEGO BAY MARINE PARK see NATIONAL PARKS

MONTPELIER
Once one of the largest sugar plantations in Jamaica, Montpelier in ST JAMES Parish became noted for its fine CATTLE after the collapse of sugar. In the 1890s, the owner, a member of the famous BRITISH Ellis family, brought in Indian Zebu cattle that he crossed with native stock to produce a hardy breed of draft animal. At the end of the 20th century the main crop at Montpelier was ORANGES.

Opposite the railway station can be seen Montpelier GREAT HOUSE and New Works. Old Montpelier was one of the estates burnt by slaves during the great slave rebellion in the western PARISHES in 1831-32 (see SHARPE, Samuel), after the colonel of the MILITIA had retreated to Montego Bay. The highway in fact goes through an area that was in the middle of the activities of 1831-32. Several skirmishes took place on the road from Montego Bay to Darliston and many estates tucked into the surrounding hills were burnt. The present great house dates from 1832. St Mary's Church (ANGLICAN) is on the site of Montpelier Old Works.

New Montpelier was studied archaeologically by the UWI Department of History, the Jamaica National Trust Commission and the INSTITUTE OF JAMAICA from 1973-80. This represented the first plantation archaeology site excavated in Jamaica and the second in the CARIBBEAN where the object was to look at the slave society thereon. Professor Barry Higman has recently published a book on the subject.
[Higman 1998]

MOONSHINE BABY
Also known as Moonshine Dolly, the central figure in a once-popular game played by country children on full moon nights. One child would lie down flat on the ground, the rest would outline his or her body with objects that would shine in the moonlight such as stones, bits of glass, mirrors, broken crockery, etc. The fun was derived from making the figure and then leaving it on the ground to frighten passersby. Claude McKay recalled making Moonshine Baby with his friends and noted in *My Green Hills of Jamaica*:

'To us children, it was very weird, something like a great enlarged china doll, which we had made ourselves. We would hold hands, form a circle, dance around it and sing.

'Sometimes our parents would come out to see what we were doing, and tell us whether our efforts were good or bad.

'I am not sure but I think my father told us that the making of these moonshine babies was an old African custom, and that different villages used to compete in the making of them.'

This was only one of the many amusements country people derived from the bright light of the moon – called by some, 'The Parish Lantern' – in the days before electricity. Older folk would dance out of doors in events that were called 'Moonshine Darling'. One folk song – 'Banyan Tree' – records such an event:

Moonshine tonight, come make we dance and sing
Me a rock so, you a rock so, under banyan tree.

[Cassidy 1971, DJE, McKay 1979]

MORANT BAY
Capital of ST THOMAS Parish, population 9,600 (1991). One of the most historic towns in Jamaica because of its association with the so-called MORANT BAY REBELLION in which most of the buildings were burnt including the courthouse which was the focus of the rebellion. The courthouse was rebuilt in 1867 and extensive repairs were carried out after the HURRICANE of 1951.

Edna Manley's statue of Paul BOGLE, one of the leaders of the rebellion, stands in front of the courthouse and was erected in 1965, a hundred years after the rebellion. (See ART.) Near the statue is the 1865 memorial that commemorates those who died in the struggle. Between the courthouse and the tombs of those who died can be seen the old fort. (See FORT MORANT.) Behind the walls of the fort, excavations were undertaken in 1965 to locate the remains of the rebels who had been executed. Seventy-nine skeletons were found in a mass grave on old refuse dumps.

MORANT BAY REBELLION

MORANT BAY, capital of ST THOMAS Parish, was the scene of an uprising in 1865 known as the 'Morant Bay Rebellion' though it covered a much wider area than the confines of the town. In a way the rebellion was the culmination of a series of events in the disastrous post-Emancipation period. But it was in this Parish that long-standing grievances between the poor black population and the repressive local government authorities came to a head, led by a small farmer named Paul BOGLE. Also implicated was a COLOURED legislator and property owner, George William GORDON. The rebellion and its suppression by the island's governor, Edward Eyre, were to have far-reaching repercussions, and came to be regarded as a watershed in Jamaica's history. Effectively, it represented the common people's assertion of their rights to consideration, fair representation, and justice. Today, Bogle and Gordon are National Heroes and Jamaica's National Heritage Week in October coincides with the anniversary of that fateful week at Morant Bay.

Governor Eyre

The Background In the 1860s economic depression affected all sectors of the population, but the suffering of the poor people was extreme. Wages were low and irregular, unemployment rose and so did the price of imported goods as a result of the American Civil War (1861-65) as well as high import duties. There were local factors such as floods followed by drought that destroyed PROVISION GROUNDS. A great divide existed between the white ruling class that controlled the economy, the legislature and the courts, and the ex-slaves who formed the majority of the population. They had been given freedom almost 30 years earlier, but had little to show for it. (See SLAVERY, EMANCIPATION, FREE VILLAGES.)

Without work, land, or a future, much of the population by this time was half-naked and starving and social ills such as crime, prostitution, and juvenile delinquency were alarmingly on the rise. So was petty theft of food crops from the plantations – a source of ill will and animosity between the landed and the landless. The planter-run magistracy was used to punish severely even the smallest infractions, and land disputes centering on ownership, trespass, and evictions, took up much of the court's time.

Prominent among those who spoke out publicly was Gordon, a KINGSTON businessman and large property owner and the elected member of the Assembly for St Thomas-in-the-East as the Parish was then called. Gordon was active in both politics and religious affairs and notorious for his criticism of the authorities, including Governor Eyre who was seen as completely out of touch with the mood of the country and the conditions of the day.

The Underhill Letter Eyre blamed outside interference for the state of rising unrest in the country, specifically the so-called Underhill Letter. This was a letter that had been sent in January 1865 by Dr Edward Underhill, Secretary of the BAPTIST Missionary Society in Great Britain to the British Secretary of State for the Colonies. In it he outlined his concerns regarding the dire conditions on the island (which he had earlier visited). He emphasized the increasing poverty and extreme distress of the poor black population, stated some of the reasons behind the island's current problems and made suggestions for improvements that involved more government initiative. When the contents of the letter became widely known on the island, many responsible civic and religious leaders agreed with the assessment. Eyre blamed the situation of the poor on their own apathy and laziness.

The letter was followed by a series of public meetings called 'Underhill Meetings' held around the island in response to the issues raised. They provided a means for public expressions of protest and resulted in resolutions and further petitions to the governor. Gordon himself presided over huge meetings in Kingston and elsewhere, often using language that was highly condemnatory of the governor and some that was called inflammatory.

'The Queen's Advice' Meanwhile, the poor people of ST ANN Parish had sent a petition to Queen Victoria (fondly known as 'Missis Queen', the woman who had freed them, many believed – see BRUCKINS). They referred to their suffering and requested that unused Crown Lands be leased to them for cultivation. Eyre forwarded the petition accompanied by his own unsympathetic observations. The reply that was sent back, Eyre had printed on 50,000 placards and circulated throughout the country as 'The Queen's Advice', requesting that it also be read aloud in churches and chapels. The non-conformist clergymen refused to read it. Basically (in a reply drafted at the Colonial Office), the Queen told the labouring classes that hard work on their part would solve their difficulties and that they should look for an improvement in their condition through their own 'industry and prudence'.

Many were affected by the insensitive language of the document and interpreted it as their abandonment by the Queen. It is said that people became fearful even of re-enslavement. The letter certainly contributed to the growing mood of desperation and resentment and fuelled the anger against the local ruling class.

Public meetings continued, Gordon presiding over one at Morant Bay that was attended by Paul Bogle and others who would become leading figures in the rebellion. There was increasing bitterness at the knowledge that no help would be forthcoming from official quarters and there were signs throughout the island that violent clashes were inevitable in the wake of the failure of the Underhill meetings to bring about any of the changes sought. Whether or not Bogle and his followers had planned an armed uprising, it was the specific local conditions of abuse in the operations of the justice system that ignited the fuse at Morant Bay.

Bogle of Stony Gut   Bogle was a prosperous small farmer of Stony Gut, St Thomas, who had both religious and political connections with Gordon, having been his local election agent. Gordon had also ordained him a deacon of the Native Baptist Church and Bogle had established his own chapel at Stony Gut. While not much is known about Bogle's activities, the chapel became a centre for political as well as religious activities and, some said, for military-style indoctrination and training. Bogle and his followers also demonstrated their loss of faith in the justice system by setting up their own court system, appointing magistrates and constables. The immediate cause of the violent outbreak was an incident at the courthouse in Morant Bay.

Violent confrontation   On 7 October, Bogle had been part of a mob involved in loud protests at judgments handed down at the courthouse that day, resulting in scuffles with the police. As a result, arrest warrants were issued against 28 people for assaults on the police. When the police tried to arrest Bogle at Stony Gut, a huge crowd gathered and routed them. The police returned to Morant Bay with the news that Bogle planned to march on the town the next day, 11 October, when a meeting of the Vestry, the local government authority (see PARISH), was due to take place. As a result, the CUSTOS sent a message to the governor asking for military assistance and called out the volunteer MILITIA. Bogle and some 400 followers arrived in the town and in a violent confrontation with the militia, the courthouse was burnt to the ground and some important citizens, including the custos, were killed. In all, 18 officials or militia were killed and three wounded while seven were killed in the crowd.

From Morant Bay, mobs spread out across the parish of St Thomas, attacking property, taking prisoners and issuing threats. Two white plantation owners were killed and others wounded. As the news travelled, the eastern parishes, and then the entire island, were gripped by hysterical rumours and fears of a general uprising, a 'race war' of blacks against whites.

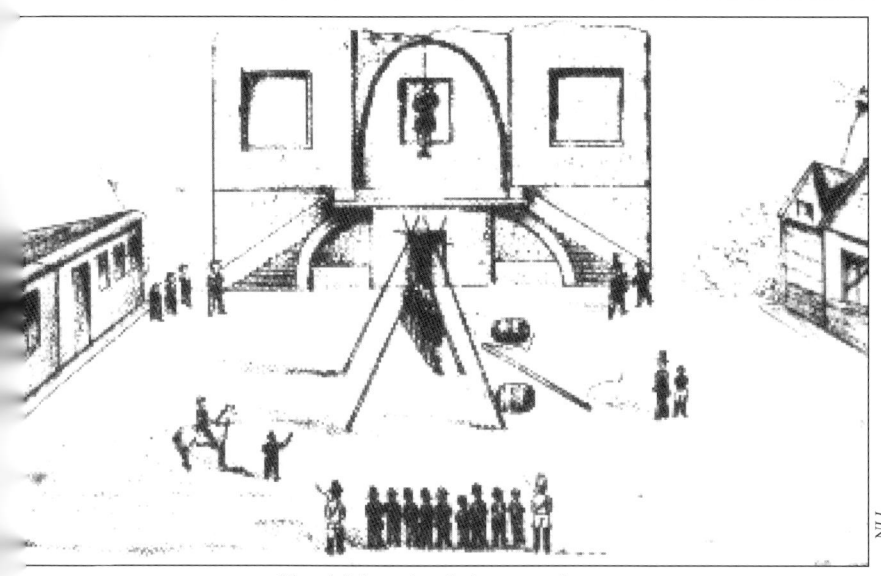

The rebels hanged at the burnt courthouse

The uprising suppressed By 12 October governor Eyre had the first troops despatched from Kingston to Morant Bay by ship. These were black soldiers of the 1st WEST INDIA REGIMENT, under white officers. Eyre also requested white troops from the garrison at NEWCASTLE and they marched eastwards over the mountains. A few hundred MAROONS also offered their services and were quickly armed. Some oral history notes that the sound of the ABENG aroused even greater terror than the marching squadrons of white soldiers.

By 13 October, a state of emergency, called martial law, had been declared over the County of Surrey, with the exclusion of Kingston, and the rebellion was quickly suppressed.

Gordon's arrest and Bogle's capture On 17 October Eyre had a warrant issued for the arrest of George William Gordon who had been at his home in Kingston all this while. When Gordon surrendered to the authorities, Eyre ordered him taken by ship, the HMS *Wolverine*, to Morant Bay where martial law was in force and where the fate of most became summary execution without trial. Gordon was charged with high treason and sedition as well as complicity with the rebels and sentenced to death, though there was no evidence of his implication in what had occurred. He was hanged on Monday 23 October from the yardarm of HMS *Wolverine*. Two days later Bogle and his chief lieutenants were captured and they too were hanged, on 25 October.

But the indiscriminate punishment of the poor people of St Thomas was to continue for several more weeks of what has been described as 'calculated terror'. Martial law was not lifted until a month after the outbreak, on 13 November. The white battalions despatched to the scene included battle-hardened veterans of the Indian Mutiny and its severe repression eight years previously; some of the officers were veterans of the Crimean War. (See Mary SEACOLE.) Captain Gordon Ramsay, the police inspector who oversaw the reign of terror at Morant Bay was a veteran of the war and a survivor of the Charge of the Light Brigade. Citizens throughout St Thomas were at the mercy of ordinary soldiers and Maroons. Hundreds were seriously wounded, thousands flogged and brutalized with no distinction made between the innocent and the guilty. The Custos of Vere commented that the soldiers flogged people 'for looking sulky or for speaking a hasty word or for nothing at all. In short, the dogs of war are let loose and there is no holding them in'.

Morant Bay courthouse with Bogle's statue

Over 430 men and women were killed by the soldiers or executed by court martial and over 1,000 homes as well as crops burnt by government forces. One man who took part in the repression estimated the number killed as closer to 1,500.

With no radio or telegraph, garbled news of the atrocities travelled slowly across the island by newspapers and word of mouth, spreading fear among Jamaicans of every class and colour. Gordon's was only one of many arbitrary arrests and detentions of those who had been prominent opponents of the governor and his policies, and several others were put to death. Many who had dared to speak out went into hiding and lived in fear for some considerable time. Gad Heuman quotes one observer saying 'the times were such that no man could open his mouth, you were almost afraid to hear your own breathing, such was the state of things'.

The Jamaica Case The 'rebellion' and the governor's response had significant repercussions and it became headline news in Britain. A commission of enquiry sent out from England found Eyre prompt and vigorous in his immediate response but condemned as excessive his use of martial force and the severity of the punishments. He was removed from his post and in August 1866 returned to England. But that was not the end of the matter. What became known as the Jamaica Case split the British parliament and intelligentsia: the fundamental question was whether Eyre was a hero or a murderer. The debate raged in parliament and outside in the streets for the next three years. One group wanted to prosecute Eyre for the murder of George William Gordon and formed the Jamaica Committee. Leading members included John Stuart Mill, Charles Darwin, Thomas Huxley, John Bright and other members of the scientific establishment, radicals, non-conformists, academics and clergy. Those who believed in a strong imperial rule formed the Eyre Defence Committee. This group included famous people like the writers Thomas Carlyle, Charles Kingsley, Alfred Lord Tennyson, Charles Dickens, 'backed by 71 peers, 20 members of Parliament, 40 generals, 26 admirals and 400 clergyman, mostly Anglican'.

A grand jury decided that there was insufficient evidence to indict Eyre but he did not secure a post with the government again and retired to rural England and obscurity. He died in 1901 and was buried in Whitchurch, Devon, where the inscription on his tombstone reads: 'Edward John Eyre, Australian explorer and governor of Jamaica. He did his duty in that state of life into which it pleased God to call him.'

Eyre's previous record as the enlightened and devoted protector of the aborigines in Australia disappeared. Eyre himself had been less than popular with the white Jamaican ruling class, yet in 1865-66 he became the hero of those Jamaicans who had feared a civil, racial war.

Crown Colony At Eyre's urging, the Jamaica House of Assembly believed itself unable to deal with the crisis and after 200 years as an independent law-making body, surrendered its power to the Crown. Jamaica became a Crown Colony, which meant direct rule from Britain. The Assembly was replaced by a governor who answered directly to the Colonial Office in England. A Legislative Council was appointed to rubber-stamp his decisions. But the new colonial governors were charged with representing the rights of all citizens, not just those of the ruling class. The planters had capitulated, but in a sense the people had won. While some saw the planters' surrender as a retrograde move, in the wake of the rebellion many steps were taken to improve the socio-economic conditions of Jamaica in the first few years under the leadership of a dynamic governor, Sir John Peter Grant. It also introduced a system of governance without ties of nepotism or favouritism to local families. The new civil servants were harder to bribe. What they lacked in ignorance of Jamaica, they made up for in a strict if narrow adherence to professional duty. From this basis grew the Jamaican Civil Service which, by the late 20th century, was among the best of its kind.

Nevertheless, Jamaicans still continued to chafe under white imperial rule, and political agitation of every sort continued over the years. The Morant Bay Rebellion became not an end but a defining moment, the first step on the road to self-government and independence.

The Legacy of '65 Bogle and Gordon are now NATIONAL HEROES of Jamaica. The Morant Bay 'rebellion' lives on in folk memory and in several folk songs, such as 'War O':

War down a Monkland
War down a Morant Bay
War down a Chigger-foot
The Queen never know
War, war, war O. War O, heavy war O

Another song states in part,

Oh General Jackson
Oh you kill all the black men them
Oh what a wrongful judgement
Oh what an awful mourning
You bring on St Thomas people

(Major General Charles Forbes Jackson was a retired Indian Army officer who had settled down as a planter at Mahogany Vale. He joined the Sixth Royal Regiment in pursuit of rebels.)

Contemporary artists continue to be inspired by the memory of '65. The popular REGGAE group Third World dedicated their 'Ninety-six degrees in the shade' to the martyrs of the rebellion and the Jamaican author V.S. Reid wrote a novel *New Day* based on the events as seen through the eyes of a young boy. Poet Lorna Goodison in her 'Name Change: Morant Bay Uprising', noted how people were afraid to be identified with Bogle after his hanging and changed their names. Indeed, the people involved were to repress their memories of these hard times, and Bogle and Gordon were almost forgotten or were seen as 'troublemakers', until a reassessment at Independence. The celebration of the 100th anniversary of the rebellion in 1965 brought them fully into public consciousness once again.

Although a great deal has been written about the events of '65, including the voluminous report of the Royal Commission, there is still no agreement on certain basic issues. These include the motives of the main instigators and whether the event was a localized, spontaneous riot that got out of hand or a planned, wide-scale rebellion. Earlier scholars on the whole saw the action as 'riot' and downplayed Bogle's activist role. New evaluations of the evidence are leading to different conclusions. Don Robotham (1981) emphasized Bogle's role as the leader of a revolt that was pre-meditated and had some degree of planning and organization. In a book published in 1994, *"The Killing Time": The Morant Bay Rebellion in Jamaica*, historian Gad Heuman concluded that the uprising was indeed a rebellion. He stated: 'the outbreak was a rebellion, characterized by advance planning and by a degree of organization. The leader of the rebellion was Paul Bogle, who, with other associates, organized secret meetings in advance of the outbreak. At these meetings oaths were taken and volunteers enlisted in expectation of a violent confrontation at Morant Bay. The meetings were often held in Native Baptist chapels or meeting houses; this was important since the Native Baptists provided a religious and political counterweight to the prevailing white norms of the colonial society.'

[Dutton 1967, Hart 1972, Heuman 1994, Jekyll 1907, Morris 1970, Reid 1949, Robotham 1981, Wynter 1965]

MORANT CAY see CAY

MORANT POINT LIGHTHOUSE

This lighthouse, located at the easternmost point of Jamaica, is the oldest in the island. It consists of a cast iron tube 30m long that has a diameter of 5m at the base and 3m at the cap. This is listed as one of the historic monuments of ST THOMAS Parish, being 'of considerable interest to historians of industrial technology'. The lighthouse was cast in London and erected in 1841, the labour being provided by Kru men, among the indentured AFRICANS who were brought to Jamaica in the period following EMANCIPATION. Sir George Grove who was later to become famous as the compiler of Grove's *Dictionary of Music and Musicians*, was the engineer who came from Britain to supervise its construction.

Morant Point lighthouse

MORAVIAN

The Moravians were the first Christian MISSIONARIES to come to the island with the express purpose of Christianizing the slaves. (See SLAVERY.) They were not very successful at first:

Count Zindendorf

arriving in 1754, by 1800 they had baptised less than 1,000 AFRICANS in the whole island.

The sect was founded by Count Nikolaus von Zindendorf in Moravia in central Czechoslovakia. They began ministering to the slaves in the West Indies in 1732 and came to Jamaica at the invitation of two landowning brothers in ST ELIZABETH, Joseph Foster Barham and William Foster.

The Moravians are still active today, especially in MANCHESTER, St Elizabeth and WESTMORELAND Parishes, with 27,589 listing themselves as adherents in the 1991 census. Bethlehem Teacher's College in the Santa Cruz mountains is operated under the auspices of the church. There are a number of Moravian cemeteries in these parishes that attest to the high death rate among the missionaries.

[Linyard 1969]

MORGAN, Henry (1635-88)

The most famous of the BUCCANEERS who became a landed proprietor in later life. King Charles II appointed him lieutenant governor of Jamaica. Morgan is supposed to have been born in Glamorgan, Wales and gone to Barbados as a bond servant (see IRISH, SCOTS, WELSH). There he joined the fleet that had stopped to collect men for the CAPTURE OF JAMAICA (1655).

He started out in a small way as crew on a privateer vessel, but soon rose to be captain and then leader of all the buccaneers of PORT ROYAL.

Henry Morgan

He carried out many daring raids on Spanish towns in the CARIBBEAN, bringing in millions of dollars worth of booty. His most famous exploit was the capture of the City of Panama in 1671. But around this time England and Spain had made peace and England ceased to licence privateers (as those pirates sanctioned by the state were called). Those who continued in the trade were now regarded as pirates or outlaws.

For his capture of Panama, Morgan was knighted and he returned to Jamaica as lieutenant governor (his friend the governor, on the other hand, was interned in the Tower of London in punishment for the Panama raid – to appease the Spaniards).

Morgan bought several properties in Jamaica and tried to be respectable. For a while he ruthlessly acted against his old comrades, helping to stamp out privateering in the area. Still, Morgan's heart was in Port Royal and he spent his last days there in the taverns. He died in 1688 and was buried near the present naval cemetery but his grave like the rest in the public cemetery was washed beneath the sea by the EARTHQUAKE which devastated the 'wickedest city on earth' which he had helped to build.

MORGAN'S HARBOUR

Hotel at the entrance to PORT ROYAL, sited in 1950 within the walls of the old naval dockyard. Here, from the 18th century onwards, ships of the Royal Navy were repaired. The dockyard was closed down in 1905.

MORTAR

A large domestic utensil which, along with a pestle ('mortar stick'), was once found in nearly every household since it was vital for pounding foods such as CORN, COCOA for chocolate, COFFEE, CASSAVA, and YAM. The wooden mortar was often home made, hollowed out vertically from a solid block of wood such as LIGNUM VITAE. The heavy mortar stick (sometimes as much as 1.5m long and 5-10cm in diameter) was also used as a weapon.

Old mortar and pestle

'MOSQUITO INDIANS' see MISKITO

MOTH see BUTTERFLIES AND MOTHS

MOUNT DIABLO

Highest point on the main road between KINGSTON and OCHO RIOS, the land rising to 914m where the highway crosses it. Mount Diablo ('Devil Mountain') was aptly named by the Spaniards who had one of their trails from SPANISH TOWN to Sevilla la Nueva (see SEVILLE, New) going across it via MONEAGUE, the same as the road today. The hill affords a spectacular view of the valley below, and of BAUXITE mining operations carried out by Alcan Jamaica Limited, Ewarton Works. The huge Mount Rosser red mud pond represents waste from the bauxite mining operations, beginning in 1959. (See RED MUD 'LAKE'.)

MOUNTAIN MULLET see MULLET

MOUNTAIN PRIDE (*Spathelia sorbifolia*)

Endemic tree that bears a huge crown of bright magenta flowers June to November and is the subject of the LEGEND OF MOUNTAIN PRIDE. Although Adams describes it as 'rather common in open thickets or woodlands on well drained shale or limestone' from sea level to 700m, it is most visible on LIMESTONE cliffs and is therefore rarely seen close up or photographed. A number of trees can be seen during the flowering months in the area surrounding GORDON TOWN, and on the SPUR TREE cliffs.

Spathelias are monocarpic, that is, plants which live for several years but are able to flower and seed only once. The plant has a very narrow trunk (around 8cm in diameter) but grows 6-16m tall; it produces its enormous flower cluster after 8-10 years and the entire plant dies once the seeds ripen.
[Adams 1972, Huxley 1978]

Mountain Pride

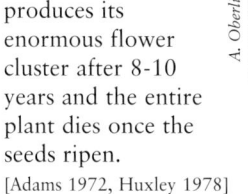

MOUNTAIN PRIDE, Legend of

The legend relates that MOUNTAIN PRIDE was a beautiful TAINO girl about to wed a CACIQUE or chief. However the chief priest wanted her for himself and poisoned the cacique at the wedding feast. Rather than submit to him, Mountain Pride threw herself over a cliff, falling to her death on a ledge below. Where she fell, there soon grew up a beautiful tree with a crown of magenta blossoms, representing the crown of feathers that Mountain Pride wore. The tree still grows near LIMESTONE cliffs in her memory. (See also LOVERS' LEAP, Legend of.)

MULBERRY GARDENS
An area of SPANISH TOWN whose name reportedly dates from the time when the Spaniards grew mulberry trees here to support a SILK spinning industry. At Mulberry Gardens there stood, until blown down by the 1951 hurricane, a TAMARIND tree under which, tradition has it, the English colonels Raymond and Tyson were shot for mutiny in 1660. Tyson was a brave officer, commander of a regiment quartered in Guanaboa Vale. Raymond was a neighbour. For various reasons, they led the regiment in a mutiny. The soldiers were eventually promised amnesty if they handed over their colonels and they did so. Raymond and Tyson were court martialled, sentenced to death, and shot. The mutiny arose partly because the soldiers, five years after their CAPTURE OF JAMAICA, were anxious to settle down as civilians. There was also a great deal of hostility between the factions who supported the restoration of the monarchy and those who supported Cromwell. Twelve days after Raymond and Tyson were shot, news came that King Charles II had been restored to the throne. The army in Jamaica was officially disbanded in 1661 and General Edward D'Oyley appointed the first civil governor.
[Black 1974]

MULLET
Small river FISH including Calipever and Mountain Mullet. Earlier chroniclers listed these mullets among the finest delicacies of Jamaican cuisine (along with Mountain or Black CRAB and Ring-tail PIGEON) but they, like the others, are now rare.

Charles Rampini (1873) was introduced to Mountain Mullet (and PEPPER-POT) in Chapelton, CLARENDON Parish and said it well deserved its fame as 'the delicatest fish that swims in Jamaican rivers'. But, he advised, it must be eaten the minute it is taken from the water, having been immediately wrapped in PLANTAIN leaves, or better still, in note paper, and lightly heated on a gridiron over a clear wood fire. He was told that the largest and best his informant ever tasted weighed 680g and had green and yellow fat, like a turtle. The fish, alas, is hardly to be seen nowadays though the appreciation lingers on. A modern cookbook writer, Norma Benghiat, recorded purchasing a string of river mullet from a vendor along the FLAT BRIDGE on the RIO COBRE, taking them home and barbecuing them, finding them 'exquisite'. She has been on the lookout ever since for a man holding a string of fish at Flat Bridge, but has not been able to repeat the experience.
[Benghiat 1985, DJE, Rampini 1873]

MUNRO COLLEGE see BLACK RIVER ANGLICAN CHURCH

MUSGRAVE MEDALS
Medals awarded by the INSTITUTE OF JAMAICA for achievements in the fields of Literature, Science and Art. The gold medal is awarded for 'distinguished eminence', the silver for 'outstanding merit' and the bronze for 'merit'. Since 1897, Musgrave Medals have been

Sir Anthony Musgrave (left) on medals

awarded annually. The award was instituted as a memorial to Sir Anthony Musgrave, Governor of Jamaica, who founded the Institute of Jamaica, Jamaica's leading cultural institution, in 1879.

MUSIC
It is perhaps not surprising that in the 20th century Jamaica gave to the world a completely new musical form called reggae, for music and song have played central roles in people's lives throughout the island's history. In the past, music for Jamaicans was not a leisure-time affair, but an integral element in the daily round, an accompaniment for work as for play, a component of rituals from BIRTH to death, a means of communication, criticism and comment, and an essential ingredient in religious worship. Above all, down to the present, music has served as a release from the pressures of daily living – whether these result from enslavement (see SLAVERY), poverty, social indifference or political corruption – and as a way of affirming life under the most trying conditions. As the popular song (embodying the REVIVAL chorus 'Never get weary yet') affirms:

I was walking on the shore and they took me
   in the ship
And they throw me overboard
And I swam right out of the belly of the whale
And I never get weary yet
They put me in jail and I did no wrong
And I never get weary yet
(Toots and the Maytals 1981).

Music has been so pervasive in the social, economic, and religious life of Jamaicans that it is perhaps not accidental that many of the folk tales or ANANSI stories feature song as a critical element of the tale, with central roles often assigned to music and musicians.

African Patterns Plantation slavery might have silenced or driven underground many of the cultural expressions of the West Africans who were forcibly brought to the island, including the playing of those MUSICAL INSTRUMENTS such as DRUMS which the masters feared could be used for communicating revolt. But voices could not be silenced, and even when the drums were, the rhythm was carried by the instrument of the body in song and dance. Percussion was provided by the tapping of feet, clapping of hands and anything that served as noise-maker – shak-shaks from dried seed pods, the rookaw (two jagged sticks) or clappers (two stones clapped together).

'Hallelujah' by Osmond Watson

Early observers such as Hans Sloane in the late 17th century identified African patterns in the musical forms and expressions and these patterns continued to shape the music over the next hundreds of years. This music in the early days owed a debt to many African ethnic groups. As Kenneth Bilby has observed of Caribbean music in general, a given musical event among slaves might have included different groups, e.g. Kromanti (see COROMANTEE), NAGO, etc., and a number of African languages. Over time, songs developed in the local creole (see LANGUAGE), incorporating a wide variety of African-derived musical forms.

Characteristic African features are the interest in vocal music and the rhythmic interaction of call and response, consisting of a solo part and an answering response from a chorus. (See GAMES, folk MUSIC, WORK SONGS.) Observers in the plantation era also noted that a good deal of the singing was impromptu and consisted of songs of derision, 'not infrequently at the expense of the overseer if he happens to be listening', according to Edward Long. J.B. Moreton recorded this one in his book published in 1793:

Tink dere is a God in a top,
No use me ill, Obissha
Me no horse, me no mare, me no mule,
No use me ill, Obissha

Another planter-historian, Bryan Edwards, added that the slave songs were 'fraught with obscene ribaldry' and accompanied with dances that were 'in the highest degree licentious and wanton', accusations that continued to be hurled at Jamaican popular music from MENTO to DANCEHALL. It was noted that while the musicians were usually male, women were frequently the singers:

Hipsaw! My deaa! You no do like a-me!
You no jig like a-me! You no twist like a-me!
Hipsaw! My deea! You no shake like a-me!
You no wind like a-me! Go, yondaa!
Hipsaw! My deea! You no jig like a-me!
You no work him like a-me! You no sweet him
   like a-me!
(Moreton, 1793)

European influences Like everything else, music became creolized, new forms arising from a fusion of the many different African styles with the European music to which the Africans were increasingly exposed. This was not just the music played at the GREAT HOUSE, at the balls and assemblies of the elite (and witnessed by the slaves). European

Young musicians, Orrett Rhoden (1973) and Stephen 'Cat' Coore, (1966)

music was also brought by the poor whites such as sailors who formed a large part of the population of the ports at any given point in time; British and American sea shanties and ballads no doubt came via this route. The European influence on secular folk music is still strong. The repertoire of Jamaican music over time gained from the large infusions of settlers from other countries, especially the Gaelic influence of the IRISH, SCOTS and WELSH. A FRENCH influence through the influx of émigrés (masters and slaves) arriving during the Haitian Revolution is harder to quantify. Many songs taught in schools and ring games played in the schoolyard also originated in the British Isles, the latter undergoing transformations over time.

Popular British and American songs of the day were brought to the island with every ship, many becoming a part of the cultural repertoire (e.g. 'Danny Boy', 'My Bonnie Lies Over the Ocean') a process helped in later years by the sheet music that was sold. Of course, in more recent times, these foreign influences gained with the introduction of radio, television and recorded music.

Given the old and rich tradition of THEATRE in Jamaica, the urban population, slave and free, was also exposed to and no doubt influenced by a wide variety of musical events by foreign performers who passed through. In addition, in the days of sail, many slaves and freedmen travelled widely to other countries, especially, in the early days, to Latin American ports and nearby CARIBBEAN countries such as Cuba and Haiti. From the mid-19th century onwards, there were the influences arising from large-scale emigration of wage labourers to neighbouring countries in Latin America (see COLÓN MAN), and later to North America and Europe. Sailing ships from America also had many black sailors among their crews and this might have contributed an African-American element from early times. A significant number of slaves also arrived with their white loyalist owners who were fleeing the American War of Independence in the 1780s.

Some elements of the population during slavery were always on the move, with opportunities for gatherings or mixing provided by jobbing GANGS, road works, transporting crops to the ports, manning coastal droghers, transporting goods in CANOES and FISHING. MARKET days, funerals, gatherings at the courthouses and churches, and the big holiday celebrations of CHRISTMAS, CROPOVER and 'Pikni Christmas' (EASTER) all provided the means for exchanging news and gossip as well as music.

At first, European social dance music was performed by Europeans on European instruments but these seemed gradually to have given way to black and COLOURED musicians who provided a bridge between the GREAT HOUSE and the hut in music, musical instruments and performance style. In his study of theatre in Jamaica, Errol Hill has noted that musicians to accompany travelling companies were always recruited locally.

'Creole Airs' The creolization process was not one-way, for the Europeans were not averse to adopting from the African-Jamaican, and in the 19th century, 'creole airs' became popular. In the 1820s, according to Errol Hill, J.F. Edelman published in London musical arrangements called 'West Indian Pot Pourri' – pianoforte selections of 'creole airs as sung and danced by the Negroes of Jamaica'. They were collected by Frances Egan, a church organist, who also published *The Negro Vocalist*, a book of folk songs, in 1834, and other volumes.

Not to be overlooked as a powerful European influence was religious music over the years, but especially through MISSIONARY activities in the 19th century, and the hymns that they introduced. 'Sankeys' became especially popular. These are hymns from the book *Sacred Songs and Solos* by Ira D. Sankey (1840-1908), singer and organist, who backed up Dwight L. Moody (1837-99), evangelical preacher. They were both Americans whose work

Cornwall College choir, Festival 1973

Jazz musicians, L-R, Lloyd Knibbs (drums), Steve Lauz (bass), Jerome Walters (conga), Aubrey Adams (piano), Lennie Hibbert (vibe)

achieved great popularity in Britain and the colonies. These Christian hymns were much sung at the Great Revivals of the late 19th century and became incorporated into African-Jamaican religious music.

While the ancestral African worldview is a vital influence, especially regarding the use of rhythm for communication between the spirit world and the tangible world, the music and symbolism of the indigenous religions such as REVIVAL also draw on Christian sources, as in the popular chorus:

Noah build the Ark an' gawn
Anadda generation come.

And while RASTAFARIAN ideology, drumming and musical styles owe much to Africa, the words to many Rasta songs also reveal a close perusal of the Bible:

We're going to leave this Babylon world
King Rasta lead us home
Glory to God in Zion
We are going home
To Ethiopia, we are going home

Classical and Choral Nor was classical music neglected. Jamaicans heard such music from the touring opera companies and other visiting theatrical performers in the early days and similar groups and performers brought in by local impresarios in the 20th century. Classically trained music teachers (like dance teachers) were always in demand, for the acquisition of such skills has been *de rigueur* for the bourgeoisie up to the present day. Music was taught especially in girls' secondary schools. By 1920, the examinations of the Associated Boards of the Royal Academy of Music and the Royal College of Music in England, were established in the island. However, the audience for classical music has always been small and the emphasis has been on performance rather than composition (though there has been a great deal of composition in the areas of jazz and popular music).

Jamaica can perhaps lay claim to one significant classical musical composition. The work of an American, Dr Thurston Dox, recently revealed the existence of an oratorio, *Jonah*, by the Jamaican-born Samuel Felsted. It is believed to be the first complete work of its kind to have been composed and performed in the New World. The score was published in KINGSTON in 1775, followed by the first performance there in 1779. The work was thereafter performed several times in the United States. Born of English parents, Felsted seems to have received his musical training in the island and was organist at both ST ANDREW and Kingston Parish churches.

The churches have nurtured the development of choral music; a foremost name in this field for over fifty years until his death was George Goode (1882-1960) who was associated with several groups, the most important of which was the Dioscesan Festival Choir, under the auspices of the ANGLICAN church. SCOTS KIRK from 1947 until recent times was the home of the St Andrew Singers.

Secular choral music has also been developed and sustained by theatrical activities such as the annual PANTOMIME and by the folk singing groups (see MUSIC, Folk).

Being self-taught, many early musicians could not sight read, though training in tonic solfa was

Hatfield singers

widespread and facilitated reading of vocal music that is still operative. According to newspaper reports, Jamaican farm workers who went in 1944 to the USA as part of Roosevelt's Good Neighbour policy, astounded their American hosts in such places as Wisconsin and Pennsylvania by purchasing violins and guitars within days of their arrival, and putting on church concerts with considerable skill. Their gift as singers was also remarked upon.

A musical training ground since the 1890s has been the band of ALPHA Boys School, part of a complex run by ROMAN CATHOLIC nuns who have used music to instil discipline in their charges. Many of Jamaica's leading musicians have been beneficiaries, including several of those of the 1940s and 1950s who were responsible for creating the new popular musical sound of Ska. (See REGGAE.) Since 1976, the Jamaica School of Music (now part of the EDNA MANLEY COLLEGE) has offered musical training in popular music and jazz as well as classical.

[Baxter 1970, Bilby 1985a, Clerk 1978, Hill 1992, Lewin 1968, 1970, 1984, 1994, 2000, O'Gorman 1986, 1989b]

MUSIC, Folk

The traditional MUSIC of Jamaica that has developed over the past 350 years is the music made by the common people, frequently a marriage of lyrics, instruments and accompanying DANCE styles. (See, e.g. MENTO.) However, this music did not gain widespread respect or acceptance until the closing years of the 20th century.

The recognition of Jamaican traditional music as a valid art form has come about through a number of factors, including a government initiative in the 1960s to begin field collections of such music that was in danger of disappearing. Collection and classification of folk music has continued through the Jamaica School of Music and arrangement and dissemination through the excellent folk-singing groups that have emerged, principal among them the JAMAICAN FOLK SINGERS, the NATIONAL DANCE THEATRE COMPANY Singers and the University Singers. All of these groups have taken the traditional music to the concert stage in Jamaica and internationally with a sophistication of interpretation and choreographed performance styles, building on the popularity of an earlier group of the fifties and sixties, the Frats Quintet. The Jamaica Festival movement has also helped to keep some of the traditional music alive by recognizing and giving a platform to traditional groups from villages and towns all over the island and also contributing to field research.

Many field recordings of Jamaican folk music as well as recordings by the various groups are now available. There are also several published folk music collections, including those dating from the early 20th century by Martha Warren Beckwith, Walter Jekyll, Astley Clerk (unpublished) and, in more recent times, Tom Murray and Olive Lewin.

Some of the ongoing discoveries of Jamaican traditional music in recent years have been associated with anthropological research into Jamaican religious expressions such as Revival

Frats Quintet

and Rastafari or groups such as Kumina practitioners and the Maroons. This has helped to contextualize the music and provide a better understanding of its functions not just as an amusing pastime but as an agent of survival. Even today, some of the more esoteric music used in religious rituals would be hidden from outsiders. Other songs have become part of the popular lore of all Jamaicans, handed down from generation to generation:

A chi chi bud, O
Some a dem a hollar some a bawl

Many of the popular songs are the 'newspapers' of the group, recording happenings of significance to the world or simply to those of a particular locality. 'War O' is the people's record of the MORANT BAY REBELLION. (See also NEWCASTLE.)

Folk songs have also provided the opportunity for gossip, scandal or chastisement as in this song recorded by Jekyll:

I have a news to tell you all about the Mowitahl Men
Time is harder every day and harder yet to come
They make a dance on Friday night an fail to pay the drummer

Say that they all was need of money to buy up their August pork.
Don't let them go free drummer! Don't let them go free drummer!
For your finger cost money to tickle the poor goat-'kin

Dr Olive Lewin, who was the first government-appointed Folk Music Research officer (and is the founder/leader of the Jamaican Folk Singers), has suggested dividing this traditional music into three broad categories:

(1) Work songs. (See DAY WORK, JAMMA, WORK SONG.)

(2) Ceremonial and ritual music arising out of religious beliefs and practices such as funeral processions and burial ceremonies, the invocation of ancestral spirits and spirit possession in the African-Jamaican religions. (See CALEMBE, DEATH RITUALS, DINKI MINI, ETU, GERREH, GOOMBAY, HOSAY, KUMINA, MAROON, RASTAFARI, REVIVAL, ZELLA.)

(3) Social and recreational music as performed and experienced during leisure hours at weekends and holidays, the music concerned with the stages of life as well as the day-to-day activities of the group. (See BRUCKINS, BURU, CROPOVER, CHRISTMAS, FESTIVALS, GAMES, JONKONNU, MENTO, 'PLAY', QUADRILLE, TAMBU.)

[Baxter 1970, Beckwith 1924, 1928, Brathwaite 1979, Jekyll 1907, Lewin 1968, 1970, 1984, 1994, 2000, Murray 1953, O'Gorman 1987a, Ryman 1985, 1989]

MUSIC, School of see EDNA MANLEY COLLEGE

MUSICAL INSTRUMENTS

Though the traditional instruments of western MUSIC are popular in Jamaica, there have developed a number of instruments that, along with the songs, DANCES and musical styles, represent the CARIBBEAN penchant for creation and improvisation.

Local musicians have for a long time made their own instruments, some in the African tradition. (See CALABASH, CATTA STICK, CONCH, BANJO, BENTA, DRUM, ETU, JAWBONE, RUMBA BOX.) Others are copies or interpretations of western musical instruments like the violin or a flute made from BAMBOO or the TRUMPET TREE branch. (See also COROMANTEE.) Ivy Baxter noted an account of a village band contest that mentions a 'piccolo' made from a steel rod, a 'saxophone' built from bicycle handlebars, and home-made violins with bows strung with fibres from unravelled twine instead of cat gut (later constructions would use lengths of plastic thread of varying diameters). MENTO bands often made their instruments from local material. 'Sugar Belly' Walker and his bamboo 'saxophone' was a well-known fixture of the urban musical scene for many years, the saxophone constructed, according to Marjorie Whylie, with bamboo 'collected during the "dark of the moon". The bell was shaped from a discarded commercial thread spool, and the reeds carefully shaped from the wild cane originally. In later years the reed was commercially acquired. Its several parts were put together with closely wrapped thread'.

Players of penny whistles, graters, accordians, paper-covered combs and musical saws used to be popular at country gatherings. The basic instruments for popular music-making up to recent years remain the drum, the rattle (shak-shak or maraccas) and the banjo or fiddle. QUADRILLE bands played their waltzes and reels on violin or fiddle and fife and sometimes trumpet and saxophone. In recent years the acoustic guitar has also become popular.

The musical instrument of the orthodox churches has always been the organ and some fine examples of pipe organs are to be found in the island. The non-traditional churches have favoured the tambourine and the drum, though nowadays the instruments might be electronic, a combination of the traditional and the popular.

Whylie has pointed out that 'The organization of traditional instrumental ensembles in Jamaica shows a complexity and sophistication which is not obvious at first glance, but becomes evident under close scrutiny. Instrumental organization follows set patterns that are often determined by the aesthetics of African music. There are distinctly functional groups or categories of instruments, the melodic, the chordal and the

Musical instruments by Everald Brown

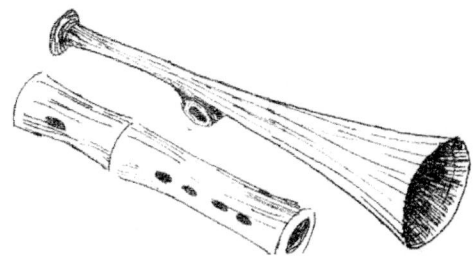

Koramanti flute and bamboo flute

Mouth organ and bamboo trumpet

percussive, and they are selected according to their effectiveness in playing specific functions and established roles. Those instruments which are grouped to provide a more communal sound are no less important to the overall sound of the ensemble than are the solo instruments.'

The TAINOS had as their main musical instruments, *fotutos* or trumpets carved from shells, flutes of reeds and bone, maracas of wood or calabash gourds, dance sticks, shell castanets and shell rattles, and drums including a slit-drum made of a hollow log. (See AREITO.)

[Baxter 1970, Bilby 1985a, Clerk 1975, 1978, JSM 1972, 1976, Whylie 2000, Whylie and Warner-Lewis 1994]

MUSLIM

Muslims – followers of the religion of Islam – have been represented in Jamaica both during SLAVERY and after, though their numbers have never been large. Muslims in plantation Jamaica included the Mandingo as well as some Hausa and Yoruba slaves. The Muslim religion demands that believers perform set duties every day, such as praying at fixed time periods five times a day while facing Mecca, weekly attendance at a mosque, fasting during the month of Ramadan and observing dietary and other restrictions. Given the relentless demands of the plantation routine, Muslim slaves were unable to maintain the practice of their religion, and most appear to have been converted to Christianity. Still, some never gave up their original faith, or forgot their homelands, as was evident with some of the Mandingo who were also literate in Arabic. The religious and political role of literacy in Arabic among Muslim Africans surfaces with respect to a pastoral letter written in Africa in about 1780 which circulated and was sent via Kingston and hand-delivered to Robert Peart (Muhammad Kaba) of MANCHESTER in 1831. (See MANDINGO.) Because Peart's wife perceived the physical evidence capable of implicating them in sedition, she destroyed the letter during the searches that followed the 1831-32 Rebellion (see SHARPE, Samuel) in western Jamaica.

As the 19th century progressed, there were few overt indications of the practice of Islam among the African-descended population. In the second half of the 19th century Islam gained visibility through the arrival of INDIAN indentured workers, 10 per cent of whom were Muslims, but even among them the rate of conversion to Christianity was high. Nevertheless, the Shi'a Muslim observance called HOSAY was kept alive in areas of high Indian population density. Among these were SAVANNA-LA-MAR in WESTMORELAND Parish, VERE, Gimme-me-bit, Racecourse and Kemps Hill in CLARENDON Parish, Bog Walk in ST CATHERINE Parish, ANNOTTO BAY in ST MARY Parish and Cockburn Pen in western KINGSTON.

In 1981 the Islamic Council of Jamaica estimated the number of Muslims to be 3,000 with the majority being of African descent, the result of the rise of the Black Muslim faith in the 1960s in the United States and, more recently, because of Islamic missionary activity. Expatriate Indians constitute a minority of the present Islamic population. A mosque near Savanna-la-mar is abandoned, the one operational mosque being on Camp Road in Kingston.

[Afroz 1995, Wilks 1967]

MYAL

An old religion concerned with healing in Jamaica. Although Myal seems to have undergone many changes throughout the centuries, and perhaps suffered from misleading descriptions by those who understood little of its ritual, what has remained at the core of Myal has been the inseparable linkage between healing (see MEDICINE, Folk) and RELIGION. Belief in such a linkage was brought from Africa. As John S. Mbiti notes: 'Major illnesses and troubles are usually regarded, treated and explained as religious experiences in African societies.' The Myalist then, might be seen as the restorer of order or health to both the individual and the community.

Although Myal as a separate religion probably no longer exists, core elements survived in later developments such as REVIVAL and KUMINA, in the practice of BALM and GOOMBAY and the MAROON heritage. In Kumina, 'Myal' is the name given to possession by an ancestral spirit or Zambi.

The origin of the word myal has not been traced, though the DJE cites the Hausa *maye*, which means: '1. Sorcerer, wizard; 2. Intoxication; 3. Return. (All of these senses are present in the Jamaican use of the word.)'

Our knowledge of Myal is based mainly on the observation of outsiders. It was first identified as a 'secret society' within OBEAH and continued to be identified with obeah by early writers. Later, it was identified as a cult for undoing the work of Obeah. Myal cultists under the influence of Christianity were in the forefront of religious frenzy associated with the Great Revival and the casting out of evil by the 'taking up' of Obeah. In the 1860s, the Myalists or 'Angelmen' as they called themselves were described as wheeling, dancing and in the spirit – characteristics that today would describe Revival ceremonies.

African Origins The Myalist seems to have been a direct descendant of the African medicine-man or, as he became known on the estates during SLAVERY, the 'Black doctor'. This was the man (or woman) who had knowledge of medicines and herbs and used them for healing and protection. In Africa, the medicine-man was also a spiritual and political leader, and the early Myal men seemed to have played that role, being involved in the struggles to break the chains of slavery. It was they who formed secret societies, administered oaths, conducted the rites and provided the CHARMS that worked magic to make warriors invulnerable to bullets. They worked for the good of the community, as opposed to the Obeah-man who worked at the behest of the individual, and part of their work might well have been combating that of the Obeah-man. But in the early days, few observers made that distinction. Indeed, in New World plantation societies, the distinctions between the different religious specialists that were maintained in Africa might not have been possible, and different roles might have been undertaken by the same individual. Edward Long who was the first to describe Myal (1774) wrote about it as a new development or 'society' within Obeah. He described the 'Myal Dance' by which initiates underwent 'death' and 'resurrection' at the hands of the Myal 'doctor', both induced by plants he administered. (See CALALU, SPIRIT WEED.)

Myal leaders were implicated in the TACKY uprising of 1760 and as such, they were identified with Obeah, which from that date was declared illegal. From then on, Myalists, like Obeah-men and -women, were frequently imprisoned. R.T. Banbury recorded a song they sang on being released:

Mial nigga, we come, oh!
We go da jail, we come out
Mial nigga, we come, oh!
We work again, we come back
Mial man we come, oh!

The distinction between Myal-men and Obeah-men seemed to have been observed by the African-Jamaicans themselves, who feared the power of both. The fear, and the power, is based on the belief, still current, that illness often has a spritual cause. Both Obeah-men and Myal-men claimed to derive their power from being able to contact the spirits or 'deaths', the difference lying in the purpose to which this knowledge was put. In the 19th century, Banbury observed that the Obeah-men were seen as 'shadow-takers', or those who stole people's souls or spirits (which resulted in illness, disorder or death); the Myalists as 'shadow-catchers', i.e. those who were engaged in the capture and restoration of souls (and health to the individual). While the Obeah practitioner conducted his secret rituals in the graveyard where he called up spirits, the Myalist's locus of power was the COTTON TREE around which he conducted his ceremonies and communicated with the spirit world. He 'travelled' to that world where he was given the information he needed for diagnosis and healing. In a communal rite with his group of initiates, he undertook the healing ritual.

Christian Influences Myalists, like other Jamaicans, from the late 18th century came under the influence of MISSIONARIES, especially the BAPTISTS from whom they adopted certain Christian rites such as Baptism. Other water rites conducted at the fountainhead of streams (see WATER SPIRITS) were also important.

Myalism seemed to have moved away from the 'secret society' role and became increasingly Christian in mission. The ending of the slave trade in 1807 meant that practices such as Myal were no longer revitalized by new arrivals from Africa. Or perhaps the practice had separated into the private that was unseen by outsiders and a more public manifestation. Banbury makes a distinction between the earlier Myalists and those who came to prominence around the 1840s whose 'work' was no longer concerned with the recovery of lost souls, but with 'taking up obeahs'. Their finding and uprooting of 'obeah' began to be conducted in the daytime as public demonstrations and attracted large groups of people flocking to see it, including white overseers and BOOK-KEEPERS on the estates. The Myalists sang,

> Dandy obeah de ya, oh
> Me wi' pull he, oh
> A any way him run, oh
> Me wi' pull he oh.

There were Myalist 'outbreaks' in the western parishes as they went about their 'divine mission'. The songs recorded at this stage clearly show the Christian influence:

> Lord have mercy, oh!
> Christ have mercy, oh!
> Obeah pain hot, oh!
> Lord we come fe pull he, oh!
> A no we put he, oh!
> A 'pirit tek he, oh!
> An we come fe pull he, oh!

The 'obeah' could be taken from the ground or from the body of the patient, the substances extracted from the body by the Myal-man or woman by 'sucking, sneezing, or retching'.

As a religious cult, Myalism reached its zenith after EMANCIPATION to around the time of the Great Revival of 1860-61 and seems to have become absorbed into what is now called Revival.

Goombay and Jonkonnu Myal in what appeared to be its earlier form was encountered in the 1920s by M.W. Beckwith in the COCKPIT COUNTRY. In ritual ways, she said, the Myal men corresponded exactly with West African medicine men and their secret societies. She described their practices as concerned with 'medicine' or healing. The 'myal dance', a song-dance ritual, was still employed in cases of 'baffling illness'. The Myal cultists would gather at the sick person's yard, the GOOMBAY and another drum would be played and songs sung to induce spirit possession, the Myal doctor or medium would go into a trance in which the 'spirit' would reveal the nature of the illness and what herbs to use for a cure. Later observers including Katherine Dunham connected Myalists with the Maroons and she described a 'myal dance' at ACCOMPONG that harked back to the earlier 'death and resurrection' theme. More recently, Kenneth Bilby has described 'Gumbay Play' from Upper ST ELIZABETH Parish as the contemporary version of the Myal healing ceremony. Bilby also noted the connection between Myal, Goombay and JONKONNU.

Myal and Shamanism While this connection has not been made in the literature, at the core of Myal is a practice which bears a striking resemblance to that of the specialist known throughout the world as the Shaman. Such a specialist, under different names, was known in Africa as well as in the pre-Colombian Caribbean (see MEDICINE, Taino). Spiritual 'travel', the ability to journey between worlds to obtain the help of guardian spirits, is one of the characteristics that distinguishes the Shaman from ordinary healers or magicians. Shamanic practice is remarkable in that it is standardized, with a template of characteristic features, as described by Mircea Eliade, among others. In the descriptions of Myal over the centuries, many correspondences with the Shamanic are apparent though little investigation has been done in this area. A short list of some of the common features might include: (1) 'work' that is community-based, (2) the leadership role, i.e as mediator between the cultural heritage of the past and the contemporary situation, (3) the mastery of a canon – knowledge of history, ritual practice, DANCE, MUSIC, songs, herbs, etc., (4) the experience of 'ecstacy' or out-of-body experience or spiritual 'travel' (which the Myal man expressed in astounding feats of climbing, 'flying', etc., in order to effect cures by securing spirit helpers and capturing lost souls), (5) the 'death and resurrection' theme, (6) significance of a 'cosmic tree' or centre pole as the passage between worlds, (7) the ability to 'see' beyond ordinary reality – such clairvoyance in Myal being described as 'four-eye', (8) experience of and control of possession rituals ('the Myal dance') to induce helping spirits for healing, and (9), the nature of the healing. The Myal man, like the Shaman, was described as a specialist in diagnosis and treatment of 'spirit disorders' as (a) the restorer of lost souls and (b) the practitioner of specific healing techniques for putting back lost objects into the body or removing objects (the sickness – called 'obeah' by the Myalist) that should not be there.

[Banbury 1894, Beckwith 1928, 1929, Bilby 1999, Dunham 1948, Eliade 1964, Kerr 1952, Long 1774, Mbiti 1975, Parrinder 1961, Seaga 1969, Williams 1934, 1938]

N

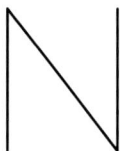

NAGGO HEAD
Place name of a headland along the coast in ST CATHERINE Parish, part of HELLSHIRE, at which an extensive TAINO site is located. (A)Nago is the name of a south westerly sub-group of the YORUBA people of western Nigeria who were among the West Africans forcibly brought to Jamaica as slaves (see SLAVERY). The Dahomeans used Nago as a generic term for Yoruba-speakers, a name adopted also by the French. The Yoruba were known by other names as well: Aku in Sierra Leone and Guyana, Lukumi in Cuba.

NAGO
YORUBA-based group in Waterworks, WESTMORELAND Parish whose ancestors lived in the hills at Abeokuta. This Jamaican place-name replicates the name of a southern Nigerian town, the name of which means 'under the rock', reference to a massive inselberg. The site at Waterworks is similarly dominated by a large rock. Nago music and dance are performed for set ups on the ninth and fortieth nights following a person's death (see DEATH RITUALS) which is similar to the practice of the ETU people of nearby HANOVER Parish.
[Adetugbo 1996, Lewin n.d., Lewin 2000, Ryman 1980]

NANNY, Rt Excellent
MAROON military tactician and chieftainess, National Hero of Jamaica. Although we know very little about the person called Nanny, she is nevertheless a genuine culture hero, the subject of a large body of LEGENDS and stories in the oral tradition, especially among the Maroons for whom she is 'Grandy Nanny', their ancestral grandmother. As poet and historian Kamau Brathwaite has pointed out, although Nanny is mentioned only four times in the written official records and in a fragmented and contradictory manner, 'Her name, actions and influence are at the core of Maroon (oral) tradition'.

But Nanny's symbolic importance goes far beyond the Maroons, representing as she does the female warrior spirit. She has inspired many CARIBBEAN writers and artists, including Sistren Theatre group.

Nanny is identified with NANNY TOWN, the Maroon stronghold in the BLUE MOUNTAINS. After the British government negotiated peace treaties with CUDJOE for the Leeward Maroons and QUAO for the Windward Maroons in 1739, a land patent of 1741 granted to Nanny and 'the people residing with her' 200ha in PORTLAND Parish on terms similar to those agreed with Cudjoe and Quao.

Scholars believe that like the majority of the Maroons Nanny was of Ashanti origin (see COROMANTEE). She was the spiritual and military leader of her people and did not

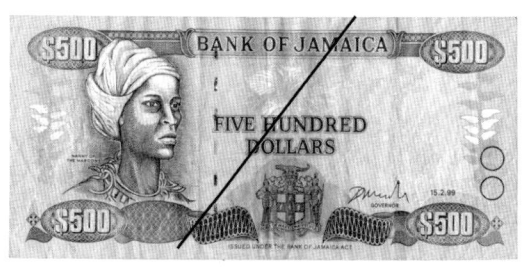

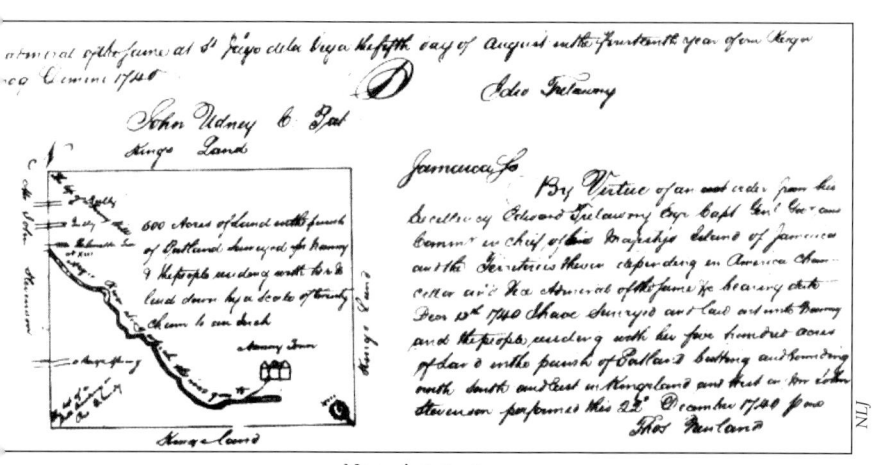

Nanny on banknote

Nanny's patent

herself take part in the fighting but worked out the strategies of the campaigns. The oral tradition has attributed to her fantastic powers and military exploits. She was supposed to have been a great magician with supernatural gifts. The fact that a separate treaty was signed with her after the one with Quao suggests that she herself reluctantly agreed to the peace. After the treaties the Eastern Maroons split in two, one group following Quao to found Charles Town near the coast, the other stayed with Nanny to found New Nanny Town (now Moore Town). She is believed to have been buried on a hill in Moore Town that is known as 'Bump Grave' and is regarded as sacred ground. There is a memorial to Nanny in NATIONAL HEROES PARK.

The likeness of Nanny that appears on the $500 banknote is an artist's imaginative rendering as we do not know what she looked like.

[Agorsah 1994, Bilby 1984, Brathwaite 1977, Mathurin 1975]

NANNY TOWN

The legendary MAROON stronghold in the BLUE MOUNTAINS of PORTLAND parish was once a large village of over 140 houses. It existed for some time before it was discovered by BRITISH soldiers, although they had continuously searched for it over many years. Around 1728, they were led there by an African who aided them in their fight against the Maroons. The town was named after the Maroon leader, NANNY, now a National Hero. It was repeatedly attacked by British troops between 1730 and 1734 until it was destroyed. The Portland Maroons signed peace treaties with the British and established Charles Town and Moore Town. Nanny Town soon faded from sight. Many LEGENDS, however, sprung up about it. One was that any European who visited the site would die, since it was a sacred place. Nanny Town is said to be protected by white birds, the spirits of dead Maroon warriors. In recent years, Nanny Town has become better known. A part of it was excavated by a joint Institute of Jamaica/Scientific Exploration Society team in 1973-74. The UNIVERSITY OF THE WEST INDIES has also begun to conduct archaeological explorations there.

[Agorsah 1994]

NASEBERRY (*Manilkara zapota*)

Small brown pulpy fruit, piercingly sweet and much esteemed, which grows on a medium size tree (15 to 18m high) found from sea level to 400m. In other countries it is better known as sapodilla or sapote. The Jamaican creole name

Naseberry

'niizberry' comes from the Spanish word for the tree – *níspero*, while standard pronunciation 'naseberry' is based on Spanish *néspera*, the name of the fruit. Naseberry is native to tropical America and was esteemed 'the best fruit in the Indies' by the Spaniards in 1657, and described by the naturalist P.H. Gosse in 1851 as 'one of the richest and most agreeable of West Indian fruit'. The fruits vary considerably in size and flavour.

[Adams 1971, DJE]

NATIONAL ANTHEM

The national anthem was introduced at the time of INDEPENDENCE to replace the BRITISH national anthem, 'God Save the Queen'. The words were by the Revd Hugh Sherlock, the music composed by the Hon Robert Lightbourne and rearranged and refined by professional musician Mapletoft Poulle. But in the words of Theodore Sealy, the chairman of the Independence Celebrations Committee, 'the anthem has no specific author, it belongs to the nation'.

[Sealy 1982]

NATIONAL AWARDS

The Jamaica national honours and awards, given to persons who have made an outstanding contribution to public life, were introduced in 1969, replacing BRITISH honours. There are five orders: the Order of National Hero, the Order of the Nation (ON), the Order of Merit (OM), the Order of Jamaica (OJ) and the Order of Distinction, Commander and Officer Ranks (CD and OD). There is also a Medal of Honour (uniformed services) and a Badge of Honour (civilians). The awards are usually made on INDEPENDENCE Day.

The National Anthem

Eternal Father bless our land
Guard us with thy mighty hand
Keep us free from evil powers,
Be our light through countless hours.
To our leaders, Great Defender,
Grant true wisdom from above.
Justice, Truth be ours forever,
Jamaica land we love,
Jamaica, Jamaica, Jamaica land we love.

NATIONAL DANCE THEATRE COMPANY

Founded in 1962, the year of Jamaica's INDEPENDENCE, Jamaica's premier dance company is inextricably associated with the development of national consciousness arising from that event, as it continues to mine and express in dance the rich resources of the Jamaican people.

The NDTC is particularly noted for the fusion of traditional forms (see DANCE) with the elements of modern dance discipline, developing in the process a unique pattern of dance movement. The repertoire, which grows every year, consists of numerous dance works by several choreographers which reflect both European and AFRICAN elements. The company has also helped to bring to public attention previously hidden cultural traditions such as KUMINA and POCOMANIA.

Music is a notable feature of NDTC performances, including the songs by the NDTC Singers. The company's annual Season of Dance in KINGSTON has come to be a much anticipated cultural event, and the company tours widely internationally, sometimes with the support of the Jamaican government as cultural ambassadors. The Company's influence is evident in the areas of dance education (through the Jamaica School of Dance which it founded – see EDNA MANLEY COLLEGE), community dance (through the Jamaica Cultural Development Commission – see FESTIVAL), and research (through the field investigations and publications of Sheila Barnett, Cheryl Ryman, Joyce Campbell, Marjorie Whylie and Rex Nettleford).

Company members are drawn from a wide cross section of Jamaicans who bring with them local and overseas training in modern and CARIBBEAN dance, European classical ballet, and the craft of performing. All the dancers pursue other occupations, and like the numerous volunteers who have served the company in key positions over the years, come together for the love of dance.

The NDTC from the start was able to build on a rich tradition of dance and dance-theatre activities, and in turn has contributed to the development of dance on an island-wide basis through dance workshops and the training of young dancers. The 'NDTC style' is evident in many of the younger groups that have since emerged.

The main founders of the NDTC were Rex Nettleford and Eddy Thomas, who were co-directors until Thomas left the company in 1967. Nettleford, a Rhodes Scholar, is frequently labelled Jamaica's 'Renaissance man', his work as dancer, choreographer and leader of the NDTC only one strand of his cultural and professional life, which includes work as an author, commentator, and university professor, his university career culminating in the Vice-Chancellorship of the UNIVERSITY OF THE WEST INDIES.

[Barnett 1982, Nettleford 1978, 1986]

NATIONAL DISH

Although not officially proclaimed, the national dish by consensus is 'ACKEE and salt fish'. For its supporting role, RICE AND PEAS is referred to as the national COAT OF ARMS.

NATIONAL HEROES PARK

Principal park in KINGSTON laid out as a memorial to Jamaica's National Heroes. This was formerly named George VI Memorial Park after the late King of England. But even before that, the 29ha park was a large open space known as KINGSTON RACE COURSE. National Heroes Park was renamed after INDEPENDENCE, and suitable monuments have been erected in their honour. The name of the road surrounding the park was changed from Race Course to National Heroes Circle.

Of the National Heroes, Rt Excellent Sir Alexander BUSTAMANTE, Rt Excellent Norman

NDTC performing

M. LaYacona

Tomb of the Rt Excellent Sir Alexander Bustamante

MANLEY and Rt Excellent Marcus GARVEY are buried here. Garvey died and was buried in London but in 1964 the body of the National Hero was brought back to Jamaica and reinterred in the park with full state honours. A memorial was erected to commemorate the 1865 MORANT BAY REBELLION and the two National Heroes associated with it, Rt Excellent Paul BOGLE and Rt Excellent George William GORDON. There are also monuments to the other two National Heroes – Rt Excellent Samuel SHARPE and Rt Excellent NANNY.

Entrance to the tomb of the Rt Excellent Norman Manley

Tomb of the Rt Excellent Marcus Garvey

In addition to those designated National Heroes, other outstanding Jamaicans are also buried in the park. Up to the time of writing, they included two former prime ministers: Sir Donald Sangster (1911-67) and the Most Hon Michael Manley (1924-97). The Hon Edna Manley (see ART, EDNA MANLEY COLLEGE), mother of Michael Manley and wife of Norman, is buried in the vault beside her husband, and a piece of her sculpture adorns the outside of the vault.

Others buried in the park include Kenneth George Hill (1909-89) trade unionist and patriot; Bishop Mallica Reynolds – 'Kapo' (1911-89) Revivalist leader and artist (see ART, REVIVAL); Randolph Samuel Williams – 'Ranny' (1912-80), folklorist, actor, playwright, journalist, TV and radio personality, comedian; Mrs Agnes McLaughlin – 'Aggie Bernard' (1910-80), heroine of the Kingston Waterfront Strike of 1938 during which she fed thousands; Dennis Brown (1957-91) singer, legendary 'Crown Prince' of REGGAE.

Tomb of Sir Donald Sangster

Memorial to the Rt Excellent Paul Bogle and the Rt Excellent George William Gordon

The Cenotaph

Also in the park is the War Memorial or Cenotaph. It was erected in 1922 to honour those who died in the First World War and formerly stood on Church Street, but was removed to its present location when HM Queen Elizabeth II visited the island in 1953 and officially opened the George VI Memorial Park. The memorial now honours those who died in both WORLD WARS.

A bust to the Cuban hero-patriot General Antonio MACEO also stands in the park. It was presented in 1952 by the government and people of Cuba to the government and people of Jamaica in gratitude for their aid and hospitality to the great Cuban Independence leader. Maceo was one

Most Hon Michael Manley's tomb

of the outstanding heroes of the Cuban Wars of Independence against Spain in the 19th century, and like the other revolutionary leaders found refuge in Jamaica.

NATIONAL PARKS

The extent of plant and animal species unique to the island is quite remarkable (see FAUNA, FLORA), but much of this rich natural heritage is under threat from pollution, deforestation and other forms of inappropriate exploitation.

The rapid deterioration of Jamaica's natural heritage has led to the belated establishment of protected areas designated as national parks. These are, so far, the Montego Bay Marine Park and the Blue and John Crow Mountains National Park. They are really national wildlife and biological reserves and are the responsibility of the National Resources Conservation Authority (NRCA). Such parks are in their infancy and there are plans for the establishment of several more. There were marine parks in OCHO RIOS and MONTEGO BAY in the 1970s, but the infrastructure was not in place for the enforcement of these protected areas.

The Blue and John Crow Mountains National Park covers the Blue Mountain Forest Reserve, which is over 78,000ha of forested area within the parishes of ST ANDREW, ST THOMAS, PORTLAND, and ST MARY. It is one of the few pristine areas of FOREST remaining. The Park area is the most biologically diverse in the island, with a range of climate and a variety of vegetation from tropical to near temperate (see BLUE MOUNTAINS). It is home to the Jamaican Hutia (see CONEY), SNAKES, tree FROGS, the Giant Swallowtail BUTTERFLY, BIRDS such as the Jamaican TODY and other species. The park also includes important watersheds, such as the YALLAHS Basin that supplies KINGSTON and most of the eastern parishes with water.

The Montego Bay Marine Park opened in 1992, with the main aim of protecting the area's CORAL reefs that are under severe pressure. The protected area is located on the northwest coast of Montego Bay and extends approximately 9km from the Sangster International Airport to just east of the Great River, covering an area of 15.3km^2 with a depth of 100m. Within the park, dumping, excavating or filling operations as well as indiscriminate cutting and chopping of trees in the MANGROVE forests are prohibited. The mangrove wetlands are important to the marine life on the coral reefs, the root systems of these mangroves providing a nursery ground for 80 percent of the life on the reefs.

Investigations are underway for the establishment of other protected areas, such as the COCKPIT COUNTRY.

NATIONAL STADIUM

Home of major national and international sporting events, the stadium was opened in 1962 to celebrate Jamaica's INDEPENDENCE. The first public event in the stadium was the lowering of the BRITISH Union Jack and the raising of the Jamaican flag (see NATIONAL SYMBOLS). The first major sporting event held here was the Ninth Central American and Caribbean Games in 1962.

The statue at the entrance to the stadium by Jamaican sculptor Alvin Marriott (see ART) is in aluminium made from Jamaican BAUXITE, and set on a plinth of Jamaican marble. The casting was done in England. The figure is based on a photograph of Olympic gold medallist Arthur Wint. The statue, however, is not meant to

National arena. Statue honouring athletic heroes by Alvin Marriott

represent Dr Wint but is a composite of the athletes in Jamaica's relay team that won a gold medal at the 1952 Olympic Games in Helsinki (see ATHLETICS). The road leading to the stadium is named after Dr Wint. The National Arena which is part of the stadium complex was built in 1966. The stadium's capacity is 32,000.

NATIONAL SYMBOLS

The following National Symbols were adopted at the time of Jamaica's INDEPENDENCE, 6 August 1962:

National Bird: the Swallow-tail or Streamertail HUMMINGBIRD (*Trochilus polytmus*).

The Jamaican flag

National Flag: The flag has a diagonal cross or saltire with four triangles in juxtaposition. The diagonal cross is in gold and one-sixth of the length of the fly of the flag; the top and bottom triangles are in green; and the hoist and fly triangles are in black. The exact shade of green used in the flag is emerald green T8 17, British Admiralty Bunting Pattern. The flag follows the Admiralty Pattern and the proportion is 2x1.

'Hardships there are but the land is green and the sun shineth' was the symbolism of the flag's colours. As described by the committee that chose it at Independence: 'Black stands for hardships overcome and to be faced; gold for the natural wealth and beauty of sunlight, and green for hope and agricultural resources.' Over the years, there has been widespread criticism of the equation of 'hardship' with black, especially when black people make up the majority of the island's population. In 1997, a special committee of the House of Representatives re-examined the national symbols and concluded that black in the national flag should represent 'strength and creativity'. The committee recommended that the overall interpretation of the flag should be, 'the sun shineth, the land is green and the people are strong and creative.'

National Flower: The LIGNUM VITAE (*Guaiacum officinale*).

National Fruit: The ACKEE (*Blighia sapida*).

National Motto: 'Out of Many, One People', chosen by the Legislature in 1962 to replace the previous motto, the only change that was made to the COAT OF ARMS.

National Tree: The Blue MAHOE (*Hibiscus elatus*).

[GOJ Handbook of Jamaica 1961, Jampress, JIS]

NAVEL STRING TREE

The term 'where your navel string is buried' symbolizes spiritual attachment to a place. It derives from a formerly widespread practice of burying the navel string (umbilical cord) of the newly born and planting a tree over it. The tree was known as the 'Navel String Tree' or 'Birth Tree' and became the property of the child, the tree and its fruit descending to his or her children and their progeny. It helped to reinforce the concept of 'family land', that is land owned in common and passed down from generation to generation.

Katherine Dunham described the practice among the MAROONS of ACCOMPONG in the 1940s when she visited. Sometimes the tree would be provided by the parents, sometimes by god-parents or other relatives or friends; a COCONUT or BREADFRUIT tree was most popular. 'While a man may have much property and several single trees in various parts of the village, he always points to his birth tree with much pride,' she noted.

The practice of planting the navel string and a tree on the BIRTH of a child was brought to Jamaica by West Africans during SLAVERY, but is known elsewhere and reflects the universal notion that the umbilical cord is still intimately connected with the fate of the child. M.W. Beckwith attributed a more materialistic motive in Jamaica where she claimed the tree was a symbol to the child of property and its returns and 'introduces the child to his economic education'. She quoted an aged informant as saying, 'if they know that it belongs to them, they learn to sell and make money for themselves – learn to be careful [saving] . . . It is a birthmark to show him [the child] that it is the beginning of his life and he must take care of it. After you christen him you show him [the tree] again'.

[Beckwith 1929, DJE, Dunham 1946]

NAVY ISLAND

Islet about 0.8km long located in West Harbour, PORT ANTONIO, PORTLAND Parish. It was originally called Lynch's Island and was the first site chosen for the town. But when FORT GEORGE was being built, the island was acquired by the BRITISH navy as a place for careening ships and erecting wharves and warehouses. British sailors were sent to clear the island – a task that resulted in the death of many from fever (see YELLOW FEVER). They persisted and a naval station was eventually built there. Navy Island has in recent times been developed as an exclusive resort.

NEGRIL

The area known as Negril extends from Half Moon Bay in HANOVER Parish to Negril lighthouse in WESTMORELAND Parish. It contains at least 8km of white sand beaches and is one of Jamaica's leading resorts (see TOURISM).

Negril Harbour was once known as Bloody Bay, probably from the fact that whales were butchered there. It was also in this bay that BRITISH ships assembled in convoys to travel under the protection of men of war to England. British ships were also in the habit of lying in wait in the MANGROVE swamps here to attack any Spanish ships that strayed too far off course on their way to Havana, Cuba.

The bay is associated with certain notable battles, including the Battle of New Orleans during the American War of Independence. It was in Negril harbour that a fleet of 50 British warships and over 6,000 men secretly assembled in 1814 under the leadership of Sir Edward Packenham with the objective of seizing Louisiana. The outcome was the Battle of New Orleans where the British were routed by Andrew Jackson and their leader slain. There is a local tradition that the American general was alerted about the attack by an American trader in KINGSTON. Among the soldiers on this engagement were 1,000 men from the First and Fourth WEST INDIA REGIMENTS. (The Battle of New Orleans was recalled by a hit song of the same name in 1959 – sung by Jimmy Horton, written by Jimmy Driftwood.)

It was on Negril beach too that the famous British Admiral BENBOW assembled his squadron for his engagement against the French Admiral Du Casse in 1702. Another famous habitué of Negril Beach in the old days was the notorious pirate 'Calico Jack' (see Jack RACKHAM).

[Wright and White 1969]

Negril lighthouse

Negril before development

NEGRIL POINT LIGHTHOUSE

This lighthouse is situated at south NEGRIL point, WESTMORELAND Parish, which is the extreme western end of the island. The concrete tower is 20m above the ground and the light is elevated 30m above sea level. The lighthouse has an automatic white light that flashes every two seconds. It was built in 1894 by the French engineering firm of Bertier and Benard.

NELSON, Admiral Horatio (1758-1805)

Admiral Nelson, probably Britain's greatest naval hero – he was BRITISH Naval Commander during the Revolutionary and Napoleonic wars – is associated with old PORT ROYAL. He was twice stationed at the naval headquarters there, a plaque on 'Nelson's Quarterdeck' at FORT CHARLES reminding visitors: 'In this place dwelt Horatio Nelson. You who tread his footprints remember his glory.'

Nelson spent a total of 30 months on the Jamaica station but suffered from illness most of the time and requested to be transferred back to

Admiral Nelson

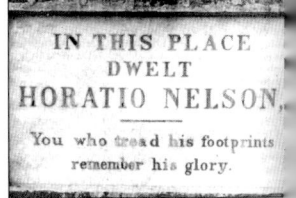

Plaque on 'Nelson's Quarterdeck', Port Royal

England, where he soon regained his health. The future hero of Trafalgar wrote to a friend: 'I return to England hope revives within me (sic). I shall recover and my dream of glory be fulfilled. Nelson will yet be an Admiral. It is the climate that has destroyed my health and crushed my spirit. Home and dear friends will restore me.' He was 22 years old.

Nelson first came to Jamaica on the *Badger* from a North American posting. On 11 June 1779 he was promoted to Post-Captain and appointed to the *Hinchinbrooke*, a 28-gun frigate. While he was waiting for the *Hinchinbrooke* to return from a cruise, the island was 'turned upside down' with fear of invasion from a strong FRENCH fleet that had assembled in the area. This was during the American War of Independence when Spain, France and the Netherlands had also declared war on England.

Although Nelson was not yet 21 years old, he was put in charge of the batteries at Fort Charles and 500 men. The island's defences were all mustered but Nelson did not believe it could withstand a strong attack. He spent his time pacing up and down and gazing out to sea from the raised wooden platform on the south side of Fort Charles, which is still known as Nelson's Quarterdeck. The French threat did not materialize and in September the *Hinchinbrooke* arrived. Nelson then took part in an ill-fated expedition to Nicaragua in which most of the British forces were to die of sickness (see YELLOW FEVER) and only 10 of the *Hinchinbrooke*'s 100 men were to survive. Nelson himself was so weak on his return to Port Royal that he had to be carried ashore on a cot. He was taken to the lodging house of a coloured woman named CUBAH CORNWALLIS, a 'doctoress' who helped to nurse him back to health. He afterwards recuperated at Admiral Parker's country house in the hills, but lamented that he was not back at Port Royal.

A representation of Nelson and the HMS *Hinchinbrooke* appears on two souvenir coins: the $10 silver coin and $100 gold coin.

[Goffe 1980, Oman 1996]

NETBALL

Netball is the national sport for women in Jamaica, officially recognized as such since 1963. The development of the sport has been spearheaded by the Jamaica Netball Association formed in 1958, and owes much to the commitment to the sport by the late Leila Robinson.

Jamaica's netballers have come to dominate the regional championships and the national team has placed consistently high at world tournaments, never ranking below fifth at any time and ranked fourth at the time of writing. In 1991 they finished third, and Janet Johnston became one of only three women ever to play in five world championships.

The seven-a-side ball game is played mostly in English-speaking countries by girls and women. It was introduced into England from the USA as the indoor game of basketball in 1895 (basketball having been invented in 1891 by a Canadian living in America). It quickly spread among women's schools and colleges. By 1905, English rules were established and became the ones used in other countries.

Elaine Davies in action for the Jamaica Netball team

The game was brought to Jamaica at the beginning of the 20th century by teachers from England hired by the girls' secondary schools. Netball was initially confined to these schools and teacher training colleges, but later the alumnae of these institutions started teams and began to play friendly matches among themselves. Over the years, organized inter-school competitions developed with both secondary and primary school leagues. In 1997 there were 58 teams associated with the Jamaica Netball Association.

Jamaica hosted the third World Tournament in 1971 and is scheduled to host the eleventh tournament in 2003.

[Arlott 1975, JNA]

NEWCASTLE

Jamaica Defence Force camp in ST ANDREW Parish. The complex of red-roofed buildings ranged in tiers down the mountainside is a striking sight from afar and a popular goal of hill excursions. Newcastle was established in 1841 as a hill station for BRITISH troops. British soldiers sent to the WEST INDIES used to regard the posting as a death sentence because so many of them died there (see YELLOW FEVER AND

Newcastle

MALARIA). In 1840 when 189 soldiers and their families from one regiment died shortly after arrival, the commander of the British forces in Jamaica put pressure on the British government to establish the station. By this time it had been demonstrated that people living in the hills were less subject to the various fevers than those on the plains. The Newcastle cemetery nevertheless bears testimony to the high death toll among whites: midshipmen aged 12 or 14, young mothers and their babies, soldiers in their teens and twenties. The dates on most of the tombstones range from the mid to late 19th century.

Newcastle was established on an old COFFEE plantation. The first soldiers lived in tents and huts and constructed the first roads and buildings in the camp. The substantial buildings to be seen today were erected gradually over the years. In the old days the soldiers (wearing their hot red coats) usually walked the 25km from KINGSTON harbour to the camp carrying all their personal belongings on their backs. Officers rode HORSES. Supplies for the camp were brought up by mule pack. Once when the soldiers were called out to quell a riot in Kingston, they marched down to the harbour in three hours. Soldiers from this camp were also active in suppressing the MORANT BAY REBELLION, as the song 'War O' proclaims:

Soldiers from Newcastle
Come down a Monkland
With gun and sword
Fe kill sinner, O!

During the Spanish-American war when Britain sent extra soldiers to bolster the island's defence, the overflow from Newcastle was accommodated at the next ridge, called Greenwich (which was later sold back to private individuals). But after that, Newcastle declined in importance and became a 'change-of-air' camp. Apart from British regiments, Canadian regiments were stationed there during the Second WORLD WAR (1939-45). Between 1958 and 1962, Newcastle was the training school for the soldiers of the Regiment of the West Indies Federation. Since 1962, it has been part of the Jamaica Defence Force establishment and new recruits spend part of their training there.

The main square was in 1965 named the Sir William Gomm Square after the commander who established Newcastle. On the wall facing the square can be seen the insignias of various regiments stationed there. It is not a complete collection, having been started in 1884 by the North Staffordshire.

The name of the district immediately below Newcastle – Red Light – dates from the days when the camp was first established. The Irish Town road from Cooperage to Newcastle was begun in 1896 and completed around the turn of the century. Before that, the usual means of travel was by a bridle track via GORDON TOWN. A Piquet House was therefore maintained at Gordon Town where horses could be changed.

Newcastle is situated on the south side of the hill and the vegetation on this side is quite different from that on the other side of the mountain (facing PORTLAND Parish) mainly because the Portland side is in an area of much higher rainfall. In the Newcastle area can be seen growing wild many plants that are not normally associated with a tropical climate. Many of these 'escapees' from cultivation were introduced by a planter named Matthew Wallen, who lived at Cold Spring estate nearby. Among the plants introduced by him were many varieties of lily, crocus, hyacinth, pinks, larkspur, geranium, nasturtium, sweet violet and many herbs, as well as wild strawberries and raspberries. A great deal of fodder had to be imported from Europe to feed the horses of the soldiers at Newcastle and many weeds arrived as 'passengers' in this fodder and became established in the area. Botanists have found that some of these weeds occur nowhere else in the New World.

NEWMARKET

A village that grew up around a new MARKET established after EMANCIPATION that has remained one of the largest markets in the west.

Newmarket was entirely flooded for a full year (1979-80). The source of the temporary lake that covered the village has not been established but it is believed to have risen from underground water, the normal outlet of which was blocked during heavy flood rains. This was not the first time that such a lake had arisen. The villagers have been resettled a short distance from the old village.

Some years earlier, Newmarket was the subject of a dispute between the parishes of ST ELIZABETH and WESTMORELAND. By custom, the village was regarded as part of St Elizabeth. However, in 1960 it was transferred to Westmoreland as a survey carried out by the Survey Department and earlier maps showed it to be part of that parish. After widespread protests of residents, a special Bill to amend the Counties and Parishes Law was passed in the House of Representatives in December 1960 that enabled Newmarket to officially remain a part of St Elizabeth.

NINE NIGHT

The period of mourning after death (see WAKE) ends with ceremonies on the ninth night, when it is believed the spirit of the dead finally departs. Thus the 'nine night' is the most important night and draws on both African and European Christian traditions. From Christian beliefs, the soul's journey to Heaven is emphasized and there will be hymns and sermons and references to Heaven. From the African tradition, the emphasis is on placating the spirit of the dead. Either way, the objective is to give the deceased a good departure from this world (see DEATH RITUALS). Often the religious ceremony will take place first, to be followed by other rituals to ensure that the dead spirit understands that severance has taken place and it should depart from its old home. Unless this is done, the spirit becomes a malignant DUPPY and will hang around to haunt the living.

NUNU BUSH (*Ocimum*)

A kind of wild basil used as TEA and for ritual purposes in Jamaica, especially in connection with DEATH, and to ward off evil spirits. The name comes from the Twi language of the Ashanti; called *nunum*, R.S. Rattray recorded it as a common medicine to drive away ghosts. Used as a substitute for basil (called 'Tulsi' by INDIANS and pronounced 'baazli' by the folk), it is also used in 'bush baths' (see BUSH) for efficacious purposes. Two bushes have been identified by C.D. Adams, *O. gratissimum* or African Tea Bush, described as 'very rare in Jamaica and occasional in the West Indies' and *O. micranthum*, which is common in open ground from sea level to 1,200m.

Folklorist Louise Bennett captured its ritual significance in her poem 'Sweepstake', in which the purchaser of a sweepstake (lottery) ticket announces that:

Me wrap it up wid Noonoo bush
Same sweet bazley, yuh know –
keiba it eena sardine pan
An' bury it a me doa.

[Adams 1972, Bennett 1942, Hall-Alleyne 1996, Rattray 1927, Robertson 1990]

NUTMEG (*Myristica fragrans*)

This spice was first introduced into Jamaica in 1788 by a Dr Marter, who was awarded £1,000 by a grateful Assembly for the introduction of the Nutmeg as well as Clove and Black Pepper plants. Such a high value was placed on these plants because at the time spices were literally worth their weight in gold. The Dutch had captured the Moluccas or Spice Islands, origin of the Nutmeg and other spices, in 1616, and used every possible means to protect their treasures. Quantities of crops were frequently destroyed to create shortages and maintain astronomical prices. Export of plant or seed of the Nutmeg or Clove was a treasonable offence. Some of these spices were believed to have been aboard a French ship that was captured in Caribbean

Nutmeg

waters in 1782. The captured plants, which included the MANGO, were sent to Jamaica, thus introducing many useful varieties. But the spices were not found. It is believed that the French captain had them illegally and threw them overboard when captured.

The Nutmeg tree grows up to 8m or more in height and is found mainly on sheltered hillsides and wet areas at low and middle elevations. The plant is dioecious, i.e. there are separate 'male' and 'female' trees. The female tree bears the blossoms that will produce fruit. When the fruit appears, it bears no resemblance to the Nutmeg in the market. It is ovoid and creamy yellow, about 5cm long. The nut is really the kernel of the fruit and will spend the next six months or so developing inside it. When ripe, the fruit will split in two, disclosing the nut, which comes surrounded by a scarlet lace-like covering called mace, which is easily removed. Mace is also used as a spice.

Aside from its culinary uses, Nutmeg is widely employed in folk MEDICINE, though it can be dangerous in large doses. A small amount of freshly grated Nutmeg applied to a bleeding cut will slow or stop bleeding. Grated Nutmeg used to be given to women to ease labour pains and at the baby's birth it was applied to the navel. Nutmeg is also used as a CHARM, worn around the neck, or held in the mouth in court cases to counteract the oath taken. Nutmeg also used to be worn on a string around children's necks to counteract eczema and other sores.

Nutmeg is grown commercially in some CARIBBEAN islands, especially Grenada.

[Adams 1972, Cundall 1915, Robertson 1990]

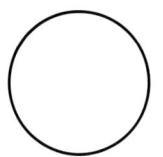

OBEAH

The word used in Jamaica to denote witchcraft, evil magic or sorcery by which supernatural power is invoked to achieve personal protection or the destruction of enemies. The word is also used in other parts of the CARIBBEAN though it conveys different meanings to different people. Obeah was first made illegal in 1760. The fact that the law is on the books up to the present time is an indication of its persistence.

In Jamaica the word 'obeah' has been used somewhat loosely to describe any non-Christian beliefs, practices, and rituals. Differentiation would lie in the purpose of the rite; whether it is used to do harm (obeah, sorcery or 'black magic') or to achieve beneficial ends or 'healing' (see MYAL, BALM, etc.). Some practitioners are obeah-men or -women exclusively and practise sorcery. Some will undertake any kind of 'work' (called 'Two-hand'). Others are mainly religious practitioners or 'healers' or 'bush-doctors' (the equivalent of the African priests, priestesses, and medicine-men) who might undertake some 'left hand work' on the side or as necessary.

Obeah is 'worked' by both men and women. The traditional obeah practitioner utilizes his or her powers for destructive purposes or to counteract the work of other obeah-men. Generally, obeah is undertaken in secret, for a fee, and is used to solve personal problems. A 'patient' will approach an obeah-man or -woman for a 'consultation' about a problem and will be given certain instructions to follow. Obeah very often is employed purely out of envy, hatred or malice and to obtain revenge. A patient can get an obeah-man to 'put', 'work' or 'set' obeah, i.e. to cast a spell on another. If the victim believes in obeah and becomes aware of what is happening, he or she will literally get sick, go insane or suffer in some way – unless a more powerful obeah-man can be secured to 'take it off' or 'turn it back'. At its most extreme, obeah can be used to cause death: poison or ground glass being widely used in the past; obeah-men were once recognized as being exceptionally skilled in their knowledge of poisons.

In Jamaica, many people would never utter the word 'obeah' or 'obeah-man', perhaps for fear of the power inherent in naming. Thus numerous euphemisms have sprung up, such as those listed in the DJE: guzu-man, zuzu-man, bunguzzu, science man, bush-man, doctor, do-good-man, duppy catcher, fini man, samfai man, professor, puller, jege or jiggey-man, knife and scissors man, meki-man, service man, weed man, jumbi man, siman-kwengkwe. Some of these words are derived from West African words, the last from the Twi *suman-kwafo*, or medicine man.

Obeah Today Since the practice of obeah is illegal and hence secret, it is difficult to know what percentage of the population supports it, though it is in no sense a dying art. No one admits to practising obeah, and those who engage in any occult practice will claim benign objectives. Obeah might be used to discover or foil thieves or enemies, to ensure success, e.g. in business, love or in passing examinations, to influence court cases, etc. Nowadays the more famous obeah practitioners seem to specialize in pragmatic objectives, such as 'guaranteeing' the acquisition of American visas and green cards by applicants. Although popularly associated with the lower classes, people of all classes do consult obeah-men. This is similar to the situation which prevailed during the plantation era, when the African bush doctor was patronized by the whites as well as blacks, both for medical treatment and to secure charms, etc. (See MEDICINE, Folk.)

'Science' and DeLaurence Two forms of obeah are practised in Jamaica today and some practitioners might combine both methods. Both practices lie in control of the spirit world. An obeah-man or -woman claims to be able to control spirits (see DUPPY) that will do his or her bidding concerning the 'work' to be carried out. Each obeah practitioner has his or her own method of capturing such duppies, usually from GRAVEYARDS. Once the spirit is captured, it can be 'used' by the obeah-man in return for being fed.

The older method employs rites that were brought from Africa and have remained practically unchanged over the centuries. This practitioner uses only indigenous material in his or her work – BUSH, i.e. roots and herbs, and other natural substances such as blood, feathers, ashes, bone, grave dirt, eggs, snakes, etc. as well as man-made artefacts such as small coffins and objects used as guzu (see CHARM) associated with the spirit world.

Obeah-men in the 20th century, especially those in urban areas, have been very much influenced by books and paraphernalia on the occult that come out of the Hebrew-Indo-European magical tradition. This branch of obeah is sometimes called 'science'. It relies on books and other material most often obtained from a mail order company, the DeLaurence Company of Chicago, USA. The company was started in the late 19th century by Lauron William de Laurence (1868-1936) – he used the lower case de – a white American, selling 'occult and spiritual books'. It then branched into other occult and mystical material and equipment. The DeLaurence Company is still operated as a family business with a worldwide clientele (their Catalogue – catering to 'the Mystic community' – has over 400 pages) so the legendary status of their name is not confined to Jamaica. The early books on offer were written by DeLaurence himself, promoted as the 'master' mystic – with such titles as *The Master Key*. Or they were translations of 'ancient manuscripts' e.g. *The Greater Key of Solomon*. However, the most famous is *Sixth and Seventh Books of Moses*, billed as 'Rare old Mosaic Books of the Talmud and Cabala . . . published under personal supervision of de Laurence' and 'translated from the original German'. This book has come to be a 'Bible' of sorts for people in the Caribbean, black America and the African continent especially, but it is also said to be popular among some segments of the population in Europe and other parts of the world, since it exists in many editions. Purporting to be 'The wonderful and spiritual arts of Moses and Aaron and the old wise Hebrews' as well as ancient Egyptians, the book tells how to conjure and evoke spirits to avert evil, to heal, how to make amulets and charms, including harmful spells, etc.

The fact that the colonial authorities included the DeLaurence books among those officially banned (a ban still in place) has only contributed to their legendary status on the island. They were first banned by the British authorities during the Second WORLD WAR, according to Erna Brodber. She adds: 'The British government gave as its reason that it did not want to have the minds and pockets of its people polluted by occult nonsense imported from abroad.' It is not clear why the books became so visible at that time. Since Jamaican men went to the United States in large numbers during the war as munitions workers and farm workers, it is possible that they were responsible for the importation of DeLaurence books in noticeable quantities. (See also REGGAE for their contribution to popular music.)

Although DeLaurence does not advocate witchcraft or sorcery, Jamaican obeah-men came to regard him as the greatest 'science-man' in the world (and still alive, presumably). 'DeLaurence' is sometimes used as a euphemism for obeah. His name alone will generate fear. Poltergeist activities (e.g. the stoning of houses by 'invisible' agents) are popularly attributed to the fact that the householder had DeLaurence books and failed to pay for them or was trying a DeLaurence 'recipe' that was too strong and got out of hand.

Brodber has written that like many Jamaicans, in her childhood she had heard the name DeLaurence, but 'had difficulty figuring out whether DeLaurence was a man, a set of books, or both . . . If a set of books, did DeLaurence write those books and sell them in Jamaica or was he just the sales agent, residing where? And how did he manage to get razor blades into people's wardrobes to shred the clothes of those who owed him money? How about the stones showered on people's houses and fires lit by unseen hands?' Brodber goes on to add that in doing research, she discovered that DeLaurence was 'alive and well' in Jamaica, citing a newspaper report in the early 1980s of an obeah-man caught with DeLaurence books, but also finding him 'alive and well too in upper St Andrew', the residential enclave of the elite. DeLaurence, and especially *The Sixth and Seventh Books of Moses*, has also been found to resonate in African-Jamaican practices such as POCOMANIA, REVIVAL and KUMINA, as Donald Hogg found spirits from this book among those invoked.

'Science' also uses paraphernalia such as crystal balls, playing cards or tarot cards, and so on. Such objects as well as 'power rings' and other jewellery, candles, talismans, etc. can be obtained from the Chicago company though nowadays they are more widely available from different sources. 'Medicines' compounded by druggists or obtained from a drugstore are also prescribed. Obeah prescriptions include oils and substances such as laundry blue, sulphur, camphor and harmless compounds given exotic names like 'compellance powder' or 'oil of come back'.

The Power of Obeah No doubt what is called 'obeah' exists in many forms and includes many quacks and money-making opportunists, yet, in Jamaica, obeah first and foremost remains an instrument of terror. The reaction of victims who believe themselves obeahed today is very much the same as it was in earlier times. As J.J. Williams describes it: 'they no sooner find Obi set for them near the door of their homes or in the path which leads to it, than they give themselves up for lost . . . No recourse is left but to the superior skill of some more eminent Obeah-man of the neighborhood who may counteract the magical operation of the other.' Should this fail, the victim 'falls into a decline, under the incessant horror of impending calamities. The slightest painful sensation in the head, or in any other part of the body confirms his apprehensions and he believes himself the victim of an invisible and irreversible agency. Sleep, appetite and cheerfulness forsake him, his strength decays, his disturbed imagination is haunted without respite, his features wear the settled gloom of despondency . . . he contracts a morbid habit of body and gradually sinks into the grave'.

During SLAVERY, obeah was so much a part of the social fabric that it was believed every estate had an obeah-man or two. They were both revered and feared, sought after for the 'obis' or guzus they sold and the revenge they could wreak on enemies. The practice was brought from West Africa and all of the early obeah practitioners were African. A suggested origin of the word obeah is the Akan *bayi* (witchcraft) or *obayifo* (witch or female sorcerer). The word for male sorcerer, *bonsam*, lived on in 'sasabonsam', a devil or evil spirit residing at the COTTON TREE root, not much mentioned today. Although it is the Ashanti word that is used in Jamaica, Africans of other tribal origins would also have influenced the Jamaican practice and indeed, during slavery those from Pawpaw or Popo country (the Ewe people of Dahomey) were the most highly rated, as they were in West Africa.

Obeah vs Myal In the historical literature, no distinction was made between those elements of the African religious complex brought to the Caribbean that included medicine men, priests, and other practitioners. All came to be designated 'obeah-men' by Europeans and their practice as 'obeah'. However, the Africans themselves maintained a distinction between those practices that were used for healing and which came to be called Myal, and the practice of sorcery or 'bad magic' based on the use of 'Obi'.

Collectively dismissed by the authorities as 'African superstition', such activities were taken seriously only when they were identified with revolutionary activity and hence seen as a threat to public order and safety. Following TACKY'S Rebellion of 1760, the first laws against obeah were passed and the word 'obeah' entered the English language. Obeah became proscribed and went underground, where it remains to this day. It became common practice for Jamaican planters to ship out so-called 'obeah-men' to neighbouring countries. Boukman Dutty, who conducted the ritual that led to the start of the Haitian Revolution was described as 'an obeah-man from Jamaica' but was more likely a Myal priest, as is suggested by the close parallels between the Haitian ceremony at Bois Caiman in 1791 and that for Tacky's followers.

[Banbury 1894, Bisnauth 1989, Brodber 1999, Cassidy 1971, DJE, Long 1774, Mbiti 1975, Parrinder 1961, Patterson 1973, Rattray 1927, Seaga 1969, Schuler 1980, Williams 1933]

OCHO RIOS

'Ocho Rios' is believed to be derived from the Spanish for 'eight rivers', but the place name is actually a corruption of *Las Chorreras* which is

Ocho Rios before development

what the Spaniards called the stretch of coastline in which the town of Ocho Rios (ST ANN Parish) is now located. As late as 1841 old inhabitants still called it 'cheiveras', its early and appropriate name. *Chorreras* means waterfall or spout, and there was a series of such falls along this coast. The character of the rivers flowing down from the hills would change on nearing the shoreline, where they suddenly left the LIMESTONE country and met other kinds of rocks. Beautiful falls and cascades resulted, as the White River, ROARING RIVER, Dunn's River and others bubbled down to the sea, giving to this area an overpowering beauty. DUNN'S RIVER Falls is the now the island's major tourist attraction. The other falls are not as accessible and Roaring River has been harnessed to provide electricity.

Like many small coastal towns, Ocho Rios in the old days used to be visited by pirates who made themselves at home on the coast. Many apparently respectable people supported piracy, and the planters in these parts seemed to have invested a great deal of money in underwriting the expense of one pirate. He was John Davis, who made a fortune for himself and his backers, retiring in the area as a rich man when piracy was stamped out in the CARIBBEAN. He was probably the same John Davis, described as an Englishman born in Jamaica, who commanded the fleet of seven or eight pirate ships that once sacked the city of St Augustine, Florida, USA.

Ocho Rios is now a major tourist area but just a few decades ago, it was a quiet fishing village with some private holiday homes on its fringes. Then the government of Jamaica formed the St Ann Development Company under the umbrella of the Urban Development Corporation and in the 1960s acquired the Ocho Rios bay area and several large tracts of land in the immediate vicinity. The harbour was dredged and a 30m crescent-shaped strip of white sand beach reclaimed. The beach frontage has been developed since that time.

While the town itself is a recent development, this part of the beautiful parish of St Ann was one of the cradles of the tourist industry, starting with the MONEAGUE Hotel, built in the 1890s and surviving as a hotel until the 1940s. Another early hotel was the Shaw Park, a great house transformed into a small hotel in 1923 by Flora Stuart. The creation of the famous Shaw Park Gardens added to its lustre and attracted international celebrities such as the Canadian Prime Minister William McKenzie King, Lord Lonsdale, and famous baritone Paul Robeson. The Shaw Park Beach hotel was later built on the beach. Other hotels of the 1940s were the Sans Souci, Silver Seas and Plantation Inn.
[Cundall 1915, Wright and White 1969]

OCHO RIOS FORT

The fort which is located on the main highway west of the town of OCHO RIOS, ST ANN Parish, was built in the late 17th century and strengthened, like all the forts around the island, in 1780, when an attack from the FRENCH was feared. In 1795, an enemy vessel appeared off Ocho Rios harbour but fearing the guns there, it made an attack at Mammee Bay along the coast, west of ROARING RIVER. It was beaten off by the guns of this little fort under the leadership of a MILITIA officer who was also overseer of DRAX HALL plantation. He was given a reward by the parish authorities. The Ocho Rios Fort was rebuilt by Reynolds Jamaica and contains two of the original guns from Ocho Rios and two of the guns that nobly defended the town at Mammee Bay.
[Wright and White 1969]

OKRA (*Abelmoschus esculentus*)

Vegetable known elsewhere as Gumbo or Lady's Fingers, this is a member of the HIBISCUS family, as can be seen from its yellow flower which develops into pod-like finger shaped fruit tapering at one end. The interior when cooked is soft, with glutinous seeds. Okra was brought from tropical Africa where it originates.
[Adams 1972]

Okra

OL'HIGE

Creature of LEGEND, a witch or sorceress who destroys people while they are asleep by shedding her skin and flying in the form of an OWL ('Kin Oul') to suck their breath; an especial threat to young babies. Lock-jaw, once a prevalent childhood disease, was taken as a sign of her suck. Young children are often protected with an open Bible, the sign of the cross, crossed knife and fork or open scissors, foul-smelling substances such as asafoetida and by general use of CHARMS and protective blue. Belief in Ol'Hige (also known as Ol'Suck) is a West African one, especially among the Yoruba, and is still widespread among people of African descent in the Americas. Ol'Hige is known elsewhere as Loup-garou, Legarou or Lagaru (French-speaking islands), Sukuyan (Trinidad) and Azeman (Surinam). While the Ol'Hige persona is African, the bat-witch or owl-witch combination is also European.

Ol'Hige takes more or less the same form in most cultures, and the methods for discovery are similar. The skin she leaves behind when she flies must be found and salt and pepper applied to it with (in Jamaica) the formula: 'Salt and pepper fe yu, Mammy!' When the witch returns and tries to resume her skin it will be too painful to do so, though she will piteously cry: 'Skin, yu no know me?' In her undisguised form she can be found and killed.

[Banbury 1894, DJE]

OLD HARBOUR BAY

Now a busy fishing village, 3km south of the town of Old Harbour, ST CATHERINE Parish, this is one of Jamaica's historic bays. It was originally called Puerto de Vaca ('Cow Bay') by Christopher COLUMBUS who visited it on his way home after discovering the north coast of Jamaica in 1494. The 'cows' were MANATEES or sea cows. Columbus found many TAINO villages surrounding Old Harbour Bay. Here he met what he described as the most intelligent and civilized of all the aborigines he encountered in the CARIBBEAN. This was a stately CACIQUE who travelled in a CANOE as large as a sea-going ship and painted all over. In full regalia, the chief and his party boarded Columbus' ship and distributed presents of island produce among the crew. It is believed that this was the paramount cacique of Hamaika (as Jamaica was called), based at White Marl, the chief bohío on the island. During the period of BRITISH settlement, Old Harbour became the principal port for the area.

OLD HOUSE OF ASSEMBLY

At the SPANISH TOWN square, the building that occupies the eastern side opposite to old KING'S HOUSE, was built around 1762 as the House of Assembly. The Supreme Court also sat here. Over the years, the building has undergone much

Old House of Assembly

alteration and now houses the offices and mayor's parlour of the ST CATHERINE Parish Council.

Previous to the construction of this building, the Assembly met in various places, including the church. Meetings of the legislative body were sometimes marked by heated tempers and the exchange of strong words. After one such debate, someone tore up the Journals (records of the proceedings) and threw them into the street. The culprit was never exposed though a reward was offered. On another occasion, heated tempers indirectly caused a death. During a debate in 1710, Peter BECKFORD Jr, the Speaker, repeatedly called the meeting to order and finally adjourned it. But when he rose to leave his chair the members drew their swords and held him there forcibly while the question was put and carried. During this time the doors to the chamber were barred. Peter Beckford the elder, the Speaker's father and a former lieutenant governor, heard the general commotion and his son's voice calling for help. He rushed for the governor who arrived with his guards who forced the door open, and the governor dissolved the Assembly in the Queen's name. In the general excitement the elder Beckford slipped and fell down the stairs and died as a result of this fall.

[Black 1974, Cundall 1915]

OLD NAVAL HOSPITAL

Cast-iron structure in PORT ROYAL dating from 1818, the oldest prefabricated cast-iron building in the Western hemisphere and one of Jamaica's oldest monuments. The iron framework was cast in England and shipped to Jamaica; the bricks were made of local clay. It was built on the foundations of an earlier hospital erected in 1740 and destroyed in 1815 by a fire. The

Old Naval Hospital

building is 115m long by 17m wide with an upstairs balcony 4.5m wide.

The site is surrounded by a high brick wall that kept the hospital patients in – and the townsfolk out. The hospital gradually went out of use after 1905 when the naval dockyard was closed down. In 1951, the townspeople washed out of their homes by HURRICANE Charlie found shelter here. In 1968 the Old Hospital became the headquarters of the Port Royal Centre for Archaeological and Conservation Research.

OPIYEL GUOBIRÁN

One of the 12 principal ZEMIS of the TAINOS, Opiyel Guobirán was a dog-like figure regarded as the guardian of the dead; believed to be the alter ego of MAQUETAURIE GUAYABA. The Taino told Father PANÉ that this animal has four feet like a DOG, comes out of the house at night and goes into the forest where the spirits of the dead (*opía*) live. The people will catch and tie him and bring him back but he always runs away. He is said to have escaped into a morass when the Spaniards arrived and never returned. See also DOG IN FOLKLORE. [Arrom 1990]

Taino carving, Turks & Caicos Islands (from Fewkes)

ORACABESSA

Former BANANA LOADING port in ST MARY Parish now being developed as a resort. The name is supposedly derived from the Spanish *ora cabeza* or 'golden head'. Among famous residents of Oracabessa were English author Ian Fleming (1908-64), creator of the James Bond thrillers, and Sir Noel Coward (1899-1973), English dramatist, actor and composer, whose former home 'Firefly' is now owned by the Jamaica National Heritage Trust and is open to the public.

Fleming first came to Jamaica in 1944 in connection with his work with MI5, the British espionage agency. He bought property in Oracabessa and, returning in 1946, built his home 'Goldeneye', staying there from 15 January to 15 March each year until his death. It was at Goldeneye that he wrote the 13 'James Bond' thrillers that would make him world famous, taking his hero's name from the author of a classic on ornithology, *Birds of the West Indies*, which Fleming described as 'one of my Jamaican bibles'. Fleming later noted that the real James Bond and Mrs Bond arrived at Goldeneye one day 'out of the blue and couldn't have been nicer about my theft of the family name. It helped at the customs, they said!' During Fleming's lifetime the house saw many illustrious visitors, including a British Prime Minister, Sir Anthony Eden who, with Lady Eden, stayed for three weeks during his convalescence in the winter of 1956 after the Suez crisis. The head of the Jamaica Special Branch at the time, David Godfrey, in charge of local security, gives an account of the visit in his reminiscences, *Reckoning with the Force*, which coincides with Fleming's account regarding the police guards shooting at the rats.

Noel Coward, the foremost theatre man of his day, first came to stay with his friend Ian

Banana Port, Oracabessa

Ian Fleming at Goldeneye in 1958

Fleming, then bought property and built two homes, ending up at 'Firefly' on the hill with the spectacular view which inspired his song, 'A Room With A View'. Like Fleming, he entertained at Oracabessa the titled, the rich, and the famous, including HM the Queen Mother when she was on an official visit in 1965 and HRH Princess Margaret. Sir Noel died at Firefly in March 1973 and is buried in the garden there. For an account of the Coward-Fleming friendship and their Jamaican sojourn, see the book edited by Morris Cargill, *Ian Fleming Introduces Jamaica*.

'Goldeneye' today is owned by Christopher Blackwell, entrepreneur and founder of Island Records. He has established the Oracabessa Foundation to integrate tourism development and the local community.

[Cargill 1965, Godfrey 1998]

ORANGE

The sweet orange (*Citrus sinensis*) was brought from Spain in the 16th century and thrives in Jamaica. Since the 19th century it has been grown as an orchard crop for export though nowadays it is shipped mainly in the form of canned fruits and juices. It is one of the fruit trees found in most backyards. This popular tree is also valued in folk MEDICINE, orange or LIME leaf tea being used to cure upset stomachs and headaches; orange seeds being used for diarrhoea. The dried peel is used in cooking, especially in cakes and puddings.

The most popular varieties of sweet oranges cultivated are the Valencia, Parson Brown, Hamlin, Navel and Pineapple.

The sour orange (Seville or 'Civil' orange – *Citrus aurantium*) is most valuable for making marmalade and lemonade, and the ripe fruit was once cut and used to scour floors, imparting a rich shine to beautiful woods such as MAHOGANY. (See FLOOR CLEANING.) Rich in Vitamin C, orange and other CITRUS fruits were a vital ingredient in the days of sail for their use in combating scurvy on board ship.

[Asprey and Thornton 1953-55, Baccus and Royes 1988, Robertson 1990]

ORANGE VALLEY ESTATE

Located off the main coastal highway in TRELAWNY Parish near to FALMOUTH, the Orange Valley compound includes well preserved ruins of a slave hospital, the factory buildings, brick chimney stack and boiling houses, BARBECUES for drying PIMENTO and copra, and a lime kiln. Irrigation came from a 'never-failing' spring from which water was pumped in times of drought to neighbouring estates such as Kent. Said to have been discovered during Spanish times, the spring vanished after an EARTHQUAKE

Old steam machinery, Orange Valley estate

in 1957. Although the estate continued in SUGAR production until the mid-20th century, the buildings date from the late 18th century. The property then was owned by a Jarrett, one of whose descendants married a Kerr. From them are descended the Kerr-Jarrett family of ST JAMES, one of the major landowners of the parish. The mausoleum of the Jarrett family still exists near to the ruins of the great house.

ORCHID

Jamaica has an impressive orchid flora, with about 237 species, of which about 60 species or 25 per cent are endemic, i.e found nowhere else. The orchid family is one of the largest and most diverse families of flowering plants in the world. It was the arrival and successful flowering of two species of Jamaican orchids at Kew Gardens in England during the 18th century that awakened interest in the cultivation of orchids outside of their natural environment.

Jamaica's own orchids are usually small flowered and their attraction is revealed in close up. They are epiphytic (grow on top of other plants) or terrestrial (i.e. live on the ground). Many large trees such as COTTON TREE are often seen festooned with orchids and Wild Pines (BROMELIADS). The most famous Jamaican species are in the genera *Broughtonia* and *Oncidium* that are used in hybridization by horticulturists.

Orchid growing has achieved widespread popularity in recent years, encouraged by the Jamaica Orchid Society, and a great deal of hybridization is undertaken by growers. Nevertheless, many of Jamaica's native orchids

Oncidium luridum

are in danger of disappearing, threatened by the encroachment on their natural habitat of development and land exploitation, and sometimes by the pressures of demand from abroad for orchid exports. At the same time, many Jamaican orchid fanciers import orchids for their collections.

[Gloudon 1995, Terry 1992]

ORTANIQUE

(*Citrus reticulata* x *C. sinensis*)
A unique Jamaican CITRUS fruit, a cross between the sweet ORANGE and TANGERINE, but juicier than the sweet orange, with an easily peeled skin. It was first propagated in MANCHESTER Parish, at a property called Manchester Pastures. It is said that the first person to create the fruit was Charles Jackson, owner of 'Dunkell' in the Mile Gully area, around 1920. The name of the fruit was derived from the words '*or*ange', '*tan*gerine' and 'un*ique*'. Mr Jackson is said to have died with the secret of propagation, but the headman and overseer by many trials and errors rediscovered how to reproduce the hybrid.

Ortanique

OSNABURGH

Word frequently met with in the historical literature, describing the work-day clothing of slaves (see SLAVERY) made from a coarse linen originally manufactured near Oznabruk in Germany. Genovese, writing of its use in plantation America, noted that osnaburgh had the advantage of durability and sturdiness but the disadvantage of roughness.

'Dat ole nigger-cloth', protested a slave from Virginia, 'was jus' like needles when it was new. Never did have to scratch our back. Jus' wriggle yo' shoulders an' yo' back was scratched.' Osnaburgh was provided by the masters; slaves bought their own clothing for their leisure hours. In the post-EMANCIPATION period, osnaburgh continued to be used by officialdom for some time; it was the material for the prescribed clothing of inmates of the lunatic asylum, for instance, and probably was also used to clothe prisoners.

From the late 18th century, the Jamaican slave laws required that masters provide 'proper and sufficient clothing' or face penalties. The annual clothing allowance on 'well regulated estates' was 9-18m for every man, 6.5-14m for every woman, with proportional amounts to children. Hats or caps were also provided. Elite slaves were given extras. On some plantations the owners also provided 'Handkerchiefs, Knives,

Examples of slave clothing drawn by W. Berryman c. 1810 (from Higman 1998)

Scissors, Thread, Needles, and short Tobacco Pipes' (see JACKASS ROPE). The slaves were expected to sew their own clothing and presumably it was the women who made the loose fitting shifts and petticoats that females wore and the loose tops and trousers which seemed to have been the everyday garb of the men. The fact that the clothing shipments arrived just before CHRISTMAS added to the excitement of that festival.

Pennistone, a coarse woollen cloth like a flannel, manufactured in the Yorkshire town of that name, was made into jackets worn in cold and wet weather. Cotton checks were also imported, mainly for children's clothing and for head-ties, and some estates provided blankets. As in Africa, babies were often carried in a cloth tied to their mothers' backs.

In their leisure hours, those slaves that could afford it wore their own fine clothing and body adornment as an expression of personal taste and, for some, to announce their status. White was the preferred colour for dressing up. Women all assumed the West African custom of the head-tie (see BANDANA). Easy-going masters (such as 'Monk' Lewis – see HORDLEY) were sometimes solicited for extra finery in clothing, or reminded – as in the old song, 'Christmas a come me want me lama' – that the time for the clothing allowance was near.

[Brathwaite 1970, Genovese 1976, Higman 1998]

OTAHEITE APPLE (*Syzygium malaccense*) Beautiful fruit tree that was introduced to Jamaica in 1793 by Captain Bligh on the same ship that brought the BREADFRUIT. The fruit is named after the island from which it came – O taheite or Tahiti. It originates in Malaysia.

The tree itself grows to quite a large size (up to 20m or more in height) and is commonly cultivated from sea level to 500m or higher. It is an attractive garden specimen all year round, with its straight grey trunk topped by dark green glossy leaves arranged in a fairly symmetrical shape, like a triangle. But the real glory of Otaheite occurs in the bearing seasons, February-March and June-July, when not only the fruit but the tree's spectacular display can be enjoyed.

Otaheite apple

First, crimson pompom-like flowers appear all over the trunk and limbs, and as the pear-shaped fruits begin to appear, flowers, young fruit (pale green or white) and mature crimson fruit will be seen, all at the same time. The blossoms retain their colour for a few days after falling and so for several weeks the ground underneath the tree will be carpeted with rose pink, a truly breathtaking sight. The fruit has a very thin skin that is usually eaten along with the sweet and snowy white flesh that surrounds a large seed. It is a close relative of the Rose APPLE.

In cooking, Otaheite is used in making preserves and wine. In folk MEDICINE, the dried peel is infused in water and drunk; it is believed to have the same health-giving properties as other apples.
[Robertson 1990]

OVERLOOK BEAN (*Canavalia ensiformis*)

A climbing plant, native of the tropics, that in former times was planted at the corners of a field to 'overlook it', i.e. protect it from thieves, probably because the vine climbs higher on poles than any other. The large bean is also called Horse-Eye (from its resemblance to that object), Sword-Bean, Jack Bean or Cut-Eye Bean. It is also planted on graves to keep down spirits (see DEATH RITUALS).
[Beckwith 1928, DJE]

OWL

There are two families of owl resident in Jamaica. One is the Common Barn Owl (*Tyto alba*) which also occurs in the CARIBBEAN and world wide. The other is the endemic Jamaican Owl (*Pseudoscops grammicus*) also called the Brown Owl or PATU (also Patoo).

The belief in the owl as an evil spirit is widespread here as elsewhere. Its connection with sorcery or evil magic is expressed most strongly in the belief in OL'HIGE. The screeching of the Barn Owl is considered an omen of death, probably due to the nocturnal habit of the bird and to its other 'supernatural qualities' – its strange cry, its silent flight, and its ability to turn its head almost all the way around on its shoulder. Owls are also (erroneously) believed to be blind in daylight.
[Jeffrey-Smith 1972]

Jamaican Owl

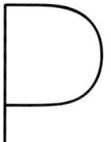

PALISADOES, The

A 16km spit of land that joins the town of PORT ROYAL to the city of KINGSTON. The spit forms a natural breakwater that protects Kingston harbour, one of the finest natural harbours in the world. The Palisadoes was created over the years by the westerly drift of sand and gravel and silt brought down by nearby rivers.

The name 'Palisadoes' apparently derives from a breastwork of 'pallisades' or wooden staves which was built at a point between Port Royal and the rest of the peninsula to cover any land approach. It was part of the general fortifications of Port Royal that existed before the 1692 EARTHQUAKE. According to David Buisseret, the 'Pallisadoe' consisted of a stout wall with a six-gun redoubt in the middle of it. In time the whole spit of land came to be referred to as 'The Palisadoes'.

For centuries the only contact between Kingston and Port Royal was by boat, until 1936 when the road along the Palisadoes was completed. During the course of the Second WORLD WAR the new road made the building of an airstrip feasible, rendering the old flying boat terminal at Harbour Head redundant. (See AVIATION.) Norman Manley International Airport (formerly Palisadoes Airport) is located at the widest point of the Palisadoes. Also located on the Palisadoes is the PLUMB POINT LIGHTHOUSE.

Although the whole area presents an arid appearance, it was at one time the scene of a flourishing coconut plantation. (See COCONUT TREE.) Palisadoes is still noted for its fascinating plants, including many native species of CACTUS and MANGROVE. The mangroves are vital to the preservation of the peninsula and provide a breeding ground for oysters, SHRIMP and fish.

[Buisseret 1971b]

The Palisadoes

PALM

Many species of palm occur in Jamaica, including 10 indigenous species (i.e. not introduced) of which about half are endemic (found nowhere else). Among the well-known introduced species are the Date Palm and the Oil Palm. One of the spectacular introduced ornamental palms is the Talipot that flowers once, then dies. Fine specimens can be seen in HOPE GARDENS.

Most palms are useful, some producing food, virtually all yielding material which is used for thatching and to make string, ropes, bags, hats, BASKETS, mats, ornaments and other items. The outer part of the trunk of many palms is also used to make rough boarding. The trunks of the COCONUT palm were found especially useful in former times to make stockades as they repelled cannon balls.

Palms are found virtually everywhere except for the higher reaches of the Blue Mountains. The Coconut is the most common.

There are several species of Royal Palm (*Roystonea*), easily identified by the large flower heads that arise from the stem several feet below the crown, and not from between the leaves, as in the Coconut. The leaves are used for thatching and the leathery sheaths for making water vessels. The flattened sheaths are also used as sleds by children to ride downhill. The best known Royal Palm is an introduction from Cuba, a tall, stately tree with a bulging trunk up to 70cm in diameter, frequently planted out in avenues as an ornamental. The endemic Jamaica Royal Palm (*R. altissima*), has a thinner trunk. It is more widely distributed, found mainly on hilltops and mountain slopes, especially in central and eastern parishes. It is also known as Mountain Cabbage because the heart, i.e. folded young leaves, can be eaten.

The closely related Morass Royal Palm or Swamp Cabbage (*R. princeps*) grows in moist and rocky woods at low elevations, usually in stands. It is found only in western Jamaica, being the dominant species of the wetlands of BLACK RIVER and formerly of NEGRIL; with the draining of the Negril wetlands, it is now found within the Negril Royal Palm Forest Reserve. Its large feathery leaves – called 'long thatch' – are especially valued as roofing material.

Talipot palm in flower

There are many different species of the useful THATCH palms. These are usually described as long thatch, i.e. those with feather-shaped leaves, or round thatch, i.e. those with leaves resembling a circular opened fan. Their use in house construction dates back to the TAINOS who used thatch palms to roof their *caneys* and *bohíos*.

'Short thatch' is a name applied to a number of different species that are superficially alike. These are fairly small trees, 3-6m in height, with slender stems. The mature leaves are used for thatching while palm fibre rope is made from the central unopened leaves. There are the Bull Thatch or Big Thatch (*Sabal maritima*), Broad Thatch (*Thrinax excelsa*), Broom Thatch or Thatch Pole (*Thrinax parviflora*) and the Bullhead or Sea Thatch (*T. radiata*). The Broad Thatch and Broom Thatch are endemic while the Bull Thatch and Bullhead Thatch are found in other parts of the CARIBBEAN. Long Thatch (*Calyptronoma occidentalis*) is also endemic. Finally, there is the Silver Thatch (*Coccothrinax jamaicensis*) which gets its common name from the silvery underside of its leaves. It is common in the HELLSHIRE HILLS and south coast and is widely used to make woven bags and baskets.

The Macca Fat or Gru-gru (*Acrocomia aculeata*) is a fairly common palm, its tall, swollen stem (up to 15m) covered with large black spines or MACCA.

Royal palms, Ocean Boulevard, Kingston

Acrocomia spinosa (A. aculeata)

Macca Fat, young plant to the left

Roystonea princeps, Swamp Cabbage

Bactris jamaicana, Prickly Pole, the rarest of the Jamaican palms

Sabal jamaicensis (S. maritima), Bull Thatch

Roystonea altissima, Mountain Cabbbage

Left: *Coccothrinax jamaicensis (C. argentata)*, Silver Thatch. Above: Silver Thatch inflorescence

Macca Fat is found mainly on the dry plains and foothills of the south coast from 15-400m as scattered individuals or in colonies. The outer covering of the yellow fruit (3.8-5cm) is edible. The wood is tough and hard and can be used for inlay work and other ornamental purposes and for walking STICKS. Another armed palm is called Prickly Pole (*Bactris jamaicana*). It has spines on both its trunk and leaves. It is a small palm and not very common, being found mostly in LIMESTONE districts, always growing in clumps. Wild PIGS feed on its berries.

The naturalized Oil Palm (*Elaeis guineensis*) is a native of West Africa from whence came the name Abbay by which it is also known in Jamaica. It yields oil ('palm oil') from the outer covering of the reddish date-like fruit though neither the oil nor 'palm wine' is produced in Jamaica. The Date Palm (*Pheonix dactylifera*) used to be widespread in Jamaica, but does not bear edible fruit here.

Although many people consider the Jippi-Jappa or Lady Fan a palm because of its appearance, it does not belong to the palm family at all, though it is closely related. Its heart is used to make 'Panama' or 'Jippi-Jappa' hats.

[Adams 1971, 1972, Cassidy 1971, DJE, Hodges 1986, NHSJ 1949, Wade 1984]

PALM SUNDAY

Christian Festival. The sixth and last Sunday in Lent and the beginning of Holy Week. Jamaica shares with other countries the practice of using PALMS to symbolically celebrate the victorious entry of Christ into Jerusalem. Churches are decorated with palm fronds and worshippers carry or wear small crosses made from palm leaves that are usually hung up in homes afterwards.

PANAMA

Up to a generation or two ago, so many Jamaicans had active 'Panama connections' that the death notices in the *Gleaner* would often say, 'Panama Papers Please Copy', the English-language Panamanian papers carrying notices saying the reverse. Many of the links have since weakened as new generations of West Indian ancestry in Panama have become integrated into that culture.

Much of the Panama connection was established during the years of construction of the Panama Canal. But Panama also represents earlier ties with Latin America that were much stronger in former times than they are today.

The Spanish Main Historically, the route

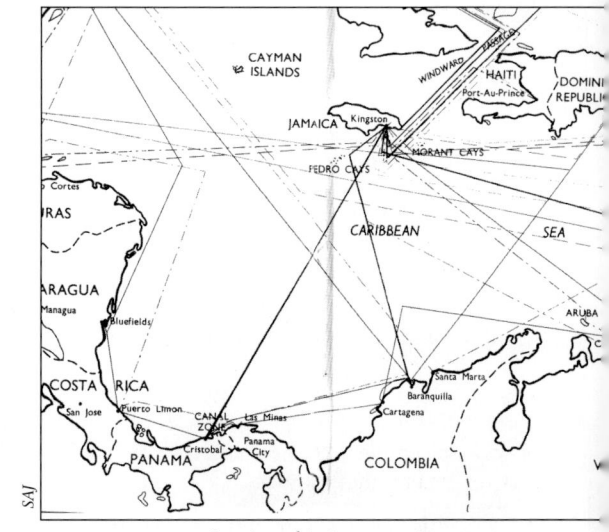

Jamaican shipping connections

between Jamaica and Panama was a well-trodden one as the island was positioned as a take off point for the so-called Spanish Main. The island lies 885km NE of Panama and a fast sailing ship could make the journey down in about a week (though the return journey, beating up against the wind, could take much longer) and steamships reduced the time to 36 hours. (The first commercial air flight from Jamaica was to the Panama Canal Zone in 1930 – inaugurating a regular Miami-Kingston-Cristóbal route. See AVIATION.)

During the Spanish conquest of the Americas, Jamaica became a provisioning depot for many of the *conquistadores* travelling to the mainland; as early as 1521 Jamaica was supplying meat to the new colony of Panama (see SPANISH JAMAICA). Among those provisioned was the *conquistador* Vasco Nunez de Balboa. Throughout the Spanish period, the Isthmus of Panama remained one of the key trade routes.

Early Central American Connections Although from the 16th century Spain claimed all of Central America, the Spanish presence on the Atlantic coast remained weak and English-speaking enclaves came to be established, mainly from Jamaica. (See MISKITO.) After the English took Jamaica in 1655, they used it as a base for infiltration and attack against the Spanish empire, at first by pirates and BUCCANEERS based at PORT ROYAL. The most famous exploit was the attack by Henry MORGAN on the city of Panama in 1671. When piracy ceased, merchants from Jamaica continued to trade illicitly with the Spaniards. The trade was legitimized in 1766 when Jamaica became a free port and the centre of British trade with the Spanish American colonies, and **KINGSTON** achieved its greatest prosperity as a trans-shipment port during the Napoleonic Wars. Traders assembled in convoy at Port Royal or Negril to sail under the protection of British men o' war for the Atlantic ports, including Chagres in Panama. Such trade ceased as the five Central American territories won their independence from Spain in the 1820s. Jamaican merchants then moved to establish themselves in Panama and elsewhere, creating business and family connections that continue to this day. During the 19th century, Jamaicans were particularly active in the commercial life of the country and there were very strong connections between West Indian and Panama business houses.

The Atlantic Coast From earliest times there was also constant traffic between the island and the Central American coast on the part of logwood cutters, turtle fishermen and seamen as well as traders. Traffic was facilitated by the establishment of English colonies on the islands of San Andres and Providencia off the Columbian coast which, over the years, were peopled with settlers from Jamaica. The English also founded settlements at Belize, Bluefields and the Bay Islands of Honduras with labour provided by African slaves. In the 18th century, Jamaican turtle fishermen founded settlements on the Atlantic coast at Bocas del Toro (now in Panama) and the Talamanca coast of Costa Rica. In the 19th century, descendants of these Jamaicans from the coastal areas would contribute labour for the establishment of banana plantations and railroad construction in this region. The capitalist enterprises in the 19th and early 20th centuries also attracted large numbers of black workers from the Antilles. Together with the earlier populations, now known as 'Creoles' –

Clearing a landslide in Culebra Cut

a mixture of blacks, white settlers and native peoples, they were to form the predominantly Anglicized enclaves in the midst of Latino cultures that are still found all along the Atlantic coastal areas.

Emigration The first large scale emigration of Jamaicans to Panama took place during the construction of the Panama Railroad 1850-55 (see **COLÓN MAN**). Much larger numbers went during the peak years of the French Canal construction (1880-1889) and smaller numbers continued work on the canal until the Americans took it over in 1904.

Many of the French Canal workers stayed on in Panama, some establishing farms and business enterprises in a country that was then sparsely settled. Panama at the time was the northernmost State of Colombia (then known as the Federation of New Granada) until it secured its Independence and established the Republic of Panama in 1903.

Recruitment During the US construction of the Panama Canal 1904-14, Jamaicans were among the West Indians who formed the largest single body of workers. Their numbers ranged from a

West Indian workers carrying dynamite boxes during canal construction

The tugboat 'Gatun' - the first boat to transit the locks, 1913

few thousand at the start of construction to some 45,000 in the peak years. Some 150,000 West Indians poured into Panama in that decade.

Jamaican workers were the first choice of the American government, but the British governor (for various spurious reasons) refused to allow recruitment on Jamaican soil by the Canal Company. (It was believed that a strong lobby by the BANANA industry which feared losing its work force was a contributory factor.)

The recruiters then turned to the eastern CARIBBEAN and in time contract labourers from Barbados formed the largest single national group employed in the US Canal Zone. However, a significant number of Jamaican workers did go on their own and Jamaicans formed the majority in the Republic of Panama itself. Because they had to find their own fare, plus deposit twenty-five shillings with the government of Jamaica before departure, a process of self-selection took place among the Jamaicans. The majority of those who went were not agricultural workers or the poorest in the land, as many were in places where they were recruited, but consisted at first of those who could raise the amount required for emigration. Thus there was a high proportion of educated professionals, craftsmen and the like.

After the canal opened, Jamaicans and other West Indians (called *Antillanos* in Panama) continued to be the main workforce in the Canal Zone and by the 1930s, they represented a new generation. From 1940, another set of West Indians was recruited for the construction of a third set of locks and for defence works on the canal. In 1943, some 77,000 West Indians were working in the US Canal Zone.

Construction Workers The Canal Zone was an enclave 8km wide on either side of the canal which cuts across the narrowest point of Panama to link the Atlantic and Pacific Oceans. This Zone was completely under United States control. While in time the Zone would embrace the canal works and residential areas built according to American mainland standards, this paradise was constructed out of the hell that the earliest canal workers had to endure. They worked under the most horrifying conditions, hacking their way through untamed jungle and malignant swamps, confronting nature in the raw and diseases that were endemic (see YELLOW FEVER AND MALARIA). They suffered from the oppressive heat and humidity and a rainy season that lasted for eight months. For the first few years, before the Americans brought such matters under control, there was little fresh food, drinking water, sanitation or housing. The workers laboured 10 hours a day to literally dig down a mountain, the black workers tackling the rock with pick and shovel, at constant risk from dynamite blasts, landslides and other accidents. But they persisted in their share in what was to be one of the greatest engineering feats of all time. The wage to black workers of ten cents US an hour was more attractive than unemployment and starvation at home.

Racial Segregation During construction and after, the Antillean workers had to contend with another factor that sapped their energy and their self-esteem, the rigid racial segregation imposed by the Americans on the Canal Zone. The black workers were not only assigned inferior pay and inferior status, but they and their families were provided with inferior facilities in every way. There were white towns and black towns, with housing, schools, and health and recreational facilities to match, and black workers were exposed to insults and racism on the job and off. 'Boy' was the workers' usual designation. There was a high level of racial antagonism on both sides, but like black Americans of the time, black Canal Zone workers were not expected to show resentment or answer back – if they wanted to keep their jobs, their freedom or even their lives. The full force of the Zonian police and judicial system was arrayed against them. Opportunities were severely limited, for there were restrictions on the kinds of jobs black Antilleans could hold as well as the amount they could earn.

Instead of the 'black' and 'white' signs of the Jim Crow south, the euphemisms 'silver' and 'gold' were used. This referred to the fact that

The Panama Canal and Canal Zone

the black workers were paid in silver coins, the white in gold coins. White workers were paid significantly more than blacks, even for the same work. The white Zonians were to become a privileged minority, enjoying wages and facilities far superior to those on the American mainland.

The racism, segregation and exploitative labour practices that characterized Canal Zone labour during construction days continued up to the 1970s when the gradual relinquishing of control of the Panama Canal by the Americans began. It culminated in the formal handing over of the canal to the government of Panama in 2000. Given the history of the Canal Zone, it is only in recent years that there has been some recognition of the contribution of the black West Indians to the building and maintenance of the canal.

The Republic The West Indians in Panama were effectively divided into two sets of people, those that both worked and lived in the restrictive atmosphere of the Canal Zone (about one-half of the canal workers) and those that lived in the Republic of Panama. These included many that had been settled there for generations. Here, West Indians were also part of the progressive element, engaged in businesses large and small, establishing schools and churches, organizing sporting, recreational and cultural activities.

Because the business of the Canal Zone was conducted in English, West Indians had a distinct advantage over native Panamanians in providing the main work force on the canal. But as Conniff observes, their attachment to the canal 'hindered their adjustment to the Latin American society in which they would eventually remain'.

On the Canal Zone and off, the mostly black immigrants had banded together and created what Mike Conniff has called a 'defensive sub-culture', exaggerating their West Indian-ness and their British connections. To a great extent, social life in Panama became a replica of life 'back home' in the islands. There were BWI schools, businesses, churches and associations. The first and second generation of West Indians moved back and forth between the islands and Panama and continued to identify themselves as British.

After the economic boom of construction days and the onset of the world-wide depression in the 1920s, there was increasing resentment of the *Antillanos* (or '*Chombos*', the more offensive term) and they became the targets of hostility and racist attacks throughout the thirties. In the Republic, restrictive laws were passed against them and a new constitution took away citizenship from many born there. West Indians born in Panama at this time told stories of how their parents kept a trunk packed since they were never sure whether or not they would be expelled. Some returned to the West Indies or emigrated to the United States.

But in the face of prejudice and hostility, many came to adopt a policy of assimilation – they made a commitment to stay in Panama, gave up their British citizenship, hispanicized their names, spoke Spanish, converted to Catholicism, ended ties with the islands, married Latin spouses, in short, became 'Panamanian'. In the 1930s and 1940s, acceptance could come only through rejection of their traditional culture. After the Second World War, Panama rescinded laws against the West Indians. The process of handing over the Canal to Panama which began in 1977 itself led to many changes both on the Zone and in the Republic itself, contributing to better racial tolerance between Latins and people of West Indian stock and the creation of a more unified culture.

[Conniff 1985, LACC 2000, Newton 1984, Senior 1977-78, 1980]

PANÉ, Friar Ramón

Pané is the author of a work of tremendous significance to Caribbean scholarship since it is the main source of information about the TAINO world views and beliefs. Pané, a Jeronymite monk (of the order of San Jeronimo), arrived in the Caribbean in 1494 and shortly afterwards started on an assignment from Christopher

COLUMBUS to write down the beliefs of the Tainos. He thus became the first European that we know of to learn a Native American language.

With an Amerindian guide and translator – Guaicabanu who was given the Christian name Juan – Pané went to live on the island of La Española (Hispaniola) for two years with the powerful CACIQUE Guarionex who is the source of many of the tales he recorded. However, Pané was assured (and modern scholars have found it to be true) that the beliefs and practices of the Tainos in all four islands of the Greater Antilles were almost identical, so the myths reflected the beliefs of all. The result was a book called *Relación acerca de las Antigüedades de los Indios*, the first written in the New World in a European language and the first to record the beliefs and myths and religious practices of indigenous peoples. It is the major record we have of the Taino myths.

The original manuscript of the *Relación* was lost; it was included in Fernando Colón's biography of his father but that was unpublished and lost after his death. The *Relación* survived only in an Italian translation; parts were also included in the account by LAS CASAS. The Cuban scholar José Juan Arrom in the 1960s went to Spain and undertook a scientific reconstruction of the text from the various versions. His notes to the work benefited from his study of the Taino names and a re-examination of Taino artefacts in the light of new knowledge. Arrom's translation of this work, with his notes, has added greatly to our knowledge of the Tainos. Up to the time of writing, this valuable work was not easily available in English. In 1906 Edward G. Bourne published a translation of a transcript of the work in English as 'Columbus, Ramon Pane and the Beginnings of American Anthropology' in *Proceedings of the American Antiquarian Society*, Vol 17, pp 310-48.

[Arrom 1990, Stevens-Arroyo 1988]

PANTOMIME

The LTM Pantomime is an annual theatrical event that has become a national institution, since 1941 opening on Boxing Day (the day after CHRISTMAS) every year and running for several months thereafter. In recent decades pantomime has attracted an average of 75-80,000 theatregoers before it ends its run in late April. Each pantomime is new and a wide cross-section of Jamaicans eagerly look forward to what the year's theme will be. It will certainly be topical, reflecting (and gently satirizing) current events

Greta and Henry Fowler

and values, and incorporating the latest elements from popular culture and the social environment in a mixture of drama, MUSIC, DANCE against a backdrop of scenic designs. Above all, 'panto' will be family entertainment.

The pantomime continues to be produced by the LITTLE THEATRE Movement (LTM) which brought the first one, *Jack and the Beanstalk*, to the WARD THEATRE stage. Like much else in modern Jamaican THEATRE, the development of pantomime for its first three decades, owes much to Greta and Henry Fowler, founders of the LTM.

The pantomime tradition was brought by BRITISH expatriates and was modelled on the English pantomimes that in their turn had descended from the Italian *commedia del arte*. The trajectory of the local pantomime can be taken as a reflection of Jamaica's social history, moving from the European fairy tales of the early years (*Cinderella, Jack and the Beanstalk, Babes in the Woods*) to a wholly Jamaican production. Cast and crew have changed accordingly too, the earliest casting reflecting the upper crust of society exclusively. The pantomime production has become more professional over time, both drawing on, developing, and providing opportunities for a pool of local theatrical talent. Whereas the casting in the past relied on annual auditions, the LTM has now created a permanent group, The Pantomime Company.

Like the English prototype, the Jamaican pantomime incorporates archetypal figures, chief of which are the Mother figure and the Samfi Man or ANANSI. The 'Anansi' series flourished from the 1950s, bringing to pantomime for several decades the much-loved leads of Ranny Williams and Louise Bennett. After 1960, according to Ivy Baxter, pantomimes were called pantomime-musicals, a progression that

Panto favourites, L-R: Louise Bennett, Ranny Williams, Lois Kelly-Miller

continued in the 1970s. The modern pantomime has moved closer to the musical theatre with 'more integrated and genuinely original works in terms of book, lyrics, music and choreography'. It also reflects more of the social environment – as some of the recent titles indicate: *Johnny Reggae, Ginneral B, Trash, King Root, Schoolers*. While many writers have been involved with pantomime, the most prolific creator in recent times has been Barbara Gloudon. But pantomime is ultimately a collective work, bringing together actors, singers, dancers, designers of sets and costumes, choreographers, musical composers, lyricists, and directors.

The show is also a vehicle for the original music that is composed each year and it has utilized the talent of many leading musicians in the classical, pop and folk genres. A number of pantomime songs have passed into the 'folk' repertoire, without attribution to their panto roots, among them the well-loved 'Evening Time' which was composed by Barbara Ferland with lyrics by Louise Bennett for *Busha Bluebeard* (1957). Pantomime has also provided a vehicle for the development of Jamaican dance, with a progression from the staged classical ballet numbers of the past to the current integration of choreography and dance movement.

Although its primary goal is to entertain, the pantomime has played a leading role in the development of Jamaican expression and self-possession. As Professor Rex Nettleford has written: 'A history of the Jamaican pantomime is in many ways a history of the theatre and Jamaican social development since 1941, including the changes in the ways in which Jamaicans perceive themselves.'
[Baxter 1970, Nettleford 1993]

PANYA JAR

'Panya jar' is the Jamaican creole rendition of 'Spanish jar', an enchanted jar of LEGEND. It is believed the fleeing Spaniards buried their treasure at the time of the English conquest (see CAPTURE OF JAMAICA) in large earthenware jars in the expectation of their returning to the island. Great hopes reside in finding such a jar that is supposedly filled with gold coins. Thus someone with a 'Spanish jar' outlook expects to be blessed with sudden mysterious wealth for which he or she has never worked.

OBEAH-men claim to know the secret of finding a Panya Jar and have secured large payments in advance for doing so. However, even if this enchanted jar is located, as in the case of the Golden Table (see GOLD, Legends of) or spectacularly large fish, there is always a problem of securing it before it disappears. Some say the enchantment can only be broken if the seeker quickly casts over the jar his or her hat, knife, handkerchief, etc. The fact that occasionally Spanish jars have been found buried in fields or caves only adds fuel to the legend.

The original Spanish jar – of a characteristic style – was used to carry olive oil and wine from Spain to the colonies. Over the centuries they have been used for water storage, etc. and small decorative replicas are still made.

Panya jar

Scene from 'Queenie's Daughter', 1967

PAPAW or Papaya (*Carica papaya*)
This is a native plant, the word papaya coming from the TAINO language; COLUMBUS on encountering it called it a 'tree melon'. Papaya is indigenous to the CARIBBEAN and Central America, originating in Panama.

Naturalized from sea level to 750m, this popular fruit tree is found in yards and gardens all over Jamaica and is also cultivated in orchards for export, a hybrid producing a small fruit called 'Solo' being the variety grown for this purpose and seen increasingly in local markets. The native papaw usually bears much larger fruits that vary in size, shape, colouring and flavour. The papaw is actually a fast-growing giant herb, producing fruit in a year. The fruits are borne close to the trunk among the umbrella-like cluster of deeply-lobed leaves at the top and the tall, unbranched, hollow trunk bears leaf scars all along it.

The ripe papaw is eaten as a fruit and the unripe can be cooked and eaten as a vegetable, though this is hardly done. All parts of the plant contain a product known as papain, a digestive enzyme that is a tenderizer. Tough meat wrapped in papaw leaves before cooking will become tender, as will meat cooked with green papaw.

All parts of the tree are used in folk MEDICINE – leaves, fruits, seeds, stem and milky latex. The latter has been used to treat CHIGGERS. The juice of the green papaw is used to treat intestinal disorders as well as skin ailments such as ringworm and warts. The skin of the green fruit is used for ulcers and wounds. The ripe fruit is used as a digestive aid and to prevent constipation, and the seeds are eaten to get rid of worms.

In its wild state, the papaw tree is dioecious, i.e. male and female flowers are borne on separate trees; the male tree produces pollen-bearing flowers and the female fruit-bearing flowers so both are necessary for pollination. Occasionally a hermaphrodite bearing both (called 'perfect' flowers) occurs and will bear fruit. In commercial breeding programmes, it is trees with 'perfect' flowers, such as the Solo variety, that have been developed.

Many superstitious beliefs are associated with the papaw, the most common being that if it is planted too near to a house, it will 'draw' the occupants, i.e. sap their sexual powers or physical strength. Animals should not be tied under this tree. It is also believed that if a CUTLASS is used to cut a papaw tree and is not cleaned immediately, it can never be made sharp again. The power of the tree is legendary: the story is told of the pirate who fell asleep on a beach near a papaw tree and covered himself with the leaves for shade. He was tenderized to nothing by the leaves; all that was left of him were the metal buttons of his coat, his shoe buckles and cutlass.

[Adams 1971, 1972, Asprey and Thornton 1953-55, Lovén 1935, Robertson 1990]

PARADE see PARK, St William Grant

PARAKEET see PARROT

PARATEE
Place in coastal ST ELIZABETH Parish (spelled Parottee on current road maps), which is listed on a 1670 map as 'Parathe Bay'. Edward Long says it was originally 'Palléta', a Spanish village destroyed by Cromwell's soldiers and in his time described as swampy, occupied mainly 'by Mulattoes, Quaterons and other Casts'. He said they were poor but peaceable and industrious, living by fishing and raising poultry. The word Paratee also seemed to have been used to describe a particular community of people from the bay and surrounding areas, regarded as 'different' from other Jamaicans.

Rampini, who lived in Jamaica in the mid-19th century, wrote about them as follows: 'In the great savanna of St Elizabeth's resides a curious colony of blacks whose origin has puzzled most travellers. They go by the name of Paratees, and build their huts in the little clumps of bush with which the plain is dotted . . . they are extremely shy, and shun the society of, or even intercourse with, white men. From their long coarse hair, their narrow almond-shaped eyes . . . and thin well-chiselled, though broad-lobed noses, it is supposed that they are of Indian origin. Parchment is a common name amongst them, – a word which contains the prefix Para, which is also found in Paratee . . . They form a curious and by no means uninteresting problem to the ethnologist.'

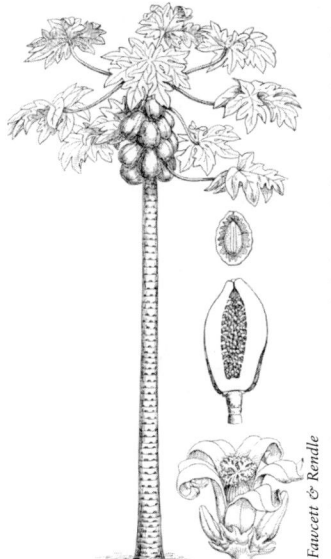

Papaw tree, cut fruit and flower (Fawcett & Rendle)

It is commonly believed that the area was settled by the remnants of the native peoples, the TAINOS. Others believe that it was settled by Amerindians of the Miskito Coast after their term of duty here ended. (See MISKITO.) Paratee Bay is believed to be the site of the original Spanish town of Oristan before it was moved c. 1513 to BLUEFIELDS.

[Long 1774, Rampini 1873, Taylor 1965]

PARDNER

'Pardner' is a Jamaicanized form of the word 'partner' and refers to an informal and widespread cooperative saving system. A pardner is sustained by a group of people who, each week (or other set period of time), 'throw pardner' or 'throw hand', i.e. lodge a fixed sum of money with one member who is the 'banker' (also called 'captain' or 'treasurer'). The total of weekly contributions, called a 'hand' is paid to each member in rotation, referred to as 'draw pardner' or 'draw'.

The practice is common in many parts of the Caribbean under different names, including 'susu', derived from *esusu*, the name for a similar system among the YORUBA people of Nigeria. Susu in Trinidad is recognized by law. The system is called a 'Meeting' in Barbados, 'Boxi money' or 'Box' in Guyana, 'Sam' on the Dutch islands, 'Syndicate' in Belize, etc. The practice has been taken by Caribbean immigrants to North America where it is known as 'susu'. Note that this term is not the same as the word 'susu', meaning gossip, derived from Twi *susuw kaw*.

[Cassidy 1971, DCEU, DJE]

PARISH

The parish is the unit of local government in Jamaica. The island is divided into 14 parishes but Kingston and St Andrew are combined into a single area, called the CORPORATE AREA, hence there are 13 local government authorities. Each is administered by a Parish Council elected in islandwide local government elections that are to be held every third year. Each council is chaired by a mayor who is elected by fellow councillors.

The Parish Councils must work closely with the central government; direct responsibility lies with the Minister of Local Government. The central government exercises control over the organization and administration of these councils whose power has been seriously eroded over the years. As the name implies, they are concerned with strictly local matters, providing public services and amenities including parochial roads and works, water supplies, public health, social welfare and fire brigades.

The division of Jamaica into parishes dates from the earliest days of BRITISH settlement. The parish was an ecclesiastical division and reflected the close union between Church and State. (See ANGLICAN.) Each parish was mandated to have a parish church and the church authorities (the vestry) were put in charge of local matters.

In 1691 an Act was passed whereby justices of the peace selected in each parish 10 vestry-men and two churchwardens, all members of the Anglican Church. Their duties included levying of a tax for the support of the clergy, maintenance of the church, relief of the poor and maintenance of the roads. Public work-houses and jails were established and provision was made for public health, postal services, preservation of order, public safety and protection from fire. The fact that such social services were mandated by law does not mean that they were necessarily provided or adequately serviced. The CUSTOS of each parish

Map of Jamaica showing parishes and main towns

was chairman of the vestry and head of the lay magistracy.

The vestry system continued until 1866 when the House of Assembly was abolished and power placed in the hands of the colonial governor in the wake of the MORANT BAY REBELLION. Indeed, the unpopularity of the local vestry was a contributory factor to that event. The vestries and lay magistracies were seen as representing the interests of the established clergy and the planter class and abusive and unjust to the poor. The vestries were abolished and municipal and road boards appointed to run parochial affairs.

In 1886 local government was reorganized and the parish authorities renamed parochial boards with members elected by local taxpayers. After 1947, election was by universal adult suffrage (introduced in 1944). In 1956, the parochial boards were renamed parish councils.

Jamaica was divided into seven parishes by the first settlers, the numbers of parishes and their boundaries changing over time. The parishes in existence today were fixed in 1867 when the number was reduced from 22 to 14 as part of the general reforms following the Morant Bay Rebellion. The Parishes are (counter clockwise from Kingston): KINGSTON and ST ANDREW, ST THOMAS, PORTLAND, ST MARY, ST ANN, TRELAWNY, ST JAMES, HANOVER, WESTMORELAND, ST ELIZABETH, MANCHESTER, CLARENDON, ST CATHERINE.

In 1758 the parishes were grouped into the three counties that exist today – Cornwall, Middlesex and Surrey – in order to facilitate the holding of courts of justice.

[Cundall 1915, GOJ STATIN 1999a]

PARK, St William Grant

Formerly named Victoria Park, after Queen Victoria, this park in the centre of KINGSTON was in 1977 renamed in memory of a notable labour leader and black nationalist, St William Grant, OD (1894-1977). Grant was a Garveyite (see Marcus GARVEY) who came to national attention by preaching his message of African redemption to crowds at many locations, chief of which was the park which now bears his name. It was from a St William Grant platform that Alexander BUSTAMANTE first addressed a public gathering in Jamaica.

St William Grant

In the 1930s, Grant joined with Bustamante as a labour leader and activist and was in the forefront of the 1938 upheavals during which both were arrested (see TRADE UNIONS). Bustamante went from strength to strength but Grant, who broke with the Bustamante Industrial Trade Union in the early 1940s, sank into poverty and obscurity. However, the role that Grant played in the development of modern Jamaica was not forgotten and he was awarded the Order of Distinction in 1974.

The area surrounding the park is still known as 'Parade' which reflects its original use as a drilling ground for BRITISH regiments and the MILITIA, and a promenade for local folk. In the plan of the city of Kingston, the whole area including the park and surrounding streets was an open rectangle and here a great deal of the life of the early town was centred. At various times there were located around the Parade the church, a theatre, a jail, and nearby a free school, market and hospital. Barracks for soldiers stood on the north side. It was also the place where public hangings were carried out. When the island was in a state of hysteria over a threatened FRENCH invasion in 1694, a fort was erected at the Parade with guns pointing down King Street. After UP PARK CAMP was established as headquarters for the troops in 1784, the Parade was no longer used by the soldiers except on ceremonial occasions.

At the Parade, a beautiful garden was laid out in 1870 and officially named Victoria Park in 1914, though the roads surrounding it still retained the old name of Parade. Until Independence, the area was dominated by the statue of the Queen (see VICTORIA STATUE) on the site on which the statue of the Rt Excellent Sir William Alexander Bustamante now stands. The other important statue is that of the Rt Excellent Norman Washington MANLEY which faces north. The Queen's statue is now on the eastern side of the park. Other statues in the park are those of Edward JORDON and Sir Charles METCALFE.

[White 1981]

PARROT (*Psittacidae*)

Four members of the Parrot family are found in Jamaica. They are two parrots and a parakeet that are found nowhere else, and the much smaller Guyana Parrotlet that is an introduction. Of the four, the more commonly observed are the endemic Jamaica Parakeet (*Aratinga nana*) and the Guyana Parrotlet (*Forpus passerinus*) which was introduced to the island around 1918 in the Old Harbour area (ST CATHERINE Parish) and has spread rapidly. In the past, a beautiful Macaw was also found in Jamaica but it is now a vanished species.

The two endemic parrots prefer mid-level wet limestone FORESTS, and as destruction of forests increases, the birds may become increasingly threatened. The main distinction between them is the colour of the bill, the two species being the Yellow-billed Parrot (*Amazona collaria*) and the Black-billed (*Amazona agilis*). In flight, they are similar, especially as they are mainly of the same bright green colour that provides them with excellent cover when they hide in the foliage of trees or among the corn. But they can be distinguished from the parakeet by their tails, the parrot having a short tail that is spread fanwise, the parakeet a long and sharply pointed tail. It also has a more slender body. These birds are also distinguished by their cries, according to the ornithologist James Bond, 'parrots squawk (waak-waak), parakeets screech (creek-creek) and parrotlets "chatter softly".' They all tend to travel in flocks, screeching as they go, and all alight on the same feeding tree, to disappear as if by magic among the foliage. P.H. Gosse described a flock of these birds on the wing as 'vociferous if not musical; and brilliant if not beautiful; particularly when the sun shines on their green backs and crimsoned wings'.

Their beautiful plumage as well as the fact that parrots can be taught to speak, led to their widespread capture in the past for sale as pets, particularly the Yellow-bill. Additionally, parakeets and parrots have been regarded as a nuisance as they feed not only on wild seeds and fruit but occasionally on crops such as CITRUS, CORN and PIMENTO and their consequent destruction by farmers has contributed to their decline.

The parrots of the Greater Antilles are more closely related to Central American parrots than to those of the Lesser Antilles. Many species of these beautiful birds were found in the pre-Columbian Antilles, valued by the TAINOS as pets that could be taught to speak, for their ornamental feathers, and as food. Called *Guacamayos* or *Papagayos*, multicoloured parrots were especially valued and were considered suitable gifts between CACIQUES. Parrot feathers were used by the Tainos as adornment; a chief and his retinue who met COLUMBUS at OLD HARBOUR BAY were described as wearing magnificent cloaks of parrot feathers.

When young, parrots were eaten boiled or roasted, caught by Taino boys in an ingenious way. A boy would climb a tree with a male parrot on his head while hunters covered with leaves quietly approached. The boy would make the bird cry out and this attracted all the parrots in the vicinity. He would pass a noose around each bird to choke it and throw it down to the hunters below.

[Fewkes 1907, Gosse 1984, Jeffrey-Smith 1972, Saur 1966, Taylor 1955, Wilson 1990]

PASSAGE FORT

A port once located at the mouth of the RIO COBRE, ST CATHERINE Parish, notable in Jamaican history as the spot where the English landed in 1655. (See CAPTURE OF JAMAICA.) Under BRITISH rule, Passage Fort for a long time remained the port for SPANISH TOWN which until 1872 was the island's capital. The actual location of Passage Fort cannot be identified today as the Rio Cobre silted up over time, discharging further east into KINGSTON harbour. In the 19th century, PORT HENDERSON replaced Passage Fort.

The Red Macaw, now extinct
JJ - drawing by A. Wiles

Amerindian parrot trap, 16th century (from Drake)

Green Parrot

PASSION FRUIT (*Passiflora*)

Several members of this large family (some 660 species) occur in Jamaica, all popular fruit growing on vine-like plants. They include Sweet Cup (*P. maliformis*) in which the characteristic seeds and jelly-like pulp are enclosed in a spherical, hard-rind fruit. Granadilla (*P. quadrangularis*) produces huge, melon-like fruit growing on a high climbing, robust vine. The smaller Passion Fruit (*P. edulis*) has either a purple or yellow skin when ripe, and Golden Apple (*P. lauri*) turns yellow-gold.

Passion fruit (Sweet Cup)

The name 'passion fruit' comes not from its supposed aphrodisiac qualities but from the unique shape of the flower, the arrangement of the floral parts said to symbolize the crucifixion, a LEGEND started by Jesuit priests who accompanied the early explorers who first discovered the plants in the New World. The purple flowers are associated with Christ's passion on the cross. The petals and sepals, which form a star, always number ten, the number of faithful apostles at the Crucifixion (Judas and Peter being absent). A corona of 72 filaments in the centre represents the Crown of Thorns. The five stamens symbolize the five wounds, the ovary symbolizes the hammer, three styles with rounded stigma the three nails. Some also see in the twining vines the cords and whips used to scourge Christ, as well as other manifestations symbolic of the crucifixion.

[Adams 1972, Bourne et al. 1988]

PATTY

Favourite convenience food of Jamaicans, widely eaten as lunch or a snack and exported to places overseas where Jamaicans have settled; patties are now manufactured and available in larger cities in North America. The Jamaican patty consists of a circle of pastry folded over to enclose a highly spiced filling, somewhat resembling an English Cornish pasty from which it might have originated. However, claims have been made that patties were first brought by the FRENCH refugees who arrived from Haiti in the late 18th century.

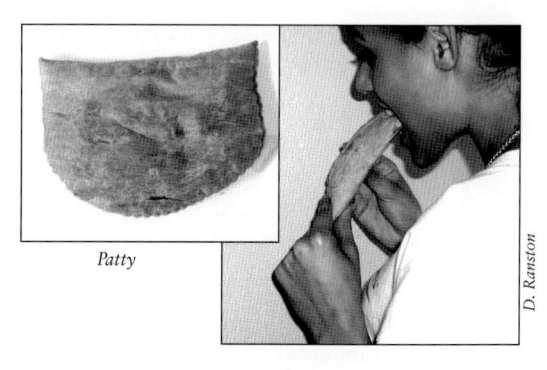

The DJE cites the first OED reference to 'patty' as 1870 though 'pasty' for a meat pie dates from Middle English. In Dr Johnson's 1756 *Dictionary*, 'patty' is derived from the French pâté and means 'a little pie'; as, 'a veal-patty'. 'Pattypan' is identified as: 'A pan to bake a little pie in.' This is probably the meaning intended in Caroline Sullivan's 19th century Jamaican cookbook which gives a recipe for 'salt fish patties' with the instruction: 'Put in patty-pans lined with pastry. Cover and bake.' There is no mention in her book of the patty as we know it. And the 'patty pan' of later times was a square metal box in which patties for sale were kept warm.

Patties formerly had a much thinner and softer crust (coloured with ANATTO) than the flaky pastry currently offered by commercial bakeries. Beef suet was the main shortening used. The regular patty filling is made with ground beef and bread crumbs with lots of pepper and thyme but now fillings of chicken, shrimp or lobster, vegetables and legumes are also available. Small 'cocktail' patties are made as appetizers; the patty is called a tart when enclosing fruit, as in 'plantain tart'.

[Benghiat 1985, DJE, Sullivan 1893]

PATU

Jamaican name for the OWL (also spelled patoo), the same name that is used for the Barn Owl in West Africa, particularly Ghana; many of the beliefs surrounding it are similar in both countries. The patu is regarded as an object of great superstition; its cry is taken to mean that someone will die. It is also a symbol of ugliness, and 'ugly like patu' is a common expression.

'Patu' is actually applied to two species of owls in the island. One is the white Common Barn Owl (*Tyto alba*) of worldwide distribution, which is also known as 'Screech Owl' from the sound it sometimes makes. The other is the Jamaican Brown Owl (*Pseudoscops grammicus*), a genus and species known only from Jamaica. The Brown Owl is 31-36cm in length and dwells in woodlands or in urban areas with large trees. It feeds on insects, SPIDERS, moths, LIZARDS and mice.

The name patu is also sometimes applied to a species of Nightjar (*Nyctibius jamaicensis*) which is sometimes mistaken for the owl. This other bird is known as the Common Potoo or the Patoo and is an endemic sub-species.

PATWA see LANGUAGE

PEAKA-PEOW

Gambling game introduced and run by the CHINESE, like DROP PAN, once widely popular – though illegal. From a paper with 120 numbers, 30 are secretly chosen by the throw of a dice; the player marks 8 numbers on a piece of paper and wins if any of these numbers correspond to any of the 30 chosen.

[Cassidy 1971, DCEU, DJE]

PEANUT (*Arachis hypogaea*)

A New World food crop cultivated by the TAINOS (who called it *maní*) and other native Americans, taken to the Old World and later used as provision on the slave ships. (See SLAVERY.) A native of Brazil, the plant is now cultivated widely throughout the tropics. It is also known as Ground Nut from an unusual feature: the plant, a small annual, produces pea-like flowers above ground and after the flower has been pollinated, it buries the seed pods (peanuts) below ground to ripen.

The plant is one of the most useful in the world – the African-American scientist George Washington Carver (1860-1943) alone discovering hundreds of uses. The mature nuts are eaten and made into peanut butter; yield oil that is used for cooking and in soaps and margarine; the residue from the oil forms groundnut cakes – an animal feed; the leaves and plant remains are used as manure.

In Jamaica the plant is cultivated mainly on the southern plains of ST ELIZABETH Parish.

[Adams 1971, Bourne et al. 1988, Lovén 1935]

PEAS AND BEANS

In Jamaica the fine distinction between peas and beans is not usually observed but pulses (as the edible seeds of pod-bearing plants are called) are very popular in the dietary, whether freshly picked or dried.

Jamaican pulses are from both the Old and the New World though with over 1,000 species, origins are sometimes hard to trace. Certainly Red Pea or Red Kidney-Bean as well as Broad Bean, the island's most popular pulses today, originated in the Americas and were grown in TAINO gardens. Red Kidney-Bean (*Phaseolus vulgaris*), an annual, is also known as French, Haricot, Snap or String Bean. The tender young pods can be eaten green as 'string bean' or the mature beans (green or dried) are consumed in soups and stews and form the main ingredient in the island's most popular starchy accompaniment, RICE AND PEAS. This combination of rice and beans is common throughout the CARIBBEAN and Latin America under different names, but has also been a West African staple. Red Pea soup, like many Jamaican soups, is often a complete meal in itself, with the addition of meat and starches such as YAM and flour or cornmeal DUMPLINGS.

Butter, Broad, or Lima Bean (*Phaseolus lunatus*), a climbing annual, is also native to Jamaica. Popular dishes are created from a combination of these beans with Trotters, Tripe, Oxtail or Cowfoot to make a rich stew. The beans are also eaten as a side dish. One other bean of this family that is not as well known is the Jerusalem Pea (*Phaseolus mungo*); it bears a very small red or brown pea that can be used like its larger relative.

Of the introduced beans, the GUNGO or Congo Pea (*Cajanus cajun*) is by far the most popular. An annual, it comes into bearing at the end of the year and is often used at that time instead of Red Peas as the main ingredient of soups and rice and peas.

Other edible pulses include Bonavist (*Lablab purpureus*), also called Banner Bean or Bannabis, a native of tropical Africa introduced by the Spaniards and found growing wild when the

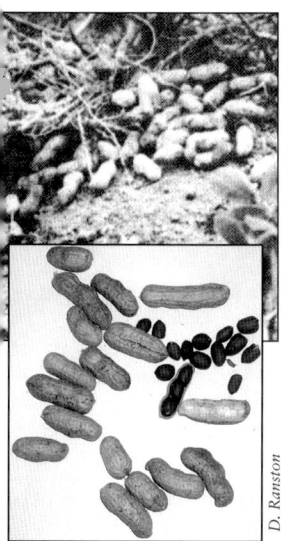

Peanuts, attached to roots, above, and shelled and unshelled, below

English arrived in 1655. According to the DJE, the name indicates its Portuguese origins: it was first imported into the New World from the island of Boa Vista, one of the Cape Verde Islands. The saying: 'Time nevva too long for bannabis bear bean' tells us something about its growing habit, and its other name of 'Bruck-pot' refers to the length of time it takes to cook. Also among locally grown legumes are two varieties of *Vigna*: Cow Peas, a brown bean with white markings and Black-Eye Pea, a white bean with black markings used in the same way as Red and Gungo Peas.

Aside from culinary uses, peas and beans play other roles in Jamaican folk life, being used as garden plants, personal decoration, in folk MEDICINE and in ritual practices. See also BEADS, COWITCH (Horse-Eye Bean), GRAVE PLANT, OVERLOOK (Horse Bean) and JOHN CROW BEAD.
[Adams 1972, Benghiat 1985, Crosby 1972, DJE]

PEDRO CAY see CAY

PEDRO SEAL
The Pedro CAYS that lie south of Portland Bight were once the haunts of the West Indian or Pedro Seal, one of the few tropical seals. They were plentiful when COLUMBUS first came, but were profitably hunted in the 17th and 18th centuries and by the 19th were virtually exterminated. Now, almost none exist. The seal was last taken from Caribbean waters in 1952. As an endangered species, it is protected under the wildlife law of Jamaica.

PELICAN, Brown (*Pelecanus occidentalis*)
Although eight species of pelicans occur throughout the world, the Brown Pelican is the only one that occurs in Jamaica. A sea bird that is commonly seen around coasts and harbours, it flies at low levels, becoming airborne by a few flaps of the wings, followed by gliding. It preys on fish, diving and scooping them up from on or near the surface. It nests in coastal lagoons, on branches of low trees and on the ground.

The Pelican is the symbol of the UNIVERSITY OF THE WEST INDIES. As the bird most common to the islands and territories that support the university, it was chosen to surmount the university's coat of arms. The lectern in the chapel also depicts a Pelican (carved in a tropical hardwood by Alvin Marriott). But the bird in other places is also associated with education and the nurturing of the young, probably derived from its Christian symbolism of self-sacrifice.

PENITENTIARY, General
The governor of Jamaica, Lord Elgin (see SPANISH TOWN CATHEDRAL), laid the foundation stone of this prison in February 1845; it was completed some years later, replacing what was called the Workhouse, dating from SLAVERY. 'GP', as it is popularly known, was built on 4.5ha of land on the southern portion of the old estate ironically named HOPE, near the harbour in KINGSTON. The high brick walls surrounding the cellblocks and lookout towers ensure that GP continues to be a dominating structure on the eastern side of the downtown area.

It has been in continuous use since its opening, the largest prison in the Commonwealth Caribbean. Built to hold 580, the prison in recent times has often held three times that number of prisoners in its antiquated cell blocks. GP is one of seven 'correctional centres' (as they are now officially called) in the island. The other main prisons are the St Catherine District Prison in SPANISH TOWN (like GP a maximum security institution) and the women's prison located in the old FORT AUGUSTA.

In earlier times, the prisoners condemned to hard labour at GP and other island prisons were employed in public works activities such as quarrying, making bricks and road works. (See

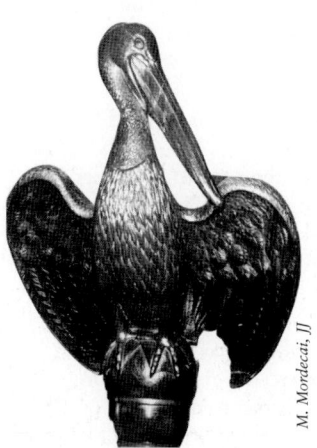

Carved lectern   *General Penitentiary*

FALMOUTH POLICE STATION.) It was prison gangs that started the first road along the PALISADOES to PORT ROYAL (completed by the Public Works Department and opened to vehicular traffic in 1936). GP itself was built by convict labour. A Quaker visitor in 1850 noted that the 500 male convicts in a 'temporary prison' were employed in 'making bricks, hewing stone, and in building the new Penitentiary, and the Lunatic Asylum'. He added: 'The new Penitentiary will take many years to complete, and will cost a large sum of money, as it is intended to furnish a separate sleeping cell for each prisoner.' He also pointed out that 'The Sugar act of 1846 has so far parylised (sic) the country that legislative grants have been suspended and buildings, in consequence, go slowly forward'.
[Candler 1850, Human Rights Watch 1990, Jacobs 1976]

PENN, Admiral William

The joint leader of the expedition that took Jamaica from the Spaniards in 1655 (see CAPTURE OF JAMAICA) was also father of Quaker William Penn (see FRIENDS) whose name the state of Pennsylvania, USA, commemorates. To liquidate a debt of £16,000 owing to the admiral, King Charles II of England settled land in America on Penn's son. Penn Jr who founded a Quaker colony there, wanted to call it 'Sylvania'. The king, in gratitude for the services of the late admiral, added the 'Penn' in his memory, much to the anger of his son. This lack of filial piety is understandable since his father once had him 'whipped, beaten and turned out of doors' for his religion.

PENTECOSTALISM

Jamaica's fastest growing religious movement, reflecting a CARIBBEAN and indeed world-wide trend. While the census of 1943 recorded only 4 per cent of the population as Pentecostals, this had grown to 20 per cent in 1970, and in 1992 consisted of over half a million persons, represented in the census by both 'Church of God' (487,988) and 'Pentecostal' (175,235).

Pentecostalism is not a single organization or denomination. The term embraces many different religious groups, both national and international, that emphasize the charismatic aspect of Christianity and regard the Bible as fundamental, i.e interpret every word of the Bible as literal truth. This includes, for instance, 'Apostolic' churches such as the Apostolic Church of God, Church of Jesus Christ Apostolic, Shiloah Apostolic Church, as well as 'Churches of God' such as The New Testament Church of God, Pentecostal Church of God, Church of God of Prophecy and the Four Square Church of God.

A 20th century phenomenon, the movement originated in the United States in 1901 in Topeka, Kansas, under the leadership of C.F. Parham, a former METHODIST minister. It was born from a desire to return to the original simplicity of the Christian religion. The basic doctrines centre on being 'born again', i.e. conversion and adult baptism as well as speaking in tongues. The name of the movement derived from the events of the Day of Pentecost when the Holy Spirit descended on the disciples, possessed them and inspired each of them to speak in unknown tongues. Especially important are the first five books of the New Testament, particularly the Book of Acts. The emphasis is not on doctrine but on the experience of the Holy Spirit.

In America, the movement gained such success among both black and white adherents that after 1906 they embarked on a vigorous missionary programme. There were evangelical missions in Jamaica as early as 1918 and they found a ground already prepared in the indigenous Jamaican REVIVAL and the Native BAPTIST churches which married Christianity with the black religious expressions brought from Africa. These included spirit possession and the centrality of music and song in worship. The Pentecostals gave new impetus to these religions that were then on the decline though it has also drawn members away from Revival in recent years.

Pentecostalism has also grown at the expense of the established churches. A Jamaican UNITED CHURCH minister argued in the 1970s that the emergence and growth of the early movement was a direct response to the alienation from the established churches felt by mainly poor and ordinary Jamaicans. Pentecostalism was perceived as offering a more democratic and egalitarian form of worship and church membership.

While Jamaican Pentecostalism at its start catered mainly to the poor and was built around charismatic but largely uneducated leaders, the movement today has grown to embrace a much wider cross-section of the population, with a trained ministry. In its early days, adherents, like the earlier adherents of Revival Zion and POCOMANIA, were derided by the rest of the population for their noisy and enthusiastic form of worship. For, as J.B. Hopkin says: 'While in more decorous churches worshippers gather to praise and worship the Lord, Pentecostals everywhere gather to experience the Lord, and in their rejoicing in that experience is the praising.'

Coupled with the nature of their religious expression that offers to worshippers a kind of personal freedom not experienced in the established churches is the marked attitude and personal lifestyle of these 'born-again' Christians that includes rejection of many aspects of the secular world and the banishing of earthly pleasures. This is often expressed in conservative dress and demeanour. While leadership in the church is usually male, a significant number of worshippers are female (80 per cent in the 1970s).

[Austin-Broos 1997, Calley 1965, Crim 1981, Hopkin 1978, Smith 1978]

PEPPER

Condiment that has been a vital ingredient in Jamaican cooking since the TAINOS cultivated peppers in their Caribbean gardens or *conucos* and used them liberally; their main meal was called PEPPER-POT. The peppers of the Americas are Capsicums, otherwise known as cayenne, chilli, green, sweet pepper, etc. and grow on small shrubs. They are quite different from 'black pepper' (*Piper nigrum*) which grows on a vine; the grains are usually dried and ground before consumption. What is called 'Jamaica Pepper' internationally (but not by Jamaicans) is not a pepper at all but the spice PIMENTO.

Capsicums are native to tropical America and were cultivated by the Mexicans as early as 7000 BC; they were introduced to Europe by the SPANISH explorers. All capsicum peppers are varieties of one valuable species but it is divided into two main types, the chillis that are small and hot in taste and the large, often bell-shaped 'sweet peppers' that are mild in taste and eaten as a vegetable raw or cooked.

Referring to Capsicum which was then called 'Indian-Pepper', Edward Long (1774) said about 15 varieties were grown in the island, and listed among them bell, goat, bonnet, bird, olive, hen, barbary, finger, and cherry – some of the names still in use. 'Bonnet' is presumably today's 'Scotch-Bonnet' (so-called from its resemblance to a Scotsman's beret). The Scotch-Bonnet is claimed to be the hottest pepper in the world and is the most esteemed by Jamaicans. Also popular is 'Country Pepper' which is larger and milder. In cooking, one or other of these peppers is usually dropped whole into soups and stews to impart its special flavour, but must be taken out before it bursts. Hot peppers are also eaten raw as an accompaniment to a meal. Jamaicans believe that the seed is the hottest part of the pepper so these are usually avoided by all but the most fanatic pepper-lover. The small, colourful 'Bird Pepper' is avidly eaten by birds as well as humans and is popular in pickles. (See also POCO-MUNGEE.)

Hot peppers are widely cultivated in home gardens, the bushes bearing prolifically. A large variety of condiments, pickles and sauces are made from peppers, some commercially, others put up by the housewife for home use. Many varieties of Jamaican peppers and sauces are now exported. Pickled peppers were popular with the early settlers, as they are today. Long described 'Man-Dram' as a mixture made of sliced cucumber, shallots or onions cut very small with lime juice or Madeira wine added and a few pods of bird or bonnet peppers, mixed well, adding that 'It seldom fails to provoke the most languid appetites'.

Piper nigrum – black pepper – comes from a jungle vine native to India and Sri Lanka (and cultivated on a small scale in Jamaica). The black pepper corn is the dried unripe fruit while white pepper is made from fully ripe fruit from which the skin is removed. The term 'peppercorn rental' attests to the former high value of the spice. Though today a peppercorn rent is minimal, in medieval times in Europe, some landlords preferred payment in pepper, so scarce and valuable was it as a commodity. (See also NUTMEG.)

[Adams 1971, Bourne et al. 1988, Facey 1993, Huxley 1991, Long 1774]

PEPPER, Village of

This village at the foot of SPUR TREE HILL, ST ELIZABETH Parish, takes its name from a nearby livestock pen which was once one of the largest horse-breeding establishments in the world. The hey-day of Pepper Pen was the period 1820-40 but the pen was famous as a stud farm from the 18th century. It is said that horses from here raced successfully on the great English racecourses. (See HORSE, HORSE-RACING.)

[Wright and White 1969]

Hot peppers

PEPPER-POT

Name given to both a meat stew made with cassareep (see CASSAVA) and a thick soup made with CALALU and other greens; the soup is now the only dish called pepper-pot in Jamaica.

Pepper-pot was the traditional stew pot of CARIB and ARAWAK-speaking peoples – including the TAINO – who used cassava or yuca as a staple. Into the pot would go fish or meats from the hunt, seasoned with PEPPERS and a thick flavourful sauce called cassareep. The pepper-pot was kept on the fire to be dipped into as needed. The Europeans and Africans adopted the pepper-pot which became popular throughout the CARIBBEAN as a mainstay of plantation cookery (the earliest Jamaican reference cited in the DJE is 1698).

The dark-coloured cassareep is made from boiling down the juice expressed from grated bitter cassava and skimming from the surface a thick froth that is believed to contain the poison found in bitter cassava (hydrocyanic acid). Cassareep is not only flavourful but acts as a preservative, and with its addition, the stew can be kept going indefinitely with new meats added, as long as it is boiled up each day. That dark rich 'pepper-pot' – a stew of meats made with cassareep – is still cooked in Guyana and some of the islands but is certainly not widespread in Jamaica today although it continued to be made until well into the 20th century. *The Jamaica Cookery Book* published in 1893 under 'Soups', gives a recipe for both 'Callilu soup' and 'Pepper pot' made with 'casseripe'.

Today, Pepper-pot or Calalu in Jamaica and some other Caribbean countries is a thick, rich soup made with chopped greens, especially calalu, OKRA and dasheen leaves (see COCO), and corned beef, pork, or crab.

A 19th century visitor, Charles Rampini, waxed lyrical after his first taste of pepper-pot soup in Chapelton, CLARENDON Parish. Not, said he, 'the Demerara [i.e. Guyana] pepper-pot with its evil-smelling and still more evil-tasting cassareep sauce and its hereditary pipkin; but a rich succulent potage, a very Meg Merrilees broth of pork and beef and fowl, ochroes and calaloo (the West Indian spinach), peppers, cray fish and negro YAM; in colour a dark green, with the scarlet prawns appearing through the chaotic mess not unpicturesquely'. Rampini also noted that the pepper-pot of the poor was a more heterogenous mixture with whatever meat kind was available plus 'bamboo tops, cotton-tree tips, cabbage, pimpernel, pulse, and even the heads of the night-blooming cereus'.

While the main characteristic of pepper-pot today is the use of calalu and other greens, a pepper-pot served to the finicky governor's wife Lady Nugent (and recorded in her *Journal* 1801-5) is a protein-rich stew. It featured Black CRABS, formerly available in great abundance and a great delicacy. The recipe for 'Black crab pepper-pot' that she was served at HORDLEY estate in ST THOMAS Parish was as follows: 'a capon stewed down, a large piece of beef and another of ham, also stewed to a jelly; then six dozen of land crabs, picked fine, with their eggs and fat, onions, peppers, ochra, sweet herbs, and other vegetables of the country, cut small; and this, well stewed, makes black crab pepper-pot.'

Pepper-pot is also used figuratively to refer to any diverse mixture.

[DJE, Nugent 1839, Rampini 1873, Sullivan 1893]

PERIWINKLE (*Catharanthus roseus*)

Popular flowering plant grown as an ornamental and used in folk MEDICINE especially in the control of diabetes, a practice discouraged by doctors as dangerous since it masks some symptoms of the disease. In the 1950s, a Jamaican country doctor who had observed its widespread usage sent the plant to Canada to test its efficacy in treating diabetes. A medical research laboratory got negative results in testing it as a substitute for insulin, but out of that research came the discovery of its anti-cancer properties. So far drugs for the treatment of leukaemia and Hodgkin's disease have been extracted from this plant and research continues. Periwinkle originates on the island of Madagascar and is now widespread throughout the tropics. It has many popular names in Jamaica including Ram Goat Roses, Brown Man's Fancy and Old Maid.

Periwinkle

PETCHARY AND LOGGERHEAD

Both Petchary (*Tyrannus dominicensis*) and Loggerhead (*Tyrannus caudifasciatus*) are birds of the family of Tyrant Flycatchers. They are similar in size, appearance, and habits, but can be distinguished by a number of features, of which the most distinct is the Loggerhead's very dark, less rounded head. The Loggerhead is resident in Jamaica and does not migrate while the Petchary (also known as the Grey Kingbird) is found in the island from March to the end of September or October when it returns to its winter quarters in South America. The MOCKINGBIRD (Nightingale) may imitate the call 'Pit-cheer-y', thus causing humans to believe, erroneously, that the Petchary has arrived.

Pugnacious birds, both Petchary and Loggerhead like to sit on the highest, most exposed spots, such as telegraph poles and wires, from which they dart to seize the insects or LIZARDS on which they feed, or to launch a vicious attack on other BIRDS. The Petchary is well known for its aerial attacks on high-flying hawks and vultures, and has been seen to 'catch a ride' on the back of one of these larger birds. The Loggerhead is noted for feeding on Bird PEPPERS.

Petchary (from Gosse)

[Jeffrey-Smith 1972, Roberts 1955, Taylor 1955]

PIABA (*Hyptis brevipes*)

A MINT-like, annual herb that grows wild near pond margins and swamps in low-lying areas, used in Jamaican folk MEDICINE as 'TEA' for colds, headaches, and as a poultice for wounds. It is immortalized in the folk song 'Man piaba, woman piaba' celebrating the West Indian 'weed woman' (see BALM, folk MEDICINE) and made popular by Harry Belafonte. An important bush of West Africa, *piaba* was listed by Rattray as one of the sacred plants of the Ashanti and is used in OBEAH practices in Jamaica. Interestingly, the historic and modern Lokono ARAWAKS of Guyana refer to their shaman as piaiman.

[Adams 1971, Campbell 1974, Rattray 1927]

'PIKNI CHRISTMAS'

Also spelled 'pickney' and 'pickaninny' in the historical literature, this referred to EASTER celebrations during SLAVERY which, as the name (creole for 'child') suggests, were briefer and less elaborate than the grand CHRISTMAS celebrations.

PIG (*Sus scrofa*)

Along with other domestic animals, pigs were introduced to the CARIBBEAN by COLUMBUS on his second voyage in 1493. After that date, Amerindian culture and traditions had to adapt to the sudden presence of six major animals – CATTLE, sheep, GOATS, pigs, DONKEYS and HORSES, all of which (except for sheep) thrived in the islands, forever altering the FLORA and way of life.

As Alfred W. Crosby Jr tells us, the pigs were the 'lean, fast, tusked boars and sows of Medieval Europe', omnivorous eaters that adapted easily in the ANTILLES with devastating effect on the human inhabitants: 'they rooted the TAINOS' manioc tubers out of the ground, stole their guavas and their pineapples, gobbled lizards and baby birds – every thing went down their maws.'

In a few years, pigs were running wild on the islands in infinite numbers. Early in the conquest, pairs were deposited on uninhabited islands to provide food for the future – giving a name and a way of life to the BUCCANEERS who smoked the flesh over a fire on a contraption of sticks called a *boucan*. Pork was in any case the preferred meat in the diet of the SPANISH *conquistadores* (though it continued to be avoided as a taboo animal by the CARIB – apparently because they thought their own eye sight as hunters would be affected if they ate an animal with such tiny eyes).

Soon, the expeditions being outfitted to conquer the American continent took lard from the Antilles as well as swine and other animals on the hoof. For the SPANISH settlers in Jamaica, the export of lard to the American mainland was an important economic activity. Espinosa (1628) tells us that the swine got fat in July-August and great battues were held to slaughter them and obtain lard from the fat. The lard was loaded into casks for shipment to the Spanish Main, a practice which gave its name in Jamaica to Manteca or Lard Bay – now Montego Bay. The wild pigs in the forests provided meat not only for the colonists and the buccaneers but sustenance for runaway Amerindians and AFRICANS. (See JERK PORK, MAROONS, PIG HUNTING.)

With the development of the plantations (see SLAVERY, SUGAR PLANTATION), domestic pig rearing became important, especially by slaves for sale in the MARKETS. Pig rearing has continued to be a popular activity for small farmers to this day though a segment of the population, RASTAFARI, do not eat pork. Farmers nowadays buy prepared feed for their animals (and most are raised on commercial farms), but part of the attraction of pig rearing for the small farmer in the past was the ease with which the animal could be fed. A *Jamaica Almanack* for 1879-80 contained much advice on hogs and the variety of their feed: 'Feb: Tame your wild hogs now, that they may not run wild during the mango season, sour cornmeal is good for the purpose, the hogs eat it voraciously . . . April: Feed your hogs on cocoa-heads, hog-slip [a vine] and plantain leaves, till guavas and mangoes come in . . . breadfruits, young and many falling withered from the trees, and are good feeding for hogs . . . August: Pears are plentiful, pull the common sort and feed the hogs, eat the best . . . October: Cut your small patch of canes, boil into sugar, or feed your hogs with them and plant the tops . . . November: Feed your hogs on canes, sour cornmeal, cocoa-heads, and plantain leaves, as there are no fruits for them to feed on, they will become very tame; December: Manage your sows, so that they may farrow in April. . . when mangoes, guavas, and cherries will be getting ripe.'
[Crosby 1972, Espinosa 1628, Jamaica Almanack 1986]

PIG, Hunting The Wild

The African-American anthropologist Zora Neale Hurston visited Jamaica in the 1930s and persuaded a party of ACCOMPONG MAROONS to take her on a hunt for the wild PIG. In her book, *Tell My Horse*, she describes her experience. The hunting party, she said, usually consisted of four hunters, the dogs, and the baggage boys. In preparation, old machetes were filed to spear point and made razor sharp and attached to long handles to form spears. This was done the day before since the Maroons said if cutting weapons were sharpened the day of the hunt, their dogs would be killed by the hog. At daybreak on the day of the hunt, the party went to the GRAVEYARD and the ancestors of all the hunters invoked, to strengthen their arms. Afterwards they left before anyone in the town could speak to the party. This was regarded as the worst of luck – portending even death – and they would have turned back if it happened. In addition to their spears, the hunters carried guns. The leader said it sometimes took four days before they picked up signs of hog. Meantime they marched into the cockpits, singing 'Karamantee songs'. The baggage boy carried an iron skillet and coffee pot and food for the trip: CORN pone, cassava BAMMY, green PLANTAIN and salt, PIMENTO and other spices for curing the meat. The wild hog is still occasionally hunted. (See JERK.)
[Hurston 1938]

PIGEON see DOVE AND PIGEON

PIGEON PEAS see GUNGO

PIMENTO (*Pimenta dioica*)
Jamaica's only indigenous spice and the only spice native to the New World that is produced in commercial quantities. It was called *pimienta* by the Spaniards and internationally is known as Allspice, the name under which it is marketed. This latter name comes from the fact that the berry is said to combine the flavours of Cinnamon, Clove, and Nutmeg. Pimento grows in Mexico, Central America, Cuba and Hispaniola and was used by the TAINOS. It has been introduced elsewhere in the tropics, but Jamaican pimento is regarded as best, and up to recently had a virtual monopoly on world markets. Jamaica still supplies dried pimento berry, berry oil and leaf oil internationally to be used in the meat processing, confectionery, and pharmaceutical industries. Locally, it is a vital ingredient in JERK seasoning and is otherwise widely used in cooking.

Pimento

The handsome tree of the myrtle family (closely related to the Bay tree) occurs throughout the island up to 1,000m but is widespread on the LIMESTONE derived soil of central parishes, especially ST ANN, thriving at lower elevations. The tree grows 7-15m in height and its characteristic light-coloured bark peels easily from the trunk. All parts of the tree – wood, flower, berry, and leaf – are aromatic. The spice is made from the immature berries that are about the size of black pepper grains but are green when harvested, turning dark brown when dried after reaping; each berry contains one or two small seeds. An aromatic oil is also extracted from the leaves.

It is only in recent times that the pimento has been cultivated. Since 1969, grafted pimento plants have been produced by the Ministry of Agriculture. Previously, the plants were grown from seeds. Earlier landowners depended on the movement of birds that feed on the ripe berries that will take root where they are excreted. As R.C. Dallas (1803) observed: 'This elegant child of nature, mocks the attempts of art to extend or improve its growth.'

The trees are dioecious, i.e. with male and female reproductive structures on separate trees. The Ministry of Agriculture recommends planting one male for every eight female trees in order to ensure successful pollination. Previously the male trees were thought to be useless for any purpose but propagation but they are now considered valuable in the production of pimento leaf oil. The berries are borne on the female trees and harvested while green. Pimento oil is distilled from unripe berries that are dried and crushed. The berries that ripen on the tree turn dark purple and are used to make Pimento Dram or liqueur. Dried berries steeped in rum are also used to produce a medicinal draught much used for stomach aches. Crushed pimento leaves are used as a fever remedy.

Pimento blossoms January to August and the berries are ready for picking August to September when the air is filled with their aroma. In the past they were reaped by the wasteful practice of breaking the berry-laden limbs from the tree and then picking off the individual berries into baskets; nowadays the small twigs that bear the berries are clipped from the tree. The small round berries are spread out on a flat paved surface called a BARBECUE to dry and are covered or taken up during rain and at nights and turned regularly for several days. When pimento is dry, the tiny seeds can be heard shaking inside the hull. The dried berries will be cleaned by fanning and hand picking to get rid of bits of stem, broken leaves, gravel, etc.

[Adams 1971, 1972, Baccus and Royes 1988, Beckwith 1928, Dallas 1803]

PINEAPPLE (*Ananas comosus*)

A member of the BROMELIAD family, the pineapple does not grow on a tree like most fruits, but on the ground on a spiny rosette, each plant producing a single fruit topped with a headdress of sharp-pointed leaves. The fruit, which can grow up to 30cm tall, is the product of about 100 compacted flowers. The plant is perennial, new plants arising as side shoots from the old, or replanted from cuttings taken from the fruit top. Commercial varieties are seedless; those in the wild are pollinated by HUMMINGBIRDS.

Now grown throughout the tropics, this popular fruit is a native of Central and South America and was first met with by the Spaniards on the CARIBBEAN islands from where it was taken to Europe. In the Old World as in the New, the fruit became extremely popular for its beauty as well as taste, and was widely used as a motif in art, its name deriving from its resemblance to a pine cone of temperate climates. Ligon in his *History of Barbados* (1657) deemed the pineapple 'all that is excellent and superlative . . . for beauty and taste' and John Evelyn recorded in his diary of 9 August 1661 the excitement attending the arrival of the first pineapple in England – 'the famous Queen Pine brought from Barbados'. Also noted was the presentation by Mr Rose, the royal gardener, of the first pineapple grown in the British Isles to King Charles II.

Pineapple in Europe soon became a symbol of hospitality – an idea borrowed from the TAINOS – and it was fashionable to have gate piers or four poster beds topped with pineapple-shaped finials (traditional to Jamaican four-posters – see GREAT HOUSE).

Pineapples (with banana tree) carved c tortoiseshell. Port Royal 1677

The fruit also caught on in American decorative arts. It is said that sea captains returning home from their Caribbean voyages stuck a pineapple on their gatepost to signal that they were home.

The pineapple's long historic association with Jamaica is symbolized in several ways, the fruit appearing on the shield of the island's COAT OF ARMS. A pineapple watermark appears on the paper used for printing the island's MONEY and was used in Jamaica's earliest postage stamps.

It is believed that Jamaica supplied the first commercial varieties of pineapple to Hawaii, now the world's largest producer of the fruit. Plants of the variety Cayenne, were shipped from Jamaica to Hawaii between 1885-95. Tradition has it that these pineapples were sent from a plantation called Lilyfield in ST ANN Parish though Temple Hall, ST ANDREW Parish also makes this claim.

Today, pineapples are grown by Jamaican farmers as a quick cash crop. The varieties Cayenne and Red Spanish (or Cowboy) are canned. Both varieties are also popular as a fresh fruit, as is the Sugar Loaf, among others.

PINGWING see BROMELIAD

PIRATES see BUCCANEERS

PIRATES, Women
Two young women in male disguise, Anne Bonny (also spelled Ann Bonney) and Mary Read, shared the pirate life of 'Calico Jack' (see RACKHAM), and were caught with him at NEGRIL beach in 1720 and brought to trial at SPANISH TOWN. Rackham and the women were sentenced to death, but while Jack swung from the gallows, both women pleaded pregnancy and their sentences were never carried out. Mary Read died in childbirth in prison; no one knows what became of Anne Bonny though it is believed that

Women pirates

Woman pirate triumphs in a duel

after she gave birth, her release was obtained by local influential business associates of her father who was a wealthy planter of Charleston, South Carolina, USA.

At the trial it came out that both women were as fierce and bloodthirsty as their companions, and Anne Bonny displayed stinging contempt for Rackham, her former lover and captain, after he was sentenced: 'Had you fought like a man', she told him, 'You would not hang like a dog.' One witness at the trial, Dorothy Thomas, said she was at sea in a CANOE with provisions when she was taken by Rackham's sloop and stated that the reason for her believing and knowing them to be women was 'the largeness of their breast'. The two women, she said, 'were then on board the said sloop . . . and wore men's jackets, and long trousers, and handkerchiefs tied about their heads . . . each of them had a machete and pistol in their hands, and cursed and swore at the men to murder [her]'.

There was even more damaging evidence from two other witnesses. They said that the women had been active on the sloop, that Anne Bonny handed gun powder to the men, that Anne Bonny had a gun in her hand, that both women were 'very profligate, cursing and swearing much, and very ready and willing to do anything on board'. At their trial, both women said 'Mi Lord, we plead our bellies' – the usual phrase for expectant mothers sentenced to execution.

Each of these women was exceptional for her times and for their paths to cross was extraordinary. They both came from very different backgrounds: Mary Read was in her twenties at the time of her trial and had lived most of her life disguised as a man; Anne Bonny was in her teens and had taken to male disguise only when she joined Rackham.

Mary Read was born in London out of wedlock and was dressed by her mother as a boy to take the place of an older brother who had died and who stood to come into an inheritance. Read first became a page to a gentlewoman of fashion, then worked as a cabin boy on a British man-of-war. She fought as a foot soldier in the Low Country (Holland) and then in a squadron of dragoons. She ended up marrying one of her fellow troopers, the other soldiers passing the hat around to give them a wedding present. The newlyweds resigned from the service and set themselves up as the proprietors of a tavern – *The Three Horseshoes* – at Breda. When their business was destroyed by the Peace of Utrecht and her husband died, Mary put on male disguise again and shipped out on a Dutch vessel to the West Indies. When her ship was taken by pirates, she joined them.

She fell in love again – with one of the pirates' prisoners, and they were, according to her, 'married in the eyes of God'. So much in love was she that when her lover was challenged to a duel by a pirate, she made sure to pick a fight with the pirate and call him out earlier, so that she could kill him. At her piracy trial she refused to reveal the name of her lover and he never came forward, though as a 'forced man' on the pirate ship he would have been among those freed.

Anne Bonny was born in Kinsale, Ireland, near to Cork, the illegitimate daughter of a lawyer and his servant who together fled the country when the scandal of their relationship broke. They settled in Charleston where he became a wealthy and influential plantation owner. Anne's mother died and the father seemed unable to control his daughter who even at an early age had a 'fierce and resolute temper'. She must have been attractive nonetheless, for she had several suitors, one of whom she thrashed till he nearly died when he attempted to 'compromise her'.

She took off with a good-for-nothing sailor, James Bonny, and when they married her father disinherited her. They went to New Providence in the Bahamas. There she met the dashing Captain Rackham when he came ashore. She attempted to get a divorce by sale, an ancient English practice whereby, with the consent of the parties, a wife could be transferred by bill of sale from one man to another. This infuriated the governor who accused them all of 'lewdness', had them arrested, and threatened to have Anne publicly stripped and flogged. Disguised in seaman's clothes, Anne and her lover stole a sloop and set out to live the pirate life on the shipping lanes between Jamaica and Cuba. Of the crew, only Rackham knew she was a woman.

One day they were joined by a young sailor recruited from a captured Dutch vessel and he caught Anne's eye. But she was in for a shock for 'he' proved to be Mary Read. Mary was forced to reveal her secret to Rackham who had threatened to kill her in a jealous rage.

Anne Bonny's maiden name was not revealed at her trial and her father was not identified nor was her subsequent fate known.

[Black 1989, Woodbury 1951]

PLANTAIN (*Musa acuminata x balbisiana*)
Fruit that is popularly thought of as a large BANANA though it is of a different species. Plantains are larger than bananas and are cooked before consumption, whether ripe or green. Like the banana, the plantain is a massive herb, believed to be of Asian origin but well established in West Africa by the 15th century. Although in Jamaica the banana was scorned as an article of diet until well into the 20th century, the plantain has been eaten from earliest times and was a staple – and favourite food – of the enslaved AFRICANS. It was also popular with the planters; Rampini claims the phrase 'Born near the plantain root' referred to those born in Jamaica.

Caroline Sullivan who wrote the first published Jamaican cookbook (1893) waxed lyrical about the plantain: 'Green roasted plantains are de rigueur with the planter's cheese, served up in a folded napkin. Boiled they are eaten too as vegetable, but not when very ripe . . .

Plantain leaf used as umbrella by Taino (from Oviedo)

"Turned" is when they are between green and ripe, and they go excellently well with salt fish or eaten boiled or roasted with butter put inside them. Ripe, they are very good indeed roasted and particularly good when cut in thin slices and fried or cut in pieces with butter inside. A breakfast dish is made of either green plantains or turned plantains roasted, then chopped in dice, or fried if preferred, and sent to table with melted butter poured over them.'

Today, plantains ripe or green are cooked in a variety of ways to accompany a meal, grated or mashed to make porridge and desserts and confections such as Plantain Tart which consists of mashed and seasoned ripe plantains enclosed in a pastry shell.

There are many varieties of plantain, the two most popular being Horse Plantain, one of large size, and Maiden Plantain, the smallest.

[Rampini 1873, Sullivan 1893, Viola and Margolis 1991]

PLANTAIN GARDEN RIVER

This river in ST THOMAS Parish is unusual in that while most major Jamaican rivers flow north or south from the main central mountain ridges, the Plantain Garden flows mainly eastwards. It rises in the Cuna Cuna Mountains and runs southerly in its upper courses, then on meeting the coastal range of hills it turns easterly and flows through a large fertile valley to which it gives its name before it empties in the sea at Holland Bay. In the old days, sugar from the various estates in the parish would be carried down this river by boat to be shipped at Rocky Point. One of its tributaries is the Sulphur River that is the source of the BATH FOUNTAIN. The Plantain Garden River Valley is one area that was settled by some of the indentured AFRICANS who were brought to the island after EMANCIPATION. Not surprisingly, researchers have found that African religious and other practices are very strong in this area.

PLANTATION SYSTEM see SUGAR PLANTATION

PLANTER'S PUNCH

Rum-based drink popular for hundreds of years. The traditional recipe that originated as a planter's drink is:

one of sour (LIME juice)
two of sweet (SUGAR or syrup)
three of strong (RUM)
four of weak (water and ice)

Sometimes Angostura bitters, soda water or fruit juices are added.

PLATO, The 'Courtly Bandit'

A folk hero of plantation days, Plato was a runaway slave who operated as a highwayman in the western side of the island, particularly in WESTMORELAND Parish. The handsome and dashing Plato gathered around him a band of other runaways including women and, as the visiting plantation owner M.G. Lewis described it: 'no Creole lady would venture out on a visit, without running the risk of having her bandbox runaway with by Plato for the decoration of his sultanas; and if the maid who carried the bandbox happened to be well-looking, he ran away with the maid as well as the bandbox.' After escaping capture for some time, Plato was finally betrayed by a slave from whom he had arranged to buy RUM. Before he was executed, he told the judge that the whole of the island would be laid waste by a storm the next year (1780), which indeed happened. He also told his jailor that he would not live long after the execution and sure enough, he 'withered away' and died within the year.

[Lewis 1818]

'PLAY'

Word used to describe amusements during SLAVERY and after. Singing, dancing and feasting, especially during holidays and WAKES were referred to by the African Jamaicans as 'play', suggesting the interactive nature of these events.

A character called 'Actor Boy' was part of the Christmas JONKONNU carnival from at least the late 18th century (and is depicted in one of the beautiful drawings by Belisario), suggesting the presence of actors among the revellers. There are several accounts of plays or fragments of plays actually being performed. Some of these plays might have been learnt from observing the travelling players in the THEATRE of the times. The plays were sometimes fragments of English plays (Shakespeare's *Richard the Third* being especially popular) or 'Doctor Plays'. Most plays ended with a sword fight, the triumph of one antagonist and the death of the other, a resurrection scene (with or without the intervention of the 'Doctor') and a reconciliation in which all joined in the dance. Plays about kings, queens and princes were especially popular and while many think these refer to the English throne, there is other evidence that suggests a strong CONGO influence, Africans from the Kingdom of the Kongo (and elsewhere) also having a strong tradition of royalty.

'Ring-play' continued into the contemporary period, referring to the playing of games by a ring of players, e.g. at NINE NIGHT celebrations. (See GAMES.) The ring-play stone-passing song, 'Manuel Road', underscores the distinction between play (or 'pretend') as opposed to real life, by cautioning: 'Mash yu finger no cry, Gal an' Bwoy, Play we a play you know.'

The word 'play' is also used to indicate someone's assumption of acting out behaviours, e.g. 'to play bad' – to act rudely or aggressively, 'to play big woman/man' – to be precocious, 'to play big' – to pretend to be bold. 'Play fool to catch wise' is a well-known saying. In Trinidad Carnival (and now by extension in the Jamaica Carnival), the term 'play mas' is used to indicate one who plays masquerade, i.e. participates by playing in a costumed band.

PLUM see APPLE, HOG PLUM, JEW PLUM, PLUMB POINT

PLUMB POINT LIGHTHOUSE

This lighthouse that guards the entrance to KINGSTON harbour is located at Great Plumb Point on the PALISADOES road. It was built in 1853 and its light has gone out only once since then. This was during the EARTHQUAKE of 1907. The 21m stone and cast iron tower of the lighthouse shows a white light visible for about 40km over the entrance of the eastern navigable channel and a red light over the south channel that is visible for 20km. The name 'plumb' is an early spelling of 'plum'; during Spanish times this locality was called *Cayo de los Icacos* or Plum Tree Cay. It referred to the Coco-plum (*Chrysobalanus icaco*), a shrub or bushy tree bearing a reddish-purple plum-like fruit that is edible but hardly eaten and which – presumably – grew in abundance here.

Plumb Point lighthouse

[Adams 1972, GOJ Handbook of Jamaica 1961, Pietersz 1938]

POCOMANIA

The accepted spelling is now Pukumina, both forms are shortened in speech to 'Poco'. An African-Jamaican traditional religion, Pukumina along with Revival ZION forms the religious grouping classified as REVIVAL.

POCO-MUNGEE

Salt ground with bird PEPPER, referred to by Hans Sloane as 'Cayan butter – the universal Indian sauce'. Long described Cayan butter as made of ripe bird peppers dried in the sun then pounded with a mixture of salt. It was kept tightly closed in a bottle and sprinkled on food as a relish. The name 'poco-mungee' was apparently given by the MAROONS to the mixture that they ground together between two river stones.

[DJE, Long 1774]

POINCIANA (*Delonix regia*)

One of the most beautiful trees of the tropical world, this leguminous ornamental will grow up to 15m. Since its introduction from Kew Gardens in 1858 it has spread all over the island from sea level to 800m and is a conspicuous feature of the summer months when its huge umbrella-shaped crown becomes completely covered with clusters of scarlet, gold or orange-coloured blossoms. Before flowering, the tree sheds its leaves and the blossoms start to emerge against the black of last year's seed pods and the green of fern-like new leaves gradually appearing. Of the five petals on each orchid-like flower, the frontal petal is white with tiny yellowish specks. Huge clusters of as many as 40 blooms are followed by the large leathery seed pods about 30cm in length which change from bright green when young to black.

Poinciana originated in Madagascar but quickly became naturalized throughout the tropics where it is also known as Flamboyant. Like other tropical favourites BOUGAINVILLEA and BAUHINIA, it was named after a Frenchman, in this case M de Poinci, a 17th century governor of the French Antilles.

Associated with this tree is a dark brown caterpillar. These are the young of the moth *Melipotis*, and they are often seen at the base of the trunk of the trees during the daytime. The caterpillars can defoliate a large tree in a few days if their numbers get large enough.

[Adams 1972]

POINSETTIA (*Euphorbia pulcherrima*)

What Christmas trees are to northern climes, the red 'Christmas flower' or Poinsettia is to the tropics, though nowadays potted Poinsettias increasingly signal the Christmas season in northern countries too and hybrid varieties in many different colours are competing with the traditional red. The plant is named after Joel R. Poinsett (d 1851), American Ambassador to

Euphorbia cotinifolia

Mexico who introduced it to the United States. Horticultural selection has resulted in single, double and triple poinsettias, the latter being the most common today for hedge and garden arrangements.

Euphorbia punicea

The brilliant colour of the plant actually comes from large, showy bracts that surround a rather inconspicuous flower, the bracts being the means by which the plant lures visitors for pollination. The poinsettia bracts are green for half the year, turning red near to CHRISTMAS. Then KINGSTON and other towns are considerably brightened by the showy splendour of this plant which is sometimes planted with a white euphorbia (*E. leucocephala*) to present a striking contrast of red and white throughout the Christmas season.

While the poinsettia originated in Mexico, Jamaica has many interesting endemic species of the genus *Euphorbia* to which it belongs, the most popular of which is the Wild Physic Nut (*E. punicea*). An interesting introduction is the Crown-of-thorns (*E. milii*). Common weeds, popularly called 'milkweed', are also species of *Euphorbia*. They are so called from the milky sap or latex that is stored in the bark and leaves of all these plants. Milkweed and certain other species of *Euphorbia* are used in folk MEDICINE.
[Adams 1971, 1972, Huxley 1978]

POND TURTLE
This Pond Turtle (*Pseudemys* or *Chrysemys terrapen*) occurs only in Jamaica though there are closely related species in other nearby CARIBBEAN islands. It is a terrapin or land

Pond Turtle

TURTLE and lives in swampy areas and along rivers and ponds; the name 'hicatee' (derived from the TAINO *hicato*) is still sometimes used for these fresh-water turtles.
[Schwartz and Henderson 1991]

PONE
A kind of pudding made with sweet POTATO, CASSAVA or cornmeal mixed with sugar, COCONUT, and spices – thus 'potato pone', 'cornmeal pone', etc. The pone is baked in a covered round iron pot (DUTCHIE) either in the oven or on top of a COAL STOVE with fire placed both underneath and on top. Coconut milk is sometimes poured over the pone before baking, so that the top will be custardy. The word is a Native American one but of long usage in Jamaica.

PORT ANTONIO
Capital of PORTLAND Parish, population 12,675 (1991). The town was described by the American poet Ella Wheeler Wilcox who vacationed there, as 'the most exquisite port on earth'. Port Antonio has twin harbours that are among the finest in the island, the western harbour protected by NAVY ISLAND. The harbours – Port Antonio (the eastern) and Port St Francis – were originally named by the Spaniards. The date of the transfer of the name of the eastern harbour to the region is uncertain but probably took place from common usage.

The town was not developed until it became the capital of Portland when that parish was formed in 1723. The town was first named TITCHFIELD, the second title of the Duke of Portland, used by his son. Navy Island was originally Lynch's Island. Up to the 1880s, Port Antonio was a sleepy coastal town. Then the BANANA TRADE began and it became a 'boom town', highly Americanized from the influx of employees of the American banana companies, and from the American tourists who came in the banana boats. The banana trade was once so large that at one time, it is claimed, weekly sailings from Port Antonio were greater than

Twin harbours of Port Antonio

weekly sailings from the great English port of Liverpool. At the height of the trade, 17 lines of steamers were operating from the port.

Tourists came on the banana boats and the international set arrived on their yachts. The old TITCHFIELD Hotel was their watering place and people like Rudyard Kipling, Randolph Hearst, Paul Whiteman (of jazz fame), Bette Davis, Ginger Rogers and Clara Bow were familiar in the town. J.P. Morgan Jr, reputedly the world's wealthiest man, would winter every season in his yacht *Corsair III* in the harbour. Errol Flynn sailed in one day and never wanted to leave, buying property in the area including Navy Island and Boston. But with the decline of the banana trade, Port Antonio also fell into decline and the illustrious visitors found other fashionable places. In recent years, Port Antonio has undergone a revival as a tourist resort.
[Brown 1976, Wright and White 1969]

PORT HENDERSON

Historic 18th century village community in ST CATHERINE Parish. The port was named after the original landowner, John Henderson (d 1811), a colonel in the MILITIA. It was once the port where passengers for SPANISH TOWN (then the capital) were landed, superseding PASSAGE FORT which had silted up. At that time, Port Henderson was a thriving community with warehouses, shops and storehouses. When a mineral spring was discovered, it rapidly became a fashionable spa and health resort. The spa no longer exists as the underground source of water has shifted owing to EARTHQUAKES.

Some of the buildings of Port Henderson are regarded as fine examples of Jamaican architecture of the 18th and 19th centuries and were restored by the JNHT. These include the 'Two Sisters', twin cottages that were used by vacationing families up to 1914; the 'Longhouse' which was once an inn; the chapel, and the old Water Police Station.

In the Port Henderson area are several interesting ruins, including 'Rodney's Lookout', an old signalling station on the west of Port Henderson that was named after Admiral George RODNEY who was once commander-in-chief of the Jamaican naval station and who had the lookout established. Nearby is 'Grasspiece Lookout', a cut-stone structure that was used as a platform from which work in the canefields below could be observed. On Port Henderson hill also are a number of TAINO sites.

PORT MARIA

The capital of ST MARY Parish, Port Maria (population 7,196 in 1991) was originally named by the Spaniards 'Puerto Santa Maria'. Port Maria was the location for TACKY'S rebellion, regarded as one of the most serious slave uprisings in Jamaica. (See SLAVERY.) In the early 20th century it became a busy BANANA LOADING port.

In the Victoria Gardens next to the churchyard can be seen a monument to Sir Charles Price, a wealthy 18th century planter and speaker of the House of Assembly. The monument was removed to this site in 1933 from 'The Decoy', Price's estate higher up in St Mary. Price's tomb is in the cathedral churchyard at SPANISH TOWN. Price was unusual among the wealthy men of his day in that he chose not to be an absentee proprietor but to live in Jamaica where he took over the family estates. The Price family were at one time the owners of WORTHY PARK estate.

Gray's Charity is an old people's home established in 1897 under the will of John William Gray, a Port Maria merchant who died in 1849.

PORT ROYAL

Historic city of the Americas. Now a fishing village, Port Royal is interesting for two main reasons. First, for its brief life as a rich merchant city and home port of pirates and BUCCANEERS who made it the 'wickedest city on earth' and its subsequent destruction by EARTHQUAKE in 1692. Second, for its importance as an English naval station for two and a half centuries.

Located at the tip of the PALISADOES peninsula that joins it to KINGSTON, Port Royal started out as a separate island, one of a string of CAYS. The SPANISH settlers named it Cayo de Carena (Careening Cay) after the use they found for it – to beach their ships and scrape barnacles from

Port Royal

the hulls. When the BRITISH captured Jamaica, they immediately saw the strategic importance of the cay, which they called Cagway or The Point. They built a fort and named it Fort Cromwell but as soon as the monarchy was restored, it was renamed FORT CHARLES after King Charles II.

The town that grew up around the fort became known as Port Royal. At this stage Port Royal was still an island, but the English settlers filled in the marshy swamps and joined it to the Palisadoes. After the great earthquake that destroyed the town in 1692, Port Royal again became an island – of less than 5ha. It has been joined and separated from the Palisadoes at various other times in the past – notably after HURRICANES in the 1700s and 1903.

In the early history of Jamaica as an English colony, Port Royal was by far the most important place in the island, as a rich merchant town grew up there. For a while the governor had his residence there, though SPANISH TOWN was the capital. When Port Royal was one of the most important cities in the New World, Kingston across the harbour was not even thought of: the site on which that city eventually grew was being used as a hog crawle.

In its heyday, it is estimated that Port Royal had about 6,500 inhabitants of whom perhaps 2,500 were slaves (see SLAVERY) and a significant number of the whites were indentured servants bound to their masters and mistresses for a period of 10 years. (See also 'PRINCESS OF PORT ROYAL', IRISH, SCOTS.) Some were shipped for criminal misdemeanours and some were political prisoners, for instance in 1685-86, some 355 convicted rebels from Monmouth's Rebellion were sent out; all were sold into bondage as soon as the ships arrived. They probably contributed to the large number of artisans at work, including the expected ones – COOPERS, carpenters and shoemakers – but also sail makers, gold and silver workers, tortoise-shell workers (see TURTLE), ivory-tuners, pewterers and pipe-makers (see JACKASS ROPE). According to Pawson and Buisseret, some of these craftsmen were 'producing work which competed with the best which could be imported'. Some of these locally manufactured artefacts have been recovered in archaeological explorations.

The houses of Port Royal became more elaborate as time went on, and the wealthier inhabitants were supplied with the very latest fashions from Europe in clothes and everything else. In 1687 a visitor observed that the merchants were living 'to the hight of splendor, in full ease and plenty, being sumptuously arrayed, and attended on and served by their Negroa slaves, which always waits on them in liverays, or otherwise as they please to cloath them'. The Port Royal merchants did not become 'creolized' as the planters later did, but transplanted their English way of life. Thus Pawson and Buisseret concluded that 'everyday life in Port Royal seems to have been very similar to what might have been observed in any English seaport of similar size . . . food, clothes, buildings, and recreations all obstinately followed English norms, however unsuitable these might be. Because of the restricted area of

THE EXPLANATION

A. The Houses falling.
B. The Churches.
C. The Sugar Works.
D. The Mills.
E. The Bridges in the whole Country.
F. The Rock and the Mountains.
G. Captain *Ruden's* House Sunk first into the Earth with his Wife and Family.
H. The Ground rolling under the Minister's *Feet*.
I. The great Church and Town Falling.
K. The Earth Opening and Swallowing Multitudes of People in *Morgan's* Fort.
L. The Minister Kneeling down in a ring with the People in the Street at Prayers.
M. The Wharf covered with the Sea.
N. D'. *Heath* going from Ship to Ship to visit the bruised people, and do his last Office to the dead Corpses that lay Floating from the Point.
O. Thieves Robbing and Breaking open both Dwelling Houses and Ware-Houses during the Earthquake.
P. Dr. *Trapham*, a Doctor of Physick, hanging by the hands on a Rack of the Chimney, and one of his children hanging about his Neck seeing his wife and the rest of his children a-Sinking.
Q. A boat coming to save them.
R. The Minister Preaching in a tent to the People.
S. The dead Bodies of some Hundreds floating about the Harbour.
T. The Sea washing the dead Carkasses out of their Graves and Tombs, and dashed to pieces by the Earthquake.
V. People swallowed up in the Earth, several as high as their Necks, with their Heads above Ground.
W. The Dogs eating of Dead Men's Heads.
X. Several Ships Cast away and driven into the very Town.
Y. A Woman and her two daughters beat to pieces one against the other.
Z. Mr. *Beckford* : His Diging out of the Ground.

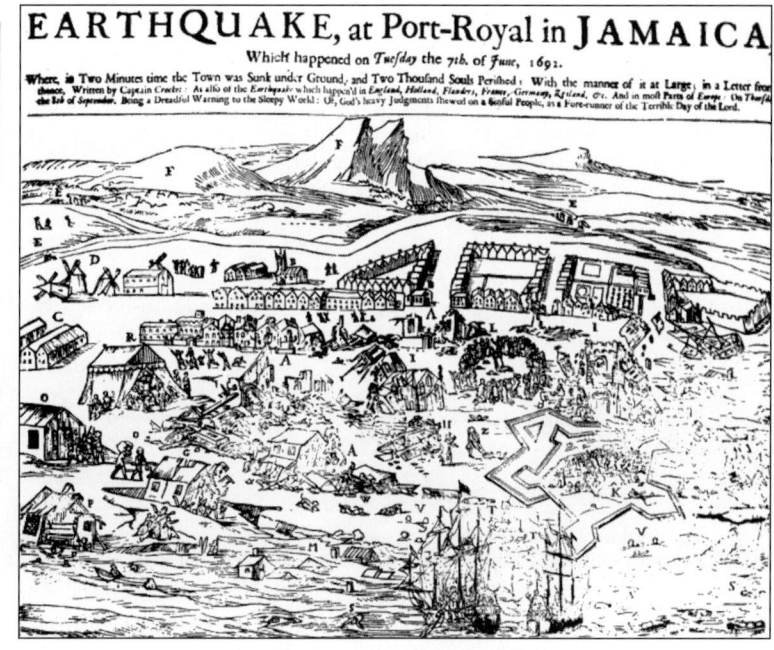

Broadsheet issued in England after the earthquake

the site, and the ever-increasing pressure of business, the concentration of people was probably greater than in any English town, except for parts of London'. More than 2,000 buildings came to be jammed together, some of them on pilings driven into the soft sand, many of several stories, factors contributing to the great devastation of the earthquake.

The town was well supplied with taverns, markets, prisons and forts. At the time of the earthquake, in addition to St Paul's Church (ANGLICAN), there was a PRESBYTERIAN church, a Quaker meeting house (see FRIENDS), a ROMAN CATHOLIC chapel and a Jewish synagogue (see JEWS), reflecting the cosmopolitan character of the early settlement. Port Royal was full of drinking places – in 1661 the Council issued 40 new licences for rum shops, taverns and punch houses. It had two prisons – the Marshallsea for men, and the Bridewell, a 'house of correction for lazie strumpets' – in addition to forms of public punishment common in the 17th century – stocks on the High Street, a cage for the 'strumpets' not jailed, a ducking-stool, a pillory, and a gallows.

The external defence of the city was also important – there were over 1,500 volunteers in the armed MILITIA in 1688. Port Royal was extremely well fortified, being ringed by six forts – Charles, James, Carlisle, Rupert, Walker and Morgan – with 145 guns. The guns seemed to have been fired more for warnings and celebrations than defence: arriving friendly ships as well as those of the enemy were announced by cannon fire and guns were set off to announce sales of black slaves and white bond servants as well as other public events. Gunners at Fort Charles got their practice in by firing at a cask set up on the islet that is now called Gun Cay. Public proclamations by the authorities were announced by the Town Crier who was preceded on his rounds by a drummer to attract attention.

'The Wicked Period' What brought the greatest wealth to Port Royal in the first place was its establishment as a base for the buccaneers from the 1650s. Licensed by the governor as a way of providing protection for the island, and called 'privateers' until they were officially criminalized in 1671, the buccaneers were encouraged to strike at England's traditional enemies, the Spaniards. They brought so much wealth into the port that soon everyone in the town was busily investing money to outfit expeditions – in return for a share of the booty. Though officially called something else, piracy was really the town's source of wealth and Henry MORGAN, their most famous leader, would retire as one of Port Royal's (and Jamaica's) leading citizens.

The buccaneer fleets would sail off to raid Spanish settlements or attack ships on the high seas, capturing massive fortunes in gold and silver, precious stones, silks, and spices. When the expedition returned to Port Royal, the whole town celebrated. As soon as the lookout at Fort Charles spotted the ships returning, a cannon salute would be fired and everyone dropped everything else to rush down to the waterside. Merchants would close their shops and the courts would sometimes stop in mid-session. As soon as the ships dropped anchor, the king's official would be the first person aboard to claim one-tenth of the booty. The rest of the takings would immediately be auctioned off to the highest bidders. Then everyone would flock to the taverns where the crews of the triumphant vessels would be quickly parted from their share of the booty – usually pieces-of-eight (see MONEY) – by women and drink.

Duels, drunkenness and 'all kinds of vices' were common. It was a case of easy come, easy go: men who were rich one day would lose everything at the gambling tables or the taverns in one night. The authorities had no control over the lawless buccaneers and they took over the town completely when they were in port. The townspeople welcomed them for they were big spenders. The buccaneers in turn loved the facilities for trade, sport, and amusement offered by the town, as well as the facilities for repairing their ships. But after 1671 and a treaty between England and Spain which ended that old enmity, the buccaneers were no longer welcome and those who continued their old way of life were outlawed as 'pirates' and were ruthlessly hunted and hanged. The island was by this time developing as a planting colony and the English saw the opportunity for much legitimate trade with their former Spanish enemies. Port Royal soon developed into a rich mercantile city in its own right, the clearing house for the slave trade with the Spanish Indies. But the 'wicked ways' continued and many prophesied that it would end in destruction. This period of Port Royal's history lasted for only three decades before earthquake and tidal waves destroyed most of the town.

Destruction by Earthquake The earthquake occurred at a few minutes to noon on Tuesday 7 June 1692. The third shock was followed by a huge tidal wave that wrecked ships in the harbour and flung one ship, The *Swan*, into the middle of the town. Like Noah's Ark, it came to rest on top of the ruined houses and over 200 persons climbed aboard it for shelter. Fewer than one-tenth of the buildings were left in the town and part of Port Royal sank forever beneath the sea. Over 2,000 people died as a result of the disaster. Many of the victims were swallowed by the earth that opened before them, one man was thrown up again and survived. (See GALDY.)

After the earthquake, the survivors went across the harbour and many eventually settled in the new town that was called Kingston. For a while settlement on Port Royal was forbidden, but the town refused to die and people continued to build there. The earthquake drove away many of the criminals and cut-throats who had infested Port Royal – they plundered the dead before fleeing the stricken town – and it became a quieter place. Despite repeated disasters, such as the great fire in 1703 and several hurricanes which devastated it, Port Royal continued for a long time to be a rich merchant town until it was eclipsed by Kingston.

The Sunken City Since the earthquake, the story of the 'sunken city' of Port Royal has fascinated people all over the world, and many legends still persist of fabulous treasure beneath the seas. Although archaeological work has been carried out in the area in recent years, unearthing many interesting and important relics in the process, a disappointing amount of 'treasure' has been found. It is believed that after the earthquake, valuables were carried away by looters.

The most recent attempts to explore the sunken city began in the 1950s. In 1954 Cornel Lumiere, a well-known producer of underwater

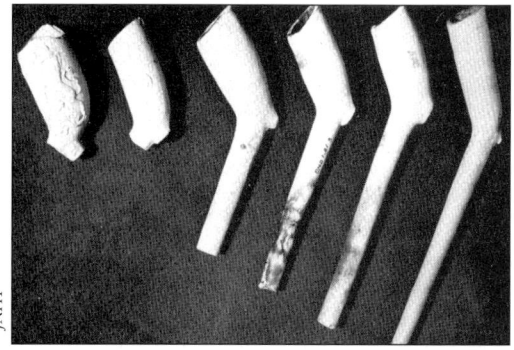

Artefacts recovered in archaeological excavations at Port Royal

Port Royal children

films, and Mr and Mrs Alexis DuPont, carried out a series of dives in the area but recovered very little. In 1956 the noted inventor and treasure-hunter Edwin Link also undertook underwater explorations at Port Royal. He returned in 1959 with a special vessel, the *Sea Diver*, which he had designed and built for the purpose. The expedition was under the sponsorship of the National Geographic Society, the Smithsonian Institution and the INSTITUTE OF JAMAICA. The Link Expedition located a number of buildings beneath the sea and brought up some artefacts. Since 1965 the government of Jamaica has been undertaking marine explorations at Port Royal. (See OLD NAVAL HOSPITAL.) Ongoing research work is also being undertaken by Texas A&M University, Port Royal being the only archaeological site of its type in the western hemisphere.

The Naval Period During the 18th and 19th centuries, Port Royal was Britain's naval base in the CARIBBEAN. The foundations of Fort Charles were laid in 1655 although the fort was several times rebuilt and enlarged. The other forts in the town were thrown into the sea by the earthquake. The ruins of Fort James and Fort Carlisle lie in deep water but that of Fort Rupert has been discovered in a lagoon.

When Fort Charles was built, two sides of the fort were washed by the sea. The inland side gradually silted up and today forms what is the Parade Ground (formerly used by the Police Training School that was located there up to 1982). In the 18th century when the maritime nations fought for supremacy in the Caribbean, Fort Charles became the headquarters of the Royal Navy in the area and carried a full complement of 104 guns. Probably because of its strength, the fort was never once attacked in its history. Despite lack of engagement from the enemy, the fort was never idle, for it was from here that the morning and evening guns and the ceremonial salutes were fired. In 1739, it was computed that over 7,718kg of powder were used in firing salutes. Many of the legendary admirals of British history were connected with Port Royal. (See BENBOW, NELSON, RODNEY, VERNON.)

David Buisseret notes that by the early 20th century, the focus of British sea power shifted with the development of a powerful fleet of steam warships based at dockyards in Britain and the Mediterranean. The chain of small dockyards (including Port Royal) serving the North Atlantic were shut down, only Halifax and Bermuda remaining. The naval dockyard at Port Royal was closed in 1905. The Port Royal defences were, however, maintained during both WORLD WARS.

From time to time there has been talk of devloping Port Royal as a heritage TOURISM site.
[Aarons, 1990, Black 1988, Buisseret 1971b, Marx 1967a,b, Pawson and Buisseret 1975]

PORTLAND, Parish of

Area: 814.0km^2, population 79,000 in 1997. North-eastern parish extending from the coast to the highest reaches of the BLUE MOUNTAINS, having a lush, green appearance from relatively high rainfall throughout the year.

The parish was named after the Duke of Portland who was governor when it was formed in 1723 by combining the original parish of St George with a part of eastern ST THOMAS and a part of ST MARY. Great efforts were made to encourage settlers in this difficult and mountainous terrain that provided a natural refuge to escaping slaves and was a stronghold of the MAROONS. Laws were passed offering inducements to anyone who came to settle including attractive land grants and freedom from land tax for seven years. The Receiver General was authorized to provide two barrels of beef and one of flour to be delivered without charge to each person settling so that he could feed himself until he had planted and reaped his own crops.

Eventually many prosperous SUGAR PLANTATIONS were developed near the coast and the parish experienced a later period of prosperity during the banana boom (see BANANA LOADING, BANANA TRADE) which also contributed to the development of the capital of PORT

ANTONIO as one of Jamaica's first tourist resorts. (See TOURISM.) Today Portland remains mainly an agricultural parish and a low-key tourist destination, with one of the island's popular attractions, rafting on the RIO GRANDE, and an annual Blue Marlin FISHING tournament.

PORTLAND POINT LIGHTHOUSE

Situated on the summit of Portland Ridge, CLARENDON Parish, near the southernmost part of the island, the tower is an open framed steel structure 40m high. It has a white revolving light, giving two flashes in quick succession every 15 seconds.

PORTUGUESE

A few hundred Portuguese were among the immigrants brought to Jamaica as part of a scheme to acquire white labour and establish white settlers in the highlands in the post-EMANCIPATION period. Jamaica was competing with the other British West Indian SUGAR islands for immigrants, and a bounty was offered from public funds and an agent sent to Europe to recruit settlers. About 4,000 BRITISH, GERMANS and Portuguese arrived in the four year period 1834-38 (See also IRISH, SCOTS) but the schemes were a failure with high sickness and mortality rates among the immigrants. Often the survivors deserted the country parts for the towns where many died, 'assisted by the climate and the abundance of rum'. More success was obtained with indentured AFRICAN, CHINESE and INDIAN workers.

Little is known about the Portuguese who came, except that most were from the Portuguese Atlantic island of Madeira and a smaller number from the Azores and the mainland. Many of the early immigrants seem to have died, and another set came from Madeira in 1846 at a time of serious famine there. They were all hired by large estate owners in the western parishes, including Howard de Walden who brought in some Portuguese for MONTPELIER; there were 47 there in 1847, and like the other immigrants they were put to work as field labourers, planting and cutting sugar cane.

A significant employer of these immigrant workers was Charles Moulton-Barrett, then head of the BARRETT family in Jamaica, who owned Retreat in ST ANN Parish, and Cinnamon Hill and Oxford estates. Converted to the ROMAN CATHOLIC faith, he facilitated the missionary activities of that church, Retreat becoming the headquarters of the Jesuit missionary, and the Portuguese workers on Barrett's estates forming the earliest Catholic congregations in the western part of the island. We have some idea of the distribution of the Portuguese from the records left by the missionary priest: In 1866, in TRELAWNY Parish, there were 130 Catholics, mostly Portuguese, located at Oxford and George's Valley estates. In ST JAMES, Portuguese at Cinnamon Hill and Content constituted most of the 95 Catholics in that parish. In HANOVER, most of the 135 parishioners, living in the capital of LUCEA and on the three sugar estates of New Milns, Chester Castle and TRYALL, were Portuguese.

Of course the Portuguese had a much longer association with Jamaica, Portuguese JEWS being among the earliest SPANISH settlers. With the joining of Portugal to the Spanish Crown in 1580, other Portuguese Jewish families emigrated to Jamaica, forming the nucleus of a long line of settlers.

[Higman 1998, Laurence 1971, Osborne 1988]

PORUS

Village in MANCHESTER Parish, stretched out along the main MAY PEN to MANDEVILLE highway, clearly identified by the array of fruits, especially CITRUS, skilfully hung and invitingly arranged for sale along both sides of the road. The name Porus dates back to Spanish times and is probably derived from the family name Porras.

During the early years of English settlement, Porus represented the outer limits, for the land in the mountains beyond it had not been explored. In later years, Porus was developed as a CATTLE estate. After EMANCIPATION of the slaves, the land of the estates in the area was sub-divided and Porus became a village of small settlers. (See FREE VILLAGE.)

Porus was the location of one of the first two community centres to be established in Jamaica

Porus fruit stand

(1939) under the pioneering social welfare scheme, JAMAICA WELFARE.

POSTAL SERVICE

Jamaica was the first English colony to establish a post office with the appointment in 1671 of a postmaster, Gabriel Martin, who set up two post offices, one situated at St Jago (SPANISH TOWN), then the capital, and the other at the port of PASSAGE FORT. However the service seems to have proven unsatisfactory at some stage, for there are records of several efforts being made by the authorities over the next few decades to establish a proper service. One such attempt was the appointment in 1687 of James Wale (or Wales), 'Merchant Adventurer of London', to be postmaster for the island. But Wale was accused by the merchants of PORT ROYAL of profiteering (charging 7½d current money for every letter) and the merchants and planters went back to relying on sea captains to carry their mail to and from the island.

Since the island was well served with ports all around the coast, sending letters externally was much easier than internally since there seems to have been no internal postal system outside of the capital. Sending letters abroad was hazardous and became even more so by the mid-18th century as Jamaica grew into a wealthy sugar colony. As well as the risk of natural hazards such as storms, ships ran the risk of capture by enemy ships and pirates, so important letters would be duplicated many times and sent by different ships in the hope that one would get through.

There was no internal system until the 1750s when Edward Dismore was sent out from Britain as postmaster general to organize the service. He established a network of 5 mail routes and 42 post offices around the islands. But this was still 'snail mail' for up to the 19th century there were only five post roads along the main highways. On three of these roads, the mail was conveyed by pack mule, often through swollen rivers, landslides, and other hazards. Still these posts were probably better served than the other two where the mail was carried the entire distance by three slaves on foot. These were the routes from KINGSTON to PORT MARIA via Highgate (67km) and Kingston to MANCHIONEAL (102km). The carriers were instructed not to linger or loiter on their journey and the postmasters had the power to bring them before the local magistrates in case of negligence.

The postal service was reorganized in 1859 when responsibility for postal affairs was transferred from Britain to the local legislature. The developments were largely based on the report submitted by Anthony Trollope sent out by the British Post Office – before he become a famous novelist. (He wrote a book of his travels called *The West Indies and the Spanish Main* – 1860.)

Post Offices   Currently there are 313 post offices in Jamaica and 379 postal agencies.

Telegraph Service   The government's Inland Postal Telegraph system was inaugurated in 1879 and involved 1755km of lines and 47 offices.

Air Mail   This service was inaugurated in December 1930. (See AVIATION.)

Parcels Post   Jamaica was the first country with which the United States established a parcels post service. The service was inaugurated on 1 October 1887 and parcels cost 12 American cents (or sixpence) per pound plus a charge for internal service and delivery.

The first parcel sent from Jamaica was addressed to Mrs Cleveland, wife of the United States president, and contained a gift from the Women's Self-Help Society of Kingston.

Postage Stamps   In 1858 the postage stamp was first used in Jamaica, 18 years after Rowland Hill invented them for use in Britain. Before that time, the recipient, not the sender, had to pay the postal charges when the letter was delivered. At first the island used British stamps but from 1860 Jamaica issued its own adhesive postage stamps, bearing a PINEAPPLE water mark in the paper; the stamps were produced by De La Rue and Company in England. All issues portrayed the head of Queen Victoria wearing a laurel wreath, until 1900 when Jamaica issued its first real pictorial stamp – a view of Llandovery Falls based on a photograph by Dr James Johnston. (See BROWN'S TOWN.) The stamp was regarded as unattractive and proved unpopular. Jamaica's first real pictorial stamps were issued in 1919-21 and depicted aspects of the island's history.

The most valuable stamp with collectors is a one-shilling showing the statue of Queen Victoria, one sheet of which was printed with the frame inverted so the Queen appears to be standing on her head. According to John Ingledew, in 1990 two copies were auctioned by Sotheby's and fetched over £13,000 each; the whereabouts of 18 of the sheet of 60 are known, so 42 are still unaccounted for.

[Hopwood 1971, Ingledew 1990, Johnson 1964]

POTATO

In Jamaica, the white potato (*Solanum tuberosum*) is called 'Irish potato' or in the markets simply 'Irish' to distinguish it from 'Sweet potato' (*Ipomoea batatas*) which is called 'yam' in North America. The usage 'Irish potato' was for a long time regarded as a mark of the colonial, an anecdote from 1793 showing how West Indian planters trying to pass for Englishmen in England were unmasked when they asked for 'Irish potatoes'. 'They are English potatoes', retorted the landlord, 'pray gentlemen are you not CREOLES?'

The sweet potato tuber is actually a large swollen root while Irish potato tubers grow underground from the plant stem. The flesh of the sweet potato varies in colour, texture and sweetness, but all have a reddish skin. The plant is rich in carbohydrates and is eaten baked, boiled, and made into confections and puddings. It is popular with small farmers because of its quick yield, resistance to drought, and tolerance of poor soils.

The Irish potato is grown mainly in the cool hills of MANCHESTER and other central parishes while sweet potato is cultivated all over the island as a popular root crop. It was grown by the TAINOS in their *conucos*. They had two different species, the sugary ones called *batatas* and those that were not so sweet, called *ajes*. LAS CASAS noted that the tops were eaten like greens; today the leafy green parts of the vigorous climbing vine are a favourite food for animals, especially PIGS.

Sweet potato

Like the sweet, the Irish potato is a New World crop, originating in the Peruvian highlands thousands of years ago. The native peoples of the Andes had developed an enormous number of varieties by the time the Europeans arrived, and it was the principal food of the Incas. It was taken to Europe around 1570 but was not developed as a food crop for a very long time. It was in Ireland that the plant first found the right conditions for its development.

'Irish' potato

Within a hundred years of its arrival in the late 16th century (brought by fishermen from Spain), it was widely cultivated and soon became the country's chief food, resulting in the Great Famine of 1845-46 after a blight caused the crops to fail.

The Irish potato was introduced to North America by SCOTS-IRISH immigrants arriving from Europe in 1718. It is probably from this source that it arrived in Jamaica.

Over time, the Irish potato became widely cultivated throughout the world and is today one of the leading food crops.

[Bourne et al.1988, Crosby 1972, DJE, Huxley 1991, Sauer 1966, Viola and Margolis 1991]

POTTERY see ART, MONKEY JAR, YABBA

POUI (*Tabebuia*)

Called Pink Poui or Yellow Poui from the brilliant colours of its blooms, poui is cultivated as a beautiful garden ornamental, especially in KINGSTON. In other countries, poui is known as a valuable timber tree, yielding strong and beautiful wood. Pink Poui (*T. rosea*) is also used in some countries as a shade tree for crops such as COFFEE and COCOA. It will grow up to 20m and bears clusters of pink trumpet-shaped flowers with crepe-like petals, followed by a cylindrical fruit pod bearing papery seeds. Like the Yellow Poui (*T. serratifolia*), it blooms erratically April-May and achieves its most spectacular flowering after it has shed its leaves. The plants are native to tropical America; one species of *Tabebuia* is endemic to Jamaica.
[Adams 1972]

PRESBYTERIAN

Now a part of the UNITED CHURCH, the Presbyterian is one of the oldest denominations in Jamaica. A Protestant church governed by presbyters or lay elders and adhering to varying modified forms of Calvinism, the church had its beginnings in the preaching of John Knox in Scotland. In 1688 the Church of Scotland became the Established Presbyterian Church of Scotland but there were many breakaway groups, brought by the SCOTS to the different countries to which they emigrated.

A Presbyterian meeting house is recorded at PORT ROYAL before the EARTHQUAKE of 1692, but little is known about this congregation or any other until 1800 when the Established Church of Scotland despatched three MISSIONARIES to commence work in Jamaica. Two of them – the Revd James Bethune and the Revd William

Clarke – died of fever within three weeks of arrival. The third, Ebenezer Reid, a teacher, survived but the opposition to his work was so intense that he joined the staff of WOLMER'S Boys School where he taught for many years.

In 1813, the many Scots residing in KINGSTON began a drive to build a church and the island's first Presbyterian church was opened on 4 April 1819 as the SCOTS' KIRK, later to become St Andrew's Scots Kirk. Because this church was a local effort and not attached to any Mission Board abroad, the congregation asked the Church of Scotland to send a minister and the Revd John Brown arrived.

In 1824 two Scottish planters in the west, Archibald Sterling and William Stothert, requested the Missionary Society of the Church of Scotland to send someone to minister to their slaves, and the Revd George Blyth arrived, later joined by five more missionaries. Churches were built at Sterling's Hampden estate (which straddles ST JAMES and TRELAWNY Parishes) in 1828, at FALMOUTH (1832), Mt Zion (1838) and the MAROON town of ACCOMPONG. Sterling also welcomed a Presbyterian minister to his estate at Frontier in ST MARY, the present church at Port Maria dating from this effort, around 1830. All of these churches are now part of the United Church.

Blyth and the other missionaries were all linked to the Edinburgh Presbytery of the United Session Church and not the Church of Scotland. This led to two Presbyterian groups working in Jamaica: Scots Kirk and its satellite congregations in Retirement and Giddy Hall (ST ELIZABETH Parish) and Medina (MANCHESTER Parish) and the other group working in western, northern, and southern parishes.

Bisnauth has observed that 'It can be safely assumed that the doctrines taught by the Scottish missionaries were Presbyterian in nature. But the congregations which developed in Jamaica as a result of the Presbyterian missionary outreach were not organized along Presbyterian lines until after 1836. That year, ruling elders were elected and ordained for the first time in Jamaica. On 10 February 1836, the first local Presbytery was constituted in Montego Bay'. In 1931 the groups united to become the Presbyterian Church of Jamaica.

The Presbyterian church played a leading role in the post-EMANCIPATION era especially in the area of education among INDIAN indentured workers.

[Bisnauth 1989, Thomas 1999, 1999a, Wright and White 1969]

'PRINCESS OF PORT ROYAL'

Among the notorious residents of PORT ROYAL during the time of the BUCCANEERS was a woman named Mary Carleton who styled herself 'The German Princess'. Her career in crime and imposture began in London at an early age. In 1663 she married one John Carleton and was soon tried for bigamy but was acquitted 'by public proclamation'. She took to the stage and had a play, *The German Princess*, specially written for her. Soon she was arrested for theft, tried and found guilty and sentenced to be transported to Jamaica in 1671. Unrepentant, she published in the same year her famous 'News from Jamaica in a letter from Port Royal to her famous collegiates and friends at Newgate' – Newgate being the English prison. She shortly afterwards returned to London and resumed her old way of life but was eventually executed at Tyburn in 1673.

Mary Carleton

[Black 1988]

PRISON see FORT AUGUSTA, PENITENTIARY, ST CATHERINE DISTRICT PRISON

PROVERB

Proverbs are brief, didactic statements that in Jamaica, as in other parts of the world, form an important element in the oral culture. They are still widely used, though probably much less than formerly, and appear in many African-derived folktales. Sometimes the ending of the tale is in the form of a proverb, or proverbs are quoted by the characters.

Proverbs give spice to everyday conversation but also serve an educational and social function, assisting children to learn the norms of the society for, after all, 'What you don't know older than you'. Proverbs can also be used to influence the behaviour of others, suggesting a course of action or passing judgement through criticism, ridicule, warning, derision or defiance. 'You sleep with dog, you rise with flea' warns about choosing one's companions wisely. 'One finger can't catch louse' affirms the value of cooperation. 'Fowl scratch up too much dirt, him find him granny skeleton' suggests one should let sleeping dogs lie. 'If you want good, yu nose have fe run' reminds that success comes from effort.

Some proverbs are simply sayings or statements of fact, enshrined in school and Sunday school as MEMORY GEMS, e.g. 'Honesty is the best policy'. The language is often metaphorical: 'Don't cut off your nose to spite your face.'

Although many of Jamaica's proverbs show parallels with those of the two main cultures from which they originated – the West African and the European – some are purely Jamaican in origin. Proverbs reflect the wit and wisdom of the folk as well as the colour and vitality of 'Jamaica Talk'.

While proverbs and sayings are not as common in everyday speech as they once were, the wisdom of 'Grannie' continues to be deeply inscribed in the memories of successive generations, appearing frequently in the new forms of popular culture, especially in MUSIC. Countless REGGAE songs over the past few decades that employ old-time sayings bear this out. For instance, 'Mawga Dog', ('Sorry fe Mawga dog, mawga dog turn roun' bite you'), 'Nanny Goat' by Larry and Alvin 1968 ('What sweet Nanny Goat a go run her belly'), 'Everything Crash' by the Ethiopians 1968 ('What gone bad a morning can't come good a evening').
[Anderson and Cundall 1910, Beckwith 1924, Morris-Brown 1993, Watson 1991]

PROVISION GROUND

The 'provision ground' which is still the province of the small farmer today (see AGRICULTURE, GROUND), originated as the small plot of land assigned by the estate owner to each slave, who was expected to grow his or her own food. (See SLAVERY.)

When the SUGAR PLANTATIONS were first established, special areas were cultivated to feed the slaves. But the responsibility was more and more transferred by the masters to the slaves themselves, and the provision ground system was well developed by the end of the 17th century. However, not all slaves were taken care of by the system and some starved, 'scuffled', or lived by stealing. The slaves' plots were also subject to natural and other disasters like the rest of the plantations. In the years 1780-88, some 16,000 slaves died from a combination of many disasters besetting the island and creating extreme food scarcity – drought, and a series of HURRICANES, as well as the American War of Independence which affected imports.

At first, slaves had Saturday afternoons, and Sundays, and CHRISTMAS and EASTER holidays to work in their grounds, but as the prosperity from SUGAR increased, so did the demands of the industry and the slave's only time for personal cultivation was limited to Sunday. Later, alternate Saturdays, out of crop, were added.

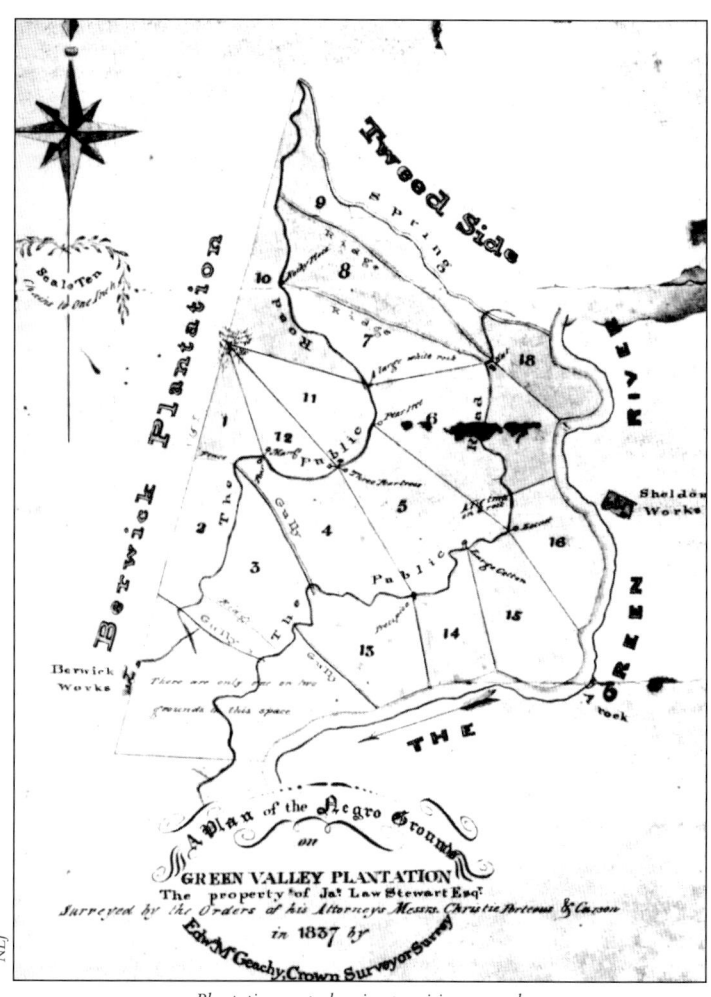

Plantation map showing provision grounds

Some went to work in their fields during the lunch break from plantation labour, others, at night. During croptime when all hands were required to quickly reap and grind the cane, and labour continued around the clock, there was little time for the ground. (See SEASONS.)

Despite these difficulties, by the mid-18th century many of the slaves were not only providing for themselves but were selling their surpluses at the Sunday MARKETS. Edward Long (1774) estimated that the slaves controlled 20 per cent of the cash circulating in the island.

Some slaves also kept small stock, although there were laws prohibiting this practice. By the 19th century they were described as owning cows, and provided much of the island's poultry and livestock. (See CATTLE, GOATS, PIGS.) Fowls roosted in trees about the huts, and chickens were hung up in baskets to protect them from rats. Pigs were allowed to roam at night and feed on the master's property – to be recalled home with a special whistle. Sometimes cows were owned collectively by several slaves; they were allowed pasturage on the master's property in the expectation that they would be sold to him at below market price.

The 'grounds' were originally called polincos or polinks (transferred from the Spanish-American word for stockade – *palenque*) and located on the backlands. The size of the plot varied, with an average of .8ha per slave. The 'ground' was cleared by fire (even after a law of 1807 which outlawed the practice) and worked with the assistance of friends and close relatives. Couples living together usually united their grounds and even small children helped. Root crops such as YAM and COCO as well as PUMPKIN, PLANTAIN, and ACKEE were staples of the provision ground, similar to the plot of a small farmer today. As is the case today, there was a separate kitchen garden around the dwelling where OKRA, CALALU, vegetables, culinary and medicinal herbs, COCONUT, CALABASH, ORANGE, shaddock, PEPPER, and 'abbeh' or oil PALM might be planted.

It is believed that the skills in agriculture and marketing that the Jamaican slaves developed through the provision ground system and the money they earned were invaluable in contributing to the development of rural life in the post-EMANCIPATION years. (See FREE VILLAGE.) Comparing their situation to that of the North American slaves, Genovese notes that 'The palinkas and related Sunday markets transformed the slaves into part-time peasants and petty traders. When emancipated, they had already acquired the habits, experience, and talents of an independent peasantry and petty bourgeoisie . . . The slaves of the Old South did not have an equivalent. The other side of the slaveholders' boast that their slaves were well fed was that they did not, anywhere near to the extent of the Jamaican slaves, learn to take care of themselves in a world of production for market'.

[Genovese 1976, Mintz 1985, Mintz and Hall 1960, Patterson 1973]

PUMPKIN (*Cucurbita*)

The West Indian Pumpkin or Calabaza is a member of the gourd family that includes Cucumber, CERASEE, CHOCHO, WATERMELON and ANTIDOTE CACOON. Originating in Central America, pumpkin was cultivated in the islands before the arrival of COLUMBUS. The bright orange-coloured flesh is much thicker and denser than pumpkins of temperate climates that are of

Pumpkin

a different family. In the market, pumpkin is often cut up and sold in pieces. It is a favourite vegetable, forming the base of a rich soup, boiled or baked as a side dish, and used in pies. In addition to the pulp, the leaves, fruits, flowers, and seeds are used in folk MEDICINE, the seeds being thought good for expelling worms.

Its rounded shape and growth habit have imbued pumpkin with a mystical quality exemplified in the saying 'where water walk go a pumpkin belly'. This is symbolic of a deep mystery, since the water gets to the pumpkin via the stem, an enormously twisted vine that spreads over the ground in convoluted fashion, making it difficult to unravel. The phrase is often used when threatening children with the most dire punishment that will leave a lasting impression – 'You will find out where water walk go a pumpkin belly'! 'Pumpkin vine' is also used to symbolize complex family connections.

Certain planting rituals surround pumpkin. Old time farmers would sit quietly after planting pumpkin seeds so the vine wouldn't run around too much but would settle down and bear. It is believed that a pregnant woman walking all over a pumpkin patch will encourage bearing. Also, one should not point at pumpkin blossoms or the young fruit will drop off. When transporting pumpkin, a small nick should be cut in it or the vehicle will get a flat tire.

[Adams 1972, Asprey and Thornton 1953-55, Beckwith 1928, Robertson 1990]

PUSS-BOOTS

Former name for rubber-soled, laced-up canvas shoes in which one could walk softly as a cat, early version of what the Americans called 'sneakers' and the English 'plimsolls'. These were the shoes required for high school gym classes and games (called by the elite 'tennis shoes') and as such they had to be cleaned a gleaming white before each school appearance. For poor children, these were often their only shoes, and aside from 'puss boots', they were given many other names such as 'crepe soles', 'crepe', 'buggas', and 'rubbers'.

Q

QUACO
The Twi DAY NAME for a boy born on Wednesday; like other African names, used nowadays in an insulting or derisive sense to denote an ignorant or stupid person. 'If you can't catch Quaco, yu catch him shirt' is a PROVERB. J.J. Williams, a Jesuit priest who lived in Jamaica and wrote several books on Jamaican culture, noted that in his time, Quaco was a common nickname, 'not relished by the recipient'. He suggested that the Jamaican use of Quaco from the Twi *Kwaku* may have been originally a play on words with reference to the Ashanti *kwa* which means worthless. (See also QUASHIE.)
[DJE, Williams 1934]

QUACO BUSH see GUACO BUSH

QUACO POINT
Located on the ST THOMAS coast, this place name celebrates an African leader of a MAROON band in the area (see also QUAW HILL).

QUADRILLE
A European DANCE that acquired African-Jamaican elements soon after its introduction into the island in the early 19th century. It is still danced today by enthusiasts, though like many traditions, it is a dying art. Public performances of Jamaican quadrille are most often seen nowadays as part of Festival. (See FESTIVAL, Jamaica.) In the past, anyone (white or black) who aspired to be in society learnt the complicated movements of this dance that is done by couples in a group. The etiquette instilled by quadrille dancing (which begins with bows and curtseys all round) was not lost on older heads who cautioned the younger, 'Howdy and tenky nuh bruck no square' – suggesting that politeness facilitates the dance (of life).

Quadrille began as a popular dance of the European aristocracy, originating in France at the end of the 18th century and spreading throughout Europe and to the colonies. In the colonies it was first danced by the gentry but was soon taken up by the Africans who added their own distinctive touches. Jamaican Quadrille has up to eight set figures, each with its distinct movement and music, though European country dances such as Schottische, Mazurka, Polka, Valse etc. which vary according to the region in Jamaica, might also be included. Typically Jamaican is the 5th figure that is danced to MENTO music.

Quadrille as danced today has been handed down from generation to generation and varies in detail of style from one locality to the next. The quadrille is a set dance with two basic variations, the ballroom style and the camp style. The ballroom style is more formal and elegant,

Quadrille dancers, Festival 1965

closer to the European, with dress to match. The camp style is rustic and lively with couples standing in two lines instead of a square and adding their own uninhibited footwork. It shares some elements with the 'square dance' of North America that also originated from the European quadrille. The band accompanying a quadrille group usually consists of a violin, fiddle, and fife, and sometimes trumpet, though other instruments such as RUMBA BOX, drums, banjos, are also used.

Olive Lewin has suggested that while there is enthusiasm among young people to dance Quadrille (an enthusiasm fostered by Festival), the disappearance of the village band is a seriously inhibiting factor: 'Taped and mechanical music just cannot motivate dancers or generate the excitement stimulated by the human interchange between musician and dancer.'
[Baxter 1970, Lewin 2000, Ryman 1980]

QUASHIE

An African DAY NAME from the Twi *Kwesi* (male born on a Sunday) which, like the others, acquired derogatory overtones. (See also QUACO.) J.J. Williams claimed that quashie was a generic term for the black man as backra was for the white. But centuries before, at the time of Edward Long (1774) quashie was being used to refer to a country bumpkin or someone stupid. Sociologist Orlando Patterson uses the term 'quashie mentality' to describe a grovelling, subservient type of person produced by the system of SLAVERY. 'Quashiba', the female version, was formerly used to describe a woman considered foolish or stupid, but also referred to the black or COLOURED mistress of a white man. As the planter Moreton (1793) claimed:

> When pepper-pot and wine his blood alarms,
> He takes a quashiba into his arms.

With the growing interest in the African heritage since the 1960s, some parents now proudly choose to give their children these names. In some other CARIBBEAN islands, African Day Names such as Quashie and Cuffy are well-known family names.
[DCEU, Patterson 1973, Williams 1934]

QUASSIA, Jamaica (*Picrasma excelsa*)

Jamaican bitterwood, the source of quassia chips of commerce. Up to the Second WORLD WAR, small quantities were shipped to Europe for use in the beer industry, as a substitute for hops in brewing 'bitter' beer. The wood has also been exported for use in the manufacture of insecticides. Quassia contains a bitter principle that has medicinal properties and has been much used in Jamaica in the past as a TONIC and for making a drinking cup ('bitter cup') which transferred the medicinal property of the wood to water which was left in it overnight. Several other species of trees are also called 'Bitterwood' and have similar properties. The Jamaica Quassia was so called after the discovery that it had the same properties as the Quassia tree of Surinam.

The name Quassia was originally given to a small tree found in northern South America, *Quassia amara*, after an African healer who first used it in treatments. According to the *Dictionary of Phrase and Fable*, the plant was named after 'Quassi . . . who in 1730 was the first to make its medicinal properties known' and, quoting Lindley and Moore, *Treatise of Botany*: 'Linnaeus applied this name to a tree of Surinam in honour of a Negro, Quassi . . . who employed its bark as a remedy for fever.' The English soldier Capt Stedman who wrote of his experiences in Surinam, spoke of Quassi in his book, calling him 'Gramman Quacy'. He said Quassi was a slave from Guinea who had been given his freedom and practised as a famous 'lokoman', selling 'obias' to the black population, including those which made soldiers invulnerable. Stedman, while obviously disapproving, wrote that by the blacks he was 'adored and respected like a God' hence his honorific 'Great-man'. He records Quassi's discovery of the valuable root and its naming by the Swedish naturalist to whom it was made known in 1761.

Quassia, like QUASHIE, is a corruption of *Kwesi*, an Akan (Twi) DAY NAME.
[NHSJ 1949, Stedman 1796]

QUATTIE see MONEY

QUAW HILL

Place in ST THOMAS Parish that commemorates the name of the MAROON chief QUAO who was leader of the eastern Maroons and established a settlement in this area. *Quao* is the African DAY NAME for a boy born on Thursday.

QUEEN'S COLLEGE

Jamaica's first university, established by the government in 1873, was called Queen's College. It was located at the OLD KING'S HOUSE, SPANISH TOWN. The previous year, the seat of government had been transferred from Spanish Town to KINGSTON, and the expectations for the college were obviously very high. By Law 25 of 1873 the Public Square in Spanish Town, with the public buildings and public lands surrounding it, were reserved exclusively for the college. A principal, Mr William Chadwick, and a tutor, Mr Grant Allen, both Oxford educated, were appointed.

Queen's College was one of the projects of the reforming governor Sir John Peter Grant who administered Jamaica as a Crown Colony after the MORANT BAY REBELLION. But while Grant contributed a great deal to the development of the island's educational system, this idea was perhaps too far ahead of its time. The college was a dismal failure from the start – when it opened 22 September, only three students were enrolled – and it lasted for only one academic year. Over time, a number of tertiary institutions were successfully established, but Jamaica had to wait another 75 years for a university. (See UNIVERSITY OF THE WEST INDIES.)

The Canadian-born Queen's College tutor, Grant Allen, went on to achieve fame as an author and novelist. One of his novels, *In All Shades*, was set in Jamaica (disguised as Trinidad) and was popular in the early decades of the 20th century.
[Marsala 1972]

QUEEN'S HIGHWAY
Northcoast stretch of highway from Bengal Bridge over the RIO BUENO to DISCOVERY BAY, which was opened by HM Queen Elizabeth II on 25 November 1953. Bengal Bridge was built in 1789 by a Scottish contractor and marks the boundary between the Parishes of TRELAWNY and ST ANN.

QUICK-STICK (*Gliricidia sepium*)
Plant used to make a live fence, so called because a branch will quickly sprout if stuck into the ground. Also called 'Growing Stake'. Different species of plants are used, but *Gliricidia* is the most popular. A native of tropical America, *Gliricidia* grows up to 6m high and is common from sea level to 800m. From January to April it bears pendant clusters of pink pea-like flowers.
[Adams 1972]

R

RACKHAM, Jack, 'Calico Jack'
Notorious pirate who haunted Jamaican waters in the early 18th century. Rackham's name will linger in history because after his capture it was discovered that two of his most bloodthirsty crew were women disguised as men – Anne Bonny and Mary Read (see PIRATES, Women). Rackham was actually captured while enjoying a RUM punch party at NEGRIL in November 1720. He was tried in SPANISH TOWN and executed at Gallows Point off the PALISADOES. His body was then squeezed into an iron frame and hung up on the sandy islet that still bears his name – Rackham Cay. Rackham supposedly got his nickname from his preference for calico clothes.

RAFTING see MARTHA BRAE, RIO GRANDE

RAILWAY

For nearly 150 years, rail travel was a significant part of Jamaica's transportation system. Regular train service began in 1845 and ceased in 1992 when the government-owned railway was shut down. Although there has been talk of reviving it, at the time of writing the only lines in use were the Ewarton and Kirkvine lines, by arrangement with the BAUXITE company Windalco.

The first steam engine

In 1845, the Jamaica railway became the first line outside of Europe and North America to be opened to traffic. The line at first ran from KINGSTON to SPANISH TOWN, a distance of 22.5km, most of it through swamps. (See FERRY.) Top speed of the train was 48kph.

In those pioneering days, farmers objected to the coming of the railway on the grounds that they would be deprived of their supplies of manure, a by-product that was supplied by the

Kingston station

pack mules and HORSES that would be replaced by the 'iron horse'. Indeed, the main means of transportation in the island before the coming of the railway was by carriage or horse and buggy, and livery stables which supplied both did a roaring business, as did lodging house keepers.

Although rail travel might have been more comfortable than road travel then, it too had its hazards. A visitor in the 1870s – when the line had been extended to Old Harbour, ST CATHERINE Parish – complained bitterly of the danger from sparks flying into his carriage. The train took 2 hours to travel the 37km from Kingston to Old Harbour, stopping frequently to avoid cows on the tracks and to take on water for the steam engine. The introduction of diesel engines in the 20th century made the trains speedier and cleaner.

The railway was started by English brothers William and David Smith. It was bought by the government in 1879 and the line was extended to Ewarton, St Catherine Parish. In 1890 the railway was sold to another private company, the West Indian Improvement Company, which laid the line over the mountains to MONTEGO BAY (182km from Kingston) in 1894 and PORT ANTONIO (121km from Kingston) in 1896. By then the company had run out of money and the government again took over the railway, running lines into the interior from MAY PEN to Frankfield (CLARENDON Parish) and LINSTEAD to New Works (St Catherine Parish). This service was important in opening up the interior – the coastal areas were served by coastal steamers and other vessels.

The railway expansion coincided with the BANANA boom and gave access to new areas for banana cultivation as it created freight. It became known as the 'Banana Railway' as the fruit destined for export consisted of 75 per cent of the total tonnage handled per annum. The saying 'bananas are the First Class passengers' seems justified from the complaints that the trains would always stop and pick up wagons of bananas regardless of passenger inconvenience. In 1937 the railway carried some 60 per cent of the island's maximum output of 27,000,000 stems of bananas. But the Second WORLD WAR which broke out shortly afterwards severely curtailed production as fruit could not be shipped to England, and it never regained such heights. The railway, however, benefited from the development of bauxite freight in the post-war years.

The railway eventually had 330km of track, much of it through difficult mountain terrain (up to 510m) and a large number of tunnels had to be made. The longest is the Gibraltar Tunnel outside Bog Walk that runs for 668m.

For several generations, the rail service was a significant element in travel between the rural parishes and Kingston and other towns, and children who used the train to travel back and forth between country homes and schools in the towns knew the names of the stations like a litany . . . Balaclava . . . Maggotty . . . Ipswich . . . Stonehenge . . . Catadupa . . . Cambridge.

Although the design of each station was similar, each had its own character due mainly to the type of food that was vended there, purchasers and buyers eagerly meeting through the open train windows for the exchange. For the hungry traveller the purchase could be fruits, popular 'aerated water' such as cream soda and orange crush, home-made drinks such as GINGER BEER, and foods such as roast corn, PEANUTS or fish fritters (STAMP-AND-GO).

The boredom of travel (the Kingston-Montego Bay train took the entire day) was not only relieved by slow, perilous climbs, breathtaking mountain scenery, hair-raising bends, and frequent tunnels, but was also enlivened by the itinerant vendors. Vendors of trinkets or home made confections travelled on the train and cried their wares as they walked through. Preachers and WARNERS also boarded from time to time. Usually there was one first-class carriage attached to each train with a firmly closed door that casual intruders never breached for it was strictly the domain of the elite. Before the line was closed down, train travel with its spectacular scenery and local colour also provided an attraction for tourists. The introduction of a new diesel rail coach service in 1952 finally enabled travellers to make a round trip between Kingston and Montego Bay in one day.

The passenger and cargo rail service between Kingston and Port Antonio was affected by flood rains in 1979 and owing to damage to the lines, the service to Port Antonio was shut down. Trains travelled from Kingston to Buff Bay up to 1982 but service on this line was eventually

Station vendors

On track in Portland

terminated in 1985 and on the Kingston to Montego Bay line in 1992. The lines from May Pen and Linstead to the interior had been closed a long time before.

The major accident recorded by the railway was the Kendal crash of 1 September 1957 when an excursion train derailed, killing 175 and injuring 400. In August 1938, a 10-coach train derailed at the Oxford embankment, 2.4km from the Balaclava station, leaving 32 dead and more than 70 injured. In 1942, 12 died and 32 were injured when a freight train collided with a trolley coach packed with passengers on the Frankfield line, between May Pen and Sevens siding.

[GOJ Handbook of Jamaica 1961, KSAC 1952, Porter 1990, Rampini 1873]

RAIN FLY

A winged creature that swarms around lights during rainy weather, especially March to May. It is the wood-boring termite (*Cryptotermes brevis*) called 'chichi', which acquires wings in one phase of its life cycle; it later sheds them and bores into wood.

RALLY

A method of fund-raising once widely practised in churches. Members competed with one another to see who could collect the most money, the total amount being announced at a rally that usually took the form of a sacred concert. Some months before, church members would be given cards marked in rows with a sum assigned to each row (e.g. $10, $20) and dots that could be punched by a pin to indicate the sum donated by each contributor. The aim was to fill one or more cards. The rally would sometimes be given a name, e.g. The Rally of the Rainbow, the Rally of the Twelve Apostles etc., and competing teams formed accordingly. Congregations of different churches often attended each other's rallies and the highlights were often the visiting choirs and soloists. For rural dwellers especially, rallies provided much anticipated entertainment and outlets for talented singers and musicians.

The DCEU records this type of rally for Jamaica and Guyana. This Caribbean usage does not appear in standard dictionaries but is probably derived from the sense of organizing for a common cause or purpose.

RASTAFARI

Millennial movement originating in Jamaica which is both ideological and religious, becoming in the sixty-odd years of its existence the focus of the search for identity by the black man in the New World. Though a new and original movement, Rastafari nevertheless evolved out of a persistent though often latent spirit of Ethiopianism that has flowered from time to time, expressed in the 20th century through movements such as Bedwardism and Garveyism (see **BEDWARD, GARVEY**). Rastafari (which is the term adherents use to describe the movement as a whole) continues to evolve, appealing to people of different nationalities, economic and social backgrounds, and educational status.

Though relatively small in number, Rastafari today is a highly visible force, internationally influential in music (Reggae), fashion (dreadlocks, etc.), food, and language. The 'peace and love' philosophy of some segments of the early Rasta movement is said to have influenced the American 'Hippie' movement of the sixties. Of course, many today might be called 'designer Rastas' since their adherence is limited to fashion ('dreadlocks' or 'locksing') or using the Rasta image as a marketing tool, e.g. the 'Rent-A-Dread' phenomenon in which spurious Rastas hire themselves out to female visitors in search of novelty. Nevertheless, the overall reach and influence of Rastafari today is profound as well as astonishing, considering that the movement began as a 'cult of outcasts' who were much derided and persecuted in their homeland.

Origins and Development The precise origins of the movement are obscure, but an acknowledged leader of the Rastafarian cult that came to national attention in the early 1930s was Leonard Howell, along with Robert Hinds, Joseph Hibbert, and Henry Dunkley. Marcus Garvey's teachings provided an inspiration for the movement and its icon (and eventual

Rastafarian

Leonard Howell

messiah) was Haile Selassie who was crowned Emperor of Ethiopia in 1930. It is often said that this fulfilled a prophetic statement of Garvey's that the black man should 'Look to Africa where a black King shall be crowned' though scholars have been unable to pin down the source. Rastafari (meaning 'Crown Prince' in Amharic) refers to Selassie's title prior to his coronation. For the orthodox and theocratic Rastas, Haile Selassie was the black reincarnated Christ. A central goal of the early movement became redemption through repatriation to Africa (Ethiopia) which is seen as the spiritual home of all black peoples.

When Selassie himself visited the island in April 1966, thousands of Rastafari swarmed the airport and the plane and gave him such an exuberant welcome, the emperor wept. Despite the fall and demise of the emperor in the temporal world, his spirit is embodied in the proud African lion (one of his titles was 'Conquering Lion of Judah') which has become a totemic animal for Rasta, signifying natural pride, wholeness, and power. The lion image, along with the colours of red ('ites'), green and gold, are identifying symbols of Rastas everywhere.

For the original, religious wing of Rastafari, the Bible is the sacred book that is interpreted literally, a continuous source of guidance for daily living and inspiration for the collective 'reasonings' or discussions which take the place of formal worship. Early Rastas identified with the 'chosen people' of Israel, particularly the Zionists. Taking their inspiration from the Babylonian captivity which the Jews endured, they identified themselves as 'exiles' and 'captives' in their own BABYLON which is represented by the western capitalist system and the individual countries, such as Jamaica, to which their ancestors were forcibly brought. (See AFRICAN HERITAGE, SLAVERY.)

There is no Rasta church as such; groups come together to worship with their unique style of drumming, dancing, singing and exhortations and reasonings based on Bible readings. Rastafari as it began and in many of its branches today, is male-dominated, based on Biblical notions of the patriarchy. In 1970 a branch of the ETHIOPIAN ORTHODOX CHURCH was established and some Rastas belong to this. Groups have gathered around leader-visionaries such as Prince Emmanuel Edwards (founder of the communal sect called the Bobos) and Prophet Gad, founder of the Twelve Tribes of Israel, which was the most powerful group of the seventies, attracting a large number of middle-class adherents.

Rastafari today seems to have moved away from its early Messianism and Biblical mysticism which were coupled with the desire for a physical return to Africa. The early, poverty-stricken Rastas on more than one occasion purchased tickets for the ship that was expected to come to take them off the island. In 1959, 15,000 such 'tickets' were distributed by the Revd Claudius Henry and many Rastas sold their possessions and camped out at his church to await the vessel. This event, coupled with a 21-day GROUNDATION held by Prince Emmanuel the previous year, which attracted some 3,000 Rastas, focused increasing public attention on the 'Brethren'. As they became more visible, Rastas were increasingly perceived as a threat to national and personal security and became a special target for police attention. Rasta's cultivation and use of GANJA (marijuana) as the 'sacred herb', their sometimes extreme expressions of alienation, and their assertion of blackness and 'dreadness', contributed to the negative public perception of Rasta as a frightening phenomenon.

Claudius Henry became involved in other events that added to the widespread fear of Rastafari. In 1960 he was tried for treason and sentenced to a long prison term. His son and several American blacks who had come with him from America were alleged to have set up a guerrilla base in the Red Hills. They were captured and tried and several were executed.

In light of these events, leading Rastafarians asked scholars at the UNIVERSITY OF THE WEST INDIES to investigate and report on their movement to show their peaceful intentions. The report was quickly undertaken (Smith et al. 1960) and had maximum impact as it was first published serially in the *Gleaner* newspaper. Among its recommendations was one that a mission should be sent to Africa to investigate the possibility of settling Jamaicans there. The government of the day did send such a team and it included three Rastafarians. The report, and the mission to Africa, were the first official attempts to understand the phenomenon of Rastafari. An earlier study had in fact been undertaken by sociologist G.E. Simpson, who in 1953 had done field work among Rastafari groups in West Kingston as part of his study of religious cults in the CARIBBEAN.

By the 1960s Rastafari was becoming less of a cult of outcasts drawing membership almost exclusively from the poor and dispossessed, and more of a widespread national religious-cultural movement with a growing world view. It began to attract adherents from the middle class youth and intellectuals who were themselves alienated politically and culturally. The emergence at that time of the 'Black Power' movement in the United States as well as the 'tune in, turn on, drop out' philosophy of a growing generation of youth, helped to make the Rasta alternative lifestyle an attractive one.

Beliefs Rastafari is a very visible movement since adherents on becoming Rasta assume a different 'livity' or lifestyle, adopting different codes of behaviour, dress, speech, diet, etc. from 'Babylon', i.e. the rest of society. Most religious Rastas also follow certain Biblical injunctions quite literally, particularly those relating to codes of behaviour. While in the past only one extremist group of Rastas – called 'Locksmen' – wore their hair long and uncombed, 'locksing' or 'dreadlocks' is now almost synonymous with Rasta. Indeed many non-Rastas, especially entertainers, wear 'dreads' as a fashion statement.

Although there is no central organization and Rastafari embraces a wide diversity of belief and expression, some commonalities may be identified. These include a conscious recognition of African roots; a philosophy based on the natural relationship between man and his environment; and arising from this, a consciousness of the physical body and foods eaten, preference being given to those which are natural or 'Ital' (vital); certain foods such as pork are taboo. A central part of the philosophy is the use of the 'sacred herb', ganja, which is seen as the means of communicating with God or gaining insight or wisdom – a view not shared by the Jamaican authorities for whom ganja is still a proscribed drug.

The ability to tap into a formerly repressed African consciousness provided by Rasta has produced an outstanding body of creative work by adherents. Rasta artists, painters, craftsmen, poets, and musicians, started to come to the fore in the 1960s and have remained in the forefront of Jamaican cultural life. (See ART.) Certainly, traditional Rasta music, especially its slow powerful drumming, has had a profound effect on the development of popular music in Jamaica, beginning with the ska. (See REGGAE.)

Many talented performing artists have either come from Rasta ranks or been converted to Rastafari, so much so that Rasta and Reggae music became closely identified, and it is the spread of the music internationally that has brought Rastafari to international attention. The identification of prominent musicians such as Bob MARLEY with African liberation movements, especially in Southern Africa, also helped to garner awareness of the movement's black liberation role. The Rastafarian influence on the Jamaican LANGUAGE in recent years has also been pronounced.

The movement has spread throughout the Caribbean and the rest of the world and attracts considerable attention from scholars and other researchers as an authentic 'New World religion'. Its connection with popular music has helped to generate numerous papers, books, and films on the phenomenon.

In describing its appeal, Rastafarian psychologist Leahcim Semaj wrote in 1985 that 'In a generic sense a Rastafarian is one who is attempting to restructure identity so that s/he can consciously live from an Africentric perspective. This covers the physical, mental and spiritual dimensions of life. Rastafari therefore provides a vehicle through which and by which the African in the Diaspora can recreate an African identity'.

[Campbell 1985, Chevannes 1994, 1998, CQ monograph 1985, Hill 1983a, Murrell et al. 1998, Owens 1976, Pollard 1994, Simpson 1970, Smith et al. 1960]

RED MUD 'LAKE'

Huge ponds – popularly called 'lakes' – created to store the waste from BAUXITE mining operations, the most visible being the Mount Rosser pond of the West Indies Alumina Company's Ewarton Works which can be seen from the main road at MOUNT DIABLO. This 'lake' was formed from a natural depression aided by a large man-made dam on the south side. At the time of writing, the pond covers some 36ha and was over 76m deep at the deepest point. This red mud lake might be the most visible but is not the largest, that being the Battersea red mud pond on the outskirts of MANDEVILLE.

The red mud is a by-product of the process of refining alumina from bauxite and was first produced in 1952 at Jamaica's first processing plant at Kirkvine Works, Shooters Hill. Approximately one tonne of red mud is generated for every tonne of alumina produced. Over the years various proposals have been made for the disposal or productive use of 'red mud', but none of these has proved feasible. Meanwhile, the ponds continue to grow with, many believe, deleterious environmental effects.
[Porter 1990]

REGGAE

Jamaica's contribution to world music. 'Reggae' originally referred to the beat that became popular from 1969 onwards but is nowadays used as a generic term for all Jamaica's popular music since 1960. This music is generally classified from the prevailing beat as Ska (roughly 1960-66), Rock Steady (1966-68) Reggae (1969 to the present) DANCEHALL (1983 to the present). Outside of Jamaica, Dancehall is often called 'Ragga' or 'Dub'.

The word reggae (originally spelled 'reggay') has been attributed to many sources, but the song 'Do the Reggay' by Toots and the Maytals in 1968 is acknowledged as the first use of the word musically.

In an interview for the book *Reggae Routes*, Toots Hibbert told the authors: 'it was just a word you would hear on the streets. I don't remember why I apply it to the music . . . At first reggae sort of mean untidy or scruffy. But then it start to mean like coming from the people.' The *Dictionary of Jamaican English*, published in 1967, cites rege-rege as 1. 'ragged clothing' and 2. 'A quarrel'. The *Dictionary of Caribbean English Usage* notes of 'reggae' that apart from its application to music, 'The word may have a wider coverage in other areas of folk-life' in the Caribbean, spreading through the music from Jamaica. The DCEU cites Yoruba *rege-rege* meaning 'rough', in a 'rough manner', Hausa *rega* meaning 'to shake', Tobago *rege-rege* meaning 'rough, uncultured'.

It is precisely from the so-called 'rough', 'uncultured' people of the KINGSTON ghettoes that the music that has captured the world was born, and the poverty-stricken neighbourhoods continue to be the wellspring from which it continually renews and reinvents itself. Reggae has grown directly out of the experiences of the Jamaican people and it is perhaps this visceral quality which has enabled it to connect with people everywhere. Reggae is heard (and played) in every country of the world, and its fundamentally revolutionary stance has been an inspiration for the world's liberation movements, in Zimbabwe and South Africa as in China's Tienanmen Square.

Chang and Cheng in their book *Reggae Routes* cite a CNN report 'of an astronomer in the American midwest who was trying to make contact with extraterrestrial life by beaming radio signals into outer space. His music of choice was reggae, because of its universal appeal'. As Toots said: 'reggae is just a name. Where music is concerned, reggae is a combination of communication . . . reggae means real music, music that tells a good story, music that you can relate to, music you can make sense out of.'

DANCE and MUSIC have always been avenues of exploration for Jamaicans trying to 'make sense' of their lives, often providing the only means for a collective emotional release. So it seems appropriate that the new Jamaican music was not born in a studio but evolved from the dances to which ordinary people flocked. At its heart, Jamaican popular music is always the music that keeps one dancing. At the same time, popular music has also provided the most witty, scandalous, painful, and acute commentary on social and political events over the years.

Up to the 1950s, dance music was provided by the live orchestras that played American-inspired ragtime and swing music. According to Verena Reckord, in the immediate period after the First

Toots and Maytals, 1966

WORLD WAR, the big band was the rage. Popular bandleaders included Eric Deans, Redver Cook, Ivy Graydon, Roy Coburne, Roy White, Milton McPherson, and Carlisle Demetrius and his Alpha Boys Band. These bands were usually Kingston-based and played for the upper and middle class.

The rest of the population danced to 'fife and drum' music at village fetes or 'wined' to MENTO played by local village bands. Mento was the music of the Jamaican heartland, the lyrics often risque or scandalous, the dance salacious, as earthy as the countryside where it had rooted. In Kingston, several individuals from the big band aggregations would do occasional 'gigs' with the mento players in the less affluent areas of the city.

Sound Systems and Deejays In the early 1950s two developments occurred to introduce Jamaicans to something new. The first commercial radio station (Radio Jamaica) began BROADCASTING in 1950 and its reach was essentially middle class, but on their newly acquired radio sets, many began to listen to American rhythm and blues (R&B), which they could pick up on stations such as WINZ in Miami, Florida. Especially popular was the version from New Orleans and black stars such as Fats Domino, LaVerne Baker, Nat Cole, Lloyd Price, the Drifters, the Coasters, the Platters. It is said that Jamaicans took to R&B because it had a similar beat to Mento.

At the same time, farm workers who had gone to America to cut sugar cane in the late forties began bringing back record players and records to the island. Up to that time, a record player was a luxury item, a Victrola wind-up gramophone (often brought back by earlier migrants – see COLÓN MAN), is still a treasured item in many homes. By the early fifties, a few enterprising promoters began to put together what became known as the 'sound system', giant portable record playing sets that were trucked around the island to dance halls as needed. Soon, rivalry erupted between the sound system owners as to who could acquire the latest and hottest records that would draw the crowds to the 'lawn' or 'dance hall'.

A crucial figure of the 'dance hall' was the 'disc jockey', shortened to 'DJ' or 'deejay', who played and introduced the records, developing a kind of patter over the music to keep the fans happy – a style that persisted and came fully into its own in Dancehall. And the sound system, born out of necessity, never went away, becoming an entrenched part of Jamaican life.

A 'set' or two is now a permanent fixture not just on every city block but even in the remotest parts of the island. Legislation was introduced in 1997 to control what those who aren't fans describe as 'noise pollution' but enforcement is another matter. As Bob MARLEY expressed the ethos long ago in 'Bad Card':

I want to disturb my neighbour
Cause I'm feeling so right
I want to turn up my disco
Blow them to full watts tonight

The Ska As R&B caught on, local singers began to cut records in that style and two of the biggest sound system promoters – Duke Reid and Clement 'Coxone' Dodd – got into the recording business too, using fairly primitive and sometimes improvised equipment. Keith and Enid, Laurel Aitken, Jackie Edwards were a few of the singers of this early period. The backing musicians in the late 1950s began to create a sound that was characterized by the use of percussion instruments, guitar riffs, and horns. The music, like the dance that it generated, was high energy, and it came to be called the 'Ska'. These first studio musicians included many of Jamaica's most outstanding instrumentalists, a number coming together to form the seminal band Skatalites which featured the legendary trombonist, Don Drummond. Unlike the singers who were for the most part raw talent, many of the musicians had been trained at ALPHA Boys School and/or had a background playing jazz with the big dance orchestras, and it was they who shaped the music.

Ska was essentially instrumental, drawing from the sources that had nurtured the musicians, including the traditional music of Mento, the religious music of REVIVAL, American swing, bebop and rhythm and blues, some Latin influences, and the new, explosive BURU drumming which had been taken up by Rastafarians. (See RASTAFARI.) Oswald 'Count Ossie' Williams' backing for the Folkes Brothers 'O Carolina' (1961) is acknowledged as one of the crucial elements in the new sound. By this time it was being carried around the island by the juke box, introduced after vinyl 7-inch 45s started to be manufactured at the end of the 1950s.

Ska was unquestionably the music of the poor and dispossessed, expressed especially in the melancholy of the horns. Gordon Rohlehr has suggested that this peculiarly Jamaican sound derived from the musicians' awareness of the increasing pressure of life in Kingston. 'The Ska

The Ska

was an extremely aggressive and tedious beat, requiring a great deal of energy and producing a great deal of sweat. People danced it every weekend to the point of exhaustion, as if they found in its almost military rigidity, both a perfect expression of their own unalterable position at the bottom of society, and an opiate, a release from the daily inferno of their highly regimented lives.' Others saw it as reflecting the exuberance arising from the promise of Jamaica's INDEPENDENCE in 1962.

At first, the new music stayed in the downtown dance halls; it was taken uptown and popularized by the big bands such as Byron Lee and the Dragonaires. The fact that the new indigenous music coincided with Independence contributed to its official promotion and dissemination; it was something that the new nation could proudly claim as 'ours'. The new Minister of Culture, Edward Seaga, had himself been a record producer, which no doubt contributed to both its recognition and its appropriation by officialdom. Jamaica had its first big international hit with Millie Small's 'My Boy Lollipop' in 1964 (produced by Chris Blackwell who went on to found the influential Island Records).

Rock Steady and 'Rude Boy' Ska peaked in the mid-sixties, the driving beat slowing down to what came to be called 'rock steady', with its accent on the bass and drum rhythm and a more laid-back style, encouraging the artistry of 'legs men' or virtuoso dancers. The singer also began to assume greater importance, ushering in the era of social commentary and introducing many who would become the great reggae stars. Locally, the introduction of a Festival Song as part of the annual islandwide celebration (see FESTIVAL, Jamaica) from 1966 onwards helped to give legitimacy to what was still seen by the elite as a marginal form.

An important element was the 'rude boy' that emerged in the early sixties as the euphoria associated with Independence subsided. The ghettoes were even more overcrowded with the youth flocking in from the country in search of bright lights, work, and opportunity. As hopes of the latter faded, tensions rose and rachet knives and guns came into play. 'Dissing' authority, 'rude boy' emerged as the ghetto idol, modelling himself on the heroes of 'spaghetti' westerns and James Bond movies. This spawned a whole series of 'rudie' records celebrating or chastising rudie. Several, such as Prince Buster's 'Judge Dread' in 1967, also satirized the justice system that was vainly trying to keep rudie in check. The Wailers' first hit, 'Simmer Down' (1963), was a direct message to rudies.

Reggae By the late sixties the music was again changing, the tempo speeded up, and the Maytals 'Do the Reggay' in 1968 gave it a name that stuck. Barrow and Dalton in *Reggae: The Rough Guide* have observed that 'It's fitting that the word "reggae" has endured as the favoured label for all Jamaican popular music, because reggae began in a period of extraordinary experiment, in which almost all later styles were prefigured and all previous styles absorbed'.

Recording studios had become more sophisticated and in this period the music also caught on overseas, forging linkages with the international pop scene as foreign stars also began to record reggae. Jamaica's first feature-length film, *The Harder They Come* (1972), featuring Jimmy Cliff and a brilliant reggae sound-track, also helped to promote the music internationally. In the seventies many of the Jamaican performers achieved international recognition, of whom the most notable remains Bob Marley. By 1975, Rastafari had become both the dominant influence on the music and the life style of many of the artists, leading to a proliferation of 'roots' records. Burning Spear's *Marcus Garvey* (1975) helped to promote the Rastafarian-influenced 'cultural' music of this period.

'Cultural' or 'Roots' reggae faded into the background following the death of Marley in 1981 and Dancehall took over as Reggae's latest manifestation.

Dancehall and Dub Technological change has been very much a part of the music. Dancehall itself has utilized 'computer riddim' – digitalized

Reggae icon, Burning Spear

music that has allowed the exposure of almost limitless 'VERSIONS' of the old Ska and Rock Steady classics to new generations.

One of the early technological manipulations was called 'dub'. Originating in Jamaica in the 1960s, dub is now part of the vocabulary and practice of dance culture world-wide. With the introduction of multi-track recording studios, rhythm and other instrumental tracks could be recorded independent of vocals. At first these instrumental 'versions' were released for sound system play. But these dub 'versions' became so popular that by 1970 they were introduced on the flip sides of virtually all singles released in Jamaica, providing the base for deejays to talk over and for further manipulation by the studio engineers to create reverbs and remixes. King Tubby (Osbourne Ruddock) is regarded as the undisputed father of the radically remixed version.

Dub in Jamaica gave rise to the genre of Dub Poetry where a poet speaks over the instrumental reggae rhythm. Though they might not claim the name 'dub poet', the most popular exponents of this art form have been: (in Jamaica) Mutabaruka, Oku Onora, Michael Smith and Jean 'Binta' Breeze; in England, Linton Kwesi Johnson, and in Canada Lilieth Allen and Clifton Joseph.

In 1993, the International Reggae Studies Centre was established at the UNIVERSITY OF THE WEST INDIES to facilitate research and teaching on reggae and its social history.

[Barrow and Dalton 1997, Chang and Chen 1998, Cooper 1998, DCEU, DJE, Reckord 1977, 1982, Richards 1999, Rohlehr 1992, White 1984]

RELIGION

Jamaica has an enormous number of churches for its population and size; it is commonly believed that this has earned the island a place in the *Guinness Book of Records*. Of the 2.3 million Jamaicans counted in the census of 1991, over 1.47 million listed themselves as belonging to a congregation (though there is no indication of attendance).

Every variety of religion is represented, ranging from all the orthodox denominations to the fundamentalist to the home-grown. Many who are members of indigenous religions, cults, and sects will also attend one or other of the orthodox churches as that is considered 'respectable'. What Elizabeth Thomas-Hope has noted of the CARIBBEAN as a whole, also applies to Jamaica: 'with little that is uniform in the Caribbean, it is hardly surprising that diversity should also be a feature of the religious scene. As imprints upon the cultural landscape, the Christian cathedrals and churches, the meeting houses of numerous Afro-Christian sects, Hindu temples and prayer flags, MUSLIM mosques and JEWISH SYNAGOGUES, all bear witness to the plurality of Caribbean religions.'

Taino The religion of the earliest Amerindian inhabitants has been described as animist, that is, belief in a natural world animated by spirits. But the TAINOS, like almost all peoples, posited a high god. Their supreme deity was YAYA, who was remote from everyday affairs.

A pantheon of benevolent spirits were invoked through the intermediary of ZEMIS to harness divine power and blessings for man and the environment.

African The beliefs of many of the AFRICANS who were forcibly brought as slaves to replace the vanishing Tainos might also be described in similar terms, including animism, belief in a supreme being (under many different names) as well as many subordinate deities, and a belief in the continued power of departed ancestors. Many observers claimed of Africans both in Africa and the Caribbean that they had 'no religion', but religion in fact permeated every aspect of traditional African life; it was not limited to worship on one day of the week but was part of everyday affairs. Central to this was the idea of power in the universe that could be harnessed for good or evil purposes, to affect the outcome of decisions or to guide in times of crisis. Song and dance were part of ritual worship as was possession by the ancestors or by a deity. Healing and magic were intrinsic elements of African religion and there were religious specialists such as priests and priestesses, medicine men, diviners, mediums and seers, rainmakers, and so on. Many of these beliefs along with the specialists were brought to the Caribbean. However, the institution of SLAVERY and the requirements of the plantation system made it impossible for African religion as it was known on the continent to flourish.

Church goers in downtown Kingston

African beliefs and practices were misunderstood by Europeans, and were either rejected as 'superstition' or seen as dangerous. Consequently they were abandoned, transformed, or forced to go underground, e.g. OBEAH, MYAL. A strong African element nevertheless persisted, manifested today in such cultural expressions as KUMINA, REVIVAL and RASTAFARI, and in the way in which Christianity has been reinterpreted in African terms.

European The first orthodox Western religion of the island was the ROMAN CATHOLIC, brought by the SPANISH settlers who erected churches at Sevilla La Nueva (see SEVILLE, New) and, later, SPANISH TOWN when they moved their capital there in 1534. The centre of Roman Catholic worship in the island today is the HOLY TRINITY CATHEDRAL in Kingston. After the capture of the island by ENGLISH forces in 1655 a group of PORTUGUESE (called Portugals or Marranos) among the Spanish colonists soon revealed that they were JEWS and were allowed by the British to remain and practise their religion openly. The ANGLICAN church (then known as the Church of England) became the state religion and remained so until 1872. The SPANISH TOWN CATHEDRAL (built on the site of the Spanish church) is the oldest cathedral in the former British colonies and ST ANDREW PARISH CHURCH and ALLEY CHURCH are among the earliest Anglican foundations.

The need to attract settlers to the new colony of Jamaica led to a kind of religious tolerance that was unusual for the times. Early PORT ROYAL, remarkably, had places of worship for Anglicans, Presbyterians, Quakers, Catholics, and Jews. But such tolerance vanished as the plantation system took hold, and while Jews never lost their right to worship, the only Christian faith tolerated in a plantocratic society was the Church of England. The first challenge to the state church came in 1754 when the MORAVIANS arrived, to be followed later by other non-conformist MISSIONARIES, including PRESBYTERIANS, Wesleyans (now METHODISTS), and BAPTISTS. Quakers from America (see FRIENDS) in the late 19th century reintroduced this religious group which had existed much earlier and then vanished from the scene. From the late 19th century and into the 20th came many newer faiths such as the SEVENTH DAY ADVENTIST, SALVATION ARMY, African AME, Jehovah's Witnesses, Bahai and Mormons. The ETHIOPIAN ORTHODOX CHURCH also came in the 20th century in response to a request by Rastafari. The fastest growing religious movement in Jamaica today is a 20th century phenomenon – the many fundamentalist churches collectively grouped under PENTECOSTALISM.

As remarkable as the diversity of religious practice in Jamaica is the ecumenical movement which has been far in advance of similar movements elsewhere. The Jamaica Council of Churches was formed in 1941 when representatives of ten branches of the Christian churches came together, joined since then by other churches. The United Theological College for the training of ministers of the gospel is a result of such collaboration. The JCC has also cooperated in providing a number of social services. The Christian churches in Jamaica also collaborated in assisting local Rastafari to establish a branch of the Ethiopian Orthodox Church in 1970. The UNITED CHURCH in Jamaica and the Cayman Islands is also an expression of religious ecumenism, being formed from a union of the Presbyterians, Congregationalists and Disciples of Christ.

Formal worship

Street meeting

The churches as a whole have made an outstanding contribution to EDUCATION in Jamaica and to the development of social welfare services, including hospitals.

Political Activism One salient feature of grassroots Jamaican religion is its connection with political activism, expressed in such episodes as the 'Christmas Rebellion' (see SHARPE, Samuel) and the MORANT BAY REBELLION, and in cultural resistance, as expressed in, e.g. BEDWARDISM, Rastafari, and Revival. Indeed, as Barry Chevannes has expressed it: 'The most central institution to the tradition of resistance in Jamaica has been religion. Whether resistance through the use of force, or resistance through symbolic forms such as language, folk-tales and proverbs, or resistance through the creation of alternative institutions . . . Even in those areas of socio-cultural life where resistance has lost meaning, having successfully brought colonial domination to an end, religion still flourishes as the guardian of public and private morality.'
[Bisnauth 1989, Chevannes 1995, GOJ API 1972, Osborne 1988, Pawson and Buisseret 1975, Thomas-Hope 1980]

REVIVAL

A distinctly Jamaican RELIGION created by a synthesis of European and African religious influences. Revival embraces two different branches: Revival Zion and Pukumina (also called POCOMANIA or Poco). Revivalists are noted for their colourful dress (robes and turbans in different colours depending on the ceremony), for their powerful drumming and singing, and their characteristic wheeling dance to induce spirit possession. In recent times the general public has been more exposed to Revival ceremonies such as their elaborate 'Tables' and to some of their imagery through art and MUSIC.

Once sidelined as small bands of deluded and derided cultists, Revival bands nowadays are organized as churches with pastors and bishops, conventions and communion services. These churches are increasingly associated with PENTECOSTALISM.

Possession by spirits is central to Revival worshippers and powerful rituals, DANCE, and music induce the spirits to come. Power derived from the spirit world is used for both physical and spiritual healing and the enhancement of the worshipper's life and well being.

Although its various elements existed long before in MYAL and native BAPTIST movements, Revival as a distinct folk religion gained impetus and its name from the Great Revival of 1860-61 which started in Christian churches but was increasingly taken over by African elements. Revival groups dating their origin to that time refer to themselves as the '60 Order' (Revival Zion representing those at the more Christian end of the spectrum) or '61 Order' (Pukkumina or Poco, representing the more 'African' element in worship and practice).

At the time of the Great Revival, the orthodox church leaders, alarmed by what they saw as over-emotionalism and 'heathenism', roundly denounced the Revivalists, and this attitude has influenced popular perception to this day of what are generally referred to as 'Poco people'. Revivalists are usually poor, working class people and have always been frowned on or ridiculed by the rest of society, 'Poco' people especially being regarded as noisy, deluded and dangerous. 'Pocomania', many have been quick to point out, translates to 'little madness' though there is no evidence to suggest the slightest association with Spanish. Scholars nowadays believe the word is derived from Pu-Kumina.

With the ongoing re-evaluation of Jamaican culture since INDEPENDENCE in the 1960s, there has been increasing recognition of the validity of such indigenous religions as Revival and their value in preserving the cultural traditions of Jamaica. Their colourful ritual involving dance-drumming-singing has inspired the NATIONAL DANCE THEATRE COMPANY to choreograph one of their more spectacular dances, 'Pocomania'. One Revival Shepherd, Kapo (Mallica Reynolds) gained international recognition as an 'intuitive' artist and many of his works can be seen on permanent exhibition at the National Gallery of Jamaica (see ART); the art, like Revival music, is full of original symbolism and imagery.

Indeed, Kenneth W. Bilby claims that Revivalists 'have invented an entirely new musical form'. They have done so 'by blending Protestant devotional songs (many of them taken from nineteenth century British and American hymnals) with polyrhythmic clapping and, in the case of Revival Zionists, forceful drumming'. The language employed is sometimes rich in symbolism and imagery such as the song, 'Parakeet in the Garden' which likens Judas the betrayer of Jesus to a chattering and destructive parakeet.

Origins Revival origins may be traced to Myal, which embodied traditional West African beliefs. With the introduction of the enslaved Africans to Christianity through non-conformist MISSIONARY activity, the Baptist church became a powerful influence from the beginning of the 19th century. Over time, the native element in the Baptist church began to reinterpret Christianity in ways they believed were more appropriate to their lives and set up their own churches, becoming known as 'Native Baptists'; by the 1860s they were stronger than the European organizations and fuelled the 'Revival' element. Early Revivalist leaders often came from the ranks of 'daddies' or Baptist church leaders. From the Baptists, Revivalists adopted certain practices such as baptism with which Africans, accustomed to water rites, could easily identify.

Beliefs Like KUMINA, Revival is based on the African belief that the spiritual and temporal worlds are not separate but form a unified whole, therefore the living can become possessed and influenced by the spirits of the dead. According to G.E. Simpson who was one of the first scholars to study this religious expression, Revivalists have adopted from Christianity the belief that God the father is the creator of the universe and Jesus Christ, his son. The former never comes to service; the latter comes but does not usually manifest himself. Most important is the Holy Spirit (sometimes called 'Messenger' or 'Spirit') who attends services and possesses followers. Revival spirits also include: Old Testament prophets, New Testament apostles and evangelists, archangels, Satan and his chief assistants, beings from Hebrew magical tradition, other assorted mystical figures, and the dead: great Revival leaders – shepherds and shepherdesses.

Revival Bishops

Dreams and visions in which spirits appear are important. 'Getting into the spirit' or possession, is brought about by the use of a specific ritual which involves singing, drumming, dancing, clapping, groaning, and prayers. Most followers 'travel under' (are possessed by) one spirit but some claim they receive messages from and are possessed by many spirits.

Poco and ZION are alike in many respects, their basic difference having to do with ritual and doctrine and with the types of spirits they invoke, Zion deals only with sky spirits, i.e. God, archangels, angels. Poco spirits are the 'ground spirits', i.e. human dead, or 'earthbound spirits', i.e. fallen angels. Zion is closer to Christianity and Poco to African traditions though sometimes the distinction is not so clearly observed. Unlike European beliefs that see 'good' and 'evil' as two separate and distinct forces, Revivalists are concerned with harnessing the unseen forces of the universe that are not good or bad in themselves but can be utilized by man for different purposes.

Organization Revival groups or 'bands' are organized around a strong leader. Male leaders are called 'Captain' in

Revivalists by Osmond Watson

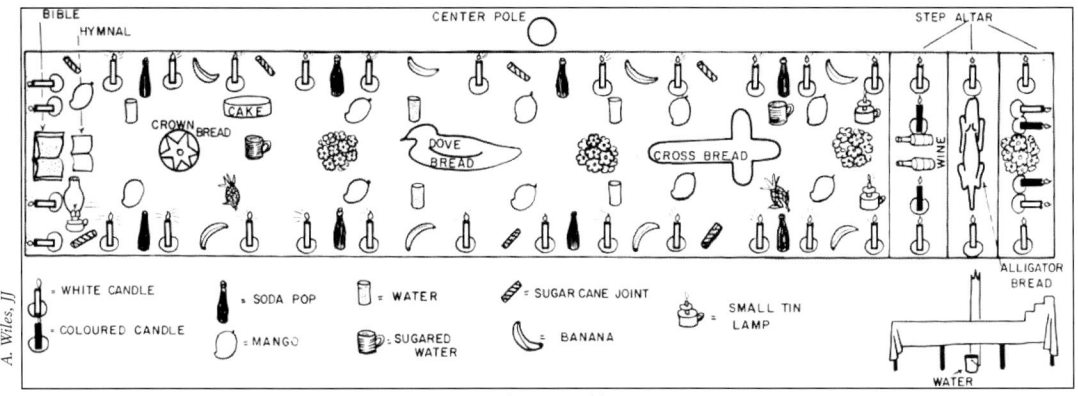

Pukumina Table

Zion and 'Shepherd' in Poco, female leaders are called 'Mother'. Each 'bands' has many titled officers with different duties including responsibility for the rituals and care of devotees who are possessed.

The 'mission ground' where meetings are held is usually part of the leader's YARD. The leader, outside of services, also serves as a temporal adviser and counsellor to his flock. A mission ground is usually marked by a tall pole or poles on which flags of a solid colour are flown. This is both to identify the ground and attract spirits.

Revivalists usually hold three distinct types of meetings – prayer meetings (divine worship), rituals for special occasions, and street meetings – in addition to 'baths' for healing. The special services include baptismal rites, death rites, dedication of new church, installation of new officer.

The rituals are usually elaborate ceremonies – each held for a specific purpose, and might last for days. 'Tables' are held for special events such as anniversaries or for specific purposes such as healing, mourning, etc. and can last for a week. A 'feasting table' is held as thanksgiving for deliverance from trouble. The Table is laid with spirit conductors such as rum, flowers, fruits, water and candles. These along with the colour theme will indicate to initiates the purpose of the ritual. Each spirit – like the orishas or deities in other African-Caribbean religions, such as Santería or Vodun – has a special colour, food preference, music, etc. which must be used if it is to respond to the summons.

Revival for its adherents is a way of life. Leaders dress in long flowing robes and wear characteristically styled turbans. Members dress soberly with their heads tied turban-style. For meetings, leaders and members will wear clothing of specific colours, depending on the ceremony. Ivy Baxter has commented on the elegance of dress and regalia, and careful adornment of the table in pukumina that is 'often in striking contrast to the stark appearance of poverty that exists in the surrounding area'.

Ceremonies A Revival ceremony will start with singing, preaching, Bible reading led by the Shepherd, and build up to a pitch where certain members will become possessed or get 'into the spirit'. Practices called 'trumping and labouring' will help to induce such possession. In trumping (or tramping) and labouring, members led by the Shepherd dance counter-clockwise around the table, seal or altar in the process of which evil spirits are trampled or expelled, Zionists maintaining a circle, Poco adherents preferring a horseshoe shape to leave space for the spirits to enter. While moving their bodies forward, Revivalists bend, expelling the breath, and utter a groaning sound on the upswing, all in 2/4th rhythm, a movement that causes dizziness in some persons and facilitates the onset of spirit possession.

The Shepherd orchestrates the proceedings by 'cymballing', i.e. chanting in 'unknown tongues'. Trumping will continue till the drums are suddenly stopped and the only sounds heard are vocal – the gutteral sounds of the trumping and the Shepherd's 'cymballing' chant. A wheeling stage will follow in which members turn around rapidly on the same spot, their gowns billowing. Members will become possessed and 'travel' to the spirit world. Each member imitates the particular spirit in movement or sound, e.g. 'dove', 'bell ringer' etc. The leader himself receives and interprets spirit messages.

Outside of their regular services, Revivalists will sometimes hold street meetings that are usually brief affairs held to attract members.

Revival music, dress, and behaviour have inspired novels, poems, plays, dance-theatre, and REGGAE music. In recent times, numerous popular songs utilizing Revival rhythms and satirizing 'Poco people' have made the charts, such as 'Revival Time' by Chalice and 'Pocomania Day' by Lovindeer.

[Baxter 1970, Bilby 1985a, Chevannes 1998, Lewin 2000, Ryman 1980, Seaga 1969, Simpson 1956, 1970, 1978]

RICE AND PEAS
Popular dish made from rice cooked with beans (see PEAS AND BEANS), especially 'red peas' (kidney beans) or GUNGO peas, and COCONUT milk, and seasoning. For many people Sunday dinner without rice and peas is unthinkable: it is jocularly referred to as the 'Jamaican coat of arms'. Variants of the dish (called 'Peas and Rice' and 'Peas and Beans' in some territories) are popular throughout the Caribbean.

RICHMOND-LLANDOVERY
Located in ST ANN Parish, this was one of the oldest SUGAR estates in Jamaica in continuous production until closed in 1970, both Llandovery and Richmond having been settled in 1674 by the BRITISH. Llandovery is also believed to have been occupied during the SPANISH period, part of the Sevilla la Nueva settlement (see SEVILLE, New). Richmond and Llandovery were amalgamated in 1952 and until 1972 produced a famous rum called TTL; the estates are now mainly in COCONUTS and CATTLE as well as SUGAR CANE. At the old Llandovery factory, a coat of arms (origin unknown) can be seen over the doorway. For much of the 19th century Richmond estate was owned by the Dukes of St Albans, according to Wright and White 'a branch of the family of DeVere which has held the hereditary office of Lord Great Chamberlain of England for eight centuries'.

[Wright and White 1969]

RIDDLE
One of the oldest forms of verbal art, riddles are still popular in Jamaica, representing an element of folk knowledge easily transmitted from generation to generation. Riddles are actually metaphors, often humorous and witty, the humour arising from unexpected associations. In Jamaica, riddles used to be an important element in story-telling and entertainment sessions among adults as well as children, and are still a part of the repertoire of such events as NINE NIGHT and DINKI MINI.

Jamaican riddles take two forms. Some riddles are couched in the form of a statement, that is, the question who or what is implied. An example is: 'Little Miss Nancy tear her pretty yellow gown and no one to mend it.' Answer: A ripe banana skin. Other riddles begin with the formula: 'Riddle me this, riddle me that, guess me this riddle and p-raps not.' Some common examples:

> Why are a tailor and a plantain alike?
> Ans: One cut to fit, the other fit to cut (i.e. is ready for reaping).

> Send boy to call doctor, doctor come before boy
> Ans: Coconut picked by a boy climbing the tree.

[Beckwith 1924, Brown 1996, Dance 1985]

RIO BUENO, Town of
Like FALMOUTH, Rio Bueno (TRELAWNY Parish) with its fort, warehouses, and old churches reminds us of the BRITISH period of settlement. Convincing evidence has been advanced to support the view that this is the bay where COLUMBUS first landed, although claims have been made for DISCOVERY BAY.

Rio Bueno used to be one of the many active ports around the island in the days when coastal traffic was important. The two-storey building in the town on the side away from the sea (with wrought iron balconies) was used in the filming of *A High Wind in Jamaica* (1964). It was once a sugar warehouse. Before that, it was probably a hotel. In the early 19th century a visitor claimed that Rio Bueno had the best lodging house on the north side of the island. However, by the 1870s, at a time of economic decline of the entire island, another visitor found Rio Bueno to be a ghost town. The hotel (probably the same building) he found quite empty and unprepared for visitors. 'Up in the crazy room where I slept I lay upon an antique bed in the company of LIZARDS, and gazed through holes in the roof upon the twinkling stars. Providentially it didn't rain.' The stone building on the seaward side housing an art gallery was once a warehouse. Ruins of FORT DUNDAS can be seen behind the government school.

[Rampini 1873, Wright and White 1969]

Rio Bueno

RIO BUENO ANGLICAN CHURCH

St Marks, in the town of RIO BUENO, TRELAWNY Parish, on the edge of the sea, was consecrated in 1833 after the inhabitants of the town had petitioned the Assembly for the establishment of a church.

Legend has it that before the church was built, services were held on the top floor of a three-story building. The first floor housed a tavern and the second a courthouse. Local wits said that one could commit oneself on the first floor, be tried on the second, and gain absolution on the third. The fact is that the upper part of a house belonging to one Jas Uten was rented out in 1820 for the purpose of worship. The rental was £50. Apparently there was some disagreement with Mr Uten, for after the present church was built in 1832, the Vestry had to order the clerk to write to him demanding the return of the church organ. In that year too, the vestrymen instructed the parish solicitor to take action on the estate of one Charles Lewis, planter, to recover his subscription to the church. In those days, maintenance of ANGLICAN churches depended largely on the funds guaranteed by estate owners.

[Wright and White 1969]

RIO BUENO BAPTIST CHURCH

The original BAPTIST church in RIO BUENO, TRELAWNY Parish, was burnt down in 1832 by the COLONIAL CHURCH UNION, a group hostile to non-conformist MISSIONARIES. In November 1834 a new chapel was opened on the site, twice the size of the former building. It was the first of the churches destroyed in the anti-missionary riots to be reopened. The present church was erected on the site of the old in 1901.

Rio Bueno Baptist Church

RIO COBRE

This is the major river of ST CATHERINE Parish and one of the largest in Jamaica. The river disappears at a place called River Sink at WORTHY PARK and runs underground for 5km before it emerges from Riverhead Grand Cave in St-Thomas-in-the-Vale. Some 50.9km long, it traverses the entire parish and enters the sea at Hunts Bay on the western side of KINGSTON harbour. In earlier times the river used to enter the sea at PASSAGE FORT, famous in history as the place the BRITISH first landed in Jamaica in 1655.

The river has changed course many times and some of these ancient courses can still be traced on the landscape. At one time it entered the sea at Great Salt Pond south of PORT HENDERSON. At another time its mouth was at Galleon Bay near OLD HARBOUR BAY. The river has created many fertile alluvial valleys including St-Thomas-in-the-Vale and the areas around SPANISH TOWN. Its waters have been used to provide hydroelectricity and to irrigate the plains.

Spanish Town, LINSTEAD and Bog Walk are three of the principal towns on the banks of this river. At Bog Walk it receives water from a number of tributaries including the Thomas River which enters from the west and the Rio D'Oro and the Rio Pedro from the east. The Rio Pedro is its chief tributary.

Two of Jamaica's most interesting bridges span the Rio Cobre – the FLAT BRIDGE in the RIO COBRE GORGE and the old IRON BRIDGE near to Spanish Town.

Rio Cobre is Spanish for 'Copper River' and one of its tributaries is Rio D'Oro – 'River of Gold' – though there is no evidence that these minerals were actually associated with these rivers. During early SPANISH times the river was called *Caguaya* (or *Cahauya*) and was important in many ways to the Spaniards. Their main town (Villa de la Vega, later Santiago de la Vega) was on its banks and main port *Caguaya* (Passage Fort) at its mouth. In the early 17th century there was a fortified embankment at Passage Fort.

In his book *The West Indies*, published in 1628, Vasquez de Espinosa says that the river water was considered curative because of SARSAPARILLA and other medicinal plants that grew on its banks.

RIO COBRE GORGE

The highway from SPANISH TOWN to OCHO RIOS runs for several kilometres alongside the RIO COBRE gorge, also called Bog Walk Gorge. It was discovered in the 1660s by a man named Carey Helyar who hacked his way down the stream. Helyar patented land near what is now Bog Walk and called it Bybrook, the name it still bears. Before Helyar discovered the gorge, the area beyond the point where the river enters it (Angels or Los Angeles) was unknown territory. The first road through the gorge was opened around 1770. The FLAT BRIDGE was originally constructed of logs. Many of the huge rocks in the riverbed were probably thrown there by the EARTHQUAKE of 1692 that destroyed PORT ROYAL. It is believed that so much rock was thrown into the river that it was blocked for a while until the water rose to such a height that it burst a way through.

RIO GRANDE

Large river (34.3km long) in the parish of PORTLAND, rising nearly 900m on the northern slopes of the BLUE MOUNTAINS. The Rio Grande and its main tributaries – the Back and Stony Rivers – rise in areas of torrential rainfall and have carved out a spectacular and rugged terrain. The area is identified with the history of the Windward MAROONS.

The Rio Grande is also identified with one of Jamaica's most popular visitor attractions – rafting. The two- or three-passenger rafts are poled downstream by skilled raftsmen who spend many years as apprentices. The 2½ hour trip begins at the village of Berrydale and ends at Rafter's Rest, 8km west of PORT ANTONIO where

Rafting on the Rio Grande

the Rio Grande enters the sea.

Rafting originated among the river communities not as a sport but as their principal means of transportation, especially in the days before the river was bridged. The many cataracts on the river preclude the use of conventional boats and villagers fashioned rafts from the wild BAMBOO and WIS (lianas). The movie star Errol Flynn is said to have been the one who first encouraged rafting as a sport. Rafting as a visitor attraction also takes place on the MARTHA BRAE.

RIO MINHO

At 92.5km in length, the Rio Minho is officially listed as Jamaica's longest river. It was originally called Rio de la Mina (River of the Mine) by the Spaniards who found traces of GOLD in the sands, and had a small mine at Longville, CLARENDON Parish. Gold, however, was never found in any quantity in Jamaica to the great disappointment of the Spaniards. The Minho rises in the mountains near to Spaldings and flows the entire length of the parish of Clarendon, discharging in the sea at CARLISLE BAY.

The river divides the parish into two. In what is called Upper Clarendon, it is fed by many tributaries. This is a lush green district in an area of productive small settlers and was known as 'the bread basket of Jamaica'. Between 1913 and 1925 the RAILWAY was extended into this area from MAY PEN to Frankfield. It opened up these areas so that farmers could get their produce to market and also facilitated the development of extensive BANANA cultivation since the perishable fruit could now be shipped by rail.

After passing through the mountains, the water in this river tends to sink in its sandy bed as it flows to the sea, hence its other name of 'Dry River'. Although the river beneath the bridge at May Pen is dry for most of the year, in times of flood it can become a raging torrent. At such times it is unpredictable and very dangerous: waters dammed in the upper reaches suddenly break through in a floodwall, carrying everything in the riverbed out to sea. Before it was bridged, communications between the south side of the island and the east were completely cut when the river was in spate.

The first bridge to span the river was an iron bridge opened to traffic in 1870. The iron structure was then considered 'the finest in the world' but by the 1940s it was taken down as the iron in some parts had turned to rust, and the present structure was erected.

RIO NUEVO, Battle of

The site of the most important battle ever fought in Jamaica lies at the point where the Rio Nuevo (in ST MARY Parish) enters the sea. A memorial erected by the National Trust Commission marks the spot where the English decisively defeated the Spaniards in their bid to retake the island in 1658 (see CAPTURE OF JAMAICA). When the English soldiers marched on the SPANISH capital of Villa de la Vega (SPANISH TOWN) in 1655, the governor surrendered. But many Jamaican-born young men refused to leave and under a leader called Cristobal YSASSI continued to harass the soldiers for another five years, effectively holding up settlement by the English.

Aiding Ysassi were three groups of former Spanish slaves who had established their own communities in the hills. However, one of them, Juan de Bolas (see LUBOLO) turned traitor to Ysassi and made terms with the English, a factor that contributed to Ysassi's defeat. Nevertheless the decisive battle was the one at Rio Nuevo. In 1657 the King of Spain finally heeded Ysassi's pleas for reinforcements and sent troops that landed at OCHO RIOS. Before they could reach Ysassi they were found by the English and routed. In May 1658 more Spaniards arrived from Cuba. A contingent of 557 men was landed by boat at Rio Nuevo and they quickly built a stockade and a fort on the cliffs overlooking the bay. They were spotted by English warships and the English governor D'Oyley quickly sailed round from PORT ROYAL.

D'Oyley landed after some fighting and built a camp across from the stockade. He politely sent his drummer boy across the bay to ask the Spaniards to surrender (the drummer boy at the same time testing the depth of the water to see if D'Oyley's men could get across the bay). The Spaniards just as politely refused to surrender, but gave the drummer boy a present of money and a gift of sweetmeats for D'Oyley. The next day D'Oyley caused his ships in the harbour to fire on the fort as a distraction (they were too far away to do any damage). In the meantime, the main body of his men marched inland, crossed the river higher up and came upon the fort on the other side where they were least expected. They captured the fort after a short fight, killing 300 Spaniards and taking 100 prisoners. Not more than 50 Englishmen died.

Although Ysassi (who was in the fort) escaped with some men and continued guerrilla warfare for two more years, after Rio Nuevo they were never again able to obtain reinforcements to take the island. Ysassi and his men finally made canoes and used them to leave the island for good. It is believed the place from which they left is DON CHRISTOPHER'S COVE, St Mary.
[Osborne 1971]

RIVERMAID see WATER SPIRITS

ROARING RIVER, St Ann Parish
This river marks the start of a stretch of coastline that was known by the Spaniards as *Chorreras* (see OCHO RIOS). The Roaring River consists of two tributaries of equal length – the Roaring and Little Rivers – which come together a little above the spectacular but not very accessible falls. A hydroelectric station has harnessed much of the water in the river below the falls for electricity.

ROARING RIVER, Westmoreland Parish
This river's source near a modern filtration plant at Shrewsbury is said to be 'the best-known example of the rise or emergence of a Jamaican river in full flow from a subterranean channel'. Water gushes up from the ground, then joins another mountain stream to form the Roaring River. An old aqueduct takes off some of the water.

ROCKFORT
Located on the WINDWARD ROAD, Kingston, this area takes its name from the fort that once stood there, remains of which can still be seen. The main highway once passed through the fort. Rockfort was first fortified against an expected FRENCH invasion in 1694. However, the French avoided the fort and attacked further west at CARLISLE BAY. The fort was later enlarged to hold a total of 17 large guns, all covering the approaches from the east. It was last fortified during the MORANT BAY REBELLION of 1865.

Near the fort is a spring that was first used to supply water to the naval base at PORT ROYAL by Admiral Edward VERNON in 1739 and later to the whole town. The water was carried on a sailing ship specially fitted for the purpose until around 1902 when water pipes were laid along the PALISADOES from Rockfort to Port Royal.

Rockfort is now the centre of industrial activity including a power barge, a flour mill, and a cement factory. When the cement factory was established by private enterprise in 1952, it marked the first large industrial undertaking in Jamaica. One of the backers was Sir William Stephenson who under the code name 'Intrepid' during the Second WORLD WAR was in charge of the Anglo-American intelligence and counter-espionage network. Stephenson's work was revealed in the best-selling book, *A Man Called Intrepid* (1976). After the war, Stephenson, a Canadian, acquired a house at Reading, MONTEGO BAY, and lived there for some time.
[Cundall 1915, Wright and White 1969]

ROCKFORT MINERAL SPRING
This mineral spa at ROCKFORT on the WINDWARD ROAD has been a big attraction for generations of Kingstonians. The water rises from cold mineral springs in the hills above, and flows through the

Rockfort in the late 19th century

bath and into the sea under the main road. The water is slightly saline and is more radioactive than BATH, St Thomas. Rockfort was a well-known place for watering ships from the mid-17th century.

RODNEY, Admiral George (1718-92)

Famous BRITISH admiral who was regarded as a hero in 18th century Jamaica because he saved the island from almost certain capture by the FRENCH. During the American Revolution when France and Spain also declared war on England, France attempted to seize British possessions in the West Indies. Rodney led the resistance from PORT ROYAL and eventually defeated the French fleet.

By 1782 the American colonists aided by the French had virtually won the War of Independence and Britain was badly defeated elsewhere. Of all the British West Indies, only Jamaica, Barbados, and Antigua were still in British hands. The French commander, Admiral de Grasse, decided to join forces with the Spaniards and invade Jamaica. De Grasse's fleet first assembled at the French island of Martinique with Rodney and his fleet keeping close watch. Because of the lack of communication, the island of Jamaica in the meantime had no way of knowing what was happening, and the inhabitants spent weeks waiting tensely for the expected invasion. Then, Rodney appeared at Port Royal as the victor of the 'Battle of the Saints' with the French

Admiral Rodney

admiral's flagship *Ville de Paris* in tow and the admiral himself as prisoner. In the final battle only de Grasse himself and two of the men on his ship remained unwounded. Jamaica went wild with joy and for many years thereafter, Rodney was regarded as a great hero. The Assembly voted over £1,000 to commission the RODNEY MEMORIAL.
[Cundall 1915]

RODNEY MEMORIAL

This elaborate structure at the northern end of the SPANISH TOWN SQUARE is a memorial erected by a grateful House of Assembly to the BRITISH naval hero Admiral George RODNEY after he saved the island from almost certain capture by a FRENCH fleet led by Admiral de Grasse in 1782. The memorial consists of an eight foot statue of Rodney on a square pedestal, set in an octagonal temple featuring eight circular columns supported by buttresses. Curving colonnaded walkways link the temple to buildings on either side of it.

John Bacon (1740-99), the most important English sculptor of the day, was commissioned to create the statue and is supposed to have made two trips to Italy before he found a block of marble large enough for the design. The statue eventually weighed 204t. Rodney is shown in the dress of a Roman emperor because this was the artistic convention of the time. The House of Assembly had voted £1,000 for the statue but the entire project ended up costing nearly £31,000.

The 'temple' over the statue was made locally. The panel at the rear of the statue shows de Grasse's flagship striking the flag of surrender. Two other panels have symbolic reliefs featuring Britannia. The Latin inscription translated reads:

> To George Brydges Rodney
> Baron Rodney
> victor in a sea fight
> on the day before the ides of April
> in the year of our Lord 1782.
> He restored peace to Britain.
> The legislature and the people of Jamaica presented [this memorial].

In front of the monument, typifying the spoils of war, are two brass cannon that were taken from the French flagship *Ville de Paris*. They were cast in the French Royal Foundry in 1748 and are finely decorated and hand-finished. They bear the motto of King Louis XIV. Over the front arch of the superstructure is the Rodney coat of arms.

Rodney memorial

When the inhabitants of KINGSTON and PORT ROYAL heard that the statue was to be placed in SPANISH TOWN (then the capital), they petitioned the House of Assembly to have it placed at the Parade in Kingston. The petition was rejected only by the casting vote of the Speaker. The statue was, however, temporarily located in Kingston (1872-89).

ROLLING CALF
Legendary calf-like monster-animal with red, fiery eyes, trailing a clanking chain and capable of growing to huge size, rolling over and over as it moves around the countryside at nights. R.T. Banbury, writing in the mid-19th century, portrayed 'Rollen Calf' as more of a shape-shifter, an evil spirit that could assume different shapes and dispute the path at night with travellers. Rolling Calf can be beaten with a tarred whip (held in the left hand) which it fears more than anything else. Beaten, it will echo the familiar cry of all DUPPIES when they are chastised: 'Me dead two time, oh.' If one believes one is being followed by a Rolling Calf (one's head 'growing big' is a sign), one should prepare to 'tek foot in hand' and run, or at the very least, employ the usual CHARMS. These might include dropping objects for it to count, cutting the sign of the cross, etc., and trying to get to a cross-road before it does (this spirit is always portrayed as male). Sticking an open penknife in the ground and running without looking behind you is also advisable.

In the daytime, the Rolling Calf like other duppies is said to live at COTTON TREE roots, in CAVES, or BAMBOO roots, and can only be seen by 'four-eye' people who are specially equipped to see spirits. It is said that people who are particularly wicked in life turn into Rolling Calf, a category that in the old days consisted mainly of butchers and shopkeepers who cheated their customers. Or, says another account, when a man is too wicked for Heaven and not bad enough for Hell, he turns into a Rolling Calf. The Rolling Calf is also encountered in Guyana.
[Banbury 1894, DJE, Hurston 1938, Mico 1896, Rampini 1873]

ROMAN CATHOLIC
This was the first Christian denomination to be established in Jamaica. On 6 May 1494, COLUMBUS took possession of the island for the Catholic Spanish monarchs and renamed it Santiago in honour of the Spanish St James of Campostela (though it reverted to its TAINO name – see JAMAICA). The historian Fr Francis Osborne, SJ, has suggested that the honour of the second Mass celebrated in the New World probably belongs to Jamaica. Columbus had a chaplain with him on the voyage who more than likely would have celebrated Mass some time between the 6 and 9 of May. (Mass was said for the first time in Hispaniola, 6 January 1494.)

The SPANISH settlers who began to arrive in 1509 brought their religion with them and the first Roman Catholic church was built at Sevilla la Nueva (see SEVILLE, New), the site of the present Catholic church, followed by two churches in what is now SPANISH TOWN. After Jamaica became a BRITISH possession (see CAPTURE OF JAMAICA), the Church of England (ANGLICAN) became the established church and Roman Catholicism was not allowed. There is evidence that there were secret Catholic worshippers, especially in a chapel in PORT ROYAL established at his house by James Castillo, the agent for the *asiento* (the contract by which Britain supplied Spanish settlements in the New World with slaves).

For a brief time when there was a Catholic monarch on the English throne (James II) Catholics were able to worship openly, but the religion did not gain official sanction again until 1791 when the English parliament removed

Roman Catholic Archbishop the late Samuel Carter

some disabilities on Catholics. In Jamaica their numbers were from that year augmented by FRENCH refugees fleeing the slave revolt in nearby Hispaniola (Haiti) along with their priests, and for a long time the church remained French speaking. The first names recorded in the funeral register of the new Catholic chapel in KINGSTON were of Pierre Sicard, a French planter from Hispaniola, and François Porissard, a slave, buried side by side, 20 August 1795.

The Haitians were mostly planters and as a result, many Catholic churches were established in rural areas. After EMANCIPATION, the church received a boost with the arrival of white settlers who were Catholics in their homelands, including GERMANS, IRISH, and PORTUGUESE. The church was also active in the conversion of CHINESE immigrants.

Like other religious groups in Jamaica, the Catholic church has played a major role in the development of EDUCATION and social welfare institutions in the island and remains a leading religion, with 93,401 listed as Catholics in the census of 1991.

[Bisnauth 1989, Osborne 1988]

St Joseph's Roman Catholic Church, Falmouth

ROSE APPLE see APPLE

ROSE HALL GREAT HOUSE

Now a tourist attraction, Rose Hall offers visitors a tour of a beautifully restored GREAT HOUSE as well as contact with Jamaica's most powerful LEGEND, that of the White Witch.

Located in ST JAMES Parish, near to MONTEGO BAY, this was regarded as the most magnificent planter's residence ever built in Jamaica. The house fell into ruin in the early 20th century and in the 1960s was faithfully restored with authentic period furnishings under the supervision of Tom Concannon, who did much work in historic restoration in Jamaica. It is part of a development that was undertaken by John Rollins, a former lieutenant-governor of Delaware, USA.

Rose Hall Great House

The great house was built between 1770 and 1780 by the Hon John Palmer, CUSTOS of St James, whose wife was Rosa Palmer, to all accounts a loveable and gracious lady. Her beautiful marble tomb can be seen in the ST JAMES PARISH CHURCH, Montego Bay. For a long time, it was believed she was the legendary White Witch (see ROSE HALL, White Witch of) and the words on her tombstone were therefore considered ironic. Only recently have Rosa Palmer's name and reputation been cleared and 'Annee Palmer' designated the 'wicked witch'.

While Rosa and John Palmer were alive, the magnificent Rose Hall was the setting for the most elaborate balls and assemblies on that side of the island. After the death of the couple, Rose Hall was neglected for some years until it was inherited by John Palmer's grandnephew, John

Rose Palmer. In 1820, John Rose Palmer married; his marriage certificate to Annee Palmer is in the Jamaica Archives. Since the record of his burial has also been found in the St James Parish Register, his 'disappearance' at the hands of his wife, as the legends say, is unlikely.

According to the legend, the woman who became mistress of Rose Hall was Annee May Patterson who was born of an English mother and an Irish father and grew up in Haiti where, it is said, she was schooled in vodun. Though Annee Palmer has been identified as the 'White Witch', it is possible that in time her name, like Rosa Palmer's, will be cleared, since no one so far has managed to unravel fact from fiction.

ROSE HALL, White Witch of
Subject of Jamaica's most famous LEGEND. It tells of Annee Palmer, the mistress of Rose Hall plantation who is said to have dabbled in witchcraft, murdered four husbands and had countless lovers. She was finally murdered by the slaves whom she had terrorized. Killed in her bedroom at the ROSE HALL GREAT HOUSE, she was buried in the garden where her grave can still be seen. Across from the present great house, four palm trees together on the beach are said to symbolize Annee Palmer's four husbands. The legends say she wore a ring inscribed: 'If I survive I shall have five.'

Psychic researchers from time to time have visited Rose Hall to establish contact with the White Witch. In the 1950s, Mrs Eileen Garrett, described as 'the famous sensitive', came to Jamaica with the intention of laying Annee's ghost. She was accompanied by her secretary and other witnesses and a transcription of the proceedings was made (and published in the *West Indian Review*). She went into a trance immediately on arrival and claims to have accomplished her mission. However, her success may be judged by the fact that Annee is also supposed to have appeared to a psychic named Bambos, at a seance held Friday, 13 October 1978.

Annee has been the subject of more than one novel, the first and most famous of them being H.G. DeLisser's *The White Witch of Rose Hall*. More recently, she gave her name to the White Witch Golf Course attached to the Ritz-Carlton Rose Hall Hotel that opened in 2000.

ROWE'S CORNER
Small village about 5km from Alligator Pond on the southern coast of MANCHESTER Parish. It is of historic interest because the first elementary school established in Jamaica for black children was located here (see EDUCATION). The school, called 'Somerset', was established by the MORAVIANS in 1823. Three years later it was transferred to LITITZ where the Moravians were given 200ha of land by Mr Ellis, a member of the Assembly, and they founded a mission and school there. In 1979 during the 225th anniversary of the Moravian mission in Jamaica, a monument was unveiled at Rowe's Corner to mark the historic spot. Nearby is an important TAINO site, part of the Alligator Pond Redware Complex which, dated AD 600, represents the earliest Taino settlement thus far found in Jamaica.

RUM
Jamaica's most famous export, an alcoholic drink industrially distilled from molasses which is derived from the juice of the SUGAR CANE. Molasses is the dark brown syrup that remains from the process that extracts the crystals of raw sugar from the cane. The molasses is fermented and with the addition of water and yeast, undergoes chemical changes that break down the sugar into alcohol that is then blended and aged.

Jamaican rums are heavy, dark and full-bodied, the oldest type of rum made; dry and light-bodied rums being manufactured only from the late 19th century. Rum is colourless when distilled; the amber colour characteristic of refined rum comes through ageing in barrels or oak casks from 3 to 20 years, depending on the type required. 'White rum' produced by some countries is rum that is blended but not aged and is a light rum preferred by many. Jamaica's white overproof rum, on the other hand, is regarded as the purview of the serious 'rummer' or for cooking, health and ritual purposes. While most rums contain 40-46 per cent alcohol by volume, white overproof rum contains 57-63 per cent.

Although Jamaican rums have been famous for centuries, the first mixture was developed by the planters of Barbados who added an extra 'kick' to the process that was used by the Brazilians to make a liquor which they called *agua ardente*.

There is speculation about how rum came to be named. A derivation from *Saccharum officinarum*, the Latin name for SUGAR has been suggested. 'Kill-devil' was the original name given to rum when it was first made in the 17th century for, says one chronicler, 'a man who imbibed it promptly became boisterous, reckless and daring'. After a time the liquor came to be called rumbullion – 'a hott, hellish liquor'. By 1667 it had been shortened to 'rum'. Richard

Allsopp in the DCEU points out that 'rum' in the 16th-17th century was cant for 'good, fine, excellent' and 'bullion' from the French bouillon for 'a boiled drink' – hence 'rumbullion'.

Rum was at first the drink of pirates, BUCCANEERS, sailors, servants, and poorer folk, the rich planters importing the spirits they were accustomed to drink in Europe. But gradually rum crept into everyday local life, often in the form of Rum Punch or PLANTER'S PUNCH, and other mixed drinks.

The American colonies were at first large importers of West Indian rum, but after a time they imported the molasses instead and set up their own distilleries. Britain was always a large consumer of rum, in 1810 importing over three million gallons from Jamaica. Part of this might have gone to the British navy, since a daily ration of rum was given to sailors from the 18th century up to 1970. (See GROG.) The military were also supplied with rum which, it is believed, contributed to their high mortality in the tropics, especially those who resorted to raw, unrefined bootleg rum. It was discovered much later that bootleg rum was often contaminated with lead.

The popularity which rum assumed in Europe is reflected in a ditty penned by the English poet Lord Byron (1788-1824):

There is naught no doubt the spirit cheers
As rum and true religion.

And at the height of the slave trade came the often-quoted verse from the English poet William Cowper (1731-1800):

I own I am shocked by the purchase of slaves
And fear those who buy them and sell them
    are knaves.

What I hear of their hardships
Their tortures and groans
Is almost enough to draw pity from stones.
I pity them greatly but I must be mum
For how can we do without sugar and rum?

In Jamaica, jocular names for rum such as 'Rude to Parents', 'Search my Heart' and 'Raise my Thoughts' have all been used by drinkers especially in reference to white overproof rum, called 'whites', a favourite at the 'rum shop', the poor man's meeting place throughout the Caribbean. Usually part of a small shop selling other goods, a rum shop exists in almost every village and is the gathering place for males, the scene of lively arguments and loud DOMINO games. A 'rummarian', 'rummer' or 'rum-bibber' is one who is thought to indulge too much, and can be identified by a 'rum bump', a prominent Adam's apple. 'Rum talk' means chatting nonsense.

White rum is widely used in folk MEDICINE. Rum is used with LIME juice and honey as a favourite antidote for coughs and colds or simply as a night cap. It is also applied externally to cuts, bruises, and for headaches. It is sopped on the body to ward off chills and colds if one is caught in the rain, especially on the 'mole' on top of the head which is thought to be particularly susceptible. Rum is used ceremonially in folk customs, for instance as an offering to the earth by workmen before undertaking such jobs as digging a grave, excavating the foundations for a house, cutting down a COTTON TREE or building a tank. Rum is sprinkled in the corners of a new house before occupation to ward off evil spirits. DUPPIES are said to be fond of rum; it is one of the 'gifts' given as payment by the OBEAH-man or -woman. White rum is essential in some religious rituals. In KUMINA, it is used to bless the drums.

Rum is also widely used in cooking, in mixed drinks and desserts, and is an essential ingredient in CHRISTMAS PUDDING and wedding cake. (See WEDDING, Country.)

[Buckley 1979, Cassidy 1971, DCEU, DJE]

Rum retailer

RUMBA BOX

MUSICAL INSTRUMENT, a bass version of the African thumb piano known variously as *likembe, kalimba, nsansa, mbira*. Elsewhere it is known as the marimba box (Belize), *marímbula* (Cuba), *marimboula* (Haiti). Styles vary but the instrument basically consists of a wooden box with four metal tongues held in position at one end by a bar, the free ends corresponding to

Rumba Box

strings that vibrate when plucked. The player sits on the box and plucks the keys between his or her legs. More primitive versions are made with tongues of BAMBOO or split cane over a box or even a gourd resonator.

The rumba box is a key instrument in MENTO, providing not only rhythmic integrity but an elementary bass line to the Mento ensemble.

RUN DUNG
Popular thick flavourful sauce made of COCONUT milk boiled down with seasoning to the point where it begins to form a custard. Usually salt fish – shad, cod or mackerel – is added, thus 'mackerel run dung', etc. (See FISH, Salt.)

While Run Dung (run-down) seems the most popular name today, the dish had many common names (as listed in the DJE), attesting to its widespread popularity. It was also named 'Dip and Fall Back', because (suggests the DJE), the dish was served in a bowl in the middle of the table in which one dipped starchy food (YAM, boiled green BANANAS, BREADFRUIT, etc.) before 'falling back' and allowing another person to dip. The name 'Dip and Fall Back' probably gained prominence over the others by a song now in the folk repertoire that was popularized and probably composed by the itinerant singing duo Slim and Sam, during the Second WORLD WAR. One verse of the song (a version is quoted in its entirety in Lewin 2000) affirms: 'An if the war should come ya/An bomb begin to drop/I woulda face a tank or a long range gun/fe me dip and fall back.' The final verse quotes 'Mass John' who says:
> Take me land
> Take me mule and take me dray
> Take me married wife and me three sweetheart away
> Take away me house, and take me burial spot
> But don't skylark, I will bus' yu head
> Fe me dip and fall back.

[DJE, Lewin 2000, Taylor 1983]

RUNAWAY
Running away was a form of resistance to SLAVERY that was widely practised, especially before 1740. After that date the MAROONS returned captured runaways to their masters as one of the terms of their peace treaties. According to the Slave Act of 1696, a slave who was absent for less than 12 months was a runaway, punished by severe flogging; after 12 months he or she was classified as a rebel, punishable by death or transportation to another country.

Most of the runaways were newly arrived Africans; men were more likely to run away than women. Runaways often hid on other estates or with lovers; sometimes couples ran off together. Some were audacious: one slave produced a false ticket of freedom and joined in the search for himself. Some ran to Cuba and Haiti since these could be reached in CANOES. Some evaded the Maroons and set up villages; for instance it was reported in 1818 that there were considerable numbers of runaways in the hills between KINGSTON and OLD HARBOUR BAY under a leader called Scipio.

The custom existed where a runaway would ask a neighbouring estate owner or overseer to plead with his master on his behalf when he (or she) wished to return. Many slaves habitually 'pulled foot' for days, weeks, or months so as to visit relatives, spouses, or shipmates from Africa. Others just wanted to have a good time as is suggested by this newspaper advertisement of 1820: 'Runaway creole negro named Caesar, otherwise called Darby, who was well known as a leading character at Dances, Maypols [sic] and Christmas Sets.' (See MAYPOLE, SET GIRLS.)

[Mathurin 1975, Patterson 1973]

RUNAWAY BAY
Town in ST ANN Parish, active in the tourist trade. People like to say that this north coast town got its name because the last Spaniards ran away from the island from this point when the English came. This is not so. (See RIO NUEVO.)

The people who ran away from here were probably African slaves who fled in CANOES to Cuba, only 144km away.

In the early 18th century, there was a great deal of traffic between Cuba and Jamaica's north coast, mostly by traders in mules and CATTLE, who carried the animals in open boats. So it was easy for slaves to travel the same route. Once they arrived in Cuba, their return by the Cuban authorities was highly unlikely. On one occasion, the authorities there turned down a request from the governor of Jamaica for the return of some slaves. The slaves, said the Cubans, had been baptized as ROMAN CATHOLICS and could not be allowed to return to live among heretics.

RUNAWAY CAVE
Although Jamaica has many extremely spectacular CAVES, this is one of the few that has been developed as a visitor attraction. Officially known as Hopewell Cave, it is situated right beside the road about 5km east of DISCOVERY BAY, ST ANN Parish, and is a dry shallow labyrinthine cave with many complex passages and what is called a 'green grotto'.

RUSEA'S SCHOOL
This school in LUCEA, HANOVER Parish, owes its origin to a grateful Frenchman who found a home in Jamaica. Martin Rusea was a protestant (Huguenot) in Catholic France and came as a religious refugee. By his will of 1764 he left his entire estate for the establishment of a school in Hanover in gratitude for the hospitality shown him in Jamaica. Although his relatives contested the will for ten years, the Rusea Trust was eventually established. (See EDUCATION.) The main school building is part of what was originally the old barracks attached to FORT CHARLOTTE.

S

SALLY WATER

One of the most popular ring GAMES played by girls, with one girl – 'Sally' – standing in a ring of players who sing the words of the song while she mimes the actions which end with her choosing a partner who will then replace her:

> Little Sally Water
> Sprinkle in a saucer
> Rise Sally rise and wipe your weeping eyes.
> Sally turn to the east, Sally turn to the west,
> Sally turn to the very one you love the best.

The chorus encourages Sally to 'shake it' to the one she loves the best, providing the opportunity for Sally and the one she has chosen to 'wine' their bodies. Lomax and Elder point out that this is the most popular of all African-American children song games, played in all the southern United States and the West Indies. The song is nevertheless steeped in British lore since it seems to refer to a marriage ceremony in which a water rite played a part, a relic perhaps of pre-Celtic peoples, according to folklorist Alice Gomme (*Traditional Games of the British Isles*). Some versions of the song do have verses referring to 'Sally' being married, e.g.

> Now you are married we wish you joy
> First a girl and then a boy
> Seven years after son and daughter
> Kiss together come out of the water.

In the past the term 'Sally Water' was used to refer to the playing of ring games and similar diversions and was so used by Jekyll in his collection of Jamaican songs and stories.
[Jekyll 1907, Lomax et al. 1997]

SALT

As one of the earliest preservatives known to man, salt has come to assume symbolic importance everywhere and is an emblem of immortality. In many countries, salt is associated with holiness and is thus used to repel evil spirits. In Jamaica, many of the European superstitions regarding salt persist. For example, spilling salt is regarded as bad luck that can be deflected if a pinch is thrown over one's shoulder. Salt is also widely used in African-Jamaican DEATH RITUALS. Spirits do not like salt, hence food offered to ancestral (benevolent) spirits must be prepared without salt. Salt is used to repel evil spirits (see DUPPY) and in death rituals to 'tie' or keep the dead spirit from wandering. If one has the misfortune to see a duppy, it is believed salt should immediately be taken as an antidote.

Salt is symbolically associated with the enslavement of Africans in the New World, perhaps the means by which they were spiritually 'tied' by their captors (see SLAVERY); it was widely held that slaves who did not eat salt in captivity would on their deaths be able to return to Africa. Modern back-to-Africa believers or RASTAFARI also do not eat salt. Those enslaved Africans who were born in Africa were called 'Salt Water Negroes', having crossed the Atlantic (see MIDDLE PASSAGE), to distinguish them from the CREOLES, i.e. those born on the islands.

Salt was nevertheless important during the plantation era. 'Salt provisions' or 'salt' for short was the allowance of salted herring or salt fish (see FISH, Salt) provided for each slave, adding relish to a normally bland diet of starches. A liking for salted food – salt pork, fish or meat – persists in Jamaica to this day. The phrase 'to be in one's salt', like 'to be in one's GUNGO', means having plenty to eat and, by extension, being happy. To 'be salt' means to be disappointed. To 'suck salt' is to endure hard times when, presumably, salt is the only food available.
[DJE, Hurston 1938, Opie 1992, Puckett 1926]

SALT FISH see FISH, Salt

SALVATION ARMY

An international religious and charitable movement founded in England in 1865 by William Booth (1829-1912) on semi-military lines, with the leader called a general and members wearing uniforms to signify the fight for Jesus Christ. Booth's original group was known as the Christian Mission; the present name was adopted in 1878. The movement spread throughout the world and its uniformed brass bands, open air meetings, and collection kettles are familiar features. The Salvation Army is noted for its social work among the poor, sick, and unemployed.

The movement in Jamaica was started by W. Raglan Phillips, an Englishman living in WESTMORELAND Parish who in 1887 asked General Booth to send officers to Jamaica. Their first activities were centred at BLUEFIELDS in Westmoreland.

In the 1920s, Phillips (who was also for some time a BAPTIST minister) founded a breakaway offshoot of the Salvation Army, at first called The Light Brigade and later called the City Mission; it still exists with a number of congregations in Jamaica and overseas. Although it shared with the Salvation Army the system of rank and the use of uniforms, the City Mission became increasingly PENTECOSTAL.
[Bowker 1997, Calley 1965]

SAMAN see GUANGO

SAMUEL SHARPE SQUARE
This MONTEGO BAY square was in 1981 renamed to honour the great slave-leader and National Hero, Rt Excellent Samuel SHARPE. A memorial sculpture by Kay Sullivan was erected on the spot where Sharpe and over 300 slaves were hanged for their part in the uprising known as the 'Christmas Rebellion' of 1831-32. Previously it was known as Charles Square after Charles Knowles, a former governor of the island. But even before that, the square, like similar open spaces in other Jamaican towns, was known as the Parade. This dated from the days when all coastal towns had defensive measures, including a local volunteer MILITIA, and a complement of regular soldiers. The St James Regiment that was scattered all over the parish held their quarterly musters at the Parade and it was also the venue for public events.

SANDBOX TREE (*Hura crepitans*)
Large tropical tree (10-25m high) noted for its round, deeply grooved segmented seedpods which burst explosively into sections when ripe, scattering the seeds for quite a distance (up to 14m) hence the name in some countries of Monkey Dinner Bell. The sound of the popping fruit in Jamaica is taken to signify that a 'lizard wedding' is taking place. The popular name 'Sandbox' refers to the large seed pod (up to 8cm in diameter) which in the old days was dried and used to hold sand for blotting ink when blotting paper was not available. The tree is native to the West Indies and Central America and is found in Jamaica at elevations 20-800m. Its trunk and limbs are covered with hard, sharp conical spines. Like other members of the Euphorbia family it has a milky sap. The plant bears both male and female flowers, the female a large-lobed corolla, the more insignificant male grouped on a spike.
[Adams 1972, Huxley 1978, NHSJ 1949]

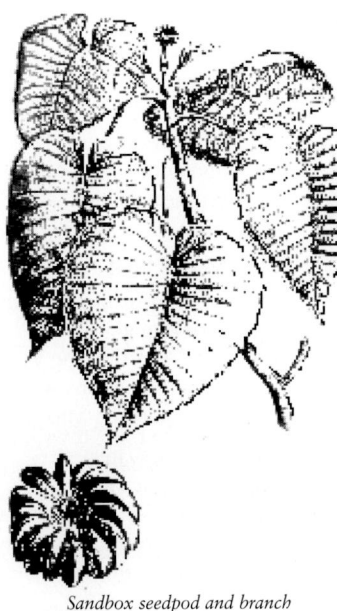

Sandbox seedpod and branch

SANGAREE
Like RUM punch or PLANTER'S PUNCH, a popular drink of plantation days, a mixture of Madeira wine diluted with water and fruit juice and sweetened, probably a derivation of the Spanish sangría. A slave song recorded by J.M. Phillippo (1843) went:

Sangaree kill de captain,
O dear, he must die;
New rum kill de sailor,
O dear, he must die;
Hard work kill de neger,
O dear, he must die.

A 19th century Jamaican cookery book gives the following recipe for sangaree:

'one wine glass and a half of sherry
two wine glasses of water
Nutmeg, lime peel, sugar

Put the water and about a dessert spoonful of sugar into a tumbler first. Grate nutmeg upon it; stir. Then put in a long strip of lime peel. Stir well, adding the sherry last. Mix and serve with a bit of ice in it. This is for one person.'
[Sullivan 1893]

SANTA CRUZ
Place name in ST ELIZABETH Parish (Spanish for Holy Cross), referring to the town of Santa Cruz as well as the Santa Cruz Mountains which bisect the lower part of the parish. This town gained some prosperity from the development of BAUXITE in the area. It is well linked by road to BLACK RIVER and the southern part of the parish

as well as to MANDEVILLE, the business centre of the south western parishes, and capital of MANCHESTER Parish. One road from Santa Cruz leads to Malvern in the cool Santa Cruz Mountains, an area that has long been popular as a holiday resort and residential area. In the Malvern area are located several well-known educational institutions, including Bethlehem Training College, Munro College for Boys, and Hampton School for Girls.

SARSAPARILLA (*Smilax regelii*)
The most popular of the 'roots' used in Jamaican folk MEDICINE, Jamaican Sarsaparilla is sometimes combined with another WIS, Chainy Root (*S. Balbisiana*). Dried pieces of the root are boiled in water and sweetened, the resultant red-coloured drink regarded by many as an excellent TONIC. It is commonly used to 'build strength' and by some males as an aphrodisiac. It is also used as a poison antidote, acting as a diuretic.

A climbing vine that is native to the Guyanas and Brazil, sarsaparilla is found in Jamaica between 200-700m. It was exported to Spain by the SPANISH settlers from the 16th century.
[Adams 1972, Espinosa 1628, Robertson 1990]

SAVANNA-LA-MAR
'The plain-by-the-sea', Savanna-la-mar is the capital of WESTMORELAND Parish, with a population of 16,340 in 1991. It was founded about 1730 as the chief town, displacing Queen's Town which was then the chief settlement and located at a crossroads some miles inland, now called Cross Path.

Savanna-la-mar has been almost completely destroyed by natural disasters many times in its history and old-timers used to recall an incident from the HURRICANE of 1912 when the sea rushed inland for half a mile, leaving the schooner *Latonia* in the middle of Great George

Savanna-la-mar by J.B. Kidd

Great George Street, Savanna-la-mar

Street. In a hurricane of 1748 the sea surge also left ships beached on dry land after the storm. In 1780, the sea rushed inland for nearly a mile, a scene described by William BECKFORD in his *Descriptive Account of the Island of Jamaica*. Part of the town of that date remains underwater, like the more famous town of PORT ROYAL. The hurricane of 1780 was predicted by a slave bandit named PLATO who terrorized travellers on the highway between Westmoreland and ST JAMES.

Edward Long noted that the town carried on a considerable trade with Truxillo, Honduras and the MISKITO Shore (now in Nicaragua), the passage to which was 'short and speedy' from the trade wind.

The Savanna-la-mar Parish Church was built in 1904 on the foundation of an older church dating to 1797, and the courthouse in 1925. Remains of FORT GEORGE can be seen at the end of Great George Street. In 1755 when the admiral inspected this fort he pronounced it the very worst in the island; although the inhabitants had laid out a vast sum of money for defence, the fort had never been finished and one-third had already collapsed into the sea. On the west side of the fort is the West Indies Sugar Company pier from which SUGAR from the central factory at FROME is loaded into lighters for transporting to the ships anchored offshore. This pier is used mostly in the crop season, from January to June.
[Cundall 1915, Long 1774, Wright and White 1969]

SCHOOLGIRL
Term used to describe an old custom whereby a girl child from a poor family was sent to the home of a better-off person to perform light housekeeping duties in the hope that she would derive some advantage from the exchange, such as an education. The custom was called 'caretaker' in Trinidad, *kweki* in Dutch Guiana and *ti-moun* in Haiti. Herskovits said it was an African tradition that persisted in the New World.

In some upper class families, the schoolgirl was an attendant to the ladies of the house, often sleeping on the bedroom floor on a mattress or a truckle bed placed under the high four poster bed. This practice ensured the physical and moral safety of both the lady and the schoolgirl, who might earn more favour than was accorded to a maid by her employer-keeper.

Although similar arrangements were made for boys, the term 'schoolboy' was not used, 'yard boy' perhaps serving as the corresponding expression.

[Herskovits 1976]

SCOTS

The earliest arrivals from Scotland were mainly prisoners of war, taken during the uprisings against Cromwell's rule. Thousands were forcibly transported to the American colonies to be sold as bond servants to the settlers; they were said to be 'barbadosed' from the numbers sent to that colony. Those taken in 1653-54 were sent to Jamaica after its capture by Cromwell's forces in 1655 (see CAPTURE OF JAMAICA). Hundreds of Scots were shipped off to the colony in 1745-46 after the failure of the last Jacobite uprising (Jacobites being supporters of King James II and his descendants who claimed the throne of England). Also transported from Scotland in the late 17th century were 'idle' beggars, gypsies and criminals, to Virginia, Barbados, and Jamaica.

The number of Scots in the island considerably increased with the arrival in 1700 of the remnants of the failed Scottish settlement of Darién (See CAMPBELL.) There was also considerable voluntary emigration from Scotland, some for religious reasons, some by young men in search of adventure, but more in search of fortune. In addition to those forcibly shipped, poor men and women from the British Isles also voluntarily signed up to work for a designated master in the Caribbean and North American colonies for a fixed period of time, in exchange for passage and maintenance during the term of contract. Jamaica continued to be an important destination for white indentured servants from the late 1600s to the 1750s. Skilled Scottish servants were in especial demand and many planters specifically requested them. (See also IRISH.) White indentureship preceded the widespread institution of black slavery and there were far more white servants in the early days of the plantation system, but as slavery proved a more economic solution to the labour problem, the whites were priced out of the market. Over time, black slaves also took over many of the skilled jobs on the plantations formerly held by white tradesmen. After the mid-18th century, few continued to be recruited, except as BOOK-KEEPERS and the like. Those whites that chose to remain found other means of earning a living outside of the plantations, the Scots being best equipped to move up in society.

Professionals Alan Karras in his book on Scottish migrants to Jamaica and the Chesapeake makes a distinction between the permanent Scottish immigrants who were almost universally drawn from the lower echelons of Scottish agricultural society in the highlands and lowlands and most of those arriving after 1740 whom he describes as 'sojourners'. These were well educated, middle class men who came with the intention of making their fortune and returning home as quickly as possible. A high proportion of these Scots were professionals, especially doctors and lawyers. Many became attorneys, as estate managers were called. One doctor, at least, achieved notoriety (see EDINBURGH CASTLE).

Those with professional and mercantile qualifications generally made a speedier entry into the plantocracy, though many a poor Scottish lad who started in the lowest ranks of managerial whites on an estate rose to become its owner.

By 1750 Scots made up about one-third of the white population of Jamaica. It was noted that 'Jamaica, indeed, is greatly indebted to North-Britain, as very near one third of the inhabitants are either natives of that country, or descendants from those who were. Many have come from the same quarter every year, less in quest of fame, than of fortunes; and such is their industry and address, that few of them have been disappointed in their aim'. The planter-historian Edward Long concluded: 'To say the truth, they are so clever and prudent in general, as by an obliging behaviour, good sense, and zealous services, to gain esteem.' Education also helped, 'the good education, which the poorest of them receive, having great influence on their morals and behaviour'. Lady Nugent in 1801 observed that 'almost all the agents, attorneys, merchants and shopkeepers, are of that country, and really do deserve to thrive in this, they are so industrious'.

The Scots also encouraged others of their families to emigrate and were noted for helping their own countrymen. Long had heard of one hundred Campbells resident in Jamaica, 'all claiming alliance with the Duke of Argyle'. An anonymous writer in 1780 quotes a black as saying: '*England* must be a large place and Scotland a small one; for *Scots Bacceroes* (which they call all white Men) all know one another, *but English Bacceroes no know one another.*'

The Scots' support of one another reaches a kind of climax in *Marley*, an anonymous novel published in 1828 but believed written by someone with intimate experience of the island. The hero hears of a Mr Campbell who hires only Gaelic-speaking highlanders: 'The very negroes . . . so well understand his predilection for the language of his clan, that when they see a walking buckra seeking employment . . . they accost him with the question, "Can you talk Gaelic? for, if you can't massa no employ you".'

Post-emancipation   In the 19th century, Scots immigrants were brought into the island as part of a scheme (largely unsuccessful) to import Europeans to fill the expected labour shortage on the plantations following EMANCIPATION of the slaves and to establish a white yeoman class in the mountains. (See also GERMAN, IRISH, PORTUGUESE.) The last of these immigrants arrived in 1845. Some were imported by planters and their agents, under inducement of a bounty. Most of the Scots, like the other Europeans, were expected to work in the SUGAR CANE fields and COFFEE plantations.

Others were recruited by official government agents and the plan was to place them in European townships to be created in the mountainous interior, one to be established in each county. The German settlement of Seaford Town was one of these, established in the county of Cornwall; plans to create a township in Middlesex were abandoned. The Surrey township of Altamont was established on the upper RIO GRANDE, near to the MAROON settlement of Moore Town. It was believed the Highland Scots would take readily to the mountainous terrain and misty climate of PORTLAND Parish. Houses were built on the 200ha allotted and Maroons were hired to plant crops for each family before their arrival. In 1837, one group of Scots arriving from Aberdeen was sent to the township. They prospered initially, but within a few years, many were dead from illness, including most of the family heads. The remaining women and children went to live in the Maroon villages of Moore Town and Mill Bank. Over time, the remnants of this Scottish outpost became absorbed into Maroon culture, family names of Brodie, Keller, Hepburn, Stevenson, Allan, Christian and Mitchell attesting to their presence, according to Maroon historian Beverly Carey.

Many place-names in other parts of Jamaica recall the Scottish influx: Auchenbreck and Auchendown (WESTMORELAND Parish); Blackstonedge (ST ANN Parish); Carlisle Bay (CLARENDON Parish); Dressikie (ST MARY Parish); Edinburgh Castle (St Ann Parish), and so on through the alphabet.

Cultural customs   During the plantation era, it was noted that the free COLOUREDS tended to imbibe Scottish customs, especially in recreation, but so did the slaves, the narrator in the song 'Quaco Sam' (see DANCE) asserting:

> Me wi dance de shay-shay, me wi dance de cotch reel,
> Me wi dance till ebry craps a me foot-battam peel.

This is one thing the anonymous slave woman had in common with the governor's wife, as Lady Nugent's *Journal* mentions dancing highland reels more than once, on one occasion recording, 'after supper, I forgot all my dignity, and with all my heart joined in a Scotch reel. – Many followed my example and the ball concluded most merrily'.

The Scots in Jamaica continued their customs up to recent times, such as the celebration of St Andrew's Day with a traditional menu ending with the 'national dish' of Haggis brought in to the strains of the bag-pipes.

Like the Irish, the Scots also influenced Jamaican speech patterns (see LANGUAGE). According to D'Costa and Lalla: 'Living in daily contact with slaves, the speakers of regional English, Hiberno-English and the Celtic languages of Ireland, Scotland, and Cornwall (Cornish was extinct by the end of the eighteenth century), provided the models of English for Africans and creoles alike.'

[Carey 1970, D'Costa and Lalla 1989, Galenson 1981, Karras 1992, Long 1774, Nugent 1839, Patterson 1973]

SCOTS KIRK

St Andrew's Scots Kirk, located on Duke Street, KINGSTON, was the principal PRESBYTERIAN church in the island; today it is a congregation of the UNITED CHURCH in Jamaica and the Cayman Islands.

Originally founded as Scots Kirk, it was rebuilt after the EARTHQUAKE of 1907 on the foundations of the original church that had been erected in 1819 at a cost of £12,000. Funds for the rebuilding came from Scotland and local persons as well as a grant from the Jamaican

Scots Kirk

government. The original building, designed by James Delaney, was a brick and stone octagonal with a gallery supported by tall, stately mahogany pillars. In 1821, visiting artist James Hakewill found it 'the handsomest building in Jamaica'. In reconstruction, the height of the original building was reduced.

In December 1939 the membership of St Andrew's Kirk (corner of East Queen St and John's Lane) which had also been badly damaged in the earthquake united with Scots Kirk, thus ending a separation that had been based largely on the class and social status of the founders of each. The church then became St Andrew's Scots Kirk.

The church has made a major contribution to choral music in Jamaica, having been home to the St Andrew Singers from 1947 till recent times. The church organ is said to be one of the finest in the West Indies.
[Anon 1998, JJ 21:1 1988]

SEA GRAPE
(*Coccoloba uvifera*)
A tree (also called Seaside Grape) that is characteristic of Caribbean beaches but also grows inland, easily identified by its almost circular, smooth, leathery leaves with prominent red veins and its green, fleshy fruits hanging in narrow bunches like European grapes. The fruits are edible though hardly eaten, remaining hard and green for a long time. When they turn purple – which they do one at a time – they can be used to make jelly. The plant's habit depends on its environment; on beaches it often remains a sprawling shrub but in more sheltered locations it will grow into a large tree. It is a native of the Caribbean and tropical America. The hard wood is sometimes used for boat building and making furniture.
[Adams 1971, Bourne et al. 1988, Kingsbury 1988]

SEA SHELL see SHELL

SEACOLE, Mary (1805-81)
Jamaican woman of colour (see COLOURED) who lived an exceptional and adventurous life. Like Florence Nightingale, she achieved her greatest fame as a nurse during the Crimean War (1854-56) though under very different circumstances. She wrote a book called *Wonderful Adventures of Mrs Seacole in Many Lands* that was published in England in 1857 and became a bestseller.

Born in 1805 in Kingston as Mary Jane Grant, she was the daughter of a free black woman and a Scottish army officer. Her mother ran a boarding house called Blundell Hall where her clientele included many British naval and army officers and their families, to whom she also provided medical services, being a notable 'doctoress' (see MEDICINE, Folk.) It was from her mother that Mary gained her earliest knowledge of treatments of tropical diseases and ailments that would later bring her fame, knowledge vastly augmented over her lifetime by her natural curiosity and eagerness to grasp all opportunities to learn about medicine.

Mary Seacole

Of an adventurous spirit, she travelled abroad several times before marrying in 1836 Edwin Horatio Seacole, an English merchant and godson of Lord NELSON, as she stated in her will. After his death, soon followed by that of her mother, she took over Blundell Hall and built it into a much larger establishment. She became a noted doctoress in her own right, especially during the CHOLERA epidemic of 1850. Shortly after that, she undertook travels in Central America, including a spot of gold prospecting. She spent three years in PANAMA while the

Sea Grape

railroad was being built, and functioned as doctoress and hotelkeeper. (See COLÓN MAN.)

In 1854, she read with interest of the start of the Crimean War (which was fought on the Crimean peninsular, a part of Russia on the Black Sea, between Russia on the one hand and Turkey, France, Sardinia and England on the other). One of the British regiments sent there had once been stationed in Jamaica, and she regarded the officers as 'her boys'. When she read of the terrible death toll and the need for medical help, to the Crimea she decided to go.

'I never stayed to discuss probabilities, or enter into conjectures as to my chances of reaching the scene of action,' she says in her *Wonderful Adventures*. 'I made up my mind that if the army wanted nurses, they would be glad of me, and with all the ardour of my nature . . . I decided that I would go to the Crimea; and go I did, as all the world knows.'

The soldiers were being ravaged by tropical diseases such as cholera, YELLOW FEVER AND MALARIA as well as dysentery. Based on her extensive experience of such diseases in Jamaica and Panama, Mrs Seacole on arrival in England had confidently applied to the British War Office to go as a nurse; Florence Nightingale was then assembling her first ever team of nurses. But there was no room for a woman of colour.

Undaunted, at the age of 49, Mrs Seacole bought up a stock of goods to sell and set out for the battlefield. In these times, before the army established its own catering system, it was people like Mrs Seacole – called 'sutlers' – who catered to the men. But Mrs Seacole went well beyond that service, establishing a store, canteen, and the British Hotel two miles from Balaclava, which became a home away from home for the officers and soldiers. For the duration of the war, she herself went on to the battlefields to care for the wounded and dying, becoming a familiar figure to the soldiers and a household name to the British public through newspaper accounts of her activities. She travelled to the front by mule back, medicines of her own preparation on one mule, baskets of wines and hams on another. She moved around as the war shifted, bringing comfort as she could and catering to the soldiers whether they could pay her or not.

One doctor remembered that she 'out of the goodness of her heart and at her own expense, supplied hot tea to the poor sufferers . . . She did not spare herself if she could do any good . . . In rain and snow, in storm and tempest, she was at her self-chosen post, with her stove and kettle, in any shelter she could find, brewing tea for all who wanted it'. Even without waiting for a cease-fire, she went on to the battlefield to care for the sick and dying, of enemy or ally, becoming known to all as 'Mother Seacole'.

She returned to London penniless at the end of the war in 1856, but was befriended by royalty and people in high places and seems to have become a well-known 'character' on the London scene. She travelled back and forth to Jamaica but died and was buried in London in 1881.

Despite enormous fame during her lifetime, Mrs Seacole seems to have been forgotten soon after her death and so remained until the centenary of the Crimean War rekindled interest. In 1954, the headquarters of the Jamaican Nurses' Association was named in her honour, to be followed by a hall of residence for women at the UNIVERSITY OF THE WEST INDIES, and a ward at the Kingston Public Hospital. In England, in 1973, a group of West Indian women undertook to focus public attention on this remarkable woman with a public re-consecration of her grave in St Mary's Catholic Cemetery, Harrow Road, London. Since then, interest in Mrs Seacole has revived and her book, *Wonderful Adventures* is again in print, in several editions.
[Fryer 1984, Seacole 1857]

SEAFORD TOWN see GERMAN HERITAGE

SEASONING
The process of becoming acclimatized, in colonial times used in relation to Europeans first coming to the tropics, but more significantly, to those forcibly brought from Africa as slaves (see SLAVERY).

Mary Seacole in a hospital on the Crimea, as depicted in 'Punch', 30 May 1857

After enduring the horrors of the MIDDLE PASSAGE and (in the early days) the ordeal of being sold by scramble, the slave was taken to the estate to which he or she would belong, to be branded (by a hot silver brand) and given a new name. Slaves would then be expected to undergo a period of 'seasoning' that lasted from one to three years. The purpose was to enable them to become acculturated to plantation life. This included not just the work routine but learning a new LANGUAGE by which to communicate with fellow slaves and the master.

During this time, the newcomer was theoretically assigned light tasks to enable him or her to adjust. However, the death rate was between one-quarter and one-third of the new arrivals. They often died from amoebic dysentery and other diseases contracted on the Middle Passage, malnutrition exacerbated by a drastic change in diet on arrival, and environmental factors such as the chilly Jamaican nights to which they were exposed without proper clothing. Some were set to labour too early, before they had physically recovered their strength. The mental state of the new arrivals was a significant factor; depression was common and the rate for RUNAWAYS was highest for this group; yet they were the ones least able to survive on their own in the new environment. Not surprisingly, the newly arrived and traumatized slaves were described (by the planter-historian William BECKFORD) as totally indifferent: cold, unfeeling and unpredictable.

Newcomers would be placed under the supervision of an older slave of his or her own country. While this might have been advantageous to both, the young slave was sometimes cruelly exploited by the older. In other cases, the new slave would be given a PROVISION GROUND already planted with some food and be forced to work on it on Sundays, under supervision of a driver. As a third option, some masters gave the slaves provisions from the stores for a year.

In the early days, the tribal divisions of the slaves was marked, and newcomers tended to seek out their own. In addition, the CREOLES or Jamaican-born slaves tended to stick together, regarding themselves as superior to the 'Salt-water Negroes', as the African-born were called (see SALT).

[Patterson 1973]

SEASONS

In the CARIBBEAN, the 'seasons' have acquired different meanings from those in the temperate zones. The four seasons are not clearly marked, and seasons are usually designated as 'dry' and 'wet'. The term is also applied to 'HURRICANE season' and 'CHRISTMAS season', both of which have marked weather and vegetal patterns.

The word 'season' is applied to rains that fall at the time they are needed, i.e. at the start of planting. In Jamaica and the rest of the Greater Antilles, the wet season (coinciding with spring) usually commences in May and is characterized by heavy rain and thunderstorms every day, sometimes for weeks. At the end of this time, 'planting season' begins. Summer usually begins in July when the days are very hot and the skies cloudless, the nights clear with a brilliant sky; the heat is somewhat moderated by the sea breeze which blows inland on most days though it is often absent in September. There is also a land breeze by night that is especially felt blowing down the river valleys. The peak hurricane season is from August to October and some rain will fall, culminating in October which is another wet month. The months of November to April are usually dry and cool, considered the most comfortable time and coinciding (more or less) with the winter tourist season.

'Season' is often equated with 'time'. Cassidy and LePage in the DJE define 'Time' as follows: 'A season; a period of time considered in terms of the prevailing weather, or some effect thereof.' Thus 'season' is used metaphorically to designate food surplus or food scarcity, identified by what crop is bearing, e.g. TAMARIND season (hard time), MANGO season (time of plenty), and 'Hungry time' or 'Hungry season'. Season is also applied to the animal world, as in 'BIRD shooting season'.

In the plantation era, the word 'season' was applied to the year's work on the SUGAR estate. 'Croptime', beginning after the Christmas celebrations, was the most important, the 'season' around which plantation life revolved. According to Philip Curtin: 'The planters' year began and ended on August 1. By that date, the previous crop was shipped and the books were closed,' hence First of AUGUST became an important seasonal marker. During the actual 'crop' which lasted for three or four months, all the canes had to be cut, transported to the mill, ground and made into sugar and RUM. Although crop-time was the busiest time of year, for the slaves it was the healthiest as they had free access to cane juice, regarded as a source of nourishment and vitality.

The 'planting season', then as now, took advantage of the rains expected in the spring and

autumn months and 'out of crop' or 'dead season' signified the period between September to Christmas when the factories were not operating and many food crops were scarce. (For the 'social season', see SPANISH TOWN.)
[Curtin 1955, DJE, GOJ Handbook of Jamaica 1961]

SEATING, Ceremonial
The TAINOS had elaborately carved ceremonial seats called *duhos* that were regarded as status symbols (their use limited to the elite) and said to be among their most valuable possessions. Like other elite items, they were probably important for trade and exchange among the nobility.

The *duho* was part of the ritual paraphernalia of the shaman-CACIQUE who sat on it during religious and other ceremonies. When he died, he was buried seated on his *duho*, inside a crypt of sticks, over which earth was thrown.

Many of these beautiful objects (usually of dark EBONY wood but also of CEDAR, MAHOGANY, LIGNUM VITAE and stone) have been found. They are usually carved at one end with the head of a ferocious animal or ZEMI. Fernando Colón (son of COLUMBUS) noted one such wooden stool 'made of one piece, in very strange shapes, almost resembling some living creature with four very short legs. The tail was lifted up, and as broad as the seat, to serve for the convenience of leaning against; and the front was carved into the resemblance of a head, having golden eyes and ears'. Such carvings of ferocious creatures are a feature of these stools elsewhere in tropical America where they are also used ritually, for example the Maya, the Chibcha of Costa Rica and Panama, and the Arawak and Warrau of Guyana.
[Alegría 1985, Bercht et al. 1997, Fewkes 1907, Lathrap 1970, Rattray 1927, Roth 1901, Rouse 1992, Wilson 1990]

Ceremonial seating is also part of African culture as seen in this Bameleke chief's stool, Cameroon, Africa

Taino duho

SENSEH FOWL
The senseh or sensay is a type of domestic fowl that used to be very common in Jamaican YARDS because it was used as a guard against 'tricks' or conjuration, supposedly being able to detect and 'scratch up' such objects. (See CHARM, OBEAH.) The name comes from the Twi (West African) word *asense*, which means a hen without a tail, a fowl with ruffled feathers. Senseh fowls have 'peel neck', i.e. no neck feathers. They were also highly regarded because they would fight off the MONGOOSE, the scourge of the barnyard. The bird is also called Jack Panya (Jack Spaniard) according to the DJE because its sparse feathers are reddish.

The name 'Jack Panya' is also applied to a native bird, the Greater Antillean Bullfinch (*Loxigilla violacea*), also known as 'Jack Sparrow'.

SENSITIVE PLANT see MIMOSA

SET GIRLS
Carnivalesque processions of beautifully dressed young women which formed a central part of the elaborate CHRISTMAS celebrations in the late 18th and early 19th centuries and which were also associated with JONKONNU. Most of the participants were slaves or free blacks and COLOUREDS. The prints by Belisario (1837) show some of the set girls in their splendour in the early 19th century. But there is little reference to them after that time; the set girls too seemed to have faded away when Jonkonnu itself, under pressure from authorities and MISSIONARIES, ceased to occupy centre-stage. One element, the rivalry of two 'sets' dressed in red or blue, seemed to have been preserved or revived in BRUCKINS Party.

Each 'set' consisted of a group of young women who would be dressed identically and elaborately in the same colour. Thus each set would be known as the 'Yellow set', 'Blue set', etc. In their lavish clothing, they would parade the streets singing and dancing and trying generally to outdo each other. Often the sets were led by an older woman called a 'Maam' whose duty was to keep order.

These sets have been cited as early as 1776

Set girls by Belisario

and probably began in KINGSTON and then spread to other towns and throughout the countryside. The 'Blue' and 'Red' set girls of Kingston are said to have arisen from among the female guests invited to the separate balls hosted by the military and the naval officers. The Reds represented the Red-coats or army billeted on the island and the Blues, the Blue-jackets or sailors of the navy.

Errol Hill suggests that the islandwide engagement with things military at the time of the Anglo-French wars and the celebrations following RODNEY'S return to the island after his defeat of the French fleet in 1782, might have given an impetus to the rise of the 'set girls'. The rivalry perhaps originated in the taverns frequented by the sailors or soldiers and their respective female attachments.

The early sets were later reinforced by the FRENCH creole sets consisting of Haitian refugees, and a host of other sets based on location (e.g. a set from each plantation), skin pigmentation and other status distinctions. The set girls at their height represented a wide range of female power and – it might be added – ritualized contest and competition, elements that are expressed today in the DANCEHALL environment.
[Belisario 1837, Hill 1992, Ryman 1984a]

SET UP
Custom of sitting up all night with the family of a dead person. The length of the 'set up' varies – it might be only the first night, all the nights immediately after death until the burial, the night of the burial, the ninth night after death or it might last for all nine nights after death. (See NINE NIGHT, WAKE.)

SEVENTH-DAY ADVENTIST
Protestant church that started out as one of the group of Adventist sects expecting the Second Coming of Christ ('advent') in 1844. They began to observe the seventh day of the week (Saturday) as the Sabbath, although the name 'Seventh-day Adventist' was not adopted until 1861. The Bible forms the basis of Adventist faith and practice and members are expected to live a life of strict temperance, abstaining from alcohol and tobacco and observing dietary laws from the Old Testament. They observe the Sabbath from sunset on Friday to sunset on Saturday. Adventists still believe the return of Christ is imminent, though they set no date for that event.

The church was first organized in KINGSTON in 1894 and is now one of the most popular and fastest-growing religions in Jamaica. There were 208,173 adherents in the 1991 census. In addition to churches around the island, Adventists established a number of educational institutions, including West Indies Training College in Mandeville (MANCHESTER Parish) in 1919 (now Northern Caribbean University), and Andrew's Memorial Hospital in Kingston.
[Bowker 1997, GOJ Handbook of Jamaica 1961]

SEVILLE GREAT HOUSE
This GREAT HOUSE in ST ANN Parish dates from the English period of the historic New SEVILLE area. Richard Hemming, the first owner, had come with the English army of conquest in 1655. His grandson built the great house in 1745 on the site of the original 17th century house and it has been subjected to many changes. The last proprietor of Seville, Henry Smallwood Hoskins, who died in 1915, arranged for the property to be put in the hands of the Administrator General of Jamaica and is buried with two of his three sisters in a small burial plot on the grounds of the great house. It is now owned by the JAMAICA NATIONAL HERITAGE TRUST which administers the New Seville site.

SEVILLE, New (Sevilla la Nueva)
The area along the northcoast highway that is now known as Seville (starting at Priory and continuing eastwards to ST ANN'S BAY) stands on the site of the old SPANISH capital of Jamaica, Sevilla la Nueva (New Seville). It was one of the first cities to be founded by Europeans in the New World. The highway now runs through the site and much of it is buried beneath the cane fields and coconut trees. The site and the archaeological explorations taking place there

Carvings from New Seville

are now under the supervision of the JAMAICA NATIONAL HERITAGE TRUST

At New Seville all the historic periods of Jamaica are represented: the pre-Columbian by at least five TAINO village sites; the Spanish colonial, including the island's first SUGAR mill (1515) and arrival of the first AFRICANS; and the ENGLISH colonial by SEVILLE GREAT HOUSE and associated industrial buildings.

Archaeological interest in the site is enhanced by the fact that COLUMBUS beached his caravels *Santiago de Palos* and *Capitana* here in 1503, eventually abandoning them in 1504 (see COLUMBUS IN JAMAICA). Remains of the city beneath the earth and of Columbus' ships have been the focus of an extensive ongoing search, survey and excavation project. The JNHT/INSTITUTE OF JAMAICA in collaboration with the Spanish Archaeological Mission of the government of Spain and the Institute of Nautical Archaeology at Texas A&M University, USA have been involved. Syracuse University, New York, USA, has been investigating the Anglo-African period.

The Rediscovery of New Seville The city of New Seville was started in 1509 and abandoned in 1534. It fell into ruin, eventually disappearing from view. The ruins were rediscovered after an accident in September 1937. The then manager of Seville property, Mr Gerraint Casserly, was riding his horse over the estate when the horse suddenly stumbled into what on investigation turned out to be an old Spanish well (later determined to be within the so-called governor's house or 'castle'). This well was the starting point for excavations first undertaken by the local archaeologist, Captain Charles Cotter. Although much work has been done, most of New Seville still remains underground, and the remains of Columbus' ships have been so far undetected. A great deal of information on New Seville has nevertheless come to light.

The Colonists New Seville was laid out on the orders of Columbus' son Diego who was appointed governor of the Indies. He sent Don Juan de ESQUIVEL as the island's first governor with orders to found a settlement on the site where Columbus spent a year on the island in 1503-04. Esquivel – who had been with Columbus on that previous occasion – arrived in November 1509 with 60 to 70 colonists, their livestock and supplies. Soon a substantial town of cut-stone and brick buildings with tiled roofs was laid out, using forced Taino labour.

Named after the Spanish city of Sevilla, New Seville covered some 6ha and was planned on a large and splendid scale, though it was never completed. It had brick-paved streets, wells, a 'castle' where the governor lived, a grand church, sugar mills and forts. But its location on the north side of the island placed New Seville off the beaten track since ships travelling between the South American mainland and Cuba and Hispaniola, the nearest Spanish colonies, sailed pass the south coast. The land was low and swampy and the colonists never kept good health. In 20 years they managed to raise only 10 children.

The Spaniards set out to find a better site for their capital city and, crossing the mountains, came to a broad plain near a large river. They built their new capital there and called it Villa de la Vega, the Town on the Plains. Today it is known as SPANISH TOWN.

New Seville was abandoned as a city in 1534, 25 years after its founding, but continued as a settlement till the English took the island in 1655 (see CAPTURE OF JAMAICA). The area was given to one of the English army officers who quickly developed it as a sugar plantation. The Spanish ruins could still be seen for some time after English settlement, being mentioned by Sloane in 1688, the Duke of Portland in 1723, and Edward Long in 1774. But after that New Seville became lost in the cane fields and vanished from memory – until that day in 1937 when a horse accidentally stumbled on a Spanish well.

The Buildings The area called Priory (on the site of what was a Spanish monastery) marks the eastern end of New Seville. The Columbus monument is located on the site. The bronze figure of the explorer is the work of Michele Guerisi of Rome and was cast in Columbus' native city of Genoa. Three small bronze plaques on the sides of the pedestal depict the three small ships that Columbus first set sail in. The coral rock forming the base was raised from OCHO RIOS when a deep-water pier was being built by Reynolds Jamaica Mines and presented by the company. The monument was erected in 1957 largely through the efforts of Fr Neil Donahue SJ and stands on the premises of the ROMAN CATHOLIC Mission. The Roman Catholic Shrine was built by Fr Ray Sullivan SJ in 1939-40. For its construction, some of the stones from the old foundations of the church of Peter Martyr at New Seville, now beneath the cemetery of the present Roman Catholic Church, were used. Other stones came from historic estate buildings in the area.

The governor's house was about 457m north of the church site in the coconut grove between the main road and the sea. It had walls about 1m thick. In 1937 a number of carvings done in Jamaican limestone were discovered on the New Seville site, within the well and scattered over the castle's site. They were intended to decorate the governor's house. Some of the carvings are now in the National Gallery of Jamaica. The inscription of the church of Peter Martyr was found in 1957 in the old fort at St Ann's Bay that was constructed of material from the Seville ruins.

Sevilla la Nueva Church dedicated to Peter Martyr, abbot, stood about 91m west of where Columbus High School now is. It was never finished but was planned as a large building of stone and bricks. Some of the bricks were brought from Spain, others made on the spot. The foundations of the church remained on the site until the 1940s when it was dismantled to provide stones for the construction of the present church. The sugar mill was first excavated by Charles Cotter (1887-1972), in the 1960s, and there are many other traces of Spanish buildings scattered around the estate. Near the shore are the remains of fortifications for the town.

[Aarons 1983-84, Osborne 1988, Wright and White 1969, Wynter 1984]

SHARK PAPERS

These are among the most fascinating documents in the manuscript collection of the National Library of Jamaica. In 1799 when Britain was at war with France, a ship called the *Nancy* was seized by the British and taken to PORT ROYAL on the grounds that she was engaged in illicit trading. The captain swore that his vessel was American and that he was on legitimate business. While the case was in progress and the captain had almost convinced the court of his innocence, another British ship arrived in port and dramatically produced documents that showed that the captain was lying. The documents were the true ship's papers, which had been found inside a shark captured off the coast of Haiti. Apparently the captain had thrown the incriminating papers overboard when he was captured, only to have them swallowed by the shark, which was then caught.

SHARPE, Samuel, Rt Excellent (1801-32)

National Hero of Jamaica. Samuel Sharpe was a 19th century slave leader and BAPTIST deacon, leader of the 'Christmas Rebellion' that engulfed the western parishes from 28 December 1831 – 5 January 1832 and which undoubtedly speeded up the date of the EMANCIPATION of the slaves in the British West Indies. (See SLAVERY.)

Although he acknowledged his role as leader and was hanged, Sharpe had in fact not advocated the violent rebellion that broke out. What he had envisaged a century before Mahatma Gandhi or Martin Luther King, was a movement of passive resistance, a sit-down strike of all the slaves of the western parishes to force the plantation owners to pay them for their work and thus affirm their freedom. He (and many others) believed that the King of England had already given this freedom ('Free Paper') which the plantation owners were withholding. On each of the estates, a driver who was part of the plan, was delegated to tell the overseer when they returned after the three-day CHRISTMAS holidays that the slaves would work no more without wages.

Artist's impression of Samuel Sharpe

But militant elements took over, and on the last night of the holidays, set fire to Kensington estate, located on the highest hill in ST JAMES Parish. By midnight, 16 other estates in the west were burning and rebellion was underway, led by some of Sharpe's most trusted lieutenants.

The rebels easily routed the volunteer MILITIA and roamed over the countryside, gathering

Montpelier Old Works in flames, January 1832. Lithograph by A. Duperly

force and destroying estates, though there was no central plan or military organization. But the terrified planters and their families fled, leaving for a while 50,000 slaves suddenly freed and uncertain what to do. Sharpe himself moved among the estates, counselling and praying, though there was little he could do to control the situation. The rebellion engulfed the west and created panic and fear in the rest of the island, and was not subdued until early January by superior military force.

Then the reprisals against the slaves began. For six weeks, trials were held under martial law at the MONTEGO BAY courthouse and day after day the magistrates handed out sentences of 'guilty'. The slaves were led out and hanged in twos at a gallows on the Parade (now SAMUEL SHARPE SQUARE). They were left hanging until another lot were brought out to be hanged, then they were cut down and thrown into mass graves.

It is estimated that 312 slaves were executed and over 1,000 killed by soldiers, while 16 white colonists were killed. But most historians now agree that if it did nothing else, the rebellion forced the authorities to speed up the process of freeing the slaves, full freedom coming in 1838.

Samuel Sharpe gave himself up to the authorities but even in jail he never lost his composure, praying and preaching to his fellow prisoners.

On 23 May 1832, Sharpe was hanged, the last of the executions. He had admitted responsibility and cleared of any blame the white MISSIONARIES who were themselves in great danger, having been accused of fomenting the rebellion which was called the 'Baptist War' from the number of members of that church who were involved. (See COLONIAL CHURCH UNION, KNIBB MEMORIAL CHURCH.)

'Daddy' Sharpe was held in such high esteem that he was hanged and buried in a suit made and sent to him by the women of the family that owned him and his owner also tried in vain to obtain his body for a decent burial. Instead, he was ordered buried in the sands near the harbour. But Sharpe was loved and respected even in defeat, for many years afterwards, his grave was opened and his bones taken out by three church members and reverently buried in the vault at the old BURCHELL MEMORIAL CHURCH where he had been a deacon.

Although Jamaica was the most rebellious of the New World slave colonies, what made this particular rebellion remarkable is that it was entirely the work of CREOLE slaves, that is, those born in the island and who were, presumably, socialized into European values. Earlier revolts and marronage had involved mainly the African-born community.

Sharpe was a literate man who read the newspapers of the day and his sense of urgency was fuelled by his belief that freedom had been granted but was being withheld by the planters. Contributing to this fear was the violent language used by the planters who were opposed to Emancipation, and the threats by some to hand the island over to the Americans if the Emancipation Act went through. Since slavery still existed in the United States, that would have left no hope for speedy Emancipation.

[Brathwaite 1977, Hart 1985, Senior 1835]

SHAY-SHAY

A dance of past days, equated by some with MENTO, which probably superseded it. The dance is referred to in the song 'Quaco Sam'.

(See DANCE.) The DJE quotes a source as late as 1949 in Manchester Parish: 'Shay-shay, an African dance still practised in the wild areas of the island'; it was also described (1963) as 'a kind of shuffle dance'. A description by H.G. DeLisser sounds very much like what was later called Mento and indeed DeLisser made that connection. As DeLisser described the Shay-Shay, it was danced by two people, always accompanied by song, and consisted of slow movements of the lower part of the body only, as the dancer shuffled over the ground, hence described as 'erotic', 'wild', etc. As late as the 1940s, an outraged grandmother at a village dance called out to her granddaughter to 'shay-shay decent, gyal!' The term comes from French *chassé*, a dance common in the 18th century.

Cheryl Ryman describes Shay-Shay as 'a generic term for any lively or vigorous dance generally considered to be of African origin' and she cites it as referring specifically to a lively figure ('sashay') in QUADRILLE and a particular dance-music style in TAMBU.
[Beckwith 1929, DJE, Lalla and D'Costa 1990, Ryman 1980]

SHELLS (*Mollusca*)
Some 497 species of marine molluscs have so far been found in Jamaican waters, according to Michael Humfrey in his *Sea Shells of the West Indies* (1975). There are many beautiful small species as well as some rather spectacular and equally attractive large shells: queen conch, flame helmet, king helmet, emperor helmet, and trumpet triton. The olive shells, the cowries, and the murexes are also favourite collectors' items.

One of the rarest Caribbean sea shells, Adanson's Pleurotomaria (*Perotrochus adansonianus*) was collected in 1972 at depths of 107m and 153m using the grappling arm of a two-man submersible. The collection site was DISCOVERY BAY, ST ANN Parish. Of interest also, are the tree oysters (*Crassostrea rhizophorae*), that cling to the MANGROVE roots and are exposed when the tide is out. These are collected and sold by street vendors, a pepper sauce being poured on the oyster in the half shell.

Shells of sea snails (*Gastropoda*) account for the largest number of marine shells found in the Caribbean and include the CONCH shell family. Most are simple spiral shells that usually coil to the right. 'Freak' left coiling shells are regarded as especially valuable by collectors.

Scientists regard Jamaica's roughly 555 species of land snails to be about the largest concentration of snail species for any land area of comparable size. The large amount of LIMESTONE (providing calcium carbonate for their shells), isolated hills and valleys, as well as the relatively rapid rate of reproduction probably account for this rather startling speciation. Some 514 species or 93 per cent are endemic.

The most spectacular and numerous of the land shells is the Operculate ('door bearing snails') which is represented by over 300 species worldwide. The snail of this family comes equipped with a lid or door that it closes tightly when it withdraws inside its shell, offering it snug protection from animals and the elements. Many sea snails share this same feature. The door is attached to the animal's foot, which is the last part of the body to be drawn inside.
[Farr 1990, Humfrey 1975]

SHIPMATE
Term used to designate Africans who came over on the same ship. (See SLAVERY.) The bonds formed on the MIDDLE PASSAGE were the most lasting of bonds, like those of blood relatives. Children called their parents' shipmates 'Aunt' and 'Uncle' and shipmates regarded each other's children as their own. The term was also used by INDIAN indentured immigrants. (See also ADDRESS, Terms of.)

SHOEBLACK see HIBISCUS

SHRIMP
In the lower BLACK RIVER morass, shrimping is a major activity. Pots are set in the river banks and open marshes and many of the fishermen still use dugout CANOES. The design of the shrimp pot originated on the Niger and has undergone little change in more than 300 years since its introduction to Jamaica. The shrimps are sold at MIDDLE QUARTERS, ST ELIZABETH Parish, parched and peppery hot.

SHUT PAN
Cylindrical vessel of tin, its tight-fitting cover made with a handle for lifting. Formerly used for carrying food but also employed by Myalists and Obeah-men ('sheppon') to capture spirits. (See MYAL, OBEAH.)

SILK
The Chinese art of using silkworms to produce silk has been tried in Jamaica more than once, including an effort in the early 1900s encouraged by the Jamaica Agricultural Society.

The most ambitious attempt, however, was made in the 1840s at Metcalfeville, near

Claremont, ST ANN Parish (now Whitehorn's Thickets). Bostonian Samuel Whitmarsh established the Jamaica Silk Company and planted out 80ha of mulberry trees for the silk worms to feed on. (The 'worm' is actually a caterpillar that spins itself into a cocoon that can be unwound into a single silk thread.) The company imported thousands of worms and 20 Bostonians to run the industry. Mrs Nancy Prince, the black American freedwoman who wrote a book of her life and travels, actually came to Jamaica on the same ship as the silk experts. Her narrative tells us: 'I left America, November 16th, 1840, in the ship *Scion*, Captain Mansfield, bound for Jamaica, freighted with ice and machinery for the silk factory. There were on board a number of handicraftsmen and other passengers.' Samples of the silk found acceptance in London and enthusiasm ran high. However, the industry never really got off the ground and foundered five years later, mainly for lack of capital. Over the years since then, several other efforts have been made to get a silk industry going.

MULBERRY GARDENS in SPANISH TOWN attests to the long history of this effort. It is said that the name harks back to once extensive mulberry plantations on the bank of the RIO COBRE planted out by the SPANISH settlers with the intention of starting a silk industry.

[GOJ Jamaica 1946, Prince 1850, Wright and White 1969]

SILK COTTON see COTTON TREE

SINKLE BIBLE see ALOE

SLAVERY

To Jamaicans (and other peoples in the Americas of African descent), slavery is still an emotive word and a painful concept, despite the experience of freedom by many generations since slavery ended. While slavery continued in the United States of America until 1865, in Brazil until 1888 and in Cuba until 1890, full freedom was achieved in the British West Indian colonies in 1838.

Yet in Jamaica, even today, from juke boxes and dance halls comes the cry: 'Do you remember the days of slavery?' (Burning Spear). The strong undercurrent of 'Ethiopianism' or identification with an African motherland continues to be expressed in song (see MUSIC, REGGAE), in ART, and other political and cultural manifestations such as the GARVEY movement and RASTAFARI. And yet, though the shackles are off, many will argue that mental slavery remains,

Cape Coast slave fort or 'castle'

with some Jamaicans still unwilling to embrace the idea of an African past because of the identification of Africa with slavery.

The institution of slavery and the politics of colonialism touched every aspect of Jamaican life for hundreds of years. And in the Americas, the institution of slavery came to be identified with the black race, though the system of humans holding others in bondage appears to be as old as human society. Orlando Patterson states: 'There is nothing notably peculiar about the institution of slavery. It has existed from before the dawn of human history right down to the twentieth century, in the most primitive of human societies and in the most civilized. There is no region on earth that has not at some time harbored the institution. Probably there is no group of people whose ancestors were not at one time slaves or slaveholders.'

Pre-Columbian slavery did indeed exist in the Western hemisphere. In the Aztec empire, slaves were persons fallen into bondage as a result of poverty or crime, according to Patterson. It is possible that other Amerindian societies also

Slave coffle

practised slavery in some form, at some time. None, however, practised the wholesale enslavement brought by the Spaniards in the 16th century, a bondage that helped to wipe out the native peoples of the CARIBBEAN. Forced labour in mining (see GOLD) and agriculture helped to destroy the TAINOS.

When COLUMBUS arrived in 1492, the native Caribbean population may have numbered in the hundreds of thousands. By 1570, Amerindians totalled only about 22,150 in Jamaica, Cuba, Hispaniola and other Spanish islands, making up only 26 per cent of the population of the Spanish Caribbean. In the 1570 census, the largest section of the population (56,000) was made up of Africans and the enslaved descendants of slaves: slaves descended from Amerindian and African unions, from African and European unions, and from other combinations of the three races.

The first African slaves to arrive in Jamaica were Iberian blacks brought to Spain and Portugal from West Africa by the Portuguese, the first Europeans to engage in the African slave trade. The Portuguese created forts and permanent trading posts on the African coast, places in which a trading pidgin language probably developed. Africans were imprisoned in such forts as Elmina in present-day Ghana for long periods awaiting transportation.

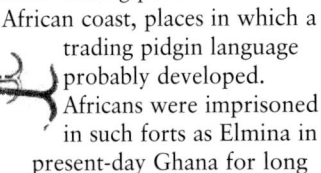

Slave punishment

Prior to the Portuguese venture, African slaves had been sold north and eastwards to the Arab powers. Slave trading on the coast in the 15th and 16th centuries was slow; the great trade routes crossed the Sahara northwards, and went eastwards past Lake Chad, taking slaves, gold and ivory. By the late 17th century, however, routes out to the Atlantic coast developed, as African traders realized the opening of a new and profitable market. Today, at least one West African country, Benin, has formally apologized 'for their country's role in once selling fellow Africans by the millions to white slave traders' according to a report from Richmond, Virginia, USA (The *Sun-Sentinel* newspaper, Florida, 1 May 2000).

The first stage of African enslavement was capture, whether by warfare or by abduction, or by being condemned for crimes. Prisoners of war, criminals and kidnapped villagers made up the

Branding iron used on slaves

In the stocks

majority of those marched down to the coast or taken there by river. Yoked by the neck, the slave 'coffle' formed the second stage, the forced march. Then came confinement in a trade post or fort, the third stage in which they found themselves among strangers, many of whom spoke languages unknown to one another. After weeks or months, the Africans were herded on to the hideously overcrowded ships for the infamous MIDDLE PASSAGE to the Americas. This was the fourth stage, which many did not survive. Those who lived called each other shipbrothers and shipsisters (see SHIPMATE). They formed deep and lasting relationships, as strong as family bonds, which endured across generations in their places of exile. On arrival, they were prepared like cattle for sale, which marked the fifth stage.

The sixth and final stage was SEASONING, a period in which each one was attached to a slave knowledgeable in the work and LANGUAGE of the plantation, and responsible for training the newcomer. Such was the experience of the vast majority.

The white slave traders of the 16th and 17th centuries were mainly the Dutch, English and Portuguese. By the 1690s, the English rose to prominence in the trade and continued to hold a major place in the 18th century.

Up until 1693-94, when the first great influx of Africans arrived in Jamaica, the white and black populations were almost equal, with the white outnumbering the black between 1655 and about 1670. White indentured servants performed much of the labour later performed by blacks as the plantation system became established. (See IRISH, SCOTS.) Among the first slaves brought to Jamaica by the English were people from Madagascar: this venture failed because no diet could be found to keep these slaves in working trim. Thereafter, Africans from the Gold Coast (Ghana) and the Slave Coast (Nigeria) predominated. Yet many came from nations and clans far removed from their ports of exit, and represented many different cultures. (See AFRICAN HERITAGE, CONGO, COROMANTEE, IBO, MANDINGO, YORUBA.)

Due to the development of the SUGAR PLANTATION – and to the lucrative promise of crops such as indigo, COFFEE, COCOA and TOBACCO – African slavery became the mainstay of the Caribbean economy. Jamaica was to receive hundreds of thousands of enslaved Africans over the next century, as deaths consistently outstripped births, and infant mortality soared. The island earned the reputation of being the most rebellious slave colony in the Western Hemisphere. (See NANNY, MAROONS, Samuel SHARPE, TACKY.) Jamaica also became a great centre of the slave trade, with huge warehouses in KINGSTON in which slaves were kept for purchase and transhipment to other parts of the Americas.

In 1807 the abolitionist movement in Britain influenced the government to end the slave trade, and to outlaw anyone, of any country, caught trading in human flesh. The abolitionists brought about the end of British slavery in 1834, substituting APPRENTICESHIP, an unsuccessful arrangement by which slaves of working age remained bonded to their masters for a set period of years, and those too young or too old were sent off to fend for themselves. Full EMANCIPATION came in 1838, after which a great majority of former slaves were forced off the plantations (see FREE VILLAGES) and the reconstruction of the society began. By this point, black and COLOURED in Jamaica outnumbered whites by about ten to one, and Jamaican-born apprentices had begun to outnumber those born in Africa.
[Patterson 1973, 1982]

SLIGOVILLE
Village in the hills of ST CATHERINE Parish, which is of historic interest because it was the location of the first FREE VILLAGE to be established in the West Indies after the EMANCIPATION of the slaves. It was started by the BAPTIST minister at SPANISH TOWN, the Revd J.M. Phillippo, who bought the land in 1835. The property was a wilderness but even before SLAVERY ended, it was

Sligoville free village

cleared by church members who also started to build a church and school there. The land was sub-divided into lots and sold, and eventually 200 families were settled. The purchaser of the first lot of land in June 1838 was a man named Henry Lunan who had been a slave and a head driver on an adjoining estate. The settlement was officially opened on 12 July 1840.

The village was named Sligoville after the 2nd Marquis of Sligo, Howe Peter Browne, who was governor of Jamaica 1834-36 during the period of APPRENTICESHIP. Sligo had inherited Jamaican properties through his grandmother, including Kelly's Estate in the Old Harbour area of ST CATHERINE Parish. Sligo was not popular, however, with members of the House of Assembly or the majority of the Jamaican planters who adhered to the letter of the Abolition Act, which forced the slaves to provide 40½ hours per week of free labour to their former masters for a period of years before they could achieve 'full free'. In this turbulent period, Sligo was often accused of invariably interpreting the law "in favour of the Negro". He was also regarded as

Candelabrum with inscription: "Presented to the Most Noble Howe Peter Marquis of Sligo by the Negroes of Jamaica in testimony of the grateful remembrance they entertain for his unremitting efforts to alleviate their sufferings and to redress their wrongs during his just and enlightened administration of the Government of the Island and of the respect and gratitude they feel towards His excellent Lady and Family for the kindness and sympathy displayed towards them 1837"

a friend of the non-conformist MISSIONARIES, and sympathetic to their activities, factors that contributed to the brevity of his governorship. The apprentices of Jamaica were to subscribe over one thousand dollars to provide a mark of gratitude to Sligo, and in 1837 he was presented on their behalf with a magnificent silver candelabrum. In January 1996, Sligo's descendant, the 11th Marquis of Sligo and his wife, visited Jamaica and attended a memorial service at Sligoville church.

Sligoville was also at one time the summer residence of the governor, who had a mansion at Winchester. The Anglican church in the village was originally built by Sir John Augustus O'Sullivan, Chief Usher of the Black Rod and Provost Marshall General of Jamaica from 1825-71, as a private chapel for his family and servants. The enormously wealthy O'Sullivan who resided at Highgate Park in Sligoville, also introduced to Jamaica the English sport of hunting with hounds and the Highgate Park Hunt became a well established social event, the imported hounds following an artificial scent.
[Phillippo 1843, Tamlyn 1969]

SMALLPOX

Once deadly viral disease (official name: variola) which left disfiguring pock-marks on the survivors. Introduced into the New World in the early 16th century from Europe, smallpox remained a killer for centuries until its control by widespread vaccination in the 20th century.

The smallpox virus was common in European cities in the Middle Ages, so most Europeans developed an immunity to it. But the native peoples of the New World had no immunity to this and other Old World diseases, such as measles, and their introduction by the early explorers contributed to the catastrophic population declines. Smallpox first appeared in Santo Domingo around Christmas 1518, and from there spread through the Greater Antilles, and to Yucatan and the rest of the mainland. The Spaniards reported that it killed one-third to one-half of the Amerindians in Hispaniola and had similar swift and devastating effects elsewhere. It is now recognized that the decimation from smallpox was one of the factors that contributed to the easy conquest of the Aztec and Inca Kingdoms of Mexico and Peru.

During the slave trade, smallpox continued to reach the West Indies from Africa where it had been present for centuries. While large numbers in Jamaica continued to die from this disease in the 17th and much of the 18th century, it began

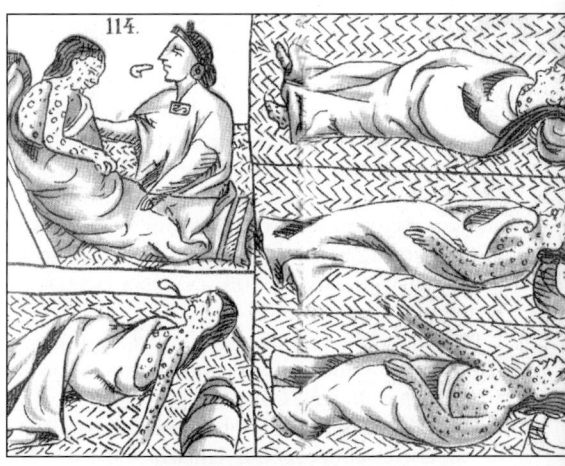

Smallpox victims, from the Aztec codex

to wane from the last quarter of the 18th century due to massive efforts at inoculation. These were spearheaded by a local doctor, John Quier, who had perfected the technique for inoculation. By the first decades of the 19th century there was widespread vaccination of both blacks and whites, using Jenner's vaccine, Lady Nugent, the governor's wife, recording in her *Journal* her anxiety over the vaccination of her child.

After EMANCIPATION, vaccination seems to have declined among the population. There were smallpox epidemics in 1861 and 1874, and though vaccination was made compulsory in 1865, there was little enforcement until the 20th century.
[Craton 1975, Craton and Walvin 1970, Crosby 1972, Kiple 1984, Viola and Margolis 1991]

SNAIL see SHELLS

SNAKE

Snakes are rarely encountered except in remote areas like the COCKPIT COUNTRY. They are frequently killed on sight though none of the seven species found on the island is harmful. Six of the snakes found here are endemic (i.e. are found nowhere else) and one, *Tropidophis haetianus*, is indigenous (found naturally in Jamaica but also elsewhere). The scientific names of the six endemic snakes are *Alsophis ater, Arrhyton callilaemum, A. funereum, A. polylepis, Epicrates subflavus, Typhlops jamaicensis*.

Some snakes were far more common before the introduction of the MONGOOSE in 1872. The Black Snake probably became extinct early in the 20th century directly as a result of predations by the mongoose.

Since the Yellow Snake (*Epicrates subflavus*) is nocturnal, it seldom encounters the mongoose. Also known as 'Nanka', this boa is the island's largest snake. This particular species is found only in Jamaica though close relatives occur in the other CARIBBEAN islands. Secretive and nocturnal, it spends its day resting in trees or in holes in rocky terrain and comes out at night to feed on BIRDS and rats. The young are born as many as 18 at a time. This non-aggressive species is the only Jamaican snake that attains any size, commonly reaching a length of 2m though there are reports of much longer individuals – up to 3.5m. It is beautifully patterned in yellow and black with iridescent blue-black on its tail. Vulnerable to extinction, it has been successfully bred in captivity by the Jersey Wildlife Preservation Trust in the UK.

There are three species of snakes in Jamaica called Grass Snake, all belonging to the same genus (*Arrhyton*) and about 30cm in length. One of the species is brown on top and whitish underneath, the others are slate-grey. They are insect- (and perhaps snail-) eaters that are usually found under logs or in piles of vegetable trash. Sometimes they are found under boards lying on the ground near residences.

The Two-headed or Worm Snake (*Typhlops jamaicensis*) is a burrowing, nocturnal reptile in which the tail and the head are hard to distinguish. It is seldom seen even though it exists in residential Kingston.

Snakes were much used in OBEAH and other occult practices in the past and this has probably contributed to the great fear with which they are viewed. The Jamaican pronunciation 'si-nyake' comes directly from the West African language, Twi, in which /sn/ or /sm/ are always broken apart by an /i/, and /n/ often becomes /ny/.

[NHSJ 1949, Oliver 1986, Schwartz and Henderson 1991]

Yellow Snake

SNOWBALL

A popular cooler that was sold by street vendors. Snowball consisted of ice shaved and compressed into a ball (white like snow) over which red fruit-flavoured syrup was poured; also known as 'shave ice'. In the days before widespread refrigeration, the arrival of the 'snowball man' was eagerly awaited by rural children while city children and adults patronized the dazzlyingly colourful snowball carts on the street.

The 'snowball man' travelled the countryside by donkey cart or bicycle with a large block of ice kept cool by being wrapped in CROCUS BAGS and surrounded with sawdust. He peeled back the crocus bag and used a metal ice-shaver to shave the ice and compress it into a ball. For many children, this was their first introduction to ice. In former times, the snowball was placed directly into the hand of the purchaser who would immediately start sucking it; later, it was

Snowball cart

sold in a cone-like paper cup and came to be called 'snow-cone'. Still later, it was placed in a transparent plastic bag, sucked with a straw, and called 'sky juice'.

SOAP PLANTS

Several plants are known as 'soap plants' from the fact that some part of the plant will yield lather and has cleansing properties, and thus was formerly used in washing. The best known is Soapberry (*Sapindus saponaria*), the seed coating or pericarp being used. A seaside plant (*Phyllanthus angustifolius*) also known as Seaside Laurel, Rock Rush, Soap Plant, Sword Bush, is also used for cleansing, soap being made from its ashes. Some forms of cactus are also used for cleansing, e.g. TOONA (swipple pole). ACKEE pods have been used by the poor as a cleanser, Louise Bennett humorously recalling this fact in her poem 'Soap Vacation' which laments a shortage of washing soap:

Soapberry

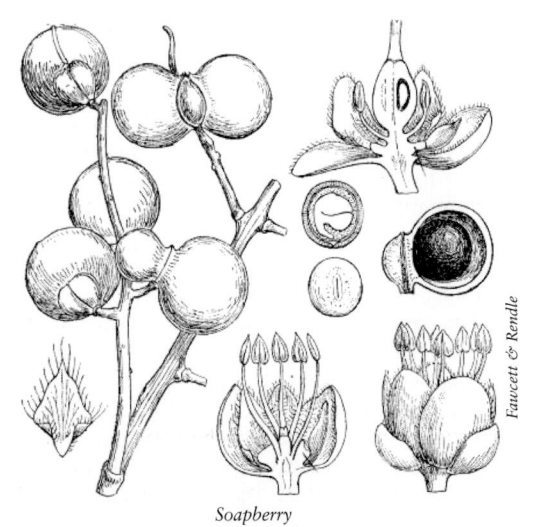

Ackee-skin and ashes is me
Dutty clothes dem only hope,
For me hear Pooto dah-tell Jane
Sey dem meck good washin' soap.

She say fe meck de clothes an ashes
Soak eena de tub,
Den start rub awn de ackee-skin
An so yuh rub, yuh scrub.

The Jamaica Cookery Book (1893) noted that 'Wild Parsley' was used by the washerwomen 'to rub the clothes as well as soap. It appears to possess cleansing properties'. (See LAUNDRY.)

The TAINOS used a plant for washing called *digo* but its identity has not been established. Like other Amerindians, the Tainos utilized soap plants to wash their bodies on a daily basis, but also engaged in ritual washing in connection with ceremonies, especially to remove the black stain derived from GUINEP during initiation and other rites.

[Arrom 1990, Bennett 1966, Sinha 1977, Sullivan 1893]

SOCCER see FOOTBALL

SOLDIER'S STONE

Old tombstone on the roadside at Struie, WESTMORELAND Parish, which is the subject of LEGEND. The monument is to Obadiah Bell Chambers, a soldier who was killed during the great slave rebellion of 1831-32. (See SHARPE, Samuel.) The stone was erected by officers and men of his company. According to the legend, Obadiah was one of a detachment of soldiers who rode out against the slaves on mule and horseback. Meeting strong resistance, the soldiers retreated, all except Obadiah whose mule carried on. The rebels cut off the soldier's head but the head ran back to a place called Kew Park (near Struie) where it was eventually found. People walking past this area used to hear the clash of steel, and it is said that Obadiah's headless ghost still walks.

[Wright and White 1969]

SOLITAIRE

The Rufous Throated Solitaire (*Myadestes genibarbis*) is a songbird of the mid-to high-level forests which descends to lower elevations during the winter months, returning in summer to nest in the heights where it sings. Its dawn songs are heard around August when most other BIRDS are silent. One observer commenting on its name, noted that though seldom seen, the bird 'can scarcely be said to be solitary, since it rarely sings alone, but in harmony or concert with some half-dozen others . . . Occasionally it strikes out such an adventitious combination of notes, as to form a perfect tune'.

Many have been affected by its musical song, describing it in such terms as 'heavenly concert', 'mournful beauty', 'poignant and pure'. Celebrated by the poets of the region, the solitaire is called 'musicien' and 'organiste' in the French-speaking islands, since 'only an organ can reproduce and give breath to the sustained flute-like notes'. In Jamaica it is known as the Mountain Whistler or Fiddler.

The bird is a member of the thrush family, 19cm in length, of dark slate grey with lighter underparts and a rufous patch under the throat and the tail.

[Gosse 1984, Roberts 1955, Taylor 1955]

SOLOMON GUNDY

Popular hot and spicy paste (also 'Salmagundy' or 'Gundy' for short) made of ground-up salted red herring, oil, vinegar, hot peppers, onions and spices. Usually served on crackers as a starter or relish and now made commercially. The name is derived from *salmagundi* which first appeared – along with the dish – in the 17th century according to Brewer's *Dictionary of Phrase and Fable*, the origins of both being unknown. The dish became popular in 18th century England where it was more of a salad, including chopped meats as well as pickled herrings and chopped onions. It is believed that pirates brought the word – and dish – to the West Indies.

SORREL (*Hibiscus sabdariffa*)

Hardy annual shrub commonly cultivated from sea level to 800m that provides Jamaicans with their favourite CHRISTMAS drink. After flowering, the petals drop off, leaving the sepals (fleshy seed pods) behind. These become enlarged and turn crimson as the fruit matures in December, and they are used to make the drink.

The custom of brewing a red drink from Sorrel dates back hundreds of years. There are many recipes, but generally, the fleshy sepals are stripped from the stems, washed, and placed in hot water with PIMENTO, GINGER and other spices, and left to steep for about 24 hours. A few rice grains are sometimes added to aid fermentation. It is then decanted, and SUGAR and (if desired) RUM added, the rum helping to preserve it. Sorrel is also made into a jelly and a jam. In folk MEDICINE, it is regarded as diuretic and digestive. Although most people associate sorrel with the red variety, a white sorrel is becoming popular.

In other places sorrel is known as Jamaica Sorrel, Roselle or Sudanese Tea. The plant originated in the Sudan. It belongs to the HIBISCUS family, which includes Seaside and Blue MAHOE, and OKRA, and was introduced into Jamaica by the BRITISH soon after 1655.

[Adams 1972, Facey 1993, Robertson 1990]

SOURSOP (*Annona muricata*)

A native of the American tropics, Soursop is commonly cultivated in lowland and hill gardens up to 800m and is popular as a fruit and in folk MEDICINE. The tree grows 5-8m high, and fruits September to January.

The large kidney-shaped fruit (weighing between 1-3kg) is one of the most popular in the Caribbean. The prickly green skin encloses a snowy-white, sweet, and somewhat fibrous flesh that is rich in Vitamin C. It is often made into a drink (with condensed milk or LIME juice) or into ice cream.

The glossy green leaves give off a slightly aromatic scent when crushed and are used to make a TEA which is widely used for hypertension and 'calming the nerves', and also to reduce fever, to induce perspiration, for colds, and for worms. The heart of the fruit (not usually eaten) is a traditional cure for bed-wetting.

Soursop is a member of the Annona family in which the fruits are composed of the joined products of many flowers, each flower represented by a hard black seed that is embedded in the pulp. SWEET SOP, CUSTARD APPLE and Cherimoya are members of this family, all consumed from the time of the TAINOS.

[Adams 1971, Asprey and Thornton 1953-55, Baccus and Royes 1988, Kingsbury 1988, Robertson 1990]

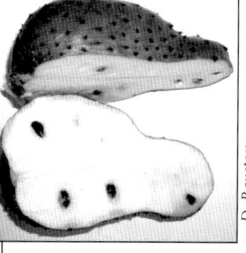

Soursop

SPANISH JAMAICA

Jamaica was a settled Spanish colony for 146 years, 1509-1655. Christopher COLUMBUS claimed the island for the King and Queen of Spain in 1494 and the first settlers arrived in 1509. They established a settlement at Sevilla la Nueva (see SEVILLE, New) but abandoned it in 1534 and founded Villa de la Vega (SPANISH TOWN). Although the colonists opened trails across the island, most of their settlements and *hatos* (ranches) were on the south side, in present-day ST THOMAS Parish, principally at Morante and Ayala (Yallahs), on the LIGUANEA and CLARENDON plains, in the BLACK RIVER area, and in WESTMORELAND at Oristan near present-day BLUEFIELDS.

The settlers established large ranches for open grazing, and raised CATTLE – principally for hides, and HORSES, donkeys and mules. They also had small tanneries and sugar mills. The PIGS that had run wild and multiplied provided vast quantities of lard. These, along with some island produce such as SUGAR, COTTON, PIMENTO, COCOA, CASSAVA flour and some hardwoods, were the principal exports to Spain.

The island also served as a provisioning depot for the Spanish ships going to and from South America, and provided horses and supplies for most of the colonizing attempts in Central America. The colonists, their African slaves, and the remnants of the fast-vanishing TAINOS, supplied cassava bread (BAMMY), lard, and what was described as 'barbecued pork' – perhaps JERK PORK.

The colony was never at any stage prosperous, and the Spaniards, disappointed by the lack of precious metals, made little effort to develop it. The population remained small, consisting after

Spanish ships unloading animals brought to the New World (from the Aztec codex)

a while of only a few families, and there was a great deal of intermarriage. But the colony's lack of development also owed something to its peculiar status.

Family Estate In 1536, Jamaica was handed over to Don Luis Colón, Columbus' grandson and heir, as his personal property. While Columbus had been promised magnificent titles and lands as rewards for his great discoveries, these had not been forthcoming and he died in poverty. His son Diego had married into a powerful Spanish family and, after his death, his widow, Doña Maria de Toledo carried on the struggle to secure the promised inheritance on behalf of their son, Luis. The settlement that was finally reached with the Spanish Crown, gave the heir of Columbus very little of what was claimed. He ended up with titles (including a dukedom), land on the mainland, and the island of Jamaica. The Colón titles were Marquis de Jamaica, Conde de la Vega, and Duque de Veragua, Veragua being the property on the mainland.

The island was given precisely because it lacked value. Sylvia Wynter quotes the President of the Indies Council as recommending Jamaica 'because it is small, and up till now has been of no advantage whatsoever, seeing that it possesses neither gold nor silver nor pearls nor anything else, besides cattle pens'. While the island became the personal property of the Colón family, by the terms of the agreement, the King of Spain remained 'the supreme authority'. This led to what Wynter has called divided rule and dual authority and contributed to the colony's neglect and poor administration. It was reflected in the frequent clashes between the church and state authorities, who were loyal to one or the other faction. It also led to the island's poor defences.

By the terms of the agreement, the Colón family was not allowed to put up fortifications, and the coasts were infested with smugglers and BUCCANEERS. The island had few men to defend it – perhaps never more than 500 – and even the capital of Villa de la Vega was plundered by sea rovers several times. It was easily taken by Cromwell's English forces in 1655 (see CAPTURE OF JAMAICA), and the surviving Spaniards were shipped off to nearby Spanish colonies, leaving behind some former slaves and guerrillas (see LUBOLO, YSASSI) as well as some settlers who revealed themselves to be JEWS and were allowed to remain. The English soldiers destroyed many of the Spanish buildings, but the English settlers rebuilt on Spanish foundations, for instance, those surrounding the SPANISH TOWN SQUARE.

Spanish Heritage In addition to these foundations and the archaeological site of New Seville, the Spanish legacy today consists of a number of words from the Spanish language, a few places that retain their Spanish names or derivations (e.g. RIO COBRE, RIO MINHO, ORACABESSA, MONTEGO BAY, OCHO RIOS), artefacts such as olive jars and other ceramics, water filters (see FILTERING STONE) and SPANISH WALL. Also still alive is the memory of Spanish coins and their names (see MONEY) and folk tales and LEGENDS of Spanish treasure hidden in PANYA JAR. (See also GOLD.)

There are many compound words with 'Spanish' and in the DJE, Cassidy and LePage make this interesting point in their entry on 'Spanish' used as an adjective: 'As a colour word in early general and present dial use: bright yellow or gold: cf Spanish Carnation, Coot, Elm, etc. In reference to weapons it usually means very sharp, sharpened on both sides: cf Spanish Bill, Machete.' Some of these terms might have come about through Jamaica's long connection with Spanish America. A much larger number of words came into the language from the TAINO via Spanish (e.g. JAMAICA).

The most important legacy remains the animals and the economic plants the Spaniards introduced that have continued to be of great significance to Jamaica's economy, among them all the domestic animals and major crops such as BANANA, SUGAR CANE, and CITRUS. The Spaniards also brought the ROMAN CATHOLIC faith that did not become prominent again under English rule until 1792, although there was a papist (Roman Catholic) chapel in PORT ROYAL until 1692. The Spanish settlers also included members of the Jewish faith. Called 'Marranos' or 'Portugals', they worshipped secretly, and remained after the English takeover, making Judaism the oldest religion practised continuously on the island.

Spanish America   Over time, and especially in the 19th and 20th centuries, Jamaica's Spanish connections continued to be mainly with Latin America. First, through trade with the Spanish American colonies, later with the contact established by tens of thousands of wage labourers, professionals, and business people who emigrated to Latin American countries in search of work and opportunities (see COLÓN MAN, PANAMA). With the establishment from the 19th century of a strong Roman Catholic presence in Jamaica, it was also the practice for many years for wealthy Latin American families to send their children to Catholic boarding schools in the island. Jamaica has also had varied connections over many centuries with Spanish-speaking Cuba, its nearest neighbour.

[Aarons 1983b, 1984, Buisseret 1983, Espinosa 1628, Morales Padron 1952, Osborne 1988, Wynter 1969, 1984, 1994]

SPANISH TOWN

The island's capital from 1534-1872, Spanish Town is Jamaica's second largest urban area with a population of 110,379 (1991). The original town is about 2.6km² in area and many of its 40 streets and lanes are still lined with old brick buildings and shuttered jalousies of a bygone era, most in a dilapidated condition. The SPANISH established their capital here after the failure of Sevilla la Nueva (see SEVILLE, New) and called it Villa de la Vega – the town on the plain. The Columbus heir had for a second title Conde de la Vega, after this town.

Jamaica was not a prosperous Spanish colony and the capital was a small town with never more than a few hundred inhabitants. Spanish Town was sacked several times by English adventurers who landed at PASSAGE FORT and marched the 9.5km inland. As was the case with other Spanish settlements near the coast throughout Latin America, at the cry of 'Inglesa! Inglesa', all the inhabitants would grab whatever possessions they could and flee to the hills, until the invaders left. (See ST JAGO.) One of the invaders, the privateer Captain William Jackson, described Spanish Town in 1643 as consisting of 'four or five hundred houses, built for ye most part with canes, overcast with morter and lime, and covered with Tyle. [See SPANISH WALL.] It is beautified with five or six stately churches and chappels, and one Monastery of Franciscan Fryers'. So attractive was Jamaica to the sailors that many deserted the raiding fleets to remain on the island.

Spanish Town was weakly defended and easily taken when the BRITISH arrived in 1655. (See CAPTURE OF JAMAICA.) But the first five years were ones of misery and famine for the English soldiers who refused to plant crops and had to face constant harassment from the Spanish MAROONS and the guerrillas led by YSASSI. The political turmoil in England was played out here as well, between the Cavaliers (supporters of the King) and the Roundheads (supporters of Cromwell's Commonwealth) and the military governor Edward D'Oyley had to put down at least one mutiny. With the defeat of Cromwell and the restoration of the King of England, D'Oyley also became the first civil governor.

Although at first eclipsed by the rich city of PORT ROYAL, Spanish Town developed as the social and administrative capital of the island. Its main civic buildings were erected at the height of the plantation era, the splendid Georgian square being built on the *plaza real* of Villa de la Vega. Here met the House of Assembly, the Courts of Justice, and here resided the governor.

The town was a hive of activity during the 'dead season' on the SUGAR estates, that is, from October to Christmas. Then the legislature met, and planters, their wives, and servants would come in from all over the island to stay for the social 'season' that included the races. (See

Georgian Square, Spanish Town

HORSERACING.) Spanish Town boasted one of the earliest newspapers, the *St Jago de la Vega Gazette*, published by William Daniels who, like other journeymen in the newly developed print shops in the West Indies, was trained at the printery of the famous American, Benjamin Franklin, in Philadelphia.

However, KINGSTON, which was established after the 1692 EARTHQUAKE destroyed Port Royal, was the great mercantile centre and Kingstonians enviously sought to have their city become the capital. In 1755, the merchants 'curried favour' with the governor, Sir Charles Knowles, and persuaded him to force a bill through the legislature for the removal of the capital to Kingston. As soon as the bill was passed, the ARCHIVES were taken there.

The people of Spanish Town lodged a swift protest with the King of England and Knowles was replaced by Sir Henry Moore. The bill was eventually proclaimed illegal since the king had not given his assent and in 1758 the Archives were loaded up on 30 heavily armed wagons and trundled back to Spanish Town. One overturned and was lost in the swamp at FERRY. The jubilant citizens greeted the wagons with dancing and cheering and burnt the former governor in effigy. However, the decline of Spanish Town had already started, accelerated by the decline of the plantations. Anthony Trollope who visited in the 1850s (see POSTAL SERVICE) described it as 'stricken with eternal death'. The capital was peacefully removed to Kingston in 1872. With this move, the town lost much of its former grandeur though it has developed as a busy commercial centre for St Catherine and surrounding parishes, and the location for modern light industries.

[Baxter 1970, Black 1974, Cundall 1915, Osborne 1988]

SPANISH TOWN BAPTIST CHURCH

This BAPTIST church has been designated a national monument. It is better known as Phillippo's Church after the Revd J.M. Phillippo, one of the celebrated Baptist MISSIONARIES who was pastor here for 50 years until his death in 1879. The Revd Phillippo arrived in Jamaica in 1823 and was first denied a licence to preach. However his work progressed and he was instrumental in founding churches over a large area, as well as FREE VILLAGES. A tablet in the churchyard marks one of the historic graves in which the black congregation buried the instruments of SLAVERY on the achievement of full freedom in 1838.

The building dates from 1827 though the congregation was in existence from 1819. The church was built on part of the old artillery ground. Outstanding features of the interior are the beautiful woodwork of the banisters and staircases and domed wooden ceiling of the choir loft. The building was badly damaged by the HURRICANE of 1951 but was faithfully restored with some assistance from Mr Harold de Phillipeaux of Canada, a descendant of the missionary. Phillippo is the author of the work, *Jamaica: Its Past and Present State* (1843).

[Phillippo 1843, Sibley 1965; JJ 16:1]

SPANISH TOWN CATHEDRAL

The ANGLICAN Cathedral Church of St James is the oldest cathedral in the former BRITISH colonies and stands on the site of the SPANISH Chapel of the Red Cross built around 1525, one of the first ROMAN CATHOLIC cathedrals to be established in the New World. The Spaniards had two chapels in the town, a 'Red Cross' and a 'White', so-called after the habits worn by the monks, the Franciscans and the Dominicans. The Franciscans were located on this site while the Dominicans' Chapel of the White Cross was probably at the northern end of Monk Street on the site of the Rio Cobre Approved School.

When the English took the island (see CAPTURE OF JAMAICA), Cromwell's Puritan soldiers destroyed the original chapels. The Anglican Church (the Parish Church of St Catherine) was built on the foundations and with materials from the original Red Cross church in 1666. The church was destroyed in the HURRICANE of 1712, rebuilt in 1714, fell into disrepair and restored in 1901, damaged in the EARTHQUAKE of 1907 and restored 1908. The church became the cathedral of the Jamaican diocese in 1843, the first Anglican cathedral outside of England. It is dedicated to St James who is also the patron saint of Spain. The cathedral is, after FORT CHARLES, the oldest English foundation on the island. The Baptism

Spanish Town Cathedral

and Marriage Registers date from 1668, and the Burial Register from 1671.

The cathedral was intimately associated with all the events and personalities in the early history of the island, and many of the famous people of the 17th and 18th centuries are buried within its precincts, with elaborate marble monuments to several governors and their wives. Among the interesting monuments is one by the celebrated English sculptor Bacon, to the Earl of Effingham, a former governor, and his countess. Another beautiful monument is that to the Countess of Elgin (d 1843). Her husband was the governor of Jamaica and subsequently went on to become a celebrated governor-general of Canada and viceroy of India. It was Lord Elgin's father who brought the 'Elgin Marbles' from Greece to the British Museum. The monument to the countess was executed by Sir John Steell, a Scottish sculptor. There are also many interesting monuments in the churchyard.

[Black 1974, Lewis 1972]

SPANISH TOWN COURTHOUSE

This Georgian building at the southern end of the SPANISH TOWN SQUARE was gutted by fire in 1997 and stands now as a ruin. Built in 1819, it was formerly used for the courts and the town hall. The site was originally a cemetery and was later a chapel and armoury.

SPANISH TOWN SQUARE

This splendid square surrounded on all four sides by relics of Georgian buildings is a monument to the 'Golden Age of SUGAR' when Jamaica was the richest colony of Britain. The square was then called 'The Parade'. It was originally laid out by the Spaniards for whom it was the *plaza mayor* or *plaza real* though no SPANISH buildings remain above ground, the Royal Audencia being beneath the OLD KING'S HOUSE. The other buildings surrounding the square are the courthouse, OLD HOUSE OF ASSEMBLY, the ARCHIVES and the RODNEY MEMORIAL.

SPANISH WALL

Masonry of rocks held together with a mortar of WHITE LIME and sand (also called 'stone nog'), commonly used in building before the widespread use of Portland cement and block-and-steel construction, the lime mortar becoming hard and durable if properly done. The construction method was introduced by the SPANISH settlers – part of the medieval Iberian-North-Africa-Islamic tradition – and passed

Spanish Wall

down virtually unchanged from generation to generation. A more primitive method of Spanish Wall uses only rocks with red clay and water as the mortar. Aside from stone nog, lime mortar was also used in brick nog (the traditional English form) and concrete nog, as well as WATTLE AND DAUB. Lime, mortar, and stone were also used for constructing water tanks using a method known as 'kick and buck'.

In making Spanish Wall, each wall of the prospective building is first framed up in wood, the nog frame being of two wooden flats many inches or feet apart so that the stony mixture can be rammed between the flats and held until it dries. A finishing layer of mortar is then put on and smoothed over. When dry, the wall can be washed with a solution of plain lime and water ('whitewash'), or one mixed with charcoal powder to produce grey, or with other colouring matter. Glue is added to give the wash greater permanence. Properly done, such construction could last for generations. Many of these colourful Spanish Wall houses could once be seen, especially on the ST ELIZABETH plains, but most have vanished with the times. The method of construction, however, was still well known by village builders up until the 1940s and 50s.

[Buisseret 1980a, Hodges 1987, Williams 1972]

SPATHODEA (*Spathodea campanulata*)

Also known as African Tulip Tree, Flame of the Forest and Flame Tree, this is one of the most striking of trees. At the end of branches at the top of the tree, it bears clusters of swollen green buds that open into brilliant red tulip-like flowers that can be seen from a great distance. As the flower buds develop, they fill with water, giving the tree its other names of Water Man or Man Water; children use the bulbs like water pistols, and the dried opened boat-shaped seed pod (19-25cm) is good for floating on water.

A native of Africa, Spathodea was first introduced to Jamaica around 1850 at the same time as two other showy ornamentals,

POINCIANA and BOUGAINVILLEA. The tree is now widespread at lower elevations up to 800m and flowers and fruits most of the year. The huge spreading ornamental grows up to 20m tall.
[Adams 1972]

SPIDER
Jamaica's spiders include one of the largest orb web makers in the world (*Nephila clavipes*). The orb web is the classic flat spider's web most people are familiar with. The spider is commonly called the silk spider and the web might get up

Orb webmaker

to 1m in width, with attachment lines extending out 2m or more. It is claimed that small birds can become trapped in these webs. Sometimes tiny species of spiders will become squatters on the nets, feeding on small insects trapped there.

Jamaica also has the Black Widow and Brown Widow spiders. Their bites can cause some discomfort, though they are not as dangerous as portrayed and are in fact rarely met with. Another interesting spider is the Trap Door Spider, that digs a burrow in the ground which it plasters with mud and saliva to make it watertight, then lines it with silk. The spider enters and leaves by a tiny hinged trap door that closes automatically. The outside of the door is usually disguised with scraps to hide it from curious eyes.

A large brown spider (*Heteropoda venatoria*), which frequents homes and carries its eggs in a packet wherever it goes, is called 'Nansi' and is associated with ANANSI, the spider of the folk tales. It is also known as 'Banana spider' from its habit of stowing away on shipments of BANANAS.
[Farr 1970]

SPIDER IN FOLKLORE
All SPIDERS in Jamaica are commonly called ANANSI or Nansi though the one associated with the trickster-hero of the stories is the common house spider, which carries its young ones in a sac, like Anancy's ever-present 'namsack'. It is considered bad luck to sweep a spider from the ceiling. In folk MEDICINE, cobweb is used to stop bleeding, a practice that is also known in the British Isles.

SPIRIT WEED (*Eryngium foetidum*)
Also called Fit-weed and Myal-weed, this pungent smelling herb is rubbed over the body to revive people from fits and fainting spells. A decoction is also used for colds and fits in children. The plant (which grows on a small bush about 40cm high) is also much used in ritual practice as an antidote to bad spirits or DUPPIES. It is believed to be the plant used by Myalists (see MYAL) to revive those they had put in a coma

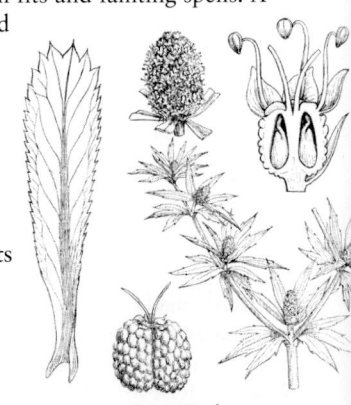

Spirit Weed

with branched CALALU. Zora Neale Hurston was told by her ACCOMPONG informant that drinking TEA made from Spirit Weed would render one perfectly safe from duppies, and the plant was one of the ingredients used in the protective ritual Katherine Dunham underwent at the hands of an obeah-man there (see OBEAH). In Caribbean East Indian cookery, the weed, known as *shado beni* (Bastard Coriander) in Trinidad, is said to be a standard ingredient in talkaris and chutneys.
[Asprey and Thornton 1953-55, Dunham 1946, Hurston 1938, Mahabir 1992, Robertson 1993]

SPRING GARDEN
The place in PORTLAND Parish where the MONGOOSE was first introduced into Jamaica. This was once a SUGAR estate owned by the English family named Hogg. (A direct descendant, Quintin Hogg, Conservative British MP and cabinet minister, renounced his title in 1963. His father was First Viscount Hailsham.) In the 1880s, Spring Garden was bought from the family by the former overseer, William Bancroft Espeut, of a Jamaican family of Huguenot (FRENCH) origin. He was active in local and national politics and introduced certain innovations in sugar planting, such as a tram line to carry the canes on his estate. But Espeut is chiefly remembered as the man who introduced the mongoose.

SPUR TREE HILL
Prominent hill in MANCHESTER Parish, traversed by the southern highway, probably named for the Ceiba or COTTON TREE that throws out huge buttresses or spurs. The road rises at a

breathtaking 304m per .8km, as it crosses the Don Figuerero Mountains, which were named during Spanish times. Spectacular views can be obtained. Spur Tree Hill was a great obstacle to travellers in the old days. At the foot of the hill, carriages had to be hitched to strong draught mules or oxen to pull them over. Many people left their carriages to ride up the hill on the sturdy Jamaican ponies that were used to the terrain. The journey from the foot of the hill to MANDEVILLE would take five hours under these conditions. Now there is a well-graded asphalt three-lane road.

STAMP-AND-GO

Popular fried fritter made with codfish (see FISH, Salt). It is said to be so called from the fact that as a 'fast food' it could be bought at wayside shops and stands by impatient travellers. However, according to F.G. Cassidy, the expression 'stamp-and-go' was an order given to sailors in the old days to perform certain actions, such as haul on a line. In the days of sail and active ports all around the island, nautical language was popular (e.g. WINDWARD ROAD) and the sailors' phrase might well have caught the popular fancy and been transferred to the travellers' food.
[Cassidy 1961]

STAND-PIPE

Piped water is often brought to a village or settlement via one pipe that is usually mounted on a concrete stand for communal use. From the 'stand-pipe', the inhabitants collect their water in a variety of vessels. Water piped to homes is replacing these community fixtures but they still exist in poor urban as well as rural areas and serve as a gathering place. 'Stand-pipe' is frequently used as a literary device to portray the meeting place for the collective or community voice.

Stand-pipe

STARAPPLE (*Chrysophyllum cainito*)

Large fruit tree (up to 15m high), which is distinguished by its leaves of two colours – green above and bronze below – and its large round fruits like apples, which appear November to March amidst its dense foliage. The fruits are purple or green-skinned when ripe, depending on the variety. The purple fruit has purple flesh and the green-skinned fruit, white flesh. When cut crossways, the fruit reveals a star-shaped pattern. Starapple flesh is sweet and gelatinous when fully ripe (stainy otherwise) and is eaten as a fruit or combined with oranges and condensed milk to make a dessert called 'matrimony'.

A member of the Sapodilla family, the tree is a native of the Greater Antilles and was introduced from these islands to the rest of the tropical world, *caymito* being its TAINO name. In Jamaica it grows at lower-lying elevations up to 500m. The reddish-brown wood is hard and heavy.

Starapples with leaves

In FOLKLORE, the Starapple tree is regarded as 'cubbitch' (mean) because it never drops its fruit and is difficult to climb. A two-sided Starapple leaf is a symbol of deception; a person who is lying, hypocritical or deceitful would be compared to it.
[Adams 1972, Rashford 1993a]

ST ANDREW, Parish of

This parish covers 430.7km². For administrative purposes it is combined with KINGSTON (21.8km²) to form the CORPORATE AREA, administered by the Kingston and St Andrew Corporation (KSAC). Generally, distinctions are not made between the two parishes in everyday speech and 'Kingston' is usually used to refer to the entire metropolitan area. However, St Andrew goes from the densely populated areas contiguous to Kingston to the highest reaches of the BLUE MOUNTAINS. Its principal urban centres were and still are villages centrally located on the highways into the city – HALFWAY TREE, GORDON TOWN and Stony Hill.

St Andrew was one of the earliest areas of settlement, first by the TAINOS who had several villages there. The name *Liguania* was first given by Spanish settlers to a large ranch they established on the plains and was retained by the English as Liguanea – the first name for the Parish of St Andrew, which originally included the plain on which the city and Parish of Kingston were established. It is believed to be derived from IGUANA. The ST ANDREW PARISH CHURCH was founded by English settlers in 1666.

ST ANDREW PARISH CHURCH

Popularly known as 'Half Way Tree Church', this ANGLICAN church is one of the oldest in the island. The first church in ST ANDREW Parish was erected shortly after the English CAPTURE OF JAMAICA, on a site nearer to Waterloo Road. The first church on the present site dates from the 1680s but was destroyed in the EARTHQUAKE of 1692. The foundation stones of the present church were laid that same year and the building completed in 1700. Over time, many changes and additions have been made. The church registers date from 1666.

There are a number of interesting monuments in the church including some prominent United States connections. The son of one of the signers of the United States Declaration of Independence in 1776 got married here. He was Philip Livingston (named after his father) who in 1768 wed Miss Sarah Johnson of St Andrew. Livingston was a merchant in Jamaica. He was at one time a member of the Assembly for PORTLAND Parish but was expelled from that body for non-attendance. The Livingstons originated from a distinguished Scottish family, some of whom emigrated to New York where they played a prominent part in the social and political life of the new state. Descendants of the British side still live in Jamaica. Col Harrison, the first US Consul to Jamaica and his wife are both buried in the cemetery, close by the north door of the church. He was the brother of US President Benjamin Harrison (1833-1901).

[Cundall 1915]

ST ANN, Parish of

St Ann covers 1,212.6km^2 with a population of 163,700 (1999) and is one of the largest, most beautiful and most historic parishes in Jamaica. Named Santa Ana by the Spaniards, it is also known as the 'Garden Parish' because of its natural beauty. (See FERN GULLY.) In this parish, Christopher COLUMBUS first set foot on Jamaican soil. Columbus also spent a whole year on this coast, the longest time spent in one place on any of his voyages to the New World. The first capital of Jamaica – Sevilla la Nueva (see SEVILLE, New) – was built in St Ann. It was one of the earliest European settlements in the Americas. The first black AFRICANS to come to Jamaica also landed in this parish. They came as body servants to the Spaniards. St Ann is one of the places where the famous PIMENTO or allspice grows. It is also one of the principal areas of BAUXITE mining in the world and contains the important tourist resort of OCHO RIOS.

In earlier times there was a great deal of traffic between St Ann and the south coast of Cuba. Mules and CATTLE were carried in small-decked vessels or open boats; it is also said the Cuban settlers kidnapped slaves from here though some undoubtedly went voluntarily (see RUNAWAY BAY).

ST ANN'S BAY FORT

The old fort (west of the town of ST ANN'S BAY, ST ANN Parish) was built about 1750 with stone blocks taken from Sevilla la Nueva (see SEVILLE, New). In 1795 the fort was declared useless because of encroachment from the sea and a new fort was built at Windsor Point on the opposite side of the bay. The old fort was adapted as a jail and 'house of correction', as slave prisons were called. (See FALMOUTH POLICE STATION.) The jail had solitary cells, a TREADMILL, a separate room for lunatics, a room for debtors, a 'hospital', and jailor's quarters. When a traveller visited the town in 1850 he found that the jail had been closed for six months for lack of patronage. At that time, he reported, there was no burglary, brigandage or highway robbery in even the most unsettled parts of the island.

[Candler 1850, Wright and White 1969]

ST ANN'S BAY, Town of

Capital of ST ANN Parish, population 10,961 (1991). The bay was originally called Santa Gloria by COLUMBUS. Cotter's wharf at the end of Bravo Street was used in the filming of the James Bond film, *Dr No*.

The courthouse was erected in 1860. Previously, the courthouse and church shared the same building. This was at a time when there was a close alliance between church and state (see ANGLICAN). Religious conflict reached its height in this parish in the 19th century. At the centre of the controversy was the Revd George Wilson Bridges, Anglican Rector of St Ann from 1823 to 1837 who was violently opposed to the EMANCIPATION of the slaves and became a leading light in an anti-MISSIONARY organization called the COLONIAL CHURCH UNION. In St Ann, Bridges lived first at Tydenham some miles out of the town and then bought a property called the Cloisters on Winders Hill overlooking the Bay. In a strange twist of fate, the Cloisters ended up as the property of the Wesleyans, one of the missions attacked and shot up by an armed mob in the anti-missionary riots. National Hero Marcus GARVEY spent much of his childhood next door to the Cloisters at Winders Hill. His father was a mason and a member of the Wesleyan church.

[Wright and White 1969]

ST CATHERINE, Parish of

Large parish named after the consort of Charles II, who was on the throne of England when it was formed in 1660. St Catherine covers 1,192.4 km² and has a population of 411,600 (1999). The present parish boundaries were established in 1867 when the smaller parishes of St Catherine, St Dorothy, St John, and St Thomas-in-the-Vale were amalgamated. It embraces many areas of historic association with both English and Spanish settlers, including SPANISH TOWN, the parish capital and, until 1872, capital of Jamaica.

Once mainly rural, St Catherine now contains the fastest growing urban areas in Jamaica, with the recent development of residential communities in the HELLSHIRE HILLS linked to both KINGSTON (by a causeway across the harbour) and Spanish Town. The new development of Greater Portmore grew from 5,100 in 1970 to 93,799 in 1991, representing a growth rate of 19.6 per cent per annum, and much development has taken place since then. In the same period, the population of Spanish Town increased from 39,204 to 110,379 representing an annual growth rate of 5.1 per cent.
[GOJ STATIN 1999 a,b]

ST CATHERINE DISTRICT PRISON

Located in SPANISH TOWN, ST CATHERINE Parish, this started out as the Middlesex and Surrey County Gaol. The original building was erected from the proceeds of a will of George Fletcher dated 1714. A maximum security prison, this is where hangings are carried out.

ST ELIZABETH, Parish of

Size: 1,212.4km², population 148,900 (1999). The parish was probably named after Elizabeth, Lady Modyford, wife of Sir Thomas Modyford, the governor from 1664-71. One of the oldest parishes, St Elizabeth originally included much of the western end of the island, but part of it became the Parish of Westmoreland in 1703, and a part was carved out to create Manchester Parish in 1814. The capital is the town of BLACK RIVER that once enjoyed a brief prosperity on the proceeds of LOGWOOD.

This parish has many features that make it different from the rest of the country, including the vegetation. Most of the southern part of the parish consists of dry savannas divided into two by the SANTA CRUZ Mountains that run north to south. Up to the early 20th century, the economy of this area was based on the raising of CATTLE and HORSES, growing CASSAVA, and FISHING. The area has at times been subject to unrelenting

Treasure Beach, St Elizabeth

drought – on occasion no rain falls for over a year. Thus one area is called 'Labour in Vain Savanna'.

As a result of the harsh conditions of life here, the migration out of this parish has been higher than elsewhere in Jamaica. In the mid-19th to early 20th century some of the young men simply left for more prosperous parts of Jamaica such as the BANANA parishes in the east. Many thousands headed for Latin America when there was heavy demand for wage labour on projects such as the construction of the PANAMA Canal (see also COLÓN MAN) and for railway construction and banana cultivation in places such as Costa Rica, Guatemala, Mexico and sugar cultivation in Cuba. In more recent times, the United Kingdom, Canada, and the United States have been the destinations of the migrants. The impact of recent emigration is seen in the substantial new houses being built throughout the parish, replacing the characteristic old-style SPANISH WALL thatch-roof dwellings.

The droves of HORSES and CATTLE that used to roam the plains are no more. Much of the livestock died out in successive droughts and the demand for horses was sharply curtailed with the advent of the motor car. As the population has grown, the land has been divided into smaller and smaller units, reducing the large areas necessary for free ranging and grazing.

Fertile soil in parts of southern St Elizabeth consists of the top 15cm of clay loam. The land below is infertile red clay. The residents of places such as Pedro Plains have to be extremely careful

Traditional St Elizabeth house

about their methods of cultivation and have devised techniques to conserve what they have. As described by Eyre, the main technique is fly penning and mulching using the savanna grass that grows rapidly after the rain. The farmer cuts the grass and spreads it thickly in an enclosed field where he puts his livestock to provide manure. He plants his crops in the enclosure and removes the animals when the plants appear. The process will be repeated in another small plot as there is savanna grass available. By this means several crops can be grown during the year with even a little rain. In recent years, fly penning has been giving way to the use of artificial fertilizers. The savannas are noted for the production of certain crops, notably tomatoes, melons, carrots, escallion, sweet PEPPER, TOBACCO, and CORN.

In the northern part of the Parish, SUGAR is widely grown and Appleton Estate is the home of famous RUMS. In recent years, BAUXITE mining and low scale TOURISM have helped to diversify the economy. Popular visitor attractions include YS FALLS and boat tours through the MANGROVE forests on the Black River tributaries.

A striking factor is the racial mix of St Elizabeth that has a significantly large proportion of light-skinned people. Many explanations have been offered for this. Some say it was settled by remnants of the TAINO, by Spanish people of mixed blood, or resulted from the activities of three virile Devon men who came as settlers! Some of the ethnic mix undoubtedly comes from Amerindians who were brought in to help track down the Maroons (see MISKITO). They were given lands to settle in the southern part of the parish (especially the PARATEE region). People of ARAWAK stock also came with settlers from Suriname in the 17th century (see SURINAM QUARTERS.) SCOTS retreating from the failed Darién expedition of 1699 (see CAMPBELL) also settled along the coast of St Elizabeth. All these people, as well as GERMAN settlers who came in the 19th century, have probably contributed to the mixture.
[Eyre 1972, Wright and White 1969]

ST GEORGE'S COLLEGE
Boys' secondary school in KINGSTON, founded in 1850 as 'St George's Colonial College' by ROMAN CATHOLIC Jesuit Priests, with 38 day students and 30 boarders. Since then, the school has become a leading institution, in the forefront of academic achievement as well as sports and extra-curricular activities.

ST JAGO
Early name for SPANISH TOWN, ST CATHERINE Parish, a corruption by the English of the name of the patron saint of Spain, Santiago (Saint James). The name Santiago had been given to the island by the Spanish Crown, though the original Amerindian name was to prevail (see JAMAICA).

The Spaniards attributed miraculous powers to St James who had first appeared in militant form, on horseback, leading their forces to victory in battle against the Moors; this iconic image of conquest was transferred to Spanish America. Here also arose many legends of St James' miraculous appearance at opportune moments, once in SPANISH JAMAICA.

During the governorship of Don Fernando Melgarejo in 1603, the English pirate Christopher Newport arrived with a large fleet. He demanded supplies, threatening to land 1,500 men and raze the town if refused. The governor marshalled the town's defence and though few in number, they managed to rout the English who had landed 500 men, killing some, including the officer leading the attack. This stunning victory was made possible by the strategy employed by the governor, which included sending 100 cattle into the English ranks at a critical moment. But soon the victory passed into LEGEND, the Spanish Carmelite missionary Antonio Vásquez de Espinosa a little over twenty years later attributing the English rout to the vision of a friar mounted on a powerful horse and singing a hymn of victory, recognized as St James. According to this report, the town said prayers, made him their patron saint, and annually held a fiesta and general celebration in honour of his day.
[Espinosa 1628, Osborne 1988]

ST JAGO HIGH SCHOOL
School in SPANISH TOWN, ST CATHERINE Parish, formed from a merger in 1956 between Beckford and Smith's School for Boys and Cathedral School for Girls. Beckford and Smith's was partly endowed by Peter BECKFORD, speaker of the Assembly 1707-11 and 1711-13.

ST JAMES, Parish of
Size: 594.9km^2, population 178,800 (1999). St James was named not after the saint but after James, Duke of York, and was formed as a parish in 1664-65. It was much larger at that time since it included what are now the separate parishes of TRELAWNY and HANOVER.

There are many remains of the TAINOS in this

coastal area. All the north coast Amerindian inhabitants have been called the 'Fairfield People' after a site near to MONTEGO BAY where some of their characteristic pottery has been found, a later derived version of the 'White Marl' ceramic type, after a site near to SPANISH TOWN.

The Spaniards also had a highway through St James, from Oristan in WESTMORELAND to the region around MARTHA BRAE. There are still many legends in the parish about treasure that is supposed to have been left by the SPANISH colonists (see PANYA JAR).

For many years after the English conquest, the north side of the island including St James was sparsely settled. In 1673 only 146 persons resided in the entire parish. One year the parish was so poor its citizens were excused from paying taxes. The north coast was far from the seat of government in Spanish Town and the interior of the parish was inhabited by the MAROONS. The roads were in shocking condition and communications were poor. From Montego Bay to Spanish Town would have been a three- or four-day coach journey, undertaken in stages.

However, St James was quickly developed by the SUGAR planters and grew to great wealth in the mid-18th century. By the 1780s, the capital of Montego Bay was regarded, next to KINGSTON, as the most flourishing town in the island. In 1982 it officially became Jamaica's second city. With the decline of sugar, the parish's prosperity came from BANANAS, the Montego Bay based J.E. Kerr shipping the fruit on his own vessels. TOURISM, which began at the beginning of the 20th century, is now a major industry.

In 1795 the Parish was turned upside down by the Maroons in the interior who took up arms again after decades of peace. Montego Bay became the headquarters of the governor, the Earl of Balcarres, who came to personally direct operations against them, and it was from here that the Trelawny Maroons were put aboard ships in the harbour that eventually sailed to Halifax, Nova Scotia, Canada. Montego Bay also witnessed the final act of the last slave uprising, the 'Christmas Rebellion' of 1831-32 that engulfed the western parishes. Under martial law, the slaves were tried in the courthouse and over 300 of them were hanged at the Parade, now called SAMUEL SHARPE SQUARE, where there is a memorial to the leader Samuel SHARPE.
[Cundall 1915, Wright and White 1969]

ST JAMES PARISH CHURCH

This ANGLICAN church in the ST JAMES parish capital of MONTEGO BAY is dedicated to St James the Great, the patron saint of Spain. It was built between 1775-82 and was regarded by the visiting artist Hakewill as the finest church in Jamaica. In 1957 the building was wrecked by an EARTHQUAKE but was restored with few changes from the original. The structure is in the form of a Greek cross with a bell tower at the western end. The earliest baptism recorded in this church was in 1771, the earliest marriages and the earliest burials, in 1774. Inside the church are some interesting monuments, including two marble monuments by the famous English sculptor, John Bacon. One of them (left of the altar) is to Mrs Rosa Palmer, erected by her husband; it was for a long time mistakenly believed to be a monument to the White Witch of Rose Hall (see ROSE HALL).
[Cundall 1915]

ST MARY, Parish of

Area: 610.5km^2, population 113,000 (1999). The parish was one of the earliest to be formed and today includes the former parish of Metcalfe and part of the former parish of St George. It might have been named from the Spanish port called Puerto Santa Maria – now the capital of PORT MARIA. Many of the early settlers were part of the conquering English army of Penn and Venables (see CAPTURE OF JAMAICA) and were given land in the area. The most prominent was Francis Price whose grandson Sir Charles Price created one of the grandest colonial establishments at the Decoy, high in the mountains, where he kept open house in true plantation style (see GREAT HOUSE); there is a monument to him in Port Maria. The wealthy Price family remained prominent in Jamaican political life for many generations. They were the original owners of WORTHY PARK estate in ST CATHERINE Parish. Also associated with this Parish was the Hibbert family, Thomas Hibbert (d 1780) of Agualta Vale being the builder of the town house which is now called HEADQUARTERS HOUSE in Kingston. Fort George near Annotto Bay was owned by the Ellis family, who owned many other estates, including MONTPELIER.

In the 20th century, sugar gave way to BANANAS and COCONUTS in this parish, and a new aristocracy arose, chief among them the Pringle family, builders of a new Agualta Vale great house on the ruins of the old. The founder, Sir John Pringle (1848-1923), a Scottish physician who was once medical officer to the lunatic asylum in Kingston, owned over 50 properties, having bought up derelict sugar plantations at rock-bottom prices and planted them with bananas at a time when that crop was Jamaica's most flourishing.

The island's first large American-style hotel, the Tower Isle (now Couples), was opened in 1949 near the parish border with ST ANN, initiating tourism development along that stretch of coast. The beautiful and still largely unspoilt St Mary coastline attracted some famous residents to the area around ORACABESSA in the mid-20th century.

ST PETER'S CHURCH, Port Royal

The present church was built in 1725-26 and was the fifth ANGLICAN church to be erected in PORT ROYAL. Earlier churches were destroyed in the EARTHQUAKE of 1692, the fire of 1703, and the 1721 HURRICANE. The present church was originally of brick but the walls were later faced with cement to simulate concrete blocks. Restoration work has been carried out on the interior more than once. The organ loft was erected in 1743 and is an interesting example of Jamaican woodwork of the period. The brass candelabrum was given to the church by Christopher Terry in 1743. The communion plate is said to have been a gift from BUCCANEER Henry MORGAN.

The most interesting monument inside the church is that to Lt Stapleton of the HMS *Sphinx* – carved by the sculptor, Louis François Roubiliac (1695-1762). Stapleton was killed in MORANT BAY when a cannon he was firing exploded, a circumstance dramatically recalled on the monument. Among the interesting tombs

St Peter's Church

Church plate

in the churchyard is that of earthquake survivor Lewis GALDY, who was one of those responsible for the rebuilding of the church in 1726.
[Black 1988]

ST PETER'S CHURCH (Clarendon) see ALLEY CHURCH

ST THOMAS, Parish of

Size: 742.8km², population 91, 900 (1999). Historic eastern parish, one of the earliest areas of settlement, with a large TAINO population at the time of COLUMBUS' arrival. The Spaniards established cattle ranches at 'Morante' where the principal town of MORANT BAY later grew up, as well as 'Ayala', now YALLAHS. The earliest English settlers included soldiers sent to colonize the Morant area shortly after the conquest (see CAPTURE OF JAMAICA) and a group of 1,600 arriving from the Eastern Caribbean (see STOKES HALL GREAT HOUSE). The earliest church seems to have been one at Yallahs, the church patten (communion plate) inscribed with the date 1683. This parish was formerly called St-Thomas-in-the-East, to distinguish it from St-Thomas-in-the-Vale that was a separate parish until incorporated into ST CATHERINE in 1867. St Thomas itself absorbed the former Parish of St David.

St Thomas is one of the most mountainous parishes, and its many large rivers flowing swiftly to the coast for a time remained unbridged, hindering effective communications and development. The parish was the scene of the so-called MORANT BAY REBELLION, the most serious social protest of the immediate post-EMANCIPATION years. Still largely rural, St Thomas was at first a major producer of SUGAR, the plantations later turned into BANANA and COCONUT production.

STEWART CASTLE

An old estate in TRELAWNY Parish, settled by James Stewart of Scotland. His ruined 18th

century mansion that included a fortified tower is listed as a national monument. On this property, interesting TAINO artefacts have been found, Cundall stating that where the middens are located was known by the locals as 'Indian Town'.
[Cundall 1915]

STEWART TOWN
Hill village in TRELAWNY Parish that was laid out as a market town during the War of 1812 between the US and Britain (fought chiefly along the Canadian border 1812-14) when food, lumber, and other supplies that normally came from America were cut off. The Trelawny planters argued that a market town on the main interior road would encourage settlers in the nearby hills to supply lumber and provisions for their slaves. Twenty hectares were purchased by the civic authorities and the town laid out, named after the Hon James Stewart (1766-1828), then CUSTOS of the parish and owner of STEWART CASTLE.

Just outside the village is Westwood High School for girls which was founded in 1882, on the initiative of the Revd William Mendez Webb (1839-1912), a Jamaican trained at CALABAR who served as pastor of the Baptist church (now the Webb Memorial Church) for 50 years. During his ministry he went to England and secured the interest of Dr and Mrs Trestrail of Bristol in 'higher education for coloured girls', resulting in the founding of Westwood which until 1913 continued to be supported by Baptists in Bristol. The school nevertheless was run on non-sectarian lines, with various Protestant denominations represented on the school board.
[Sibley 1965, Wright and White 1969]

STICK
A stick, rod or wand as the standard equipment of the magician or powerful leader is found everywhere in FOLKLORE, and Jamaica is no exception. Such 'power' objects that immediately come to mind are the shepherd's crook of REVIVAL – some of them elaborately carved, sometimes braided and hooked – and OBEAH or 'dealing sticks'. In more recent times, there was the symbolic 'Rod of Correction' introduced into the election campaign of 1972 by Michael Manley (who went on to become prime minister). Also called 'stick' are weapons such as coco-macca, supple jack, 'cudjoe' and mortar stick, and implements such as the hook stick or 'garabata' used by farmers.

Revival leader with stick

Much feared in the past were the 'obeah sticks' in the hands of practitioners who supposedly endow them with magical properties so they are able to 'deal' with spirits, hence the other name of 'dealing stick'; they are also known as 'ebolite'. These sticks are of African origin: the missionary Waddell records a riot in 1842 at Running Gut estate caused by the new Africans having prepared what the Christians called an 'obeah stick'. Part of the fear came from the fact that some of these sticks were identified with SNAKES (another 'weapon' of the obeah-man), the obeah-man supposedly able to turn the stick into a snake and vice versa. Two sayings (recorded from Guyana) perhaps refer to this practice: 'Wha deh a stick head, deh a snake head' and 'Wha sense deh a snake head, the same deh a bostick-head.'

In the past, sticks were used for swagger and as weapon and as such were called 'Botick' (beau-stick), 'Cudjoe' and 'Supple Jack'. The

Westwood High School

'Stick-lickery' by A. Brunias, 1779

Supple Jack was made from climbing plants (*Paullinia barbadensis* and *P. Jamaicensis*) with flexible knobby stems, which would be cut into pieces, stripped of bark, and made into cudgels that were once shipped to England as walking sticks; the slender stems were used to make riding switches. The Cudjoe was similar, but was perfectly straight and smooth, without knobs. The DJE suggests that the word comes from the English 'cudgel' perhaps influenced by CUDJOE, the great MAROON leader.

The most famous was the Coco-Macca stick, made of jointed palmwood (the trunk or stem of the tree *Bactris plumeriana*, noted for its hardness). It was the attribute of the dandy as well as his weapon. Known in Haiti as *coco-maque* (deriving from the CARIB/TAINO *macana*, meaning 'stick' or 'club'), the heavy cane (often topped with metal knobs) was believed to have been brought to Jamaica by Haitian refugees (see FRENCH). It was used by them – and others – as a weapon, passing into local use and folklore. A Slim and Sam song from the Second WORLD WAR has the verse:

> Jamaica ready to go to war, To ra, ra ra
> We need no gas or man-o-war, To ra, ra ra
> For we have coco macca stick
> De razor an' de half a brick
> To rip, to rip, to ra ra ra

The Coco-Macca had other uses, not recorded from Jamaica, which put it in the ranks of the 'dealing stick'. The definition given in the Funk and Wagnalls *Dictionary of Folklore* notes that it is 'a magic stick found among Haitians that walks by itself. The owner can send it on errands, especially punitive ones. If he hits an enemy with it, the man will die before morning'.

But sticks were also commonplace objects. In the days before public transportation, those who had long distances to travel invariably walked with sticks, and slaves were often so portrayed in ads for RUNAWAYS, the stick also serving as a potential weapon. Slaves and sailors used them to display their skills at 'stick fights', a test of manhood and courage leading to the saying: 'If you can't stand the lick, don't play stick.' Stick-fights are also recorded as part of the WAKE tradition and sticks play a role in dances associated with wakes, e.g. CALEMBE and LIMBO. Two traditional stick-fighting dances, 'Warrick' and 'Kittihalli', have been recorded. Warrick has been found among the KUMINA people of ST THOMAS Parish and is included in the NATIONAL DANCE THEATRE COMPANY'S dances, 'Kumina' and 'Plantation Revelry'. The name is derived from a British Mummers/JONKONNU character noted for his brilliant sword-play. The INDIANS also brought a stick-dance as part of HOSAY.

Of course sticks – like WHIPS – were also used as instruments of punishment and torture during SLAVERY and after, flogging or caning being pervasive up to recent times in boys' schools and prisons.

Sticks used for other purposes can also be turned into weapons, such as the heavy 'mortar stick' which used to accompany the large wooden MORTAR, a once essential equipment in every kitchen. Sticks and mortar sticks feature as weapons in several folk tales.

[Alegría 1985, Cassidy 1971, DJE, Fewkes 1907, Hurston 1938, Leach and Fried 1972, Ryman 1980, Speirs 1902]

STOKES HALL GREAT HOUSE

Ruin near to Golden Grove, ST THOMAS Parish, which is probably the oldest foundation of a house in Jamaica from the English period. It was built with four two-storeyed towers at the corners and a main building, all of solid stonework 76cm thick. The towers and the main building all had loopholes, a common feature of many of the old buildings near the coast, which had to be prepared for defence against pirates, foreign enemies, and potentially rebellious slaves.

Stokes Hall and nearby Stokesfield, commemorate a group of people from the Caribbean islands of Nevis and St Kitts who first colonized the area. Their names still survive in place names in the parish such as Phillipsfield and Rowlandsfield.

One year after the English conquest in 1655 (see CAPTURE OF JAMAICA), Cromwell, the Lord Protector, issued a proclamation to other colonies inviting settlers for the new colony of Jamaica. In December 1656, the governor of Nevis, Major Luke Stokes, his wife, and teenage sons arrived with 1,600 colonists from Nevis and St Kitts. They were settled in the MORANT BAY area. At that time, the only other inhabitants were a garrison of English soldiers since the earlier SPANISH settlers had fled the country when the English arrived.

On the low-lying coast, the new settlers started to die of fevers as soon as they arrived (see YELLOW FEVER AND MALARIA). By March, two-thirds of them, including Major Stokes and his wife, had been buried. But the survivors managed to establish SUGAR plantations in the area, and many of them prospered. Among those who became wealthy were the Stokes' children, the eldest of whom was only 15 when their parents died. It was they who eventually established the two outstanding houses in the area – Stokes Hall and Stokesfield.

[Cundall 1915]

STONY GUT

In this village in ST THOMAS Parish was located the home and chapel of National Hero Rt Excellent Paul BOGLE. His congregation formed the nucleus of those who fought against oppression in the parish, culminating in the so-called MORANT BAY REBELLION. At the site of Bogle's chapel, the JNHT has erected a commemorative plaque.

STREET CRIES

Nowadays seldom heard, the cries of street vendors were a part of old Jamaica. Before refrigeration, one's daily food needs could be met by the vendors who passed by city streets, some on a regular schedule. Others plied their wares in certain districts, while others – as they do today – sat on the sidewalk waiting for customers. But even sidewalk vendors used to keep up a steady patter to attract passers-by. Louise Bennett in several of her poems has immortalized the verbal art of these street sellers (e.g. 'Candy Seller', 'South Parade Peddler') who indulged in wheedling, charm, and – for some who did not buy – abuse.

Not all street criers were vending products. Some, like the knife grinder, were selling services, while others, like the bottle woman or man, were buying: 'Any wi-pi, any chapai-pi, any whiskey bottle' would be understood as 'any wine pint, any champagne pint, any whiskey bottle.'

Items sold by vendors have varied over time. Charles Rampini in the late 19th century observed East INDIANS with baskets of vegetables on their heads; girls with cedar boxes full of sugar cakes of every kind; boys with bundles of walking sticks; vendors of tripe and 'chickling';

Stokes Hall ruin — J. Tyndale-Biscoe

men with trays of king fish; a woman with a basket of parched corn on her head; a woman selling 'rosy apples which the ice-ship had just brought over from America'; a woman selling a saucerful of Alpine strawberries 'brought down that morning from the Newcastle hills' and 'magnificent artichokes' – also grown in the mountains.

Each vendor, Rampini noted, had his or her speciality, each selling one item exclusively – a situation that would not hold today: 'He who sold booby eggs had nothing to do with the vendor of eggs of ordinary poultry. The dealer in radishes sold neither carrots nor turnips. If you wanted fruit, you had to buy your bananas from one person, your oranges from a second, and your pineapples from a third.' Each vendor, presumably, had his or her own distinctive cry. Rampini found the street cries 'neither very musical nor very amusing. They seemed all to be uttered in a whining, nasal, discontented tone, and at the shrillest possible pitch'.

The Jamaican, Astley Clerk, disagreed in a lecture he gave at the INSTITUTE OF JAMAICA on the subject of street cries in the 1920s. Clerk's lecture was accompanied by Mr Granville Campbell, noted musician of his day, who had set 'Kingston street cries' to music.

All who have written on the subject seem to agree on one thing, the common use of the phrase 'gwine pass' (passing by) by the fruit and vegetable sellers. 'Again and again', said Clerk, 'throughout the day's work our ears are vocally saluted with the cry:

Yellow-heart breadfruit gwine pass
Lucy yam gwine pass, eh, de dry Lucy yam gwine pass
Sweet orange gwine pass
Green banana gwine pass, etc.'

Clerk also recalled, 'As a boy listening to similar chants, I was as much struck with the slip-slop of the san-pattas [sandals] on the feet of the women as with their song. To me it was an accomplishment which has ever been associated with the memory of the cry'.

Among the most popular vendors were those of BOOBY eggs raw or cooked and of roasted PEANUTS or 'pindars' as they were also called. Even now, one can almost hear the cry of the peanut boy, 'Pea-nuts, pea-nuts, nuts, pea-nuts, penny nuts' or 'Pea-nuts, ladies, pea-nuts gents, while laughing and talking crack peanuts, hot peanuts'. Clerk noted that the shrill steam whistle of the peanut cart was prohibited on city streets in his time though it is a sound that is still heard in KINGSTON.

Also popular were vendors of SNOWBALLS and ice cream. The latter, says Clerk, were seldom vocal but 'make the welkin ring with the continual "tin-tin-nabulation of the bells" they carry to attract attention'. Today, vendors of ice cream and fudge are among the only ones to be heard on suburban streets with sometimes a straightforward cry of 'fudgee' and sometimes the continual ringing of their bicycle bell to attract attention. Commercial ice cream carts have more elaborate bells and a mobile ice cream cart plays a tune to summon customers.

While the streets cries were once a colourful part of Jamaican life, street vending and hawking or higglering were usually frowned upon by the authorities who enacted numerous laws over the years to prevent such activities, often subjecting the vendors to arrests and fines. Higglers today seem still in control of the streets but their cries, alas, are no more.

[Bennett 1966, Clerk 1985, Rampini 1873]

Milk vendor by Isaac Mendes Belisario

SUGAR CANE (*Saccharum officinarum*)

The major source of processed sucrose, sugar cane is a perennial giant grass that grows to 5m high and forms clumps as it grows. The round stalk is about 5cm in diameter with a hard exterior rind covering a softer fibre that contains the sugar that is extracted by crushing.

In harvesting, the ripe cane is cut down but the suckers or 'stools' at its base will send up

Cane being loaded at factory

fresh canes the following year, called 'ratoons'. However, the yield per acre from ratoons diminishes each year, so in commercial operations the fields are usually dug up and replanted every five or six years. For planting, the cane is cut into short lengths with three buds or 'eyes', a new cane springing from each bud and taking root.

There are many modern varieties of sugar cane and research is ongoing in sugar growing countries to improve the species. The modern varieties are generally derived from hybrids of two or more of the six species of the genus Saccharum which is thought to have originated in southern Asia, the islands of south east Indonesia, and the New Guinea area. The best known cultivar of the 18th and 19th century was the 'Bourbon' but when this was attacked by disease it was replaced by new types. For a long time it was believed that sugar cane did not set seeds but when it was discovered that it did, sugar cane breeding began and still continues, with the accent on improvement in yield and disease resistance. The cane seeds are produced in the flower or 'arrow', a tall feathery plume that is sent up 10 to 24 months after planting (depending on the variety), a signal that the cane is ready to be reaped. Cane is usually harvested between early December and late May.

While today there is some mechanical harvesting, sugar cane is traditionally reaped by hand, the cane cutter using a sharp 'bill' or machete (or CUTLASS) to cut the stalk at ground level and strip it of leaves and flowers. (Jamaican cane cutters have developed such expertise that they are much in demand as reapers of cane in the USA under the Farm Workers, also called the H-2 Workers, Scheme.)

The cut cane is immediately transported from field to factory where the stalks are squeezed between rollers to extract the maximum amount of juice (about 80 per cent of their content). The juice will be put through a complicated process including boiling and evaporation, ending with the raw sugar crystals being separated from the dark syrup that is called molasses from which RUM is produced. The raw sugar will be further refined before consumption. The fibre remaining after the juice is extracted is called 'bagasse', and is used as fuel for the factories and to make particle board and other products. However, as Hagelberg points out, although we speak of sugar 'factories', 'what actually takes place there is not a manufacturing process, in the sense of a transformation such as that taking place in a shoe factory, but rather a series of liquid-solid separations to extract and purify the sucrose made in the cane and transfer it from the solution to the solid phase'.

The cultivation of sugar cane is of great antiquity: the 'sweet cane' is mentioned twice in the Bible (Isaiah 43:24, Jeremiah 6:20). From Asia, the crop was brought steadily westward over the centuries, arriving with COLUMBUS on his second voyage, and planted in Santo Domingo in 1493. From there it was taken by the Spaniards to their other possessions, including Jamaica. (See SPANISH JAMAICA.)

The Spaniards grew sugar on a small scale in Jamaica and erected mills: the ruins of the

Cane cutters c. 1890

earliest one has been discovered at Sevilla la Nueva (see SEVILLE, New). But it was not until the 1660s that an attempt was made to put the sugar industry on a regular footing by the English governor, Sir Thomas Modyford. The industry grew rapidly, reaching its peak in the early 19th century and though in decline since then, has remained a dominant force in Jamaican life. (See SUGAR PLANTATION.)

[Hagelberg 1985]

SUGAR PLANTATION

SUGAR CANE was for centuries Jamaica's most important economic crop, the sugar islands of the Caribbean being at one time the most important possessions in the BRITISH Empire, and Jamaica, the 'jewel in the crown'. In 1805, the peak year, Jamaica produced almost 101,600t of sugar, making it the leading individual sugar producer in the world. So rapid were the returns from sugar that where in 1672 there were 70 plantations producing 772t per annum, by the 1770s there were well over 680 plantations. The industry entered a rapid decline by the third decade of the 19th century and was revived somewhat in the 20th when the remaining small factories were consolidated into large central factories. However the industry has continued to contract and at the time of writing only eight factories are in operation. Though of much less importance than formerly, sugar is still a significant employer of labour and the major agricultural source of foreign exchange earnings.

The institution of New World SLAVERY grew in response to the demand for workers for the labour-intensive sugar plantations, and the two trades – in sugar and slaves – thereafter went hand in hand. Following EMANCIPATION, indentured workers were brought to the Caribbean to work the plantations in conditions of semi-slavery. (See AFRICANS, Indentured, CHINESE, INDIANS.) Hence sugar is still an emotive issue for many Caribbean people. As the saying goes, 'Cane is bitter'.

Loading sugar

From the late 17th century the sugar plantation became the centre around which most of island life revolved. As Barry Higman notes: 'Throughout the eighteenth and nineteenth centuries the plantation was not only a dominant institution but also provided the spatial context within which a large proportion of the Jamaican population lived and worked. During slavery this existence went together with literal physical confinement, slaves being forced to spend the greater part of their lives within the close community defined by a single plantation's boundaries.' The Jamaican sugar estates were the largest in plantation America. Higman states that 'Around 1830, for example, 36 per cent of Jamaican slaves lived in units of more than 200, compared to 5 per cent in the sugar-producing regions of Louisiana and a mere 1 per cent in Bahia'.

The plantations were an early development of the factory system. Each estate was a self-contained entity, growing its own sugar cane, processing it, and shipping the by-products of sugar, molasses and RUM. The demands of the sugar cane itself determined the structure of the industry, since the cane must be processed as soon as possible after cutting or lose much of its sugar content. Each plantation required a vast number of workers, especially during croptime when the work of harvesting, replanting and processing continued non-stop. (See CHRISTMAS, SEASONS.)

Appleton estate and canefields

While the layout of each plantation varied considerably, from a distance each appeared 'like a small town', according to the planter-historian William Beckford, with the GREAT HOUSE and the village where the slaves lived, and the stockhouse, hospital, COOPER'S, wheelwright's, carpenter's, and blacksmith's shops. It is significant that for the most part, the most expensive and imposing structure on each plantation was the factory complex, the domestic residences being a minor part of the whole. The sugar works consisted of the mill-house, curing-house, still-house, and trash-houses. The overseer's offices usually comprised a stable and a corn house, a kitchen, a wash house, a buttery and a store, and there were pig-sties, poultry yard, and a pigeon house. In addition to the sugar cane fields, there were several gardens including that of the slaves (see YARD), as well as their PROVISION GROUNDS in the mountains.

The plantation system in Jamaica was defined by absenteeism. The majority of the wealthy proprietors lived in great splendour 'at home' in Britain, leaving their plantations to be managed by a small number of white tradesmen and indentured servants (see IRISH, SCOTS) under the charge of an attorney (estate manager). The more successful attorneys presided over many estates. It was the white BOOK-KEEPERS, sometimes little more than boys, who were given the task of supervising the vast body of enslaved workers (see GANG, SEASONING, STICK, WHIP).

The production of sugar consumed vast quantities of people (see AFRICAN HERITAGE, MIDDLE PASSAGE, SEASONING), and engrossed the best and most productive lands, relegating the slave and later free 'small settlers' to the least desirable. (See FREE VILLAGE.) This division between plot and plantation, export AGRICULTURE and the small farmer, still persists to some extent. This historically-determined and skewed economic structure has engaged the attention of Jamaican scholars over many decades, resulting in the formation of the influential New World Group in the 1960s and 70s, and many analytical studies, George Beckford's *Persistent Poverty* being among the best known.

The heyday of the sugar planters reached its peak in the late 18th century and began to decline by the 19th. Its demise was hastened by cheaper beet sugar coming to European markets, the ending of the slave trade in 1807, the Emancipation of the slaves in 1838, and the introduction of tariffs such as the Sugar Duties Equalization Acts of 1846. This no longer gave West Indies sugar a monopoly in England.

Ironically, sugar produced by slaves and later freed people in their provision grounds and sold in the local markets, for a long time supplied the needs of most of Jamaica's people (see SUGAR, Wet). The factory product was regarded as too valuable for the local market; hence theft of sugar was a serious offence on any plantation.

Sugar is particular as to soil and climate and grows best in the southern plains of WESTMORELAND, CLARENDON, and ST CATHERINE where the 'sugar belt' is still located. One exception is WORTHY PARK, the oldest estate in Jamaica, which has been in continuous production since 1670, located inland at Lluidas Vale, near the centre of the island.

Conditions in the ownership and operations of the factories as well as those respecting sugar cane workers underwent many changes in the 20th century, assisted by the rise of TRADE UNIONS and the establishment of political parties linked with these unions.

Slavery, the production of sugar, and plantation society have been much studied but only recently have there been studies of specific plantations (e.g. Craton and Walvin 1970), of plantation layout (Higman 1988), and more especially of the African-Jamaican populations thereon (e.g. Armstrong 1991, Craton 1978, Higman 1998). Douglas Hall's presentation of the diaries of Thomas Thistlewood, a planter-penkeeper of modest means, has also provided a unique picture of the intimate interaction between slave and master.

[Beckford 1972, Beckles and Shepherd 1996, Brathwaite 1971, Curtin 1969, GOJ STATIN 1999a, Hall 1989, Higman 1976, Mintz 1985, 1991, Patterson 1973, Post 1978, Sheridan 1985]

SUGAR, Wet

Using the simplest type of mill, ('mill and copper'), small settlers throughout Jamaica once produced their own sugar, known as 'wet sugar' from the high molasses content (see SUGAR CANE). If allowed to harden, it was known as 'head sugar'. It was cheap, healthy, and the preferred sweetener throughout the countryside. For domestic use, bits of the 'sugar head' would be shaved with a knife as needed, and used to make a particularly delicious lemonade called 'berridge'. Head sugar was also eaten as a confection or put between slices of hard dough BREAD. Wet sugar was also sold in kerosene tins to bakeries that used it in bun-making.

Charles Rampini in 1873 noted that there were 5,415 sugar mills throughout the island, most using horse power, 240 dependent on

A 'John Crow' sugar mill (from James Johnston)

manual labour. Home production of sugar contributed greatly to the development of an independent peasantry, especially in such areas as Upper CLARENDON. In 1942, some 590,000 tons of wet sugar were made using these mills, equivalent to approximately 12,444t. These mills fell out of use for various reasons. With the reorganization of the sugar industry, more and more farmers turned to supplying their canes to the factories. It also became increasingly difficult for the farmer to obtain his most important vessel, the 'copper', as he found they were no longer being imported.

These mills were once a common sight, with motive power sometimes provided by manual labour but most often by an old mule or HORSE that spent all day pulling a long arm attached to the mill around a circle 7-9m in diameter. At the hub would be three vertical rollers geared together and mounted on a central post. The arm or sweep attached to the animal turned the axle of one so the rollers crushed between them the sugar cane stalks that were fed in. The cane juice fell into a gutter or wooden trough that led to a barrel or directly into a 'copper' or large iron pot in which the juice was boiled until it was sufficiently crystallized, with WHITE LIME thrown in to 'temper' it – the same as in the factories. The boiling required a great deal of skill since the speed with which the juice crystallized would depend on the weather. The boiling juice, which gave off the sweet-sour smell characteristic of sugar factories, was turned constantly with a long stick and a ladle and skimmer used to take off the scum that rose to the surface.

Once it reached the right consistency, the hot sugar would be ladled into containers. If left fairly liquid, it was 'new sugar' or 'wet sugar'. If the sugar overcooked and got tough it would become 'tie-teeth', a much loved confection. Head sugar would be formed by pouring sugar boiled fairly dry into a cylindrical tin (or clay pot) and allowing it to harden; when turned out, the 'sugar head' (as each one was called) would keep the cylindrical shape. For protection on the way to market, each would be completely wrapped in dried BANANA leaves and tied up with banana trash.

Accidents were a sad by-product of the industry, especially to those given the task of feeding the cane into the mills. A hand or both upper limbs frequently got caught up in the rollers and were severed; the victims were often children. At first, the mills were simple wooden ones, known as 'John Crow', a name derived, it is said, from the number of mules and horses they wore out, to be eaten by the JOHN CROW or scavenger bird. A more sophisticated development was the Chattanooga iron mill popularly known as the 'Exhibition mill' since it was first shown at the Great Exhibition in Jamaica in 1891.

[Beckwith 1928, GOJ Jamaica 1946, McKay 1979, Rampini 1873]

SURINAM QUARTERS

Area between BLUEFIELDS and Whitehouse in WESTMORELAND Parish, named after a group of people who were resettled here from the former English colony of Surinam after it was captured by the Dutch in 1667. By the terms of the peace treaty, England allowed the Dutch to keep Surinam. In exchange, they were given the North American Dutch colony of New Amsterdam, which they renamed New York.

The English settlers in Surinam were sent to Jamaica that was greatly in need of colonists, the island having been taken from the Spaniards just twelve years previously, in 1655 (see CAPTURE OF JAMAICA). About 1,200 people came, including servants and slaves. These settlers made a great contribution to the early development of Jamaica, for they had a good knowledge of SUGAR production and brought their know-how with them. Although the Spaniards had left behind a few primitive sugar mills, there was as yet no sugar industry. The settlers helped to develop the Westmoreland plains into one of the premier sugar-growing areas of the island, a position it retains to this day. Surinam remained a Dutch colony until (as Suriname) it gained independence in 1975.

SUSU see PARDNER

SUSUMBA (*Solanum torvum*)
Small, spherical green berry (about 1.5cm in diameter) found on a bush which grows wild or occasionally cultivated, relished by some people especially when cooked in a dish with salt fish, avoided by others for its bitter taste. Also known as Gully Bean or Turkey Berry, it comes from the same family as the Deadly Nightshade or Gooma, and the Eggplant and Tomato. It is sometimes used for grafting tomatoes.

Susumba

SWEETS

Homemade sweets and confections (called 'sweeties' by children) are still sold, but sweet-making is becoming a dying art. A notable feature of the towns used to be the candy seller who arranged her wares attractively in a portable cabinet, called a 'show case', 'glass case' or 'candy bowl', although it is definitely box-like with a wooden frame and bottom and glass top and sides. These women were located on the sidewalks or near to school gates and usually made the goods they sold, though most sweets in recent times are made commercially. Although tastes change and sweets come and go in fashion, a number have survived and are still made and sold. But, as Charles Hyatt recalled: 'Them times the food that yuh use to get in or aroun' the school yard did have personality because them use to be baked, boiled, roast or prepared by the people who sell them.'

Norma Benghiat has pointed out that in the past, making peppermint candy was an art shrouded in secrecy, a fact that has perhaps contributed to its decline along with the rise of commercial manufacture.

Popular hard sweets (some of which are still made) include candy-striped Peppermint Stick, Candy Bump made from twisted sticks cut into one-inch lengths (also called Farden (farthing) Bump from its former price) and round red and white striped Mint Ball (sometimes with a hint of green stripe). Paradise Plum is an almond shaped sweet coloured bright pink on one side and orange on the other. Bustamante Backbone (named after Alexander BUSTAMANTE) is an extremely tough confection (also known as Stagger-Back) made of brown sugar and grated COCONUT, boiled down until it became 'tie-teeth' and cut into cubes for sale. 'Tie-teeth' is applied to any confection made of brown sugar that is cooked until it becomes tough, sticky, and difficult to chew.

Several popular confections are coconut-based: Coconut Drops are made from boiling diced coconut meat with brown SUGAR, GINGER and other spices and dropping it into lumps that coalesce and harden. GRATER CAKE is made by the same method but the coconut is grated and nowadays, white sugar is used; the mixture is dropped on to a baking sheet and spread out; once it gets hard, it is cut into triangles or squares. Food colouring is often added to part of

Pulling peppermint

the mixture and the two combined into a pretty assembly of pink and white. GIZADA is a round pastry shell or tart filled with grated, sweetened and spiced coconut, then baked, also called Pinch-Me-Round from the characteristic crimped edges. Plantain Tart is not a tart but a pastry shell filled with a mixture (usually coloured pink) of mashed ripe PLANTAIN and spices that is baked.

Sweet and sour Tamarind Balls were probably brought by INDIAN immigrants; they are made by kneading TAMARIND pulp and sugar, forming into balls and allowing to harden by air drying. Pinda Cake is a confection made of peanuts mixed with boiled brown sugar; with sesame seeds added, it is also known as Wangla.

In the category of cakes or biscuits are Cut Cake, BULLA, and Toto. Cut Cake (though sometimes used to refer to Grater Cake), is more often a cake made with flour and coconut and very little raising agent. Baked in a large pan, it is cut into squares for sale. Cake made with baking powder is often referred to as 'light cake' to distinguish it from its poor cousin. Toto is made of flour, brown sugar and grated coconut and is also baked in a pan and cut in pieces for sale. Bulla is a small, flat, round cake (about five inches wide) made with flour, molasses and soda, known for its sweetness and toughness, as is JACKASS CORN. Also popular are the various foods made from corn such as Asham, Brown George, Coction, Tie-Leaf, Pone. (See also BREAD, CORN, DOKUNU, PONE.)

[Benghiat 1985, Cassidy 1971, DJE, Donaldson 1993, Hyatt 1989]

SWEET POTATO see POTATO

Sweet sop

SWEET SOP (*Annona squamosa*)

Small tree (5-8m high) of the same family as SOURSOP and CUSTARD APPLE, like them having a white, sweet pulpy flesh and black seeds; the sweet sop is small and rounded with distinct segments outlined on its skin. Also called Sugar Apple, it is commonly cultivated in lowland gardens from sea level to 300m but also grows wild, having been a fruit tree of the TAINOS. It fruits April to July and sporadically. In folk MEDICINE, the crushed leaves are a home remedy for fainting and the fruit is made into syrup for coughs.

[Adams 1972, Asprey and Thornton 1953-55, Robertson 1990]

SYRIAN see LEBANESE

TACKY

Freedom fighter and folk hero of Jamaica renowned for his personal courage and daring. Tacky led a slave uprising in ST MARY Parish in April-September 1760 that is known as 'Tacky's War'. The uprising began at Frontier estate and spread to other estates in the parish before it was defused, but it was part of a much wider uprising of enslaved Africans (see SLAVERY) planned for the entire island. However, the plans were betrayed by fellow slaves and the conspiracy suppressed by the authorities.

It was from this uprising that the authorities first became aware of the role played by African religion in such events. The word 'obeah' went into the official records and from thence into dictionaries from this time though there is now evidence that the spiritual specialists involved might have been Myalists (see OBEAH, MYAL). The 1760 Law passed as a result of Tacky's rebellion stated: 'Obeiah-men, pretended conjurors, or priests, upon conviction before two justices and three free holders of their practising as such, to suffer death, or transportation, at the discretion of the court.'

The slaves involved in the rebellion were virtually all COROMANTEES. The historian Bryan Edwards says that Tacky 'was a Koromantyn Negro ... who had been a chief in Guiney'. At Frontier estate he displayed outstanding qualities and had been made a driver. He secretly planned the uprising with slaves of his own and neighbouring Trinity estate.

On Easter Monday of 1760, Tacky led about 50 slaves from Frontier to the town of PORT MARIA, where they killed the storekeeper of FORT HALDENE and seized arms and ammunition. They also armed themselves with lead weights from fishing nets to be used as bullets. The insurgents went through the plantations in the area, burning, killing and looting, being joined by other slaves as they went along. By this time the owner of Trinity plantation had been alerted and like the legendary Paul Revere he rode out to warn as many of the other planters as he could.

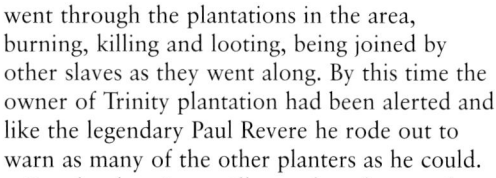

But the slaves' guerrilla war lasted a month before most of them were killed or captured by overwhelmingly superior military force, including the local MILITIA, loyal slaves, the MAROONS and soldiers dispatched from SPANISH TOWN, the capital.

Tacky and a small band were captured and his head was cut off and taken to Spanish Town on a pole where it was displayed, but his followers came in the night and spirited it away. Many of his followers committed suicide rather than surrender. Those who did surrender were either executed or sold to the LOGWOOD cutters of Honduras. In all, 300 slaves were killed, 50 were executed and 300 shipped off the island. Sixty whites were killed. In his bold bid for freedom, Tacky became a legendary figure whose exploits made him a folk hero for a long time afterward. Remains of the battles of this war have been found at Whitehall estate, St Mary Parish.
[Edwards 1794]

Iron gibbet like the ones in which insurrectionists were hung up alive to await a slow and painful death by starvation

TAINO MUSEUM

Opened in 1966 under the auspices of the INSTITUTE OF JAMAICA at White Marl, SPANISH TOWN. The site is significant because it was once a large TAINO village located on the bank of the RIO COBRE.

TAINOS

The Tainos were the people of the northern CARIBBEAN islands who greeted COLUMBUS on his first voyage in the late 15th century, and were historically referred to in the English-speaking world as ARAWAKS. Few physical traces of them are to be found today. Flourishing in the islands when they were first encountered by Europeans (Jamaica's population, for example, has been estimated at 600,000) the Tainos were virtually extinct as a people within 30 years of that contact.

The Tainos and their neighbours (after Rouse)

According to the noted archaeologist Irving Rouse: 'The Taino people emerged during the latter part of the first millennium AD and reached maturity about 1200. They were still evolving when Columbus arrived, but soon succumbed to the effects of overwork, malnutrition, epidemics of introduced diseases, rebellion, emigration, and outmarriage. By 1524 they had ceased to exist as a separate population group.'

When the English captured Jamaica from the Spaniards in 1655, they claimed that no Tainos were to be found. A census of 1611 counted 'seventy four Indians' and as a separate group they vanished from the Jamaican scene – and the history books – until a recent awakening of interest in these first inhabitants, spurred on by the 500th anniversary of Columbus' arrival in the New World.

MAROON oral history has always claimed they had 'Arawak' ancestors alongside African freedom fighters, and Taino artefacts have been found recently in ongoing archaeological excavations of the 18th century Maroon stronghold of NANNY TOWN. Given the ruggedness of the terrain of the Greater ANTILLES and the difficulty of communications, it is easy to believe that the Tainos contributed to a 'maroon' element in Jamaica and the other islands for a long time after their official extinction.

In the islands that remained Spanish (Hispaniola, Cuba and Puerto Rico) much stronger elements of Taino culture survived and Hispanic Caribbean natives claim such an element in their culture: there are communities with people of Taino ancestry in these countries. Hispanic Caribbean scholars have also been at the forefront of investigations into the Tainos.

Who were the Tainos? Although the people Columbus met on these islands beginning in 1492 were of the Arawak language group, over time they had become sufficiently distinct from the Lokono Arawaks of South America to be regarded as a separate people speaking their own language or languages. Many of the objects first encountered by Europeans in the Caribbean still bear their Taino-derived names. Among these are artefacts such as hammock, CANOE, BARBECUE; plants such as maize, CASSAVA, tobacco, POTATO, YUCA, mammee (APPLE), PAPAW, GUAVA; animals such as hicotea (land TURTLE), IGUANA, MANATEE, cayman (CROCODILE); natural phenomena such as HURRICANE, savanna and CAY, and many place names, including Haiti, Jamaica and Cuba (Aiti, Hamaika or Haymaica, Colba).

The people of the islands shared a similar language and culture but each set of islanders called themselves by a different name. Some referred to themselves as *taino* (meaning 'good' or 'noble' – and pronounced tie-ee-no) to distinguish themselves from their enemies the Cariban people (commonly known as CARIBS), and Taino is what they came to be called. Taino is the name that was used by the SPANISH chroniclers, and which survived in the Spanish-

Taino Houses (from Oviedo)

and French-speaking islands. In the English-speaking world, 'Taino' in the past was used exclusively by archaeologists. However, Taino is now the term generally accepted by scholars and is used throughout this book, unless the Arawak language or continental Arawaks are being referred to. (See also INDIAN.)

The Tainos occupied the Bahamian archipelago, the islands of the Greater Antilles – Cuba, Hispaniola (now shared by Haiti and the Dominican Republic), Jamaica and Puerto Rico – and the northernmost islands of the Lesser Antilles. Lokono Arawaks as well as mainland Caribs occupied Trinidad and Tobago, and Caribs occupied some of the southern islands of the Lesser Antilles by 1492, thus separating the Tainos from South America, the continent from which both sets of people are believed to have migrated. Close contact was however maintained between the Tainos of the various islands, and there were also trading and other contacts with the peoples of the Yucatan peninsula and what is now Florida. Since the Island Carib warriors were in the habit of killing Taino men on their raids and capturing the women, many of their children were in fact of mixed Carib and Taino stock.

Origins of the Tainos Like other Arawak-speaking peoples, the Tainos originated in the tropical rain forests of South America and spread out from there via the river systems to the northern part of the continent. From what is now Venezuela some travelled in the period 300-100 BC, via the Orinoco River, to the Caribbean Sea and began to populate the islands, starting in Trinidad. As they moved northwards from island to island by canoe, the Tainos displaced or absorbed earlier peoples, of whom little is known except that they were stone-age hunters and gatherers believed to have themselves migrated from South America.

The Tainos eventually settled in the fruitful islands of the northern Caribbean. Over time they developed a distinct culture based on some of the traits they brought with them from South America, enhanced by distinct new creations and embellishments of their own and as a result of contact with Amerindian groups in Mexico and Central America, notably the Maya. Thus while the Tainos share many elements in common with Lokono Arawaks, they are distinct enough to be considered a separate cultural group.

With the tribes of the tropical lowlands of South America, the Tainos shared the following: cultivation of yuca (cassava) as their staple (see also BAMMY) as well as CORN, cultivation and use of tobacco in religious and curing rituals (see TOBACCO, COHOBA); mortuary practices, shamanism (see MEDICINE, Taino); a social structure based on chiefdoms (see CACIQUE); and a linguistically related language. Artefacts such as the canoe, GOURD, duho (see SEATING, Ceremonial), clay vessels, use of ANATTO and GUINEP as sacred plants also point to their South American origin, as does their style of architecture. Many elements in their myths (see PANÉ) can also be traced to that continent, so can the plants that they brought to the islands. However, it is tantalizing to note that some Taino culture traits can also be found in both Meso-America (Mexico) and North America and scholars are divided as to how much contact there was between the Tainos and these regions.

Tainos in the Caribbean In the Greater Antilles, the Tainos first settled the most eastern island, Puerto Rico, and over time, migrated in a westerly direction to the other islands, arriving in Jamaica around AD 600. The Jamaican Tainos, like the Cuban and Puerto Rican are thought to have arrived via Hispaniola where they had been established for a long time, as they referred to that island as *bohío* or home. Although archaeologists originally believed each island was a separate culture, they are now considered together as representing one culture, with higher

Hammock (from Oviedo)

development in the east where the Tainos first settled, i.e. Hispaniola and Puerto Rico.

The Tainos' early settlements can be traced through their pottery styles, the first settlers on Puerto Rico employing a style called Saladoid – that is similar to pottery found on a site in the Lower Orinoco Basin. It features geometric designs of white over red (like Greek pottery) and is dated from 600-100 BC. With a movement between AD 600-1200 westward into Western Hispaniola (Haiti), Jamaica, and eastern Cuba, two completely new styles of pottery emerged. Called the Ostionioid and the Melliacoid, they displayed few or none of the features of the Saladoid and featured moulded faces. By around 1200 a third major ceramic style emerged – the Chicoid – that combined the moulded faces with the geometric style of the earliest settlers – the Saladoid.

It should be borne in mind that since the main evidence of Taino culture today comes from the archaeological record, new information is constantly coming to light, which leads to ongoing revision of what is known of the Tainos of each island.

The Taino way of life The Europeans regarded the Taino way of life as representative of the Lost Paradise, and indeed the world they occupied was one that was peaceful, healthy, and yielded bounty from sea and land. They were skilful hunters, fishermen and farmers, living in large village settlements with established forms of social organization (see CACIQUE) and religious beliefs and rituals (see AREITO, ZEMI). To the conquering Spaniards they also displayed many positive qualities – their hospitality and generosity were legendary and they were fundamentally peaceful and gentle, resorting to violence only in the face of extreme provocation.

The Tainos cultivated a variety of food crops of which cassava was the staple. They also grew corn (maize), sweet potato, YAMPI, ARROWROOT, squashes, beans, PEANUTS, tomatoes and PEPPERS as well as PINEAPPLES. They cultivated tobacco and anatto. They made permanent fields called *conucos* and planted their root crops in mounds, a practice still continued by Caribbean farmers today.

They were knowledgeable about the properties and uses of plants for medicinal and religious purposes. They cultivated the CALABASH to provide containers and utensils of every kind but they also made and traded in pottery, copper, gold and cotton items, Jamaica being notable as a centre for COTTON production. They carved bowls from wood and sculpted ornamental and ceremonial objects from wood and stone, and fabricated them from cotton. They made musical instruments such as trumpets and drums. Their principal tool was an axehead made from stone and a digging tool called *coa*. They felled huge trees like the COTTON TREE using fire and stone implements and hollowed out the insides to make canoes, some large enough to hold 100 people. The largest that Columbus saw was one from Jamaica that measured over 30m from stem to stern, larger than Columbus' flagship the *Santa Maria* by 5m.

Carrying burdens with a balance pole (from Oviedo)

There was a division of labour in Taino villages. Women grew the crops and made cassava bread, pottery, hammocks and bowls, carried loads, fetched water, cared for the livestock and garden plots in addition to their child rearing and domestic tasks. The men felled trees and cleared the land for planting, made canoes, hunted and fished and organized defence and religious ceremonies. Each village had a headman (or woman) called a *cacique*, and a religious leader or shaman called a *behique*. Descent and inheritance was matrilineal, that is, through the mother's side. A man always lived in the village of his mother's people, his wife joining him there after marriage.

The Tainos and their way of life were doomed with the coming of the Europeans, the islands becoming what the bio-historian Alfred W. Crosby Jr has called 'death camps'. By the 1520s, the population of Hispaniola was decimated, but nothing was learned from this experience to save the Amerindians of the other islands – such as Jamaica, which was settled by the Spaniards after the populations had begun to decline in the islands settled earlier. After Columbus' earlier visit to Jamaica in 1494 and his later year-long sojourn 1503-4 (see COLUMBUS IN JAMAICA) Spanish settlers had begun to arrive in 1509. Here too the Amerindians began to die off from a combination of ruthless exploitation – overwork or wanton cruelty – as well as food shortages, or from the newly introduced diseases such as SMALLPOX and measles. Many killed themselves, and women aborted their children.

Before the arrival of the Europeans, the only threat to the Tainos' existence came from the Island Caribs who had been their traditional enemies on the mainland. Jamaica's isolation at first protected the Tainos from Island Carib raids, but by the time of the European's arrival, the Island Carib had begun to penetrate the northern Caribbean including, possibly, Jamaica. But in a short time, very few of the race described by all who met them as gentle, generous and peaceful would have been found.

The Jamaican Tainos The only visible reminders today of the Tainos in Jamaica are the two 'Arawaks' depicted on the COAT OF ARMS. The name of the country also serves as a reminder of their presence, the Taino naming the island 'Hamaika' or 'Haymaica' (meaning 'land of wood and streams') which was hispanicized as XAYMAICA, or variants thereof, the English further changing it to 'Jamaica'.

Taino rubbish dumps called 'middens' have yielded up some information on their presence and way of life to archaeologists. They also left behind them in caves, some burial sites, paintings and carvings on rock walls (pictographs and petroglyphs) and carved ceremonial objects. The most famous of these carvings are the so-called 'bird man' carvings that were found at Spots in the Carpenter's Mountain in MANCHESTER Parish in June 1792, and are in the British Museum (with copies at the INSTITUTE OF JAMAICA). A more recent find consists of three figures found in a cave at Aboukir, ST ANN Parish, and brought to official attention in 1992.

In Jamaica, as in the other islands, the Tainos lived in village settlements near to rivers and the sea. Jacks Hill, ST ANDREW Parish, is the highest point in Jamaica in which signs of village settlements have been found. The largest Taino village site found was at White Marl, near Central Village in ST CATHERINE Parish, continuously occupied for over 1,000 years. The most important pictograph/petroglyph cave discovered so far is the Mountain River Cave near Guanaboa Vale in St Catherine Parish, and the most important burial caves are the Cambridge Hill caves in ST THOMAS Parish and the cave at White Marl.

Fire-making (from Oviedo)

There are at present some 300 known Taino sites in Jamaica. The parish with the largest number is St Ann while PORTLAND is the only place where none has been found. Three main complexes – all based on styles of pottery – have been identified for Jamaica: Little River (the earliest redware site), White Marl, and Fairfield near MONTEGO BAY, thought to be the latest.

[Aarons 1983,1984, 1988, 1994, Agorsah 1994, Alegría 1978, 1985, Alexander 1920, Arrom 1975, 1990, Bercht et al. 1997, Campbell 1989, Clerk 1978, Crosby 1972, 1991, deGoeje 1943, Fewkes 1907, Fuson 1987, García Arévalo 1977, Harrington 1921, Im Thurn 1883, Jane 1960, Karsten 1926, Las Casas 1974, Lathrap 1970, Lopez-Baralt 1976, Lovén 1935, Morales Padron 1952, Olsen 1974, Parry and Keith 1984, Radin 1942, Reichel-Dolmatoff 1971, 1975, 1978, Roth 1901, Rouse 1992, Saur 1966, Steward 1948, Viola and Margolis 1991, Watson 1988, Wilbert 1987, Wilson 1990, Wright 1910]

TAMARIND (*Tamarindus indica*)

Majestic tree (up to 16m or more in height) with pale green, delicate leaves, now naturalized throughout the tropical and sub-tropical world, probably a native of tropical Africa. The tamarind has been recorded in Jamaica since the 17th century and is found in the drier areas, from sea level to 700m. Though grown as a shade tree and for its wood, Tamarind is most valued for its fruit. From October to June, the tree bears long segmented brown pods 5-13cm long, the easily cracked skin of the ripe fruit revealing a brown acidic pulp covering flat seeds, one in each segment. Tamarind is loved by some as a fresh fruit, the pulp being sucked off, though others dislike its extreme sourness. It can be preserved in syrup or macerated and made into a refreshing drink or into Tamarind balls (see SWEETS). Commercially, the pulp is used in the manufacture of sauces such as Jamaica's Pickapeppa. (Tamarind is also used in Trinidad's famous Angostura bitters as well as internationally popular commercial sauces including HP and Lea and Perrins Worcestershire Sauce.)

In folk MEDICINE, bathing in a tamarind leaf infusion is a well known remedy for the itching of chicken pox. The long flexible tree branches are very hard to break and are used to make switches. 'Tamarind switch' was formerly a favourite implement of punishment in prisons and boys' schools.

The expression 'tamarind season' or in folk pronunciation 'tambran' – the period

Tamarind pods

January to March when most food crops have not yet come in but Tamarind is ripe – means hard times.

There is also a tree called Wild Tamarind (*Pithecellobium arboreum*) a different species that is indigenous.

[Adams 1972, Bourne et al. 1988, Robertson 1990]

TAMARIND TREE CHURCH

Popular name for the historic Church of St Dorothy near OLD HARBOUR, one of the oldest churches in the island. It was the Parish Church (ANGLICAN) when this area was the separate parish of St Dorothy. It is now part of ST CATHERINE Parish. The church was built in the 17th century, shortly after the English conquest (see CAPTURE OF JAMAICA), on lands donated by an early settler, Colonel Fuller, one of the officers of the English army which took the island in 1655 from the Spaniards. Like the other officers who wished to settle, he was given large tracts of land. Inside the church there is a monument to Fuller, who died in 1690.

Up to 1845, the church had red brick walls and wooden window shutters and was known as the 'Old Harbour Barn'. In 1845-46 it was renovated and a belfry put on the roof by Alexander Bravo (1797-1868), a plantation owner who lived at Knights, about 24km from MAY PEN. He was the first JEW to be elected to the Jamaica House of Assembly, in 1835, though four years prior to this he and his family had converted to Christianity.

[Cundall 1915]

TAMBU

Type of dance-music reported from Wakefield area, TRELAWNY Parish, performed by a group that refers to themselves as 'Kongo people'. They claim both a family and ethnic connection with practitioners of KUMINA in ST THOMAS Parish, who also claim CONGO origins. Tambu was formerly used to contact ancestral spirits but as the older practitioners have died off, nowadays it seems to be performed purely for entertainment, being described as 'a lively, somewhat flirtatious' dance-music.

Tambu drumming in Wakefield, Trelawny (from J.S. Roberts)

Tambu (sometimes spelled 'tambo' or 'tamboo') takes its name from the drum, the complex rhythms of which have been identified with Congo drumming tradition. The drummer applies the heel of his foot to the head of the drum to change pitch while another musician uses CATTA STICK on the back of the drum to beat out another rhythm. Such use of percussion sticks on the drum is found in other African-Caribbean traditions.

A French connection has been suggested by several observers, and the Tambu tradition might have been brought by the FRENCH who came in the late 18th and early 19th century as refugees fleeing the Haitian Revolution. Ivy Baxter links the word tambu to the French *tambour* (meaning 'drum') and points to French words in one of their songs: 'Mama Rey lookoo tamboo, Ay Mama Rey, Me Muma e joli oh.' Olive Lewin in her research also found one characteristic feature that was similar to Haitian practice. The drums when not in use were partially dismantled and hung in an anteroom – a leftover, she suggests, from the days when drumming and the rituals they accompanied had to be done in secret, so the drums were disguised.

It is believed that the tambu drum is a remnant of the old Ka drum which may also be found accompanying the Bamboula dance of Louisiana, the French islands and the Virgin Islands, for death celebrations (called 'turn tanks'). The dance also shows French connections, resembling the Bele found in Louisiana, Guadeloupe and Trinidad. Baxter also found the dance to be similar to the Chica described from St-Domingue (Haiti) in the 18th century, and attributed to the Congo people.

[Baxter 1970, DJE, Lewin 2000, Roberts 1972, Ryman 1980]

TANGERINE (*Citrus reticulata*)

A native of China, where it is known as Mandarin, this CITRUS plant like the others found in Jamaica was introduced by the Spaniards in the early 16th century (see SPANISH). The tree is a small one, with spines mainly on the inner branches. The fruit is smaller than an orange and slightly flattened at both ends, with a loose skin that is easily peeled without a knife.

[Adams 1971]

TEA

The word 'tea' in Jamaica usually refers to any kind of hot drink or infusion, e.g. 'fish tea', 'mint tea', 'cocoa tea', 'ganja tea', and is

Workers at the Ramble Tea factory, c. 1903

sometimes used by older folk to refer to the first meal of the day. A herbal tea taken for medicinal purpose, e.g. MINT, is called 'bush tea' (see BALM). Oriental tea is referred to as 'green tea'.

Several efforts have been made in the past to establish oriental tea plantations in Jamaica; the most ambitious of these projects were at CINCHONA in ST ANDREW Parish and at Ramble, near Claremont, ST ANN Parish. The latter was started by Herbert Edward Cox, an Englishman who first came to Jamaica as a tourist in 1892. Having seen tea plantations in the East, he was struck with the suitability of Jamaica for tea cultivation and returned in 1894 to start his plantation, using plants from the Cinchona stock. In 1902 he founded the Ramble Tea Company and built a factory. When he died in 1914, *Who's Who in Jamaica* noted that 'the venture proved a commercial success'. Cox was for 16 years the CUSTOS of St Ann.

On his death the business passed to his son James and then to the Archdeacon of Surrey, the Ven Archdeacon Herbert Sharpe. It apparently thrived but, according to an informant of Anthony Johnson, in 1920 when a breakthrough order was received from overseas and after the shipment was prepared, a fire broke out in the stores and all was lost. The business never recovered.
[Johnson 1995, Who's Who 1921-24]

Tea fruit and flowers

TEA MEETING

Traditional form of entertainment and fund-raising that emerged in the post-EMANCIPATION period, once very popular. The Tea Meeting varied from place to place, but basically would consist of a concert, auctions, set speeches or 'speechifying', dancing, food and drink.

Usually, a COCONUT booth (made of the leaves of the palm) was constructed with a platform and seating, including a 'throne' for the queen. The big moment would be the arrival of the queen and her retinue, ushered in by the song, 'The Queen just arrive/Every money must show'. The elaborately gowned and veiled queen – a young woman of the area – and her attendants were often dressed in a prearranged colour. For a feature of the event was the elaborate clothes worn by the principal participants – top hats and tail coats for the men, gowns and gloves for the women. Another important element was the 'showbread' (hard-dough BREAD baked into elaborate shapes but especially that of a crown – in which case it was called Crown Bread) and/or an elaborate cake. These, like the queen, would remain covered or veiled until the highlight of the proceedings, the auction.

During the auction, the honour of being the one to unveil the queen would be enthusiastically bid for, and so would the right to unveil the showbread or cake, which would then be sliced up and the pieces sold. In some cases, the audience would also bid for items on the concert programme, some paying to take a performer off the stage, others to 'put them back up'.

Part of the success of the Tea Meeting rested on the ability of the chairman chosen to conduct the proceedings, including the unveilings and auctions. He had to be verbally adroit, as he was also expected to keep the company amused with 'speechifying' (talk in flowery, elaborate language), and recitations.

A concert programme might consist of favourite songs of the period and recitations of popular poems learnt by heart in school. There would be musical selections by village fiddlers or talented locals, who sang or performed musical renditions on the comb, saw, or home made MUSICAL INSTRUMENTS such as the BANJO.

The Tea Meeting ended in GAMES and dancing which sometimes lasted until sunrise, when the party paraded through the main street of the village.

Claude McKay, who described the social functions of a Tea Meeting in his novel *Banana Bottom*, also noted its economic importance in the early part of the century: 'For the peasants it was a kind of practical lottery which was often resorted to, to replenish an empty coffer or help out in an emergency such as finding the funds for an unfortunate lawsuit. The trousseau of many a village bride and the cost of the wedding feasts had been paid for by means of a tea meeting.'

Martha Warren Beckwith described the Tea Meeting as 'Perhaps the most elaborate entertainment borrowed from English sources', and she identified such borrowings from English seasonal festivals as the veiled queen, hidden cake or showbread, and mock bidding. Ivy Baxter has suggested a more satirical purpose: 'A fairly late social innovation, the Tea Meeting was influenced in respect to dress by the style and dress of the masters and the growing elegance in the attire of the free COLOURED. It has been said that the bidding element imitated the bidding for slaves; and the speechifying was a copy, in ridicule, of the long speeches which were made in the Assembly and public gatherings.'

Reports from Jamaica and other West Indian islands suggest that the Tea Meeting might have been introduced into the region by METHODIST and other MISSIONARIES in the mid-19th century. The practice seems to have been taken up in many parts of the West Indies by entrepreneurs seeking a way of raising funds, and the character of the meetings changed. In later days, Tea Meetings became purely secular affairs and were frowned upon by the rising bourgeoisie, who considered them not respectable.

In Jamaica, the Tea Meeting seemed to have been one of the elements of the old style BRUCKINS Party. Both are now a part of vanishing Jamaica, though some form of Tea Meeting was recorded up to the 1980s. The spirit of Tea Meeting might also be said to live on in the concerts and fairs held to raise funds for schools and churches.

[Baxter 1970, Beckwith 1929, Lanigan 1844, Lewin 2000, McKay 1933]

TELEPHONE SERVICE

Telephone service is provided by Cable and Wireless Jamaica Ltd under licence from the Jamaican government. In April 2000, the number of telephone lines totalled a little over half-million. Cellular service is also provided by several private companies.

The first telephone was installed in KINGSTON in 1878 and the first directory of subscribers, 50 in all, was distributed in 1883. The Jamaica Telephone Company, which was incorporated in 1892, took over responsibility for the all island system in 1945 at which time there were 7,700 subscribers. The telegraph system was introduced to Jamaica in 1859 and in 1869 cablegraphic communication with Europe was established.

TENNIS, Lawn

The game was first played in Jamaica at Sabina Park in KINGSTON in 1883 and the Jamaica Lawn Tennis Association founded in 1899. Since then, tennis has remained a popular sport though with a lack of public courts, it has been limited mainly to the elite. TOURISM has encouraged the development of courts in resort areas and in the past several outstanding players came to the island as tourists and returned as tennis pros, among them Donald Budge, the US Davis Cup player who was a professional at the Montego Bay Racquet Club, and Fred Perry, the British tennis and golf pro who was associated with Runaway Bay Hotel.

In the first half of the century, B.M. Clark (see GOLF) and Donald Leahong often played creditably against foreign opposition. Up to the time of writing, the most successful Jamaican player has been Richard Russell who was the first Jamaican to go on the international circuit. In 1966, Russell and Lance Lumsden as a doubles pair, beat Arthur Ashe and Charlie Passarell of the USA in a Davis Cup match. Russell's son Ryan has had good success as a junior.

The game is derived from Real or Royal Tennis, an old aristocratic sport, and burst into sudden popularity in the mid-Victorian era. Like CYCLING, it became a popular social sport partly because it was a game in which women also participated. In 1874 a Major Wingfield invented and patented a system for 'a new and improved portable court for playing the ancient game of tennis'. While Major Wingfield's efforts spurred on development of the game, his hour-glass shaped court did not catch on, and the rectangular court was the one used in the first lawn tennis championship in the world held at Wimbledon in 1877.

[Arlott 1975, J. Carnegie, personal communication]

TETHERING POSTS

Some old metal posts seen in downtown KINGSTON, e.g. at the corner of Water Lane and East Street and the corner of Duke and Charles Street, near to GORDON HOUSE, refer to a past era when the HORSE was the popular mode of transportation and the posts were used to tether the animal. There were formerly many such posts dating from the time of the Napoleonic Wars (1799-1815) when a great deal of captured cannon were brought into Kingston by the Royal Navy. The cannon barrels were driven into the ground at street corners to provide tethering

posts called bollards. The one at the corner of Peters Lane and Water Lane is not a cannon but an imitation specially made for tethering.
[Jacobs 1976]

THATCH

Tree leaves were widely used as a roofing material in Jamaica from the days of the TAINOS until about the 1950s, when concrete and various types of shingles became popular and more people could afford them as their economic status improved. Thatch roofs became associated with dire poverty and have been largely discarded in favour of more modern (and expensive) materials. A few thatched residences might still be seen (especially covering houses of the SPANISH WALL type in ST ELIZABETH Parish) but thatch is nowadays used mainly for recreational buildings, out-buildings, temporary shelters and sheds for drying TOBACCO.

Leaves for thatching are provided by different species of 'thatch PALMS'. The most prominent in Jamaica are Silver Thatch (*Coccothrinax jamaicensis*), Crab Thatch, Broom Thatch or Thatch Pole (*Thrinax parviflora*), Broad Thatch (*Thrinax excelsa*), Bullhead or Sea Thatch (*Thrinax radiata*), Bull Thatch or Big Thatch (*Sabal maritima*) and Long Thatch (*Calyptronoma occidentalis*). COCONUT palms and certain grasses are sometimes used for more temporary shelter.

The method of preparing and fixing the thatch to the roof is Amerindian (see TAINO) while the construction method of using a centre ridge supported by poles, or erecting a circular roof around a centre pole, betray both West African and Amerindian influences.
[Adams 1971, Hodges 1986]

Thatched houses, Duperly c. 1905

Thatchers at work

THEATRE

What many regard as the poverty of the Jamaican theatre at the beginning of the 21st century belies the history of theatre in the island which shows it was once the most flourishing of the arts. At the time of the American Revolution, the theatre in Jamaica had such a reputation that the highest recommendation for plays opening in New York was, 'straight from success in Jamaica'. Of course much of this theatrical activity itself consisted of visiting players and a diet of classical plays. What was important in the early days was the existence of theatre buildings and audiences that made travelling to the island a worthwhile venture. Additionally, there was a great deal of local theatrical activity that kept the playhouses open in between visits by travelling players.

However, in considering the contemporary situation as well as the historical, it is well to bear in mind that western dramatic arts, that is, text-based drama and theatre, as the terms are conventionally understood, are merely one aspect of Jamaican (and Caribbean) performance. Popular performances (primarily incorporating music, dance, design and role play) have always been an important part of Jamaican culture and must therefore be considered an important element of what constitutes theatre.

At the time of writing, what might be regarded as the theatre in the classical western tradition is

Playwright Trevor Rhone

in serious decline in Jamaica. Aside from the PANTOMIME which remains a popular annual event, much of the theatre fare today consists of a genre called 'Roots' theatre, a vibrant though often deliberately vulgar and coarse popular theatre that is commercially successful.

Other forms of theatre, particularly those that are not comic, are rarely commercially successful and their output is therefore erratic. Production is expensive and downright backbreaking for individual producers because of the lack of funding and of professional systems of support. Theatre criticism is mostly journalistic or superficial, failing to develop critical standards appropriate to different forms. This is the view of people who grew up with a theatre that was strong and innovative up to the 1980s. Some of the resources available for theatre and drama in Jamaica have disappeared in the decades of financial crises affecting the entire economy. The growing popularity of home entertainment in the form of broader offerings through television, cable and satellite, combined with issues of personal security, have also kept potential audiences at home.

Nevertheless, if theatre is conceptualized more broadly as 'performance', then this element of Jamaican life is still vital, ranging from the rites of popular religions, sermons, ritualized kas-kas, tracing matches, DANCEHALL music, dress and dance, carnival and the staging of official functions. Indigenous dance, originally a by-product of theatre, has developed as dance-theatre; and FOLK MUSIC has acquired a performance dimension which makes it a popular visual as well as musical entertainment on the stage.

Two books on the history and development of theatre in Jamaica by Richardson Wright (1937) and Errol Hill (1992) demonstrate that the formal theatre was firmly established in Jamaica from the 17th century. Alongside it, the Africans were practising their own style of performance and were also taking elements from the established theatre, reshaping and satirizing them. Over time, each influenced the other, leading to the creation of a theatre which, though deeply embedded in its BRITISH roots, has thrown up many new indigenous elements and styles. Ultimately, the theatre has been, and remains, an arena in which the link between the formal and informal, between 'low' and 'high' culture, is played out.

Theatre in the Early Colonial Period The SPANISH *conquistadores* described a kind of theatrical performance by the aboriginal TAINOS in the form of their sacred AREITOS, which was a kind of pageant that included recital of the deeds of heroic ancestors. Though Cundall refers to a Spanish theatre at Seville (see SEVILLE, New) we have no record of theatre during Spanish times (1509-1655).

Jamaica was taken over by the English in 1655 during Cromwell's puritanical rule when the theatre was frowned upon, but this changed with the Restoration of King Charles II five years later. A visitor, Francis Hanson, noted 'the Plays at a Publick Theatre' in 1682 which 'demonstrate the flourishing condition of the island'. Unfortunately, we are not told if this theatre was located at SPANISH TOWN (the island's capital until 1872) or PORT ROYAL, the flourishing mercantile city. And while theatrical activity continued over the next hundred years, little is known about it.

What is known is that from its earliest days as an English colony, Jamaica attracted touring professional actors and acting companies from England, mostly provincial troupes. Errol Hill notes that: 'They lived a frugal existence and were drawn across the Atlantic by stories of affluent New World settlements in need of cultured entertainment. Jamaica had the added inducement of storied buccaneers in their haven in Port Royal tossing around pieces-of-eight as if they were penny-farthings. Players coming over to Charleston (South Carolina) or Williamsburg (Virginia) would be tempted to make the journey further south to the largest and most prized English colony in the Caribbean.'

Planter's Punch

The first known theatre building in Kingston

John Moody, who managed the first theatrical troupe to play in Jamaica (from Wright)

The Plantation Era
The heyday of the theatre not unnaturally coincided with the most flourishing days of the plantation – the mid 1700s to the early 1800s. The brevity of life in the tropics contributed to the pursuit of pleasure, and the theatre had the patronage and sanction of the English governors. Festivities were controlled by the Master of the Revels, an office dating back to the time of Henry VIII in England. The Master licensed plays and companies of actors and gave permission for fetes and public entertainments. The most notorious holder of the position (in the 1750s) was actually a Mistress of the Revels, Teresa Constantia Phillips. She had come to the island after publishing her memoirs in London that she used to blackmail former lovers by charging them huge sums to have their names removed from the text. In the island she secured the patronage of several wealthy men (and five wealthy husbands whom she 'married and buried') and was reportedly the object of affection that led to the contest to build Kingston's finest town house (see HEADQUARTERS HOUSE).

The most famous of the early players was John Moody (c. 1727-1812) who was to become the great comedian of Garrick's London farces but before that, had a successful company in Jamaica. Moody came in 1745.

By the middle of the century there were three flourishing centres of theatre. In the 1740s a playhouse was erected in Spanish Town and a theatre built in 1776. A MONTEGO BAY theatre was built in 1777. KINGSTON from 1754 had a regular playhouse in rented premises on Harbour Street and a permanent theatre from 1774 when the Kingston Theatre was built north of the Parade, the first of a number of theatres on the site culminating in the present WARD THEATRE.

Performers consisted of the visiting English and American players, operatic and other companies from Spain who stopped over on visits to and from Cuba and Spanish-America, and visiting solo performers and popular acts such as circuses, acrobats, gymnasts, etc.

Additionally, there were in Jamaica a small cadre of professionals who had taken up residence and a large number of resident amateurs who sometimes joined the professionals in theatrical productions.

The high point of the colonial theatre occurred during the American Revolutionary War (1775-83) when Puritan sentiments drove out companies from America and closed the theatres. Arriving from American shores was the Company of Comedians under Lewis Hallam, famed in the early annals of American theatre. Between 1755 and 1758 and 1775 and 1785, this company and its successor, the American Company of Comedians, was to spend a total of 13 years in the island. The Hallam company's sojourn confirmed the island's reputation as a

Lewis Hallam and Mrs Hallam (from Wright)

theatre-conscious venue and attracted many others. When, following the war, George Washington encouraged the reopening of American theatres, productions were billed as 'straight from success in Jamaica'.

The 19th Century After the Revolutionary and Napoleonic Wars, the economic recession and subsequent decline of the plantations led to a lull in professional theatre, though the amateurs kept it going. In the early 19th century the Kingston stage seems to have been dominated by FRENCH refugees. The Kingston theatre was closed for a while but reopened in 1812. But while theatre remained active (and successive new theatre buildings were constructed on the same site in Kingston) it seems to have lost its wealthy audience and its impetus. The composition of players and audience was changing too. While in the early days theatre seating and sometimes performances were segregated, the increasing power of the COLOURED class led to a more egalitarian theatre. Whereas black Jamaicans had their own type of theatrical performances outside the precincts of the theatre (see, e.g.

Mistress of the Revels, Teresa Constantia Phillips

DANCE, JONKONNU, 'PLAY', SET GIRLS), by the mid-19th century at least they had entered the theatre as players. Hill notes that performing in the new Kingston theatre in 1849 were two clearly black groups, the Ethiopian Amateur Society and the Numidian Amateur Association.

The issues of SLAVERY, plantation society and race had featured in several of the early plays written for the Jamaican stage, and indeed performed on English ones, the rich West Indian in England and the highwayman THREE-FINGER JACK being favourite subjects. But even when Jamaican creole speech or dialect was put in the mouths of some of the characters (see LANGUAGE), these plays were all written from a European perspective. The first local playwrights that we know of emerged in the 19th century. They were followed by monologists and reciters who wrote their own material. The most popular were a family of black Jamaicans called Murray (Henry Garland Murray, the father and his sons Andrew C. Murray and William Coleman Murray) who wrote and performed much of their work in the Jamaican vernacular from the 1870s to the early 20th century.

Twentieth Century After 1866 touring companies from abroad had again started to appear (presumably in the wake of the economic and social reconstruction following the MORANT BAY REBELLION), offering light entertainment, variety shows and popular operas. Such visits continued into the 20th century, especially after the new Ward Theatre opened in 1912. The most popular was the Florence Glossop-Harris company which came between 1914 and 1931 on regular visits, members of the troupe continuing the tradition as the Empire Players after the founder's death, touring from 1933-39. This was the last of the regular visiting companies, and the post-war years were to see the flourishing of local theatre.

From the 1920s the local production of musical and dramatic performances, vaudeville and variety shows and locally written plays revealed a growing nationalism and a movement towards a Jamaican theatre that would marry the theatrical traditions of Europe with ideas rooted in Jamaica. Much of the indigenous theatrical activity was aimed at translating the popular on to the stage, drawing on western dramatic structures. Writers and directors up to the present have continued to create and stage scripts that combine the popular with the genres of formal drama and theatre in an ongoing dialectic between the oral and written, the formal and informal theatre.

Central to this early development were people like MARCUS GARVEY, whose Edelweiss Park became a venue for locally produced plays and entertainment. Also popular was the CHRISTMAS Morning Concert in Kingston, which was first centred on Astley Clerk's music store and later moved to the Ward Theatre where Louise Bennett was first introduced. Several local variety and vaudeville performers, the most popular being Cupes and Abe (Cupidon and Ableton) appeared at concerts throughout the year. The formation of the LITTLE THEATRE Movement (LTM) and the introduction of the Pantomime in 1941 created opportunities for the employment of a wide range of artistic and production talent on a regular basis.

In the 1960s a small experimental theatre called The Barn was founded by Trevor Rhone (b 1940) and Yvonne Jones Brewster. The Barn produced a number of plays authored by Rhone on themes such as tourism, race and social mobility and issues of partnership. Rhone's work, particularly his *Smile Orange*, was extremely popular and commercially successful. Audiences streamed into the theatre to enjoy his combination of social critique with comedy and his deploying familiar figures such as the storyteller and the trickster in new ways.

Alongside this development, a theatre of ritual and the grotesque developed, heavily influenced by the work of Jamaican playwright and director Dennis Scott (1939-91). Scott, who was also a poet, in 1972 produced a ritual play commemorating slavery called *Echo in the Bone*. *Echo* marked a stylistic shift to a serious theatre that incorporated bare stage, non-chronological scenes, character transformations, and shifting scenic spaces. In the classroom at the Jamaica School of Drama, Scott developed the implications of this kind of writing for the actor, going for a mode of acting that relied on social gesture, physical transformation and the serious use of the creole language. Scott's approach influenced the work of groups like Sistren, who infused into the theatre of ritual, compelling dramas woven from the testimonies of working class women's existence and social histories which had not received much attention previously. The work of playwright Rawle Gibbons drew on Scott's initiatives and extended the search for a performance language rooted in ritual to explorations of the Orisha religion in his native Trinidad.

Systematic research into indigenous cultural forms and their utilization and translation to a wider public on stage began in the 1930s, but came to full flowering in the 1970s and 1980s and fed the later developments in theatre. The research has been carried out through institutions such as JAMAICA WELFARE, the INSTITUTE OF JAMAICA, AFRICAN CARIBBEAN INSTITUTE OF JAMAICA and the Jamaica Memory Bank, the Schools of Art, Dance, Drama and Music now constituting the EDNA MANLEY COLLEGE, the JCDC and the Jamaica FESTIVAL, the NATIONAL GALLERY, UNIVERSITY OF THE WEST INDIES, among others, and by performing groups such as the JAMAICAN FOLK SINGERS, the Little Theatre Movement and its Pantomime tradition, the NATIONAL DANCE THEATRE COMPANY and the NDTC Singers.

[Baxter 1970, Bennett 1974, Ford-Smith 2000, Fowler 1968, Hill 1992, Wright 1937]

THREE-FINGER JACK

Slave bandit-outlaw who was once 'the terror of Jamaica'. A roadside marker near to Eleven Miles on the Kingston to St Thomas highway commemorates this daring 18th century rebel whose hideouts in the BLUE MOUNTAINS appeared on official maps and whose name struck fear into many hearts up to half a century after his death.

Jack was active for some months during 1780 until his capture and death in January 1781, but stories about him continued to be written, told and circulated for many years, his fame having spread far beyond the island. In England he was the subject of plays, musicals, pamphlets and, according to L. Alan Eyre who has sought to untangle some of the facts from the LEGEND, was written about more than any other West Indian of the time. A pantomime fancifully based on his life (*Obi – or Three Fingered Jack*) had a nine year run at London West End theatres. The surname Mansong often attributed to him also seems to have been a foreign fabrication, according to Eyre.

One account suggests that Jack took to the wilds after he led his fellow slaves in ST MARY Parish in a failed attempt at revolt. He was sentenced to be executed but tore apart the bars of his prison with his bare hands and escaped into the mountains, where he became an outlaw, protected by powerful OBEAH. Jack's exploits occurred only ten years after the most serious slave insurrection of the period (see TACKY), also in the eastern section of the island, and he was seen not simply as an outlaw bandit but as someone plotting a slave uprising. The leading role played by the obeah-man or myalist, as

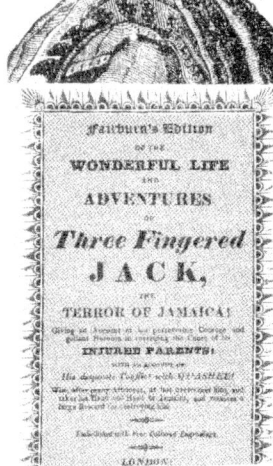

Sistren theatre group

Three-Finger Jack as subject of a play

in Tacky's rebellion, and rumours of blood oaths among his followers, lent credence to these fears.

His first hideout was in the Cane River area but he later retreated to the Queensbury Ridge of the Blue Mountains, living in a cave that came to bear his name. He and his band of runaways would lie in wait on the highway in the vicinity of Eleven Miles where they robbed and killed travellers on the WINDWARD ROAD that linked Kingston with the eastern part of the island. Wild stories circulated about the highwayman. He was believed to be a giant in stature and able to absorb bullets in his body without harm. He was especially cruel to soldiers say the legend, but he never harmed a woman or child.

Three-Finger Jack (so-called because he had lost two fingers of one hand in a fight) was hunted by the soldiers, the MILITIA, other slaves and MAROONS, for there was a reward of £300 on his head plus the promise of immediate freedom for any slave who captured him. Jack was eventually trapped and killed after a bloody fight by a Maroon named QUASHIE and two others. The rebel's head was stuck on a pole and the proud captors marched with it to MORANT BAY, ST THOMAS Parish, followed by a large crowd. Then they marched with it all the way to SPANISH TOWN to collect the reward offered, again followed by a crowd of people, beating drums and singing a chorus that might well have been written for the play:

> Beat big drum – wave fine flag
> Bring good news to Kingston Town, O!
> No fear Jack's Obeah-bag –
> Quashie knock him down, O!

[Black 1952, Eyre 1973]

THREE-FOOT POT see DUTCHIE

THREE-FOOT HORSE
Spirit horse of LEGEND with three legs, one in front and two behind, which haunts the roads on moonlit nights. He kills on sight by 'blowing' on the victim a bad 'breeze' (his breath). The only safety lies in reaching a crossroad before the monster and crawling under a fence, since he can't follow, but to jump over the fence is fatal since he can jump too. Zora Neal Hurston, who heard of 'Three-legged-Horse' from the Accompong MAROONS, got a different version. Their claim that the spirit was a masked dancer who appeared at CHRISTMAS and accompanied the JONKONNU masqueraders suggested to her that it was a remnant of a West African secret rite. She felt it might have been a puberty ceremony for boys, since 'all the women feared it . . . But none of the men were afraid at all'.
[DJE, Hurston 1938, Mico 1893, 1896]

THUNDER-BALL
In times past, Jamaicans kept family drinking water stored in earthenware jars and frequently put inside a beautifully polished triangular-shaped stone picked up in the fields. This was known as a 'thunder-ball', 'thunder-bolt' or 'thunder-stone', and was believed to keep the water cool. The belief that these stones fell from the sky – hence their names – used to be common in many parts of the world. Various cult groups in the CARIBBEAN regard such stones as sacred and use them in rituals. We now know these stones to be stone tools (called 'celts') left behind by earlier peoples. Thunder-balls found in Jamaica were TAINO stone celts which they made by selecting a stone of the general shape from the riverbed, and grinding it into shape by rubbing with sand. Handles were sometimes attached.

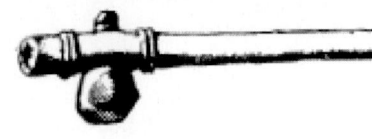

'Thunder-ball', above, and attached to handle, below

[Porter 1990, Simpson 1978]

TIKI-TIKI
Minnows or other minute fresh-water FISH that swarm in enormous numbers in ponds and streams; called 'millions' or 'guppy' in other Caribbean islands. The DJE notes as possible sources for the name the West African Ewe word *tikitiki* and the English word 'thick' ('tick' in Jamaican creole) both meaning 'crowded'.

TITCHFIELD
Name of the hilly section of the town of PORT ANTONIO, PORTLAND Parish, which was the name given to the town itself at the time of English settlement. It was named after the English estate of Lord Portland, the governor after whom the parish was named. However, the town itself reverted to its earlier SPANISH name of Port Antonio.

On Titchfield is located TITCHFIELD SCHOOL and it was also the site of the once-famous Titchfield Hotel, one of the earliest large hotels in the island (see TOURISM). The original hotel was built in 1897 by the Boston Fruit Company,

Titchfield Hotel (from Johnston)

spearheaded by Captain Lorenzo Dow Baker, one of the pioneers of the BANANA TRADE, who encouraged Americans to visit the island (and travel on his ships). The hotel was rebuilt several times, the last building (renamed Jamaica Reef Hotel) burnt down in 1969. One famous owner was the film star Errol Flynn who sailed his yacht into Port Antonio harbour by accident one day and fell in love with the place. He became involved in the life of the town, acquiring a great deal of property that he planned to develop, but died before doing so.

TITCHFIELD SCHOOL

High school in PORT ANTONIO, PORTLAND Parish, founded in 1785, supported by income from the Titchfield Trust. The Trust owned most of the common land of the town that it used to raise funds for the education of the children of the parish. In 1969 an act was passed to allow the Trust to be taken over by the government to encourage the development of the town.

At first, only boys were educated at Titchfield School. When a girls' school was started in 1884, the governors of the Trust did not approve and the headmaster was forced to teach the girls in his spare time until the girls' section was recognized in 1886. The co-educational school is partly housed in the old barracks of FORT GEORGE, the remains of which can be seen.

TOAD see BULLFROG

TOBACCO (*Nicotiana tabacum*)

The tobacco plant is an annual herb native to the CARIBBEAN and South America and was unknown in Europe before the time of COLUMBUS. When the explorer first landed in the Bahamas on 12 October 1492, the TAINOS offered him dried shrivelled leaves and he witnessed their habit of tobacco smoking. LAS CASAS later reported the strangeness of seeing the Amerindians smoking cigars:

'On their journey these two Christians saw many people in their villages, men and women. The men all had firebrands in their hands and certain plants from which they get smoke. The plants are dry and are put on a certain leaf which is also dry. It is like [the barrel of] a musket made of paper, like those the boys make at Easter time. It is lighted on one end, and they suck or draw or inhale that smoke from the other. As a result of this, they become drowsy and almost drunk. These muskets, or whatever we call them, are called tabacos by the Indians.'

The Europeans were to discover that the native peoples of the Americas also chewed tobacco, smoked it in pipes, used it as snuff and inhaled it. Everywhere a sacred plant, the favourite food of the spirits, tobacco was used ritually by religious practitioners; the shaman of the Taino and other groups would intoxicate himself with tobacco smoke during curing rituals (see also COHOBA). Ritual smoking was also indulged in by the Island CARIBS, who blew the smoke from cigars some 1-1.5m long on warriors dancing in a circle to give them courage.

Johannes Wilbert notes that tobacco use by South American peoples at the time of the conquest was near universal. The drug was indulged in by men for social purposes – to seal friendships, conduct palavers, war councils, war dances and to fortify warriors; for fertility – to predict good weather for fishing, lumbering, planting, successful courtship; and for spiritual purposes – vision quests, trances, spirit consultation and magical curing. After the

Tobacco workers

Tobacco drying shed

conquest, tobacco use lost its mystical properties for many peoples and consumption solely for pleasure became a popular and widespread pastime. However, in many Amerindian and African-American religions today, tobacco smoke still plays a mystical role, being regarded as a spirit conductor or food for the spirit helpers. Tobacco leaves are also used in folk MEDICINE in Jamaica as elsewhere, Diane Robertson citing it in the treatment of mumps.

Tobacco is of the nightshade family that includes food plants like POTATO, tomato, PEPPER and eggplant and hallucinogens like thornapple (DATURA) and belladonna. *Nicotiana* is of South American origin. There is prehistoric evidence for its use going back 3,000 years but according to Wilbert, evidence of its ritual use is much older, to the beginning of lowland South American agriculture some 8,000 years ago, possibly antedating the cultivation of food plants.

Tobacco has been grown commercially in Jamaica from SPANISH colonial times. It was cultivated extensively during the English plantation era, both for export of the leaves and by the local population for its own consumption, much of it in the form of JACKASS ROPE. The modern industry dates from the 1870s when Cuban refugees fleeing the wars of independence in their country settled in Jamaica (see MACEO), the most prominent among the tobacco producers being the brothers B. and J.B. Machado who in 1875 founded the firm that bore their name. The Cubans engaged in growing tobacco and, more importantly, in making cigars and cigarettes. Jamaica is still regarded as among the top cigar producing countries in the world, the others being Cuba, the Dominican Republic, Honduras and Nicaragua. Jamaican cigars are regarded by connoisseurs as full bodied, with a mild aroma. Leading brand names of the top quality, handmade Jamaican cigars include Macanudo, 8-9-8 Collection, Royal Jamaica, Temple Hall and Palomino. Tobacco is still grown extensively, especially in CLARENDON.

[Chapman 1958, Espinosa 1628, Long 1774, Lovén 1935, Reichel-Dolmatoff 1971, Robertson 1990, Roth 1901, Wilbert 1987]

TODY (*Todus todus*)

An endemic bird, the Jamaican Tody is particularly fascinating because it is one of the few BIRDS that goes underground to make its nest. A Tody couple will dig a long curving tunnel 61cm or more, usually on the side of a bank, in which one to four eggs will be laid. Both male and female take turns at digging. All five species of Tody are found only in the Greater ANTILLES. The Jamaican Tody is sometimes called 'robin redbreast' though it bears little resemblance to the bird that is so called in England.

A local belief (recounted by *BirdLife Jamaica*) is that the Tody got its red breast at the crucifixion of Christ when a drop of blood fell while the bird gazed up at the cross. The story does not say how this tiny bird made it halfway across the world from the Middle East to the Caribbean. However, it does draw on the fact that the Tody is often seen looking upwards, which it does as it searches under leaves for insect food.

Tody (from Gosse)

[BirdLife Jamaica 1999]

TOKEN

A sign or warning of coming events; thus a rat eating someone's clothes would be taken as a 'token' of a death in the family. That the notion is an old one is suggested by R.T. Banbury's report of the great MYAL procession of the 1840s that coincided with the appearance of an 'extraordinary' comet. The Myalists took this as a 'token', an affirmation of their divine mission

and referred to it in their songs, such as:
   Token show da night, oh
   Da fe you day da behine oh!
   Sinna O, no mine, oh
[Banbury 1894]

TOLL GATE

The name of this village in CLARENDON Parish bears witness to the fact that a toll used to be collected here from travellers using the main road. Tolls were in use in other parts of Jamaica to collect money that was used to maintain the roads. They were not very popular and more than one toll-gate riot has been recorded.

TOM CRINGLE'S COTTON TREE

Historic landmark that stood for centuries at FERRY, ST CATHERINE Parish and collapsed with a mighty crash on the night of 18 January 1971, blocking the main road. It was said to have been damaged by a truck, though it might have been weakened by activities to widen the roadway, and from old age. It was one of many COTTON TREES around Jamaica that became famous for their great age and size (similar ones, for instance, giving their names to HALF WAY TREE and SPUR TREE HILL). Tom Cringle's Tree was so called after the hero of a popular 19th century novel, *Tom Cringle's Log* (1833) by Michael Scott. The Ferry tree was mentioned in an episode in the book, much of which deals with the hero's adventures in Jamaica. Until its demise, the tree (across from the police station) was a popular and much photographed attraction.
[Black 1974, Scott 1833]

'TONIC'

Generic name for a variety of drinks made from extracts from roots and other plant material, still widely used as a home remedy for promoting vitality, strength and – in some cases – sexual potency.

The ingredients and combinations vary but usually include the roots of WIS, especially SARSAPARILLA, Chainy Root and Bryal Wis. A 'tonic' recipe from a Jamaica FESTIVAL culinary arts competition in 1972 included as main ingredients: Sarsaparilla, dried leaves, stem and roots of Strong Back, Bryal Wis, bits of green wis, young BANANAS. Another recipe used Sarsaparilla, COCONUT root, Chew Stick, Bryal Root, 'nerve wis', gum arabic, Strong Back. Spices such as NUTMEG, PIMENTO, CINNAMON, and cloves are added. (The term Strong Back is applied to a number of different bushes believed able to strengthen the back or aid sexual performance.) Many of these ingredients can be obtained from herbalists in the markets.

In making 'tonic drink', the ingredients are boiled until the water is substantially reduced in quantity, thus extracting the vital minerals and salts. It is then cooled, drained and stored. The tonic is sweetened immediately before use, with white overproof RUM or brandy often added. A small amount ('a wine glass' is the usual prescription) is taken once or twice daily to achieve the desired results.

In recent times, the addition of commercial malt-based alcoholic drinks to the mixes has become popular, aided by suggestive advertising that links them to male sexual vigour. The addition of liquefied PEANUTS as well as canned milk-based dietary aids is also of recent popularity.

The suggestive names given to these drinks (some of which can be purchased in markets and from roadside roots vendors) reflect the creators' or the purchasers' high expectations: Keep me Fit, Tallawah (meaning 'strong' or 'tough'),

Tom Cringle's cotton tree

Depth Charge, Young Gal Tempter, Three Foot, Stagger Back, Power Plus, Ital Juice, Strong Back.
[Campbell 1974, Robertson 1990]

TOONA (*Opuntia spp.*)
The name 'Toona' or 'Tuna' is applied to several species of CACTUS (*O. dillenii*, *O. tuna*, *O. jamaicensis*). Toona is a popular plant in folk MEDICINE and as a cosmetic aid, especially as a hair rinse against dandruff. Baked, sliced Toona leaves are used against swellings and bound on the head for vomiting, fever and headaches. Sliced and rubbed with salt, it is used as a poultice for soreness and pain. The word 'toona' comes via the TAINO language
[Asprey and Thornton 1953-55, Robertson 1990]

TORCH-WOOD
Several plants burnt to provide lights at night are called Torch-wood or Candle-wood. From the time of the TAINOS, fishermen have used the dried fibrous inside of the dildo CACTUS (*Harrisia gracilis*) as torches, putting them at the end of their CANOES to attract fish at night. The resinous wood of several trees has also been used to provide light, principal among them Amyris sp. (*A. elemifera* and *A. balsamifera*) known as Torch-wood, Candle-wood and by the local name Kantu, derived from a Twi word. *A. balsamifera* is also called Burn-eye or Blind-eye because unless care is taken, its resin will irritate the eye; it gives off a pleasant smell when burnt. Several other species of trees are used for lighting purposes, such as Ebolite (*Erythroxylum areolatum*).
[Adams 1971, DJE]

TOURISM
Tourism is one of Jamaica's major industries, making a substantial direct economic contribution to the country by way of employment and foreign exchange inflows.

While visitors from COLUMBUS to the present have waxed lyrical about the island's compelling natural beauty, Jamaica as a destination has otherwise had mixed reviews. It might be said that the early visitors were not tourists, but travellers, some of them rather unwilling. Many on arrival felt threatened by the lush tropical vegetation, the bizarre nature of social life in a slave colony, the lack of civic amenities and the reputation for unhealthiness (see YELLOW FEVER AND MALARIA). Added to that were the inconveniences of the travel experience itself. A ship from England to the colony could take up to three months in the days of sail. Coach travel around the island was a painful bone-rattling experience on practically non-existent roads. The offerings of the taverns, lodging houses and inns (few and far between) rested entirely on the whims and eccentricities of the proprietors, many of them women of colour. Indeed, up until the 19th century, hospitality to visitors centred on the GREAT HOUSE and the lavish generosity of the planters and merchants, to which both Lady Nugent and Tom Cringle, the hero of Michael Scott's novel, among many others, could attest.

Jamaica has hosted many of the world's celebrities, including Marilyn Monroe, here arriving for her honeymoon with Arthur Miller

The island became popular in the late 19th century as a destination for visitors who could now be described as 'tourists'. They came solely for pleasure, for the sea cruise on comfortable steamers catering to their every whim, and to enjoy the island's beauty and growing reputation as a health resort. The earliest hotels were connected with the development of the BANANA TRADE, the sea captains having to fill their ships on the journeys to the island. Thus one of the earliest promoters was Captain Lorenzo Dow Baker, who built the TITCHFIELD Hotel and made PORT ANTONIO the centre of the early tourist trade. MONTEGO BAY soon followed.

But the major impetus for the construction of large hotels came with Jamaica's hosting of a Great Exhibition in 1891 and the passage of the Jamaica Hotels Law of 1890, the island's earliest incentive legislation to promote tourism. It provided government assistance for the construction of hotels by private investors. Five hotels were built, three in KINGSTON and ST ANDREW – Myrtle Bank, Queens, CONSTANT SPRING (then 9.5km outside the city), and two in rural areas – at Rio Cobre near SPANISH TOWN, and MONEAGUE. The Queen's (at the corner of Heywood and Princess Streets) was built by the benefactor Colonel Ward (see WARD THEATRE) with the specific purpose 'of providing a comfortable lodging for the respectable peasantry of the island'. The Constant Spring was noted for its 18 hole GOLF course.

What was to become the famous Myrtle Bank was built on Harbour Street in Kingston on the site of an earlier small hotel by that name, established in 1857 by an eccentric Scotsman and newspaper publisher named James Gall. The Myrtle Bank, like the Titchfield, also came to be owned by United Fruit Company, which brought in passengers on their Great White Fleet of boats, travel by steamship being the height of luxury at that time. Many pleasure cruise boats and private yachts also brought in the very wealthy and for many decades the island continued to be a favourite destination of the rich and famous from the United States, Canada and England.

The Jamaica Tourist Association was formed in 1910 to publicize the colony abroad and provide information to prospective visitors and holidaymakers, and it issued the first illustrated guide book to the island, probably to counteract some of the wildly imaginative information being peddled by visiting travel writers. The Jamaica Tourism Development Board was established in 1922 and was later succeeded by the Jamaica Tourist Board, the agency in charge today.

A significant feature of the early industry was the large number of female proprietors. While the early lodging houses and inns were run mainly by COLOURED women, some like CUBAH and Mary SEACOLE achieving near-legendary status, by the early 20th century a number of white women had established hotels that also made them famous. They included the MANDEVILLE HOTEL of Jane Brooks established in 1898, the Ethelhart, Casa Blanca and Sunset Lodge in Montego Bay run by Ethel Hart, Maybelle 'Ma' Ewen, and Carmen Pringle, respectively, and the Shaw Park and Plantation Inn, ST ANN (see OCHO RIOS) operated by Gloria Stuart. Some of these were to continue as family businesses beyond the passing of their proprietors.

Up to the end of the Second WORLD WAR, Jamaica attracted the international elite. It was not until the construction of airports in Montego Bay and Kingston in the 1940s and the development of air travel that the middle classes could also travel to the CARIBBEAN, and what is now called 'mass tourism' did not develop until the 1970s. Montego Bay, Ocho Rios and NEGRIL continue to be the main tourist destinations.

The tourist industry has undergone many changes, both in structure and ownership, Jamaicans now having a substantial stake in the industry. The latest development has been the creation of what are called 'all-inclusives' in which one price is charged and all services are included. This is the fastest growing sector and represents gated communities in which the tourist's needs are catered to in one location. While this appeals to many, some visitors also come to enjoy less organized 'alternative tourism' in places such as Negril, ST ELIZABETH and the BLUE MOUNTAINS.
[Booth 1985, Hanna 1988, Murray 2000, Olley 1952]

TRADE UNIONS

The trade union movement was a significant element in Jamaica's economic, social and cultural development in the 20th century. Through the formation of trade unions, Jamaican workers gained economic improvement and developed a sense of their own collective power. Even more important, the rise of the labour movement was closely allied to the growing political movement and workers fought not only for better wages and working conditions but for political reforms. This movement led to the transition from Crown Colony government (see MORANT BAY REBELLION) to the granting of a new constitution in 1944 which restored elected government and gave voting rights to all adults.

Trade unions provided the mass base for the two major political parties, the People's National

'Adult Suffrage', woodcut by Judith Salmon

Party (PNP) and the Jamaica Labour Party (JLP), that have dominated Jamaica's political life since the 1944 election. From the Bustamante Industrial Trade Union (BITU), founded in 1938 and closely allied with the JLP, have come two prime ministers – founder-president Alexander BUSTAMANTE, and Hugh Shearer and other elected members of parliament. In like manner, the National Workers Union (NWU) since its founding in 1952 has been closely allied with the PNP. Many NWU officers, including former island supervisor Michael Manley have run for office under the aegis of the PNP, Manley twice serving as prime minister.

While the concept of worker militancy was part of post-EMANCIPATION Jamaica, the modern trade union movement dates from the mass disturbances of the 1930s that marked the rise of labour to political power. What happened in Jamaica was not isolated but should be seen as part of a movement that swept all the British colonial territories in the West Indies and Guyana at the same time.

Early worker militancy During the plantation era (see SLAVERY), the enslaved workers were not free to bargain for wages but the concept of worker mobilization was not unknown. The 'Christmas Rebellion' of 1831-2 was originally conceived by Samuel SHARPE as a peaceful sit-down strike. The APPRENTICESHIP period was a time of bitter conflict between employers and workers. As Swithin Wilmot and others have shown, while some of the ex-slaves abandoned the plantations, a significant number remained to struggle with the proprietors for better wages and working conditions. Although the Masters and Servants Act of 1841 was aimed at preventing strikes, these did occur from time to time on the sugar plantations. The incoming indentured workers too withheld their labour to protest conditions. One of the earliest sit-down strikes recorded was among CHINESE indentured workers. However, while there was militancy, there was no real organization and the so-called unions that were formed were transitory.

Early Unions The Jamaica Union of Teachers was organized in 1894 but was a professional organization rather than a union. Several short lived unions were formed, including the Carpenters Bricklayers and Painters Union (popularly known as the Artisans Union – 1898) and the Tailors and Shoemakers Union (1901). Two unions formed in 1907 by printers and by cigar makers, became affiliated with the American Federation of Labour (AFL). They called strikes that were unsuccessful but note would be taken of two of their leaders – A. Bain Alves, a cigar maker, and Marcus GARVEY, then a printer. Bain Alves was later to help other categories of workers form unions and united them in a Jamaican Federation of Labour. But by 1910 all of the first batch of unions formed had ceased to exist.

There was another tide of worker militancy following the First WORLD WAR as the ex-soldiers returned disillusioned and radicalized. Many workers also returned or were repatriated from PANAMA and other places in Latin

Headline after Frome riots

America in similar frame of mind. Their experiences of racism combined with the new racial consciousness inspired by Garvey and the UNIA contributed an ideological base to their protests. Over several years there was general unrest and several strikes, but the climate was not right to sustain a movement, and the momentum died by the mid-1920s.

This post-war militancy did lead to the enactment of legislation on 25 October 1919 making trade unions lawful in Jamaica. However, the legislation was limited, and strikes were easily crushed, since picketing remained illegal and employers could sue strikers for damage and summon troops and the police for assistance. It was after the disturbances of 1938 that legislation was enacted to bring trade union rights in line with those of British unions, based on recommendations of the Moyne Commission.

The Thirties In the 1930s, several factors combined to create the conditions on which mass movements could be built and led to the development of the modern unions. They included the frustration and growing militancy of the working class arising from the devastating impact of the world-wide economic depression that began in 1929. In Jamaica it led to a dramatic fall in price of the leading crops of SUGAR and BANANAS. Wages for the working man and woman were well below the minimum needed to maintain their families. There were also significant demographic factors including rapidly rising population increases. Migration outlets were cut off and thousands repatriated at the same time as unemployment rose. Many of the returnees as well as the jobless rural labourers who had drifted to KINGSTON swelled the city's population and contributed to the growth of the urban and disaffected working class. A final factor was the politicization and rise of an educated anti-colonial middle-class leadership that was to ride on the crest of the worker movement.

What Richard Hart has called the third wave of unrest throughout the Caribbean was to become a major social upheaval that led to dramatic changes in these societies. In Jamaica in 1934 there were strikes at the outports of FALMOUTH and ORACABESSA and of banana carriers at a wharf in Kingston. Throughout 1936 there were marches and strikes involving banana workers, dock workers, sugar workers and ex-servicemen. In 1937 there were disturbances at Serge Island estate in ST THOMAS Parish. Then came the disorder regarded as the most critical, a disturbance in May 1938 at FROME sugar factory where four workers were shot and killed in clashes with the police, several wounded and many arrested and charged. This was to be followed by further turmoil and labour unrest that engulfed the island. The British government appointed a Royal Commission of enquiry, the Moyne Commission, and some of its recommendations, especially those relating to labour, were instituted, laying the foundations for the modern trade union movement.

In 1938, Alexander Bustamante emerged first as a mediator between employers and labour then as leader of the workers' movement after his arrest and that of his associate St William Grant (see PARK) sparked off an island-wide revolt. Bustamante had been associated with A.G.S. Coombs, an ex-soldier who had formed the Jamaica Workers and Tradesmen Union in 1935. But Bustamante broke with Coombs and on his release from jail in 1938 formed what was to become a blanket union representing a wide array of workers, the Bustamante Industrial Trade Union. This was to be the dominant union at the time, allied with the JLP, though several other unions were formed. On the side of the PNP, were the Trade Union Advisory Council formed in 1939, later to become the Trade Union Council (TUC), to be later followed by the National Workers Union (NWU).

Recent Developments Until recently, the two mass unions, the BITU and the NWU continued to dominate the labour scene. They divided the major industries between them and in the case of sugar, once the largest employer of labour, shared representation of the workers. Rather than challenging the two monoliths, other unions for the most part have worked in specialized areas, such as local government, education and transport. One union that has made a bid to move into the major industries is the University and Allied Workers Union (UAWU) which was originally associated with the now defunct Workers Party of Jamaica (WPJ).

While trade unions continue to fight for workers rights, their power to effect changes has been blunted by several factors, such as the wage guidelines imposed by the government as a condition for successive IMF programmes. Even when such guidelines were lifted, inflation and other factors have contributed to the serious erosion of gains by workers. Difficult relations continue to exist between labour and management, but in a changing economic climate, the heyday of mass movements

organized by the unions seems to have passed. And while trade union support is still important to the political parties, other factors than that support now appear far more significant.
[Bolland 2001, Hart 1998, Post 1978, Sewell 1981, White 1981]

TRAFALGAR HOUSE
The residence of the British High Commissioner to Jamaica (located behind the office on Trafalgar Road, KINGSTON) is one of 15 houses in the overseas estate of the British and Commonwealth Office that have been designated as being of historical importance or architectural merit.

Trafalgar House

Trafalgar House was built on land that was first settled by Col Henry Archbould of the English Army of Conquest in the mid-17th century and called Snow Hill Pen (the residential area of Trafalgar Park and commercial New Kingston now occupy part of it).

The present house dates from 1911, having been built on the strengthened foundations of the earlier house that was destroyed in the EARTHQUAKE of 1907. The design is light, airy and tropical with the upstairs surrounded by louvered galleries. The previous house was built at the turn of the 19th century as a private residence and sold by its owners to the British Secretary of State for War in 1895; it has remained the property of the British government. It was the official residence of the senior British army officer in the island until 1962, when it became the official residence of the high commissioner.
[Reid 1985]

TRAMCAR
Tramcars provided KINGSTON'S main means of transportation for 70 years from 1876 to 1948.

The first trams were drawn by mules along steel rails on a 7.25km long route, the mules wearing bells around their necks to warn of their approach. In 1898 the West India Electric Company was established to develop a system using electricity, having bought the lines from the Street Car Company that had established the tramway. The new company extended the lines and acquired the system for electrical generation, bringing the electric tramway system into operation in 1899. Once people got over their initial fear of being shocked by electricity, the tram enjoyed great success. In 1923 the operations were taken over by the newly formed Jamaica Public Service Company. By the 1930s, the company was feeling the competition from motor buses and closed the service in 1948.

The electric tramway facilitated the geographical expansion of the city and acted as a lure for rural migrants. It opened up for residential settlement areas such as Constant Spring Road, Hope Road and Windward Road. Eventually, there were nine lines. The main routes were from Harbour Street up King Street to Constant Spring, Paradise Street to May Pen cemetery, Harbour Street to Race Course (NATIONAL HEROES PARK), Rae Town to the Railway station. Tramcar routes were distinguished by the different coloured boards on which were painted the name of the car's destination.

Many writers have attested to the role the tramcar played in commuters' lives, most notably Louise Bennett in a series of poems including 'Rough Riding Tram', 'Tan-Up Seat' and 'Ole Time Tram'. Despite the growing complaints about the inadequacies of this form of transport, including the overcrowding from passengers and HIGGLERS' baskets, the trams became part of the city's identity. Their passing (to be replaced by gleaming new 'chi-chi' buses which in their turn were replaced by overcrowded 'mini-buses') was

Tramcar

greeted with sadness and nostalgia. As Bennett noted,

> De bus drive sweet, but massa, it
> Noh sweet me like de Tram!

Another observer of urban life, actor and comedian Charles Hyatt also recorded in his memoirs the passing of the tramcar, for him as a small boy the 'last tram ride' representing the end of an era. Hyatt notes: 'The most fascinatin' thing 'bout the tram was the way it did versatile. Monday to Friday it loaded with office worker and school children, Saturday is market people and basket and Sunday is pure dress up Sunday-go-to-meetin'.' Riding the tram to HOPE GARDENS was a popular Sunday outing.

[Bennett 1966, Hyatt 1989, C. Morrissey 1983]

TREADMILL

Method of torture introduced into the slave prisons or 'work houses' during the APPRENTICESHIP period between the abolition of

Treadmill

slavery in 1834 and 'full freedom' in 1838 (see EMANCIPATION). In this unsettled period of extreme antagonism to abolition by the planters, even the most trivial of offences could result in incarceration. The treadmill was introduced by the governor, Lord Sligo (see SLIGOVILLE), as a more humane punishment than the WHIP; but flogging was merely added to punishment on the treadmill.

The treadmill consisted of a large hollow wooden cylinder with steps on the outside. Prisoners were forced to walk on the steps, their weight causing the cylinder to revolve. As it turned, they were forced to move quickly from step to step, their hands tied to overhead handrails. Those who slipped or fainted were battered by the contraption.

The treadmill was invented by an engineer named Cubitt in 1818 and first used in English prisons. It continued to be used in Jamaican prisons until 1908.

[Black 1965, Bryan 1991]

TRELAWNY

Northcoast parish, size 874.6km^2, population 72,600 (1999) formed in 1770 from the eastern portion of ST JAMES, after the wealthy sugar planters of the coast complained that the parish capital of MONTEGO BAY was too far away for them to conduct business. MARTHA BRAE was the first capital of Trelawny with Rock as the shipping port, but this was superseded in 1790 when the town of FALMOUTH was laid out. The parish was named after Sir William Trelawny, who was governor at the time it was formed.

Lower Trelawny continued as a leading sugar area for some time while the upper or hill areas were opened up by small settlers in the post-EMANCIPATION period. The parish embraces part of the COCKPIT COUNTRY.

TRUMPET TREE (*Cecropia peltata*)

Unusual forest tree with an extremely slender trunk growing up to 20m in height, topped by a crown of large palmately lobed leaves, dark green on top with a whitish underside. Found below 1000m, it is native to tropical America and the CARIBBEAN.

It is called the Trumpet Tree in Jamaica because

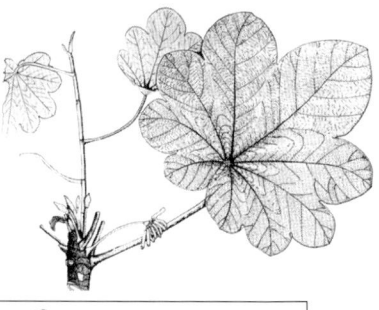

Trumpet tree with close-up (top) of leaves and flowers

MUSICAL INSTRUMENTS – fifes and flutes – were formerly made from its hollow trunk or branches, when cleared of septa. Patrick Browne (1756) noted: 'The smaller branches . . . serve for wind instruments, and are frequently heard many miles among those echoing mountains; they yield an agreeable hollow sound: I have seen some cut and holed in the form of a German flute, and have not been displeased with their notes.'

The tree is also known as Snakewood, no doubt in reference to its long slender trunk and curving branches. It is of the family Moraceae that includes the fig, BREADFRUIT and JACKFRUIT. The fruit is edible (though hardly eaten in Jamaica) and is said to taste like the fig. BIRDS feed on it and contribute to the tree's wide dispersal. The Trumpet Tree grows readily wherever natural vegetation has been removed.

The soft, hollow wood is used for many purposes including matchsticks, boxes, crafts and paper pulp; the branches are used to make floats for fishnets; the trunks split lengthwise can be used for gutters. The strong fibrous inner-bark is used for making ropes and hammocks and has some value in tanning. The dry wood is used for producing fire by friction and was so used by the TAINOS to start their fires. The tree also serves as a weather prognosticator: when the light-coloured underside of the leaf is seen to turn up, it is taken as a sign of impending rain. The tree is associated with DUPPY in Jamaica and is imbued with magical properties elsewhere. In folk MEDICINE, the leaves are used to make a tea for colds and sore throats and in the treatment of high blood pressure.

The Trumpet Tree is a good example of what biologists call symbiosis in plants – it provides a home for ants and for aphids and scale insects. The ants herd and milk these, in exchange, it is believed, for the protection afforded by the ants against herbivores and climbing plants.
[Adams 1971, Campbell 1974, Huxley 1978, JJ 24:3 back cover]

'TRUNK FLEET'
Term used to describe a string of slaves – men and women – who carried the wardrobes of their masters and mistresses from place to place as they went visiting, an important part of social life in plantation days (see GREAT HOUSE). Sometimes it was the waiting maids who carried the trunks and bandboxes of their mistresses on their heads, walking long distances – up to 40km – along the roads and paths in single file. The 'trunk fleet' would be dispatched early in the morning to arrive in time to announce the arrival of their owners and prepare their dress.
[Brathwaite 1971, Lewis 1834]

TRYALL
Hotel complex with a championship GOLF course, formerly an old SUGAR PLANTATION in HANOVER Parish. The old water wheel can still be seen, turned by water brought from the Flint River by aqueducts and stone gutters. The original sugar works here were destroyed by the slaves during the slave rebellion of 1831-32 (see SHARPE, Samuel).

TURTLE
Six species of sea turtles are found world-wide. These are the Loggerhead, Green, Hawksbill, Leatherback, Kemps Ridley and Olive Ridley. Five of these are found in CARIBBEAN waters and four are usually reported from Jamaican waters. These are the Loggerhead (*Caretta caretta*), the Hawksbill (*Eretmochelys imbricata*), the Green (*Chelonia midas*) and the Leatherback (*Dermochelys coriacea*).

Ruthless hunting over the centuries of both the turtles and their eggs has resulted in severe reduction of their numbers. These turtles migrate each year hundreds of miles to their breeding grounds. They were numerous in Jamaican waters in former years but are now on the endangered list. Hunting and trading in turtles and turtle parts are prohibited.

Caricature of 'West Indian fashionables' by William Holland, 1807 showing 'Trunk fleet' at left

The Loggerhead is the largest turtle, equipped with a tough flexible carapace instead of a true shell; its flesh is inedible. The Hawksbill is not good to eat either but its shell provides the beautifully ornamental 'tortoiseshell' from which ornaments are made. The most important is the vegetarian Green Turtle. Big and slow moving, it was in earlier times easily harpooned as it swam near the surface or was caught by remoras (sucking fish). This was a method used by the TAINOS who had huge pens or turtle crawles by the seashore in which the animals were kept alive until required, sometimes hundreds at a time. The crawle consisted of a hollowed out basin of water with a channel to the sea to allow the water to circulate. Such crawles were common around Jamaica's coastline in colonial times and Turtle Crawle River in Portland Parish recalls the practice.

Turtles were also captured when they came ashore to lay their eggs, or the long grass of the river marshes was set on fire to drive them into the water to be killed by spear fishermen, a method used till recent times.

The Tainos ate turtle flesh but valued turtle fat as the greatest delicacy, a taste transmitted to the colonists. Hans Sloane said Green Turtles were so-called from their fat being of that colour. (Blue MAHOE is sometimes called Turtle-fat Mahoe from the resemblance of the wood to turtle fat.) In the 19th century, Charles Rampini noted: 'Turtle steak, turtle fins stewed, turtle liver, turtle tripe, and above all, turtle eggs, are delicacies which it is almost worth while taking a journey to Jamaica to procure.'

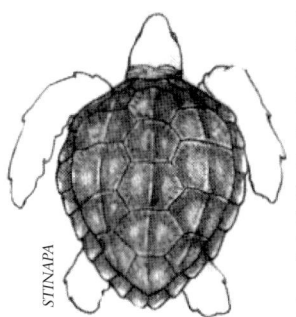

In the colonial period, turtle meat enjoyed great popularity as a luxury dish in Europe. A large number of turtle crawles existed in PORT ROYAL and elsewhere in the early years of English settlement when turtling was a big industry, especially in the Cayman Islands, then a dependency of Jamaica. The animals would be shipped live, tipped over on their backs and lashed on decks with no food or water for the entire voyage to England. Turtle was also a part of the diet of sailors.

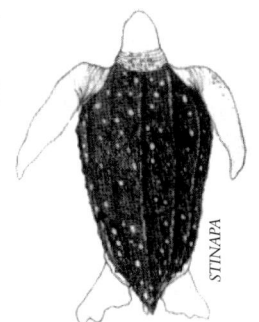

Salt-water turtles are sometimes called 'coots' from the Gambian name, and a 'cooter', a floating decoy made of cottonwood with a head to simulate the sea turtle, was used in connection with a net when turtle hunting was permitted.

Some of the most beautiful artefacts from 17th century Port Royal in the collection of the INSTITUTE OF JAMAICA are the carved and decorated boxes and comb cases made from turtle shell.

[DJE, Grohall and Jones 1992, Rampini 1873, Sloane 1725]

TURTLE, Pond see POND TURTLE

UGLI

Hybrid CITRUS fruit (a cross between a GRAPEFRUIT and a TANGERINE) developed in Jamaica at Trout Hall, ST CATHERINE Parish. The name refers to the irregular warty shape of this fruit. It is larger than a tangerine with a loose skin and large, juicy segments inside. Ugli is now a trade name under which the fruit is exported.

Ugli fruit

UNITED CHURCH

The United Church represents a union of three Protestant denominations: Presbyterian, Congregationalist and Disciples of Christ.

In 1965, the PRESBYTERIAN Church of Jamaica and the Congregational Union of Jamaica merged to become the United Church of Jamaica and Grand Cayman. The church in Grand Cayman was founded by the Presbyterian Church of Jamaica and was a part of the Jamaica church. In 1992, a further union took place between the United Church and the Disciples of Christ in Jamaica. This latter group was a part of the Disciples of Christ in the USA. The official name of the three united denominations is now The United Church in Jamaica and the Cayman Islands.

The United Church consists of 202 congregations in Jamaica and Grand Cayman. The census of 1991 showed 63,971 adherents in Jamaica.

UNITED CONGREGATION OF ISRAELITES see JEWS

UNIA see GARVEY, Marcus

UNIVERSITY CAMPUS, Mona

The campus of the UNIVERSITY OF THE WEST INDIES at Mona, ST ANDREW Parish, is one of the most scenic anywhere, spread over some 263ha on the LIGUANEA Plain with the magnificent Long Mountain in the background and the ever-changing foothills of the BLUE MOUNTAINS in the distance. The campus is beautifully landscaped, the historic ruins of an old stone aqueduct running through it betraying its origins as a SUGAR estate. While the aqueduct once carried water to turn the mills on the former Mona estate, the campus also encompasses parts of the former Papine and HOPE estates. The most striking building is the cut-stone UNIVERSITY CHAPEL near the main entrance.

The original wooden buildings of the university were called Gibraltar Camp, since they originated during the Second WORLD WAR as a temporary residence for refugees who had to be evacuated from Gibraltar. Over 4,000 refugees lived there from October 1940 to October 1944. The majority were ROMAN CATHOLICS but there were also some ANGLICANS and over 1,000 JEWS – some from Holland and Portugal – who arrived from London and Gibraltar during the war; they had their own synagogue in the camp barracks. Later residents included prisoners of war – Italians and a few Germans as well as enemy aliens from the Axis powers. A number of the Italians began manufacturing ceramic fixtures for bathrooms as well as ornamental benches from cement, and some remained in Jamaica after the war and set up businesses.

The building housing the Philip Sherlock Centre for the Creative Arts has won an architectural award. The metal bird on Ring Road is savacou, a mythical Carib Indian war bird. It is the work of noted sculptor Ronald Moody, a Jamaican (see ART). The murals on the walls of the main administrative building and the Caribbean Institute of Mass Communications were executed by Belgian artist Claude Rahir with the help of Jamaican art students.

[Osborne 1988]

Philip Sherlock Centre

UNIVERSITY CHAPEL

Located near the main entrance to the UNIVERSITY CAMPUS, MONA, the chapel of the UNIVERSITY OF THE WEST INDIES is a striking cut-stone building, a magnificent example of Georgian architecture (see GREAT HOUSE). It was formerly an old sugar warehouse at Gales Valley estate in TRELAWNY Parish that was dismantled stone by stone and moved to Mona where it was rebuilt. The name of the original owner and date of the building – 'Edward Morant Gale 1799' – can be seen along the top of the pediment just under the roof. The portico, also stone from Trelawny, was added later. The chapel was presented to the university by the owner of Hampden estate, the late Mrs C.M. Kelly-Lawson, JP, at the urging of Princess Alice, Countess of Athlone and first chancellor of the new university.

University Chapel

The interior of the chapel is decorated with material contributed by all the territories served or formerly served by the university, including MAHOGANY from Belize, Greenheart wood from Guyana, coral LIMESTONE from Barbados (forming the font) and pulpit and rails carved from Jamaican hardwoods. Sunken panels in the ceiling show the coat of arms and seals of all the member territories; of the University of London, the parent university of what began as the University College, and of HRH Princess Alice, moving spirit behind the relocation of the building.
[Richards et al. 1998]

UNIVERSITY OF TECHNOLOGY

Formerly CAST (College of Arts, Science and Technology), this institution became fully

University of Technology

chartered as a university on 29 June 1999. From just over 50 students and four programmes in 1958, when CAST was first established, 'UTech' now has a student population of over 7,000 and offers more than 100 different programmes at certificate, diploma and degree levels. The university is organized into five faculties: Built Environment, Business and Management, Health and Applied Science, Engineering and Computing, and Education and Liberal Studies. Its academic offerings and development have been modelled on the English polytechnic system with emphasis on flexibility of approach, work-based learning and professional linkages. It offers full-time and part-time (day release, evening) courses and cooperative work-based programmes.

UNIVERSITY OF THE WEST INDIES

The University of the West Indies (UWI – familiarly referred to as 'Yuwi') is a multi-campus, regional institution serving 14 countries of the Commonwealth Caribbean and providing some services to Guyana. There are three main campuses: Mona in Jamaica, St Augustine in Trinidad, and Cave Hill in Barbados. There is also a Centre for Hotel and Tourism Management in the Bahamas and university centres in the non-campus countries. These provide access to educational resources and facilities through distance education. The UWI also collaborates with other tertiary institutions in the Caribbean in developing joint programmes.

The university is funded mainly by the governments of the countries from which students are drawn. It offers a wide range of undergraduate, masters and doctoral programmes in arts and education, humanities, agriculture and natural sciences, science and technology, pure and applied sciences, engineering, law, medical sciences and social sciences. Certificates and diplomas in many fields are also offered. The university also offers facilities for continuing studies.

The UWI began at Mona, Jamaica on 3 October 1948 with 33 medical students from across the region, then added the sciences, humanities, education, social sciences and an extra-mural department. Known first as the University College of the West Indies, it was founded by a consortium of British universities and offered a curriculum supervised by the University of London up until 1965, when the new University of the West Indies began granting its own degrees and created its own curriculum. The campus in Trinidad was established in 1960, and Barbados in 1963.

Since its founding UWI has played a leading role in the development of the region and, as importantly, in helping to define a Caribbean identity. It has done this through teaching as well as the significant body of research and publications conducted under its auspices. Outstanding work in the medical and scientific fields and in such areas as Caribbean economics, history and CREOLE languages have gradually changed various aspects of Caribbean life. The CXC schools curriculum and examinations system (see EDUCATION) are a direct result of collaboration between UWI staff and secondary school systems across the region.

Even more important, the university in its early days provided the only means by which WEST INDIANS from all over the region were brought together, at the first campus at Mona, Jamaica, giving them a chance to know each other and helping to develop a sense of a common identity. While the majority of students at the Mona Campus today are Jamaicans, the institution as a whole still remains strongly pan-Caribbean and maintains its focus on Caribbean issues. Its 50,000 alumni are represented at the highest levels of government, corporate and professional life; a number of them are prime ministers and one, Derek Walcott, is a Nobel Laureate. The other West Indian Nobel Laureate, Sir Arthur Lewis, while not a graduate, led the university in its transition from college to university.

The UWI is no longer the only university serving the region. In 1999 the former CAST (College of Arts, Science and Technology) became the UNIVERSITY OF TECHNOLOGY (UTech) and the West Indies College in Mandeville was upgraded to the Northern Caribbean University. Several overseas universities have also established linkages with private education and training institutions to offer degree courses, especially in the area of business. The UWI also has to compete with prestigious American universities that make attractive financial offers to bright school leavers; most sixth form (final year) high school students are now encouraged to sit the SAT exams to qualify them for entry to these schools.

Over time, the profile of the UWI student has also changed, with 50 per cent of students at the Mona Campus now over 25 years of age. The campus has also moved from a significant majority of male students to a student body that is 70 per cent female. In 1998/9 the Mona campus had approximately 11,000 students enrolled.

The UWI operates on a two semester system with teaching beginning in August and ending in May.

A comprehensive look in words and pictures at the first 50 years of this important regional institution is provided by three distinguished medical alumni in: *UWI A Photographic Journey*, photographs by Ken Richards and Owen Minott with text by Henry Fraser (1998).

UP PARK CAMP

'Camp', the popular name of the military headquarters in Jamaica, was established in the late 18th century as the home of BRITISH regiments stationed in the island. Since INDEPENDENCE, it has been the headquarters of the Jamaica Defence Force. The name of the camp derives from Up Park Pen, the property on which it was established. The southern gate to the camp is known as 'Duppy gate' because, the LEGENDS say, members of the WEST INDIA REGIMENT keeping guard at the gate were at night regularly visited by a ghostly officer.

UWI Mona campus

VALE ROYAL

Located at Montrose Road, ST ANDREW Parish, not far from KING'S HOUSE and JAMAICA HOUSE, Vale Royal can be seen from the road and is a striking example of a grand colonial house. Formerly the residence of British colonial secretaries, it has been much refurbished and put to various official uses by successive governments since INDEPENDENCE, serving at various times as the residence of the prime minister and of the minister of finance. Since 1989 Vale Royal has been used as a protocol house, made available to visiting heads of state and government heads of international organizations and other VIPs. It is also used by the prime minister and deputy prime minister for meetings and functions.

Vale Royal was once owned by Simon Taylor, said to have been the richest man of his day (see LYSSONS). The property was then known as Prospect Pen and saw many illustrious visitors through its portals. One of the more memorable entries in the *Journal* of the governor's wife, Lady Nugent, concerns dinner at Vale Royal as guest of Simon Taylor at which she was the only woman present. On 5 March 1802, she records: 'A most profuse and overloaded table, and a shoulder of wild boar stewed, with forced meat, &c. as an ornament to the centre of the table. Sick as it all made me, I laughed like a ninny and all the party thought me the most gay and agreeable lady they had ever met with.' Later, she returned to her room 'surrounded by the black, brown and yellow ladies of the house and heard a great deal of its private history. Mr. Taylor is the richest man in the island, and piques himself upon making his nephew, Sir Simon Taylor, who is now in Germany, the richest Commoner in England, which he says he

Simon Taylor

Vale Royal

shall be, at his death.' Taylor's nephew did inherit, but died only two years after his uncle.

The house has been frequently refurbished over the years but has been in continuous use as a residence since its construction, which is believed to be in the late 17th or early 18th century. In 1928, Vale Royal was acquired by the BRITISH government and became the official residence of the colonial secretary, next to the governor the most important official of the day. It is one of the few remaining houses in KINGSTON that has a lookout tower on the roof. This was a feature of many buildings in the old days as it enabled the owners to keep track of the movement of ships in the harbour. The road leading from Trafalgar Road to Vale Royal was once part of the private driveway to the estate and became public property in the 1920s.
[GOJ STATIN 1999a, Shields 1983]

VENABLES, General Robert
Joint commander of the English forces that took Jamaica from the Spaniards in 1655. (See CAPTURE OF JAMAICA).

VERE
The southern part of CLARENDON Parish, which was once a separate parish. It was named after Vere, wife of a governor, Sir Thomas Lynch, who with her twin sons died on a voyage out from England.

This district was once one of the wealthiest in Jamaica. The source of wealth was at first indigo dye, a major industry in the 17th century. The root of the indigo plant (*Indigofera tinctoria*) produces the blue dye which was once favoured for use in Persian rugs and carpets. The extraction of the dye was a complicated process, and special indigo works had to be set up. At one time, land on both sides of the RIO MINHO was taken up with such works and the profits allowed the settlers here to live in much splendour; it is said that there were more gentlemen's carriages here than anywhere else outside the capital of SPANISH TOWN. However, the English introduced a high tax on indigo, production became unprofitable and the works were abandoned. Although indigo still grows wild in the area, the art of production has been lost.

The settlers then turned to SUGAR which became another source of wealth (and is still the economic mainstay of the area). Before the introduction of steam engines, they used windmills to provide motive power for their sugar factories. The windmills in this area were built with stone towers and the remains of a few can still be seen, the foundation of the one at Braziletto estate now housing the local library.

TOBACCO and COTTON were also extensively grown in this area in the past. (See also ALLEY and ALLEY CHURCH.)
[Long 1774, Taylor 1976]

VERNAMFIELD
Located in CLARENDON Parish, this was a United States Air Force base (named Fort Simonds) during the Second WORLD WAR. It was leased under the 'bases for destroyers' deal arranged between British Prime Minister Winston Churchill and US President Franklin Roosevelt in 1941 and was one of several such bases in the island (see GOAT ISLANDS). Mrs Eleanor Roosevelt, the president's wife visited the base for a few hours on 6 March 1944 while on a brief visit to the island. Most of the land has long since been returned to cultivation. Vernamfield became, for a while, the base for organized motor racing in the island. In the 1960s and 1970s, it was a favourite spot for illegal GANJA flights by light aircraft smuggling marijuana to the USA.

VERNON, Admiral Edward (1684-1757)
One of the famous British admirals who commanded at PORT ROYAL (1739-42) when this was the headquarters of the BRITISH fleet in the CARIBBEAN. Vernon gave his name to Mount Vernon, home of George Washington, the first president of the United States and his nickname to GROG, a RUM and water mixture which served as a regular beverage in the British Navy for over two centuries.

During a war with Spain (known as 'The War of Jenkins's Ear') Vernon boasted that he could take Porto Bello with six ships. Porto Bello on the Spanish Main was then the strongest city in the Americas and one of the richest. Vernon fulfilled his boast and became the toast of London, where the Portobello Road was named in honour of his feat.

George Washington's older brother, Lawrence Washington, captained a Virginia Regiment that served under Vernon during the war. When Lawrence settled on the family estates in 1743, he changed the name from Little Hunting Creek to Mount Vernon in honour of the admiral. The Mount Vernon property was inherited by the future president and became his home and burial place.

While stationed at Port Royal, it was Vernon who first developed ROCKFORT as a naval watering place.
[Black 1988, Cundall 1915]

'VERSION'

Term in Jamaica that denotes a second or additional variation on the original, deriving from a practice in the music industry (see DANCEHALL, REGGAE) in which the flip side of a record would include an instrumental version or 'mix' of the song on the other side. In the 1960s, DJs at dances began to improvise 'toasts' or 'raps' over these instrumentals, thus giving birth to a poetic and musical style that became known as 'Dub'. Dub now also refers to experimentation with new sound recording technologies. As anthropologist Kenneth Bilby reminds us: 'Today the concept of "version" is that any piece of music can be used as the starting point for an endless series of variations – all of them performed "in a different stylee" and thus bearing an individualized stamp.' The concept remains central to Jamaican popular music and reflects the penchant for variation and experimentation.
[Bilby 1985]

VICTORIA CROSS

Two members of the WEST INDIA REGIMENT won the first awards to non-European soldiers of the Victoria Cross, the highest award in Britain and the Commonwealth for bravery in the face of the enemy. One of them was a Jamaican, Sgt William Gordon of the 1st Battalion. He was awarded the VC on 13 March 1892 for bravery during action in West Africa. He was the second recipient, the first being Private Samuel Hodge of the British Virgin Islands who was awarded the VC on 30 June 1866 for bravery while serving in Gambia, West Africa with the 4th Battalion WIR.

Sgt Gordon was invited to be a member of the Jamaican delegation to Queen Victoria's jubilee celebrations in England in 1897. The Queen invited him to Windsor Castle to meet her and gave him the dubious honour of calling him 'Zouave boy' (see JAMAICA MILITARY BAND). She requested that he be given due recognition for the rest of his life and expressed the wish that Gordon should never be tried by court-martial if such a contingency should arise. Sgt Gordon died in 1922 and was buried at the military cemetery of Up Park Camp.

In 1939 Major-General Henry Douglas, described by the *Gleaner* as 'Jamaica's only surviving V.C.' died in England, having won the award for gallantry as a 24-year-old subaltern during the Boer War in 1899. Of British ancestry, he was born in Kingston and educated at ST GEORGE'S COLLEGE and the Collegiate School, his father for some years having been superintendent of the General PENITENTIARY; his sister became matron of the Kingston Public Hospital. He later went to England and studied medicine and joined the Royal Army Medical Corps in 1899, becoming a career officer.

Sgt William Gordon (from Wilkin)

The Victoria Cross was instituted by Queen Victoria 'for most conspicuous bravery, or some pre-eminent act of valour or self-sacrifice or extreme devotion to duty in the face of the enemy'.
[NLJ]

VICTORIA MARKET

Where King Street, the city of KINGSTON'S main street, met the sea was the site of one of Jamaica's oldest MARKETS, called the Negro or Sunday market during the plantation era, Sunday being the only day the slaves were free from labour. Here they would come to buy and sell, and the market would be a colourful mixture of slaves, free people of colour and white hucksters who brought along imported goods for sale. At the beginning of the 19th century, more than 10,000 people used to come to this market from all over the eastern parishes. Stores in Kingston stayed open on Sundays to benefit from the crowds the market attracted.

An iron building was constructed on the site in 1872 and later became the Victoria Crafts Market. It remained so until the redevelopment of the waterfront in the 1960s and the relocation of the crafts market. Beside the market was the Victoria Pier, another historic spot, for in the days before air transport, this was the public landing place and the spot where all important visitors to the island – kings, queens, presidents, prime ministers, or movie stars – first set foot on Jamaican soil.

Victoria Market

VICTORIA STATUE

The statue of Queen Victoria which is now located at the eastern end of St William Grant PARK formerly stood at South Parade where the statue of Sir Alexander BUSTAMANTE now is. During BRITISH colonial days, all important announcements, including the accession to the throne of British monarchs, were traditionally proclaimed from its base. In the EARTHQUAKE of 1907, Victoria's statue – which normally faced down King Street – was turned on its base to face the opposite direction.

The statue, by Geflowski, was erected by a vote of the legislature to commemorate the Queen's diamond jubilee in 1887. It is a replica of one erected in the hall of the Colonial Office at Singapore. Queen Victoria for many generations was a popular folk figure in Jamaica, since it was during her reign that the slaves were freed. Thus an old folk song claims, 'Queen Victoria set we free'. (See BRUCKINS.)

VILLA DE LA VEGA

This was the original name for SPANISH TOWN, meaning 'the town on the plain'. It was the name the Spaniards gave to the capital they founded after they abandoned Sevilla la Nueva (see SEVILLE, New) in 1534. The island itself was called Santiago de la Vega – after St James (San Diego) the patron saint of Spain. When the English took the island they pronounced Santiago 'St Jago' and applied it to the town which then became St Jago de la Vega. Eventually the name was changed to Spanish Town, but the old name of ST JAGO is still sometimes used in reference to the town, e.g. St Jago High School.

VOMITING, Ritual

A practice common among the TAINOS (and other Native Americans) to purge the body of impurities before significant religious and ceremonial events and healing rites. Specially carved and decorated spatulas were sometimes used to induce vomiting and these objects have been found in significant quantities by archaeologists. Some vomiting spatulas also contained rattles to summon the ZEMIS to the ritual.

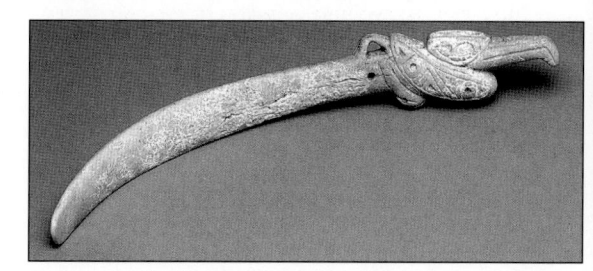

Vomiting spatula, (from Fundación García Arévalo, Santo Domingo)

VOMITING SICKNESS see WILLIAMS, Dr Cecily

WAG WATER RIVER

The Junction Road between KINGSTON and ANNOTTO BAY runs along the bank of this river which rises in the BLUE MOUNTAINS near Hardwar Gap and flows across ST MARY Parish, entering the sea at Annotto Bay. It flows by CASTLETON GARDENS. Junction Road itself seems to have existed as a track for a long time but a carriage road 'passable in rainy weather' was begun in 1856 and completed in 1869.

The Wag Water is the source of a large portion of the CORPORATE AREA'S water supply. As early as 1770 an act was passed giving permission to Daniel Moore, the owner of CONSTANT SPRING estate in ST ANDREW Parish, to bring water from this source to supply his needs. This he did by means of a tunnel and aqueduct through the mountain that are still in use. In modern times the headwaters of the Wag Water have been impounded at Hermitage Dam.

This river is sizeable as Jamaican rivers go and along its length (36.2km) it is joined by many tributaries that drain a large area. These are the Iron River that joins the main stream at Golden Spring, Plantain River, Ginger River that joins near Castleton, Tom's River that flows into the Wag Water at Tom's District, Roaring River, Brae's River and Ugly River. The Flint River which extends over a wide area in the parish of St Mary also flows into the Wag Water. However, the volume of water in the river has declined in recent times and the river mouth has become blocked with silt, occasionally flooding the town of Annotto Bay where dredging and engineering works have had to be undertaken.

The river was originally named by the TAINOS *Guayaguata*. The Spaniards heard and wrote this as *Agua Alta* that was corrupted to Wag Water by the English. The place name Agualta Vale harks back to the earlier pronunciation.
[Cundall 1915, STATIN 1999a]

WAKE

Throughout Jamaica, the custom of family, friends, well wishers and neighbours gathering at the home of a dead person (called 'dead yard') every night or specific nights after death is still observed by many people. (See DEATH RITUALS.)

What actually goes on at a wake will be modified by the religious beliefs and desires of the family and their social status. Nowadays, though all Jamaicans will usually observe some modified form of a 'wake', among the elite it will probably be limited to the reception of guests who call at the house on hearing of the death and a reception for family and close friends immediately after the funeral.

Elaborate wake-keeping is usually undertaken by the folk, especially in the rural areas where there are still families who have perfected the unique style of wake-singing – called 'tracking' – and will travel from funeral to funeral in their district to participate in what is essentially a community event. In tracking, one person calls out a verse from the Scriptures or a sankey (hymn), one line at a time, and the line is sung by the rest in a kind of harmony that creates a unique and memorable kind of music.

Communal singing, testimonies, ring GAMES, RIDDLES, story-telling, ritual music and dance, food and drink, are all elements of the traditional wake which nevertheless varies considerably from one location to the next.

The wake might be held on one or several nights after death, or on all nights up to the ninth. Thus the most widespread name for these events is NINE NIGHT, possibly based on the

Wake song performed at Festival by Islington Secondary School, 1981

belief among the enslaved Africans (see SLAVERY) that it took nine nights for the spirit of the dead to travel back to 'Guinea' or Africa to join the ancestors. The term SET UP is used in some places. Special ceremonies survive in specific localities; called DINKI MINI and ZELLA in eastern parishes, GERREH in the west.

Usually there is a gathering but little activity on the first night, sometimes called a 'silent wake' when the bereaved are urged to cry and mourn. The third night is critical, for it is the night when the dead person is believed to come out of the grave to join the mourners in spirit. An all-night vigil will keep the dead amused and entertained until dawn when he or she must return to the grave. In the old days, on this night a game called 'Baakiny' was played and songs sung to stone-pounding games (e.g. 'Manuel Road' and 'Cobally') along with ring play and dances such as CALEMBE or stick-dance, and LIMBO.

Activities on other nights might be restricted to singing until the nine night ceremony. This is the night of final separation when rituals are undertaken to convince the dead that it is time for it to leave the world of the living forever and join the world of the ancestors. Such a leave-taking in some places is called CROPOVER, a metaphor from the celebrations held to mark the end of the SUGAR harvest. Food (cooked without salt) is provided for the dead inside the house and a formal leave taking by family and other participants is followed by activities – such as rearranging the furniture – intended to signify the breaking of ties and to confuse the dead should it return. (In some places this is done immediately the body leaves the house.) There will also be speechmaking and singing and ritual dance and music.

The wake, then, is basically a vigil kept by the living not only to comfort the bereaved but to entertain (and flatter) the dead so it will not stay around to harm the living. The dead must be convinced that proper respect has been paid so that when the time comes for final leave-taking (on the ninth night), the shadow will remain with the body in its grave and not become a wandering spirit (see DUPPY) that can do, or be employed to do, great harm to the living.

There was also a practical aspect to the keeping of the wake. In the days before refrigeration and professional undertakers, the body was prepared for burial at home and the funeral took place the following day. With open windows and doors in the tropics, the body needed to be watched and protected from animals until burial. The DJE records the term 'watch dead' as the name for a funeral wake on the first night.

Refreshments are an important element of the wake. Depending on the family resources, food and drink will be provided every night or only on the important nights, but it is expected at the Nine Night. Those attending are not averse to making up songs to complain of the absence or inadequacy of the feast:

From me come ya me nuh see no founder
Me a go mash up de booth and go weh
  home a me yard.
From me come ya me so see no cawfee
Me a go mash up de booth and go weh
  home a me yard
From me come ya me no get no white rum
Me a go mash up de booth and go weh
  home a me yard
Me a go pull down de booth an go weh
  home a me yard

The fact that many people will pitch in and contribute to making the wake a success by providing supplies and generally assisting with cooking and serving modifies this attitude somewhat. All understand that, even with the complaints, tradition is being observed. COFFEE and COCOA tea (and white proof RUM for those requiring it) are the expected drinks, along with hard dough BREAD, fried fish and BAMMY. These are the basic wake foods in rural Jamaica.

[Beckwith 1929, Genovese 1976, Hurston 1938, Kerr 1952, Lewin 2000, Pigou 1987b, Simpson 1957]

WANGLA (*Sesamum indicum*)

The oily seeds of the sesame plant have been used for culinary, medicinal and magical purposes over a long period of time. Called Wangla or Wangra in Jamaica, it is probably best known today for its association with the practice of OBEAH. To 'burn wangla' is to obeah someone by burning Wangla seeds with salt and pepper on a path he or she frequents, used especially as a punishment for thieves. It was formerly believed the thief would catch the 'King's evil' or COCOBAY. R.T. Banbury in the 19th century observed that so great was the fear of this practice, that if the intention was announced beforehand, it would make the thief return the stolen goods.

According to F.G. Cassidy, 'wangla' is probably derived from the Kongo word for sesame – *wangila*. It is also known in Jamaica as Beniseed or Benne – its popular name in the rest of the Caribbean (probably derived from the Mandingo word for sesame). Other local names are Gingelly, Oil-plant, Soongah, and Wolongo. Zezegary is the name under which the seeds were imported in the 18th century, Hockalenah an early name recorded by Hans Sloane who also noted that it was 'frequently sown in the fields by the negroes'. Patrick Browne in the 18th century said that the plant was grown in many parts, 'the seeds are frequently used in broths, by many of our Europeans; but the Jews make 'em chiefly into cakes'. Though Wangla is hardly grown or used today, many generations of Jamaicans enjoyed it combined with peanuts to make the popular 'pinda cake' or 'wangla'. The confection is still made but often without sesame. In earlier times, the leaves and seeds were also used in folk MEDICINE, principally in the treatment of dysentery.

Sesame has been a part of the dietary for a very long time, having been one of the earliest plants to be domesticated in Africa, first developing on the southern shore of the Sahara and recorded at Sumer before 2350 BC.

[Banbury 1894, Browne 1756, Cassidy 1971, DCEU, Viola and Margolis 1991]

WARD THEATRE

'The Ward' is the fourth theatre to be built on a site in downtown KINGSTON that has been in continuous use for that purpose since the 1770s, when Kingston's principal venue for entertainment moved from Harbour Street. The first theatre on the North Parade site was the Kingston Theatre (built 1774) that attracted many American and English touring companies (see THEATRE). The theatre was also at one time used as a lockup for rebellious MAROONS. It was eventually torn down in 1838 and the Theatre Royal built on the site. This theatre was rebuilt in 1897, but was destroyed in the EARTHQUAKE of 1907 and was replaced by the Ward. The Ward has a special place in the hearts of Jamaicans, probably because of its association with the development of an indigenous theatre and as the home of PANTOMIME. It has recently undergone extensive renovation.

Ward Theatre was built at a cost of £12,000 and presented to the city in 1912 as the gift of Col Charles Ward, a colonel in the volunteer MILITIA, CUSTOS of Kingston, and a partner in the RUM firm of J. Wray and Nephew Ltd (he was the nephew).

The tavern next door to the theatre occupies the site of the Shakespeare Tavern where in 1825, John Wray, a wheelwright from the country, started a business as a liquor dealer. Eventually he went into rum making, his firm in time becoming one of the island's largest rum manufacturers and his nephew the city's benefactor.

[Baxter 1970, Hill 1992, Wright 1937]

Ward theatre interior

Colonel Ward

Ward Theatre

WARRI

Board game of West Africa brought by enslaved AFRICANS to the CARIBBEAN where it is still played in some places. The game has different names in Africa and the name Warri is a YORUBA one. The wooden board has holes (called 'houses') in which small

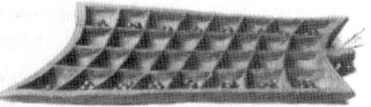

Warri board

round objects – balls, beads or stones – are moved around, the objective being to capture as many of the opponent's houses as possible. There are records of Warri being played in Jamaica with nickols (see BEADS) used as counters. The Yoruba say the game was invented by the orishas or deities.

WARNER

A man or woman who suddenly appears along roads, in towns, or on city streets, to loudly warn the inhabitants of impending doom. The Warner-man or Warner-woman is usually dressed in robes and head-wrap like a Revivalist (see REVIVAL), and is believed to be in communication with the spirit world from which he or she receives direct messages. Warners will cover long distances in delivering their message to the populace at large and warning them to repent from sin and mend their ways. Edward Baugh has captured the feeling associated with the Warner suddenly appearing:

> Bell-mouthed and biblical
> she trumpeted out of the hills,
> prophet of doom, prophet of God,
> breeze-blow and earthquake,
> tidal wave and flood

There are many stories of Warners correctly forecasting major disasters so they have always been regarded as figures of dread, from the time of the Port Royal EARTHQUAKE of 1692.
[Baugh 2000, Chevannes 1994]

WATER BIRDS see GAULIN

WATER HYACINTH (*Eichhornia crassipes*)

Plant bearing an attractive blue flower like a hyacinth that floats on rivers and waterways. It is regarded as a pest since it will end up choking a water course, blocking out light and using up all the oxygen in the water so that aquatic life is destroyed. The botanical name *crassipes* means 'fat foot', referring to an inflated bladder at the base of each leaf which forms a rosette, keeping the plant afloat and growing by simple division. The only way of destroying the plant is by keeping it out of the water.
[Huxley 1974; Proctor 1968]

WATER SPIRITS

Jamaican FOLKLORE provides many illustrations of the belief that water is inhabited by powerful spirits – usually female, since water is a female element. If offended, these spirits will punish the guilty: by drowning them in a stream, by catching them in a storm at sea, by preventing them from catching fish, etc. Thus rituals were held to propitiate these spirits. There is also the universal belief that powerful gods and goddesses came out of the sea to teach crafts or give cultural instruction to humankind. In Guyana it was the water spirit Orehu who taught the first Lokono ARAWAK medicineman certain secrets, giving him the CALABASH tree (from which he made sacred rattles) and a similar myth is found among the TAINOS (see GUAHAYONA). In Taino mythology, the chief female deity or ZEMI is the water mother, ATABEYRA, associated with fresh water and human fertility. YÚCAHU, her son, is associated with the fertility of crops and the harvest of the sea. A number of other zemis controlled water for crops (see WEATHER SPIRITS) and regulated HURRICANES and floods (see COATRISCHIE, GUABANCEX, GUATAUBÁ).

In Jamaica today, the principal water spirit is Rivermaid, which is the name given to both a powerful spirit in REVIVAL and a mermaid-type of seductress or river guardian in secular stories. In Revival, Rivermaid is a female spirit associated with rivers, sometimes brought into worship, especially during rainstorms. Like the Taino water deity Guabancex, she has her assistants – Water Shepherd and Shepherdess, and Water Boy and Water Girl. When Rivermaid appears, she might become the most important spirit at a ceremony.

The Revival practice of offering sacrifices to Rivermaid at the riverhead might derive from an earlier widespread belief in a powerful female river spirit or deity called River Maid or Ribba Mumma. R.T. Banbury writing in the 19th century tells us that it was believed the sources of streams were inhabited by a powerful female deity. She was worshipped and sacrifices offered

Water hyacinth

M. LaYacaona

to her. Slaves on waterworks would sometimes persuade their masters to sacrifice an ox to her in times of drought so water would come flowing again to turn the sugar mill. They would go to the fountainhead and sing a song and perform the 'Mial dance' (see MYAL) for the Ribba Muma. Fish of such rivers would not be touched since they were believed to be children of the river goddess and whoever ate them would suffer.

M.W. Beckwith tells us more about this being: dances would be performed and sacrifices of a white goat, a black cock, and silver money made to the water being called 'Mamajdo' who also cured disease, especially YAWS. Mamajdo seems close to the name of such a spirit in the French islands – *Maman de l'eau* sometimes corrupted to *Mammadillo*. Similar beliefs in a water spirit are found in other parts of the Caribbean.

The spirit that is variously called River Maid, Ribba Mumma, Ribba Missis, Ribba Mammy, might have originated as a religious being but, outside of Revival, is nowadays better known as the subject of folk tales and legends. Rivermaid by whatever name is the guardian of the river and makes her home at the riverhead or in deep BLUE HOLES. Here she is said to appear sometimes at noon, combing her long black flowing hair. If she is seen, she will 'call' the person, who will be forced to go with her and she will drag him or her down to the depths. She is sometimes associated with another LEGEND, that of the Golden Table that rises out of the water, sometimes at noon, to tantalize watchers who will attempt to drag it from the depths, only to be themselves dragged into the water, a sacrifice to the water spirit. In some tales, Rivermaid is the guardian of GOLD left behind by the Spaniards (see PANYA JAR) often in caves where the fountainheads of many rivers are located. In this guise she is always a Taino woman.(See e.g. MARTHA BRAE.)

As the guardian of rivers, the water spirit in folk tales demands propitiatory offerings before a successful crossing can be made. Several stories tell of her varying responses to obedient and disobedient children (see Tanna 1984). A spirit of the sea called Sea Mammy also appears in some folk tales and ANANSI stories. Jamaican fishermen, like fishermen everywhere, do have rituals to propitiate the spirit of the sea in order to obtain a good catch and ensure a safe return, though these have not been studied.

In summary, water spirits in the current guise of Rivermaid might be the clearest example we have of creolization or cultural mixture, since the beliefs embody African, European and Amerindian elements. The fact that the secular Rivermaid often appears combing her hair (leaving her golden comb behind to lure victims in some versions) suggests an old European form of magic.

There is no doubt, however, that many of the beliefs also have an African origin; on that continent, water is the most precious element and the belief is widespread that all bodies of water are inhabited by living spirits. According to John Mbiti, in many parts of Africa, rivers, lakes and waterfalls 'are regarded with religious awe. People make sacrifices and take offerings there, as a sign of wishing to be in harmony with their waters, especially if they wish to fish in them or cross them'. Water is also used in many sacred rituals, symbolizing 'purification and cleansing, not only of bodily but also of mystical impurities'.

Thus Africans in the New World could readily identify with Christian baptism by immersion that was introduced by BAPTIST missionaries in the 19th century. Both Myalists and Revivalists readily incorporated this practice into their rites. Water remains a significant element in African-Jamaican worship and cultural practices. (See also BEDWARD.)

[Banbury 1894, Baxter 1970, Beckwith 1928, Mbiti 1975, Moore 1953, Seaga 1969, Tanna 1984]

WATER SQUARE, Falmouth

The fountain at Water Square, FALMOUTH, TRELAWNY Parish, stands on the site of the stone reservoir that supplied the town with water for 150 years. Water was raised from the MARTHA BRAE RIVER by the use of a water wheel (a replica of which tops the fountain) and piped to Falmouth, where it was stored in the reservoir to be distributed by the water carrier, as only the homes of the rich had pipes. Before that, people depended on wells dug in their backyards or water brought by CANOES from the Martha Brae. In 1902 the government took over the water supply from the private company that had operated it before. In 1953 the reservoir was removed. The town is now fully supplied with piped water.

WATERMELON (*Citrullus vulgaris*)

Annual vine, a member of the Cucurbit or gourd family, which bears a large smooth fruit with bright pink flesh and numerous black seeds. A native of tropical Africa, watermelons are grown mostly in the dry southern parishes and are commonly offered for sale on the highways.

Wattle and daub

WATTLE AND DAUB

A method of construction used in Jamaica from the 16th century, in which red clay is plastered over a wood framework of woven wattles, formerly much used for house construction, now used mainly for storage sheds and other out-buildings. The framework of timber is first constructed and the wattles – usually split BAMBOO or other flexible round wood – are interwoven in panels between the uprights and braces. They are left to dry and shrink, then a plaster of lime, earth, mortar or clay is daubed on. When the plaster is applied on both sides of the wattled wall and smoothed over, the wattles are not visible. The surface can be painted or lime wash applied. The method is ancient and was widely used in Europe, and was probably introduced in Jamaica by the earliest settlers.
[Hodges 1987]

WEATHER SPIRITS

Among the twelve principal ZEMIS of the TAINOS, the weather spirits are known as MÁROHU and BOINYAEL, often represented as twins. In Taino art, they are usually carved of wood and represented as twins that 'sweat', that is furrows were engraved on their faces to collect condensed water drops and simulate tears (rain), hence they are also known as the 'crying twins'. On the different Taino islands, their images were kept in caves, and rites were performed for them to provide favourable weather for agriculture. Twins

'The crying twins' (from Fewkes)

are associated with weather and rain in many cultures.
[Arrom 1990, Campbell 1989, Fewkes 1907]

WEDDING, Country

Weddings in Jamaica follow the pattern of those in the western world, the majority borrowing from both English and American practices. (Of course, people of non-Christian religions also follow their own traditions and practices.)

In the past, traditional 'country' weddings had many unique features that have vanished with the times. One was the custom of 'bringing home the wedding cake'. The main cake of several stories and smaller 'side cakes', would usually be baked some distance from the bride's home. The day before the wedding, a procession of women

Carrying the wedding cakes, early 20th century

dressed all in white would set off for the bride's home carrying the cakes covered in snowy white cloths borne on trays on their heads. They were not supposed to speak to anyone on the way.

But other preparations for the wedding took place long before. Both the bride and groom would have sponsors, called 'godparents', who would help with the wedding preparations. The godmother usually accompanied the bridegroom to church. The bride, dressed in satin and lace, would be accompanied by her godfather and the bridesmaids. In the old days the whole party would travel on horseback.

The celebrations usually took place at the bride's home. The day before, family and friends would have constructed a COCONUT booth in the yard where the ceremony would be held. The booth, made of BAMBOO uprights and PALM fronds interwoven to form the walls, usually had an ARCHWAY at the entrance and would be decorated with flowers such as BOUGAINVILLEA and FERNS. The coconut booth might be built over a BARBECUE (flat paved area used for drying crops) or beaten earthen floor.

At the wedding reception the cakes would be unveiled – and the main cake cut as a highlight of the evening. There would be feasting – on curried GOAT usually – and wine would be drunk. The speeches would be long, flowery and elaborate in a form known as 'speechifying'. The wedding would end with GAMES and dancing to a fiddler or MENTO band.

The Sunday after the wedding, the entire wedding party would attend the regular church service for what was called the 'turn thanks', i.e to return thanks.

[Beckwith 1928, Mills 1969]

WELSH

Thanks to the privateer-turned-governor, Sir Henry MORGAN, the Welsh presence in Jamaica was clearly established from the 17th century, although the Welsh people have left less of a mark on the island's history than other groups such as the SCOTS and IRISH. Most were sailors, labourers and artisans. From the Welsh came the method of building low walls of free stone to enclose pastures and fields, altering the landscape of ST ANN and TRELAWNY in particular, and handing down a skill that still survives. The slate that covered the roofs of many 18th and 19th century sugar works came from Wales, and probably so did the slates and slate pencils used in elementary schools up until the 1950s. From Wales also comes the name and practice of *eisteddfod*, an ancient national festival at home, in Jamaica a competition in music, poetry, drama and the fine arts that was once popular in schools and arts groups and was probably introduced by Welsh teachers and ministers.

Welsh place names account for only 16 items listed in Inez Sibley's *Dictionary of Place Names in Jamaica*, but many others exist as this list shows: Anglesey (WESTMORELAND); Bangor Ridge (PORTLAND); Bryan Castle (two in St Ann); Bryan's Bay (Portland); Bryan's Hill (CLARENDON); Bryan's retreat (ST MARY); Deeside (Trelawny and St Mary); Cardiff Hall (St Ann); Denbigh and Denbigh Crawle (Clarendon); Flint River (St Mary); Jones Depot (Clarendon); Llandewey (ST THOMAS); Llandillo (Westmoreland); Llandovery (St Ann); Llandruff Pen (Trelawny); Llanrumney River and Llanrumney estate (St Mary, once owned by Henry Morgan); Lloyds (ST CATHERINE); Lloyds, and Lloyds Great House (St Thomas); Morgan's Bridge, Morgans, Morgan's Pass and Morgan's Valley (all named after the buccaneer, in Clarendon); Morgan's River (St Thomas); Pencarne (St Mary, owned by Morgan); Penrhyne Castle (Clarendon); Phantillanda (ST ELIZABETH); Phantillands (St Elizabeth); Vaughnsfield (ST JAMES); Powell Drain (St Mary); Vaughan's Rock (St Mary); Wales (MANCHESTER); Welsh Woman's Point (Portland); Williams Park (St Mary); Williamsfield (Clarendon); and Ythanside (Portland).

In addition to these, one of the old parishes of 17th century Jamaica was named St David, after the patron saint of Wales. On a map of the County of Middlesex, 1804, one finds several small estates owned by Welsh proprietors: Griffiths, Howell, Lloyd, Powell, Penrhyn, Welsh, and Williams, many of the names occurring in more than one parish. The Welsh may have made up something of a middle class of small estateholders, and of middle men in general. Their names are not among the millionaire class of 18th century Jamaica. Curiously, up to the 1950s, suburban house names in KINGSTON and ST ANDREW included Abergavenny, Aberystwyth, Brecknock, Llandudno, Pontypridd, and Radnor, a fading echo of the Welsh presence.

Although Scottish surnames far outnumber Welsh in Jamaica, 'Williams' appears on a ratio of three to two when compared with 'CAMPBELL', the commonest Scots name in the Kingston telephone directory, and outnumber all others.

Welsh surnames in Jamaica include Boyd, Bryan, Bryce/Brice, Conway, Davis, Davies, Evans, Griffiths, Ellis, Ewan/Ewen, Howell, Hughes, Jones, Meredith, Morgan, Owens, Parry, Powis, Price, Rice, Rhys/Reece, Rhynie, Thomas, Vaughan, Welsh/Welch, as well as Williams.

WESLEYAN see METHODIST

WEST INDIA REGIMENTS

Historic BRITISH regiments of black soldiers who were uniformed, armed and trained along European lines, originally formed for the defence of the British West Indian territories during the French and Napoleonic Wars in the late 18th and early 19th centuries. Despite hostility to them by the colonial planter class who dominated the island Assemblies, the soldiers proved themselves superior to British troops posted to the islands, being much more adapted to the climate and with a far lower mortality rate. Throughout the 19th century, WIR soldiers were employed on various campaigns in West Africa, including the Ashanti Wars. Their outstanding campaigns include Dominica 1805, Martinique 1809, Guadeloupe 1810 (Napoleonic Wars) and in Africa, Ashanti 1873-4, West Africa 1887 and 1892-4, Sierra Leone 1898. During operations in West Africa, two WIR soldiers won

A Private of the Fifth West India Regiment, 1814

the highest military honour, the VICTORIA CROSS for bravery, one of them a Jamaican, Sgt W.J. Gordon. During the First WORLD WAR, the WIR was posted to Cameroons 1915-16, and East Africa 1916-18.

The WIR was finally disbanded in 1927 as an economy measure. In that year the Jamaica Regiment was formed, and no doubt included many who had served in the WIR. In January 1959 the West India Regiment was reformed as part of the short-lived WEST INDIES Federation, replacing the Jamaica Regiment that formed the nucleus of the new force which recruited men from all the islands of the British West Indies. When the Federation was dissolved in 1962, the Jamaica Defence Force was formed, consisting of the Jamaica Regiment and the Jamaica National Reserve.

UP PARK CAMP, now the JDF headquarters, was home to the 1st, 2nd, and 3rd Battalions of the WIR, which were stationed in Jamaica from time to time. The only reminder today of the historic WIR is the zouave uniform worn by the JAMAICA MILITARY BAND, which was formed on the breakup of the WIR in 1927.

Origin While blacks in the Caribbean, both slave and free, were often used in the islands' defences as needed, the use of regular black soldiers dated to the American War of Independence. Both black and white loyalists were formed into corps to fight on the side of the British, some of them coming to the Caribbean after their defeat in the war. When war broke out with France in 1793 and threatened the British West Indies, the first black corps was raised in the Windward Islands in 1795 from free blacks and purchased slaves, to be followed by seven more (all led by white officers). These black troops were to take part in the fierce fighting that raged in the islands during the Anglo-French wars, and thereafter became a permanent part of the British garrison. Eventually there were twelve regiments.

The original black regiments were given several designations before the title West India Regiment was universally adopted. Individual regiments were frequently identified by the name of the commanding officer, hence the first regiment was known as 'Whyte's Regiment of Foot' and included members of the Black Carolina Corps that had been formed earlier from the black American soldiers who had come to the islands.

The WIR was the direct responsibility of the British War Office and regarded as part of the British army, treated the same as white regiments in the West Indies regarding pay and conditions of employment. No black, however, was allowed to enter the officer class; the regiments were all commanded by whites.

The idea of a permanent black army was not popular with the white settlers but was pushed through by the British government, which saw it as the solution to island defences. The British had no permanent army in the islands, white troops being sent out as needed. These were often raw and unsuitable recruits and conscripts who died on the crowded and unsanitary troopships, their deaths on the islands hastened by the unaccustomed climate, tropical diseases, unsuitable accommodation, poor leadership and over-consumption of raw rum. (See, e.g. FORT GEORGE, NEWCASTLE, YELLOW FEVER.) The Jamaican planters strongly resisted when the newly raised 2nd WIR, consisting of 500 men and officers, was sent to be part of the garrison which hitherto had consisted entirely of white regiments.

African Recruits The British Army at first hoped to secure enough recruits locally through the planters but when this approach failed, they took to purchasing the fittest specimens arriving on the slave ships from Africa (see SLAVERY, AFRICAN HERITAGE), and eventually these African recruits were preferred over the creole or Caribbean-born. By 1798, the WIR was almost entirely African. Even after the abolition of slavery in 1807, for a long time free Africans continued to be recruited. (See AFRICANS, Indentured.) Lady Nugent, wife of the governor of Jamaica, in 1804 went to FORT AUGUSTA to see the new recruits and recorded in her *Journal*: 'See the West India regiment out, and all the new recruits. They made a most savage appearance, having only just arrived from Africa; all their names were written on cards, tied round their necks!' Like the other enslaved blacks, the new arrivals were given European names. Communication remained difficult; not only did the new recruits have no English, they had a multiplicity of African languages among themselves. In the early days, a minimal effort was made to make them literate and teach them

English, but somehow the army made itself understood. Out of such unpromising material came what all impartial observers regarded as excellent soldiers; the regiments were to win the highest praise from every commander under whom they served.

The young newcomers had no ties on the islands and so were easily moulded into military life and indoctrinated with the idea of their superiority to plantation slaves. The army did its best to isolate them from the general population, though interaction did take place, especially with the females. In time, to be a soldier in the WIR was regarded as a highly attractive occupation.

First Freedmen The social and legal status of these 'slaves in red coats', as Roger Buckley calls them, was an ambivalent one. As he points out: 'Within the walls . . . of British garrisons, the West India soldier lived under egalitarian conditions of military discipline, implying at least that he was a freedman. But no similar pronouncement covered him once he stepped beyond the gates of the post.'

The legal problem was solved in 1807, when the British by an Act of Parliament declared the soldier-slaves of the British West Indies to be freedmen, 26 years before the EMANCIPATION of the rest of the slaves. According to Buckley, this affected about 10,000 soldiers. With Britain ending the slave trade in that year, recruits continued to come from Africa, but from among those liberated from slave ships of nations still engaged in the trade.

With the end of the Napoleonic Wars (1815) and the removal of a major threat to West Indian security, seven of the original twelve regiments were disbanded. By 1870, three more were disbanded. In 1887, the remaining 1st and 2nd were amalgamated as the 1st and 2nd Battalions of the West India Regiment. A 3rd Battalion, added in 1897, was disbanded in 1903. The WIR was finally disbanded in 1927.

During the First World War, the volunteer force that was raised in the West Indies to fight for Britain was known as the British West Indies Regiment and should not be confused with the historic West India Regiments.

[Buckley 1979, Cundall 1915, Nugent 1839]

WEST INDIES

The islands COLUMBUS encountered in the Caribbean Sea came to be called (in the English language) 'West India' from his belief that he had found a new passage to India, a belief reinforced by the brown-skinned peoples, similar to the inhabitants of India, that he found there (see TAINO). West India is the older form of West Indies. Over time the term came to be applied to the English-speaking islands. The DCEU defines 'West Indian' in the contemporary period as: '(A person or thing) of or belonging to any of the English-speaking islands, including the Bahamas archipelago, and the mainland territories that enclose the Caribbean Sea.' The term 'Commonwealth CARIBBEAN' is coming increasingly into use to denote these countries.

In the 1950s there was an attempt to form the ten Anglophone Caribbean island states (then colonies of Britain) into a political union known as the West Indies Federation. Created in January 1958, the Federation was dissolved in February 1962 when Jamaicans voted against it in a national referendum. As Jamaica was by far the largest and most populous of the islands, it led to the sardonic comment by Trinidadian Premier Eric Williams: 'One from ten leaves nought.'

Since the breakup of the Federation, most of the islands have become Independent nations. Some have formed their own regional groupings, such as the Organization of Eastern Caribbean States (OECS) and all are now members of the Caribbean Community, known widely as Caricom. Caricom was established to facilitate cooperation in several essential fields of national economic development, and for the coordination of foreign policies. This regional grouping was first established by the Georgetown Accord of 1973 and later expanded. It now includes the 12 member states of Carifta (the Caribbean Free Trade Area that was established in 1965). They are Antigua, Barbados, Belize, Dominica, Grenada, Guyana, Jamaica, Montserrat, St Kitts-Nevis, St Lucia, St Vincent and the Grenadines, Trinidad and Tobago. They have been joined by the Bahamas and, more recently, Suriname and Haiti, representing a first step outside the Anglophone territories.

Outside of Caricom, the most potent symbols of West Indian unity today are the UNIVERSITY OF THE WEST INDIES, the West Indies CRICKET team and the CXC – Caribbean Examinations Council, the official body responsible for organizing terminal examinations for secondary schools in the English-speaking Caribbean (see EDUCATION). It is perhaps in the area of culture, especially LITERATURE, that a West Indies sensibility is most clearly identifiable, all the islands sharing a common history and LANGUAGE. Carifesta – a Caribbean Festival of Creative Arts inaugurated in 1972 and held occasionally since then – has served as a means of bringing together

creative artists and performers not only from the English-speaking West Indies but from all the other languages and cultures of the wider Caribbean. (See also ANTILLES.)
[DCEU, Mordecai 1968]

WESTMORELAND, Parish of

Area: 807km², population 139,000 (1999). Jamaica's westernmost parish, created in 1703. The capital is SAVANNA-LA-MAR. About a quarter of the parish consists of a rich alluvial plain on which sugar has been grown for centuries; CATTLE raising has also been important and TOURISM is now the main activity in the area around NEGRIL.

When the West Indies Sugar Company (WISCO) built the FROME Central Sugar Factory in 1939, it also bought out many small antiquated plantation-factory combines which in the 18th century had provided the foundation of the huge fortunes of English families such as the BECKFORDS and Vassalls. The best known member of the Vassall family was Elizabeth, Lady Holland, a famous Whig hostess of Regency London who was born in Jamaica in 1770 and inherited several estates, including Friendship in Westmoreland, though she never returned to the island.

Other historical figures associated with this rich sugar belt included Matthew Gregory 'Monk' Lewis (see HORDLEY) who owned Cornwall (one of the properties later bought by WISCO) which he described in his book *Journal of a West India Proprietor* (1834).

Westmoreland seems to have inspired much literary activity in the past. In addition to Lewis and William Beckford, who wrote a history of the island, author-residents for longer or shorter periods have included the naturalist P.H. Gosse (see BLUEFIELDS House); Dr Henry Barham, owner of Barham Estate who wrote a botanical treatise *Hortus Americanus* (1726) and who introduced LOGWOOD to the island; a retired army officer called Bernard M. Senior who published (anonymously) an account in 1835 called *Jamaica as it was, as it is and as it may be*, and the overseer/penkeeper Thomas Thistlewood, inveterate 18th century diarist whose work was edited and published (1989) by noted Jamaican historian Douglas Hall (himself a son of Westmoreland).
[Hall 1989, Wright and White 1969]

WHIP

Whipping or flogging is identified not only with punishment – or as a spur to greater activity – but also functions as a magical device. Thus in African-Caribbean practices, a whip is often used to deflect potentially evil forces. For instance, in JONKONNU, 'Pitchy-Patchy' and sometimes other characters (Oxhead, Devil) crack a cattle whip along the route. In REVIVAL, officers in charge of protection from evil forces sometimes carry a whip. Whipping or scourging as a religious rite is often an act of purification.

Whips are also used in DEATH RITUALS: where death is believed caused by the activity of someone, the dead will sometimes be armed with a whip and instructed to go and avenge himself by beating his enemy.

The use of the whip – and floggings – is associated with SLAVERY and its aftermath, the police state. Until recently, flogging with the cat-o-nine tails (a whip with nine lashes) was often legally added to punishment of certain types of offenders in prison. Schoolboys were punished by a strap or TAMARIND switch (in addition to similar punishment at home). Not surprisingly, children will imply punishment in a gesture of snapping the wrist while bringing thumb and forefinger together sharply to imitate a cracking whip and taunt the wrongdoer, 'Eee-he now'.

During slavery, the driver or man in charge of a slave GANG (usually a privileged slave himself) would have as part of his equipment a 'knotted stick and a whip flung carelessly over his shoulder'. Often the fear of the whip was enough. 'Fire!' was the term used to denote cracking a whip loudly as a threat. The fictionalized planter 'Marly' noted in the 1820s: 'The whip was sometimes fired behind them (i.e. cracked loudly like gunfire) to keep them in line, but seldom did any require to be touched with it.' Brutal floggings were nevertheless frequently inflicted. The sugar estate manager whose symbol of office included a cowskin whip was derisively known as 'Cowskin hero'.

Even the sick were not immune to being subjected to 'planter's medicine' described by McMahon in 1839 (and quoted in the DJE): 'All persons in the hospital afflicted with ulcers . . . were flogged every Monday morning until the ulcers got better, and the patient was enabled to leave . . . discipline

Overseer with whip

of this kind was customary on every estate . . . it was called planter's medicine.' The beatings of slavery live on in the name Fum-Fum Spring near Buff Bay, PORTLAND, 'fum-fum' being the African word meaning flogging, or the whip itself. The sound of the whip was also heard as part of everyday affairs, such as herding CATTLE.

But the whip was a product not only of plantation society. In the MAROON village of Accompong, Katherine Dunham in the 1940s was shown what was in the old days a whipping post but was at the time of her visit a place where offenders (after a public hearing) were tied to one of the trees at the parade 'to be flogged by "Big John".'

Not surprisingly, the whip is also heard and felt in FOLKLORE, for instance in the ANANSI story 'Do-Mek-Me-See' and in popular music, e.g. Junior Byles – 'Beat Down Babylon' (1972):

> I and I a go beat down Babylon
> I and I go whip them wicked men
> I and I go beat them, whip them

[DJE, Dunham 1946, Hurston 1938]

WHITE HORSES

Area along the sea coast in ST THOMAS Parish. According to Thomas Coke (1808) the name was given by sailors to the white cliffs of exposed marl that stood out above the coastline, though others have thought the 'horses' to be the white crests of the waves racing into the shore.

WHITE LIME

White lime is made from burning LIMESTONE and wood, and was formerly much used in house construction (see SPANISH WALL). In former times, 'lime kiln parties' would be held to mark the building of a lime kiln, so important was this event in community life. Today, lime is rarely burnt, but lime mortar was once used widely, as it becomes hard and durable if properly done.

To make a lime kiln, large pieces of green wood are laid in a circle with a hole in the centre, and wood chips used to fill the spaces. Broken white limestone rocks are laid on top. The hole is filled with dry wood that is fired to generate extreme temperatures in the pile, causing the limestone to crumble and mix with the ash of the wood. Limestone is made of calcium carbonate, and when brought to 950° C gives off carbon dioxide and leaves the brittle white solid known as 'quicklime'. The actual process takes up to a week. The lime then has to be 'cured' by slaking, i.e. rain is allowed to fall on the heap before it is considered cured (known as 'slaked lime' or 'white lime') and ready for use.

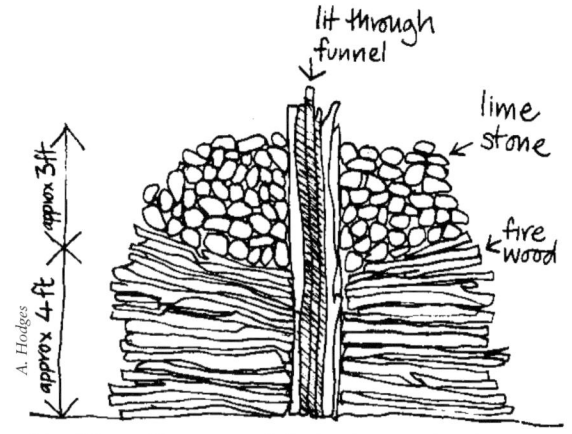

Lime kiln on old sugar estate (below) and cross-section of contemporary kiln (above).

A Westmoreland planter, R.F. Williams, described his method of making mortar as follows: After the lime was burnt 'it was slaked and mixed on the spot with marl by two men with hoes, two of marl and one of lime – heaped up and smoothed over with spades to mellow for six to twelve months in the open and when wanted for actual building it was carted to the house site and remixed again . . . which ensured good quality mortar.'

While most communities constructed a lime kiln as needed, more solid kilns were built on the SUGAR estates where lime was used in the sugar-boiling process; the ruins of an 18th century kiln at Prospect, ST THOMAS is listed among the historic structures of that parish.

[Buisseret 1980a, Hodges 1987, Williams 1972]

WHITE RIVER

This river for its entire length forms the boundary between the parishes of ST ANN and ST

MARY. It is the only long river in St Ann since all the others rise a short distance from the coast. The river once possessed beautiful falls at Cascade, which used to be a well-known beauty spot, but is now the site of a hydroelectric station.

WHITE WITCH see ROSE HALL

WHOOPING BOY
Ghostly creature of LEGEND – also called Whistling Cowboy – who appears only at certain times and places, cracking his WHIP. He is said to be the rider of THREE FOOT HORSE, whooping like a human being and dancing on twigs in the wood. He is supposed to be the DUPPY of the man who penned the CATTLE during SLAVERY. Others have said that he is heard and seen only during August as he pens his ghost cows, frightening real cows in the process.
[Beckwith 1928, Hurston 1938, Mico 1893,1896]

WILD PINE see BROMELIAD

WILLIAMS, Dr Cecily (1893-1992)
One of Jamaica's most distinguished doctors, Dr Williams was a major international contributor to the revolution in mother and child care that occurred in the 20th century. She first described the condition Kwashiorkor in Africa, and in Jamaica headed the team that in the early 1950s identified the cause of 'vomiting sickness' as due to the hypoglycaemic effects of unripe ACKEES on poorly nourished children. She worked in over 70 countries and was the first maternal and child health adviser to the World Health Organization.

Born into a remarkable family of the Jamaican plantocracy, the Williamses of Kew Park, WESTMORELAND, she first developed her interest in medicine as a child, at the clinic her mother had organized on the veranda of the family home. She would continue to lecture to medical students until she was 92 years old. She died at the age of 99, having been awarded Jamaica's highest honour, the Order of Merit, as well as honorary doctorates from the UNIVERSITY OF THE WEST INDIES and the University of Ghana. She was the first woman to be given the Honorary Fellowship of the Royal Society of Medicine.

Dr Williams studied medicine at Oxford University and had to struggle against the prejudices of the day against women doctors. She was eventually sent by the colonial office to Ghana where, struck by the signs of malnutrition, she devoted herself to nutrition, maternal and child health. Her revolutionary findings regarding Kwashiorkor, a Ga word meaning 'neglect of the deposed', the deposed child being the one 'deposed' from the mother's milk (and affection) by the arrival of another child and thus becoming the more susceptible to malnutrition were eventually published in *The Lancet*.

Later, she was to lead the international campaign in favour of breast milk and against baby food manufacturers, in the process incurring the wrath of officialdom and 'punishment' transfers to remote places. Her courage and humour served her in good stead when she was captured by the Japanese in Malaysia in the Second WORLD WAR and spent a year in a prisoner of war camp, first as a doctor and women's camp commander, later in solitary confinement in a metal cage.

In Jamaica, where she returned to recover from her ordeal, she was appointed by the government director of a committee set up 'to improve child care and investigate the causes of food poisoning'. This work between 1951-53 resulted in the findings which made the connection between 'vomiting sickness' and the Ackee.
[Golding 1994]

Dr Cecily Williams

WINDWARD ROAD, Kingston
The name dates from the days of sailing ships when the eastern side of the island was referred to as the 'windward' side as opposed to the 'leeward' or western side. In the past, words and phrases derived from sailing were widely used in Jamaica. Many sailors were among the early settlers and there was active shipping all around the island in the heyday of SUGAR. Edward Long (1774) also claims that many of the early settlers followed alternately privateering (see BUCCANEER) and planting. The journey from Europe to Jamaica in the days of sailing ships was so long that the planters and their servants absorbed the vocabulary of the sailors and applied the words to other things on land. Thus, in the early days of the sugar industry, for example, a foreman was called the 'bosun of the mill', a kitchen was called the 'cook-room' and 'bread-kind' referred to substitutes for that

product. It was probably from sailors that the slaves arriving in the New World adopted the term SHIPMATE to denote the relationship to someone who came over on the same ship. (See also DAY, STAMP-AND-GO.)
[Cassidy 1971, DJE]

WIS
Jamaican name (derived from the English word 'withe') applied to any flexible stem, vine or root that can be used for tying. Wis also provides skipping ropes, medicinal drinks, WHIPS, material for making BASKETS and a host of other useful things.

Types of wis include Johncrow Packer, used for tying up bundles of firewood, and Supple Jack (*Paullinia*), a flexible stem which when stripped has round knobs every 15cm or so and is used to make whips. Pudding Wis, also called Travellers Joy, Wild Yam or Snake Wis (*Cissus sicyoides* and other sp.) is used to tie rails and in former times the leaves were applied to sores, especially from YAWS. According to Asprey and Thornton, the leaves were chopped and mixed with fat, or 'quailed' and rubbed with castor oil to provide a plaster for boils, bruises and itching skin conditions. The plant climbs over trees and rocks and sends down long cord-like fibres (hence: 'Snake Wis'), that root when they touch the ground. Some species, especially *Tournefortia* and *Chamissoa*, provide the split stems used for making hampers and other baskets and are called Basket Wis. Hoop Wis or Cooper Wis (*Trichostigma octandrum*) has a tough and flexible stalk which, as its name implies, was used by COOPERS to make hoops for barrels when imported material was not available.

Various folk names are used for several similar Wis with long aerial roots that are used to make wicker and in housebuilding, for lashing the THATCH to roofs. Some are called Coco Wis from the resemblance of the divided leaves to the COCO plant, also Five Finger or Seven Finger, the latter names being usually applied to *Syngonium auritum*. The aerial roots of the Coco Wis or China Wis are cut, boiled and stripped before being used to make wicker. This vine grows a long way from the root and is also known as Vine Walk or Mile Walk. House Wis is used in roofing to tie the thatch. China or Chainy Wis (Smilax family) was called *boschiuchi* by the TAINOS and used to tie wild canes to the walls of their huts; they also used the roots medicinally, as is done today (see 'TONIC', SARSAPARILLA). Finally there is the remarkable Water Wis, a wild grape vine (*Vitis tiliifolia*). It grows on the dry hillsides and when cut yields copious quantities of clear drinkable water.
[Adams 1972, Asprey and Thornton 1953-55, Cassidy 1971, DJE]

'Supple Jack'

Cissus species

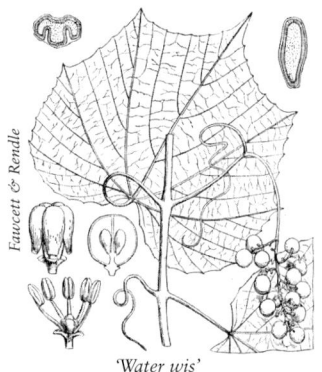

'Water wis'

Wis hanging from tree

WOLMER'S SCHOOL
One of the island's oldest secondary schools, founded in 1736. A wealthy Kingston goldsmith, John Wolmer, left £2,300 in his will to found a school in whatever parish he should happen to

die. Wolmer died in 1729 and the boys' school was founded in KINGSTON, next to the Parish Church. The boundary with MICO COLLEGE of the current school campus is the boundary of Kingston and ST ANDREW parishes. Wolmer's is now a government-funded school for boys and girls. There is a monument to Wolmer at KINGSTON PARISH CHURCH, erected as an expression of public gratitude 60 years after his death.
[Cundall 1915]

WOMAN'S TONGUE (*Albizia lebbeck*)
A native of the Far East, this plant is a close relative of the GUANGO though it is a much smaller tree (growing 5-12m high). Like the Guango, it grows in low-lying country between 100 and 800m. It was brought to Jamaica in 1782 at the same time as the MANGO and since then has become naturalized, often found near to dwellings, including city yards. Its long seed pods that are pale green when young turn beige when dry, and rattle in the slightest breeze – hence the tree's popular name.
[Adams 1972, NHSJ 1946]

WOODPECKER (*Melanerpes radiolatus*)
The Jamaican Woodpecker is the only woodpecker resident in the island. It is widespread and occurs at all elevations. It inhabits woodlands and forests, but may also be seen in pastures with tall trees. A visitor, the smaller North American Yellow-bellied Sapsucker is sometimes seen as it winters in the Greater Antilles and the Bahamas.

The local woodpecker is olive-grey below with an orange patch on the abdomen, but a distinctly red head, white face, and black beak. The rest of the bird is mainly black, the wings and the tail streaked with white markings. It best reveals its presence by sounds – by its very loud harsh cries, especially in spring and summer when it is courting and nesting, and by its steady drumming noise as it bores into trees – hence the woodpecker's name in other islands of Carpenter Bird.

Lady Taylor

Woodpecker

The woodpecker comes equipped with a strong beak that it uses for hammering holes in rotten trees to find insect larvae and to create nesting holes. It licks up insects with its strong, sticky tongue, which it also uses to hollow out fruit on trees, and to consume ants and seeds. May Jeffrey-Smith notes that the tongue is so strong that country folk sometimes dried it and used it as a toothpick! Woodpeckers also have powerful claws and their toes are arranged in pairs – with two toes pointing backwards – unlike most birds. This enables them to get a good grip on the wood to which they cling lengthwise.

A pair of woodpeckers usually returns to the same nest each year.

This is a significant bird in the mythology of Native Americans and other peoples. The TAINOS named it *Inriri Cahubabayael* – Son of Mother Earth (*Itiba Cahubaba*). In a Taino myth, it was the woodpecker that used its strong beak to peck at tree trunks to create women.
[Arrom 1990, Gosse 1984, Jeffrey-Smith 1972, Taylor 1955]

WORK SONGS
Singing once lightened virtually all communal labour activities, giving rise to a large body of FOLK MUSIC categorized as 'work songs'. These songs follow the call-and-response pattern of traditional African-American work songs in that a leader sings or calls out the first line while the work gang sing out a one-line chorus (called the 'bobbin') to the rhythm of the task, the sound of their activities providing a natural background rhythm. In Jamaica, the lead singer (who does not take part in the work) is called the 'bomma' or 'singerman'.

Often, these songs are improvised on the spot, or new words composed to old melodies to reflect local happenings and concerns. The more popular will move beyond the confines of the village to become part of the national body of 'folk songs'. Jamaican work songs reflect African patterns as well as the influence of West European harmonies and melodies and American work songs. Those sung in the fields were also called digging songs or JAMMA SONGS, perhaps from the rhythm of 'jamming' the forks or other implements into the ground. (Jamma songs are also sung at WAKES.)

Charles Hyatt has given us an inimitable picture of the digging songs performed by men working on the streets of KINGSTON in the 1930s, a reminder that work songs flourished in the city too:

'Yuh have a line of up to say twelve man with pick-axe an one leader or shouter. His job is to keep a rhythm goin' an the diggin' men work to that rhythm. To see twelve pick-axe raised in unison an come down on a beat with the accompanying 'Hhhhm' is a joy to watch and listen to. People, young and old, would stan up an watch it for hours.

'Then, of course, the more the people enjoy it

the better the diggers perform. That time yuh get all the fancy trimmin's. When the pick-axe go up in the air yuh see it spin roun' and when it come down is the right point it land pon. Then the song is not only melodious but harmonious as well.

'Put on top a that, it funny. There is no way that yuh can leave without hearin' the next verse or seein' the next dance step of the shouter who is not only keepin' the rhythm goin' but also directin' the diggers where to throw the axe. The only time yuh get a chance to be released from the hypnotism is when them stop to drink water.'

Work songs formerly accompanied every kind of labour, whether digging in the field, building a house, rowing a boat, cutting and hauling timber, building railways or roads, and for women, washing clothes, cleaning floors, or beating food in a MORTAR. Although most of the work songs are from the African-Jamaican tradition, musicologist Olive Lewin has brought to light work songs of ethnic groups such as the itinerant cloth vendors from the Middle East ('Quattie a Yard O, Salo') and East Indian rice threshing songs.

While many of the work songs, especially the Jamma songs, could be quite salacious, some work groups sang hymns or improvised to religious music. Communal labour activity and song, sponsored by a church group, was called a 'Wesleyan' (see METHODIST).

Work songs originated in the days of SLAVERY when group singing was used as a means of relieving the backbreaking toil. Singing was also used to communicate where talking was prohibited, and a good deal of information was sometimes conveyed in seemingly simple or 'nonsense' songs, sometimes right under the nose of the overseer. News, gossip and social commentary were also exchanged in these songs – characteristics of folk songs that still persist. In the post-slavery days, songs associated with virtually all aspects of daily life continued to be made and sung. The cooperative labour exchange known as DAY WORK or Digging Match helped to keep many of these songs alive.

While work songs have faded with the times, the significance of music to workers has not. Lileth Sewell in her 'Music in the Jamaican Labour Movement' has traced the role of music and song in the development of the labour movement from the 1930s (see TRADE UNIONS) as well as their expression in contemporary politics.

[Baxter 1970, Bilby 1985a, Hyatt 1989, Lewin 1968, 1970, 2000, Patterson 1973, Sewell 1981]

WORLD WARS

Jamaicans today probably think of the two World Wars of the 20th century as remote conflicts that affected Europe and other places far from their home. However, the West Indian islands were not only seriously affected by the wars economically and in the second war threatened by enemy boats, but directly participated in the wars on the side of Britain, then the 'Mother Country'. In the First World War, over 15,000 men from the British WEST INDIES served as soldiers, 11,000 of them from Jamaica. Of the total, 1,256 West Indians died – 1,071 from sickness, 185 were killed or died of wounds, and 697 were wounded. Numerous others came home suffering from war related illnesses. In the Second World War, approximately 10,000 served, including 600 West Indian women who volunteered for the Auxiliary Territorial Service (ATS).

The First World War, fought between Britain and its allies against Germany, lasted from 1914 to 1918. Britain's declaration of war on 4 August immediately put the entire British Empire at war. Jamaica was next to New Zealand in the overseas empire in adopting compulsory military service, which by the Conscription Act made every male between the ages of 16 and 41 liable for military service. However, it was unnecessary to enforce conscription in Jamaica or the other West Indian islands because so many volunteered. Among them were nearly 2,000 men who came from PANAMA, having gone there to work on the Canal.

The sailing of a Jamaica contingent

The Contingents The first contingent of men from Jamaica sailed in November 1915, to be followed by 10 other contingents. Jamaica was to supply 7 of the 11 battalions of the newly raised British West Indies Regiment (BWIR) which consisted of 15,601 officers and other ranks. Many West Indians resident in Britain also joined the British Army there, among them Norman MANLEY, then a law student at Oxford, and his brother Roy who was killed in the war.

The young and enthusiastic BWIR troops were to conduct themselves bravely, but experienced such racism during the war that it became a contributing factor to the post-war unrest that led to political decolonization in the islands and final independence from Britain. Many ex-soldiers would be in the forefront of the political agitation that culminated in the 1937-38 riots (see FROME) which engulfed Jamaica and the other West Indian islands. Several well known post-war labour leaders such as St William Grant (see PARK) and A.G.S. Coombs (see TRADE UNIONS), came from their ranks. Two of the soldiers who won Military Medals, Norman Manley and Capt Arthur A. Cipriani of Trinidad, were to become post-war political leaders in their respective countries.

The men who volunteered for service did so for many reasons, some purely for the adventure and the chance to travel overseas. The enlisted soldiers were promised pay of one shilling per day, with free rations, housing, fuel and light, a disability pension of 9d per day for those rendered totally incapable by war service, and separation allowances to be paid to legal wives. But the propaganda of the day in all the islands made a heavy appeal to the natural sense of patriotism people then had, and it was considered a matter of honour to fight for 'King and Country'. Jamaicans of all races and classes volunteered. Because a literacy test was at first applied, the majority of the first 4,000 to go were skilled tradesmen with carpenters and cabinet-makers (356) and bakers (245) having the highest numbers, though all occupations were represented, including clerks, printers, teachers, engineers and other professionals. Later recruits included more rural agricultural workers as the literacy requirement was dropped.

The War However, while the British wanted soldiers, they did not want black soldiers. As C.L. Joseph has written: 'In the Colonial Office the major issue was how to recognize and encourage West Indian participation, and to appease their aspirations for helping in the imperial struggle in the face of strong resentment in the War Office against using black troops. Both the Colonial Office and the War Office accepted the argument that black West Indians should not be opposed to white forces.'

One immediate result of this attitude was the shabby treatment of the WEST INDIA REGIMENT (WIR), which consisted of black soldiers who had a proud tradition and brave record of service as regular troops for over 200 years. In 1914 the WIR consisted of two battalions of black soldiers commanded by white officers, administered directly by the War Office. The WIR was kept out of the war theatres by the War Office – the First Battalion in Jamaica and the Second in East Africa where it saw only limited action.

The volunteers of the BWIR were similarly kept away from the European theatres of war, and in Europe were assigned to labour and construction duties. Of these, two battalions served in Egypt and in the Palestine campaign, smaller units participating in the East African and Mesopotamian campaign. The rest were employed as labour battalions in France.

According to Joseph, the battalions in France were attached to the British Expeditionary Force and were employed in all the main operations that had taken place, including the battles of the Somme, Arras, Messines and Ypres. Their work consisted chiefly of handling ammunition at the railheads and carrying it to the batteries both day and night, digging cable trenches and emplacement for guns, often under heavy shell fire occasioning heavy casualties. Sometimes detachments were involved in loading and unloading at the docks at Boulogne, and in the construction of light railways. The 3rd battalion was in France from September 1916 up to the armistice, working through both the winters of 1916-17 and 1917-18. Other battalions, like the 4th, spent one winter in France, and the other winter between France and Taranto, Italy, where they worked on the quays in construction work, unloading stores, and loading lighters for ships. The black contingent from Bermuda also served in the same capacity on the ammunition dumps for some time with the Canadian Corps subsequent to the capture of Vimy Ridge, May 1917.

In his report on these battalions, Field-Marshall Sir Douglas Haig, Commander-in-Chief of the British Armies in France, stated that in spite of casualties the men had shown themselves 'willing and cheerful' and had rendered valuable services at times of great pressure. He commented on their 'exceptional' physique, excellent discipline and high morale. Nevertheless, black Bermudans and West Indians were never allowed to be actively engaged in the fighting on the western front whereas white Bermudans were. Only whites were commissioned as officers.

By March 1916 the first three battalions had arrived in Egypt and were sent to the Imperial School of Instruction, Zeitoun, for specialist training, working alongside men from all parts of the Empire. Some men also saw active service in Jordan. However, Joseph noted that 'mainly for racial reasons the Regiment was not allowed to serve as a brigade but was deliberately scattered over the various theatres'. He adds: 'Not a single incident was reported that could question the courage, steadiness, and soldierly bearing of the men of the British West Indies Regiment under fire, even in their capacity as ammunition carriers.' They amassed a total of 123 war medals.

Demobilization Following demobilization in 1919, black soldiers in Britain were subjected to racist attacks and rioted in a number of areas including London. There were major anti-black riots in Cardiff and Liverpool. Many black seamen from around the world were left stranded in Britain. No black troops were allowed to participate in London's victory celebrations, the Peace March of 19 July 1919. The racist treatment of the ex-soldiers heightened tensions throughout the West Indies and Guyana, to which many returned angry and disgruntled.

Between May and September 1919 the surviving Jamaican soldiers returned home and were greeted with tumultuous public welcomes. Three memorial crosses (cenotaphs) in honour of the war dead were erected – one for each county – in KINGSTON, SPANISH TOWN and SAVANNA-LA-MAR. The ex-soldiers were given some assistance, including help with employment, loans, and the issuing of free permits for Cuba (then enjoying a sugar boom) for those who wanted to go there. But many were affected by the economic depression and unemployment of the post-war years, and became active during the 1938 disturbances.

At home, the war had had devastating effects on the economy. While sugar production soared, the BANANA industry was brought close to ruin for lack of shipping. There were severe shortages of vital food and supplies normally imported, and rationing was introduced.

Second World War The Second World War (1939-45) also had a considerable impact on the West Indies. Once again the islands contributed fighting men. Approximately 10,000 served, all volunteers, recruited mainly for the Royal Air Force (RAF). While there was still racism in the services, the men were treated differently and reported much less racial tension. Generally, Jamaicans served in every aspect of the war effort. Jamaicans were among West Indian women who volunteered for the Auxiliary Territorial Service (ATS) of whom 300 served in the Caribbean, 200 in Washington and 100 in England. Jamaicans were also recruited as workers in munitions factories. As German submarines were active in Caribbean waters, a Home Guard was established for local defence and Jamaicans also served at lookout points such as lighthouses across the island. A shortage of farm labour in the USA during the war led to the creation of the Farm Labour Scheme for men and the recruitment of the first farm workers. Jamaica also accepted some refugees from the war in Europe, as well as prisoners of war (see UNIVERSITY CAMPUS).

Lend-lease Bases When the US entered the war, the US Air Force assumed defence of the Panama Canal, establishing a chain of 55 airfields and bases throughout the Caribbean between 1940-42, and patrolling the Caribbean Sea for German U-boats. In 1941, British Prime Minister Winston Churchill signed the Anglo-American Agreement with US President Roosevelt which included the lease of areas in some of the West Indian territories for 99 years for the establishment of bases. In Jamaica, bases were established on the south coast (see GOAT ISLANDS, VERNAMFIELD) and at Montego Bay and Kingston, the latter two developing into the present international airports. (Following negotiations in 1960, the 'lend-lease' land in Jamaica which consisted of some 9,300 hectares was released by the US government, except for a small parcel near Portland Ridge.)

Rationing The Second World War, like the First, caused severe hardships and led to rationing of scarce food items as well as gasoline and other products. Nevertheless, the Jamaican population contributed considerable funds to the war effort and continued to rally around the 'Mother Country'. As they do with any disaster, Jamaicans met the hard times with humour, exemplified by the songs of Slim and Sam and the poems of Louise Bennett. Bennett wrote several wartime poems, and some of their titles are suggestive, such as 'Rice Gawn' and 'Soap Vacation'. 'Obeah Win de War' was one Jamaican's solution to Hitler. Given an airplane to fly over Germany,

> Me hooden haffe drop bomb
> Nor leaflet deh at all
> Jus shillin ile-o-kill-him-dead
> An shillin buck-pon wall.

At the political level, the war put a temporary halt to the movement towards self-government in the islands. Following the riots of 1937-38 a Royal Commission headed by Lord Moyne was sent out to the West Indies to investigate conditions, but their far-reaching report, which revealed the appalling conditions under which the majority of people lived, was not released until after the war. Some local politicians agitating for improved conditions adopted a conciliatory attitude to Britain during the war years and there was suppression and imprisonment of those considered 'agitators', e.g. BUSTAMANTE.

[Amin-Addo 1995, Bennett 1966, Black 1965, Bousquet and Douglas 1991, Fryer 1984, Joseph 1971, Post 1978, Who's Who 1921-24,]

WORTHY PARK

Jamaica's oldest sugar estate in continuous production, Worthy Park was founded in 1670 by Francis Price, an English soldier with the conquering army (see CAPTURE OF JAMAICA). Price patented 340ha acres in the fertile inland valley of Lluidas Vale, ST CATHERINE Parish, almost the exact centre of the island. Over time, this SUGAR PLANTATION came to encompass 4,900ha.

Remarkably, Worthy Park survived the recurrent crises in the sugar industry that claimed other producers, and today has diversified into CATTLE and CITRUS. Worthy Park's success is usually attributed to two significant factors: its ideal geographical location and the fact that, aside for a brief period in the 19th century, it has been owned by only two families.

Six generations of Prices owned the estate, and while most of them lived in England as absentee proprietors, a junior family member always resided locally. They built the estate into one of the largest in the island. By 1820 Worthy Park was one of a dozen estates with more than 500 slaves. But the factors affecting the entire sugar industry also affected Worthy Park, and in 1863 the Prices sold it. The estate continued in sugar production under two subsequent owners, though at a much reduced level. In 1918 it was acquired by Frederick Clarke, who ushered in the second family ownership, the estate continuing in Clarke hands to the present. The fact that the papers relating to the history of this estate have been preserved, led to the publication of two books by Michael Craton. These have given us the most comprehensive picture so far of a Jamaican sugar estate and the people, slave and free, associated with it over an extended period of time.

But even before the establishment of the estate, Lluidas Vale played a central role in early Jamaican history. It was discovered by the English while in pursuit of SPANISH guerrillas who resisted them for five years after the conquest, aided by the black slaves they had freed. One set of slaves led by LUBOLO (Juan de Bolas) was discovered cultivating food in this valley for the Spanish freedom fighters. Lubolo was persuaded to cross over to the English side, which led to the ultimate defeat of YSASSI and his forces and the departure of the Spaniards from the island. Lubolo and his people were granted their freedom, and land in this valley, thus becoming a free black settlement. However, following Lubolo's death his followers were ousted by the English settlers and the valley passed from peasant cultivation to plantation. Lubolo's name lives on in Juan de Bolas Mountain that overlooks the valley.

[Craton 1978, Craton and Walvin 1970, Taylor 1965]

WRITERS see LITERATURE

X

The 'X' is usually the sign of the cross or the crossroads, the meeting of lines at a central point and thus a space filled with power, the site of many rituals. Aside from its religious symbolism, the X sign is imbued with magical power in other practices and can stand for both life and death. Among the superstitious, the gesture of 'cutting ten' (crossing the index and second fingers) is used to ward off evil spirits such as DUPPIES and can also be expressed by crossing objects such as kitchen utensils. Often, X symbols will be chalked on the walls of a room, in the dirt or on roads as protection from evil spirits. Crossing one's fingers can also be used as a sign of wishing for luck or in the hope of nullifying a negative outcome. In witchcraft or OBEAH, an X cut into the ground will be taken as a sign of imminent death ('erasure') of the one obeahed.

An X marked by an illiterate person is accepted as his or her signature (in legal documents accompanied by the words 'his mark' and the signature of a witness).

XAYMAICA

Early name for Jamaica, a TAINO word (*Hamaika* or *Haymaica*) which occurs in many variations in the 16th and 17th SPANISH documents and was adopted by the early English settlers.

YABBA

An earthenware vessel of West African origin, in the past used for a wide range of domestic purposes, especially for storing and holding water, and cooking and serving food. Various types of Yabbas were made, but nowadays the word is most commonly applied to a large bowl, usually glazed on the inside, which is used for mixing cakes and puddings and for salting or corning and storing meat. These vessels are highly valued by their owners since they are hardly made today, having been replaced by containers and cooking vessels of metal, plastic or glass. The name 'yabba' is from the Twi *ayawa* meaning 'earthen vessel, dish'. According to the DCEU, the word Yabba is also used for an earthenware vessel in some other Caribbean islands including Antigua, Montserrat, Nevis and the US Virgin Islands.

The ceramic type in Jamaica dates to the early 16th century. Archaeological explorations at the OLD KING'S HOUSE, SPANISH TOWN, have revealed a highly developed Yabba culture and this has been confirmed by excavations done at PORT ROYAL, Old NANNY TOWN, DRAX HALL, HELLSHIRE HILLS, New SEVILLE, etc. The tradition of Yabba-making continued up to the late 20th century and led directly to the development of modern ceramics (see ART), through Jamaica's master potter Cecil Baugh, who learnt his craft from the traditional Yabba makers he encountered in KINGSTON. 'Ma Lou' (Mrs Louisa Jones) of Spanish Town, believed to be the last of the Yabba-makers in the African-Jamaican tradition, died in 1992.

The ceramic heritage in Jamaica includes work by the TAINOS (AD 500-1600), the Africans, the Europeans (SPANISH and later BRITISH) and what is regarded as a syncretic style, a combination of European and African traditions.

[Ebanks 1984, Mathewson 1972, Tanna and Baugh 1999]

Yabba

YALLAHS

The name of this village and surrounding area in ST THOMAS Parish comes from the SPANISH family Ayala, who owned a cattle ranch in the area before the English takeover of the island in the 17th century. The area was called *Hato de Ayala*, i.e. ranch of the Ayala family.

YALLAHS PONDS

Large ponds that can be seen from the main highway in the vicinity of YALLAHS, ST THOMAS Parish. There are really two ponds that are enclosed by sand spits. The large pond is 425ha of surface water while the small one is about 100ha.

The only entrance to the sea is a barmouth (sandbar) at the southeastern side of the little pond. It is a seasonal opening, usually open for not more than a month at a time. The big pond does not have an opening to the sea but it is sometimes connected to the little pond, in the north.

This is the only permanent hypersaline ecosystem in Jamaica. The salinity of the water in the ponds is at least twice that of sea water and can get as high as five times that of sea water for long periods.

Early settlers in this area got their salt from these ponds and had salt works there. Some years ago, a pre-TAINO stone axe was found near the channel between the two ponds. There is also the ruin of a small stone tower nearby. It is

Yallahs Ponds

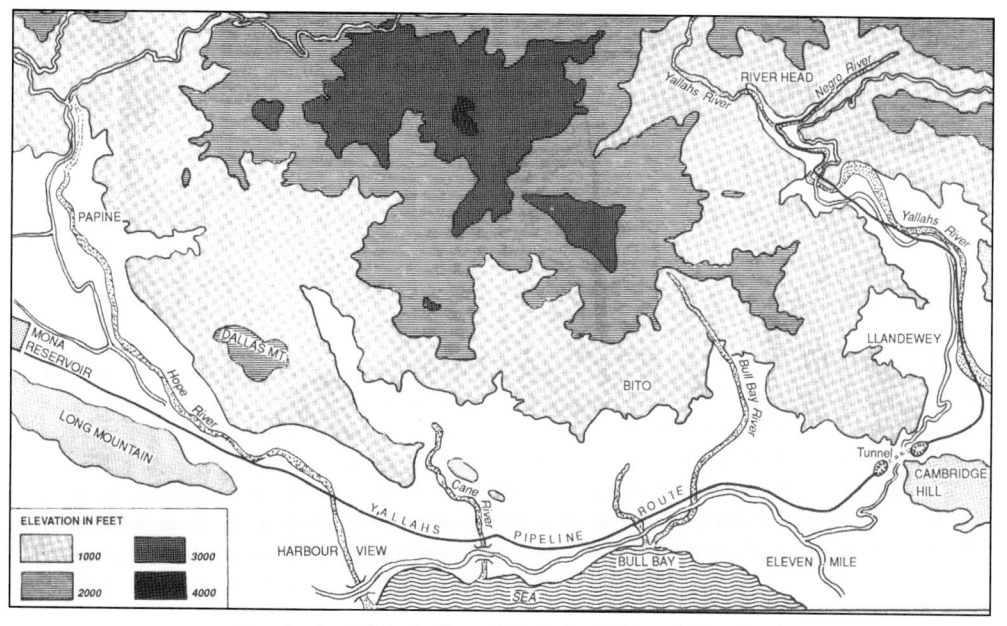

Map showing Yallahs pipeline and Cambridge Hill tunnel (from Porter)

believed to have been built in the 1770s to establish communication between the eastern parts of the island and naval forces at PORT ROYAL. The ruin is listed as a National Monument. Most recently Yallahs Ponds have provided a habitat for the study of viruses in a natural environment.

Yallahs is the only place in Jamaica where *Artemia* (brine shrimp) seems to have occurred naturally. There are many stories as to how they may have gotten there. Some pet fish hobbyists claim to have introduced *Artemia* into the ponds by throwing in bad cysts that they had for feeding their fish. *Artemia* could also have been introduced naturally from the feet and stool of wading migratory birds. Scientists believe *Artemia* in the ponds are most likely the San Francisco strain, like many of the populations all around the western hemisphere.

There is a local LEGEND attached to the ponds. It is said that long ago, there were no ponds; the property belonged to a wealthy landowner and was prime farmland, rich in crops and herds of GOATS and cows. The man died without making a will and his two sons quarrelled because they could not decide how to divide the property. The fighting between them became more and more bitter, and one night they swore they would kill each other the following morning. However, when they arose, they found the land was completely flooded over, drowning all the disputed property and creating the ponds.

[Personal communication Gillian Young and G.A. Aarons.]

YALLAHS RIVER

At 36.9km, this is one of the longer rivers in Jamaica. The Yallahs rises 1,371m up in the BLUE MOUNTAINS and flows through eastern ST THOMAS Parish. In recent years it has become a source of water for KINGSTON. The water is gravity fed through an overland pipeline to the Mona Reservoir, previously fed exclusively by the HOPE RIVER.

The lower part of Yallahs River is usually dry since water sinks in its loose sandy bed, and it is forded without difficulty where the main highway crosses it. But rivers such as these rise at

Yallahs River

high elevations in areas of very high rainfall, and in times of flood can become raging torrents, causing a great deal of damage, especially since cultivation on the steep slopes in the valley and surrounding ridges takes place on shale soil. The upper valley of the Yallahs was one of the most devastated areas in a HURRICANE of 1951. The Yallahs Valley Land Authority was established to assist people here in rehabilitation and conservation measures.

The river in former times symbolized more than a geographical boundary. The DJE notes the expression 'to drink Yallahs water' as follows: 'An expression from St Thomas parish, alluding to the Yallahs River at its western boundary: to come into the parish (as a stranger – not altogether welcome).'
[DJE, GOJ Handbook of Jamaica 1961, STATIN 1999a]

YAM (*Dioscorea spp.*)

This edible tuber is one of the most commonly consumed starches in Jamaica, and is also exported. It should be noted that what is called 'yam' in North America is the sweet POTATO (*Ipomoea*) – an unrelated species that is native to the New World.

Yam field

Although wild varieties of yam are native to the island (or were brought by the TAINOS from South America), the yams that are commonly grown and consumed were brought from Africa; the first wild yam was cultivated in sub-Saharan Africa around 5000-4000 BC. Yams were used as ships' stores from earliest times because of their ability to weather long sea voyages well. They also provided vitamin C which was important in the sailors' diet to combat scurvy. Yams were an important part of the diet of many of the enslaved AFRICANS shipped across the Atlantic (see SLAVERY), especially the IBO, and were first brought to the New World on Portuguese slave ships. About 200 yams per person was regarded as adequate provision for the MIDDLE PASSAGE.

Though perhaps not as important in the diet as formerly, given the rising popularity of other starches, yam has been a staple food in Jamaica up to the present time, especially for country people. Rural Jamaicans even today identify 'food' with root crops or 'ground provisions' (see GROUND), so it is perhaps not surprising that the English word 'yam' comes from the African word *nyam*, meaning 'to eat'. 'Nyam', like 'yam' is common throughout the CARIBBEAN.

Richard Allsopp in the DCEU points out that the word 'nyam' is found in a large number of West and Central African languages as a noun ('meat', 'food') and a verb ('eat'). He concludes, 'The sound would have occurred, with high frequency among Africans in the slave era, with the basic meaning "food".' It is from the Senegalese word – *nyami* – meaning 'to eat' that the Portuguese word *inhame* derived, leading to the Spanish *ñame* and French *igname*, from which came the English 'yam', for the root vegetable.

There are over 600 species of yams but only a small number of these are edible. A few of the African names for the edible yams still persist; the most popular yam in Jamaica retaining its African name is Afu, also known as Yellow yam. Also popular in the marketplace are White yam and Negro, which is a species of white yam but of coarser texture. Hard white yam is also sometimes called White Afu. Other popular yams are Lucea, which is soft and white, Trinidad or Renta, Taw, Mozella, and St Vincent. White yam and Renta are valued for their keeping qualities, for most yams must be consumed soon after reaping.

Yams come in an enormous variety of shapes and sizes. They are portions of underground stems or tubers, the top part of the stem forming the climbing vine. The plant is an annual, and

Yams

Yam vendor

dies down after each growing season. When the yam is harvested, the portion of the tuber closest to the stem (the 'yam head') is cut off and retained. It is allowed to sprout in a dark place and will be planted out to produce the next year's crop. However, yam can also be sprouted from cut-up bits of the whole yam, from the whole tuber in multiple-tuber varieties such as YAMPI, and by the more modern method of plantlets developed by tissue culture.

Although modern agricultural techniques have been introduced to yam cultivation, many still grow the crop the traditional way. Usually a yam field is prepared in advance: holes are dug and filled back lightly with earth and manure to form a mound or a continuous bank. The yam cuttings are planted in the mound – 'yam hill' or 'yam bank' as it is called – two or three to each hill. The hill is usually covered with banana trash or other mulch to keep it cool, and sometimes another quick crop, such as peas, is planted on it. The vines are provided with poles ('yam sticks') to run on. The tuber will mature over seven months to a year. Once dug, the yam will keep for a few days or weeks, depending on the variety, but if left in the ground, it can remain there for a long time without spoilage. Usually the farmer will take yams from successive hills, covering them up afterwards so that more yams can be reaped in the future. A second crop can be harvested from the same planting but is never as strong as the first.

The first oral contraceptive pills were developed from a species of yam from which both the female hormone progesterone and the male hormone testosterone can be synthesized. The first pills were produced in Mexico from yams cultivated on a large scale, though nowadays most pills are synthetic. However, in India and China, yams are still produced for this purpose.

[Baccus and Royes 1988, Beckwith 1928, DCEU, Huxley 1978, 1991, JAS 1954, Viola and Margolis 1991]

YAM FESTIVAL

In the plantation era, a YAM festival was observed in Jamaica by those AFRICANS who were accustomed to doing so in their homelands, e.g. the IBO of Nigeria and Ewe of Togo. It took place in September when the first yam was reaped, and slaves would get permission to go to different estates to join in the celebrations. In West Africa, an annual festival in honour of the ancestors marked the beginning of the yam season, the spirit of the ancestors appearing as masked dancers (called *Egungun* in some places) and it is believed that this masquerade tradition continued in Jamaica and became part of JONKONNU. The offering of first fruits to the ancestors also continued for a long time: in the mid-19th century, R.T. Banbury noted that when Negro yam was cut, none of it would be touched until it was offered, along with boiled fowl, to spirits at the graves of the departed.

The Yam Festival was only one of the religious rituals brought by African peoples that acknowledged the role of agriculture in their lives and invoked blessings for these vital activities. Many of these rituals continue to be practised, though in fragmented form. They include rituals when first clearing the bush to plant a field, when first cutting into the earth, planting rituals to ensure a good crop (see e.g. PUMPKIN) and harvest rituals (see e.g. CROPOVER). In the past too, rituals to invoke rain were also performed (see e.g. WATER SPIRITS) and the rainmaker was an important personage (as he or she still is in Africa).

With the conversion to Christianity of a substantial segment of the slave population in the 19th century (see MISSIONARY) some of these rituals of thanksgiving were incorporated into church observance (e.g. Harvest Festivals).

[Banbury 1894, Beckwith 1929, Mbiti 1975, Patterson 1973]

YAMPI or YAMPEE (*Dioscorea trifida*)

The only common species of YAM in Jamaica that did not come from Africa. It is a native of the New World, originating in South America, and in former times was called 'Indian yam'. However, F.G. Cassidy suggests a Vai origin for the name Yampi – *dzambi* – that means wild yam. (Vai is spoken in Liberia.) Two other New World species are found here but are little known. They are Bitter Jessie or Wild Yam, and *D. pilosiuscula* that seems to have no common name. Yampi differs from other yams in two important respects. In the first place, it bears many tubers in clusters instead of one large tuber as yam does. Secondly, while all other species of yam twine right to left, the Yampi twines left to right.

Yampi is a highly prized delicacy, cultivated by fewer and fewer farmers today as it requires skill and patience and a fairly high altitude. It commands good prices both at home and overseas among Jamaican expatriate communities.

YANGA

Word used to describe a swaying motion of the body considered provocative or 'stylish'. The DJE suggests a derivation of the word from a West African word, *nyanga* which means 'ostentatious', 'giving oneself airs'. Cheryl Ryman lists it as a DANCE style or specified dance steps in her survey of traditional dances in Jamaica. A version of the once-popular folk song 'Ada' alludes to the dance step: 'Me cyan yanga, jigger gwine spwile mi toe.'

The word is known elsewhere in the Anglophone Caribbean, with the same idea of a stylish or provocative walk or dance.

[Baxter 1970, DCEU, DJE, Ryman 1980]

YARD

In Jamaica the word 'yard' in general usage defines one's dwelling and the space around it. More specifically, it is used to refer to a type of urban living arrangement associated with low-income groups. This urban 'yard' corresponds to a 'tenement'.

In either usage, 'yard' is a powerfully emotive word that defines one's spatial as well as social relationships and is used by expatriate Jamaicans in reference to the homeland, Jamaica. 'Back a yard' means back home; 'Yardie' is a term used in England to define those who share a Jamaican and, to some extent, a CARIBBEAN origin, i.e. coming from the same yard.

The Private Yard The yard space symbolically establishes one's private space, as opposed to the road (public space), and is recognized as such by everyone, even if the yard is not physically enclosed with a barrier – hedge, fence, or gate. In many cases, several houses will be set inside one yard ('family land') to comprise a 'family yard'. The house and yard are governed by rules and regulations and in rural families especially, are regarded as the domain of the women. In households with conservative child-rearing practice, the 'yard' serves to define the physical and social boundaries for the children of the household, 'school' and 'church' being the only other arenas permitted them even into adolescence. While boys might be permitted more freedom as they grow older, a young woman who is seen too often outside her yard is automatically given a bad reputation as a 'walk bout'.

Often the yard space immediately in front of the house is bare ground, and keeping the yard cleanly swept (with a 'yard broom') is the job of children. Better-off homes in the past had what was referred to as a 'yard boy' who was employed to do this and other outdoor domestic chores. The character of the woman of the household is often judged on how immaculate this yard is kept.

Etiquette demands that no one should enter the yard of another without permission. Since so many householders keep a DOG, 'Hol' Dawg!' is commonly called out as a signal that a visitor is approaching. Often the yard space and veranda serve as the extension of the house and visitors will be entertained here, instead of inside the house. The term 'yard' in the rural context also embraces the crops that are grown in close proximity to the house, separate and apart from one's cultivated field or GROUND. These will include medicinal herbs, seasonings, vegetables such as tomatoes and peppers, smaller fruit trees such as CITRUS, and – depending on space – other tree crops such as BREADFRUIT, ACKEE and SOURSOP. Even city householders will try to grow some fruit trees; houses advertised for sale up until the 1960s often carried the tempting line 'Well-fruited yard'.

Archaeological work on the African-Jamaican settlements at New MONTPELIER and DRAX HALL have shown that the 'yard' developed from the pre-EMANCIPATION period and had West African origins. The fact that among Africans and their descendants, family members were (and to a limited extent still are) buried within the family compound or yard has reinforced the concept of equating 'yard' with one's roots. In times past, this connection was made even stronger with the planting of one's NAVEL STRING TREE. This Jamaican pattern also harks back to the original meaning of the word *geard* which in the Old English period (c. AD 500-1000), denoted an enclosure contained by dwellings and outhouses.

Urban Yards In the urban areas of Jamaica, where the poor did not have access to land, a different type of yard arrangement developed from the earliest days of settlement. Town lots would often consist of one large house fronting on the street where the owner lived. In the back of the premises, and usually invisible from the streets, would be a warren of rooms that at first provided accommodation for slaves and servants and the 'outhouses' for cooking, LAUNDRY, and ablutions. Later, as the wealthier owners moved out of the town centres to the more salubrious suburbs, the premises were rented out to tenants who shared the communal (and usually substandard) facilities of the outhouses. In time, the main house itself would be divided into rooms.

In recent times, apart from privately owned 'yards', there have also developed 'government yards', usually barrack-type structures with centrally shared facilities, erected by the government to house the poor. The song 'No woman no cry', sung by Bob MARLEY, evokes the camaraderie of a Trench Town 'guvvament' yard of his early years.

The urban yard and its occupants are usually looked down on by the elite. But studies of these yards (such as Erna Brodber's) have shown them to be providing not just an address but a social unit, substituting to a certain extent for the family unit of poor rural migrants who usually end up as residents. The urban yard has a life and social organization of its own. Roger Mais has presented graphic pictures of 'yard life' in his novels *The Hills Were Joyful Together* and *Brother Man*, and Orlando Patterson in his *Children of Sisyphus*.

Grass Yard The term 'yard' has also been applied to other defined areas used for commercial purposes: 'Grass yards' were places in the city where DRAYS and carts bringing HIGGLERS in from the country would stop and unload. Grass would be available for the animals and cheap overnight accommodation for man and beast. Before the establishment of the big city markets, the grass yard was also a kind of open air market in which goods were exchanged between city and country people. Food and charcoal brought in from the country were bartered for goods made by city artisans such as cabinet-makers, YABBA makers and dressmakers. The grass yards (some known by the names of the owners of the land) were also where city folk went to meet their poor kin coming in from the country on the market drays and trucks. Today coal is sold at the one 'grass yard' remaining, in western KINGSTON.
[Brodber 1975, DCEU, DJE]

YAWS

An infectious disease (also called Framboesia) of tropical climates that afflicted slaves and other plantation workers; frequently met with in the historical literature and in FOLKLORE. The word is from the CARIB language. The bacterium that causes yaws is *Treponema pertenue*, which closely resembles *Treponema pallidum* that causes the sexually transmitted infection, syphilis. Most laboratory tests still cannot distinguish between these two bacterial species and over the years some persons with yaws have been falsely diagnosed as having syphilis, causing much confusion and family conflict. Yaws was characterized by skin eruptions and because of its infectious nature, those with the disease were isolated. It was once so widespread that as late as 1932 a Yaws Commission established that about 50 per cent of the population had had yaws at some time. A control programme mounted in Jamaica with the aid of the Rockefeller Foundation eradicated yaws in 1965.

In many CARIBBEAN folk tales, a character called 'Yawsy Boy', whose skin shows the scars of the disease, appears; he represents the hero who is at first ostracized or ignored and then manages to save the day.
[DJE, Golding 1994, Kiple 1984]

YAYA

In the TAINO myths YaYa is the High God or supreme being; also known as Giaia. His name has been translated by José Arrom as 'spirit of spirits'. Like other supreme spirits he is also said to be nameless. In contemporary Jamaica, YaYa is a common name for mother or grandmother, from the Africa Ewe *ya*; Yoruba *iya*.
[Arrom 1990, DJE]

YELLOW FEVER AND MALARIA

A slave song recorded in 1799 was an accurate observation of the progress of the killer disease of the time:

> New-come buckra
> He get sick
> He tak fever
> He be die
> He be die

Newcastle Military graveyard

The main fever was Yellow Fever (also called 'Yellow Jack'), an acute infectious tropical disease, its primary victims the newly-arrived whites ('buckra'). In former times, a trip to the West Indies was not greeted with the effusions of today's tourist – it was regarded as a death sentence, especially by naval and military forces. (See NEWCASTLE.)

Raw recruits sent out on overcrowded transports to fight European battles abroad were most susceptible, disease usually proving the strongest enemy. One of the most appalling examples occurred in 1741. Of 13,000 troops sent out under Admiral Edward VERNON, naval commander at PORT ROYAL, to take Cartagena, then the Spanish stronghold on the Central American coast, 600 died in battle. Most of the rest died from malaria and yellow fever that broke out on the troop ships; only 1,700 returned to Jamaica fit for duty. They continued to die and by the end of the year only 300 men were left. The Scottish novelist, Tobias Smollett (1721-71), was a surgeon's mate on one of the ships, and in his novel *Roderick Random* exposed the mismanagement of the enterprise that was part of the so-called 'War of Jenkins's Ear'. (Smollett lived in Jamaica for a while and married a Jamaican heiress, Anne Lassells or Lascelles.)

No doubt the greater survival rate of the BUCCANEERS was due to their hardiness derived from long residence in the CARIBBEAN. People who lived all their lives in regions susceptible to yellow fever seemed to build up some immunity against a first attack. Thus, when an epidemic broke out it was the recent arrivals who fell. (See KINGSTON BUTTERCUP.) While the CREOLE population did not succumb to yellow fever as rapidly, it was more susceptible to the effects of another 'fever' – malaria.

Both yellow fever and malaria are transmitted by mosquitoes, yellow fever by the female *Aëdes aegypti*, malaria by the *Anopheles*. To put it in simplest terms, mosquitoes of certain species will suck the blood of a victim with the disease and, if the timing is right, pass it to another victim by biting. In the 20th century, these diseases were controlled by the simple expedient of destroying the breeding ground of the mosquitoes.

Until the late 19th century the cause of these 'fevers' was unknown; they were blamed on foul air (hence '*mala aria*'), poisons in the atmosphere, or the moral qualities of the victims, not on environmental factors.

Yellow fever occurs in tropical and sub-tropical areas. It broke out from time to time as a virulent epidemic and swept through an area, lasting probably a few months. The onset of the disease was sudden and its progress swift. It attacked the liver, causing jaundice, and hence the victim turned 'yellow'. There was no real treatment and no cure; the patient either lived or died. Once he or she survived an attack, the victim did not contract the disease again.

Unlike yellow fever, malaria is endemic in low-lying tropical regions of the world and has no definite season. It occurs more or less all the while and if not checked, sooner or later

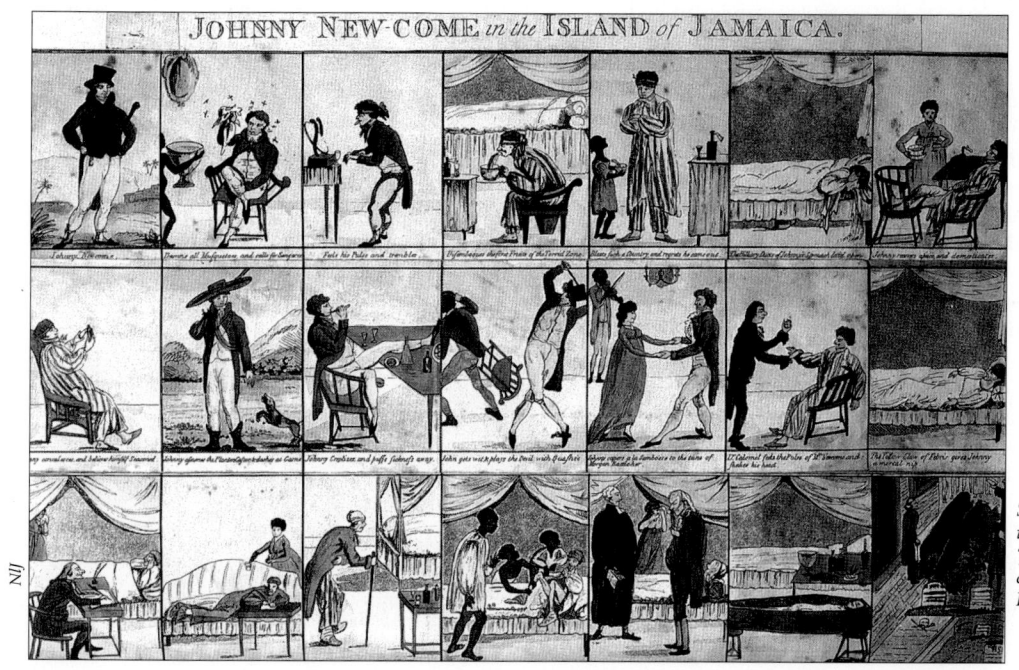

Satirical view of the progress of 'Johnny New-come' by William Holland, 1800

virtually all the inhabitants will become chronic victims. After the first attack, it recurs throughout a person's life, often leading to persistent debility. The sickness usually takes the form of violent shivering and chills, followed by a raging fever. Each attack is followed by a period of physical debility and mental depression.

Before a World Health Organization eradication campaign began in 1956, the global incidence of malaria was estimated at 300 million cases annually, with at least three million deaths. In Jamaica, in 1952, there were 724 deaths from the disease, but it was eradicated in 1961 as part of the WHO campaign. Although Jamaica is relatively free of malaria today, the disease continues to be a world-wide threat, especially with the prevalence of air travel.

Serious attention was paid to eradication of yellow fever by American army doctors stationed in Cuba during and after the Spanish-American war (1898). The lessons they learnt there were to be applied to making the environment safe for the construction of the PANAMA Canal; failure to control disease had contributed to failure of the previous French Canal effort.

It was a Cuban doctor, Juan Carlos Finlay, who gave the world the theory that a mosquito – the *Stegomyia fasciata* (renamed *Aëdes aegypti*) – was the vector or carrier of yellow fever. It was left to an American doctor, Col William Gorgas, to work out how the disease was transmitted and to take steps to eradicate it from the Panama Canal Zone. Meanwhile, in another part of the world, an English army doctor named Ronald Ross had in 1898 succeeded in working out how another disease – malaria – was spread by the *Anopheles* mosquito. Eradication or control of these diseases on the Canal Zone was one of the triumphs of modern medicine and contributed to the successful completion of the Panama Canal in 1914. The techniques Gorgas pioneered were then applied in many countries, including Jamaica, freeing the country of yellow fever and keeping malaria in check. Quinine (derived from the CINCHONA bark) was for a long time used as a treatment and preventative against malaria attack, and in Jamaica the tablets were sold throughout the rural areas at post offices.

While the yellow fever mosquito is a domestic variety and easily controlled (having a range of a few hundred metres), the malaria mosquito is more wide ranging and much more difficult to eradicate.

[Augier et al. 1960, Cundall 1915, Kiple 1984, Rawlins et al. 1988].

YORUBA

Ethnic and linguistic group among the enslaved Africans brought to Jamaica. The Yoruba are peoples of SW Nigeria and the neighbouring Republics of Benin (Dahomey) and Togo. The Yoruba language and people are subdivided into many regional subgroups. The Yoruba culture is one of the most elaborate and urbanized in West Africa. Religions based on their Orisha tradition (that is, a pantheon of gods and goddesses) still flourish in many parts of the Americas, such as Brazil (Candomble and Macumba), Cuba (Lucumi or Santería, and Bembe), Trinidad and Grenada (Shango or Orisha), St Lucia (Kele) – all places to which either large numbers of Yorubas came or where cohorts of Yoruba-speaking immigrants established communities. Yoruba-based funeral rites exist also in the Itutu of Cuba and the ETU of Jamaica.

The influx of Yoruba-speaking people to Jamaica began in the 1770s. Many of the free Africans who came in the late 19th century were also Yoruba (see AFRICANS, Indentured). The Yoruba were called Anago by the Dahomeans, referring to both the group and their language. The name, shortened to Nago, is still retained in Jamaican place names such as NAGGO HEAD and NAGO Town, and old people of Yoruba ancestry up to recent times still referred to themselves as 'Nago people'.

Traces of Yoruba culture have been found in the WESTMORELAND village of Abeokuta (called 'Bekuta' by the people of the area) as well as in HANOVER Parish, among the Etu people. Monica Schuler notes that Abeokuta (named after the original in Africa) was founded after 1841 by Yoruba from Waterworks Pen and adjoining Dean's Valley estate, along with others from Shrewsbury and Bluecastle estates. Abeokuta (and some of its old Yoruba inhabitants) was 'rediscovered' in the 1970s by Olive Lewin, then undertaking an islandwide survey of Jamaican folk music (see MUSIC).

[Adetugbo 1996, Bilby 1998, Lewin n.d., Schuler 1980, Tanna 1983, Warner--Lewis, 1991]

Yoruba carving representing the god Shango

Lagos Museum

YS

Estate and river in ST ELIZABETH Parish, the YS being a tributary of the BLACK RIVER. The beautiful YS Falls (on private property) are now a tourist attraction, the falls consisting of a series of drops and terraces. According to Anthony Porter, the combined vertical height of the drops is 33m, with a beautiful pool at the base.

The origin of the name YS is uncertain. One suggestion is that it derives from an ancient Gaelic word formed by these two letters and meaning 'crooked' or 'winding'. On old maps it is spelled Wyess. It is possible that YS was the estate mark that would have been stamped on hogsheads of SUGAR. The estate was first settled by Thomas Scott, who had come from Suriname. (See SURINAM QUARTERS.)

[Porter 1990, Wright and White 1969]

YS Falls

YSASSI, Don Cristobal Arnaldo de

Spanish-Jamaican freedom fighter who led a courageous guerrilla war against the English for five years after the official SPANISH surrender, following the CAPTURE OF JAMAICA in 1655. Ysassi was a fifth generation Jamaican. His great-great-grandfather had come to Jamaica from Spain to command the fort that had been built at SEVILLA LA NUEVA, the first Spanish settlement (see SEVILLE, New). His father had for a time acted as governor. One brother was Lieutenant-Governor of Santiago de Cuba and another was Bishop of Puerto Rico.

After the English capture and the departure of the Spanish governor and most of the Spanish citizens, who were transported according to the terms of surrender, Ysassi gathered around him those Spaniards who refused to surrender, to continue guerrilla warfare. He was eventually appointed governor by the King of Spain, becoming the last Spanish governor of Jamaica.

With the help of former black slaves like LUBOLO who formed settlements in the hills, Ysassi was to wage guerrilla warfare against the English settlers for five more years, until the defection of Lubolo and the decisive battle of RIO NUEVO. He left the island only after all hope for its recapture had faded. Although RUNAWAY BAY is commonly said to be the place of his departure, it is now believed that the brave Ysassi departed Jamaica elsewhere on the coast (see e.g. DON CHRISTOPHER'S COVE).

[Osborne 1971, Taylor 1965]

YUCA see CASSAVA

YÚCAHU

TAINO male spirit of fertility, a sky-dwelling spirit, associated with yuca (CASSAVA) and the sea which provided fish. His full names of Yúcahu Guama Bagua Maorocote have been translated to mean 'Spirit, without male ancestor, of the yuca and the sea', suggesting that he is the supreme ZEMI. His mother was ATABEYRA or Atabey, the female spirit of human fertility and fresh water.

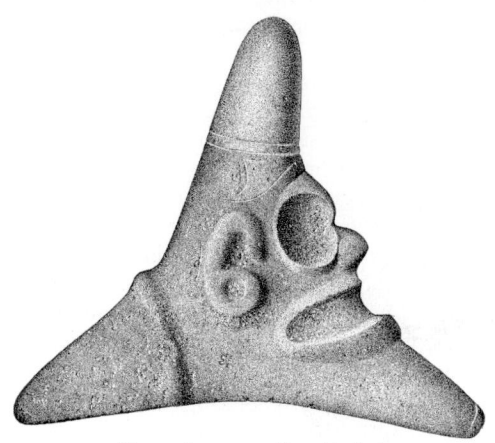

Three pointer stone (from Fewkes)

The so-called 'three-pointer stones', Taino artefacts found in great numbers in the ANTILLES and which for a long time puzzled archaeologists as to their meaning, are now believed by some to represent Yúcahu.

[Arrom 1990]

ZELLA

Name for WAKE or Nine-night celebration held in PORTLAND Parish, similar to DINKI MINI of ST MARY Parish. The DJE cites as a possible source for the name the Ewe *zeli*, a funeral drum.

ZEMI

Zemeism was the religion of the TAINOS in which specially created images (zemis) were used to represent and invoke the blessing and protection of deities or benevolent spirits. Zemis (*cemís* on the Spanish-speaking islands) have been described as the intermediaries between the high god (YAYA) and the world of humans, and should be regarded as religious objects imbued with the power of the spirits that they represented. These could be familial or mythic ancestors or deities. Zemis therefore were treated as living beings and were 'fed' spiritual food – offerings of TOBACCO smoke, CASSAVA flour or cassava juice – just as statues of saints or representations of orishas are presented with gifts and 'fed' by worshippers in other religions.

Zemeism is believed to have been peculiar to the Tainos and is one of the characteristic features that sets them apart from other Amerindians.

'Weeping Figure'. Zemi from Jamaica

The basic elements of their religion are clearly derived from beliefs shared by peoples in the Amazon basin where the Tainos are thought to have originated, especially reverencing the bones of ancestors and using priests as intermediaries between men and spirits. But the use of the images in their worship was developed by the Tainos as central to a coherent system of belief that developed on the islands. The zemis were given the most prominent place in their religious rites relating to fertility, healing, divination and the cult of ancestors. According to the Puerto Rican scholar Antonio M. Stevens-Arroyo: 'The rites were celebrated to communicate with the invisible power of the cosmos, and the cemis were the conduits of these exchanges that maintained the coherence of life.' First fruits of the harvest were offered to them, they served as ancestral memorials and were used as protection against various omens.

Zemis were of different sizes and made of different materials. The largest were kept in the CACIQUE'S house that also served as the spirit house or temple of the Tainos. COLUMBUS reported that most of the caciques had three great stones to which they and their people showed great devotion – one helped corn or other grain, one helped women in painless childbirth, the other procured rain or fair weather.

Images of zemis were often carved in miniature and were worn as personal adornment. They were painted on bodies, celebrated in masks, amulets or other ornaments as well as household utensils, and painted in CAVES or carved on rocks. Taino warriors going into battle wore images of zemis tied to their foreheads. Public festivals – AREITOS – were held in their honour and pilgrimages were made to zemi images placed in caves or shrines.

Not surprisingly, zemis were the most prominent motif in Taino art and many of these religious objects have been found throughout the ANTILLES, including a wide range of 'three pointer stones', so called from their basic shape. More elaborate zemi carvings are among the most prized examples of Taino art, and include

Cotton Zemi (Dominican Republic) now in the Museo di Antropologia, Turin

several fine pieces found in Jamaica. Among them are five works in the British Museum, including the so-called 'bird man' carvings, one in the Metropolitan Museum of Art in New York, and three pieces recently discovered at Aboukir in ST ANN Parish and now in the possession of the JNHT.

The work of the Cuban scholar José J. Arrom has enabled identification of the images representing the powerful zemis that were named in PANÉ'S narrative, beginning with YÚCAHU and ATABEYRA, the sky-god and earth-goddess. Below them were the powerful secondary deities, each representing a different domain: BAIBRAMA, MÁROHU and BOINAYEL, GUABANCEX, GUATAUBÁ, COATRISCHIE, MAQUETAURIE GUAYABA, OPIYEL GUOBIRÁN, BARAGUABAEL, COROCOTE.

[Aarons 1994, Arrom 1975, 1990, Bercht et al. 1997, Fewkes 1907, Stevens-Arroyo 1988]

ZINC
Name applied to objects made of different metals, such as 'zinc fence' or 'zinc roof' (made of corrugated metal sheets coated with zinc to prevent rust, also known as galvanized iron or 'galvanize') and 'zinc pan' (metal or 'kerosene' tin).

ZION
Revival Zion or Zion Revival, forms, with pukumina (see POCOMANIA), the indigenous African-Jamaican religion known as REVIVAL that takes its name from the Christian Great Revival that started in Ireland and spread to England and the United States before reaching Jamaica in the 1860s. Zion is known as the '60 Order' and is the more Christianized form of Pukumina, which is known as the '61 Order', reflecting the ascendancy of more African elements by 1861.

ZAMBI
Ancestral spirit of the KUMINA, probably CONGO-derived. Also referred to as 'zombi'. Kumina practitioners refer to the supreme spirit as Nzambi Mpungu, 'the highest nzambi'. In Angola, Zambi is the supreme being who lives in the skies.

[Schulyer 1980]

ZOUAVE see JAMAICA MILITARY BAND

Bibliography

Aarons, G.A. 1983. 'Archaeological Sites in the Hellshire Hills'. *JJ* 16:1.

Aarons, G.A. 1983-84. 'Sevilla la Nueva: Microcosm of Spain in Jamaica'. Pt 1, *JJ* 16:4, 1983. Pt. 2, *JJ* 17:1, 1984.

Aarons, G.A. 1988. 'Feedback: The Mountain River Cave'. *JJ* 21:3.

Aarons, G.A. 1990. 'Port Royal: An Archaeological Adventure – the last Fifteen Years 1974-1989'. *JJ* 22:4.

Aarons, G.A. 1994. 'Tainos of Jamaica: The Aboukir Zemis'. *JJ* 25:2.

Aarons, John A. 1989. 'Musgrave Medals'. *JJ* 22:2.

Acworth, A.W. 1951. *Buildings of Architectural or Historic Interest in the British West Indies*. London: HM Stationery Office.

Adams, C. Dennis 1971. *The Blue Mahoe and Other Bush: An Introduction to Plant Life in Jamaica*. Kingston: Sangster's in association with McGraw Hill.

Adams, C.D. 1972. *Flowering Plants of Jamaica*. Mona: UWI.

Adams, C. Dennis 1976. *Caribbean Flora*. Surrey: Nelson Caribbean.

Adams, Dennis, K. Magnus, and C. Seaforth. 1963. *Poisonous Plants in Jamaica*. Mona: UWI Extra Mural Studies.

Adetugbo, Abiodun. 1996. 'The Yoruba in Jamaica'. *ACIJ Research Review* 3.

Afroz, Sultana. 1995. 'The Unsung Slaves: Islam in the Plantation Society'. *CQ* 41:3 & 4.

Agorsah, E. Kofi (ed.). 1994. *Maroon Heritage: Archaeological and Ethnographic and Historical Perspectives*. Mona: Canoe Press.

Aiken, Karl. 1984. 'Lobsters: Their Biology and Conservation in Jamaica'. *JJ* 17:4.

Alegría, Ricardo E. 1978. *Apuntes en torno a la mitología de los Indios Taínos de las Antillas Mayores y sus orígenes Suramericanos*. San Juan: Centro de Estudios Avanzados de Puerto Rico y el Caribe.

Alegría, Ricardo E. 1985. 'Christopher Columbus and the Treasure of the Taino Indians of Hispaniola'. (Trans. James W. Lee). *JJ* 18:1.

Alexander, Hartley Burr. 1920. *Latin-America*. Vol 11 of *The Mythology of All Races* (ed. Louis Herbert Gray). Boston: Marshall Jones.

Alleyne, Mervyn. 1980. *Comparative Afro-American. Theoretical Issues in Caribbean Linguistics*. Ann Arbor: Karoma.

Alleyne, Mervyn. 1988. *Roots of Jamaican Culture*. London: Pluto Press and Karia Press.

Allsopp, Richard. 1996. *Dictionary of Caribbean English Usage*. Oxford: Oxford UP.

Ammar, Nellie. 1970. 'They Came from the Middle East'. *JJ* 4:1.

Anderson, Izett and Frank Cundall. 1910. *Jamaica Negro Proverbs and Sayings*. Kingston: IOJ.

Andrade, J.A.P.M. 1941. *A Record of the Jews in Jamaica*. Kingston.

Anim-Addo, Joan. 1995. *Longest Journey: A History of Black Lewisham*. London: Deptford Forum Publishing.

Anon. 1993. 'Drug Producing Plants. From Use to Abuse'. *JJ* 24:3.

Anon. 1998. 'Scots Kirk – Church of Scotland, 1851'. Anniversary feature, *Sunday Outlook*.

Arlott, John (ed.). 1975. *The Oxford Companion to Sports and Games*. Oxford: Oxford UP.

Armstrong, Douglas V. 1991. 'The Afro-Jamaican Community at Drax Hall'. *JJ* 24:1.

Arrom, José J. 1975. *Mitología y artes prehispánicas de las Antillas*. Mexico City: Siglo Veintiuno Editores.

Arrom, José J. 1990. *Fray Ramón Pané: Relacion acerca de las antigüedades de los Indios* (new ed.). Havana: Editorial de Ciencias Sociales.

Ashcroft, Michael. 1969. 'Caves in Jamaica'. *JJ* 3:2.

Ashcroft, Michael. 1980. 'Robert Charles Dallas Identified as the Author of an Anonymous Book about Jamaica'. *JJ* 44.

Asprey, G.F. and Phyllis Thornton. 1953-55. 'Medicinal Plants of Jamaica', Parts 1-4. *WIMJ* Vol. 2 No. 4, Vol. 3 No.1, Vol. 4 Nos. 2 & 3.

Asprey G.F. and R.G. Robbins. 1953. *The Vegetation of Jamaica*. Ecological Monographs 23:4.

Augier, F.R., S.C. Gordon, D.G. Hall, and M. Reckord. 1960. *The Making of the West Indies*. London: Longman.

Augier, F.R. and S.C. Gordon. 1962. *Sources of West Indian History*. London: Longman.

Austin, Diane J. 1984. *Urban Life in Kingston, Jamaica: The Culture and Class Ideology of Two Neighbourhoods*. Caribbean Studies Series 3. New York and London: Gordon and Breach Science Publishers.

Austin-Broos, Diane J. 1997. *Jamaica Genesis: Religion and the Politics of Moral Order*. Jamaica: Ian Randle.

Baccus, Gillian and Heather Royes (eds.). 1988. *The Jamaica Farmer's Guide*. Kingston: Selectco Publications.

Bain, J.R. 1985. *Recognizing and Understanding the Bats of Jamaica*. Kingston: Natural Resources Conservation Department.

Baker, R.J. and H.H. Genoways. 1978. 'Zoogeography

of Antillean Bats'. *Zoogeography of the Caribbean.* Academy of Natural Sciences Special Publication 13.

Balandier, Georges. 1968. *Daily Life in the Kingdom of the Kongo.* (Trans. Helen Weaver). New York: Meridian Books.

Banbury, Revd R. Thomas. 1894. *Jamaica Superstitions: or, The Obeah Book.* Kingston: DeSouza.

Bannochie, Iris and Marilyn Light. 1993. *Gardening in the Caribbean.* London: Macmillan.

Barnes, M.J.C. 1988 'Some Aspects of Jamaica's Butterflies and Moths'. *JJ* 21:2.

Barnett, Sheila. 1980. 'Jonkonnu: Pitchy Patchy'. *JJ* 44.

Barnett, Sheila. 1982. 'Notes on Contemporary Dance 1930-1982'. *JJ* 46.

Barrett, Leonard. 1973. 'The Portrait of a Jamaican Healer: African Medical Lore in the Caribbean'. *CQ* 19:3.

Barrett, Leonard. 1976. *The Sun and the Drum.* Kingston: Sangster's.

Barrow, Steve and Peter Dalton. 1997. *Reggae: The Rough Guide.* London: Rough Guide Limited.

Baugh, Edward. 2000. *It Was the Singing.* Toronto: Sandberry Press.

Baxter, Ivy. 1970. *The Arts of an Island.* Metuchen: The Scarecrow Press.

Beckford, George. 1972. *Persistent Poverty.* Oxford: Oxford UP.

Beckford, William, Jnr. 1790. *A Descriptive Account of the Island of Jamaica.* London.

Beckles, Hilary and Verene Shepherd (eds.). 1996. *Caribbean Freedom: Economy and Society from Emancipation to the Present.* Princeton: Marcus Weiner.

Beckles, Hilary McD. 1998. *The Development of West Indies Cricket.* Vol. 1 *The Age of Nationalism.* Mona: The Press UWI.

Beckwith, Martha Warren. 1924. 'Jamaica Anansi Stories'. *Memoirs of the American Folk-Lore Society*, 17.

Beckwith, Martha Warren. 1928. *Jamaica Folk-Lore.* The American Folklore Society XXI. New York. Kraus Reprint, 1969.

Beckwith, Martha Warren. 1929. *Black Roadways, A Study of Jamaican Folk Life.* New York: Negro Universities Press, 1969.

Belisario, I.M. 1837. *Sketches of Character.* Kingston: The Artist.

Bell, Hesketh J. 1889. *Obeah: Witchcraft in the West Indies.* New York: Negro Universities Press, 1970.

Benghiat, Norma. 1985. *Traditional Jamaican Cookery.* UK: Penguin.

Benghiat, Norma. 1987. 'Bread – Jamaican Style'. *Skywritings* 52.

Benítez-Rojo, Antonio. 1992. *The Repeating Island. The Caribbean and the Postmodern Perspective.* Durham: Duke UP.

Bennett, Louise. 1942. *Jamaica Dialect Verses.* Kingston: Gleaner.

Bennett, Louise. 1966. *Jamaica Labrish.* Kingston: Sangster's.

Bennett, Louise. 1979. *Anancy and Miss Lou.* Kingston: Sangster's.

Bennett, Wycliffe. 1974. 'The Jamaican Theatre: A Preliminary Overview'. *JJ* 8:2 & 3.

Bercht, Fatima, Estrelita Brodsky, John Alan Farmer, and Dicey Taylor (eds.). 1997. *Taíno: Pre-Columbian Art and Culture from the Caribbean.* New York: El Museo del Barrio and The Monacelli Press.

Bettellheim, Judith. 1976. 'The Jonkonnu Festival: Its Relation to Caribbean and African Masquerades'. *JJ* 10:2, 3, 4.

Bettelheim, Judith. 1999. 'Costume Types and Festival Elements in Caribbean Celebrations'. *ACIJ Research Review 4.*

Bilby, Kenneth M. 1984. ' "Two Sister Pikni" Historical Tradition of Dual Ethnogenesis in Eastern Jamaica'. *CQ* 30:3 & 4.

Bilby, Kenneth M. 1985a. 'The Caribbean as a Musical Region', in *Caribbean Contours* edited by Sidney W. Mintz and Sally Price, Baltimore: Johns Hopkins UP.

Bilby, Kenneth M. 1985b. 'The Holy Herb: Notes on the Background of Cannabis in Jamaica'. *CQ Rastafari Monograph.*

Bilby, Kenneth. 1998. 'Across the Ocean: West African Gods in the Americas'. *The Yoruba/Dahomean Collection: Orishas Across the Ocean.* Ryodisc 10405 CD, Library of Congress.

Bilby, Kenneth. 1999. 'Gumbay, Myal and the Great House: New Evidence on the religious background of Jonkonnu in Jamaica'. *ACIJ Research Review* 4.

Bilby, Kenneth and Elliott Leib. 1986. 'Kumina, the Howellite Church and the emergence of Rastafarian traditional Music in Jamaica'. *JJ* 19:3.

Binder, Pearl. 1972. *Magic Symbols of the World.* London: Hamlyn.

Binney, Marcus, John Harris, and Kit Martin. 1991. *Jamaica's Heritage: An Untapped Resource.* Kingston: The Mill Press.

BirdLife Jamaica. 1999. *A Teachers' Guide to the Birds of Jamaica.* Kingston.

Bisnauth, Dale. 1989. *History of Religions in the Caribbean.* Kingston: Kingston Publishers.

Black, Clinton V. 1952. *Tales of Old Jamaica.* London: Collins.

Black, Clinton V. 1965. *The Story of Jamaica.* London: Collins.

Black, Clinton. 1968. 'The Jamaica Archives'. *JJ* 2:1.

Black Clinton V. 1974. *Spanish Town, the Old Capital.* Parish Council of St Catherine.

Black, Clinton. 1983. *History of Jamaica.* London: Longman.

Black, Clinton V. 1988. *Port Royal, Jamaica.* Kingston: IOJP.

Black, Clinton V. 1989. *Pirates of the West Indies.* Cambridge: Cambridge UP.

Bligh, William. 1792. *The Mutiny on Board H.M.S. Bounty.* New York: Signet Classic, 1961.

Bolland, O. Nigel. 2001. *The Politics of Labour in the British Caribbean: The Social Origins of Authoritarianism and Democracy in the Labour Movement.* Kingston: Ian Randle.

Bolster, W. Jeffrey. 1997. *Black Jacks: African American Seamen in the Age of Sail.* Cambridge, Mass: Harvard UP.

Bond, James. 1960. *Birds of the West Indies.* London: Collins.

Booth, Karen. 1985. 'When Jamaica Welcomed the World. The Great Exhibition of 1891'. *JJ* 18:3.
Bourne, M.J., G.W. Lennox, and S.A. Seddon. 1988. *Fruits and Vegetables of the Caribbean*. London: Macmillan.
Bousquet, Ben and Colin Douglas. 1991. *West Indian Women at War: British Racism in World War II*. London: Lawrence and Wishart.
Bowker, John (ed.). 1997. *The Oxford Dictionary of World Religions*. Oxford: Oxford UP.
Boxer, David. 1990. *Edna Manley: Sculptor*. Kingston: Edna Manley Foundation and National Gallery of Jamaica.
Boxer, David and Veerle Poupeye. 1998. *Modern Jamaican Art*. Kingston: UWI/Ian Randle.
Brathwaite, Augustus. 1979. 'The Cudjoe Minstrels'. *JJ* 43.
Brathwaite, Edward K. 1970. *The Folk Culture of the Slaves in Jamaica*. London: New Beacon.
Brathwaite, Edward. 1971. *The Development of Creole Society in Jamaica 1770-1820*. Oxford: Oxford UP.
Brathwaite, Edward. 1973. *The Arrivants: Islands*. Oxford: Oxford UP.
Brathwaite, Edward K. 1974. *Contradictory Omens: Cultural Diversity and Integration in the Caribbean*. Mona: Savacou.
Brathwaite, Edward K. 1977. *Wars of Respect: Nanny and Sam Sharpe*. Kingston: API.
Brathwaite. E.K. 1978. 'Kumina: The Spirit of African Survival in Jamaica'. *JJ* 42.
Brathwaite, E.K. 1984. *History of the Voice*. London: New Beacon.
Brathwaite, E.K. 1986. 'The African Presence in Caribbean Literature' in *Roots*. Havana: Casa de las Americas.
Breiner, Laurence A. 1998. *An Introduction to West Indian Poetry*. Cambridge: Cambridge UP.
Brett, W.H. 1880. *Legends and Myths of the Aboriginal Indians of British Guiana*. London.
Bretting, Peter. 1983a. 'Jamaica's Flowering Plants: The Five Endemic Genera'. *JJ* 16:1.
Bretting, Peter. 1983b. 'Jamaica's Flowering Plants Revisited'. *JJ* 16:2.
Bretting, Peter. 1983c. 'The "Secret lives" of Jamaican Plants and Animals'. *JJ* 16:3.
Bridges, Revd G.W. 1828. *The Annals of Jamaica*. (2 vols) London.
Britton, N.L. and J.N. Rose. 1963. *The Cactaceae*. New York: Dover Publications Inc.
Brodber, Erna. 1975. *A Study of Yards in the City of Kingston*. Mona: UWI ISER.
Brodber, Erna. 1999. 'Brief Notes on DeLaurence in Jamaica'. *ACIJ Research Review* 4.
Brooks, A.A. 1917. *History of Bedwardism or the Jamaica Native Baptist Free Church*. Kingston: Gleaner Co.
Brown, Beryl. 1975. 'The History of Portland 1723-1917'. *JJ* 9:4.
Brown, Beryl. 1976. *A Short History of Portland*. Kingston: Ministry of Education.
Brown, Cudelia (Comp.). 1996. *Riddles of Jamaica*. Kingston: Jamworld Publications.
Brown, F. Martin and Bernard Heineman. 1972. *Jamaica and its Butterflies*. London: E.W. Classey.
Brown, Lloyd. 1978. *West Indian Poetry*. Boston: Twayne. London: Heinemann 1984.
Brown, Wayne. 1975. *Edna Manley: The Private Years 1900-1938*. London: Andre Deutsch.
Browne, Patrick. 1756. *The Civil and Natural History of Jamaica*. London.
Bruckner, Andrew. 1993. 'The Threatened Coral Reefs of Jamaica'. *Jamaica Naturalist* 3.
Bryan, Patrick. 1973. 'Conflict and Reconciliation: The French Émigrés in Nineteenth Century Jamaica'. *JJ* 7:3.
Bryan, Patrick. 1991. *The Jamaican People 1880-1902: Race, Class and Social Control*. London: Macmillan.
Buckley, Roger. 1979. *Slaves in Red Coats. The British West India Regiments 1795-1818*. New Haven: Yale UP.
Buisseret, David and Jack Tyndale-Biscoe. 1969. *Historic Jamaica from the Air*. Barbados: Caribbean Universities Press.
Buisseret, David. 1971a. 'Edward D'Oyley'. *JJ* 5:1.
Buisseret, David. 1971b. *The Fortifications of Kingston 1566-1914*. Kingston: Bolivar Press.
Buisseret, David. 1975. 'The Windmills of St Thomas'. *JJ* 9:4.
Buisseret, David. 1980a. *Historic Architecture of the Caribbean*. Kingston: Heinemann.
Buisseret, David. 1980b. 'The Iron Bridge of Spanish Town'. *JJ* 44.
Buisseret, David. 1983. 'The French Invasion of Jamaica'. *JJ* 16:3.

Cabrera, Lydia. 1984. *La Medicina Popular de Cuba*. Miami: Ediciones Universal.
Cabrera, Lydia. 1992. *El Monte*. Miami: Ediciones Universal, 7th edition.
Cadbury, H.J. 1971. 'Quakers and the Earthquake at Port Royal, 1692'. *JHR VII*.
Caldwell, David L.K. 1966. *Marine and Freshwater Fishes of Jamaica*. Kingston: IOJ.
Calley, Malcolm J.C. 1965. *God's People: West Indian Pentecostal Sects in England*. Oxford: Oxford UP.
Campbell, Carl. 1996. 'Social and Economic Obstacles to the Development of Popular Education in Post-emancipation Jamaica, 1834-1865', in *Caribbean Freedom* edited by Hilary Beckles and Verene Shepherd. Princeton: Marcus Weiner.
Campbell, Horace. 1985. *Rasta and Resistance: from Marcus Garvey to Walter Rodney*. UK: Hansib.
Campbell, Joseph. 1989. *Historic Atlas of World Mythology, 2:3, Mythologies of the Primitive Planters: The Middle and Southern Americas*. Harper and Row.
Campbell, Mavis C. 1976. *The Dynamics of Change in a Slave Society: A Socio-political History of the Free Coloreds of Jamaica. 1800-1865*. Rutherford, N.J. Fairleigh Dickinson UP.
Campbell, Mavis C. 1990. *The Maroons of Jamaica 1655-1796*. Trenton, NJ: Africa World Press.
Campbell, Sadie. 1974. 'Folk Lore and Food Habits' and 'Corollary: "Bush Teas: A Cure-All"'. *JJ* 8:2 & 3.
Candler, John. 1850. 'A Good Friend in our midst'. *JHR* 3:2, 1959.

Carey, Beverly. 1970. *Portland and the Rio Grande Valley*. Montego Bay: Public Relations Advisory Service.

Carey, Beverly. 1997. *The Maroon Story*. Kingston: Agouti Press.

Cargill, Morris (ed.). 1965. *Ian Fleming Introduces Jamaica*. London: Andre Deutsch.

Caribbean Quarterly. 1995. The Indian Presence: Arrival and After. 41:1.

Carnegie, Charles V. (ed.). 1987. Afro-Caribbean Villages in Historical Perspective. *ACIJ Research Review* 2.

Carnegie, J. 1983. 'Cricket' in *Jamaica. Insight Guides* No. 16. edited by Hans Hoefer and Paul Zachs, Hong Kong and Kingston: APA Productions.

Carnegie, Jimmy. 1996. *Great Jamaican Olympians*. rev. ed. 1999. Kingston: LNH Publishers.

Carnegie, J., Hubert Lawrence, and Mike Henry. 1998. *Reggae Road to Soccer Glory*. Kingston: Kingston Publishers.

Carrington, Sean. 1993. *Wild Plants of Barbados*. London: Macmillan.

Carson, Peter. 1994. 'Cabinet-Making in Jamaica 1670-1870'. *The Jamaican*. December.

Carson, Peter. 2000. 'Jamaican Regency Furniture 1815-1840'. *The Jamaican Annual*.

Carter, Hazel. 1996a. 'The Language of Kumina and Beele Play'. *ACIJ Research Review 3*.

Carter, Hazel. 1996b. 'Annotated Kumina Lexicon'. *ACIJ Research Review 3*.

Cassidy, F.G. and R.B. LePage. 1967. *Dictionary of Jamaican English*. Cambridge: Cambridge UP.

Cassidy, Frederic G. 1971. *Jamaica Talk, Three Hundred Years of the English Language in Jamaica*. London: Macmillan.

Chamberlin, J. Edward. 1993. *Come Back to Me My Language: Poetry and the West Indies*. Urbana: University of Illinois Press.

Chang, Kevin O'Brien and Wayne Chen. 1998. *Reggae Routes: The Story of Jamaican Music*. Kingston: Ian Randle.

Chapman, Esther (ed.). 1958. *Pleasure Island: The Book of Jamaica*. Kingston: The Arawak Press.

Chevannes, Barry. 1989. 'Drop Pan and Folk Consciousness'. *JJ* 22:2.

Chevannes, Barry. 1994. *Rastafari Roots and Ideology*. Syracuse: Syracuse UP.

Chevannes, Barry (ed.). 1998. *Rastafari and other African-Caribbean World Views*. New Brunswick: Rutgers UP.

Chinsee, Helen. 1968. 'A Chinese in Jamaica'. *JJ* 2:1.

Chubb, L.J. 1975. 'Early History of Geology in Jamaica'. *JJ* 9:4.

Clarke, Colin G. 1975. *Kingston, Jamaica: Urban Development and Social Change 1692-1962*. Berkeley: University of California Press.

Clarke, Edith. 1957. *My Mother Who Fathered Me*. London: Allen and Unwin.

Clerk, Astley. 1975. 'The Music and Musical Instruments of Jamaica'. *JJ* 9:2-3.

Clerk, Astley. 1978. 'The Musical Instruments of the Arawaks'. *JJ* 11:3-4.

Clerk, Astley. 1985. 'Kingston Street Cries c. 1927 and something about their Criers'. *JJ* 18:2.

Coke, Thomas. 1808. *A Journal of the Rev Dr Coke's visit to Jamaica. . .* London 1789.

Collett, J.H. and Patrick Bowe. 1978. *Gardens of the Caribbean*. London: Macmillan.

Concannon, T.A.L.1965. 'The Great Houses of Jamaica', in *Ian Fleming Introduces Jamaica* edited by Morris Cargill. London: Andre Deutsch.

Concannon, T.A.L. 1967. 'Houses of Jamaica'. *JJ* 1:1.

Concannon, T.A.L. 1974. 'Kenilworth Ruins'. *JJ* 8:1.

Conniff, Michael L. 1985. *Black Labor on a White Canal. Panama 1904-1981*. Pittsburgh, Penn.: Pittsburgh UP.

Cooper, Carolyn. 1993. *Noises in the Blood: Orality, Gender and the 'Vulgar' Body of Jamaican Popular Culture*. London: Macmillan.

Cooper, Carolyn (ed.). 1998. *Reggae*. Special Issue SES 41:1.

Cotter, C.S. 1970. 'Sevilla Nueva: The Story of an Excavation'. *JJ* 4:2.

Courlander, Harold. 1973. *Haiti Singing*. New York: Cooper Square.

Cozier, Tony. 1995. 'Cricket: The National Religion'. *Insight Guide to Barbados*. Apa Publications.

Crahan, Margaret E. and Franklyn W. Knight (eds). 1979. *Africa and the Caribbean: The Legacies of a Link*. Baltimore: Johns Hopkins UP.

Craton, Michael and James Walvin. 1970. *A Jamaican Plantation: The History of Worthy Park 1670-1970*. London: W.H. Allen.

Craton, Michael. 1978. *Searching for the Invisible Man: Slaves and Plantation Life in Jamaica*. Cambridge, Mass: Harvard UP.

Crim, Keith (gen. ed.) 1981. *Abingdon Dictionary of Living Religions*. Nashville: Abingdon.

Cronon, E.D. 1955. *Black Moses: The Story of Marcus Garvey and the UNIA*. Madison: University of Wisconsin Press.

Crosby Jnr., Alfred W. 1972. *The Columbian Exchange. Biological and Cultural Consequences of 1492*. Westport: Greenwood Press.

Crosby Jnr., Alfred W. 1991. 'Metamorphosis of the Americas' in *Seeds of Change* edited by Herman J. Viola and Carolyn Margolis. Wash. DC: Smithsonian Institution Press.

Cundall, Frank. 1915. *Historic Jamaica*. Johnson Reprint 1971.

Curtin, Marguerite. 1984. 'The Kingston Parish Church', *JJ* 17:4.

Curtin, Philip D. 1955. *Two Jamaicas. The Role of Ideas in a Tropical Colony 1830-1865*. Cambridge: Harvard UP.

Curtin, Philip D. 1969. *The Atlantic Slave Trade: A Census*. Madison: University of Wisconsin Press.

Dallas, Robert Charles. 1803. *The History of the Maroons*. 2 vols. London.

Dance, Daryl C. 1985. *Folklore from Contemporary Jamaicans*. Knoxville: University of Tennessee Press.

Dancer, Dr Thomas. 1801. *The Medical Assistant; or Jamaica Practice of Physic*. Kingston.

Davidson, Marjorie. 1971. 'Ackees and Avocadoes'. *JJ* 5:4.

Davis, Stephen. 1984. *Bob Marley*. London: Panther.
Dawes, Kwame. 1999. *Natural Mysticism: Towards a New Reggae Aesthetic in Caribbean Writing*. Leeds: Peepal Tree Press.
D'Costa, Jean. 1975. *Escape to Last Man Peak*. UK: Longman.
D'Costa Jean and Barbara Lalla (eds). 1989. *Voices in Exile: Jamaican Texts of the 18th and 19th centuries*. Tuscaloosa and London: The University of Alabama Press.
Delapenha, Lindy. 1993. 'Understanding the Origins of Afternoon Tea, or A Beginners Guide to Cricket'. *Skywritings* 85.
Dello Strologo, Sergio. 1984. 'Devon House: House of Dreams'. *JJ* 17:2.
DeGoeje, C.H. 1943. *Philosophy, Initiation and Myths of the Indians of Guiana and Adjacent Countries*. Leiden: IAE 44.
Diesel, R., G. Bäuerle and P. Vogel. 1995. 'Cave breeding and froglet transport: a novel pattern of anuran brood care in the Jamaican frog, *Eleutherodactylus cundalli*'. *Copeia* 354-360.
Donaldson, Enid. 1993. *The Real Taste of Jamaica*. Kingston: Ian Randle.
Downer, Audrey and Robert Sutton. 1990. *Birds of Jamaica – a Photographic Field Guide*. NY: Cambridge UP.
Dunham, Katherine. 1946. *Journey to Accompong*. New York: Negro Universities Press, 1971.
Durant-Gonzalez. V. 1983. 'The Occupation of Higglering'. *JJ* 16:3.
Dutton, G. 1967. *The Hero as Murderer; The Life of Edward John Eyre*. Sydney and Melbourne: Collins and Cheshire.

Eaton, George. 1975. *Alexander Bustamante and Modern Jamaica*. Kingston: Kingston Publishers.
Ebanks, Roderick. 1984. 'Ma Lou and the Afro-Jamaican Pottery Tradition'. *JJ* 17:3.
Edwards, Bryan. 1794. *The History, Civil and Commercial of the British Colonies in the West Indies*. 2 vols. 2nd ed., London.
[Edwards, Bryan]. 1796. *The Proceedings of the Governor and Assembly of Jamaica in Regard to the Maroon Negroes*. Published by order of the Assembly. London.
Edwards, David. 1961. *An Economic Study of Small Farming in Jamaica*. Mona: UWI ISER.
Eisner, Gisela. 1961. *Jamaica 1830-1930*. Manchester: Manchester UP.
Eliade, Mircea. 1964. *Shamanism. Archaic Techniques of Ecstasy*. Princeton: Princeton UP.
Emery, Lynne. 1972. *Black Dance in the United States from 1619 to 1970*. Palo Alto: National Press Books.
Equiano, Olaudah. 1789. *The Interesting Narrative of the Life of Olaudah Equiano or Gustavus Vassa the African*. Abridged and edited by Paul Edwards. Heinemann, 1967.
Espinosa, Vásquez de, Antonio. 1628. *The West Indies*. (Trans. Charles Upson Clark). Wash, D.C.: Smithsonian Institution. 1948.
Esquemeling, A.O. 1678. *The Buccaneers of America*. London: Allen and Unwin, 1951.
Evans, H.L. 2001. *Inside Jamaican Schools*. Mona: The Press UWI.
Eyre, Alan. 1966. *The Botanic Gardens of Jamaica*. London: Andre Deutsch.
Eyre, L. Alan. 1972. *Geographic Aspects of Population Dynamics in Jamaica*. Florida Atlantic UP.
Eyre, L. Alan. 1973. 'Jack Mansong: Bloodshed or Brotherhood'. *JJ* 7:4.
Eyre, L. Alan. 1996. 'The Tropical Rainforests of Jamaica'. *JJ* 26:1.

Facey, Valerie (ed.). 1993. *Busha Browne's Indispensable Compendium of Traditional Jamaican Cookery*. Kingston: The Mill Press.
Facey, Valerie and Jackie Ranston. 1996. *The Founding of Sligoville*. Kingston: The Mill Press.
Farr, T.H. 1967. 'Jamaican Insects'. *JJ* 1:1.
Farr, T.H. 1970. 'Seven Spiders'. *JJ* 4:3.
Farr, T.H. 1983. 'Wild Pine Aquaria'. *JJ* 16:2.
Farr, T.H. 1984a. 'Land Animals of Jamaica'. *JJ* 17:1.
Farr, T.H. 1984b. 'Fireflies'. *JJ* 17:1.
Farr, T.H. 1990. 'Land Snails'. *JJ* 22:4
Fawcett, W. and A.B. Rendle. 1914-1936. *Flora of Jamaica*. London: British Museum.
Fewkes, J.W. 1907. *The Aborigines of Porto Rico and Neighbouring Islands*. Bureau of American Ethnology 25. Johnson reprints, 1970.
Fincham, Alan G. 1997. *Jamaica Underground. The Caves, Sinkholes and Underground Rivers of the Island*. Mona: The Press UWI.
Foner, Philip S. 1977. *Antonio Maceo: 'The Bronze Titan' of Cuba's Struggle for Independence*. New York and London: Monthly Review Press.
Ford-Smith, Honor. 2000. 'Performing the Nation: the pedagogy and politics of Jamaican Theatre 1972-1988'. Unpublished paper produced for Ontario Institute for Studies in Education. Toronto.
Fowler, Henry. 1968. 'A History of the Theatre in Jamaica'. *JJ* 2:1.
Francis-Jackson, Chester. 1995. *The Official Dancehall Dictionary*. Kingston: Kingston Publishers.
Fraser, Henry, Sean Carrington, Addinton Forde, and John Gilmore. 1990. *A-Z of Barbadian Heritage*. Kingston: Heinemann.
Fryer, Peter. 1984. *Staying Power: The History of Black People in Britain*. London: Pluto Press.
Fuson, Robert E. 1987. *The Log of Christopher Columbus*. Camden, Me, International Marine Publishing Co.

Galenson, David. 1981. *White Servitude in Colonial America: An Economic Analysis*. Cambridge: Cambridge UP.
García Arévalo, Manuel. 1977. *El Arte Taíno de la República Dominicana*. Santo Domingo: Museo del Hombre Dominicano.
Garraway, Eric and Audette J.A. Bailey. 1993. 'The Ecology and Conservation Biology of Jamaica's Endangered Giant Swallowtail Butterfly, Papilio Homerus'. *Jamaica Naturalist* 3.

Garvey, Amy Jacques. 1970. *Garvey and Garveyism.* New York: Collier Books.

'Garvey Centenary'. 1987. Special Issue, *JJ* 20:3.

Gastmann, Albert L. 1978. *Historical Dictionary of the French and Netherlands Antilles.* Metuchen: The Scarecrow Press.

Gayle, Clement. 1982. *George Liele: Pioneer Missionary to Jamaica.* Jamaica Baptist Union.

Georgian Society of Jamaica. n.d. c. 1970. *Falmouth 1791-1970.*

Genovese, Eugene D. 1976. *Roll Jordon Roll: The World the Slaves Made.* NY: Vintage Books.

Girvan, D.T.M. 1993. *Working Together for Development 1939-1968* compiled and edited by Norman Girvan. Kingston: IOJP.

Gloudon, Ancile and Cecily Tobisch. 1995. *Orchids of Jamaica.* Mona: The Press UWI.

Godfrey, David. 1998. *Reckoning with the Force: Stories of the Jamaica Constabulary Force in the 1950s.* Kingston: The Mill Press.

Goffe, Anthony. 1980. 'The Search for HMS Hinchinbrooke'. *JJ* 44.

Golding, John S.R. 1994. *Ascent to Mona: A Short History of Jamaican Medical Care.* Mona: Canoe Press.

Golesworthy, Maurice. 1988. *Encyclopedia of Boxing.* 8th ed. London: Robert Hole.

Goodwin, R.E. 1970. 'The ecology of Jamaican bats'. *J. Mamm.* 51:571-579.

Goodwin, William B. 1946. *Spanish and English Ruins in Jamaica.* Boston: Meador Publishing.

Gordon, Shirley C. 1998. *Our Cause for His Glory: Christianisation and Emancipation in Jamaica.* Mona: The Press UWI.

Gosse, Philip Henry. 1984. *Gosse's Jamaica 1844-45* edited by D.B. Stewart. Kingston: IOJP.

Goucher, C. 1990. 'John Reeder's Foundry: A Study of Eighteenth Century African-Caribbean Technology'. *JJ* 23:1.

GOJ. 1961. *Handbook of Jamaica.*

GOJ. 1971. *A National Physical Plan for Jamaica 1970-1990.*

GOJ. API. n.d. *The Geography of Jamaica.*

GOJ. API. 1972. *Religion in Jamaica.*

GOJ. Central Bureau of Statistics. 1946. *A Fact a Day About Jamaica.* Vol. 1.

GOJ. Geological Survey Department. 1973. *The Mineral Resources of Jamaica.*

GOJ. JIS. 1968. *The Banana Industry in Jamaica.*

GOJ. Ministry of Education. 1996. *Jamaica Education Statistics 1994-5.*

GOJ. Office of Disaster Preparedness. 1990. *Hurricanes.* Historical notes, National Library.

GOJ. STATIN. 1999a. *Statistical Yearbook of Jamaica 1998.*

GOJ. STATIN. 1999b. *Demographic Statistics 1999.*

Green, Lena. 1968. 'Uses of Gracilaria verrucosa "Irish Moss" '. *JJ* 2:1.

Gregory, Joe. 1964. 'Link with past is broken'. *Sunday Gleaner* Magazine, 12 January, p. 9.

Grohall, Gene and Margaret A.J. Jones. 1992. 'Sea Turtle Nesting'. *Jamaica Naturalist* 2:1.

Habekost, Christian. 1993. *Verbal Riddim. The Politics and Aesthetics of African-Caribbean Dub Poetry.* Cross/Cultures 10. Amsterdam/Atlanta: Rodopi.

Hagelberg, G.B. 1985. 'Sugar in the Caribbean – Turning Sunshine into Money', in *Caribbean Contours* edited by Sidney W. Mintz and Sally Price. Baltimore: Johns Hopkins UP.

Hall, D.G. 1953. 'Sir Charles Metcalfe', *CQ* 3:2.

Hall, D.G. 1959. *Free Jamaica 1838-65: An Economic History.* New Haven: Yale UP.

Hall, Douglas. 1974-75. 'Bountied European Immigration with Special Reference to the German Settlement at Seaford Town up to 1850'. Pt.1 *JJ* 8:4, 1974, Pt. 2 *JJ* 9:1, 1975.

Hall, Douglas (ed.). 1989. *In Miserable Slavery. Thomas Thistlewood in Jamaica.* London: Macmillan. The Press UWI, 1999.

Hall-Alleyne, Beverley. 1982. 'Asante Kotoko: The Maroons of Jamaica'. *ACIJ Newsletter* 7.

Hall-Alleyne, Beverley. 1996. 'An Ethnolinguistic Approach to Jamaican Botany'. *ACIJ Research Review* 3.

Hamilton, Beverley. 1991. 'The Legendary Marcus Garvey'. *JJ* 24:1.

Hamilton, B. St J. 1978. *Anthology of a Hero.* Kingston: Publications and Productions Ltd.

Handler, Jerome S. 1971. 'History of Arrowroot and Peasant Origins'. *Journal of Caribbean History* 2.

Handler, Jerome S. and Charlotte J. Frisbie. 1972. 'Aspects of Slave Life in Barbados: Music and its Cultural Context'. *Caribbean Studies* 11:4.

Handler, Jerome S. and Frederick W. Lange. 1978. *Plantation Slavery in Barbados: An Archaeological and Historical Investigation.* Cambridge, Mass: Harvard UP.

Hanna, W.J. 1988. 'Tourist Travel to Jamaica in the 1890s'. *JJ* 22:3.

Hanna, W.J. 1992. 'Early Days of Commercial Aviation in Jamaica'. *JJ* 24:2.

Hannau, Hans W. and Jeanne Garrard. n.d. *Flowers of the Caribbean.* Miami: Argos Inc.

Hargreaves, Dorothy and Bob Hargreaves. 1965. *Tropical Trees found in the Caribbean, South America, Central America, Mexico.* Kailua, Hawaii: Hargreaves Co.

Harrington, M.R. 1921. *Cuba Before Columbus.* New York: National Museum of the American Indian.

Harries, H.H. 1980. 'The Natural History of the Coconut'. *JJ* 44.

Harris, Wilson. 1981. 'History, Fable and Myth in the Caribbean and Guyana' in *Explorations: A Selection of Talks and Articles, 1966-1981.* Denmark: Dangaroo Press.

Hart, Ansell. 1953-1964. *Monthly Comments.* Newport, Jamaica.

Hart, Ansell. 1954. 'The Banana in Jamaica: Export Trade'. *SES* 3:2.

Hart, Ansell. 1972. *The Life of George William Gordon.* Kingston: IOJ.

Hart, Pansy Rae. 1993. 'Norman Manley – Out to Build a New Jamaica'. *JJ* 25:1.

Hart, Richard. 1980. *Slaves Who Abolished Slavery.* Vol. 1 *Blacks in Bondage.* Mona: UWI ISER.

Hart, Richard. 1985. *Slaves Who Abolished Slavery.*

Vol 2: *Blacks in Rebellion*, 1985. Mona: UWI ISER.
Hart, Richard. 1998. *From Occupation to Independence. A Short History of the Peoples of the English-Speaking Caribbean Region*. London: Pluto Press.
Hawkes, Alex D. 1974. *Illustrated Plants of Jamaica*. Kingston.
Hawkes, Alex D. and Brenda C. Sutton. 1974. *Wild Flowers of Jamaica*. Kingston: Collins Sangster.
Henderson, George E. 1931. *Goodness and Mercy. A Tale of a Hundred Years*. Kingston: Gleaner.
Henriques, Fernando. 1953. *Family and Colour in Jamaica*. London: McGibbon and Kee.
Henry, Adina. 1984. 'Bruckins Party' collected and transcribed by Laura Tanna. *JJ* 17:3.
Herskovits, M.J. 1958. *The Myth of the Negro Past*. Boston: Beacon Press.
Herskovits M.J. 1976. *Trinidad Village*. Octagon.
Herskovits, Melville J. and Francis S. Herskovits. 1936. *Suriname Folk-lore*. New York: Columbia UP.
Heuman, Gad. 1981. *Between Black and White. Race, Politics and the Free Coloureds in Jamaica. 1792-1865*. Westport, Conn.: Greenwood.
Heuman, Gad. 1994. *'The Killing Time'. The Morant Bay Rebellion in Jamaica*. London: Macmillan.
Higman, B.W. 1976. *Slave Population and Economy in Jamaica 1807-1834*. Cambridge: Cambridge UP.
Higman, B.W. 1979a. 'Slave Family Patterns in Trinidad', in *Africa and The Caribbean* edited by Margaret E. Crahan and Franklyn W. Knight. Baltimore: Johns Hopkins UP.
Higman, B.W. 1979b. 'Slavery Remembered: The Celebration of Emancipation in Jamaica'. *Journal of Caribbean History* 12.
Higman B.W. 1988. *Jamaica Surveyed, Plantation Maps and Plans of the eighteenth and nineteenth centuries*. Kingston: IOJP.
Higman, B.W. 1998. *Montpelier, Jamaica. A Plantation Community in Slavery and Freedom 1739-1912*. Mona: The Press UWI.
Hill, Errol. 1992. *The Jamaican Stage 1655-1900*. Amherst: University of Massachusetts Press.
Hill, Frank. 1975. *Bustamante and His Letters*. Kingston: Kingston Publishers.
Hill, Robert. 1983. 'Leonard P. Howell and Millenarian Visions in Early Rastafari'. *JJ* 16:1.
Hill, Robert (ed.). 1983-1990. *The Marcus Garvey Papers*, University of California Press. 7 vols.
Hoagland, D.B., G.R. Horst, and C.W. Kilpatrick. 1989. 'Biogeography and population biology of the mongoose in the West Indies', in C.A. Woods (ed.), *Biogeography of the West Indies*. Gainesville: Sandhill Crane Press.
Hodges, Ann. 1986. 'Thatch: Traditional Jamaican Building materials and techniques'. *JJ* 19:4.
Hodges, Ann. 1987. 'Lime and Earth: Traditional Jamaican Building Materials and Techniques'. *JJ* 20:1.
Hodges, Margaret (ed.). 1993. *Blue Mountain Guide*. Natural History Society of Jamaica.
Hogg, Donald W. 1961. 'Magic and "Science" in Jamaica'. *Caribbean Studies* 1.
Holm, John. 1988. *Pidgins and Creoles*, Vols. 1 and 2. Cambridge Language Surveys. Cambridge: Cambridge UP.
Holzberg, Carol S. 1987. *Minorities and Power in a Black Society: The Jewish Community of Jamaica*. New York: North-South Publishers.
Honychurch, Penelope N. 1986. *Caribbean Wild Plants and their Uses*. London: Macmillan.
Hopkin, John Barton. 1978. 'Music in the Jamaican Pentecostal Churches'. *JJ* 42.
Hopwood, Stephen. 1971. 'Three Hundred Years of Postal Service in Jamaica'. *JJ* 5: 2-3.
Hose, H.R. 1950. *The Geology and Mineral Resources of Jamaica*. Colonial Geology and Mineral Resources. Kingston: IOJ reprint, 1951.
Hoyte, Clyde. 1975. *The Life and Times of Willie Henry*. Kingston, IOJ.
Human Rights Watch. 1990. *Prison Conditions in Jamaica*: An Americas Watch Report.
Humfrey, Michael. 1975. *Sea Shells of the West Indies*. London: Collins.
Hurston, Zora Neale. 1938. *Tell My Horse*. NY: Harper and Row, 1990.
Huxley, Anthony. 1978. *Plant and Planet*, rev. ed. UK: Penguin.
Huxley, Anthony. 1991. *Green Inheritance, The World Wildlife Fund Book of Plants*. Canada: Grolier Ltd.
Hyatt, Charles. 1989. *When me was a Boy*. Kingston: IOJP.

Im Thurn, Everard F. 1883. *Among the Indians of Guiana*. New York: Dover, 1967.
Ingledew, John. 1990. 'Stamps of Jamaica'. *JJ* 23:1.
Ingram, K.E. 1992. 'Furniture and the Plantation: Further Light on the West Indian Trade of an English Furniture Firm in the Eighteenth Century'. *Furniture History*. The Journal of the Furniture History Society. XXVIII.
Issa, Suzanne. 1994. *'Mr Jamaica': Abe Issa. A Pictorial Biography*. Kingston: Suzanne Issa.

Jackson, Bruce. (ed.). 1967. *The Negro and his Folklore in Nineteenth Century Periodicals*. Austin and London: University of Texas Press.
Jackson, Trevor. 1983. Geological Society of Jamaica. *Daily Gleaner*, letter, 19 February.
Jacobs H.P. 1973. *Sixty Years of Change*. Kingston: IOJ.
Jacobs, H.P. 1976. *A Short History of Kingston*. Jamaica: Ministry of Education.
Jacobs, Charles C. 1980. 'Jamaica and the Cuban Ten Years War 1868-1878'. *JJ* 44.
Jamaica Agricultural Society. 1954. *The Farmer's Guide*. Kingston: JAS.
Jamaica Alphabet. 1990. Jamrite Publications.
'Jamaica Almanack 1879-80'. 1986. *JJ* 19:1.
Jamaica Chamber of Commerce *Journal*. 1970. 26:1
Jamaica Cultural Development Commission. 1988. *The Jamaica Festival Story* 25th anniversary publication.
Jamaica School of Music. 1972. 'Traditional Instruments Exhibition'. *JJ* 6:2.
Jamaica School of Music. 1976. Jamaican Traditional Music and Dance (record with notes). *JJ* 10:1.

James, C.L.R. 1938. *The Black Jacobins*. Vintage, 1963.
Jane, Cecil (Trans.) 1960. *The Journal of Christopher Columbus*. New York: Clarkson N. Potter.
Jeffrey-Smith, May. 1972. *Bird Watching in Jamaica*. Kingston: Bolivar Press.
Jekyll, Walter (ed.). 1907. *Jamaican Song and Story*. New York: Dover Publications 1966.
Jobes, Gertrude. 1961. *Dictionary of Mythology, Folklore and Symbols*. Metuchen: The Scarecrow Press.
Johnson, Alfred N. 1964. *Jamaica: A review of the Nation's Postal History and Postage*. The American Philatelic Society.
Johnson, Anthony. 1993. *Kingston: Portrait of a City*. Kingston: TeeJay Limited.
Johnson, Anthony. 1995. *Ocho Rios, St Ann. Portrait of the Garden Parish*. Kingston: TeeJay Ltd.
Johnston, James. c. 1903 *Jamaica: the New Riviera*. London: Cassell & Co.
Jones, Evan. 1986. 'Song of the Banana Man' in *The Penguin Book of Caribbean Verse in English* edited by Paula Burnett. UK: Penguin.
Joseph, C.L. 1971. 'The British West Indies Regiment 1914-1918'. *Journal of Caribbean History* 2.

Karras, Alan L. 1992. *Sojourners in the Sun: Scottish Migrants in Jamaica and the Chesapeake 1740-1800*. Ithaca: Cornell UP.
Karsten, Raphael. 1926. *The Civilization of the South American Indians*. New York: Knopf.
Katzin, Margaret Fisher. 1959. 'The Jamaican Country Higgler'. *SES* 8:4.
Kerr, Madeline. 1952. *Personality and Conflict in Jamaica*. Liverpool: Liverpool UP.
Kerr, Rhema. 1996. 'Jamaica's Sea Turtles'. *JJ* 26:1.
Kightly, Charles. 1986. *The Customs and Ceremonies of Britain. An Encyclopedia of Living Traditions*. London: Thames and Hudson.
Kingsbury, John M. 1988. *200 conspicuous, unusual, or economically important tropical plants of the Caribbean*. Ithaca: Bullbrier Press.
Kingston and St Andrew Corporation. 1952. *Sesquicentennial anniversary of the granting of a charter to the City of Kingston, 1802-1952*.
Kiple, Kenneth F. 1984. *The Caribbean Slave: A Biological History*. Cambridge: Cambridge UP.
Kopytoff, Barbara K. 1976. 'The Development of Maroon Ethnicity'. *CQ* 22:2-3.
Kopytoff, Barbara K. 1976. 'Jamaica Maroon Political Organizations: The Effects of the Treaties'. *SES* 25:2.
Kurlansky, Mark. 1997. *Cod: A Biography of the Fish that Changed the World*. Toronto: Vintage Canada.

Laguerre, Michael. 1987. *Afro-Caribbean Folk Medicine*. Granby, Mass: Bergin and Garvey.
Lalla, Barbara. 1981. 'Quaco Sam: A Relic of Archaic Jamaican Speech'. *JJ* 45.
Lalla, Barbara and Jean D'Costa. 1990. *Language in Exile: Three Hundred Years of Jamaican Creole*. Tuscaloosa, Alabama: University of Alabama Press.
Lalla, Barbara. 1996. *Defining Jamaican Fiction: Marronage and the Discourses of Survival*. Tuscaloosa, Alabama: University of Alabama Press.
Lanigan, Mrs. 1844. *Antigua and the Antiguans*, 2 vols, London.
Langford, Mary Jones. 1997. *The Fairest Isle: History of Jamaica Friends*. Richmond, Ind.: Friends United Press.
Larousse Encyclopedia of Mythology. 1987. New York: Crescent.
Las Casas, Bartolomé de. 1552. *Brevissima relación de la destrucción de las Indias. The Devastation of the Indies*. A Brief Account (Trans. Herma Briffault). New York: Seabury Press 1974.
Lathrap, Donald W. 1970. *The Upper Amazon*. New York: Praeger.
Latin American-Caribbean Centre (LACC) UWI, Mona. 2000. 'West Indian Participation in the construction of the Panama Canal'. Proceedings of symposium held at UWI, Mona, Jamaica, 15-17 June 2000.
Laurence, K.O. 1971. *Immigration into the West Indies in the Nineteenth Century*. Barbados: Caribbean Universities Press.
Leach, Maria and Jerome Fried (eds.). 1972. *Standard Dictionary of Folklore, Mythology and Legend*. New York: Funk and Wagnalls.
Leader, Alfred. 1907. *Through Jamaica with a Kodak*. London: Bristol J. Wright & Co.
Leaf, Earl. 1948. *Isles of Rhythm*. New York: A.S. Barnes.
Lecky, T.P. 1996. *Cattle and I: An Autobiography*. Kingston: Ian Randle.
Lee, Easton. 1998. *From Behind the Counter: Poems from a Rural Jamaican Experience*. Kingston: Ian Randle.
Lee Tom Yin. 1963. *The Chinese in Jamaica*. Kingston: Chung San News.
LePage, R.B. and David DeCamp (eds.). 1960. *Jamaican Creole. Creole Language Studies* 1. London: Macmillan.
Lethbridge, John. 1996. *The Yachtsman's Guide to Jamaica*. Jamaica: Zone Publishing.
Leslie, Charles. 1740. *A New History of Jamaica*. London.
Lévi-Strauss, Claude. 1955. *Tristes Tropiques* (Trans. John and Doreen Weightman). Atheneum 1974.
Lévi-Strauss, Claude. 1966. *Mythologies: From Honey to Ashes*. New York: Harper and Row. 1973.
Levy, Jacqueline. 1972. 'Chinese Indentured Immigration to Jamaica during the latter part of the nineteenth century'. Paper presented to the fourth conference of Caribbean Historians. Mona, Jamaica.
Lewin, Olive. n.d. 'An Old Man Dies, a Book is Lost'. *Jamaican Folkart*, IOJ.
Lewin, Olive. 1968. 'Jamaican Folk Music'. *CQ* 14:1 & 2.
Lewin, Olive. 1970. 'Folk Music of Jamaica: An Outline for Classification'. *JJ* 4:2.
Lewin, Olive. 1973. *Forty Folk Songs of Jamaica*. Wash. DC: Organization of American States.
Lewin, Olive. 1974a. *Brown Gal in de Ring*. Oxford: Oxford UP.
Lewin, Olive. 1974b. 'Helena'. *JJ* 8:2 & 3.
Lewin, Olive. 1984. 'Emancipation songs and festivities'. *JJ* 17:3.
Lewin, Olive. 1994. 'Music on that long, rocky

"freedom road" '. Spotlight on Music, *Sunday Gleaner*, 31 July.
Lewin, Olive. 1998. 'Traditional Jamaican Music: Mento'. *JJ* 26:3.
Lewin, Olive. 2000. *Rock it Come Over: The Folk Music of Jamaica*. Mona: The Press UWI.
Lewis, C.B. 1976. 'Judgement Cliff'. *JJ* 10:2.
Lewis, Gordon K. 1983. *Main Currents in Caribbean Thought*. Kingston: Heinemann.
Lewis, Leslie. 1972. *English Commemorative Sculpture in Jamaica*. Kingston: JHR monograph 9.
Lewis, Matthew Gregory. 1818. *Journal of a West-India Proprietor*. London: Murray, 1834, 1845.
Lewis, Rupert and Patrick Bryan. 1988. *Garvey, His Work and Impact*. Mona: UWI ISER.
Linyard, Fred. 1969. 'The Moravians in Jamaica'. *JJ* 3:1.
Lomax, Alan, J.D. Elder, and Bess Lomax Hawes. 1997. *Brown Girl in the Ring: An Anthology of Song Games from the Eastern Caribbean*. New York: Pantheon.
Long, Edward. 1774. *The History of Jamaica*. 3 vols. London.
Look Lai, Walton. 1998. *The Chinese in the West Indies, 1806-1995: A Documentary History*. Mona: The Press UWI.
Lopez-Baralt, Mercedes. 1976. *El mito Taíno*. Rio Piedras: Ediciones Huracán.
Lovén, Sven. 1935. *Origin of the Tainan Culture, West Indies*. Göteborg: Elanders Bokfryckeri Äkfiebolag.
Lowe, H.I.C. 1972. 'Jamaican Folk Medicine'. *JJ* 6:2.
Lowe, H.I.C. 1977. 'Periwinkle: From Folklore to Super-medicine'. *JJ* 11:1 & 2.

Macmillan, Allister. 1922. *The Red Book of the West Indies*. London: W.H. & L. Collingridge.
Macmillan, Mona. 1957. *Land of Look Behind – A Study of Jamaica*. London: Faber & Faber.
Madden, Robert R. 1835. *A Twelve Month's Residence in the West Indies During the Transition from Slavery to Apprenticeship*. 2 vols. London.
Mahabir, Kumar. 1992. *Caribbean East Indian Recipes*. Trinidad: Chakra Publishing House.
Mahon, R. and K. Aiken. 1977. 'The establishment of the North American Bullfrog, *Rana catesbeiana* (*Amphibia, Anura, Ranidae*) in Jamaica'. *J. Herpetol.* 11.
Manley, Michael. 1995. *A History of West Indian Cricket*. Kingston: Ian Randle.
Manley, Norman Washington. 1993. Centenary Issue. *JJ* 25:1.
Manley, Norman W. 1973. 'The Autobiography'. *JJ* 7:1
Manley, Rachel. 1996. *Drumblair*. Kingston: Ian Randle.
Mansingh, Lakshmi and Ajai Mansingh. 1976. 'Indian Heritage in Jamaica'. *JJ* 10: 2-4.
Mansingh, Ajai and Laxmi Mansingh. 1995. 'Hosay and its Creolization'. *CQ* 41:1.
Mansingh, Laxmi and Ajai Mansingh. 1999. *Home Away from Home: 150 years of Indian Presence in Jamaica 1845-1995*. Kingston: Ian Randle.
Marks, Jeannette. 1938. *The Family of the Barretts: A Colonial Romance*. New York: Macmillan.
Markus, Julia. 1995. *Dared and Done: The Marriage of Elizabeth Barrett and Robert Browning*. New York: Knopf.
Marsala, Vincent John. 1972. *Sir John Peter Grant Governor of Jamaica 1866-1874*. Kingston: IOJ.
Marshall, W. Taylor. 1952. 'Cactus' in *Guide to Jamaica* edited by Philip P. Olley. Kingston: Tourist Development Board.
Martin, Tony. 1976. *Race First: The Ideological and Organizational Struggles of Marcus Garvey and the UNIA*. Westport: Greenwood Press.
Marx, Robert F. 1967a. 'The Last Day of Port Royal'. *JJ* 1:1.
Marx, Robert F. 1967b. *Pirate Port: The Story of the Sunken City of Port Royal*. Cleveland: World Publishing.
Mathewson, R. Duncan. 1972. 'Jamaican Ceramics: An Introduction to 18th century Folk Pottery in the West African Tradition'. *JJ* 6:2.
Mathurin, Lucille. 1975. *The Rebel Woman in the British West Indies during Slavery*. Kingston: ACIJ IOJ.
Matley, Charles Alfred. 1951. *Geology and Physiography of the Kingston District*. Kingston: IOJ.
Mbiti, John S. 1975. *Introduction to African Religion*. London: Heinemann.
McKay, Claude. 1933. *Banana Bottom*. NY: Harcourt Brace Jovanovich, 1961.
McKay, Claude. 1979. *My Green Hills of Jamaica*. Kingston: Heinemann.
Mercatante, Anthony S. 1988. *The Facts on File Encyclopedia of World Mythology and Legend*. New York and Oxford: Facts on File.
Mendes, Judith. 1994. 'Coral Reefs and Coastal Pollution'. *JJ* 25:2.
Mico College 1893, 1896. *Folklore Collection*. National Library of Jamaica.
Miller, Errol. 1989. 'Educational Development in Independent Jamaica', in *Jamaica in Independence* edited by Rex Nettleford. Kingston: Heinemann.
Mills, J.J. 1969. *His Own Account of His Life and Times* edited by R.N. Murray. Kingston: Collins and Sangster.
Milne-Home, Pamela. 1890. *Mamma's Black Nurse Stories: West Indian Folklore*. Edinburgh: Blackwood.
Mintz, Sidney W. 1976. 'From Plantations to Peasantries in the Caribbean', in *An Anthropological Approach to the Caribbean Past* edited by Sidney W. Mintz and Richard Price. ISHI.
Mintz, Sidney W. 1991. 'Pleasure, Profit and Satiation', in *Seeds of Change* edited by Herman J. Viola and Carolyn Margolis. Wash. DC: Smithsonian Institution Press.
Mintz, Sidney W. and Douglas Hall. 1960. *Origins of the Jamaican Internal Marketing System*. Yale University Publications in Anthropology 57.
Mintz, Sidney W. and Sally Price (eds.). 1985. *Caribbean Contours*. Baltimore: Johns Hopkins UP.
Montejo, Esteban. 1970. *Autobiography of a Runaway Slave*. UK: Penguin Books.
Moore, Brian L. 1995. *Cultural Power, Resistance and Pluralism. Colonial Guyana 1838-1900*. Mona: The Press UWI.
Moore, Joseph G. 1953. 'Religion of Jamaican

Negroes: A Study of Afro-Jamaican Acculturation'. Unpublished Ph.D. dissertation, Northwestern University.

Morales Padron, F. 1952. *Jamaica Española*. Seville: Escuela de Estudios Hispano-Americanos de Seville.

Mordecai, Sir John. 1968. *The West Indies: The Federal Negotiations*. London: Allen and Unwin.

Mordecai, Martin. 1984. 'Cinchona: "The Nearest Place to Heaven" '. *JJ* 17:2.

Mordecai, Martin. 1991. 'The Challenge of Media Divestment and State Policies: Regulating the Electronic Media Landscape in Jamaica 1950-1990'. Unpublished paper.

Mordecai, Martin and Pamela Mordecai. 2001. *Culture and Customs of Jamaica*. Westport: Greenwood Press.

Moreton, J.B. 1793. *West India Customs and Manners*. London.

Morgan, Jacqueline. 1979. 'Coins of Jamaica', eight-part series, *Sunday Gleaner*, June-July.

Morgan, Jacqueline. 1984. 'The Advent of the Christian Quattie'. *JJ* 17:3.

Morris, James. 1970. 'Eyre: Between Duty and Murder'. *Encounter*, July.

Morris, Mervyn. 1986. 'Anancy and Andrew Salkey'. *JJ* 19:4.

Morris, Mervyn. 1999. *Is English We Speaking and Other Essays*. Kingston: Ian Randle.

Morris-Brown, Vivien. 1993. *The Jamaica Handbook of Proverbs*. Mandeville: Island Heart Publishers.

Morrissey, Carol. 1983. 'Trams and the Tramway Era in Jamaica'. *JJ* 16:4.

Morrissey, Mike. 1983. *Our Island, Jamaica*. London: Collins Educational.

Morrison, Samuel Eliot. 1955. *Christopher Columbus, Mariner*. New York: Mentor Books.

Munro, J.L. 1969. 'The Sea Fisheries of Jamaica: Past, Present and Future'. *JJ* 3:3.

Murphy, Veronica and Rosemary Crill. 1991. *Tie-dyed Textiles of India*. New York: Rizzoli in association with the Victoria and Albert Museum.

Murray, Lorraine (ed.). 2000. *The Jamaican*: special Tourism issue.

Murray, Tom. 1953. *Folk Songs of Jamaica*. Oxford: Oxford UP.

Murrell, N.S., W.D. Spencer, and A.A. McFarlane (eds.). 1998. *Chanting Down Babylon. The Rastafari Reader*. Kingston: Ian Randle.

Musical Instruments of the World. 1976. An Illustrated Encyclopedia by the Diagram Group. New York: Facts on File.

National Library of Jamaica. 1983. 'The National Library of Jamaica: Storehouse of the Nation's Memory'. *JJ* 16:2.

Natural History Society of Jamaica: 1946. *Glimpses of Jamaican Natural History*. 2. Kingston: IOJ.

Natural History Society of Jamaica. 1949. *Glimpses of Jamaican Natural History*. 1. (2nd ed.) Kingston: IOJ.

Nettleford, Rex. 1969. *Roots and Rhythms: Jamaica's National Dance Theatre*. London: Andre Deutsch.

Nettleford, Rex (ed.). 1977. *Manley and the New Jamaica: Selected Speeches and Writings*. London: Longman.

Nettleford, Rex. 1978. *Caribbean Cultural Identity: The Case of Jamaica*. Kingston: IOJ.

Nettleford, Rex. 1986. *Dance Jamaica: Cultural Definition and Artistic Discovery*. New York: Grove Press.

Nettleford, Rex. 1993. 'Fifty Years of the Jamaican Pantomime 1941-1991'. *JJ* 24:3.

Newman, A.J. 1968. 'The Story of Mico College'. *JJ* 2:2.

Newton, Velma. 1984. *The Silver Men. West Indian Labour Migration to Panama 1850-1914*. Mona: UWI ISER.

North, Marianne. 1892. *Recollections of a Happy Life*. 2nd. ed. London: Macmillan.

Nugent, Maria. 1839. *Lady Nugent's Journal of her Residence in Jamaica from 1801 to 1805* edited by Philip Wright. Kingston: IOJ 1966.

Nunley, John W. and Judith Bettelheim. 1988. *Caribbean Festival Arts*. Seattle: University of Washington Press.

O'Callaghan, Evelyn. 1993. *Woman Version: Theoretical Approaches to West Indian Fiction by Women*. London: Macmillan.

Ogilvie, Dan. 1954. *History of the Parish of Trelawny*. Kingston: United Printers.

O'Gorman, Pamela. 1986. 'Jamaican Music: Cultural Modes and Composers'. *JJ* 19:1.

O'Gorman, Pamela. 1987a. 'From Field to Platform: Jamaican Folk Music in Concert'. Part 1, *JJ* 20:1. Part 2, *JJ* 20:2.

O'Gorman, Pamela. 1987b. 'Jamaica School of Music'. *JJ* 20:1

O'Gorman, Pamela. 1987c. 'On Reggae and Rastafarianism – and a Garvey Prophecy'. *JJ* 20:3.

O'Gorman, Pamela. 1989a. ' "Gilbert" Songs'. *JJ* 22:2.

O'Gorman, Pamela. 1989b. 'Jonah: An Eighteenth Century Jamaican Oratorio'. *JJ* 22:4.

O'Gorman, Pamela. 1991. 'Drumming in Jamaica: Marjorie Whylie's contribution'. *JJ* 24:1.

Oliver, William L.R. 1983. 'Looking for Conies'. *JJ* 16:2.

Oliver, William L.R. 1986. 'Nanka or Yellow snake: A Jamaican Boa'. *JJ* 19:2.

Olivier, Lord. 1936. *Jamaica the Blessed Island*. London: Faber.

Olley, Phillip (ed.). 1952. *Guide to Jamaica*. Kingston: Tourist Development Board.

Olsen, Fred. 1974. *On the Trail of the Arawaks*. Norman: University of Oklahoma Press.

Oman, Carola. 1996. *Nelson*. Annapolis: Annapolis Naval Institute Press.

Opie, Ione. 1992. *A Dictionary of Superstitions*. Oxford: Oxford UP.

Osborne, Francis J. 1971. 'Ysassi: Last Spanish Governor of Jamaica'. *JJ* 5:1.

Osborne, Francis J. 1988. *History of the Catholic Church in Jamaica*. Chicago: Loyola UP.

Oviedo y Valdés, Gonzalo Fernández de. 1851-55. *Historia general y natural de las indias*. 4 vols.

Natural History of the West Indies (Trans. Sterling A. Stoudemire). Chapel Hill: University of North Carolina Press, 1959.

Owen, J. 1976. *Dread: The Rastafarians of Jamaica*. Kingston: Sangster's.

Paget, Hugh. 1954. 'The Free Village System in Jamaica'. *CQ* 1:4.

Parboosingh, Ivan K. 1985. 'An Indo-Jamaican Beginning: A Fragment of Autobiography'. *JJ* 18:2.

Parkes, E.T. and R. Stewart (Comp). 1999. *Jamaica Seismic Network Catalogue of Located Events 1976 and 1998*. Earthquake Unit, UWI.

Parrinder, E.G. 1961. *West African Religion*. London: SPCK.

Parrinder, E.G. 1967. *African Mythology*. London: Hamlyn.

Parry, John H. and Robert G. Keith. 1984. *New Iberian World: The Caribbean*. Vol. 2. New York: Times Books.

Patterson, James B. 1964. 'Fishing in Jamaica'. 9th International Game Fishing Conference, Runaway Bay Jamaica, 21 November.

Patterson, Orlando. 1973. *The Sociology of Slavery*. Kingston: Sangster's.

Patterson, Orlando. 1982. *Slavery and Social Death*. Cambridge, Mass.: Harvard UP.

Patterson, Patricia and Maxine McDonnough. 1997. *Edward Rasheed Hanna: The man and his times 1894-1978*. Kingston: Ian Randle.

Patteson, Richard F. 1998. *Caribbean Passages: A Critical Perspective on New Fiction from the West Indies*. Boulder: Lynne Rienner.

Pawson, Michael and David Buisseret. 1975. *Port Royal, Jamaica*. Oxford: Oxford UP.

Payne, Nellie. 1990. ' "Grenada Mas" 1928-1988'. *CQ* 36:3 & 4.

Perkins, Lilly G. 1969. 'Duppy Plants in Jamaica'. *JJ* 3:1.

Phillippo, James Mursell. 1843. *Jamaica: Its Past and Present State*. London.

Pietersz, J.L. 1938. Letter to the *Daily Gleaner* 20 April.

Pigou, Elizabeth. 1987a. 'Western Responses to Death in a Jamaican Context'. *JJ* 20:2.

Pigou, Elizabeth. 1987b. 'A Note on Afro-Jamaican Beliefs and Rituals'. *JJ* 20:2.

Pinto, G. de Sola and Anghelin Phillips. 1982. *Jamaican Houses*. Montego Bay: De Sola Pinto Publishers.

Pollard, Velma. 1993. *From Jamaican Creole to Standard English: A Handbook for Teachers*. New York: Caribbean Research Center, Medgar Evers College, CUNY, New York.

Pollard, Velma. 1994. *Dread Talk: The Language of Rastafari*. Mona: Canoe Press.

Pollard, Velma. 1995. 'A Language or Languages for Jamaica'. *Vistas*. 2:4, December.

Porter, Anthony R.D. 1990. *Jamaica: A Geological Portrait*. Kingston: IOJP.

Post, Ken. 1978. *Arise Ye Starvelings: The Jamaican Labour Rebellion of 1938 and its Aftermath*. The Hague: Martinus Nijhoff.

Poupeye-Rammelaere, Veerle. 1991. 'Garveyism and Garvey. Iconography in the Visual Arts of Jamaica'. *JJ* 24:1, 24:2.

Poupeye-Rammelaere, Veerle. 1995. 'A Concise Guide to Publications on Jamaican Art'. *Tribute to David Boxer: Twenty Years at the National Gallery of Jamaica 1975-1996*. Kingston: NG and IOJP.

Poupeye, Veerle. 1998. *Caribbean Art*. London: Thames and Hudson.

Powell, Dulcie. 1972. *The Botanic Garden, Liguanea, with a revision of Hortus Eastensis*. Kingston: IOJ.

Powell, Dulcie. 1973. *The Voyage of the Plant Nursery HMS Providence 1791-1793*. Kingston: IOJ.

Powell, Dulcie. 1974. 'The Preservation of Fern Gully'. *JJ* 8:2 & 3.

Price, Richard (ed.). 1973. *Maroon Societies*. New York: Anchor Books.

Prince, Nancy. 1850. 'A Narrative of the Life and Travels of Mrs Nancy Prince' in *Collected Black Women's Narratives* edited by Anthony G. Barthelemy. Oxford: Oxford UP 1988.

Proctor, George R. 1968. 'Jamaican Aquatic Plants'. *JJ* 2:3.

Proctor, George R. 1972. 'Ferns'. *JJ* 6:1.

Proctor, G.R. 1985. *Ferns of Jamaica*. London: British Museum (Natural History).

Puckett, N.N. 1926. *Folk Beliefs of the Southern Negro*. New York: Dover 1969.

Raboteau, Albert. 1978. *Slave Religion*. New York: Oxford UP.

Radin, Paul. 1942. *The Indians of South America*. New York: Doubleday.

Raffaele, H.A. et al. 1998. *A Guide to the Birds of the West Indies*. Princeton: Princeton UP.

Ramchand, Kenneth. 1970. *The West Indian Novel and its Background*. London: Faber.

Rampini, Charles. 1873. *Letters from Jamaica the Land of Streams and Woods*. Edinburgh.

Ranston, Jackie. 1972. *The Best of Bustamante*. Kingston: Twin Guinep.

Ranston, Jackie. 1993. 'Jamaica's Horse-Breeding Heritage'. *Skywritings* 85.

Ranston, Jackie. 1998. *Lawyer Manley*. Vol.1: *First Time Up*. Mona: The Press UWI.

Rashford, John. 1984. 'Plants, Spirits, and the meaning of "John" in Jamaica'. *JJ* 17:2.

Rashford, John. 1985. 'The Cotton Tree and the Spiritual Realm in Jamaica'. *JJ* 18:1.

Rashford, John. 1988a. 'Packy Tree, Spirits, and Duppy Birds'. *JJ* 21:3.

Rashford, John. 1988b. 'Leaves of Fire: Jamaica's Crotons'. *JJ* 21:4.

Rashford, John. 1989. 'Barringtonia'. *JJ* 22:2.

Rashford, John. 1993a. 'The Star Apple'. *JJ* 24:1.

Rashford, John. 1993b. 'Arawak, Spanish, and African Contributions to Jamaica's Settlement Vegetation'. *JJ* 24:3.

Rashford, John. 1995a. 'The Past and Present Uses of Bamboo in Jamaica'. *Economic Botany* 49:4.

Rashford, John. 1995b. ' "Those that do not smile will kill me": The Ethnobotany of the Ackee in Jamaica'. Paper presented at the 1995 meeting of the Society for Economic Botany, September 28.

Rastafari. 1985. CQ Monograph.

Rattray, R.S. 1927. *Religion and Art in Ashanti*. Oxford: Oxford UP.

Rawlins, S.C., Peter Figueroa, and Marcia Mundle. 1988. 'Malaria: Past Scourge or Continued Threat?' *JJ* 20:4.

Reckord, Verena. 1977. 'Rastafarian Music: An Introductory Study'. *JJ* 11:1 & 2.

Reckord, Verena. 1982. 'Reggae, Rastafarianism and Cultural Identity'. *JJ* 46.

Reichel-Dolmatoff, Gerardo. 1971. *Amazonian Cosmos*. Chicago: University of Chicago Press.

Reichel-Dolmatoff, Gerardo. 1975. *The Shaman and the Jaguar*. Philadelphia: Temple UP.

Reichel-Dolmatoff, Gerardo. 1978. *Beyond the Milky Way*. Los Angeles: UCLA Latin American Center.

Reid, C.S. 1983. 'Early Baptist Beginnings'. *JJ* 16:2.

Reid, V.S. 1949. *New Day*. NY: Knopf.

Reid, Jane. 1985. 'Trafalgar House'. *JJ* 18:2.

Richards, Tereza. 1999. *Bibliography on Reggae, Rastafari and Jamaican Culture*. CQ Monograph.

Rickford, John, ed. 1978. *A Festival of Guyanese Words*. Georgetown: University of Guyana.

Roberts, George W. 1957. *The Population of Jamaica*. Cambridge: Cambridge UP.

Roberts, John Storm. 1972. *Black Music of Two Worlds*. New York: Praeger.

Roberts, Kenneth and Philip Shackleton. 1983. *The Canoe: A History of the Craft from Panama to the Arctic*. Toronto: Macmillan Canada.

Roberts, W. Adolphe. 1955. *Jamaica: The Portrait of an Island*. New York: Coward-McCann.

Robertson, Diane. 1982. *Jamaican Herbs, Nutritional and Medicinal Values*. Kingston: Jamaica Herbs Ltd.

Robertson, Diane. 1990. *Live Longer Look Younger with Herbs*. Kingston: Stationery and School Supplies Ltd.

Robertson, E. Arnot. 1959. *The Spanish Town Papers*. London: Cresset Press.

Robertson, Glory. 1985. 'Some Early Jamaican Postcards, their Photographers and Publishers'. *JJ* 18:1.

Robinson, Carey. 1969. *The Fighting Maroons of Jamaica*. Kingston: Collins Sangster.

Robinson, Carey. 1987. *Fight for Freedom*. Kingston: Kingston Publishers.

Robotham, Donald. 1981. *The 'Notorious Riots': The socio-economic and political bases of Paul Bogle's Revolt*. Mona: UWI ISER.

Rodney, Walter. 1970. *A History of the Upper Guinea Coast 1545-1800*. Oxford: Oxford UP.

Rohlehr, Gordon. 1992a. *My Strangled City and other essays*. Port-of-Spain: Longman Trinidad.

Rohlehr, Gordon. 1992b. *The Shape of that Hurt and other essays*. Port-of-Spain: Longman Trinidad.

Ross, Frank. 1985. 'Aquaculture in Jamaica'. *JJ* 18:4.

Roth, Walter E. 1901. *An Inquiry into the Animism and Folklore of the Guiana Indians*. Wash. DC: Bureau of American Ethnology 13. Johnson Reprints 1970.

Rouse, Irving. 1992. *The Tainos: Rise and Decline of the People who Greeted Columbus*. New Haven: Yale UP.

Roy, Namba. 1961. *Black Albino*. UK: Longman, 1986.

Rubin, Vera and Lambros Comitas. 1976. *Ganja in Jamaica: The Effects of Marijuana Use*. New York: Doubleday Anchor.

Ryman, Cheryl. 1980. 'The Jamaica Heritage in Dance'. *JJ* 44.

Ryman, Cheryl. 1984a. 'Jonkonnu: A Neo-African Form'. Part 1, *JJ* 17:1. Part 2, *JJ* 17:2.

Ryman, Cheryl. 1984b. 'Kumina: Stability and Change'. *ACIJ Research Review* 1.

Ryman, Cheryl. 1985. 'Astley Clerk 1868-1944: Patriot and Cultural Pioneer'. *JJ* 18:4.

Ryman, Cheryl. 1989. 'The Frats Quintet'. *JJ* 22:1.

Sauer, Carl O. 1966. *The Early Spanish Main*. Berkeley: University of California Press.

Schuler, Monica. 1980. *'Alas Alas Kongo'. A Social History of Indentured African Immigration into Jamaica 1841-65*. Baltimore: Johns Hopkins UP.

Schwartz, A. and R.W. Henderson. 1991. *Amphibians and reptiles of the West Indies: descriptions, distributions, and natural history*. Gainesville: University Press of Florida.

Schwartz, A. and D.C. Fowler. 1973. 'The anura of Jamaica: a progress report'. *Stud. Fauna Curaçao and Carib.* Is. 43. University of Texas Press.

Scott, Michael. 1833. *Tom Cringle's Log*. London: Dent, 1969.

Scott, Rosemarie DePass. 1981. 'Spanish and Portuguese Jews of Jamaica: mid-16th to mid-17th century'. *JJ* 43.

Seacole, Mary. 1857. *Wonderful Adventures of Mrs Seacole in Many Lands* edited by Ziggy Alexander and Audrey Dewjee. London: Falling Wall Press, 1984.

Seaga, Edward. 1955. 'Jamaica's Primitive Medicine'. *Tomorrow*.

Seaga, Edward. 1968. 'Healing in Jamaica' in *True Experiences in Exotic ESP*. New York: Signet.

Seaga, Edward. 1969. 'Revival Cults in Jamaica: Notes Towards a Sociology of Religion'. *JJ* 3:2.

Sealy, Theodore. 1982. 'How We Celebrated our first Independence: A Personal Remembrance'. *JJ* 46.

Semmel, Bernard. 1962. *The Governor Eyre Controversy*. London: McGibbon and Kee.

Senior, Bernard Martin. 1835. *Jamaica as it was, as it is, and as it may be*. New York: Negro Universities Press, 1969.

Senior, Carl. 1978. 'The Robert Kerr Emigrants "Irish Slaves" for Jamaica'. *JJ* 42.

Senior, C.H. 1997. 'Asiatic Cholera in Jamaica 1850-1855'. *JJ* 26:2.

Senior, Olive. 1977-78. 'The Colon People', Pt. 1, *JJ* 11:3, 1977, Pt. 2, *JJ* 42, 1978.

Senior, Olive. 1980. 'The Panama Railway'. *JJ* 44.

Sewell, Lileth. 1981. 'Music in the Jamaican Labour Movement'. *JJ* 43.

Shaul, Wendy and Ann Haynes. 1986. 'Manatees and their Struggle for Survival'. *JJ* 19:3.

Shepherd, John B. 1968. 'Earthquakes in Jamaica'. *JJ* 2:1.

Shepherd, V.A. 1985. 'Transients to Citizens: The Development of a Settled Indian Community in Jamaica'. *JJ* 18:3.

Shepherd, V.A. 1989. 'The Apprenticeship Experience on Jamaican Livestock Pens'. *JJ* 22:1.

Shepherd, V.A. 1994. *Transients to Settlers: The*

Experience of Indians in Jamaica 1845-1950. University of Warwick and Leeds: Peepal Tree Press.

Shepherd Verene, Bridget Brereton, and Barbara Bailey (eds). 1995. *Engendering History: Caribbean Women in Historical Perspective.* Kingston: Ian Randle.

Shepherd, Verene and Glen Richards (eds.). 1998. 'Konversations in Kreole: Essays in Honour of Kamau Brathwaite'. *CQ* 44:1 & 2.

Sheridan, Richard B. 1985. *Doctors and Slaves: A Medical and Demographic History of Slavery in the British West Indies 1680-1834.* Cambridge: Cambridge UP.

Sherlock, Philip. 1954. *Anansi the Spiderman.* New York: Thomas Crowell.

Sherlock, Philip. 1966. *West Indian Folk Tales.* Oxford: Oxford UP.

Sherlock, Philip. 1980. *Manley: A Biography.* London: Macmillan.

Shields, Enid. 1983. *Vale Royal: The House and the People.* Kingston: JHS.

Shields, Enid. 1991. *Devon House Families.* Kingston: Ian Randle.

Shields-Brodber, Kathryn. 1997. 'Requiem for English in an "English-speaking Community": The Case of Jamaica', in *Englishes Around the World* 2 Edited by Edgar Schneider. Amsterdam/Philadelphia: John Benjamins Publishing Co.

Shore, Joseph and John Stewart. 1911. *In Old St James.* Kingston: Sangster's, 1970.

Sibley, Inez Knibb. 1965. *The Baptists of Jamaica 1793 to 1965.* Jamaica: The Baptist Union.

Sibley, Inez Knibb. 1978. *Dictionary of Place Names in Jamaica.* Kingston: IOJ.

Simmonds, Lorna. 1987. 'Slave Higglering in Jamaica 1780-1834'. *JJ* 20:1.

Simpson, G.E. 1956. 'Jamaican Revivalist Cults'. *SES* 5:4.

Simpson, G.E. 1957. 'The Nine Night Ceremony in Jamaica'. *Journal of American Folklore*, Oct-Dec.

Simpson, G.E. 1970. *Religious Cults of the Caribbean.* Rio Piedras: University of Puerto Rico, Institute of Caribbean Studies.

Simpson, G.E. 1978. *Black Religions in the New World.* New York: Columbia UP.

Sinha, S.C. 1972. 'Plant Collections before 1900 with a Biography of Sir Hans Sloane'. *JJ* 5:1.

Sinha, S.C. 1977. 'Soap, Syndet and Soapberry'. *JJ* 11: 1 & 2.

Sloane, Sir Hans. 1725. *A Voyage to . . . Jamaica, with the natural history.* London Vol. 1, 1707; Vol. 2, 1725.

Smith, Revd Ashley. 1978. 'Pentecostalism in Jamaica'. *JJ* 42.

Smith, M.G., Roy Augier, and Rex Nettleford. 1960. *The Ras Tafari Movement in Kingston, Jamaica.* Mona: UWI ISER.

Smith, Pamela Coleman. 1905. *Chin-Chin: Folk Stories from Jamaica.* London.

Smith, Roger W. 1968. 'Jamaica's Own Birds'. *JJ* 2:4.

Soares, Dave. 1989. 'Cricket in Jamaica. A Brief Sketch of its Development in the Nineteenth Century'. *JJ* 22:2.

Sobel, Dava. 1995. *Longitude.* New York: Walker and Co.

Speirs, James. 1902. *The Proverbs of British Guiana.* Georgetown: Argosy.

Stedman, Capt. J.G. 1796. *Narrative of a Five-years' Expedition Against the Revolted Negroes of Surinam.* London.

Stevens-Arroyo, Antonio M. 1988. *Cave of the Jagua: The Mythological World of the Tainos.* Albuquerque: U of New Mexico Press.

Steward, Julian H. (ed.). 1948. *Handbook of South American Indians*, vol. 4. Wash DC: US Government Printing Office.

Stolzoff, Norman. 2000. *Wake the Town and Tell the People: Dancehall Culture in Jamaica.* Durham: Duke UP.

Stoppelman, Francis. 1962. *Jamaica.* London: Ernest Benn.

Straw, Petrine Archer and Kim Robinson. 1990. *Jamaican Art. An overview with a focus on fifty artists.* Kingston: Kingston Publishers.

Stubbs, Jean. 1995. 'Social and Political Motherhood of Cuba: Mariana Grajales Cuello' in *Engendering History* edited by Verene Shepherd, Bridget Brereton, and Barbara Bailey. Kingston: Ian Randle.

Sullivan, Caroline. 1893. *The Jamaica Cookery Book.* Kingston: Aston W. Gardner and Co.

Tamlyn, Peter. 1969. 'John Augustus Sullivan and the Highgate Park Hunt'. *JJ* 3:1.

Tanna, Laura. 1983a. 'Anansi: Jamaica's Trickster Hero'. *JJ* 16:2.

Tanna, Laura. 1983b. 'African Retentions: Yoruba and Kikongo Songs in Jamaica'. *JJ* 16:3.

Tanna, Laura. 1984. *Jamaican Folktales and Oral Histories.* Kingston: IOJP. 3rd. ed. Miami, Fla: DLT Associates.

Tanna, Laura. 1984. *Jamaican Folk Tales and Oral Histories.* 104 minute two-part colour video. Miami, Fla: DLT Associates.

Tanna, Laura. 1987. *Jamaican Folk Tales and Oral Histories.* 60 minute audio cassette. Miami, Fla: DLT Associates.

Tanna, Laura. 1992. *Maroon Storyteller.* 60 minute audio cassette. Miami, Fla: DLT Associates.

Tanna Laura with Hazel Ramsay. 1987. 'Dinki Mini'. *JJ* 20:2.

Tanna, Laura and Cecil Baugh. 1999. *Baugh: Jamaica's Master Potter* (rev. ed.). Miami, Fla: DLT Associates.

Taylor, Godfrey. 1983. 'Slim and Sam: Jamaican Street Singers'. *JJ* 16:3.

Taylor, Lady. 1955. *Introduction to the Birds of Jamaica.* London: Macmillan.

Taylor, S.A.G. 1965. *The Western Design.* Kingston: IOJ.

Taylor, S.A.G. 1976. *A Short History of Clarendon.* Kingston: Ministry of Education.

Terres, John. 1980. *The Audubon Encyclopedia of North American Birds.* (Reprinted 1987) New York: Knopf.

Terry, Shaughan I. 1992. 'Wondrous World of Orchids - Jamaica'. *Jamaica Naturalist* 2:1.

Thomas, Carmen J. 1999a. *A History of the Presbyterian Church in Jamaica and Cayman 1824-1965.* Kingston: United Church office.

Thomas, Carmen J. 1999b. *East Indian Mission of the Presbyterian Church in Jamaica. 1894-1951.* Kingston: United Church office.

Thomas, Herbert T. 1890. *Untrodden Jamaica*. Kingston.
Thomas, Mary Elizabeth. 1974. *Jamaica and Voluntary Labourers from Africa, 1840-66*. Gainesville: University Press of Florida.
Thomas-Hope, Elizabeth. 1980. 'The Pattern of Caribbean Religions' in *Afro-Caribbean Religions* edited by Brian Gates. Ward Lock Educational.
Thompson, D.A., P.K. Bretting, and Marjorie Humphreys (eds). 1986. *Forests of Jamaica*. Kingston: Jamaica Society of Scientists and Technologists.
Thompson, Robert Farris. 1981. 'African Influence on the Art of the United States'. *Journal of African Civilizations* 3:2.
Thompson, Robert Farris. 1984. *Flash of the Spirit: African and Afro-American Art and Philosophy*. NY: Vintage.
Thompson, R.L. 1996. 'Larval habitat, ecology, and parental investment of *Osteopilus brunneus* (Hylidae)' in *Contributions to West Indian herpetology: A tribute to Albert Schwartz* edited by R. Powell and R.W. Henderson. Ithaca, NY: Society for the Study of Amphibians and Reptiles. 12.
Trollope, Anthony. 1860. *The West Indies and the Spanish Main*. London.
Tyrrell, Esther Q. and Robert A. Tyrrell. 1984. *Hummingbirds, their life and behavior*. New York: Crown Publishers.
Tyrrell, Esther Q. and Robert A. Tyrrell. 1990. *Hummingbirds of the Caribbean*. New York: Crown Publishers.

Underwood, Garth and Ernest Williams. 1959. *The Anoline Lizards of Jamaica*. Kingston: IOJ.

Van Sertima, Ivan. 1976. *They Came Before Columbus: The African Presence in Ancient America*. NY: Random House.
Vansina, Jan. 1966. *Kingdoms of the Savanna*. Madison: University of Wisconsin Press.
Vansina, Jan. 1990. *Paths in the Rainforests: Towards a history of political tradition in Equatorial Africa*. London: James Currey.
Varner, John Grier and Jeannette Johnson Varner. 1983. *Dogs of Conquest*. Norman: University of Oklahoma Press.
Vincent, Theodore. 1975. *Black Power and the Garvey Movement*. Berkeley: Ramparts Press.
Viola, Herman J. and Carolyn Margolis (eds). 1991. *Seeds of Change, Five Hundred Years Since Columbus*. Wash. DC: Smithsonian Institution Press.
Vogel, Peter. 1993. 'Rotifers in Bromeliad Watertanks'. *Jamaica Naturalist* 3.
Vogel, P. 1994. 'Evidence of reproduction in a remnant population of the critically endangered Jamaican Iguana, *Cyclura collei* (Lacertilia, Iguanidae)'. *Caribbean J. Sci.* 30.
Vogel, Peter and Rema Kerr. 1992. 'The Conservation Status of the Jamaican Iguana'. *Jamaica Naturalist* 2:1.
Vogel, P., R. Nelson, and R. Kerr. 1996. 'Conservation strategy for the Jamaican Iguana, *Cyclura collei*', in *West Indian Herpetology* edited by R.W. Henderson and R. Powell. Society for the Study of Amphibians and Reptiles.
Wade, Barry. 1984. 'The Black River'. *JJ* 17:4.
Walcott, Derek, 1986. *Selected Poems 1948-84*. NY: Farrar, Straus & Giroux.
Waldron, Eric. 1926. *Tropic Death*. NY: Collier Books, 1972.
Walmsley, Anne. 1992. *The Caribbean Artists Movement 1966-1972*. London: New Beacon.
Waring, Philippa. 1978. *A Dictionary of Superstitions*. New York: Ballantine.
Warner-Lewis, Maureen. 1977. *The Kikuyu: Spirit Messengers of the Kumina*. Kingston: Savacou.
Warner-Lewis, Maureen. 1991. *Guinea's Other Suns: The African Dynamic in Trinidad Culture*. Dover, Mass.: The Majority Press.
Warner-Lewis, Maureen (ed.). 1996. African Continuities in the Linguistic Heritage of Jamaica. *ACIJ Research Review* 3.
Watson, Karl. 1988. 'Amerindian Cave Art in Jamaica: Mountain River Cave'. *JJ* 21:1.
Watson, G. Llewellyn. 1991. *Jamaican Sayings*. Tallahassee: Florida A & M Press.
Webster, Aimee DeLisser. 1965. *Caribbean Gardening and Flower Arranging*. London: Spottiwoode, Ballantyne and Co.
White, Garth. 1984. 'The Development of Jamaican Popular Music: The Urbanization of the Folk. The Merger of the Traditional and Popular in Jamaican Music'. *ACIJ Research Review* 1.
White, Noel. 1981. 'St William Wellington Grant – A Fighter for Black Dignity'. *JJ* 43.
White, Timothy. 1983. *Catch a Fire: The Life of Bob Marley*. London: Corgi.
Who's Who in Jamaica 1921-24.
Whylie, Marjorie. 1994. 'When August Morning Come Again'. *Sunday Gleaner*, 31 July, p. 3c.
Whylie, Marjorie. 1998. 'Jamaican Drumming Styles'. *CQ* 44:3 & 4.
Whylie, Marjorie. 2000. 'Mento. The What and the How'. Kingston: Whylie Communications.
Whylie, Marjorie and Maureen Warner-Lewis. 1994. 'Characteristics of Maroon Music from Jamaica and Suriname' in *Maroon Heritage* edited by E. Kofi Agorsah. Mona: Canoe Press.
Wiggins-Grandison, Margaret D. (ed.). 1996. The Jamaica Earthquake of 13 January 1993. *The Journal of the Geological Society of Jamaica* Vol. XXX.
Wilbert, Johannes. 1987. *Tobacco and Shamanism in South America*. New Haven: Yale UP.
Wilkin, P.A. 1904. *History of the Victoria Cross*. London: Constable.
Wilkins, L. 1991. 'Notes on the Jamaican Hutia, *Geocapromys brownii* and a reintroduction of a captive bred population'. *Jamaica Naturalist* 1.
Wilks, Ivor. 1967. 'Abu Bakr Al-Siddiq of Timbuktu' in *Africa Remembered: Narratives by West Africans from the Era of the Slave Trade* edited by Philip Curtin. Madison: University of Wisconsin Press.
Williams, R.F. 1972. *R.F. Looks Back*. Kingston.
Williams, Joseph J. 1932. *Whence the "Black Irish" of Jamaica?* NY: Dial Press.

Williams, Joseph J. 1933. *Voodoos and Obeahs, phases of West India Witchcraft*. London: Allen and Unwin.

Williams, Joseph J. 1934. *Psychic Phenomena of Jamaica*. Westport: Greenwood 1979.

Williams, Joseph J. 1938. *The Maroons of Jamaica*. Anthropological Series of the Boston Graduate School. 3:4.

Wilmot, Swithin. 1984. 'Not "full free": The Ex-slaves and the Apprenticeship System in Jamaica 1834-1838'. *JJ* 17:3.

Wilson, Samuel N. 1990. *Hispaniola: Caribbean Chiefdoms in the Age of Columbus*. Tuscaloosa: Alabama UP.

Woodbury, George. 1951. *The Great Days of Piracy in the West Indies*. NY: Norton.

Woodley, J.D. 1968. 'A History of the Jamaican Fauna'. *JJ* 2:3.

Wright, I.A..1910. *The Early History of Cuba 1492-1586*. USA: Octagon Books Edition, 1970.

Wright, Philip. 1966. *Monumental Inscriptions of Jamaica*. London: Society of Genealogists.

Wright, Philip and Paul F. White. 1969. *Exploring Jamaica: A Guide for Motorists*. London: Andre Deutsch.

Wright, Raymond M. 1976. 'Earthquake Risk and Hazard'. *JJ* 10:2, 3, 4.

Wright, Richardson. 1937. *Revels in Jamaica*. Kingston: Bolivar Press, 1986.

Wynter, Sylvia. 1965. *The Morant Bay Rebellion*. GOJ API.

Wynter, Sylvia. 1969. 'Bernardo De Balbuena. Epic Poet and Abbot of Jamaica 1562-1627'. Part 2. *JJ* 3:4.

Wynter, Sylvia. 1970. 'Jonkonnu in Jamaica'. *JJ* 4:2.

Wynter, Sylvia. 1971. *Jamaica's National Heroes*. JNTC.

Wynter, Sylvia. 1984. 'New Seville and . . . Bartolome de Las Casas'. *JJ* 17:2 and 17:3.

Wynter, Sylvia. 1994. *New Seville: Major Facts, Major Questions*. Kingston: JIS.

Young, Sir William. 1795. *An Account of the Black Charaibs in the island of St Vincent's*. Cass reprint, 1971.